"In the past few decades discourse analysis has been making inroads, albeit slowly, into the practice of New Testament studies, but the approaches have been anything but uniform, easily accessible, or widely applied to the process of exegesis. Yet, with this volume we have varied applications across the New Testament, with voices as diverse as Robert Longacre, Daniel Patte, and Stephen Levinsohn. The collection capitalizes on more recent developments in discourse analysis, while putting on display the power and potential of the approach. Through the years younger New Testament scholars have contacted me to ask concerning discourse analysis, "Where do I begin?" I now have a ready answer."

George H. Guthrie
Professor of New Testament, Regent College, Vancouver, BC

"The analysis of discourse is one of the most developed branches of New Testament Greek studies at present. But it is also clear that the analysis of discourse has many kinds of methodologies. This much-needed book examines in some detail the application of discourse analysis to the books of the New Testament. Readers of this volume will immediately be struck by the diversity of approaches employed by the various contributors. Nevertheless, I believe this book succeeds in making discourse analysis immediately relevant to the modern exegete. I therefore commend it to all who believe in the integration of traditional grammar and modern linguistics."

David Alan Black
M. O. Owens Jr. Chair of New Testament Studies, Southeastern Baptist Theological Seminary

"Pastors and students frequently have some vague familiarity with Discourse Analysis (DA). They know that DA aids in determining the structure of the biblical text and thus can help us to read, preach, and teach the text more faithfully. But, where is the accessible introduction for the non-specialist? Where are understandable essays that will assist with the structure of each book in the New Testament? Todd Scacewater has assembled just such a set of essays by a team of specialists in DA. I am glad to know of *Discourse Analysis of the New Testament Writings* and look forward to using the volume and recommending it to others."

Robert L. Plummer
Collin and Eveyln Aikman Professor of Biblical Studies, Chairman, New Testament Department, The Southern Baptist Theological Seminary

"Finally, we have as close to a head-to-head comparison of approaches to discourse analysis as could be conceived, and more importantly, to the exegetical utility of the results achieved. Scacewater's volume brings together leading advocates of varied approaches, along with some employing eclectic blends, to provide readers with analyses of every New Testament book. Some succeed more than others, but that is the point of such a volume—to allow you to critically evaluate these approaches in practice rather than in a theoretical vacuum."

Steven E. Runge
Research Associate, John W. Wevers Institute for Septuagint Studies, Trinity Western University; Scholar-in-Residence, Faithlife Corporation, Bellingham, WA

"This is one of the most helpful volumes on the use of linguistics in New Testament exegesis to appear in many years. It not only showcases the value of discourse analysis for interpreting the New Testament, but it does so in a manner that allows readers to easily compare the relative strengths and weaknesses of a range of approaches to discourse analysis. Scholars and pastors alike will find this an important resource for discovering how the linguistic choices of each biblical author elucidates the structure, and thus the message, of each New Testament book."

Martin M. Culy
Founding Editor, Baylor Handbook on the Greek New Testament

Discourse Analysis of the New Testament Writings

Discourse Analysis
of the New Testament Writings

TODD A. SCACEWATER

Editor

Fontes Press

FONTES PRESS

DALLAS, TX

www.fontespress.com

To all the Bible translation servants

PREFACE

L inguistics offers an array of insights about the structure and use of human language that would profit any student of the New Testament. However, linguistics remains a rather intimidating discipline to students of the Bible, even to most biblical scholars. The field has its own history, its own technical jargon, and its own broad curriculum including phonetics, phonology, morphology, syntax, semantics, pragmatics, and since the 1960s, discourse. But while linguistics is formidable to the uninitiated, many scholars have sought to bridge the gap by making these insights available to biblical scholars and applying them to their own analysis of Scripture. Some of the most fruitful of these insights have come from discourse analysis.

Some of the earliest authors to bring linguistic insights about discourse into the world of biblical exegesis and interpretation were SIL Bible translators and consultants. After some years, it became apparent that discourse studies had much to offer biblical scholars, whose passion is to study written discourses. In the 1980s and 1990s, a variety of authors from different backgrounds showed that discourse analysis held great potential for helping us analyze NT writings as holistic units rather than linear series of verses or sentences. By now, textbooks on the discourse features of NT Greek are available, most NT writings have been subjected to a complete discourse analysis (often as dissertation projects), articles that use discourse analysis in some way or another continue to appear, and it seems that discourse analysis is here to stay.

Yet, not everyone is drawn to study and use discourse analysis, and many questions about it remain. What exactly is discourse analysis? Is it a field of study, a tool, a method, or something else? Why does each use of discourse analysis look different? Why do some authors use complicated charts and figures that are nigh uninterpretable? Does discourse analysis really improve our interpretation of texts, or is it only a very methodical application of exegetical rules we already practice? Can discourse analysis really be understood and practiced responsibly without studying other fields of linguistics? By this point, should it be considered essential for students and pastors to learn, or is it just a premium tool for the exegete's workshop? This book is intended to allow readers to form their own answers about these questions. It is one thing to read about the theory of discourse analysis; another to see it in action.

My purpose in this book is twofold. First, I wanted to display a variety of discourse-analytical methods in order to show the possibilities and drawbacks of each method. As the introductory chapter will demonstrate, discourse analysis includes dozens of topics, which cannot all be brought to bear on any one text. Each method is therefore selective, based on what the author is trying to achieve with the analysis. My hope is that one or more of these methods will prove attractive and worthwhile to the reader, who might then be inspired to pursue the study of discourse further. Second, I believe that each chapter serves as a useful analysis of a NT writing that will help the reader understand that writing as a holistic unit rather than a "string of pearls." I especially hope that pastors will consult this book profitably to better understand how a passage at hand fits into and functions within the entire discourse in which it is found.

I have many people to thank for the completion of this book. My wife, Dezi, has graciously supported me through the years of its strenuous completion. Cliff Kvidahl has been a constant support and voice of encouragement as well. David Clark has been an inspiration for me as I have finished this project. Many friends and colleagues have helped by reading and providing feedback and corrections on chapters, including Kyle Keesling, Andrew Simpson, Cary Smith, Jacob Cerone, David Fish, Mark Giacobbe, and several others. Many authors signed on immediately and completed their chapters swiftly. I thank them for their enthusiasm and their grace as the volume was completed. Some authors were called upon at the last hour, either because a previous author dropped out, or because even after more than a year of searching, I had yet to find someone to take on that chapter. I thank them for agreeing to a tough assignment with an intimidating deadline. Those at Dallas International University have supported this project even as I was just transitioning onto the faculty.

Finally, I must admit that at several key moments in this project, I wondered if I would be able to complete it. I was pushed to prayer, being reminded that self-sufficiency is not a virtue no matter how natural and satisfying it may seem. At each of these moments, God was faithful to provide what was needed. You are holding this book because it was the Lord's will, and not my own. As I write these words, the book is in its final stages of production and, Lord willing, only the parousia would hinder its publication. May these chapters provide a clearer window into the oracles of God, so that the gospel it contains and the Christ it proclaims shine brighter than before.

CONTENTS

CONTRIBUTORS

David L. Allen is Distinguished Professor of Preaching at Southwestern Baptist Theological Seminary.

Isaiah Allen teaches Bible courses at Asbury University and Booth University College.

Michael Aubrey is a linguist specializing in Ancient Greek serving with Wycliffe Bible Translators.

Todd R. Chipman is Assistant Professor of Biblical Studies at Midwestern Baptist Theological Seminary.

David J. Clark is a retired Bible Translation Consultant (UBS 1971–2002; IBT 2002–2009).

Christopher J. Fresch is Lecturer in Biblical Languages and Old Testament at the Bible College of South Australia.

Thomas W. Hudgins teaches at Gordon College and Liberty University.

J. Gregory Lawson is Professor of Christian Education at Southeastern Baptist Theological Seminary.

Stephen Levinsohn is a Senior Linguistic Consultant with SIL International and a member of Wycliffe Bible Translators.

Frederick J. Long is Professor of New Testament and Director of Greek Instruction at Asbury Theological Seminary.

Robert Longacre was Professor Emeritus at the University of Texas at Arlington.

Daniel Patte is Professor Emeritus of Religious Studies, New Testament and Christianity at Vanderbilt University.

Stephen Pattemore is Translations Director at Bible Society New Zealand.

Jenny Read-Heimerdinger is Visiting Research Fellow at Newman University, Birmingham, UK.

Michael Rudolph is a Theological Educator with World Venture in Kyiv, Ukraine.

Todd A. Scacewater is Assistant Professor of International Studies at Dallas International University.

Aaron Sherwood is a former professor and an independent scholar of biblical studies, specializing in Paul and New Testament.

Ervin Starwalt is Assistant Professor of Applied Linguistics at Dallas International University.

R. Bruce Terry is Professor of Bible and Humanities at Ohio Valley University.

William Varner is Professor of Bible and Greek at The Master's University.

Ernst Wendland is Professor in Ancient Studies at Stellenbosch University, South Africa.

Cynthia Long Westfall is Associate Professor of New Testament at McMaster Divinity College.

LIST OF FIGURES

ABBREVIATIONS

AAW	Approaching the Ancient World
AB	Anchor Bible
ABRL	The Anchor Yale Bible Reference Library
AJEC	Ancient Judaism and Early Christianity
AnBib	Analecta Biblica
ANRW	*Aufstieg und Niedergang der römischen Welt*
AnBib	Analecta Biblica
ANTC	Abingdon New Testament Commentaries
ASCP	Amsterdam Studies in Classical Philology
AUSDDS	Andrews University Seminary Doctoral Dissertation Series
AUSS	Andrews University Seminary Studies
BBC	Blackwell Bible Commentaries
BBR	*Bulletin for Biblial Research*
BDAG	W. F. Bauer, W. Danker, W. F. Arndt, and F. W. Gingrich, *Greek-English Lexicon of the New Testament and Other Early Christian Literature*, 3rd ed. (Chicago, IL: University of Chicago, 2001)
BDF	F. Blass, A. Debrunner, and R. W. Funk, *A Greek Grammar of the New Testament and Other Early Christian Literature*
BECNT	Baker Exegetical Commentary on the New Testament
BETL	Bibliotheca ephemeridum theologicarum lovaniensium
BHGNT	Baylor Handbook on the Greek New Testament
BibSac	*Bibliotheca Sacra*
BIS	Biblical Interpretation Series
BNTC	Black's New Testament Commentary
BR	*Biblical Research*
BSL	Biblical Studies Library
BST	The Bible Speaks Today
BT	*The Bible Translator*
BTB	*Biblical Theology Bulletin*
BTL	Blackwell Textbooks in Linguistics
BZAW	Beihefte zur Zeitschrift für die alttestamentliche Wissenschaft
BZNW	Beihefte zur Zeitschrift für die neutestamentliche Wissenschaft
CBQ	*Catholic Biblical Quarterly*
CBR	*Currents in Biblical Research*
CC	Condordia Commentary
CDA	Critical Discourse Analysis
CDS	Continuum Discourse Series
CEB	Commentaire Évangélique de la Bible
CILT	Current Issues in Linguistic Theory
CLiP	Cognitive Linguistics in Practice

CSL	Cambridge Studies in Linguistics
CTL	Cambridge Texts in Linguistics
CTS	Critical Theory Series
DA	Discourse Analysis
DEL	Describing English Language
EB	Etudes Bibliques
EBNS	Etudes Bibliques Nouvelle Serie
EBS	Encountering Biblical Studies
EFN	Estudios de Filología Neotestamentaria
EGGNT	Exegetical Guide to the Greek New Testament
EGT	Expositors Greek Testament
EKKNT	Evangelisch-Katholischer Kommentar zum Neuen Testament
ETL	*Ephemerides Theologicae Lovanienses*
EC	*Early Christianity*
ELL	*Encyclopedia of Language and Linguistics*
ESV	English Standard Version
GBS	Guides to Biblical Scholarship
G-E	Franco Montanari, *The Brill Dictionary of Ancient Greek* (Brill 2015)
GNS	Good News Studies
GNTE	Guides to New Testament Exegesis
GTJ	*Grace Theological Journal*
HBM	Hebrew Bible Monographs
HBT	*Horizons in Biblical Theology*
HNT	Handbuch Zum Neuen Testament
HNTC	Harper's New Testament Commentaries
HTR	Harvard Theological Review
HTRDR	Harvard Theological Review Dissertations in Religion
ICC	International Critical Commentary
IJSELL	*International Journal on Studies in English Language and Literature*
ISI/RR	*ISI Research Report*
IVPNTC	IVP New Testament Commentary
JAAR	*Journal of the American Academy of Religion*
JBC	The Jerome Biblical Commentary
JBL	*Journal of Biblical Literature*
JETS	*Journal of the Evangelical Theological Society*
JGRChJ	*Journal of Greco-Roman Christianity and Judaism*
JIBS	*The Journal of Inductive Biblical Studies*
JLAS	*Journal of the Linguistics Association of the Southwest*
JLing	*Journal of Linguistics*
JLTR	*Journal of Language Teaching and Research*
JOTT	*Journal of Translation and Textlinguistics*
JPrag	*Journal of Pragmatics*
JSNT	*Journal for the Study of the New Testament*
JSNTSup	Journal for the Study of the New Testament Supplement Series

JSOTSup	Journal for the Study of the Old Testament Supplement Series
JT	*Journal of Translation*
JTS	*Journal of Theological Studies*
JTT	*Journal of Translation and Textlinguistics*
KEK	Kritisch-exegetischer Kommentar über das Neue Testament
KTSP	Key Topics in Semantics and Pragmatics
LBRS	Lexham Bible Reference Series
LEC	Library of Early Christianity
JILS	*Journal of Interdisciplinary Literary Studies*
L&N	J. P. Louw and E. A. Nida, eds., *Greek-English Lexicon of the New Testament: Based on Semantic Domains*, 2 vols. (United Bible Socities, 1988–1989)
LCL	Loeb Classical Library
LNTS	Library of New Testament Studies
LPS	Library of Pauline Studies
LS	Language in Society
MJTM	*McMaster Journal of Theology & Ministry*
NA	Nestle-Aland
NAB	New American Bible
NAC	New American Commentary
NASB	New American Standard Bible
NCBC	New Century Bible Commentary
Neot	*Neotestamentica*
NET	New English Translation
NIBC	New International Biblical Commentary
NICNT	New International Commentary on the New Testament
NIDNTTE	Moisés Silva, ed., *New International Dictionary of New Testament Theology and Exegesis*, 5 vols. (Zondervan, 2014)
NIGTC	New International Greek Testament Commentary
NIV	New International Version
NIVAC	New International Version Application Commentary
NL	Notes on Linguistics
NLT	New Living Translation
NovT	*Novum Testamentum*
NovTSup	Supplements to Novum Testamentum
NT	New Testament
NTG	New Testament Guides
NTL	New Testament Library
NTM	New Testament Monographs
NTTSD	New Testament Tools, Studies, and Documents
NTS	*New Testament Studies*
OG	Old Greek
OHO	Oxford Handbooks Online
OILS	OILS

OLS	Open Linguistic Series
OPTAT	Occasional Papers in Translation and Textlinguistics
OSSM	Oxford Surveys in Syntax and Morphology
OT	Old Testament
P&B	Pragmatics and Beyond
P&BNS	Pragmatics and Beyond New Series
PL	Publications in Linguistics
PLAL	Perspectives on Linguistics and Ancient Languages
PNTC	Pillar New Testament Commentary
PRSt	*Perspectives in Religious Studies*
RB	*Revue Biblique*
RHLT	Routledge History of Linguistic Thought
RNT	Regensburger Neues Testament
RST	Rhetorical Structure Theory
RT	Relevance Theory
SBD	Society of Biblical Dissertation Series
SBLDS	Society of Biblical Literature Dissertation Series
SBLSS	The Society of Biblical Literature Semeia Studies
SBLSymS	Society of Biblical Literature Symposium Series
SFL	Systemic Functional Linguistics
SKG	Studies in Koine Greek
SHBC	Smyth & Helwys Bible Commentary
SIL	Summer Institute of Linguistics
SILeB	SIL e-Books
SIS	Studies in Interactional Sociolinguistics
SNT	Supplements to Novum Testamentum
SNTSMS	Society of New Testament Studies Monograph Series
SNTSup	Society of New Testament Studies Supplement Series
SP	Sacra Pagina
SSA	Semantic Structural Analysis
SSBT	Studies in Scripture and Biblical Theology
SSS	Syntax and Semantics Series
STDJ	Studies on the Texts of the Desert of Judah
SwJT	*Southwestern Journal of Theology*
TDNT	*Theological Dictionary of the New Testament*, 10 vols., ed. Gerhard Kittel, trans. Geoffrey W. Bromiley (Eerdmans, 1964)
TESOL	Teaching English to Speakers of Other Languages
THGNT	Tyndale House Greek New Testament
THKNT	Theologischer Handkommentar zum Neuen Testament
TLSM	Trends in Linguistics. Studies and Monographs
TNTC	Tyndale New Testament Commentaries
TSAJ	Texts and Studies in Ancient Judaism
TynBul	*Tyndale Bulletin*
UBS	United Bible Societies

UBSMS	United Bible Society Monograph Series
UCLWPL	UCL Working Papers in Linguistics
VT	*Vetus Testamentum*
WBC	Word Biblical Commentary
WUNT	Wissenschaftliche Untersuchungen zum Neuen Testament
ZB	Zürcher Bibelkommentare
ZNW	*Zeitschrift für die neutestamentliche Wissenschaft*

INTRODUCTION

DISCOURSE ANALYSIS:
HISTORY, TOPICS, AND APPLICATIONS

TODD A. SCACEWATER

D iscourse analysis (henceforth, "DA"), despite attempts by some biblical scholars to integrate it into a standard exegetical method, remains one of the most unfortunately misunderstood and underutilized tools that the student, pastor, and scholar could employ. The present volume seeks to demonstrate the usefulness of DA when applied to written documents, particularly the NT writings, and to motivate biblical students and scholars to study DA and linguistics in general.

Indeed, linguistics is one of many modern disciplines that have begun to be integrated into general hermeneutical theory, but not one of the more popular ones. Several scholars since the 1990s have emphasized the "hermeneutical triad" of history, theology, and literature.[1] That is, all biblical texts have historical, theological, and literary qualities that require attention for adequate interpretation. This triad is helpful heuristically, but other academic disciplines more or less influence our ability to read ancient texts properly, especially philosophy

---

[1] On the hermeneutical triad, see N. T. Wright, *The New Testament and the People of God* (Fortress, 1992), 1–144; Andreas J. Köstenberger and Richard D. Patterson, *Invitation to Biblical Interpretation: Exploring the Hermeneutical Triad of History, Literature, and Theology* (Kregel Academic, 2011); Craig G. Bartholomew, *Introducing Biblical Hermeneutics: A Comprehensive Framework for Hearing God in Scripture* (Baker Academic, 2015), 281–462. Additionally, Wright and Bartholomew rightly include philosophy as a fourth discipline to include in a proper hermeneutical theory.

and linguistics. The potential impact of integrating modern linguistics into a standard hermeneutical theory is evident from the oft-cited impact of J. Barr's *Semantics of Biblical Language*, whose linguistic-based critiques of *TDNT* and works in the first biblical theology movement were significant.[2] Linguistics deserves to be integrated into standard hermeneutical theory. I hope this volume will demonstrate that DA is a practical linguistic tool that aids in our comprehension of ancient texts, particularly the NT texts. Secondarily, I hope that the usefulness of DA demonstrates the need to integrate linguistics more broadly into our hermeneutical arsenal. Without understanding at least the broad contours of how language works, it will be difficult for us to engage responsibly with written texts.

What is Discourse Analysis?

Before defining DA, we must define "discourse" and "text." For most authors, there is a distinction between the two terms.[3] A text is any record of language use; hence, it is an artifact. But texts are always produced for some purpose. Since texts themselves do not have purposes (only authors do), we can define discourse as the entirety of a language producer's communicative purposes intended to be achieved through a text or utterance.[4] Thus, DA "cannot be restricted to the description of linguistic forms independent of the purposes or functions which those forms are designed to serve in human affairs."[5] For this reason, DA must involve language-in-use rather than constructed examples, and we must speak not of rules of discourse, but regularities, which are observed and described.[6]

Definitions of DA vary widely, but they may be boiled down to the three common elements of the study of (1) language beyond the level of the sentence;

---

[2] James Barr, *The Semantics of Biblical Language* (Oxford University Press, 1961). For a summary of the issues, see Peter Cotterell and Max Turner, *Linguistics and Biblical Interpretation* (InterVarsity Press, 1989), 106–128. D. A. Carson's influential *Exegetical Fallacies* (2nd ed. [Baker Academic, 1996]) is another work that demonstrates how a basic understanding of linguistic concepts goes a long way toward being responsible with interpreting texts.

[3] Unfortunately, linguists do not define the terms consistently, which can cause some confusion. See a brief analysis of the problem in Konrad Ehlich, "Text and Discourse," in *The Discourse Studies Reader: Main Currents in Theory and Analysis*, ed. Johannes Maingueneau, Dominique Maingueneau, and Ruth Wodak (John Benjamins, 2014), 282–285.

[4] H. G. Widdowson, *Discourse Analysis*, OILS (Oxford University Press, 2007), 6. Some authors reverse these definitions, but at least for Americans "text" seems more appropriate for designating the artifact.

[5] Gillian Brown and George Yule, *Discourse Analysis*, CTL (Cambridge University Press, 1983), 1.

[6] Ibid., 20–23.

(2) language use; and (3) the social and interpersonal aspects of communication.[7] It is in the combination of these three elements that DA may be fully described, even if it cannot be adequately defined.[8] These three elements are interrelated. First, texts are generally composed of more than one sentence, and many linguistic concerns cannot be explained adequately at the restricted level of the sentence, such as anaphora, coherence, and conversational exchanges. Second, while one may study language-in-use at the sentence level (e.g., how deixis functions within an isolated sentence), the relationship between linguistic forms and their users becomes more complex above the level of the sentence, thus prompting studies on the pragmatics of discourse. Third, discourse always has a communicative function, and studying the social and interpersonal aspects of communication can help resolve many of the questions about language functions at levels higher than the sentence.

The initial concern of discourse analysts was not to create a method for better analyzing texts. The concern was to understand discourse as a linguistic entity, just as traditional grammarians have sought to understand the sentence as a linguistic entity. Once the linguistic characteristics of discourse, its production, and its reception are understood, one might apply these theoretical insights to the study of a text to better understand its structure, meaning, and function.[9] DA

---

[7] Deborah Schiffrin, Deborah Tannen, and Heidi E. Hamilton, "Introduction to the First Edition," in *The Handbook of Discourse Analysis*, 2nd ed., ed. Deborah Tannen, Heidi E. Hamilton, and Deborah Schiffrin (Wiley Blackwell, 2015), 1:1. For further definitions, see James Paul Gee and Michael Handford, "Introduction," in *The Routledge Handbook of Discourse Analysis*, ed. James Paul Gee and Michael Handford (Routledge, 2012), 1, and Adam Jaworski and Nikolas Coupland, *The Discourse Reader*, 3rd ed. (Routledge, 2014), 1–3, which catalogues ten different definitions.

[8] Sometimes the term "discourse analysis" is used to refer to "Critical Discourse Analysis," which was developed by N. Fairclough and his followers. Critical Discourse Analysis ("CDA") is interested in the use of language (at any level, sentence or higher) as a social practice, particularly practices that relate to power, racism, discrimination, politics, and other related social phenomena. According to CDA practitioner Ruth Wodak, it is built on Marxist and Frankfurt School critical theory, which means that the surface level of a text cannot be taken at face value ("Critical Discourse Analysis," in *The Bloomsbury Companion to Discourse Analysis*, ed. Ken Hyland and Brian Paltridge [Bloomsbury, 2013], 50). See Norman Fairclough, *Discourse and Social Change* (Polity, 1992); idem, *Analyzing Discourse* (Routledge, 2003). For an updated introduction, see James Paul Gee, *An Introduction to Discourse Analysis: Theory and Method*, 4th ed. (Routledge, 2014). None of the authors in this volume have utilized a critical discourse model, so I will not explain it further.

[9] Similarly, Teun A. van Dijk stresses that "discourse analysis is *not* a method but a discipline.... Even when studying the 'same' object, such as a news item or a parliamentary debate, we may have recourse to many 'methods', also depending on the kinds or structures we want to focus on, and especially also depending on our aims of study" ("The Study of Discourse: An Introduction," in *Discourse Studies*, ed. Teun A. van Dijk [Sage, 2007], 1:xix–xlii, emphasis original).

should therefore not be seen as a golden key to unlocking the meaning of a text. It is simply an array of linguistic insights that helps us understand what discourse is and how it works. Once we better understand discourse, then as we examine texts, those insights about what discourse is and how it works may help us to better understand texts as holistic entities (not as a linear sequence of sentences), to resolve exegetical problems, and to better discover communicative intent.

Consider a brief text:

(1)   I ate dinner. I brushed my teeth. We went to bed.

Traditional grammarians would be concerned with these three sentences as autonomous units. The entire sequence would be no more than the sum of its parts, each well-formed and self-contained. But DA is concerned with how we receive this sequence as a whole. Why does this sequence appear "normal" to us, and why do we believe the speaker is cognitively well, rather than schizophrenically incoherent? Notice that there are no explicit connectors between these sentences, and thus no explicit signals to co-interpret these sentences. There are still several factors that cause us to receive this sequence as a coherent discourse, of which I observe only a few. First, this sequence describes a typical order of events for an evening (even if it omits other events) and therefore fits with our experience. Second, there is continuity of referents (I, I, we), and even though the third referent shifts to the first plural pronoun, our assumption of coherence will cause us to seek an explanation for the shift (the person must have eaten and brushed alone, and then joined his or her spouse for sleep). Third, we assume that there is some reason for uttering such a bland recollection of events (otherwise, we would ask, "ok, so?"). We might construct an overarching purpose for the discourse such as "X wants to inform Y that X's evening was boring." The assumption of this communicative purpose helps us to make better sense of the entire sequence (e.g., if it was unclear that eating dinner was boring, it now becomes clear in light of the entire sequence's communicative purpose). These are only a few of the linguistic, cognitive, and social factors that help us process discourse, and a fuller array of these factors will be explored further below.

The History of Discourse Analysis

While definitions orient us to a field, we may better understand it by exploring its origins.[10] The study of grammar traces back to the Greeks, from whom we

---

[10] The following sources were helpful to me in this area: Teun A. van Dijk, "New Developments. Discourse Analysis (1978–1988)," *JILS* 1 (1989): 119–145; idem, "Introduction: Discourse Analysis as a New Cross-Discipline," in *Disciplines of Discourse*, vol. 1 of *Handbook of Discourse*

have several extant works analyzing Greek grammar under the categories of lex-icography, philology, and syntax.[11] The domain of grammar, though, was limited to the level of the sentence.[12] The ancient study of rhetoric dealt with the organi-zation of whole discourses, but mostly with their arrangement and delivery for maximal impact on the audience.[13] Stylistics, which was one of the five depart-ments of rhetoric, also shared concerns with DA, such as how language varies (or should vary) across sequences of sentences.[14]

At the turn of the nineteenth century, modern linguistics began to bloom with the founding of philology and comparative grammar.[15] F. Diez's *Grammar of the Romance Languages* (1836–1844) came closer to studying language rather than languages, while F. de Saussure founded semiology at the beginning of the twentieth century and set the course for the modern discipline of linguistics.[16] One hallmark feature of these earlier linguistic approaches is that, as with the Greeks, investigation was still limited to the maximum level of the sentence.[17]

The Interdisciplinary Origins of Discourse Analysis

Interest in language beyond the level of the sentence arose in the 1950s and 1960s with the rise of structuralist analyses of texts, especially narrative analy-sis.[18] Studies in this vein necessarily evaluated writings as a whole and the

---

Analysis, ed. Teun A. van Dijk (Academic Press, 1985), 1–10; Robert de Beaugrande and Wolf-gang Dressler, *Introduction to Text Linguistics* (Longman, 1981), 14–29.

[11] Dionysius Thrax, *Téchnē Grammatikē*; Apollonius Dyscolus, *On Syntax*; cf. Aristotle, *Rhetoric*. See further, Franco Montanari, Stephanos Matthaios, and Antonios Rengakos, eds., *History Disciplinary Profiles*, vol. 1 of *Brill's Companion to Ancient Greek Scholarship* (Brill, 2015); Pieter A. M. Seuren, *Western Linguistics: An Historical Introduction* (Blackwell, 1998), 3–37; R. H. Robins, *A Short History of Linguistics*, 4th ed. (Longman, 1997), 12–57.

[12] Dionysius Thrax, *Téchnē Grammatikē*, §12–13.

[13] De Beaugrande and Dressler, *Introduction to Text Linguistics*, 15; Teun A. van Dijk, *Macrostructures: An Interdisciplinary Study of Global Structures in Discourse, Interaction, and Cognition* (Erlbaum, 1980), 130.

[14] De Beaugrande and Dressler, *Introduction to Text Linguistics*, 17.

[15] F. A. Wolf was a major founder of philology, while works such as Franz Bopp's *Über das Conjugationssystem der Sanskritsprache* (Andreäischen, 1816) helped establish comparative grammar.

[16] Friedrich Diez, *Grammatik der romanischen Sprachen*, 3 vols. (Eduard Weber, 1836–1844); Ferdinand de Saussure, *Course in General Linguistics*, ed. Charles Bally and Albert Sechehaye, trans. Roy Harris (Open Court, 1986), which is a compilation of his students' notes from three courses he taught at the University of Geneva between 1906–1911.

[17] Most famously, Leonard Bloomfield, *Language* (Holt, Rinehart and Winston, 1933), 170.

[18] Influential for structuralism was the structure of Russian folktales by Vladimir Propp, published in 1928 and translated into English in 1958 (*Morphology of the Folktale* [Indiana University Press, 1958]).

function of their parts, since it tied textual form to meaning in one way or another. These approaches were also influenced by the ideas of linguist
Bronislaw Malinowski, who viewed language as a human activity, and anthro-
pologist Claude Lévi-Strauss, who posited the symbolic nature of aspects of
human culture and studied the functional similarities of myths from different
cultures.[19] In the 1960s and 1970s, sociolinguists began investigating the effect
of social context on speakers within their own speech communities. Interest in
the social context of speech was furthered in these same decades by the innovation of Speech Act Theory by J. L. Austin and J. Searle, as well as the theories
of implicature and conversational maxims developed by H. P. Grice.[20] These
theories all fed into DA in the 1970s and 1980s so that, while the textual level of
a discourse was still significant, it was greatly enriched by exploring the
communicative context and the way that language producers used linguistic
forms to create or signal meaning, especially across sequences of sentences,
paragraphs, etc.

By the end of the 1970s and the beginning of the 1980s, discourse analysts
were integrating insights from cognitive psychology and artificial intelligence.
Both disciplines helped develop ideas about how humans process and receive
discourse, store it in memory, and integrate this knowledge with pre-existing
knowledge.[21] The concept of a "mental model" helped to explain in part how
people process discourse as coherent, and helped to turn attention to the *way*
that people receive discourse, store it in memory, and recall it. Thus, the origins
of DA lie in a multitude of disciplines including at least anthropology, structuralism, philosophy of language, sociology, cognitive psychology, and artificial intelligence.

---

[19] Bronislaw Malinowski, "The Problem of Meaning in Primitive Languages," in *The Meaning of Meaning*, ed. Charles Ogden and Ivor Richards (Harcourt, Brace & World, 1923), 296–
336; Claude Lévi-Strauss, *Anthropologie Structurale* (Paris: Plon, 1958); idem, "La structure et la
forme," in *Cahiers de l'Institut de Science Économique Appliquée* 99 (1960): 3–36; idem, *Myth
and Meaning* (1978; repr., Routledge, 2001). See De Beaugrande and Dressler, *Introduction to
Text Linguistics*, 18.

[20] J. L. Austin, *How to Do Things with Words*, 2nd ed., ed. J. Urmson and M. Sbisà (Harvard
University Press, 1962); J. Searle, *Speech Acts: An Essay in the Philosophy of Language* (Cambridge University Press, 1969); H. P. Grice, "Meaning," *The Philosophical Review* 66, no. 3 (1957):
377–388; idem, "Logic and Conversation," in *Syntax and Semantics, 3: Speech Acts*, ed. P. Cole
and J. Morgan (Academic Press, 1975), 41–58; idem, *Studies in the Way of Words* (Harvard University Press, 1989).

[21] See especially *Introduction to Text Linguistics* by De Beaugrande, originally published in
1972 and translated by Dressler in 1981; P. N. Johnson-Laird's *Mental Models* (Cambridge University Press, 1983); Teun A. van Dijk and Walter Kintsch, *Strategies of Discourse Comprehension*
(Academic Press, 1983).

The Development of Discourse Analysis

Early attempts at formally analyzing language at levels above the sentence were not entirely successful but sparked the discussion. Z. Harris first used the term "discourse analysis" as a technical term in 1952.[22] He analyzed the recurrence of morphemes across an entire text to better perceive its structure, so that (as he puts it) we learn nothing new about what a text says, but only about how it says it. His method did not catch on. By the end of the 1960s, analysts began focusing on cohesion (the binding together of a text by explicit linguistic features).[23] In his 1968 monograph, Roland Harweg argued that "syntagmatic substitution" is the basic means of producing texts across successive sentences.[24] Also in 1968, Longacre published the results of SIL linguists' research on minority languages in the Philippines, focusing on cohesion, peak, and discourse types.[25] In Britain, M. Halliday and R. Hasan in their *Cohesion in English* (1976) categorized five types of cohesive devices necessary for textual coherence.[26] J. Grimes in 1975 explored a wider variety of discourse features, especially semantic features and information structure, but still mostly to the exclusion of extra-textual factors.[27] This early stage of DA (or text-linguistics) tended to focus on explicit linguistic features in the text and tended to treat the text in isolation from non-linguistic features arising from the communicative event and reception of the text. The earliest fruit from these new studies in discourse resulted in text-grammars (especially in Europe), whose purpose was not to consider the structure of isolated sentences. Rather, they sought to explain the role of discourse context for the construction of local sentences, and to explain textual phenomena that cannot be explained properly by sentence grammar (e.g., anaphora and coherence).[28]

---

[22] Zellig Harris, "Discourse Analysis," *Language* 28, no. 1 (1952): 1–30.

[23] Special mention should be made of James Loriot's 1958 paper, not published until 1970, that explored cohesive ties and discourse features that mark the beginning and end of paragraphs in the Shipibo language of Peru. It was jointly published with Barbara Hollenbach as "Shipibo Paragraph Structure," *Foundations of Language* 6, no. 1 (1970): 43–66.

[24] Roland Harweg, *Pronomina und Textkonstitution* (Fink, 1968); idem, "Substitutional Text Linguistics," in *Current Trends in Textlinguistics*, ed. Wolfgang Dressler (de Gruyter, 1978), 247–260, esp. 253.

[25] Robert E. Longacre, *Discourse, Paragraph, and Sentence Structure in Selected Philippine Languages* (Summer Institute of Linguistics, 1968). Further results were published on languages of Papua New Guinea (1972) and Central/South America (1976). Longacre focused on how explicit surface features of the text signaled deep structures.

[26] Michael Halliday and Raqaiya Hasan, *Cohesion in English* (Longman, 1976).

[27] Joseph E. Grimes, *The Thread of Discourse* (Mouton, 1975).

[28] This line of inquiry extended into what is now referred to as information structure. See Nomi Erteschik-Shir, *Information Structure: The Syntax-Discourse Interface*, OSSM (Oxford University Press, 2007).

With the integration of sociolinguistics, cognitive psychology, and pragmatics in the 1970s–1990s, attention in discourse studies shifted from lexically-based cohesion studies to the study of discourse coherence and communicative context. The ethnography of speech, which analyzes the interpretive rules used by members of a speech community, led some linguists to analyze oral discourse, resulting in a field called Conversational Analysis.[29] The oft-cited 1983 textbook of G. Brown and G. Yule summarized the field up to that point, covering the topics of context, topics, theme and staging, information structure, reference, and coherence.[30] Systemic Functional Linguistics (henceforth, "SFL"), developed by M. Halliday, also provided a theoretical framework in which both textual and social factors could be analyzed from different perspectives.[31]

From the 1990s to the present, the insights of the nature of discourse have been applied across the social scientific disciplines including linguistics, sociology, anthropology, political science, gender studies, pedagogy, literature, communication studies, rhetoric, business, marketing, natural language processing, and more. To give only one example, insights on the nature of discourse coherence have been used to help teach English language learners how to produce coherent essays. Because every social science involves language and discourse in its own way, the insights of DA are applicable to the social sciences. In this way, DA became truly interdisciplinary, with insights from the social sciences illuminating the nature of discourse, and the enhanced understanding of discourse further illuminating the linguistic aspects of the social sciences.

New Testament Discourse Analysis

Just as DA has been applied to many of the social sciences, so it has been applied to the NT documents in two different ways: first to apply insights from DA to NT texts, and second to research the discourse features of NT Greek.

Applying Discourse Analysis to New Testament Texts

DA was initially employed in NT studies in the 1980s. These early studies analyzed entire NT writings to better understand their structure or some of their discourse features.[32] While these studies covered entire NT writings, they focused on only

---

[29] Malcolm Coulthard, *An Introduction to Discourse Analysis* (Longman, 1977).

[30] Brown and Yule, *Discourse Analysis*.

[31] On the two ways Systemic Functional Linguistics has been developed in discourse studies by Ruqaiya Hasan and J. R. Martin, see Mary J. Schleppegrell, "Systemic Functional Linguistics," in *The Routledge Handbook of Discourse Analysis*, 21–34.

[32] David J. Clark and J. de Waard, "Discourse Structure in Matthew's Gospel," *Scriptura Special Issue* S1 (1982): 1–97, reprinted in David J. Clark, *Analyzing and Translating New Testament*

one or several features of the text throughout the document (predominantly lexical cohesion, discourse markers, and coherence relations). These types of studies do not seem to have been very influential in making NT scholars aware of DA. Also helpful but relatively unknown outside of the SIL world has been the Semantic Structural Analysis series, inaugurated in 1987 and intended to provide a semantic structural analysis of every NT writing.[33] The most influential demonstration of DA for NT scholars came at the end of the decade in two separate books. Each introduced linguistic principles to biblical scholars and included a section on textually-based semantic analysis along the lines of Semantic Structural Analysis.[34] These two volumes, given their accessible presentation, helped to show the value of DA to NT scholars. Several journal articles and book chapters using DA also appeared in the 1980s—some arising from Bible translation workshops—but the scattered nature of the sources resulted in no forceful cumulative effect.[35]

In the 1990s, several works tried to promote DA among NT scholars, one edited by D. Black and two arising from the SBL study group on Biblical Greek Language and Linguistics.[36] In 1994, G. Guthrie published his DA of Hebrews, applying cohesion shift analysis to determine the writing's structure.[37] In 1997, J. Reed published a significant study applying DA to Philippians from a SFL perspective in order to contribute to the discussion of the epistle's literary unity.[38] This oft-cited study promoted DA to NT scholars in three helpful ways: it (1) provided an application of DA to a specific NT problem (2) from a specific linguistic tradition

---

Discourse (Fontes, 2019), 13–111; J. P. Louw, *A Semantic Discourse Analysis of Romans* (University of Pretoria, 1987); Stephen Levinsohn, *Relationships between Constituents Beyond the Clause in the Acts of the Apostles* (PhD thesis, University of Reading, UK, 1980), parts of which were published in his *Textual Connections in Acts*, SBLMS (Scholars Press, 1987).

[33] The first volume was John Banker, *A Semantic and Structural Analysis of Titus* (SIL, 1987). The theory on which the series is based, and which is explained later in this chapter, was developed by John Beekman, John Callow, and Michael Kopesec, *The Semantic Structure of Written Communication* (SIL, 1981). The series is not yet complete, but SIL plans to finish it.

[34] Peter Cotterell and Max Turner, *Linguistics and Biblical Interpretation* (IVP Academic, 1989); David A. Black, *Linguistics for Students of New Testament Greek: A Survey of Basic Concepts and Applications* (Baker, 1988; 2nd ed. published 1995).

[35] E.g., arising from a Bible translation seminar was Robert E. Longacre's "Exhortation and Mitigation in First John," *Selected Technical Articles Related to Translation* 9 (1983): 3–44.

[36] David A. Black, ed., *Linguistics and New Testament Interpretation: Essays on Discourse Analysis* (B&H, 1992); Porter and Carson, eds., *Discourse Analysis and Other Topics in Biblical Greek*; Stanley E. Porter and Jeffrey T. Reed, eds., *Discourse Analysis and the New Testament: Approaches and Results*, JSNTSup 170 (Sheffield Academic, 1999).

[37] George H. Guthrie, *The Structure of Hebrews: A Text-Linguistic Analysis*, NovTSup 73 (Brill, 1994).

[38] Jeffrey T. Reed, *A Discourse Analysis of Philippians: Method and Rhetoric in the Debate over Literary Integrity*, JSNTSup 136 (Sheffield Academic, 1997).

(3) in a comprehensive and methodical study. While his use of SFL as a specific linguistic tradition is a positive feature of the study, it is also a double-edged sword, since NT scholars are unlikely to master a linguistic tradition (especially one as complex as SFL) in order to add one tool to their exegetical belt.[39] Since Reed's study, several other monographs have provided a DA of an entire NT writing, and each has been to some extent helpful in demonstrating the usefulness of DA.[40]

By 1995, S. Porter observed that DA had not yet been used heavily in NT studies and wondered whether the discipline would remain.[41] He suggested a fourfold taxonomy of analytical theories that had been applied to the NT: the SIL model with its emphasis on Bible translation, the SFL model with its integrated linguistic model, the Continental European model that distinguished semantics and pragmatics, and the South African school with its colon analysis. Since Porter's essay, it seems that the SIL camp has become the most influential in biblical studies, while the SFL camp has mostly been promulgated by those in Porter's circles. The South African camp never made much headway into biblical studies, while the Continental European model has probably involved too much linguistic theory to attract biblical scholars.

While the twenty-first century has seen some further DA studies applied to the NT, there have been few if any advances in how biblical scholars use DA. Biblical scholars have been attracted to semantic discourse features that are marked by explicit linguistic features, such as cohesive ties and discourse markers, and most of those insights came in the 1960s and 1970s. Insights into the nature of discourse that arose from sociolinguistics, pragmatics, and cognitive psychology have by and large not been integrated into the DA methodologies of biblical scholars. Partially, this tie to explicit linguistic features is understandable, since the communicative context of ancient letters is less accessible than modern conversations or texts from our own culture. But to the extent that these additional insights about discourse can be integrated into the study of ancient texts, they should be, if the DA is to be fully exploited for the benefit of students of Scripture.

---

[39] The standard textbook on SFL is now M. A. K. Halliday and Christian Matthiessen, *Halliday's Introduction to Functional Grammar*, 4th ed. (Routledge, 2014).

[40] Jakob K. Heckert, *Discourse Function of Conjoiners in the Pastoral Epistles* (Summer Institute of Linguistics, 1996); Ralph Bruce Terry, *A Discourse Analysis of First Corinthians* (SIL, 1995); Stephanie L. Black, *Sentence Conjunctions in the Gospel of Matthew: καί, δέ, τότε, γάρ, οὖν, and Asyndeton in Narrative Discourse*, LNTS 216 (T&T Clark, 2002); Cynthia Long Westfall, *A Discourse Analysis of the Letter to the Hebrews: The Relationship between Form and Meaning*, LNTS 297 (T&T Clark, 2005); William Varner, *The Book of James—A New Perspective: A Linguistic Commentary Applying Discourse Analysis* (Kress, 2011); Mark E. Taylor, *A Text-Linguistic Investigation into the Discourse Structure of James*, LNTS 311 (T&T Clark, 2011).

[41] Stanley E. Porter, "Discourse Analysis and New Testament Studies," in *Discourse Analysis and Other Topics in Biblical Greek*, 24–35.

In sum, DA in NT studies seems to have gained little ground since the flurry of studies and essays in the 1980s and 1990s, which mostly utilized discourse insights from the 1960s and 1970s. But the field of discourse studies has advanced greatly since its early decades, and many insights about discourse are ripe for applying to NT texts. There is room (and a need for) genuinely interdisciplinary scholars to get a firm grasp on the wide field of discourse studies and to help the rest of the biblical studies community see the great potential that linguistics, and DA in particular, has to offer.

Discourse Features of New Testament Greek

While the earliest uses of DA in NT studies were applications of a method to a text in order to analyze it more systematically, at least two scholars have published major works that aim to lay out the discourse features and information structure of NT Greek. In 1992, Stephen Levinsohn published the first edition of his *Discourse Features of New Testament Greek*, which was later updated in 2000 (2nd ed.).[42] Steven Runge published his *Discourse Grammar of the Greek New Testament* in 2010.[43]

Levinsohn's textbook focuses on discourse features and information structure in NT Greek, the latter being the analysis of how language is organized in discourse and how context affects linguistic choices. He focuses on the constituent order of sentences, the discourse function of conjunctions, patterns of reference (including how they are introduced and tracked), ways to background and highlight information, default and marked ways of reporting speech, and discourse boundary features. These topics provide useful ways of discerning a type of prominence (or markedness) within sentences and paragraphs, finding topic shifts and discourse boundaries, noting backgrounded and foregrounded information through default and marked forms, analyzing intersentential conjunctions in a way that accounts for semantics and pragmatics, tracking participants across a discourse and the way they are introduced and highlighted, and more. This "functional" approach to grammar deals with the explicit features of the text and how they are ordered, as well as the linguistic choices that are made and how those choices are affected by context at the local and the global level.

Levinsohn's work is a major advance for linguistically attuned analyses of NT writings at the local level of discourse especially and, in a way, at the global level. His method is especially helpful for tracing the development of the discourse

---

[42] Stephen H. Levinsohn, *Discourse Features of New Testament Greek: A Coursebook on the Information Structure of New Testament Greek* (SIL, 1992; 2nd ed. 2000).

[43] Steven E. Runge, *Discourse Grammar of the Greek New Testament: A Practical Introduction for Teaching and Exegesis* (Hendrickson, 2010).

and prominent information throughout the discourse. One should beware, however, that this specific work (Discourse Features of New Testament Greek) does not lay out a DA method. Rather, it provides an array of insights about discourse in the Koine Greek language specifically, which can then be applied to texts in order to better understand how they hold together, shift, and function. Levinsohn has demonstrated how his functional grammar approach can be applied to texts in his analysis of Galatians in ch. 9 of this volume.

Steven Runge's discourse grammar has a similar aim as Levinsohn's textbook. Runge also works with a functional grammar perspective, which relies on default and marked grammatical choices. He covers the discourse function of conjunctions, forward-pointing devices, information structuring devices, and thematic highlighting devices. One of the unique and helpful aspects of Runge's work is that, for each discourse feature, he gives both the traditional grammatical explanation of that feature, followed by his own functionally-oriented explanation. One is therefore able to see how a linguistic perspective enhances the explanatory power of discourse features. While Runge reinforces much of what Levinsohn covered in his textbook, he also adds some unique insights about Koine Greek discourse that are especially helpful at the local level. Like Levinsohn's work, Runge's discourse grammar is not intended to provide a DA method. Rather, it gives us the tools we need to understand how Koine Greek discourse flows and functions, and what choices were available to Koine Greek authors to express their ideas.[44] These foundations enable us to perform DA in Koine Greek more accurately.

Topics in Discourse Analysis

While every chapter in this volume begins with a methodology section, the reader will be served well by first being introduced to the vast array of topics in the field of DA. There is not space to treat every DA topic, so I will explain briefly the more common concepts, especially the ones that are employed in this volume.

Context, Semantics, and Pragmatics

In October 1854, British general Lord Raglan positioned himself on high ground from where he directed his military against a Russian army. From his context, he could see the Russians retreating with captured British artillery, so he issued a text with instructions for the cavalry:

---

[44] For a more comprehensive review of the work of Levinsohn and Runge, see Constantine R. Campbell, *Advances in the Study of Greek* (Zondervan, 2015), 163–191.

(2) Lord Raglan wishes the cavalry to advance rapidly to the front, follow the enemy and try to prevent the enemy carrying away the guns—Troop horse artillery may accompany. French cavalry is on your left. Immediate. R. Airey.

The definite articles show that Lord Raglan assumed his audience would share his situational context, but they did not. The only "front" they could see was one where Russian troops were safely entrenched. The result was a massive loss for the British army.[45] Communicative purposes are only successful insofar as context is shared.

Context may be of two kinds: communicative context, which is the social and situational context of the discourse producer and receiver, and textual context (often called co-text), which is the text surrounding an utterance. In DA, both kinds of context are essential for interpreting an utterance efficiently and according to the intentions of the producer. Communicative context involves pragmatic considerations, while co-text largely involves semantic considerations. Pragmatics is the study of the relationship between linguistic forms and the users of those forms. Semantics is the study of the relationships between linguistic forms, their referents, and truth conditions.[46]

Co-text largely involves semantic considerations because the semantic dimension of discourse lies in its concepts (or ideas) and their relation to one another, which are encoded in the textual dimension. Exegetes are well acquainted with how co-text constrains the interpretation of utterances in a discourse, so much so that "context" in commentaries or biblical studies publications almost always refers to a verse's co-text. The communicative context involves pragmatic considerations, because the pragmatic dimension of discourse lies in the way that the speaker uses language in a specific situation to interact with the recipient, and how the recipient receives the language as coherent. Most studies that have applied DA to NT documents have unfortunately focused on the semantic dimension of discourse to the exclusion of the pragmatic dimension. Since discourse has both dimensions, to ignore the pragmatics of discourse "leads to inadequate or at most partial accounts of discourse and discourse processing."[47]

Contextual pragmatic factors of discourse include at least the relevant features of the language producer and receiver, presuppositions, implicatures, inferences, and shared contextual objects.[48] Analyzing discourse for these factors relating to language production and reception are paramount for understanding not only a fuller meaning of the discourse, but also its purpose. When analyzing the context

---

[45] This example is taken from Widdowson, *Discourse Analysis*, 23.

[46] Pragmatics and semantics, along with syntax, compose the main branches of linguistic analysis.

[47] Van Dijk, *Macrostructures*, 25.

[48] Brown and Yule, *Discourse Analysis*, 28–35; J. R. Firth, *Papers on Linguistics* (Oxford University Press, 1957), 182; Widdowson, *Discourse Analysis*, 21.

of discourse, the principle of local interpretation says one should not expand the context any larger than is needed to interpret an utterance ("open *the* door" means open the closest door or the one in focus). The principle of analogy says that context involves an assumed normality of the world, and discourse will only be received coherently insofar as it coheres with that normality.[49]

Pragmatics also considers how language functions as action. Speech act theory distinguishes between locution (the utterance itself), illocution (the force of the utterance), and perlocution (the effect of the utterance). The five main types of illocutions are declarations, representatives, expressives, directives, and commissives. Initially, speech act theorists paid attention to explicit performatives (words that recognizably perform an act) in certain circumstances, such as "I hereby pronounce you husband and wife." It later became apparent, though, that any utterance could be converted into a speech act by artificially adding before it a "performative prefix" such as "I state that…" or "I demand that…" or "I commit that…," etc. The artificial addition for the sake of analysis makes explicit the kind of illocution that the sentence carries.[50] Thus, when someone says, "the weather is nice today," we may analyze it as "I inform you that the weather is nice today," making it a declarative speech act. In this way, every utterance may be considered an act with a certain type of illocution. Thus, discourses not only have ideas and relations between them, but also acts and relations between them. Analyzing these pragmatic relations between utterances is an essential part of understanding the fullness of meaning in a discourse.[51]

Cohesion

Cohesion occurs on the surface level of a text and binds a discourse together in explicit ways through grammatical or conceptual ties.[52] In the seminal English

---

[49] Brown and Yule, *Discourse Analysis*, 58–67. Cf. text (1) discussed above.

[50] In declarative sentences, though, it can change the semantic truth value of the overall sentence. While "the sky is green" is false, "I declare to you that the sky is green" is true. This problem is part of what is called the "performadox," and demonstrates that illocutionary force lies outside the traditional domains of phonology, syntax, and semantics (and therefore, within the domain of pragmatics). Thus, performative prefixes should only be used to determine the pragmatic macrostructure of the discourse, not the semantic macrostructure. See further in Stephen C. Levinson, *Pragmatics*, CTL (Cambridge University Press, 1987), 226–283; Coulthard, *An Introduction to Discourse Analysis*, 11–29; Sandrine Zufferey, Jacques Moeschler, and Anne Reboul, *Implicatures*, KTSP (Cambridge University Press, 2019).

[51] The most developed theory of analyzing the relations between speech acts is van Dijk, *Macrostructures*, 133–199. For the original publications developing speech act theory, see note 20.

[52] Robert A. Dooley and Stephen H. Levinsohn, *Analyzing Discourse: A Manual of Basic Concepts* (SIL International, 2001), 27; Yuan Wang and Minghe Guo, "A Short Analysis of Discourse Coherence," *JLTR* 5, no. 2 (2014): 464.

study on cohesion, Halliday and Hasan categorized cohesive ties into five types: conjunctions, lexical relationships, reference, ellipsis, and substitution.[53] One could consider ellipsis and substitution as two types of syntactical cohesive techniques, reducing the types to four.

These four categories can be further sub-divided. Conjunctions may be sub-categorized as (1) additive, adversative, causal, temporal, or as (2) conjunctive, disjunctive, contrajunctive, and subordinate. Co-referential forms (or pro-forms) may be exophoric (referring outside the text) or endophoric (referring within the text). Endophoric forms may be anaphoric (referring backward) or cataphoric (referring forward). Pronouns are probably the most common co-referential forms. Lexical relationships include hyponymy (generic to specific class), metonymy (part-whole relationships), collocability (words that tend to occur together), synonymy, syntactical repetitions, consistency of tense or voice or mood, stylistic choices, comparisons, and clausal substitutions. Syntactical forms of cohesion include substitution, ellipsis, paraphrase, parallelism, recurrence or partial recurrence of elements or patterns, and iconicity (an outward resemblance between surface expressions and their content).[54]

Cohesive ties provide useful data for analyzing discourse. Cohesive ties between contiguous sentences suggest that they are somehow related. On the contrary, when cohesive ties are lacking between contiguous sentences, the topic may be shifting. Cohesive links can be explicit indicators of information that would otherwise be implicit, including relations between sentences or larger discourse units. Co-referential forms can help to maintain focus on a specific topic. M. Hoey's method for analyzing networks of cohesive relationships in a text allows for implications about semantic content and prominence, and may be the most focused cohesive analytical method to date.[55]

But while cohesion is a useful and explicit means for helping a text be received as coherent, cohesion is neither necessary nor sufficient for creating a coherent or a well-formed text.[56] Consider the following sequence of sentences from a schizophrenic patient:

---

[53] Halliday and Hasan, *Cohesion in English*.

[54] Brown and Yule, *Discourse Analysis*, 191; De Beaugrande and Dressler, *Introduction to Text Linguistics*, 71.

[55] Michael Hoey, *Patterns of Lexis in Text* (Oxford University Press, 1991).

[56] Brown and Yule, *Discourse Analysis*, 194–197; Dooley and Levinsohn, *Analyzing Discourse*, 33; Wang and Minghe, "A Short Analysis of Discourse Coherence," 460–465; J. R. Martin, "Cohesion and Texture," in *The Handbook of Discourse Analysis*, ed. Tannen, Hamilton, and Schiffrin, 71; Patricia L. Carrell, "Cohesion is Not Coherence," *TESOL Quarterly* 16 (1982): 479–483; Widdowson, *Discourse Analysis*, 49. By "well-formed," I mean that it would sound natural to native speakers of the language.

(3)   I am thinking of Paisley. It is a nice town, it is quite warm. There are houses
       being built. They pull down houses there, and are building fifteen- and
       twenty-story flats. I think in Scotland and Glasgow there are twenty-story
       flats because people are so crowded in houses and they can't breathe.[57]

This sequence exhibits multiple types of cohesion, but it is incoherent for many
reasons; e.g., there seems to be no point, and it is not clear what the sequence is
"about."[58] Thus, cohesion is not sufficient to create a coherent text.

      Cohesive ties are also not *necessary* for coherence. Consider the sequence of
sentences, "I'm hungry. What time is it?" Such a discourse is perfectly natural;
context would help the receiver understand that the second sentence is a speech
act that requests information so that a plan can be formed to solve the hunger
problem. It is easy to see, then, how cohesion is not a necessary contributor to
coherence in a text. One study even found no correlation between the statistical
occurrence of cohesive ties and the resulting coherence of a text.[59] Nevertheless,
the examples to prove that cohesion is neither necessary nor sufficient for coherence are rather extreme and sometimes artificial. In natural discourse, cohesion is common. On balance, then, cohesion is a useful concept of discourse
studies, but it should be considered less important than other aspects such as
context and coherence, to which we now turn.

Coherence

According to W. Bublitz, while coherence began as a vague concept, studies on
coherence abounded in the 1980s and 1990s so that, by 1999, it was perhaps the
key concept in DA.[60] It is one of the most fascinating aspects of discourse analysis because of its complexity, which is evident from the numerous definitions
the concept is given.[61] Perhaps an agreeable definition to most would be that

---

[57] Quoted from Tanya Reinhart, "Conditions for Text Coherence," *Poetics Today* 1, no. 4
(1980): 166.

[58] In other words, one might ask both "what are you talking about?" (semantics) and "why
are you telling me this?" (pragmatics).

[59] Robert J. Tierney and James H. Mosenthal, *The Cohesion Concept's Relationship to the
Coherence of Text. Technical Report* 221 (University of Illinois, 1981). See also van Dijk, *Macrostructures*, 105.

[60] Wolfram Bublitz, "Introduction: Views of Coherence," in *Coherence in Spoken and Written Discourse: How to Create It and How to Describe It*, ed. Wolfram Bublitz, Uta Lenk, and Eija
Ventola (John Benjamins, 1999), 1.

[61] See De Beaugrande and Dressler, *Introduction to Text Linguistics*, 4; Dooley and Levinsohn, *Analyzing Discourse*, 23; Reinhart, "Conditions of Text Coherence," 161–180; Giora,
"Notes toward a Theory of Text Coherence," 707–708.

coherence is a cognitive concept according to which a hearer or reader receives a text as somehow connected in all its parts and relevant for a communicative situation. While not all discourse is coherent, receivers generally are conditioned through their social interactions with others to expect coherent discourse. It is an axiom that when listening to others or reading text, our minds will do their best to seek a coherent interpretation, simply because phrases and sentences are contiguous. This quest for coherence involves many factors, all of which have been explored by linguists from textual and cognitive perspectives.

Global Patterns

While receiving a discourse, readers or hearers engage in bottom-up and top-down processing. "In one part of the processing, we work out the meanings of the words and structure of a sentence and build up a composite meaning for the sentence (i.e. bottom up processing). At the same time, we are predicting, on the basis of the context plus the composite meaning of the sentences already processed, what the next sentence is most likely to mean (i.e. top-down processing)."[62] Our ability to do top-down processing greatly depends on our stored background knowledge, which some linguists and psychologists surmise is stored in chunks of information that are associated by what we may call global patterns. The following global patterns are essential for receiving texts as coherent.

Frames are slots in our memory that store data structures related to specific concepts. If a speaker mentions an office, our mind will assume the existence of a chair, a desk, pens, etc. Scripts are mental plans that specify the roles of participants and their expected actions. Scripts explain why in the sentence "Tim was injured and taken to the X," the hearer will expect the X slot to be filled by "hospital," "doctor," or something similar. Schemata are high-level knowledge structures by which people interpret their experiences. As we approach a setting with events and states, our schemata cause us to expect or predict certain things as we interpret the discourse. Because global patterns are constructed from experience, they are culturally relative, a fact for which effective speakers must account.

Global patterns allow for different types of inferences that create coherence in texts. These inferences may require more or less processing effort, depending on how culturally normative the assumption is. Since all language is underdetermined (i.e., not all meaning is explicit and semantic), coherence depends on inferences to greater or lesser degrees. In one study, subjects who were read a number of sentences that allowed for inferences reported later that the inferences

---

[62] Brown and Yule, *Discourse Analysis*, 234.

were verbatim sentences in the text.[63] In written texts, although we may see that the assumptions are not in the text, discovering them can lay bare some of the author's assumed knowledge, what is presumed that the audience knows, and other pragmatic aspects of context.

Coherence Relations

One of the most significant aspects of coherence is the ability of receivers to infer coherence relationships between units of language at the sentence level and above. For instance, there is a clear "ASSERTION-evidence" relationship between the two following sentences:

(4)   I'm losing lots of weight. I only weighed 160 pounds today.

Cohesion (I'm/I; weight/weighed; losing/only), as well as their juxtaposition, signals that these sentences belong together somehow. But without an explicit connector or phrase that signals the relationship between the sentences, we are left to infer that relationship. Receivers generally have little problem making these inferences, which is a significant factor in how discourse is received as coherent. Experiments have shown that receivers not only inferred coherence relations, but sometimes even reported that their inferred coherence relations were a part of the text.[64]

Coherence relations are more basic than surface features that may indicate them, such as conjunctions or discourse markers. Even when connectors or conjunctions join sentences together, coherence relations are not signaled unambiguously. The Greek conjunction γάρ can signal four different logical relationships between propositions (reason, cause, explanation, and conclusion).[65] Note also how a surface conjunction adds no semantic content to a sequence of sentences, but only constrains how one processes the coherence relation:

(5a)   I need an A in this course. I'm going to stay home to study tonight.
(5b)   I need an A in this course. So, I'm going to stay home to study tonight.

Both (5a) and (5b) have a clear reason-ACTION relationship, but a speaker might use (5b) if it seems possible that the receiver's pragmatic knowledge does not easily allow for the inference required by (5a). The only difference in meaning

---

[63] Marcia K. Johnson, John D. Bransford, and Susan K. Solomon, "Memory for Tacit Implications of Sentences," *Journal of Experimental Psychology* 98, no. 1 (1973): 203–205.

[64] De Beaugrande and Dressler, *Introduction to Text Linguistics*, 102; Watson Todd, *Discourse Topics*, 193–240.

[65] BDAG, s.v. γάρ

between (5a) and (5b), then, is purely pragmatic, not semantic. While discourse markers and surface particles may help guide the inferential process, context and co-text are the key factors in determining the coherence relations that a producer intends between propositions or units.[66]

Coherence relations can be either semantic or pragmatic. Example (5a) has a semantic relationship between facts. A pragmatic relation would hold between speech acts, as in (6).

(6) I need an A in this course. So, I need your help with my homework.

In this case, the first sentence is a declarative speech act. The second sentence is another declarative speech act. The first act functions as a rationale for the second. If the second sentence is considered an implicit request (rather than a command), then the relationship is rationale–REQUEST, a pragmatic relationship between speech acts.

It seems to me that pragmatic relationships exist more often when one of the speech acts is a command or question.

(7) Open the door. Our guest is here.
(8) Will you hold the door for me? This stuff is heavy.

In (7), the second sentence is a rationale for giving the command. In (8), the second sentence is a rationale for the request. In (8) we have a good example of how recognizing speech acts can explain coherence in seemingly disconnected utterances. What does the "stuff" being heavy have to do with opening the door? When the pragmatic coherence relation is inferred, the two utterances then obviously cohere. Van Dijk has most consistently distinguished between semantic and pragmatic coherence relations, and some have given a nod to the idea, but this distinction has not been as fully explored as it could be, nor has it been utilized much in DA.[67]

---

[66] For students of the NT, a small lexicon lists the different coherence relations that can be signaled by various Greek words: G. K. Beale, Daniel J. Brendsel, and William A. Ross, *An Interpretive Lexicon of New Testament Greek: Analysis of Prepositions, Adverbs, Particles, Relative Pronouns, and Conjunctions* (Zondervan Academic, 2014).

[67] Van Dijk, *Text and Context*, 205–231; idem, *Macrostructures*, 175–199. Cf. Dooley and Levinsohn, *Analyzing Discourse*, 92–95. There is growing literature on "pragmatic markers," which are surface forms that serve some type of pragmatic function, either signaling a coherence relation between speech acts, or creating a cognitive constraint on interpretation, or something else. For a helpful summary of research on pragmatic markers, see Bruce M. Fraser, "What are Discourse Markers?" *JPrag* 31 (1999): 931–952. As Fraser notes (p. 932), these markers can also be called cue phrases, discourse connectives, discourse operators, discourse particles,

Coherence relations have been one of the most popular and fruitful aspects of DA, for linguists and for biblical scholars.[68] The two most influential expositions of coherence relations are Semantic Structural Analysis (SSA), created by SIL linguists, and Rhetorical Structural Analysis (RST), developed by linguists at the University of Southern California's Information Sciences Institute.[69] Both methods divide the text into units (the smallest unit being a proposition), and then label the coherence relationship between them. One unit may be related to one contiguous proposition, or to a contiguous sequence of propositions. Most relationships recognize one unit as more semantically prominent (SSA) or as more essential to the producer's communicative purpose (RST). Once propositions are related to one another, they form a higher-level unit, and the analysis may be carried on recursively to successively higher levels of the discourse. At the top of the hierarchical network of relations will be the most prominent or essential proposition, with its immediately subordinate propositions being the main supporting points of the discourse.

The two main weaknesses of these approaches are the inherent subjectivity of inferences and the neglect of the pragmatics of discourse discussed above.[70] But when analyzing the semantics of discourse, these methodologies focus on perhaps the most important aspect of coherence. The analysis of coherence relations is likely so popular because it can be applied to every unit in a discourse, whereas other aspects of discourse (such as frames, discourse markers, or marked prominence) are not evident in every unit. Its recursive manner also allows the discourse to be represented graphically, which helps to see how the text fits together and functions as a whole. Yet, however helpful SSA and RST

---

discourse signaling devices, indicating devices, phatic connectives, pragmatic connectives, pragmatic expressions, pragmatic formatives, pragmatic operators, pragmatic particles, semantic conjuncts, and sentence connectives.

[68] Coherence relations have also been called rhetorical predicates or relations, functional relations, propositional relations, and interclausal or intersentential relations. I use the term "coherence relations" to emphasize that these relations are a key aspect of establishing coherence in a text.

[69] SSA: Beekman, Callow, and Kopesec, *The Semantic Structure of Written Communication*. The method has been applied to many NT writings in SIL's Semantic and Structural Analysis series.

RST: William C. Mann and Sandra A. Thompson, "Relational Propositions in Discourse," *ISI/RR-83-115* (1983): 1–28; idem, "Rhetorical Structure Theory: Description and Construction of Text Structures," *ISI/RS-86-174* (1986): 1–15; idem, "Rhetorical Structure Theory: A Framework for the Analysis of Texts," *ISI/RS-87-185* (1987): 1–22; idem, "Rhetorical Structure Theory: Toward a Functional Theory of Text Organization," *Text* 8, no. 3 (1988): 243–281; William C. Mann, Christian M. I. M. Matthiessen, and Sandra A. Thompson, "Rhetorical Structure Theory and Text Analysis," *ISI/RR-89-242* (1989): 1–60. The last mentioned 1989 essay lays out the mature theory of RST and provides a sample analysis of a brief fundraising letter from a political organization.

[70] Likewise, van Dijk, *Macrostructures*, 88; Brown and Yule, *Discourse Analysis*, 113–114.

might be, they are not comprehensive DA methods. Coherence relations are only one aspect of coherence, which is only one aspect of discourse. [71]

The relations posited by SSA and RST (respectively) are listed below in full as a reference, since they are used so commonly in the essays of this volume. Units in small capitals are more prominent.

I. Addition (all of equal prominence)
   A. Chronological
     1. Sequential
     2. Simultaneous
   B. Non-Chronological
     1. Alternating
     2. Conjoined
     3. Progression
II. Support-HEAD
   A. Chronological
     1. Progression ($step_n$–GOAL)
     2. Stimulus-RESPONSE
     3. Speech (remark, proposal, or question–EVALUATION, EXECUTION, ANSWER or COUNTER)
     4. Non-speech (occasion, problem, complication–OUTCOME or RESOLUTION)
   B. Non-Chronological
     1. Orientation
       a. circumstance/setting–HEAD
       b. time–HEAD
       c. orienter–CONTENT
       d. opening–HEAD
       e. HEAD–closing
       f. introduction–HEAD
       g. preliminary incident–HEAD
     2. Clarification
       a. Overlapping Information
         i.   HEAD–equivalent
         ii.   HEAD–amplification
         iii.   GENERIC–$specific_n$

---

[71] Indeed, Robert E. Longacre lists his eight "holistic concerns" of DA, of which only one is the analysis of coherence relations, or "intersentential relations" as he calls them ("Some Implications of Zellig Harris's Discourse Analysis," in *The Legacy of Zellig Harris: Language and Information into the 21st Century*, ed. Bruce E. Nevin, CILT 228 [John Benjamins, 2002], 126).

           iv.   specific$_n$–GENERIC

     b. Non-overlapping Information

           i.   HEAD–comparison

           ii.   HEAD–illustration

           iii.   HEAD–manner

           iv.   contrast–HEAD

3. Logical

     a. reason–RESULT

     b. RESULT–means

     c. MEANS–purpose

     d. grounds–CONCLUSION

     e. condition–CONSEQUENCE

     f. concession–CONTRAEXPECTATION

     g. HEAD–grounds (HEAD = implication/conclusion, exhortation, or question)

4. Associative

     a. HEAD–comment

     b. HEAD–parenthesis

Relations between Concepts

I. Delimitation

     A. CONCEPT–identification

     B. CONCEPT–description

Figure I.1: Semantic Structural Analysis Relations

Many of the same coherence relations are laid out in RST, although not as exhaustively or with the nucleus and satellite labeled.

Circumstance	Non-Volitional Cause	Otherwise
Solutionhood	Volitional Result	Interpretation
Elaboration	Non-Volitional Result	Evaluation
Background	Purpose	Restatement
Enablement	Antithesis	Summary
Justify	Concession	Sequence
Volitional Cause	Condition	Contrast

Figure I.2: Rhetorical Structure Theory Relations

Pragmatic Features of Coherence

Many pragmatic factors allow us to receive discourse as coherent. We have already discussed features of context, such as the assumption of coherence, the principle of analogy, the principle of local interpretation, general features of context and co-text, inferences, and presuppositions. We have also seen that socio-cultural knowledge helps to construct global patterns for producers and receivers. Gricean pragmatic theories postulate maxims according to which discourse takes place; if those maxims are flouted, there are likely implicatures that may be understood or discovered so that the discourse is received as coherent. Similarly, Speech Act Theory helps to explain how seemingly disconnected contiguous utterances are received coherently.

Another pragmatic factor is information structure, which helps to explain how receivers interpret discourse as it is encountered. There are different approaches to information structure: given–new, theme–rheme, and topic–focus. A given–new approach is psychologically based and analyzes the text for information that has the status of given and new. When a producer brings information into the discourse, it will be presented differently based on its activation status. By contrast, theme–rheme and topic–comment, generally different terms for the same concepts, are syntactically based. Theme/topic are the left-most part of the sentence (excluding—according to some theories—any adjuncts placed before it), while rheme/comment contain what the producer wants to say about the theme/topic. The linguistic choices made by producers are affected by context and co-text, which can enable us to analyze marked prominence, presuppositions, and more.

Macrostructures and the Representation of Discourse

At the global level, discourses must have some organizational principle in order to be received as coherent. Consider sequence (10):

(10) I went to New York. New York is in the United States, and the United States is in a trade war with China. Mandarin is the official language of China.

Despite its cohesive ties, this sequence is incoherent because the topic continues to shift. In other words, there is no macrostructure, or global organizing principle, in this discourse.

Earlier investigations of the representation and organization of discourse focused on the notion of "discourse topic," which typically refers to a single noun, noun phrase, or proposition that represents "what the discourse is about." T. van Dijk most fully developed the idea of a "macrostructure" of discourse, which is a more holistic representation of the entire discourse (not just the highest-level or most prominent idea).[72] Generally, "macrostructure" as used by biblical scholars has a broader meaning, namely, any representation of an entire discourse, often given in chart or outline form. We are interested here in the more restricted, linguistic definition, according to which macrostructures are necessary conditions for coherent discourse. However one construes a macrostructure, any part of the discourse that is unrelated to the macrostructure will be received as incoherent.

Macrostructures are also crucial for the interpretation of microstructures.[73] Consider text (11):

(11)   The process may seem complicated but actually it is not really, so long as you prepare things in advance and know what has to be done in what order. Some of the things you need you may already have, but others, of course, you may need to get. They are not always readily available and when they are they can be quite expensive. But the final result will make all the effort and cost worthwhile.

There are many cohesive devices in this text, but it is not interpretable (or perhaps even coherent) until one learns that the macrostructure of the discourse includes "cooking chicken biryani."[74] Hence, if one will properly interpret or exegete a unit within a discourse, one by necessity must have a rough idea of the discourse's macrostructure.

The linguistic status of discourse topics and macrostructures is debated. Proposals have included that they are nouns, noun phrases, concepts, clusters of concepts, propositions, or implicit questions that the discourse answers. Single nouns, concepts, and noun phrases are too limited to be an organizing principle for an entire discourse.[75] The two most viable options, then, are clusters of concepts and propositions. The former allows for a wider number of concepts—the most frequent, salient, or prominent—which provide nodes to which the rest of the discourse can connect. Propositions are semantic constructions that represent surface structures. For van Dijk, a macrostructure is a proposition or a string of propositions containing the most salient content of the discourse, from which the entire surface text may be entailed. An example of a propositional macrostructure could be "John wrecked his car, which led to his transport to the hospital

---

[72] Van Dijk, *Macrostructures.*

[73] Van Dijk calls macrostructures a "necessary condition for the interpretation of sentences and the establishment of local coherence at the microlevel" (*Macrostructures*, 26).

[74] Example from Widdowson, *Discourse Analysis*, 50. For another good example, see Richard Watson Todd, *Discourse Topics*, P&BNS 269 (John Benjamins, 2016), 8.

[75] See, e.g., Giora, "Notes toward a Theory of Text Coherence," 702, 711; van Dijk, *Macrostructures*, 94–98.

so that he could be treated by a doctor." The concept cluster view of macrostructures is amenable to lexical approaches (e.g., computational linguistics). The propositional view more accurately represents the way humans receive and remember discourse by creating and storing semantic representations of the surface text.

Macrostructures occur at the global level and the local level. The smallest unit within a discourse is one that has its own macrostructure.[76] The question is then whether and, if so, how these local macrostructures combine to form a global macrostructure. One approach is to make a linear analysis of all the local macrostructures in the discourse, including the drifts and shifts between them.[77] Another approach is to create clusters of salient or prominent concepts or events from each of the macrostructures and somehow combine them together. A third and most frequently used approach is to combine them hierarchically. The highest-level macrostructure becomes the global macrostructure that functions to organize and create coherence for the entire discourse. Since the hierarchical approach is the most commonly used, I will focus further on it by explaining four different types.

The first two hierarchical approaches have already been discussed: RST and SSA. The main differences are that (1) RST includes pragmatic relations and also demands the rhetorical function of each structure, and (2) RST analyzes the surface text while SSA promotes converting the text into semantic propositional representations. The latter difference means that RST's resulting macrostructure is composed of surface text, while SSA's macrostructure is a semantic representation (called the "Theme" of each unit).

The third method is discussed at length and tested by Watson Todd.[78] "Topic-based analysis using relations" creates a hierarchical network of concepts within a paragraph using either logical relationships (e.g., hyponymy and meronymy) or schemata, which creates slots into which concepts from the paragraph fall (e.g., a "film" schema has slots for title, characters, plot, etc.). Although Watson Todd considers the method "impractical" beyond a short text, I do not see any reason why the highest-level concept that generates the schema cannot be combined hierarchically with other high-level concepts into a global concept.[79]

---

[76] Some might want to say that the paragraph is the smallest discourse unit, but "paragraph" may be defined variously, making it a problematic term unless one defines it specifically as a unit of text that has its own macrostructure. See further in Brown and Yule, *Discourse Analysis*, 95–100.

[77] E.g., Watson Todd, *Discourse Topics*.

[78] Watson Todd, *Discourse Topics*, 123–137.

[79] For his discussion of a longer text and the impracticality of these types of analyses using the five methods that he tests, see *Discourse Topics*, 234–240. His Figure 34 on p. 236 shows his graphical analysis of Text 7 and, while it looks complex, it is barely more complex than a typical

The fourth method is van Dijk's, which uses macrorules to reduce a discourse into a semantic propositional representation that retains the most prominent information.[80] First, delete all propositions of the text that are irrelevant for interpreting the other propositions in the text. Second, generalize by abstracting semantic detail from sequences of sentences to construct a proposition that is conceptually more general. Third, use global patterns to construct a new proposition that denotes a global fact of which the micropropositions are normal components, conditions, or consequences. Fourth, delete each proposition or any information that is relevant only locally and not to the global macrostructure. What remains is a semantic representation of the most prominent or important information in the discourse, akin to a summary or upshot, which entails the entire discourse. Van Dijk proposes making a semantic analysis to discover the global meaning of the discourse and a separate pragmatic analysis, which analyzes sequences of speech acts to find a global speech act that represents the purpose of the discourse.[81]

The major advantages of the hierarchical approach are its ability to represent the entire discourse with its organizational structure, its ability to be operationalized recursively at all levels of the discourse, and its basis in human reception of discourse, which is the locus of coherence.[82] One disadvantage of the approach is that it is unable to handle any units of text that do not relate to contiguous units, perhaps inserted for rhetorical purposes (e.g., the repetition of a key phrase at equally spaced points in a speech). Another is that it becomes difficult to develop a hierarchy when boundaries are not entirely clear, which leads us to the next aspect of macrostructural analysis: discourse unit boundaries.

In order to develop a macrostructure for each lowest-level unit, one must determine discourse unit boundaries. A unit boundary occurs when an utterance is not organized under the macrostructure of the preceding unit. At this point,

---

SSA or RST graphical analysis. What matters is how one combines the higher-level items together hierarchically.

[80] Van Dijk, *Text and Context*, 143–147; idem, *Macrostructures*, 46–91.

[81] Special mention should be given to Longacre, who in the 1960s had developed a hierarchical view of language from Kenneth Pike's tagmemic theory. But he focused more on discourse types and superstructures (to be discussed below) than on macrostructures. He did not employ van Dijk's macrorules, but he did take from van Dijk the understanding of "macrostructure" as the "overall meaning" of a text and as "the overall thrust and import of a discourse" (*The Grammar of Discourse*, 2nd ed. [Plenum, 1996], 4, 33).

[82] For cognitive evidence supporting the hierarchical nature of macrostructures, see W. Kintsch and J. Keenan, "Reading Rate and Retention as a Function of the Number of Propositions in the Base Structure of Sentences," *Cognitive Psychology* 5 (1973): 257–274; David Ausubel, "The Use of Advance Organizers in the Learning and Retention of Meaningful Verbal Material," *Journal of Educational Psychology* 51, no. 5 (1960): 267–272; De Beaugrande and Dressler, *Introduction to Text Linguistics*, 195–206; van Dijk, *Macrostructures*, 1–10.

there is a "coherence break." Unit boundaries can be signaled by different types of markers. The most prominent marker may be lexis; when one clustering of lexis is replaced by another clustering, there is likely a discourse boundary. Discourse particles may explicitly signal a new unit in the discourse. There may be more explicit or marked forms at the beginning of a discourse unit, since there is an increased cognitive load when shifting to a new topic. An array of literary features can signal the beginning of a new section, including the vocative, imperative, asyndeton, a formula, a newly expressed topic, the use of definite noun phrases instead of anaphoric substitutes, and the complete lack of anaphora.[83]

While unit boundaries are sometimes clear because the coherence break is either marked or intuitively obvious (in which case we have "topic shift"), sometimes boundaries are not so obvious, in which case there may be "topic drift."[84] The most common type of topic drift includes broadening and narrowing a topic (i.e., a GENERAL–specific relationship).[85] Sometimes with topic drift there is a "discourse pivot," which is a concept or lexeme that occurs in a unit and then persists in the succeeding unit after a topic drift.[86] When a drift occurs, one must decide whether the unit drifted into belongs together with the preceding unit or should be subordinate or superordinate to the preceding unit.

Macrostructural organization is not arbitrary or random, but rather is conditioned by discourse types and their associated superstructures. There are a limited number of discourse types (or genres) into which discourses may be categorized, including the four major types of narrative, expository, procedural, and hortatory.[87] These four types differ by the four parameters of (+/-) agent orientation, (+/-) temporal succession, (+/-) tension, and (+/-) projection.[88] In the 1960s and 1970s, Longacre and his SIL colleagues analyzed minority languages in the Philippines, Papua New Guinea, and Central/South America. The results showed that each discourse type had a general template that could vary slightly from language to language, or from text to text, but that overall characterized the

---

[83] Watson Todd, *Discourse Topics*, 29–47; Ernst Wendland, "The Johannine Epistles," ch. 21 in this volume.

[84] I am using Watson Todd's terminology of "maintenance" within units and "shift" or "drift" between units (*Discourse Topics*, 67–82).

[85] Ibid., 70.

[86] Ibid., 72; Jerry R. Hobbs, "Topic Drift," in *Conversational Organization and Its Development*, ed. Bruce Dorval (Ablex, 1990), 3–22.

[87] Minor discourse types include at least dramatic, activity, epistolary, and instruction. Longacre, *Philippine Languages*, 1:3; idem, "Building for the Worship of God: Exodus 25:1–30:10," in *Discourse Analysis of Biblical Literature: What It Is and What It Offers*, ed. Walter Ray Bodine, SBLSS (Scholars Press, 1995).

[88] For the most recent and complex representation of the four major discourse types, see Robert E. Longacre and Shin Ja J. Hwang, *Holistic Discourse Analysis*, 2nd ed. (SIL International, 2012), 34–37. Their chart is reproduced in this volume in ch. 20, "2 Peter."

broad structure of texts within that type.[89] For example, a typical narrative may include a stage, rising action, climax, falling action, and *dénouement*. This general template of each discourse type is what van Dijk later termed "superstructure."[90] Some elements of the superstructure are obligatory, while others are optional.

Discourse types and superstructures have important implications for discovering a text's macrostructure.[91] First, once a discourse has been classed as a certain discourse type, a rough outline of the text is already set.[92] Second, superstructures put constraints on macrostructural operations (i.e., van Dijk's macrostructural rules). For example, the macrostructure of a conflict schema unit must maintain a human component. Third, superstructures help determine what is most important or relevant for the text as a whole. For example, introductions to epistles are far less important than the body, so the latter's macrostructure will be higher in the hierarchy. Fourth, assigning sentences to units, and units to schemas within the superstructure, helps to make clear the function of those sentences and units within the wider discourse. If a sentence falls within a *dénouement* schema, then it in some way contributes to the resolution of the storyline. Fifth, certain discourse types may have their own conventional ways of shifting topics, so that identifying the discourse type makes it easier to discern topic shifts.[93] Finally, it becomes easier to group the lowest-level discourse units into higher-level units if a broad superstructure is kept in mind.

Prominence and Peak

Prominence is a linguistic feature of discourse that highlights certain parts of the discourse in different ways. As Longacre put it, a discourse without prominence would be like a black camel walking across a desert on black sand at night.[94] It is natural in language for certain elements to be more prominent than others, because some elements are naturally supportive. Intonation in oral speech provides evidence of the information that speakers find prominent, while in written discourse the analyst must follow guidelines of discourse semantics, pragmatics, and context. These factors lead to different types of prominence that analysts identify, and each type is generally tied to a different method of macrostructural analysis.

---

[89] Longacre, *Philippine Languages*, 1:3–192.

[90] See his *Macrostructures*, 107–132.

[91] For much more elaboration, see van Dijk, *Macrostructures*, 107–132.

[92] Robert E. Longacre, *Hierarchy and Universality of Discourse Constituents in New Guinea Languages* (Georgetown University Press, 1972), 1:133.

[93] Brown and Yule, *Discourse Analysis*, 94–100.

[94] Robert E. Longacre, "Discourse Peak as Zone of Turbulence," in *Beyond the Sentence: Discourse and Sentential Form*, ed. Jessica R. Wirth (Karoma, 1985), 83.

The first type of prominence is binary and hierarchical. Contiguous units of discourse are connected through a coherence relation, with one unit being more prominent than the other. The second type is discovered through information structure. Persistent 'given information' or topics/themes may be taken as prominent because the majority of the 'new information' or comments/rhemes are "about" the persistent given information/topic/theme.[95] Particles may also mark prominence (e.g., ἰδέ). This type of prominence analysis is not hierarchical, but linear. The third type of prominence is based on where a concept or lexeme falls in a network of relations. One might rank prominence based on the amount of grammatical or conceptual ties it has, or on how high a concept sits in a hierarchy of schematic structures.[96] In either case, prominence is relative rather than binary. A fourth type of prominence is based on frequency of lexis or concept, with higher frequency correlating to higher prominence. This type is the most problematic, because certain words are necessarily common but obviously not prominent (e.g., definite articles and connectives), and because it ignores the importance of where words occur in discourse.

Peak is a concept of global prominence that is distinct from these previous types of prominence. There may be one or more peaks in a discourse, in which the author concentrates attention or leads to a sort of climax. Although, according to Longacre, who popularized the notion of peak, a discourse need not have a peak at all.[97] One of the values of discovering a discourse peak is that it can be used to classify surrounding portions of the text.[98] If one knows where a peak typically falls in the superstructure of a discourse type, then one can know what the pre-peak and post-peak schemas are likely to be.

The superstructure of the discourse can assist in finding the peak. In a narrative text, one peak will appear in the "climax" section. In a hortatory text, there may be one peak in the argument section and another peak in the hortatory section, with the latter being the more prominent peak. There are several other features of a text that may signal a peak, including tense shifts, special conjunctions or particles, concentration of participants ("crowding the stage"), rhetorical features, extra-long sentences, repetition or elaboration of events, embedded discourse, a change of location, unique and concentrated grammatical and syntactic features, a slowdown of narrative movement, extensive wordiness, and a change of genre.[99] Longacre's research focused on how different languages and

---

[95] For an extended treatment of this method, see Watson Todd, *Discourse Topics*, 87–106.

[96] De Beaugrande and Dressler, *Introduction to Textlinguistics*, 95–110; Watson Todd, *Discourse Topics*, 123–147.

[97] Longacre, *New Guinea Languages*, 1:134.

[98] Ibid., 135.

[99] Longacre, *New Guinea Languages*, 1:134–140; idem, *Grammar of Discourse*, 25–28; Peter Cotterrell, "A Question of Peak," *BT* 49, no. 1 (1998): 139–148; Richard and Karis Mansen, "The

discourse types manifested these linguistic features to signal discourse peaks. Some of these features are amenable to statistical analysis, which provides a more objective method of determining peak. A statistical analysis of peak is modeled by R. Bruce Terry in his essay on 1 Corinthians in this volume.

The concepts discussed in this section do not exhaust the field of DA by any means, but hopefully they give enough information so that the reader can understand the concepts as they are applied in the essays in this volume. I also hope that the reader has seen enough of the richness of DA that he or she is motivated to implement more of these concepts into the analysis of biblical texts.

Structure of Sentence and Paragraph in Guajiro Narrative Discourse," in *Discourse Grammar: Studies in Indigenous Languages of Colombia, Panama, and Ecuador* (Summer Institute of Linguistics, 1976), 1:153; Randall Buth, "Functional Grammar, Hebrew, and Aramaic: An Integrated Textlinguistic Approach to Syntax," in *Discourse Analysis of Biblical Literature: What It Is and What It Offers*, ed. Walter R. Bodine (Scholars Press, 1995), 90–93.

1

MATTHEW

DAVID J. CLARK AND TODD A. SCACEWATER

Human language is patterned activity. Prior to the 1970s, scholars concentrated on the patterns occurring in the phonological, morphological and syntactic levels of language at the maximum level of the sentence. Since the 1970s, however, greater interest has been shown in the patterning of larger stretches of language.[1] This essay analyzes the structure of the Gospel of Matthew and its constituent parts.

A major concern of the authors is with the translation of Scripture into other languages. It is often necessary for them to put themselves in the place of people reading the Gospel for the first time, bringing to it little or nothing in the way of Christian background. But however little people in this category may bring to the reading of Matthew by way of theological presuppositions, they must necessarily bring certain linguistic presuppositions.

These would include at least: 1) that the Gospel was put purposefully into the form in which it now stands, and 2) that it is a coherent whole. The naïve reader does not start by asking questions about sources, oral traditions, redactions, and so on. He normally assumes a text to be a coherent whole unless and until he finds that within his particular frame of reference and at his level of interpretation, it is not. In this study, therefore, we shall attempt to understand what the Gospel says as a literary unit in itself. Despite its clear relationships with other pieces of writing, including Mark and Luke, it does not make direct cross-

---

[1] See the introduction to this volume for a history of DA.

reference to them.[2] Matthew also has a close relationship with the OT, but this again does not alter its status as an independent unit in literary terms.

The labels for the analytical units proposed in this study are largely taken from drama. But before these terms are applied, the Gospel is divided into "blocks," which separate the "narrative" from the "discourse."[3] The discourse blocks are each analyzed as their content demands, and no regular scheme of internal labelling is applied to them. The dramatic terms of Act, Scene, and Episode are applied primarily to the narrative material. These terms are hierarchically related: a Scene consists of two or more Episodes; an Act consists of two or more Scenes. In addition to these Scenes, an Act contains also one or more of the five discourse blocks, though these stand outside the Scene structure.

In considering the semantic structure of the Gospel, it is much less easy to set up a hierarchy of terms. We might suggest such terms as Plot, Theme, Motif and Topic (in roughly descending order) but this is not a rigorous categorization. In this essay, the terms Theme and Motif are used quite frequently, but there is no clear-cut relationship established between them.

Macrostructure

The division of the Gospel into five discourses and alternating narrative sections is now standard.[4] These sections we call "blocks." The Gospel begins with a narrative block ("N block"), continues with a discourse block ("D block"), and continues alternating. Matthew intentionally signals the end of each D block with

---

[2] Scholars have sometimes tended to outline Matthew based on Mark's Gospel as a template, with Matthew's own additions appended somehow. E.g., W. C. Allen, *A Critical and Exegetical Commentary on the Gospel according to S. Matthew*, 3rd ed., ICC (T&T Clark, 1912), lxiii. A discourse analysis, however, should consider the work as it is and not start with preconceived notions of its structure. Even if Matthew did use Mark (and any other sources), he has compiled them into the form we now have for his own specific communicative purposes. Source- and redaction-critical concerns and discourse concerns are not mutually exclusive, but should not create *a priori* assumptions about the Gospel's structure. Otherwise, see U. Luz, *Matthew 1–7*, trans. J. E. Crouch, Hermeneia (Fortress, 2007), 2.

[3] In this context, the word "discourse" is used in the relatively non-technical sense familiar in Matthaean studies. It is not to be confused with the relatively technical usage within the discipline of linguistics in such expressions as "discourse analysis," "discourse structure," etc.

[4] The initial division of Matthew into five discourses was noticed by B. W. Bacon, "The 'Five Books' of Matthew against the Jews," *The Expositor* 15 (1918): 56–66 and especially his *Studies in Matthew* (Henry Holt & Co., 1930). Bacon supposed the Evangelist composed the Gospel into five books of the commandments of Jesus (mimicking the five books of Moses) to combat lawlessness in his own community. Chapters 1–2 and 26–28 were considered a preamble and epilogue, respectively. Much of Bacon's hypothesis has been abandoned, but the delimiting of five D blocks alternating with N blocks has remained.

the formula καὶ ἐγένετο ὅτε ἐτέλεσεν ὁ Ἰησοῦς ... (7:28; 11:1; 13:53; 19:1; 26:1). Though Jesus speaks, sometimes at length, within the narrative sections, Matthew only uses this formula at the end of the D blocks, thus signaling their function as units in the Gospel's structure.

All the remaining sections of the Gospel are regarded as N blocks. The N blocks form the framework into which the D blocks are embedded, since the latter are neither independent nor self-explanatory, and need the surrounding narrative to supply their context. However, the D blocks are easier to identify first, since they are, so to speak, the marked units.

Giving only the chapter numbers for simplicity's sake, the blocks are identified in Figure 1.1.

	N	D	N	D	N	D	N	D	N	D	N
chs.	1-4	5-7	8-9	10	11-12	13	14-17	18	19-22	23-25	26-28

Figure 1.1: N and D Blocks in Matthew's Gospel

Alongside this alternating pattern of N and D blocks, the Gospel provides literary clues to a division into three Acts. At the end of the first N block, Matthew records that Jesus was "teaching in their synagogues and preaching the gospel of the kingdom and healing every disease and every affliction" (4:23). This statement gives a map of the rest of Act 1 particularly, and more broadly also to the rest of the Gospel. The Sermon on the Mount is the first D block, which exemplifies his "teaching" and "preaching," while the N block immediately after the Sermon is filled with healing episodes.[5] The same phrase from 4:23 is then repeated in 9:35, giving a summary of Jesus' activity up to that point in his ministry. The repetition of the ministry outline brings a formal closure to Act 1, with all of 9:35–38 summarizing progress thus far and opening the way for the wider possibilities chronicled in subsequent chapters. Since chs. 1–9 constitute about one third of the Gospel, we see a fine balance in the posited three-fold division.

The transition from Act 1 to Act 2 is signaled not only by the literary clues from Matthew, but also by a major transition in Jesus' ministry. Just as in 4:23–25, so also in 9:35–38 the statement that Jesus was healing every disease and

---

[5] W. Weren makes the same observation ("The Macrostructure of Matthew's Gospel: A Proposal," *Biblica* 87, no. 2 [2006]: 192). Sometimes διδάσκων...καὶ κηρύσσων...καὶ θεραπεύων are taken as three coordinate elements signaling a three-fold ministry, but there is no clear evidence for a dichotomy between διδάσκων and κηρύσσων. So 4:23 is construed to mean that κηρύσσων τὸ εὐαγγέλιον τῆς βασιλείας is the *content* of διδάσκων ἐν ταῖς συναγωγαῖς αὐτῶν, not a parallel activity. In other words the construction is a hendiadys. This fits the succeeding chapters much better and is paralleled by the construction in 4:17, where the καὶ λέγειν· Μετανοεῖτε cannot be taken as anything but the content of κηρύσσειν.

affliction is followed by the observation that large crowds gathered to him. Jesus tells his disciples, "The harvest is plentiful, but the laborers are few; therefore pray earnestly to the Lord of the harvest to send out laborers into his harvest" (9:37–38, ESV). Act 2 then opens with the answer to that prayer. Jesus gives his disciples "authority over unclean spirits, to cast them out, and to heal every disease and every affliction" (10:1). Thus, Act 2 begins with the expansion of Jesus' ministry to include his disciples in order to better care for the "sheep without a shepherd" for whom Jesus had compassion (9:36). Act 2 begins with a D block (ch. 10) providing instruction for his disciples' sending, and contains five blocks total (with the alternating pattern D-N-D-N-D).

No "formulaic" evidence signals a transition to Act 3, but there is a semantic transition at the end of ch. 18. In 19:1, there is a decisive change of location. Apart from the brief excursion to Phoenicia in ch. 15, the record from 4:12 on is largely set in Galilee. The mention of leaving Galilee in 19:1 initiates the events leading to the climax of the record, and it therefore seems an appropriate point for a crucial structural break.[6] Formally it is unobtrusive, but this can be taken as a product of Matthew's literary craftsmanship. In a symphony or concerto, one movement sometimes leads into another without the music actually stopping, so may there not be something analogous in literature?[7]

---

[6] This break is also significant because Matthew, like Mark, refrains from recording any trips of Jesus to Jerusalem until this final journey begins at 19:1. Surely Jesus would have made pilgrimages to Jerusalem for religious observances, as John's Gospel records. That Matthew omits any journeys to Jerusalem prior to 19:1 shows that Matthew wants to create extra narrative drama and signal a final turning point in the Gospel. See also R. T. France, *Matthew*, NICNT (Eerdmans, 2007), 3–4.

[7] Another proposed three-part structure is 1:1–4:16; 4:17–16:20; 16:21–28:20, based on the formula "from that time on Jesus began to" (4:17; 16:21), which supposedly opens Part 2 and Part 3. See J. D. Kingsbury, *Matthew: Structure, Chronology, Kingdom* (SPCK, 1975), 7–8; D. R. Bauer, *The Structure of Matthew's Gospel: A Study in Literary Design*, JSNTSup 31 (Sheffield, 1988), esp. pp. 73–108. This division, however, creates three very uneven parts, cuts across the N blocks, and ignores the evidence we have presented for the transition between our proposed three Acts. For further criticisms, see esp. Frans Neirynck, "ΑΠΟ ΤΟΤΕ ΗΡΞΑΤΟ and the Structure of Matthew," *Ephemerides Theologicae Lovanienses* 64, no. 1 (1988): 21–59.

Another possibility is that we cannot discern any overall literary plan, an understandable position but perhaps too cautious and overly-dependent on redaction-critical observations. See, e.g., W. D. Davies and D. C. Allison, *The Gospel According to Saint Matthew*, ICC (T&T Clark, 1988), 1:58–72; R. H. Gundry, *Matthew: A Commentary on His Handbook for a Mixed Church under Persecution*, 2nd ed. (Eerdmans, 1994), 10–11.

Finally, one might attempt a narrative structure, such as Weren ("Macrostructure"). He views 1:1–4:11 as an overture, 26:17–28:20 as a finale, and 4:12–26:16 as the corpus. Rather than taking the N and D blocks as structural markers, he uses five "hinge texts" (4:12–17; 11:2–30; 16:13–28; 21:1–17; 26:1–16). The outer hinge texts connect the overture and finale with the corpus, while the inner four hinge texts divide the corpus into two divisions, each with two sections. The

The resulting discourse structure is as follows in Figure 1.2:[8]

Act 1	Narrative	chs.	1–4
	Discourse	chs.	5–7
	Narrative	chs.	8–9
Act 2	Discourse	ch.	10
	Narrative	chs.	11–12
	Discourse	ch.	13
	Narrative	chs.	14–17
	Discourse	ch.	18
Act 3	Narrative	chs.	19–22
	Discourse	chs.	23–25
	Narrative	chs.	26–28

Figure 1.2: The Discourse Structure of Matthew's Gospel

Within Act 1 and Act 3 there is a "key" pattern as it may be called, of blocks:

N D N

Within Act 2 there is a more elaborate version of the same pattern:

D N D N D

Acts 1–3 evince a key pattern again on a larger scale, with Acts 1 and 3 being of identical internal structure, and Act 2 a variation of the same structure:

Act 1 Act 2 Act 3

---

resulting structure is balanced and takes serious account of temporal and topographical data, but again the cutting across of N and D blocks seems unsatisfactory. There are also some problems in the structure, such as viewing 17:1 as the beginning of his journey toward Jerusalem, when Matthew does not signal such until 19:1. Other narrative approaches that also cut across the N and D blocks include F. Matera, "The Plot of Matthew's Gospel," *CBQ* 49 (1987): 233–253; W. Carter, "Kernels and Narrative Blocks: The Structure of Matthew's Gospel," *CBQ* 54 (1992): 463–481; H. Combrink, "The Structure of the Gospel of Matthew as Narrative," *TynBul* 34 (1983): 61–90.

[8] The precise boundaries of the blocks will be discussed below. Here only the chapter numbers are given for simplicity.

Notice also the balance in the distribution of the discourse blocks. Acts 1 and 3 each contain a single 3-chapter long block of discourse. Act 2 also contains a comparable amount of discourse, but here it is split into three single chapter blocks. These patterns are too symmetrical and too aesthetically pleasing to be either accidental or imaginary.[9]

Microstructures

With this larger structure in mind, we will now present a more detailed analysis of the three Acts of the Gospel. The analysis will help the reader better understand how each Act, Scene, and Episode fits into the larger structure and contributes to Matthew's literary plan for telling the story of Jesus.

Act 1: First N Block

The first N block of Act 1 breaks up fairly readily. The genealogy of 1:1–17 stands apart from the rest of the section, and perhaps ought not to be included.[10] It seems to be just as much a prologue to the whole Gospel as is John 1:1–18.

The birth narrative and associated events (1:18–2:23) constitute the next section (labelled Scene 1). It opens in 1:18 with a clear announcement of the content of the section and ends in 2:23 with a reference to the OT, which is a common way for Matthew to clinch a point. The scene divides into three episodes (1:18–25; 2:1–12; 2:13–23). Each of these is initiated with a genitive absolute construction, which throughout the Gospel commonly marks a transition to a new section. The third episode further divides into three sections: the flight into Egypt (2:13–15), the murder of the children (2:16–18), and the return from Egypt (2:19–23). All three close with an OT formula quotation peculiar to Matthew.

Scene 2 opens with a new topic, introduced by a rather vague temporal marker (3:1) and concludes with the important transitional paragraph, 4:23–25, which leads into the Sermon on the Mount. The scene is best analyzed as having three episodes. The first deals with the activities and preaching of John the Baptist and closes with the end of the direct quote of John's words (3:1–12). The second consists of a two-part preparation for Jesus' ministry, first his baptism in which the Father approves of the Son, and then the wilderness temptation, in which Jesus

---

[9] These patterns also fit with Matthew's penchant for three-part sections and for chiastic arrangements, noted by commentators such as Luz, *Matthew*, 5–8; Davies and Allison, *Matthew*, 1:58–72.

[10] Similarly, C. R. Smith, "Literary Evidence of a Fivefold Structure in the Gospel of Matthew," *NTS* 43 (1997): 549.

demonstrates his Spirit-empowered ability to overcome temptation and worship God alone.

The third episode (4:12–25) details the beginning of Jesus' ministry. It opens both with a link reference back to the (now completed) work of John and with a setting in terms of place. Verses 18–22 give the first (positive) response to the preaching of Jesus. Verses 23–25, as noted earlier, summarize the content and effects of Jesus' early ministry and set the stage for the rest of the Gospel, and of Act 1 especially. In the following D block (chs. 5–7), we are given an extended example of the διδάσκων (see 5:2; 7:28, 29); and in chs. 8–9 various examples of θεραπεύων (see 8:2, 3, 7, 8, 13, 16; 9:21, 22, 25, 30, 33), though other themes are also present in this section.

To sum up, then, Scene 2 shows a chain pattern (Figure 1.3).

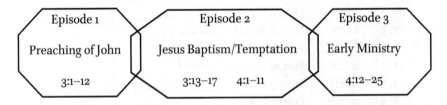

Figure 1.3: The Chain Pattern of Act 1, Scene 2

The first N block, then, follows a prologue that sets the Gospel in its cultural and historical context. The two following scenes exhibit Jesus' divine approval, his preparation for ministry and its inauguration, and also introduce the message of the kingdom of God and John's role in heralding its coming. The heavy use of OT citations throughout this first N block parallels the equally heavy use of the OT in the final N block (particularly the crucifixion, Scene 11, on which see below). Matthew therefore grounds the beginning and the conclusion of Jesus' ministry in OT prophecy and pattern.

Act 1: First D Block (The Sermon on the Mount)

This analysis sees the Sermon on the Mount as an exordium (the Beatitudes of 5:1–10), a series of seven principles (5:11–7:23), each accompanied by illustrations and/or applications, and a peroration (7:24–27). The exordium and peroration are both in the third person, while the principles and illustrations are all in the second person. Another key pattern arises, with brief opening and closing sections balancing each other on either side of the main body of the discourse (Figure 1.4).

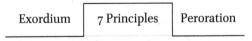

Figure 1.4: The Key Pattern of the Sermon on the Mount

The introductory words of 5:1–2 give the setting, and ἐδίδασκεν (5:2) evokes the διδάσκων aspect of Jesus' ministry stated in 4:23. The eight beatitudes immediately follow. They are totally asyndetic and have a balanced internal structure, all having the form of μακάριοι οἱ... ὅτι αὐτῶν/αὐτοί. The second clause of the first and last beatitudes (vv. 3 and 10) is identical, and all the intervening ones are different.[11] In the second halves of the six central beatitudes (vv. 4–9) there is a balance of active and passive verbal forms. The passive (avoiding the mention of God) predominates but the active occurs in the second and fifth places, thus giving a pattern of inverted parallelism, as diagrammed in Figure 1.5.

v. 3	αὐτῶν	Present
v. 4	αὐτοί	Future Passive
v. 5	αὐτοί	Future Active
v. 6	αὐτοί	Future Passive
v. 7	αὐτοί	Future Passive
v. 8	αὐτοί	Future Active
v. 9	αὐτοί	Future Passive
v. 10	αὐτῶν	Present

Figure 1.5: Inverted Parallelism in the Beatitudes

Next come the seven principles. The first (5:11–12) is usually tacked awkwardly onto the end of the beatitudes but should be considered the first principle. His disciples are blessed when they are persecuted for his sake, a principle that is supported in v. 12 and illustrated twice in vv. 13–16 (or three times, if the city on the hill is taken as a separate one). Persecution of this type arises because a follower of Jesus stands out against his background, often opposing its values and assumptions (like the prophets, 5:12).

While Jesus and his disciples must differ from the Tradition, the second principle states that there will also be continuity: they are not antinomians. The Law will not be abolished but given a fullness it never had before (5:17). Verses 18–20 expand on this principle, while 5:21–48 give six illustrations of how the Law is to be fulfilled in the new era (each illustration beginning with ἠκούσατε ὅτι ἐρρέθη, followed by the contrastive ἐγὼ δὲ λέγω ὑμῖν). These six illustrations constitute the longest section of the sermon, which presumably indicates the importance of this teaching for Matthew. A concluding comment (οὖν) summarizes the preceding teaching (5:48; cf. 6:31–34; 7:12).

---

[11] For a more detailed analysis of the discourse structure of the beatitudes, see Howard A. Hatton and David J. Clark, "From the Harp to the Sitar," *BT* 26, no. 1 (1975): 132–138.

The third principle (6:1–6:18) turns from the Law to religious practices, stating that religious activity should be directed toward God, not toward people (6:1). This principle is then applied in the three areas of almsgiving (6:2–4), prayer (6:5–15), and fasting (6:16–18). The application to prayer is much longer than the outer two, thus providing another key structure.

The fourth principle (6:19–34) deals with possessions and money. Worldly wealth is contrasted with heavenly, and the latter extolled (6:19–20). The rest of ch. 6 enlarges on this principle, with both illustrations (6:22–24) and applications (6:25–34).[12] A summary (vv. 31–34) introduced by οὖν wraps up this principle.

The fifth principle is laid down in 7:1 ("Judge not in order that you may not be judged"), and its reason added in 7:2. Verses 3-5 illustrate the point, while v. 6 gives a rider that while one must not judge, one also should not fail to discriminate. Thus, another key pattern emerges (Principle, Illustration, Rider).

The sixth principle ("Ask and it will be given to you," 7:7) is grounded in 7:8, illustrated in 7:9–11a, and concluded in 7:11b (cf. 7:6). Jesus uses an *a fortiori* argument—if even sinful human beings give good things to their children, how much greater is God's willingness to do the same for those who ask him. Verse 12 summarizes the principle by extending it to the general realm of communal life.

If the first six principles speak of the ethics of the kingdom, the seventh principle speaks figuratively of entry into the kingdom. The principle is given very tersely in v. 13a, while vv. 13b–14 give a contrasting parallel. Both false leaders (7:15–20) and false followers (7:21–23) fail to enter the narrow gate. The vivid dialogue scene and the high stakes of kingdom entry may suggest that this scene is the climax of the sermon.

The last few verses of the sermon (the peroration) give the final, overall summary of the entire discourse (μου τοὺς λόγους τούτους, 7:24, 26), again introduced by οὖν (cf. 5:48; 6:31–34; 7:12). In their position as a final challenge, they invite a response from *all* who hear. The introductory words of 5:1–2 are balanced by the narrative comment of 7:28–29, which contains the D-block closing formula, and a note on the reaction to Jesus' words. The recurrence of διδάσκων (v. 29) is another glimpse back to 4:23. But whereas in 4:24–25, the reaction to Jesus' activities is rather neutral, here it is recorded as the more positive one of amazement, because of his authoritative pronouncements.

Summarizing this D Block, it consists of an exordium of eight beatitudes, a main section of seven principles, and a peroration. Within the main section, each principle is reinforced by various illustrations and/or applications. With

---

[12] The "light of the body" (6:22–23) seems like an intrusion, but Matthew may here use a Jewish idiom that "a good eye" is a metaphor for liberality, while "an evil eye" refers to greed. See Clark, *Analyzing and Translating*, 29. Matthew 6:24, the following verse, may be an explanation of the "light of the body" saying in less cryptic language.

one major exception (the six applications of the second principle), these are distributed symmetrically, balanced around the fourth principle, as shown in Figure 1.6.

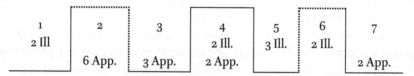

Figure 1.6: The Seven Principles and Their Illustrations in the First D Block

If the function of the first N block was to establish Jesus' divine approval, the preparation and inauguration of his ministry, and to introduce the kingdom and John's role in announcing its coming, this first D block functions to expound on the kingdom, both its ethics and its entry by genuine disciples.

Act 1: Second N Block

The second N block (8:1–9:38) divides into four scenes, numbered 3-6, continuing the numbering from the first N block. With 4:23 outlining the program for the Gospel as teaching/preaching and healing, and with Jesus just having concluded his first main teaching block, he now proceeds with his first dense section of healing.

Scene 3 (8:1–17) begins with a change of location (8:1) and concludes with an OT formula quotation peculiar to Matthew (8:17). The three healing episodes in Scene 3 create another key pattern, signaled in several ways.[13] Scene 4 (8:18–8:34) then records three reactions to Jesus. Whereas to this point the reaction has been positive (4:18–22; 4:23–25; 7:28–29), now the reactions become mixed (positive, 8:18–22; neutral, 8:23–27; negative, 8:28–34). Scenes 5 and 6 are set somewhat vaguely in "his own city" (9:1), presumably Capernaum. Scene 5 (9:1–17) contains three episodes detailing opposition to Jesus over his forgiving sins (9:1–8), his association with sinners (9:9–13), and his disciples' lack of fasting (9:14–17). Scene 6 (9:18–34) has three further episodes of healing (9:18–26; 9:27–31; 9:32–34). Of note is the blind men's recognition of Jesus as "Son of David" (9:27)—a theme fully suppressed by Jesus here—and the opposition of the religious leaders, who make their first charge of Jesus' empowerment by Satan (9:34).

The remaining verses (9:35–38) form an epilogue to round off this N Block and the whole of Act 1, while also pointing toward the widening ministry of Act 2. As noted earlier, Jesus' sight of the helpless crowds is the stimulus to his prayer for more workers to gather the lost into God's kingdom. In this thought lies the

---

[13] See Clark, *Analyzing and Translating*, 36–37.

link with the opening section of Act 2, in which the disciples are sent out to share in and enlarge the reach of Jesus' ministry.

The function of this second N block of Act 1 is therefore to follow up the first main teaching block about the kingdom (chs. 5–7) with detail on his healing ministry, and also to establish certain themes, such as mixed reactions to Jesus' ministry, including especially the opposition of the religious leaders, who charge Jesus with demonic influence (see Figure 1.7).

Scene 3	Scene 4	Scene 5	Scene 6		
3 Eps. of healing	3 Eps. of reaction	3 Eps. of opposition	1 Ep. healing	1 Ep. reaction	1 Ep. opposition

Figure 1.7: The Relationship between the Scenes in the Second N Block

Act 2: First D Block

Act 2 (chs. 10–18) has the pattern D-N-D-N-D. The three D Blocks are roughly chs. 10, 13, and 18. Prominent themes include those of John the Baptist and of the demand for a sign. The first demand for a sign is in 12:38, and initiates a lengthy response from Jesus. The demand is repeated at the beginning of ch. 16, and is again refused. Yet almost all the narrative material between these two points consists of dramatic signs. The two-fold demand for a sign in Matthew suggests it has structural significance. John the Baptist is mentioned at the beginning of both chs. 11 and 14 (cf. Act 1, Scene 2). John is also mentioned in ch. 17 (near the end of an N block), following the transfiguration, where he is identified with the Elijah of the eschatological interpretation of the scribes.

The first D block in Act 2 (10:1–11:1) opens and closes with setting material (10:1–4; 11:1) to set up the monologue (10:5–42). After Jesus' choice of twelve disciples to join his harvesting efforts (10:1), Matthew gives the names of the twelve in a way that evokes the genealogy that begins Act 1.

The actual monologue of 10:5–42 can be divided into four sections three of which have the phrase ἀμὴν λέγω ὑμῖν in their final sentence.[14] The first section (10:5–15) is concerned with the practical aspects of the mission. The second section (10:16–23) deals with the psychological aspects of the mission. The οὖν at the beginning of v. 26 suggests that vv. 24–25 should be closely linked with vv. 26–31, so the third section is 10:24–31. It gives the disciples the intellectual equipment

---

[14] On the use of ἀμὴν λέγω ὑμῖν as a discourse marker, esp. in Matthew, see Clark, *Analyzing and Translating*, 195–210.

for reconciling their impending rejection with the message that kingdom of heaven has come near (10:7). If the king himself will be rejected, so will the kingdom message. The final section (10:34–42) speaks of the spiritual demands of the mission upon its proponents. The closing verses (vv. 40–42) are something like an epilogue summarizing the results of the mission. Despite the opposition mentioned earlier, there will be those who receive and in their reception will find present blessing (v. 40) and future reward (v. 42).

A certain amount of parallelism can be observed between sections 1–2 and between sections 3–4. Perhaps this will be seen most easily if set out in parallel columns (Figure 1.8).

Some of the labels in Figure 1.8 are perhaps a bit vague, but the parallels are evident enough to be significant. Also important is the prominence of eschatological content at the end of each of the four sections, which is unlikely to be accidental.

vv.	Section 1	Section 2	vv.
5–6	Imperatives Animal Analogy πρόβατα	Imperatives Animal analogies πρόβατα λύκοι, ὄφεις, περιστεραί	16–17a
7–8	Content of the mission	Reaction to the mission	17b–18
9–10	Absence of physical anxiety	Absence of emotional anxiety	19–20
11–14	Reactions to the messenger	Reactions to the messenger	21–22
15	Eschatological implications	Eschatological implications	23
	Section 3	Section 4	
24–25	Analogies from human relationships	Analogies from human relationships	34–36
26–31	Whom to fear	Whom to love	37–39
32–33	Eschatological implications	Eschatological implications	40–42

Figure 1.8: Parallelism between Sections in Act 2, D Block 1

The function of this D block is thus to prepare the disciples for their mission to preach the kingdom of heaven to "the lost sheep of the house of Israel" (10:5–6). They have now been enlisted as workers in the great harvest, equipped with Jesus' authority, and sent out with instructions on how to go about their journey and how to deal with their impending rejection.

Act 2: First N Block

Each N block in Act 2 can be said to constitute a scene. Thus, Scene 1 is coterminous with the first N Block (11:2–12:45). It may be divided into five episodes, after the third of which there occurs a brief editorial comment which we label an interlude.

Episode 1 is the longest and most complex (11:2–30). A question to Jesus from the imprisoned John through his disciples ("Are you he who is to come?") triggers a lengthy response from Jesus. In Isaianic language, he gives a veiled "yes." As the disciples return to John, Jesus addresses the crowd about the significance of John (11:7b–19), the woeful response of certain towns to his miracles (11:20–24), and a prayer of thanksgiving for the Son's unique role in salvation history with an offer for the weary to come to him for rest (11:25–30). If John the Baptist closed the old era, here is something of what the new era holds.

The next two short episodes are both concerned with Sabbath observance. In episode 2 (12:1–8), the Pharisees object to the disciples plucking grain (working) on the Sabbath, and Jesus defends them from the OT. In episode 3 (12:9–14), the Pharisees object to Jesus healing on the Sabbath, to which Jesus responds by proving their hypocrisy and thus prioritizing man over the Sabbath. In response, the Pharisees plot to do away with Jesus, which is both the logical outcome of the attitude that crowned Act 1 (9:34), and a forward look to the climax of the Gospel in Act 3.

After an interlude (12.15–21) in which Matthew describes Jesus withdrawing to another place and healing many—an activity which Matthew connects with the Servant of Isa 42—episode 4 (12:22–37) narrates a blind and dumb man being healed (v. 22), which sets up another charge of demonic inspiration by the Pharisees. (The crowds, on the other hand, draw potential Messianic implications from the miracle.) Jesus retorts that a divided kingdom cannot stand (12:25–26), that the kingdom is present through his works (12:28), and that the Pharisees' evil hearts will witness against them on judgment day (12:31–37).

In episode 5 (12:38–45), we reach the climax of the scene in the demand for a sign, which Jesus scathingly rejects (except for a veiled reference to the resurrection via the analogy of Jonah's experience). In this he links two themes which have been increasingly prominent in this scene: the superiority of the new over the old and the certainty of future judgment (12:41–42).[15] The Pharisees' lives should have been purified and adorned by their religion, but they had in fact become worse than those who knew nothing of it. And through their influence the whole nation/generation (γενεά) had become similarly infected.

Thus, the scene ends with a head-on confrontation between the old and the new. Figure 1.9 shows the five episodes, divided into three parts based on their

---

[15] Judgment has been mentioned specifically in 10:15, 11:22, 24; 12:36, 41 and 42, and referred to also in 10:23, 26, 32–33, 42; 12:32. The superiority of the new over the old has occurred in 11:11–14, 21, 23, 12:6, 8, 28; this theme can also be traced in Act 1, e.g. at 3:11 and 9:16–17, as well as the six ἐρρέθη ... ἐγὼ δὲ λέγω ὑμῖν occurrences in ch. 5.

foci. From here the account moves into the somewhat calmer waters of the next D Block, which elaborates on the spread of the new, namely, the coming of the kingdom of heaven.

Episode 1	Episodes 2–3	Episodes 4–5
11:2–30: John – the end of the old era	12:1–21: Jesus – the Lord of the new era	12:22–45: the break between old and new

Figure 1.9: Episodes in Act 2, Scene 1

Act 2: Second D Block

This D block (12:46–13:58) includes wider setting material (12:46–50; 13:53–58) and more immediate setting material (13:1–3a, 51b–52a). The internal setting especially differentiates this D block from the previous two (13:10–11a, 24a, 31a, 33a, 36–37a, 51b–52a). In the wider setting material, members of the immediate nuclear family of Jesus are featured (12:46–50). In the first, Jesus uses their presence to show how spiritual relationships transcend physical ones. In the second (13:55-56), the people of Nazareth use their presence as an excuse for recognizing nothing beyond Jesus' natural relationships. These two incidents, then, form a complementary and appropriate setting for the D block whose main elements concern the growth of the kingdom of heaven, i.e., the manner in which human relationships can be changed and transcended.

On the basis of its internal setting material, the remainder of the block, 13:1–52, can be divided as in Figure 1.10.

Setting 1–3a	Setting 24a	
Parable 3b–9	Parable 24b–30	Parables 44–48
Setting 10–11a	Setting 31a	Interpretation 49–50
Comment 11b–17	Parable 31b–32	Setting 51–52a
Interpretation 18–23	Setting 33a	Comment 52b
	Parable 33b	
	Comment 34–35	
	Setting 36–37a	
	Interpretation 37b–43	

Figure 1.10: Divisions of Chapter 13 with Internal Setting Material

Why there is so much apparently trivial setting material is hard to determine. If we omit it and concentrate on the rest, a pattern becomes clearer (Figure 1.11).

Parable	Parables	Parables
Comment	Editorial comment	Interpretation
Interpretation	Interpretation	Comment

Figure 1.11: Divisions of Chapter 13 without Internal Setting Material

This is the first use of parables in this Gospel (later than in the framework of Mark and Luke). Perhaps the deliberate concentration of parables in ch. 13 compelled the author to comment on their nature and use.

The first parable is given to the crowds (v. 2) whereas the interpretation is for the disciples alone (v. 10). In v. 24 we are given the impression that the next three parables are for the disciples alone, but v. 34 makes it clear that the crowds have been in view again. The interpretation is again only for the disciples (v. 36), and so it seems, in the light of v. 51, are the final three short parables (vv. 44–48). The setting pieces are then much more concerned in this block with audience than with location and time as is usual elsewhere. The frequent change of audience perhaps accounts in part for the frequency of the setting pieces, though in vv. 31 and 33 they seem simply to mark the end of one parable and the beginning of the next.

Just as in Mark's Gospel, the parable of the sower is foundational because of the explanation given to the disciples about the purpose of the parables (Matt 13:10–17; cf. Mark 4:1–20). When his disciples ask him why he speaks in parables (13:10), Jesus answers that he does so "because seeing they do not see, and hearing they do not hear, nor do they understand" (13:13). He then says that Isa 6:9–10 is fulfilled among his Jewish audience. His disciples, however, are blessed because they perceive and hear, for it has been given them to know the mystery of the kingdom of heaven (13:11). The interpretation of this explanation by Jesus is difficult and has been handled in various ways, but two things are clear. First, the parables somehow expound the "mystery of the kingdom." Second, the true meanings of the parables are (generally or to the fullest extent) revealed to those who have not merited the same judgment as those who rejected Isaiah's message (Isa 6:9–10; 53:1; cf. John 12:37–43).

In the second section of the chapter (13:24–43) there are six parables in two groups of three. The first group of parables all begin with a statement of their figurative nature, "the kingdom of heaven may be compared to [or 'is like']" (vv. 24, 31, 33). In the second group there are three very short parables emphasizing the value of the kingdom and its eschatological newness that surpasses that of the old order. The wider setting material sets up an implied response for the reader: one may choose familial and earthly relationships as supreme, or transcendent kingdom relationships, preeminently with its king, Jesus.

In summary, this D Block contains a long didactic section embedded in briefer narrative settings. Thus, there is a key pattern (Figure 1.12).

Setting	Teaching	Setting
12:46–13:3a	13:3b–52	13:53–58

Figure 1.12: The Key Pattern of Act 2, D Block 2

If the function of the first D block (chs. 5–7) was to expound the ethics of the kingdom and an invitation to it, and the next D block (ch. 10) functions to prepare Jesus' followers for preaching the message of the kingdom and being rejected, then this D block (ch. 13) provides extensive parabolic teaching on the nature of the kingdom. They must know what exactly the kingdom is as they go out to preach it, especially if they are to suffer persecution for the sake of Jesus and his message. The parables also give further explanation of why the message will be rejected.

Act 2: Second N Block

This second N block of Act 2 (14:1–17:23) includes two scenes (14:1–15:39; 16:1–17:23). The first (Scene 2 of Act 2) is enclosed by the two demands for a sign and contains six episodes, all but the first marked off by a change of location (14:13, 22, 34; 15:21, 29).

First, the narrative reintroduces John the Baptist and relates his death at the hands of Herod Antipas, signaling the end of the old era (14:1–12; cf. 11:11–14; 17:12–13). On hearing the news of John's murder, Jesus seeks solitude but is followed by crowds, the 5,000 of whom he heals and feeds miraculously (14:13–21). Jesus then sought again his lonely prayer time, which was only interrupted by the storm at sea, through which he walked to his disciples. When the storm ceased, the disciples declared, "You really are the Son of God" (14:33, cf. ἐγώ εἰμι in 14:27). Later, in spite of Jesus' healing abilities and their widespread value, the Pharisees complain that Jesus' disciples do not follow the handwashing "traditions of the elders" (14:34–15:20). In contrast with the Pharisees' opposition, the fifth episode (15:21–28) gives an example of outstanding faith—by a Gentile (cf. 8:5–13)!

The sixth and final episode (15:29–39) combines a rehearsal of Jesus' general healing powers with another feeding miracle (the 4,000). Verses 29–31 provide the final and most detailed of all the general summaries of healing (4:23–24; 8:16; 9:35; 14:34–36). Again, the crowd's positive response (15:31) contrasts with the opposition of the religious establishment. The repetition of a feeding miracle combined with the final summary of the healing miracles thus forms a suitable culmination to the section on signs, and a poignant contrast with the renewed demand for a sign which follows.

Scene 2 throughout connects thematically with many parts of Matthew, as Figure 1.13 illustrates.

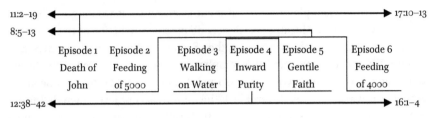

Figure 1.13: Thematic Connections with Act 2, Scene 2

Scene 3 (16:1–17:23) is difficult to divide clearly into episodes, but four are possible, each falling into two phases (a scheme that is admittedly somewhat arbitrary): 16:1–12; 16:13–28; 17:1–13; 17:14–23. The first and last episodes are both concerned with lack of adequate faith, while the two central episodes are both concerned with various aspects of Messiahship.

The first episode renews the demand for a sign by both the Pharisees and the Sadducees (16:1; cf. 12:38–39). The joint appearance of both Jewish parties (not mentioned together since 3:7) indicates the buildup of opposition to Jesus.

The focus then shifts to Jesus' Messianic identity. Jesus asks his disciples who they believe he is, and Peter responds with direct revelation that Jesus is "the Christ, the Son of the living God" (16:16). Jesus then entrusts the Twelve with his authority on earth (16:18–20), a deepened role from 10:1, and invites them to join his Messianic destiny of glory through death and resurrection (16:24–28). This episode brings to a close the development of Jesus as teacher and healer while also opening up the avenue to the cross and resurrection. Jesus' private acceptance of a Messianic title is a new development, but even so he immediately redefines it.

In the third episode (17:1–8), Jesus' true nature is finally seen directly. The mention of Moses and Elijah is a clear connection with God's purposes in the old era, and the voice from the cloud gives divine approval to the course of the ministry, as in 3:17 it gave approval to its inception. When he tells the disciples not to reveal this vision until his resurrection, they ask about Elijah's eschatological role, which Jesus claims has already been fulfilled by John the Baptist. Jesus reminds them that he would suffer the same fate as John, thus continuing to temper their understanding of Messiahship.

The fourth episode (17:14–23) is somewhat surprising since the disciples are rebuked for their inability to cast out a demon just after the two previous climactic episodes. They are chastised as faithless and "of little faith" (ἄπιστος v. 17; ὀλιγοπιστία v. 20), with ὀλιγόπιστος used elsewhere as a harsh reproach (6:30; 8:26; 14:31; 16:8). By contrast, if only they could have genuine faith, they could move mountains (16:20). The next two verses reiterate Jesus' passion prediction. The gloomy reaction of the disciples (16:23) shows how very far they still were from understanding the true nature of Jesus' Messiahship. Perhaps we can take this as a further example of their "little faith," and if so, it would go some way towards explaining the location of the second passion prediction at this point.

If this structural analysis is correct, then Scene 3 is chiastic, with the Messianic episodes in the center (and thus emphasized), with the center of the Scene acting as the thematic pivot of the Gospel. While Jesus' identity has been revealed in private, his disciples still lack the faith to accept Jesus' own definition of Messiahship, and have yet to embrace their call to die with him. Perhaps now that the invitation to join Jesus has become a call to die, Matthew's implicit participation of the reader in Jesus' invitation is stronger than at any other point in the Gospel.

The main function of Scene 3, then, is to wrap up the initial phase of Jesus' ministry, to reveal his true identity to his disciples (and the Gospel reader), to strengthen opposition to Jesus, and to set the course for the rest of Jesus' mission: death, resurrection, and glory. Figure 1.14 gives an oversimplified visual of this scene.

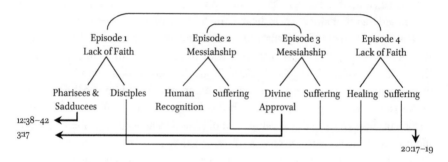

Figure 1.14: The Structure of Act 2, Second N Block

Act 2: Third D Block

This block, including setting material, extends from 17:24 to 19:2. The incident of the temple tax (17:24–27) is unique to Matthew and is taken here as setting up the discourse. Jesus submits to the temple tax voluntarily rather than as a duty, and this attitude exemplifies the kingdom values that Jesus will teach in the discourse. That Peter is singled out by the tax collectors as perhaps the most prominent of Jesus' followers may set up the occasion for the question: "Who is the greatest in the kingdom?" (18:1), i.e., "Why is Peter assumed to be the chief among us?" Support for this possibility is, first, that 18:1 says this question came in the same hour as the temple tax episode, and second, the question begins with a post-positive ἄρα, which elsewhere in the Gospels refers backwards.[16]

---

[16] A check of the twenty occurrences of ἄρα in the Synoptics and Acts shows that in 17 cases ἄρα refers backwards to a previous point in the argument, or draws a conclusion from a set

The monologue section of this block (18:3–35) is dominated by two questions, the first posed by the disciples in 18:1, and the second by Peter in 18:21. The "secondary setting" of v. 2, Jesus setting a child in the midst of the disciples in response to their question, is crucial for the whole of this first section of the monologue. Those who want a part in the kingdom and to be great in it must become like a child. God cares even for the least (self-)important, as a shepherd cares for even one lost sheep (18:10–14). The following section on brotherly reconciliation may deal with the question of greatness as shown by the handling of discord in personal relationships. After Peter's second question in 18:21, Jesus gives a direct answer ("not seven times, but seventy times seven," v. 22), which he expands on for the rest of the discourse in the parable of the unforgiving servant (18:23–35).

The terminal setting (19:1–2) contains the D block closing formula, and the important change of location into Judea "beyond the Jordan" which is taken as marking the end of Act 2. Involved in the journey from Galilee to Transjordan are crowds still seeking healing. Thus is the stage set for the third and final act.

We summarize this D Block in Figure 1.15, where arrows show the links of thought.

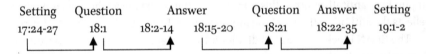

Setting	Question	Answer		Question	Answer	Setting
17:24-27	18:1	18:2-14	18:15-20	18:21	18:22-35	19:1-2

Figure 1.15: Flow of Thought in Chapter 18 Discourse

This D block functions to provide an important check on the disciples' future ministry. While they have been given divine insight into Jesus' identity, granted Jesus' authority, and given the keys to bind and unbind on earth, they must remember that the measure of greatness in the kingdom of heaven is not power but humility. They must become as children if they wish to be great. They must be reconciled with their brother when necessary and forgive innumerable times. They should never forget what they have been forgiven, so that they will not lord it over others. In short, this discourse functions to begin preparing the disciples to take up Jesus' ministry—with Jesus' own attitude and spirit—once he is crucified.

---

of events or circumstances. In the three residual examples, the ἄρα follows εἰ in the protasis of a conditional clause, but even in these places, the condition is based on information given in the earlier part of the same sentence. The six other instances of ἄρα in Matthew all contain a clear reference to what has preceded (7:20; 12:28; 17:26; 19:25, 27; 24:45) and it is probable therefore that the same is true here. The ἄρα in 18:1 looks back not only to the ἄρα of 17:26, but to the whole argument of 17:25–27, which, as suggested before, provides the setting for the question in 18:1.

Summary of Act 2

Act 2, bearing the structure D-N-D-N-D, advances Jesus' ministry through the pivotal confession of Peter and Jesus' prediction of his death and resurrection. The three discourses prepare the disciples for their gospel-preaching role, teach them more about the nature of the kingdom they will be heralding, and remind them that their greatness depends on their humility and service. The N blocks advance themes such as the gradual revelation of Jesus' identity, the growing opposition to Jesus, the end of the old era and the inauguration of the new, and include sufficient signs to implicitly provide the evidence demanded by the religious leaders, which are rejected anyway. All that is left is for Jesus' prediction to be fulfilled, but first he must lock horns a few more times with the religious leaders and equip his disciples even more for the near and distant future.

Act 3: First N Block

Act 3 embraces the rest of the Gospel, chs. 19–28. Its structure is N-D-N (chs. 19–22; 23–25; 26–28). All three are considerably longer than any previous block and give a total of 450 verses, as against approximately 350 for Act 2 and 270 for Act 1. In purely quantitative terms, this may seem rather unbalanced, but presumably it reflects the author's estimate of the importance of the last period of Jesus' ministry.

   The first N block (19:3–22:46) divides into six scenes, each containing three or four episodes. In the first scene (19:3–9), Jesus clashes again with the religious leadership and their tradition. When they ask him about divorce, Jesus presents marriage as an indissoluble union. While the disciples struggle to accept this teaching, Jesus commends celibacy for the sake of the kingdom (19:10–12). Lest this teaching create false expectations, Jesus goes out of his way to bless some children nearby, showing that marriage (the usual result of which is children) is the natural and typical state even for kingdom workers (19:13–15).

   In Scene 2, the rich young man seeks the requirements for eternal life. Jesus' reply to sell all he has and give it to the poor is an *ad hominem* challenge to break down the barriers that prevented his full commitment to the kingdom. The young man's (presumable) failure to accept the challenge (19:22) leads Jesus to proclaim the difficulties of the rich entering the kingdom of heaven, along with the blessings that come to those who are able to enter it (19:23–30). The following parable supports Jesus' call to abandon trust in riches by portraying God (represented by the householder) as one who will ensure that each kingdom worker has what he or she needs.[17]

---

[17] This seems to be the point of the parable; not so much that the householder may do what he wants with his money, but that the workers surely lived at subsistence level and required a full day's pay to survive. Especially since those who were hired last were not being

Scene 3 opens, significantly, with "as Jesus was going up to Jerusalem..." (20:17). While Matthew does not structure his Gospel around Jesus' journey to Jerusalem as does Luke (see Luke 9:53–19:44), certainly once the journey has begun there is no turning back. That the third passion prediction is included here is apropos. Its detail provides a roadmap for the rest of Act 3 (cf. 4:23 for Act 1): Jesus will be betrayed, condemned, "mocked and scourged and crucified," and then will rise on the third day (20:17–19). Ironically, just afterwards the mother of James and John requests that they be first in the kingdom, to which Jesus responds that they must share his suffering in order to share his glory (20:20–28). Finally, when two blind men again address Jesus as "Son of David" (cf. 9:27), he no longer denies it but rather substantiates it symbolically (but not yet explicitly) in the triumphal entry.

The fourth scene (21:1–22) includes three episodes linked to Jesus' ministry in Jerusalem. First (21:1–11), Jesus receives the Messianic title "Son of David" not only from two men, but from an entire crowd in Jerusalem. Second (21:12–17), Jesus prophetically disrupted the business activities of the temple in order to demonstrate the need for restoring its proper spiritual purpose, which brings a further challenge from the chief priests and scribes. Third (21:18–22), Jesus used the wonder of the disciples about the cursing of the fig tree to teach a lesson on the potential of believing prayer.

The two remaining scenes consist almost entirely of a dialogue in which Jesus and his opponents are in open confrontation. This has been foreshadowed in 9:1–17 and developed in 12:1–14, 22–45; 15:1–20; 16:1–4. The fifth scene (21:23–22:14) opens with an attack on Jesus by the establishment, who inquire about his authority (21:23–27). Jesus stifled their criticism by pinning them into a corner about John the Baptist's authority. He uses the parable of the two sons and that of the vineyard tenants to portray his opponents as spiritually dull and near to judgment (21:28–32, 33–46). The parable of the wedding feast emphasizes that the rejection of unbelieving Israel is based on their own willful and persistent refusal to accept God's invitation (22:1–14).

The sixth and final scene (22:15–46) includes three questions put to Jesus by his enemies attempting to trap him, followed by a question put by him to them. First, the Pharisees with the Herodians try to trap Jesus on the matter of taxes, but Jesus neatly turned their attack into an unforgettable lesson on the twin responsibilities of man to God and to society (22:15–22). The Sadducees concoct an improbable marital situation with metaphysical implications, but Jesus sidesteps their question, declaring it to reveal the defectiveness of their knowledge both

---

lazy, but were waiting for work, the householder is happy to pay them enough to survive, even though they did not "earn" it. So God will be with his children. For this interpretation see Joachim Jeremias, *The Parables of Jesus*, 2nd rev. ed. (Charles Scribner's Sons, 1972), 37.

scripturally and experientially (22:23–33). When asked about the greatest commandment, Jesus answered masterfully that the thrust of the law and the prophets
is the twofold duty of love to God and to man (22:34–40). Finally, Jesus asks his
interrogators (22:41–46) why it is that the Messiah, who comes from David's line,
will be David's "Lord." Their dullness could not be penetrated, but they at least
recognized their theological impotence and ceased their subtle questions.

In the six scenes of this N block, Jesus deals with a variety of topics, mostly in
dialogue with his disciples or his opponents. Jesus has begun to accept Messianic
ascriptions, but only in a veiled and symbolic way, and not yet explicitly. The
block functions to heighten the tension between Jesus and the establishment, to
move closer toward Jesus' open acceptance of the Messianic title, and to demonstrate his theological superiority over the tradition of the Jewish leaders. Figure
1.16 represents the N block thematically.

Scene 1	Scene 2	Scene 3	Scene 4
Divorce	Wealth	The Suffering Servant	Triumphal Entry
Celibacy	Its Significance	The Serving Lord	Cleansed Temple
Children	Rewards	The Coming King	Cursed Fig Tree

Scene 5		Scene 6	
	Obedience	Taxes	
Authority	Fruitfulness	Resurrection	The Messiah
	Responsiveness	Love	

Figure 1.16: The Structure of Act 3, N Block 1

Act 3: First D Block

This block (23:1–26:2) is set in the temple in the last week of Jesus' ministry
(21:23), and in 23:1 Matthew adds that the audience initially included both disciples and "the crowds." In 26:1 the discourse closing formula occurs, and is linked
with an announcement of the imminence of the passion. This serves both as a
backward glance to the three passion predictions, and as a topical link with the
plot against Jesus that immediately follows. The block divides into two, based on
changes of location (to the Mount of Olives), audience (narrowed down to the
disciples), and topic (eschatology) signaled in 24:1–4.[18]

[18] Whether this final D block includes ch. 23 is debated. See an extensive list of those who
include or exclude it in J. Hood, "Matthew 23–25: The Extent of Jesus' Fifth Discourse," *JBL* 128,
no. 3 (2009): 529–530. In favor of excising ch. 23 is the change of setting and partial change of
audience (so argues, e.g., Kingsbury, *Matthew*, 4–5 and other sources cited therein). Howev-

The first section (23:2–39), like the Sermon on the Mount, has an introductory section (23:2–12), a longer central section (23:13–36), and a concluding brief lament over Jerusalem (23:37–39). The first section states generally that the scribes and Pharisees "sit on Moses' seat," so the people should therefore observe whatever they say, but not what they do (23:2–3). Verses 4–12 expand to state what the leaders do and what the crowds and his disciples should do instead. The final saying that the greatest must be a servant echoes the last D block (ch. 18). The main section (23:13–36), like the main section of the Sermon on the Mount, has seven parts, each opening with "Woe to you, scribes and Pharisees, hypocrites" (23:13, 15, 23, 25, 27, 29; 23:16 varies with "Woe to you, blind guides who say...").[19] Each woe formula except the third is followed by a reason introduced by ὅτι. The concluding lament (23:37–39) connects this D block with the preceding and following N blocks that narrate the journey toward the Jerusalem-based crucifixion. Verse 39 must in its present position refer to the Parousia, which would then connect with the eschatological material in the following chapter.

The second section of this D block (24:1–25:46) is the most difficult section of the Gospel, and preconceived eschatological schemes make it even more difficult. Yet, a thematic structure is clear and will be kept in focus. Jesus' words on the destruction of the Temple (24:2) seem to provoke the disciples' question in v. 3, which is the key to the structure of the next two chapters. The disciples ask two questions, the first simple in form ("when will these things be?"), and the second complex ("what will be the sign of your coming and of the close of the age?"). Chiastically, in 24:36–25:30, the second question is taken up first, with the transition from addressing the second question to addressing the first signaled by περὶ δὲ in 24:36.[20]

Answering the second question first, Jesus gives initially the negative indications of his coming (24:4–6), then its positive indications (24:7–14), all practical

---

er, the discourse clearly begins in ch. 23 and the discourse-ending formula does not occur until 26:1. Chapter 23 occurs in the temple, while chs. 24–25 are spoken in response to the disciples pointing out the buildings of the temple to Jesus (24:1–3). Chapters 23 and 24 both contain judgments on the religious authorities. The change of location therefore does not override the thematic continuity between the chapters and the structural signal by Matthew. The disciples are also a constant part of the audience in both sections. Hood also notes the change of setting in ch. 13, which is not taken to signal two distinct discourses ("Matthew," 531).

[19] On the possibility of including v. 14 as original, and on the resultant discourse structure, see Clark, *Analyzing and Translating*, 83–85.

[20] The phrase περὶ δὲ is used in various writings to signal a change in topic, sometimes as a response to a previously asked question. E.g., 1 Cor 7:1, 25; 8:1, 12:1, 16:1, 12; 1 Thess 4:9; 5:1; Did. 6.3; 7.1; 9.1; 11.3. See Todd Scacewater, "Economic Ethics in the Didache," in *Written for Our Instruction: Essays in Honor of William Varner*, ed. Abner Chou (Fontes, forthcoming); also R. Bruce Terry, "1 Corinthians," pp. 234–239 in this volume.

in nature and ethical in import. Verses 15–31 narrow the focus to the tribulation (θλῖψις vv. 9, 21, 29) and its after-effects. These verses seem to begin with descriptions applicable to the siege of Jerusalem in AD 66–70, and end with material which can only be futuristic. The transition happens somewhere within vv. 21–22. Verses 32–35 zoom out again to give a symbolic lesson on the indications of his coming. Just as in nature there are clear signs of the advancing temporal seasons, so the discerning should be able to detect signs of the spiritual season.

Verse 36a marks a transition to answering the first question ("when will these things be?"), but whereas in v. 3 the disciples seemed to be asking when the destruction of the Temple (v. 2) would take place, in his answer Jesus seems to be dealing with when the Parousia will take place (vv. 37, 39, 44). It seems the fall of Jerusalem is somehow symbolic of the end time (as it seems to be in vv. 15–27). Jesus first answers the question negatively ("no one knows...but the Father," 24:36). Nevertheless certain general characteristics can be given, in descriptions that are so mundane as to be unhelpful. This ordinariness suggests that the end could come at any time, which is consistent with the morals drawn. The morals are that believers must be watchful (γρηγορεῖτε, v. 42 and ἕτοιμοι, v. 44) and faithful (πιστὸς...καὶ φρόνιμος, v. 45). These two needs are illustrated, respectively, by the parable of the ten girls (25:1–13) and that of the talents (25:14–30).

Jesus brings the discourse to a climax in 25:31–46, which moves from the Parousia to judgment. The opening phrase "when the Son of man comes" connects with the disciples' first question ("when will these things be?" [24:3]), while the separation of faithful from unfaithful connects with much of the rest of the discourse. The judgment scene is in two contrasting and closely parallel halves (25:31–40, 41–46), both concluded by a sentence beginning with ἀμὴν λέγω ὑμῖν (25:40, 45).

To sum up the Olivet section of this final D block, each question is first answered negatively and then positively, and in each answer the second half expands on some particular feature(s) of the first. The first answer (to the second question) contains a brief summary to which there is no parallel in the second answer. The final section on the judgment draws together themes from both answers, and goes beyond what the questions originally asked. (Figure 1.17 gives a visual summary of this final D block.) Though these chapters have often been used in the construction of programs for the end-time, we should note again the heavy ethical emphasis that pervades them (24:4, 6, 13, 23, 42, 44, 46; 25:13, 21, 23, 35, 36, 42, 43). It can hardly be repeated too often that what Scripture says about the future, it says so that we may be equipped with right attitudes rather than right answers.

The function of this final D block is to prepare his disciples to carry out their mission on Jesus' behalf once he has been crucified, has risen again, and has ascended. The discourse brings to a head many themes from the Gospel, including Jesus as the Son of Man who is here revealed as the eschatological judge. The disciples are warned against false prophets and false messiahs and given general indications of the Son's returning. They may take solace in the judgment, when all their persecution (ch. 10) will be recompensed. They should also be motivated to spread the gospel of the kingdom so that men and women everywhere may escape this terrible eschatological judgment.

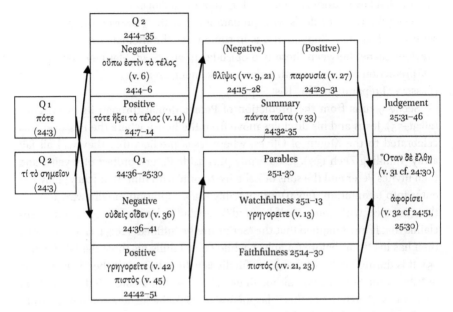

Figure 1.17: The Structure of the Eschatological Discourse. Arrows indicate the connections of thought.

Act 3: Second N Block

This final N block (chs. 26–28) concludes the Gospel and divides into six scenes (numbered 7–12) with a short epilogue. The narrative is much more continuous in this section than in any previous section and, to that extent, any division into scenes is rather more arbitrary than previous divisions. However, in most cases there is some credible unity of theme to hold the scene together and the key pattern is often evident. The scenes divide as follows:

Scene 7: 26:1–16
Scene 8: 26:17–30
Scene 9: 26:31–75
Scene 10: 27:1–14
Scene 11: 27:15–61
Scene 12: 27:62–28:15
Epilogue: 28:16–20.

Scene 7 (26:1–16) opens with Jesus' prediction to his disciples that "after two days the Passover is coming, and the Son of Man will be delivered up to be crucified" (26:2). At the end of the scene, the authorities plot his arrest and carry it out, but in between the two episodes is the anointing of Jesus to prepare him for his burial. A key pattern is evident (Plot, Anointing, Plot).

Scene 8 (26:17–30) deals with preparations for the Passover and then a description of the Last Supper, and is in some ways the thematic converse of the previous scene. Between these two episodes in 26:20–25, Matthew narrates Jesus' prediction of the plot with Judas' involvement, creating another key pattern (Passover Preparation, Plot, Last Supper).

Scene 9 runs from the prediction of Peter's denial through its occurrence (26:31–75). Jesus and his disciples move from the house where the Passover was celebrated to the Mount of Olives, where Jesus predicts that they will all fall away (fulfilling Zech 13:7). Jesus firmly puts aside Peter's protest of loyalty, and then invites Peter and the sons of Zebedee to pray with him "that [they] may not enter into temptation" (26:41), presumably the temptation to fall away. Jesus is then arrested with some (half-hearted?) resistance by the disciples, but Jesus claims that it must happen that the "Scriptures be fulfilled" (26:54; cf. v. 56). Jesus then has his "trial" before Caiaphas, while Peter fulfills his three denials (26:57–75). It is during his "trial" that Jesus finally is willing to accept the identification of "Christ, the Son of God," although even here he still answers indirectly ("You have said so," 26:64). For this "blasphemy" (26:65), the leaders condemn him to death (26:66).

Scene 10 (27:1–14) forms another key pattern, with the death of Judas (27:3–10) intervening between Jesus' transfer to Pilate (27:1–2) and his interrogation by Pilate (27:11-14). Even the traitor's conduct and demise is related to God's purposes (Zech 11:12–13 and Jer 32:7–9 in Matt 27:9–10). It is worth noting here how many of the characters in this N block, including Judas, are introduced and withdrawn quickly in the narrative, only to serve the purposes of the chief priests. Note in Figure 1.18 how Judas, Pilate, and the guards are all present for a short time, sometimes overlapping briefly, but the religious authorities are present in every scene as the villains masterminding the whole disreputable business. The placement of Judas' death pericope (unique to Matthew) immediately after Jesus is in Pilate's hands may be Matthew's way of closing off one aspect of his narrative as he takes up the next.

Scene 11 (27:15–61) is the most continuous in narrative and loosely knit in theme. It may be divided into five episodes. First (27:15–26), the episode about Barabbas emphasizes both the determination of the authorities to have Jesus executed (v. 20) and Pilate's reluctance to do so (v. 24). Second (27:27–31), Jesus is handed over to the governor's soldiers for further degradation prior to the crucifixion. Third (27:32–44), Matthew gives a brief but poignant picture of the actual

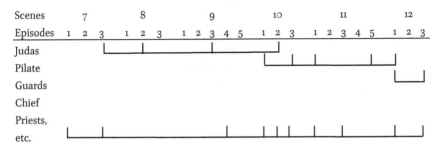

Figure 1.18: The Presence of Characters in Act 3, N Block 2

crucifixion. Fourth (27:45–56), Matthew relates the death of Jesus with minimal detail, for the interest is heavily upon its significance and interpretation. The darkness and earthquake are evidently suggestions of divine confirmation of Jesus' actual identity (vv. 51–54). Fifth (27:57–61), Joseph of Arimathea obtains Jesus' body and gives it respectable burial. The stone across the grave entrance must have given the setting an air of awesome finality as the two Marys took up their lonely vigil (v. 61).

Just as the Gospel's first N block (chs. 1–4) was peppered with OT quotations and allusions, so also this final N block—specifically Scene 11 depicting Jesus' crucifixion—is saturated with them. Obvious quotations and allusions are shown in Figure 1.19, but the list is not exhaustive.

Thus, both the beginning and the end of Jesus' life are portrayed as fulfilling Israel's Scriptures. The pervasiveness of Ps 22 (a Davidic psalm), and Jesus' existential use of it, suggests how deeply he had internalized his role as Son of David. The density of OT quotations and allusions are one reason to see this Scene as a peak, if not the peak of the Gospel. That this scene is the longest uninterrupted narrative in the Gospel, and that the opposition with the religious authorities has finally reached its outcome, also suggest that Scene 11 is the peak of the Gospel.[21]

Figure 1.20 shows the structure of Scene 11. The broken line indicates a possible key pattern and the square with dotted internal lines indicates the close unity of the scene.

Scene 12 (27:62–28:15) gives a rather clear key pattern. First (27:62–66), the Jewish authorities get guards from Pilate to prevent any possibility of a resurrection myth (even noting the importance of the third day), which shows how widely known Jesus' prediction of his resurrection was. Next comes the resurrection

---

[21] Weren's structure takes chs. 26–28 as the Gospel's "finale" (with 26:1–16 as a "hinge" text)—the climactic conclusion to the story's drama ("Macrostructure," 188–190). It is possible, though, to narrow the finale or climax down to this specific Scene (11), based on the evidence presented here.

Matthew	Old Testament
27:29	Ps 22:7[22]
27:30	Isa 50:6
27:34	Ps 69:21
27:35	Ps 22:18
27:39	Ps 22:7 / Ps 109:25
27:43	Ps 22:8
27:45	Amos 8:9 / Jer 15:9 (?)
27:46	Ps 22:1
27:48	Ps 69:21
27:52	Ezek 37:12 / Isa 26:19 / Dan 12:2

Figure 1.19: OT Quotations and Allusions in Act 3, Scene 11

Release of Barabbas Episode 1 27:15–26	Mockery by Soldiers Episode 2 27:27–31	The Crucifixion Episode 3 27:32–44	Death of Jesus Episode 4 27:45–56	Burial of Jesus Episode 5 27:57–61

Figure 1.20: The Structure of Act 3, Scene 11

The Guard Set Ep. 1, 27:62–66	The Resurrection Ep. 2, 28:1–10	The Guard Bribed Ep. 3, 28:11–15

Figure 1.21: The Key Pattern in Act 3, Scene 12

account (28:1–10), in which an angel tells the women that Jesus is risen and promises them a meeting with Jesus in Galilee. Third (28:11–15), the guards report to the high priests, who make one last attempt to discredit Jesus. Setting the resurrection account in-between the accounts of the guards, both of which are unique to Matthew, seems deliberately to throw the resurrection into higher relief. We represent this scene with a simple key diagram in Figure 1.21.

---

[22] OT references in this chart use English versification.

The last five verses of the Gospel (28:16–20) are considered an epilogue (rather than another episode in the previous scene) for several reasons. First, there is a clear break of time and place, moving from Jerusalem back to Galilee. Second, these verses have the typical function of an epilogue in that they pull together some loose ends, including the sending out of the disciples to preach the kingdom and, more notably, the thrice repeated promise of the resurrection (16:21; 17:23; 20:19). These promises are here fulfilled not only to the women (as in 28:9–10) but also to the disciples to whom the promises were given. Third, the inclusion of these verses with the previous scene would not simply fail to yield a coherent pattern, but would actually obscure the one which is otherwise there. Fourth, taking these verses as an epilogue gives the whole Gospel a nicely rounded balance both of structure and of theme. The Prologue of 1:1–17 links Jesus with Israel's historic past; this epilogue, especially in its closing words, links him with the open-ended future of the new community that his ministry has formed. Whereas before Jesus' birth, God's purposes were narrowly channeled through one particular nation and through successive members of it, now in the resurrection era, they can embrace all nations through the authority and perpetual presence of the one representative Man. Thus will come the completion of God's purposes in the consummation of the age.

To summarize this final N block, there are six scenes, each carefully constructed by Matthew as demonstrated in Figure 1.22. The block begins with preparations for Passover, the Last Supper, and Jesus' betrayal. It concludes with the Gospel's climactic portrayal of Jesus' crucifixion, which is viewed as fulfilling many OT passages, and the resurrection. The block therefore functions to bring all of the Gospel's themes to a climax and finally to a resolution with Jesus' resurrection and his commissioning of the disciples.

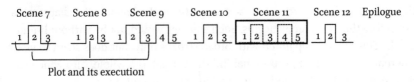

Plot and its execution

Figure 1.22: The Structure of Act 3, N Block 3

Summary of the Gospel

We summarize the Gospel's structure by looking at the development of the N and D blocks separately. Figure 1.23 shows the development of themes throughout the N blocks, although we can give only the main themes and cannot do full justice to the complexity of the Gospel. In Act 1, the first N block is now seen to be the *setting* for the whole Gospel, but a setting in which both opposition (derived ultimately from Satan) and human response (e.g. from Herod, the Magi, or the first four disciples) are latent. The second N block gives the *establishment* of the main themes, with the healings bringing a challenge that evokes varying reactions from the beholders. The opposition from the establishment begins to make itself felt.

In Act 2 Jesus is led, through the questions from John the Baptist, to make a private but explicit self-identification. The opposition to his ministry grows and hardens, but through the confession at Caesarea Philippi and the transfiguration, there is a corresponding growth in understanding and conviction on the part of at least some of the disciples. Thus, Act 2 can be said to give the *development* of the main themes.

Act 3 sees the culmination of the ministry in the public recognition of Jesus at the triumphal entry. This naturally brings the opposition to a head and leads to its final action in the crucifixion. In the resurrection, however, God gives an open vindication of Jesus' life and work which is of universal and eternal application. Thus, the Gospel reaches its *consummation*.

If the above outline is a reasonable presentation of the Gospel's themes, then we can categorize Matthew as being basically polar in its outlook. Jesus' life and ministry provoke fundamentally only two types of response: acceptance or rejection. Both are manifested in different ways, but the variety of expression conceals what is essentially a dichotomy.

A general movement forward from the setting, through the establishment and the development to the consummation, is now visible. The only large break in this scheme comes in chs. 19 and 20 at the beginning of Act 3. Until the healing of the two blind men at the end of ch. 20, this section does not carry the action forward at all. Rather, we are simply given more examples of Jesus' teaching on issues such as family life and wealth. If this section is to be integrated into the outline, it has to be regarded as a sort of plateau (the label in the diagram), a pause before the final climax begins. Such a device would not be without literary parallels. This outline is painted with broad strokes only, but does seem to yield a coherent direction and purpose behind the Gospel as a whole, into which the various sections fit fairly readily, each making its contribution.

Turning to the D blocks, Figure 1.24 provides a visual summary with general labels. All of the D blocks make considerable mention of the Kingdom of Heaven, and so we use this as a basis for the labels. The first D block, the Sermon on the Mount, with its frequent "You have heard ... but I say to you ..." sets up the Kingdom of Heaven in contrast with life under the Law as in the past. They are in contrast, but not in opposition, since in Jesus' ministry, the Law is not destroyed but fulfilled. The three separate D blocks in Act 2 give three windows into the kingdom as Jesus expounds it, specifically the kingdom's propagation, growth, and ethos. Since they expound especially the nature of the kingdom as

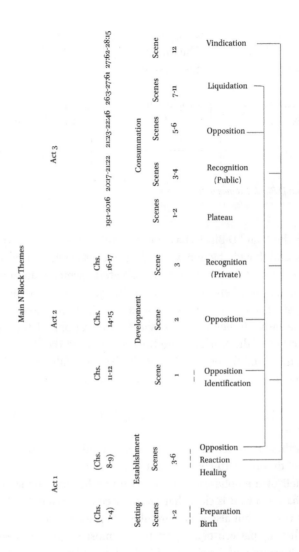

Figure 1.23: Main N Block Themes in the Gospel

inaugurated in Jesus' ministry, the label "The Kingdom and the *Present*" seems not inappropriate. In the final D block, with its two distinct parts, the two previous aspects of teaching are picked up. The practical rejection of the New Era by those who preferred life under the Law leads to the denunciations of ch. 23. The spread of the Kingdom through the life and witness of its members leads naturally to teaching on its consummation as found in the predictions of chs. 24 and 25. Hence this section is labeled "The Kingdom and the *Future*."

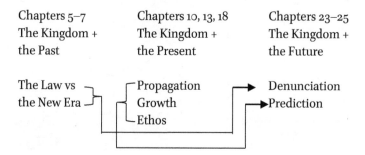

Figure 1.24: Main D Block Themes in the Gospel

Now, though the N and D Blocks have been considered separately with regard to their themes, and though the removal of the D Blocks would still leave an orderly narrative, we can see that the D Blocks hold material which is appropriate to the stage of the narrative where each is placed. The Sermon on the Mount, with its broad contrast of old and new, is consonant with its position in the section where the narrative is being *established*. Considerations of the propagation, growth and ethos of the Kingdom are fittingly set amid the *development* of the narrative themes. And to set teaching on the future fulfillment of the Kingdom in the *consummation* of the narrative is natural and congruent.[23]

Conclusion

A DA of Matthew's Gospel helps one to understand better how each episode, scene, and act fit into Matthew's larger scheme. Everyone tells a story their own way, with their own emphases, inclusions, and exclusions, and some use more literary art than others. It is clear that Matthew constructed not only the overall design of his Gospel, but also a large number of episodes and scenes at the local level, with the key pattern being perhaps his most frequently used structural device. The alternation of the N and D blocks gives a pleasing flow to the Gospel, and our analysis has suggested how the D blocks are appropriately placed to fit with the topics and functions of the surrounding N blocks. If even the high levels of analysis are kept in mind when reading, studying, or teaching episodes or scenes in the Gospel, the meaning and function of these microstructures will be better illuminated.

---

[23] There is confusion over whether each D block belongs to the preceding or following N block, and how the D blocks connect with their surrounding N blocks. E.g., Luz's judgment is that "a unified coordination of the discourses with their narrative context is not possible" (*Matthew*, 3). Our approach of fitting the D blocks into the broader theme of each Act overcomes this difficulty.

2

MARK

ROBERT E. LONGACRE

Methodology

Narrative analysis is necessarily dependent on the basic characteristics of narrative. What makes a story a story? A story is not an essay or a sermon or a food recipe or a set of procedures. It has a storyline, that is, a succession of happenings which are recounted. It involves a certain departure from the routine and expected. But nevertheless, it takes the stuff of life, sometimes with great detail and apparent arbitrariness, and weaves it into what Ricoeur calls an *emplotment*, or *plot*[1] for short. It necessarily has participants involved in some sort of struggle, however refined or crude. It has to bring such struggle to a head and resolve it someway, even if the resolution is not a happy one.

Obviously, there is some sort of narrative *template* according to which stories are made. Since classical times (beginning with Aristotle's writing on drama) such a template has been recognized, although various writers have expressed it differently. The schema I have held to for some time now[2] (but cf. Labov and

---

[1] P. Ricoeur, *Time and Narrative*, 3 vols., trans. Kathleen McLaughlin and David Pellauer (University of Chicago Press, 1984–88). The material of special interest to us here is vol. 1, Chapter 3.

[2] Cf. R. E. Longacre, *An Anatomy of Speech Notions* (Peter de Riddler, 1976), and idem, *The Grammar of Discourse*, 2nd ed. (Plenum, 1996). The particular form in which I have expressed the narrative schema is taken from W. Thrall, A. Hibbard, and H. Holman, *A Handbook to Literature* (Odyssey Press, 1961).

Waletzky,[3] Rumelhart,[4] and others) has the following elements: (1) *Stage*, (2) *Inciting Incident*, (3) *Mounting Tension*, (4) *Climax*, (5) *Denouement*, (6) *Closure*.

The purpose of (1) Stage is to lay the foundation for creating the storyworld, time, place, circumstances and participants (not necessarily the ones dominating the ensuing story). Element (2) brings in that which is unexpected and routine-breaking, so that "thereby hangs a tale." Element (3) typically involves a series of *episodes* which complicate the plot. Elements (4) Climax and (5) Denouement are further episodes which are somewhat correlative. The French terms *nouement* "tying it up" and *denouement* "untying it" capture this reciprocity quite well. The last element, Closure, brings the curtain down. It may, however, be preceded by one or more episodes of *Lessening Tension* or even *Final Suspense* which are consequent on the preceding denouement. The latter reports an event which makes resolution *possible*; it may leave many details to be worked out.

But while this is the underlying template, the actual story which is produced is like a theme with variations which it is the privilege of narrators to develop to their liking. Narrators elaborate the episodic *surface structure* of the story. They cannot tell all there is to tell at every stage of their narrative or the story would be both infinitely long and infinitely tiresome. They must be highly selective. They will, in fact, have portions of their story that they present summarily and other parts concerning which they give considerable detail. The latter are the great moments of the story, which I will call *action peaks*[5] in this essay. These great moments typically involve such sections of the underlying template as the Inciting Incident, the Climax and the Denouement. Narrators may also prepose a *Title* and/or *Aperture* to their story and may postpose a *Finis*. Aperture and Finis are characteristically formulaic and culture-determined.

A story of any length will typically have plots and subplots, that is, it may have story-within-story. Or narrators may find it necessary, if they are to guide the hearer/reader skillfully through the tale, to group the happenings in wavelike successive units. In either case the template is applied recursively.[6] It is quite improbable to find a story of any length that is a simple linear string of happenings reported in successive episodes. Furthermore, narrators may group certain episodes of their story so as to suggest a special parallelism of one account with

---

[3] W. Labov and J. Waletzky, "Narrative Analysis: Oral Versions of Personal Experience," in *Essays on the Verbal and Visual Arts*, ed. J. Helm (University of Washington Press, 1967), 12–44.

[4] D. E. Rumelhart, "Notes on a Schema for Stories," in *Representation and Understanding*, ed. D. G. Bobrow and A. M. Collins (Academic Press, 1975), 211–236; idem, "Understanding and Summarizing Brief Stories," in *Basic Processes in Reading: Perception and Comprehension* (Erlbaum, 1977), 265–304.

[5] Longacre, *Grammar*, ch. 1; idem, "Discourse Peak as Zone of Turbulence," in *Beyond the Sentence*, ed. J. R. Wirthe (Karoma, 1985), 81–98.

[6] Longacre, *Grammar*, ch. 7.

another account which consists of similar incidents. Narrators may even (especially if from a Semitic background) use a chiastic arrangement which suggests that there is a central episode which is pivotal. At all events the narrator is likely to echo at beginning and end—and maybe also in the center—certain themes.

The above brings us to the consideration that a story has not simply happenings and participants but *themes*. The latter can surface in various ways in a story: in background material which is not on the storyline, in the simple recurrence of certain "key" words, and in reported speech. The latter is so important that a story may contain a *Didactic Peak*,[7] that is, an episode in which action ceases and themes are developed via monologue and/or dialogue. Thus every novel or story of Ayn Rand[8] contains a sermon, by its chief participant, on the virtue of self-reliance and the perniciousness of all forms of altruism and collectivism. In the book of Genesis the Flood Narrative[9] contains besides the action peak in ch. 7, a didactic peak in ch. 9 whose themes are covenant and promise. In the Joseph story[10] with which the book of Genesis terminates, Joseph's call to prepare himself for an audience with Pharaoh and his installation as grand vizier after the interview are elements of an action peak that bracket a didactic peak in which Joseph interprets Pharaoh's dreams and develops as theme the providence of God (total passage, Gen 41:14–45). Thus, a didactic peak may occur in a distinct section of narrative from the action peak, or it may occur in conjunction with the latter.

Analytically all this implies that a narrative analyst can proceed somewhat as follows in the preliminary approach to a text.[11]

1. Search for natural fissures, joints, or seams in a narrative. This search requires both an intuitive following of "hunches" and a sensitivity to formal marking

---

[7] Longacre, *Grammar*, ch. 1.

[8] For example, *Atlas Shrugged* (New American Library, 1943) and *Fountainhead* (New American Library, 1957).

[9] R. E. Longacre, "The Discourse Structure of the Flood Narrative," *JAAR* 47, no. 1 (1979): 89–133.

[10] R. E. Longacre, *Joseph, a Story of Divine Providence* (Eisenbrauns, 1989).

[11] This top-down, template-driven analysis amounts to a beginning sketch; to be more adequate the analysis needs to be extended downward to include relations within the paragraph in which sentences and groups of sentences are related according to what I term "interclausal relations" (*Grammar*, chs. 3–4); or according to the system of "rhetorical relations" formulated by W. Mann and S. Thompson, *Relational Propositions in Discourse*, Technical Report ISI/RR-83-115 (Information Sciences Institute, 1983); and by the same two authors, "Rhetorical Structure Theory: A Theory of Text Organization," *Technical Report ISI/RS-87-190* (Information Sciences Institute, 1987); "Rhetorical Structure Theory: A Framework for Analysis of Texts" (International Pragmatics Association Papers in Pragmatics 1.79–105). For a narrative analysis that is both top-down and template-driven and also carried down through interclausal relations within component paragraphs, see Longacre, *Joseph*.

by occurrence of conjunctions and other sequence signals, by cyclic recurrence of staging (time and locational expressions, change of participant slate, or radically changed circumstances), and by markers that an action sequence is slowing down or terminating.

2. Try to match underlying template segments with surface segments. In general, the latter will be episodes of the story. A valid match between a template segment and a surface segment establishes the *function* of the surface segment.

3. Apply the template recursively as much as necessary so as to obtain a coherent picture of what is going on semantically and structurally. There is no point in trying to establish the moons of Jupiter in solar orbits, nor in viewing the hand as a direct appendage of the body instead of as an appendage of the arm which is attached to the body. Hierarchical structuring[12] must be recognized in astronomy, biology and in textlinguistics. We can expect, therefore, to find within a story *embedded discourses* up to several layers—as many layers as seem necessary to obtain a plausible grouping.

4. Watch for peak-marking whether in respect to actions or themes. Action peaks are marked by a variety of means[13] which I will summarize here as (a) augmentation of the storyline (verb forms, sentence lengthening or shortening, crowding the storyline with a rapid sequence of happenings, with minute components of actions, or even with paraphrase of actions as pseudo-happenings); (b) immediacy (detail and dialogue); and (c) maximum interlacing of participants, that is, the "crowded stage" effect.[14] As mentioned above we can expect to find peak-marking applied to surface units which correspond to the Inciting Incident, the Climax or the Denouement. Didactic peaks are large segments of reported speech in which thematic material is developed.

5. Watch for parallelism and chiasm in the development of the story. The former can determine a *compound discourse*, where successive events in two sections of a story are developed in a parallel fashion not generally characteristic of the rest of the story. While detailed use of chiasm is often best analyzed as an overlay over the successively episodic structure,[15] a looser chiasm can be employed

---

[12] Longacre, *Grammar*, ch. 9.

[13] Longacre, *Grammar*, ch. 2.

[14] R. E. Longacre, *Storyline Concerns and Word-Order Typology in East and West Africa*, Studies in African Linguistic Supplements 10 (University of California, 1990), 8–9.

[15] Thus, my template-driven, linear-recursive analysis of the Genesis Flood Narrative ("Discourse Structure") can be fruitfully compared with Wenham's chiastic analysis of the same (G. J. Wenham, "The Conference of the Flood Narrative," *VT* 28 [1978], 336–348). Likewise my analysis of Mark in this article may be compared with M. P. Scott's masterful chiastic analysis in "Chiastic Structure: A Key to the interpretation of Mark's Gospel," *BTB*, 17–26. I do not feel that a linear-recursive analysis and a chiastic analysis are ultimately incompatible; rather, they reflect different modes of linguistic structuring. The linear-recursive analysis is an

so that one episode which cross-references both to the beginning and also to the end is developed as a *Pivot* in the episodic structure of the story. Such a pivot may take peak-marking.

Narrative Analysis of the Gospel According to Mark

It is assumed here that Mark's Gospel can be analyzed as a narrative. The broad category "narrative" embraces both fact and fiction. But even a story rooted and grounded in fact—as I believe this one to be—must be shaped according to narrative conventions if it is to be successful with its readers.[16] We could, of course, argue that the Gospel is a special genre developed in order to present the mighty words and works of Jesus. But even the recognition of a specifically Gospel genre—with, for example, approximately a quarter of its bulk devoted to the last week in Jesus' life—can hardly escape classification as narrative. At any rate, common to all four canonical Gospels is the plot that turns on the struggle between Jesus and the establishment of his day—a struggle that culminates in trial, crucifixion, death and resurrection. And the presence of plot is a diagnostic trait of narrative.

I have set about to develop a top-down, template-driven and functional analysis of Mark's Gospel with application of the assumptions of the previous section to the analysis of the text. The editors (Aland *et al.*) present us with a Greek text of Mark neatly divided into 91 pericopes, but it may be regarded as a foregone conclusion that the Gospel is not a simple linear sequence of these pericopes. Most assuredly there is a higher organization into bigger blocks. Most of the pericopes have, however, an introductory element that may be temporal, locative, circumstantial or participant-presentative. Very frequently motion verbs

---

extrapolation from the grammar of the clause and the sentence. Chiastic analysis addresses itself to the content and colligational characteristics of a text, what the Pikes call "referential structure." Cf. K. Pike and E. Pike, *Grammatical Analysis*, Summer Institute of Linguistics Publications in Linguistics 53 (SIL and the University of Texas at Arlington, 1977). I believe, therefore, that the type of analysis that is presented here and chiastic analyses such as those proposed by Wenham and Scott are *complementary* rather than contradictory. Ethel Wallis of the Summer Institute of Linguistics also has published a chiastic analysis of Mark: "Mark's Goal-Oriented Plot Structure," *JOTT* 10 (1995): 30–45. One matter of considerable interest is that even my linear-recursive analysis presented here by setting up EPISODE 3 as pivotal makes the Transfiguration account central and in this respect agrees with Scott's taking Mark 9:7 as central to his chiastic structuring. We have, in effect, a two-map problem with a central piece of topography common to the two maps and thus facilitating the relating of the two.

[16] Ricoeur's discussion (*Time*, III) of the mutual relationships of fact and fiction within the overall narrative genre is a good contribution to this contemporary issue. Cf. also R. E. Longacre, "Paul Ricoeur's Philosophy and Textlinguistic Analysis," in *The Nineteenth LACUS Forum 1992* (The Linguistic Association of Canada and the United States, 1993), 47–55.

with given participants as subject introduce a pericope. While in my organiza-tion of the text of the Gospel into a hierarchy of units I do not always mention the introductory elements of a pericope in the discussion below, they are care-fully catalogued in the display that constitutes an appendix to this paper. I do not make much use of the term "pericope" in this analysis; rather I recognize them as episodes, which are typically on the lowest level of discourse embedding.

In that the Gospels present both the works and words of Jesus, I frequently posit didactic peaks on various levels of organization in the text. Outstanding works (miracles) are frequently found marked as peaks in various ways; such a marked account of a miracle I posit as *climactic* on various levels of structure. While the Gospel of Mark as a whole has a climax with a matching denouement, most of the embedded discourses end in a climax without a corresponding de-nouement. Typically an embedded discourse ends with an outstanding work which is reported in vividness and detail; each such climax further complicates the overall plot and makes increasingly urgent the thematic question "Who is he?"

The use of the historical present in this Gospel has long been considered to be a prime analytical concern.[17] No amount of local contextual explanation in terms, for example, of continuity and discontinuity, can answer the simple question as to why it is used at all and especially why *clusters* of historical pre-sents characterize the text at certain points. In keeping with my assumptions regarding peak-marking, according to which tampering with the tense of the verb is a specially sensitive area in many languages, I take the historical present, when occurring other than pericope-initial, when not limited to speech verbs, and when clustering within a passage, to be a peak marker. This has sometimes turned my analysis in unexpected directions. For example, I tried at first to handle the episode of Christ's prayer in the garden of Gethsemane as simply another episode in the progress towards the cross, but the proliferation of his-torical presents in the passage, Mark 14:32–42, forced me to change my analysis at this point. Ralph Enos's suggestive article is of special relevance in this regard;

---

[17] A considerable bibliography could be cited at this point. Stephen Levinsohn's work has attempted to go at the matter of the historical present in the Gospels and Acts largely in terms of local cohesion, in what I could characterize as a "bottom-up" approach in contrast to my "top-down" analysis as illustrated in this article. Cf. S. H. Levinsohn, "The Historical Present and Speech Margins in Mathew," in *Language in Context: Essays for Robert Longacre*, ed. S. Hwang and W. Merrifield (SIL and the University of Texas at Arlington, 1992), 451–474, and the same material presented as Chapter 10 in S. H. Levinsohn, *Discourse Features of New Testa-ment Greek: A Coursebook* (SIL, 1992). I also want to cite here an excellent but little-known work by R. Enos, "The Use of the Historical Present in the Gospel According to Saint Mark," *The Journal of the Linguistic Association of the Southwest* 3, no. 2 (1981): 281–298. Enos's article is especially noteworthy for its extensive bibliography of work done on the historical present prior to the writing of his article, including some earlier work of Levinsohn.

he, however, discusses isolated uses of the historical present which I do not consider here.

A suggested gross segmentation of the Gospel follows immediately below (Figure 2.1) with further discussion following and with a more detailed analysis displayed in the appendix to this essay. In both analyses, capital letters signify primary constituents, that is, constituents of the Gospel as a whole. Capitalization of only the first letter of a word indicates constituents on the first level of discourse embedding. Italics symbolize constituents on a lower level of discourse embedding.

TITLE/APERTURE of whole 1:1	
STAGE:	The ministry of John the Baptist 1:2–8
EPISODE 1	(INCITING INCIDENT): 1:9–13 (either a brief embedded discourse or a compound paragraph)
	The Spirit comes on Jesus and confirms his Sonship; the heavens are "split" 1:9–11
	The Spirit "drives" him out to be tempted by the Devil 1:12–13
EPISODE 2	The rise to prominence 1:14–5:43
EPISODE 3	At full tide; Jesus a power figure and nurturer 6:1–8:26
EPISODE 4	(PIVOTAL): "Who is he?" 8:27–9:50
EPISODE 5	The last journey to Jerusalem 10:1–52
EPISODE 6	(PEAK): 11:1–16:8
Episode 1	(Inciting Incident): The Triumphal Entry 11:1–11
Episode 2	(The DIDACTIC PEAK of the whole book): Teaching amid controversy 11:12–13:37
Episode 3	(The ACTION PEAK of the whole book): Events which culminate in the crucifixion (CLIMAX) and resurrection (DENOUEMENT) 14:1–16:8

Figure 2.1: Macrostructure of Mark according to a Narrative Analysis

I will not comment on here nor attempt to justify the segmentation above but will reserve such comment for the sections below which discuss EPISODES 1–6 in order. I do, however, mention briefly here the way in which I have analytically disposed of the first 13 verses of Mark's Gospel. The ambiguity of v. 1 as to TITLE/APERTURE is discussed extensively by Cranfield.[18] It structures plausibily either way. John the Baptist's ministry as forerunner is cited by Mark as fulfillment of Mal 3:1 and Isa 40:3. This resort to OT quotation is noteworthy in Mark

---

[18] C. E. B. Cranfield, *The Gospel according to St. Mark* (Cambridge University Press, 1959), 34–35. I take occasion here to commend Cranfield's sensitivity to the flow and structure of Mark's Gospel; he is not as slavishly verse-by-verse in his approach as are many traditional commentaries.

since he is not given to as frequent a use of such quotations as is Matthew. The Baptist's own words in vv. 7 and 8 underline the preparatory nature of his own ministry: "After me will come one more powerful than I...." In terms of narrative structure the presentation of the Baptist and his ministry qualify as STAGE for all that follows. Nothing of the main story happens in its stage, but the groundwork is laid for what follows. Later in his Gospel Mark felt obliged to recount the imprisonment and death of John the Baptist in the flashback account which is found in Mark 6:14–29 even though the account does not integrate too well into the ongoing story.

Microstructures

EPISODE 1 (INCITING INCIDENT): 1:9–13

The passage 1:9–13 qualifies well as EPISODE 1, the INCITING INCIDENT of the whole Gospel. While the Greek text of Aland et al. makes vv. 12–13 a separate pericope, probably because of the parallelism with Mt. 4:1–11 and Luke 4:1–12, Mark here abbreviates and makes vv. 12–13 one compound unit with vv. 9–11. The only transition particle is Mark's omnipresent εὐθύς. There is, however, a new locale, the wilderness. The Holy Spirit does not enter the scene as a new participant but is carried over from v. 10. Satan is the new participant in the new locale. It seems simpler neither to compromise the ongoing unity of vv. 9–11 with vv. 12–13 nor to disregard their differences. Whether to consider the whole one compound paragraph or a short, embedded discourse is somewhat irrelevant; the two seem to go together as the INCITING INCIDENT of the Gospel. As the Spirit descends on him the heavenly voice declares him to be the Son of God, thus preparing us as readers for the works and words of power that follow. Furthermore, such an explicit word as to the identity of the man Jesus does not occur again until we hear it in the voice from the cloud Mark 9:7, and finally from Jesus' own mouth at the time of the trial in 14:61–62—although this is implied in Peter's confession in 8:29 as well. Indeed, the passage before us sheds light on the whole central and theologically pivotal portion EPISODE 4 (8:27–9:50), which I have entitled "Who is he?"

Similarly, the temptation of Jesus prepares us for the heavy emphasis on exorcism which characterizes Mark's Gospel as well as for the conflict with the establishment of his day. We are, as it were, taken behind the ensuing scenes along the lines indicated later by Paul: "For our struggle is not against flesh and blood, but against the rulers, against the authorities, against the powers of this dark world, and against the spiritual forces of evil in the heavenly realms" (Eph 6:12).

Therefore, in a fundamental sense 1:9–13 sets us up for all that follows and may plausibly be considered to have the characteristics of an inciting incident.

EPISODE 2: The Rise to Prominence 1:14–5:43

It is plausible to consider that the balance of ch. 1 and the entire four chapters that follow constitute an embedded discourse with 1:14–15 patterning as Stage, ch. 4 as Didactic Peak and ch. 5 as Action Peak. The latter recounts in great detail three miracles of Jesus, the exorcism of the demons in the Gadarene demoniac and the raising of Jairus's daughter, interrupted by the healing of the woman with a long-term disturbance of her menstrual cycle. The last is itself unique, no other recorded miracle has such a story interrupting and bracketed by another story. Moreover, the argument that ch. 5 is to be regarded as the Action Peak of the first part of the book is reinforced by the consideration that special peak-marking features are present as well. The second half of the chapter, the miracle-within-miracle, is well marked by special verb forms. To begin with, the case history of the afflicted woman is given in a long string of participles culminating in the verb ἥψατο, "she touched" (v. 27). This is an unusually long chain of participles preceding the finite verb and is reminiscent of medial-final chaining in languages of Papua New Guinea.[19] Then there is a clustering of historical presents in the bracketing story, the raising of Jairus's daughter. It is noteworthy that Luke Johnson in his recent commentary on Luke also considers that Luke's recounting of these miracles constitutes the end of a major section of Luke.[20] With the performance of this exorcism, the healing, and a raising of one from the dead this part of Mark's Gospel comes to a climax and is given appropriate surface development as such.

Chapter 4, concerning Jesus' teaching in parables and giving a sample ensemble of the same, can be considered to be an embedded discourse which constitutes the didactic peak of this second main section of the Gospel. The internal structure of this one-chapter embedded discourse ends with an action episode, the calming of the storm (4:35–41). It is closely spliced onto the teaching that precedes by the connective expression in v. 36 "And sending away the crowds they took him as he was in the boat [where he had been seated teaching]."

Episodes one to three of the embedded discourse which manifests main EPISODE 2 likewise pattern as embedded discourses whose constituents are on a still lower level of embedding (represented with italic letters). Thus, within EPISODE 2, Episode 1 (1:16–45) is the story of Jesus' initial ministry in and around Capernaum; it is an embedded narrative with five *episodes*, the last of which may be its *action peak*. These *episodes* recount, presumably in chronological order,

---

[19] Among the various works that could be cited here I take my 1972 monograph as an introduction to languages of this type: Robert E. Longacre, *Hierarchy and Universality of Discourse Constituents in New Guinea Languages* (Georgetown University Press, 1972).

[20] L. T. Johnson, *The Gospel according to Luke* (Liturgical Press, 1993). Johnson makes tracing the discourse-structure and flow one of the main concerns in his commentary.

the calling of the four fishermen (1:16–20), an exorcism in the synagogue (1:21–28), healings and exorcisms at the house of Peter (1:29–34), a preaching tour which begins the next morning (1:35–39) and, finally, his healing of a leper which provoked such a large following of people that he could no longer openly enter a town (1:40–45). The latter is certainly climactic but may perhaps lack the specific marking which we expect to find in a peak. It is not implausible to suggest that this embedded narrative is of Petrine origin.[21]

Episode 2 of the embedded discourse which constitutes EPISODE 2 of the main story is considered by some to reflect a topical arrangement of stories[22] which are concerned with the beginnings of Jesus' conflict with the authorities of his day. This, of course, does not deny the possibility that whatever their principle of selection they could have occurred substantially in the order in which they are introduced. The Episode is set off locationally by indicating a return to Capernaum and temporally by δι' ἡμερῶν, "after some days." The lower level *episodes* of this embedded discourse which manifests Episode 2 are five of which the first may be the *inciting incident* and the last is at least the climax and may have some peak marking: *Episode 1*: Jesus heals a paralytic and presumes (?) to forgive his sins (2:1–12 with several historical presents serving as peak marking in an inciting incident); *Episode 2*: Jesus encounters criticism by calling Levi and attending a banquet with him and his friends (2:13–17); *Episode 3*: (unfriendly) questions about fasting (2:18–22); *Episode 4*: the disciples are criticized for plucking and eating grain on the Sabbath (2:23–27); *Episode 5*: Jesus heals a man with a withered hand on the Sabbath and there is first mention of a plot to kill him (3:1–6, plainly climactic; the fact that all speech verbs are in the historical present may be peak marking in this instance).

EPISODE 3: Jesus a Power Figure and Nurturer 6:1–8:26

This major episode, which pictures Jesus at full tide, has a compound structure with two parts each expounded by an embedded discourse. In each of the parallel discourses which constitute the compound structure, there is a feeding miracle. Furthermore, each embedded discourse ends with miracles of healing which are told in typically Markan (Petrine?) detail accompanied by scintillating dialogue and the use of the historical present for non-speech verbs. These similarly peak-marked endings of the parallel discourses make it awkward to attempt to account for all of 6:1–8:26 as one linear string of episodes on the same level. The

---

[21] So Cranfield, *Mark*, 61. In respect to the first four episodes he remarks that they are a "closely articulated group of four narratives of Petrine origin." What I consider the climax of this section he considers simply "a link to what follows" (p. 90).

[22] Cranfield, *Mark*, 61.

first of the two embedded discourses also embeds some lower-level discourses in two of its episodes.

Part 1 (6:1–7:37) has four episodes, a didactic peak and an action peak. The first three Episodes are somewhat disparate but probably belong here to a new main EPISODE after the clearly marked and brilliant climax that constitutes ch. 5. Episodes 1 and 2 are the rejection at Nazareth ("his own country") 6:1–6 and the sending out of the Twelve 6:7–13. Episode 3 (6:14–29) reports Herod's conjecture that Jesus was John the Baptist come back from the dead; it then gives in a flashback the death of the latter. It thus for the first time raises the question "Who is he?" that is thematic in EPISODE 4. Episode 4 (6:30–56) of this embedded discourse appears to be an embedded discourse with three *episodes*; the whole could be entitled "Miracles performed back and forth across the lake." Two non-healing miracles are reported here; both emphasize Jesus' power over nature. In *Episode 1* (6:30–44), the disciples return from their mission and Jesus feeds the 5000. In *Episode 2* (6:45–52), Jesus walks on the water. These supremacy-over-nature miracles are told with great clarity and vividness, but do not otherwise have peak marking nor are they positioned in their discourses where we might expect a peak to be positioned. *Episode 3* (6:53–56), compared to what precedes, is more of a summary statement of healings in and around Gennesaret. Mark's Gospel is not characterized by large teaching blocks as is Matthew's, but 7:1–23 is a large section of teaching by Markan standards. I consider this passage to be Episode 5, didactic peak of the whole embedded discourse which constitutes Part 1 of EPISODE 3. This stretch of teaching deals with Jesus' impatience with criticism of his disciples having eaten with unwashed hands and asserts that what comes out of a person's inner being defiles him, not what descends into one's stomach. Perhaps this is not inappropriately located here by Mark in a section where Jesus is pictured as one providing food.

I find it plausible in regard to 7:24–37 to believe that the two pericopes which are found here are meant to be taken together in that they have cross-referencing settings in 6:24, which refers to Jesus' going away to the environs of Tyre, and in 6:31, which refers to his leaving the environs of Tyre, coming through the environs of Sidon, and eventually proceeding towards the Sea of Galilee through the Decapolis. On this ballistic movement out of the land of Israel and returning around its northern fringe, two miracles of healing are performed: *Episode 1*, the healing of the Syrophoenician woman's daughter, and *Episode 2*, the healing of the deaf and dumb man. Both miracles are recounted in vivid detail with reported dialogue; in addition the account of the second miracle features the verbs "bring" and "beseech" in the historical present (v. 32) and reports the popular evaluation "He's done all things well; he makes the deaf to hear and the dumb to speak." I therefore label this whole passage 7:24–37 as action peak of the discourse which constitutes Part 1 of EPISODE 3. As we see from here and the conclusion of Part 2 of this compound discourse—as well as from the placement of ch. 5, at the end of EPISODE 2—a typically Markan way of bringing a discourse to a close is by giving its last pericope special peak marking, reserving the historical present of non-speech verbs for the second of two such accounts if two are found in the overall unit. Part 2 of the compound unit that manifests EPISODE 3 has a somewhat simpler structure but is in certain ways parallel to the discourse found in Part 1. Its Episode 1 (8:1–9) recounts the feeding of the 4000; Episode 2 (8:10–12) depicts the Pharisees demanding a sign and getting Jesus' enigmatic answer; Episode 3 (8:13–21) records the disciples' confusion on receiving Jesus' warning against the "leaven" of the Pharisees and the Herodians; again the food motif occurs reinforced with Jesus' explicit back reference to the two feeding miracles (vv. 19–20). Finally, Episode 4 (8:22–26) is an action peak in many ways marked like the action peak of the preceding part of this compound discourse: both in respect to the detail, the dialogue, and the use of the historical presents of the verbs "bring" and "beseech." Only in this account, among all of Mark's miracle accounts, do we find a man reported as being healed in two stages!

EPISODE 4 (PIVOTAL): 8:27–9:50

While there is no reason to believe that this block as a whole is not consecutive upon what precedes and anterior to what follows, it has certain unique properties which lead me to characterize it as in some sense central and pivotal in the narrative. The theme of the whole major EPISODE 4 seems to be "Who is he?" first raised in effect by Herod in EPISODE 3, Part 1, Episode 1 (6:14). But here the matter of Jesus' identity is peculiarly foregrounded. The answer given is twofold: (1) he is the Messiah, the Christ; and (2) he is to be a suffering Messiah. In Episode 1 (8:27–9:1) of the embedded discourse found here, Peter understood the first point but resisted the second and was summarily rebuked by his Lord, who not only identified himself with suffering but extended "cross-bearing" to be the lot of all his true disciples. Christ's rebuke of Peter is very severe. In addressing Peter as "Satan" it is as if Jesus is recalling the temptation in the wilderness— although Mark gives none of the cross-avoiding nature of the temptations as do the parallels in Matthew and Luke.

But if we are in doubt as to whether there is an allusion here to the INCITING INCIDENT in respect to both the Baptism and the Temptation, the central episode of this embedded discourse, that is, Episode 2 (9:2–13), the transfiguration and the immediately following incident, removes this doubt. In the Transfiguration the voice from the cloud "This is my beloved Son" echoes the baptismal voice "You are my beloved Son"—and anticipates the trial scene where Jesus is forced to confess his identity as "The Christ, the Son of the Blessed One" (14:61).

Furthermore, just as the Baptism is followed by the Temptation in the INCITING INCIDENT, so the transfiguration is followed by a conflict with Satan in the exorcism of the evil spirit from the child in 9:14–29—which is represented as a difficult exorcism which the disciples could not perform in spite of their having been empowered to exorcise demons in 3:15.

Two further Episodes conclude this major EPISODE 4. In Episode 3 (9:30–32) of this embedded discourse, Jesus foretells his death and resurrection a second time, and Episode 4 (9:33–50) records further teaching arising out of the quarrel as to who would be the greatest. Episode 3 further reinforces the point that Jesus as Messiah will prove to be a suffering Messiah. Episode 4, probably a hortatory discourse with three points, may well qualify as a didactic peak. Only the motion verb and the new locality mentioned in 9:33 keep us from joining the two Episodes. But Episode 3 is relatively unelaborated and could perhaps be grouped with what follows. If we were to make such a grouping then the whole embedded discourse which constitutes EPISODE 4 could be reduced to three episodes with the transfiguration and its aftermath as central, that is, pivotal in the pivotal section of the Gospel. The didactic material at the end of ch. 9, brings in a new motif, speaking or acting "in my name" (vv. 37–41) which is at this juncture quite congruent with the identification of who Jesus is as developed in the previous passages. Granted who he is, the Messiah, the suffering Messiah, and the beloved Son of God, then words and deeds performed "in his name" are appropriate.

Taking EPISODE 4 as pivotal to the whole Gospel, we see that Mark has constructed it well with Peter's confession and the Transfiguration as the two main pieces but with congruent material combined with them. There is a backward look at the INCITING INCIDENT and an insistent forward look towards the momentous events, suffering, death and resurrection, the recounting of which constitutes the ACTION PEAK of the Gospel. Verse counting is revealing—in spite of the lateness and occasional arbitrariness of verse division. I count 316 verses preceding EPISODE 3, PIVOTAL, and 312 verses following it!

EPISODE 5: The Last Journey to Jerusalem 10:1–52

I take 10:1a to signify the beginning of the last journey: "Jesus then again left that place and went into the region of Judea and across the Jordan." Cranfield[23] chooses to consider that the last journey begins in 8:27 in the neighborhood of Caesarea Philippi, but I do not see how the detour over to the Mount of the Transfiguration fits this too well. At all events, making 8:27–9:50 a pivotal portion distinct from what precedes and what follows makes it more convenient to believe that the fateful journey begins with 10:1. Note also 10:17, "As Jesus started

---

[23] Cranfield, *Mark*, 266.

on his way," and the somewhat more explicit reference to their being on their way to Jerusalem in 10:32, and, of course, the arrival in Jericho in 10:46. The travelogue discourse which constitutes ch. 10 has a clear Stage in 10:1, three Episodes, a further Episode 4 which is a complex Didactic Peak, and Episode 5, which is an Action Peak. The latter, exploiting a device previously noted in Mark, consists of a healing miracle told with vivid detail and dialogue and with a historical present in its interior.

In this embedded discourse, Episode 1 (10:2–12) recounts a question concerning divorce and Jesus' answer; Episode 2 (10:13–16) recounts his blessing the children; and Episode 3 (10:17–31) gives the story of the rich man who inquired concerning eternal life but found the price too high—along with ensuing teaching. Episode 4 patterns as Didactic Peak, 10:32–45; it is an embedded discourse with two subepisodes. Episode 1 (10:32–34) pictures Jesus resolutely leading the way towards Jerusalem while the disciples follow in fear. The first part of v. 32 may be the stage for what follows. Jesus teaches them in vv. 32b–34 even more explicitly concerning his betrayal, his rejection and death at the hand of the Gentiles, and his resurrection. Episode 2 (10:35–45) recounts the request of the sons of Zebedee that they be given pre-eminence in the coming glory along with Jesus' solemn answer that they will indeed drink from his cup and be baptized with his baptism. All this could possibly be regarded as a distinct episode from what follows in vv. 41–45. Notice however, that in trying to calm the indignation of the other disciples against James and John, Jesus utters a saying fraught with deep meaning concerning his coming death: "For even the Son of Man did not come to be served, but to serve, and to give his life as a ransom for many" (10:45). It seems plausible that this final reference by Jesus to his death forms with vv. 33–34 an inclusio which unites all 10:32–45 into one unit, namely Episode 4 of the embedded discourse which constitutes EPISODE 5 in the larger context. The contrast is exquisite: Jesus is preoccupied with his coming death, while the two disciples are preoccupied with their possible coming prerogatives and pre-eminence; even Jesus' answer to them is couched in symbolic figures of grief and suffering!

Finally, all the above is followed by a typically Markan action peak (10:46–52), the healing of blind Bartimaeus. Note the wealth of detail and the dialogue. Even the giving of the blind man's name is of itself noteworthy. His yelling for help in an attempt to gain Jesus' attention, his calling him "Son of David," the attempts of the crowd to quiet him, his making all the more of a scene, and finally Jesus' stopping in his tracks and asking for the man to be brought to him—all this is high drama. But more is to come: they call to the blind man (historical present); he throws aside his rags and springs to his feet to have his royal audience; Jesus makes him state his need and then heals him on the spot. So Bartimaeus becomes one of the many in the crowd following Jesus. All this is first-rate storytelling and is delivered by Mark in a style reserved for great moments in his

Gospel. If the many vivid details here and in other such passages are from Mark's having heard such incidents first hand from Peter—as many suggest—then we are bound to commend Mark's placement of the incidents which are told in this vivid storytelling style; his placement of them so as to close out structural sections of his story, reflects the skill of a major craftsman.[24] As already mentioned, each such vividly described miracle properly functions as a climax in terms of increasing the confusion and embarrassment of Jesus' adversaries—and thus making inevitable the final CLIMAX and DENOUEMENT.

EPISODE 6 (DIDACTIC PEAK and ACTION PEAK): 11:1–16:8

I assume that this extensive embedded discourse has three major Episodes, the first of which is Episode 1, the Triumphal Entry (11:1–11); the second of which is Episode 2, the DIDACTIC PEAK (11:12–13:37); and the third of which is Episode 3, the ACTION PEAK (14:1–16:8). An alternative analysis in which the two peaks would each be separate major structural EPISODES of the entire Gospel is precluded by the fact that the triumphal entry seems to be the Inciting Incident for *all* that follows while the embedded discourses which encode the two peaks each have their own inciting incidents. Nevertheless, while structural concerns of this sort must be given their proper weight the two peaks which are so introduced must be considered to be high points of the entire Gospel. Here structural and semantic concerns are somewhat askew, and it is best not to sacrifice one set of concerns to the other. I therefore accept the anomaly that the twin peaks of the entire Gospel are encoded as episodes of an embedded discourse. This necessitates a further layer of embedding than I have used earlier in the analysis. Thus, while I will continue to use EPISODE for a major section of the entire Gospel, Episode for the next lower level of embedding, and *Episode* for the layer below that, I will need to refer to a still deeper level of embedding as Episode.

Episode 1, The Triumphal Entry into Jerusalem (11:1–11)

This is clearly the inaugural event of Passion week. Furthermore, the account is marked as a great moment of the story by the use of the historical present not

---

[24] Cranfield (*Mark*, 11–12) believes that "there are four different kinds of narrative material": (1) narratives with vividness of detail which may be of Petrine origin, (2) narratives "which give the impression of being units of oral tradition which have been worn smooth by frequent repetition," (3) narratives which although based on tradition were possibly constructed by Mark himself, and (4) "brief summary statements indicating in general terms what was happening during a certain period." I rather suggest that, whatever the variation in source, the narratives have been subtly shaped and adapted by Mark himself to fit the varying needs of particular contexts in which they are found.

only at the opening in v. 1: "And when they draw near to Jerusalem ... he sends two of his disciples" (v. 2 "and says to them"); but also in the interior of the account in vv. 4 and 7: "And they loose it [the colt] ... And they bring the colt to Jesus, and they throw their garments up onto it." It is plausible to take 11:1–11 as the inciting incident of all that follows in the Gospel from 11:12 to the conclusion. The triumphal entry provoked the debates of the last week and its salvific events.

Episode 2, DIDACTIC PEAK (11:12–13:37).

I have combined three pericopes into Episode 1, the Inciting Incident of the embedded discourse which constitutes Episode 2, in that they form an ABA chiastic sequence: the cursing of the fig tree Episode 1, the cleansing of the temple Episode 2, the withering of the fig tree Episode 3. The three pericopes are closely tied chronologically, with the cursing of the fig tree and its withering taking place on successive mornings, and the cleansing of the temple on arrival at Jerusalem the first of the two days. As a chiasm, presumably the center section dominates and may shed some light on the interpretation of the surrounding segments. Is the fig tree meant to symbolize the nation of Israel here? But, although Jesus ends this whole Episode 2 DIDACTIC PEAK with a prophecy of the desolation of Jerusalem and the nation, he never in any place curses the city and its people. Eliminating the curse from the metaphor as possibly not germane to the comparison, there may still be symbolism in the apparently flourishing but fruitless tree and its withering.[25] In terms of the narrative template I take this to be an inciting incident on the grounds that the chiastic structure, even in absence of historical presents except in v. 15, amounts to a kind of peak-marking, that is, the Inciting Incident of the discourse which constitutes Episode 2. A similar chiastic unit (14:1–11) patterns as the Inciting Incident of Episode 3, the ACTION PEAK. It is the parallel use of these two chiastic structures to mark inciting incidents, as well as the strongly marked account: of the Triumphal Entry as also an inciting incident, that provides the clue that a complicated situation of discourse embedding is present here. We have various intertwined structures that need to be untangled so as to permit the assignment of the proper inciting incident to its appropriate structure.

Episode 2, the DIDACTIC PEAK, once past *Episode 1*, its inciting incident, unrolls as a series of controversial exchanges between Jesus and his opponents and culminates in the Olivet Discourse which is an answer to an inquiry on the part of the disciples. In some of the controversial exchanges the opponents of Jesus take the initiative in propounding questions, in other exchanges Jesus himself

---

[25] For discussion concerning this incident and its possible symbolic value, see Cranfield, *Mark*, 254–257, and W. L. Lane, *The Gospel According to Mark* (Eerdmans, 1974), 398–402.

takes the initiative. In the latter case, here and in the accompanying display in the appendix, I mark with an asterisk * *Episodes* in which Jesus takes the initiative. Perhaps the shifting inititatives indicate a further dialogue-like structure of proposal and response between certain of the episodes, but I have not at present recognized any such groupings. I proceed now to present what follows in Part 1 as *Episodes 2–11* below.

Episode 2, 11:27–33:	Jesus silences a question regarding his authority by countering with a question regarding what authority lay behind the ministry of John the Baptist.
*Episode 3, 12:1–12:	Jesus, taking the initiative, gives the parable of the Tenant Farmers which his opponents recognize as having been spoken against them and incites their desire to arrest him (v. 12).
Episode 4, 12:13–17:	Jesus answers the question about paying tribute to Caesar with, "Render unto Caesar the things that are Caesar's and unto God the things that are God's."
Episode 5, 12:18–27:	Jesus answers a *reductio ad absurdum* argument of the Sadducees regarding the resurrection by teaching that there is no sex in the afterlife while nevertheless stoutly affirming the resurrection and the life to come.
Episode 6, 12:28–34:	On being questioned regarding the greatest commandment Jesus reaffirms love to God and other humans and commends his interrogator.
*Episode 7, 12:35–37:	Jesus, seizing the initiative, questions them as to how the Messiah can simply be called David's son when the latter addresses him as Lord in Ps. 110:1.
*Episode 8, 12:38–40:	Jesus denounces the scribes.
* *Episode 9*, 12:41–44:	Jesus commends the widow's offering.
Episode 10, 13:1–2:	In response to a remark of the disciples, Jesus foretells the destruction of the Temple.
Episode 11, 13:3–36:	Didactic peak of the whole discourse which is DIDACTIC PEAK. This is a hortatory discourse (the Olivet Discourse) given in response to further inquiry from the disciples. It has at least three or four points and is not analyzed here.
Episode 3, ACTION PEAK, chs. 14, 15, and 16:1–8	A narrative discourse pivoting around *Episode 3*, 14:32–42 (see below).

Episode 1, Inciting Incident 14:1–11:	This is a chiastic structure ABA with the plot to kill Jesus as **Episode** 1, 14:1–2; the anointing at Bethany as **Episode** 2, 14:3–9; and Judas's agreeing to betray Jesus as **Episode** 3, 14:10–11. In this little embedded discourse Mary's anointing of Jesus, told with great detail and pictured as provoking considerable discussion and criticism, is clearly the central piece. It stands as an example of reckless, abandoned worship, even though surrounded by plotting and betrayal. In commending her Jesus said, "She came beforehand to anoint my body for burial"—thus focusing even Mary's act of devotion on his coming suffering and death. Not once does the narrator break step in the remorseless march towards the finale.
Episode 2, 14:12–31:	The Last Passover. Here there are subepisodes marked by temporal expressions and verbs of motion; with the first two subepisodes, the introductory verbs of motion are historical presents.
Episode 1, 14:12–16:	Preparations.
Episode 2, 7–21:	Prophecy of betrayal.
Episode 3, 14:22–26:	Institution of the Lord's Supper.
Episode 4, 14:27–31:	Peter's denial foretold.

Figure 2.2: Controversial Exchanges between Jesus and His Opponents. Each * *indicates that Jesus takes the initiative in verbal dueling.*

Episode 3, Pivotal 14:32–42: Jesus prays in Gethsemane. This episode cannot simply be treated as another in the ongoing string of successive episodes. It contains nine verbs in the historical present, three of which are speech verbs (and hence not very evidential of special marking) but six of which are motion verbs. These verbs occur scattered through the passage not merely at its head. We do not find a similar spate of historical presents until the portrayal of the mocking and crucifixion in *Episode 8* below—where again nine examples of this tense occur. The final spate of historical presents is in *Episode 11* below, the resurrection, where three such verbs occur. Taking *Episode 8* below as climax marked for Action Peak, and *Episode 11* as denouement marked for Peak, we raise the question as to the status of this episode, *Episode 3* (the ordeal in Gethsemane).

What is happening narrative-wise is not hard to explain: the narrator is, as it were, gathering his feet under him for the final sprint. But it occurs late in the total stretch of the discourse expounding the ACTION PEAK for an inciting incident, and besides we have already assigned this function to 14:1–11. We simply have to view Mark's narrative as marking, in addition to the Inciting Incident, three great moments in the Passion Narrative: Gethsemane, Calvary and the Empty Tomb. I label the first of the three Pivotal along with the Climax and Denouement, represented in the latter two. Mark pictures the sufferings of Christ as beginning in Gethsemane and properly underscores that point. The concept of pivotal has also been used in reference to the total structure of Mark's Gospel in our setting up of main EPISODE 3 in this function.

Episode 4, 14:43–52: The betrayal and arrest of Jesus. The verb tenses again merit comment here. Curiously enough, not only is there a verb in the historical present in the first verse of this passage, "And immediately while he was still talking, up comes Judas," but also in its last vv. 51–52: "And a young man, wearing nothing but a linen garment was following along, and they seize him. And he fled away naked." While it is not unusual to have historical presents of verbs of motion and speech which initiate a section or which occur both initially and in the interior of a section, it is somewhat rare to find them closing out a passage. Two explanations are possible: (1) the verses in question are in reality not an addendum to what preceded but a separate section (as punctuated by Aland *et al.*), or (2) Mark writes of himself in these verses and the historical present is resultant on his own vivid personal recollection of the incident.[26] It is also noteworthy that a perfect occurs in pluperfect sense in 14:44: "The one who betrayed him had given a sign (δεδώκει)."

Episode 5, 14:53–65: Jesus before the Council.

Episode 6, 14:66–72: Peter's denials.

Episode 7, 15:1–15: Jesus is sentenced by Pontius Pilate.

Episode 8 Peak, 15:16–32 (maybe two subepisodes): Jesus is mocked and crucified. Nine historical presents are found in this passage. No longer is the historical present simply limited to motion, transportation, and speech verbs. The verbs in the historical present here are συγκαλοῦσιν "they call together" v. 16; ἐνδιδύσκουσιν "they clothe [him] in" v. 17; περιτιθέασιν "they place upon" v. 17; ἐξάγουσιν "they lead [him] out" v. 20; ἀγγαρεύουσιν "they commandeer" v. 21; φέρουσιν "they take away" v. 22; σταυροῦσιν "they crucify" v. 24; διαμερίζονται "they divide" (in an Old Testament quotation) v. 24; σταυροῦσιν (two thieves) v. 27.

Thus, not only do we have an impressive number of historical presents but a more unrestricted domain of their occurrence. The crucial verb "crucify" occurs

---

[26] Cranfield, *Mark*, 438–439; Lane, *Mark*, 526–528.

twice in the historical present in the passage. Historical presents dominate the action part of the episode until the action merges into reporting of speech acts (mockeries and taunts) in vv. 29–32, where no more historical presents are found.

Episode 9, 15:33–41: The death of Jesus.

Episode 10, 15:42–47: The burial.

Episode 11, 16:1–8: The resurrection. There are three historical presents in this passage: ἔρχονται "they come" v. 2; θεωροῦσιν "they see" v. 4; λέγει "he says" v. 6. Again these verbs characterize three out of the eight verses in this brief account.

In regard to the almost universally felt problem regarding the abrupt ending of the Gospel according to Mark—a problem felt from the earliest centuries when at least two attempts were made to "finish" the Gospel—I adopt the suggestion that Mark himself terminated the Gospel in this abrupt manner. Just as the Gospel starts abruptly so it by his intention ends abruptly with denouement as peak—without further wind-down or closure.[27]

Evaluation of the Exegetical Worth of Such an Analysis

What then? Is the analysis offered here simply another tedious example of over-structuring on the part of the analyst? In sidestepping this accusation I point out here some theological implications of the analysis. To begin with, however, let us recognize that our bracketing and labeling is no more a part of the authorial intent of the author Mark than phonological and grammatical analytic conventions figure with us in our immediate intuitive use of language. All such analytical devices—including those invoked in this essay—are attempts to make the message of a text explicit. But in invoking the narrative template as the starting point we appeal to something rooted in our cognitive structure. We know, for example, from how people react, that pointless stories, plots without resolution and ceaseless rounds of events without prominence or progress are not tolerated by listeners or readers. Furthermore, in invoking recursion, story-within-story or simply pause-for-station-identification breaks we tread again on ground provided by basic facts of language structure. From these cognitive and linguistic concerns the present analysis has come about.[28]

---

[27] For a brief bibliography of older authorities (prior to 1955) that accepted the view here suggested, see Cranfield, *Mark*, 471—although he himself rejects this explanation.

[28] I also note here the appearance of Mark Wegener's book *Cruciformed: The Literary Impact of Mark's Story of Jesus and His Disciples* (University Press of America, 1995). Wegener's

I point out here as of special interest several analytical results of considerable exegetical import: (1) The setting up of a compound discourse in EPISODE 2 elevates the two feeding miracles of Jesus above the nagging doubt that we have here simply a source-motivated doublet. Each feeding miracle is in a separate but parallel embedded discourse with startlingly similar closures in 7:31–37 and 8:22–26. By thus twice presenting Jesus as nourisher/provider a strong theological point is implicitly made (cf. Gen. 41:32) which another Gospel writer, John, explicitly develops in ch. 6 of his Gospel: Christ the bread of life. (2) Miracles of healing told in detail with sparkling dialogue mark climaxes in several parts of the ongoing work, namely ch. 5, 7:31–37 along with 8:22–26, and finally 10:46–52. Each such climactic display of Jesus' supernatural power makes more acute and agonizing the challenge to the establishment of his day and makes more crucial the question "Who is he?" (3) The putting together of 8:27–9:50 as central and pivotal to the whole work, connecting plausibly with the baptism and temptation in the Inciting Incident and with the trial scene at the end, foregrounds the question of the identity of Jesus: the claim is made that the historical Jesus is a supernatural figure, the Christ. All this is vindicated by the denouement of the Gospel, the resurrection. Even a linear/recursive analysis such as that here presented yields at this point to the presence of chiastic elements in Mark's composition. (4) The recognition of didactic peaks in Mark is a way of showing how larger blocks of teaching are deployed characteristically before action peaks, as in ch. 4, the parables; 7:1–23, clean and unclean foods; 10:32–45, servanthood in the light of Jesus' sufferings; and especially 11:12–13:37, the controversy-enveloped last teachings. (5) The manner in which Mark underscores the scene of Jesus' praying in the garden constrains us to recognize that the grand action finale has three great events: Gethsemane, Calvary and the empty tomb—with profound theological implications. (6) The recognition of local chiastic structures in 11:12–26 and in 14:1–11 has further import. With the former, the cleansing of the Temple is surely inciting and provocative of much of the following controversy, but it is wrapped up in the enacted parable of the cursed and withering figtree. In the latter passage, while conspiracy and betrayal lead to all that follows, Mark gives the story a wonderful twist by putting in, as the key of the chiasmus, the anointing of Jesus at Bethany—implying that devotion to the wonderful figure revealed in his Gospel will in the end outweigh conspiracy and dark betrayal.

---

study and mine have in common a concern for holistic analysis and discourse movement. His book is especially to be commended for its further concern with reader impact of the Gospel.

Appendix: Display of the Discourse Structure
of the Gospel according to Mark

Basic Assumptions

A. Very probably Mark is not a simple linear sequence of pericopes—91 according to Aland *et al.*—such as we might obtain by attention to breaks based on all possible transition markers, e.g. time expressions (T), locative expressions (L), or introduction of new participants. Very probably a series of more inclusive blocks is present, and these should have some relation to the typical narrative template.

B. Inciting incidents and peaks, both didactic and action, are very probably involved—as well as certain episodes which may be called *pivotal.*

C. Multiple occurrences of the historical present (HP), especially when not limited to verbs of speech or to verbs of speech and motion, may contribute to such marking as suggested in B above. Ralph Enos's suggestion (1981), that pericope-initial HP's may mark material of special theological importance, is of possible relevance. For this reason, a pericope-initial HP is labelled below with the sign #. Typically, these are motion verbs or verbs of speech.

APERTURE of whole book 1:1

STAGE of whole book (ministry of John) 1:2–8

EPISODE 1 (INCITING INCIDENT) 1:9–13. A brief embedded discourse or a compound paragraph:

> The Holy Spirit comes on Jesus and confirms his sonship; the heavens are "split"
>
> The Holy Spirit drives# him out to be tempted by the Devil

EPISODE 2 The rise to prominence 1:14–5:43:

> Stage: Time, place, circumstances, Jesus and his message 1:14–15
>
> Episode 1 An embedded discourse with five episodes, the last of which may constitute an action peak: 1:16–45.
>
>> *Episode 1* Calls four fishermen 1:16–20
>>
>> *Episode 2* (motion verb#, place name) Exorcism in the synagogue 1:21–28
>>
>> *Episode 3* Healings and exorcisms at the house of Peter 1:29–34
>>
>> *Episode 4* (T, motion verb) Preaching tour begins next morning 1:35–39
>>
>> *Episode 5* (*action peak?*) (motion verb#, participant) Heals a leper and great crowds follow so that he can no longer openly enter a city 1:40–45

Episode 2 (Capernaum, T "after some days") Tangling with critics (embedded discourse with five episodes, the first of which is Inciting Incident and the last of which is Peak) 2:1–3:6:

Episode 1 (Inciting Incident) (several HP's) Jesus heals a paralytic and pre-sumes (?) to forgive his sins. (The latter is the big point according to Mat-thew who omits all the interesting details.) 2:1–12

Episode 2 (motion verbs, L, and πάλιν) Jesus calls Levi and eats with sin-ners 2:13–17

Episode 3 (motion verb#, speech verb#, participant switch) Questions about fasting 2:18–22

Episode 4 (motion verb, L) Plucking and eating grain on the Sabbath 2:23–27

Episode 5 Action Peak (πάλιν, all speech verbs are HP) Jesus heals a man with a withered hand on the Sabbath; first mentioning of a plot to kill him 3:1–6

Episode 3 Increasing confrontation and misunderstanding (embedded dis-course with four episodes):

Episode 1 (many place names, Jesus, motion verbs) Attempted withdraw-al, great crowds, teaches from a boat 3:7–12

Episode 2 (motion verb#, verb "call"#, L) Choosing of the Twelve 3:13–19

Episode 3 (2 motion verb#, L, and πάλιν) Great crowds; his family sets out to fetch him home; those who ascribe his power to Beelzebub receive a solemn warning 3:20–30

Episode 4 (motion verb#, participant switch; all verbs of speech are HP) Arrival of his family; Jesus says that his disciples are his true family—is this a peak? 3:31–35

Episode 4 didactic peak (motion verb#, L, and πάλιν) Parables and aftermath 4:1–41. Internal structure? Two episodes, the second of which is an action peak which concludes a hortatory discourse:

Episode 1 One long compound paragraph with clear aperture and clo-sure—reinforced by a mid-paragraph reference in vv. 11–12; the theme is teaching in parables 4:1–34

Episode 2 (action peak) This section is tightly connected to what precedes by "evening of same day" and "they take# him as he was in the boat" (L, internal HP's). Jesus stills a storm on the lake; for the first time the ques-tion is raised "Who is he?" 4:35–40

Episode 5 action peak of whole embedded discourse (i.e. of 1:14–5:43) Great miracles in great detail. All of ch. 5 is an embedded discourse with two episodes the second of which has more explicit peak-marking:

> *Episode 1* (L, motion verb) Healing of Gadarene demoniac 5:1–20

> *Episode 2* (L, motion verb, proper names Jesus and Jairus; story within a story with woman's case history given in string of participles, HP's in the bracketing story) 5:21–43

EPISODE 3 compound narrative discourse with two somewhat parallel parts, Jesus at full tide as power figure and nurturer 6:1–8:26:

Part 1 embedded discourse with four episodes, didactic peak and action peak.

Episode 1 (2 motion verbs#, L) Rejection at Nazareth 6:1–6

Episode 2 ("calls"#, new participants) Jesus sends out the Twelve 6:7–13

Episode 3 (new participant, Herod raises question of Jesus' identity) flashback records death of John the Baptist 6:14–29

Episode 4 embedded discourse with three episodes 6:30–56 (back and forth across the lake):

> *Episode 1* (motion verb#, participants, name Jesus) Disciples return and Jesus feeds the 5000 6:30–44

> *Episode 2* (motion verb, L) Jesus walks on water 6:45–52 (motion verb# in v. 48)

> *Episode 3* (motion verb, L) Healing in and around Gennesaret 6:53–56

Episode 5 didactic peak (motion verb#, new participants) Disputation about the "clean" and the "unclean" 7:1–23

Episode 6 action peak, Miracles performed on excursus through territory of Tyre and return; the two subepisodes have cross-referencing settings, dialogue and detail:

> *Episode 1* (motion verb, L, participant) The faith of Syrophoenician woman 7:24–30

> *Episode 2* (motion verb, L, participant, πάλιν) Healing of the deaf and dumb man 7:31–37 ("bring"# and "beseech"# in v. 32; cf. 8:22–26 below)

Part 2 embedded discourse with three episodes and action peak:

Episode 1 (time, participants, πάλιν) Feeding of the 4000 8:1–9

Episode 2 (motion verb, L, participants) Pharisees demand a sign 8:10–12

Episode 3 (motion verb, πάλιν) The "leaven" of the Pharisees and Herod 8:13–21

Episode 4 action peak (motion verb#, "bring"#, "beseech"# L, participant) Blind man healed in two stages! (unique in miracles of Jesus) 8:22–26

EPISODE 4 (CENTRAL AND PIVOTAL) "Who is He?" 8:27–9:50 (316 verses precede this passage; 312 verses follow), embedded discourse with four episodes:

Episode 1 (L—on the road to Caesarea Philippi, name Jesus) Peter's confession, Jesus predicts his death, rebukes Peter, and teaches on cross-bearing 8:27–9:1

Episode 2 (time, L, "takes"#, motion verb#, names of Jesus and three disciples) Transfiguration and aftermath, embedded discourse with two episodes:

> *Episode 1* Transfiguration 9:2–13 (the voice from the cloud, cf. 1:11)

> *Episode 2* (motion verb, L, participants) Jesus heals the boy with the evil spirit 9:14–29 (motion verb# in v. 25)

Episode 3 (motion verb, L) Jesus foretells his death a second time 9:30–32

Episode 4 (motion verb, L) Teaching arising out of the quarrel as to who would be the greatest 9:33–50 (new theme "in my name" vv. 36, 38, and 39–41)

EPISODE 5 The last journey to Jerusalem, embedded discourse with six episodes ch. 10:

Stage (2 motion verb#, πάλιν [2×]) 10:1

Episode 1 (participant?—textual variation) Questions on divorce 10:2–12

Episode 2 (motion verb, participants) Jesus blesses the children 10:13–16

Episode 3 (motion verb, participant) The rich young ruler; resultant teaching 10:17–31

Episode 4 didactic peak, compound discourse with two subepisodes 10:32–45:

> *Episode 1* (motion verb, L—in the road going up to Jerusalem, name Jesus) Jesus leads the way up to Jerusalem and for third time predicts his death 10:32–34

> *Episode 2* (motion verb#, proper names) Request of James and John provokes further teaching on servanthood, culminating with an insightful saying on the meaning of his death 10:35–45

Episode 5 action peak (motion verb#, participant) Healing of blind Bartimaeus. Story told with dramatic detail and dialogue ("call"# in v. 49) 10:46–52

EPISODE 6 DIDACTIC PEAK and ACTION PEAK 11:1–16:8:

Episode 1 Inciting Incident (motion verb#, "send"#, "say"# L, T, three more HP's occur internal) The triumphal entry 11:1–11

Episode 2 DIDACTIC PEAK 11:12–13:37, In the verbal dueling below * marks where Jesus takes the initiative:

Episode 1 Inciting Incident, a chiastic structure ABA

Episode 1 (motion verb, T, L) The cursing of the fig tree 11:12–14

Episode 2 (motion verb#, L) The cleansing of the Temple 11:15–19

Episode 3 (motion verb, T) The withering of the fig tree; lesson on faith 11:20–26

Episode 2 (2 motion verbs#, T, participants) The authority of Jesus is questioned 11:27–33

*Episode 3 Parable of the Tenants 12:1–12

Episode 4 (motion verb#, T, L, participants) Question regarding paying tribute to Caesar 12:13–17

Episode 5 (motion verb#, participants) Question regarding the resurrection 12:18–27

Episode 6 (motion verb, participants) Question regarding the greatest commandment 12:28–34

*Episode 7 (L) Jesus questions them about David's son 12:35–37

*Episode 8 Jesus denounces the scribes 12:38–40

*Episode 9 (L) Jesus commends the widow's offering 12:41–44

Episode 10 (motion verb, L, response to a remark of his disciples) Jesus foretells the destruction of the temple 13:1–2

Episode 11, didactic peak of this embedded discourse (motion verb, L, answer to a question put by three disciples) "Olivet discourse" (hortatory, with at least three or four points; analysis not given here)

Episode 3 ACTION PEAK, chs. 14, 15 and 16:1–8:

Episode 1 (T) Inciting Incident in a chiastic structure ABA

Episode 1 (T, participants) The plot to kill Jesus 14:1–2

Episode 2 (motion verb, L, participants) The anointing at Bethany 14:3–9

Episode 3 (motion verb, participants) Judas agrees to betray Jesus 14:10–11

Episode 2 The Last Passover 14:12–31

Episode 1 ("send"#, long T) Preparations 14:12–16

Episode 2 (motion verb#, T) Prophecy of betrayal 14:17–21

Episode 3 Institution of the Lord's Supper 14:22–26

Episode 4 (Proper name Jesus) Peter's denial foretold 14:27–31

Episode 3 pivotal (motion verb#, L, eight HP's) Jesus prays in Gethsemane 14:32–42

Episode 4 (motion verb#, participants-Judas) Betrayal and seizure 14:43–52 (HP in the isolated incident mentioned at the close in v. 52)

Episode 5 (motion verb#, proper name Jesus, participants) Jesus before the council 14:53–65

Episode 6 (motion verb#, participants) Peter's denials 14:66–72

Episode 7 (motion verb, T, L, participants) Jesus is sentenced by Pontius Pilate 15:1–15

Episode 8 Action Peak (motion verbs, both initial and internal, new participants, nine HP's) (maybe two subepisodes) Jesus is mocked and crucified 15:16–32

Episode 9 (T marked twice, darkness, proper name Jesus) Jesus dies 15:33–41

Episode 10 (motion verb, T, participant) The burial 15:42–47

Episode 11 Peak (denouement) (motion verb, T marked twice, L, participants, three HP's) The resurrection 16:1–8

3

LUKE

TODD CHIPMAN

"The way or the manner, i.e., the structure, in which a notion is communicated, is the heart of its effectiveness. Although the structural pattern may not be obtrusive (and effective communication usually *does not* reveal its structure obtrusively) it is a necessary prerequisite for any sensible discourse that it should be based on an underlying structural pattern."[1]

Methodology

The discipline of discourse analysis seeks to identify patterns of language in a text. Robert E. Longacre, Peter Cotterell, Max Turner, Stanley E. Porter and Jeffrey T. Reed are among those who have joined J.P. Louw in applying discourse analysis to texts of Christian Scripture. Their perspectives influence my presentation of the Gospel of Luke in what follows. Reed notes that discourse analysis has the potential to bring the grammarian and the commentator closer together as they work to identify the functional use of language in the whole of a text.[2] Porter writes that literary disciplines influence discourse analysis, including anthropology and sociolinguistics.[3] Applying discourse analysis to an historical

---

[1] Johannes P. Louw, "Discourse Analysis and the Greek New Testament," *BT* 24, no. 1 (1973): 101–02 (italics original).

[2] Jeffrey T. Reed, "Discourse Analysis," *Handbook to the Exegesis of the New Testament*, ed. Stanley E. Porter (Brill, 2002), 194.

[3] Stanley E. Porter, "Discourse Analysis: Introduction and Core Concepts," in *Linguistic Analysis of the Greek New Testament: Studies in Tools, Methods and Practice* (Baker, 2015), 142.

text like the Gospel of Luke[4] confirms Porter's observation. I suggest four steps for analyzing a discourse.[5]

Identify the Genre of the Discourse

Discourse analysis has the capacity to explain why a text is placed in a certain genre.[6] By identifying the genre of a text, an interpreter can apply the best tools for analyzing said text and explaining its character. The interpreter will need to have the right expectations about the text—even if those expectations are superficial—if he is to present the structure of the text to its readers. As Robert E. Longacre and Shin Ja J. Hwang note, the interpreter working in a hortatory text should not bring the expectations appropriate for a procedural text.[7] Longacre's table of notional discourse types distinguishes narrative, procedural, behavioral, and expository texts.[8] Each of these is (+) or (−) agent orientation and (+) or (−) contingent temporal succession. Narrative, procedural, behavioral, and expository texts can also be analyzed along the parameters of (+) or (−) projection (future or past temporal reference) and tension (struggle of participants).

I recognize the Gospel of Luke as an historical narrative offering a biographical portrait of Jesus of Nazareth. As such, it displays characteristics of Longacre's narrative notional discourse type. The Gospel of Luke is (+) agent orientation in that participants like Jesus, John the Baptist, the disciples, the Jewish

---

[4] Unless noted otherwise, all references to and citations of the Greek text are from NA[28] and English quotations are from the ESV.

[5] Reed proposes four steps in the discourse analysis process: distinguishing the various linguistic and extra-linguistic levels which influence discourse production and interpretation, analyzing the semantic content of discourse, investigating the interpersonal dimensions of discourse, and studying the cohesive structures of discourse (Reed, "Discourse Analysis," 189–217). My schema in what follows reflects but does not mirror Reed's process. Porter notes that discourse analysis has at least three goals: (1) establishing the boundaries of a text unit, (2) identifying phenomena that provide cohesion of the units of said text and provide coherence of meaning therein, and (3) articulating the ideas, persons, or events an author makes prominent in a text (Stanley E. Porter, "Linguistics and Biblical Interpretation," in *Linguistic Analysis of the Greek New Testament*, 90–91).

[6] "A linguistic analysis of a literary text aims at explaining the interpretation and evaluation that are put upon that text. The role of linguistics is to say how and why the text means what it does to the reader or listener, and how and why he evaluates it in a certain way" (M.A.K. Halliday and Ruqaiya Hasaan, *Cohesion in English* [Longman, 1976], 328).

[7] Robert E. Longacre and Shin Ja J. Hwang, *Holistic Discourse Analysis*, 2nd ed. (SIL International, 2012), 153–84.

[8] Robert E. Longacre, *The Grammar of Discourse*, 2nd ed. (Plenum, 1996), 10, and Longacre and Hwang, *Holistic*, 37. In *Holistic*, Longacre and Hwang note that discourse types like drama, persuasion, description, and indictment need special attention (Longacre and Hwang, *Holistic*, 37–38).

leadership and others described in the text participate as voluntary actors in relation to one another. It is (+) contingent temporal succession in that the events Luke describes are also presented in relation to one another. One event leads to another event as Luke scaffolds the text toward the climax. In his prologue, Luke writes that he has investigated the events of Jesus' life, events that occurred far enough in the past that others had already written about them (Luke 1:1–4). Luke's Gospel is thus (–) projection, temporally situated in the past even though the events of Jesus' life, death, and resurrection would have implications for the moment of Luke's writing and the future of the world. Finally, the Gospel of Luke, in accord with the other canonical Gospels, is (+) tension. Jesus' death and resurrection at the conclusion of the Gospels necessitates identifying anticipatory scenes of conflict.

Determine Unit Boundaries within the Discourse

Once the interpreter has established the genre of the discourse in view, he is ready to embark upon the primary focus of discourse analysis, determining the breaks that mark units within the discourse.[9] Identifying the boundaries of a discourse positions the interpreter to explain how the ideas in the text flow one to another. For larger texts, often narrative, a top-down approach might be the first step. A bottom-up analysis often suits shorter texts, especially epistolary literature like that found in the New Testament.[10]

Longacre proposes that a top-down analysis of narrative is conducive to identifying the notional structure slots of the text.[11] What Longacre labels slots resemble the components of the storywriter's plot schema.[12] Most narrative texts begin

---

[9] Discourse analysis, as Longacre and Hwang note, operates on the presupposition that both the main structure and embedded discourse units are identifiable—even though not every analyst will arrive at the same conclusion (Longacre and Hwang, *Holistic*, 39, 43). This can be demonstrated even from the fact that NA[28] marks 245 paragraphs and the THGNT has 358.

[10] See Porter, "Discourse Analysis: Introduction and Core Concepts," 137–38 for advantages and disadvantages of each method.

[11] Longacre and Hwang (*Holistic*, 45) suggest that narrative is conducive to macro analysis because a story has well-delineated participants, and actions that can be viewed through a who, what, when, where, why, and how scheme. The flow of the narrative is identified by marking what Longacre calls Episodes. He suggests that the schematic slots like exposition, inciting incident, climax, denouement, and conclusion are consistent in the narrative genre.

[12] Longacre, *Grammar*, 33–35; Longacre and Hwang *Holistic*, 54–55. In analyzing the Gospel of Mark according to notional structure slots, Longacre labels slot one "Stage," slot three "Inciting Incident", and combines slots six and seven under the heading "Closure" (Robert E. Longacre, "A Top-Down, Template-Driven Narrative Analysis, Illustrated by Application to Mark's Gospel," in *Discourse Analysis and the New Testament: Approaches and Results*, ed. Stanley E. Porter and Jeffrey T. Reed, JSNTSup 170 [Sheffield Academic, 1999], 140–168). Longacre notes

with information on time, place, and main participants, information Longacre places within the Exposition or Stage of the discourse. The second phase of a discourse is the Inciting Moment, when some event or participant takes an unexpected turn and pricks the reader's curiosity. Longacre notes that the next slot, Developing Conflict, portrays an intensification of action, often requiring several embedded episodes. As these episodes unfold the reader recognizes mounting tension and reads on to discover how the major problem(s) will be resolved. The scenes portraying final confrontation Longacre labels Climax. In the Climax slot, the major characters of the plot fulfill their roles in the narrative, their true colors shine forth. The fifth notional slot Longacre identifies in narrative he labels Denouement. Here the author expresses the resolution that proceeds from the final confrontation in the Climax slot. Longacre identifies the portion of text where the author further unwinds the results of the Climax as Final Suspense. In the Conclusion, the seventh and final notional slot of narrative, the story comes to an end.

Longacre's notional slot structure resembles Cotterell and Turner's list of six sections typically found in narrative discourse: (1) Title: a formula introducing or clarifying genre, (2) Stage: identification of the problem, conflict or question of the discourse, (3) Pre-Peak Episodes: the explication of the issue, increasing tension, (4) Peak: the solution as it develops, (5) Post-peak episodes: clarification, tying-up loose ends, and (6) Closure.[13] Approaching the Gospel of Luke via a synthesis of Longacre's and Cotterell and Turner's schemata for narrative discourse, I identify the following units. These units are visualized in the Profile in Figure 3.1 that follows.[14]

Title and Introduction (1:1–4)

Stage (1:5–2:52), the Births of John and Jesus, and the Hopes of Israel

Inciting Incident (3:1–4:13), the Identification of John and Jesus in Salvation History

Mounting Tension 1: Galilean Ministry (4:14–9:50), Confirmation of Jesus as God's Messianic Prophet

Mounting Tension 2: Mission to Jerusalem (9:51–19:44), Confrontation of Israel's Religion

---

that hortatory, persuasive, expository and procedural discourse also have identifiable notional slots useful for identifying the structure and progress in the text (Longacre, *Grammar*, 34, n. 2).

[13] Peter Cotterell and Max Turner, *Linguistics & Biblical Interpretation* (InterVarsity, 1989), 247–48.

[14] Longacre and Hwang describe Profile as a "visual representation of the overall discourse progression from aperture, stage, prepeak, peak, postpeak to closure and finish; surface structure realization of mounting and declining tension within a discourse" (Longacre and Hwang, *Holistic*, 221).

Climax (19:45–24:12), Jerusalem ministry: Condemnation of Temple-Centered
    Religion, and Jesus' Triumph

Denouement and Closure (24:13–53), Resurrection Appearances: Confirmation
    of Jesus as God's Victorious Messiah

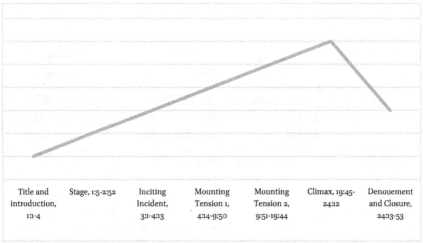

| Title and introduction, 1:1-4 | Stage, 1:5-2:52 | Inciting Incident, 3:1-4:13 | Mounting Tension 1, 4:14-9:50 | Mounting Tension 2, 9:51-19:44 | Climax, 19:45-24:12 | Denouement and Closure, 24:13-53 |

Figure 3.1. Profile of the Gospel of Luke

The macro-structure I offer here resembles those presented in recent commentaries on Luke's Gospel. Though I. Howard Marshall, Darrell L. Bock, Joel B.
Green, and I differ in some exact verse designations for the units we observe in
the Gospel of Luke, our macro-outlines are similar (Figure 3.2).[15] Scenes from
John's and Jesus' childhood dominate 1:5–2:52. These scenes differ from the early
ministries of John and Jesus recorded in 3:1–4:13. Jesus' ministry in the northern
regions around Galilee (4:14–9:50) is differentiated from his mission to Jerusalem
(9:51–19:44). And obvious is the break between the crucifixion of Jesus and the
account of Jesus' resurrection and subsequent ministry in chapter 24.

    Some might diminish the value of discourse analysis because it does not offer
novel interpretations of a text. I reply with two comments. First, as Longacre, Cotterell and Turner, and others note, because discourse analysis is based upon principles that humans have used to communicate across the ages, often the results
of a discourse analysis will reflect non-discourse-analysis based divisions of a
text. Nonetheless, as M. A. K. Halliday and Ruqaiya Hasan note, linguistic analysis

---

[15] I. Howard Marshall, *The Gospel of Luke: A Commentary on the Greek Text*, NIGTC (Eerdmans, 1978); Darrell L. Bock, *Luke 1:1–9:50*, BECNT 3A (Baker, 1994) and Darrell L. Bock, *Luke
9:51–24:53*, BECNT 3B (Baker, 1996); Joel B. Green, *The Gospel of Luke*, NICNT (Eerdmans, 1996).

Marshall	Bock	Green	Chipman
1:1–4, Preface	1:1–2:52, Luke's Preface and the Introduction of John and Jesus	1:1–4, Prologue	1:1–4, Introduction
1:5–2:52, The Birth and Childhood of Jesus		1:5–2:52, The Birth and Childhood of Jesus	1:5–2:52, The Births of John and Jesus, and the Hopes of Israel
3:1–4:13, John the Baptist and Jesus	3:1–4:13, Preparation for Ministry: Anointed by God	3:1–4:13, The Preparation for the Ministry of Jesus	3:1–4:13, The Identification of John and Jesus in Salvation History
4:14–9:50, The Ministry in Galilee	4:14–9:50, Galilean Ministry: Revelation of Jesus	4:14–9:50, The Ministry of Jesus in Galilee	4:14–9:50, Galilean Ministry: Confirmation of Jesus as God's Messianic Prophet
9:51–19:10, Progress towards Jerusalem	9:51–19:44, Jerusalem Journey: Jewish Rejection and the New Way	9:51–19:48, On the Way to Jerusalem	9:51–19:44, Mission to Jerusalem: Confrontation of Israel's Religion
19:11–21:38, The Ministry in Jerusalem	19:45–24:53, The Innocent One Slain and Raised	20:1–21:38, Teaching in the Jerusalem Temple	19:45–24:12, Jerusalem Ministry: Condemnation of Temple-Centered Religion, and Jesus' Triumph
22:1–24:53, The Passion and Resurrection of Jesus		22:1–23:56, The Suffering and Death of Jesus	
		24:1–53, The Exaltation of Jesus	24:13–53, Resurrection Appearances: Confirmation of Jesus as God's Victorious Messiah

Figure 3.2. Comparison of Macro-Structural Outlines

of a text seeks to explain why a text is interpreted as it is.[16] The value of discourse analysis is not solely in its potential to offer new interpretations of a text—though at times it does—but in its ability to explain the unit breaks in a text and the various lexical and grammatical features that serve as cohesive ties for those units.[17] I offer here an explanation of how the various units of Luke's Gospel fit together in and of themselves and contribute to the whole of Luke's narrative about Jesus.

Locate Cohesive Features within Units of the Discourse

Having identified the main divisions in a discourse, the discourse analyst then scours these units of text to discover features providing cohesion within each unit.[18] That is, after the discourse analyst working in narrative completes a top-down investigation of the text, he is ready to work bottom-up, unit by unit. Much of what follows in my analysis of Luke's Gospel carries out this third step in discourse analysis.

Reed's categorization of cohesive elements proves helpful for moving between macro- and micro-analysis of the text.[19] Reed proposes that cohesive linguistic items be identified as either organic or componential. He places units of language that mark transition—especially, conjunctions, particles, prepositions, and certain lexical items—under the heading of organic ties. These linguistic features provide a sense of interdependence in the clauses, phrases, and sentences in both the macro and micro units of a text. Organic cohesive features help the reader to understand the extent of one idea in relation to another. Differentiating between organic and componential cohesive elements, Reed writes, "Whereas organic ties generally concern various paratactic and hypotactic, logico-semantic relationships *between clauses and paragraphs* (and phrases), COMPONENTIAL TIES generally concern the meaningful relationships between *individual linguistic components* in the discourse (e.g. repetition of words)."[20] The linguistic elements Reed identifies as

---

[16] Writing broadly of the value of linguistics, within which he discusses discourse analysis in relation to biblical studies, Porter notes that though we may not always find new insights, we will have analyses that are based upon data derived from investigating the texts themselves (Porter, "Linguistics and Biblical Interpretation," 92).

[17] "Cohesion expresses the continuity that exists between one part of the text and another" (Halliday and Hasan, *Cohesion*, 299).

[18] Porter notes that nearly any linguistic feature—including morphological elements like verbal-tense forms, voice, and mood—in a text can contribute to the cohesion of that text. Discourse analysis is especially concerned with these cohesive features because they can be quantified (Porter, "Discourse Analysis: Introduction and Core Concepts," 139–40). For examples of quantification schema, see Halliday and Hasan, *Cohesion*, 333–55 and Longacre, *Grammar*, 269–96.

[19] Jeffrey T. Reed, "The Cohesiveness of Discourse: Towards a Model of Linguistic Criteria for Analyzing New Testament Discourse," in *Discourse Analysis and the New Testament*, ed. Porter and Reed, 28–46.

[20] Reed, "Cohesiveness of Discourse," 36.

componential ties serve the bottom-up analysis of a text. Reed notes three sub-categories of componential ties: co-reference, co-classification, and co-extension. Concerning reference, Reed writes that a text must be analyzed to identify the personal, temporal, and spatial linguistic elements that point to other elements in a unit.[21]

Thus, the various sub-units in Luke 1:5–2:52 can be recognized by the individual speakers (the angel Gabriel, Zechariah, Elizabeth, Mary, etc.) and their settings. Together, these speakers and their activities present the births and childhood experiences of John the Baptist and Jesus. Likewise, units of text can be identified by observing words of the same class or genus, what Reed labels co-classification. For instance, as will be noted in what follows, nearly half of Luke's references to how the crowds respond to Jesus are found in Mounting Tension 1: Galilean Ministry (4:14–9:50). These serve as cohesive ties for Jesus' ministry before he sets out toward Jerusalem.

Distinguish Peak Units within the Discourse

"Peaking in narrative text is always marked, so as to ensure that the reader is aware that the peak has been reached."[22] Longacre describes peak units in narrative discourse as "zones of turbulence."[23] These are places in the text where lexical and grammatical features noted for their cohesive force throughout the text occur with a higher degree of density. Longacre suggests that peak micro-units can be labeled as Action Peaks or Didactic Peaks.

---

[21] Longacre and Hwang offer a ten-fold schema to track the storyline of a text via its participants: First mention, Integration into the story as central, Tracking routinely, Restaging or reinstatement, Boundary marking episode or sub-episode, Confrontation and/or role-change, Locally contrastive/thematic status, Evaluation or comment by the narrator, Addressee in dialogue, and Exit (Longacre and Hwang, *Holistic*, 84). They conclude that major participants tend to be the subjects of verbs and are qualified by a full noun phrase while minor participants are often the objects of those verbs (Longacre and Hwang, *Holistic*, 92).

[22] Cotterell and Turner, *Linguistics*, 246. Peak units might be recognized by observing what Porter notes as linguistic features that are emphasized in a section of a discourse. These are referred to as marked forms—a shift from the normal course or the style of the text. A unit with several marked forms becomes prominent, a peak. "Prominence is motivated by markedness. That is, it involves marked features that are (by whatever means) shown to be motivated in a particular context, so that a given dimension of a text is brought to the fore" (Porter, "Discourse Analysis: Introduction and Core Concepts," 141).

[23] Longacre, *Grammar*, 38–48. See also Longacre and Hwang, *Holistic*, 53–54. In his discourse analysis of Mark, Longacre notes that peak-marking features can be summarized under three headings: "(a) augmentation of the storyline (verb forms, sentence lengthening or shortening, crowding the storyline with a rapid sequence of happenings, with minute components of actions, or even with paraphrase of actions as pseudo-happenings); (b) immediacy (detail and dialogue); and (c) maximum interlacing of participants, that is, the 'crowded stage' effect" (Longacre, "A Top-Down, Template-Driven Narrative Analysis," 143–44).

Longacre describes six characteristics of these zones of turbulence. First and most frequent is rhetorical underlining. Here the narrator uses extra words, detail and description to make sure the reader gets the point. Second, concentration of participants. In the peak units, characters (or characters representing particular classes) prominent throughout the narrative interact with each other in relation to the primary problems or conflicts of the story.[24] Third, heightened vividness. What Longacre means is that shifts in noun/verb concentration and verbal tense-forms— together with concentration of first and second person pronouns—create a zone of turbulence, drawing the reader into the story at that point. Fourth, peak units are characterized by a change of pace. Turbulence is observed via a shift to shorter or longer sentences and paragraphs, polysyndeton or asyndeton, or the sudden use of extended adnominal or adverbial clauses.[25] Fifth, the change of vantage-point or orientation. If a story is told in the third person and then shifts to first, the place at which the shift takes place may be the beginning of a peak unit. Longacre's final characteristic of peak units is the use of particles and onomatopoeia, rhetorical features that might cause the reader to pause and feel the story.

In the analysis of the Gospel of Luke that follows, I note four Action Peaks. The various participants and events in these scenes confirm that Jesus is who he claims to be, God's Son, the Messiah. First is 2:41–51, when Jesus stays behind in Jerusalem in the temple while his parents begin to travel home to Galilee (the final scene of Stage). Second is 13:10–17, when Jesus heals a crippled woman in the synagogue on the Sabbath (during Jesus' Galilean ministry, which I identify as Mounting Tension 1). Third is 19:1–10, Jesus' visit to Zacchaeus' home (toward the end of Jesus' mission to Jerusalem, which I identify as Mounting Tension 2). The final Action Peak is 24:1–12, the discovery of the empty tomb (which I identify as the end of Climax). Three of the four Action Peaks I identify here are unique to the Gospel of Luke.

I recognize four Didactic Peaks in Luke's Gospel. In each of these, Jesus is positioned or positions himself as a divine figure, speaking to his opponents in view of Scripture with the result that his teaching confirms his identity as the Messiah. First is 4:1–13, Jesus' dialogue with devil in the desert (the final scene of the Inciting Incident). Second is 16:19–31, Jesus' story of the Rich Man and Lazarus (in the latter portion of Jesus' mission to Jerusalem, Mounting Tension 2). Third is 20:20–47, Jesus' diatribe with the Jewish leadership (during Climax) as he teaches in the temple in the presence of both the crowds and his disciples. Finally, in 24:44–49 Jesus teaches the eleven and the Emmaus disciples (toward

---

[24] Cotterell and Turner note that the peak unit is marked by a shift in participant reference. If the story consistently has a crowded stage, a scene that involves just one character may feature as a peak unit (Cotterell and Turner, *Linguistics*, 246).

[25] Cotterell and Turner suggest that the key peak-marking feature here is also shift. If the pace is normally slow, peak is characterized by a sudden quickening of pace. The converse is also true (Cotterell and Turner, *Linguistics*, 246).

the end of Denouement and Closure). Two of the four Didactic Peaks in Luke are unique to his Gospel.

Macrostructure

Title and Introduction (Luke 1:1–4)

Luke begins his Gospel with a formal statement of provenance and purpose. He places himself in a stream of tradition, noting that he has investigated matters that others before him have also examined. Luke's offer of an orderly account of the things fulfilled concerning Jesus assures his initial reader, Theophilus, that he can trust what he will read. Luke's statement opens the door for formal analyses of his discourse, making the Gospel of Luke a prime text for discourse analysis.

Stage (1:5–2:52): The Births of John and Jesus, and the Hopes of Israel

I suggest that Luke employs elements of Stage in Luke 1:5–2:52. By the end of Luke 2, Luke casts Jesus—who will be the main character of his discourse—as a noble young adolescent esteemed by God and man. "How did Luke carry his readers to that point?" becomes the question that must be addressed. In Stage, an author will often use the notional element of time/sequence as the basis of the circumstantial, geographical, and other components that provide the setting for the main characters introduced therein. Luke does just that in Luke 1:5–2:52, beginning each major division (1:5, 26, 39, 57; 2:1, 21, 39) with a prepositional phrase or noun case designation identifying temporal or sequential progress.

He begins by noting in Luke 1 the various individuals and events that precede Jesus' birth. In Luke 2, he notes the birth of Jesus and events that follow. By first giving an account of Zechariah and Elizabeth's barrenness and the subsequent miraculous conception of John, Luke delays Jesus' entry into the narrative. Luke initially casts Jesus' birth as an event within a stream of divine activity already in progress. The repetition of temporal markers in Luke 1:5–2:52 contribute to the coherence in the Stage unit and keep the scenes therein moving and connected.

Other cohesive devices in 1:5–2:52 include the repetition of participants, themes, and places. References to David direct the flow of thought in 1:5–2:52 (1:27, 32, 69; 2:4[2x], 11) with just seven references in the remainder of the Gospel. Geographical regions surface frequently in Stage. In 1:5–2:52, Luke notes key events taking place in Judea (1:5, 65; 2:4 with six subsequent references in the Gospel), Jerusalem, (2:25, 38, 41, 43, 45, noted more than thirty times in the remainder of the Gospel), and Nazareth (1:26; 2:4, 39, 51, mentioned just one more time in 4:16). Finally, references to the temple (2:27, 37, 46 with eleven references to come in the Gospel) provide specific historical and theological lenses for the subsequent chapters of Luke's narrative. The way that Luke collocates the aforementioned terms in 1:5–2:52 exemplifies Stage in that they together lay a foundation of thought common to Luke and his readers. Readers of Stage expect that God will fulfill his promises to redeem his people by intervening in history in Jerusalem in accord with the activities of the temple.

Luke introduces a diverse array of figures through whom God begins to carry out his plan. Zechariah, Elizabeth, Mary, Joseph, Jesus, Simeon, Anna, angelic messengers, and the Holy Spirit begin to enact God's redemptive purposes. In Stage (1:5–2:52), iterative speeches and songs of praise provide windows into the expectations Luke establishes with his audience. The angel of the Lord announces to Zechariah that his son would be a figure announcing redemption and calling for repentance (1:13–17). Luke notes the presence of the Holy Spirit in 1:15, 35, 41, 67; 2:25, 26, and 27 and will reference the work of the Spirit ten times in the remainder of his Gospel. The angel Gabriel announces to Mary that her son, Jesus, would be a Davidic ruler (1:30–33). Mary praises God for the forthcoming deliverance he will accomplish by freeing Israel from her enemies (1:46–55). Zechariah likewise praises God with a song of redemption whose dual themes of victory over enemies and forgiveness of sin (1:67–79) frame the Gospel of Luke through chapter 24.

In 1:5–2:40, the human participants and angelic figures speak about John and Jesus. In 2:41–50, Jesus begins to speak for himself as he dialogues with the teachers in the temple. This is the first Action Peak that I identify in Luke's Gospel (Figure 3.3). Jesus accompanies his parents to Jerusalem for the Passover and remains there teaching in the temple and identifying himself as God's Son.

Luke uses this scene in Jesus' adolescence to foreshadow the statements and actions of John and Jesus in 3:1–4:13. Grown up, these men speak for themselves. I suggest that Luke's description of the ministry of John the Baptist and presentation of Jesus' genealogy serve as a protracted thesis statement, confirmed in the chapters that Luke writes through the remainder of his Gospel.

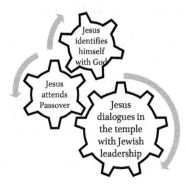

Figure 3.3. Action Peak 1: Jesus in the Temple in Jerusalem after the Passover (2:41–51)

Inciting Incident (3:1–4:13): The Identification of John and Jesus in Salvation History

The identification of Jesus is a central theme in the Gospel of Luke. So, what Inciting Incident might, to use Longacre's phrase, "get something going?"[26] Jesus' endurance of temptation in the wilderness is his first adult confirmation that he is God's Son (4:1–13). I identify 4:1–13 as the first didactic peak in the Gospel of Luke (Figure 3.4). The presence of the Spirit and Jesus' statements of Scripture confirm him as God's Son, despite the devil's efforts to thwart Jesus' mission.

Divine Authority

· The Spirit leads Jesus into the wilderness

Opposition

· The Devil tempts Jesus to exploit his identity as God's Son

---

Confirmation

· Jesus authenticates his identity as God's Son by citing and obeying Scripture

---

Figure 3.4. Didactic Peak 1: Jesus' Responses to the Devil's Temptations (4:1–13)

Luke arranges his Gospel such that the temptation of Jesus immediately follows his presentation of Jesus' genealogy, which identifies Jesus as the Son of God (3:38). The genealogy follows John's baptism of Jesus—during which the divine voice establishes Jesus' identity as God's beloved Son (3:22). John's self-identification as the forerunner and his identification of Jesus as the Messiah in 3:1–18 anticipate the temptation sequence in 4:1–13. Jesus' endurance of temptation in 4:1–13 validates what John announces in 3:7–18. Luke's brief editorial of John's fate with Herod Antipas (3:19–20) reinforces John's prophetic identity and integrity as one who is willing to suffer for his words—words that confirm Jesus as the Messiah.

Luke gets his Gospel going in the Inciting Incident slot (3:1–4:13) by setting out the words and deeds of the central characters introduced in Stage (1:5–2:52). John and Jesus speak and act for the purpose of establishing their identities in salvation history. They operate by the Spirit (3:16, 22; 4:1; noted later in 4:14, 18; 10:21; 11:13; 12:10, 12; 24:49) and the word (3:4–6; 4:4, 8, 12; which Jesus references in 4:18–19; 7:27; 8:10; 12:53; 13:35; 18:20; 19:46; 20:17, 37, 42–43; 22:37; 23:30, 46; 24:27, 44–47). Their ministries confront human opponents (3:7–20; cf. 4:23–27; 7:31–35, 43–48;

---

[26] Longacre, *Grammar*, 33–35; Longacre and Hwang, *Holistic*, 54–55.

10:13–16; 11:37–52; 12:49–53; 13:15–18, 34–35; 19:41–47; et al.) and the anti-God force of evil operating behind them in the world (4:1–13; cf. 4:31–41; 5:12–14, 17–25; 6:6–10, 17–19; 7:1–10, 11–15; 8:26–39, 40–55; 13:10–17; et al.).

Mounting Tension 1: Galilean Ministry (4:14–9:50), Confirmation of Jesus as God's Messianic Prophet

Each of the commentators in Figure 3.1 above note boundaries marking 4:14–9:50 as a unit. The geographical frames of Galilee in 4:14 and journey toward Jerusalem in 9:51 justify these divisions. Discourse analysis seeks to identify not just geographical themes that might be used as cohesive mechanisms but also lexical, grammatical, and ideational phenomena that provide a sense of coherence to a discourse unit. In what follows, I describe 4:14–9:50 as its own story. Here I wish to identify the plotline that provides coherence to 4:14–9:50 and how this unit follows the Inciting Incident unit (3:1–4:13) described above.

I suggest that Jesus undertakes specific ministry activities in and around Galilee in 4:14–9:50 to confirm his self-proclaimed identity as God's messianic prophet à la Isa 61:1–2. At the outset of this unit, Luke places Jesus in a synagogue in Nazareth. There Jesus takes the scroll of Isaiah and reads Isa 61:1–2, stating that in that moment this Scripture was fulfilled. This is no small statement.

Isaiah 61:1–2 describes a Spirit-anointed figure who would preach the gospel to the poor, free those held captive, and heal those suffering from disease and oppression. Together, these three activities would signal to the masses that a time of God's favor had come. For Luke, this tri-fold rubric of prophetic ministry becomes a table of contents for Jesus' ministry through 9:50 (Figure 3.5).

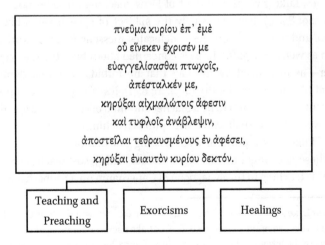

Figure 3.5. Themes of Isa 61:1–2 (Luke 4:18–19) used as Cohesive Ties in Mounting Tension 1: Galilean Ministry (4:14–9:50), Confirmation of Jesus as God's Messianic Prophet

And Luke notes along the way that the crowds are watching. Figure 3.6 shows the percentage of references in 4:14–9:50 that relate to the three themes from Isa 61:1–2 and to the crowds. The lexical basis of these themes is synthesized in what follows.

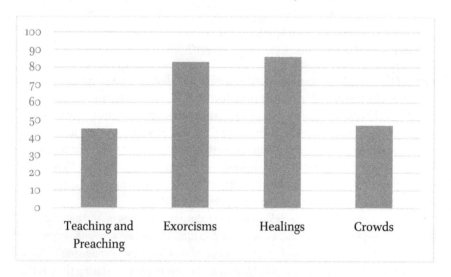

Figure 3.6. Percent of Lucan Cohesive Themes in Mounting Tension 1: Galilean Ministry (4:14–9:50), Confirmation of Jesus as God's Messianic Prophet

In 4:14–9:50, Luke presents Jesus' Spirit-anointed teaching as the base, compelling activity of Jesus' ministry. Jesus teaches in synagogues (4:15, 17, 32, 44), by the lake of Gennesaret (5:1), in a private home (5:17), and on a Galilean plain (6:17, 20). At times, Luke gives the content of Jesus' teaching but does not specify the location (7:29; 8:1, 4). Jesus is usually the subject of speech verbs like διδάσκω, εὐαγγελίζω, and κηρύσσω,[27] but Jesus delegates messengers to go forth speaking about him as well (8:39; 9:1ff.). Jesus is concerned about both the message and the messenger—as evidenced by the fact that he forbids exorcised demons from speaking of his messianic identity (4:34, 41; 8:41). Jesus' dependence upon God in prayer accentuates his claim to be a teacher anointed of God. In 5:16 and 6:12, Jesus' private prayer habits are collocated with public teaching and the call of the twelve.

Five of Luke's six reports of Jesus casting out demons occur in 4:14–9:50.[28] Some of these accounts of exorcism collocate with Jesus' teaching ministry, as when Jesus is teaching in the synagogue of Capernaum on a Sabbath day (4:31–37).

---

[27] Eight of Luke's twenty-seven uses of the lexeme διδάσκω with Jesus as the subject or addressee of the vocative occur in 4:14–9:50. Five of Luke's seven references to Jesus as the functional subject of the lexeme εὐαγγελίζω occur in 4:14–9:50. Five of Luke's six references to Jesus as the functional subject of the lexeme κηρύσσω occur in 4:14–9:50.

[28] The only other report of an exorcism occurs in 13:10–17.

There an unclean demon had control of a man's body. Jesus cast the demon from the man, freeing him before the eyes of those in attendance at the synagogue service that day. And news spread. Luke reports that while Jesus is in Capernaum, he cast out many demons (4:41). Likewise, Jesus' famous Sermon on the Plain (6:20–49) is anticipated by many instances in which Jesus frees those held in spiritual bondage (6:18–19). While Jesus is in the Gerasenes opposite Galilee, he frees a man who was possessed by a legion of demons and lived among the tombs (8:26–39). The final exorcism report during Jesus' Galilean ministry occurs in 9:37–43. Luke emphasizes Jesus' unique authority over demonic forces. While Jesus is with Peter, James, and John on a mountain, transfigured in their presence, the other disciples attempt to cast a demon from a young boy but cannot. The demon holds the boy in physical bondage until the moment when Jesus rebukes it.

Luke records fourteen statements of Jesus' healing miracles. Twelve of these occur in 4:14–9:50, underscoring the notion that Luke portrays Jesus' Galilean ministry as a fulfillment of Isa 61:1–2. Several episodes of Jesus' healing miracles collocate with Jesus' prophetic and exorcism ministries. In 4:38–39, Jesus heals Peter's mother-in-law of a fever. While yet in Capernaum that evening, Jesus performs many other healings and exorcisms (4:40–41). The next day, Jesus departs to preach in other Galilean towns despite the crowds wanting him to stay in their town (4:42–44). Likewise, in 5:17–25, Jesus performs a healing miracle in the context of teaching in a private home as a delegation of Pharisees and teachers of the law look on. In 6:6–10, Jesus heals a man with a paralyzed hand while he is in a synagogue on a Sabbath day teaching as some Pharisees look on. Just before Jesus' Sermon on the Plain (6:20–49), he heals many of their diseases (6:18–19). In 9:6, 11, Jesus' healing ministry also collocates with teaching episodes. But at times in his Galilean ministry, Jesus' healing miracles do not occur in accord with episodes of teaching or exorcism. Faith and desperation on the part of the needy prompt Jesus to heal—as in the case of the Centurion's servant (7:1–10), the widow's son (7:11–15), the synagogue leader's daughter, and the woman suffering from bleeding (8:40–55).

Iteratively throughout 4:14–9:50, Luke presents Jesus' ministry endeavors as fulfillment of his synagogue statement of Isa 61:1–2 in 4:18–19. And Luke notes that many are watching as Jesus goes about Galilee confirming his messianic status. Nearly half of Luke's references to crowds (often signified by ὄχλος) of people surface in 4:14–9:50. Though Luke describes the reactions of the crowds surrounding Jesus as he heads toward Jerusalem in Luke 11–13, in 4:14–9:50, twenty-one times Luke notes how crowds respond to Jesus' teaching, exorcisms, and healings.[29] These lexical references, together with general descriptions of people assembled to behold Jesus, serve as lexical cohesive phenomena for Jesus' Galilean ministry. So prominent are the crowds in Luke's arrangement of Jesus' Galilean ministry

---

[29] 4:30, 40, 42; 5:1, 15, 19, 29; 6:17; 7:9, 11, 24; 8:4, 19, 40, 42, 45; 9:11, 12, 13, 16, 18.

that near its conclusion, Jesus asks the disciples, "Who do the crowds (ὄχλοι) say that I am?" (9:18). At the theological level, Jesus' question elicits Peter's confession that Jesus is the Messiah. But that question rests on a discourse observation: the crowds would have a basis for understanding Jesus because—as Luke empha-sizes—Jesus publicly enacts the messianic activities of Isa 61:1–2, confirming for all that he is God's eschatological anointed prophet. Jesus' messianic acts in 4:14–9:50 are so noteworthy that those who behold his ministry spontaneously spread the news of what they see (4:32, 37; 5:15; 7:16–17).[30] The crowds and individuals who experience Jesus' ministry respond with amazement and intrigue.[31] In his rec-ord of Jesus' Galilean ministry, Luke notes the attitudinal or emotional response of those who observe Jesus' teaching, exorcism or healing ministries (θαυμάζω, 4:22 and 8:25; ἔκστασις, 5:26; rhetorical question in 7:49; ἐξίστημι in 8:56; ἐκπλήσσω in 9:43).[32]

Mounting Tension 2: Mission to Jerusalem (9:51–19:44), Confrontation of Israel's Religion

As I noted in the Methodology section above, discourse analysis identifies the the-matic, lexical, and grammatical elements that provide cohesion to macro-units of a text. The section I label as Mounting Tension 2: Mission to Jerusalem (9:51–19:44) is Luke's account of Jesus' mission to Jerusalem. Luke's statement that Jesus reso-lutely set out for Jerusalem (9:51) anticipates Jesus' arrival in the city in 19:41. Com-mentators identify these geographic references as literary frames in Luke's Gospel.

I suggest that 9:51–19:44 can be read as its own story, an episode. Here Jesus judges and condemns the religious practices of Israel's leaders and their followers. Jesus' statements of judgement and condemnation function either as a response to or result in the Jewish leadership's rejection of Jesus' ministry. In the midst of this tension between Jesus and the Jewish leadership, Luke notes with increasing frequency that Jesus is referred to and addressed as Lord. Jesus' disciples often address him as Lord—the role Jesus fulfills in setting forth the demands of disci-pleship for all that would follow him. The percentages of references to these themes are listed in Figure 3.7. In what follows, I synthesize the lexical stock and context of these references.

---

[30] Though already in 4:14, even before Jesus' statement of Isa 61:1–2 in Nazareth (4:16–19), Luke notes that news about Jesus is spreading among the people in the region.

[31] Luke records only two such responses (11:14 and 38) in Jesus' journey to Jerusalem (9:51–19:44), just one (20:26) when Jesus teaches in Jerusalem during passion week (19:45–23:56), and two others (24:12, 42) in his account of Jesus' resurrection (24:1–53).

[32] "Astonishment (cf. Fear; Miracle; Stir Up)," *NIDNTTE* 1:25; "Surprise, Astonishment (25.206–25.222)," L&N 1:310–312.

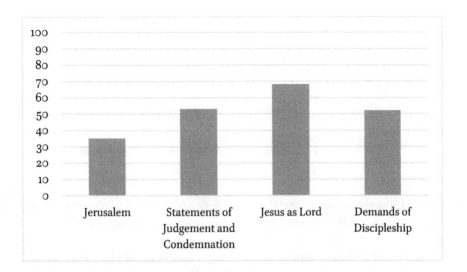

Figure 3.7. Percent of Lucan Cohesive Themes in Mounting Tension 2: Mission to Jerusalem (9:51–19:44), Confrontation of Israel's Religion

In the Methodology section above, I note that verbal tense-forms can be used as a cohesive element in macro-units.[33] This brings us to the issue of pacing in narrative discourse. Because narrative is normally past-time oriented, the aorist and imperfect tense-forms are used to provide oppositional aspectual frames.[34] Both tense-forms describe a past event but differ in aspect. The aorist encodes perfective aspect while the imperfect provides imperfective aspect. The imperfect is lively, framing scenes in a more rapid pace. Figure 3.8 shows that the use of the imperfect nearly equates to the aorist in 13:1–19:44. The increasing frequency of the imperfect as Jesus approaches Jerusalem provides a dramatic flow in the storyline of 9:51–19:44.

The perfective aspect of the aorist tense-form dominates the initial sentence in paragraphs in 9:51–12:59. Many of these paragraphs begin micro units, labeled with headings in English translations such as the ESV. In 9:51–12:59, nineteen times the aorist is used as the first verbal tense-form to begin a labeled micro unit[35]

---

[33] Longacre, *Holistic*, 17–20; Reed, "The Cohesiveness of Discourse," 28–46; Porter, "Discourse Analysis: Introduction and Core Concepts," 139–40.

[34] I advocate the view that the Greek verbal system is aspectually prominent but not void of morphological and semantic temporal reference. See Nicholas J. Ellis, "Aspect-Prominence, Morpho-Syntax, and a Cognitive-Linguistic Framework for the Greek Verb," in *The Greek Verb Revisited: A Fresh Approach for Biblical Exegesis*, ed. Steven E. Runge and Christopher J. Fresch (Lexham, 2016), 122–60, and Peter J. Gentry, "The Function of the Augment in the Hellenistic Greek," in *The Greek Verb Revisited*, ed. Runge and Fresch, 353–78.

[35] 9:51, 57; 10:1, 13, 17, 21, 25, 38; 11:1, 5, 24, 27, 29; 12:1, 13, 22, 33, 41, 49.

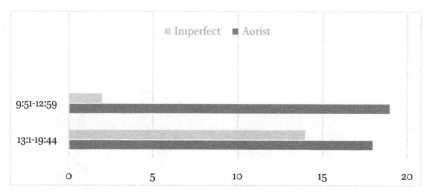

Figure 3.8. Imperfect and Aorist Tense-Form Initial Verbs in Labeled Micro Sections of the ESV in Mounting Tension 2: Mission to Jerusalem (9:51–19:44), Confrontation of Israel's Religion

In this same section of text, only two imperfects begin labeled micro units.[36] In 13:1–19:44, Luke progressively uses the imperfect tense-form, as pictured in the visual profile of the imperfect in Luke 9:51–19:44 in Figure 3.9.

Often Luke uses the imperfect tense-form as the initial verb in sentences that begin labeled micro units. In 13:1–19:44, eighteen times Luke employs the aorist as the first verbal tense-form to begin a labeled micro unit in the ESV. In this same section of text, the imperfect tense-form begins labeled micro-units fourteen times. The result is that many of the micro units in 13:1–19:44 are to be understood as links in a chain of events—as opposed to individual events separated from a sequence. The use of the imperfect tense-form in these places serves to quicken the pace of Jesus' movement to Jerusalem. The reader of the Greek text catches an increasing sense of drama as Jesus approaches Jerusalem, judging and condemning his opponents and calling his disciples to radical commitment. In Figure 3.10 below, I note the ESV micro units that begin with an imperfect tense-form, a tense-form that frames these units in a progressive aspect and related to the previous context.

Jerusalem

In 9:51, Luke states that Jesus sets his face to Jerusalem.[37] This reference to Jerusalem provides a launchpad for the cohesive themes I recognize in 9:51–19:44.

---

[36] 11:14; 12:54.

[37] Though the announcement of Jesus' forthcoming death in Jerusalem iterates throughout 9:51–19:44, it surfaces in 4:14–9:50 as well. When Jesus is transfigured, Moses and Elijah speak with Jesus about what would come upon him in Jerusalem (9:30). In 9:21–22 and 43–45, Jesus prophesies to the disciples that he would suffer and die at the hand of his opponents. In 18:31, Jesus predicts his death for the third time in the Gospel of Luke, specifying that it would take place in Jerusalem.

The crucifixion of Jesus in Jerusalem at the hands of the Jewish leadership is the result of Jesus' consistent confrontation of their selfish religious practices. Four of the eleven references to Jerusalem in 9:51–19:44[38] note the city as the place where Jesus would be killed. In 13:31–34, Luke reports that the Pharisees warn Jesus that Herod Antipas desires to kill him. Jesus responds to the Pharisees by noting that, for him, a prophet, Jerusalem is the greater threat (13:31). Despite Jerusalem's rejection of him, Jesus laments the city with the double vocative Ἰερουσαλὴμ Ἰερουσαλήμ (13:34). Jesus predicts the demise of Jerusalem because the people of Jerusalem, he knows already, will reject his ministry.

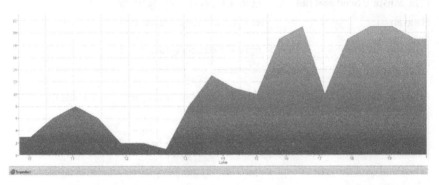

Figure 3:9. Profile of Imperfect Tense-Form Verbs in Mounting Tension 2: Mission to Jerusalem (9:51–19:44), Confrontation of Israel's Religion[39]

As 9:50–19:44 progresses and Jesus nears Jerusalem, the disciples expect to witness the arrival of the kingdom of God in the city (19:11). And they do—even though it differs from their expectations. Their stewardship in God's kingdom is related to Jesus' death in Jerusalem, not the conquering of Israel's opponents there. As Jesus approaches Jerusalem, he prophesies that the city would be conquered—and weeps at the thought (19:41–44). The scene provides a geographical and theological concluding frame for the announcement of Jesus' resolute departure for the city in 9:51.

Statements of Judgement and Condemnation

At the outset of Jesus' Galilean ministry in 4:14–9:50, he condemns the synagogue crowd because they mock his claim that he is God's Spirit-anointed Messiah (4:16–27). Jesus first condemns the Jewish leadership in a village in Galilee when

---

[38] 9:51, 53; 10:30; 13:4[2], 33, 34; 17:11; 18:31; 19:11; 19:41.

[39] From Accordance Bible Software, Version 11.2.5, January 2017, Oak Tree Software Inc.

Heading in the ESV	Reference
Repent or Perish	13:1 Παρῆσαν δέ τινες ἐν αὐτῷ τῷ καιρῷ ἀπαγγέλλοντες αὐτῷ περὶ τῶν Γαλιλαίων
The Parable of the Barren Fig Tree	13:6 ῎Ελεγεν δὲ ταύτην τὴν παραβολήν
A Woman with a Disabling Spirit	13:10 ῏Ην δὲ διδάσκων ἐν μιᾷ τῶν συναγωγῶν ἐν τοῖς σάββασιν.
The Mustard Seed and the Leaven	13:18 ῎Ελεγεν οὖν· τίνι ὁμοία ἐστὶν ἡ βασιλεία τοῦ θεοῦ καὶ τίνι ὁμοιώσω αὐτήν;
The Narrow Door	13:22 Καὶ διεπορεύετο κατὰ πόλεις καὶ κώμας διδάσκων
The Parable of the Wedding Feast	14:7 ῎Ελεγεν δὲ πρὸς τοὺς κεκλημένους παραβολήν
The Cost of Discipleship	14:25 Συνεπορεύοντο δὲ αὐτῷ ὄχλοι πολλοί
The Parable of the Lost Sheep	15:1 ῏Ησαν δὲ αὐτῷ ἐγγίζοντες πάντες οἱ τελῶναι καὶ οἱ ἁμαρτωλοὶ ἀκούειν αὐτοῦ.
The Parable of the Dishonest Manager	16:1 ῎Ελεγεν δὲ καὶ πρὸς τοὺς μαθητάς·
The Law and the Kingdom of God	16:14 ῎Ηκουον δὲ ταῦτα πάντα οἱ Φαρισαῖοι φιλάργυροι ὑπάρχοντες καὶ ἐξεμυκτήριζον αὐτόν.
The Rich Man and Lazarus	16:19 ῎Ανθρωπος δέ τις ἦν πλούσιος , καὶ ἐνεδιδύσκετο πορφύραν καὶ βύσσον εὐφραινόμενος καθ᾽ ἡμέραν λαμπρῶς.
The Parable of the Persistent Widow	18:1 ῎Ελεγεν δὲ παραβολὴν αὐτοῖς πρὸς τὸ δεῖν πάντοτε προσεύχεσθαι αὐτοὺς καὶ μὴ ἐγκακεῖν,
Let the Children Come to Me	18:15 Προσέφερον δὲ αὐτῷ καὶ τὰ βρέφη ἵνα αὐτῶν ἅπτηται· ἰδόντες δὲ οἱ μαθηταὶ ἐπετίμων αὐτοῖς.
Jesus and Zacchaeus	19:1 Καὶ εἰσελθὼν διήρχετο τὴν Ἰεριχώ.

Figure 3.10. Labeled Micro-Units in the ESV that Begin with an Imperfect Tense-Form Verb in 13:1–19:44

they scoff at his claim to forgive sins (5:17–26). Though Jesus continues to judge and condemn the scoffing crowds and Jewish leadership at points during his Galilean ministry (5:31; 6:5, 9–10; 7:31–35; 7:43–48), the rate at which he confronts those who oppose him accelerates as he heads toward Jerusalem in 9:51–19:44.[40]

As Jesus sets out for Jerusalem, he sends ahead seventy disciples to announce the message of the kingdom of God. He notes that they would be rejected just as those in towns like Chorazin, Bethsaida, and Capernaum reject him. Because the people of these towns misjudge Jesus, he judges them, pronouncing woe (οὐαί) statements against Chorazin and Bethsaida (10:13).[41] M. Silva lists οὐαί under the concepts "Judge, Judgment, Condemn, Decide,"[42] and Louw and Nida under the domain of "Trouble, Hardship, Distress (22.1–22.14)" stating, "In some languages there may not be a noun for 'disaster,' but one can express the meaning of the Greek term οὐαί as 'how greatly one will suffer' or 'what terrible pain will come to one.'"[43]

Along the way to Jerusalem, Jesus also condemns the crowds that flock to him. Their tepid response to his message of the kingdom of God places them in a more dire situation than those who reject God's messengers in the days of the old covenant. In 11:31–32, Jesus states that the Queen of Sheba and the Ninevites would rise at the judgement (ἐν τῇ κρίσει) to condemn (κατακρινεῖ, κατακρινοῦσιν respectively) the obstinate crowds that reject Jesus' ministry. When a man in the crowds asks Jesus to arbitrate an inheritance, Jesus condemns all forms of greed (12:15). The crowds were full of those who could judge the weather patterns but fail to respond to Jesus' message (12:54–56). If these hard-hearted ones do not make peace with Jesus along the way, Jesus assures them that they will not escape when God, the final judge (ὁ κριτής) passes sentence upon them (12:57–59). When crowds inform Jesus that Pilate murdered some worshippers from Galilee, Jesus interprets Pilate's act as a basis that all should repent and believe upon him (13:1). Jesus' hearers are guilty and in danger of eternal destruction (ἀπόλλυμι).[44] As Jesus makes his way to Jerusalem, someone in a town asks if only a few are being saved (13:23). Jesus warns that—in light of the eternal consequences of the coming judgement—all should seek to enter through the narrow gate (13:24–30).

But Jesus reserves his sharpest statements of condemnation for the Jewish leadership he encounters on the way to Jerusalem. Just as Jesus pronounces οὐαί

---

[40] There are twenty-two instances of lexemes from the lemma κρίνω in Luke, fourteen of which occur in Mounting Tension 2: Mission to Jerusalem (9:51–19:44) (κρίνω: 12:57; 19:22; κρίσις: 10:14; 11:31, 32, 42; κριτής: 11:19; 12:14; 12:58[2]; 18:2, 6; κατακρίνω: 11:31, 32).

[41] Of the fifteen instances of Jesus' use of οὐαί in Luke, nine occur in Mounting Tension 2: Mission to Jerusalem (9:51–19:44).

[42] *NIDNTTE* 1:52–52.

[43] L&N 1:242.

[44] Silva lists ἀπόλλυμι as the primary lexeme for the concept range "Destroy, Ruin, Perish" (*NIDNTTE* 1:36).

upon Chorazin and Bethsaida (10:13), he pronounces οὐαί upon the Pharisees (11:42, 43, 44) and scribes (11:46, 47, 52) for their hypocrisy. While teaching in a synagogue one Sabbath day (13:10–17), Jesus sees a woman disabled by a demonic spirit for eighteen years (13:11–16). Jesus heals her—and the synagogue leader becomes indignant that the Lord would do such a thing on the Sabbath. Jesus confronts him and his fellows for caring about their animals on the Sabbath but castigating him for freeing a daughter of Abraham of her physical and spiritual bondage on the Sabbath (13:16). Luke concludes the scene by noting the reaction of all who observe the miraculous event. Jesus' opponents are humiliated, and the rest rejoice in Jesus' acts (13:17). Themes that pervade the Gospel of Luke intensify in Jesus' healing of the woman in the synagogue in 13:10–17, qualifying it as an Action Peak (Figure 3.11).

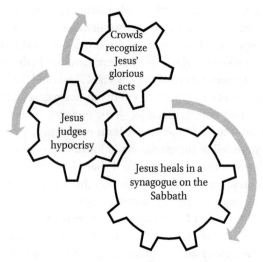

Figure 3.11. Action Peak 2: Jesus Heals a Daughter of Abraham on the Sabbath (13:10–17)

When a Pharisee invites Jesus to dine with him in Luke 14, Jesus observes a scene worthy not of celebration but condemnation. Jesus judges the Pharisee host and his guests because they act arrogantly at the expense of those truly in need (14:5, 7–11, 12–14). Luke notes that the Pharisees—being lovers of money—are offended by Jesus' teaching on generosity and the use of wealth for kingdom purposes (16:14). Jesus condemns them for valuing that which is detestable to God (16:15). Jesus' story of the Rich Man and Lazarus (16:19–31) follows the rubric of a Didactic Peak (see Figure 3.12 below) noted in the Methodology section above. Jesus positions himself in the place of God. He employs the historical figure Abraham in a setting of eschatological judgement and confirms Old Testament Scripture in his verdict against the Rich Man and his family.

Divine Authority
· Jesus describes Abraham in a scene of eschatological judgement

Opposition
· The Pharisees oppose Jesus because of his teaching about money and power

Confirmation
· Jesus authenticates his identity as God's Son by pronouncing judgement that is consistent with God's judgement and Scripture

Figure 3.12. Didactic Peak 2: Jesus' Parable of the Rich Man and Lazarus (16:19–31)

The Pharisees' love of wealth is consistent with their love of self and self-righteousness. Jesus condemns their attitude in the Parable of the Pharisee and the Tax Collector (18:9–14). Jesus' condemnation of Jerusalem—that the city's enemies would come against Jerusalem and not leave one stone on another (19:42–44)—serves as a statement of condemnation of the Pharisees and the institutions of their religion.

Jesus as Lord

Twenty-three of the thirty-four total references to Jesus as Lord in Luke occur in 9:51–19:44. As Jesus approaches Jerusalem, condemning and judging those who would oppose his ministry, followers and inquirers address him as Lord. And so does Luke. Jesus' followers and inquirers address Jesus as Lord (nearly always with the vocative, κύριε) twelve times, and ten times Luke reports Jesus' actions and speech as that of article plus some inflection of the lexeme κύριος. These references to Jesus as Lord are cohesive ties for the story of Jesus' journey to Jerusalem in 9:51–19:44.

Luke reports several references to Jesus as Lord as Jesus sets his face toward Jerusalem. When James and John observe the Samaritan village rebuff Jesus' campaign, they turn to Jesus saying κύριε, "do you want us to tell fire to come down from heaven and consume them?" (9:54). As Jesus and his disciples travel on the road a man asks to join the group and follow Jesus. Though the conscript addresses Jesus as κύριε (9:59), his desire to return and bury his father demonstrates that he knows little of Jesus' dominion. Another man addresses Jesus, calling him κύριε (9:61), but wanting to follow with the disciples only after saying good-bye to his family. Jesus makes clear to the home-hearted man that following the Lord requires valuing the kingdom of God above all domestic interests (9:62).

Five times in 9:51–19:44, Luke collocates his references to Jesus, ὁ κύριος, with instances when followers or inquirers address Jesus as Lord, often using the formal vocative κύριε.[45] Luke's pairing of his own titular references with statements where followers or inquirers recognize Jesus as Lord serve to confirm the ascription on the part of the follower or inquirer. Luke, from the narrator's perspective, references Jesus as Lord alongside statements of the same made by followers or inquirers so as to help his readers grasp how they, as followers or inquirers, might follow Jesus as Lord

The first pairing occurs in 10:1 and 17. Luke notes that ὁ κύριος (10:1) sends out the seventy, and then reports that the seventy return saying, "Lord (κύριε), even the demons are subject to us in your name!" (10:17). Second, Luke writes that in the village of Mary and Martha, Mary sits at the feet τοῦ κυρίου listening to his word (10:39). Though Martha addresses Jesus, κύριε, in 10:40, her request for Jesus to incite Mary to help her with the hospitality chores publicizes the shallowness of her understanding of the title as it applies to Jesus. Luke notes that it is ὁ κύριος (10:41) who replies, "Martha, Martha, you are anxious and troubled about many things, but one thing is necessary" (10:41b–42).

Third, after Jesus' message about the need for watchfulness and urgency in 12:33–40, Peter inquires "Lord (κύριε), are you telling this parable for us or for all?" (12:41). Luke writes that ὁ κύριος (12:42) answers Peter with the story of a κύριος who will come to inspect his slaves, recompensing each based upon their faithfulness (12:42–46). In nearly all of Luke's accounts of the disciples' addresses to Jesus, they use the vocative κύριε. In the fourth pairing, however, Luke reports indirect discourse between the disciples and Jesus. The disciples make a request τῷ κυρίῳ (17:5) to increase their faith. Luke writes that ὁ κύριος (17:6) replies with the figures of the mustard seed and the mulberry tree.

Luke's fifth and final paring of his own titular attribution of ὁ κύριος to Jesus alongside a follower's reference to Jesus as Lord in 9:51–19:44 occurs in Jericho, at the house of Zacchaeus. At the moment of Zacchaeus' confession, he "stood and said to the Lord (τὸν κύριον)" that he would give half of his goods to the poor and fourfold to any he had defrauded (19:8). Jesus' pursuit of Zacchaeus, an unclean tax collector, and Zacchaeus' public repentance and restoration qualify 19:1–10 as an Action Peak (Figure 3.13).

As Jesus leads his disciples toward Jerusalem, he proclaims his Lordship for himself. Luke notes that Jesus sends two disciples to secure a colt for him to ride into the city. In 19:31, Jesus tells them that that if the owners of the colt ask what

---

[45] Only in 11:39, 13:15, and 18:6 does Luke use ὁ κύριος as a title for Jesus without a paired reference of a follower or inquirer recognizing Jesus as Lord. In both 11:39 and 13:15, Luke uses ὁ κύριος in reference to Jesus as Jesus confronts the Pharisees for their hypocrisy. Luke presents Jesus as ὁ κύριος when Jesus tells the Parable of the Persistent Widow (18:6).

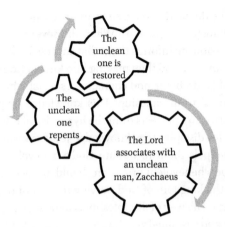

Figure 3.13. Action Peak 3: Jesus Visits Zacchaeus' House (19:1–10)

the disciples are doing, they need only reply that "the Lord has need of it" (ὁ κύριος αὐτοῦ χρείαν ἔχει). When the owners (οἱ κύριοι) of the colt ask what the two disciples are doing untying their colt (19:33), the disciples reply with the exact phrase Jesus had given them, ὁ κύριος αὐτοῦ χρείαν ἔχει (19:34), and bring the colt to Jesus.

Teachings on Discipleship

It is difficult to identify the specific group(s) Jesus has in mind as he teaches in 9:51–19:44. Though I recognize that Jesus' statements to an individual, crowd, group of the Jewish leadership or group of disciples (including the twelve) might reverberate beyond the specific target audience, Jesus' teachings on the theme of discipleship provide cohesion to Jesus' ministry as he travels toward Jerusalem. As Jesus approaches the city—and the cross—he sets out the blessings and demands of following him in discipleship.

At the outset of Jesus' mission to Jerusalem in 9:51–19:44, Jesus emphasizes the difficulties of discipleship. To the man who promises to follow wherever Jesus would go, Jesus states the homeless, transient nature of his earthly ministry (9:57–58). Others are reluctant to follow Jesus because they are unwilling to forgo family allegiances (9:59–62)—a theme to which Jesus returns in 14:22–25. There Jesus turns to the large crowd following him and states that allegiance to the kingdom of God requires hating all family and personal commitments in comparison. Jesus states that whoever would not take up his cross and follow Jesus is not able to be his disciple (14:27).

Jesus informs the seventy that discipleship involves a vision for laborers and intercession that God might increase the number of disciples spreading the kingdom message (10:2). In order to spread the kingdom message effectively, disciples must eliminate the distractions caused by excessive possessions or pursuit of better ministry circumstances (10:3–9). When the seventy report to Jesus the successes of their mission, he informs them that successful discipleship is motivated more by being known of God than making him known (10:18–20).

Knowledge of God's Being and character, especially his omniscience and benevolence, is central to discipleship. This knowledge helps disciples endure in prayer (11:1–13; 18:28–29), protects from the hypocrisy of the Pharisees and scribes (11:37–12:3), enables disciples to acknowledge Jesus even at the risk of their lives (12:4–12), and compels them to imitate God's benevolence (12:22–34; 16:9–13). Knowledge of God's benevolent provision should motivate Jesus' disciples to give full attention to the kingdom of God, serving in view of the Son of Man's return (12:35–48; 19:11–27). The way of discipleship is narrow (12:23–30) and requires initial commitment and sustained zeal (14:28–35). That zeal is to be demonstrated in concern for right relationships with other disciples—as expressed by a willingness to forgive (17:1–4).

Climax (19:45–24:12), Jerusalem Ministry: Condemnation of Temple-centered Religion, and Jesus' Triumph

Some of the cohesive themes noted in Inciting Incident (3:1–4:13), Mounting Tension 1: Galilean Ministry (4:14–9:50), and Mounting Tension 2: Mission to Jerusalem (9:51–19:44) surface in Climax (19:45–24:12) as well. For instance, 9:51–19:44 includes eight references to Jesus as Lord. But in 19:45–24:12, references to Jesus as Lord are part of a cohesive matrix ordered around Jesus' death and victorious resurrection. Jesus uses Ps 109:1 (LXX) in 20:42 and 44 to proclaim his Lordship—a fact the Jewish leadership rejects and the grounds by which they lead Jesus to Pilate for crucifixion. Peter addresses Jesus as κύριε (22:33), telling Jesus that he is willing to die with him. But in 22:61, when Peter denies for the third time, ὁ κύριος looks at Peter and Peter remembers the word τοῦ κυρίου spoken to him that he would deny knowing Jesus. When Jesus teaches the eleven about the dangers that will come upon them for their discipleship (20:35–37), they address Jesus as κύριε (20:38, 49), proclaiming that they are sword-ready to defend his cause. These references to Jesus as Lord permeate the thematic cohesive ties in Climax (19:45–24:12). Here Jesus proclaims his supremacy, confronting Israel's temple-centered religion. The Jewish leadership will have none of it, conspiring to put the Lord to death. But—as the profile in Figure 3.14 displays—these cohesive ties lead to the climax of Luke's gospel, Jesus' victorious death and resurrection. The arrow pointing forward prompts us to think about the implications of Jesus' victory. In 24:13–53, which I label as Denouement and Closure, Jesus appears to the Emmaus disciples and the eleven confirming his status as God's anointed prophet and setting in motion the events that would lead to the foundation of the church in Acts.

Condemnation of Temple-Centered Religion

In Stage (1:5–2:52), the temple is esteemed. Simeon—guided by the Spirit—enters the temple, takes Jesus in his arms, and prophesies that God's salvation had come (2:27–32). The prophetess Anna remains in the temple ministering to God day and night with fasting and prayer (2:37). When the adolescent Jesus attends the Passover festival with his parents, he remains in Jerusalem in the temple after they depart. There Jesus dialogues with the Jewish leadership, asking them questions and answering theirs (2:41–48). Jesus calls the temple his Father's house (2:49), a claim he objectifies in Climax (19:45–24:12).

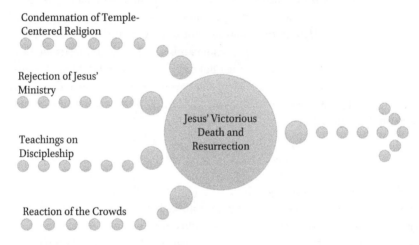

Figure 3.14. Profile of Cyclical Cohesive Acts in Climax (19:45–24:12), Jerusalem Ministry: Condemnation of Temple-Centered Religion, and Jesus' Triumph

Jesus' claims of authority in the temple in 19:45–24:12 bring Luke's Gospel full circle. Eight of the fourteen instances of ἱερόν in the Gospel of Luke occur here. The temple is both the location of and the reason for Jesus' battle with the Jewish leadership. Jesus teaches in the temple, confronting the Jewish leadership for centering Israel's religion upon it—and therefore upon their position of power—instead of God's power and his program to be recognized as the God of all peoples.

Luke notes that Jesus' first activity in 19:45–24:12 takes place in the temple. Jesus, on a mission, enters the temple and casts out those turning God's house into a marketplace (19:45). Luke places an *inclusio* at 19:47–48 and 21:37–38 to frame Jesus' ministry in the temple. Here Luke weaves together three of the four cohesive themes I observe in 19:45–24:12: Jesus teaches, in the temple, in the presence of the crowds of people. "And he was teaching (διδάσκων) daily in the temple (ἐν τῷ ἱερῷ). The chief priests and the scribes and the principal men of the people were seeking to destroy him, but they did not find anything they could do, for all the people (ὁ λαός) were hanging on his words" (19:47–48). "And every day he was teaching (διδάσκων) in the temple (ἐν τῷ ἱερῷ), but at night he went out and lodged on the mount called Olivet. And early in the morning all the people (ὁ λαός) came to him in the temple to hear him" (21:37–38).

Between 19:47–48 and 21:37–38, the Jewish leadership rejects Jesus' ministry. Jesus confronts their temple-centered religion and teaches his disciples what it will mean to follow him in the days to come. Of note here is the Parable of the Vineyard owner (20:9–18). The Jewish leaders understand that Jesus tells the parable against them, prophesying that their days as stewards of God's vineyard have reached their conclusion. Throughout Luke 21, the temple—including its central importance in the city of Jerusalem—provides lessons on discipleship (discussed in what follows). Yet, these teachings are not unrelated to the judgement Jesus brings upon the temple, the Jewish leadership, and Jerusalem. Jesus views his teaching ministry in the temple as the final indictment against the Jewish leadership. When the cohort of Jewish leaders and temple police—led by Judas—come to arrest Jesus, Jesus chides them because they are coming to arrest him at night, away from the crowds.

Rejection of Jesus' Ministry

The Jewish leadership reject Jesus' ministry throughout the Gospel of Luke. They are thus poised to oppose Jesus as he approaches Jerusalem. Their concerted rejection of Jesus' ministry serves as a necessary antecedent to his victorious resurrection. As noted in Figure 3.15 below, the priests, rulers, and elders serve as cohesive participant references in 19:45–24:12. And Luke presents these groups acting in concert—just as the Pharisees, scribes, and lawyers co-mingle in Mounting Tension 1: Galilean Ministry (4:14–9:50) and Mounting Tension 2: Mission to Jerusalem (9:51–19:44). Luke notes that when Jesus begins his teaching ministry in the temple, "The chief priests and the scribes (οἱ δὲ ἀρχιερεῖς καὶ οἱ γραμματεῖς) and the principal men of the people were seeking to destroy him" (19:47). As Jesus continues to teach, the elders join with the chief priests and scribes to oppose Jesus' evangelistic efforts (20:1). When the scribes and chief priests recognize that Jesus' Parable of the Vineyard Owner is directed at them, "The scribes and the chief priests (οἱ γραμματεῖς καὶ οἱ ἀρχιερεῖς) sought to lay hands on him at that very hour" (20:19). Their posture remains unchanged as Passover draws near: "And the chief priests and the scribes (οἱ ἀρχιερεῖς καὶ οἱ γραμματεῖς) were seeking how to put him to death, for they feared the people" (22:2).

After having arrested Jesus at night—away from the crowds of people gathering in the temple to listen to Jesus' teaching—"When day came, the assembly of the elders of the people (τὸ πρεσβυτέριον τοῦ λαοῦ) gathered together, both chief priests and scribes (ἀρχιερεῖς τε καὶ γραμματεῖς). And they led him away to their council" (22:66). So zealous are οἱ ἀρχιερεῖς καὶ οἱ γραμματεῖς that they accompany Jesus to Herod Antipas for the purpose of accusing Jesus before the Galilean governor (23:10). Pilate's act of calling together various divisions of the Jewish leadership, like τοὺς ἀρχιερεῖς καὶ τοὺς ἄρχοντας, is redundant (23:13). These groups rarely act alone in opposing Jesus. In Figure 3.15, I identify Luke's references to the various groups of Jewish leadership, marking with an asterisk (*) those references where groups are named together.

	Inciting Incident (3:1–4:13)	Mounting Tension 1: Galilean Ministry (4:14–9:50)	Mounting Tension 2: Mission to Jerusalem (9:51–19:44)	Climax (19:45–24:12)	Denouement and Closure (24:13–53)
ἀρχιερεύς	3:2	9:22*		19:47*, 20:1*, 20:19*, 22:2*, 22:4, 22:50, 22:52*, 22:54, 22:66*, 23:4, 23:10*, 23:13*, 24:20*	24:20*
ἄρχων			18:18	23:13*, 23:35, 24:20*	24:20*
γραμματεύς		5:21*, 5:30*, 6:7*, 9:22*	11:53*, 15:2*	19:47*, 20:1*, 20:19*, 20:39, 20:46, 22:2*, 22:66*, 23:10*	
νομικός		7:30*	10:25, 11:45, 11:46, 11:52, 14:3*		
νομοδιδάσκαλος		5:17*			
πρεσβύτερος		7:3, 9:22*	15:25	20:1*, 22:52*, 22:66*	
Σαδδουκαῖος				20:27	
Φαρισαῖος		5:17*, 5:21*, 5:30*, 5:33, 6:2, 6:7*, 7:30*, 7:36 (3x), 7:39	11:37, 11:38, 11:39, 11:42, 11:43, 11:53*, 12:1, 13:1, 14:1, 14:3*, 15:2*, 16:14, 17:20, 18:10, 18:11, 19:39		

Figure 3.15. Table of References to Groups of Jewish Leadership in Climax (19:45–24:12), Jerusalem Ministry: Condemnation of Temple-Centered Religion, and Jesus' Triumph

Teachings on Discipleship

Jesus turns the Jewish leadership's attacks into opportunities to teach about discipleship. After Jesus endures attacks from the chief priests and scribes (20:1–2, 19–22), the Sadducees (20:27–33), and a group of scribes (20:39–40), he turns to his disciples with a word of warning (20:45–47). I identify 20:20–47 as the third Didactic Peak in Luke's Gospel (see Figure 16 below). Here Jesus answers the questions of the various divisions of the Jewish leadership and then turns the table on them. Jesus' use of Ps 109:1 (LXX) in 20:42–43 silences the Jewish leadership and confirms his identity as the Messiah.

Divine Authority

· Jesus is recognized as an influential teacher in the temple, worthy of direct discussion with the Jewish leadership

Opposition

· Divisions of the Jewish leadership question Jesus in turn, attempting to trap him in speaking against their interpretations of Scripture

Confirmation

· Jesus confirms his status as an authoritative teacher by citing and interpreting Scripture

---

Figure 3.16. Didactic Peak 3: Jesus' Responses to Jewish Opponents (20:20–47)

Jesus commands the disciples, προσέχετε ("beware of") the danger of the hypocrisy of the scribes. They use the temple for displays of religious pomp without reference to God (20:46). Jesus' use of προσέχετε in 20:46 serves as an *inclusio* with προσέχετε in 21:34, where Jesus warns the disciples to beware lest their hearts get attached to the world and they lose focus on the day of his return. Jesus' ten second-plural imperatives in 20:46–21:34 serve as cohesive devices for the various ideas of considerate, thoughtful, perceptive discipleship that Jesus sets out here. These terms are noted in Figure 3.17.

Jesus' next use of the second-person plural imperative serves as a summary and application of his teaching on discipleship in Climax (19:45–24:12): "But stay awake (ἀγρυπνεῖτε) at all times, praying that you may have strength to escape all these things that are going to take place, and to stand before the Son of Man" (21:36).

Reaction of the Crowds

Crowds accompany Jesus both in Galilee (4:14–9:50) and as Jesus traverses the road to Jerusalem (9:51–19:44). In Jerusalem, the reaction of the crowds becomes

Reference	Gloss, Domains, and Subdomains in L&N	Concepts in *NIDNTTE*
Luke 20:46 προσέχετε	27.59 προσέχω: be alert for[46] (27. Learn: F. Be Ready To Learn, Pay Attention (27.55–27.60)	προσέχω: Hear, Heed, Obey[47]
Luke 21:8 βλέπετε	27.58 βλέπω: watch out for[48] (27. Learn: F. Be Ready To Learn, Pay Attention (27.55–27.60)	βλέπω: Think, Consider, Reckon[49]
Luke 21:14 θέτε	37.96 τίθημι: appoint[50] (37. Control, Rule: E. Assign to a Role or Function (37.96–37.107)	τίθημι: Determine, Appoint[51]
Luke 21:19 κτήσασθε	21.20 κτάομαι τὴν ψυχήν: to save oneself from grave danger or death[52] (21. Danger, Risk, Safe, Save: E. Cause To Be Safe, Free from Danger, 21.17–21.24)	κτάομαι: Possessions, Treasure, Mammon, Wealth, Money, Debt[53]
Luke 21:20 γνῶτε	28.1 γινώσκω: to possess information about[54] (28. Know: A. Know, 28.1–28.16)	γινώσκω: Knowledge/Ignorance; Proclaim; Revelation[55]
Luke 21:28 ἀνακύψατε	17.33 ἀνακύπτω: to straighten up from a bent over position[56] (17. Stances and Events Related to Stances: H. Bend Over, Straighten Up, 17.29–17.33)	---

[46] L&N 1:332.
[47] *NIDNTTE* 1:49.
[48] L&N 1:332.
[49] *NIDNTTE* 1:76.
[50] L&N 1:482.
[51] *NIDNTTE* 1:36.
[52] L&N 1:240.
[53] *NIDNTTE* 1:63.
[54] L&N 1:333.
[55] *NIDNTTE* 1:575.
[56] L&N 1:219.

Luke 21:28 ἐπάρατε	25.160 ἐπαίρω τὴν κεφαλήν: (an idiom, literally 'to raise up the head') to demonstrate courage in the face of danger or adversity[57] (25. Attitudes and Emotions: N. Courage, Boldness, 25.156–25.166)	ἐπαίρω: Carry; Destroy[58]
Luke 21:29 ἴδετε	24.1 ὁράω: to see, sight, seeing[59] (24. Sensory Events and States: A. See, 24.1–24.51)	ὁράω: Experience; Hide; Knowledge/Ignorance; Prophesy; Revelation; Vision[60]
Luke 21:31 γινώσκετε	28.1 γινώσκω: to possess information about[61] (28. Know: A. Know, 28.1–28.16)	γινώσκω: Knowledge/Ignorance; Proclaim; Revelation[62]
Luke 21:34 Προσέχετε	27.59 προσέχω: be alert for[63] (27. Learn: F. Be Ready To Learn, Pay Attention (27.55–27.60)	προσέχω: Hear, Heed, Obey[64]

Figure 3.17. Table of Jesus' Ten Second-Person Plural Imperatives in 19:46–21:34

the fulcrum upon which Jesus' fate turns. The Jewish leaders resist answering Jesus' query about John the Baptist. They know that the people consider John a prophet. If the Jewish leaders counter the claim, they are afraid that all the people (ὁ λαὸς ἅπας) will stone them (20:6). When the scribes and chief priests recognize that Jesus' Parable of the Vineyard Owner (20:9–18) is directed at them, they want to put their hands on Jesus but fear how the people might react (20:19). I have already noted the *inclusio* in 19:47 and 21:38. In both places, Luke writes that the people attend to Jesus' teaching in the temple and in 21:38 he notes that all the people (πᾶς ὁ λαός) gathered to Jesus in the temple to hear him. In 22:1, Luke writes that as the Passover draws near, the chief priests and scribes want to do away with Jesus but did not because they were fearing the people (τὸν λαόν). After Judas agrees to betray Jesus, in 22:6 Judas begins to look for a time when he might hand Jesus over apart from the crowd (ὄχλου).

---

[57] L&N 1:306.
[58] *NIDNTTE* 1:177.
[59] L&N 1:276.
[60] *NIDNTTE* 3:526.
[61] L&N 1:333.
[62] *NIDNTTE* 1:575.
[63] L&N 1:332.
[64] *NIDNTTE* 1:49.

But the crowds described in 19:54–24:13 are not all of the same frame of mind about Jesus. The crowds that the Jewish leaders assemble before Pilate cry out to the Roman governor demanding that he crucify Jesus (23:4–5, 18, 21, 23). The crowd gathered around Pilate's headquarters is the first crowd in 19:45–24:12 that is not sympathetic toward Jesus. But that is all that is necessary to bring about Jesus' victorious death and resurrection. The final references to crowds in 19:54–24:13 demonstrate the divisive nature of Jesus' mission. One crowd—yet under the sway of the Jewish leadership and in the company of the Roman soldiers—mocks Jesus as he is crucified (23:35–36). The other crowd grieves over the events unfolding before them. On the way to Golgotha, the Roman soldiers compel Simon of Cyrene to carry Jesus' cross and Luke notes that a large crowd of people (πολὺ πλῆθος τοῦ λαοῦ) followed Jesus (23:27)—including a gathering of women that mourn and lament what is being done to Jesus. Crowds observe every move of the crucifixion of Jesus, watching him breathe his last. After Jesus dies, all the gathered crowds (πάντες οἱ συμπαραγενόμενοι ὄχλοι ἐπὶ τὴν θεωρίαν ταύτην) depart beating their chests (23:48).

Jesus' Victorious Death and Resurrection

Jesus' death is understood to be a victory because he had repeatedly predicted his death[65] and because he rose from the grave. Jesus' detailed predictions of his death must be kept in mind when reading Pilate's final verdict that Jesus is to be crucified (23:25). Pilate—catering to the Jewish leadership and the crowds under their influence—acts in step with what Jesus says will come about. When Jesus is crucified between two criminals (23:33), mocked as the king of the Jews (23:38), takes his last breath, and commits his spirit to the Father (23:46), he is not a victim. He is victorious.

The empty tomb confirms the victorious nature of Jesus' death and itself becomes the symbol of his victory. The pacing of 24:1–2 signifies the passage as an Action Peak (see Figure 3.18 below). Luke relates with great brevity the events confirming Jesus' predictions that he would rise from the dead. In Climax (19:45–24:12) to

---

[65] Even in his Galilean ministry (4:14–9:50), Jesus predicts the general nature of his death, what would result, and why. Upon Peter's confession that Jesus is the Messiah, Jesus tells his disciples that it is necessary for him to be rejected by the Jewish leadership, to die, and to be raised up (9:22). Jesus' statement here is the first of three references to Jesus' death in Luke 9 (see vv. 30, 44). Jesus explicates that he is to die in Jerusalem—the place of danger and destruction for God's prophets throughout Israel's history (13:32–33). In 18:31–33, Jesus offers his most detailed prophecy of his death and resurrection. He states that it will take place in Jerusalem, according to the scriptural prophecies about the suffering Son of Man, at the hands of the nations, after which he will rise on the third day. In Climax (19:45–24:12), Jesus predicts his death at the Passover meal (22:14–20).

this point, Luke provides extensive back and forth between Jesus and the Jewish leadership, the Jewish leadership and Judas, Jesus and the disciples, the Jewish leadership and Roman officials, the crowds and the Roman officials, Jesus and the women, Jesus and those crucified with Jesus. The rapid pacing of 24:1–12 sets this passage off from the protracted activity and dialogue reports Luke offers in 19:45–23:56.

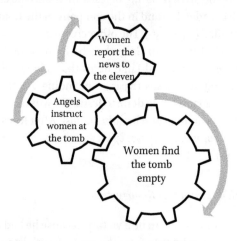

Figure 3.18. Action Peak 4: Women Discover the Tomb Empty and Witness of Jesus' Resurrection (24:1–12)

Denouement and Closure (24:13–53): Resurrection Appearances: Confirmation of Jesus as God's Victorious Messiah

In narrative, the Climax slot does not resolve all the issues the characters face to that point in the story. Implications, explanations, and further actions must be explored. Luke does this in 24:13–53. Jesus' interactions with the Emmaus disciples (24:13–35) and the disciples that remain in Jerusalem (24:36–49) demonstrate the reality of Jesus' resurrection. But Luke is not here concerned just with confirming Jesus' predictions of victory—as noted especially in Climax (19:45–24:12)—but also to bring his Gospel full-circle. In 24:13–53, Luke describes the implications of Jesus' resurrection in light of two motifs that surface throughout his account of Jesus' life, death, and resurrection. Here in 24:1–12 the city of Jerusalem and Jesus' use of meals for didactic purposes shape the narrative.

At the end of Luke's Gospel, the city of Jerusalem yet plays a pivotal role in the cohesion of a unit. Luke notes that after Jesus' resurrection, the Emmaus disciples leave Jerusalem for their home village (24:13). Jesus joins them on the journey to Emmaus, playing coy about the recent events in Jerusalem (24:18). Once

```
┌─────────────────────────────────────────────────────────────────────────┐
│  Divine Authority                                                          │
│    · Jesus states that Scripture testifies to him                          │
└─────────────────────────────────────────────────────────────────────────┘

┌─────────────────────────────────────────────────────────────────────────┐
│  Opposition                                                                │
│    · The disciples fail to understand Jesus' death and resurrection in light of │
│      Scripture                                                             │
└─────────────────────────────────────────────────────────────────────────┘

┌─────────────────────────────────────────────────────────────────────────┐
│  Confirmation                                                              │
│    · Jesus authenticates his identity by opening the minds of the disciples to │
│      understand his sufferings as fulfillment of Scripture                 │
└─────────────────────────────────────────────────────────────────────────┘
```

Figure 3.19. Didactic Peak 4: Jesus' Post-Resurrection Message to the Jerusalem Disciples (24:44–49)

they recognize Jesus, the Emmaus disciples head back to Jerusalem to inform the disciples there of Jesus' resurrection (24:33). After revealing himself to the disciples in Jerusalem, Jesus states that the message of the kingdom is to be preached first in Jerusalem and then to the nations (24:46). I note that in Stage (1:5–2:52), Jerusalem and the temple serve as settings upon which Luke builds his narrative. Luke concludes his Gospel noting that the disciples remain in Jerusalem, in the temple, praising God (24:53). References to Jerusalem and the temple in the final verse of Luke's Gospel bring the narrative full circle.

Meals, always more significant than just the consumption of food, serve as occasions for Jesus to teach. The same meal can be an occasion of celebration and confrontation—especially if the Pharisees are the hosts. During Jesus' Galilean ministry (4:14–9:50)[66] and his mission to Jerusalem (9:51–19:44),[67] meals become occasions for Jesus to confront his opponents and instruct the invited guests in the ways of God's kingdom. Though the meals in Denouement and Closure (24:13–53) do not include the Pharisees or any opponents, Jesus still uses them as occasions to teach. The meals in 24:13–53 reflect Jesus' meal and instruction at the home of Martha and Mary (10:38–42), where Jesus gives understanding to those who are inclined to follow him. In the two meals described in 24:12–49, Luke emphasizes the role of Scripture in Jesus' teaching. It is during a meal—after a period of walking and dialogue—that Jesus speaks and acts in such a way that the Emmaus disciples understand Jesus' death as fulfillment of Scripture (24:30–31). Likewise, Jesus uses the occasion of a meal—or at least some on-hand fish—to confirm his identity for the disciples in Jerusalem (24:36–42). There Jesus opened their minds to comprehend what was said of him, the suffering Messiah, in the Scriptures (τὰς γραφάς) (24:45). Jesus' focused instruction to the disciples in Jerusalem is the final Didactic Peak in the Gospel of Luke (Figure 3.19).

---

[66] 5:29–30 and 7:36–50.

[67] 11:37–54 and 14:1–14.

Conclusion

One value of discourse analysis is that it provides a basis for synthesizing a text. I suggest that Luke writes his Gospel to show how Jesus confirms himself to be God's Messiah, the Son of God come near, promised in the Scriptures. The Figures that I offer here demonstrate the capacity of discourse analysis to visualize the synthetic features of a text. Consistent graphics represent Action Peaks and Didactic Peaks so that readers can identify these micro units and their prominence in the discourse.

By the end of Stage (1:5–2:52), Jesus is in Jerusalem in the temple dialoguing with the Jewish leadership. Jesus' authoritative activity as an adolescent establishes a frame for understanding 3:1–4:13, which I identify as the Inciting Incident of the Gospel of Luke. Here John the Baptist clarifies his role and the role of Jesus in salvation history, and Jesus confirms his special status by using Scripture to counter the devil's temptations in the wilderness. From here the tension begins to mount.

I label 4:14–9:50 as Mounting Tension 1: Galilean Ministry. Jesus travels throughout Galilee preaching, teaching, healing, exorcising demons, and confirming that he is God's Spirit-anointed prophet. The one promised in Isa 61:1–2 is here! Luke writes that Jesus' ministry is fulfilled in Jerusalem and so to Jerusalem Jesus sets his gaze in 9:51. During Mounting Tension 2: Mission to Jerusalem (9:51–19:44), Jesus confronts the Jewish leadership and their associates for employing Israel's religion for their own ends. The pace of the text quickens as Jesus moves toward Jerusalem. While the adherents of Israel's religion oppose Jesus along the way, many individuals address him as Lord and hear his messages of discipleship.

Jesus' ministry reaches its Climax (19:45–24:12) in Jerusalem. Here Jesus confronts the Jewish leadership for centering their religion on the temple and not on God and Scripture. Though the Jewish leadership conspires together to pressure Pilate to condemn Jesus to death as a political insurrectionist, their actions are the means of Jesus' victory. Jesus' resurrection from the dead recalls his many predictions that he would suffer, die, and rise. In Denouement and Closure (24:13–53), Jesus appears to the Emmaus disciples and those remaining with the eleven in Jerusalem. Jesus teaches them that his death fulfills the scriptural prophesies that God's Messiah would suffer. The disciples' minds are opened to understand and witness that Jesus is the Messiah.

4

John

Michael Rudolph

Structural analysis is a glaring weakness of NT studies. The absence of any structural consensus for most NT texts is frequently admitted; the Gospel of John is no exception.[1] The failure to resolve this issue can be attributed to one of two opposite extremes: a dismissive attitude that mistakenly minimizes the significance of structural analysis, or a reliance upon complex terminology and intricate diagrams that obscures the analytical impotence and fundamental flaws of the underlying linguistic paradigm. Both extremes are roadblocks to exegetical clarity.[2] Since *how* an author shapes a message is often as critical for

---

[1] For an extensive survey of various structural proposals for the Gospel of John from 1907 to 2007, see George Mlakuzhyil, *Christocentric Literary-Dramatic Structure of John's Gospel*, 2nd ed., AnBib 117 (Rome: Gregorian & Biblical Press, 2011), 51–278.

[2] For examples of the latter roadblock, see Mlakuzhyil's work noted above, ibid. For scholars who dismiss, or minimize structural analysis, see e.g., Andreas J. Köstenberger, *Encountering John: The Gospel in Historical, Literary, and Theological Perspective*, EBS (Baker Academic, 1999), 30–31, who states, "Recent years have witnessed a deplorable de-emphasis upon theology. Literature is a medium, a vehicle to convey a message. Once the study of the medium ... has overshadowed the apprehension of the message ... biblical priorities have been reversed.... [F]aithfulness to the intentions of the authors of Scripture demands that the historical and theological dimensions of biblical narratives are given their due and the literary investigation of a given text be kept in proper perspective." To this one must respond that the "apprehension of the [author's] message" *requires* an accurate literary analysis prior to drawing historical or theological conclusions. See also D. A. Carson, *The Gospel according to John*, PNTC (Eerdmans, 1991), 103–104, or Craig S. Keener, *The Gospel of John: A Commentary* (Hendrickson, 2003), 1:427, who states, "Any modern outline of the Fourth Gospel is somewhat arbitrary....

interpretation as *what* the author's explicit message is, one should wonder why this state of affairs is tolerated regarding such a foundational issue.

Methodology

The approach of this study is pragmatic. While the appearance of a certain eclecticism must be acknowledged—no one is immune from the influence of one's scholarly heritage—the foundational linguistic paradigm underlying those influences is, nevertheless, here rejected. Thus, to those who yet work within the perspective of this fading paradigm, the approach of this analysis may appear radical in its simplicity and in the conclusions of the academy that it rejects. Specifically, when Saussure rendered irrelevant the tedious work of nineteenth-century philologists (i.e., the diachronic search for the *Ursprache*), he, nevertheless, in following the academic trends of his own day, built the foundation of twentieth-century linguistics on flawed synchronic footings that were just as irrelevant and just as ineffective.[3] In particular, Saussure exiled the human will (the source of meaning) from interpretive consideration and elevated in its place an artificial (i.e., non-existent), socially-constrained construct (*langue*) as the only proper *scientific* object of consideration.[4] In effect, the independent exercise of the human will in isolated, historical events was now to be interpreted solely through the ever-shifting and unbounded kaleidoscope of societal experience or expectation. Rather than sharpening the focus of interpretation with overwhelming data, as Corpus Linguistics suggests, the solitary voice has been drowned out by the cacophony of the masses.[5] The Sausurrean paradigm, with

---

But given the expectation that a commentary will divide sections, we have offered a division as likely as any."

[3] For a discussion of factors shaping nineteenth-century philology, see Tuska Benes, *In Babel's Shadow: Language, Philology, and the Nation in Nineteenth-Century Germany* (Wayne State University, 2008). For Saussure's arguments that rendered nineteenth-century philology irrelevant, see Roy Harris and Talbot J. Taylor, *Landmarks in Linguistic Thought: The Western Tradition from Socrates to Saussure*, RHLT (Routledge, 1989), 182. For societal factors shaping Saussure's thinking, see Jonathan Culler, *Ferdinand de Saussure*, rev. ed. (Cornell University Press, 1986), 15–16, 85–94; or Harris and Taylor, *Landmarks in Linguistic Thought*, 180–81.

[4] J. E. Joseph, "Saussurean Tradition in Twentieth-century Linguistics," *ELL* 7:3665.

[5] *Contra* Michael Stubbs, *Text and Corpus Analysis: Computer-assisted Studies of Language and Culture*, LS 23 (Blackwell, 1996), 44–45. Linguists have been forced to acknowledge that distinctions in language use are discernible to the level of idiolect; in fact, in many cases one must appeal to the presence of diglossia or code-switching. See e.g., Ronald Wardhaugh, *An Introduction to Sociolinguistics*, 4th ed., BTL 4 (Blackwell, 2002), 5, 87–94, 100–114. The position becomes wholly untenable when one factors in the additional parameters of individualized life experience and belief systems that form the basis for formulating inferences necessary in the process of communication (see further below).

its multiplied offspring, must be, and is being, replaced.[6]

The proper object of study for the NT exegete is not a contrived system of language (or language use), but rather, individual acts of human communication. For this reason, this study draws primarily from the insights of Relevance Theory. Sperber and Wilson, in their ground-breaking study of human communication, demonstrated that communication is successful not because of shared semantic knowledge between communicative partners, but because of shared, in fact, innate processes of human communication. In the process of communication, partners draw the appropriate inferences on an ongoing basis consistent with what is conceived to be the most relevant interpretation requiring the least processing effort. The meaning that one intends to convey is never fully expressed (for the sake of efficiency), nor fully shared (due to the fact that communicative partners share neither identical dialects nor draw inferences from identical experiences or beliefs); rather, meaning is negotiated.[7] The text does not convey meaning, but rather serves as evidence of the author's meaning. On the basis of that evidence, the recipient seeks to re-create a mental representation of that meaning. Since both parties view that evidence through their own unique lenses of experience, beliefs, and history of language use, the message must be structured, and continually modified as needed, to address its perceived or anticipated reception.[8]

In keeping with the individualized perspective of the solitary human will, as highlighted by Relevance Theory, this study focuses upon the unique ways that the author shapes and develops his message utilizing certain principles of

---

[6] It is critical to note, as Harris states, "[I]n spite of the divisions and changes of emphasis that have marked the development of linguistics throughout this [twentieth] century, the basis of linguistic theory has remained in all essentials unchanged since it was first laid down in Saussure's Geneva lectures of 1907–1911.... [T]he fundamental error in contemporary linguistics is still the fundamental error of Saussure's original thesis. It involves a crude process of abstraction by which certain phenomena are segregated from the continuum of human communication, and these segregated phenomena are then, rather capriciously, set up for academic purposes as constituting the *linguistic* part of communication" (Roy Harris, "On Redefining Linguistics," in *Redefining Linguistics*, eds. Hayley G. Davis and Talbot J. Taylor [Routledge, 1990], 20–22). See also Perry L. Blackburn, *The Code Model of Communication: A Powerful Metaphor in Linguistic Metatheory*, SILeB 4 (SIL International, 2007), 132–67, who demonstrates the common, underlying foundation of seemingly competing schools of linguistics that may appear radically different and that pride themselves in those distinctions, but who are, nevertheless, essentially the same.

[7] For an entrance to the field of Relevance Theory, see the original presentation, Dan Sperber and Deirdre Wilson, *Relevance: Communication and Cognition*, 2nd ed. (Blackwell, 1995); or, a more recent summary, Billy Clark, *Relevance Theory*, CTL (Cambridge University Press, 2013).

[8] Blackburn, *The Code Model of Communication*, 218–28.

communication as the foundation for its analysis. The process of interpretation, as communication itself, is intuitive and will not appear radically different to most scholars—divide the text, trace the theme, etc. The lens through which that analysis is made, however, differs remarkably in the details that are allowed to shape the conclusions.

First, *all communication is dialogical*—i.e., there is, even in what appears to be a one-sided communication, such as a written text, a constant interaction between communicative partners providing clues that can be detected regarding the author's purpose, the overall message, and the situational context.[9] Certain mechanisms available for the writer serve both to preserve and to guide the intended dialogue. For example, a parenthetical statement provides off-line information at the precise time when the recipient needs to receive it. These statements do not represent the main point, but provide relevant information to answer questions or objections that have been, or will soon be, raised in the recipient's mind. The absence of such statements would impede or, possibly even, terminate reception of the author's message. Their presence shows *what* the author believed the recipient needed to hear at that precise moment in order to understand or accept the message.[10] Another example is the authorial comment in which the author steps outside of the narrative to speak directly to the recipients. In these cases, the text is not *marked* as a parenthetical statement, nevertheless, the flow of the narrative is interrupted to some degree. It may take the form of a summary statement, ensuring that the author's point was understood, an evaluation of what has just been presented, or a statement (often more disconnected) to place the message in a certain context.[11] In the Gospel of John it often appears to serve a structural role to indicate the conclusion of a section (see further below).

Second, "[*communication*] *is a patterned activity ... the patterning of patterns.*"[12] This statement should *not* be understood in the sense that modern NT

---

[9] Ruqaiya Hasan, *Linguistics, Language, and Verbal Art* (Deakin University Press, 1985), 103, states, "The present emphasis on the private nature of writing and reading tends to obscure the fact that both are a form of dialogue, in which the turns are separated by the social import of time and place. In dialogue, you are never free to say just what you like; the nature of the other's turn acts upon the nature of your turn.... [I]n the writing turn, the ... reader is the other."

[10] Diane Blakemore, "*And*-Parentheticals," *JPrag* 37 (2005): 1167–68, 1175–79; Diane Blakemore, "Divisions of Labour: The Analysis of Parentheticals," *Lingua* 116 (2006): 1684–86. Parenthetical information provided *before* the recipient needed to hear it would only obscure more relevant points, serve as a distraction, and add to the required effort of the recipient to listen to, and follow, the author's message. Too much too soon or too little too late are both devastating for communication.

[11] See e.g., John 5:1, 5, 9b; 6:2–4; 11:1, 2, 4, where each proposition is marked by δέ.

[12] Hasan, *Linguistics, Language, and Verbal Art*, 15. In keeping with her Saussurean perspective, Hasan specifically states, "Language ... is a patterned activity.... [D]iscourse is fashioned by

scholars have abused this principle, but rather in a sense as rich and vibrant as communication has always existed. It is the modern reader, rather than the ancient recipient, who has become lazy in verbal communication. In a society where resources for writing were scarce so that words were recorded without spaces or headings, a society where literacy was rare so that the message was more often received aurally than visually, the full spectrum of human imagination was utilized in a way that the message stood out and was heard. It is a serious mistake to think that ancient societies thought (or wrote) primarily in terms of a complex chiasm or an extended *inclusio*, but it is just as serious of a mistake to dismiss or overlook the more subtle patterns that the author does give. These patterns were intentional and often carried the backbone of the message or marked significant divisions of the text. Rather than hearing and properly interpreting these patterns, modern scholars, in their rush to address more weighty theological or historical questions, often dismiss or distort these subtle signals, especially when they prove to be inconvenient for their own preconceived and foreign structural expectations.

Third, *the reception of communication is directed by discourse markers*. There are two types of words utilized in communication: words that convey concepts and words that signal how the following text is to be processed (i.e., discourse markers). While conceptual words are, to some degree, semantically fluid (e.g., operating on a spectrum from literal to metaphorical to ironic), procedural words (i.e., discourse markers) are not.[13] It is regarding these easily-overlooked words that NT scholars have committed, and continue to commit, inexcusable semantic malpractice. In so doing, they render an accurate structural analysis nearly impossible. Scholars have mistakenly assumed that these words *conjoin* syntactical units.[14] On the basis of perceived (and frequently debated) coherent

---

the general device of the patterning of patterns." (The pragmatic term *communication* is chosen here as the more appropriate term, consistent with the author's discussion and examples of *discourse*. Communication is an activity; language is not.) Hasan notes three important types of patterning (i.e., repetition, parallelism, and contrast, pp. 3–15) and suggests that the presence of significant patterns should "point toward the same general meaning" (p. 95).

[13] *Contra* J. D. Denniston, *The Greek Particles*, 2nd ed. (Clarendon, 1954), lvi. For a discussion of procedural meaning, see Diane Blakemore, *Relevance and Linguistic Meaning: The Semantics and Pragmatics of Discourse Markers*, CSL 99 (Cambridge University Press, 2002).

[14] See e.g., A. T. Robertson, *A Grammar of the Greek New Testament in the Light of Historical Research*, 4th ed. (Broadman, 1934), who described these words as "the hinges of speech, the joints of language" (p. 1144; see also p. 1177). Much of the work of SIL scholars in the twentieth century pursued this flawed (coherence-based) perspective. See e.g., John Beekman, et al., *The Semantic Structure of Written Communication*, 5th ed. (SIL, 1981); or Kathleen Callow, *Man and Message: A Guide to Meaning-Based Text Analysis* (University Press of America, 1998). More recent work from the SIL school of thought has recognized the subjectivity and inconsistency of this approach. See Stephen H. Levinsohn, "The Relevance of Greek Discourse Studies to

relationships between these supposedly conjoined units, scholars have mistakenly offered a wide range of meanings, often mutually contradictory, for words that are, by nature, monosemic.[15] A radical re-thinking of the words that fall within the classification of *procedural* is necessary if NT scholarship is to make any progress toward structural consensus regarding the NT text. For example, δέ is a marker of discontinuity—nothing more, nothing less, nothing else.[16] Καί conjoins two elements and should not be overlooked as insignificant. Γάρ signals a response to a perceived, or anticipated, question or objection to the author's message. While δέ and καί function on a broad vertical spectrum from marking words to marking sections, γάρ functions on a sentential level and is rarely (and never appropriately in the Gospel of John) found at the paragraph level.[17] In this

---

Exegesis," *JT* 2 (2006): 11–21. Blass appropriately states, "[C]onnectivity in discourse is a pragmatic rather than semantic matter: it results from relevance relations between text and context rather than from relations linguistically encoded in the text." Regina Blass, *Relevance Relations in Discourse: A Study with Special Reference to Sissala*, CSL 55 (Cambridge University Press, 1990), 1. See also Diane Blakemore, *Semantic Constraints on Relevance* (Basil Blackwell, 1987), 105–25.

[15] The nineteenth-century grammarian, George Winer, condemned his peers for this "imbecil[ic]" excess (p. 565) that allowed Scripture to be twisted "as a waxen nose" (p. xxii). George Benedict Winer, *A Treatise on the Grammar of New Testament Greek Regarded as a Sure Basis for New Testament Exegesis*, trans. W. F. Moulton, 3rd rev. ed. (T&T Clark, 1882), xxii, 565. Nothing has changed since Winer's criticism. Even within the Gospel of John, καί is commonly translated with a connective ('and'), contrastive ('but'), concessive ('yet'), and even a disjunctive ('or'; ESV, John 3:8) sense. (The issue extends far beyond these examples and plagues every discourse marker utilized in the Greek text.) Scholars in the secular field of linguistics have long recognized what biblical scholars continue to ignore. These signals are monosemic. For a recent discussion, see, Deirdre Wilson and Dan Sperber, "Pragmatics and Time," *UCLWPL* 5 (1993): 277–98.

[16] For a similar conclusion, see Kathleen Callow, "The Disappearing Δέ in Corinthians," in *Linguistics and New Testament Interpretation: Essays on Discourse Analysis*, ed. David Alan Black with Katharine Barnwell and Stephen Levinsohn (Broadman & Holman, 1992), 192–93, who suggests δέ always marks the "next step."

[17] Michael Rudolph, "Reclaiming Γάρ: Correcting the Conjunctive Errors of New Testament Lexicography," in *Getting into the Text: New Testament Essays in Honor of David Alan Black*, ed. Daniel L. Akin and Thomas W. Hudgins (Wipf and Stock, 2018), 55–76. Γάρ can be found at a paragraph division in combination with δέ where δέ signals a new paragraph while γάρ signals that this new thought is in response to an implied question or objection raised by the previous text. See e.g., Justin Martyr, *Dial.* 13. Γάρ may also be used in what has been described as an inchoative sense to mark an embedded narrative following a declaration of the topic or the request to speak (e.g., Heb 5:1 where the new topic was introduced in Heb 4:16)—answering, "What is it that you have to say?" For a discussion of this use, see Irene J. F. de Jong, "ΓΑΡ Introducing Embedded Narratives," in *New Approaches to Greek Particles: Proceedings of the Colloquium held in Amsterdam, January 4–6, 1996, to Honour C. J. Ruijgh on the Occasion of His Retirement*, ed. Albert Rijksbaron, ASCP 7 (Amsterdam: Gieben, 1997), 175–85.

study, the monosemic communicative signals of discourse markers are honored, even where the author's intended signal forces the interpretation of the text in a direction contrary to the established consensus (limited as it is) of modern scholarship (see further below).

Fourth, *communication is linear.* There is a starting point (i.e., the impetus for communication) and a purpose relentlessly prodding the message forward along a chosen (i.e., thematic) path to a goal as of yet, most often, unseen. The message may march forward in an orderly, almost mechanical fashion, or appear to wander aimlessly through repetition and seemingly unrelated interruptions or stories that the author connects only later in the message. Some parts are more prominent than others, but all serve to advance the author's purpose. These features are the aspects of communication that give a message its contour, or structure. As such, they represent important clues for interpretation.[18] All of this is locked in time, both in the sense of a historical, communicative event, but also as an unavoidable progression as one statement must follow another while the author seeks to relay the meaning in his mind and simultaneously adjust the parameters of the message in response to perceived or imagined responses. In the case of the Gospel of John, this 'event' is complicated further by multiple levels of communication: the primary (i.e., most relevant) level of the author to the original recipients, the secondary level of characters in the narration that the author is utilizing to make a point, and the tertiary level of author to the modern reader which more often provides interpretive noise rather than clarity. Finally, where possible, the perspective one uses to describe this contoured line (i.e., the structure) should be that of the author. Thus, in the structural analysis below, the words of the text are used, where practical, to reflect that perspective. Ultimately, the test of a structural analysis is measured by its ability to retrace the trajectory of the author's message and by its consistency with the evidence of the text.

Finally, *prominence,* a critical feature for structural analysis, *is not primarily an inherent characteristic of language or syntax, but rather a recognizable, often spontaneous, feature of communication.* Hasan notes that prominence is measured by the contrast it establishes with the norms, or background, created by the text itself. As such, the prominent feature is highlighted because it serves an important and specific role in the author's message.[19] Prominence is characterized

---

[18] See Callow, *Man and Message,* 158, 187–200, who discusses three communicative schemas (informational, volitional, and expressive [i.e., emotive]) and the impact of the recipient's perceived receptivity (contested or uncontested) upon the shaping of the author's message.

[19] Hasan, *Linguistics, Language, and Verbal Art,* 94–95. Hasan appears here (appropriately) to step outside of the normal position of Saussurean and, specifically, Systemic Functional Linguistics, by measuring prominence from the internal perspective of an individual text (i.e., historical act of communication), rather than from the perspective of a larger, poorly-defined, societal norm.

both by the intensity and range of its impact (e.g., a prominent feature may have high intensity with limited range or a somewhat lesser intensity but extensive range). Typically, lexical or syntactical prominence will have less impact than a rhetorical element, but both will be surpassed by elements of surprise or deep emotion, especially where the range is likewise extensive. Authors utilize prominence first to activate certain contextual assumptions and beliefs that will be addressed in the subsequent text. Frequently, it is also necessary to motivate an emotional frame-of-mind more conducive to receiving what the author has to say. The primary purpose of prominence, however, is to trace the thematic development of the author's message. The intensity of the prominent elements along this trajectory will vary, often reaching a peak or climax at the most critical juncture(s) of the text.[20]

Macrostructure

Consensus is normally, although not universally, reached regarding the broad contours of the Gospel of John. These are as follows:

1. an introduction;
2. a lengthy narrative interspersed with dialogue generally within a public setting covering approximately three years;
3. a private supper with an extended monologue from Jesus directed to his disciples;
4. events surrounding the death, burial, and resurrection of Jesus; and
5. an epilogue.

Other than the explicit purpose statement (20:30–31), whose meaning is itself a point of debate, there is scarce evidence bold enough to demand the attention of most modern scholars.[21] It is, after all, a gospel and gospels are, as Bauckham claims, relatively open texts written for an indefinite audience.[22] The Gospels, however, are *not* devoid of historical context nor necessarily as *open* as Bauckham suggests. The restriction of a geographic community, which Bauckham appropriately rejects, does not demand the restriction of a chronological context. The

---

[20] For a discussion of prominence, see Callow, *Man and Message*, 181–85.

[21] For differing views regarding the meaning of the purpose statement in the Gospel of John, see e.g., D. A. Carson, "Syntactical and Text-Critical Observations on John 20:30–31: One More Round on the Purpose of the Fourth Gospel," *JBL* 124 (2005): 693–714; or Gordon D. Fee, "On the Text and Meaning of John 20:30–31," in *To What End Exegesis? Essays Textual, Exegetical, and Theological* (Eerdmans, 2001), 29–42.

[22] Richard Bauckham, "For Whom Were Gospels Written?" in *The Gospels for All Christians*, ed. Richard Bauckham (Eerdmans, 1998), 44–48.

intentional shaping of the narrative structure may be indicative of a situational context beyond what Bauckham allows and should not be so quickly dismissed.[23]

In the Gospel of John, it is ironically the lowly καί ('and') that offers an important key to unlock the mystery of this text. Its presence as an intersentential (discourse) marker at John 7:1 indicates that the use of the expression μετὰ ταῦτα has been intentional and that this expression has a more significant function in the text than scholars generally perceive.[24] The use of καί, in fact, suggests, and the text confirms, that μετὰ ταῦτα has been marking sectional boundaries for some time and that the series (A ..., B ..., C ..., D ..., *and* E) ends following the events linked to John 7:1 (i.e., 7:1-10:42) only to be resumed at a later point to mark the final sections of the text. Μετὰ ταῦτα occurs within the Gospel of John at 3:22; 5:1, 5:14; 6:1; 7:1; 13:7; 19:38; and 21:1; the singular form, μετὰ τοῦτο, occurs at 2:12; 11:7, 11; and 19:28. Of these occurrences, most mark a clear sectional boundary and both series of μετὰ ταῦτα are preceded by a section marked with μετὰ τοῦτο such that one finds divisions at the following points in the text:

2:12 Μετὰ τοῦτο
3:22 Μετὰ ταῦτα
5:1   Μετὰ ταῦτα
6:1   Μετὰ ταῦτα
7:1   Καὶ μετὰ ταῦτα

Extended Interlude

19:28 Μετὰ τοῦτο
19:38 Μετὰ δὲ ταῦτα
21:1 Μετὰ ταῦτα.

---

[23] *Contra* Bauckham, who states, "[T]he way in which a creative writer is influenced by and responds to his or her context is simply not calculable. The chances of being able to deduce from an author's work what the influences on the author were, if we have only the work to inform us, are minimal." Ibid., 45. See, however, further below.

[24] See e.g., Carson, *John*, who describes this phrase as "vague" (p. 267), "a frequent connective between narratives in John" (p. 175) that "establishes sequence, but not tight chronology" (p. 267). While Carson does note the occurrences of μετὰ τοῦτο/ταῦτα throughout the Gospel of John, he fails to perceive the true structural significance of this phrase (even missing the division marked at 19:28; pp. 108, 608–22), to note the added significance of καί at John 7:1 (p. 305) or δέ at John 19:38 (pp. 628–29), and to distinguish the non-structural uses at John 11:7, 11 (pp. 408–9; both of which are used in that passage to emphasize the delay of Jesus in going to Lazarus) and John 13:7 (this use is mid-sentential in a statement made by Jesus). For a discussion of μετὰ ταῦτα at John 5:14, see further below.

Hence, following the introduction, one finds six sections progressing in some fashion but not extending to the end of the public ministry, an extended interlude, and a resumption of this series of discourse markers prior to what might understandably, but mistakenly (in this text), be called the climax of the resurrection (see further below). Furthermore, within each section there are multiple events for which a structural account must be given.

Reference to Cana as a structurally-defining *inclusio* for the early chapters of this text is an excellent example of the weakness of structural analysis among NT scholars. The evidence of the text stands against this position.[25] First, one should note that John 2:1–11 was introduced by καὶ τῇ ἡμέρᾳ τῇ τρίτῃ. This phrase links this paragraph to the previous paragraphs by the use of καί to mark the end of a series and by the repetition of marking the paragraph with chronological precision versus the unspecified references (μετὰ τοῦτο/ταῦτα) that follow. Second, the disciples have been the focus of each paragraph since 1:29, culminating here with the concluding statement: "and his disciples believed in him" (John 2:11b), but play a much more minor role in the text that follows. Third, the structurally-defining feature of both 2:1–11 and 4:43–54 is not 'Cana' but the concluding authorial comments suggesting that these paragraphs mark the end of their respective sections rather than form an *inclusio*.

This, the first of his signs, Jesus did in Cana of Galilee.
Ταύτην ἐποίησεν ἀρχὴν τῶν σημείων ὁ Ἰησοῦς ἐν Κανὰ τῆς Γαλιλαίας.

This, the second sign Jesus did when he came again from Judea to Galilee.
Τοῦτο [δὲ] πάλιν δεύτερον σημεῖον ἐποίησεν ὁ Ἰησοῦς ἐλθὼν ἐκ τῆς Ἰοθδαίας εἰς τὴν Γαλιλαίαν.

While 'Cana' is repeated in the second paragraph, it is not found at the end, but toward the beginning of the paragraph (4:46), distinct from the repeated phrase ("this the first/second sign ..."). To claim that these texts mark a geographical cycle is to make an unfounded assumption regarding what motivated the author's structuring of the text, an assumption that encounters further difficulties for some scholars in chapters five through seven.[26]

---

[25] See also Joseph R. Dongell, "Discerning Segment Boundaries within John 1:19–4:54," *JIBS* 1 (2014): 116–21.

[26] On the basis of a perceived geographical displacement in chapters five through seven, scholars have offered various contrived explanations. See Raymond E. Brown, *An Introduction to the Gospel of John*, ed. Francis J. Moloney, ABRL (Doubleday, 2003), 40–69; or Andrew T. Lincoln, *The Gospel According to Saint John*, BNTC (Hendrickson; Continuum, 2005), 50–55.

There is a notable difference between the texts marked by μετὰ τοῦτο/ταῦτα and the extended interlude. The difference is not just a matter of narrative versus monologue/dialogue, nor is it a matter of public versus private settings since each of these elements is present in the intervening text. Nevertheless, scholars instinctively begin to feel a difference in the narrative when chapter eleven is reached.[27] What distinguishes this intermediate section is narrative pace. Biblical scholars are quick to criticize those who would *borrow* the features of modern fiction to analyze a text as theologically significant as the Gospel of John. Surely such *tools* are both anachronistic for the analysis of the ancient text and inconsequential in light of the importance of theological or historical analysis.[28] This criticism is void of merit since story-telling is an ancient craft inherent to the human experience, since it is clearly evident in ancient texts pre-dating the Gospel of John by several centuries, and, more significantly, since the text itself provides this evidence (see below).[29]

---

[27] See e.g., Keener, *John*, 1:xvii–xviii, 2:833, who treats John 11–12 as the introduction to the Passion; or Richard A. Burridge, *Four Gospels, One Jesus?: A Symbolic Reading*, 2nd ed. (Eerdmans, 2005), 139, who describes John 11–12 as an interlude.

[28] See e.g., Francis J. Moloney, "Into Narrative and Beyond," in *What We Have Heard from the Beginning: The Past, Present, and Future of Johannine Studies*, ed. Tom Thatcher (Baylor University Press, 2007), 200, who states regarding narrative criticism, "This theory had its birth within the academic analysis of the English novel, a relatively recent phenomenon. There is much that we can learn from that approach, but the texts that responded so well to it were modern and contemporary fiction, not ancient texts written in Hebrew and Greek. The biblical narratives emerged from social, religious, and historical settings that were very different from the modern and contemporary world and claimed to be something other than 'fiction.'" For an alternative view, see e.g., R. Alan Culpepper, *Anatomy of the Fourth Gospel: A Study in Literary Design* (Fortress, 1983), 79–98. While there is much to criticize in Culpepper's study, he is correct to state, "Each of the evangelists tells essentially the same story, but the plots and emphases of the gospels differ greatly. The difference is due ... to the peculiar social and religious struggles of their intended readers" (p. 85).

[29] See Christopher Pelling, *Literary Texts and the Greek Historian*, AAW (Routledge, 2000), 1–17, who states, "Rhetoric is the craft of persuasion.... One instance is narrative, where an author selects and presents material in such a way as to persuade the audience that these were the facts, that they happened like this and in this sequence, and that this is the right way of looking at them ... [i.e.,] to adopt a particular attitude to a state of affairs (p. 1).... Much of our task as historians is to proceed from the literary text and infer what we can about the other ingredients in that performance [i.e., oral presentation], the presumptions which the author must have been making about the audience and the ways in which he must have hoped his persuasion would work (p. 2).... [I]t is unsurprising that modern narratological techniques, forged for analysing novelistic fiction, are proving so fruitful when applied to ancient historiographic texts.... [H]istorians ... orchestrated [i.e., selected, arranged, and emphasized, rather than made up] the narrative in such a way as to direct the receptive reader to put the best questions to the past and render it intelligible" (pp. 8–9).

Text			Words	Days	Words/Day
1:29–2:11			608	6	101
2:12–10:42			7206	1240	6
	2:12	μετὰ τοῦτο			
	3:22	μετὰ ταῦτα			
	5:1	μετὰ ταῦτα			
	6:1	μετὰ ταῦτα			
	7:1	μετὰ ταῦτα			
11:1–12:50			1840	30	61
13:1–19:27			4165	1	4165
19:28–21:24			1443	42	34
	19:28	μετὰ τοῦτο			
	19:38	μετὰ ταῦτα			
	21:1	μετὰ ταῦτα			

Figure 4.1: Narrative Pace in the Gospel of John

While this data is, at best, approximate, it nevertheless illustrates in broad fashion a marked slowing of narrative time and, inversely, the quickening of the narrative pace.[30] Within the trial itself one can also see a pronounced quickening of scenes, first, through the alternation of Jesus before Annas and the denials of Peter outside in the courtyard (18:12–27), and then, through Pilate moving out of the Praetorium to speak with the Jews and then back inside to deal with Jesus (18:28–19:16a). Following these events are three scenes upon the cross narrated in an almost surreal fashion reminiscent of earlier statements:

Come and see the King (19:16b–22)
> (Pilate places a sign upon the cross: Jesus of Nazareth, King of the Jews [19:19–22; cf., 1:46b, 49b; Matt 27:37; Mark 15:26; Luke 23:38])

Who fulfilled Scripture (19:23–24)
> (the soldiers cast lots for his clothing [19:24; cf., 12:38; 13:18; 15:25; 17:12; 18:9, 32; Matt 27:35; Mark 15:24; Luke 23:34b])

---

[30] Harold W. Hoehner, *Chronological Aspects of the Life of Christ* (Zondervan, 1977), 143; C. J. Humphreys and W. G. Waddington, "The Jewish Calendar, a Lunar Eclipse, and the Date of Christ's Crucifixion," *TynBul* 43 (1992): 331–51.

And loved his own unto the end (19:25–27)

("Woman, behold your son," [19:26b; cf., 13:1; unique to John's gospel]).

The tension of the trial (and conflict of the text itself) is gone (with only the brief, minor dispute regarding Pilate's sign as an exception). Absent in the Gospel of John are the following:

the ominous warning of Jesus to the mourners (Luke 23:27–31),

the mocking of the crowd and Jewish leaders (Matt 27:39–44; Mark 15:29–32; Luke 23:35–37),

the drama of a last-minute conversion (Luke 23:39–43),

the fearful display of nature (an earthquake, Matt 27:51b; the darkness: Matt 27:45; Mark 15:33; Luke 23:44),

the significant symbolism of a rent Temple curtain (Matt 27:51a; Mark 15:38; Luke 23:45b),

the supernatural raising of the saints (Matt 27:52–53), and

the awe of the centurion (Matt 27:54; Mark 15:39; Luke 23:47).

The mood is broken only by the return of μετὰ τοῦτο restarting the narrative clock to mark the event and affirmation of Jesus' death (19:28–37). In the Gospel of John, as presented by the author, the events surrounding the death, burial, and resurrection of Jesus—while central to the Gospel message—appear to *follow* the climax. The turning point in this text appears to have been reached when the Jews exclaimed with words that have reverberated throughout the centuries, "We have no king if not Caesar!"[31]

The proper identification of the climax of this text establishes a second, clear structural landmark. Indeed, as the climax, one should attach even more structural

---

[31] Wayne A. Meeks, *The Prophet-King: Moses Traditions and the Johannine Christology*, NovTSup 14 (Brill, 1967), 76–78, states, "Rejecting the 'King of the Jews', 'the Jews' cease to be 'Israel', the special people of God, and become only one of the ἔθνη subject to Caesar.... [A]nyone familiar with the Passover Haggadah cannot fail to be reminded by the cry of the high priests, 'We have no king but Caesar', of the *Nišmat*, the hymn sung at the conclusion of the Greater Hallel:

From everlasting to everlasting thou art God;

Beside thee we have no king, redeemer, or savior,

No liberator, deliverer, provider

None who takes pity in every time of distress and trouble.

We have no king but thee....

[B]ecause God the king and judge, who appears in the person of his son and ἀπόστολος enthroned on the tribunal, is rejected, then the judges who reject him become themselves the condemned."

significance to this statement than to the purpose statement. While John 20:31 records the author's purpose in writing, the climax (19:15c) represented the critical element, or turning point, necessary for achieving that purpose. The identification of this unexpected climax is indicative of a more definitive situational context than Bauckham's gospel definition would seem to allow and raises the question of what issue the author perceived to warrant shaping his message in this fashion.

Tracing the Trajectory

Conflict and the spiritual nature of that conflict are introduced into the message of the Gospel of John almost from the beginning: "The light shines in the darkness and the darkness has not overcome it (1:5)." The battleground between these two spiritual forces comes into sharper focus as the author engages the reader:

> "He was in the world;
>> And (καί) the world was made through him;
>> And (καί) the world did not know him.
> He came unto his own;
>> And (καί) his own did not receive him" (1:10–11).

In these statements, the author *does not state* what modern translators and commentators feel compelled to provide. Καί is neither concessive nor adversative in these texts—nor is it ever truly concessive or adversative in *any* text. By leaving unsaid what the recipient would naturally expect, the author establishes a dialogue, soliciting a response, even an objection, to what seems incongruous: "Why did creation not recognize its Creator?" and, more significantly, "Why did God's chosen people not receive their God?"

The proper significance of καί is also ignored in setting the limits of the Prologue. John 1:1–18 certainly provides fertile soil for theological discussion before the more mundane and apparently time-bound details of John 1:19–28, but the author has not yet finished his opening remarks.[32] Bracketing what is arguably a

---

[32] While a modern reader would naturally assume that John 1:19–28 should be included with the paragraphs that follow, since it appears to relate time-bound events and the phrase τῇ ἐπαύριον at John 1:29 would cause one to make this connection, the original recipients would have heard the text differently. First, the authorial comment—"these things took place in Bethany ..." (1:28)—would have been heard as a concluding remark preparing the recipients for a transition. (Note, if the author was merely establishing the geographic context, this statement would have been given at the beginning of the paragraph. The use of an authorial comment to mark the conclusion of one section before the transition to another is a common

thematic statement shaping much of this gospel (1:10–13), καί marks a parallel expansion at both 1:14 *and* 1:19:

> In the beginning was the Word....
>> And (καί) the Word became flesh (1:1, 14);

> There was a man sent from God who came as a witness....
>> And (καί) this is the testimony of John (1:6-7a, 19).

In the final paragraph of the Prologue, the author further specifies the earthly participants (priests, Levites, and, more significantly, Pharisees) directly involved in this spiritual conflict:

> Make straight the way of the Lord ... [who] stands among you ... [*whom*] *you do not know* (1:23b, 26b)!

His own did not receive him, because the very people responsible for their spiritual guidance did not themselves even know him.

The faith of the disciples (1:29–2:11) and the limited examples of faith given by the author in the subsequent text (chapters four and nine) serve as the counter-balancing theme in the trajectory of the author's message (i.e., isolated faith and emerging faithfulness in the midst of unexpected hostility). For the disciples, what begins as a directive to "Behold the Lamb of God" becomes a personal invitation among friends ("Come and see ...") and finally a life-changing experience of faith ("We beheld his glory ... and believed [2:11; cf., 1:14]). The experience for most of the Jews was much different. The first two sections marked by μετὰ τοῦτο/ταῦτα relate two very different reactions to the coming of the Light into the world: first, his own, who would not receive him (2:12–3:21), and second, those who unexpectedly did (3:22–4:54). When Jesus came to his own, he found worship replaced by commerce (2:12–17) and the honor due him replaced by

---

structural device utilized by the author [see further below].) Second, the author does not introduce chronological precision until he states τῇ ἐπαύριον in John 1:29, a phrase that is now repeated in a series (1:35, 42) culminating with καί (indicating the last in a series) τῇ ἡμέρᾳ τῇ τρίτῃ. No such phrase is found at John 1:19. Third, with John 1:29, the author introduces a new topic ("Behold, the Lamb of God who takes away the sin of the world") and new characters (i.e., the disciples), who become the focus of the narrative while John the Baptist disappears. Finally, there is a thematic change in the author's message at John 1:29. Specifically, the theme of John 1:1–28 has been the unexpected non-reception of the Word, including the fact that, though he stood among them, even the Jewish leaders did not know him (1:26), while the theme introduced in John 1:29 relates the disciples coming, seeing, and eventually believing (1:29–2:11).

demands imposed upon him (2:18–22). There is little reason to wonder why he would therefore not entrust himself to them (2:23–25). Even among the religious leaders, where one would expect the Light to have been received, there was only darkness (3:1–21). The purpose of the Son of God coming into the world was not to condemn the world, but to save the world (3:17–18). The vast majority of his own, however, would not admit that they, even as the surrounding Gentiles, whom they despised, also stood condemned. Their exposure to the Light not only revealed their sin, it fueled their hatred for having been exposed.[33]

In the next section (3:22–4:54) the author once again utilizes the testimony of John the Baptist to validate the subsequent text. Knowing that the bridegroom is above all (3:31–36) and that he would, and should, become more prominent as the friend of the bridegroom faded into the background (John 3:22–30), the Baptist declares, "*Whoever* receives his testimony ... *whoever* believes in the Son has eternal life" (3:33, 36). The breadth of what *whoever* meant (i.e., reaching even to a Samaritan woman of ill-repute; 4:1–42; cf., 10:16; 12:20–21) was no doubt offensive in its original context, but arguably affirmative for those who later received the author's message. The impact of this new reality was highlighted against a backdrop of limited reception among "his own" where "a prophet is without honor" (4:43–54).[34] (Note: The authorial comment concluding this section [4:54; parallel to the concluding comment in 2:11] prepares the recipient to expect a transition.)

In the next two sections (5:1–47 and 6:1–71), once again marked by μετὰ ταῦτα, the author reveals why the chosen people of God, who had experienced the power of God (historically, through the events of the Exodus and now, personally, through the ministry of Jesus), failed to receive, or even recognize, the Son of God.[35] The healing of the paralytic and Jesus' subsequent claim of divinity

---

[33] The dialogue between Jesus and Nicodemus extends through verse eighteen. (Note: the final use of the second person (3:12) is followed by, and linked with, two statements marked by καί, followed by two clarifying remarks introduced by γάρ and a final, unmarked (asyndeton) summary statement. John 3:19–21 represents an authorial comment to the recipients in which the verbal tenses are significant: verse nineteen, introduced emphatically, points to the rejection of Jesus, emphasizing, in particular, that the deeds of the Jews (i.e., his own people and, specifically, the leaders) were (imperfect tense) evil. Verses twenty and twenty-one address the recipients directly (present tense) with a general principle likely relevant for their own current milieu (i.e., opposed by those who hate the Light, cf., 7:7; 15:18–19; 17:14) and an implied exhortation for their appropriate response (i.e., do not retreat from the Light within you, but embrace the Light even more so that in the darkness of your own circumstances the works of God will be clearly known).

[34] The author's point is not to distinguish the reception of Jesus in Judea versus Galilee, but in the broader world versus among his own people.

[35] Cf. the theme activated in the Prologue: "The Law through Moses was given; grace and truth through Jesus have come" (1:17).

serve as the backdrop for Jesus' monologue to answer his critics.[36] The Jews (in this case primarily referring to the Pharisees—note their objection regarding breaking the Sabbath) did not receive his message, because they did not have the word of the Father abiding in them. They claimed to have set their hope in Moses, but he himself would accuse them, because they had not believed what Moses wrote, seeking instead the glory of men rather than the glory of God (5:44). In the events recorded in chapter six, Jesus shows that he is the Prophet like Moses who was to come—not just in that he provided bread or that he could deliver his own through the sea, but that he himself *was* the bread that imparted eternal life. In these events, Jesus did what the Jewish leaders could not do because of their own sinfulness: confront the people with their need of a Savior. Yet, once again, his own people failed to receive his words.[37]

The last section before the shift in narrative pace (7:1–10:42, marked by καὶ μετὰ ταῦτα) begins and ends with a challenge for Jesus to show himself clearly to the world (7:4b; 10:24). This demand could not be met in terms of what his challengers expected, first, because his hour had not yet come, but also, because he refused to reveal himself in terms of what they demanded of him (cf., 6:15). The purpose and impact of his earthly ministry (and of the gospel message itself) was always that he would reveal himself, but his invitation (7:37–39) was met primarily with division rather than genuine faith (7:40–[53]). Ultimately, although he bid them come, they did not because they were slaves to sin (8:1–59a) and because they would not acknowledge his works or believe his words (8:59b–10:42). The miracle of healing the man born blind ironically captured the essence of Jesus' ministry and an important thematic element in the author's message. Those who claimed that they could see were blind; those who acknowledged their blindness would be made to see, yet at the cost of losing their place in a sinful world (9:34–41).

Throughout this section, the conflict with the Jewish leaders has continued to escalate. Having shattered the false piety of their self-identification with Moses

---

[36] In this section, μετὰ ταῦτα occurs at both John 5:1 and 5:14. The first occurrence marks the sectional division of the text; the second occurrence marks a relatively brief passing of time, but it also serves to focus attention on the following monologue in which the author's *primary* point is made.

[37] Cf. Deut 18:15, 19. Note also that the absence of an authorial comment at the end of chapter five is indicative that chapters five and six are intended to function together as two parts of one unit. In chapter six, a concluding authorial comment closes the end of the public events and discussion (6:59). The author, however, continues recording a private conversation among first, a broader group of disciples, who, being offended, largely abandon Jesus, and then, second, with the twelve disciples, who affirm their commitment (although, even here, one was a διάβολος). This is a pattern that is prevalent throughout the Gospel of John (see esp., 8:30–59a): although many are attracted to the Light, the Light continues to probe, even offend, until only those who truly believe, if any, remain.

by exposing their sinful motivation to seek their own glory (5:44; cf., 12:42–43), the author returns to this theme through the words of Jesus charging them with not keeping the Law (7:19). When his words and deeds create division among the people, the Pharisees strike back: first, by condemning those whom they viewed as deceived, ignorant of the Law, and accursed (7:45–48), and then, by seeking to trap Jesus in a test regarding the Law (8:1–11; the *Pericope Adulterae*).[38] The words of Jesus in response ("Let whoever is sinless among you cast the first stone") serve a double purpose: they expose the sinfulness of the leaders ("they went away, one by one, beginning with the older ones"), but they also establish an ironic contrast ("which of you [who are slaves to sin; 8:34] convicts me of sin" [8:46]). Although unable to make a case, "they (who were *not* without sin) picked up stones to throw at him" (8:7b, 59a; 10:31).

In the growing darkness, the Light continued to shine. The ultimate sign of raising Lazarus after four days in the grave, while stirring a reaction among the fickle crowd, induced primarily a murderous rage among the Jewish leaders. Confronted by inevitable defeat (whether the loss of power to a popular Jesus or the loss of everything to a Roman dynasty [11:47–48]), the leaders embraced the prophecy of Caiaphas: "it is better that one man should die for the people" (11:49c).[39] The author declares, in these final moments before this literary (and spiritual) sunset, "Now is the judgment of the world" (12:31a). He asks, with Isaiah, "Who has believed our message and to whom has the arm of the Lord been revealed" (12:38b; cf., Isa 53:1)? He concludes, "although he had done so many signs before them, they did not believe in him ... and [would therefore] be judged on the last day by the word which [he] had spoken" (12:37, 48).

Nearly one-fifth of the author's message is uncharacteristically devoted now to a discourse delivered exclusively to the disciples.[40] The message, generally known as the Upper Room Discourse, is intended to strengthen their faith by

---

[38] The authenticity of the *pericope adulterae* is primarily a textual issue that cannot be resolved here. For a recent discussion of this issue, see David Alan Black and Jacob N. Cerone, eds., *The Pericope of the Adulteress in Contemporary Research*, LNTS 551 (T&T Clark, 2016). The pericope is included here because it does, in fact, fit the thematic trajectory.

[39] In the three paragraphs immediately following the raising of Lazarus, the common element contrasting the thematic trajectory (Will he come [John 11:55–57]? He is coming [John 12:1–10]. He is here [John 12:11–19]!) is the reaction of the Jewish leaders, who seek to arrest Jesus (John 11:57), who plot to kill Lazarus also (John 12:10), and who complain in frustration that "the world has gone after him" (John 12:19).

[40] Eighteen percent (2,835 out of 15,671 total words) of the Gospel of John is devoted to this discourse. In contrast, the same events in the Synoptics are given one percent in Matthew (Matt 26:20–35; 268 out of 18,363 total words), two percent in Mark (Mark 14:17–31; 239 out of 11,312 total words), and two percent in Luke (Luke 22:14–38; 419 out of 19,495 total words). (Some of the statements generally included within the upper room discourse in the Gospel of John were likely made after leaving that specific location [cf. the synoptic accounts].)

preparing them for the events that would soon transpire, for the ministry that would soon be set before them, and for the spiritual and physical hostility they would soon face. In this section, Jesus first sets an example for the disciples to follow (13:1–20), foretells the outcome of the coming events (13:21–38), and then addresses their fears (chapter fourteen). In chapters fifteen and sixteen— structured by the pattern of an imperative linked to a purpose statement by the phrase, "these things I have spoken to you"—Jesus shows the disciples how they will be able to do what he has called them to do.

> "Remain in me ... so that your joy may be full" (15: 4a, 11).
> "Remember the word that I spoke to you
>> [a servant is not greater than his master],...
>> so that you will not fall away" (15:20a, 16:1).
> "Be courageous ... so that in me you might have peace" (16:33).

In the final chapter of this discourse (John 17), Jesus prays for the perseverance and sanctification of not only his disciples after he has left them, but also for those who would believe on account of their testimony (17:20–21).

Following the climactic courtroom confession of the Jewish leaders and the scenes upon the cross, as discussed above, the narrative clock resumes for three more sections (19:28–37; 19:38–20:31; and 21:1–24). The first two are parallel, as signaled by their concluding purpose statements: "so that you might believe" (19:35d; 20:31a). The first section lays the foundation for the second and both together illustrate in deed what Jesus proclaimed earlier through words (12:24):

> (μετὰ τοῦτο) The Reality and Confirmation of the Death of Jesus;
>> "unless a grain of wheat falls to the ground and dies, it remains alone";

> (μετὰ δὲ ταῦτα) The Burial and Resurrection of Jesus;
>> "if it dies, it bears much fruit."

The distinct division marked by the second μετὰ ταῦτα is emphasized by the additional discourse marker, δέ. The placement of these two structural markers together at this point in the text defies expectations of modern historians and theologians and is thus generally, and inappropriately, ignored.[41] Within this section there are three paragraphs with certain conceptual parallels demonstrating that the author's intended focus is not upon the events, as one would naturally suppose, but upon the reaction of certain characters to those events—i.e.,

---

[41] See e.g., Carson, *John*, 108; and Keener, *John*, 1:xxiii–xxiv, who mark John 20:1–31 as a distinct unit from John 19:38–42 functioning on a higher structural level.

upon fruit produced by Jesus' death. The burial and resurrection of Jesus inspired faith: in Joseph of Arimathea, who believed in spite of his fear of the Jews (19:38–42; cf., 12:42–43); in Peter and the disciple whom Jesus loved, who believed in spite of their lack of understanding (20:1–10); and in Mary, who believed in spite of not being able to cling to his physical presence (20:11–18).[42] The parallelism of these three paragraphs stops and a second subsection further developing the author's point is continued in John 20:19–31. The presence of faith (19:38–20:18) demands the exercise of faithfulness (20:19–31)—a point suggested by the general commission of the disciples (20:19–23) and the later command to Thomas, "do not be unbelieving, but believing" (20:24–29).

The final section of the text focuses upon Peter, not because it represents an epilogue, but because he served as an example. The Gospel of John was obviously written after the death of Peter (21:19a). These three scenes regarding both his life and death were necessary to make the author's final point. As is typical in any narrative, the characters and events in the text serve as examples for the purpose of motivating the reader in some fashion.[43] In this case, these three final paragraphs (before the conclusion in 21:25) provide in detail for the reader what John 20:21b described in general for the disciples—i.e., their commission.

Come, eat: God provides what you could not provide for yourselves.
Feed my sheep: God commissions in spite of your past failures.
Follow me: God directs even unto death.

Once again, these scenes illustrate the words of Jesus at a critical point as he neared the end of his public ministry: "if anyone wishes to serve me, he must follow me" (12:26a).

Conclusion

Structural analysis, properly applied, provides clarity regarding the author's message and restraint in the face of over-zealous theologians, or overly critical historians. The analysis presented here, however, being constrained by the limitations of a brief chapter, is far from complete. Probing the subtle situational clues found in the text, within the larger framework outlined in this study, will have to

---

[42] The author does not specify if Nicodemus, who accompanied Joseph of Arimathea, was likewise a disciple of Jesus.

[43] Pelling, *Literary Texts and the Greek Historian*, 8, who states, "Greek historians prefer to allow their big ideas to emerge *through* the narrative, to allow readers to infer the leading themes through recurrent patterning, selective emphasis, ... and sometimes through the speeches of the characters themselves. 'Show, not Tell': that is the historian's craft."

wait for another day. Nevertheless, while Carson is correct to state that the recipients of this text were biblically well-versed, it appears doubtful that the text was primarily intended for Jewish evangelism.[44] In the Gospel of John, the author provides the reader with a glimpse of what sustained the disciples and what now will sustain them.

An Outline of the Gospel of John

1A. Introduction: In the Beginning Was the Word (1:1–28).

    1B. In Him Was Life, the Light of Men ... and the Darkness Has Not Overcome It (1:1–5).

    2B. There Was a Man Sent from God Who Came as a Witness ... So That All Might Believe (1:6–9).

    3B. To All ... Who Believed ... He Gave the Right to Become the Children of God (1:10–13).

    4B. And the Word Became Flesh ... And We Beheld His Glory (1:14–18).

    5B. And John Testified: Among You Stands ... [One Whom] You Do Not Know (1:19–28).

    Authorial Comment: These things happened in Bethany (1:28).

2A. The Light Shines in the Darkness ... (1:29–12:50)

    1B. We Beheld His Glory ... and Believed (1:29–2:11).

        1C. Behold the Lamb of God Who Takes Away the Sin of the World (1:29–34).

        2C. Come and See the Messiah (1:35–42).

        3C. Come and See the King of Israel (1:43–51).

        4C. His Disciples Believed in Him (2:1–11).

        Authorial Comment: This, the first of his signs, Jesus did in Cana in Galilee (2:11).

    2B. God ... Sent His Son ... [so] that the World Might Be Saved through Him (2:12–4:54).

        1C. He Came unto His Own and His Own Did Not Receive Him (2:12–3:21).

            1D. Light Has Come into the World ... (2:12–25)

                1E. Do Not Make My Father's House a House of Trade (2:12–17).

                2E. Destroy This Temple and in Three Days I Will Raise It Up (2:18–22).

---

[44] Carson, *John*, 89–95.

3E. Authorial Comment: Jesus Would Not Entrust Himself to Them Because He Knew What Was in Man (2:23–25).

2D. [And] Men Loved Darkness Rather than the Light (3:1–21).

  1E. God Did Not Send His Son to Condemn the World but that the World Might Be Saved through Him (3:1–18).

  2E. Authorial Comment: This is the Judgment: Light Has Come into the World and Men Loved Darkness Rather than the Light (3:19–21).

2C. To All Who Did Receive Him, He Gave the Right to Become the Children of God (3:22–4:54).

  1D. John Testifies: Whoever Receives His Testimony ... Whoever Believes in the Son Has Eternal Life (3:22–36).

    1E. Everyone Is Going to Him ... and I Rejoice Greatly (3:22–30).

    2E. The One Who Comes from Above is Above All (3:31–36).

  2D. Many Samaritans Believe on Account of His Word (4:1–42).

    1E. The Setting: Jesus Leaves Judea for Galilee by Way of Samaria (4:1–6).

    2E. Jesus Reveals Himself to the Samaritan Woman (4:7–38).

      1F. Her Need Exposed: Give to Me This Water that I Might Not Thirst (4:7–15).

      2F. Her Invitation Extended: The Father Is Seeking Those Who Will Worship Him in Spirit and Truth (4:16–27).

      3F. Her Belief Expanded: Lift Up Your Eyes and See the Fields Are White for Harvest (4:28–38).

    3E. Many of the Samaritans Believed that This One is Truly the Savior of the World (4:39–42).

  3D. A Prophet Is Without Honor in His Own Country (4:43–54).

    1E. The Setting: He Departed for Galilee (4:43–45).

    2E. Unless Signs and Wonders You See, You Will Certainly Never Believe (4:46–50).

    3E. When He Knew [the Wonder Jesus Had Done] the Man Himself and His Whole Household Believed (4:51–54).

    Authorial Comment: This again was the second sign which Jesus did when he came from Judea to Galilee (4:54).

3B. The Law through Moses Was Given, Grace and Truth through Jesus Have Come (5:1–6:71).

1C. If You [the Jews] Do Not Believe His [Moses'] Writings, How Will You Believe My Words (5:1–47)?

  1D. Jesus Heals the Paralytic Man (5:1–13).

    1E. The Setting: A Feast of the Jews; A Pool Called Bethesda (5:1–4).

    2E. The Event: Jesus Heals the Paralyzed Man (5:5–9a).

    3E. The Issue: That Day Was a Sabbath (5:9b–13).

  2D. Jesus Exposes the Unbelief of the Jews (5:14–47).

    1E. Jesus Incites the Jews (5:14–18).

    2E. Jesus Answers His Critics (5:19–47).

      1F. The One Who Does Not Honor the Son Does Not Honor the Father Who Sent Him (5:19–23).

      2F. The One Who Hears My Word and Believes Has Passed from Death [Judgment] into Life (5:24–30).

      3F. You Do Not Have [the Father's] Word Abiding in You Because You Do Not Believe the One Whom He Has Sent (5:31–40).

      4F. Moses, in Whom You Have Set Your Hope, Will Accuse You Because You Would [Not] Believe (5:41–47).

2C. Truly This is the Prophet Who Is to Come into the World, ... [But Who Will Listen (Deut 18:15, 19)?] (6:1–71).

  1D. Jesus Shows He is the Prophet Foretold by Moses (6:1–21).

    1E. By Feeding the Five Thousand (6:1–15).

      1F. The Setting: By the Sea of Tiberias, a Crowd Follows Jesus (6:1–4).

      2F. Jesus Tests His Disciples: Where Can We Buy Bread So That We Might Feed Them (6:5–11)?

      3F. When the Crowd Had Eaten Their Fill ... They Were About to ... Seize Him by Force ... [and] Make Him King, but Jesus Withdrew by Himself (6:12–15).

    2E. By Delivering His Disciples across the Sea (6:16–21).

  2D. Jesus Tests to See Who Has Heard Him (6:22–59).

    1E. Jesus Addresses the Crowd Who Seeks for Food (6:22–29) and for a Sign (6:30–40).

      1F. The Work of God is That You Would Believe in the One Whom He Has Sent (i.e., Work for the Food That Remains) (6:22–29).

2F. The Will of God Is That Everyone Who Beholds the Son (the Sign) and Believes in Him Will Have Eternal Life (6:30–40).

2E. Jesus Addresses the Jews Who Grumble About His Claims ... (6:41–59)

1F. To Be the Bread of Life that Comes Down from Heaven: Unless the Father Who Sent Me Draws Him, No One Can Come to Me (6:41–51);

2F. To Be the Living Bread Given as an Atonement: Unless You Eat the Flesh of the Son of Man and Drink His Blood, You Will Not Have Live in Yourselves (6:52–59).

Authorial Comment: These things he said while he taught in the synagogue in Capernaum (6:59).

3E. Jesus Addresses the Disciples Who Wrestle with His Message (6:60–71).

1F. To the Disciples (in a Broader Sense) Who Turn Back: Does This Offend You (6:60–65)?

2F. To the Twelve Who Remain (Though One is a Devil): And Do You Not Want to Go (6:66–71)?

Authorial Comment: He was speaking of Judas ... [who] was going to betray him.

4B. Among You Stands One Whom You Do Not Know (7:1–10:42; cf., 1:26).

1C. They Did Not Know Him Though He Bid Them Come (7:1–[53]).

1D. The Brothers of Jesus Challenge Him: Show Yourself to the World (7:1–13).

1E. Jesus: My Time Has Not Yet Come (7:1–9).

2E. There Was Much Murmuring about Him among the Crowd (7:10–13).

2D. In the Middle of the Feast Jesus Defends Himself before the People (7:14–36).

1E. To the Jews: If Anyone Desires to Do [God's] Will, He Will Know Whether [My] Teaching is of God (7:14–19).

2E. To the Crowd: Do Not Judge According to [Those Who Appear to Keep the Law], But Judge [According to One Who Does Keep the Law] (7:20–24).

3E. To Some of the People of Jerusalem: You Do Not Know from Where I Have Come, Because You Do Not Know the One Who

Sent Me (7:25–30).

4E. To the Jews: You Will Seek Me and Not Find [Me]; Where I Am You Are Not Able to Come (7:31–36).

3D. On the Last Day of the Feast Jesus Invites the People to Come (7:37–[53]).

1E. Let Anyone Who Thirsts Come to Me and Let the One Who Believes in Me Drink So That Out of His Heart Will Flow Rivers of Living Water (7:37–39).

2E. There Was a Division among the Crowd on Account of Him: "Is This the Christ?" versus "He Should Be Arrested" (7:40–44).

3E. There Was a Division among the Leaders on Account of Him: "No One Ever Spoke Like This Man" versus "Have You Also Been Deceived?" (7:45–[53]).

Authorial Comment: And they left, each one to his own house ([7:53]).

2C. They Did Not Know Him Because They Were Slaves to Sin ([8:1]–59a).

1D. Jesus Exposes the Sin of Those Who Claim to Follow the Law ([8:1]–29).

1E. Let Whoever is Sinless among You Cast the First Stone;… Where Are Those Who Condemn You ([8:1–11])?

2E. I Am the Light of the World … [and] You Know Neither Me Nor My Father (8:12–20).

Authorial Comment: These words he spoke in the treasury as he taught in the Temple and no one arrested him because his hour had not yet come (8:20).

3E. I Am Going Away and You Will Seek Me and You Will Die in Your Sin (8:21–29).

2D. Jesus Exposes the Unbelief of Those Who Claim to Believe in Him (8:30–59a).

1E. Everyone Who Practices Sin is a Slave to Sin (8:30–34).

2E. If You Were the Children of Abraham, the Works of Abraham You Would Be Doing (8:35–39).

3E. If God Were Your Father, You Would Love Me (8:40–44).

4E. Which of You Convicts Me of Sin (8:45–49)?

5E. There is One Who Seeks [My Glory] and Judges [Those Who Oppose Him] (8:50–59a).

Authorial Comment: So They Picked Up Stones in Order to Stone Him (8:59a).

3C. They Did Not Know Him Because They Refused to Believe His Words or Acknowledge His Works (8:59b–10:42).

  1D. Jesus Displays the Works of God (8:59b–9:41).

    1E. Jesus Heals the Man Blind from Birth (8:59b–9:7).

    2E. Answers to Questions Raised by the Healing (9:8–34).

      1F. The Blind Man Answers the Question of His Neighbors: "Where Is He [Who Healed You?] ... I Do Not Know" (9:8–12).

      2F. The Blind Man Answers the Question of the Pharisees: "What Do You Say About This [Man Who Healed You on the Sabbath?] ... He is a Prophet" (9:13–17).

      3F. The Blind Man's Parents Avoid the Question of the Pharisees for Fear of 'the Jews': "Ask Him; He is of Age" (9:18–23).

      4F. The Blind Man: "If This Man Were Not from God, He Would Not Be Able to Do Anything" and They Cast Him Out [of the Synagogue] (9:24–34).

    3E. And Jesus Said, "For Judgment I Have Come into This World, So That Those Who Do Not See May See and Those Who See May Become Blind (9:35–41).

  2D. Jesus Condemns the False Shepherds (10:1–21).

    1E. The Sheep Hear the Shepherd and Follow, But They Flee from the Voice of Strangers (10:1–6).

    2E. I Came That the Sheep Might Have Abundant Life, But the Thief Comes Only to Steal and Destroy (10:7–10).

    3E. I Lay Down My Life for the Sheep, But the Hired Hand Leaves the Sheep and Flees When the Wolf Comes (10:11–18).

    Authorial Comment: There was a division again on account of these words (10:19–21).

  3D. Even Yet the Jews Do Not Know Him: "If You Are the Christ, Tell Us Plainly" (10:22–42).

    1E. Jesus Responds: "I and the Father Are One,... But You Do Not Believe Because You Are Not of My Sheep" (10:22–30).

    2E. The Jews Again Pick Up Stones to Stone Him and Jesus Responds: "If Not My Words, Believe [My] Works That You May Know ... That the Father is in Me and I Am in the Father" (10:31–38).

3E. The Jews Were Seeking to Arrest Him and He Escaped from Their Hands (10:39–42).

Authorial Comment: He went away across the Jordan … and many believed in him there (10:40–42).

5B. In Him Was Life and the Life Was the Light of Men (11:1–54).

  1C. Lazarus Was Ill … So That the Son of God [Would] Be Glorified Through It (11:1–4).

  2C. Jesus Showed His Love … (11:5–17)

    1D. By Going in spite of His Enemies (11:5–10);

    2D. By Waiting So That His Disciples Might Believe (11:11–17).

  3C. Jesus: "I Am the Resurrection and the Life; He Who Believes in Me, Though He Die, [Yet] Shall He Live" (11:18–29).

  4C. Some: "Could He Who Opened the Eyes of the Blind Not Do Something So That This Man Also Would Not Have Died?" (11:30–36).

  5C. Jesus: "Did I Not Tell You That If You Would Believe, You Would See the Glory of God?… Lazarus, Come Out!" (11:37–45).

  6C. The Chief Priests and Pharisees Decide: "It Is Better That One Man Should Die for the People … So … They Made Plans to Kill Him" (11:46–54).

  Authorial Comment: From that day, they [the Jews] made plans to kill him. So Jesus no longer walked openly among the Jews (11:53–54).

6B. Now Is the Judgment of the World (11:55–12:50).

  1C. Who Has Believed Our Message and to Whom Has the Arm of the Lord Been Revealed (11:55–12:19)?

    1D. While the Crowd Wondered if Jesus Would Come to the Passover, the High Priests and Pharisees … [Were Seeking to] Arrest Him (11:55–57).

    2D. While Mary Anointed Jesus in Preparation for His Burial, They [the Jews] Made Plans … Also to Kill [Lazarus] (12:1–11).

    3D. While the Crowd Shouted, "Hosanna, Blessed Is He Who Comes in the Name of the Lord, the King of Israel," the Pharisees Murmured, "[We] Are Not Gaining Anything; Behold the World Has Gone After Him" (12:12–19).

  2C. The Hour Has Come for the Son of Man to Be Glorified (12:20–36).

    1D. Unless a Grain of Wheat, Falling to the Ground, Dies, It Remains Alone (12:20–26).

    2D. Should I Say, "Father, Save Me from This Hour?" No, For This Reason I Have Come to This Hour (12:27–30).

      3D. If I Am Lifted Up from the Earth, I Will Draw All People to Myself (12:31–34).

      4D. While You Have the Light [Believe] So That the Darkness Does Not Overtake You (12:35–36).

    3C. He Has Blinded Their Eyes and Hardened Their Hearts (12:37–50).

      1D. *Although* He Had Done So Many Signs Before Them, They Did Not Believe in Him (12:37–43).

      2D. Jesus Declares, "The One Who … Does Not Receive My Words … [Will Be Judged] By the Word Which I Have Spoken (12:44–50).

      Authorial Comment: These last two paragraphs serve as an authorial coment to mark the end of the first half of the gospel.

3A. … And the Darkness Has Not Overcome It (13:1–21:24).

  1B. He Loved His Own to the End … (13:1–17:26)

    1C. By Preparing His Disciples for the Crucifixion (13:1–14:31);

      1D. By Setting the Example for Them to Follow (13:1–20).

        1E. Unless I Wash You, You Have No Share with Me (13:1–11).

        2E. Do [Forgive] As I Have Done to [Forgiven] You (13:12–20).

      2D. By Foretelling the Outcome of the Coming Events (13:21–38).

        1E. Glory Will Overcome Betrayal (13:21–32).

        2E. Love Will Overcome Denial (13:33–38).

      3D. By Addressing Their Fears: Let Not Your Hearts Be Troubled … Believe in Me (14:1–30)

        1E. Because I Am the Way to the Father (14:1–6);

        2E. Because to Know Me Is to Know the Father (14:7–14);

        3E. Because the Father Will Send an Advocate to Those Who Love Me (14:15–26).

        4E. Reprise: Let Not Your Hearts Be Troubled When You See These Things Come to Pass (14:27–31).

    2C. By Preparing His Disciples for Future Ministry (15:1–16:33);

      1D. Remain in Me … So That Your Joy May Be Full (15:1–11).

      2D. Remember the Word That I Spoke to You [That a Servant is Not Greater Than His Master] … So That You Will Not Fall Away (15:12–16:4a).

        1E. Love As I Have Loved You: Laying Down My Life for My Friends (15:12–17).

     2E. Know That You Will Face Persecution: Even unto Death (15:18–16:4a).

    3D. Be Courageous … So That in Me You Might Have Peace (16:4b–33).

     1E. The Holy Spirit Will Come to You (16:4b–11).

     2E. The Spirit of Truth Will Guide You into All Truth (16:12–15).

     3E. Your Sorrow Will Turn to Joy and No One Will Take It Away from You (16:16–24).

     4E. I Have Overcome the World (16:25–33).

   3C. By Praying for His Disciples (17:1–26).

    1D. Glorify Your Son So That the Son May Glorify You (17:1–5).

    2D. Keep Those [Whom You Gave to Me] in Your Name (… [and] from the Evil One) So That They Might Be One (17:6–15).

    3D. Sanctify Them in Truth … So That the World Might Believe That You Sent Me (17:16–23).

    4D. May They Be with Me So That They Might See My Glory (17:24–26).

 2B. Shall I Not Certainly Drink the Cup the Father Has Given to Me (18:1–19:27)?

   1C. The Jews Prepare for Trial (18:1–27).

    1D. I Am the One Whom You Are Seeking (18:1–11).

    2D. They Bound Him and Led Him to Annas … [So That] One Man Could Die for the People (18:12–14).

    3D. Peter Gains Entrance to the Courtyard and Immediately Denies Christ (18:15–18).

    4D. Jesus: Why Do You Strike Me? … You Can Not Bear Witness to Anything I Have Said Wrongly (18:19–24).

    5D. Peter Denies Christ Twice More and the Cock Crows (18:25–27).

   2C. The Trial of the Jews (18:28–19:16a).

    1D. Pilate: What Accusation Do You Bring (18:28–38a)?

     1E. The Jews Charge: He [Jesus] Is Worthy of Death [by Crucifixion].... It Is Not Lawful for Us to Put Anyone to Death (18:28–32).

     2E. Jesus: I Have Come Into the World to Bear Witness to the Truth … [But Only Those Who Hear My Voice Will Know the Truth] (18:33–38a).

    2D. Pilate: I Find No Basis for an Accusation.... [Whom] Should I Release to You (18:38b–19:3)?

     1E. The Jews Choose: [Do] Not [Release] This Man, But Barabbas (18:38b–40).

  2E. Pilate Responds by Having Jesus Flogged and by Allowing the Soldiers to Mock "The King of the Jews" (19:1–3).

 3D. Pilate: Behold the Man.... [I Have Beaten an Innocent Man to Appease You] (19:4–11).

  1E. The Jews Demand: He Should Die Because He Claimed to Be the Son of God (19:4–7).

  2E. Jesus Responds to Pilate: He Who Delivered Me to You Has the Greater Sin (19:8–11).

 4D. The Conviction: Pilate: Behold Your King!... Shall I Crucify Your King (19:12–16a)?

  1E. The Jew's Rebuttal: If You Do Not Crucify This Man, You Are No Friend of Caesar (19:12).

  2E. The Chief Priests Declare [Expose Their Guilt]: We Have No King If Not Caesar (19:13–16a).

3C. When I Am Lifted Up, I Will Draw All People to Myself (19:16b–27).

 1D. Come and See the King ... [Pilate Wrote an Inscription in Aramaic, Latin, and Greek: "Jesus of Nazareth, the King of the Jews"] (19:16b–22)

 2D. Who Fulfilled Scripture ... [They Cast Lots for His Clothes] (19:23–24)

 3D. And Loved His Own Until the End [Woman, Behold Your Son] (19:25–27).

3B. So That You Also Might Believe (19:28–20:31).

1C. Unless a Grain of Wheat Falls to the Ground and Dies, It Remains Alone (19:28–37).

 1D. The Reality of the Death of Jesus: Jesus Said, "It Is Finished," and He Bowed His Head and Gave Up His Spirit (19:28–30).

 2D. His Death, as a Fulfillment of Scripture, Was Confirmed by an Eyewitness So That You Also Might Believe (19:31–37).

2C. If It Dies, It Bears Much Fruit (19:38–20:31).

 1D. The Burial and Resurrection of Jesus Inspire Faith (19:38–20:18).

  1E. You Must Overcome Your Fear: Joseph of Arimathea Believes in Spite of His Fear of the Jews (19:38–42).

  2E. You Will Not Understand All That You Would Like: Peter and the Disciple Whom Jesus Loved Believe in Spite of Not Yet Understanding Scripture (20:1–10).

  3E. You Cannot Cling to What is Secure: Mary [Believes] in Spite of Not Being Able to Cling to His Physical Presence (20:11–18).

2D. The Resurrection of Jesus Demands Faithfulness (20:19–31).

    1E. Just As the Father Has Sent Me, I Also Am Sending You (20:19–23).

    2E. Do Not Be Unbelieving, But Believe (20:24–29).

    3E. These Things Are Written So That You Might Believe ... and ... Have Life in His Name (20:30–31).

4B. If Anyone Wishes to Serve Me, He Must Follow Me (21:1–24).

    1C. Come, Eat: God Provides What You Could Not Provide for Yourselves (21:1–14).

    2C. Feed My Sheep: God Commissions in Spite of Your Past Failures (21:15–17).

    3C. Follow Me: God Directs Even Unto Death (21:18–24).

4A. Epilogue: There Are Many Other Things that Jesus Did [and Will Yet Do] (21:25).

5

ACTS

JENNY READ-HEIMERDINGER

There is an inherent and inevitable connection between the disciplines of linguistics and textual criticism: for any analysis of the language of a book, it is clearly of importance to know what the text actually says. The difficulty with regard to the text of Acts is that there is an exceptionally high degree of uncertainty as to what the author wrote. For many practical purposes, the edition of the Greek New Testament[1] generally serves well enough as a reference tool, based as it is on a consideration of a range of early witnesses by an international committee of expert textual critics. The published text represents what, in their judgement, is the earliest form of the text, if not the original form, with a small selection of variant readings noted in the critical apparatus.[2]

One particular manuscript of Acts, Codex Bezae (D05), stands out.[3] Its text is

---

[1] Barbara and Kurt Aland et al., eds., *Novum Testamentum Graece*, 28th ed. = NA[28] (Deutsche Bibelgesellschaft, 2013). The same text is reproduced in *The Greek New Testament*, 5th ed. (Deutsche Bibelgesellschaft/United Bible Societies, 2014).

[2] For a fuller account of the extent and complexity of the variation, see: Holger Strutwolf, Georg Gäbel, Annette Hüffmeier, Gerd Mink and Klaus Wachtel, eds., *The Acts of the Apostles* (5 parts), Vol. 3 of *Novum Testamentum Graecum: Editio Critica Maior*, ed. Institut für Neutestamentliche Textforschung (Deutsche Bibelgesellschaft, 2017).

[3] Codex Bezae is a bilingual Greek-Latin uncial manuscript copied around 400 C.E., of which numerous pages, including some in Acts, are missing. For a thorough examination of its external features, see David C. Parker, *Codex Bezae: An Early Christian Manuscript* (Cambridge University Press, 1994), esp. p. 284. A digital copy can be viewed online at https://cudl.lib.cam. ac.uk/view/MS-NN-00002-00041. Retrieved in Lyons, France, by the French Protestant leader Théodore de Bèze in 1562, the manuscript was given to Cambridge University Library in 1581.

by and large rejected by textual critics as secondary because it is seen as the result of emendation carried out by a succession of somewhat capricious scribes who, careless of the authority of the original text, supposedly modified and expanded it to make it more colourful and to bring it into line with their own later, Gentile, church context.[4] Successive editors and translators of the Greek New Testament since the end of the 19th century have preferred to adopt the text of a family of manuscripts known as the Alexandrian text and represented by Codex Sinaiticus (א01) and Codex Vaticanus (B03). In comparing Acts in D05 with the Alexandrian manuscripts, attention is usually focused on the amount of material read by D05 that is absent elsewhere, with the figure of ten percent often cited to refer to D05's longer length.[5] The impression this gives is misleading, for the situation is both more complex and more interesting. First, the extra material is only part of the picture, since there is also material absent from D05 that is present in the Alexandrian text so that, taking B03 for comparison, D05 is longer by only 6.6% overall. Further, in addition to a difference in length, there is as much material that is present in both manuscripts but either in a different form (syntactical or lexical) or in a different word order.

My own motivation to study the text of Acts in more detail was prompted not by the quantity of variation but by the nature of numerous readings in D05 that I identified as sophisticated allusions to Jewish traditions, presented moreover from an inner Jewish perspective.[6] If these findings were accurate, they tended to go against the frequently repeated notion that D05 was a re-writing in a Gentile context.[7] In order to get a clear and objective picture, an analysis of the

---

The association of its text with Lyons may date from at least the second century; see Louis Holtz, "L'écriture latine du Codex Bezae," in *Codex Bezae: Studies from the Lunel Colloquium June 1994*, ed. D.C. Parker and C.-B. Amphoux, NTTSD 22 (Brill, 1996), 14–55.

[4] For recent consideration of D05 as a Greek representative of what is mis-named the "Western Text," see Strutwolf et al., eds., *The Acts of the Apostles*, Part III, *Studien*. A rationale of the decisions taken by the earlier editors of NA[27] is presented in Bruce M. Metzger, *A Textual Commentary on the Greek New Testament*, 2nd ed. (Deutsche Bibelgesellschaft, 1994), a volume that informs much of the textual discussion found in commentaries on Acts.

[5] Metzger, *Commentary*, 223.

[6] I have set out in numerous publications the justification for identifying the Jewish context of Bezan readings in Acts, supported by further extensive evidence in the Bezan form of Luke's Gospel, summarized in Josep Rius-Camps and Jenny Read-Heimerdinger, *The Message of Acts in Codex Bezae. A Comparison with the Alexandrian Tradition*; 4 vols., LNTS (T&T Clark, 2004–2009). An early date for the text of D05 tallies with the high number of early forms of Greek among its readings, see Edouard Delebecque, *Les deux Actes des Apôtres*, EBNS 6 (Gabalda, 1986).

[7] Eldon J. Epp in *The Theological Tendency of Codex Bezae Cantabrigiensis in Acts*, SNTSMS 3 (Cambridge University Press, 1966) identified a series of readings (several taken from witnesses other than D05) which, he maintained, intensified criticism of the Jews. My analysis of the Bezan readings leads me to a similar conclusion but I believe that close scrutiny of the

language of the Bezan form of Acts in its entirety was essential, as continuous text rather than as a string of variant readings and comparing it with the language of B03 as a representative of the Alexandrian manuscripts.[8]

Methodology

The first task was to look at the variant readings that involved differences, whether lexical or syntactical or of word order and regardless of how important they appeared *prima facie* to be.[9] The principal categories that emerged were:

Syntactical	connectives
	article before proper names
	use of noun/pronoun to refer to participants (tracking)
	prepositions
	speech introducers (dative or preposition πρός)
	participle versus finite verb
	word order within a) noun phrases b) verbal clauses c) sentences
Lexical	synonyms
	spelling
	divine titles

Figure 5.1: Classification by Linguistic Categories of Variant Readings between D05 and B03

Variants involving the above items may indeed be noted in a critical apparatus and discussed by textual scholars (even if by no means systematically), but such variables are generally viewed as features of style or scribal habit; the critic's decision to select a reading as the most likely to be authentic is generally guided by what is judged to be an author's usual practice, on the basis of statistical frequency. As a result, the printed text represents a mixture of manuscripts; it is "eclectic."[10]

---

context reveals that this criticism is made from a Jewish point of view, not a Gentile one. See, e.g, Jenny Read-Heimerdinger, "The Apostles in the Bezan Text of Acts," in *Apostelgeschichte als Kirchengeschichte*, ed. T. Nicklas and M. Tilly, BZNW 122 (Walter de Gruyter, 2003), 263–280.

[8] The work was published as Jenny Read-Heimerdinger, *The Bezan Text of Acts: A Contribution of Discourse Analysis to Textual Criticism*, JSNTSup 236 (Sheffield Academic Press, 2002).

[9] The NA critical apparatus avowedly presents a selection of the variant readings that the committee considered to be "the most important," though exactly what were the criteria for "importance" is not explicit (NA[28], "Introduction," 55).

[10] That, at least, is the theory, even if in reality the text currently printed largely reflects the editors' prejudgements in favour of the Alexandrian manuscripts, with B03 usually given preference in the book of Acts where א01 differs from it.

It is striking that this list of features that emerges from an examination of variants between Do5 and Bo3 includes many aspects of Greek that linguists adopting the approach known as "Discourse Analysis" had identified as early as the 1960s as playing a role in conveying meaning rather than expressing personal style.[11] That is, they attribute to them an objective value rather than a subjective one, one that is peculiar to the language and accessible primarily to a native speaker. They view them as much a part of the grammar of Greek as the features of a traditional grammar handbook, with the difference that whereas grammar in the familiar sense tends to consider the way a language functions within a sentence, these more recently identified features operate on a level beyond the sentence and even depend on pragmatic factors outside the verbal communication (the "discourse") itself. Thus, these features link the parts of a discourse with each other and bind it together as a whole; they give it structure; they relate the discourse to the context in which it takes place; they are a means to present a story or argument from the recipient's point of view, and to connect the author (the "speaker") with the one being addressed (the "hearer"), in such a way that the communication is truly bi-directional even if the addressee never makes an utterance.

Being familiar with such a set of linguistic features clearly has implications for textual criticism. Textual criticism (and much exegesis for that matter) typically has tended to think of scribes as copying their texts in isolation, adapting them in the process to suit their own understanding, preferences and customs. A discourse analysis approach to language breaks down this notion, viewing manuscripts as creations of both the scribe and the people for whom the text is being copied, so that the scribe is truly an editor more than a simple copyist. In the early centuries of the Church, texts would frequently be copied in order to be transmitted to another community and the location, identity and nature of the intended recipient community will inevitably have influenced the ways in which the copyist felt the need to make modifications. It is a poor story-teller who does not alter the tale when re-telling it to a new audience: leaving out information that would only make sense to previous recipients who had first-hand knowledge of the setting and characters of the story, articulating the narrative so that its purpose was clearer to an audience more distant in time and space, adding in explanations, or changing the vocabulary to suit the speech of the new hearers. The editing of texts to adapt it to a new audience was not to disrespect the earlier form but, on the contrary, was entirely in keeping with the Jewish

---

[11] Notable among the early linguists working on the biblical text, and using discourse analysis as a tool to aid translation, were Kenneth L. Pike, *Language in Relation to a Unified Theory of the Structure of Human Behavior* (Mouton, 1967; repr. 2015); Joseph E. Grimes, *The Thread of Discourse* (DeGruyter, 1975).

view of Scripture as the living voice of a living God: updating it was a way to honour his word so that it was intelligible to those who received it in changed circumstances.

Discourse analysis thus becomes a tool for navigating a way among the variants which, given their interconnectedness, have to be considered collectively rather than as a string of independent readings. The counterpoint to this is that analysis of the language of a text should ideally work from manuscripts if the results are going to be precise. Working from an edition of the Greek NT that presents an eclectic text, reconstructed without recourse to discourse analysis and according to the editors' understanding of variant readings as reflections of scribes' personal preferences or errors, means that to some extent the results will be skewed. That said, in so far as recent editions of Acts reproduce more often than not the text of B03 and/or א01, they do provide a relatively stable corpus of data that allows conclusions to be drawn, which can subsequently be checked and fine-tuned by taking variant forms of the text into account.

Structural Considerations

An important contribution that discourse analysis makes to the study of language, one that is of particular relevance to ancient written texts, is the identification of structure on both a large and a small scale. This is because discourse analysis looks not only at the sentence and its components but also at the larger units which group sentences together in an organized structure from the smallest units up to the level of the entire discourse. Discourse analysis examines how the boundaries between the various units are signaled. It is similarly concerned with the ways in which the units relate to each other, how they are ordered, and how they hold together to create a unified discourse.

Because of the concern of discourse analysis with language above the level of the sentence, it opens up the way to consider how a writing is organised, specifically what are the inherent means available in a given language to group ideas or themes together, to create a framework that makes communication more intelligible and effective than would be a formless mass of utterances. All good speakers give shape to their discourse in a bid to get the audience's attention and keep them focused on what is being said. In the case of discourses intended to be read aloud rather than privately, communication is liable to be rendered ineffective if this condition is disregarded. The business of organising discourse is generally a natural and instinctive operation for a native speaker in everyday speech, though in formal communication it may necessitate more careful effort and skill, and implies a more arduous task for a non-native speaker. For it is important to recognize that each language has its own way of building discourses; the similarities that may exist between languages are unpredictable and by no means regular, which means that ancient Greek has to be examined as a distinct language, independent of any apparent overlap with English, for example.

In modern writing, the structure of a text is greatly assisted by the use of visual devices. Books are divided into chapters, with paragraphs to mark the grouping and separation of topics. Punctuation, too, plays a critical role in conveying the speaker's intentions by the grouping of material into phrases, clauses, and sentences. In ancient Greek writing, on the other hand, there was not only no visual system in regular use for dividing the material into smaller units, there was no punctuation either. Furthermore, the extant NT manuscripts of the first centuries are written exclusively in capital letters, and usually without separation between sentences or even between words. The familiar chapter divisions were introduced as late as the 13th century and verses only in the 16th century, and cannot be relied upon in order to identify the author's intended organisation of a book. The problem with relying on other literary or rhetorical signposts—for example, changes in theme, location, time or protagonist, or the repetition of vocabulary or phrases—is that the high degree of subjectivity involved, associated with the expectations of readers in other times and other cultures, leads to not a little disagreement among exegetes as to where divisions occur.

Narrative

A primary consideration in thinking about the structure of the book of Acts is that it is a narrative discourse. It is written as a story, with the typical features of a time frame, characters, locations, and plot. As such, for discourse analysis purposes Acts is to be distinguished from writing which is overtly discursive, which presents an argument or seeks to persuade, for example. In describing Acts as narrative, however, that is not to say that the author was telling a story simply to entertain or to show off his literary skill. On the contrary, Luke said in the first volume of his work that his intention was to present his recipient, Theophilus, with a series of facts and to convince him of their truth (Luke 1:1–4; cf. Acts 1:1–2). Yet, whatever his purpose, he chose to express it as a narrative. It should be borne in mind that ancient conventions of recording factual reality allowed considerable licence with the organisation and selection of material, without the present-day demands that the details of reported events and characters correspond to literal reality. In biblical narrative, the historian's freedom to re-arrange the sequence of incidents or to change details—for example, dates or names of people and places—reflects at least in part the notion that reality is first and foremost spiritual in nature, existing outside the confines of time and space of the physical world. This is the truth that the biblical historian must seek to communicate, and in so doing may need to modify literal details in the interests of expressing it more clearly.[12]

It is perhaps a consequence of not recognizing authorial licence in the composition of Acts that the work is often seen as a collection of sources, badly pieced together with gaps in the narrative thread, careless repetition and factual errors. In this case, no well-defined structure is looked for, except possibly some clumsy scaffolding erected to hold the thing together where it was in danger of falling apart.[13] Thus, it is relatively rare to find commentators discussing the narrative structure of the book of Acts—frequently, there is not thought to be one. Recognizing a structural framework depends on accepting the writing as the production of an author who knew what he was doing, and did it deliberately. It is the contention of the analysis here that whatever sources Luke may have used, he made them his own and crafted a highly complex narrative with a carefully planned and intricate structure that is not only a model of artistic skill but also a rhetorical tool that serves to convey his message.

Direct speech

Within the narrative of Acts are passages of direct speech placed in the mouths of characters in the story. In some respects, the wording of these speeches is often closely tied to the wording of the surrounding narrative, so that on the basis of rhetorical or literary analysis there would be justification for considering their content as intertwined with the narrative content. From the point of view of discourse structure, in contrast, they are to be viewed as separate units that slot into the narrative structure as unified chunks. They have their own speaker and their own internal structure. In the presentation of the structure of the book of Acts that follows, therefore, the internal structure of the speeches will not be analysed; rather, they will be viewed as blocks embedded within the overall narrative framework.

Two principal features of *Koine* Greek identified by discourse analysis as key to the organisation of narrative are: 1) connectives between sentences, and 2) word order within the sentence. These will now be considered in turn, before looking at how they function together as indications of structure.

---

[12] For Jewish historians, including the authors of records collected in the NT, there is the further notion that the whole of the history of Israel is contained within the Torah, subsequent events being re-enactments of the earlier, paradigmatic ones. This perspective is a factor that needs to be taken into account for its contribution to the re-shaping of literal reality in Acts. For a discussion of the Jewish notion of history, see Bernard Barc, *Les arpenteurs du temps. Essai sur l'histoire de la Judée à la période héllenistique* (Lausanne: Éditions du Zèbre, 2000).

[13] This is the position adopted by, e.g., Charles K. Barrett in his *Acts of the Apostles*, 2 vols., ICC (T&T Clark, 1994), *passim*.

Connectives

Connectives is a term that refers to any means of joining together sentences, where "sentence" means a finite verb and any associated subordinate clauses or phrases.[14] Unlike in English, for example, where it is common to make no explicit connection between sentences, in ancient Greek it is far more usual to make clear the connection, which the absence of punctuation renders all the more necessary. In Acts, Luke makes use of a variety of devices to express relationships between sentences, the explicit links usually being conjunctions; when there is no kind of connecting word (asyndeton), this is sufficiently exceptional for it to be viewed as a particular type of connection. So, connectives serve to indicate the relationship of a sentence with what has gone before, and even to anticipate what will follow. Through detailed studies of connectives carried out by linguists working within the field of discourse analysis,[15] it becomes apparent that beyond their role in joining sentences together, connectives play a further critical function in determining the structure of narrative units, serving as signs of punctuation in place of capital letters, commas, semi-colons, full-stops, paragraph breaks and so on.

The following sentence connectives are found in Acts, listed here in order of frequency (others, such as ἀλλά or ὥς, are not included in this list, being viewed as subordinating conjunctions to introduce clauses that are dependent on another):

καί – δέ – τε – τότε – μέν –μὲν οὖν – γάρ – asyndeton –dem. pron. – rel. pron.

Careful and painstaking analysis of the connectives in their narrative context shows that they have quite distinct functions that go beyond an expression of style.[16]

---

[14] For this definition of a sentence, see Stephen H. Levinsohn, *Textual Connections in Acts* (Scholars Press, 1987), xviii.

[15] With reference specifically to Acts, see Levinsohn, *Textual Connections*; see also his *Discourse Features of New Testament Greek*, 2nd ed. (Summer Institute of Linguistics, 2000), 83–161, where he extends his analysis to other New Testament writings. Levinsohn's work on connectives was reviewed, and largely confirmed, in an examination of variant readings by Read-Heimerdinger, *Bezan Text*, 202–253.

[16] For reasons that are not yet altogether understood, it is clear that the patterns of connectives vary to some extent among the various books of the New Testament. Individual authors tend to use the range of connectives in their own, self-consistent ways, suggesting that there was variation in usage in different places or at different times. Consequently, what is said about the patterns in the use of connectives in Acts has to be modified when applied to the Gospels of Matthew or Mark, and especially John; even Luke's, too, though to a lesser degree, which is surprising given the many indications that the Gospel is the work of the same author as the book of Acts.

καί and δέ

καί as a conjunction[17] is used to join together sentences that are presented by the speaker as being on an equal footing with each other. The actions or events are viewed as closely tied together, part and parcel of the same larger event.

In contrast, δέ indicates that a particular action or event represents something new with regard to what has gone before. The "something new" signaled by δέ can represent a variety of distinctive information. In places, it indicates a contrast with what has just preceded the sentence. In others, it presents information that is parenthetical, operating like modern-day brackets. It is also used to switch attention between speakers in a dialogue, especially when there is an answer to a question, or a response to a command.

If two sentences can be thought of as separate pieces of rope, καί joins them together by splicing the ends and weaving them together in a bond which, as any fisher knows, is no less strong for being practically invisible. Δέ, on the other hand, unites the two ends of the rope by knotting them together with an easily detectable join. Thus, καί groups events and actions on the same plane or in parallel, whereas δέ signals something distinctive—a change of location, time, place, or the introduction of a new character or a new theme.

For the purposes of structure, the distinction between καί and δέ in Acts is a key that allows a speaker to indicate, and a hearer to recognize, the organisation of the narrative. For, whereas καί serves to join elements within an episode, expressing continuity, δέ can be used to mark a new development in some way, signalling discontinuity. A sentence introduced with καί belongs with the previous one, but δέ is used to introduce a sentence that moves the story forward. Consequently, δέ is the conjunction found at boundaries between episodes, unlike καί which unites elements within an episode.

In consequence, while the two conjunctions καί and δέ are often considered to be interchangeable, thorough analysis of the text of Acts shows that they are used in quite distinct ways and serve not least as a means to structure a narrative. Occurring frequently as variant readings in Acts, the choice between καί and δέ has nothing to do with an author's or a scribe's habit or style, but everything to do with how the elements of a story are viewed by the author or scribe as fitting together—not representing some objective reality but reflecting the speaker's organization of the narrative.[18]

---

[17] καί is also used some 20 times in Acts as a characteristic variant reading of D05 to introduce a main verb following a participle; in these cases, it serves adverbially to underline the significance of the main verb rather than to conjoin it to the participle (e.g., 2:1D05; 12:16D05; 14:14D05; 18:7D05; 20:10D05). See Read-Heimerdinger, *The Bezan Text of Acts*, 208–210.

[18] Given that connectives are subject to a high degree of textual variation, it is all the more striking that the variation in Acts is such that the essential distinctive function of each connective is maintained in the diverse manuscripts. In other words, different copyists appear to

τε

τε is the only conjunction to operate in the same way as καί to join sentences that are viewed by the speaker as having equal or parallel status and, as such, are in continuity. τε is sometimes found after one or more instances of καί where its specific role is to present a final event or action as a culminating one, inviting the translation "moreover" or "above all." There are few examples in the firm text, a telling one being 6:7 where τε introduces the last in the series of outcomes (linked with καί) following the election of the seven Hellenists, namely, the large number of priests who joined the believers. At a few places τε is, in fact, difficult to account for and it is reasonable to suspect, given the number of variant readings between τε and δέ, that in those instances τε may have arisen through phonetic confusion with δέ.

τότε

When τότε is used as a conjunction,[19] it has the same function as δέ in moving the narrative forward but, unlike δέ, it never marks a break between structural units; rather it links sentences within the same episode. It indicates a time connection with the previous material ("then") or, commonly, a response that may have the specific role of bringing a sequence of events to a close. Τότε at 13:3 illustrates this well, for it introduces the action that responds to the instruction of the Holy Spirit to appoint Barnabas and Saul for a chosen task (13:2) and concludes the setting of the context for the subsequent part of the book.

οὖν

For all that students of Greek learn to translate οὖν as "therefore," its function is not restricted to the force it has in English of direct consequence or effect. More broadly, it expresses the idea that the sentence (the action, the event) is in accordance with what has gone before: the second event "closely conforms with [the] demands and implications" of the previous one.[20] In that sense, it is retrospective, and plays a valuable role in tracking the line of argument in the speeches

---

have understood the connectives in similar ways; it was their view of the organization of the narrative that differed.

[19] Τότε is also used in Acts as an adverb but only as a variant reading (11:26 in D05; 17:41 in א01/B03) where there exists a separate conjunction (καί and δέ respectively). Its function at those places is not to join sentences but to give a time indication (Read-Heimerdinger, *The Bezan Text*, 224–225).

[20] Levinsohn, *Textual Connections*, 137–141.

of Acts. In the narrative of Acts, however, it occurs only as a variant reading, in the "we" sections (16:10 in D05, 16:11 in B03) or at the resumption of the narrative after direct speech (22.29 in B03). When it is found in the firm text of the narrative, it is in association with μέν.

μὲν οὖν ... δέ

μέν is prospective, causing the sentence that it adds to the narrative to look forward to a further sentence introduced with δέ. It is this δέ sentence that moves the narrative forward, the first one being of secondary importance for the development of the story.[21] In the firm text of Acts, μέν always occurs accompanied by οὖν, which produces an interesting two-directional movement—οὖν looking back to tie the new events or actions to the previous sentences, and μέν anticipating a further event or action after the initial sentence, one that will advance the story. Thus, at 15:30, in accordance with (οὖν) the decision of the meeting in Jerusalem to send Judas and Silas with Paul and Barnabas to Antioch with a letter of instructions (cf. 15:22), they go there (μέν) and (καί) hand over the letter; the new development that causes the story to progress (δέ, v. 31) is that the people in Antioch greet the letter with rejoicing.

γάρ

It was observed above that δέ sometimes introduces parenthetical information. This, too, is the function of γάρ; in addition, γάρ may be used to expand on something said earlier or to develop a logical argument (more so in speech than in narrative). In presenting a parenthetical comment, there is a key difference with the use of δέ: γάρ explains or comments on something that is relevant for the immediate context (e.g., at 4:3, the narrator explains that Peter and John were put in prison until the next day, γάρ it was already evening). Δέ, in contrast, makes a comment that is relevant for something that is going to follow, as if to say "keep this in mind." An example is seen at 19:7, where the narrator observes of the men whom Paul met in Ephesus that: ἦσαν δὲ οἱ πάντες ἄνδρες ὡσεὶ δώδεκα. By using δέ rather than γάρ, the narrator indicates that the number of men is not merely background information but that the figure 12, as a metaphorical reference to traditional Israel, is important for what follows, namely Paul's preaching in the synagogue.

---

[21] Saying here that something is of secondary importance does not mean that an event or action is in itself of minor significance but rather that the speaker does not accord it a primary role in moving the narrative forward.

Asyndeton

By asyndeton is meant the absence of any connecting device. It is a natural feature of direct speech, employed either when the speaker moves on to a completely new thought, or re-iterates a statement in a parallel affirmation with different words as a rhetorical device to underline the point being made. Strict asyndeton in narrative, however, whereby the next sentence begins with no connecting word at all, never occurs in the firm text of the narrative of Acts. On three occasions where there is no conjunction to join sentences together, an adverb is used, whether of time (10:44, ἔτι) or manner (17:33; 19:20, οὕτως). In these instances, the adverb itself makes the close connection between the sentences explicit. At 10:44 and 17:33, the adverb occurs at the juncture of speech and narrative to signal an abrupt development that arises from the preceding action, and at 19:20 to present an intermediate summary statement.

Relative or Demonstrative Pronoun

On other occasions in the absence of a conjunction, a relative or a demonstrative pronoun is used to link sentences. A relative pronoun usually adds further information about a character or event without introducing anything new; sometimes, however, it presents a verb that is a separate action, that is, a new sentence (e.g., 8:15). A demonstrative pronoun is used occasionally on its own, in a variety of cases, to introduce a separate sentence that expands on a previous reference to a character (1:14; 14:9; 16:3, 17).

Seeing the individual function of each connective allows the flow of the narrative to be properly recognized, such as Luke appears to have intended it. In the absence of punctuation and formatting in the hand-written documents, the various connectors show how sentences are grouped together and how the story is developed by the speaker.

So far, the present analysis of the connectives in Acts has concentrated on the immediate connection between separate sentences, though some indications have been seen concerning the grouping of sentences, bringing in notions of looking backwards and also looking forwards in anticipation of what follows. Connectives, however, serve a further important purpose, for they operate not just locally from one sentence to the next but also on a larger scale, to show where divisions in the narrative are placed. In other words, they serve as paragraph markers or chapter breaks. In order to examine their use at that level, it is necessary to look first at the matter of word order, for this comes into play at this point.

Word Order

Greek is often said to have a word order that is "free" as opposed to "fixed," and to differ in that respect from English. It is true that in a language that has case-markings, such as Greek has, word order plays a lesser role in indicating grammatical relations than in languages without case-markings. Aside from a few aspects (e.g., the second position of δέ and γάρ) that are determined by grammatical or syntactical considerations, it has usually been assumed in traditional grammar books of NT Greek that word order is largely a matter of a speaker's choice. Word order variation is ascribed to personal custom or style, whether an unconscious habit on the part of the speaker or deliberately worked for rhetorical effect.

In line with the interest of discourse analysis in looking at language in its real-life context, it is now recognized that there are, in fact, constraints operating on Greek word order but that these are of a semantic and pragmatic nature rather than a grammatical one. In other words, the constraints are connected with the function of the words and sentences within the discourse, not the grammatical relations that exist between the words or sentences. They operate on a deep level rather than a surface level. They have to do with such purposes as signaling which part of the sentence is the most important, introducing a new idea, or indicating a contrast or conflict. Word order choice is thus not a matter of style, dependent on a writer's or scribe's preference or habit, but is a device that forms an integral part of the communication of the message.

Word order plays a particularly important role in structuring narrative, where its impact is not so much on the relationship among constituents within a sentence as on the relationship between sentences themselves. It has been observed[22] that sentences in a Greek narrative typically start with the verb, followed by the subject if it is expressed, then the object if there is one. This order, referred to as VSO, is as close to ordinary speech as can be determined in the NT (e.g., from the parables). The initial position of the verb in narrative reflects the fact that a story is about actions and events first of all—unlike hortatory discourse where people, a topic or a line of argument are more likely to be the prominent concern. Besides, in a continuous story in Greek, it is often unnecessary to specify the subject since this can be encoded in the verb ending and, furthermore, it can be understood to be the same as the subject of the previous main verb if no change is explicitly indicated, e.g., at 12:1–2, the subject of successive main verbs is Herod:

12:1 ... ἐπέβαλεν Ἡρῴδης ὁ βασιλεὺς τὰς χεῖρας κακῶσαί τινας τῶν ἀπὸ τῆς ἐκκλησίας. ² ἀνεῖλεν δὲ Ἰάκωβον...

---

[22] Levinsohn, *Discourse Features*, 16–17.

It is usual to describe a typical pattern of word order of a language as the "unmarked" or "default" order, and to go from there to identify the effects of modifying that unmarked order to produce patterns that are described as "marked." With regard to the initial position of the verb in a narrative sentence, this means that the word order is marked if the verb is *not* at the head of the sentence but some other constituent occupies that place.

Now, two reasons have been identified for word order to be marked in this way. First of all, when a constituent is moved to any position further to the left than it would occupy by default (i.e. it is "fronted"), this is a means to underline it, to highlight it as being of particular importance at that point. For example, in a sentence where the subject is explicit, if the subject is placed before the verb, attention is being drawn to it for some reason such as contrast or surprise. E.g., at 12:7, two new subjects, the angel of the Lord and a light, appear quite unexpectedly:

12:7 καὶ ἰδοὺ ἄγγελος κυρίου ἐπέστη καὶ φῶς ἔλαμψεν ἐν τῷ οἰκήματι

Placing any constituent before the verb at the start of a sentence in a narrative discourse ("fore-fronting") focuses special attention on it, because it disrupts the expected pattern. E.g., at 16:3, Timothy is the object of the verb but the reference to him (with a demonstrative pronoun) is placed at the front of the sentence, which has the effect of highlighting the nature of the person just described and chosen by Paul to be his companion:

16:3 τοῦτον ἠθέλησεν ὁ Παῦλος σὺν αὐτῷ ἐξελθεῖν

In addition to focusing attention, there is another reason for placing a constituent before the verb at the start of a sentence, and it is this one that is relevant for the purpose of structure: a constituent may be fore-fronted in order to signal a new development in the narrative, one that forms a new basis for the next part of the story. This could be a change of place, time, protagonist, or topic, which acts a fresh "point of departure" for the next part of the story.[23] Continuity is the norm in narrative, and so disrupting the expected order of words is a means to signal a change in direction of some kind. As such, these fore-fronted sentences serve as boundary markers, indications of structural breaks that the narrator intended for the narrative. A few examples will serve to illustrate the discontinuity signaled by this device. At 6:8, Stephen becomes the chief protagonist:

---

[23] Levinsohn, *Discourse Features*, 7–28.

6:8 Στέφανος δὲ πλήρης χάριτος καὶ δυνάμεως ἐποίει τέρατα καὶ σημεῖα μεγάλα ἐν τῷ λαῷ.

At 10:23b, there is a change of time:

10:23b Τῇ δὲ ἐπαύριον ἀναστὰς ἐξῆλθεν σὺν αὐτοῖς

At 17:16, the change is one of place:

17:16 Ἐν δὲ ταῖς Ἀθήναις ἐκδεχομένου αὐτοὺς τοῦ Παύλου παρωξύνετο τὸ πνεῦμα αὐτοῦ ἐν αὐτῷ

It is important to distinguish between the purpose of fore-fronting for focus and the purpose for establishing a new point of departure, because only the latter instances contribute to the structure of the narrative. A general rule is that if the fore-fronted constituent is already present in the narrative, even if not explicitly stated, then the purpose should be understood as focus. In such cases, the directing of attention is also liable to be localized and short-term, without serving to develop the story on a larger scale. Thus, at 15:37–38, Barnabas and Paul are already active in the new time frame (cf. 15:36 Μετὰ δέ τινας ἡμέρας εἶπεν πρὸς Βαρναβᾶν Παῦλος...), when the narrator directs attention first to one and then the other by placing their names before the respective verbs, because of the disagreement between them:

15:37 Βαρναβᾶς δὲ ἐβούλετο συμπαραλαβεῖν καὶ τὸν Ἰωάννην τὸν καλούμενον Μᾶρκον· 38 Παῦλος δὲ ἠξίου

On some occasions, the two purposes may coalesce, as an already present participant is now brought into focus to become the main protagonist who moves the story forward—this is what happens at 6:8 cited above, for example.

The narrator of Acts employs a further technique to mark a fresh point of departure, using the verb εἶμι (γίνομαι in the aorist) to introduce a new factor into the narrative. In such sentences, the verb comes first, but by the very presentative nature of the verb the construction overall marks the importance of the new subject by setting it out in a separate sentence at the start of a new unit. The technique is a kind of fore-fronting *par excellence*. Examples of presentative sentences with εἶμι are found in the firm text of Acts at 4:5; 9:10; 13:1 and with γίνομαι at 5:7; 8:1b; 14:1; 16:16; 19:23.

Conversely, if there is a change in time, place, protagonist or topic, and it is not pre-posed, then continuity of situation is indicated. E.g., in the introduction to the dispute over the circumcision of the Gentiles in Acts 15, a paragraph break is marked in the NA text at 15:6, which most translations reproduce:

15:6 Συνήχθησάν τε οἱ ἀπόστολοι καὶ οἱ πρεσβύτεροι ἰδεῖν περὶ τοῦ λόγου τούτου.

It may seem counter-intuitive not to start a new paragraph here, because there is a clear change of subject from the previous sentences (Paul and Barnabas 15:3–4; some of the Pharisees 15:5). However, despite the change, the first position in the sentence of the verb at 15:6 indicates that this sentence belongs closely with the preceding narrative. If a break is intended, it is in the following sentence at 15:7, where the dispute is fore-fronted:

15:7 Πολλῆς δὲ ζητήσεως γενομένης ἀναστὰς Πέτρος εἶπεν πρὸς αὐτούς·

Using the criteria of word order to discern the divisions of the Acts narrative may, then, conflict with the divisions identified by noting thematic or other changes, which commentators typically look for in order to locate boundaries. However, taking account of word order, specifically fore-fronting, provides an objective basis for identifying the shifts or developments in the narrative that the narrator apparently intended. It reduces considerably the risk of anachronistically imposing on the text ways of understanding a story that derive from modern interpreters' expectations or preconceptions.

There arises, however, the difficulty of variation among the manuscripts, for there is a fair amount affecting word order at the start of sentences. Rather than dismissing this as arising from scribal preference for a different order of words, it would be more accurate, given the significance of word order as an indication of organisation of the text, to interpret it as arising from a different understanding of the structure of the narrative.

It is time to bring this criterion into contact with the choice of connectives, to see how these two factors work together to confer structure on a narrative. It has been noted that a point of discontinuity in the narrative is marked by a disruption of the default "verb first" word order of a sentence, placing something before the verb that forms the basis for the next part of the narrative. Such instances serve as points of departure for the next part, and as such occur at the beginning of a structural unit. Thus, they can be used to determine the structural organisation intended by the narrator. When they are examined systematically throughout the text of Acts, it is possible to make observations about how the connectives are used at the various stages of the structural units, whether the beginning (in combination with fore-fronted word order), the end (just before the next fore-fronted word order), or somewhere between. Figure 5.2 sets out the devices Luke uses to link sentences and classifies them according to their occurrence in a structural unit:

Connective	Beginning	Middle	End
καί	√	√	√
μὲν οὖν ... δέ	√	×	×
asyndeton	√ (vll)	√	×
οὖν	×	√	×
καί	×	√	√
τότε	×	√	√
γάρ	×	√ (rare)	√ (rare)
rel. pro.	×	√ (rare)	√ (rare)
dem. pro.	×	√ (rare)	√ (once, vl)

Figure 5.2: Distribution of Connectives within Structural Units

Only two connectives are used to open a new unit, δέ on its own and μὲν οὖν in combination with δέ. This function of δέ is in keeping with the observation that δέ as a connective between sentences marks something as new or distinctive. As explained above, with μὲν οὖν the logical connection with the preceding unit is underscored, with two events being presented as resulting from it, of which the second (δέ) is seen as the one that carries the story forward. At the beginning of a structural unit, both δέ and μὲν οὖν ... δέ present a fresh point of departure in the development of the narrative. They are found at high level boundaries that mark major divisions in the narrative, as well as at lower levels of the structure.

There are, in addition, instances of asyndeton at the start of a new structural unit, but only as a variant reading: at 2:5 in D05 (א01/B03 δέ), asyndeton underlines an important shift in register at the start of a new unit;[24] and at 18:1, the text of א01/B03 (D05 δέ) introduces Paul's departure from Athens simply with μετὰ ταῦτα, apparently viewing it as marking a break with the previous material rather than a development of it.

The other connectives only link elements in the middle of a unit or bring the unit to a close.

Macrostructure

Before presenting an analysis of the structure of Acts, words of caution are needed on several counts. The first concerns the Greek text used. As indicated earlier,

---

[24] At 2:5D05, the register changes as the narrative moves from relating a historical account to presenting a figurative one, see Rius-Camps and Read-Heimerdinger, *The Message of Acts*, I, 154.

an eclectic edition of Acts, such as the NA text, does not take account of the significance of a) connectives, or b) word order for the narrator's organisation of the text, because the editorial committee did not apply principles of discourse analysis to their decisions about variants. The text is not necessarily, therefore, a reliable basis for analysing structure. Instead, individual manuscripts should be used, and in the following discussion I have followed the text of Codex Bezae, noting variant readings in Codex Vaticanus where they impinge on matters of structure.

The second cautionary note concerns the overlapping nature of the structure of ancient narrative texts.[25] While linguistic features serve as formal markers of division at specific points, from a narrative point of view divisions are frequently accompanied by a series of carefully crafted sentences that link together two units, by anticipating at the end of one unit what will follow in the next, or by summarising at the beginning of a unit what had gone before. As a result, the content itself cannot be appealed to in looking for a boundary at a single point. It may be, in fact, that the idea of single point boundaries is anachronistic, more in keeping with modern notions of structure. That said, in so far as the linguistic features described above allow new points of departure to be marked by the narrator, these can be used to identify specific points within overlapping passages as the start of a new unit.

A third issue concerns the levels of hierarchy. It is one thing to formally identify boundaries between units by observing the linguistic features of connectives and word order, but there is then the task of identifying how the narrator organizes these units into larger units. For that purpose, there do not appear to be clear linguistic clues; the markers in themselves do not allow different structural levels to be distinguished. In other words, the device of fore-fronted sentences in combination with the conjunction δέ is important for determining boundaries, for a division will not be expected without it, but this does not give information as to whether the sentence marks the start of a new unit at a high level (the equivalent of a modern section or chapter) or a lower level (e.g., a paragraph). So, at the point of seeking to understand the hierarchical organization of units, there enters a certain amount of interpretation that depends on the recipient's understanding of the narrator's purpose. Notably, at the higher levels of the hierarchy, thematic considerations play a dominant role in identifying the interplay of divisions.

Now, interpretation of Acts may seem to be a matter that does not elicit much contention in that, following the overwhelming majority of the manuscripts of Acts that are extant today, the work can be, and is, construed as presenting the leaders of the early Church as heroes who faithfully carried out God's plan for his people. The portrayal is somewhat more nuanced in copies such as D05, whose text was reproduced to a large extent by the earliest translations in

---

[25] The rhetorical feature of overlap in ancient narrative is discussed by Jacques Dupont, *Nouvelles Études sur les Actes des Apôtres*, Lectio Divina 118 (Éditions du Cerf, 1994), 27–36.

Latin, Syriac, Middle Egyptian and even Aramaic,[26] dating from before the first standardised translations in the fourth century. In this text, the leaders are presented as fallible disciples who made mistakes as they slowly came to terms with the teaching of Jesus; by no means did either their actions or their speeches all make a positive contribution to the spread of the gospel. This is an important consideration in detecting the structure of the book because it means that, even though on the surface the narrative may appear to unfold in a sequence of time and place, logical connections of cause/effect or reason/consequence have to be anticipated. The way in which the separate units relate to each other is reflected in the way they fit into the wider organization of the book, and so the structure that can be identified inevitably differs from one form of text to another, according to their different messages. This factor adds a further complication to defining the structure of Acts, in addition to the problem posed by textual variation explained above. In the structural organization that is presented in the following discussion it is the text of Codex Bezae that is adopted, with comments made on variant readings where they do not involve lengthy exegetical expositions.

It is at the level of the overall plan of the book that work on analysing the structure of Acts has tended to be carried out. There is every reason, however, to expect in a work of the length of Acts that the author would provide a more detailed structure to aid his audience. By studying the successive sentences noted as signalling a division by their marked word order, the various levels of structure can be identified, as follows in Figure 5.3.

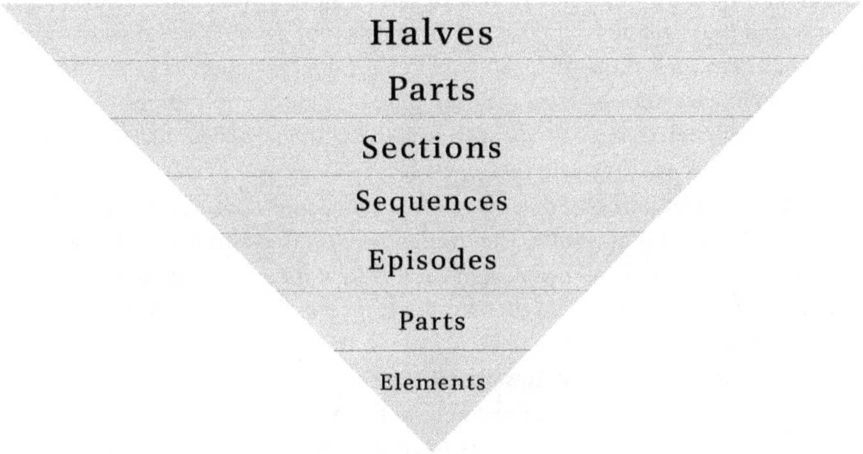

Halves

Parts

Sections

Sequences

Episodes

Parts

Elements

Figure 5.3: Hierarchical Arrangement of Structural Units

---

[26] The few extant fragments of Acts in Aramaic (10:28-29, 32-41) have readings that are otherwise only found in D05 or other early versions. See Rius-Camps and Read-Heimerdinger, *The Message of Acts*, II, 233–236.

In this arrangement, the smallest building blocks at the lowest level of the hierarchy are labelled "elements," grammatical sentences that consist of a main verb and any associated clauses or phrases, introduced with some kind of connective, as discussed above. An element is the creation of the narrator—it reflects Luke's choice of how to express actions or facts, selecting one as the chief component and making any others subordinate to it. That is not to say that the clauses (with verb forms such as participles, infinitives or subordinate verbs) or phrases (adjectival or adverbial expansions) that may cluster around a main finite verb are not important, but the narrator's choice to select one for the principal focus must be respected in analysing a sentence and seeing how the components have been fitted together to create a coherent and cohesive structure. Once again, the question of the Greek text is crucial for identifying the main finite verb of each sentence, for there is a great deal of variation affecting the verbal forms among the manuscripts.

Elements are organised into larger units, here labelled "sequences" that often (though not always, indicated by the dotted lines) are made up of "episodes" and "scenes." Sequences are grouped into "sections," which combine to make "parts" that fall into two "halves."

Halves

As far as the Bezan text of Acts is concerned, at the highest level the book divides two "halves," albeit of uneven length, for there is a clear separation between the chapters in which Peter is the main protagonist together with other leaders (chs. 1–12), and those where Paul takes over that role (chs. 13–28). The concern of the first half is to work through the story of Peter, from his imperfect grasp of Jesus' teaching in ch. 1 until his final realisation of the radical implications of it in ch. 12. Peter will make a brief appearance to speak at the Jerusalem meeting related in ch. 15 but from ch. 13 Paul takes over as the focus of the book. Paul, as Saul, had already been introduced in chs. 8–9, but it is only at ch. 13 that he replaces Peter as the main protagonist. The overlap between the two halves of the book reflects the tendency in ancient narrative to look forwards and backwards between sections as a means to tie them together closely, though in this case the anticipatory and retrospective references are some distance apart.

In the alternative text of Acts, where the characters are not, or not so clearly, presented as progressing over the course of the narrative in their understanding of the gospel, a boundary between two halves of the narrative at ch. 13 may not necessarily be identified at that point. If it is, no problems arise with the text from a linguistic point of view, for the divisions are the same whatever textual tradition is followed: ch. 13 begins with a presentative sentence, introducing a new set of characters in the Antioch church:

13:1 ῏Ησαν δὲ ἐν Ἀντιοχείᾳ κατὰ τὴν οὖσαν ἐκκλησίαν προφῆται καὶ διδάσκαλοι.

Parts

The parts into which these two halves of Acts in turn fall are each characterised by their principal location. The first half is broadly divided between Jerusalem and Judaea, on the one hand, involving only the apostles (Part 1, chs. 1–5); and on the other, Samaria and other parts of Israel where the Hellenist leaders emerge as an identifiable group (Part 2, chs. 6–12). As for the second half of Acts, chs. 13–28 concerning Paul, the place where, or even if, a division occurs is open to dispute. When a division is recognized, it is generally taken to be located somewhere between the so-called missionary journeys to other countries outside of Israel (from ch. 13 to somewhere in chs. 19, 20, 21) and Paul's trial and journey to Rome (up to the end of the book at ch. 28), but even then, the exact point at which the missionary phase of Paul's activity ended is not at all clear, and different commentators fix it differently. This point will be returned to but meanwhile, Figure 5.4 sets out the divisions so far:

Book of Acts			
First Half		**Second Half**	
Chs 1–12 Peter and the other apostles		Chs 13–28 Paul	
Part 1	**Part 2**	**Part 3**	**Part 4**
Chs. 1–5 Jerusalem and Judaea	Chs. 6–12 Samaria and the rest of Israel	Chs. 13–? Gentile nations	Chs. ?–28 Trial and Rome

Figure 5.4: The Four Parts of Acts

Concerning the division in the first part, it is worth noting that there is a clear break at 6:1, with the typically fore-fronted formula Ἐν δὲ ταύταις ταῖς ἡμέραις (ταῖς ἡμέραις ταύταις, ℵ01/B03), 'In those days...', introducing the new section that develops the theme briefly hinted at in the earlier chapters, that of the disagreement between the Hellenists and the Hebrews.[27] There then follows

---

[27] The tension between Hellenists and Hebrews is implicit in the contrast between Barnabas, a Hellenistic Jew from Cyprus, who gave the proceeds of the sale of a field for the use of the believers (4:36–37), and Ananias and Sapphira, representative of the older Jews (cf. the young men at vv. 6, 10) who retained part of the proceeds of the sale of their property with disastrous consequences (5:1–11).

a summary statement[28] in 6:7, which backtracks and brings the previous section concerning Jerusalem to a close:

6:7   Καὶ ὁ λόγος τοῦ θεοῦ (κυρίου, D05) ηὔξανεν καὶ ἐπληθύνετο ὁ ἀριθμὸς τῶν μαθητῶν ἐν Ἰερουσαλήμ...[29]

It is only after this summary statement that the theme of the Hellenists is taken any further, so that 6:1–7 constitutes a bridge between the two sections and creates a characteristic overlap.

As is often pointed out, the progression from Acts 1 to Acts 28 follows the order of the three-fold command given by Jesus to the apostles just before he left them:

1:8   ἔσεσθέ μου μάρτυρες ἔν τε Ἰερουσαλὴμ καὶ [ἐν] πάσῃ τῇ Ἰουδαίᾳ καὶ Σαμαρείᾳ καὶ ἕως ἐσχάτου τῆς γῆς

It is in part because of the three-fold nature of the command that the chapters relating to Paul can be viewed as one block, with chs. 13–28 representing the third aspect of the command, the "ends of the earth." The narrative development reflects the gradual extension of the gospel, starting from the Jews in Jerusalem and then moving out geographically to other Jews and finally Gentiles. Most commentators, however, see at least one division in the section concerning Paul at the end of his missionary journeys, even though disagreement arises over where the end is intended: is it as he leaves Ephesus and sets off on his last journey to Jerusalem (19:20)?[30] After he has spoken with the Ephesian leaders at Miletus on his way to Jerusalem (20:38b)?[31] Or once he arrives in

---

[28] There are five similar summary statements in Acts (6:7; 9:31; 12:24; 16:5; 19:20; 28:30-31), which D.L. Blood and D.E. Blood ("Overview of Acts," Notes on Translation 74 [1979]: 2–36), take as marking out two sections, the first made up of 1:12–19:20 (1:1–11 are taken as an Introduction), and the rest of the book (19:21–28:31) forming a second section. Dividing the book up in this way depends on the text of 19:21 as read by the majority of MSS.

[29] The use of καί at 6:7 tells against the interpretation of this verse as marking a new section (*contra* David Wenham and Steve Walton, *Exploring the New Testament* I, *Introducing the Gospels and Acts* [SPCK, 2001], 272.

[30] Blood and Blood, "Overview," 9–11; F.F. Bruce, *Commentary on the Book of Acts. The English Text with Introduction, Exposition and Notes* (Marshall, Morgan and Scott, 1954), 325–92. From a linguistic point of view, however, the adverbial connection οὕτως at 19:20 looks back over the previous scene. It is the next sentence at 19:21, with the connective δέ and the subordinate clause Ὡς ἐπληρώθη ταῦτα, that moves the story forward as Paul takes the decision to go to Macedonia and Achaia.

[31] J. D. G. Dunn, *The Acts of the Apostles* (Epworth Press, 1996), 212–276; I.H. Marshall, *The Acts of the Apostles*, TNTC (IVP, 1980), 299–337. The initial position of the verb tells against 20:38b being intended as starting a new unit. The fore-fronted word order of 21:1,

Jerusalem where he is confronted with the angry mob outside the Temple (21:26)?[32] The difficulty is first, that there is no definite break between Paul's mission in Ephesus and his journey to Jerusalem, and secondly, that the purpose of his journey to Jerusalem can be interpreted in various ways—was it a missionary journey, and if not, why did he go there? Codex Bezae has its own answers to these questions, seeing Paul's journey to Ephesus as the first stage on his journey to Rome, which was interrupted by his personal decision, against the guidance of the Holy Spirit, to go back to Jerusalem before finishing the journey to Rome (20:3 in Do5; cf. 21:4). Additional references in Do5 to the directions given to Paul by the Holy Spirit make it clear that Paul's work in Ephesus was at the prompting of the Holy Spirit, contrary to his own intentions to stay in Jerusalem (19:1 in Do5)[33] and, furthermore, that his return to Jerusalem was not how things were meant to be, but came about because of the Jews' plot against him (20:3 in Do5).[34]

In view of this portrayal of Paul's work and of his conflict with the divine plan, it is not surprising that a top level division in Do5 can be understood between the end of the second phase of his missionary activity in the various nations outside Israel (13:1–18:23) and his circuitous travels to Rome (18:24–28:31), which take him via Ephesus and Jerusalem (18:24-28). The text leading up to 18:24 reads as follows:[35]

v. 22 καὶ κατελθὼν εἰς Καισάρειαν, ἀναβὰς καὶ ἀσπασάμενος τὴν ἐκκλησίαν κατέβη εἰς Ἀντιόχειαν

v. 23 καὶ ποιήσας χρόνον τινὰ ἐξῆλθεν διερχόμενος καθεξῆς τὴν Γαλατικὴν χώραν καὶ Φρυγίαν, ἐπιστηρίζων πάντας τοὺς μαθητάς

---

despite considerable variation between Do5 (genitive absolute) and אo1/Bo3 (subordinate clause of time), indicates that this is where the new unit begins.

[32] B. Witherington, *The Acts of the Apostles: A Socio-Rhetorical Commentary* (Paternoster, 1998), 562–641. Τότε at 21:26 in fact marks the conclusion of a unit, and it is the fore-fronted word order of 21:27, again with variation between Do5 (genitive absolute) and אo1/Bo3 (subordinate clause of time), that introduces a new unit.

[33] 19:1 (Do5) reads: Θέλοντος δὲ τοῦ Παύλου κατὰ τὴν ἰδίαν βουλὴν πορεύεσθαι εἰς Ἱεροσόλυμα εἶπεν αὐτῷ τὸ πνεῦμα ὑποστρέφειν εἰς τὴν Ἀσίαν...

[34] While the אo1/Bo3 text has Paul's intention to sail to Syria thwarted by the plot of the Jews, in Do5 it is the plot itself that prompts his decision to sail there. The Spirit directed him to Macedonia, from where he could have continued to Rome, but instead he turned eastward to fulfil his intention of going to Jerusalem. The reading is discussed in detail in J. Rius-Camps, "The Gradual Awakening of Paul's Awareness of his Mission to the Gentiles," in *Apostelgeschichte als Kirchengeschichte: Text, Traditionen und antike Auslegungen*, ed. T. Nicklas and M. Tilly, BZNW 122 (De Gruyter, 2003), 281–296.

[35] There is little variation between Do5 and Bo3 in the text of 18:24 and the preceding sentences: Do5 reads a different word order (marked with italics): Ἰουδαῖος δέ τις *ὀνόματι Ἀπολλῶς*, γένει Ἀλεξανδρεύς, ἀνὴρ λόγιος, κατήντησεν εἰς Ἔφεσον, δυνατὸς ὢν ἐν ταῖς γραφαῖς.

v. 24   Ἰουδαῖος δέ τις Ἀπολλῶς ὀνόματι, Ἀλεξανδρεὺς τῷ γένει, ἀνὴρ λόγιος,
κατήντησεν εἰς Ἔφεσον, δυνατὸς ὢν ἐν ταῖς γραφαῖς

18:24 introduces a new character who is the basis on which the next part of
the narrative is built. The narrator highlights his Jewish ethnicity by placing
Ἰουδαῖος at the start of the sentence, and indeed, it is the fact that Apollos is Jewish that is of particular significance for his activity in Ephesus and his relationship with Paul.

Whatever may be said of the NA text, the resultant structure in D05 thus has
a division in the second half as follows in Figure 5.5:

Paul	
Acts 13–28	
Part 3	**Part 4**
13:1–18:23	18:24–28:31
Evangelisation of the Nations	Journey to Rome via Ephesus

Figure 5.5: Parts 3 and 4 in Codex Bezae

Sections

As explained above, each the four parts divides into a series of smaller sections,
identified by their specific content. A change in the main topic marks the move
from one section to the next, with various other features accompanying it to signal
the move to a new section. A change in the principal character is frequently involved, and where this is the case it is signaled by the name of the character being
placed at the beginning of the sentence that opens the new section.[36] The change
may also be marked by some reference to time, whether it be the same time as before (e.g., "In those days") or a new time (e.g., "After some days"), but it is noticeable
that time markers at the start of a new section are more common in the Bezan text
that in other manuscripts.[37] A change in place often occurs from one section to another, too. These features of boundaries between sections are criteria that are recognised by discourse analysis studies as typical signals pointing to a significant development in a narrative. Figure 5.6 sets out the sections for each part of Acts that
can be identified in D05. The identification of the exact boundary point between
sections is determined by the linguistic criteria of word order and connectives, as
will be illustrated with reference to Part 2 in the microstructure analysis that follows.

---

[36] Examples in Acts of the fronting of the names of new characters at the opening of a new
section occur at 4:36 and 18:24.

[37] Time indicators are given at the start of a new section at 6:1; 8:1; 11:27; 12:1; 14:28; 15:36;
and additionally, in D05 at 1:15; 2:1; 3:1.

		Part 1
		Acts 1:1–5:42
Prolegomena	1:1–14	
Section I	1:15–26	Replacement of the Twelfth Apostle
Section II	2:1–47	Outpouring of the Holy Spirit
Section III	3:1–4:35	The Sign of the Lame Man's Healing
Section IV	4:36–5:42	The Jerusalem Church
		Part 2
		Acts 6:1–12:25
Section I	6:1–8:1a	The Emergence of the Hellenists
Section II	8:1b–11:26	Removing the Obstacles
Section III	11:27–30	The Antioch Church
Section IV	12:1–25	Release of the Church from Israel
		Part 3
		Acts 13:1–18:23
Section I	13:1–14:27	The First Phase of the Mission to the Gentiles
Section II	14:28–15:41	Judicial Review in Jerusalem
Section III	16:1–18:23	The Second Phase of the Mission to the Gentiles
		Part 4
		Acts 18:24–28:31
Section I	18:24–19:40	The Third Phase of the Mission to the Gentiles
Section II	20:1–21:14	The Journey to Hierosoluma
Section III	21:15–27:1	Paul on Trial
Section IV	27:2–28:31	Rome

Figure 5.6: The Sections in Codex Bezae

Microstructures

In order to examine more closely the reasoning behind the structural divisions in Figure 5.6, the rest of the discussion will focus on Part 2 (Acts 6–12), explaining how the particular boundaries have been identified and pointing out where they are dependent on the readings of D05.

Within each of the four parts of the Book of Acts, the material is grouped according to theme and character following, as was pointed out earlier, a geographical path to bring about the progression of the gospel. After a preliminary account of Jesus' departure (1:1–14), Part 1 is concerned with the proclamation of the gospel in Jerusalem, where the first person to be freed from exclusion in full participation in the People of God, a Jewish lame man, is introduced.[38] In Part 2, the geographical area is expanded, as is the category of people now integrated fully into the People of God: Hellenistic Jews, Samaritans, a Jewish eunuch, sojourners among the Jews, and finally Gentiles. The expansion is reflected in the four divisions or "sections" in chs. 6–12. The topic of the first section (6:1–8:1a) is the Hellenists, starting with their election and closing with the stoning of their leader, Stephen. The marked linguistic features of word order in the opening sentence of 6:1 have been discussed above. The second section (8:1b–11:26) consists of a series of incidents that contribute to the topic of the growth of the Church, culminating in the proclamation of the gospel to Gentiles. It opens with the presentative construction mentioned above in this study, ἐγένετο δὲ ἐν ἐκείνῃ τῇ ἡμέρᾳ διωγμὸς μέγας καὶ θλῖψις.[39] There follows a brief transitional third section (11:27–30),[40] introduced with ἐν δὲ ταῖς ἡμέραις ταύταις, just like the opening of Section I at 6:1; it establishes the relationship between the Antioch church (Jewish and Gentile) and the Jerusalem (Jewish) one. Finally, Section IV (12:1–25) begins with another fore-fronted time expression (κατ᾽ἐκεῖνον δὲ τὸν καιρόν...) and brings the second part of Acts to a close with a critical presentation of the relationship of the Church with Israel.

Sequences

The sections themselves are subdivided into smaller units, "sequences." At this level of the structure, and at the lower level of episodes and scenes if a sequence is subdivided, an inner structure can be observed, created by the arrangement of the components within it. The arrangements follow recognisable and established literary patterns, for which the author would have drawn on rhetorical devices that were familiar to him, in part at least from the Jewish Scriptures.[41] Arrangements have been found in Acts that are concentric ([a b a'], organised

---

[38] The lame man in ch. 3 had been prevented by Jewish law from entering the Temple because of his physical condition, see Rius-Camps and Read-Heimerdinger, *The Message of Acts*, I, 202-72.

[39] Καὶ θλῖψις is absent from most manuscripts, including ℵ01/B03.

[40] Given the exceptional brevity of this third section, it might be preferable to think of 11:27-30 as transitional, a bridging summary rather than a separate section. It is the opening time phrase, so characteristic of major breaks elsewhere in Acts, especially in D05, that suggests that the narrator views the material as a separate section.

[41] The narrator of the Bezan text of Acts is unmistakeably Jewish, shown by the sophisticated nature of the intricate allusions to Jewish oral tradition and ways of thinking that are found within it (see Rius-Camps and Read-Heimerdinger, *The Message of Acts*, I, 2–4). Even if he were not, a first century Gentile believer of the level of education displayed by the narrator of Acts can be expected to have been familiar with the literary structural devices that are an integral part of the Jewish Scriptures. See Robert Alter, *The Art of Biblical Narrative* (Basic Books, 2011); Jerome T. Walsh, *Style and Structure in Biblical Hebrew Narrative* (Michael Glazier, 2001).

around a single centre); symmetrical ([a b b' a'], two parts matching each other with a double centre); or linear (progressing in a single line [a b c d]). For example, Section IV of Part 2, the one dealing with the separation of the Church from Israel, displays a concentric pattern of three sequences [A] [B] [A'], with Herod the topic of the outer sequences and Peter that of the central one. The analysis of Section IV is set out in Figure 5.7:

Part 2, Section IV		
Acts 12:1–25 Release of the Church from Israel		
Sequence [A]	12:1–4	Herod's Persecution of the Church in Judaea
Sequence [B]	12:5–17	Peter's Escape from Prison
Sequence [A']	12:18–23	The Death of Herod
Colophon	12:24–25	Conclusion of Part 2

Figure 5.7: Section IV in Codex Bezae: 12:1–25

The first [A] and last sequences [A'] relate the treatment of the Church by Herod, as representative of the Jews opposed to the believers.[42] They form corresponding outer frames for the middle sequence [B] which focuses attention on Peter as the object of Herod's attack. All three sequences are complete units, without further divisions of episodes or scenes. A colophon summarises the situation at the end of the three sequences to conclude both Section IV and Part 2, as well as preparing for the next section. The boundaries are justified as follows, citing from D05 though there are no variant readings in ℵ01/B03 that affect the analysis of the structure of this section:

[A] 12:1 [D05] Κατ' ἐκεῖνον δὲ τὸν καιρὸν τὰς χεῖρας ἐπέβαλεν Ἡρῴδης ὁ βασιλεὺς κακῶσαί τινας τῶν ἀπὸ τῆς ἐκκλησίας

The sequence is linked to the previous one with the conjunction δέ and is situated specifically within the time that Barnabas and Saul visited the brethren in Judaea (11:29–30). The relevance of the timing will be reinforced in the conclusion to the sequence (12:25), for it means that the persecution against the believers in Judaea coincided with the time when financial aid was brought to Jerusalem from the Gentiles in Antioch. The time is fore-fronted before the main verb ἐπέβαλεν to establish it as the basis of the new sequence and as a new point of departure. In D05, τὰς χεῖρας is also placed before the verb, anticipating the

---

[42] Throughout Acts, the Bezan narrator, speaking from an internal Jewish perspective, highlights the conflict between the growing number of Jesus-believing Jews and those who rejected their claims that Jesus was the Messiah. See Rius-Camps and Read-Heimerdinger, *The Message of Acts*, II, 331–391.

attack carried out by Herod. Herod is the topic of 12:1–4, being the subject of all the main verbs, apart from the parenthetical statement in 12:3b.

[**B**] 12:5a [D05] ὁ μὲν οὖν Πέτρος ἐτηρεῖτο ἐν τῇ φυλακῇ…

A new sequence is introduced with the connective μὲν οὖν at v. 5a, repeating the information of v. 4 but changing the topic so that Peter is now the focus of interest as the narrative develops. The connective μὲν οὖν makes this information secondary, anticipating the action (δέ) that carries the story forward in 12:5b. The prominence accorded to prayer by its fore-fronted position (πολλὴ δὲ προσευχὴ ἦν …) is crucial for the interpretation of the following part of the story, which D05 underscores by including the adjective πολλὴ, for it signifies that the church's prayer for Peter plays a key role in the events that unfold. It is by paying attention to the linguistic clues—the connective link with the previous sequence (μὲν οὖν…δέ) and the word order of the key development sentence (πολλὴ προσευχὴ at the front of the sentence)—that the narrator's intention can be seen.

[**A′**] 12:18 [D05] Γενομένης δὲ ἡμέρας ἦν τάραχος…

The third sequence returns to the day that was set for Peter's appearance before the people (cf. v.4) and picks up the story of Herod who was the main character of the first sequence [A]. The time is highlighted by the presentative construction, fore-fronted as a genitive absolute before the finite verb ἦν. Attention moves away from Peter who has disappeared (v. 17b, καὶ ἐξελθὼν ἐπορεύθη εἰς ἕτερον τόπον) to focus on his opponent, Herod, represented first by the guards before he himself takes centre stage in v. 19 where the switch of focus is indicated by the position of Herod's name at the head of the sentence. The main verb of this sentence (ἐκέλευσεν) indicates the importance the narrator accords to it, other verbs being subordinate.

Colophon 12:24 [D05] Ὁ δὲ λόγος τοῦ θεοῦ ηὔξανεν καὶ ἐπληθύνετο

The section is brought to a close with two concluding statements that bring in new topics. The first concerns the growth of the word of God, which is positioned at the head of the sentence as a boundary marker. The justification for considering that the two main verbs, ηὔξανεν and ἐπληθύνετο, constitue a single element is that they represent two complementary aspects of the same action, conjoined with καί, rather than discrete actions. The other statement in the Colophon at 12:25 picks up the trail of Barnabas and Saul, whose presence in Judaea had provided the time-frame for Section IV (cf. 11:30 and comments above). The position of their names before the verb is for the purpose of focus; they have been implicitly present in the background of this section, for it was while they were in Judaea (cf. 11:30) that the events took place.

Elements

It is at the level of the smallest structural component, the element, that the structural patterns are at one and the same time the most visible and the most complex, as will be seen by taking the final sequence [A'] for illustration.

Identifying an element is essentially a matter of noting the main verbs, as explained above. Once that has been done, the way the author has arranged the elements can be examined. Unless the events unfold in a strictly linear fashion, the centre of the arrangement is found by counting the main verbs: an equal number implies a symmetrical pattern, and an odd number a concentric one. Figure 5.8 sets out the arrangement of elements in the Sequence [A'], including the final component of Sequence [B] and the initial component of the Colophon to show how the sequences are linked to one another. The main verb in the Greek text of each element is underlined for clarity: the English translation often requires more than one verb to be rendered with a finite verb to avoid an unnatural sentence form. It should be noted how the verses do not serve to distinguish separate elements, since they often contain more than one.

All the standard components of a classical story are present in the sequence: an introduction setting the scene [a], initial action [b-c-d], steps that build the tension [e-f-e'], the climax [c'], resolution [b'] and the conclusion [a']. The structural centre [f] is located at v. 20c as the key step in the build up of tension that acts like a fulcrum, because it is the information that the Tyrians and Sidonians requested peace that is the turning point in the series of events and prepares for the acclamation of Herod as a god. The mention of Blastus at v. 20c could seem to be no more than a curious incidental detail were it not for its central position in the story, which suggests that it was meaningful to a contemporary audience.[43] Some striking correspondences between the two sides of the pattern can be observed.

[e]//[e'] at either side of the central element are placed references to the meeting of the people with the king
[d]//[d'] the dispute between the king and the people is stated and resolved
[b]//[b'] Herod orders Peter to be killed, and is himself struck dead by the angel of the Lord
[a]//[a'] the outcome of Peter who had escaped to another place (12:17d) contrasts with that of Herod who dies a dishonourable death.

---

[43] Some commentators are all too ready to dismiss details such as the apparently irrelevant naming of Blastus as evidence of a story clumsily adapted from its source (see, e.g., Barrett, *Acts*, I, 589, citing Conzelman). Some humility is called for. It is much more probable that it is we today, so far removed in time and culture from the first century context, who are poor listeners; unwilling to acknowledge our ignorance, we wrongfully set ourselves up as judges of ancient historians.

[B]	Peter's Escape from Prison	
a′	¹⁷ᵈ καὶ ἐξελθὼν <u>ἐπορεύθη</u> εἰς ἕτερον τόπον.	And he left and travelled to another place.
[A′]	The Death of Herod	
[a]	¹⁸ Γενομένης δὲ ἡμέρας <u>ἦν</u> τάραχος οὐκ ὀλίγος ἐν τοῖς στρατιώταις τί ἄρα ὁ Πέτρος ἐγένετο.	Now when day came, there was a disturbance among the soldiers over what had happened to Peter.
[b]	¹⁹ᵃ Ἡρῴδης δὲ ἐπιζητήσας αὐτὸν καὶ μὴ εὑρών, ἀνακρίνας τοὺς φύλακας <u>ἐκέλευσεν</u> ἀποκτθῆναι,	Herod searched for him and when he did not find him, he questioned the guards, and then ordered them to be killed;
[c]	¹⁹ᵇ καὶ κατελθὼν ἀπὸ τῆς Ἰουδαίας εἰς Καισάρειαν <u>διέτριβεν</u>.	and he went down from Judaea to Caesarea and stayed there
[d]	²⁰ᵃ ᵉ<u>Ἦν</u> γὰρ θυμομαχῶν Τυρίοις καὶ Σιδωνίοις	(for he was embroiled in a dispute with the Tyrians and the Sidonians).
[e]	²⁰ᵇ οἱ δὲ ὁμοθυμαδὸν ἐξ ἀμφοτέρων τῶν πόλεων <u>παρῆσαν</u> πρὸς τὸν βασιλέα	Together, the people from both towns presented themselves together to the king
[f]	²⁰ᶜ καὶ πείσαντες Βλάστον, τὸν ἐπὶ τοῦ κοιτῶνος αὐτοῦ, <u>ἠτοῦντο</u> εἰρήνην διὰ τὸ τρέφεσθαι τὰς χώρας αὐτῶν ἐκ τῆς βασιλικῆς.	and, having gained the favour of Blastus who was his chamberlain, they set about asking for peace, because their regions were provided for from the king's.
[e′]	²¹ᵃ τακτῇ δὲ ἡμέρᾳ ὁ Ἡρῴδης ἐνδυσάμενος ἐσθῆτα βασιλικὴν καὶ καθίσας ἐπὶ τοῦ βήματος <u>ἐδημηγόρει</u> πρὸς αὐτούς.	On an appointed day, Herod, clothed with a royal robe and seated upon the tribunal, addressed them.
[d′]	²¹ᵇ καταλλαγέντος δὲ αὐτοῦ τοῖς Τυρίοις.	(Note that he had been reconciled with the Tyrians.)
[c′]	²² ὁ δὲ δῆμος <u>ἐπεφώνει</u>· θεοῦ φωναὶ καὶ οὐκ ἀνθρώπου.	The crowd cried out, "The proclamations of a god and not of a man!"
[b′]	²³ᵃ παραχρῆμα δὲ αὐτὸν <u>ἐπάταξεν</u> ἄγγελος κυρίου ἀνθ' ὧν οὐκ ἔδωκεν δόξαν τῷ θεῷ	Immediately, the angel of the Lord struck him because he did not give the glory to God;
[a′]	²³ᵇ καὶ καταβὰς ἀπὸ τοῦ βήματος γενόμενος σκωληκόβρωτος ἔτι ζῶν καὶ οὕτως <u>ἐξέψυξεν</u>.	and he came down from the tribunal, and was eaten by worms while still alive, and this is how he died.
Colophon	Conclusion	
[a]	²⁴ Ὁ δὲ λόγος τοῦ θεοῦ <u>ηὔξανεν</u> καὶ <u>ἐπληθύνετο</u>.	The word of God increased and continued to grow.

Figure 5.8: Sequence [A′] in Codex Bezae: Acts 12:17–24

The detail of Herod's death is spelt out in D05 with an adverbial (epexegetic) καί before the main verb (καὶ οὕτως ἐξέψυξεν), typical of the language of D05,[44] underlining the gruesome nature of it.

In other manuscripts including B03, the comment about the reconciliation with the Tyrians [d'] is absent (cf. 12:20b).[45] Consequently, the central point of the sequence is different, since the structure is symmetrical with a double centre of vv. 20b–20c, and the parallels between the two sides of the sequence, noted above, are lost as a result.

Note that the aside in 12:21b in D05 is linked with δέ, for it looks forward to anticipate and justify the proclamation of the crowd. The unusual choice of a participle instead of a main verb in the Bezan clause serves to underline the information that it provides. The forward-looking function of the aside can be compared with that of v. 20a which, introduced with γάρ, looks back to explain that the reason for which Herod went to stay in the Roman capital of Caesarea was the need to resolve a problem with neighbouring provinces.

Further Discourse Features

Further discourse features aside from the choice of connectives and word order could be considered for the way that they contribute to the development of the story. These include the use of participles, the choice to introduce addressees of speech with the dative or the preposition πρός, participant reference, and the presence of the article before the names of persons. An analysis of the latter illustrates the discourse significance of what may otherwise seem to be an unimportant detail.

The Article before Names of Persons

The use of the article before proper nouns plays an important role in determining the status of the noun and tracking it within the course of a narrative. This is especially the case with the names of persons. Contrary to the tendency of traditional grammars and of textual critics to disregard the fluctuation between the presence and absence of the article before names, systematic

---

[44] See note 17 above.

[45] In D05, the importance of the Tyrians is brought out by a series of details (see Barrett, *Acts*, I, 589), including the observation in 12:21bD05 that the king had been reconciled with the Tyrians. Such an emphasis in D05 brings out the parallel between Herod and the ancient prince of Tyre, whom the Jewish Scriptures present as a paradigm of hubris, proclaiming himself a god and not a man (Ezek. 28:2), echoed in the acclamation of the Roman client king by the Tyrians (cf. Acts 1222). For discussion of the parallels, see Rius-Camps and Read-Heimerdinger, *The Message of Acts*, II, 382–386.

analysis shows that there is a real purpose to the variation.[46] Two principles emerge:

1. names of persons by default are preceded by the article (arthrous references);
2. omitting the article (anarthrous references) has the effect of highlighting the person.

The most common reason for which omission occurs in a narrative is to draw attention to a character when he or she is brought into the story for the first time (e.g., Herod 12:1; James, John 12:2; Blastus 12:20c). Subsequent references are usually arthrous by default, but may be anarthrous:

1. when the character returns to the story in a new scene after leaving it temporarily: Peter, Πέτρος 12:3a, cf. ὁ Πέτρος 12:5a, 6a, 7a, 7b, 11, 18; Herod, Ἡρῴδης 12:19a, cf. ὁ Ἡρῴδης 12:21a;
2. if a character who has already been introduced is viewed from the point of view of other participants in the story: Herod, Ἡρῴδης 12:11; Peter, Πέτρος 12:14b; James, Ἰακώβῳ 12:17c;
3. to highlight a person's name for contrast (e.g., Barnabas and Paul at 15:37–38, cited above) or because the character is of particular importance at that point (e.g., Stephen at 6:8 when he is singled out from among the Hellenists, having already been mentioned at 6:5).

When the first mention of a character is, contrary to expectation, arthrous, it can be presumed that the character is a person known to the recipients of the story, and is the expected name. Thus, the name of Jesus is arthrous throughout the Acts narrative when spoken by the narrator. It is important to be clear that "known" means "to the recipients of the story"—as underlined earlier, a good narrator adapts the telling of the story to make it of maximum relevance to the audience, and it is their knowledge and expectations that are constantly monitored. This is apparently the case at 12:12 where Peter goes to "the house of Mary," ἐπὶ τὴν οἰκίαν τῆς Μαρίας. The retention of the article before her name suggests that within the local context of the addressee it was known that the church praying for Peter would be meeting at Mary's house. She is further defined as the mother of John, whose name is anarthrous. Since his mother was known, it can be surmised that John was, too, meaning that the omission of the

---

[46] Jenny Read-Heimerdinger, "The Function of the Article with Proper Names: The New Testament Book of Acts as a Case Study," in *The Article in Post-Classical Greek*, ed. D. King (SIL International, 2019), 153–185.

article before his name draws attention to him. The reason becomes clear at the end of the sequence, when he is named as the one Paul and Barnabas took with them (12:25). At this point, D05 considers that his presence has already been sufficiently established in the scene, and/or that his role alongside Paul and Barnabas was sufficiently well-known, for the article to be retained, contrary to most other manuscripts which omit the article.

Conclusion

Throughout this study of the structure of Acts, it has been seen that an important contribution of discourse analysis is as a tool that provides a measure of objectivity for recognizing the way the writer constructs a text and intends it to be heard. It allows linguistic criteria to be identified that are not only generic to the particular language in question but also specific to the particular author of the text under scrutiny. Alongside a traditional grammatical understanding of the language, an approach based on discourse analysis reveals principles that operate under the surface, serving to give coherence and cohesiveness to a discourse. With regard to ancient Greek narrative in general, the main principles underlying the marking of divisions concern the choice of sentence connectives and sentence-initial word order. By analysing these aspects in the text of Acts, some insight can be achieved into the writer's organization of the narrative. At the lowest level of elements (a sentence composed of a main verb and any associated constituents), this can be ascertained with a high level of confidence, with the proviso that a single manuscript be used because of the extensive variation in sentence construction. The arrangement of elements into higher level divisions is also straightforward by applying the division-marking criteria to locate the boundaries. At this level there is little variation among the manuscripts. Going on from there to detect a hierarchy of divisions, seeing how discrete episodes fit together to form larger sections at higher levels, is more problematic because at this point it is necessary to take account of the thematic development of the narrative, which in turn depends in large measure on what is understood to be the narrator's purpose in writing the account. Some indication of the variation in purpose among the varying forms of Acts has been given, and of the way in which the viewpoint and intention of the writer affects the higher-level divisions of the story.

As underlined in the introduction to this study, discourse analysis views language as "language in use," which means that the purpose of the discourse is understood to play a crucial role in the shaping of it. There is then an inevitable difficulty that arises for us as readers today, in that we know very little indeed of the circumstances in which the book of Acts was written. Furthermore, anything we know about the original author and about the addressee, and of the relationship between them, has to be deduced from the text.[47] All these elements are bound to the context of the time when Acts was written, embedded as it was in Judaism alongside other cultures that are unfamiliar to us today. At a distance of 2000 years, and belonging to a considerably different social—and, dare I say, religious—context, we are confronted with a significant difficulty in retrieving that earlier context and there is the danger of imposing on the text not only our own context but also our preconceived ideas about what the text means.

In sum, the application of discourse analysis to an ancient text certainly provides greater access to it than is otherwise possible, but it is nevertheless important to keep an open mind and honestly acknowledge that whatever we say about a biblical text has to be viewed with some element of caution.

---

[47] In view of the consistently Jewish viewpoint that analysis of Acts in D05 tends to reveal, expressed as it is through an intricate system of allusions to Jewish traditions and ways of thinking, the natural conclusion is that the addressee of that text was a Jew, too; and the only known Jew with the name Theophilus in the first century is the High Priest of 37–42 C.E., third son of Annas, brother-in-law of Caiaphas (Tal Ilan, *Lexicon of Jewish Names in Late Antiquity: Part I: Palestine 330 Bce–200 Ce*, TSAJ 91 [Mohr Siebeck, 2002]).

6

ROMANS

AARON SHERWOOD

As the other contributors to this volume profess, DA is a terrifically useful tool in biblical studies.[1] DA studies a text and its author's purpose in writing that text in terms of one another, facilitating a better understanding of both. Unfortunately, discourse analysis is by its nature especially subjective, perhaps more than other interpretive approaches. So it often happens that readers who would not have already agreed with an interpretation may not be persuaded by even a coherent and data-driven DA.

Next, factor in how any analysis is recursive. This can be less of a problem when addressing just one piece of a document. For instance, say you wanted to publish a fresh analysis of the To-Be-or-Not-To-Be soliloquy in Shakespeare's *Hamlet*. Acceptance of the conventional view—that *Hamlet* is about a broody, indecisive prince struggling with court intrigue—provides a reference point to situate the analysis. But once you switch your task to an analysis of the whole work, then you risk either being pedantic when agreeing anyways with the standard view; or else taking on a mammoth task that may not convince anyone when proposing a radically new alternative (regardless of its merits).

Now consider the prospect of conducting a DA of the entire document of Paul's letter to the Romans.

This chapter, then, is ambitious yet measured. The aim is an appreciation of the scope, purpose and message of Romans that results from—and is therefore

---

[1] This chapter comprises excerpt(s) of my *Romans: A Structural, Thematic, and Exegetical Commentary* (Lexham, 2020). The analysis presented here (particularly all diagrams) is reproduced by permission.

substantiated by—a keen apprehension of how Paul crafted the structure of his letter, up through clauses, to pericopae, to the letter as a whole. In short, we hope for an understanding of the meaning of Romans that results from a DA of Romans.

Method

Regarding the interpretation of any document (or act of human communication), Romans included, there is admittedly a recursive relationship between decisions about what is the meaning (and/or core topic) of a given portion and decisions about the overall structure of the document. Nevertheless, it is fair to say that many interpreters bias their readings of the overall structure of Romans toward what they already reckon is the meaning of various portions of the letter. That is, analyses—or merely descriptions—of the shape of Romans are often made to conform to settled views on the meaning of its content.

But in my experience with Romans in particular, structure needs to be embraced as a control in analyzing content. So DA becomes a key resource for sound analysis, because as an approach it pays the closest attention to logical connectors, with which Romans is especially saturated: The *not-but*s, the *neither-nor*s, the *not-only-but-also*s, and the *rather*s; the *since*s and the *because*s; the *for*s, *therefore*s, and *so-then*s.

The guiding idea, here, is what might be called Paul's *communicative strategy* in Romans: It is presumed that Paul's composition is purposeful, competently written (*i.e.*, comprehensible to his original audience) and coherent. In that case, Paul wrote Romans the way that he did in order to communicate a certain message. Granted, much of the formal polish so evident in the letter is likely due in part to Paul's using some amount of previously prepared material (as many interpreters suspect). Still, Romans is an occasional document that Paul intended to be relevant to his original audience in particular. And it can be further granted also that Paul's manner of writing both facilitates the successful transfer of his message, and is itself part of his message. But again, it is still true that the way in which Paul writes Romans channels (and restricts) the meaning of his message.

Communicative strategy, then, refers to how Paul wrote and shaped Romans in order to tailor both its meaning, and the reception of that meaning by his original audience. To a significant degree, communicative strategy comes down to the structure of a document. And this is where DA proves its worth.

The notion of DA has been helpfully addressed by a number of scholars.[2]

---

[2] In addition to the DA resources noted by other contributors in this volume, see e.g. Peter Cotterell and Max Turner, *Linguistics and Biblical Interpretation* (InterVarsity, 1989), esp. pp. 188–248; Jeffrey T. Reed, "The Cohesiveness of Discourse: Towards a Model of Linguistic Criteria

Regarding Paul's meaning in Romans, DA allows a synthetic (re)construction of the structure of each pericope, and the relationship(s) between those pericopae to reveal the macro-structure of the text. In the process, Paul's structural composition of each pericope highlights its main idea—the primary point that he wants to make sure his audience takes away from a pericope, even were they to miss everything else. And in turn, the meaning of those pericopae combine to divulge what are Paul's primary interest(s) for the letter as a whole.

The process is most easily seen in action. Take, for instance, just the short pericope of Rom 6:12–14. Internally, Paul orients this thought unit around instruction regarding how his audience are to live in response to God's grace. Its structure is illustrated in Figure 6.1 below (whose busyness and spatial inefficiency, of course, preclude laying out all of Romans in this way in this essay). The approach here deals with kernels on the level of entire clauses.[3] This analysis identifies the logical relationship between each adjoining set of clauses (Argumentation; Addition; or Clarification); and as well, it at once diagnoses both which clause is *Subordinate/Modifying* versus *DOMINANT*, and the nature of the relationship between them (*Grounds-CONCLUSION*; *Contrast-HEAD*; *Condition-CONSEQUENCE*, etc.).

As Figure 6.1 demonstrates, Paul's structuring of Rom 6:12–14 discloses his main idea of the pericope. In this case, Paul's focus is found at the center, where the main idea constitutes a parallel pair ("yourselves...your members," v. 13b). Paul accentuates the (paired) main idea by contrasting it ('but instead,' using indirect parallelism) also against a pair of 'not' elements (vv. 12a, 13a). Then Paul further grounds the main idea ("present yourselves...your members," v. 13b) in an explanatory elaboration that recaptures the motif(s) of 6:1–11, the pericope that vv. 12–14 modifies. Thus, structure reveals logic, which in turn reveals the primary point (and theology). All told, what 6:12–14 is 'about,' is ***Paul's instruction to his audience that they are to live righteously before (and for) God (v. 13b)***, because God's grace has freed them from sin (v. 14a).

As regards the larger literary context, the immediately preceding material (6:8–10) rhetorically segues into 6:12–14, but this pericope is logically tied to the main idea within Rom 6:1–11, back at 6:3–4. So 6:12–14 as a thought unit functions as an application of the principle expressed in 6:3–4, in turn ensuring that the audience's lives prove Paul's claim, that his gospel does not imply that sin should be used to further the spread of grace (6:1–2; see on 6:1–11, below). The corollary

---

for Analyzing New Testament Discourse," in *Discourse Analysis and the New Testament: Approaches and Results*, ed. Stanley E. Porter and Jeffrey T. Reed, JSNTSup 170 (Sheffield Academic, 1999), 28–26; George Guthrie, "Discourse Analysis" in *Interpreting the New Testament: Essays on Methods and Issues*, ed. David Allan Black and David S. Dockery (B&H, 2001), 255.

[3] The display could work down to the level of individual words and the syntax of phrases. But that would just yield diminishing returns, buying marginally greater precision at the cost of increasing unreadability by a magnitude.

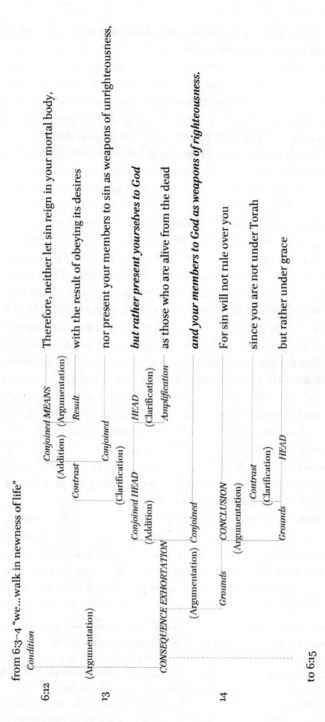

Figure 6.1: The Logical Structure of Romans 6:12–14

is that believers are not to live sinfully, or in the service of sin (vv. 12–13a). Finally, the notion of living righteously due to being "not under Torah but rather under grace" (vv. 13b–14) rhetorically flows into the start of Rom 6:15–23 (the
dashed line in the above diagram). However, 6:15 begins a new section within
the literary sub-unit of 6:1–7:6, such that 6:15 (like 6:13b) logically ties into 6:3–4,
and this section of Paul's discussion (6:1–14) finishes with 6:12–14 (see Figure 6.3
below).

One more brief example in Figure 6.2 (below) will also serve in illustrating
the method used here in the DA of Romans. Happily, the diagram in Figure 6.2
can be simplified because the procedure has already been demonstrated. But
again, the following analysis (Figure 6.2) reveals that Paul structures Rom 13:8–10
in order to highlight his opening thought as the main idea of the pericope. *He
pastorally instructs his audience to only owe the charity of love towards one
another* (v. 8a, bold lines). Paul supports the legitimacy of his command by ap-
pealing to the principle that loving each other satisfies the moral prescription(s)
of Scripture (v. 8b, semi-bold lines). And lastly, Paul explains the logic of that
connection using a quick, elaborating syllogism: that the ethical standard of Torah is satisfied by love of neighbor (v. 9)—which (Paul elaborates) does certainly
not overstep authority into the realm of judgment and harm (v. 10b; cf. 13:2,
4b)—proves the principle that loving each other indeed fulfills Torah (v. 10b).
And Rom 13:8–10 as a whole is prompted by the closing idea in the previous pericope of Rom 13:1–7, that paying what is 'owed' has a corollary within the community of faith (v. 7); all of which together leads into the summation found next
in Rom 13:11–14.

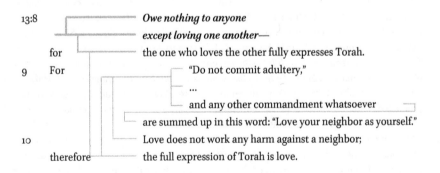

Figure 6.2: The Logical Structure of Romans 13:8–10

By treating all the pericopae that constitute Romans in this way, DA facilitates a synthetic (re)construction of the structure of the letter as a whole. This, in
turn, provides a working model for the letter, at least as a starting point. That is,

by showing how structure determines the main idea for each pericope, DA thereby helps to maintain a focus upon two questions when interpreting Romans. First, how does Paul craft a given thought unit so that it contributes to his overall agenda? And second, when the meaning and function of all those units is taken together, then what does that reveal about what Paul is saying in the letter as a whole? In this way, DA illuminates Paul's communicative strategy in Romans. And beginning with a proper understanding of Paul's communicative strategy will then guide an analytical interpretation so that it results in a sound understanding of Romans.

Macrostructure

The Historical Meaning and Literary Function of Romans 1:16–17

Current wisdom is that, of course Romans is addressed to a particular audience in a particular situation (even if some particulars remain debated). Yet there is a danger of adopting this truism only superficially, as concerns the letter structure. An overwhelming majority of interpreters (and commentaries in particular) reckon that the theme of Romans is Paul's understanding of the gospel. It is consequently surmised that letter body starts at 1:16, and that Rom 1:16–17 is thus the thesis of the letter. Commonly, the remainder is then divvied up on thematic lines, which are then (to a degree) equivocated as "structure."[4]

---

[4] For some, this goes with effectively treating Romans as Paul's *Summa Theologica*; e.g. John Murray, *The Epistle to the Romans*, NICNT (Eerdmans, 1968), 1:xxii–xxv, 2:xi–xvi; F.F. Bruce, *Romans*, TNTC (Eerdmans, 1985), 67–69; Dieter Zeller, *Der Brief an die Römer: Übersetzt und erklärt*, RNT (Regensburg: F. Pustet, 1985), 7–9; Brendan Byrne, *Romans*, SP 6 (Liturgical, 1996), 26–30; James R. Edwards, Romans, NIBC (Hendrickson, 1992), 3; Joseph A. Fitzmyer, *Romans: A New Translation with Introduction and Commentary*, AB 33 (Doubleday, 1993), 96–98; Peter Stuhlmacher, *Paul's Letter to the Romans: A Commentary*, trans. Scott J. Hafemann (Westminster John Knox, 1994), 13–16; Simon Légasse, *L'épître de Paul aux Romains*, LD 10 (Paris: Saint-Laurent, 2002), 42–44. But interpreters who focus on the occasional nature of Romans often arrive at the same structure; e.g. James D.G. Dunn, *Romans 1–8*, WBC 38A (Word, 1988), 284–288; Jeffrey A.D. Weima, "Preaching the Gospel in Rome: A Study of the Epistolary Framework of Romans," in *Gospel in Paul: Studies on Corinthians, Galatians and Romans for Richard N. Longenecker*, ed. L. Ann Jervis and Peter Richardson (Sheffield Academic, 1994), 337–338; Douglas J. Moo, *The Epistle to the Romans*, NICNT (Eerdmans, 1996), 32–35, 774; Samuel Bénétreau, *L'épître de Paul aux Romains*, CEB 17 (Vaux-sur-Seine, France: Edifac, 1997), 1:37–41; Thomas R. Schreiner, *Romans*, BECNT 6 (Baker, 1998), 24–27, 178–179, 184, 198, 200; Giusepe Segalla, *Lettera ai Romani: Traduzione Strutturata*, Sussidi biblici 69 (Reggio Emilia: San Lorenzo, 1999), 10–13; Klaus Haacker, *Der Brief des Paulus an die Römer*, THKNT 6 (Evangelische Verlagsanstalt, 1999); 14–17; Eduard Lohse, *Der Brief an die Römer*, KEK 4 (Vandenhoeck & Ruprecht, 2003), 9–11, 53–55; Romano Penna, *Lettera ai Romani, I: Rm 1–5*,

DA will helpfully inform this situation. But first, the nature of 1:16–17 is a deciding factor regarding the macrostructure of Romans. This is a literary-historical issue, and not structural or directly related to discourse. Still, given the history of interpretation (including present trends), recognizing what 1:16–17 is and is not saying is a ground-clearing step toward seeing how Paul did indeed fashion the structure of his message to his Roman audience.

Romans 1:16–17 reads,

> For I am not ashamed of the gospel, for it is the power of God for the salvation of everyone who trusts, both Jew first and Greek. For in it God's righteousness is being revealed, which is a matter beginning and ending in faith, just as it is written, "But it is by faith that the righteous person will live.

Every aspect of these verses is contested, and space does not permit a full analysis. However, a few observations will suffice to clear the way, toward identifying the macrostructure of Romans.[5]

First, when Paul uses language of *ashamed* (ἐπαισχύνομαι), he should not be misunderstood as stating either that he is unembarrassed to share his faith, or that he is proud (stated negatively) of the gospel (or God's power).[6] Instead,

---

Scritti delle origini Christiane 6 (Bologna: Edizioni Dehoniane di Bologna, 2004), 58–59; Grant R. Osborne, *Romans*, IVPNTC 6 (InterVarsity, 2004), 24–26. Finally, here can be included attempts to establish the structure of Romans using classical rules of rhetoric, nearly all of which still produce similar structures and theological analyses to those above; e.g. Neil Elliott, *The Rhetoric of Romans: Argumentative Constraint and Strategy and Paul's Dialogue with Judaism*, JSNTSup 45 (JSOT Press, 1990), passim; Marty L. Reid, "A Rhetorical Analysis of Romans 1:1–5:21 with Attention Given to the Rhetorical Function of 5:1–21," *PRSt* 19 (1992): 255–272; Robert Jewett, "Following the Argument of Romans," in *The Romans Debate*, ed. Karl P. Donfried, rev. and exp. ed. (Hendrickson, 1992): 272–275 (cf. idem, *Romans: A Commentary*, Hermeneia [Fortress, 2006], 135–137); R. Dean Anderson, *Ancient Rhetorical Theory and Paul* (Kampen: Kok Pharos, 1998), 207–238 (who critiques some rhetorical analyses as "rather extreme example[s] of disturbing trends in recent rhetorical studies, namely, the confusion of ancient and modern rhetorical theory, and the misuse...of ancient terminology"; ad loc., 193); Douglas A. Campbell, "Determining the Gospel through Rhetorical Analysis in Paul's Letter to the Roman Christians," in *Gospel in Paul: Studies on Corinthians, Galatians and Romans for Richard N. Longenecker*, ed. L. Ann Jervis and Peter Richardson (Sheffield Academic, 1994), 319–320; Thomas H. Tobin, *Paul's Rhetoric in Its Contexts: The Argument of Romans* (Hendrickson, 2004) 88–98.

[5] For detailed examination, see Sherwood, *Romans*, 122–36.

[6] Cf. Richard B. Hays, *Echoes of Scripture in the Letters of Paul* (Yale University Press, 1987), 39; Neil Elliott, *The Rhetoric of Romans: Argumentative Constraint and Strategy and Paul's Dialogue with Judaism*, JSNTSup 45 (JSOT Press, 1990), 278–290; Johannes N. Vorster, "Strategies of Persuasion in Romans 1.16–17," in *Rhetoric and the New Testament: Essays from the 1992 Heidelberg Conference*, ed. Stanley E. Porter and T.H. Olbricht, JSNTSup 90 (JSOT Press, 1993), 153–154; Reid, "Rhetorical," 124; Antoinette Clark Wire, "'Since God is One': Rhetoric as Theology and History in

ashamed relates to the honor/shame dynamic of Graeco-Roman (and Mediter-
ranean) culture, and it refers to disgrace, loss of face, and loss of status in the
eyes of others. Several scholars have shown that both Paul and his gospel suffered from a negative reputation that preceded him among some parts of the
early church whom he had not met—like the Roman believers—because wherever he preached or planted churches, the Jewish gospel concerning the Jewish
Messiah was rejected by Jews but accepted by non-Jews, the *goyim*/nations.[7]
Thus Paul's main claim in 1:16–17 is that extenuating circumstances mean that
things are not as they appear. The gospel that he proclaims—the gospel in which
he intends to help the Roman audience grow (1:15; see below)—is not shameful,
and does not by association bring shame upon himself or God.

As v. 16 continues, Paul's reason for this claim is the principle that it is by the
gospel—his gospel, which Paul preaches—that God is now saving both Jews and
Greeks (*i.e.*, non-Jews). That is, Paul preaches God's tangible, formidable activity
in the present day, when by means of the Christ-event he effects in history the
deliverance and redemption to which Israel and Second Temple Jews have so
long looked forward. And Paul explicitly states that the means of cleaving to this
salvation is πιστεύω-ing God, that is, believing and trusting (within the context of
a personal relationship) God's testimony and perspective regarding Jesus' identity and work in the Christ-event.

Finally, in v. 17, Paul supplies that this move by God reveals his righteousness
(δικαιοσύνη θεοῦ). Again, this issue is also contested, but increasingly interpreters
assent to reading "God's righteousness" as a reference to his covenantal faithfulness. That is, through the Christ-event, God fulfills his scriptural promise(s) of
salvation.[8] And as Paul further elaborates, God's methods are (while surprising)

Paul's Romans," in *The New Literary Criticism and the New Testament*, ed. Elizabeth Struthers
Malbon, JSNTSup 109 (Sheffield Academic, 1994), 214; Luke Timothy Johnson, *Reading Romans: A
Literary and Theological Commentary* (Crossroad, 1997), 9–10; Schreiner, *Romans*, 58–61, etc.

[7] For full discussion, see Aaron Sherwood, *The Word of God has not Failed: Paul's Use of the
Old Testament in Romans 9:6–29*, SSBT (Lexham, 2015), 23–27; cf. Stuhlmacher, *Romans*, 143–
144; Steve Mason, "'For I am Not Ashamed of the Gospel' (Rom. 1.16): The Gospel and the First
Readers of Romans," in *Gospel in Paul: Studies on Corinthians, Galatians and Romans for Rich-
ard N. Longenecker*, ed. L. Ann Jervis and Peter Richardson (Sheffield Academic, 1994), 280;
Byrne, *Romans*, 2–4, 9; A.J.M. Wedderburn, *Reasons for Romans* (T&T Clark, 1988), 93–94; and
Schreiner, *Romans*, 14; Rikki E. Watts, "'For I Am Not Ashamed of the Gospel': Romans 1:16–17
and Habakkuk 2:4," in *Romans and the People of God: Essays in Honor of Gordon D. Fee on the
Occasion of His 65th Birthday*, ed. Sven K. Soderlund and N.T. Wright (Eerdmans, 1999), 22–23.

[8] Taking the objective reading of *God's righteousness* in 1:17a renders this pericope internally and contextually incoherent (to say nothing of the letter structure, which depends on
1:16–17 to relate the materials to either side): It would be a sharp *non sequitur* for Paul to argue
that his gospel does not bring dishonor upon God (v. 16) because what it features is God's
imputing righteousness to believers.

consistent with precedent, as is the centrality of trusting him: First, understanding God's work within the gospel is wholly an issue of faith (according to Paul's use of the idiom ἐκ πίστεως εἰς πίστιν).[9] Second, Paul's citation of Grk. Hab 2:4 backs his reading of the present-day situation, since in Habakkuk, too, the point is that God is faithful to his people even when Israelites seem to suffer God's disfavor rather than (more) wicked *goyim*. That is, Paul endorses and reapplies Habakkuk's point. God's strategic timing is his own, and despite appearances he remains faithful to his covenant people. In the meantime, the Israelite who continues to live as a righteous Israelite will do so while trusting God's plan and his loyalty.[10]

Therefore, the role of Rom 1:16–17 is to introduce Paul's answer to the *Israelf-rage* (*i.e.*, the "question of Israel") vis-à-vis the reputation of his evangelization record, as the cause of his Roman audience's hesitancy to accept his authority and/or input. And since not all sixteen chapters of Romans are dedicated to this concern, this means that 1:16–17 is neither the thesis of the letter body, nor summarizes Paul's communicative strategy for the letter as a whole. Having established, then, what Rom 1:16f. is *not* doing, we are now able to look to a DA of Romans to see more clearly what indeed are its macrostructure and communicative strategy.[11]

Macrostructure and Paul's Communicative Strategy in Romans: Mission, Pastoral Care, and Apology

Space does not permit presenting the examination of the structure of every pericope that comprises Romans. However, those examinations do indeed lead to seeing that Paul writes Romans in the way that he does so that it is organized according to the schema in Figure 6.3 (below).

DA of all the pericopae in Paul's letter shows what is the ***main idea*** for each of them, and thus how each pericope connects to those around them. And the resulting structure (Figure 6.3) shows that Paul largely dedicates the body of Romans to his pastoral care for his audience, in addition to broaching the possibility of their

---

[9] See Wilbur A. Benware, "Romans 1.17 and Cognitive Grammar," *BT* 51 (2000): 336–338; John Taylor, "From Faith to Faith: Romans 1.17 in the Light of Greek Idiom," *NTS* 50 (2004): 341–342.

[10] See Watts, "'Not Ashamed'," 16–17; Alice Ogden Bellis, "Habakkuk 2:4b: Intertextuality and Hermeneutics," in *Jews, Christians, and the Theology of the Hebrew Scriptures*, ed. Alice Ogden Bellis and Joel S. Kaminsky, SBLSymS 8 (SBL Press, 2000), 369, 372–375; Taylor, "From Faith," 338–339; cf. Richard P. Carlson, "Whose Faith? Reexamining the Habakkuk 2:4 Citation within the Communicative Act of Romans 1:1–17" in *Raising Up a Faithful Exegete: Essays in Honor of Richard D. Nelson*, ed. K. L. Noll and Brooks Schramm (Eisenbrauns, 2010), 297–299, 301–302, 314.

[11] See below on the microstructure of 1:16–17.

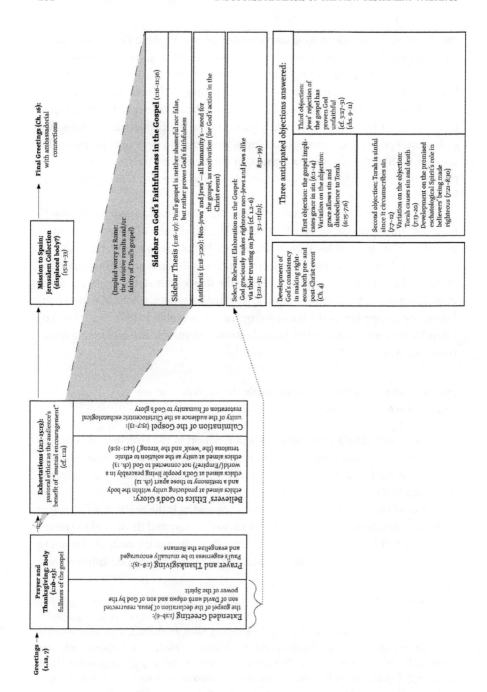

Figure 6.3: The Macrostructure of Romans

assistance in his mission to Spain. Along the way, Paul takes the time to include a meticulous and necessary formal defense of his gospel, the content of which does bear upon his pastoral instruction (once he is able to return to it). So although this structure still needs fleshing out (below), it means that Paul's communicative strategy in Romans is:

1. to introduce himself to the church at Rome and ask for their support in his evangelistic program;
2. then also to speak pastorally into the audience's context, addressing difficulties that they are negotiating (even while having no previous connection or authority over them);
3. and finally, to accomplish these goals by also addressing misgivings the audience have about the potentially divisive and shameful effects of his gospel preaching, in order that they will accept him on those other fronts.

Notwithstanding the above ground clearing exercise, this view of the structure of Romans (or the above reading of 1:16–17, itself) is not a reaction to recognizing the limited scope of 1:16–17. Instead, the impetus comes from what Paul says in 1:8–15, following (and together with) the Greetings in 1:1–7.

Rom 1:1–7 is the letter introduction, which Paul includes in all of his epistles. But in this case, his greeting elaborately details the proof and global implications of the gospel, and then relates the gospel to the letter occasion. In vv. 2–6 especially, Paul specifies that throughout the document, he means by *gospel* the good news that the Christ-event has presently realized the promises of Israel's Scriptures (and not, e.g., justification by faith). Then, the following pericope of 1:8–15 is at once the Prayer and Thanksgiving (another typical element; cf. εὐχαριστέω, προσευχή, vv. 8, 10), and the start of the letter body. Thus, **when Paul states, "I long to see you in order...to firmly establish you" (v. 11), he is articulating the core theme of Romans, the thing that he most hopes to accomplish by writing the letter, and by writing it in the way that he does (i.e., his communicative strategy).**[12] Due to that basic commitment, Paul structures 1:8–15 so that it builds toward his final, summative statement, "often I intended to come to you...in order that I might have some fruit also among you, just as among the rest of the nations.... Hence, I am obligated—and I do so enthusiastically—to proclaim the gospel also to you who are in Rome" (vv. 13–15; see Figure 6.4 below).[13]

---

[12] Cf. M. L. Reid, "Paul's Rhetoric of Mutuality: A Rhetorical Reading of Romans," *SBLSP Papers* 35 (1995), 189–190; Erwin Ochsenmeier, "Romans 1,11– 12: A Clue to the Purpose of Romans?" *ETL* 83 (2007): 398–399.

[13] On the punctuation of vv. 13b–15, see e.g. Beverly R. Gaventa, "'To preach the gospel': Romans 1,15 and the Purposes of Romans', in *The Letter to the Romans*, ed. Udo Schnell, BETL 226 (Peeters, 2009) 183–184, 187; Runar M. Thorsteinsson, "Paul's Missionary Duty towards

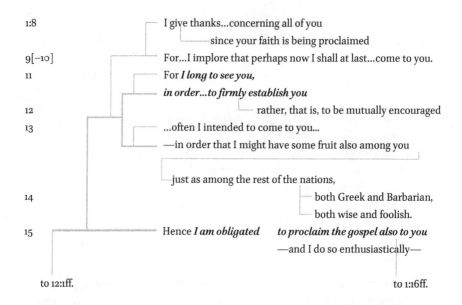

1:8   — I give thanks…concerning all of you

          since your faith is being proclaimed

9[–10]   — For…I implore that perhaps now I shall at last…come to you.

11   — For *I long to see you,*

       in order…to firmly establish you

12   rather, that is, to be mutually encouraged

13   — …often I intended to come to you…

       —in order that I might have some fruit also among you

      just as among the rest of the nations,

14   both Greek and Barbarian,

                     both wise and foolish.

15   — Hence *I am obligated*   *to proclaim the gospel also to you*

                     —and I do so enthusiastically—

   to 12:1ff.   to 1:16ff.

Figure 6.4: The Logical Structure of Romans 1:8–15

As Figure 6.4 indicates, it is in 1:8–15 that the two routes through Romans diverge. As regards a DA of Romans, it still makes the most sense to proceed linearly
through the text. But funnily enough, it is almost viable first to take chs. 12–15 together with 1:8–15, and leave 1:16–11:36 for afterward, since that traces Paul's own
interest for the letter. Were Paul and his audience unproblematically known to
one another, then the structure of 1:8–15 entails that—in accordance with the occasion of the letter—much (all?) of 1:16–11:36 might not even have been set down
(in this document, at least), since it is not directly relevant to Paul's pastoral care
regarding difficulties presently experienced by his audience. It is in 12:1ff. that Paul
is able to return to addressing his audience's situation. Thus, Paul's dedication to
pastorally care for his audience (1:11, 15a) feeds into his pastoral instructions, in chs.
12–15; and at the same time, his mention of the gospel (1:15b) makes necessary a
diversion into Paul's defense of his gospel, so that his communicative strategy for
the letter will be successful and his input not be (possibly) rejected by his audience.

Therefore, from 1:15, Paul segues into his defense of God's faithfulness in the
gospel, which comprises the material found in all of Rom 1:16–11:36. Paul's defense
of his gospel begins with its thesis, set forth in 1:16–17 (as already discussed above).
Paul's claim is that despite negative reports, his gospel is not shameful, but instead

Gentiles in Rome: A Note on the Punctuation and Syntax of Rom 1.13–15," *NTS* 48 (2002): 544–
545, passim.

proves God's covenantal faithfulness. Next comes what can be provisionally labeled the antithesis to that thesis, in 1:18–3:20, which analyzes humanity's need for the powerful salvation of the gospel. And finally, Paul expands on his thesis for the sidebar by selectively elaborating on relevant aspects of his gospel in 3:21–31; 5:1–11[21]; and 8:31–39; these passages together (especially if 1:16–17 is included) form the backbone to the sidebar that is 1:16–11:36.

Microstructures

1. Romans 1:1–15: Prayer and Thanksgiving; Start of Letter Body

In effect, the first major (albeit modest) literary unit of the letter is Rom 1:1–15, which comprises two literary sub-units. As noted above, Rom 1:1a, 7 constitutes Paul's standard epistolary Greetings, with 1:1b–6 as an extension that divulges what is the referent of *gospel* for the letter. Then, Rom 1:8–15 (esp. vv. 8–10) constitutes Paul's standard Prayer and Thanksgiving. But vv. 8–15 also begin the letter body, as Paul moves naturally into his proposal of pastoral care (which he diplomatically frames as mutual care), as if he might be part of the answer to his own prayer for the Roman church. It is here that Paul's announces his primary agenda for the letter (esp. vv. 11, 15).

2. Romans 1:16–11:36: Sidebar Concerning Paul's Defense of his Gospel

Romans 1:16–17: Sidebar Thesis

The next literary unit of the letter is quite long, that of 1:16–11:36. This piece is composed of numerous literary sub-units, the first of which is just Rom 1:16–17. As noted above, 1:16–17 begins Paul's apology of his gospel. These verses are the thesis for this portion of the document. To reiterate, ***Paul's claim is that his gospel is not shameful, but instead proves God's covenantal faithfulness, in accordance (and continuity) with Scripture and Israel's biblical history.***

Romans 1:18–3:20: Sidebar Antithesis

The next literary sub-unit is Rom 1:18–3:20 (Figure 6.5 below), which may be termed the 'Antithesis' to 1:16–17 (still within the compass of just 1:16–11:36) because its focus is a consideration of humanity's position apart from the gospel. Thus is it prompted by the principle set forth in 1:16–17, but ultimately 1:18–3:20 finds its answer in 3:21–26, when Paul resumes his consideration of the gospel vis-à-vis God's righteousness.

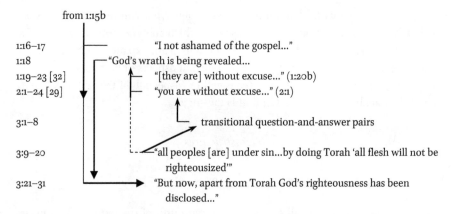

from 1:15b

1:16–17	"I not ashamed of the gospel..."
1:18	"God's wrath is being revealed...
1:19–23 [32]	"[they are] without excuse..." (1:20b)
2:1–24 [29]	"you are without excuse..." (2:1)
3:1–8	transitional question-and-answer pairs
3:9–20	"all peoples [are] under sin...by doing Torah 'all flesh will not be righteousized'"
3:21–31	"But now, apart from Torah God's righteousness has been disclosed..."

Figure 6.5: The Structure of 1:18–3:20

While not necessary to how DA identifies the structure of Romans (and thus Paul's communicative strategy), a helpful (if contested) caveat to remember is the reference point that Paul uses in 1:18–3:20. That is, he is not (for the most part) evaluating various segments of humanity according to standards of the gospel and from the perspective of an eschatological, post-Christ-event context. Instead, the Antithesis largely considers the situation in the abstract, before the gospel is considered as a factor in the equation. Accordingly, the thesis for the sub-unit of 1:18–3:20 is that all people who fall into the category of 'the unrighteous' are subject to God's "wrath." That is, *Paul finds that categorically speaking, all quarters of humanity are subject to God's eschatological judgment; hence the need for the powerful salvation available in the gospel (1:18).*

Following the Antithesis thesis of 1:18, Paul first treats the *goyim* (*i.e.,* Gentiles/nations; 1:19–32). In this section, Paul uses a profile that early Jews typically used when characterizing wicked non-Jews (a basically redundant notion)—and yet unapologetically evaluates them using the outlook of a typically Jewish, scriptural normative position: In vv. 19–23, Paul applies to them the biblical principle that *non-Jews' humanity—and that of all people—is defined by their being God's image (Gen 1:26; cf. Rom 1:23), such that being human confers sufficient innate knowledge that God is the source of their being human (Rom 1:19–20a).* Thus the reason Paul gives for why the unrighteous are subject to God's eschatological judgment, is that they did have (sufficient) knowledge of God, and yet willfully rejected what they understood to be the case—what has always been plain to everyone and even comprehensible just on the basis of familiarity with the artistry of God's craftsmanship.

From here, Paul unleashes a triptych (vv. 24–31) that details the ways in which "God handed over" (vv. 24, 26, 28) unrighteous non-Jews to their rebellion against him, to suffer the dehumanizing consequences of their choice to reject him as the source of their humanity; and then Paul pairs that triptych with a parallel evaluation that in their idolatry, unrighteous non-Jews additionally effect the uncreation of others in their own image, taking part in separating others from God as well (v. 32). Moreover, Paul's use of the present tense in 1:18, "is being revealed," indicates that God's judgment upon the unrighteous is partially a present reality. So the evaluative pairing of vv. 24–31 and v. 32 articulates how the wicked already partially suffer eschatological judgment within the context of the present eschatological age. The ungodly lives of unrighteous non-Jews are an initial stage of that judgment, the precursory punishment of living out twisted and perverse lives apart from God (vv. 21–23), all as a result of their "being without excuse" (v. 20).

In the next section (2:1–29), Paul outlines how Jews stand condemned for doing the same wicked things that they recognize non-Jews commit.[14] So still without factoring in the gospel, *Jews who fail to satisfy Torah are also—like unrighteous non-Jews—"without excuse" (2:1a).* Even, worse, they have Torah, and so are not only wicked but also hypocrites and transgressors (2:1b). Therefore, all things being equal, they too are subject to God's eschatological wrath (1:18).

Finally, a transition (3:1–8) leads to the last section (3:9–20), where Paul considers whether anyone may yet be exempt from God's judgment (v. 9a). But against this, Paul assembles a catena of Scriptures (vv. 10–18) that makes clear that *all national Israel has historically and presently (in the first century) rebelled against God, confirming that fully "all peoples" are under sin (v. 9b).* This conclusion to the antithesis of 1:18–3:20 is double-edged, since here Paul also reincorporates the fact of the Christ-event. Doing so, he finds that since rejecting the gospel is now rebellion against God, then even Torah-faithful Jews find themselves in the same position as the wicked nations, as maintaining allegiance to Torah now means abandoning devotion to God (vv. 19–20). So being righteous is no longer possible (if it ever was) through possession and/or observance of Torah alone; all categories of people are subject to God's eschatological judgment, and hence the necessity for the gospel.

---

[14] For two pericopae, Paul's interlocutor is just "you," but then in 2:17 Paul explicitly identifies him as one who is named "'Jew.'" Identifying the second-person subject of 2:1–11 with that of 2:17ff. makes the best sense of both the text and the historical context of the letter; so Murray, *Epistle*, 1:54–56; C.E.B. Cranfield, *A Critical and Exegetical Commentary on the Epistle to the Romans*, ICC (T&T Clark, 1975), 1:138–139; Leon Morris, *The Epistle to the Romans* (Eerdmans, 1987), 107–108; Osborne, *Romans*, 60; Colin G. Kruse, *Paul's letter to the Romans*, PNTC (Eerdmans, 2012), 119, etc.; cf. Fitzmyer, *Romans*, 297; Arland J. Hultgren, *Paul's Letter to the Romans: A Commentary* (Eerdmans, 2011), 111–112.

Romans 3:21–31: Part I of the Sidebar 'Backbone'

The next sub-unit (still within 1:16–11:36) comprises Rom 3:21–31, which marks the resumption of Paul's positive case following the foregoing antithesis (Figure 6.6). At 3:21, Paul begins laying out his selective elaboration of his gospel, in order to defend his claim that it proves God's covenantal faithfulness (1:16–17).

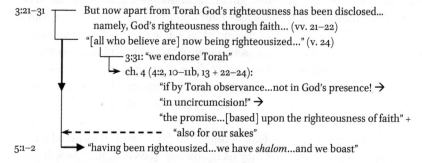

3:21–31 ⸺ But now apart from Torah God's righteousness has been disclosed...
namely, God's righteousness through faith... (vv. 21–22)
"[all who believe are] now being righteousized..." (v. 24)
3:31: "we endorse Torah"
ch. 4 (4:2, 10–11b, 13 + 22–24):
"if by Torah observance...not in God's presence! →
"in uncircumcision!" →
"the promise...[based] upon the righteousness of faith" +
"also for our sakes"
5:1–2 "having been righteousized...we have *shalom*...and we boast"

Figure 6.6: The Immediate Role of Romans 3:21–31 within Romans 1:16–11:36

Paul structures the leading pericope here (3:21–26) in a way that drives home his main idea: God is presently righteousizing sinful believers through their personal trust in Jesus; and since that is the eschatological deliverance promised by Scripture, the gospel manifests God's covenantal faithfulness. Here, Paul does use the findings of 1:18–3:20 to motivate the necessity of the gospel (vv. 23–24). But his main idea is that *God is using the Christ-event to righteousize (and redeem) sinful believers; and since that is the eschatological deliverance promised by Scripture, the gospel is the manifestation of God's covenantal faithfulness (vv. 21–22a, with v. 26b)*. In the process, Paul explicates how the gospel announces God's working through Jesus (vv. 25–26a), which supports Paul's contrast between pre- and post-Christ-event contexts: Whereas national Israel could not achieve righteousness by expressing their trust in him by observing Torah (v. 21a; cf. 3:9–20), God now—eschatologically—bestows righteousness upon his people as a result of their instead directly trusting him in Jesus.

The next pericope (vv. 27–31) adds the elaboration *that all sinful people now enjoy equal access to the righteousization (and redemption) offered by God in the gospel, since it is exclusively on the basis of faith (v. 27)*. But apparent tension between the current and pre-Christ-event states of affairs raises the concern that the exclusion of boasting threatens theological discontinuity between Scripture and Paul's gospel. So Paul also claims here that righteousization by faith affirms and upholds Torah (v. 31), leading into ch. 4.

Romans 4: God's Covenantal Consistency in the Gospel

Paul's point in 3:31—that righteousization in the gospel is in continuity with Scripture—is significant enough to make him interrupt his selective elaboration of the gospel, and to report on the nature of that continuity. So, he does just that in the sub-unit of Rom 4:1–25. Therefore, while much of what Paul covers when making this point may be theologically rich, DA demonstrates both how the position of ch. 4 with the structure of Romans is simple, and that its function within Paul's communicative strategy is straightforward (see Figure 6.6 above).

Paul starts (4:1–8) by drawing upon the authority of Scripture, which teaches that Abraham is the precedent of righteousization. Paul starts with his primary point, that *God righteousized Abraham himself in response to the personal, relational trust that he placed in God (vv. 2–3)*. In support, Paul even compares David to Abraham (vv. 7–8, citing Grk. Ps 31): David benefitted from the possession of Torah and yet was unrighteously unfaithful to it. Nevertheless, God gives David mercy and does not credit (λογίζομαι, Grk. Ps 31:2) his transgressions as unrighteousness. If God can allow for David, then surely he can also righteousize Abraham, who trusted God and did not rebel despite not even possessing Torah.

Accordingly, Paul fills out this sub-unit in two further steps. First, he extends his analysis by reiterating (4:9–12) how *Abraham's righteousization was independent of Torah, that in fact it occurred prior to even the existence of Torah or circumcision (vv. 9–10)*. Then Paul concludes (4:13–25) by arguing that God's promise to Abraham and his heirs (a cosmic legacy) was not—could not have been—based upon Torah observance. *To be a gift given by promise, by definition it is (and had to be) accomplished by God alone (v. 13)*.

In this way, Rom 4 not only supports the claim in 3:31 that the gospel does not contradict Torah, but even further proves that the gospel expresses the heart of Torah. Further, the fact that this directly impacts Paul's audience (cf. 4:24–25) rhetorically prompts Paul's return to his selective elaboration of the gospel, taking up again in 5:1 the thread of discussion from 3:21–31.

Romans 5:1–21: Part II of the Sidebar 'Backbone'

The literary sub-unit of Rom 5 resumes from 3:21–31 Paul's selective elaboration on the gospel and how it is the manifestation of God's covenantal faithfulness (even while also incorporating the material of ch. 4; see Figure 6.6 above). In particular, a DA approach highlights how there is no clear recent antecedent to "having been righteousized" in 5:1; and that ch. 4 only functions as support for the claim back in 3:31, rather than the grounds to the conclusion "Therefore...we have *shalom*...and we boast," in 5:1. Thus, insofar as the general topic of 5:1–11(ff.) is what the gospel means for believers, the clearest logical antecedent to 5:1a is

Paul's description of how he and his audience—"all who believe" (3:22a)—are in the gospel "[now] righteousized…through faith," back in 3:24–25.

Paul's main idea in the dominant pericope of the sub-unit (5:1–11) is that *faith-based righteousness results in shalom with God and participation in his immortal life, as well as assurance of rescue from future eschatological judgment and (more significantly) deliverance into God's righteous reign (vv. 1–2, 11).*[15] And regarding Paul's communicative strategy for the letter, he articulates these features specifically because they further prove that his gospel proves God's covenantal faithfulness.

And since for Paul it is through Jesus that God effects all these blessings, he finishes this portion of his selective elaboration of the gospel by reviewing Jesus' instrumentality (vv. 12–21). Specifically, Paul designates the Christ-event as "God's grace(/*charis*)" (v. 15), which builds to the main idea (in the second pericope), that *it is through Jesus that God forgives believers' sins, transforms them into his righteous royal subjects, and gives them full participation in resurrection and eternal life within his kingdom (vv. 18–19).* In this way, Paul has not wavered in his communicative strategy. DA shows that Paul continues to structure his text so that the one thing his audience is sure to hear is how his gospel proves God's covenantal faithfulness.

Romans 6:1–8:30: Responses to the First and Second Objections

In the next stage(s) in Paul's defense of his gospel (1:16–11:36), he again breaks off from his selective elaboration that is meant to show why his gospel is not shameful. Paul concluded the last portion of his elaboration by (re)stating how God's *charis* of Jesus is the solution to sin, mentioning Torah's role in defining sin and the judgment for sin (5:20–21). So, in the pair of literary sub-units of 6:1–7:6 and 7:7–8:30, Paul responds to objections that he anticipates might be raised regarding his mention of Torah and sin in such close proximity (Figure 6.7):

Throughout, Paul presents his discussion using the form of diatribe (see 6:1, 15; 7:1, 7, 13), which he also used earlier within the larger literary unit (cf. 3:3–4, 5–6, 31). The first sub-unit is 6:1–7:6 and comprises Paul's response to both the first anticipated objection (6:1–14) and a variation on it (6:15–7:6). Specifically, since 5:20–21 ended in saying how Paul's gospel states that God gave the *charis* of his son Jesus in response to human sinfulness, then the worry is, could Paul be suggesting that sin has some intended role in the spread of grace? So Paul first responds by contending (6:1–11) that, no, *his gospel does not entail that sin advances*

---

[15] The main idea (vv. 1–2) is developed by being rooted in Jesus' death (vv. 3–8); and then believers' resulting salvation from coming wrath (vv. 9–10) ties back into the main idea by connecting reconciliation with God in Jesus' resurrection (v. 11).

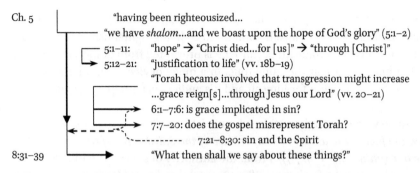

Figure 6.7: The Immediate Role of Romans 5 within Romans 1:16–11:36

the cause of grace (6:1–2). Paul explains that he and his audience are living out a new life that is no longer characterized by sin, since their identity is defined by their relationship with God in Jesus (vv. 3–4; cf. the hortatory corollary next, in vv. 12–14, per above).

Next, Paul answers the variation (6:15–7:6) that is rhetorically prompted by his concluding language of "not under Torah" and "under grace" (6:14). Namely, does Paul's gospel imply that, because believers are "under grace," they may act however they wish, without concern for sinfulness? Again, Paul ripostes, ***"Certainly not!" (6:15), based on the fact that his audience's lives are presently not characterized by sin because they have been righteousized in the gospel (vv. 17–18).*** To drive home the point, Paul next offers further elaboration (7:1–6) that invokes the principle that the audience's death in Christ frees them to join his new life of obedience (v. 4).

From here, Paul anticipates a second objection, addressing both it (7:7–12) and a variation on it (7:13–25) to start the literary next sub-unit (7:7–8:30). Like 6:1, Rom 7:7–12 also goes back to 5:20–21 (additionally reflecting the proximity of sin and Torah throughout 6:1ff.), the worry now being that Paul's gospel slanders Torah as being sinful (v. 7). Paul's response is to insist and affirm that Torah is (on the view of his gospel) good and holy (v. 12), but to confirm that ***Torah does reveal and define sin (v. 7b–8a).*** The problem, then, lies not with Torah (or Paul's gospel), but with the fact that sin exploits even Torah in bringing sinners to death (vv. 8–11).

And once again, Paul next answers a variation (7:13–25), that his gospel implies that Torah causes (sin and) death (v. 13a). And again, Paul argues to the contrary, using a persona of the "I"—an unbelieving Jew (committed to righteousness but lacking recourse to grace in the gospel)—to state unequivocally that ***it is sin that causes death, and even abuses Torah to do so (v. 13b).***

So, to date, Paul has fielded two potential objections to his analysis of how his gospel is not shameful, and instead proves God's covenantal faithfulness.

However, at the close of the last piece (7:21–25, within 7:13–25), Paul's "I" summarizes how he is himself committed to living righteously as Torah outlines, yet consigned to death because he is prevented from doing so by the sin within him (v. 25b); at the same time, in a hinge device, Paul interjects (as a believer) a celebration for himself and his audience, anticipating what comes next (v. 25a).

Namely, Paul completes this sub-unit (still 7:7–8:30) by clarifying (8:1–30) how *the fact of the audience's experience of the Spirit is proof that surely, they are free (unlike the "I" of 7:7ff.) from the authority of sin* (8:1–2 within 8:1–11; cf. vv. 10–11). In fact, he further specifies (8:12–17) that *he and his audience are free from sin because they belong to the Spirit instead of sin (vv. 12–13);*[16] and ends (8:18–30) with an explanation of how *identification with Christ in his suffering (v. 18; cf. 8:17) more vitally means participation in his life, their restoration, and God's eventual, eschatological restoration of creation itself (vv. 18–21).*

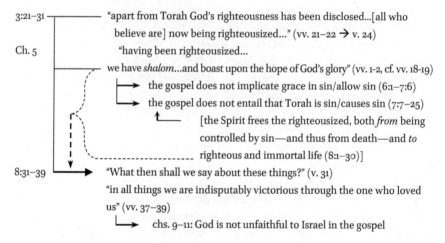

3:21–31 ———— "apart from Torah God's righteousness has been disclosed...[all who believe are] now being righteousized..." (vv. 21–22 → v. 24)

Ch. 5   "having been righteousized...
                 we have *shalom*...and boast upon the hope of God's glory" (vv. 1-2, cf. vv. 18-19)
                      → the gospel does not implicate grace in sin/allow sin (6:1–7:6)
                      → the gospel does not entail that Torah is sin/causes sin (7:7–25)
                           ↑—— [the Spirit frees the righteousized, both *from* being controlled by sin—and thus from death—and *to* righteous and immortal life (8:1–30)]

8:31–39 ——→ "What then shall we say about these things?" (v. 31)
             "in all things we are indisputably victorious through the one who loved us" (vv. 37–39)
                  → chs. 9–11: God is not unfaithful to Israel in the gospel

Figure 6.8: The Structure of Romans 6:1–8:30

As with ch. 4 (above), much of what Paul passes over in the two sub-units of 6:1–7:6 and 7:7–8:30 is compelling, rich, and theologically provocative. Yet regarding communicative strategy, Paul's purpose is evinced by the structure of his composition, as discerned through the use of DA. Namely, Paul interrupts his selective elaboration of the gospel to forestall potential miscommunication(s), and then having done so is now able to return to the main task of 1:16–11:36.

---

[16] Notably, Paul's argument is not theological (or doctrinal, or philosophical), but empirical, rooting his theological evaluation in the historical fact of the audience's experience of the eschatological spirit.

Romans 8:31–39: Part III of the Sidebar 'Backbone'

Paul focuses the (brief) literary sub-unit of 8:31–39 by starting with the rhetorical question, "What then shall we say about these things?" (8:31). Most immediately, "these things" rhetorically recalls that the future of "we" is assured (in 8:22–30) by sound understanding of the gospel and the fact of the Spirit's presence (which supports the primary point there, that present sufferings are insignificant compared to God's impending restoration; vv. 18, 21). At the same time, though, "these things" are not only the proofs that Paul's gospel does not permit sin(fullness) or malign Torah (or leave believers stranded in sin; 6:1ff.). The central topic of 8:31–39 is how Paul and his audience's connection with God is one of insoluble love—his love for them—which serves as the basis for their victory according to the gospel. This means that fundamentally, "these things" in 8:31 reaches back to Paul's account of his gospel most recently in 5:1–21.

Therefore, Rom 8:31–39 resumes (from 5:1–11) and completes Paul's selective elaboration of his gospel (Figure 6.8 above). While this pericope attends to Paul's basic interest within the 'sidebar,' his message is brief and to the point: *The results of righteousization in the gospel both entail and are proven in that Christ will (and does) overcome all threats to believers' salvation, which ultimately goes to proving how Paul's gospel proves God's covenantal faithfulness (vv. 31b, 37).*

Taken together, then, Rom 1:16–17; 3:21–31; 5:1–21; and 8:31–39 raise and address the question of whether Paul's gospel is divisive and unbiblical, and therefore (by association) brings shame upon Paul, God, and his audience should they choose to welcome Paul. Paul biblically and empirically demonstrates the contrary, that his gospel is indeed God's powerful salvation, by which it therefore proves God's covenantal loyalty. All that remains before Paul can return to giving pastoral care (his true interest in writing to the Roman church; 1:11, above) is the *Israelfrage*, the third and final potential objection, and the reason for Paul's apology in 1:16–11:36 in the first place.

Romans 9–11: Response to the Third Objection

Much like 1:16–17, virtually every aspect of Rom 9–11 is contested, and space does not permit a fair treatment of either the text or the literature. A descriptive presentation of the findings of a DA of the material has to suffice. And the most basic point to be made is that like 6:1ff. and 7:7ff., chs. 9–11 are Paul's response to the third anticipated objection to his relevantly selective elaboration of the gospel. Frankly, the last step in Paul's elaboration rhetorically prompts his discussion here (which he already raised and set aside for later, in 3:1–8). Namely, if the identity of he and his audience as God's people is secure in their relationship with Israel's God (8:31–39), then what of national Israel?

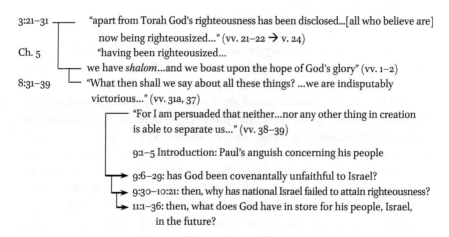

Figure 6.9: The Structure & Function of Romans 9–11 within Romans 1:16–11:36

Here Paul again uses the form of diatribe, starting the successive sections of chs. 9–11 with rhetorical questions (see 9:6, 30; 11:1; cf. 6:1, 15; 7:1, 7, 13, above). But *Paul first introduces the problem (9:1–5), framed in terms of his anguish over his people (v. 2)*. In so doing, he restates the problem: His claim is that his gospel is God's salvation first for Jews and then for non-Jews (1:17), and now such salvation is inherently among national Israel's blessings (9:4–5). Yet, Paul's primary point in this introduction is that despite appearances to the contrary, he grieves over his countrymen's negative response to his preaching (vv. 1–2).

From here, Paul responds in earnest. First, he states his thesis for chs. 9–11: *God has not been covenantally unfaithful to Israel (9:6)*. Paul's position is that the Christ-event may have been unexpected, but non-believing Jews' rejection of his gospel is not the result of God's likewise unexpected rejection of them (whether in favor of non-Jewish believers, or otherwise). Rather, within this literary sub-unit, the first section (9:6–29) demonstrates how national Israel unexpectedly responded to God by rejecting the Christ-event. Their subsequent judgment by God, then, is only in response to national Israel's prior idolatry.[17]

First, Paul demonstrates God's consistent faithfulness to Israel, throughout their history, from their identity and existence as a community of faith being predicated on his faithfulness, to his loyalty amidst their (previous) rebellion(s) and apostasy (9:6–13). Then, *Paul analyzes the sundering of first-century non-believing Jews' relationship with God in terms of consequences—God's judgment—upon their idolatry (likening them even to Pharaoh; 9:14–18)*. Finally

---

[17] For the analytical interpretation of 9:6–29—including DA—see Sherwood, *The Word of God has not Failed*, 33–132; on the remainder of chapters 9–11, see Sherwood, *Romans*, 532–636.

(9:19–29), Paul explicates how *national Israel surrendered their humanity through their idolatrous rebellion (vv. 20–21)*; they are uncreated in the image of the lifeless objects that they worship (in place of living through worshipping the living God), and inanimate objects lack the standing (or ability) to protest to which use God puts them in accomplishing his purposes (even of redeeming sinful non-Jews).

In the next section of chs. 9–11, Paul specifies the nature of non-believing Jews' idolatry (9:30–10:21). First (9:30–10:4), *Paul indicts national Israel for identifying Torah observance rather than a trusting relationship with God as the heart of right-eousization (9:32)*, which (Paul further clarifies) means that they have the implicit aim of displacing God in his role of generating righteousness for them (10:2). That is, Paul identifies Torah observance as national Israel's idol. In the post-Christ-event context, God no longer righteousizes on the basis of Torah observance. Yet even at the cost of rupturing their relationship with God, national Israel have committed to expressing trust toward God through Torah observance rather than expressing trust by directly trusting God in Jesus (v. 4). And Paul next elaborates on the character of national Israel's idolatry by speaking to the quality of their idolatry (10:5–13). In particular, *their rejection of the Christ-event is just another instance in their history of repeated unfaithfulness (in direct contravention of the deuteronomic admonition not to disregard God; vv. 6–8)*. Finally (10:14–21), Paul closes this section by expanding on that same point, that *national Israel is rejecting God's ambassadorial message of the Christ-event (vv. 16–17)* in a way similar to their recorded history of receiving and then refusing God's message and redemptive activity.[18]

The last section of Rom 9–11 concludes Paul's response to the third and final anticipated objection (11:1–32, with closing doxology in vv. 33ff.) with a consideration of God's purpose(s) for national Israel and his people. First (11:1–10), Paul cites himself as an example in maintaining that *national Israel's idolatry does not entail that God abandoned "his people" (vv. 1–2)*.[19] Next Paul interjects a comment (11:11–24) that really points downward, to what comes next (vv. 25ff.): *The present rift between national Israel and God is neither necessary nor permanent (v. 11)*, and it would be easier for their full Israelite identity to be restored than it was for it to be sundered (vv. 23–24).[20] Lastly, Paul fills out his description of God's hopes for national Israel with an eschatological revelation (11:25–33).

---

[18] *I.e.*, it is not that God has failed to deliver his message to them, having both given national Israel their Messiah, and sent Paul to faithfully discharge the truth of Jesus (vv. 14–15).

[19] "His people" is ambiguous in this context. The scriptural precedent (1 Kgdms 19:10, 14, 18 = Rom 11:2b–4) applies to the present reality, such that God's people are still partially constituted by a remnant of believing, covenantally faithful Jews within the entire nation of Israel (v. 5; implying that "the rest" in v. 7 is the remainder of national Israel repeating the sins of their forerunners).

[20] Along the way, Paul digresses with a warning to the non-Jewish portion of his audience. He decries any potential arrogance on their part, since but for grace they, too, were divided from God, and could be divided again more easily than national Israel has been (vv. 17–22).

Paul's language here is difficult (and space prevents the deserved treatment). But regarding communicative strategy, Paul is mainly concerned to get across how his audience should understand the overall landscape, that *an entity to which God is committed, called "all Israel" (v. 26a), will be saved when the full complement of the nations has become Israel-ified, over the course of the ongoing eschatological present, stretching forward from Paul's time until the final consummation of history (v. 25,* with primarily vv. 26–27 as support).

In this manner, Paul fashions his discussion in chs. 9–11 to answer the possible charge that his gospel entails God's breaking his scriptural promises to Israel, and therefore the failure of his covenantal faithfulness. Paul's response is that his gospel has neither led national Israel away from God, nor injected any element of God's replacement of the *goyim* for national Israel. Rather, their distance from God is the result of his judging their idolatry by confirming them in their choice and releasing them to its consequences (9:6–29); and national Israel's refusal to follow God from Torah observance to the Christ-event betrays their idolatry, which is ultimately a commitment to displace God with themselves in their own lives (9:30–10:21); and finally, God's desire is that national Israel would return to the covenantal faithfulness to which he is committed, and that God will in any case accomplish the eschatological restoration of his community of faith (11:1–33).

Summary of Romans 1:16–11:36

Romans 1:16–11:36 is Paul's defense of his gospel to his audience. It is made necessary by the reputation of Paul and his gospel, which preceded him to Rome. To some degree, Roman believers were committed to Jews' entitlement (even priority) to God's salvation in Jesus, and they had some awareness that Paul's preaching largely resulted in Jews' alienation from the Christ-event. Much (or all) of what Paul offers in 1:16ff. is profitable as the context for 12:1ff. (below); and likely Paul's audience already understood and agreed with some (much?) of Paul's theological views in 1:16ff. (whose formal preparation suggests previous use). Nevertheless, DA reveals how Paul positions(/interjects) and then shapes 1:16ff. in the way that he does, and how he selectively covers relevantly necessary ground, all in order to disperse for the Roman audience any cloud that might surround his gospel. Thus, regarding communicative strategy, Rom 1:16–11:36 ensures that no misunderstanding about Paul's preaching and its impact would prevent them from receiving him and his instruction.

In sum, Paul's purpose for 1:16–11:36 is to contend that his gospel proves God's covenantal faithfulness (1:16f.), because it proclaims that in the eschatological present, God is righteousizing sinful believers through the Christ-event (3:21ff.); this results in the realization of *shalom* with God, participation in his immortal life and both present and future deliverance into God's righteous reign, all of which God effects through Jesus (ch. 5); and finally, from all these things Paul concludes that their experience of God's love proves that he and his audience are indeed hyper-victorious in the gospel (8:31ff.). As well, Paul takes several necessary breaks along the way. He motivates his positive claim about the gospel by evaluating the estate of every quarter of humanity when the gospel is not factored into the equation (1:18–3:20). He pauses to demonstrate the continuity between God's relationship with his people with Israel's biblical history and in the present post-Christ-event context (ch. 4). And when needed, Paul also resolves possible misunderstandings about what is implied by his gospel (6:1–7:6; 7:7–25[8:30]; and 9[1]6–11:36).

Having dealt with the elephant in the room, in 12:1 Paul is able to return to what is his chief interest in writing the letter (cf. 1:11, above), namely, offering pastoral care to the church at Rome.

3. Romans 12:1–15:13: Pastoral Exhortation

Romans 12: Exhortation Thesis; and Unity and Love within the Community

The next major literary unit in the letter is Rom 12:1–15:13, which effectively constitutes the "spiritual gift" (1:11) that Paul hopes eventually to share with his audience in person. This unit of course presumes the nature and benefits of the gospel presented in 1:16ff., but in terms of communicative strategy, 12:1 is where Paul writes to further evangelize the Roman church (*i.e.*, bring meaning to their lives by way of the gospel; 1:15, above). And for the unit of 12:1–15:13, the opening verses of 12:1–2 both provides Paul's thesis, and heads up the first literary sub-unit of just ch. 12 (Figure 6.10).

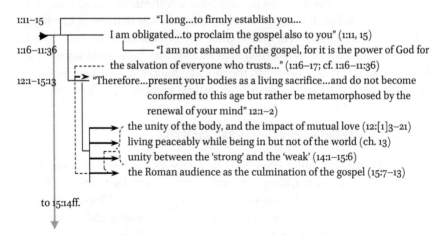

1:11–15 ——————— "I long...to firmly establish you...
——— I am obligated...to proclaim the gospel also to you" (1:11, 15)
1:16–11:36 └——— "I am not ashamed of the gospel, for it is the power of God for
the salvation of everyone who trusts..." (1:16–17; cf. 1:16–11:36)
12:1–15:13 "Therefore...present your bodies as a living sacrifice...and do not become
conformed to this age but rather be metamorphosed by the
renewal of your mind" 12:1–2)
the unity of the body, and the impact of mutual love (12:[1]3–21)
living peaceably while being in but not of the world (ch. 13)
unity between the 'strong' and the 'weak' (14:1–15:6)
the Roman audience as the culmination of the gospel (15:7–13)

to 15:14ff.

Figure 6.10: The Position and Structure of Romans 12:1–15:13

The first literary sub-unit within 12:1–15:13 is Rom 12:1–21. First, *Paul frames his instructions for the letter as a whole ("Therefore, brothers, I exhort you...," v. 1) by the opening sentence (12:1–2) that functions as his pastoral thesis:*

> ...present your bodies as a living sacrifice: holy, well pleasing to God, your appropriate act of worship; and do not become conformed to this age, but rather be metamorphosed by the renewal of your mind toward your discriminating what is God's will: the good, the well pleasing, and the perfect.

Paul's idea here is twofold. First, the audience's individually and communally living out christlikeness achieves its goal of glorifying God (cf. the cultic dimension of λατρεία; v. 1). Second, the audience are to live as distinct, peculiar creatures within their setting of an already-but-not-yet dichotomy of co-missioning with God's realization of his purposes within "this age" (v. 2; cf. 15:7–13, below). These principles proleptically preview all that Paul has to teach his audience regarding godly living.

Then, coming to the sub-unit proper of 12:[1]3–21, Paul delivers two complementary sets of instructions. First (12:3–8), *Paul enjoins his audience to individual humility, that they might view their community with God's perspective and live together accordingly (v. 3).* Toward this end, Paul uses his metaphor of the body for the variety of spiritual giftings in the church, giving such examples as "the one who teaches" being gifted "to teaching;... the leader to dedication; the one who shows mercy to cheerfulness," etc. to illustrate that the audience are complementary—positioned relative to each other—within Christ's body (vv. 4–8). Second (12:9–21), *Paul closes this sub-unit with instruction on the character and quality of the love that is to define the audience's community (vv. 9–13).* Paul's main idea in this pericope is composite, a syntactically punchy list of attributes that identifies love as the defining characteristic of those in Christ (e.g. "Detesting evil. Being joined to what is good. ...In dedication, unhesitant. In Spirit, enthusiastic," etc.; vv. 9–13). Then Paul extends his characterization with application (vv. 14–21) that describes the tangible impact of said love, including both positive elements (vv. 14–16a, 17b, 20–21) and negative (vv. 16b–17a, 18–19).

Romans 13: The Community Living within the World

The next sub-unit within 12:1–15:13 is Rom 13, which in terms of letter structure really anchors to 12:1–2, alongside (and not to) the previous sub-unit (Figure 6.10 above). If ch. 12 aimed at ethics within the community of faith, then ch. 13 aims at the community of faith (Paul's audience) living in a godly manner—emulating God's kingdom—within the wider world. This focus is borne out by the structure that Paul builds into his discourse. First (13:1–7), Paul leads with his main idea, that *each individual believer at Rome is to live in a* civilis *manner within their societal/imperial context* (*v. 1a*; with application, vv. 6–7). Paul provides two parallel arguments (vv. 1b–2, 3–4) toward the supporting conclusion (to support v. 1a), that Christian ethics and prudence both demand living rightly within society (v. 5). To this overall command Paul appends further application(s) (vv. 8–10; see Figure 6.2 above). The complement to externally paying what they owe (vv. 6–7) is that the audience are to owe only a reciprocal, growing payment of love amongst each other (v. 8). Finally, to tie off chs. 12–13, Paul offers an eschatologically contextualized summary of Christian ethics (13:11–14), *especially by highlighting their spiritual orientation* (*v. 12b*).

Romans 14:1–15:6: Resolving Tension between the "Weak" and the "Strong"

The next sub-unit is Rom 14:1–15:6, which also anchors to 12:1–2 (rather than ch. 13), and which addresses tension between the "weak" (14:1) and the "strong" (15:1; again, Figure 6.10 above). Paul ends with this issue because it is the most important. The effectiveness of his pastoral care for his audience—his primary interest in structuring the letter in the way that he has—succeeds or fails based on resolving this trouble. Just as Paul ended with the *Israelfrage* in 1:16–11:36, so he leaves this most contentious ethical issue until the end of 12:1–15:13.[21] The identities of the weak and strong remain a matter of some debate. However, since the issues of contention between them relate to former Torah observance, the best working theory is that *the weak* refers to Jewish believers at Rome, who are troubled by the disregard shown for Torah-related customs by non-Jewish believers in the audience (the larger demographic and referent of *the strong*).[22]

A DA approach to this portion of the document shows that Paul resolves the tension by *not* siding with either camp. That is, to start (14:1–9) *Paul does not condemn either the position or practices of either the "weak" or the "strong," but instead he condemns the practice of condemning* (*v. 1*). For the remainder of his opener, Paul supports this priority with the notion that each believer stands alone before the Lord (v. 4), supported in turn by the elaboration that each believer is to be confident in herself (v. 5)—all of which rests on the truth that

---

[21] Cf. Ben Witherington III, *Paul's Letter to the Romans: A Socio-Rhetorical Commentary* (Eerdmans, 2004), 325; Wedderburn, *Reasons*, 30–35; James C. Miller, *The "Obedience of Faith," the Eschatological People of God, and the Purpose of Romans*, SBLDS 177 (SBL Press, 2000), 112–113, 116, etc.

[22] Notably, this would mean that the final and most crucial topic for Paul's pastoral care relates to the reason for his extended apology in 1:16–11:36. I.e., the most significant tension among Roman believers—that relating to the relevance of Jewish ethnic background to church unity—is reflected in their concern over whether Paul's gospel is illegitimate because it is severed from its Jewish pinnings.

"Christ died and lived in order to be Lord of both the dead and living" (v. 9). Next (14:10–23), Paul likewise builds upon the fact of God's supremacy (vv. 10–12) with his positive instruction regarding the audience's (religio-)ethnic tension (vv. 13–18), culminating in the primary point here, *"So then, let us pursue for one another the things of* shalom *and of edification" (v. 19*; cf. vv. 20–23).[23] Finally (15:1–6), Paul concludes his instruction on the matter of "the weak" and "the strong" with a summary that is anchored to the preceding main point (14:19): He reiterates (in parallel) twice for emphasis (15:1–2), that *all of the "strong"—and here Paul includes himself—are to seek what is good not for themselves, but rather for their neighbors, the weak* (v. 1 ἀδύνατος, *lit.* 'un-powerful,' 'disenfranchised'). And the basis for this injunction is that by so doing, they are living out their authoritative example of Christ himself (vv. 3–6).[24]

All told, the three pastoral care sub-units so far are parallel to each other—tied to the thesis of this literary unit at 12:1–2 (Figure 6.10 above)—and therefore have equal structural weight. At the same time, Paul composes each of these sub-units in a way that accentuates their central application (12:3 with vv. 9–13; 13:1; and 14:1 with 14:19; cf. 15:1–2). And last to note is how Paul builds toward the greatest source of strain within the Roman church, addressing lastly their unity-disrupting ethnic tensions by counseling mutual care (cf. 1:12) in order to discharge his burden of pastorally caring for his audience in their present circumstances (cf. 1:11).

Romans 15:7–13: The Culmination of the Gospel in the Audience's Unification

The final sub-unit, then, within the larger literary unit is Rom 15:7–13. Rom 15:7–13 fits with the previous three sub-units in 12:1–15:13 as a whole (esp. as a conclusion to 14:1ff.), but in a way stands apart as both a summary and the culmination of Paul's exhortations in chs. 12–15 (Figures 6.3, 6.10 above).[25] Insofar as 15:7–13 completes the discussion of the "weak" and the "strong," Paul plays off of 15:1–6: He recycles the arrangement of command, christological warrant grounded in Scripture, and benediction; but whereas the worship in 15:1–6 is vocal (*i.e.*,

---

[23] Simon J. Gathercole, *Where is Boasting?: Early Jewish Soteriology and Paul's response in Romans 1–5* (Eerdmans, 2002), 39 notes that "nothing is unclean in and of itself" (v. 14; cf. v. 20) may represent Paul's view of the "correct" theological position (likely on the basis of Jesus traditions; cf. v. 14 οἶδα καὶ πέπεισμαι ἐν κυρίῳ Ἰησοῦ and, e.g., Mark 7:18–19), were he to offer it.

[24] Given the social value of reciprocity, Paul frustrates the audience's expectations with his use of obligation language and the conspicuous absence of any obligation the "weak" have toward the "strong"; cf. Scott J. Hafemann, "Eschatology and Ethics: The Future of Israel and the Nations in Romans 15:1–13," *TynBul* 51 (2000): 166–167.

[25] For a full treatment of 15:7–13, including DA, see Sherwood, *Paul and the Restoration of Humanity in Light of Ancient Jewish Traditions*, AJEC 82 (Brill, 2013), 231–247.

takes the form of sharing verbal expression of worship), in 15:7– 13 it is ethical (*i.e.*, takes the form of the audience's God-glorifying actions toward one another). Then, in the sense that Rom 15:7–13 concludes Paul's ethical teaching, the initial διό of v. 7 harkens back to the thesis in 12:1–2, and thus ultimately to 1:8–15. In a significant respect, then, 15:7–13 is within Romans both the climax to its literary structure, and the logical culmination to Paul's theology.

The structure of Rom 15:7–13 positions its main idea in its opening statement, wherein *the entire audience's mutual acceptance and unity is an act of worship that realizes God's eschatological promises in Scripture (v. 7)*.[26] In particular, Paul identifies God's promises as the worship-based unification of "the circumcision" and the *goyim* (effected by Christ's service; vv.8–9a), and then demonstrates how said unification is the realization of God's eschatological design for humanity using a catena of Scriptures (vv. 9b–12). The traditions that Paul cites (aesthetically arranged) together recount God's mighty deeds at four landmark moments in Israel's history—backward through David, the culmination of Torah and exodus (all of which contain an eschatological note), and then leaping forward to Isaiah's New Creational, eschatological coming Day of Yhwh. And each of these traditions expresses God's mighty deeds in terms of his glorification; specifically, glorification that results from Israel-nations unity in worshipping Israel's God.

All told, then, Paul caps the structure of Romans with his pastoral instruction that his ethnically mixed audience are to welcome one another, because—in accordance with Scripture—their unification in Christ instantiates God's intended eschatological restoration of humanity. A DA of Romans results in a structural analysis that funnels all of Paul's attention down to 15:7–13. And so, DA demonstrates how the audience's worship of God through their being his eschatologically restored humanity is the driving force of Paul's theology for the letter as a whole.

4. Romans 15:14–16:27: Mission to Spain and the Jerusalem Collection; Final Greetings

Romans 15:14–33: Paul's Spanish Mission

The final stage of the letter body is Rom 15:14–33 (Figure 6.3, above). Paul diplomatically resumes his rhetoric of mutuality (v. 14; cf. 1:12) and reminds of his desire to visit (v. 22), recalling his language in the body opening (1:13–14, above). Paul starts (15:14–21) by outlining the circumstances that prevented his having visited Rome before (cf. 15:22), conceding his audience's theological proficiency

---

[26] For a DA of the syntax in 15:7–9, see Sherwood, *Paul*, 326–329.

(v. 14) but emphasizing his primary point, that *he wants to go on as he has start-ed and continue reaching unreached non-Jews with the gospel (v. 20a)*, in ac-cordance with God's management and the expectations of Scripture (vv. 20b–21). In support, Paul orients his main point by speaking of how his work on be-half of the gospel is to be celebrated, referencing his previous instrumentality in God's spread of his gospel of the Christ-event (vv 15–19).

Lastly (15:22–29), Paul ties in this busyness with evangelism as the explana-tion for why he has so far been prevented from visiting the audience (v. 22). But this just leads (by contrast) into the main idea here, that *Paul intends a mission-ary trip to Spain, and seeks support from the (hopefully) now agreeable Roman church (vv. 23–24, 28)*. As above, Paul offers further support in the form of men-tioning the Jerusalem collection, whereby he has been instrumental in uniting non-Jewish Christians with their suffering Jewish fellow-believers (vv. 25–27; cf. 15:7–13, above), to whose heritage they are spiritually indebted. Finally, Paul closes the letter body with a sort of initial final greetings and benediction (with doxology; 15:31–33).

Romans 16: Final Greetings

There still remains some debate on the authenticity of Rom 16. But as regards DA and the macrostructure of Romans, ch. 16 (overlapping with 15:31–33) straightforwardly comprises Paul's Final Greeting and his closing doxology.

Conclusions

So what does the tool of DA bring to the interpretation of Romans? It was admit-ted at the outset that DA sometimes seems a subjective approach to a document. However, those examinations which space allowed produced structural analyses of pericopae that best explained both their content, and their various linguistic features. Likewise, the structures offered for the pericopae in Romans and its proposed macrostructure (Figure 6.3 above) correlate with each other. And final-ly, the overall result is a sound apprehension of Paul's communicative strategy for the letter as a whole within its historical context. Perhaps the proof of the pudding is in the eating, as it were.

In the case of Romans, the value of DA is that it offers the best chance at rec-onciling the text and occasion of the letter, thereby arriving at the best articula-tion of Paul's communicative strategy (including both his meaning and his theo-logical priorities). DA reveals how Paul structures his discourse in order to ad-dress the multiple factors that prompted him both to write the letter at all, and to write it in the way that he does. Namely, Paul first mentions and closes with his pragmatic missional purpose (1:10, 13–15; 15:14–29); which is in a sense theologically motivated by Paul's own main interest within the letter of providing his audience pastoral care (1:11–12, 12:1–15:13); and which is necessarily interrupted to ensure that Paul's audience will receive him at all (1:16–11:36). Thus Paul composes the letter so that it addresses both "the present situation of the church in Rome and the present situation of Paul."[27] Furthermore, the structure of any given pericope attests to this fact about Paul's discourse within Romans.

The present study, then, shows DA to be valuable as regards Romans because it identifies the overall structure—and therefore Paul's communicative strategy—for Paul's letter. At the very least, this safeguards against misreading (or even just missing out on) Paul's interests and theology within the letter. And potentially, DA is instrumental is showing that within Romans—and thus Pauline theology (depending how central the document is judged to be)—Paul's theological interest is most clearly expressed in his pastoral concern that the church would live out their identity as God's new humanity, and that they would accordingly share with him in bringing the reaches of the earth to participate in that same identity.

---

[27] Wedderburn, *Reasons*, 142; cf. Karl P. Donfried, "A Short Note on Romans 16," in *The Romans Debate*, 50–59; Morris, *Romans*, 7–18; Dunn, *Romans 1–8*, lv–lviii; Wedderburn, "Purpose and Occasion of Romans Again," in *The Romans Debate*, 195–202; Fitzmyer, *Romans*, 79–80; Miller, *Obedience*, 17; Brian J. Abasciano, *Paul's Use of the Old Testament in Romans 9:1–9: An Intertextual and Theological Exegesis*, LNTS 301 (T&T Clark, 2005), 30, etc.

7

1 CORINTHIANS

R. BRUCE TERRY

There are many aspects of discourse analysis which can be pursued. While my dissertation research[1] was limited to eight of them, this chapter focuses on three of those eight. In order to understand the overall thrust of the book, an attempt is made to formulate the macrostructure of 1 Corinthians. Next, based on the results of gross chunking and macrosegmentation, a constituent analysis has been done. Then a search for markers of peak is conducted throughout the book. This latter involved charting and the creation of a computer database. When these studies had been done, the data was then checked to see if there is a difference in grammatical and stylistic tendencies between the parts of this letter which were in response to the letter which the Corinthians sent to Paul and the parts that were in response to information that he received by word of mouth.

Methodology

Work on macrostructures within 1 Corinthians begins by concentrating on the macrostructures of each of the several discourses within the letter. Van Dijk's four methods have been used where possible, but in order to make the task manageable, two concepts on macrostructure have been imported from Longacre's

---

[1] Ralph Bruce Terry, "An Analysis of Certain Features of Discourse in the New Testament Book of I Corinthians" (PhD diss., The University of Texas at Arlington, 1993); published as Ralph Bruce Terry, *A Discourse Analysis of First Corinthians*, PL 120 (SIL, 1995).

work.[2] The first is that macrostructure material is more likely to be foregrounded in the text than backgrounded. Therefore the background material has been omitted from consideration for the most part. The second is that the primary material in a hortatory text consists of forms of commands, suggestions, and requests. Since most of the discourses in 1 Corinthians are hortatory, macrostructure work centers around these primary forms. The procedure is described in more detail below.

The constituent analysis has been done from two ends. For top down processing, the text has been divided using principles of gross chunking. For bottom up processing, relationships between colons (Greek linguistic sentences) and paragraphs have been considered. This is often known as micro-segmentation. A constituent display for selected passages has been prepared and from this work a preliminary salience chart for Greek hortatory text has been prepared. Ideally, material that is higher up on the salience chart should be given prominence in the constituent analysis.

A clause chart for the text of 1 Cor was prepared according to the layout shown in Figure 7.1. The passage from 1 Cor 2:1 is given to demonstrate how the chart is prepared. Information from the chart was entered into a database.

Notes	conjunct-tion	preceding dependent	independent	following dependent
sV V- ViO	1 Κἀγὼ	ἐλθὼν πρὸς ὑμᾶς, ἀδελφοί,	ἦλθον οὐ καθ᾽ ὑπεροχὴν λόγου ἢ σοφίας	 καταγγέλλων ὑμῖν τὸ μυστήριον τοῦ θεοῦ.

Figure 7.1: 1 Corinthians 2:1

That database contains information on twenty-six variables plus two other items for each clause of 1 Cor. Using the database, as well as a Greek concordance, a search is then made for markers of peak and for features (both at the clause and discourse levels) which control word ordering. Specifically, preliminary research has indicated that passive constructions and conditional sentences are found distributed throughout the letter in a manner which may indicate that the extent of their use or non-use was dependent upon whether Paul at any given point was responding to the Corinthians' letter to him or was responding

---

[2] Teun A. van Dijk, *Text and Context* (Longman, 1977), 144–146; Robert E. Longacre, "Macrostructures" in class Discourse Grammar (lecture delivered at University of Texas at Arlington, Arlington, TX, April 12, 1990).

to a report which he had received by word of mouth. Further study has been done to determine whether this distribution of these features is statistically significant and whether there are other features that show the same distributional patterns.

Macrostructure

The presupposition behind the search for macrostructures is that, for any given well-structured discourse, there exists an overall idea that the author of the text has in mind as he produces it. To the extent that the text is well-formed, that controlling idea is reproduced in the mind of the receiver as he reads or listens to the text. It is the macrostructure which is identified when a person gives a brief summary of the discourse. Where a text contains several loosely related discourses, each discourse will have its own macrostructure.

Van Dijk has suggested four procedures for isolating the macrostructure of a given discourse.[3] The first may be called *attributive deletion*, in which attributes and other less important parts of the text are irrecoverably deleted. The second may be called *predictive deletion*, in which information is deleted that is inductively recoverable. The third may be called *simple generalization*, in which information is grouped and replaced by a more generic term. The fourth may be called *integration*, in which descriptions of processes are combined into a more general term, which entails all of the processes.

Ideally, such a procedure should yield something like the thesis of the discourse, which most readers would intuitively arrive at by reading the discourse. For a lengthy discourse, however, this procedure can be quite tedious. With this in mind, a shortcut proposed by Robert Longacre can be taken.[4] Longacre has noted that the most important material for any given discourse is usually encoded in a given mode and/or tense. A chain of these tenses he calls *mainline* (*storyline* in narrative; *themeline* in other texttypes). For example, in Greek narrative text, the storyline is usually given in the aorist tense. For hortatory text, the themeline is marked by the imperative (and other methods of encoding command forms).

In this study, the following methodology has been chosen for determining the macrostructure. First, the text was divided into its major sections using both conceptual (topical) and grammatical (syntactic) concerns. Next, hortatory forms (imperative, hortatory subjunctive, and statements containing words such as *appeal* and *ought*) were identified for each section. Third, using topic sentences, key words, and the hortatory themeline, the key ideas were abstracted

---

[3] Van Dijk, *Text and Context*, 144–146.
[4] Longacre, "Macrostructures."

from the text. Then, these were reduced to macrostructural statements for each section. Finally, an attempt was made to combine these macrostructures into one overall macrostructure.

An Overall Macrostructure

The body of the letter of 1 Cor is composed of ten discourses, whose main topics are division (chs. 1–4), fornication (chs. 5–6), marriage (ch. 7), food offered to idols (chs. 8–10), head coverings (ch. 11), the Lord's Supper (ch. 11), spiritual gifts (chs. 12–14), the resurrection from the dead (ch. 15), the contribution for the saints (ch. 16), and the coming of Apollos (ch. 16). The question can be raised as to whether 1 Cor has an overall macrostructure. An analysis shows that the macrostructures of the various discourses are so diverse that no single macro-structure can be constructed for the whole book. There is a theme of Christ over culture that is found in nine of the ten discourses, but the element of cultural beliefs and practices is abstracted from studies of ancient literature and not from the writing itself.

The Macrostructures of the Discourses

From the argument summaries and listings of key ideas described in the next section, we can abstract a macrostructure for each of the ten discourses and the conclusion in 1 Cor. They are as follows:

Discourse 1 (1:10–4:17): I appeal to you to avoid division and strife due to fol-lowing men (Paul, Apollos, and Cephas), for such boasting is due to the wisdom of men, but in God's wisdom they are servants of Christ.

Discourse 2 (4:18–6:20): Flee fornication and lawsuits with one another, and deliver an incestuous fornicator to Satan.

Discourse 3 (7:1–40): Let everyone remain in the marital status in which he was when called, but it is not a sin to get married if an unmarried person cannot control his passions.

Discourse 4 (8:1–11:1): Do not eat meat offered to idols in an idol's temple, for this is not a right but idolatry and can lead a weak brother into sin; but eat meat bought at the meat market or at a friend's dinner without asking any questions.

Discourse 5 (11:2–16): A man ought not cover his head when he prays or prophesies, but a woman should.

Discourse 6 (11:17–34): When you meet to eat the Lord's Supper, wait for one another and remember the body and blood of the Lord.

Discourse 7 (12:1–14:40): Seek spiritual gifts, especially prophecy, which builds up the church, but above all, show love.

Discourse 8 (15:1–58): Just as Christ was raised from the dead, so you should believe that Christians will be raised at His coming with a spiritual body.

Discourse 9 (16:1–11): Every Sunday let each of you put something aside and store it up for the contribution for the saints at Jerusalem. I will come after Pentecost, and Timothy will come now.

Discourse 10 (16:12): Apollos will not come now.

Conclusion (16:13–18): Be subject to and acknowledge those workers who have devoted themselves to the service of the saints.

Microstructures

The Hortatory Distribution in the Letter

The letter as a whole may be treated as being a hortatory text, but the hortatory sections are not distributed uniformly throughout the letter. Shorter discourses, such as those on head coverings and the contribution, show hortatory sections throughout. In the same way, the chiastic discourse on marriage has commands in all three chiastic sections. The chiastic discourse on fornication and lawsuits has overt command forms only in the first and last sections on fornication. The hortatory force in the inner section on lawsuits is mitigated to rhetorical questions. With the exception of the appeals at the beginning (1:10) and end (4:16) of the first discourse, most of the hortatory forms there are found in the inner section of the second chiastic set about wisdom and division. Three discourses (the longer chiastic ones about meat offered to idols and spiritual gifts, and the shorter one about the Lord's Supper) have the hortatory section reserved until the last part of the discourse. The only hortatory material in the discourse about the resurrection are admonitions not to sin (15:33–34) and to remain steadfast (15:58). Both of these are in result sections that follow from the main point: that of believing in the resurrection of the dead. This discourse is primarily persuasive in nature rather than hortatory, and even then its call to belief is mitigated to a rhetorical question (15:12).

The Argument Summaries and Key Ideas of the Discourses

In the first discourse (1:10–4:17) after beginning with an appeal for the Corinthians to be united, Paul makes two main arguments. The first is that it is human wisdom, not divine, which leads people to be puffed up and boast in men. The second is that the men they are boasting in are merely servants of God and are not to be followed themselves. Rather than saying "I belong to" some man, the Corinthians should realize that they all belong to Christ (3:22).

The key ideas of the first discourse can be summarized as follows: I appeal to you by the name of Christ that all of you agree and that there be no divisions among you (1:10). In God's wisdom, the foolishness of preaching Christ crucified is wiser than the wisdom of men, so that no person might boast (1:21, 23, 25, 29). We impart a secret hidden wisdom of God revealed through the Spirit (2:7, 10). While there is jealousy and strife among you, you are fleshly, not spiritual (3:1, 3). Apollos and Paul are servants: farmers and builders for God (3:5, 6, 9, 10). The wisdom of this world is foolishness with God, so let no one boast of men, for you all belong to Christ (3:19, 21, 23). We are servants of Christ and stewards of God's mysteries (4:1). Do not be puffed up in favor of one against another or boast as if you have things you did not receive (4:6, 7).

The second discourse (4:18–6:20) begins with a rebuke because one of the Corinthian Christians is living with his father's wife (probably the man's stepmother). Paul commands that the offender should be delivered to Satan. The discourse then turns to the problem created when the Corinthian Christians sued one another in public lawsuit. Paul suggests that the church should decide such disputes; otherwise, it would be better to suffer loss. Paul ends the discourse with an admonition against fornication.

The key ideas of the second discourse can be summarized as follows: Deliver the man who is living with his father's wife to Satan (5:1, 5). When one of you has a grievance against another, he should not go to law before unbelievers instead of before the saints (6:1). The unrighteous will not inherit the kingdom of God (6:9). Flee fornication, for our body is meant for the Lord, not for a prostitute, and we are united to the Lord by the Holy Spirit in our body (6:13, 18, 19).

The third discourse (7:1–40), on marriage, seems to be in answer to a couple of questions which the Corinthians had written in their letter. Paul argues that it is best for each one to stay either married or unmarried, as they were when they became Christians. He states that celibacy can lead to a more productive Christian life than marriage, but celibacy is not for everyone. Therefore it is no sin to get married.

The key ideas of the third discourse can be summarized as follows: A husband and wife should have sex with each other to avoid fornication (7:2, 3, 5). It is best for the unmarried to remain so if they can practice self-control (7:8). The

Lord says a husband and wife should not separate (7:10). Everyone should remain in the state in which he was called (7:20). The unmarried should not seek marriage, but if passions are strong, let them marry; it is not a sin (7:25–26, 36).

The fourth discourse (8:1–11:1) is on eating meat offered to idols. This also seems to be in answer to the Corinthians' questions. He argues first of all that one must not use his Christian liberty in such a way as to lead a weaker brother into sin. Next he discusses the right he has as an apostle to be supported by the church and how he has given up this right for the sake of the gospel, implying that the Corinthians should not insist on their rights either. In ch. 10 he argues from Old Testament examples that idolatry must not be practiced. Then he argues that a Christian cannot share in the Lord's Supper and in an idol's sacrifice also, for to do so is in fact to share in the worship of demons. He summarizes by giving specific examples which show that it is not wrong to eat meat if one does not realize that it has been sacrificed to idols.

The key ideas of the fourth discourse can be summarized as follows: Take care lest the liberty which you have because of your knowledge that an idol is nothing does not cause a weak brother to fall into sin (8:4, 9). I have not made use of my right to make a living by preaching the gospel, so that I might win people for Christ (9:14, 15, 19). Do not be idolaters, but be warned by the example of what happened to the Israelites (10:6, 7). Flee from idolatry, for when you eat food offered to idols you share with demons rather than with the table of the Lord (10:14, 20, 21). Eat meat sold in the meat market or at a friend's dinner without raising questions, unless someone says, "This has been offered in sacrifice" (10:25, 27, 28).

The fifth discourse (11:2–16) on head coverings contains five arguments as to why women should cover their heads when they pray or prophesy and men should not. First Paul argues that Christ is the head of man and man is the head of woman. Then he argues from the creation that woman was created from and for man. His third argument ("because of the angels") is obscure, but perhaps refers to the belief that angels are present in worship. The next argument is from the lesson of nature. And his final argument is that the churches of God have no such custom as women praying bareheaded. From his use of the word "anyone" in 11:16, it would seem that the problem was not extensive.

The key ideas of the fifth discourse can be summarized as follows: A man ought not cover his head when he prays or prophesies, because to do so would dishonor Christ, while a woman ought to cover her head, lest she dishonor her man (11:4, 5, 7, 10).

The sixth discourse on the Lord's Supper (11:17–34), on the other hand, deals with a more extensive problem. Here, in contrast to v. 2, Paul writes "I do not commend you." He begins with an admonition not to use the Lord's Supper as a time for satisfying hunger and thirst. He then gives an account of Jesus institut-ing the Lord's Supper. Next, he admonishes them to examine themselves before they eat, and closes with instructions to wait for one another and satisfy their hunger at home.

The key ideas of the sixth discourse can be summarized as follows: When you meet to eat the Lord's Supper, wait for one another, and remember the body and blood of the Lord Jesus, as He said (11:20, 24, 25, 33).

The seventh discourse (12:1–14:40) is on the proper place of spiritual gifts. Paul begins with the argument that all the gifts come from the same Spirit of God. The gifts are different, but by analogy with the human body, he shows that all are needed. He next argues that love is more important than any of the spiritual gifts. Then he contrasts prophecy and speaking in tongues, and concludes with instructions regulating the use of spiritual gifts in the assembly.

The key ideas of the seventh discourse (12:1–14:40) can be summarized as follows: Just as the body is one and has many members, so you are one body in Christ, with each person having gifts given by the Spirit for the common good (12:4, 7, 12, 27). Love, which remains, is greater than the spiritual gifts, which will pass away (13:8, 13). Seek spiritual gifts, especially prophecy, which is greater than speaking in tongues, because it builds up the church (14:1, 5, 12). All things should be done decently and in order, which means that those who speak in tongues without an interpreter, and women, should keep silent in the assembly (14:28, 34, 40).

The eighth discourse (15:1–58) is on the resurrection from the dead. Some of the Corinthians were following Greek philosophy by saying that there will be no resurrection from the dead (15:12). Paul begins by arguing from the reality of Christ's resurrection. He repeats the Christian tradition that the death, burial, resurrection, and appearances of Christ are of first importance. Then he demonstrates that the resurrection of Christ is tied to the resurrection of Christians at Christ's coming. He next discusses the nature of the resurrection body. He writes of the events of the second coming and concludes with praise to God.

The key ideas of the eighth discourse can be summarized as follows: Just as Christ was raised from the dead, so at His coming all who belong to Him will be made alive (15:20, 22, 23). Unlike our physical body, the body which is raised will be imperishable, glorious, powerful, spiritual, and immortal (15:42–44, 53).

The ninth discourse (16:1–11) concerns the contribution for the saints. In four verses he encourages the Corinthians to put some money aside every Sunday for this purpose. If the gift they collect is worthwhile, he will accompany their representatives when they take it to Jerusalem. The letter continues with travel plans for Paul and Timothy.

The key ideas of the ninth discourse can be summarized as follows: Each of you should put something aside and store it up for the contribution for the saints at Jerusalem (16:1, 2). I will come visit you after Pentecost and spend some time with you (16:5, 7, 8). Welcome Timothy and send him back to me (16:10, 11).

The final discourse (16:12) is merely a statement that Apollos will not come at this time. After concluding exhortations, he commends Stephanas and Fortunatus and Achaicus. The letter closes with greetings and a postscript in Paul's own handwriting.

The key ideas of the tenth discourse and conclusion can be summarized as follows: Apollos will come when he has an opportunity, but not now (16:12). Be subject to and acknowledge those workers who have devoted themselves to the service of the saints (16:15, 16, 18).

Other Discourse Considerations

The Structure of the Letter

As noted above, the body of the letter of 1 Cor is composed of ten discourses, whose main topics are division (chs. 1–4), fornication (chs. 5–6), marriage (ch. 7), food offered to idols (chs. 8–10), head coverings (ch. 11), the Lord's Supper (ch. 11), spiritual gifts (chs. 12–14), the resurrection from the dead (ch. 15), the contribution for the saints (ch. 16), and the coming of Apollos (ch. 16). The discourses on marriage, meat offered to idols, spiritual gifts, and the contribution seem to be written in answer to the Corinthians' letter. The discourses on division, fornication, head coverings, the Lord's Supper, and the resurrection seem to have arisen from reports brought by some members of Chloe's household (1:11) and by Stephanas, Fortunatus, and Achaicus (16:17). There are indications of oral reports also in 5:1, 11:18, and 15:12, although there is no indication of the source of this information.

The discourse on marriage actually seems to be in answer to two questions (7:1, 25). However, the responses to both are similar, and it seems best to treat this as one discourse.

The motivation for the order in which the subjects are addressed is not entirely evident. Presumably the subjects that are introduced by περὶ δέ ("now concerning") are in the same order as in the Corinthians' letter, although even this is not certain. The sections on fornication and marriage are found together, probably because both have to do with sexual issues. In the same way, the worship concerns of head coverings, the Lord's Supper, and use of spiritual gifts are grouped together, even though the first two interrupt what would have been a continuous reply to the Corinthians' letter. Perhaps the lengthy treatment given the subject of division, the back reference to that subject in 11:18, and the primary place accorded it indicate that it was foremost in Paul's mind. In the same way, the ordering of the discourse on the resurrection as the last major discussion may indicate its importance, although it is possible that the contribution received only four verses of attention due to constraints imposed by the size of the scroll on which the letter was written (note that the subject merits two chapters in 2 Cor). But Paul may have seen the end of the scroll coming and decided to address the question of the resurrection before he ran out of room.

Now this study takes the position that only those sections that are introduced by περὶ δέ ("now concerning") are in fact Paul's answers to the Corinthians' letter. All other sections are in response to oral reports which Paul received from various sources. However, this position is not universally accepted. In perhaps the most significant study dealing with this question, Hurd has argued that some of the sections which do not begin with "now concerning" are also answers to questions in the Corinthians' letter.[5] These sections include 5:9–13a, 6:12–20, 11:2–16, and 15:1–58.[6] Let us examine each of these in more detail.

First, John Hurd argues that 5:9–13a (on not associating with fornicators) can perhaps be considered as material dealing with the written questions in the letter from the Corinthians.[7] Hurd admits that these verses occur within "the context of Paul's discussion of oral information."[8] But he argues that "this item was not based on an item of information connected with the news concerning the incestuous man and is thus free of its present context";[9] thus, since it contains information about Paul's previous letter, it can be considered to be a part of the material in the epistolary dialogue between Paul and the Corinthians. Now, it is not the purpose of this study to deny that these verses shed light on that dialogue. But there is a great deal of difference between verses shedding light on a previous stage of a dialogue and being in response to the latest stage of that dialogue. Even though Paul refers to his previous letter (5:9–11), he does not suggest that the Corinthians had written back disputing his instructions. Rather, he is here pointing out that the instructions that he has just given regarding the incestuous man are nothing new—in a general statement he said the same thing in his previous letter. The incestuous man belonged to the class "fornicator" discussed in 5:9–11 and the class "those inside the church" in 5:12 and thus is still under discussion in vv. 5:9–12a. These verses are thus properly included with the material written in response to oral reports.

Second, Hurd argues that 6:12–20 (the last major paragraph on fornication) is transitional between the responses to oral material and those to the Corinthians' letter.[10] He well points out that these verses prefigure several sections which come later in this letter: the Old Testament quotation "the two shall become one

---

[5] John C. Hurd, Jr., *The Origin of 1 Corinthians*, 2nd ed. (Mercer University Press, 1983), 93.

[6] Ibid.

[7] Ibid., 83.

[8] Ibid.

[9] Ibid.

[10] Ibid., 86–89.

flesh" (6:16; from Gen 2:24) foreshadows the discussion on marriage in ch. 7; the maxim "all things are lawful for me" and the reference to food (6:12–13) foreshadow the discussion of food offered to idols in chs. 8–10; the terminology "members of Christ" (6:15) anticipates that used in ch. 12; and in these verses is the first reference to the resurrection (6:14), a theme given fuller expression in ch. 15.[11] In addition, Fee notes that the verb form (ἐξουσιάζω) of the word for 'rights' or 'authority' (ἐξουσία) is found in this section.[12] The concept of "rights" is found again in ch. 9 and mentioned as "authority" in 11:10. That these verses contain transitional elements is not here denied; however, it may be the case that Paul is using many different persuasive techniques here that he later repeats on other topics. The sexual overtones of the one flesh quote can fit the topic of fornication as well as marriage. The resurrection is a common theme that occurs often in many parts of Paul's letters, not just in foreshadowing a major chapter on the subject. The expression "members of Christ" is similar to the concept of members of the body of Christ in ch. 12, but there the emphasis is on the body as being the church, while that concept is absent here. Certainly the semantic domains covered by ἐξουσία ("authority, rights") in chs. 9 and 11 are different from that covered by the verb form here, where it means something like *overpowered* or *mastered*.[13]

In addition, there is little or no evidence that these verses in ch. 6 were written in response to a question about fornication in the Corinthians' letter. To be sure, the two maxims "all things are lawful for me" (6:12) and "food for the stomach and the stomach for food" (6:13) are thought by many scholars to be sayings of the Corinthians that could have been in their letter.[14] The first is repeated in 10:23 in a section that is definitely written in response to the Corinthians' question about food offered to idols. Since the second also talks about food, it is possible that both maxims were in the Corinthians' letter, but in the section on food offered to idols rather than part of a question about fornication.

Actually, these verses function as a section providing justification for the command to deliver the incestuous man to Satan that Paul has given in 5:3–5. They are showing that fornication is wrong for a Christian. On this, Fee comments: "This is the standard view, found in most of the older commentaries. After an aside over the matter of lawsuits, Paul returns to the issue of sexual immorality from 5:1–13, for which he is now giving a general theological argument."[15]

---

[11] Ibid., 87–88.

[12] Gordon D. Fee, *Commentary on the First Epistle to the Corinthians*, NICNT (Eerdmans, 1987), 252.

[13] W. F. Bauer, W. F. Arndt, and F. W. Gingrich, *A Greek-English Lexicon of the New Testament and Other Early Christian Literature*, 1st ed. (University of Chicago, 1957), s.v. ἐξουσιάζω.

[14] Hurd, *The Origin of 1 Corinthians*, 67–68, 86–87.

[15] Fee, *First Epistle to the Corinthians*, 250.

While there seem to be elements that reflect statements in the Corinthians' letter in 6:12–20, the section itself is better viewed as being written in response to
an oral report that Paul had received.

Third, Hurd argues that 11:2–16 are written in response to a question in the
Corinthians' letter about head coverings, and with this Fee agrees.[16] Now many
commentators have seen 11:2 as a reflection of a statement of the Corinthians'
letter,[17] and this same position is adopted in the reconstructed letter found in
chapter two of my dissertation.[18] Most likely their letter contained a sentence
that said something like, "Now we remember you in everything and maintain the
traditions even as you have delivered them to us." As Fee notes, "how does he
know that they have 'kept the traditions' (v. 2) unless they have so expressed
themselves, most likely in their letter?"[19] In saying that this section is in response
to the Corinthians' letter, Hurd appeals to Faw's notion that δέ can introduce a
response to a letter just like περὶ δέ can.[20] The problem with Faw's position is
that not only do the sections in response to the letter begin with the postpositive
conjunction δε, so do sections like 1:10 and 11:17, which are stated to be a reaction
of a report received by Paul. In fact, with the possible exception of the second
discourse, all the discourses in 1 Cor begin with δέ, whether in response to oral
reports or to the Corinthians' letter. And if, as suggested below, the transitional
paragraph in 4:18–21 about Paul's travel plans should be taken with the second
discourse rather than the first, all discourses begin with δέ. But whether it is all
sections or just all but one, the fact that 11:2 contains a δέ is hardly an argument
in favor of the section being in response to the Corinthians' letter.

Certainly it is possible that after mentioning that they keep the traditions,
the Corinthians went on to say something like, "But we want to know why our
women cannot keep our Greek custom of uncovering their heads when they
pray?" At least three factors make this unlikely, however. First, he seems to pair
11:2–16 and 11:17–34 with "I praise you" (v. 2) and "I do not praise" (v. 17). The second of these two sections is stated as being in response to a report that Paul had
heard (11:18). Without any indication of a question by the Corinthians in 11:2–16,
it seems better to take this paired section as also a response to an oral report.
Also, the particle δέ seems to have an adversative sense "but" in 11:17.[21] Even
though Paul can praise them as a group for keeping the traditions, he has some
teaching to give on a subject that "someone" (τις) is being contentious about

---

[16] Hurd, *The Origin of 1 Corinthians*, 90–91; Fee, *Commentary*, 492.

[17] Hurd, *The Origin of 1 Corinthians*, 68.

[18] Terry, "An Analysis of Certain Features," 35–36; Terry, *A Discourse Analysis*, 19–20.

[19] Fee, *First Epistle to the Corinthians*, 491.

[20] Hurd, *The Origin of 1 Corinthians*, 90; Chalmer E. Faw, "On the Writing of First Thessalonians," *JBL* 71 (1952): 221.

[21] Fee, *First Epistle to the Corinthians*, 500–501.

(v. 16). Unlike the situation with the Lord's Supper, the problem is not extensive, and so the indefinite singular τις is used. How could Paul have known that there was only 'someone' advocating the abandonment of the Christian tradition unless he had been told? Finally, to reference the research presented in chapter five of my dissertation, the grammatical variables studied as a part of style are more like those in chs. 1–6 than like those in chs. 7–10.[22] Thus it is more likely that the specific issue of head coverings was something that Paul had heard about due to an oral report.

The final passage that does not start with περὶ δέ that Hurd argues is in response to the Corinthians' letter is 15:1–58.[23] Hurd notes that Paul "explicitly refers to at least one question that the Corinthians were asking: 'How can some of you say there is no resurrection of the dead?' (15:12)."[24] But this is not a question from the Corinthians; rather, it is a statement which 'some' (τινες) among them were making. Just as in the discussion of 11:2–16, how could Paul have known that this was the statement of some of the Corinthians without an oral report to that effect? Rather than 15:12 indicating a question in the Corinthians' letter, it provides evidence that Paul had information about the situation of a kind that does not come in letters but is transmitted in oral reports. As for Hurd's contention that the text is logical and persuasive like his answers to the Corinthians' letter,[25] suffice it to say that this is entirely due to the fact that the chapter is trying to effect a change of belief, not a change of behavior. The material is presented using persuasive texttype rather than hortatory, and this is sufficient to account for the perceived differences.

With these points in mind, it seems fair to say that it is best to treat only those sections which are introduced by περὶ δέ ("now concerning") as replies to questions in the Corinthians' letter and the other sections as responses to oral information which Paul had received. When this is done, the letter divides nicely into a cyclical structure of ABA'B'A"B", where A is a response to oral reports and B is a response to the Corinthians' letter. This is shown clearly in Figure 7.2. First, two subjects are covered in response to oral reports; then there are two subjects in response to their letter. This is followed by a two-one-one-two pattern of two responses to oral reports, one to the letter, one to an oral report, and two to the letter. The motivation for this pattern is not clear, although it may provide groupings of related topics (discourses 2 and 3 on sex; 4, 5, and 6 on pagan worship forms; and 6 and 7 on the Christian assembly). In addition, Paul's travel plans are found both between the first two discourses and the last two discourses.

---

[22] Terry, "An Analysis of Certain Features," 265–273; Terry, *A Discourse Analysis*, 159–164.
[23] Hurd, *The Origin of 1 Corinthians*, 91–92.
[24] Ibid., 91.
[25] Ibid.

If the division defended below and indicated in Figure 7.2 is correct, these travel plans are found at the beginning of the second discourse and the end of the next to last discourse, showing an even greater balance in the overall structure of the book.

Paul's Use of Chiasmus in Major Sections

Several of the discourses in 1 Cor show chiasmus of major sections in the form ABA'. The B section in these discourses has often been mistakenly identified as a digression or excursus.[26] For the moment skipping the discourse in chs. 1 through 4, we find this feature in the discourses in 4:18–6:20 (fornication, lawsuits, fornication), 7:1–40 (marriage, circumcision and slavery, marriage), 8:1–11:1 (eating meat offered to idols, right of the teacher to receive pay, eating meat offered to idols), and 12:1–14:40 (spiritual gifts, love, spiritual gifts).[27] In the latter three, a transition is made that ties the second subject in with the first in such a way that the second subject actually becomes an argument for the first. Failure to note the unity and chiastic structure of chs. 8 through 10 have led to the misunderstanding that Paul is allowing freedom to eat meat offered to idols. Chapter 8 cannot correctly be seen as independent of ch. 10. The whole thrust of the section is to confirm the ruling of the apostolic decision at Jerusalem in Acts 15, albeit presented in a persuasive way, rather than as authoritarian dogma. The relationship between fornication and lawsuits is not so obvious, although it may have been to the first readers.[28] Perhaps the lawsuits were over problems aggravated by fornication. Richardson lists eight possible scenarios for this possibility, but it remains precisely that, only a possibility.[29] More likely, the section on lawsuits is establishing the church's right to judge the offender (cf. 5:12, "those inside the church whom you are to judge").

In the same way the first discourse shows a form of chiasmus with the topics of division and wisdom, although the form is not the simple ABA'. These topics are combined with the topic of servanthood (introduced in 3:5) to form a double chiasmus. The chiasmus may be charted in the following way:

First set: division, wisdom, division (1:10–3:4)
Second set: servanthood, wisdom and division, servanthood (3:5–4:17).

---

[26] Donald Guthrie, *New Testament Introduction*, 3rd ed. (InterVarsity, 1970), 425; Paul Feine, Johannes Behm, and Werner Georg Kümmel, *Introduction to the New Testament*, trans. A. J. Mattill, Jr., 14th rev. ed. (Abingdon Press, 1966), 198–199; John Morgan-Wynne, "Introduction to 1 Corinthians," *SwJT* 26 (1983): 7.

[27] Nigel Turner, *Style*, vol. 4 of *A Grammar of New Testament Greek* (T&T Clark, 1976), 97.

[28] Guthrie, *New Testament Introduction*, 444.

[29] Peter Richardson, "Judgment, Immorality, and Sexual Ethics in 1 Corinthians 6," in *SBL 1980 Seminar Papers*, ed. Paul J. Achtemeier (Scholars Press, 1980), 347–348.

When this is done, the structure of the first discourse shows the double chiastic form of ABA' C(A"/B')C'.

Ch.	Response to Oral Report	Response to Letter
1	Introduction (1:1–9)	
	1. Church Division (1:10–4:17)	
	A. Division (1:10–17)	
2	B. Wisdom (1:18–2:16)	
· 3	A'. Division (3:1–4)	
	C. Servanthood (3:5–15)	
	D. Wisdom & Division (3:16–23)	
4	C'. Servanthood (4:1–17)	
	2. Fornication (4:18–6:20)	
	Travel Plans (4:18–21)	
5	A. Fornication (5)	
6	B. Lawsuits (6:1–8)	
	A'. Fornication (6:9–20)	
7		**3. Marriage (7)**
		A. Marriage (7:1–16)
		B. Circumcision & Slavery (7:17–24)
		A'. Marriage (7:25–40)
8		**4. Idol Food (8:1–11:1)**
		A. Idol Food (8:1–13)
9		B. Rights (9:1–27)
10		A'. Idol Food (10:1–11:1)
11	**5. Head Coverings (11:2–16)**	
	6. The Lord's Supper (11:17–34)	
12		**7. Spiritual Gifts* (12–14)**
		A. Spiritual Gifts (12)
13		B. Love (13)
14		A'. Spiritual Gifts (14)
15	**8. The Resurrection* (15)**	
	A. The Resurrection (15:1–32)	
16		**9. Contribution** (16:1–4)
		Travel Plans (16:5–11)
		10. Apollos (16:12)
	Conclusion (16:13–24)	

Figure 7.2: Discourse Structure of 1 Corinthians. * Discourses 7 and 8 are peak sections foreshadowed by the thanksgiving in 1:4–9.

The Unity of the Fourth Discourse

In the preceding section it was suggested that chs. 8 and 10 cannot be correctly understood as independent of one another. Before going further, it is necessary to examine this more closely since in fact many scholars have understood them, not only as independent, but even as contradictory. Hurd notes that a small number of scholars have divided the text of 1 Cor into two or three letters based primarily on what they see as instances of Paul changing his mind about what he should teach on the subject of food offered to idols.[30] The material in 1 Cor 10:1–22 is obviously opposed to eating meat offered to idols, first comparing it to idolatry in the Old Testament and then comparing it to sharing food with demons. This would seem to be in accord with the Apostolic Decree of Acts 15 which forbade Christians from eating food offered to idols.[31] On the other hand, the last verses of 1 Cor 10 give times when it is not wrong to eat food offered to idols (when it is bought in the meat market and when it is served by a friend at a private meal). In addition, 1 Cor 8 is often interpreted as accepting the Corinthians' argument that it is all right in itself to eat food offered to idols, but Paul argues that one must be careful in doing so not to lead a weaker brother into sin. Chapter 9 is then interpreted as a defense of Paul's apostleship because he is flying in the face of the Apostolic Decree and has to establish his right to do so.[32]

All of this is to miss the force of Paul's argument. This section deals with three different situations regarding meat offered to idols in which two principles of Christianity seem to be at odds. These two principles are that Christians are not to take part in the worship of idols and that Jesus declared all foods clean for Christians to eat. The three situations are eating idol-food in an idol's temple, at a private meal given by a non-Christian friend, and at home using food bought in the meat market. Paul argues that the latter principle takes precedence in regards to food purchased in the meat market and found on the table at a friend's house, unless of course the friend wants to make it a matter of accepting the worship of idols.

But in the situation of eating meat in an idol's temple, where the worship of an idol could be seen as being in the fore, Paul gives four arguments to support the claim that the former principle takes precedence: 1) the person eating with knowledge that an idol has no real existence may lead a weaker brother who does not know this into sin (8:1–13); 2) Paul himself has set an example of giving up his own rights for the sake of the gospel, and the Corinthians should do likewise (9:1–27); 3) the Old Testament forbids idolatry (10:1–13), and 4) one cannot eat both the Lord's Supper at the Lord's table and idol-meat at a demon's table

---

[30] Hurd, *The Origin of 1 Corinthians*, 44–45, 69–70.

[31] Charles Kingsley Barrett, "Things Sacrificed to Idols," *NTS* 11 (1965): 138–144.

[32] Ibid., 150.

without making God jealous (10:14–22). The latter two arguments in 10:1–22 are obviously opposed to the eating of meat in the temple of an idol. But the first two arguments are not so easily understood. Paul uses a conditional approach: he introduces the Corinthians' position in 8:1–6 and seems to accept it as valid for the moment. That is, Paul begins by taking the Corinthians' arguments and saying in effect, "Let's assume for a minute that you are right, that if you are not personally worshiping the idol, then you have a right to eat food offered to that idol, even in its temple." Even so, he goes on to argue, there are two problems with eating food offered to an idol: a weaker brother may be made to sin, and a Christian should be willing to give up rights for the sake of the gospel. Having noted these problems that come with accepting the Corinthians' position, he goes on in ch. 10 to argue that it is in fact wrong to eat meat in an idol's temple. When the reader sees that Paul is only conditionally accepting the Corinthians' proposition that he later tears down, it becomes clear that all four arguments are points against the Corinthians' position and in accord with the Apostolic Degree of Acts 15.

Now Paul does not explicitly state that at first he is for the moment assuming the Corinthians' argument to be valid, which is the cause for the usual misunderstanding by many scholars. As Westerners, most Bible scholars are looking for explicit markers to lay out an argument in unambiguous terms. The Oriental approach, however, is much more subtle: the listener or reader is given the argument, but is supposed to figure out what the speaker or writer is saying and what the relationship is between the parts of the discourse. As Orientals, the Hebrews often used such an approach in the Old Testament, where the setting is missing from passages and transitions are made from one item to another without explicit conceptual markers showing the relationship. But this is not just a Jewish feature of rhetoric. In speaking of Greek style, Demetrius refers to Theophrastus as his authority "that not all possible points should be punctiliously and tediously elaborated, but some should be left to the comprehension and inference of the hearer."[33] To understand the relationship requires induction on the part of the reader.

The Endings of Two Discourses

In a couple of places it is questionable whether chapter beginnings actually mark the beginnings of the major embedded discourses. It is generally agreed that 11:1 is the last statement of the discussion on meat offered to idols rather than the first on the subject of head coverings.[34] In the same way, there is some

---

[33] Demetrius, *On Style* IV [§222].

[34] Leon Morris, *The First Epistle of Paul to the Corinthians,* TNTC 7 (Eerdmans, 1958), 150.

difficulty in knowing whether to assign the transitional verses 4:18–21 to the first or second discourse.

It is traditional among commentators to carry the discussion of the first discourse through 4:21 and begin the new discourse on fornication with 5:1. This view is not without its problems. Some commentators who take this view note that 5:1 begins abruptly[35] or *medias in res*[36] or as a "sudden bursting of the storm."[37] A few note either that the discourse should begin with 4:21,[38] or that 4:21 ties the two discourses together.[39] Fee notes that there are verbal "ties" between 4:18–20 and 5:2–6,[40] and Hurd lists 4:18–21 as a transitional passage.[41] Several ancient manuscripts marked 4:21 as beginning kephalaion 2 (an ancient system of chapters) while manuscript Vaticanus marked the new section as beginning with 4:16. Various manuscripts also began paragraphs either at 4:16, 17, or 18 as well as at 4:14 and 5:1 (see NA[23] and NA[26]).

If indeed the new discourse begins at 5:1 (or even at 4:21), this would be unique among the discourses of 1 Cor, for all the other discourses (1:10; 7:1; 8:1; 11:2; 11:17; 12:1; 15:1; 16:1; and 16:12) begin with a verse containing the conjunctive particle δέ 'now'. In addition, they all end with verses that contain a transitional particle, either δέ 'but' (7:40; 11:16; 11:34; 14:40; 16:12), ὥστε 'so' (11:33; 14:39), οὖν 'therefore' (10:31), or γάρ ... δή 'for ... but' (6:20). But neither 5:1 nor 4:21 contain inter-colon transitional conjunctions (4:21 does contain ἤ ("or") and 5:1 contains καί ("and"), but both connect clauses within a colon).

For the purposes of this analysis, it is suggested that the first discourse actually ends with 4:17 and the new discourse begins with 4:18. In favor of this are the following facts: First, the verses 4:18–21 are all on a single subject—Paul's proposed visit to Corinth. This subject is picked up again in 16:5–9. It hardly seems right to begin the new discourse in the middle of this subject. This small section can fit with either the preceding discourse or the following as far as content is concerned. But when put with the following discourse it provides a meaningful introduction to the stern words of ch. 5. Second, it also contains ideas elaborated

---

[35] G. G. Findlay, *St. Paul's First Epistle to the Corinthians*, EGT 2 (1897; repr., Eerdmans, 1979), 807; Morris, *The First Epistle*, 86.

[36] Richard C. H. Lenski, *The Interpretation of St. Paul's First and Second Epistle to the Corinthians* (Wartburg Press, 1946), 205.

[37] Thomas Charles Edwards, *A Commentary on the First Epistle to the Corinthians* (Hodder and Stoughton, 1885), 118; Archibald Robertson and Alfred Plummer, *A Critical and Exegetical Commentary on the First Epistle of St. Paul to the Corinthians*, ICC, 2nd ed. (T&T Clark, 1914), 95.

[38] John Calvin, *Commentary on the Epistles of Paul the Apostle to the Corinthians: Volume First*, trans. John Pringle (Eerdmans, 1948), 177.

[39] Henry Alford, *The New Testament for English Readers*, 4 vols. (Baker, 1983), 3:1000.

[40] Fee, *First Epistle to the Corinthians*, 194.

[41] Hurd, *The Origin of 1 Corinthians*, 89.

on in ch. 5: those of being puffed up (vv. 18–19) and having power (vv. 19–20). These words are picked up in 5:2 and 5:4, respectively. Third, it contains the phrase "kingdom of God," a term which is picked up again in 6:9–10. Fourth, beginning the discourse on fornication with 4:18 would make this discourse begin with a verse containing δέ 'now' and have the discourse on division end with verses containing οὖν 'therefore' (v. 16) and διὰ τοῦτο 'because of this' (v. 17). Fifth, commentators have noted the difference in tone between 4:14, where Paul is admonishing the Corinthians as children, and 4:21, where Paul is threatening to come against the arrogant with a whip.[42] And finally, vv. 16 and 17 contain similar ideas to those found in other verses that end discourses. The idea of imitating Paul in v. 16 also brings to a close the discourse on eating meat offered to idols in 11:1 and the idea of the practice of all the churches in 4:17 closes the discourse on head coverings in 11:16. Therefore it seems best to take the first discourse as ending at 4:17 and 4:18 beginning a transition into a new section. But however one divides the text at this point, it does not affect the macrostructure, for the material in the paragraph in question is merely transitional and not central to either section.

Peak

Sometime between the first and third centuries A.D., an unknown writer whom scholars have come to call "Longinus" wrote a treatise on Greek style entitled *On the Sublime*. In chs. 23 to 29 of that work, "Longinus" discusses techniques which lend variety and liveliness to a composition through grammatical changes. Among those changes which he discusses are the expansion of the singular into the plural to convey the idea of multitude, the contraction of the plural into the singular to give an effect of sublimity, the use of the present tense in narrating past time in order to increase vividness, the change of the person addressed from the whole audience to a single individual also to give a vivid effect, the use of the first person for one of the characters to show an outbreak of emotion, and the use of periphrasis or circumlocution to give the work a far richer note. His conclusion is that these techniques "all serve to lend emotion and excitement to the style" (LCL 199: 255).

Recently, linguistic study in discourse has found that techniques such as these are used, not only by the Greeks, but by storytellers around the world in many, if not all, of the world's languages. Longacre[43] has studied this phenomenon

---

[42] Kenneth E. Bailey, "The Structure of 1 Corinthians and Paul's Theological Method with Special Reference to 4:17," *NovT* 25 (1983): 162; Charles Kingsley Barrett, *A Commentary on the First Epistle to the Corinthians*, HNTC (Harper & Row, 1968), 117.

[43] Robert E. Longacre, "A Spectrum and Profile Approach to Discourse Analysis," *Text* 1, no. 4 (1981): 337–359; idem, "Discourse Peak as a Zone of Turbulence," in *Beyond the Sentence*, ed. J. Wirth (Karome, 1985), 81–92; idem, "Macrostructures"; idem, *The Grammar of Discourse*, 2nd ed. (Plenum, 1996).

of grammatical change to increase emotional effects and labeled it *peak*. The discussion in this chapter will center on the techniques for discovering the zone or zones of peak grammatical turbulence in 1 Cor and the significance of such zones for hortatory texttype.

There are a couple of features, which elsewhere seem to mark peak,[44] which do not seem productive in 1 Cor. One is the use of vocatives at other places than the beginning of paragraphs. Seven vocatives fall in this category. They are found in 1:11, 7:16 (2x), 7:24, 15:31, and 15:55 (2x). Of these, the one in 1:11 seems to be marking the beginning of the first discourse, the three in ch. 7 are found in the final colons of their paragraphs, and the two in 15:55 occur in a quotation. The one instance of a vocative in 15:31 without another explanation can hardly be said to be determinative of peak. The same can be said of the interjection ἰδού ("behold"). It occurs only once in 1 Corinthians, in 15:51. Even though these two items occur in the same chapter, two cases do not provide much evidence.

Actually, there are two aspects of peak which jump out at the reader who is on the lookout for a zone of grammatical turbulence in 1 Cor. First, the fact that ch. 15 is primarily persuasive rather than hortatory in nature is a rather obvious difference from the rest of the book. This is indicated primarily by a noticeable lack of imperatives, which serve as the mainline of hortatory text. Second, the reader may well note the large number of verbless clauses that begin to appear in the text beginning with ch. 12. These factors give an initial impression that the text from chs. 12 to 15 may contain peak material, but that impression must be checked out in a methodical manner to confirm it.

Figure 7.3 lists three variables for each chapter in the book of 1 Cor. First, the number of clauses for each of four types of texttype is given for each chapter. Those places where more than fifty occurrences of one texttype are found in a chapter are indicated by bold print. Of special note is the strong hortatory nature of chs. 7 and 14 and the strong persuasive nature of chs. 15.

The second variable studied is the clause ordering of verbs and objects across the chapters. Considering all kinds of clauses, objects are slightly more likely to precede verbs in 1 Cor than vice versa (by a count of 370 to 331). However, in seven chapters (1, 5, 8, 12, 13, 15, and 16) there are more clauses with objects following the verbs than vice versa. These have been indicated in bold in the clause order column of Figure 7.3. An application of the chi-square test to this data shows that this distribution is statistically significant, that is, there is less than a 5% probability that it would occur due to random distribution of objects and verbs. Some of this turbulence may be analogous to that found around an inciting incident in narrative, for chs. 1, 5, 8, and 12 all begin multi-chapter discourses;

---

[44] Ralph Bruce Terry, "Some Aspects of the Discourse Structure of James," *JOTT* 5, no. 2 (1992): 121–122.

the heavy distribution of VO clauses toward the end of the book, however, would seem to point to a peak area.

The third variable presented in Figure 7.3 is the number of verbless clauses. There are three kinds of verbless clauses in 1 Cor: implied, equative, and spread. In four cases (in 1:1, 4:6, 9:10, and 15:8) a verb is omitted from a clause, but it can be supplied from the context by implication. The most common situation is that forms of the equative verbs (εἰμί, "be," and γίνομαι, "be, become," often called *copulas*) may be omitted from equative clauses.[45] The remarkable thing about this omission is that chs. 12 and 15 show 19 and 35 instances of this feature, respectively. In fact, ch. 15 has three major spans of text with no verbs (vv. 38b–41, 45b–48, and 55–56). No other chapter shows more than 12 instances. The third kind of omission of the verb occurs in clauses where the verb would have been the same as the verb of the previous clause. The verb of the previous clause "spreads" across the following clause or clauses. Again, chs. 12 and 15 stand out with 9 and 7 instances of verb spreading, respectively.

Ch.	Texttype				Clause Order		# of Verbless Clauses		
	Hor.	Per.	Exp.	Nar.	VO%	OV%	Implied	Equative	Spread
1	4	28	47	1	68%	32%	1	12	
2	1	32		8	41%	59%		1	
3	17	33	18		40%	60%		7	1
4	72				39%	61%	1	7	1
5	26		8		58%	42%		2	1
6	61				40%	60%		4	
7	132		18		44%	56%		3	1
8	8	31	4		58%	42%		6	
9	18	71	13		39%	61%	1	1	6
10	69	21	4	8	38%	62%		4	1
11	84		15	12	42%	58%		11	3
12	1	54	33		53%	47%		19	9
13		53			57%	43%		4	1
14	131	1			38%	62%		7	
15	10	139	14	14	63%	37%	1	35	7
16	38		14	14	60%	40%		4	

Figure 7.3: Indicators of Peak in 1 Corinthians

---

[45] This situation is a well documented fact of Greek grammar. See BDF §127–128; A. T. Robertson, *A Grammar of the Greek New Testament in the Light of Historical Research* (Broadman, 1934), 395–396; Nigel Turner, *Syntax*, vol. 3 of *A Grammar of New Testament Greek* (T&T Clark, 1963), 294–298.

All of these factors seem to point toward chs. 12, 13, and 15 as showing a marked difference from the rest of the text. From a wave perspective, chs. 12 and 13 may be the peak for the discourses in response to the Corinthians' letter, while ch. 15 may be the peak for the discourses in response to the oral reports. But from a particle perspective, it seems advisable to hypothesize that the region also includes ch. 14 and thus take the zone of grammatical turbulence as covering chs. 12 through 15. This would be confirmed by the high degree of embedded chiasmus found in chs. 12–14 while studying the field perspective as found in the dissertation. With this in mind, the database of clauses in 1 Cor was set to compare grammatical structures in chs. 12 through 15 against the rest of the book. When this was done, the following variables showed a highly significant difference between the peak area and the rest of the book: sentence location, clause relationship, independent relationship, clause order type, verb mode, verb tense, verb voice, verb semantic type, subject type, subject person, texttype, and statement or question form. This means that for these variables there are such grammatical differences between the peak zone of chs. 12 through 15 and the rest of the book that there is less than .5% probability that such differences could be due to random distribution factors of these grammatical features. From this list, the twenty-one most significant factors in causing these differences have been gathered in Figure 7.4.

This is not to imply that all of these factors are uniformly distributed across the peak zone. The aorist tense is still used in the peak area, but notably less frequently than in non-peak areas. But toward the end of ch. 15, from verses 38 through 48, there is a small region of very little verb use at all. Only fifteen verbs are used at all in these eleven verses, and only two (13.3%) of them are aorist. The distribution of tense is not uniform.

There is also a greater use of passive voice verbs in the peak area than in the letter as a whole. But closer examination reveals that this greater use is limited to ch. 15, where 35.9% of the verbs are in the passive voice, while chs. 12 through 14 show a 10.7% use of passive voice verbs, which is less than the average percentage of passive verbs used in the rest of 1 Cor. The point is that peak constitutes a zone of turbulence, but different factors change at different rates.

The question remains as to the significance of peak in the book of 1 Cor. Peak can hardly be said to constitute a "hortatory climax" in a region of text where the primary texttype is persuasive rather than hortatory. Of course, there is a relationship between persuasive and hortatory texttype. Persuasive text tends to influence the reader toward a different belief, while hortatory text tries to get the reader to change a course of action. This distinction is similar to that noted by Stowers in ancient letters of advice: "When advice calls for a specific course of action it is deliberative; when it only seeks to increase adherence to a

Variable	Peak	Non-Peak
Persuasive Texttype	**55.3%** (n=247)	23.2% (n=216)
Hortatory Texttype	31.8% (n=142)	**56.9%** (n=530)
Preceding Clauses	**18.1%** (n=81)	11.0% (n=102)
Following Clauses	8.7% (n=39)	20.0% (n=186)
Independent Clauses	**58.2%** (n=260)	51.7% (n=481)
Dependent Clauses	41.8% (n=187)	**48.3%** (n=450)
Verbless Clauses	**18.6%** (n=83)	8.4% (n=79)
Conditional Clauses	**12.5%** (n=56)	7.2% (n=67)
VO Clause Order	**52.5%** (n=96)	45.4% (n=235)
OV Clause Order	47.5% (n=87)	**54.6%** (n=283)
OS Clause Order (for verb-less clauses)[46]	**56.3%** (n=18)	23.1% (n=9)
Statements	**76.5%** (n=342)	63.1% (n=587)
Questions	11.9% (n=53)	**15.8%** (n=147)
Commands	11.6% (n=52)	**21.2%** (n=197)
Aorist Tense Verbs[47]	20.6% (n=75)	26.6% (n=227)
Passive Voice Verbs[48]	**19.8%** (n=72)	14.2% (n=121)
Noun Subjects[49]	**61.4%** (n=154)	44.5% (n=203)
Pronoun Subjects[50]	23.1% (n=58)	**38.2%** (n=174)
First Person Subjects	19.9% (n=89)	**24.2%** (n=225)
Second Person Subjects	9.8% (n=44)	**18.5%** (n=172)
Third Person Subjects	**69.8%** (n=312)	56.3% (n=524)

Figure 7.4: Highly Significant Peak Indicators in 1 Corinthians for Chapters 12–15 as Peak. All unmarked percentages are based on 447 clauses in peak text and 931 clauses in non-peak text.

value or to cultivate a character trait it is epideitic."[51] Just as both texttypes convey advice, so both texttypes rely on motivation to achieve their ends. These similarities between these texttypes may indicate that peak does mark a kind of "advice climax" here. Since it is in a letter, it could also be called an "epistolary climax."

---

[46] These percentages are based on 83 verbless clauses in peak text and 79 verbless clauses in non-peak text.

[47] These percentages are based on 364 verbs in peak text and 852 verbs in non-peak text.

[48] These percentages are based on 364 verbs in peak text and 852 verbs in non-peak text.

[49] These percentages are based on 251 overt subjects in peak text and 456 overt subjects in non-peak text.

[50] These percentages are based on 251 overt subjects in peak text and 456 overt subjects in non-peak text.

[51] Stanley K. Stowers, *Letter Writing in Greco-Roman Antiquity*, LEC (Westminster Press, 1986), 107.

It is also worth noting that this peak area covers two of the discourses, one in response to the Corinthians' letter (chs. 12–14) and one in response to the oral reports (ch. 15). Perhaps there is a peak for each of these response types.

However that may be, it can be said that the peak area in 1 Cor does indicate topics about which Paul felt and showed a marked increase in emotion and wanted to convey that emotion to his intended audience. He was deeply concerned about the oneness of the body of Christians as it was endowed with different spiritual gifts. Likewise, he considered the topic of the resurrection to be a matter of first importance (cf. 1 Cor 15:3).

This is further signified by the fact that these topics are the ones mentioned in the opening thanksgiving in 1:4–9. There Paul mentions that the Corinthians had "all speech" (both prophecy and speaking in tongues) and "all knowledge" and were "not lacking in any spiritual gift" (1:5–6). These themes are discussed in full in chs. 12 through 14. He goes on to say that the Corinthians were waiting "for the revealing of the Lord Jesus Christ" who would sustain them as "guiltless in the day of our Lord Jesus Christ" (1:7–8). That day is thoroughly treated in the discussion about the resurrection in ch. 15.

New Testament studies in the epistles have taken seriously Schubert's proposal that the opening thanksgiving often suggested the purpose of the letter and outlined its key topics.[52] There has been some attempt to make the opening thanksgiving of 1 Cor fit this pattern, but the efforts fall short.

The macrostructures of the ten discourses cover much more material than the few items noted in the thanksgiving.

All of this is to suggest that the themes of the opening thanksgiving in 1 Cor point primarily to the items covered in the peak material of chs. 12–15, not to the whole letter. Perhaps in other New Testament books that have a unified macrostructure, a similar relationship between thanksgiving and peak material holds, but it is masked by the fact that the peak material brings to a climax the discussion of themes that are central to the whole letter. The matter is worthy of further research.

Constituent Paragraph Structure

Now relationships between paragraphs are not always overtly marked. Rather they are often inherent only in the meaning of the paragraphs. For this reason Young, Becker, and Pike speak of a generalized plot as "a sequence of semantic slots."[53] On

---

[52] William G. Doty, *Letters in Primitive Christianity*, GBS (Fortress, 1973), 32–33; Stowers, *Letter Writing*, 21–22.

[53] Richard E. Young, Alton L. Becker, and Kenneth L. Pike, *Rhetoric: Discovery and Change* (Harcourt, Brace & World, 1970), 319.

a lower level, paragraphs also may be said to exhibit plots.[54] These plots are often marked on the surface structure of a text by what may be called *plot cues*. Plot cues are words and phrases which "indicate the relationship of one linguistic unit to another within a specific, or surface, plot."[55] Now since the term *plot* is usually reserved for narrative texttype, it is perhaps better to refer to these overt markers as *relational cues*. If paragraph B is an illustration of paragraph A, it may well begin with a relational cue such as *for example* or *for instance*. If paragraph B contains a cause for paragraph A or a reason for it, the relational cues *because*, *since, therefore*, or *consequently* may be found in the text.[56]

But even where such overt markers do not exist, the semantic relationships between paragraphs which they signify do. In commenting on a Beekman-Callow relational structure tree diagram of 1 John, Miehle has noted, "Even on the lower levels of structure, I have been prompted more by the semantic rather than the grammatical structure."[57] This is where Pike's four-celled tagmeme becomes a useful tool. The third cell is that of role, an acknowledgement that grammar is more than syntax; it contains an element of semantics even within its structure.

For example, in Greek the category *voice* is used to distinguish active, middle, and passive. These categories do not just refer to structural forms, but to semantic relationships within the sentences within which they are used. Now even when the structure of the middle and passive are the same, the relationships signified by the middle and the passive are quite different. Further, these relationships are grammatical, not merely conceptual. There is a significant semantic difference, but not an ultimate conceptual difference, between "The key turned in the lock," and "The key was turned in the lock." In both, the speaker and listener may conceptualize a person turning the key, even though neither sentence specifies such. The semantic difference is entirely due to the grammar, not to the conceptual picture drawn by word choice. Pike's inclusion of role in the grammatical tagmeme allows this semantic element to be presented as an integral part of grammar, thus emphasizing his idea that units should be treated as form-meaning composites.[58]

Longacre has taken this concept a step further by analyzing two-celled paragraph tagmemes with what can be taken as Role:Class instead of the traditional Slot:Class. This is consistent with the two-celled tagmeme since originally both were combined (e.g., Slot could be filled by *subject-as-actor*, where *actor* is a

---

[54] Ibid., 320.

[55] Ibid., 322.

[56] Ibid.

[57] Helen Louise Miehle, "Theme in Greek Hortatory Discourse: Van Dijk and Beekman-Callow Approaches Applied to 1 John" (PhD diss., University of Texas at Arlington. 1981), 105.

[58] Kenneth L. Pike, *Linguistic Concepts: An Introduction to Tagmemics* (University of Nebraska Press, 1982), 111–113.

Role[59]). Role seems to be more significant in determining relationship than slot does. Longacre has given a fairly detailed treatment of this method of analysis.[60] It is well illustrated for a biblical text in his analysis of 1 John[61] and in the fourth chapter of his book *Joseph*, an analysis of the Hebrew text of Gen 37 and 39–48.[62]

Several of the different types of paragraphs which have been identified to date based on role are listed in Figure 7.5. The terminology in the figure is generally that of Longacre, who labels the head or nucleus of the paragraph the *thesis*, although at one time he used the term *text* for some units.[63] Also following Longacre,[64] here his earlier terminology for constituent elements of the sequence paragraph has been changed from Build-up (BU) to Sequential Thesis (SeqT). The term build-up applies best to narrative material before the climax, but even in this material an item in the sequence may not build up the storyline. In the same way, the coordinate paragraph is sometimes analyzed as two items rather than two theses.[65] Amplification and clarification paragraphs are similar, but the former merely gives additional information, while the latter does so in order to make the thesis clear. Clendendon has labeled the evidence paragraph the attestation paragraph.[66] But the terminology followed here is current and understandable.

Most of the entries in Figure 7.5 are listed as right branching paragraphs, that is, paragraphs in which the thesis comes first. The exceptions are the condition paragraph and the quote paragraph, both of which are left branching, that is, paragraphs in which the thesis comes last. These are the normal (unmarked) ordering for these paragraphs, but it is possible for paragraph types which are normally right branching to be left branching and vice versa. There are three other possibilities listed in Figure 7.5. Although it may have an introduction as a left branch, the simple paragraph is often without such a branch, having only a head or nucleus. Next, the coordinate paragraph, the dialogue paragraph, and the simultaneous paragraph are usually double headed, although they may be multiple headed. Finally, the sequence paragraph is usually multiple headed.

---

[59] Ibid., 77.

[60] Robert E. Longacre, "Sentence Structure as a Statement Calculus," *Language* 46, no. 4 (1970): 783–815; Longacre, "An Apparatus for the Identification of Paragraph Types," *Notes on Linguistics* 15 (1980): 5–22.

[61] Robert E. Longacre, "Exhortation and Mitigation in First John," *Selected Technical Articles Related to Translation* 9 (1983): 3–44.

[62] Robert E. Longacre, *Joseph: A Story of Divine Providence* (Eisenbrauns, 1989), 83–118.

[63] Ibid.

[64] Robert E. Longacre, "Two Hypotheses regarding Text Generation and Analysis," *Discourse Processes* 12 (1989): 450–458.

[65] Longacre, *Joseph*, 116.

[66] Ewell Ray Clendenen, "The Interpretation of Biblical Hebrew Hortatory Texts: A Textlinguistic Approach to the Book of Malachi" (PhD diss., University of Texas at Arlington, 1989), 131.

Paragraph Type	Constituents				
Alternative	(Intro.)	+	Thesis	+	Alternative
Amplification	(Intro.)	+	Thesis	+	Amplification
Antithetical	(Intro.)	+	Thesis	+	Antithesis
Clarification	(Intro.)	+	Thesis	+	Clarification
Comment	(Intro.)	+	Thesis	+	Comment
Condition	(Intro.)	+	Condition	+	Thesis
Coordinate	(Intro.)	+	Thesis$_1$	+	Thesis$_2$
Dialogue	(Intro.)	+	(Continuation)	+	Response
Evidence	Initiation	+	Thesis	+	Evidence
Generalization	(Intro.)	+	Thesis	+	Generalization
Illustration	(Intro.)	+	Thesis	+	Illustration
Motivation	(Intro.)	+	Thesis	+	Motivation
Paraphrase	(Intro.)	+	Thesis	+	Paraphrase
Quote	(Intro.)	+	Quote Formula	+	Quote
Reason	(Intro.)	+	Thesis	+	Reason
Result	(Intro.)	+	Thesis	+	Result
Sequence	(Setting)	+	SeqT$_1$	+	SeqT$_n$
Simple	(Intro.)	+	Thesis		
Simultaneous	(Intro.)	+	Thesis	+	Simul. Thesis

Figure 7.5: Types of Paragraphs Based on Role. This figure was derived in part on work from Longacre and Clendendon.[67] *Optional constituents are listed in parentheses. SeqT = Sequential Thesis.*

In addition, paragraphs can be categorized according to structural features. Following Longacre's terminology, the question-answer paragraph can be called *rhetorical question-answer* or simply *rhetorical* for short, the question-command paragraph called *rhetorical command*, the chiastic paragraph called *chiastic*, and the parallel paragraph called *parallel*.[68] When paragraphs have rhetorical and rhetorical command structure, they often become left branching. Longacre also has identified *running quote* and *cyclic* paragraphs as further examples of what he calls *stylistic* types.[69] A paragraph can thus be identified by a combination of its stylistic structural type, its branching direction, its texttype, and its basic role relationship as listed in Figure 7.5.

Illustrations of this method of analysis are given in Figures 7.6 (for 1 Cor 1:10–17), 7.7 (for 1 Cor 2:6–16), 7.8 (for 1 Cor 3:10–15), 7.9 (for 1 Cor 6:12–20), and 7.10

---

[67] Longacre, *Joseph*, 83–116; Clendendon, "The Interpretation," 131.

[68] Robert E. Longacre, "The Paragraph as a Grammatical Unit," in *Discourse and Syntax*, ed. Talmy Givón, SSS 12 (Academic Press, 1979), 131.

[69] Ibid.

(for 1 Cor 10:23–11:1). All of these are major paragraphs according to the study of orthographic paragraphs done above.

But this method of analysis provides a much clearer picture about the relationships, the level of embedding, and even the boundaries between paragraphs than a study of orthographic paragraphs does. For example, an analysis of orthographic paragraphs in several English translations shows minor paragraphs beginning at 2:10 and 2:14; however, Figure 7.7 shows that 2:10 is actually a place where a series of right branching paragraphs ends and the relationship returns to a higher level paragraph. In the same way, 2:14 is the second half of an antithetical paragraph, and the contrast has proven a good place to mark an orthographical paragraph. The analysis also shows that 2:10b is not an ideal place to mark an orthographic paragraph (as the NIV and NEB have done) because to do so obscures the relationships.

The sample sections analyzed in Figures 7.6–10 have been chosen to give a cross-section of material from different texttypes. Figure 7.6 shows a combination of texttypes; Figure 7.7 shows a text of primarily persuasive texttype; Figure 7.8 has a text of mostly expository texttype; and Figures 7.9 and 7.10 are mainly hortatory texttype. The assignment of texttype here is arbitrary, based upon an intuitive assessment of purpose. The sections analyzed have also been chosen from material which is non-peak in nature, so that any shift in grammatical markers due to peak will not be a factor.

POINT 1: (H) Motivation ¶
    THESIS: (H) Reason ¶
        THESIS: 10 Now I appeal to you, brothers, through the name of our Lord Jesus Christ, that you all speak the same thing and that there be no divisions among you, but that you be united in the same mind and the same viewpoint.
        REASON: (E) Amplification ¶
            THESIS: 11 For it has been indicated to me about you, my brothers, by the household of Chloe that there is strife among you.
            AMPLIFICATION: 12 This is what I am saying, that each of you says, "I am of Paul," and "I of Apollos,"and "I of Cephas," and "I of Christ."
    MOTIVATION: (P) Comment ¶
        THESIS: (P) Coordinate ¶
            THESIS_1: 13 Has Christ been divided?
            THESIS_2: Paul was not crucified for you, was he?
            THESIS_n: Or were you baptized into the name of Paul?
        COMMENT: (P) Reason ¶
        THESIS: (P) Clarification ¶
            THESIS: 14 I thank God that I baptized none of you except Crispus and Gaius, 15 lest anyone should say that you were baptized into my name.
            CLARIFICATION: (N) Antithetical ¶
                THESIS: 16 Now I did baptize also the household of Stephanas.
                ANTITHESIS: For the rest, I do not know whether I baptized any other one.
        REASON: 17 For Christ did not send me to baptize but to preach the gospel, and not in wisdom of word, lest the cross of Christ be emptied of its power.

Figure 7.6: Constituent Display of 1 Corinthians 1:10–17 Mixed Texttypes
Key: E=Expository; H=Hortatory; N=Narrative; P=Persuasive

POINT X: (P) Amplification ¶
   THESIS: **6** But we do speak wisdom among the mature, but not a wisdom of
         this age nor of the rulers of this age, who are being done away with.
   AMPLIFICATION: (P) Amplification ¶
     THESIS: (P) Reason ¶
       THESIS: **7** But we speak the hidden wisdom of God...
       REASON: (P) Evidence ¶
         THESIS: for if they understood, they would not have crucified
           the Lord of glory.
         EVIDENCE: **9** But, just as it is written, "What eye..."
     AMPLIFICATION: (P) Amplification ¶
       THESIS: (P) Clarification ¶
         THESIS: **10** But to us God has revealed [them] through the
           Spirit.
         CLARIFICATION:(P) Amplification ¶
           THESIS: For the Spirit searches all things, even the depths
             of God.
           AMPLIFICATION: Rhetor. (P) Evidence ¶
             EVIDENCE: **11** For what man knows...
             THESIS: So also no one understands... the [thoughts]
               of God except the Spirit of God.
     AMPLIFICATION: Chiastic (P) Antithetical ¶
       THESIS A₁: **12** Now we have received not the spirit...
       ANTITHESIS B: **14** The soulical man does not accept...
       THESIS A2:(P) Evidence ¶
         THESIS: **15** The spiritual [person] discerns all things, but
           he himself is discerned by no one.
         EVIDENCE:(P) Comment ¶
           THESIS: **16** "For who has known the mind of the Lord
             so that he may instruct him?"
           COMMENT: But we have the mind of Christ.

Figure 7.7. Constituent Display of 1 Corinthians 2:6–16 Persuasive Texttype
Note: The punctuation of 2:7–8 follows the corrected UBS³.

POINT X:(P) Illustration ¶
    THESIS: verse 5
    ILLUSTRATION:(P) Coordinate ¶
        THESIS$_1$: vv. 6–9
        THESIS$_2$: vv. 10–15 analyzed below

THESIS2:(E) Amplification ¶
  THESIS:(E) Comment ¶
    THESIS: 10 According to the grace of God given to me, as a wise master builder I laid a foundation, but another man is building on [it].
    COMMENT:(H) Reason ¶*
      THESIS: But let each one watch out how he builds on [it].
      REASON: 11 For another foundation no one can lay than that which is laid, which is Jesus Christ.
  AMPLIFICATION:(E) Reason ¶
    THESIS: 12 Now if any one builds on the foundation with gold, silver, precious stones, wood, hay, straw, 13 each one's work will become apparent, for the Day will make [it] evident;
    REASON:(E) Amplification ¶
      THESIS: because it will be revealed with fire, and the fire itself will test each one's work [to see] of what sort it is.
      AMPLIFICATION:(E) Antithetical ¶
        THESIS: 14 If anyone's work which he has built remains, he will receive a reward.
        ANTITHESIS: 15 If anyone's work is burned up, he will suffer loss, but he himself will be saved, but [only] thus, as through fire.

Figure 7.8: Constituent Display of 1 Corinthians 3:10–15 Primarily Expository Texttype. This paragraph functions as a hortatory aside.

POINT N: (H) Reason ¶
   REASON: (H) Antithetical ¶
      INTRODUCTION: (H) Coordinate ¶
         THESIS₁: **12** All things are permissible for me, but not all things
            are expedient.
         THESIS₂:All things are permissible for me, but I will not be
            brought under authority by anything.
      ANTITHESIS: (H) Antithetical ¶
         THESIS: **13** Food for the stomach and the stomach for food--
         ANTITHESIS: but God will do away with both this and that.
      THESIS: (H) Comment ¶
         THESIS: But the body is not for fornication but for the Lord...
         COMMENT: **14** And God both raised the Lord and will raise us up
            through his power.
   THESIS: (H) Motivation ¶
      MOTIVATION: (H) Result ¶
         THESIS: **15** Do you not know that your bodies are members...
         RESULT: Rhetorical (H) Clarification ¶
            THESIS: Shall I take therefore the members of Christ...
            CLARIFICATION: (H) Reason ¶
               THESIS: Definitely Not!
               REASON: (H) Antithetical ¶
                  THESIS:(H) Evidence ¶
                     THESIS: **16** Or do you not know that...
                     EVIDENCE: For it says, "The two shall be..."
                  ANTITHESIS: **17** But the one joined to the Lord...
   THESIS: (H) Motivation ¶
      THESIS: (H) Reason ¶
         THESIS: **18** Flee fornication.
         REASON: Every sin which a man does is outside the body...
      MOTIVATION:(H) Result ¶
         THESIS: Rhetorical (H) Amplification ¶
            AMPLIFICATION: **19** Or do you not know...
         THESIS: **20** For you were bought with a price.
         RESULT: So glorify God in your body.

Figure 7.9: Constituent Display of 1 Corinthians 6:12–20 Hortatory Texttype

POINT N: (H) Generalization ¶
   INTRODUCTION: (H) Coordinate ¶
      THESIS₁: **23** All things are permissible, but not all things are expedient.
      THESIS₂: All things are permissible, but not all things build up.
   GENERALIZATION: Chiastic (H) Coordinate ¶
      THESIS A₁: **24** Let no one seek his own [good], but that of another.
   THESIS: (H) Coordinate ¶
      THESIS B₁: **25** Eat everything sold in the meat market, raising no ques-
                  tions because of conscience. **26** For "the earth [is] the
                  Lord's, and its fulness."
      THESIS B₂: (H) Antithetical ¶
         THESIS: **27** If any of the unbelievers invites you [to dinner] and you
               wish to go, eat everything set before you, raising no ques-
               tions because of conscience.
         ANTITHESIS: (H) Reason ¶
            THESIS: **28** But if someone says to you, "This is a sacred sacri-
                  fice," do not eat because of that one who informed
                  [you], and conscience—**29** but I mean not your con-
                  science but that one's.
            REASON: (H) Coordinate ¶
               THESIS₁: For why is my liberty determined by another's
                   conscience?
               THESIS₂: **30** If I partake with thankfulness, why am I slan-
                   dered because of that for which I give thanks?
      THESIS A₂: (H) Comment ¶
         THESIS: (H) Amplification ¶
            THESIS: **31** Therefore, whether you eat or drink, or whatever
                  you do, do all things to the glory of God.
            AMPLIFICATION: **32** Do not be a stumbling-block either to
                        Jews or to Greeks or to the church of God,
                        33 just as I also try to please everyone in
                        everything...
         COMMENT: **11:1** Be imitators of me, just as I also am of Christ.

Figure 7.10: Constituent Display of 1 Corinthians 10:23–11:1 Hortatory Texttype
N.B.: THESIS A₂ is chiastically coordinate with THESIS A₁.

8

2 Corinthians

FREDRICK J. LONG

Discourse of any type reflects higher organizational "structure(s)" consisting of conventionalized patterns and topics that are in varying degrees discernible to audiences. "Conventional" refers to that which is "based on or in accordance with what is generally done or believed;" "structure" refers to "the arrangement of and relations between the parts or elements of something complex."[1]

I propose that a more complete discourse analysis (DA) should ideally attend to at least four cognitively-based and conventional features that organize discourse structure from sentence level (word, phrase, clause) to larger segments (paragraphs, sections, units) to the entire discourse (books) and even to corpora (e.g., the Psalter, the canon of the ten Attic orators, Cicero's *Ad Familiares*, and the Pauline Epistles).[2] Due to space limitations, I will limit my attention to the following four organizational features of discourse:

1. Major Structural Relationships (MSR);
2. Information Structure, Discourse Grammar, & Emphasis Constructions;

---

[1] The first definitions, respectively, in Apple's *Dictionary* Version 2.2.2 (203.1).

[2] On the macro-organization of the Psalter, see recently, e.g., Ian J. Vaillancourt, *The Multifaceted Saviour of Psalms 110 and 118: A Canonical Exegesis*, HBM 86 (Sheffield Phoenix, 2019). For a discussion of the ten Attic orators in relation to the Alexandrian literary canons, see R. M. Smith, "A New Look at the Canon of the Ten Attic Orators," *Mnemosyne* 48, no. 1 (1995): 66–79. For a consideration of the macro-organization of Cicero's letter collection *Ad Familiares*, see Francesca Martelli, "The Triumph of Letters: Rewriting Cicero in *Ad Fam.* 15," *JRS* 107 (2017): 90–115.

3.   Analogues of Genre and Literary Form;

4.   Image Schemas and Conceptual Archetypes.

Certainly, these four organizational features of discourse may overlap and re-late creatively with one another. Then too, authors (and audiences) may or may not be (entirely) cognizant of the influence of such conventions in the discourse that effectively still work and "blend" together. Such blending has communicative benefit so that we should not be surprised to discover these different layers mutually informing our understanding of the discourse as a whole.[3] Important in this regard is Relevance Theory which posits that humans like to offer and receive efficient, effective, and beneficial discourse with as little effort as possible.[4] Essentially, as I say, we humans are lazy, greedy, and needy all at the same time.

On the one hand, our general lack of awareness of these discourse features simply attests both to the tremendous human capacity for discourse creation and to the ubiquity and efficiency of conventional communication patterns. On the other hand, to the extent that we do not properly recognize prominent dimen-sions of these features, we may very well miss the point(s) of the discourse. Thus, a central task for DA practitioners is to increase their awareness of the features and dynamics of discourse creation to better observe and understand them. In this respect, our DA should be "re-creative" of the discourse itself such that one should attempt, as best as possible, to reconceptualize the discursive design after the author's own designs.[5] In view of the totality of biblical materials, theologically Daniel P. Fuller has articulated the following principle: "the ultimate end of Bible

---

[3] On the blending of notions in language usage, see Gilles Fauconnier and Mark Turner, *The Way We Think: Conceptual Blending and the Mind's Hidden Complexities* (Basic Books, 2002). They argue, "we live in the blend for activities that are crucial to survival-perception, sensation, arousal, immediate reaction to basic environmental threats. In the face of such threats, global and immediate insight is the priority, and there is little survival value in check-ing step by step how that global insight is achieved" (84).

[4] See Deirdre Wilson and Dan Sperber, "Outline of Relevance Theory," *Hermes* 5 (1990): 35–56 and Dan Sperber and Deirdre Wilson, *Relevance: Communication and Cognition*, 2nd ed. (Blackwell, 2001). The theory and literature is immense and increasingly coming into transla-tion theory and biblical studies.

[5] On this recreative dimension of biblical study, see Fredrick J. Long, "Major Structural Re-lationships: A Survey of Origins, Development, Classifications, and Assessment," *The Journal of Inductive Biblical Studies* 1, no. 1 (2014): 22–58 at 31–32 (available at http://place.asburyseminary. edu/ jibs/vol1/iss1/3), and see ch. 9 "The Compositive and Re-Creative Methods," summarizing the methods of White and Howard T. Kuist in Charles Richard Eberhardt, *The Bible in the Mak-ing of Ministers; the Scriptural Basis of Theological Education: The Lifework of Wilbert Webster White* (Association Press, 1949).

study is to understand what God has said by thinking after him the thoughts which he inspired the Biblical authors to write."[6]

Methodology

Major Structural Relationships (MSRs)[7]

Central to the observation of biblical materials are Major Structural Relationships (MSRs) that are articulated within the interpretive approach called Inductive Bible Study (known as IBS).[8] Dedicated to promoting this approach is *The Journal of Inductive Biblical Studies* (2014–present).[9] The identification and depiction of MSRs to describe varying levels of discourse is grounded in Bible study principles of working with one's vernacular language (while valuing original languages), observing inductively what is present (not deductively assuming anything), asking questions of what is observed, and valuing the theology in the discourse.

The influence of Inductive Bible Study across Christian institutions (such as Asbury, Fuller, and Princeton seminaries) and parachurch organizations (such as InterVarsity, Campus Crusade [Cru], and Precept Ministry) is vast and global.[10] In addition to those leaders discussed below, notable practitioners include Irving T. Jenson (Moody Bible Institute);[11] Mary Creswell Graham (a student of Wilbert Webster White's);[12] Daniel P. Fuller (a student of White's, Fuller Theological

---

[6] Daniel P. Fuller, *The Inductive Method of Bible Study* (Fuller Theological Seminary, 1955), IV.8; cf. II.9, IV.1–2, 5 *passim*).

[7] In this section, I am summarizing my discussions in Long, "Major Structural Relationships," and idem, "Vital Relations and Major Structural Relationships: Heuristic Approaches to Observe and Explore Biblical and Other Discourse," *The Journal of Inductive Biblical Studies* 4, no. 2 (2017): 92–128 (available at http://place.asburyseminary.edu/jibs/vol4/iss2/3).

[8] See a monumental description and application of this approach in David R. Bauer and Robert A. Traina, *Inductive Bible Study: A Comprehensive Guide to the Practice of Hermeneutics* (Baker Academic, 2011), Part 2 "Observing and Asking" (chs. 11–13).

[9] Available for PDF downloads at https://place.asburyseminary.edu/jibs.

[10] On the historic influence, see the chart found in Mary Creswell Graham, ed., *Newsletter: Inductive Bible Study Network* 17 (1994): 4; this chart is reproduced in Long, "Major Structural Relationships," 28. On the history and global promise, see David R. Bauer, "Inductive Biblical Study: History, Character, and Prospectus in a Global Perspective," *Asbury Journal* 68, no. 1 (2013): 6–35.

[11] Irving Lester Jensen, *Independent Bible Study* (Moody, 1963; rev. ed. 1992).

[12] Graham, *Inductive Bible Study Explained,* rev. ed. (Mary L. Graham; Institute of International Studies, 1995); she also edited the *Newsletter-Inductive Bible Study Network* (1991–2001, nos. 1–30).

Seminary);[13] Howard G. Hendricks (Dallas Theological Seminary);[14] Oletta Wald (a student of Traina's, Lutheran Seminary);[15] and numerous graduates from such institutions, too many to note, some of whom have published works explicitly promoting Inductive Bible methodology;[16] and others actively engaged in teaching the Bible inductively at various levels of education and in church discipleship settings.[17]

Although the nomenclature for MSRs has varied—and arguably one may posit additional MSRs such as "List" and "Analogue" among the "Rhetorical Structures"—the following MSRs have arisen to the most helpful and have thus stood the test of time in Inductive Bible Study.

A. **Recurrence Structures** refer to repeated motifs, concepts, persons, literary forms, or other structural relationships across (a unit of) the discourse.

B. **Semantic Structures** "are characterized by binary or twofold progression employed to indicate sense connection: movement from something to something."

   1. CONTRAST: "the association of opposites or of things whose differences the writer wishes to stress";
   2. COMPARISON: "the association of like things, or of things whose similarities are emphasized by the writer";
   3. CLIMAX: "the movement from the lesser to the greater, toward a high point of culmination" (implicitly involves an element of contrast, and usually of causation);
   4. PARTICULARIZATION: "the movement from general to particular" (implicitly involves preparation/realization); types include identificational, ideological, historical, geographical, and biographical;

---

[13] Fuller, *The Inductive Method of Bible Study* (cited in note 6 above).

[14] Howard G. Hendricks and William Hendricks, *Living by the Book* (Moody, 1991); this book has been revised (2007) now with a workbook (2012, 2014). They describe these relations and give credit to "an unpublished chart by John Hansel. Used by permission" (p. 121–22).

[15] Oletta Wald, *The Joy of Discovery: In Bible Study, in Bible Teaching*, rev. ed. (Bible Banner Press, 1956). This work has been revised in 1972 and 2002 (Augsburg Fortress).

[16] For example, David L. Thompson, *Bible Study That Works*, rev. ed. (Evangel, 1994); T. Michael W. Halcomb, *People of the Book: Inviting Communities into Biblical Interpretation* (Wipf & Stock, 2012).

[17] With essays discussing various settings and featuring Traina's previously unpublished materials on "Method in Bible Teaching" (ch. 1), see Fredrick J. Long and David R. Bauer, *Method in Teaching Inductive Bible Study—A Practitioner's Handbook: Essays in Honor of Robert A. Traina with His Unpublished Material on the Subject*, GlossaHouse Festschrift Series 2, The Journal of Inductive Biblical Studies Monograph Series 1 (GlossaHouse, 2019).

5. GENERALIZATION: "the movement from particular to general" (implicitly involves preparation/realization); types include identificational, ideological, historical, geographical, and biographical;
6. CAUSATION: "the movement from cause to effect" (implicitly involves preparation/realization); types include historical, logical, and hortatory;
7. SUBSTANTIATION: "involves the same two components as causation, but used in reverse sequence" (implicitly involves preparation/realization); types include historical, logical, and hortatory;
8. CRUCIALITY: "involves the device of the pivot" (implicitly involves recurrence of causation and contrast);
9. SUMMARIZATION: "an abridgment or compendium (summing up) either preceding or following a unit of material";
10. INTERROGATION: "the employment of a question or a problem followed by its answer or solution" (implicitly involves preparation/realization, and often causation; problem/solution involves contrast);
11. PREPARATION/REALIZATION or INTRODUCTION: "the inclusion of background or setting for events or ideas";
12. INSTRUMENTATION: "involves the movement from means to end" (implicitly involves causation).

C. **Rhetorical Structures** "involve the arrangement of material within the text.... [They] do not include within themselves a certain sense or meaning; rather, they pertain only to the ordering or placement of elements within the text."

1. INTERCHANGE: "the exchanging or alternation of certain elements in an a-b-a-b arrangement."
2. INCLUSIO: "the repetition of words or phrases at the beginning and end of a unit, thus creating a bracket effect."
3. CHIASM: "the repetition of elements in inverted order: a-b-b'-a'. Sometimes chiasm has a middle element, in which case the order would be a-b-c-b'-a'."
4. INTERCALATION: "the insertion of one literary unit in the midst of another literary unit."

These MSRs apply to all levels of discourse (word, clause, paragraph, unit, book, corpus, even arguably, canon) and may be described using charts, pictorial representation, and diagraming. Typically in Inductive Bible Study, students begin with a "book survey," closely observing a book-as-a-whole, noting discourse breaks and transitions, describing the presence of MSRs that govern a majority of the discourse (e.g., in 2 Corinthians, an MSR must span seven or more chapters), and asking questions of the MSRs and other observations (what?, how?, why?, and implications?). Next, students will perform a "segment survey" of a shorter unit of text following the same procedure. Often, then, students will perform detailed observations (phrase-by-phrase and clause-by-clause) making all sorts of observations about word meanings, phrase modifications, MSRs, clausal relationships of implied and explicit information all the while asking questions. One particular approach that I utilize is called Semantic Diagramming and Semantic Analysis (SD/SA).[18] This detailed observation work across all levels of the discourse eventually will lead to the identification of key questions for interpretation; then gathering of evidence to answer the questions; then evaluating the interpretations (whether and to what extent it may be situation-bound or transcultural in nature); then considering best applications and appropriations of the interpretations; and finally, a move toward correlating the interpretations with other interpretations of biblical materials in the creation of biblical theology.[19] In my analysis of 2 Corinthians below, I will necessarily need to limit my approach to Inductive Bible Study to observations and a description of the presence of MSRs at different levels of discourse.

Information Structure, Discourse Grammar, and Emphasis Constructions

Recent perspectives by which to analyze Greek discourse include information structure, discourse grammar, and emphasis constructions. I will provide here only the briefest initial descriptions before suggesting how these fit together within a comprehensive model for DA as applied to 2 Corinthians. Stephen H. Levinsohn brought information structure to bear on biblical texts in numerous works.[20] Although I may disagree on his explanations of discourse features in specific pericopae due to my understanding of the historical-critical and rhetorical context, still Levinsohn's keen pragmatic insight and astute observation of the pragmatics of textual phenomenon always merits careful attention. Levinsohn's approach has been extremely influential for me and I require his *Discourse Features* in my Advanced Discourse Greek Grammar course.

---

[18] This is a discrete interpretive "step" in my exegetical workflow described in Long, *In Step with God's Word: Interpreting the New Testament with God's People*, GlossaHouse Hermeneutics & Translation 1 (GlossaHouse, 2017), ch. 4.

[19] For discussion and examples, see parts 3–5 in Bauer and Traina, *Inductive Bible Study*, 177–360.

[20] Primarily in his *Discourse Features of New Testament Greek: A Coursebook on the Information Structure of New Testament Greek*, 2nd ed. (Summer Institute of Linguistics, 2000). See also, Robert A. Dooley and Stephen H. Levinsohn, *Analyzing Discourse: A Manual of Basic Concepts* (SIL International, 2001). Then Stephen H. Levinsohn has numerous works, *Some Notes on the Information Structure and Discourse Features of …* (SIL International, 2009) on *1 Corinthians 1–4, 1 Thessalonians, 1 Timothy*, and *Luke 22 and 6:20–49*. Very helpful, too are his, *Self-Instruction Materials on Non-Narrative Discourse Analysis* (SIL International, 2011) and *Self-Instruction Materials on Narrative Discourse Analysis* (SIL International, 2012).

Then, Steven E. Runge (Levinsohn's doctoral student) has offered his *Discourse Grammar of the Greek New Testament* in 2010 along with databases across the NT: *The Lexham Discourse Greek New Testament* and *High Definition New Testament* (2008–2014).[21] What makes Runge's work accessible is its application to tagging features to create searchable databases for Hebrew, Greek, and English base texts. However, this same strength is also a weakness since arguably more discourse features and prominence constructions occur in Koine Greek than his discourse grammar describes, even as seminal as his work has been.[22] Runge's work continues to inspire my thinking on Greek discourse grammar.

In terms of attention to emphasis constructions and prominence effects in NT Greek, several works are notable.[23] I will provide a more complete and linguistically-grounded description of such devices in a forthcoming work. Such constructions include the following types of emphasis: 2nd attributive position, additive (or thematic addition), appositional, aspectual emphasis, attention getting devices, comparative, concentric patterning, correlative, demonstrative, discontinuous constituents, final placement, forward-pointing references, genitival, identical, inclusion, intensive, lexical, metacomments,

---

[21] Steven E. Runge, *Discourse Grammar of the Greek New Testament: A Practical Introduction for Teaching and Exegesis* (Hendrickson, 2010); idem, *The Lexham Discourse Greek New Testament* (Logos Bible Software, 2008); and idem, *The Lexham High Definition New Testament: ESV Edition* (Lexham Press, 2008–2014). Other significant contributions include his, "Now and Then: Clarifying the Role of Temporal Adverbs as Discourse Markers," in *Reflections on Lexicography: Explorations in Ancient Syriac, Hebrew, and Greek Sources*, ed. Richard A. Taylor and Craig E. Morrison, PLAL 4 (Gorgias, 2014), 303–23 and Steven E. Runge and Christopher J. Fresch, eds., *The Greek Verb Revisited: A Fresh Approach for Biblical Exegesis* (Lexham, 2016).

[22] I raised this and other critiques in a paper, "Emphasis and Prominence Markers in Greek: A Proposal and Case Study within 2 Corinthians," presented at the Biblical Greek Language and Linguistics Session at the Annual Meeting of the SBL, Chicago, IL, Nov 19, 2012.

[23] Joseph B. Rotherham, *The New Testament Critically Emphasized* (Samuel Bagster & Sons, 1878); John Beekman, John C. Callow, and Michael F. Kopesec, *The Semantic Structure of Written Communication*, 5th ed. (SIL International, 1981); Robert E. Smith, "Recognizing Prominence Features in the Greek New Testament," *Selected Technical Articles Related to Translation* 14 (1985): 16–25; Stanley E. Porter, "Prominence: An Overview," in *The Linguist as Pedagogue: Trends in the Teaching and Linguistic Analysis of the Greek New Testament*, ed. Stanley E. Porter and Matthew Brook O'Donnell, NTM 11 (Sheffield Phoenix, 2009), 45–74; Cynthia Long Westfall, "A Method for the Analysis of Prominence in Hellenistic Greek," in *The Linguist as Pedagogue*, 75–94. See also Porter, *Idioms of the Greek New Testament*, 2nd ed. (Sheffield Academic Press, 1994), *passim*; Frederick Long, *2 Corinthians: A Handbook on the Greek Text*, BHGNT (Baylor University Press, 2015); idem, *Koine Greek Grammar: A Beginning-Intermediate Exegetical and Pragmatic Handbook*, Accessible Greek Resources and Online Studies (GlossaHouse, 2015). For a more detailed description of these contributions (excepting Beekman, Callow, and Kopesec) and a description of many types of emphasis constructions leading to prominence within a discourse, see my *2 Corinthians*, xxxi–xxxvi.

morphological, natural prominence, over-specification, patterned (chiasm, inclusio, lists, parallelism), periphrastic, point/counterpoint sets, qualitative, quantitative, referential prominence, repetition, subjectival, and thematic address (vocative emphasis), word order (abutment, discontinuous, final placement, fronted, etc.).[24]

This list is not complete. Beekman, Callow, and Kopesec maintain that "[e]very language has its own prominence devices, which the translator needs to master. Some of the devices used in New Testament Greek to give marked prominence to propositions are briefly discussed below."[25] They discuss the following:

- a nominalized (and/or forefronted) relation (e.g., 1 Tim 1:5; the forward-pointing device in 1 Thess 2:13), which are both cataphoric;
- rhetorical questions;
- proportion of description; i.e., the "extent of development";
- direct speech in summary form;
- special devices in Greek including sandwich structures (*inclusio*) and chiastic structures.

Importantly, the various types of marked prominence—what I refer to as emphasis constructions—occur at different levels of discourse; e.g., thematic addition (traditionally called "ascensive καί" and often translated *also*) may function at the level of adding a word (2 Cor 1:11), or a phrase (1:7), a clause (1:5, 6, 10, 13), or a sentence in relation to another sentence (1:20; 2:9, 10). Likewise, working at these levels is correlative emphasis (the combination of two or more connectors or sentence adverbs). Patterned emphasis (e.g., chiasm) may work within a clause (5:21b) or a sentence (9:6 [x2]) and across sentences (9:7, 8), a unit (7:2–16), or a discourse (2 Timothy); what motivates such is orality.[26] Meta-comments—explicit statements about the act of communication itself, either from the perspective of speaking or of hearing—will orient audiences to the authorial tone or perspective of material in a unit (2 Cor 6:13), possibly the

---

[24] A comprehensive listing of types of "Emphasis" and "Pragmatic" constructions is found in the index and discussed throughout Long, *Koine Greek Grammar*, 607–8, 609–10.

[25] Beekman, Callow, and Kopesec, *Semantic Structure*, 119–120. Throughout their work, repeated attention is given to discuss both natural and marked prominence (20, 24–25, 45, 51, 60, 119–20, 130, 135).

[26] Fredrick J. Long, "The Oral, the Textual, and the Visual (or, The Good, the Bad, and the Ugly) in Jesus's and Paul's Chiastic Performance of Scripture in 2 Corinthians, Ephesians, and Mark," in *Orality and Theological Training in the 21st Century*, ed. Jay W. Moon and Joshua Moon (Digibooks, 2017). For 2 Timothy, I worked together with a former undergraduate student, April Stier, to identify this chiasm.

whole discourse and its themes (1:13; 12:19), or even the broader situational context (1:12, 17).[27]

All in all, then, emphasis constructions and marked prominence should be understood paradigmatically (as conventional construction options) and observed syntagmatically (as instantiated constructions in context) at successively higher discourse levels where they may be found, beginning with the lexeme-phoneme choices and successively at varying discourse levels, as they may so govern, and then through to the entire discourse.[28] In this regard, special attention should be given to what Robert Longacre has called the "marking of surface structure peak" or "zone[s] of turbulence."[29]

Analogues of Genre and Literary Form; Image Schemas and Conceptual Archetypes

Joseph R. Dongell had postulated another MSR that he called ANALOGUE. He defined this as "Some extra-textual entity ... chosen as a framework by which to organize the text."[30] Indeed, humans create, organize, recognize, and adapt discourses according to both Genres and Literary Forms as well as to Image Schemas and Conceptual Archetypes, i.e., activated discourse metaphors and conventionalized types of people, things, scenes, and events with networks of (possible) associated themes.[31] A complete DA of 2 Corinthians would include careful consideration of

---

[27] It is important to recognize that emphasis constructions and marked prominence are often achieved through an author's selection along a clining of options. For a more complete discussion, see Long, *2 Corinthians*, xxv–xxviii.

[28] Porter provides another taxonomy with "five categories: material, implicational, distributional, positional, and cognitive markedness" (Porter, "Prominence: An Overview," 56). For his discussion of paradigmatic and syntagmatic analysis, see pp. 58–72. For a critique of Porter's application of markedness, see Steven E. Runge, "Contrastive Substitution and the Greek Verb: Reassessing Porter's Argument," *NovT* 56 (2014): 154–73.

[29] Robert E. Longacre, *The Grammar of Discourse*, 2nd ed. (Plenum, 1996), 3 and 38. Porter and Westfall have applied Longacre's "zone of turbulence" to describe the convergence of various types of marked prominence (Porter, "Prominence: An Overview," 55). Westfall argues, "marked features that occur together with other emphatic features create 'zones of turbulence' that characterize prominence" ("A Method for the Analysis of Prominence," 76).

[30] Found only in Joseph R. Dongell's "Structural Relations" handout from 2005 (but missing thereafter in similar handouts); see the discussion and documentation in Long, "Major Structural Relationships," 49, 55–57.

[31] For the former, see, e.g., M. M. Bakhtin's "Statement of the Problem and Definition of Speech Genres," in *Speech Genres and Other Late Essays*, ed. Caryl Emerson and Michael Holquist, trans. V. W. McGee, University of Texas Press Slavic Series 8 (University of Texas, 1986), 60–102. For the latter, the cognitive grammarian Ronald W. Langacker maintains, "Image schemas and conceptual archetypes are each essential to cognition and linguistic structure"

these, but space here does not allow that. For specifics of the Genre and Literary Forms of 2 Corinthians, I will refer you to my dissertation, published with Cambridge University Press, *Ancient Rhetoric and Paul's Apology: The Compositional Unity of 2 Corinthians* (2004) that attends to the rhetorical situation and Paul's argumentative strategies shaping the discourse as a whole. In terms of Image Schemas and Conceptual Archetypes, one could explore God's leading of Paul using a Triumphal Procession Metaphor (2:14–17) that materially relates to Paul's defense of his itinerate ministry (one great cause of the Corinthians' criticism of Paul);[32] additionally, one could explore the networks of themes surrounding (Paul's) Exile, Suffering, and Covenantal Exhortation.[33] Then, too, Paul presents himself and ministry partners using lists of sufferings that evoke archetypes that include a Suffering Sage, Soldier, Psalmist, the Servant of Isaiah, and Scapegoat like Christ.[34]

("Possession and Possessive Constructions" in *Language and the Cognitive Construal of the World*, ed. John R. Taylor and Robert E. MacLaury, TLSM 82 [Mouton de Gruyter, 1995], 51–79 at 52.).

[32] See the most recent and comprehensive treatment by Christoph Heilig, *Paul's Triumph: Reassessing 2 Corinthians 2:14 in Its Literary and Historical Context*, BTS 27 (Peeters, 2017). Quite influential in my thinking has been the work of Paul Brooks Duff who has related the Roman Triumph as a type of Epiphany Procession that gives explanatory power to a number of subsequent topics, such as the glory given to Moses in the Exodus event, the prototypical Jewish epiphany procession (2 Cor 3); see especially Paul Brooks Duff, "Metaphor, Motif, and Meaning: The Rhetorical Strategy behind the Image 'Led in Triumph' in 2 Corinthians 2:14," *CBQ* 53 (1991): 79–92 at 84–86. Thus, Duff concludes, "an epiphany procession of a deity could be metaphorically portrayed as a triumphal procession. This metaphorical usage ... probably came about because many deities in the ancient world were considered victors" (83). Extending the research of Duff and others, I have identified over forty connections and/or allusions to the Roman Triumph and epiphany religious processions presented November 19, 2011 in Fredrick J. Long, "'The god of This Age' (2 Cor 4:4) and Paul's Empire-Resisting Gospel" at the Intertextuality in the New Testament Session of the Annual Meeting of SBL in San Francisco, CA. Some of this material has been published in Fredrick J. Long, "'The god of This Age' (2 Cor 4:4) and Paul's Empire-Resisting Gospel," in *The First Urban Churches: Volume 2: Roman Corinth*, ed. James R. Harrison and Laurence L. Welborn, WGRWSup 7 (SBL Press, 2016), 219–69; but the bulk will be published in Long, "Discerning Greco-Roman Political Thought and Ideology in NT Discourse: 2 Corinthians as a Case Study" in *Handbook of Historical Exegesis: The Use of Background Data in Biblical Interpretation*, ed. by Stanley E. Porter and David J. Fuller (Cambridge University Press), *forthcoming*.

[33] Jonathan Brent Ensor has recently argued that Paul in 2 Corinthians is seeking to mitigate his political displacement and secure his amiable return and participation in the community, especially regarding the Collection; see his recent dissertation "Second Corinthians: St. Paul's Political Displacement from Corinth and Rhetoric of Return" (PhD, Middlesex University/London School of Theology, 2019), who conducted this research under my supervision.

[34] For example, investigating these catalogues of sufferings as exemplifying character as seen in the Stoic or Cynic sage, see Jonathan T. Fitzgerald, *Cracks in an Earthen Vessel: An Examination of the Catalogues of Hardships in the Corinthian Correspondence* (Scholars Press,

What follows is my DA of 2 Corinthians. Although I will touch here and there on matters of genre and literary form, I will keep my comments brief. I will focus on performing a book survey using the methodology of Inductive Bible Study identifying and describing Major Structural Relationships (MSRs). Throughout, I will integrate select and illustrative discussions of Information Structure, Discourse Grammar, and Emphasis Constructions.

Macrostructure, Genre, and Major Structural Relationships (MSRs)

Second Corinthians evinces a conventionalized epistolary framework of identifying sender(s)/recipient(s) and offering a greeting (1:1–2) along with a conclusion consisting of exhortation, greetings, and (two) benediction(s) (13:11–13); these surround a letter body.[35] In the textual transmission history of extant manuscripts, no textual variants support the various partition theories that scholars have proposed for dividing 2 Corinthians into different letters or letter fragments; rather, based upon discourse themes (such as mutuality between Paul the Corinthians, commendation, and exhortations to live faithfully) and the literary convention of ancient rhetoric (specifically ancient apology), the discourse may be readily perceived as a compositional unity. This conclusion is supported by the GENERALIZATION (an MSR) in the retrospective metacomment about the discourse as a whole in 12:19 in which Paul admits that to the Corinthians it appears "all along" (πάλαι) like a formal defense. He says, "all along [πάλαι] you are supposing that we are defending ourselves [ἀπολογούμεθα] to you. Before God in Christ we are speaking. Moreover, all things, beloved, are for your upbuilding [ὑπὲρ τῆς ὑμῶν οἰκοδομῆς]." Paul here also acknowledged the political nature of the discourse for "upbuilding" (οἰκοδομή) the Corinthians.[36]

1988) and Martin Ebner, *Leidenslisten und Apostelbrief Untersuchungen zu Form, Motwik und Funktion der Penstasenkataloge bei Paulus*, FB 66 (Echter, 1991). I would extend the extent of Paul's comparison based upon the recent conference papers of Channing L. Crisler, "Answered Lament as *Sapientia Experimentalis*: Paul's Use and Reconfiguration of OT Lament for the Motif of Suffering in 2 Corinthians" and Mark Gignilliat, "Paul as the Servant's Servant: On Figural Reading and the Inherence of 2 Corinthians 5:14–6:10 and Isaiah 40–66," both presented at the Scripture and Paul Seminar at the Annual Meeting of the Society of Biblical Literature, San Diego, CA, Nov 24–25, 2019. Then, too, exploring the scapegoat archetype (or subversion of it) is Robert G. Hamerton-Kelly, "A Girardian Interpretation of Paul: Rivalry, Mimesis and Victimage in the Corinthian Correspondence," *Semeia* 33 (1985): 65–81.

[35] So, e.g., Murray J. Harris, *The Second Epistle to the Corinthians*, NIGTC (Eerdmans, 2005), 127, 930–31; for the closing material, Harris is dependent on Jeffrey A. D. Weima, *Neglected Endings: The Significance of the Pauline Letter Closings*, JSNTSup 101 (Sheffield Academic, 1994), 209–10.

[36] On this dual apologetic and deliberative/political nature, see discussions in Long, *Ancient Rhetoric and Paul's Apology*, 2, 9, 112–13, 118–19, 190–93. Paul's appeal to speaking before God is found throughout the discourse and is a judicial topos (2:17; 4:2; 5:11; 7:12; 8:21).

As will be shown below, Paul will need to defend his ministry travel itinerary (see 1:12–17), his sending of a letter and surrogates like Titus instead of being there himself in person (2:1–13; 7:2–16; chs. 8–9; 12:14–13:4), and the nature of his God-appointed and upright ministry in relation to money, denying that he had any impure motives or deceitfulness and that he was not a burden expecting financial support (3:2; 4:2; 6:3; 7:2; 8:3–5, 20; 11:6–9; 12:13–18). Paul here offered a counter-charge to "excuse" his absence: He "spared" (φείδομαι) the Corinthians a painful visit and wrote a letter instead because they were so sinful and ill-prepared for him (1:23; 2:1–3; 7:2–16; 13:2). Thus, in preparation for his imminent itinerate travel stop at Corinth, the two related political aims of 2 Corinthians are both to exhort them to turn away from idolatrous associations and immorality (6:14–7:1; 12:20–13:4) and to complete their readiness and commitment to the Collection for Jerusalem. As this is a "thanksgiving (offering) to God" (9:11–15), Paul urged the Corinthians to pray and participate with him in this thanksgiving (1:11) since this is his ethically conducted and carefully curated initiative (chs. 8–9).

I now turn to my *Inductive Book Survey of 2 Corinthians* that identifies (1) General Materials (discourse type and genre); (2) Specific Materials in which I provide a two or three word description of each "chapter" as a heuristic exercise knowing these were added subsequent to the original discourse production; (3) Book Structure including the identification of literary forms; (4) Major Structural Relationships (MSRs); and (5) Strategic Areas where each MSR is most prominent and recognizable.

Inductive Book Survey of 2 Corinthians

I. General Materials:

A. Discourse Type: Argumentative
B. Genre: Epistolary Speech (apologetic with deliberative purposes; see 12:19)

II. Specific Materials

ch.1 Paul's Comforting Intentions	ch.8 Ethically Prepared Collection
ch.2 Letter of Tears	ch.9 Giving Cheerfully
ch.3 Glorious Covenants	ch.10 Weighty, Strong Letters
ch.4 Jars of Clay	ch.11 Intrusive False Apostles
ch.5 Ambassadorial Persuasion	ch.12 Christ's Final Word
ch.6 Paul's Covenantal Call	ch.13 Authority in Christ
ch.7 Titus reports Grief	

Summarizing each chapter as accurately as possible led to some preliminary observations that helped to understand the macro-structure. Chapter 1 contains distinct materials (1:1–2, 3–7, 8–16, and 17–24). So too does ch. 2: Paul's tearful letter (2:1–11), searching for Titus (2:12–13), and Paul in God's Triumphal Procession (2:14–17). Also, the asyndeton at 3:1 isolates 2:14–17 in which Paul makes explicit a central metaphor with themes found across 2 Corinthians. Also, 7:1 was determined to belong in the distinct unit of 6:14–7:1. Then too, ch.11 is divided in content at 11:15 ending critiques and moving into 11:16 to Paul's boasting. The asyndeton in 12:11 and self-reflectivity there mark a transition to a new unit.

III. Book Structure, MSRs, and Macro-level Genre and Literary Forms

A. 1:1–16 Paul's Intention of Mutual Comfort in Sufferings 1. Epistolary Opening (1:1–2) 2. Comfort amidst Suffering (1:3–7) 3. *Narration #1* Paul's Suffering & Intentions (1:8–16) <u>MSRs</u>: INTRODUCTION WITH INSTRUMENTATION AND GENERALIZATION (1:1–16)	**Epistolary Opening** (1:1–2) *Exordium* (1:3–7) *Narratio #1* (1:8–16)
B. 1:17–24 Paul's Word Reflects God's Faithful Word 1. Paul's Decision Not to Visit (1:17) 2. Promises and God's Glory (1:18–20) 3. God's Down Deposit of the Spirit (1:21–22) 4. Paul Spared the Corinthians (1:23) 5. Paul Works for Their Joy (1:24) <u>MSRs</u>: RECURRENCE OF PROBLEM-SOLUTION WITH SUMMARIZATION	*Divisio* (1:17) *Partitio* (1:17–24)

C. 2:1–9:15 Paul is Approved New Covenant Minister
 1. Paul Writes rather than Visits (2:1–11)
    Narration #2 Paul's Search for Titus (2:12–13)
 2. New Covenant's Greater Glory (2:14–3:18)
 3. Paul Proclaims in the same Spirit (4:1–5:10)
 4. Paul's Persuades in the Fear of God (5:11–7:1)
    Narration #3 Paul's Report from Titus (7:2–16)
 5. Paul's Ethical Collection (8:1–9:15)
 <u>MSRs</u>: SUBSTANTIATION RECURRENCE OF SCRIPTURE USE and COMPARISON WITH GENERALIZATION AT 2:14–17
	Probatio (2:1–9:15)
	
	 Narratio #2 (2:12–13)
	
	 Narratio #3 (7:2–16)

D. 10:1–12:10 **Paul's Criticisms, Rivals, and Self-Praise**
  1. Paul Destroying Arguments
    a. Refuting Critics (10:1–11)
    b. Refuting Rivals (10:12–11:15)
  2. Paul's Foolish Boast (11:16–12:10)
MSRs: RECURRENCE OF CONTRAST WITH PARTICULARIZATION
	Refutatio (10:1–11:15)
	Self-Adulation (11:16–12:10)

E. 12:11–13:14 **Paul's Final Appeal and Authority**
  1. Paul's Impending Visit (12:11–13:10)
  2. Epistolary Closing (13:11–14)
MSRs: RECURRENCE OF CRUCIALITY WITH GENERALIZATION
AND CLIMAX (12:1–10) and CHIASM WITH GENERALIZA-
TION AND PURPOSE and RECURRENCES OF WORDS OR
THEMES
	Peroratio (12:11–13:10)
	Epistolary Closing (13:11–14)

IV. Major Structural Relationships (MSRs) and Interpretive Questions

The following MSRs are "major" in that they govern a majority of the text. For 2 Corinthians, this means that they must "span" seven of the thirteen chapters. All but the list of repetitious words/themes are noted above in the Book Structure.

A. INTRODUCTION WITH INSTRUMENTATION AND GENERALIZATION: The unit of 1:1–16 prepares for and INTRODUCES the remainder of the discourse in several ways:

1. the epistolary prescript identifies senders and recipients in (1:1–2);
2. the rhetorical *proemium* discloses Paul's divine understanding of reciprocation in suffering and encouragement (1:3–7);
3. the rhetorical *narratio* then describes Paul's his near-death experience during his Asian ministry (1:8–11); and
4. affirms his good intentions and upright conduct with the Corinthians (1:12–14); and
5. explains his intended travel itinerary on his way to Judea (1:15–16).

The epistolary prescript identifies the apostle Paul and the brother Timothy as senders. The recipients are "God's church being in Corinth along with all the saints being in the whole of Achaia" (τῇ ἐκκλησίᾳ τοῦ θεοῦ τῇ οὔσῃ ἐν Κορίνθῳ σὺν τοῖς ἁγίοις πᾶσιν τοῖς οὖσιν ἐν ὅλῃ τῇ Ἀχαΐᾳ). Quantitative specification with inclusive scope (πᾶσιν ... ὅλῃ) stresses the circular nature of 2 Corinthians; the unnecessary second attributive constructions with the copula εἰμί (τῇ οὔσῃ ... τοῖς οὖσιν) stress the locatedness and likely identity of the audiences in Corinth and Achaia for understanding the exhortative contours of the discourse since Paul will identify the saints as "Corinthians" precisely at 6:11 as he exhorts them to covenantal faithfulness to God rather than to idols (6:14–7:1). Paul and Timothy convey divine grace and peace of the Father and the Lord Jesus Christ through composing and sending the discourse (1:2).

Then, after beginning the *narratio* by recounting his dire circumstances, professing his hope in God's deliverance, and testifying to his ethical ministry conduct (1:8–12), in 1:13–14 Paul discloses a purpose in writing the discourse by referring to its general contents through neuter plural pronouns ("<u>other things</u> ... than <u>that which</u> [ἄλλα ... ἢ ἅ] you are reading"): namely, that the readers would understand completely (ἕως τέλους ἐπιγνώσεσθε) that Paul et al. are their boast just as they are theirs (Paul et al.) in the day of the Lord. There is mutual boasting, but first, the Corinthians would seem to need complete knowledge of Paul in order to understand first that Paul et al. are their boast. Below is my translation of 1:13–14:

> 13 For we are not writing to you any other things but than that you are reading or also understanding; moreover, I am hoping that you will completely understand, 14 just as also you partially did understand us, that we are your boast just as indeed you also are ours in the day of our Lord Jesus.

The GENERALIZING of the discourse content as "the things written" itself is the means for the end-goal of "understanding" (i.e., INSTRUMENTATION); it may be depicted as follows:

MEANS   → END
Things written

→ are read → and understood
GENERAL
MATERIALS

→ for complete knowledge of Paul et al. that
Paul hopes   they have a mutual boasting in the Lord's day

Paul "hopes" that the things written would be read for complete understanding. Paul twice elsewhere uses ἐλπίζω to express the apologetic goal of the discourse that Paul and his ministry team are known/manifest and have not failed:

> 5:11   Therefore, knowing the fear of the Lord, we try to persuade others; but we ourselves have been manifest [πεφανερώμεθα] to God, and I hope [ἐλπίζω] that we have also been manifest [πεφανερῶσθαι] to your consciences.
> 13:6   I hope [ἐλπίζω] you will know [γνώσεσθε] that we have not failed.

This use of ἐλπίζω and γινώσκω or φανερόω to refer to the audience's knowledge of Paul's ethical conduct is strategically placed in 2 Corinthians. Yet, the use of these verbs is conventional for judicial discourse—the litigants have "hope" (ἐλπίζω) that the jury will know (γινώσκω) the facts, their conduct, their innocence, etc. in order to issue a proper judgment. Such statements in speeches are found at the beginning and ending of the discourse as is the case in 2 Corinthians in anticipation of a decision expected of the audience.[37]

Contributing to the force of the MSR of INSTRUMENTATION (means to end) in 1:13–14 are several discourse features and prominence devices:[38]

1. correlative emphasis (coordinated use of two or more connectors) is observed three times: the οὐ ... ἀλλ' construction ("<u>not</u> writing anything <u>other</u> [but] than that which you are reading"); the ἢ ... ἢ καὶ construction (than ... or also..."); and the forward pointing target καθὼς καὶ ... ὅτι ("just as also ... namely that...");[39]

2. the four-fold repetition of the *γινώσκ- verb stem: ἀναγινώσκετε ... ἐπιγινώσκετε ... ἐπιγνώσεσθε ... ἐπέγνωτε that are metacomments.[40]

3. the additional metacomment of ἐλπίζω ὅτι ("I hope that");

4. thematic addition (with καί); ἢ καὶ ("or also"); καθὼς καὶ ("just as also"); καθάπερ καὶ ("just as indeed also");

5. morphological emphasis by adding περ unto καθώς in καθάπερ;

6. abutted emphasis of pronouns to communicate mutual relationship at the most stressed part of 1:14 καθάπερ καὶ ὑμεῖς ἡμῶν ("just as indeed also you are ours");

7. the natural prominence of the eschatological, divine event "in the day of the Lord"; this heightens the importance of the mutual boasting.

Overall, these prominence devices stress Paul's clearly written discursive hope that the Corinthians will certainly know Paul et al., specifically that Paul et al. are their boast and mutually they Paul et al.'s boast in the day of the Lord.

Notable, too, is the switch between first person plural (Paul et al.) and singular (Paul) with "I hope" (ἐλπίζω). Why this switch? This reflects a complexity of the rhetorical situation in that Paul is mainly the one who appears to have failed in his travel itinerary (1:15–16; 13:1–3; cf. 12:14, 20–21) and individual conduct (1:17). Also, he is the one particularly scrutinized so that he must boast about himself (11:16–12:19) after asserting his strong refutative presence at 10:1 with an overly specified pronominal subject referent (Αὐτὸς δὲ ἐγὼ Παῦλος παρακαλῶ ...

---

[37] See the discussion and ancient examples in Long, *Ancient Rhetoric and Paul's Apology*, 149–50, 154–55.

[38] See my discussion of these features in my Baylor Handbook on 2 Corinthians, s.v.

[39] On the forward-pointing target, see Runge, *Discourse Grammar*, ch. 13.

[40] On metacomments, see Runge, *Discourse Grammar*, ch. 5 and Long, *Koine Greek Grammar*, 196–97.

"Now, indeed I myself Paul am exhorting ...").[41] This "individual" nature of Paul's defense at the same time is mitigated by a "we" of ministry associates (et al.) organized freely by and with Paul who are working together with him; it is also in reference to these people (Titus, Timothy, Silvanus, and the brothers) that Paul also offers the defense (e.g., 1:12; 1:18–19, 24; 2:12–13; 7:2–16; 8:6, 16–24; 9:5; 12:16–18). So, while Paul must acknowledge his own apparent failures, these failures implicated also Paul's ministry associates to some extent. Thus, Paul appeals to their upright conduct in order to show his own careful and ethical actions—e.g., Titus in 2:12–13; 7:2–16 and Titus and the brother(s) in 8:6, 18–24; 9:6; 12:16–18. Thus, we also observe the first-person plural at times in the discourse that may include Paul et al., Paul et al. and the Corinthians, or all believers together. All in all, discursively the use of singular and plural is often strategic as the references cited above indicate.

B. RECURRENCE OF PROBLEM-SOLUTION WITH SUMMARIZATION: Paul's failure to visit as he had promised and the consequentially poor evaluation of his ministry as discussed in 1:15–17 is a PROBLEM to which Paul offers SOLUTIONS in the remainder of the letter. Specifically in 1:17, a pair of rhetorical questions focus on Paul's "intentions" (βούλομαι) in terms of "acting with flippancy" (τῇ ἐλαφρίᾳ ἐχρησάμην) and "deliberations" (βουλεύομαι [2x]) as being "according to the flesh" (κατὰ σάρκα). Then, in 2:16b Paul raises another facet of the problem, "Who is sufficient for these things [i.e., to spread about the life-death consequences of God's Triumph in Christ]"? This recurring PROBLEM is given an initial response in the material of 1:17–24 by connecting Paul's and his companions' preaching ministry to God and God's Word in these ways:

1. God himself is faithful (1:18).
2. The preaching of Paul, Silvanus, and Timothy that Jesus is the Son of God is "yes" (1:19) because all of God's promises are yes in Jesus leading to Amen and God's glory (1:20).
3. God establishes Paul along with the Corinthians through the anointing of the Holy Spirit as a down deposit (1:21–22).
4. God is Paul's witness that he chose not to visit to spare them (1:23).
5. Paul works with the Corinthians for their joy since they stand firm in the Faith (1:24).

---

[41] On subject over-specification, see Runge, *Discourse Grammar*, ch. 15. The expression ἐγὼ Παῦλος only occurs five times in the Pauline epistles: 2 Cor 10:1; Gal 5:2; Eph 3:1; Col 1:23; and Phlm 19. It is highly-marked for authorial action. Not surprisingly, then, it occurs either in transitional material at the conclusion (Col 1:23) or start of a new unit (2 Cor 10:1; Gal 5:2; Eph 3:1) or to support and assert Paul's agency when promising to repay losses (Phlm 19). Here in 2 Cor 10:1, this over-specification is further amplified by the presence of αὐτός. It is hard to translate the full effect and I have added "indeed" for stress.

These five points in 1:17–24 distill, if not SUMMARIZE, the subsequent discourse units in 2:1–9:15. Form-critically, 1:17–24 consists of a rhetorical *divisio* (the basic statement of the issue) and *partitio* (the outline of the main argumentative proofs). In rhetorical practice, the *divisio* moves directly to the argument heads, i.e., the *partitio*. As Sara Rubinelli summarizes, "Cicero clarifies that *partitio* is the part of an oration where speakers, first, guide the audience to a clear understanding of the controversy involved in a case and, second, introduce briefly the matters they will discuss in the argumentation."[42]

The information structure of 1:17–24 supports five argument heads. At 1:17, we encounter the first two inferential conjunctions, οὖν and ἄρα. Οὖν marks +inference and +distinctive development whereas ἄρα marks +inference and +consequence.[43] These connectors mark the discourse as progressing and extending consequences of Paul's narrative. Paul asks two questions: first, an emphatic negative rhetorical question with μήτι: "Therefore, then, intending this, I didn't act in a fickle/vacillating way, did I? (No!)." This is followed by another question in which no answer is explicitly marked as anticipated (unless once again assumed as negative response): "Or, is that what I am planning, am I planning according to the flesh so that with me the 'Yes, Yes,' is the 'No, No'?" Such questions produce "interrogative emphasis" and heighten the audiences' attention.[44] Critically, with these questions Paul identifies his understanding of the underlying problems or issues he faced, that is, the problems needing resolution for the audience. According to ancient rhetorical theory (especially *stasis* theory), often when analyzing a situation, the rhetor boiled the issue or basis down to a question (a *quaestio*). Space does not allow me here to explore the importance of *stasis* theory to analyze the argumentative strategy in 2 Corinthians as a matter of rhetorical genre and discourse analysis, but I have done so at some length elsewhere.[45]

Then, the next four argument heads are demarcated by three uses of δέ—a connector signaling +distinctive development—in 1:18, 21, and 23 followed by an οὐκ … ἀλλά construction in 1:24.[46] In these five heads, we observe content variation in addition to grammatical subject switches: "I" (1:17) to "God" and God's

---

[42] Sara Rubinelli, "The Invention of the Young Cicero," *The Classical Quarterly* 52.2 (2002): 612–15 at 612.

[43] For an extended discussion of pragmatic constraints of coordinating and subordinating conjunctions, see Long, *In Step with God's Word*, 121–24.

[44] For a discussion of rhetorical questions and interrogative emphasis, see Long, *Koine Greek Grammar*, 257–62.

[45] Long, *Ancient Rhetoric and Paul's Apology*, ch.9.

[46] For the view that 1:13–14 is the thesis statement on the topic of reconciliation, see Ivar Vegge, *2 Corinthians—A Letter about Reconciliation: A Psychological, Epistolographical and Rhetorical Analysis*, WUNT 2/239 (Mohr Siebeck, 2008), 106, 169–76. Kennedy and Witherington see 2:14–17 as the thesis. See note 49 below.

Word–God's Son–God's Promises through us to you (1:18–20) to "God" affirming and sealing us with you (1:21–22) to "I" sparing you (1:23) to "We" working and "You" standing in the Faith (1:24). Pulling these aspects of the information structure together, we may depict these verses as the partition heads for the main argument units (*probatio*) in 2:1–9:15 as follows:

Verses	Connectors	Grammatical Subject	Content	Probatio Units
1:17	οὖν ... ἄρα	"I"	Did Paul make his plans to come to Corinth lightly? Does he plan according to the flesh?	2:1–11 2:12–13 *narratio* #2
1:18–20	δέ	"God"	God is faithful that Paul et al.'s word and preaching of Jesus, God's Son, to the Corinthians is "YES!" As many are God's promises, they are "yes" in Christ which results in "Amen" to God in Him for glory through Paul et al.	2:14–3:18
1:21–22	δέ	"God"	God establishes Paul et al. with the Corinthians (You), the One sealing and "giving the down deposit of the Spirit" [ὁ ... δοὺς τὸν ἀρραβῶνα τοῦ πνεύματος]	4:1–5:10
1:23	δέ	"I"	Paul calls God as witness: sparing them [φειδόμενος], Paul no more came to Corinth (cf. 13:2).	5:11–7:1 7:2–16 *narratio* #3
1:24	οὐκ ... ἀλλά	"We" & "You"	Paul and companions don't lord over their faith; they are co-workers for their joy (in the Collection). The Corinthians stand in the Faith.	8:1–9:15

In rhetorical theory, the partition heads do not include the topics treated in the *refutatio* (10:1–11:15), the self-adulation "concerning oneself" which follows the *refutatio* in a defense speech (11:16–12:10), and the *peroratio* (12:11–13:10).

C. SUBSTANTIATION BY RECURRENCE OF SCRIPTURE USE: Starting with 2:1 (γάρ),[47] the discourse provides support (SUBSTANTIATION) that Paul has not "acted with flippancy" or "according to the flesh" and that the ministry of Paul and his associates' preaching and work aligns with God's Word and Gospel in Christ. The discourse sprinkles RECURRENCES of Scriptural allusion and citation as SUBSTANTIATION (depicted by an arrow ←):

---

[47] The UBS committee gives this a C rating. The reading γάρ is supported by 𝔓⁴⁶ B *passim* whereas δέ is supported by ℵ A C D¹ F G Ψ *passim*.

3:1–16	←	Exod 34:34 (strong allusion at 3:16) entails an extensive comparison (*synkrisis*) of Moses/Old Covenant and Paul/New Covenant
4:1–5	←	Gen 1:3
4:13–18	←	Ps 116:10
5:16–21	←	Isa 49:8
6:14–16	←	Lev 26:12; Jer 32:38; Ezek 20:34, 41; 37:27; Isa 52:11; 2 Sam 7:8, 14
8:1–14	←	Exod 16:18
9:6–9	←	Ps 112:9
10:12–18	←	Jer 9:24
13:1–5	←	Deut 19:15

Ten of the fourteen quotations are marked as providing argumentative support-ive (ὅτι, κατά, γάρ, καθώς), three are initiated with δέ (+distinctive development) with implied support, and one is stated with asyndeton with the sense of warn-ing and implied support. Surprisingly, the first explicit quotation is not until 4:6. Before this in 1:3–7 (*prooemium*), Paul interwove major scriptural motifs of God's compassion, comfort, and return from exile.[48]

D. COMPARISON WITH GENERALIZATION: At 2:14–17 the metaphor of God's Gospel of Christ proclaimed by Paul and ministry companions is like a Triumphal Pro-cession. This entails COMPARISON. This metaphor is deployed to explain the na-ture of their ministry and its dire consequences of life or death. In some sense, 2:14–17 GENERALIZES particulars of the following discourse as depicted below (NASB at left with key word/motif underlined):

14	But thanks be to God, who always leads us in triumph in Christ, and manifests [φανεροῦντι] through us the sweet aroma of the knowledge of Him in every place.	3:3–4 Paul is known via the letter of the Corinthians who are "manifest" as epistles of Christ. Φανερόω also occurs at 4:10–11; 5:10–11; 7:12; 11:6
15a	For we are a fragrance of Christ to God among those who <u>are being saved</u>	3:15–18 when one turns to the Lord, the veil is removed and they have the glory of the Lord, the Spirit and freedom.
15b	and <u>among those who are perishing</u>;	4:3 "among those who are perishing" (identical phrase; cf. 4:9)
16a	to the one an aroma from death to death, to the other an aroma from life to life.	4:7–5:15 the themes of life and death are found repeatedly

---

[48] Particularly helpful in showing this is Paul Barnett, *The Second Epistle to the Corinthians*, NICNT (Eerdmans, 1997), 68–69.

16b	And who is <u>adequate</u> [ἱκανός] for these things?	3:5–6 Paul et al.'s adequacy is affirmed (ἱκανός, ἱκανότης, ἱκανόω)
17a	For we are not like many, peddling the word of God, but as from sincerity,	In addition to chs. 8–9 about the collection, matters of Paul et al.'s handling of money recurs at 4:2; 7:2; 8:1–4; 11:7–11; 12:13–14
17b	but as from God, <u>we speak in Christ in the sight of God.</u>	12:19 "in the sight of God we speak in Christ" is an identical metacomment that generalizes 2 Cor.

While this network of themes addressed in the subsequent discourse is undeniable, we need not understand 2:14–17 to be the rhetorical *propositio* since we have already identified 1:17–24 as the *divisio* and *partitio*.[49] Nevertheless, the deployment of the socially prominent "triumphal procession" schema encapsulates a host of themes as an umbrella concept. This is quite significant given that Corinth had just been awarded the Provincial Imperial Cult at the ascension of Nero as emperor.[50] Thus, given the rhetorical situation of the prominence of the Imperial Cult and the temptations facing the Corinthians, Paul's usurpation of Roman Triumphal imagery is strategic.[51]

---

[49] Cf. George Alexander Kennedy, *New Testament Interpretation through Rhetorical Criticism*, Studies in Religion (University of North Carolina Press, 1984), 88–89. As one of the pioneers of applying rhetorical criticism to the NT, Kennedy understood 2:14–17 as the thesis statement (*propositio*) and partition (2:17) for the next several chapters: (A) "as men of sincerity (B) as commissioned by God (C) in the sight of God we speak in Christ." These partition heads are then realized as follows stopping at the end of ch. 6:

B "as commissioned by God" 3:4–4:1
A "as men of sincerity" 4:2–6
B "as commissioned by God" 4:7–12
A "as men of sincerity" 4:13–5:10
C "In the sight of God we speak in Christ" 5:11–6:13.

But Ben Witherington III understands 2:14–16 as the transition to the *propositio* of 2:17 (*Conflict and Community in Corinth: A Socio-Rhetorical Commentary on 1 and 2 Corinthians* [Eerdmans, 1995], 335 n. 27). For my critique of Kennedy and Witherington, see Long, *Ancient Rhetoric and Paul's Apology*, 160–62.

[50] See A. J. S. Spawforth, "The Achaean Federal Cult Part I: Pseudo-Julian, Letters 198," *TynBul* 46, no. 1 (1995): 151–68; B. W. Winter, "The Achaean Federal Imperial Cult II: The Corinthian Church," *TynBul* 46, no. 1 (1995): 169–78; idem, "The Enigma of Imperial Cultic Activities and Paul in Corinth," in *Greco-Roman Culture and the New Testament Studies Commemorating the Centennial of the Pontifical Biblical Institute*, ed. D. E. Aune and F. E. Brenk, NovTSup 143 (Brill, 2012), 49–72.

[51] See Fredrick J. Long, "'The god of This Age' (2 Cor 4:4) and Paul's Empire-Resisting Gospel," in *The First Urban Churches: Volume 2: Roman Corinth*, ed. James R. Harrison and Laurence L. Welborn, WGRWSup 7 (SBL Press, 2016), 219–69.

E. Recurrence of Contrast with Particularization: Throughout 2 Corinthians Paul's and his companions' conduct is CONTRASTED with that of others sporadically (1:12; 2:17; 4:2; 5:12, etc.). These CONTRASTS involve whether Paul et al. have ethical character or not, are preaching the Word of God for financial gain or not, offer self-commendation or not, exercise certain ministry practices and discipline or not, evidence miraculous powers or not, show divine approval or not, etc. For example, consider these individual statements throughout the discourse (NASB, underlining added) that often entail the discourse feature of point-counterpoint sets ("not this, but that").[52]

1:12 in holiness and godly sincerity, not in fleshly wisdom but in the grace of God, we have conducted ourselves in the world, and especially toward you.

2:17 For we are not like many, peddling the word of God, but as from sincerity, but as from God, we speak in Christ in the sight of God.

4:2 but we have renounced the things hidden because of shame, not walking in craftiness or adulterating the word of God, but by the manifestation of truth commending ourselves to every man's conscience in the sight of God.

5:12 We are not again commending ourselves to you but *are* giving you an occasion to be proud of us, so that you will have *an answer* for those who take pride in appearance and not in heart.

6:3–4 giving no cause for offense in anything, so that the ministry will not be discredited, but in everything commending ourselves as servants of God, in much endurance, in afflictions, in hardships, in distresses,

10:3–4 For though we walk in the flesh, we do not war according to the flesh, for the weapons of our warfare are not of the flesh, but divinely powerful for the destruction of fortresses.

10:8–9 For even if I boast somewhat further about our authority, which the Lord gave for building you up and not for destroying you, I will not be put to shame, for I do not wish to seem as if I would terrify you by my letters.

10:13 But we will not boast beyond *our* measure, but within the measure of the sphere which God apportioned to us as a measure, to reach even as far as you.

11:6 But even if I am unskilled in speech, yet I am not *so* in knowledge; in fact, in every way we have made *this* evident to you in all things.

etc.

---

[52] On the use of οὐκ ... ἀλλά versus contrast made with δέ, see Levinsohn, *Discourse Features*, 38, 48, 114–16; for point-counter point sets, see Runge, *Discourse Grammar*, ch.4.

This contrast becomes most intense and PARTICULARIZED in chs. 10–12 where Paul interweaves his reply to specific critiques pertaining to his presence versus his letters (10:1–11), then turns to critique and refute his rivals (10:12–11:15) before moving to foolishly boast about himself still contrasting himself with other rivals intermittently (11:16–12:10).[53] Form-critically, 10:1–11:15 is a *refutatio* section of a judicial speech and 11:16–12:10 is Paul's parody of self-praise that defendants performed in ancient apology after the refutation.[54]

Discursively, *narratio* #2 (2:12–13) and *narratio* #3 (7:2–16) serve as bookends to the central three argument units of 2:14–3:18, 4:1–5:10, and 5:11–7:1. These three units continue to follow the order of the central three argument heads of the *partitio* found in 1:18–20 (the faithfulness of God's Word and Promises), 1:21–22 (God's establishment of Paul and the Corinthians in view of the "down deposit of the Spirit"), and 1:23 (Paul as God's covenant agent working to "spare" and reconcile). Helping demarcate each of these central three units are four common themes at the start of each: Paul's Word/Rhetoric, Commendation, God's purview of the Activities of Paul and Ministry Companions, and References to Paul's Rivals.[55]

Theme	Rhetoric in Relation to God's Word and Paul's Proclamation	(Self-) Commendation	God's Purview of the Activities of Paul et al.	Implicit or Explicit References to Paul's Missionary Rivals
2:17–3:1	2:17a "For we are not, like the majority, peddling the word of God, but we speak out of sincerity..."	3:1a "Are we beginning to commend ourselves again? ... "	2:17b "... and [we speak] as from God before God in Christ."	2:17 "like the majority" 3:1b "... Or, it isn't that we need, as some, letters of recommendation to you or from you, is it?!"
4:1–2	4:2a "But we renounce shameful secret things, not walking in dishonesty, nor disguising the Word of God..."	4:2b "but in the manifestation of the truth, commending ourselves to every conscience of persons before God."	4:2b "but in the manifestation of the truth ... before God"	4:1 "On account of this, since we have this ministry, just as we received mercy, we do not grow weary." 4:2a "not walking in dishonesty, nor disguising the Word of God,"

---

[53] For details of this contrast, see "Table 8.10 Paul's criticism of and difference from his missionary rivals" in Long, *Ancient Rhetoric and Paul's Apology*, 182.

[54] For the *refutatio* and self-adulation as discrete forms of defensive judicial speeches, see Long, *Ancient Rhetoric and Paul's Apology*, 89–95 and 186–90, respectively. St. Augustine understood Paul's boast to begin at 11:16 (*Doctr. chr.* 4.7.12); see Edwin A. Judge, "Paul's Boasting in Relation to Contemporary Professional Practice," *ABR* 16.1–4 (1968): 37–50 at 48.

[55] Slightly adapted from Long, *2 Corinthians*, xxii; cf. Chart. 8.4 in Long, *Ancient Rhetoric and Paul's Apology*, 164.

5:11–12	5:11a "Therefore, because we know the fear of the Lord, we persuade people …"	5:12a "We are not again commending ourselves to you …"	5:11b "… moreover we are well known to God. Additionally, I hope to be known also in your consciences."	5:12b "… but we are giving to you an opportunity of boasting on our behalf, in order that you would have (something) for those who boast about reputation and not about the heart."

These sections particularly reflect the heart of Paul's crafted arguments about his integrity of speech in relation to God in implicit CONTRAST to his missionary or ministry rivals. This issue of "commendation," as many commentators have noted, creates cohesion in the discourse. In his previous letter (1 Cor 16:3), Paul had asked the Corinthians to approve of people to be sent "with letters (of commendation)" to deliver the collection with Paul. Now, in 2 Cor 3, Paul would seem himself to have been challenged and in need to have "a letter of recommendation" himself; but Paul argued that the Corinthians themselves were in fact his letter of recommendation.

F. RECURRENCE OF CRUCIALITY WITH GENERALIZATION AND CLIMAX: Throughout 2 Corinthians, Paul records various types of sufferings (1:4, 6, 8; 2:4; 4:8–12, 17; 6:4–10; 7:4–5, 9, 12; 8:2; 11:23–27; 12:10). These discourse sections are identified as lists of afflictions or *peristasis* catalogues from the Greek word περίστασις "a surrounding; circumstance."[56] Yet, such suffering frames the whole discourse (1:4, 6, 8; 2:4) and pervades it at a critical transition point (7:4–5, 9, 12; 8:2). They are RECURRENCES in the discourse. These *peristaseis* are the basis (cause) for the surprising divine provision and affirmation; this CAUSATION and surprising reversal is identified by the MSR called CRUCIALITY.

In 2 Corinthians, we find suffering met with encouragement, inadequacy with adequacy, death with life, scarcity with provision, and ultimately weakness with grace and strength. This RECURRENCE OF CRUCIALITY serves to bolster Paul's and his ministry companions' claim to integrity in general and towards the Corinthians, and especially to Paul's divine legitimization. As the discourse moves to a finale, these sufferings are GENERALIZED in the notion of "being weak" or having "weakness" (ἀσθένεια, ἀσθενέω) at 11:21, 29–30; 12:5 and then are paired paradoxically with "being powerful," having "power," or "being empowered" (δυνατός, δύναμις, δυνατέω) in the climactic and concluding statements at 12:9–10 and 13:3–4, 9. The letter reaches a CLIMAX in 12:1–10 with Paul's discussion of his heavenly experiences and his thrice offered prayer request in which there exists contrast

---

[56] See, e.g., the classic treatment by John T. Fitzgerald, *Cracks in an Earthen Vessel: An Examination of the Catalogues of Hardships in the Corinthian Correspondence* (Scholars Press, 1988).

(these experiences are inexpressible things and Paul is unable to receive healing), but are yet effectively overcome and met with a direct, cogent word of the risen Lord given to him. This "oracle-like" direct word is the capstone of divine affirmation of Paul.

> 12:9 And He has said to me, "My grace is sufficient for you, for power is perfected in weakness." Most gladly, therefore, I will rather boast about my weaknesses, so that the power of Christ may dwell in me. 10 Therefore I am well content with weaknesses, with insults, with distresses, with persecutions, with difficulties, for Christ's sake; for when I am weak, then I am strong. (my translation)

G. CHIASM WITH GENERALIZATION AND PURPOSE: At 12:11, the asyndeton and self-reflective meta-comment "I have become foolish; you yourselves forced me!" (Γέγονα ἄφρων, ὑμεῖς με ἠναγκάσατε) marks a new unit concluding a speech called the *peroratio*.[57] Used here in the conclusion of the discourse is the conventional topos of the need for self-praise in one's defense ("I was forced to do so!").[58] Most importantly, 12:11–13:10 retraces the whole discourse (CHIASM) while making general statements (GENERALIZATION) about the nature and purpose of the discourse; Moisés Silva acknowledged the merit of this recapitulation structure when reviewing my monograph.[59] This is precisely one form-critical purpose of the *peroratio*, i.e., to summarize the discourse; additionally, the litigant would self-reflect on the rendering of a decision, make a final appeal, and project the consequences of right (or wrong) actions. These Paul does while including the Corinthians as those on trial along with him. He warns of decisions needing to be made about the Corinthians' own sinfulness (12:20–13:4), saying that he "will not spare" anyone when he arrives: "on the basis of two or three witnesses, every matter will be established" quoting from Deuteronomy (17:6 or 19:15; cf. Matt 18:16). Then Paul raises the question of whether his own actions are "approved" or not (13:5–8). This is a decision for the Corinthians to make. Finally, Paul appeals to his own commitment to the truth and the authority given to him by Christ, although he appears weak, to build up the Corinthians with the hope of not needing to tear them down (13:8–10). Thus, in 12:11–13:10 we observe what is at stake for Paul and the Corinthians in response to the discourse set forth.

---

[57] Discussed in Long, *Ancient Rhetoric and Paul's Apology*, 191–97.

[58] For discussion and numerous ancient examples, see Long, *Ancient Rhetoric and Paul's Apology*, 191.

[59] Moisés Silva, review of Fredrick J. Long, *Ancient Rhetoric and Paul's Apology: The Compositional Unity of 2 Corinthians*, *Review of Biblical Literature* [http://www.bookreviews.org] (2005). He says, "Long makes a respectable case for the view that the section from 12:11 to 13:10 recapitulates (in inverted order) the major arguments of the letter" (3).

So, at 12:11 Paul begins a retrospective and inverted CHIASTIC overview of the whole discourse that GENERALIZES the content as follows:[60]

Verses	Wording of the Recapitulation	Earlier Sections Summarized
12:11–13	Paul's foolishness; commendation in light of false apostles; Paul's genuine apostleship and signs.	10:1–12:10 Paul addresses critiques; confronts the false apostles; and boasts of himself.
12:14–18	Paul's coming, seeking the Corinthians, not their money, sending Titus and the brother, not taking advantage of them.	7:2–9:15 Paul discusses Titus's report; the logistics of the collection; and sending Titus and the brother.
12:19–13:4	Paul et al.'s defense is for upbuilding; they are beloved; strong moral exhortation given.	5:11–7:1 Paul calls the Corinthians to repent, but addresses them as beloved children.
13:1–4	Paul's coming, witnesses, sin confronted; Paul's speech in Christ, weakness, life, and power.	5:11–7:1 and 2:14–5:10 Paul confronts sin in the letter of tears and calls for their reconciliation in view of life and death realities.
13:5–10	Corinthian self-examination and test; Paul's seemingly acting unapproved; his writing presently but coming soon; Paul's moral authority not with severity but for building up.	2:1–11 Paul's previous writing instead of coming and the Corinthians' proper action to recognize sin but to forgive
13:11–13	The five imperative verbs generalize Paul's particular call for the Corinthians to act consistently with the covenantal salvation offered in the Gospel of Jesus as the Son of God, specifically to be "encouraged" and to "have joy" (13:11). The closing returns to the themes of "grace" and "peace" of God in Christ (13:11b, 13) in the context of "all the saints" and "all of you" (13:12, 13).	1:1–24 Believers are to "encourage" one another and show mutuality (be united) (1:3–7). Paul and company work for the Corinthians' joy (1:24). Paul offers "grace" and "peace" through God in Christ (1:2). Also, there is the inclusive scope of "all" in reference to the Corinthians and those in the whole of Achaia (1:1).
13:14	Reference to the Lord Jesus Christ, God, and the Holy Spirit as well as to grace, love, and fellowship respectively, provides an overview of God revealed as working among Paul and the Corinthians.	God is mentioned in 1:1, 2, et *passim*. The Lord, Jesus Christ, is mentioned in 1:2, 3 *et passim*. The Holy Spirit is first mentioned in 1:22; 3:3, 6, *et passim* as a feature of the New Covenant to be enjoyed in joint fellowship.

---

[60] This chart is adapted significantly from Table 8.13 "The inverted recapitulation of 2 Corinthians in 12:11–13:10" in Long, *Ancient Rhetoric and Paul's Apology*, 196.

Here it may be helpful to discuss the epistolary closing of 13:11–14. Helping de-marcate this final unit of the discourse is asyndeton, the word Λοιπόν "the rest," the vocative ἀδελφοί "brethren," and the change of person (first person to sec-ond) with a changed verbal mode moving to imperatives. According to Jeffrey A. D. Weima, this closing has the following conventional features:

> 13:11a Hortatory Section
> 13:11b Peace Benediction
> 13:12 Greetings
> 13:12a Kiss greeting
> 13:12b Third-person greeting
> 13:13 Grace Benediction[61]

In 13:11a, the five concluding exhortations are present tense imperatives and re-late to "the problem of division in the Corinthian church" stated negatively;[62] or, stated positively, to the theme of unity: "keep rejoicing, continually be restored, keep being encouraged, be thinking alike, continue in peace" (χαίρετε, καταρτίζεσθε, παρακαλεῖσθε, τὸ αὐτὸ φρονεῖτε, εἰρηνεύετε).

In this regard, 2 Corinthians concludes similarly to the five present impera-tives of 1 Cor 16:13–14.[63] Wiema observes several elaborations (additions) from the normal Pauline convention: First, the addition of the Peace benediction (13:11b); second, the three-part nature of divine agency "the grace of the Lord, Jesus Christ, the love of God, and the fellowship of the Holy Spirit" (13:13); and, third, the addition of "all" in the final "[be] with you all." Weima argues such ad-ditions are "intimately connected with the theme of unity. In fact, every one of the closing conventions of 2 Corinthians has been written and/or adapted in such a way as to relate directly to the primary issue dealt with in this particular letter."[64]

Returning to the CHIASM, 12:19 and 13:10 contain GENERALIZED PURPOSE state-ments about 2 Corinthians as a complete discourse that is perceived by the Co-rinthians to be a formal defense but with significant aspects of admonition for the sake of their "upbuilding" (12:19):

> 12:19 All this time you have been thinking that we are defending ourselves to you. *Actually*, it is in the sight of God that we have been speaking in Christ; and all for your **upbuilding**, beloved.

---

[61] Weima, *Neglected Endings*, 209.
[62] Ibid.
[63] Harris, *Second Epistle*, 931.
[64] Weima, *Neglected Endings*, 210.

Then also, the epistle was required by the situation of Paul's absence (13:10):

> 13:10 For this reason I am writing these things while absent, so that when pre-
> sent I *need* not use severity, in accordance with the authority which the Lord
> gave me for **building** up and not for tearing down.

Both GENERAL STATEMENTS express the PURPOSE of the discourse as a whole: Paul
does everything for their upbuilding. Thus, although 2 Corinthians looks like an
apology in terms of genre, this self-defense serves the ultimate political PURPOSE
of encouraging/building up the Corinthians.

H. RECURRENCE OF KEY TERMS/IDEAS: The following terms or ideas are repeated
across a majority of the discourse. Some may relate to one or more of the MSRs
identified above.[65]

1. Encourage/exhort (e.g., παρακαλέω and cognates) 1:3–7; 2:7–8; 5:20; 6:1;
   7:4–7, 13; 8:4, 17; 9:5; 10:1; 12:18; 13:11;
2. Death: 1:8–10; 2:16; 3:7; 4:11–12; 5:14–15; 6:9; 7:10; 11:23;
3. Money or its allusion: 2:17; 4:2; 7:2; chs. 8–9 (esp. 8:5, 20–21); 11:8; 12:16–17;
4. The Corinthians' moral failures: 2:5–11; 6:1–7:1; 12:20–21; 13:5, 7;
5. Paul's intentions regarding the Corinthians (1:12–17; 2:1, 4, 9; 2:4; chs. 7–9;
   12:20–13:10) and his feelings for the Corinthians (1:15; 6:11–13; 7:2–4; 8:7, 16);
6. Grace/Thanks (χαρίς): 1:2, 12, 15; 2:14; 4:15; 6:1; 8:1, 4, 6–7, 9, 16, 19; 9:8, 14–
   15; 12:9; 13:13; (χαρίζομαι): 2:7, 10; 12:13;
7. Glory (δόξα): 1:20; 3:7–9, 18; 4:4, 6, 15, 17; 6:8; 8:19, 23; (δοξάζω): 3:10; 9:13;
8. to commend (συνίστημι): 3:1; 4:2; 5:12; 6:4; 7:11; 10:12, 18; 12:11; commenda-
   tory (συστατικός) 3:1;
9. boasting (καύχησις) 1:12; 7:4, 14; 8:24; 11:10, 17; boast (καύχημα) 1:14; 5:12; 9:3;
   to boast (καυχάομαι) 5:12; 7:14; 9:2; 10:8, 13, 15–17; 11:12, 16, 18, 30; 12:1, 5–6, 9.

V. Strategic Areas

The following are locations in the discourse that best reflect or represent the
MSRs identified above. If preaching or teaching through 2 Corinthians, these
passages would deserve special attention and/or may serve as the basis for a limited sermon or teaching series (say, over 8 to 10 weeks).

A. 1:12–14 reflects INTRODUCTION WITH INSTRUMENTATION AND GENERALIZATION
B. 1:17–24 is where there is PROBLEM-SOLUTION WITH SUMMARIZATION

---

[65] For other recurrences (such as ὑπέρ and περί cognates), see Long, *2 Corinthians, passim.*

C. 6:14–18 best represents Substantiation by Recurrence of Scripture Use
D. 2:14–17 best reflects Comparison with Generalization
E. 10:12–11:15 represents Recurrence of Contrast with Particularization
F. 12:1–10 represents Recurrence of Cruciality with Generalization & Climax
G. 12:19 and 13:10 best reflect Chiasm with General Statements of Purpose
H. 6:1–7:1 represents most of the Recurrence of Key Terms/Ideas

This ends my book survey of 2 Corinthians. I will next focus on 6:1–9:15 by investigating literary forms, emphatic constructions, and prominence devices. The material in 6:1–7:16 is a zone of turbulence and transitional to the critical appeal Paul offers for the Corinthians to finish their portion of the Collection (8:1–9:15).

Micro-Structural Analysis of 6:1–9:15 (Literary Forms, Emphasis, and Prominence)

The material in 6:1–9:15 contains a striking variety of literary forms precisely where Paul is speaking with "open mouth"; he and Timothy are showcasing their rhetorical ability having already admitted, "knowing the fear of the Lord, we are persuading people" (5:11). Consider the information structure of the lack of connectors (participles and asyndeton) as well as the following literary forms.

Connector	Units	Literary Form and Explanation
δέ	6:1–2	an exhortation (παρακαλέω) substantiated with a *pesher*-like appropriation of God's speech from Isa 49:8a. Here, Paul et al. are "coworking" with God such that God's covenantal call and Word has become Paul et al.'s covenantal call to the Corinthians.
post-nuclear explanatory participles[66]	6:3–10	an extensive list of twenty-eight items attesting to God's approval of Paul's ministry that culminates in affirming he is "possessing all things."[67]
ø asyndeton	6:11–13	a meta-commentative statement of Paul's open mouth and heart calling for mutual relational openness with the Corinthians.
ø asyndeton	6:14–7:1	a well-crafted epicheireme with its own admonitions, lists, and supportive catena of covenantal Scripture texts.
ø asyndeton	7:2–16	a distributed narrative that serves as a transition to the next *probatio* unit. While continuing the "openness" theme, Paul flatly denies any wrongdoing (7:2) and clarifies his confidence the Corinthians just before appealing for them to finish their part in the collection. This material displays a lexically tight chiasm centered in 7:8, showcasing Paul's literary and rhetorical prowess.

---

[66] For a discourse functional and information structural approach to circumstantial participles, see the discussion and examples in Long, *Koine Greek Grammar*, 326–39.

[67] For a semantic diagram and analysis of 6:1–10, see Long, *Koine Greek Grammar*, 288–90.

δέ	8:1–9:15	The δέ marks +distinctive development. This material contains a unified rhetorical disposition that begins with narrative material (8:1–6) that moves into a *partition* of three argument heads (8:7, 8, 9) and then corresponding arguments to these three heads (8:10–9:12) before then concluding (9:13–15).

To help demonstrate the value of attending to emphatic constructions and prominence devices, I will discuss a variety of those present in 6:1–7:4. After this, I will look at the epicheireme rhetorical argument form in 6:14–7:1 followed by the significance of the narrative transition of 7:2–16 and its chiastic structure.

So, within 6:1–7:4, one observes numerous places of emphasis through prominence devices that particularly underscore Paul's proximate and distal discourse messaging:

- A thematic addition of καί in καὶ παρακαλοῦμεν ("we also are exhorting") highlights the participation of Paul et al. with God's admonition (6:1).
- Metacomments about Paul's and God's speech (6:2, 11, 13, 16–18; 7:1, 2–4) heighten the prominence of the material by explicitly referring to the communicative act of speech, admonition, and the rhetorical situation.
- The attention getter, ἰδού "Behold!" (6:2) underscores Paul's repeating God's word "Behold, now is the day of salvation!" and the need for the Corinthians to respond.
- The list of 6:3–10 and its development through increasing complexity creates prominence.[68]
- The list concludes climactically in 6:10c with quantitative emphasis: "as poor, but enriching <u>many</u>; as having <u>nothing</u> and possessing <u>all</u>" (μηδὲν ἔχοντες καὶ πάντα κατέχοντες).[69]
- In 6:4, the fronted genitive θεοῦ stresses God as the one for whom Paul et al. are servants.[70]
- In 6:11, verbal aspectual prominence attends the use of the perfect tense verb forms ἀνέῳγεν and πεπλάτυνται ("is opened ... is widened").[71]
- In 6:11 also, the vocative of direct address "Corinthians" specifies their civic identity that was a major factor in their bad associations and idolatry that is confronted in 6:14–16.[72]

---

[68] For a discussion of lists along with guidelines for their interpretation, see Long, *Koine Greek Grammar*, 282–90 and Long, *In Step with God's Word*, 218–26.

[69] Long, *Koine Greek Grammar*, 221–23, 224, 541.

[70] For a discussion and examples, see Long, *Koine Greek Grammar*, 77–78, 367–68.

[71] For the relative discourse prominence of the perfect tense in relation to other tenses interacting with various authorities (like Porter), see Long, *Koine Greek Grammar*, 245–47.

- Cultural topics converge in 6:13 with numerous emphatic constructions. These topics include processional imagery, mutual exchange, parental address of children, and an emphatic subject in final sentence position. Taken together, 6:11–13 tees up the very prominent and rhetorically powerful unit, 6:14–7:1 that I will treat form-critically momentarily.
- In 6:14a, the prohibition Μὴ γίνεσθε ἑτεροζυγοῦντες ἀπίστοις ("Do not continue becoming unequally yoked to unbelievers!") is more prominent than a simple (aorist) prohibition with the subjunctive (μὴ ἑτεροζυγήσητε) would have been in four ways: 1) imperfective verbal aspect (present tense vs. aorist); 2) the periphrastic construction that stresses the verbal action as an attribute;[73] 3) the unusual use of γίνομαι rather than εἰμί in the periphrastic construction; and 4) the lexical uniqueness of the focal verb ἑτεροζυγέω.
- Interrogative emphasis in the form of a list of five questions follows in 6:14b–16a.[74] In 6:16b, subject emphasis occurs with the unnecessary subject pronoun ἡμεῖς.
- The catena of Scripture quotation in 6:16b–18 contains several points of emphasis, such as the recitative ὅτι in 16b,[75] the redundant quotative frames in 6:17 (λέγει κύριος) and 6:18 (λέγει κύριος παντοκράτωρ),[76] and the ideological prominence in the face of idolatry of "the Almighty" (6:18).
- At 7:1, we observe four points of prominence: 1) the discontinuous constituents "these ... promises" (ταύτας ... τὰς ἐπαγγελίας) are backward referencing and construe the Scripture citations as "promises"; 2) the vocative "beloved" offsets the following hortatory subjunctive ("Let us cleanse ourselves");[77] 3) quantitative emphasis attends "all defilement" (παντὸς μολυσμοῦ); 4) the post-nuclear circumstantial participle clause explains the goal and motivation for cleansing.
- At 7:2 is reference to the "openness" theme followed by three parallel statements of denial with fronted and quantitative emphasis on "nobody" (οὐδένα): "Nobody we wronged! Nobody we corrupted! Nobody we took advantage of!"

---

[72] Regarding the nature of the idolatry and the meaning of "Beliar," see Long, "'The god of This Age,'" 224, 255–60. One must understand the immediate, burgeoning influence of the Imperial Cult at Corinth to fully understand the ideological import of 2 Cor 2–7.

[73] For a discussion of periphrastic emphasis, see Long, *Koine Greek Grammar*, 374–76.

[74] For a discussion of interrogative emphasis, see Long, *Koine Greek Grammar*, 257–62.

[75] See Long, *Koine Greek Grammar*, 158–59.

[76] For a discussion of redundant quotative frames where a known speaker is identified again, see Levinsohn, *Discourse Features*, 272, 278 and Runge, *Discourse Grammar*, 151–52.

[77] For a discussion of the potency of exhortations, see Long, *Koine Greek Grammar*, 501–5.

- At 7:3 is a proximate metacomment ("I am not speaking to condemn") that reflects a possible accusatory judicial perception of the discourse. Paul clarifies this and supports (γάρ) with an anaphoric distal meta-comment and a perfect tense ("I have spoken" προείρηκα).
- In 7:4a is quantitative emphasis in a metacomment ("I have <u>much</u> [πολλή] boldness towards you"), and in the parallel "I have <u>much</u> [πολλή] boasting for you," whose dative of possession (μοι), I maintain, marks +personal proximity as distinct from the more common genitive of possession would.[78] This dative of possession implies personal involvement in the bold speech and boasting.

So, a careful study of emphatic constructions allows one to track thematic prominence and progression previously or subsequently in the discourse. These choices of constructions, as opposed to other possible ones, affect construal for rhetorical impact. I hope to have shown how the themes of 6:1–7:4 relate to core features of Paul's admonitions, Paul's defense of his ministry, Paul's paradoxical living in the face of death, Paul's speaking on behalf of God in Christ, Paul's receiving encouragement amidst afflictions, and Paul's encouragement and boasting in the Corinthians.

Three further micro-structural aspects are now my focus: the literary form of the epicheireme argument in 6:14–7:1, the chiasm of 7:2–16, and the rhetorical disposition of 8:1–9:15. First, having investigated the epicheirematic nature of Paul's argumentation in 1 Thessalonians, Galatians, and 2 Corinthians, let me provide a brief introduction here.[79] The epicheireme consists of a basic syllogistic structure consisting of five parts:

1. Major Premise (*propositio*)
2. Proof of Major Premise (*propositionis approbatio*)
3. Minor Premise (*assumptio*)
4. Proof of Minor Premise (*assumptionis approbatio*)
5. Conclusion (*conclusio*)

---

[78] See Long, *Koine Greek Grammar*, 265.

[79] Fredrick J. Long, "From Epicheiremes to Exhortation: A Pauline Method for Moral Persuasion in Hellenistic Socio-Rhetorical Context," *Queen: Rhetorics, Ethics & Moral Persuasion in Biblical Discourse* (T&T Clark, 2002); idem, "'We Destroy Arguments...' (2 Corinthians 10:5): The Apostle Paul's Use of Epicheirematic Argumentation," in *Proceedings of the Fifth Conference of the International Society for the Study of Argumentation*, ed. F. H. van Eemeren et al. (Sic Sac, 2003), 697–703; idem, "From Epicheiremes to Exhortation: A Pauline Method for Moral Persuasion in 1 Thessalonians," in *Rhetoric, Ethic, and Moral Persuasion in Biblical Discourse*, ed. Thomas H. Olbricht and Anders Eriksson, Emory Studies in Early Christianity (T&T Clark, 2005), 179–95. For 2 Corinthians, see Long, *Ancient Rhetoric and Paul's Apology*, 220.

Cicero indicates that each of these five parts need not be present, and gives examples of shorter formulations in which one or both proofs are omitted. Both Cicero and Quintilian (*Inst.* 5.14.30) also advise variety in the argument form to avoid boredom.

In literary form, 6:14–7:1 is a clear syllogistic epicheireme with powerful embellishment. A climax of sorts has been reached in the discourse:

Premise A	[14a] Do not become incompatibly joined with unbelievers;
Proof of A	[14b] for [γάρ] what partnership have righteousness and lawlessness, or what fellowship has light with darkness? [15] Or what harmony has Christ with Belial, or what has a believer in common with an unbeliever? [16a] Or what agreement has the temple of God with idols?
Premise B	[16b] For [γάρ] we ourselves are the temple of the living God;
Proof of B	[16c] just as [καθώς] God said, "I will dwell in them and walk among them, and I will be their God, and they themselves will be my people [Exod 29:45; Lev 26:12]. [17] Therefore [διό], come out from their midst and be separate," says the Lord. "And do not touch what is unclean [Isa 52:11], and I will welcome you. [18] And I will be a Father to you, and you shall be sons and daughters to Me [2 Sam 7:14]," says the Lord Almighty.
Conclusion	[7:1] Therefore [οὖν], beloved, since we have these promises [B], let us cleanse ourselves from all defilement of flesh and spirit [A/B], by perfecting holiness in reverence to God.

Premise A is supported with **Proof A** that contains five rhetorical questions, a structure also found in Cicero (*Inv.* I.69, 70) and Quintilian (*Inst.* 5.14.19). **Premise B** is marked as providing support (γάρ) because it is the more general premise and presented second. This created variety (as was recommended); it also allowed the main admonition of 6:14a to be clear. **Proof B** is quite elaborative which Cicero encouraged (*Inv.* I.58). Here Paul thrice mentions God as speaker and concludes with Paul as prophet speaking God's word, "Thus says the Lord Almighty." The Conclusion is appropriately deductive and combines thematic elements of A and B.

Why would Paul carefully compose such an epicheireme with intricate elaborated proofs? Well, in 6:14–7:1 we have reached a crucial moment in the discourse. We observe Paul presenting himself as speaking boldly God's Word to the Corinthians culminating in a very clear and logically sound, Scripture-quoted, God-spoken rhetorical epicheireme in 6:14–7:1. Paul has openly played his (card) hand; he has clearly "opened his mouth" to speak to the "Corinthians." Because of their syllogistic structure, Quintilian warned against extensive use of enthymemes or epicheiremes in speeches (*Inst.* 5.14.27–28, LCL) which rather "would resemble dialogues and dialectical controversies ... with learned men seeking for truth among men of learning; consequently they subject everything to a minute and scrupulous inquiry with a view to arriving at clear and convincing truths...." Paul spoke clearly and soundly; he honors and elevates the content by this form.

Another achievement form-critically is that 7:4–16 is structured as a chiasm centering on exact lexical correspondences mirrored in 7:8.[80] It is unmistakable. The center is Paul's possible regret of writing a grief-causing epistle.[81]

7:7b	**A** ... ὥστε με μᾶλλον χαρῆναι	"... so that I rejoiced more!"
7:8	**B** Ὅτι εἰ καὶ ἐλύπησα ὑμᾶς	"Because, if also I grieved you"
	C ἐν τῇ ἐπιστολῇ,	"in the epistle,"
	D οὐ μεταμέλομαι·	"I am not regretting [it]."
	D' εἰ καὶ μετεμελόμην,	"If also I was regretting [it],"
	C' βλέπω [γὰρ] ὅτι ἡ ἐπιστολὴ ἐκείνη	"I see yes that this epistle,"
	B' εἰ καὶ πρὸς ὥραν ἐλύπησεν ὑμᾶς,	"if even for an hour, grieved you,"
7:9a	**A** νῦν χαίρω ...	"now I rejoice ..."

Then, lexically and thematically, the chiasm extends the rest of the chapter excepting 7:2–3 that are transitional in nature:

A—7:4 Paul's comfort and "joy" (χαρά) with "confidence" (παρρησία) and boast for the Corinthians

  B—7:5 Paul's initial statement of having "fears within" (ἔσωθεν φόβοι)

    C—7:6–7a God "encouraged" (παρεκάλεσεν) Paul at the coming of Titus

      D—7:7a Corinthian response, including "longing" (ἐπιπόθησις) and "zeal" (ζῆλος)

        E—7:7b "so that I rejoiced even more" (ὥστε με μᾶλλον χαρῆναι)

          F—7:8a Grieving (λυπέω)

            G—7:8b Letter (ἡ ἐπιστολή)

              H—7:8c Regret (μεταμέλομαι)

              H'—7:8d Regret (μεταμέλομαι)

---

[80] One of my students, Joseph Driver, first observed the chiasm in 7:8; from there, I was able to see the entire chiasm; this discussion is adapted from Long, *2 Corinthians*, 141–43.

[81] Investigating the nature of grief in this context is L. L. Welborn, "Paul and Pain: Paul's Emotional Therapy in 2 Corinthians 1.1–2.13; 7.5–16 in the Context of Ancient Psychagogic Literature," *NTS* 57 (2011): 1–24; idem, "Paul's Appeal to the Emotions in 2 Corinthians 1.1–2.13; 7.5–16," *JSNT* 23 (2001): 31–60. One critique is Welborn's commitment to partition theories.

G'—7:8e Letter (ἡ ἐπιστολὴ)

F'—7:8f Grieving (λυπέω)

E'—7:9a "I now rejoice" (νῦν χαίρω)

D'—7:9b–12 Corinthian response, including "longing" (ἐπιπόθησις) and "zeal" (ζῆλος)

C'—7:13 Paul "was encouraged" (παρακεκλήμεθα) and rejoiced with Titus' joy

B'—7:14–15 The resolution of Paul's fear by renewed confidence by Titus at the Corinthians' reception of Titus "with fear and trembling" (μετὰ φόβου καὶ τρόμου)

A'—Paul's "rejoicing" in confidence for the Corinthians (χαίρω ὅτι ἐν παντὶ θαρρῶ ἐν ὑμῖν)

Why would Paul compose such a chiasm? What effect would it have on the Corinthians? I believe it shows Paul's care, anxiety, and hope for the Corinthians. This *narratio* #3 concerns Paul meeting up with Titus in Macedonia who updates Paul about the Corinthians. Retelling Titus's report affords Paul an opportunity to express his own confidence in the Corinthians; it serves the purpose of explaining Paul's careful *modus operandi* and thus prepares for his delicate appeal for the Corinthians to finish their part in the Collection (chs. 8–9).

Taking a step back and looking at the totality of 6:1–7:16, the discourse brings to culmination both Paul's response to criticism from ch.1—Paul's afflictions and need for comfort, Paul's ministry conduct, Paul's failure to visit and writing instead, and Paul's relation to God's covenant in Christ—and the Roman triumph and epiphany procession metaphor initiated at 2:14. It also serves to transition (the *narratio* #3) to the practical matter of the Collection. Observing Paul's emphasis on his speaking and the display of various literary speech forms including the urgent, logical appeals of the living God speaking from Scripture allows us to appreciate Paul's creative persuasion (5:11) and theology as God's ambassador (5:20). He represents God in Christ and acts as God's prophetic mouthpiece; he continues the Suffering Servant's ministry through embodying the ministry of Isa 49:8 (2 Cor 6:1–2). Paul's prophetic covenantal speech, while utilizing recognizable conventional literary forms and social themes (lists, epicheireme, pagan processional imagery, grieving), is theologically grounded in God's covenantal goal to have a holy people of sons and daughters who are, in their identity, the temple of the living God. The interweaving and culmination of these themes in 6:1–7:16 indicates the delicate and complex exigency of criticisms against Paul and his companions and Paul's counter charge against the Corinthians of improper relations with pagan unbelievers that involved flirting with idolatry (6:16). Paul had to write a letter that was causing grief (7:8) but now has resulted in his joy.

Once again, the narrative transition in 7:2–16 helps demarcate the final argument unit of 8:1–9:15 before the refutation of opponents (10:1–11:15), self-adulation (11:16–12:10), conclusion (12:11–13:10), and epistolary closing (13:11–13). This final argument unit of 8:1–9:15 is itself in the form of a unified mini-speech.[82] To have little "speeches" within a unified discourse is shown in narrative materials (e.g., Thucydides's *The Peloponnesian War* and the Book of Acts) and has precedent in extant forensic speeches and at other places in Paul's epistles.[83]

I. *Narratio*: 8:1–6 – The Macedonians' example in giving
- initiated with disclosure formula ("We want you to know, brethren")
- employs Paul as a witness (cf. 1:8, 12)

II. *Partitio*: 8:7–9
  A 8:7 "But [ἀλλ'] as you excel in everything—in faith, in speech, in knowledge, in utmost eagerness [σπουδή], and in our love for you—so we want you to excel also in this generous undertaking."
  B 8:8 "[Ø] I do not say this as a command, but I am testing [δοκιμάζω] the genuineness of your love against the eagerness [σπουδή] of others."
  C 8:9–10a "For [γάρ] you know the grace [χάρις] of our Lord Jesus Christ, that though He was rich [πλούσιος], yet for your sake He became poor, so that you through His poverty might become rich [πλουτέω]. And I am offering my perspective on this matter."

III. *Probatio*: 8:10b–9:12
  A 8:10b–15: The Corinthians' former readiness [προθυμία]
  B1 8:16–24: The eagerness [σπουδή] of Titus, Paul, and the brother and their readiness [προθυμία] and Paul's approval [δοκιμάζω] of the brother
  B2 9:1–5: Concerning the ministry to the saints, the readiness [προθυμία] of the Macedonians and the rest of the Achaeans
  C 9:6–12: Theological appeal to give generously since they have been enriched [πλουτίζω] by God's grace [χάρις]

IV. *Peroratio*: 9:13–15 – God's Indescribable Gift

---

[82] Pace Hans Dieter Betz, *2 Corinthians 8 and 9: A Commentary on Two Administrative Letters of the Apostle Paul*, Hermeneia (Fortress, 1985). My dispositional analysis as well as the Περὶ μὲν γὰρ τῆς διακονίας of 9:1 indicate that chs. 8 and 9 are unified.

[83] See discussions and examples in Long, *Ancient Rhetoric and Paul's Apology*, 79–81, 123, 173–77; the outline is adapted from 176. Distinct dispositional speech units in Paul include 1 Cor 7, 12–14, 15.

Key notions are God's example of grace and provision of Christ; and the eagerness, readiness, and approval of various people and groups. The purpose of this final section is to report on Paul's integrity in the steps taken for the Collection effort while also making a final appeal to the Corinthians to finish their promise.

Chapter 9 especially displays persuasive rhetorical form. Just why Paul sent Titus and the brothers—a matter of some contention according to 12:16–18—is clearly explained in 9:1–5 in the form of an epicheireme.[84] Then, in 9:6–11, Paul crafts maxims sometimes from Scripture that are masterfully chiastic.[85] These serve to urge the Corinthians to participate in the Collection by highlighting three things: (a) God's sufficient provision [8:15 ← Exod 16:18 "gathering enough [manna]"], (b) Paul's integrity [8:21 ← Prov 3:4 "what is good in sight of God and humanity"], and (c) the basis for Corinthians' giving [9:7 ← Prov 22:8 "God loves a cheerful giver"; 9:9 ← Ps 112:9 "God gave to the poor; righteousness forever"; and 9:10 ← Isa 55:10 "God furnishes seed for the sower"].

Thus, Paul's composition of 2 Corinthians is his final resolution to the problems that he faced—criticism for failing to visit as planned and appearing fickle and worldly in his intentions (1:17)—by arguing to secure the Corinthian believers' goodwill. He was about to visit them again, was prepared to confront any rebellion present, and intending to collect and carry their portion of the Collection to Jerusalem. This collection effort represented the profound realization of God's saving activity that unified Jew and Gentile in Christ as the Messiah. Because missionary rivals and certain believers at Corinth had become critical of Paul's and his companions' ministry conduct (esp. their travel), Paul and Timothy composed a unified judicial discourse that defended and accused as well as exhorted the Corinthians to demonstrate their faith through being unified with Paul and the broader church through the Collection gift. This gift was properly given as a response to God's all-gracious supply always in every way empowering all sufficiency in order that believers "would abound for every good work" (9:8).

---

[84] Long, *Ancient Rhetoric and Paul's Apology*, 220–21.

[85] These chiasms are shown and discussed in Long, *2 Corinthians*, 179–81 and set within the larger communicative environment in Long, "The Oral, the Textual, and the Visual."

9

GALATIANS

STEPHEN LEVINSOHN

1. Preliminaries

Discourse analysis (or 'Text-linguistics', to use the European term) takes into account factors that are not treated in Greek grammars (questions of morphology or syntax). In particular, it concerns features of the larger context than the individual sentence. It may simply focus on how the contents of the previous sentence affect the way the current sentence is structured. However, it also looks for ways in which the author's *purpose* influences the way the information in each sentence is presented.

This article approaches the discourse features of Galatians from a *functional* perspective; namely, one that attempts "to discover and describe what linguistic structures are used for: the functions they serve, the factors that condition their use."[1]

One basic principle of a functional approach is that *choice implies meaning*.[2] So, when an author has the option of expressing himself or herself in more than one way, the ways differ in significance; there are reasons for the variations. For example, there is often a choice as to which connective is the most appropriate way to link two sentences (see Gal 4:31, for example, where the variants include διό, ἄρα, ἄρα οὖν and [ἡμεῖς] δέ). Choosing a particular connective over against the others is not just a question of style; rather, there is a functional reason for choosing each one (see §2e).

---

[1] Stephen H. Levinsohn, *Discourse Features of New Testament Greek: A Coursebook on its Information Structure and Other Devices*, 2nd ed. (SIL, 2000), vii. The next paragraphs are based on ibid., viii–ix.

[2] *Meaning* is here used loosely to denote any semantic or pragmatic distinction (ibid., viii).

2. Methodology

The following is a series of steps that a Bible scholar might follow when considering the discourse structure of the Greek text of a New Testament book.

A) Determine the nature of the discourse.

The text of Galatians is a letter with the apostle Paul as the author (1:1) and the
churches of Galatia[3] as the recipients (1:2).

Betz argues that Galatians is in fact "an example of the 'apologetic letter'
genre,"[4] constructed according to contemporary rhetorical principles with seven
main elements (discussed in §3.1). Bruce, however, notes that, although "Betz's
analysis corresponds well enough to the development of Paul's argument... one
may wonder... if in the excitement and urgency of the crisis with which he was
suddenly confronted Paul would have been consciously careful to construct his
letter according to the canons of the rhetorical schools."[5]

Longenecker goes further and feels that "what Betz has done, in effect, has
been to push a good thesis too hard and too far."[6] In particular, he "has ignored
the influence of epistolary conventions, Old Testament rhetoric and Paul's own
Pharisaic background."[7] Instead, Longenecker concludes, "In his Galatian letter
(as elsewhere in his writings), Paul seems to have availed himself almost uncon-
sciously of the rhetorical forms at hand, fitting them into his inherited epistolary
structures and filling them out with such Jewish theological motifs and exegetical methods as would be particularly significant in countering what the Judaizers were telling his converts."[8]

B) Determine the broad genre of the letter.

The broad genre of the letter is hortatory, since its concern is to change the behaviour of the recipients.[9] Hansen describes it more specifically as having "the

---

[3] This article does not address the identity of the Galatians (see F. F. Bruce, *The Epistle to the Galatians: A Commentary on the Greek Text* [Paternoster Press, 1982], 14–18 for discussion of "The Present State of the Question").

[4] Hans Dieter Betz, "The Literary Composition and Function of Paul's Letter to the Galatians," *NTS 21* (1974–1975): 354.

[5] Bruce, *Galatians*, 58.

[6] Richard N. Longenecker, *Galatians*, WBC 41 (Word, 1990), cxi.

[7] Christopher Augustin Vaz, *Functional Equivalent Translation of New Testament Hortatory Discourse into Hill Madia* (PhD dissertation, Fuller Theological Seminary, 2011), 57.

[8] Longnecker, *Galatians*, cxix.

[9] "[T]he central purpose of the letter is to arrest the progress of the judaising propaganda ... which the Galatians were on the very point of accepting, and to win them back to faith in

'rebuke-request' form," since "[l]etters of rebuke also contained requests to set things right."[10] It follows that we can expect the rebukes and exhortations of Galatians to constitute the theme line of the letter, where the theme line "presents the backbone of the discourse—whether this be ... the main points of an argument or the main commands of an exhortation—while the supportive material provides all that is necessary as a background for understanding the story, procedure, or argument as a whole."[11]

C) Determine where there is a general consensus as to the major divisions of the text and where there are disagreements among exegetes.

This is done by consulting a representative set of commentaries and versions, since the divisions they propose will usually reflect where they perceive a change of theme. Beekman and Callow write, "The basic criterion [for delineating a unit] is that a section or a paragraph deals with one theme. If the theme changes, then a new unit has started ... what gives a section or paragraph its overall coherence as a semantic unit is the fact that one subject matter is being dealt with."[12] Stutzman's *Exegetical Summary of Galatians* summarises the divisions proposed in 21 "COMMENTARIES AND REFERENCE BOOKS" and in 11 translations into English.[13]

D) Look for surface features that support the different boundaries.

Surface features that can be cited as supporting evidence for the different boundaries that have been proposed on thematic grounds include the following:[14]

- A *sentence-initial or fronted constituent* that presents a new theme or situation.[15] See, for example, the fronting of τὸ εὐαγγέλιον τὸ εὐαγγελισθὲν ὑπ' ἐμοῦ 'the gospel that was proclaimed by me' (1:11),[16] as well as the change of situation described at the beginning of 6:1 in the conditional clause ἐὰν

Jesus Christ apart from works of law" (Ernest De Witt Burton, *A Critical and Exegetical Commentary on the Epistle to the Galatians* [T&T Clark, 1921], lv). See also James D. G. Dunn, *The Epistle to the Galatians* (Hendrickson, 1995), 46–47.

[10] G. Walter Hansen, *Galatians* (InterVarsity Press, 1994), 22.

[11] Mary Breeze, "Hortatory discourse in Ephesians," *JTT* 5, no. 4 (1992): 314.

[12] John Beekman and John C. Callow, *Translating the Word of God* (Zondervan, 1974), 279.

[13] Robert Stutzman, *An Exegetical Summary of Galatians*, 2nd ed. (SIL, 2008), 7.

[14] See Levinsohn, *Discourse Features*, 279–282.

[15] Stephen H. Levinsohn, *Self-instruction Materials on Non-Narrative Discourse Analysis* (2015, https://www.sil.org/resources/archives/68640), §8.2.

[16] Unless otherwise indicated, references are to Galatians and translations into English are from the NRSV.

καὶ προλημφθῇ ἄνθρωπος ἔν τινι παραπτώματι 'if anyone is detected in a transgression.'

- A *closure* such as ἀμήν 'Amen!' (1:5).
- A *chiastic* structure such as that found in 3:2–14 (discussed in §4.2).[17] "Chiastic structures indicate that the material concerned forms a self-contained unit... which should be treated as a block over against that which precedes and follows."[18]
- An *inclusio* structure involving "The bracketing of a pericope by making a statement at the beginning of the section, an approximation of which is repeated at the conclusion of the section."[19] See, for example, the repetition of τῷ σπέρματι αὐτοῦ 'to his offspring' in 3:16 as τοῦ Ἀβραὰμ σπέρμα 'Abraham's offspring' in 3:29.
- A *summarising expression*. "[S]ummarising expressions unite together the information to which they allude and thereby imply that the preceding material is to be treated as a block, over against what is to follow."[20] See §3.3 on the conclusion of 4:31 as a summarising expression.
- A *rhetorical question* that introduces a theme, such as τίς ὑμᾶς ἐβάσκανεν 'Who has bewitched you?' in 3:1.
- An *apparently redundant reference* to an entity, such as ἐγὼ Παῦλος 'I, Paul' in 5:2.
- A *vocative* such as ἀδελφοί 'Brothers' (1:11, 5:13, 6:18) or Ὦ ἀνόητοι Γαλάται 'You foolish Galatians!' in 3:1.
- An *orienter* verb such as Θαυμάζω 'I am astonished' (1:6) or Γνωρίζω ὑμῖν 'I want you to know' (1:11) that introduces a new theme.[21]
- A shift of two or more of the following *verbal features*: tense-aspect, mood and person. For example, the final verb of 6:10 (ἐργαζώμεθα 'let us work') is a first person plural present subjunctive, whereas the initial verb of 6:11 (Ἴδετε 'See...!') is a second person plural aorist imperative.
- *Back-reference*, which "involves reference to the preceding paragraph or paragraphs or to a point or points within preceding paragraphs. Back-reference often occurs at the beginning of a new paragraph."[22] Such references are particularly significant when they reintroduce a concept or entity

---

[17] See http://www.chiasmusxchange.com/2015/06/12/galatians-31-14.

[18] Levinsohn, *Discourse Features*, 279. Vaz (*Functional Equivalent Translation*, 63–68) discusses various proposals as to the whole epistle being constructed chiastically, but concludes that "*Paul may not have deliberately chosen a chiastic structure*" (ibid., 68—italics original).

[19] George H. Guthrie, *The Structure of Hebrews: A Text-Linguistic Analysis* (Baker, 1998), 14.

[20] Levinsohn, *Non-Narrative Discourse Analysis*, §8.4.

[21] Ibid., §8.10.

[22] Linda Lloyd Neeley, "A Discourse Analysis of Hebrews," *OPTAT* 3–4 (1987): 19.

that had not featured in the immediate context. For example, the last reference to 'you' (the Galatians) before 3:1 is in 1:13.

- *Hook words* which, according to Guthrie, are "a rhetorical device used in the ancient world to tie two sections of material together. A word was positioned at the end of one section and at the beginning of the next to effect a transition between the two."[23] See, for example, the positioning of κληρονόμοι 'heirs' at the end of 3:29, in anticipation of ὁ κληρονόμος 'the heir' becoming thematic in 4:1.

Although the surface features listed above may be cited as supporting evidence for a boundary proposed because of a perceived change of theme, there may be other reasons for them to be used. For example, vocatives are used not only at the beginning of a new section, but also as a means of highlighting an important assertion, as in 4:19, where τέκνα μου 'my little children' is "an appropriate introduction to the tender and affectionate address which follows"[24] (οὓς πάλιν ὠδίνω μέχρις οὗ μορφωθῇ Χριστὸς ἐν ὑμῖν 'for whom I am again in the pain of childbirth until Christ is formed in you').

E) Consider the implications of each inter-sentential[25] conjunction used.

Each inter-sentential conjunction conveys a particular constraint on interpretation,[26] so the presence of a conjunction at a proposed boundary will indicate how what follows is to be related to the context. The following are the constraints associated with each inter-sentential conjunction found in Galatians (listed in the order in which they appear):

- ἀλλά (first used inter-sententially in 1:8): +Countering.[27] It "is the default associative connective when a positive proposition follows negative material."[28]

---

[23] Guthrie, *Hebrews*, 12.

[24] Charles J. Ellicott, *A Critical and Grammatical Commentary on St. Paul's Epistle to the Galatians* (John W. Parker & Son, 1859), 89.

[25] I define a sentence as a "single independent clause, together with those clauses that are subordinated to it" (Levinsohn, *Discourse Features*, 295).

[26] I follow Anne Reboul and Jacques Moeschler (*Pragmatique du discours: de l'interprétation de l'énoncé à l'interprétation du discours* [Paris: Armand Colin, 1998], 77) in viewing each conjunction as a linguistic marker which "(a) links a linguistic or discourse unit of any size to its context; (b) gives instructions as to how to relate this unit to its context; (c) constrains conclusions to be drawn on the basis of this discourse connection that might not have been drawn had it been absent" (Stephen H. Levinsohn, 'Therefore' or 'Wherefore': What's the Difference? In Taylor, Richard A. and Craig E. Morrison, eds., *Reflections on Lexicography: Explorations in Ancient Syriac, Hebrew, and Greek Sources*, PLAL 4 [Gorgias, 2014], 326).

[27] Ἀλλά "instructs the recipient to process a corrective relation holding between two pieces of information... The information being corrected may be textually based, an assump-

- γάρ (first used in 1:10): +Strengthening. It "constrains the reader to inter-pret the material it introduces as *strengthening* an assertion or assump-tion that has been presented in or implied by the immediate context."[29]
- καί (first used inter-sententially in 1:14): +Associative/Additive. It "con-strains the material it introduces to be processed as being added to and associated with previous material."[30]
- δέ (first used in 1:15): +Distinctive. It "constrains what follows to be inter-preted as a distinct point that advances Paul's argument."[31]
- οὐδέ (used inter-sententially in 1:17): +Negative Additive. It adds an addi-tional proposition or group of propositions to a negated proposition.
- ἔπειτα (first used in 1:18): 'next.' It marks "chronological sequence."[32]
- ὥστε (first used in 2:13): +Inferential +Result. It "constrains what follows to be interpreted as the 'result—actual, natural, conceived, intended" of what has previously been stated.'"[33]
- οὖν (first used in 3:5): +Inferential +Distinctive. It "constrains what follows to be interpreted as a distinct point that advances an argument in an in-ferential way."[34]
- ἄρα (first used inter-sententially in 3:7): +Inferential +Consequence. It "constrains what follows to be interpreted as a consequence of what has already been stated in the context."[35]
- οὕτως (4:3): +Comparative.[36]
- διό (4:31 [NA[27]]): +Inferential +Continuative. "It contrasts with οὖν in that it does not move the argument on to a new point."[37]

---

tion, an implication, or a discourse topic — whatever is most manifest and relevant to the recipient upon processing the correction and integrating it into the mental representation (i.e., takes the least amount of processing effort)" (Christopher James Fresch, *Discourse Mark-ers in the Septuagint and Early Koine Greek with Special Reference to the Twelve* [PhD Disserta-tion, University of Cambridge, 2015], 151).

[28] Stephen H. Levinsohn, *A Holistic Approach to the Argument Structure of Romans 6* (Paper presented at the International Conference of the Society of Biblical Literature held in London, July 2011, https://www.sil.org/resources/archives/68394), 5.

[29] Levinsohn, *Discourse Features*, 69.

[30] Ibid., 124.

[31] Levinsohn, *Holistic Approach*, 4.

[32] Longenecker, *Galatians*, 27.

[33] Ibid., 334, citing Stanley E. Porter, *Idioms of the Greek New Testament* (JSOT Press, 1992), 234.

[34] Ibid., 327.

[35] Ibid., 331.

[36] Levinsohn, *Holistic Approach*, 4.

[37] Levinsohn, "'Therefore' or 'Wherefore',", 329.

- ἄρα οὖν (6:10): +Inferential +Consequence +Distinctive. Typically, "οὖν introduces a distinct point that advances an earlier theme, following material introduced with γάρ that was strengthening the previous point of the theme line, while ἄρα makes explicit that this new point is a logical consequence of the previous point, together with the strengthening material."[38]

§§3 and 4 discuss how the presence of the above conjunctions impacts both the macrostructure of the letter and the flow of the argument within pericopes.

F) Look for prominence-giving devices at various levels.

Prominence-giving devices include the repetition of clauses or sentences (e.g., in 1:8–9), the presence of particles such as ἴδε 'Behold, Listen!' (5:2), the use of cataphoric demonstratives and orienters such as τοῦτο 'this' and λέγω 'I say' (3:17), as well as a number of "devices whose rhetorical effect is to slow down the story [argument] and create the expectation that the climax is about to be presented"[39] (see §4).[40]

3. Macrostructure

This section first separates off the "Epistolary Framework"[41]—"material that provides a framework for the message without being part of the message itself"[42]—from the main body of the letter. It then discusses different proposals as to where the major divisions in the body of the letter should be placed, and argues in favor of divisions at 3:1, 5:1, and 6:11.

3.1 The Epistolary Framework

According to Breeze, the framework for a letter comprises:

---

[38] Ibid., 333.

[39] Robert A. Dooley and Stephen H. Levinsohn, *Analyzing Discourse: A Manual of Basic Concepts* (SIL, 2001), 105.

[40] This chapter does not discuss prominence-giving devices within clauses. Such devices include the omission of the article with references to cognitively identifiable entities (Levinsohn, *Discourse Features*, 162–164), the preposing of focal constituents (ibid., 37), split focal constituents (ibid., 57–60), and the violation of the "Principle of Natural Information Flow" (Levinsohn, *Non-Narrative*, 54–56). For discussion of these features in specific verses in Galatians, see Stephen H. Levinsohn, *Los rasgos discursivos comparativos aplicados a la traducción de Gálatas* (https://www.sil.org/resources/archives/68387, 2009), 25–78.

[41] Betz, "Literary Composition," 356.

[42] Breeze, "Ephesians," 314.

- the **introduction**, which "relates the author to the recipients and gives a greeting;"
- the **closure**, which "consists of personal notes and a benediction." [43]

In the case of Galatians, 1:1–5 constitute the introduction or "Prescript,"[44] while 6:18 provides the closure (the concluding benediction), leaving 1:6–6:17 as the main body of the letter.[45] As I note elsewhere, "Asyndeton is typically found at the following transitions:

- from the opening salutation to the body of each letter...
- from the body of a letter to its closure...
- from one major or minor topic to another..."[46]

3.2 Major Division 1: 3:1

I noted in §2 that Betz considered Galatians to be an "apologetic letter"[47] with seven main elements: (i) epistolary prescript (1:1–5); (ii) exordium (1:6–11); (iii) narratio (1:12–2:14); (iv) propositio (2:15–21); (v) probatio (3:1–4:31); (vi) paraenesis (5:1–6:10); (vii) epistolary postscript or conclusio (6:11–18).[48] This section argues that elements (ii), (iii), and (iv) are to be treated as a macro-unit, with the first major division in the letter not occurring until 3:1.

The following surface features can be cited as supporting evidence for a division at 3:1:

- Asyndeton, which is consistent with the shift from one major topic to another (see §3.1).
- The initial vocative ῏Ω ἀνόητοι Γαλάται 'You foolish Galatians!'
- The rhetorical question τίς ὑμᾶς ἐβάσκανεν 'Who has bewitched you?' (3:1).
- The shift from first person in 2:18–21 to second person in 3:1, which is of particular significance, given that the last reference to the Galatians as recipients of the letter was in 1:13 (᾿Ηκούσατε 'You heard').
- The labelling of the Galatians as foolish, which can be taken as an illusion (a weak back-reference) to 1:6.[49]

---

[43] Ibid.

[44] Betz, "Literary Composition," 356.

[45] Because the contents of the 6:11–17 (part of the "Postscript" [ibid.]) include a summary of the main points of the letter, I treat it as part of the body of the letter.

[46] Levinsohn, *Discourse Features*, 119.

[47] Betz, "Literary Composition," 354.

[48] Ibid., 355–374.

[49] See John Stott, *The Message of Galatians*, BST (InterVarsity Press, 1968), 69.

Whereas no overt connective is found at 3:1, γάρ is used both at 1:12 (the beginning of Betz's narratio)[50] and 1:11 (NA²⁷)[51] (the division made in many versions and commentaries).[52] The presence of γάρ in these verses and, indeed, in 1:10 and 1:13, indicates that what follows strengthens the material presented in the immediate context. Hendriksen writes about the γάρ in 1:11: "In connection with the present context 'for' must mean something like 'In justification of the facts which I have stated, namely, that my gospel is of divine origin and is the only true gospel, so that anyone who distorts it is accursed, note the following corroborative facts selected from the story of my life."[53]

The presence of γάρ in these verses indicates that the "solemn curse"[54] of 1:8, which is repeated in 1:9 to give it prominence,[55] is strengthened by 1:10. In turn, 1:11 strengthens 1:10, 1:12 strengthens 1:11, and 1:13–2:14 (or 2:21—see §4.1) strengthens 1:12. Figure 9.1 seeks to capture the constituent parts of the argument:[56]

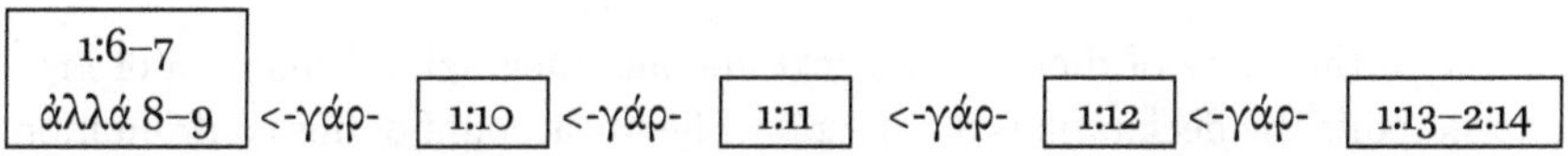

Figure 9.1: Flow-chart of Galatians 1:6–2:14 Reading γάρ at 1:11

This means that the autobiographical section that begins at 1:13 and continues until at least 2:14 is intended to strengthen the affirmations that "the gospel that was proclaimed by me is not of human origin; for I did not receive it from a human source, nor was I taught it, but I received it through a revelation of Jesus Christ" (1:11–12).

Whereas 1:11 should not be taken as the beginning of a macro-unit, the following surface features can be cited as supporting evidence for a second-level division at 1:11:

- The orienter Γνωρίζω ὑμῖν 'I want you to know.'
- The vocative ἀδελφοί 'brothers.'
- The fronting of τὸ εὐαγγέλιον τὸ εὐαγγελισθὲν ὑπ' ἐμοῦ 'the gospel that was proclaimed by me.'

---

[50] Betz, "Literary Composition," 355.
[51] See below on the variant reading δέ at 1:11.
[52] See, for example, Bruce, *Galatians*, 57.
[53] William Hendriksen, *A Commentary on Galatians* (Banner of Truth, 1968), 47.
[54] Stott, *Galatians*, 24.
[55] The introduction to 1:9 (ὡς προειρήκαμεν, καὶ ἄρτι πάλιν λέγω 'As we have said before, and now I repeat') is a slowing-down device that gives additional prominence to this curse.
[56] Many of the flow charts have been adapted from Levinsohn, *Rasgos discursivos*, 21–76.

Although the preferred reading in NA²⁷ at 1:11 is γάρ, Longnecker[57] is among a number of scholars who favour reading δέ as the connective that introduces what follows. Since δέ constrains what follows to be interpreted as a distinct point that advances the argument, it can be cited as further supporting evidence for a second-level division at 1:11.

Figure 9.2 illustrates the effect on the development of the argument of reading δέ at 1:11:[58]

Figure 9.2: Flow-chart of Galatians 1:6–2:14 Reading δέ at 1:11

As for the unity of theme in 1:6–2:21, the autobiographical material of 1:13–2:10 supports the declarations of 1:11–12,[59] while the account of this confrontation with Peter (2:11–14) supports the condemnation of those who proclaim "a gospel contrary to what you received" (1:9), as well as showing that Paul was not seeking "human approval," but "God's approval" (1:10).

We cannot know with certainty how much of 2:15–21 is a continuation of Paul's speech to Peter (§4.1 discusses this point).[60] What is certain is that these verses contribute to the rejection of those who "proclaim to you a gospel contrary

---

[57] Longnecker, *Galatians*, 22.

[58] Some commentators and versions place the second-place division before 1:10 instead of 1:11 (e.g., Herman N. Ridderbos, *The Epistle of Paul to the Churches of Galatia*, NICNT [Eerdmans, 1953], 53; R. Alan Cole, *The Epistle of Paul to the Galatians*, TNTC [Eerdmans, 1965], 81). Surface features that might support a division at 1:10 include the rhetorical questions and the repetition in initial position of the adverb Ἄρτι 'Now.' However, the presence of γάρ implies that the rhetorical questions do not in fact introduce a new theme, but are used simply to respond to "the allegation of Paul's detractors... that he was 'currying favour with men' by relaxing the terms of the gospel" (Ronald Y. K. Fung, *The Epistle to the Galatians*, NICNT [Eerdmans, 1988], 48). Guthrie makes a similar point and also writes, "The 'now' in this statement reinforces the 'now' in verse 9" (Donald Guthrie, *Galatians*, NCBC [Eerdmans, 1981], 65).

[59] "Throughout it all, Paul is emphasizing the point that the gospel he preached was of divine origin" (Leon Morris, *Galatians: Paul's Charter of Christian Freedom* [InterVarsity Press, 1996], 47–48).

[60] "Structurally speaking, these verses are a continuation of Paul's address to Peter which began with v. 14b" (Fung, *Galatians*, 112). "It is difficult to decide at what point Paul's quotation of his rebuke to Peter comes to an end and passes to his general exposition of the principle at stake. He probably summarizes his rebuke to Peter and then develops its implications, thus passing smoothly from the personal occasion to the universal principle" (Bruce, *Galatians*, 136).

to what we proclaimed to you" (1:8) 'for if justification comes through the law, then Christ died for nothing' (2:21).

I conclude that Morris is right to treat 1:6–2:21 as a single thematic unit ("The gospel"),[61] with a secondary division at 1:11.[62]

3.3 Major Division 2: 5:1

Betz classifies 3:1–4:31 as the "probation," with 5:1–6:10 as the "paraenesis" [63] or "exhortatio."[64] Other commentators include 5:1 in the second macro-unit of the letter,[65] while others again place the division between 5:12 and 5:13.[66] This section argues for the division proposed by Betz. It also argues that the 5:1–6:10 macro-unit is similar to the structure of 1:6–2:21 in that there is a second-level division between 5:12 and 5:13, with γάρ introducing 5:13–6:10.

The following surface features can be cited as supporting evidence for a division at 5:1:

- 4:31 is a summarising expression and conclusion which "is not only the résumé of the meaning of the allegory 4:21–31, but of the entire *probatio* section."[67] It is introduced with the continuative inferential connective διό (NA[27]), which is consistent with the conclusion not being a new point but, rather, expressing in other words the assertion of 4:26 that 'the Jerusalem above … is free, and she is our mother.'
- Asyndeton (NA[27]), which is consistent with the shift to a new major topic (§3.1).
- τῇ ἐλευθερίᾳ 'for [the] freedom' as a hook back to τῆς ἐλευθέρας 'of the free woman.'

"From the general theme" of not submitting 'again to a yoke of slavery' (5:1), "we come to the precise issue in vv. 2–4, which is that of circumcision."[68] Asyndeton is to be expected for such "*Generic–Specific* relations, in which the second proposition gives a specific instance of the more generic proposition that

---

[61] Ibid., 30. See also REB.

[62] See also Burton, *Galatians*, lxxii; Guthrie, *Galatians*, 65.

[63] Betz, "Literary Composition," 368, 374.

[64] Vaz, *Functional Equivalent Translation*, 62. See also Morris, *Galatians*, 30.

[65] "In 5:1 Paul sums up and applies, in non-allegorical language, the lesson of the preceding allegory and indeed the lesson of all his preceding argument from 2:14 on" (Bruce, *Galatians*, 226). See also Cole, *Galatians*, 185.

[66] For example, Fung (*Galatians*, 221) describes 5:2–12 as "this final passage of the middle, doctrinal section (III) of the epistle."

[67] Betz, "Literary Composition," 374.

[68] Stott, *Galatians*, 133.

precedes it."[69] 5:2 begins with Ἴδε 'Behold, Listen!', which "is used as a particle to give emphasis to what follows."[70] Ἴδε is followed by the fronted subject, ἐγὼ Παῦλος 'I, Paul', which does not provide supporting evidence for a new thematic unit, since it does not signal a switch of theme to Paul (he continues to address the Galatians in second person). Rather, the fronted subject and orienter λέγω ὑμῖν 'I say to you' are slowing-down devices that give further prominence to what follows.[71] The use of another orienter at the beginning of 5:3 (μαρτύρομαι δὲ πάλιν παντὶ ἀνθρώπῳ περιτεμνομένῳ 'Once again I testify to every man who lets himself be circumcised') then gives prominence to the next assertion: ὅτι ὀφειλέτης ἐστὶν ὅλον τὸν νόμον ποιῆσαι 'that he is obliged to obey the entire law.'[72]

As for the second-level division at 5:13, we have already noted the presence of γάρ which, "at the head a paragraph = 'in order to elucidate still further.' The elucidation now offered concerns the use of Christian freedom."[73]

The following surface features can be cited as supporting evidence for a second-level division at 5:13:

- The fronted subject Ὑμεῖς 'You', which signals the switch of attention from 'those who unsettle you' (5:12).
- Back-reference to the theme of freedom (ἐπ' ἐλευθερίᾳ ἐκλήθητε 'you were called to freedom'), which was last mentioned in 5:1.
- The vocative ἀδελφοί 'brothers.'

If we compare the structure of 5:1–6:10 with that of 1:6–2:21, we see that both begin with a section that contains warnings against false teaching (1:6–9, 5:2–12). Then, introduced by γάρ, follows contrary evidence for rejecting such teaching, beginning in both sections with a THESIS that is supported by what follows. In the first section, the THESIS is that "the gospel that was proclaimed by me is not of human origin; for I did not receive it from a human source, nor was I taught it, but I received it through a revelation of Jesus Christ" (1:11–12). In the second section, the THESIS is that, although you were called for freedom, you are not to "to use your freedom as an opportunity for self-indulgence, but through love become slaves to one another" (5:13).

Figure 9.3 brings out the similarity in the overall structure of 1:6–2:21 and of 5:1–6:10:

---

[69] Levinsohn, *Discourse Features*, 120.

[70] Morris, *Galatians*, 154n5.

[71] Levinsohn, *Non-Narrative Discourse Analysis*, §7.7.

[72] For discussion of the connectives used in 5:5–12, see Vaz, *Functional Equivalent Translation*, 113–116. On the vocative in 5:11, see ibid., 107.

[73] R. C. H. Lenski, *The Interpretation of St Paul's Epistles to the Galatians, to the Ephesians and to the Philippians* (Augsburg, 1937), 273.

Warning 1:6–10	<--γάρ--	EXPOSITORY THESIS 1:11–12	<--γάρ--	Support 1:13–2:21
Warning 5:1–12[74]	<--γάρ--	HORTATORY THESIS 5:13	<--γάρ--	Support 5:14–6:10

Figure 9.3: Flow-charts of Galatians 1:6–2:21 and 5:1–6:10

The internal structure of the supportive material (1:13–2:21 and 5:14–6:10) is discussed below in §§4.1 and 4.3.

3.4 Major Division 3: 6:11

Many commentaries and versions recognise a major division between 6:10 and 6:11.[75] It seems likely that, up to this point, Paul "has been dictating to an amanuensis, but now, as his custom was, he takes the pen from his secretary's hand, in order to add a personal postscript."[76] Surface features that support this division include:

- Asyndeton.
- The orienter verb ᾽Ίδετε 'See!'
- The change from first person plural (6:9–10) to singular (ἔγραψα 'I write, have written').
- 6:10 as a closure for the section ("a summary statement of the paraenesis").[77]

I follow Morris in concluding that the macrostructure of Galatians is as follows:

1:1–5	"Introduction"
	1:6–2:21 "The gospel"
	3:1–4:31 "A Christian view of the law"
	5:1–6:10 "Christian freedom"
	6:11–17 "Conclusion"[78]
6:18	Closure

Figure 9.4: The Macrostructure of Galatians

---

[74] For flow-charts of the argumentation of 5:2–6 and 5:7–12, see Levinsohn, *Rasgos Discursivos*, 63, 65.

[75] Lenski (ibid.) treats 5:13–6:16 as a thematic unit with the title, "How the Galatians Should Use their Christian Liberty," while Cole (*Galatians*, 186) has 5:2–6:18 as a thematic unit.

[76] Stott, *Galatians*, 175.

[77] Betz, *Galatians*, 376.

[78] Morris, *Galatians*, 30. Morris includes 6:18 in his Conclusion section.

4. Microstructures

This section considers the internal structure of passages from three of the macro-sections that were discussed in §3 (1:11–2:21, 3:1–4:31 and 5:13–6:10), together with the Conclusion (6:11–18).

4.1 The Internal Structure of 1:11–2:21

I proposed in §§3.2 and 3.3 that, within the macro-section 1:6–2:21, there is a second-level division at 1:11. In turn, 1:11–12 presents an expository THESIS ('the gospel that was proclaimed by me is not of human origin; for I did not receive it from a human source, nor was I taught it, but [ἀλλά] through a revelation of Jesus Christ'), which is strengthened by the autobiographical section that begins at 1:13 and continues until at least 2:14.

When, as in 1:11–12, a positive assertion is preceded by two or more negative statements, this may be viewed as a slowing-down device that gives prominence to the positive assertion (in this instance, δι' ἀποκαλύψεως Ἰησοῦ Χριστοῦ 'through a revelation of Jesus Christ').[79]

In 1:13–14 "the apostle describes his pre-conversion state 'in Judaism.'"[80] The imperfect tense (imperfective aspect) of ἐδίωκον 'I was persecuting' and προέκοπτον 'I was advancing' not only "indicates a continuing activity,"[81] but is also consistent with these activities being of a background nature in relation to his subsequent experiences.

As noted in §2(e), δέ in 1:15 introduces "a distinct point that advances Paul's argument",[82] namely, what he did after Jesus Christ first revealed himself to him (1:15–17). This unit, as well as the three introduced with ἔπειτα 'next' and a time expression (1:18–20, 1:21–24, 2:1–10), all show that "I did not receive [the gospel that was proclaimed by me] from a human source, nor was I taught it" (1:12).

The leaders of the church in Jerusalem "accepted [Paul] just as he was" because "There was no need to add anything to his message, or to his whole ministry" (2:6).[83] However, he had to correct Peter for conduct that was not consistent with the gospel that they had both accepted (2:11–14). This unit is introduced with a time expression and δέ, as it advances Paul's argument against the Judaizing teachers who were proclaiming to the Galatians "a gospel contrary to what you received" (1:9).

Figure 9.5 shows how the overall argumentation of 1:11–2:14 is developed.

---

[79] See also 1:16–17, 5:6 and 6:15.

[80] Stott, *Galatians*, 31.

[81] Morris, *Galatians*, 52.

[82] Levinsohn, *Holistic Approach*, 4.

[83] Morris, *Galatians*, 71.

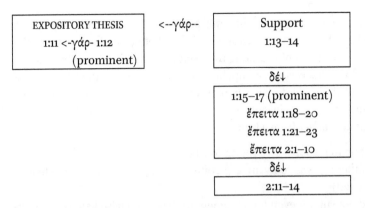

Figure 9.5: Flow-chart of Galatians 1:11–2:14

Before we discuss where 2:15–21 fits into Paul's argument, the following are observations about the internal structure of some of the units in the above flow chart, especially those that include sentences introduced with the distinctive marker δέ.

1:15–17. This unit consists of four sentences and the connectives used to link them are all associative or additive. The main clause of the first sentence is negative (εὐθέως οὐ προσανεθέμην σαρκὶ καὶ αἵματι 'I did not confer with any human being'), so οὐδέ is the appropriate connective to add a second negative proposition to it (οὐδὲ ἀνῆλθον εἰς Ἱεροσόλυμα πρὸς τοὺς πρὸ ἐμοῦ ἀποστόλους 'nor did I go up to Jerusalem to those who were already apostles before me'). Similarly, following negative sentences, countering ἀλλά is the default way of introducing a positive proposition (ἀλλὰ ἀπῆλθον εἰς Ἀραβίαν 'but I went away at once into Arabia'). The default associative connective καί introduces the final proposition of the unit (καὶ πάλιν ὑπέστρεψα εἰς Δαμασκόν 'and again I returned to Damascus').

1:18–20. This unit can be divided into three parts, with δέ introducing two distinct points that are relevant to the THESIS of 1:12 that Paul did not receive the gospel that he teaches from a human source:

- 'I did not see any other apostle except James the Lord's brother' and
- the parenthetical comment 'In what I am writing to you... I do not lie!', with ἰδού 'behold' (KJV) and ἐνώπιον τοῦ θεοῦ 'before God' giving prominence to the assertion ὅτι οὐ ψεύδομαι 'that I do not lie.'

1:21–24. This unit can also be divided into three parts, with δέ introducing two further points that are relevant to the THESIS of 1:12 that Paul did not receive the gospel that he teaches from a human source:

- 'I was still unknown by sight to the churches of Judea that are in Christ' and
- 'they were only hearing it said, "The one who formerly was persecuting us is now proclaiming the faith he once tried to destroy."'

2:1–10. The opening events of this unit are that, after fourteen years, Paul, Barnabas, and Titus went up to Jerusalem (1), laid before the leaders there the gospel that Paul was preaching among the Gentiles (2b–c), and (contrary to expectation—ἀλλά) Titus was not compelled to be circumcised (3). In turn, δέ introduces four distinct points (two parenthetical comments, followed by two groups of events) that are relevant to the THESIS of 1:12 that Paul did not receive the gospel that he teaches from a human source:

- 'I went up in response to a revelation' (2:2a).
- The gathering was 'only in a private meeting with the acknowledged leaders' (2d).
- 'we did not submit even for a moment to them [the false believers secretly brought in...], so that the truth of the gospel might always remain with you' (5).[84]
- The acknowledged leaders (James, Cephas and John) 'on the contrary [ἀλλά τοὐναντίον]...gave to Barnabas and me the right hand of fellowship, agreeing that we should go to the Gentiles and they to the circumcised...'[85] (6–9).

The combination of ἀλλά and τοὐναντίον in 2:7 may be taken as a prominence-giving device that emphasizes that "[t]hose in repute did the complete opposite of making any demand on Paul."[86]

Figure 9.6 shows how the argument of this unit develops. Καί and ἀλλά associate the events of 2:2b–c and 2:3 with 2:1, while γάρ introduces material that supports previous propositions.

2:11–14. This unit can be divided into three parts, with 2:12–13 (introduced with γάρ) supporting the assertion of 2:11, while 2:14 (introduced with ἀλλά) expands on 2:11. Within the supportive material of 2:12–13, δέ introduces a distinct point about Peter's behavior. As noted earlier, the unit as a whole supports the condemnation of those who proclaim 'a gospel contrary to what you received' (1:9), as well as showing that Paul was not seeking 'human approval', but 'God's approval' (1:10).

Figure 9.7 shows how the argument of this unit develops and also indicates material that was introduced with γάρ to support previous propositions.

---

[84] 2:5 begins with a continuative relative clause (οἷς οὐδὲ πρὸς ὥραν εἴξαμεν τῇ ὑποταγῇ 'to whom we did not submit even for a moment') which describes "an event that involves the referent of the relative pronoun and occurs subsequent to the previous event or situation in which the referent featured" (Levinsohn, *Discourse Features*, 192). "Characteristically, the information preceding the relative pronoun is *backgrounded* in relation to what follows" (ibid.). In this passage, this means that the information of 2:4 (about the 'false believers secretly brought in, who slipped in to spy on the freedom we have in Christ Jesus, so that they might enslave us') is backgrounded in relation to how we behaved towards them (2:5).

[85] "[T]he main statement of [2:7–9] is in v. 9..." (Fung, *Galatians*, 97).

[86] Lenski, *Galatians, Ephesians and Philippians*, 85.

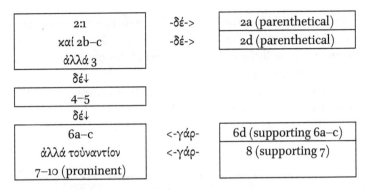

Figure 9.6: Flow-chart of Galatians 2:1–10

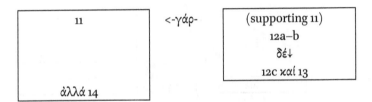

Figure 9.7: Flow-chart of Galatians 2:11–14

2:15–21. As noted earlier, we cannot know with certainty how many of these verses are a continuation of Paul's speech to Peter. Because the 'we' of 2:15 does not include Gentile Christians, though, the Gentile recipients of the letter would have assumed that Paul was still addressing Peter, together with the other Jewish Christians who were present at the time. It is noteworthy, too, that Paul switches from first person plural to singular at the point at which γάρ introduces information which supports his earlier assertions. So it would not be unreasonable to suppose that 2:14–17 constitute Paul's speech,[87] with 2:18–21 providing support for the Galatians' benefit, whether or not the words were spoken to Peter.

As to the structure of 2:15–21, the independent pronoun Ἡμεῖς signals a change of topic from σύ 'you' (Peter) to 'we' Jewish Christians in general or, more specifically, "we Jews who know that we are justified by faith [alone]."[88] If 2:15–16

---

[87] Contra Todd A. Scacewater, "Galatians 2:11–21 and the Interpretive Context of 'Works of the Law,'" *JETS* 56 no. 2 (2013): 317–318.

[88] Ibid., 318. Comments such as "'We' is emphatic—'we' as distinct from 'them' (the Gentiles)" (Bruce, *Galatians*, 137) are misleading, as it is not the pronoun itself but the rest of 2:15 (φύσει Ἰουδαῖοι καὶ οὐκ ἐξ ἐθνῶν ἁμαρτωλοί 'Jews by birth and not Gentile sinners') that indicates that the referents of 'we' are Jewish Christians. For discussion of the need to distinguish two types of "emphasis" (topical versus focal), see Stephen H. Levinsohn, "The Relevance of

are read as a single sentence,[89] then the δέ variant in 2:16 is internal to the sentence, introducing a distinct point about 'us.' The δέ in 2:17 then introduces a possible objection to 2:16 as a distinct point. Rejection of this objection is then supported by 2:17–20, with 2:21 as a separate point.[90]

Figure 9.8 shows how the argument of 2:15–21 develops (see below for discussion of the internal structure of 2:19–20).

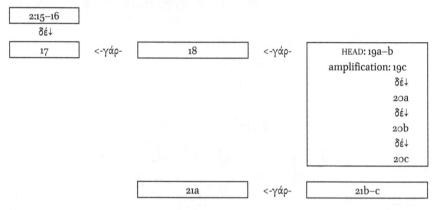

Figure 9.8: Flow-chart of Galatians 2:15–21

We now look at the internal structure of 2:19–20.

Asyndeton in 19c is consistent with 19c–20c being an "amplification" of the "HEAD" propositions 'through the law I died to the law, so that I might live to God' (19a–b).[91] The amplification itself consists of four distinct points:

- 'I have been crucified with Christ;'
- 'It is no longer I who live;'
- 'It is Christ who lives in me;'
- 'The life I now live in the flesh I live by faith in the Son of God, who loved me and gave himself for me.'

Confirmation that 'I have been crucified with Christ' is to be related to the context is the use of perfect tense-aspect (Χριστῷ συνεσταύρωμαι). Recent research on the perfect indicative in the Greek of Hebrews reveals that it "often

---

Greek Discourse Studies to Exegesis," *JT* 2, no. 2 (online at http://www.sil.org/siljot/2006/2/48004/siljot2006-2-02.pdf, 2006): §3.1.

[89] See Bruce, *Galatians*, 136–137 for discussion of this point.

[90] "A break—and climax—in the argument seems to be reached with this verse (note the asyndeton)" (Fung, *Galatians*, 125).

[91] E. Rogers, *Semantic Structure Analysis of Galatians* (SIL, 1989), 58. Rogers includes 21a in the amplification of 19a–b.

introduces restatements of past events or speeches. In passages with aorist-perfect alternation, it is also used in a marked way with added implicatures. Towards the end of a passage, assertions in the perfect often clinch the argument and/or are climactic."[92] Assuming that the perfect is used in the same way in Galatians, 'I have been crucified with Christ' is to be understood as a restatement of 'I died to the law' and, given the aorist-perfect alternation between ἀπέθανον and συνεσταύρωμαι, the assertion is more prominent than the one in the aorist.

4.2 The Internal Structure of 3:1–4:31

I discuss the internal structure of this macro-unit in four parts: 3:1–14, 3:15–4:11 (with subdivisions at 4:1 and 4:8), 4:12–20 and 4:21–31. 3:1 and 3:15 begin with asyndeton and a vocative, while 4:21 begins with asyndeton, the orienter Λέγετέ μοι 'Tell me' and the vocative οἱ ὑπὸ νόμον θέλοντες εἶναι 'you who desire to be subject to the law' which refers to a concept (ὑπὸ νόμον 'under law') which last featured in 4:5.[93]

3:1–14 "Faith or Observance of the Law" (NIV)

A number of writers have commented on the chiastic nature of 3:1–14, which may be cited as evidence that these verses form a sub-unit. For example, Sanders writes, "Verse 14 summarizes the preceding argument in chiastic fashion, the first *hina* clause ... reiterating the positive point of 3:8 (the blessing of Abraham for the Gentiles), the second, the positive assertion of 3:1–5 (the Spirit is received through faith)."[94] What is interesting is the lack of symmetry between the two parts of the chiasm. Whereas the first three elements of the first part are expressed in full sentences or groups of sentences (A: Receiving the Spirit (1–5); B: Abraham and his blessing on the nations (6–9); C: the curse of the law (10)), the second references to them are all presented in a single sentence (13–14).

Furthermore, the connectives used to link the elements of the chiasm constrain them to be related to each other in different ways. Element B (6–9) begins with καθώς 'just as', which implies that 3:6 is subordinated to 3:5. Element C (10) begins with γάρ, which indicates that what follows (10–12) supports the conclusion of 3:9. In contrast, 3:13–14 begin with asyndeton.

---

[92] Stephen H. Levinsohn, "The Perfect in Context in Texts in English, Sistani Balochi and New Testament Greek," in *Perfects in Indo-European Languages and Beyond*, ed. Robert Crellin and Thomas Jugel (John Benjamins, 2020), Abstract.

[93] See §4.2 on the sentence initial vocative in 4:19 and the sentence final vocative in 4:12d.

[94] See, e.g., E. P. Sanders, *Paul, the Law, and the Jewish People* (S. C. M. Press, 1983), 22.

In my paper on Romans 6, I raised the question as to which part of a chiastic structure is prominent. Clarke writes, "Most of the people that have studied the chiastic approach agree that the portion in the center usually contains the most important part of the chiasm."[95] However, one would not expect this to be the case when the center is introduced with γάρ, as such material is backgrounded in relation to the THESIS which it strengthens (Westfall labels γάρ "de-emphatic").[96] Rather, one would expect the edges to be prominent.[97]

So, in the case of Galatians 3:1–14, it is not the quotation from Habakkuk 2:4 (Ὁ δίκαιος ἐκ πίστεως ζήσεται 'The one who is righteous will live by faith'—11b) that is prominent.[98] Rather, it is the implied answer to the rhetorical question of 3:5 (it is by believing what you heard that God supplies you with the Spirit and works miracles among you), together with the conclusion of 3:14b (ἵνα τὴν ἐπαγγελίαν τοῦ πνεύματος λάβωμεν διὰ τῆς πίστεως 'so that we might receive the promise of the Spirit through faith') which, as Hays notes, "closes the circle of ideas that began in verse 2" and is the "linchpin of Paul's argument."[99]

The following are some notes about other connectives used in 3:1–14.

The section begins with verses that Alford describes as "solemnly severe."[100] Paul's emotional state is reflected in the absence of conjunctions throughout 3:1–4.[101] The connective οὖν 'then' in 3:5 indicates a return to the theme that was introduced in 3:2,[102] following the 'aside' of 3:4.

In 3:7, ἄρα 'so, consequently' introduces a consequence which may be deduced from 3:6. Δέ introduces distinct points in 3:8 and, within the supportive material of 3:10–12, 3:10b and 3:11. Finally, before the supportive material, ὥστε 'therefore, for this reason' introduces the conclusion of the subdivision (9).

Prominence-giving devices used in 3:1–14, other than those discussed in connection with the chiastic structure of the verses, include the following:

- In 2, the cataphoric demonstrative τοῦτο 'this' gives prominence to the rhetorical question that follows: ἐξ ἔργων νόμου τὸ πνεῦμα ἐλάβετε ἢ ἐξ

---

[95] Thomas B. Clarke, *What is a Chiasm? Understanding the Chiastic Approach.* Online at www.bible-discernments.com/joshua/whatisachaism.html (2011).

[96] Cynthia Long Westfall, "A Method for the Analysis of Prominence in Hellenistic Greek," in *The Linguist as Pedagogue: Trends in the Teaching and Linguistic Analysis of the Greek New Testament*, ed. Stanley E. Porter and Matthew Brook O'Donnell (Sheffield Phoenix Press, 2009), 85.

[97] Levinsohn, *Holistic Approach*, 8–9.

[98] Contrast http://www.chiasmusxchange.com/2015/06/12/galatians-31-14/.

[99] Richard B. Hays, *The Faith of Jesus Christ: The Narrative Substructure of Galatians 3:1–4:11*, 2nd ed. (Eerdmans, 2002), 183, 124.

[100] Henry Alford, *The Greek Testament* (Rivingtons, 1884), III.4.

[101] See Kathleen Callow, "The Disappearing δέ in 1 Corinthians, in *Linguistics and New Testament Interpretation: Essays on Discourse Analysis*, ed. David Alan Black et al. (Broadman, 1992), 192.

[102] Hendriksen, *Galatians*, 124.

ἀκοῆς πίστεως; 'Did you receive the Spirit by doing the works of the law or by believing what you heard?'

- In 7, the orienter Γινώσκετε ἄρα 'So, you see' gives prominence to the assertion that follows: ὅτι οἱ ἐκ πίστεως, οὗτοι υἱοί εἰσιν Ἀβραάμ 'that those who believe are the descendants of Abraham.'

Figure 9.9 below, which includes references to the elements of the chiastic structure (A, B, C, D, D′, C′, B′, A′), shows how the argument of 3:1–14 is developed.

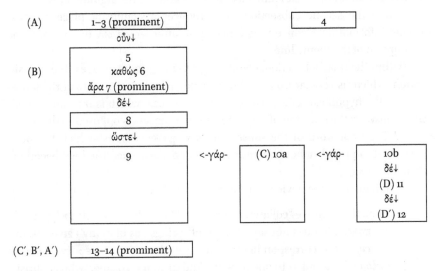

Figure 9.9: Flow-chart of Galatians 3:1–14

3:15–4:11 "The Galatians Must Know the Limitations of the Law"[103]

I follow Hendriksen in dividing this section into two principal parts (3:15–29 and 4:1–11),[104] with further subdivisions at 3:19, 3:23 and 4:8.[105] See below for the significance of introducing the second principal part (4:1–11) with δέ.

3:15–29 "Intent of the Law" (NASB)

Evidence that these verses form a section in their own right includes the *inclusio* structure involving the repetition of τῷ σπέρματι αὐτοῦ 'to his offspring' in 3:16 as τοῦ Ἀβραὰμ σπέρμα 'Abraham's offspring' in 3:29.

---

[103] Lenski, *Galatians, Ephesians and Philippians*, 155.

[104] Hendriksen, *Galatians*, 132, 154.

[105] See Fung, *Galatians*, vii.

The section may be divided into three subsections: 3:15–18, 3:19–22, and 3:23–29. The first subsection concerns the "priority and permanence of the promise"[106] and ends with supportive material that is introduced with γάρ (18). The theme of the second subsection, "The purpose of the law,"[107] is introduced with the rhetorical question Τί ὁ νόμος; 'Why the law?', together with the connective οὖν, which marks the resumption of the theme line (19). The final subsection, "The law our tutor,"[108] begins with a sentence-initial constituent, Πρὸ τοῦ ἐλθεῖν τὴν πίστιν 'before faith came', together with a switch from third to first person and the connective δέ that marks what follows as a distinct point of the argument (23).

Within the second subsection, δέ introduces a significant piece of background information[109] concerning a mediator, after which οὖν in 20 marks the resumption of the theme line.

Within the final subsection, countering ἀλλά in 3:22 introduces "the true situation" which "is very far from the law bringing people into a state of righteousness"[110] (the hypothesis of 21). The conclusion of 3:24, which is introduced with ὥστε, "answers the question of 3:21 as to whether the law is opposed to the promises."[111] The final word of the subsection is κληρονόμοι 'heirs', which has been postposed to provide a hook in anticipation of ὁ κληρονόμος 'the heir' becoming thematic in 4:1.

Prominence-giving devices used in 3:15–29 include the following:

- In 16, the negative "collateral" statement[112] (οὐ λέγει, Καὶ τοῖς σπέρμασιν ὡς ἐπὶ πολλῶν 'it does not say, "And to offsprings," as of many') gives prominence to the corresponding positive assertion: ἀλλ' ὡς ἐφ' ἑνός, Καὶ τῷ σπέρματί σου 'but as to one person: "And to your offspring," who is Christ.'
- In 17, the combination of the cataphoric demonstrative τοῦτο 'this' and the orienter λέγω 'I say' gives prominence to the following assertion: διαθήκην προκεκυρωμένην ὑπὸ τοῦ θεοῦ ὁ μετὰ τετρακόσια καὶ τριάκοντα ἔτη γεγονὼς νόμος οὐκ ἀκυροῖ 'the law, which came 430 years later, does not annul a covenant previously ratified by God...'
- In 19, the question Τί οὖν ὁ νόμος; 'Why then the law?' is used rhetorically to give prominence to the answer: τῶν παραβάσεων χάριν προσετέθη ἄχρις οὗ ἔλθῃ τὸ σπέρμα ᾧ ἐπήγγελται 'It was added because of transgressions, until the offspring would come to whom the promise had been made.' See also 3:21.

---

[106] Bruce, *Galatians*, 168.

[107] Ibid., 174.

[108] Morris, *Galatians*, 117.

[109] Levinsohn, *Discourse Features*, 90.

[110] Morris, *Galatians*, 116.

[111] Vaz, *Functional Equivalent Translation*, 104.

[112] Dooley and Levinsohn, *Analyzing Discourse*, 82.

- In 28, one rhetorical effect of a series of parallel propositions such as οὐκ ἔνι Ἰουδαῖος οὐδὲ Ἕλλην... 'There is no longer Jew or Greek...' "is to slow down the story and create the expectation that the climax is about to be presented."[113] The paraphrase of πάντες γὰρ ὑμεῖς εἷς ἐστε ἐν Χριστῷ Ἰησοῦ 'for all of you are one in Christ Jesus' (28b) in the following conditional clause (εἰ δὲ ὑμεῖς Χριστοῦ 'And if you are of Christ'—29), which includes the repeated pronoun ὑμεῖς, adds to this rhetorical effect, thereby giving prominence to the consequence that follows: ἄρα τοῦ Ἀβραὰμ σπέρμα ἐστέ, κατ' ἐπαγγελίαν κληρονόμοι 'then you are Abraham's offspring, heirs according to the promise.'

Figure 9.10 below shows how the argument of 3:15–29 is developed.

4:1–11 "Once Slaves, but Now Sons"[114]

Although I present these verses as a separate subsection, the use of the connective δέ indicates that they are to be interpreted as the next step of the argument that began in 3:15.[115] Paul "sets out an analogy meant to illustrate what he said in 3:23–25 about living 'under the law' and in 3:26–29 about new relationships 'in Christ.'"[116]

The following features may be cited as confirmation that a new sub-unit begins at 4:1: the orienter verb Λέγω 'I say', the initial time expression ἐφ' ὅσον χρόνον ὁ κληρονόμος νήπιός ἐστιν 'as long as the heir is a child' (NIV) which presents the situational frame for what follows, and the change from second to third person.

Many commentators divide 4:1–11 into two parts: 4:1–7 and 4:8–11, with countering Ἀλλά linking the two. Vaz considers 4:1–7 to be a "transitional paragraph" between chapter 3 and 4:8*ff*,[117] with the repetition in 4:7 of the singular noun κληρονόμος 'heir' in 4:1b providing "a fitting inclusio to this 'κληρονόμος' paragraph."[118]

Whereas 4:7 concludes Paul's theological exposition, in 4:8–11 he "makes another direct appeal to" the Galatians "not to return to a bondage no better than that from which they had been delivered"[119] (compare 1:6–10 and 3:1–5). The switch from second person singular to plural may be cited as evidence of a new sub-unit, as well as the temporary switch from the present to τότε 'formerly.'

---

[113] Ibid., 105.

[114] Stott, *Galatians*, 103.

[115] See H. van Dyke Parunak, "Dimensions of Discourse Structure: A Multidimensional Analysis of the Components and Transitions of Paul's Epistle to the Galatians," in *Linguistics and New Testament Interpretation*, 227–29.

[116] Longenecker, *Galatians*, 162.

[117] Vaz, *Functional Equivalent Translation*, 78.

[118] Ibid., 106.

[119] Guthrie, *Galatians*, 49.

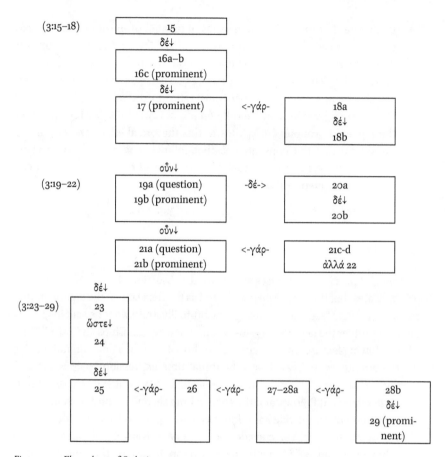

Figure 9.10: Flow-chart of Galatians 3:15–29

As for the connectives used, in 4:3, οὕτως 'so', together with additive καί 'also', introduces the principal part of the comparison of 4:1–3: a comparison between an heir who is a minor (1–2) and our own state 'while we were minors' (3). In 4:7, ὥστε introduces the conclusion of 4:1–7. In 4:8, Ἀλλά introduces a statement of the Galatians' condition which is in "striking contrast with the conclusion arrived at in the preceding verse."[120] Finally, in 4:10 and 4:11, asyndeton is appropriate, first between of the generic–specific relation between 4:9 and 4:10,[121] and then because it is normal to introduce an evaluation such as 4:11 without a conjunction.

Prominence-giving devices used in 4:1–11 include the following:

- In 7, the repetition of υἱός (εἰ υἱός 'if a child') highlights the concluding

---

[120] John Eadie, *A Commentary on the Greek Text of the Epistle of Paul to the Galatians* (1869; repr., Baker, 1979), 307.

[121] Rogers, *Semantic Structure Analysis of Galatians*, 123.

phrase: καὶ κληρονόμος διὰ θεοῦ 'also an heir, through God.'

- In 8, the particle μέν implies that the information it introduces is "of secondary importance in comparison with that introduced with δέ" in 9.[122]

Figure 9.11 shows how the argument of 4:1–11 is developed.

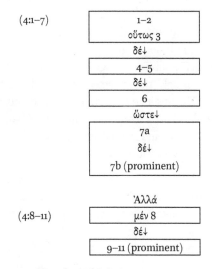

Figure 9.11: Flow-chart of Galatians 4:1–11

4:12–20 "Personal Appeal" [123]

This section begins with an imperative: Γίνεσθε ὡς ἐγώ 'Become as I am.' The final position of the vocative ἀδελφοί 'brothers' and of the orienter δέομαι ὑμῶν 'I beg you' suggests a minor sub-division after 4:12a,[124] as does the absence of a connective to introduce 4:12b.

In 4:15, the inferential connective οὖν 'then'[125] not only "indicates an inference drawn from the previous two verses,"[126] but also resumes and advances the theme that was being developed in 4:8–12a; namely, Paul's preoccupation with the current situation of the Galatians. This in turn implies that 4:12b–14, which

---

[122] Levinsohn, *Discourse Features*, 170.

[123] Bruce, *Galatians*, 207.

[124] Vaz, *Functional Equivalent Translation*, 107. The absence of an overt subject such as ὑμεῖς 'you' at the beginning of the next sentence implies that the subdivision is indeed of a minor nature.

[125] Morris, *Galatians*, 136. Some MSS have τίς instead of ποῦ οὖν.

[126] Vaz, *Functional Equivalent Translation*, 108.

concern earlier events involving Paul and the Galatians (note the aorists), should be viewed as of a supportive nature in relation to their current relationship.

The rhetorical question of 4:15a (ποῦ οὖν ὁ μακαρισμὸς ὑμῶν; 'What has become of the good you felt?') is followed by a supportive statement introduced with γάρ. The connective ὥστε introduces the conclusion of the subsection, which is also in the form of a rhetorical question (ἐχθρὸς ὑμῶν γέγονα ἀληθεύων ὑμῖν; 'Have I now become your enemy by telling you the truth?').

"Paul now draws a contrast between the attitude of the false teachers to the Galatians and his own attitude to them."[127] What is noteworthy, though, is the absence of any overt reference to these teachers as the subject changes. As Vaz notes, "Paul suddenly attacks his opponents, and surprisingly, the expected referential point of departure, such as αὐτοὶ δέ, is absent."[128] The absence of such a reference and, indeed, of an overt connective, may well reflect Paul's emotional state.[129] Vaz makes a similar point about 4:19: "best seen as an emotive and evaluative expression."[130]

Prominence-giving devices used in 4:12–20 include the following:

- In 12a, the orienter (δέομαι ὑμῶν 'I beg you') reinforces and thereby gives prominence to the preceding exhortation: Γίνεσθε ὡς ἐγώ, ὅτι κἀγὼ ὡς ὑμεῖς, ἀδελφοί 'Become as I am, for I also have become as you are, brothers.'
- In 13, the orienter (οἴδατε 'you know') gives prominence to the following assertions, which culminate with: ὡς ἄγγελον θεοῦ ἐδέξασθέ με, ὡς Χριστὸν Ἰησοῦν 'you welcomed me as an angel of God, as Christ Jesus' (14).
- In 15, the orienter (μαρτυρῶ ὑμῖν 'I testify to you') gives prominence to the following assertion: ὅτι εἰ δυνατὸν τοὺς ὀφθαλμοὺς ὑμῶν ἐξορύξαντες ἐδώκατέ μοι 'that, had it been possible, you would have torn out your eyes and given them to me.'
- In 19, the expanded vocative (τέκνα μου, οὓς πάλιν ὠδίνω μέχρις οὗ μορφωθῇ Χριστὸς ἐν ὑμῖν 'My little children, for whom I am again in the pain of childbirth until Christ is formed in you') has the effect of slowing down the discourse and thereby giving prominence to the following assertion: θελον δὲ παρεῖναι πρὸς ὑμᾶς ἄρτι καὶ ἀλλάξαι τὴν φωνήν μου 'I wish I were present with you now and could change my tone' (20).

Figure 9.12 shows how the argument of 4:12–20 is developed.

---

[127] Stott, *Galatians*, 115.

[128] Vaz, *Functional Equivalent Translation*, 109. Vaz goes on to point out that "this seems to be in keeping with Paul's attitude towards his opponents... not even once does he refer to them with an explicit pronominal subject except for vague indefinite pronouns such as τινές in 1:7..." (ibid.)

[129] Morris (*Galatians*, 136) describes 4:12–20 as "a highly emotional passage."

[130] Vaz, *Functional Equivalent Translation*, 109.

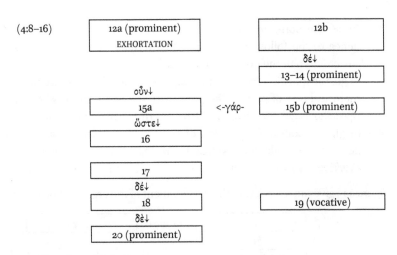

Figure 9.12: Flow-chart of Galatians 4:12–20

4:21–31 "Two Convenants"[131]

"In this section Paul resumes the argument which ended in verse 7 and which has been interrupted by his personal and intimate address to the Galatians (vv. 8–20)."[132] Textual features that confirm that a new sub-unit is beginning include the absence of a connective, the orienter Λέγετέ μοι 'Tell me,' and the vocative οἱ ὑπὸ νόμον θέλοντες εἶναι 'you who desire to be subject to the law', with its reference to a concept (ὑπὸ νόμον) which was last referred to in 4:5.

Vaz considers "the entire allegory of 4:22–27 to be subsumed under the γάρ of 4:22, since it is an attempt by Paul to justify from scripture the enslaving nature of the law."[133] In 4:28, ὑμεῖς δέ, ἀδελφοί 'Now you, brothers' "marks a shift to the specific application of the allegory to the present situation."[134] Finally, in 4:31 [NA²⁷], διό introduces a THESIS which, while inferred from the immediate context, has already been stated in other words in 4:28, with which it forms an *inclusio*.

Prominence-giving devices used in 4:21–31 include the following:

- In 21, the orienter Λέγετέ μοι ('Tell me') and the vocative (οἱ ὑπὸ νόμον θέλοντες εἶναι 'you who desire to be subject to the law') give prominence in the first instance to the question τὸν νόμον οὐκ ἀκούετε; 'will you not listen to the law?' and, thence, to the answer to that question, culminating in 4:30 and 4:31 (see below).

---

[131] Morris, *Galatians*, 143.

[132] D. C. Arichea Jr. and Eugene A. Nida, *A Translator's Handbook on Paul's Letter to the Galatians* (United Bible Societies, 1976), 109.

[133] Vaz, *Functional Equivalent Translation*, 110.

[134] Ibid., 112.

- In 28, the non-initial position of the vocative (ἀδελφοί) gives prominence to the following assertion:[135] κατὰ Ἰσαὰκ ἐπαγγελίας τέκνα ἐστέ 'are children of the promise, like Isaac.'
- In 30, the question (τί λέγει ἡ γραφή; 'what does the scripture say?') "is a rhetorical way of putting the point that 'the Scripture says'"[136]: "Ἔκβαλε τὴν αιδίσκην καὶ τὸν υἱὸν αὐτῆς 'Drive out the slave and her child...'
- In 31, the non-initial position of the vocative (ἀδελφοί) gives prominence to the following assertion: οὐκ ἐσμὲν παιδίσκης τέκνα ἀλλὰ τῆς ἐλευθέρας 'we are children, not of the slave but of the free woman.'

Figure 9.13 gives an overview of the development of the argument of 4:21–31.[137]

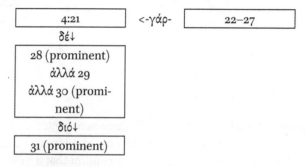

Figure 9.13: Flow-chart of Galatians 4:21–31

4.3 The Internal Structure of 5:13–6:10

I discuss the internal structure of this macro-unit in two parts: 5:13–26 and 6:1–10.[138] Surface features that may be cited as evidence of a subdivision at 6:1 include asyndeton, the vocative Ἀδελφοί 'brothers', the conditional clause ἐὰν καὶ προλημφθῇ ἄνθρωπος ἔν τινι παραπτώματι 'if anyone is detected in a transgression' which indicates a switch from the situation applicable to the end of chapter 5, and the change from first to second person.

5:13–26 "Life in the Spirit" [139]

I suggested in §3.3 that, as in 1:6–2:21, the macro-section that comprises 5:1–6:10 begins with a section that contains warnings against false teaching (5:2–12).

[135] Levinsohn, *Non-Narrative Discourse Analysis*, §7.7.

[136] Bruce, *Galatians*, 224.

[137] See Levinsohn, *Rasgos discursivos*, 59 for discussion of the development of the argument in 4:22–27.

[138] See Fung, *Galatians*, viii.

[139] Ibid.

Then, introduced by γάρ, follows contrary evidence for rejecting such teaching, beginning in 5:13 with a hortatory THESIS that is supported by what follows: although you were called for freedom, you are not to "use your freedom as an opportunity for self-indulgence, but through love become slaves to one another." These exhortations are supported first by a quotation from Leviticus 9:18 (14) and then by a warning about "what is left if his readers do not live in love" (15).[140] Δέ in 5:16 then introduces a further exhortation: πνεύματι περιπατεῖτε 'Live by the Spirit,' which is accompanied first by a promise[141] (καὶ ἐπιθυμίαν σαρκὸς οὐ μὴ τελέσητε 'and you will not gratify the desires of the sinful nature' (NIV) and then by supportive material (17–24).[142] The final exhortations of the subsection (25–26), are introduced with the conditional clause εἰ ζῶμεν πνεύματι 'If we live by the Spirit,' which "picks up where verse 16 left off."[143]

Prominence-giving devices used in 5:13–26 include the following:

- In 14, the expression ἐν ἑνὶ λόγῳ πεπλήρωται 'in a single commandment' is used cataphorically to give prominence to the following quotation: ἐν τῷ Ἀγαπήσεις τὸν πλησίον σου ὡς σεαυτόν 'in the "You shall love your neighbor as yourself."'
- In 16, the orienter Λέγω 'I say' "is used to give special prominence to the key exhortation in that verse."[144]
- At the end of 21, the introductory expression ἃ προλέγω ὑμῖν καθὼς προεῖπον '[of] which I am forewarning you, as I warned you before' may be taken as a slowing-down device to give prominence to the following assertion: ὅτι οἱ τὰ τοιαῦτα πράσσοντες βασιλείαν θεοῦ οὐ κληρονομήσουσιν 'that those who do such things will not inherit the kingdom of God.'

In contrast, the use in 5:25 and 5:26 of first-person forms makes the exhortations concerned "less potent"[145] than those in second person (13, 16).

Figure 9.14 below shows how the argument of 5:13–26 is developed, with the exhortations constituting the theme line, and the rest of the material supporting the exhortations.

---

[140] Morris, *Galatians*, 166. Vaz (*Functional Equivalent Translation*, 116) is surely wrong when he states that "The δέ in 5:15 marks the resumption of the hortatory theme line." One common function of sentence-initial conditional clauses such as εἰ δὲ ἀλλήλους δάκνετε καὶ κατεσθίετε 'If, however, you bite and devour one another' is to introduce a consequence of obeying or not obeying an exhortation.

[141] Bruce, *Galatians*, 243. Contrast NRSV, which translates the aorist subjunctive with an imperative: 'do not gratify the desires of the flesh.'

[142] "[T]he details and specific applications of this exhortation are expounded in the next several verses until 5:24" (Vaz, *Functional Equivalent Translation*, 117).

[143] Ridderbos, *Galatians*, 210.

[144] Vaz, *Functional Equivalent Translation*, 117.

[145] Levinsohn, *Non-Narrative Discourse Analysis*, §7.1.2.

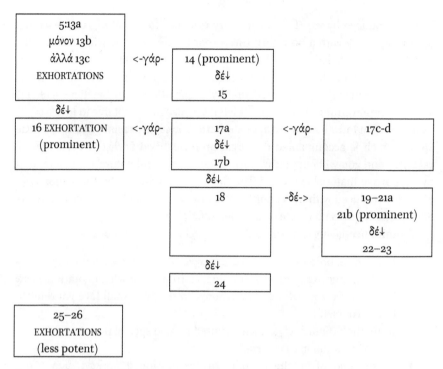

Figure 9.14: Flow-chart of Galatians 5:13–26

6:1–10 *"Mutual Helpfulness"*[146]

"The general teaching of 5:13–26 is now applied to some more specific situations,"[147] the first of which is described in the opening conditional clause of 6:1: ἐὰν καὶ προλημφθῇ ἄνθρωπος ἔν τινι παραπτώματι 'if anyone is detected in a transgression.' As in 5:13–26, the theme line is made up of exhortations, most of which are followed by supportive material introduced with γάρ.

Although 6:4 begins with an exhortation (τὸ δὲ ἔργον ἑαυτοῦ δοκιμαζέτω ἕκαστος 'All must test their own work'), I agree with Vaz that it is of a "parenthetical nature"[148] and should be treated as part of the material that supports the exhortation of 6:2, rather than being on the theme line.[149]

---

[146] Morris, *Galatians*, 177.

[147] Bruce, *Galatians*, 259–260.

[148] Vaz, *Functional Equivalent Translation*, 119.

[149] "The contrast is with the person who thinks he is something when he is nothing" (Stutzman, *Galatians*, 250); see also J. B. Lightfoot, *Saint Paul's Epistle to the Galatians*, 10th ed. (Macmillan, 1892), 217.

The final sentence of the main body of the letter, 6:10, is introduced with the connectives ἄρα οὖν 'So then.' Οὖν marks the resumption of the main theme line, following the supportive material of 6:9b, while ἄρα makes explicit that what follows is "the logical consequence of what he has just said."[150]

Prominence-giving devices used in 6:1–10 include the following:

- In 4, the adverb τότε 'then' may have been used as a slowing-down device between clauses, to give prominence to what follows:[151] εἰς ἑαυτὸν μόνον τὸ καύχημα ἕξει καὶ οὐκ εἰς τὸν ἕτερον 'that work, rather than their neighbor's work, will become a cause for pride.'
- In 7a, the orienter Μὴ πλανᾶσθε 'Do not be deceived' gives prominence to what follows: θεὸς οὐ μυκτηρίζεται... 'God is not mocked...'

Figure 9.15 shows how the argument of 6:1–10 is developed, with the exhortations constituting the theme line, and the rest of the material supporting the exhortations.

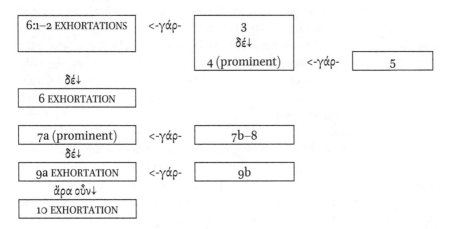

Figure 9.15: Flow-chart of Galatians 6:1–10

4.4 *Concluding Comments (6:11–17)*

Paul's concluding comments "represent a final punch in the argument, thematically related to some of the points raised in the letter..."[152] As such, they give prominence to certain themes and assertions.

The words "circumcision" (περιτομή) and "be circumcised" (περιτέμνεσθαι) were used seven times in the body of the letter (2:3, 7, 8, 9, 12; 5:3, 6, 11) and now

---

[150] Guthrie, *Galatians*, 147.

[151] Levinsohn, *Discourse Features*, 94.

[152] Vaz, *Functional Equivalent Translation*, 164.

they occur four more times (6:12, 13 [bis], 15). Of particular note is the reiteration, in 6:15, of the assertion of 5:6. In 5:6, the double negative οὔτε περιτομή τι ἰσχύει οὔτε ἀκροβυστία 'neither circumcision nor uncircumcision counts for anything' gave prominence to positive ἀλλὰ πίστις δι' ἀγάπης ἐνεργουμένη 'the only thing that counts is faith working through love.' In 6:15, the emphasis is slightly different; negative οὔτε ... περιτομή τί ἐστιν οὔτε ἀκροβυστία 'neither circumcision nor uncircumcision is anything' gives prominence to ἀλλὰ καινὴ κτίσις 'but a new creation is everything!'

In 4:17, Paul discussed the motivation of the unnamed Judaizing teachers: ἐκκλεῖσαι ὑμᾶς θέλουσιν ἵνα αὐτοὺς ζηλοῦτε 'they want to exclude you, so that you may make much of them.' In the conclusion, he returns to their motivations and makes a similar point in 6:12–13; they are ὅσοι θέλουσιν εὐπροσωπῆσαι ἐν σαρκί 'those who want to make a good showing in the flesh' who want the Galatians to be circumcised ἵνα ἐν τῇ ὑμετέρᾳ σαρκὶ καυχήσωνται 'so that they may boast about your flesh.' However, 6:12 gives another motivation; they are trying to compel the Galatians to be circumcised: μόνον ἵνα τῷ σταυρῷ τοῦ Χριστοῦ ['Ιησοῦ] μὴ διώκωνται 'only that they may not be persecuted for the cross of Christ [Jesus].' Fung comments as follows on Paul's use of μόνον: "In view of the other two motives, the expression 'their sole object' or 'the only reason' (NIV) clearly cannot be taken literally; it is probably a rhetorical device for emphasis."[153] In other words, prominence is being given to fear (rather than any deep conviction) as a motivation for the Judaizers' desire that the Galatians be circumcised.

Paul then (6:14) switches attention to himself (ἐμοὶ 'As for me'—NLT). His use of a negated verb (μὴ γένοιτο καυχᾶσθαι 'may it not be to boast') followed by εἰ μή 'if not' allows him to give prominence to the exception: ἐν τῷ σταυρῷ τοῦ κυρίου ἡμῶν 'Ιησοῦ Χριστοῦ 'except the cross of our Lord Jesus Christ.' This clause in turn is followed by a non-restrictive relative clause: δι' οὗ ἐμοὶ κόσμος ἐσταύρωται κἀγὼ κόσμῳ 'by which the world has been crucified to me, and I to the world.' The relative clause recalls Paul's earlier assertion, 'I have been crucified with Christ' (2:19) and may well be prominent, as well, since non-restrictive relative clauses often have the effect of backgrounding the information in the preceding clause.[154]

Figure 9.16 shows how the argument of 6:11–17 is developed, with 6:17 "best regarded as a separate paragraph unrelated to v. 18, which is the concluding benediction to the whole letter."[155]

---

[153] Fung, *Galatians*, 305.

[154] Levinsohn, *Discourse Features*, 192.

[155] Fung, *Galatians*, 312.

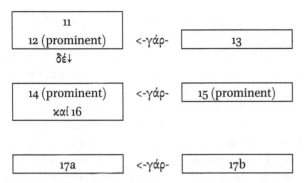

Figure 9.16: Flow-chart of Galatians 6:11–17

Conclusion

It is to be expected that the material that is given prominence in this letter relates directly to Paul's purpose in sending it; namely, to counteract the "agitators [who] were trying to get the Galatians to 'Judaize.'"[156] It was precisely to counteract their propaganda that Paul writes his solemn curse of 1:8 ('even if we or an angel from heaven should proclaim to you a gospel contrary to what we proclaimed to you, let that one be accursed!'), which he then highlights not only by repeating it in 1:9, but also by means of the extended introduction to that repetition: ὡς προειρήκαμεν, καὶ ἄρτι πάλιν λέγω 'As we have said before, and now I repeat.'

To achieve his goal, Paul needs to defend his authority to preach the Gospel,[157] so it is not surprising that he highlights the assertion that he received 'the gospel that was proclaimed by me ... through a revelation of Jesus Christ' (1:11–12) by introducing it with an orienter and vocative (Γνωρίζω γὰρ ὑμῖν, ἀδελφοί, 'For I want you to know, brothers') and by employing a series of negatives ('not of human origin; ... not ... from a human source, nor was I taught it') in the lead-up to the final, positive point.[158] See also 2:7–10 (discussed in §4.1).

Paul also gives prominence to his assertions that there is no benefit in Gentiles being circumcised (5:2–3 [see §3.3], 5:6 and 6:15 [§4.4]).

Various devices are used to give prominence to Paul's bewilderment over the Galatians' apparent abandonment of the gospel (3:2, 4:9–11, 4:13–15, and 4:20 [see §4.2]), including one of just two exhortations that are highlighted (4:12 [see §4.3]).

A number of positive assertions that further Paul's argument are also given prominence. They include the conclusion of the discussion as to whether the

---

[156] N. T. Wright, *Justification: God's Plan and Paul's Vision* (IVP Academic, 2009), 113.

[157] Vaz, *Functional Equivalent Translation*, 55.

[158] See also 1:15–17.

Galatians received the promise of the Spirit by works of the law or through faith (3:14); the conclusion that 'you are Abraham's offspring' (3:29) and, therefore, heirs of the promise given to Abraham (4:7); and of our being children of the 'free woman' (4:28, 30, 31). Various statements relating to the role of the law are also highlighted (3:17, 3:19, 3:21, 4:21ff, and 5:14).[159]

The other exhortation that is given prominence is that of 5:6 ('Live by the Spirit, and you will not gratify the desires of the flesh' [see §4.3]), which relates back to the Spirit–flesh dichotomy of 3:2. The consequence of practicing the works of the flesh is also given prominence ('those who do such things will not inherit the kingdom of God' [5:21]), as is the warning of 6:7 ('Do not be deceived; God is not mocked, for you reap whatever you sow' [see §4.4]).

All these features point to Galatians being "focused ... from start to finish on arguing a single basic point."[160] It is "a passionate letter, the outpouring of the soul of a preacher on fire for his Lord and deeply committed to bringing his hearers to an understanding of what saving faith is. ... [Paul] wrote this letter to make it very plain that the gospel is not another way of imposing the law on people. ... The gospel is about the faith that means trusting God and not relying on our own efforts."[161]

---

[159] See §4.2 for discussion of the devices used to give prominence in these verses.

[160] Douglas J. Moo, *Galatians* (Baker, 2013), 62.

[161] Morris, *Galatians*, 26–27.

10

EPHESIANS

TODD A. SCACEWATER

T he epistle to the Ephesians was, according to the document, written by the apostle Paul during an imprisonment (1:1; 3:1, 13; 6:20). If Paul wrote it, and did so from the latter part of his Roman imprisonment (rather than his Caesarean imprisonment), then he wrote it around AD 60–62.[1] If so, then we have some pragmatic information about the author, his social and historical situation, his possible audience, and potentially the occasion of the letter. But since 1792, starting with E. Evanson, scholars have challenged Pauline authorship on the basis of style, theology, the historical perspective of the epistle, and the relationship between Ephesians and Colossians as well as the Pastorals.[2] I personally do not find the arguments persuasive, and believe that Paul wrote the letter, a position not as unpopular as most think.[3] The issue is important because it determines whether we have more or less pragmatic information for our discourse analysis. The point becomes *somewhat* moot when we consider that a discourse analysis of ancient texts will necessarily focus more on semantics than pragmatics anyway, because pragmatic aspects of communication are more difficult to retrieve in ancient texts.

---

[1] On Pauline chronology, among others see L. C. A. Alexander, "Chronology of Paul," in *Dictionary of Paul and His Letters*, eds. Gerald F. Hawthorne, Ralph P. Martin, and Daniel G. Reid (InterVarsity Press, 1993), 115–123; Rainer Riesner, *Paul's Early Period: Chronology, Mission Strategy, Theology* (Eerdmans, 1998).

[2] The introductions to most commentaries will trace this history and the evidence involved, which cannot be recited here.

[3] Between 1519 and 2001, in only five decades did those who rejected it outnumber those who accepted it. See Harold Hoehner, *Ephesians: An Exegetical Commentary* (Baker Academic, 2002), 9–20.

The recipients of the letter are traditionally taken as believers in Ephesus, with the title "to Ephesus" (πρὸς Ἐφεσίους) being included in the extant manuscripts since c. 200 AD in 𝔓⁴⁶. Yet, in our extant manuscripts, ἐν Ἐφέσῳ is not included in the text until the fifth century in Alexandrinus.[4] It does seem from the available evidence that ἐν Ἐφέσῳ was not originally included in 1:1, and no conjectural reading to date has gained wide acceptance. I agree with those who believe Ephesians was intended as a general (or circular) letter for Asia Minor. If written from Rome, it would have entered through the Ephesian port and have been delivered first to the Ephesian church(es). If they made copies of the letter and perhaps helped to distribute them through Asia Minor, this could partially explain how the extant manuscripts gained the title πρὸς Ἐφεσίους. If we read Ephesians as a letter to Asia Minor generally, we gain more pragmatic information that may be useful for discerning the main purpose of the epistle.

Methodology

Since I have described the various aspects of DA in the introduction to this volume, I will explain simply my own methodology for Ephesians and the reader may refer to the introduction for explanation of terms (coherence, cohesion, macrostructures, etc.) and sources that further discuss them.

The entire process of a DA is dialectical in the sense that one must work both top-down and bottom-up simultaneously. The first step is to determine the unit boundaries at the lowest level, so that each unit has its own macrostructure (or "discourse topic"). These boundaries are provisional and may be revised as one works more closely at the exegetical level and at higher levels of the discourse. Then, by paying attention especially to discourse markers at the boundaries, one must discern how the lowest unit levels combine into higher unit levels in a hierarchical fashion. Some discourse markers will only connect sentences together, while others will connect paragraphs, and others will connect entire divisions. Again, initial decisions will be provisional as the analyst continues to work exegetically and at the highest levels, refining decisions all along. Eventually, a structure to the entire letter will be determined, showing how the lower units combine into higher level units in hierarchical fashion.

Next, lest the analysis read like a series of bullet points, one must search for prominence within each unit and between units. Each unit will have its own macrostructure, which (following Teun van Dijk) should be an entailment of

---

[4] The phrase is completely absent from 𝔓⁴⁶ and was added to the margins of Vaticanus and Sinaiticus by a second hand, until it finally forced its way from the margin into the text of Alexandrinus. There is also no sign from comments on Ephesians by Irenaeus, Clement of Alexandria, Origen, and Tertullian that their manuscripts included ἐν Ἐφέσῳ in 1:1.

every proposition within that unit, and should also function to organize those propositions and to highlight the most prominent information.[5] Once one determines the macrostructure of every lowest-level unit, these macrostructures may be combined into the next-highest level unit (combining the macrostructures of the units that were connected in the structural hierarchy). As macrostructures are combined, one must delete globally irrelevant information, generalize particulars, and construct propositions that are defined by series of propositions. In this way, macrostructures at each level should be around the same length, so the macrostructure of the entire discourse is not unwieldy.

While the work described so far is typically carried out in the realm of semantics (reference and truth), it can and should be done also in the realm of pragmatics (the relationship between linguistic forms and their users). A simple way of doing this systematically is, following RST's methodology, to posit a rhetorical function for each unit. Authors have communicative purposes, and everything they write or say is more or less connected to that purpose. One could use speech act theory to convert every unit into a micro-act (an act that is informative, commissive, directive, etc.), with prominence being determined by whether acts are auxiliary or primary. More informally, one might suggest how a unit functions in the overall structure. Pragmatic macrostructures are more difficult to discern with documents like Ephesians, for which we have only some knowledge about the letter's occasion and audience. It is much easier in Colossians, for example, to discern pragmatic macrostructures, since we have an idea of why Paul sent the letter and what he is trying to do in it. In Ephesians, the general nature of the admonitions and our lack of understanding about its communicative context requires us to infer the reasons for sending the letter, and thus engage in mirror reading to some extent. For this reason, I will focus more on semantic macrostructures, but the idea of Jew-Gentile unity in the church is such a prominent theme within the semantic macrostructure that it probably has some pragmatic implications.

Much more can be integrated into a DA, but for the purposes of this essay, these features will be enough to help the reader understand the macrostructure of Ephesians and some of its communicative purposes. The goal is that the reader will be assisted in studying, teaching, and preaching the epistle by better understanding how each microstructure contributes to the whole.

Macrostructure

Ephesians is an ancient epistle, and accordingly begins with a greeting (1:1–2) and ends with a closing (6:21–24). These units contain lexemes that evoke themes throughout the epistle (εἰρήνη, ἀγάπη, χάρις, θεός, Χριστός, κύριος), and

---

[5] On van Dijk's theory of macrostructures, see this volume's "Introduction," p. 26.

also information about Tychicus bearing news about Paul and his co-workers (6:21–22). But from a structural point of view they are formulaic. Their contents provide us some information about the letter's historical situation, but the purpose of the discourse is discerned from the letter body (1:3–6:20).

Ephesians is typically divided into two parts, chs. 1–3 and 4–6, although other structures have been proposed.[6] Despite these alternative proposals, the "amen" at the end of ch. 3, the programmatic οὖν plus imperative that opens ch. 4, and the fact that 4:1 contains the first action-oriented imperative in the epistle (cf. 2:11) all support the traditional two-part division. The οὖν in 4:1 is inferential, which means that semantically chs. 4–6 are more prominent. That is, chs. 1–3 are supportive of the communicative intent in chs. 4–6, and the latter could function on its own (even if less effectively), while chs. 1–3 on their own would be informative but one would wonder why the letter was written. For this reason, and because the discourse boundaries of chs. 1–3 are so easy to discern, the analysis of microstructures below will move more quickly through chs. 1–3, while much fuller attention will be given to chs. 4–6.

Division 1: Ephesians 1:3–3:21

The structure of the first division is easy to discern, while that of the second is not. Division 1 has a blessing or *Berekah* (1:3–14), thanksgiving/prayer (1:15–23), description of the recipients' salvation (2:1–10), an admonition to remember the meaning of that salvation (2:11–22), a discussion of Paul's apostleship and the mystery he stewards for their sake (3:1–13), another prayer for the recipients (3:14–19), and a doxology that closes both the prayer and the division (3:20–21). The units have clear boundaries, internal cohesion and coherence, and high-level discourse markers between most of the units. Some have suggested a chiastic structure to the first division, but the parallels are not convincing enough.[7]

---

[6] Some representatives of those who hold to the traditional two-part division are Andrew T. Lincoln, *Ephesians*, WBC (Word, 1990), xxxvi; Gerhard Sellin, *Der Brief an Die Epheser*, KEK (Vandenhoeck & Ruprecht, 2008), 52; Harold W. Hoehner, *Ephesians: An Exegetical Commentary* (Baker Academic, 2002), 61; Rudolf Schnackenburg, *Ephesians: A Commentary*, trans. Helen Heron (T&T Clark, 1991), 22; Robert G. Bratcher and Eugene A. Nida, *The Translator's Handbook on Paul's Letter to the Ephesians* (United Bible Societies, 1982), 2; William J. Larkin, *Ephesians: A Handbook on the Greek Text*, BHGNT (Baylor University Press, 2009), xvii.

For alternatives, Markus Barth (*Ephesians*, AB [Doubleday, 1974], 1:53–59) views 1:3–14 as a prologue and divides the rest into three parts (1:15–2:22; 3:1–4:24; 4:25–6:20). Frank Thielman (*Ephesians*, BECNT [Baker Academic, 2010], 28–30) recognizes plan and spontaneity in the letter, and while making a basic division between chs. 1–3 and 4–6, provides a linear outline with thirteen sections.

[7] Sellin, *Epheser*, 52; David J. Clark, *Analyzing and Translating New Testament Discourse*, SKG (Fontes, 2019), 263.

Division 2's boundaries are less discernible, and 4:25–5:14 in particular is divided in at least seven different ways by various commentators (as will be shown later).

Most commentaries offer a structure of the letter in outline form, which is only relevant to discourse concerns insofar as we must discern unit boundaries. A. Lincoln and G. Sellin applied rhetorical analysis to the letter, labeling chs. 1–3 epideictic (epideiktisch) and chs. 4–6 deliberative (symbuleutisch).[8] Lincoln labels 1:1–23 the *exordium*, 2:1–3:21 the *narratio*, 4:1–6:9 the *exhortatio*. Sellin agrees that the first division has a *narratio* and not an *argumentatio*, and similarly labels 4:1–6:9 the *exhortatio* and 6:10–20 the *peroratio*. While NT letters do not follow rhetorical models perfectly or perhaps even deliberately, Paul may have had at least some intuition about persuasive argumentation and modeled his writing similarly either subconsciously or to the best of his ability.

A DA of Ephesians can be more exact about semantic structure, whereas pragmatic structure (i.e., what the author is *doing* with the discourse) must be approached more tentatively because of our scarce information regarding the communicative situation. As for the semantic structure, I provide the macrostructure of each unit as well as their semantic roles within the first division. These proposals are conclusions from my own detailed analysis of the text, although they are open to refinement. In the "Microstructures" section below, I provide what is necessary to justify my analytical conclusions given in this section.

1:3–14	"May God be blessed because he has saved us in his Son, in whom we have our salvation and inheritance through the Spirit."
1:15–23	"I thank God for your salvation and ask him to further enlighten you spiritually about your calling, your inheritance, and his power."
2:1–10	"God saved you Gentiles in Christ, even when you were spiritually dead."
2:11–22	"Remember that you Gentiles were hopelessly separated from God, but now have been integrated into his people through faith, so that you are one body."
3:1–13	"Gentiles, do not be ashamed of my imprisonment because it is a necessary result of bringing Gentiles into the church, which manifests the wisdom of God to all creation."
3:14–21	"I pray that God would grant you greater spiritual comprehension and more of his presence."

The relationships between the units are as follows, with the capitalized semantic relation being the more semantically prominent unit.

---

[8] Sellin, *Epheser*, 52; Lincoln, *Ephesians*, xli.

Section 1:	1:13–14 (basis)	→	1:15–23 (INFERENCE)
Section 2:	2:1–10 (basis)	→	2:11–22 (INFERENCE)
Section 3:	3:1–13 (parenthesis)[9]	→	3:14–21 (HEAD)

The sections are discerned by grouping together units with the closest relations to one another, which the discourse markers at 1:15 (διὰ τοῦτο); 2:11 (διὸ); 3:1, 14 (τούτου χάριν) make somewhat simple.

Combining the sections by applying the macrorules again, the resulting macrostructures, are:

Section 1:   May God be blessed because he has saved us in his Son, for which I thank God and ask that he would give you even greater spiritual comprehension about your calling, your inheritance, and his power.

Section 2:   Because God made you Gentiles alive even when you were dead, remember your former condition and the work that God did to integrate you into his people so that you are one body.

Section 3:   As a prisoner for the sake of you Gentiles (which is all part of God's plan), I pray that God would grant you greater spiritual comprehension and more of his presence.

Next, the sections must be related to one another. Section 2 begins with καί, while Section 3 begins with τούτου χάριν. Sections 2 and 3 are most closely related because the description of the Gentiles' salvation prompts Paul's prayer for the Gentiles (3:1) in Section 3.[10] If the parenthesis is ignored, it is easy to see how 2:11–22 directly prompts Paul's prayer in 3:14–21 for the Gentiles to grow in spiritual comprehension. The resulting macrostructure is "I pray that God would grant you greater spiritual comprehension and more of his presence, because he has made you his one unified people."

The καί beginning 2:1, then, must connect Section 1 to all of Sections 2–3. Section 1 is a general description of God's blessings of salvation given to "us," meaning Jews and Gentiles in the church, and a prayer that all believers would receive more of those blessings. Sections 2 and 3 get more specific about those blessings, applying them to the Gentiles. The additive καί contextually functions to signal

---

[9] The function of his parenthesis is to provide a rationale for the Gentiles not to be ashamed of Paul, who is a "prisoner for [their] sake" (3:1), which is what prompts the digression. Semantically it is a parenthesis, but pragmatically it provides the basis for Paul's right to pray for them as their apostle without it being shameful (similarly, Best, *Ephesians*, 292). Thielman thinks Paul is answering in 3:2–7 the question implied in 3:1 of why he is in prison for the Gentiles (*Ephesians*, 189).

[10] Similarly, Sellin, *Epheser*, 248; Best, *Ephesians*, 292; Hoehner, *Ephesians*, 481.

an additional *specific* discussion of the spiritual benefits in Section 1.[11] The most semantically prominent unit in Division 1 is the prayer in 1:15–23, because it is the most prominent unit of Section 1 and because Section 1 contains the GENERAL information that entails the specifics of Sections 2–3. Since the most prominent units of Sections 1 and 3 are the prayers, they are almost equal, creating a chiastic effect, so the resulting macrostructure may combine the prayer elements. Both prayers ask for greater spiritual comprehension, and the second prayer adds a request that they also receive more of God's presence (3:17, 19).

The resulting macrostructure of the first division is "I pray that God would grant you more of the spiritual benefits he has already given you, particularly you Gentiles, because he has integrated you into one body with Jewish believers by saving you in Christ"

Division 2: Ephesians 4:1–6:9

The second division is primarily hortatory, although it contains some explanatory or warranting discourse as well. Given that 4:1 begins with the programmatic οὖν + imperative (the first action-oriented imperative of the epistle), a reiteration of the author's identity, and a complete topic shift from the prayer in 3:14–21 (which ends with "amen"), it is clear that Paul here begins a new division. The relationship is inferential, making Division 2 more prominent for the author's communicative purposes than Division 1.[12]

The macrostructures of this second division are as follows:

4:1–16   "Stay unified as God is, but also use your unique gifts to help the entire body mature in Christ."

4:17–24 "No longer live as the wicked and ignorant Gentiles, but instead renounce your old way of life and live as a new creation."

---

[11] Similarly, Lincoln, *Ephesians*, 85; Thielman, *Ephesians*, 121. On the difficulty of the καί, see Best, *Ephesians*, 199–200.

[12] Traditionally this relationship is referred to as the indicative-imperative structure. While this label is generally appropriate, there is at least one imperative in chs. 1–3 and there is much indicative material in chs. 4–6. The indicative-imperative structure is also not always used by Paul; see at least Galatians, the Pastorals, and the Corinthian correspondences. Outside of Paul, this structure is ignored by Peter, James, and John in their epistles. From a DA standpoint, then, the indicative-imperative structure is simply one way of structuring a letter. It is significant that the most clear-cut indicative-imperative structures are Ephesians, Romans, and (to some extent) Colossians, all letters to audiences with whom Paul is not familiar. Perhaps one pragmatic function of an "indicative" (or supporting) division is to establish rapport with an audience with whom the author is unfamiliar. This idea is supported by my analysis of Colossians in ch. 12.

4:25–32   "Renounce sin and love your neighbor, as God in Christ loved you."
5:1–14   "Imitate God and Christ by loving and forgiving one another, avoid-
           ing wickedness."
5:15–21   "Live wisely by being filled with the Spirit, because the days are evil."
5:22–6:9   "Fulfill your relational obligations at home in the Lord."

These units are connected by οὖν (4:17; 5:1; 5:15), διό (4:25), and asyndeton (5:22). The household code (5:22–6:9) is a specific instance of the more general exhortations to live by love and wisdom (5:1–21), two parallel directives that are the most general ethical concerns of the epistle, and thus the most semantically prominent. The resulting semantic structure is as follows:

$$
\begin{array}{llll}
& & \text{specific} \quad \leftarrow & \text{GENERAL} \\
& & \text{5:22–6:9} & \left\{ \begin{array}{l} \text{5:1–14} \\ \text{5:15–21} \end{array} \right\} \\
& & \text{ground} \quad \rightarrow & \text{INFERENCE} \\
& & \text{4:25–4:32} & \\
& \text{ground} \quad \rightarrow & \text{INFERENCE} & \\
& \text{4:17–24} & & \\
\text{ground} \rightarrow & \text{INFERENCE} & & \\
\text{4:1–16} & & &
\end{array}
$$

By combining the microstructures of 5:1–14 and 5:15–21, we get "Imitate God and Christ by loving each other, and live wisely in the Spirit." We may then connect this Division 2 macrostructure with that of Division 1, resulting in the following macrostructure for Divisions 1–2: "I want you to have more spiritual comprehension and more of God's presence, especially because he has already integrated you into one body with Jewish believers by saving you in Christ. So then, imitate God and Christ by loving each other, and walk wisely in the Spirit, so that you will stay unified as one body."

This proposed macrostructure of Divisions 1–2 requires some defense. First, it begins with "I want you to have" instead of "I pray that God will give you" because the inferential connection between Division 1 and 2 shows that Division 1 (and his prayers) are speech acts whose illocution is to inform his recipients about his desires for them. His prayers are truly prayers, but he *tells his recipients about his prayers* in order to inform them of his desires for them before he instructs them on how to attain his desires for them.[13]

---

[13] Also notice that the controlling verb in 1:3–14 (*may* God *be* blessed; the verb is implied) is dropped. The focus of the entire unit is clearly on the reason for God's being blessed, and

Second, I have retained the result of their salvation, which is their integration "into one body with Jewish believers." This information is in Section 2, which is less prominent than Section 3, but the integration of Gentile and Jew into one body is significant for interpreting other units of the discourse (particularly 4:1–16, 17–24), and so is globally relevant information that cannot be deleted from the discourse's macrostructure. Similarly, the phrase "so that you will stay unified as one body" at the end represents globally relevant information from 4:1–16, even though that unit is semantically the least prominent in Division 2.

Third, I have converted 4:1–16 into a result clause in the macrostructure because from a pragmatic standpoint, "stay unified" is the controlling speech act in Division 2. I base this claim on an implicit assumption that must exist to make each use of οὖν and διό in 4:17; 4:25; and 5:1 coherent.[14] Consider 4:1–16 and 4:17–24. Paul urges them to maintain unity (4:1–16), and then concludes that they should no longer live as the Gentiles (4:17–24), which he phrases as a command. It is a bit awkward in the imperative mood, to say "Stay unified as Jews and Gentiles. Therefore, don't live like the Gentiles." An implied assumption is needed for this series to be received as coherent, namely, "to live as sinful Gentiles would disrupt unity in the church."[15] Paul doesn't make this assumption explicit, but is apparently confident enough that the assumption would be shared, or obvious enough to his recipients. Likewise, the implicit assumption between 4:17–24 and 4:25–32 is "renouncing sin and loving our neighbor is the opposite of the sinful Gentile lifestyle." The assumption between 4:25–32 and 5:1–14 (or by extension, all of 5:1–21) is "to imitate God and Christ includes renouncing sin and loving one's neighbor." In this latter case, 4:32 actually makes the assumption partially explicit ("be kind...forgiving one another, *as God in Christ forgave you*"). Reading the unit relationships this way means that the core directive of each successive unit is a *means* to achieving the previous unit's core directive. Hence, the directive speech acts in 4:17–24; 4:25–32; and 5:1–21 are auxiliary speech acts that are given *in order that* his programmatic directive in 4:1–3 will be achieved, namely, the maintenance of unity in the "one new man."

1:15–23 is also inferred from these reasons (not from the phrase εὐλογητὸς ὁ θεός). The blessing is simply a formal way to introduce the thanksgiving unit of the epistle, and is not therefore actually the prominent information of the unit when higher levels are considered.

[14] On the role of assumptions for creating discourse coherence, see Gillian Brown and George Yule, *Discourse Analysis*, CTL (Cambridge University Press, 1983), 257–270

[15] Assumptions can be required for coherent inferences in other grammatical moods as well. Consider "The bank has been closed all day. Thus, we couldn't make a withdrawal." The conclusion is only coherent under the implied assumption that withdrawals can only be made when the bank is open. This example is found in Bruce Fraser, "What Are Discourse Markers," *JPrag* 31 (1999): 931–952, specifically p. 948, but the entire article is useful.

One might object that οὖν and διό cannot signal a means relationship, but that is not what I am claiming. Discourse markers (which go by a multitude of names in the linguistic literature) can serve semantically to relate facts, or pragmatically to relate speech acts or to give a rationale for a specific utterance in its context.[16] My claim is that οὖν in 4:17; 5:1 and διό in 4:25 are functioning pragmatically to signal a conclusion being drawn from the directive speech act of the preceding unit. The question is *why* Paul draws the conclusion and makes a further command, and that question is answered by the implied assumptions that I suggested in the previous paragraph. He wants to ensure that they carry out his directive, so he concludes that they should do something further; obeying the latter would entail obeying the former. The pragmatic structure of these units is more obvious if we convert the directive speech acts to informative speech acts:

> I want you to maintain the unity of the one body.
>> Therefore, I want you to avoid the Gentile lifestyle.
>>> Therefore, I want you to renounce sin and love your neighbor.
>>> Therefore, I want you to live by love and wisdom.[17]

So while semantically 5:1–21 is the most prominent concern (walk in love and wisdom), from a pragmatic perspective, Paul commands these things in the way he does for the ultimate purpose of encouraging the maintenance of the Jew-Gentile unity (4:1–3) wrought through the cross by the Spirit (2:11–22).

Finally, the proposed macrostructure suggests that Paul somehow connects spiritual comprehension and God's presence (Division 1) with the need to stay unified (Division 2). It is on the basis of his desire for them to have more of the

---

[16] On pragmatic markers, see Teun A. van Dijk, *Text and Context: Explorations in the Semantics and Pragmatics of Discourse* (Longman, 1977), 205–231; idem., *Macrostructures: An Interdisciplinary Study of Global Structures in Discourse, Interaction, and Cognition* (Erlbaum, 1980), 175–199; Manizheh Alami, "Pragmatic Functions of Discourse Markers: A Review of Related Literature," *IJSELL* 3, no. 3 (2015): 1–10, and the literature summarized therein; Bruce Fraser, "An Approach to Discourse Markers," *JPrag* 14, no. 3 (1990): 383–398; Laurel J. Brinton, *Pragmatic Markers in English: Grammaticalization and Discourse Functions* (de Gruyter, 1996). Brinton gives a list of many proposed functions of pragmatic discourse markers on p. 30. An example of a semantic use of οὖν to relate facts is found in Matt 5:19. From the *fact* that nothing will pass from the law (Matt 5:18), Jesus infers (οὖν) the *fact* that "whoever relaxes one of the least of these commandments...will be called least" (5:19).

[17] It is a tenet of speech act theory that the form of an utterance (or "locution") can accomplish different illocutions. Statements can make commands, imperatives can make requests, questions can make apologies, etc. In this case, "I want you to do X" may have the illocutionary force of a command, given the right context, and thus it is interchangeable with the hortatory locutions that Paul actually uses.

former that he directs them to unity through love and wisdom. What is the connection? Paul prays for five things in his two prayers, four of which I have subsumed under the general "spiritual comprehension," and the fifth being the presence of God (through indwelling). Each of these five prayer requests is linked to the unity of the church/body.

1. To know the hope of their calling (1:18) is to know their calling to unity (4:1–3).
2. To know about their inheritance (1:18) is to know that it formerly did not exist (2:12), but now is granted to them *along with Jewish believers* (2:13–22, esp. v. 19; "fellow citizens" implies inheritance).
3. Knowing about God's power toward "us who believe" (1:18) is to know the same power that God worked in Christ in the resurrection, which made him head *of the [unified] body* (1:23).
4. To comprehend Christ's love (3:18–19a) is achieved (3:16) by being strengthened with God's power (again related to Christ becoming head of the body, 1:23) through the Spirit (who is the agent of preparing the one body to be a "dwelling place for God," 2:22).
5. To be "filled with all the fullness of God" (3:19) is achieved by Christ dwelling in their hearts through faith (3:17)—a metonymy for the indwelling of the Spirit (1:13; cf. Rom 8:9–11)—which again is a property of the new unified temple-body (2:20–23).

So to summarize Divisions 1–2: Paul informs them in Division 1 about five things he wants for them (four noetic and one metaphysical), then directs them in 4:1–16 to the predominant action that would help them attain these five things (maintain the unity created by the Spirit), and continues with several further commands that will ensure that they achieve the maintenance of unity.

Peroratio: Ephesians 6:10–20

Concluding the two divisions is a *peroratio*, which, as I will argue later, functions to recapitulate the facts of both divisions of the epistle, and to inspire the recipients toward obedience and action. The macrostructure of the *peroratio* is "By God's empowerment, resist the attacks of the spiritual powers, praying continuously for each other and for me, that I might boldly proclaim the mystery of the gospel."

The unit is connected to Divisions 1–2 by the phrase τοῦ λοιποῦ, either "finally" or "from now on." The phrase τοῦ λοιποῦ naturally means "from now on," as it seems to mean in its only other NT occurrence (Gal 6:17). The accusative construction τὸ λοιπόν often means "finally," a concluding adverbial construction, but can also mean "from now on."[18] The genitive phrase, though, does in this context permit either the logical or the temporal meaning. In either case, Paul clearly signals the final unit of the letter, and whether or not τοῦ λοιποῦ means "from now on," the exhortations clearly bear on their lives for the future after reading the epistle. Semantically, this unit probably serves as the final, climactic exhortation in a progression of the epistle's directives. The main directives of the epistle would then be "live lovingly, live wisely, and finally, resist attacks of the spiritual powers." Pragmatically, the *peroratio* serves to recapitulate the facts and spur the audience emotionally to action, thereby serving the foundational call to unity in 4:1–3.

By combining the macrostructure of Divisions 1–2 with that of the *peroratio*, we get the macrostructure of Ephesians:

> "I want you to have more spiritual comprehension and more of God's presence, especially because you Gentiles have now been integrated into one body with Jewish believers by your salvation in Christ. So then, imitate God and Christ by loving each other, and walk wisely in the Spirit, so that you will stay unified as one body. And by God's empowerment, resist the attacks of the spiritual powers, praying continuously for each other and for my proclamation of the gospel."

Microstructures

The proposed macrostructure must now be supported by an examination of relevant microstructural details. There is not space to defend my proposed macrostructures in detail, but in the sections below I provide enough substantiation on the structure of each unit to lay bare my reasoning. Aside from the macrostructures of each unit are the boundaries of each unit and the relationships between them, for which I argue in the sections below. The result will not be exhaustive and will leave much room for the exegete to fill in the gaps and also to revise or improve on my proposed macrostructural analysis.

Section 1: Ephesians 1:3–23

The first section of Division 1 includes a blessing (*Berekah*) and a prayer. Ephesians 1:3–14 is bounded by the end of the greeting (v. 2) and the high-level discourse marker in v. 15 (διὰ τοῦτο), which connects units 1:3–14 with 1:15–23. The *Berekah*

---

[18] BDAG, s.v. λοιπός. The accusative construction appears in the second hand of Sinaiticus and in D, but the genitive construction appears in 𝔓46, Sinaiticus, A, and B. External support seems to lean in the direction of the genitive construction being original, as does the fact that the genitive construction is far less common (occurring only elsewhere in Gal 6:17) so that a scribal change to the accusative is more likely than the alternative.

divides into four parts. Verses 3–6 bless the Father for his spiritual blessings, and the final word in v. 6, "the beloved," referring to the Son, allows for three further sections all beginning with ἐν ᾧ (vv. 7–10, 11–12, 13–14). The final phrase of each section except the first includes εἰς ἔπαινον [τῆς χάριτος] δόξης αὐτοῦ. There is a Trinitarian shape to the *Berekah*, with the Father as the agent of all soteriological actions, working through Christ (mentioned at least thirteen times through nouns, adjectives, and pronouns) and the Spirit, who is the down payment (ἀρραβὼν) of our inheritance. The soteriological benefits listed (predestination, adopting, sealing, recapitulation [v. 10], etc.) can be reduced to the Pauline concept of "salvation." The unity of this section is therefore evident through the Trinitarian actors, the literary structure of the three-fold "in whom," the conceptual domain of soteriology, and more obviously the fact that the entire unit is grammatically one sentence (albeit, multiple colas).

The content of the prayer in 1:15–23 is that God would give them "spiritual wisdom and revelation"[19] in order that they might know three things. If we strip away a couple adjectives (δόξης and ὑπερβάλλον), we see fine parallelism:

	τίς	ἐστιν	ἡ ἐλπὶς	τῆς κλήσεως	αὐτοῦ,	
		τίς	ὁ πλοῦτος	τῆς κληρονομίας	αὐτοῦ	ἐν τοῖς ἁγίοις,
καὶ	τί		τὸ μέγεθος	τῆς δυνάμεως	αὐτοῦ	εἰς ἡμᾶς.

These three things that Paul hopes they are granted echo throughout Ephesians and are related to the main directive toward unity.[20] The genitive nouns are more substantive and concrete for the author's purpose than the head nouns, meaning that Paul wants them to be further enlightened specifically about their calling, their inheritance, and God's power. These three things combine with two more in the prayer in 3:14–21 for five total aspects of spiritual enlightenment and comprehension. That the Ephesians have already experienced these salvific benefits (1:3–14) helps us understand the connection between the *Berekah* and the prayer. They have already been granted these three things, and because of this (διὰ τοῦτο, v. 15) Paul prays that they would be further matured and granted even more of what they already enjoy.[21]

The final four verses of the prayer unit (1:20–23) expand on God's "power" (1:19), defined as "that which he worked in Christ" in the resurrection and ascension to the right hand of God in fulfillment of Pss 110 and 8. This installation was over

---

[19] On this translation, see Daniel B. Wallace, *Greek Grammar beyond the Basics: An Exegetical Syntax of the New Testament* (Zondervan, 1996), 90–91.

[20] Hope: 2:12; calling: 4:4; riches: 1:7; 2:7; 3:8, 16; inheritance: 1:11, 14; 5:5; power: 1:21; 3:7, 16, 20.

[21] Eadie, *Ephesians*, 76; Lincoln, *Ephesians*, 56. Commentators are split on whether "this" refers to vv. 3–14 or vv. 13–14. Even if the latter is correct, vv. 13–14 is still an integral part of the wider unit, so διὰ τοῦτο at least indirectly connects the two units as wholes.

all spiritual powers, establishing an important theme for Ephesians, even though these four verses are buried in the semantic structure of the unit as an elaboration on the concept "power."

Section 2: Ephesians 2:1–22

Ephesians 2:1–10, 11–22 constitute the two units of Section 2. The first unit involves a long sentence (2:1–7) followed by two grounds (2:8–9, 10). The fronted pronoun ὑμᾶς beginning 2:1 (καὶ ὑμᾶς...) is the direct object of the three coordinate verbs συνεζωοποίησεν, συνήγειρεν, and συνεκάθισεν (vv. 5–6), with the subject ὁ θεός in v. 4. The core of this long sentence is therefore "God made you alive, raised you, and seated you [with Christ]." The rest of these seven verses describes the recipients' former unsaved condition (children of wrath under the influence of malevolent spiritual forces, vv. 1–3), God's character as loving and merciful (v. 4), and the reason for his action (to show to believers the immeasurable riches of his grace in kindness for eternity, v. 7). How the two following grounding sentences (vv. 8–9, 10) coordinate is unclear.[22] Both may be supporting the emphasis on God's grace as the reason or impetus for the recipients' salvation. Or, v. 10 may support v. 8–9. Either way, the main concern is in the longer sentence of vv. 1–7, while vv. 8–10 are supportive. The three core actions of the main sentence may be semantically reduced again to salvation, but the συν- prefixes require us to include "with Christ" in the macrostructure.

In my macrostructure of 2:1–10, for several reasons I understood ὑμᾶς to refer predominantly to Gentiles, whom he does not explicitly address until 2:11 (ὑμεῖς τὰ ἔθνη). First, if "following the ruler of the aerial authority" (2:2) refers to idolatry, this would better relate to Gentiles.[23] Second, the repeated use of ποτέ in 2:2, 2:11 suggests the same addressee.[24] Third, if 2:1–10 spoke generally of all believers' salvation, and 2:11–22 focused in more specifically on Gentile salvation, 2:11 would naturally open with καί, δέ, or perhaps asyndeton. Instead we find διό, meaning Paul's command for the Gentiles to remember their salvation is based on 2:1–10. It seems odd to read these two units as "God saved you Jews and Gentiles, therefore, you Gentiles remember..." It makes better sense of the discourse structure, then, to see all of ch. 2 addressing predominantly Gentiles, even if Jewish believers are secondarily in mind (much in the same way the Pastorals are addressed to individuals, but with the church secondarily in mind as readers).

On this reading, 2:11–22 exhorts the Gentiles to remember what God has graciously done for them (2:1–10). Because of this gracious saving work, the Gentiles

---

[22] See the differing opinions in Lincoln, *Ephesians*, 113; Larkin, *Ephesians*, 34.

[23] Thomas M. Winger, *Ephesians*, CC (Concordia, 2015), 279.

[24] Ibid., 339.

especially among his recipients should, *therefore* (διό), "remember" μνημονεύετε (2:11). This imperative is the only one in the first division, and even it is not action-oriented, but rather noetically-oriented. While God has saved all in the church, Jew and Gentile, Paul now turns to the Gentiles specifically to tell them to remember their former condition (2:11–12) and their contrasting current status (2:13). The descriptions of their former condition amount to saying they were hopelessly separated from God's people. Verse 14 provides the contrast: but now (νυνὶ δὲ), "in Christ, you who were formerly far off were brought near by the blood of Christ" (2:14). The spatial lexemes (far off; near) express metaphorically the spiritual separation from God noted twice in v. 12 (without Christ; without God). Given Jew-Gentile relations in the first century, the idea that Gentiles could so seamlessly be "brought near" and made part of God's people requires some explanatory support, which is provided by 2:14–18 (v. 14 begins with a post-positive γάρ). Gentiles could be integrated into the church because Christ "is our peace" (v. 14). The rest of vv. 14–18 expands on this idea. Verses 19–22 then express the result (ἄρα οὖν) of God integrating the Gentiles into the church: they are no longer foreigners, but fellow citizens of the household of God, which itself is God's dwelling place, the eschatological temple that is composed of believers.

Ephesians 2:11–22, in contrast to the previous three units, focuses on the corporate aspect of the believer's existence. No longer are God's people marked by ethnicity (physical circumcision, v. 11), but now they are marked by faith in the Jewish Messiah. The result is a unified body in which racial hostilities have ceased because of their common union with Christ. They are "both one," "one new man," both reconciled "to God in one body"; they both have "access in one Spirit to the Father"; they are "fellow citizens with the saints," and members of "the household of God," built on Christ as the cornerstone in whom the "whole structure" grows into a holy "temple in the Lord" (2:14–22).

Section 3: Paul's Second Prayer and Digression

Just as 1:3–14 was the prompt for Paul's prayer in 1:15–23, so also is 2:1–22 a prompt for another prayer in 3:1–21 (signaled by τούτου χάριν in 3:1). There are two units (3:1–13; 3:14–21), based on the resumptive repetition of τούτου χάριν (3:1, 14). Paul begins to pray in v. 1, but digresses into a lengthy discussion of his apostleship (εἴ γε..., v. 2). It seems that Paul's mention being a *"prisoner* of Jesus Christ *on behalf of you Gentiles"* is what prompts his digression, since his initial clarifying statement is "assuming that you heard of the stewardship of God's grace given to me *for you."* Several clues suggest why Paul makes this digression. First, Paul may have felt that his audience would feel some shame that *their* apostle was imprisoned, especially in an honor-shame society. Verse 13 suggests so, since he asks them not to lose heart over his afflictions on their behalf, "which is your glory." But how can his imprisonment be their glory? The answer to this question is the second clue: Paul was called to steward the "mystery" that the Gentiles would be integrated into the church (3:2–6), and this mystery, when revealed to the world, makes known "through the church" the manifold wisdom of God to the spiritual powers (3:9–10). So in a rather roundabout way, Paul tries to assuage any shame or discouragement that his Gentile readers may feel when he mentions that he is a "prisoner" on their behalf. He does so by noting that he has been called to steward the mystery of Gentile integration into the church, which puts God's wisdom on display even to the invisible world. As part of the church, the Gentiles are part of the means by which God's wisdom is on display in the world, and thus they take part in this "glory." If Paul's imprisonment is an inescapable part of this whole process—indeed, a process ordained by God—then it is ironically to the glory of the Gentiles.[25]

Paul then resumes his prayer by starting over, "For this reason, I bow my knees before the Father, from whom...," i.e., "Therefore, I pray to God" (3:14). The content of this prayer, like that of 1:15–23, is that God would give (δίδωμι, 1:17; 3:16) them something. The structure of the prayer is debatable, based on how one subordinates some of the clauses. I think the best structure of the core of the prayer is to take the two aorist infinitives (κραταιωθῆναι and κατοικῆσαι) as the objects of δῷ, with the two following ἵνα clauses providing the reason for each gift, respectively. The resulting structure is:

δῷ ὑμῖν
    <u>κραταιωθῆναι</u> εἰς τὸν ἔσω ἄνθρωπον
        ἵνα <u>ἐξισχύσητε</u> καταλαβέσθαι
    <u>κατοικῆσαι</u> τὸν Χριστὸν ἐν ταῖς καρδίαις ὑμῶν
        ἵνα <u>πληρωθῆτε</u> εἰς πᾶν τὸ πλήρωμα τοῦ θεοῦ

Support for this structure is as follows. First, the underlined lexemes correspond in a cause-effect manner, suggesting they function as I have diagrammed them. Second, some take κατοικῆσαι as the purpose of κραταιωθῆναι, but being strengthened is not a prerequisite for Christ's indwelling (rather, faith is), so they function better as two coordinate gifts. Third, the ἵνα clauses are not directly related because spiritual comprehension is not a prerequisite for being filled with the fullness of God. Fourth, "being rooted and grounded in love" (v. 17) is omitted from the core of the prayer because it is only the result of the second gift.

---

[25] My understanding of this section was greatly enhanced by Aaron Sherwood, "Paul's Imprisonment as the Glory of the Ethnē: A Discourse Analysis of Ephesians 3:1–13," *BBR* 22, no. 1 (2012): 97–111.

Of the two gifts that Paul prays for, the first is again spiritual comprehension. The objects of καταλαβέσθαι ("to comprehend") are the four dimensions (width, length, height, depth), which is obscure but interpreted more concretely by the following phrase "to know the love of Christ that surpasses knowledge." The connective τε suggests a very close relationship between the clauses, which I take as HEAD–explanation, so that Paul prays for increased spiritual comprehension of the love of Christ. The second gift is Christ dwelling (κατοικέω) in their hearts, in order that they may be filled (πληρόω) with all the fullness (πλήρωμα) of God. These lexemes evoke the eschatological temple, last mentioned in 2:19–22, of which the Gentiles are now a part.[26] To be further filled with the fullness of God means to experience more of God's presence through their identity with and participation in the church. Just as in the prayer in 1:15–23, Paul prays for gifts that his audience already, to an extent, possess (1:3, 13–15; 2:20–22).

The prayer concludes with a benediction to the Father, but the mystery of the church is still in view: "to him be glory *in the church* and in Christ Jesus" forever (3:20–21). This blessing is similar to 1:3, but with the addition of the concept of God's glory being made manifest through the church (3:10).

Ephesians 4:1–16 as the Initial Hortatory Unit

We now enter the second division, which is the more prominent division for Paul's communicative purpose. Ephesians 4:1–16 is a clear unit, begun by a typical boundary marker (inferential conjunction plus an imperative), pervaded by lexemes expressing unity, and marked by an inclusio "in love" (v. 2, last word of v. 16). The main concern of 4:1–16 is that his audience walk worthily of the calling to which they were called, specifically that they remain eager to keep the unity of the Spirit (4:1–3).[27] Verses 4–6 open with asyndeton, but the oneness motif

---

[26] The semantic field of "filling" (πληρόω, πίμπλημι, ἐμπίμπλημι, and πλήρης) is used throughout the LXX to express God's habitation in the tabernacle or temple. See Exod 40:34–35; 1 Kgs 8:10–11; 2 Chr 5:13–14; 7:1–2; Isa 6:3–4; Ezek 10:3–4, 43:5, 44:4; Sir 36:13 [ET 36:19] (Christopher A. Beetham, *Echoes of Scripture in the Letter of Paul to the Colossians*, BIS 96 [Leiden: Brill, 2008], 153n41). The church was already described in 1:23 as "the fullness (πλήρωμα) of him who fills (πληρόω) all in all," which gave the hint that the church is God's new dwelling place, i.e., his new temple. After the church is explicitly identified as the temple of God in 2:21, the verb πληρόω is again used to describe the corporate church as the place of God's fullness (3:19), that is, as his temple. Similarly in 5:18, believers should not be filled with wine, but filled with God's Spirit.

[27] For multiple reasons, Paul's main concern in 4:1–3 is not the worthy walk *per se*, but rather that they maintain the unity created by the Spirit. First, unity was the main theme of 2:11–22. Second, the dominant semantic domain in 4:1–16 is "unity" or "oneness": ἑνότητα (4:3, 13), ἕν, εἷς, and μία (4:4–6), συναρμολογέω and συμβιβάζω (4:16), and σῶμα (4:16, 2x). Third, 4:4–6

("one body and one Spirit," etc.) clearly supports the command to maintain unity in 4:1–3. His audience should be unified because the Godhead is unified. Given the previous emphasis on Gentile incorporation into the "one new man" (2:15), this command is predominantly given to his Gentile recipients (as is also evident from 4:17), who must live according to their new nature to maintain the oneness of the body.

Lest they believe that unity is uniformity,[28] Paul provides a contrasting and balancing thought, that each individual within this unified body is gifted uniquely to fulfill his or her proper function for the benefit of the entire body. "Grace" (4:7), understood as a gift, brings to mind Ps 68:18 (68:19 MT), "after ascending on high, he took captive captives, he gave gifts to men." Verses 9–10 elaborate on the quotation. Verses 11–16 resume the thought of v. 7 with a simple καί and explain what exactly Christ gave to the church: apostles, prophets, evangelists, shepherds, and teachers (a list that is not exhaustive; see 1 Cor 12:28). The purpose of these gifts is obscured by the syntax, but the ultimate reason is that believers may "grow up in every way" into Christ. With Christ as their corporate *telos* toward which they all grow, they are ensured further unity.

Ephesians 4:17–24

4:17–24 is a clear unit with a simple structure of a command, followed by elaboration, followed by a negative means and a positive means to obey that command.[29] The main admonition—"this I say and testify in the Lord, that you must no longer live as the Gentiles..."—is a mitigated imperative. Verses 17b–19 elaborate on what the Gentile lifestyle is, while vv. 20–24 provide the contrast to the command: "Thus [the way of the Gentiles] you did not learn Christ." Verses 21–24 explain what exactly they learned: that negatively, they should put off their old self (or nature), while positively, they should put on the "new man" (καινὸν ἄνθρωπον, v. 24) the exact phrase used in 2:15 to refer to the unified body of Jew

---

functions as the grounds for the mention of unity, not "walking worthily," and what Paul supports shows what he deems significant.

[28] I believe I absorbed this succinct turn of phrase from Jean-Noël Aletti, *Saint Paul, Épître aux Éphésiens: Introduction, Traduction et Commentaire*, EB 42 (Paris: J. Gabalda, 2001), 214: "Paul ajoute maintenant que cette unicité n'a rien d'une *uniformité*, car le tissu ecclésial est organique et diversifié – d'une 'diversité structurée.'"

[29] 4:17–24 is commonly taken as a unit, e.g., UBS⁵; Benjamin Merkle, *Ephesians*, EGGNT (B&H Academic, 2016), 137; Larkin, *Ephesians*, 84; Best, *Ephesians*, 414. NA²⁸ and THGNT divide the unit into two paragraphs (vv. 17–19, 20–24). Hoehner uniquely divides the text into 4:17–19; 4:20–5:2 (*Ephesians*, 581), based on his idea that the five instances of οὖν with περιπατέω mark the main divisions in 4:1–6:9.

and Gentile created in Christ. To "put on the new man," whatever it means, must refer to this new unified Jew-Gentile body (2:15), with which they are to fully identify rather than identifying with their ethnic background.

The standard view of how οὖν in 4:17 (and also in 5:1) functions is based on the idea that οὖν can signal an inference, or a resumption following a digression or a supporting unit.[30] Most see οὖν here signaling a resumption of the initial command in 4:1–3, viewing 4:4–16 as a digression.[31] If 4:17 does resume 4:1–3, then the other three uses of οὖν in Division 2 may do so as well, as H. Hoehner's commentary argues based on their collocations with περιπατέω in all five instances (which is technically incorrect; see below on 5:7–8). There are multiple reasons to reject this resumptive view in 4:17 and 5:1. First, the resumptive view ignores the development of thought across the discourse units, in which each successive command is a means to achieve the immediately preceding command. Second, a resumptive conjunction such as οὖν is more likely to recapitulate or reinforce an idea from earlier in the same discourse unit, rather than across unit boundaries.[32] Third, the result of multiple uses of resumptive οὖν is a bland discourse structure with a simple series of commands. Fourth, the bullet-point discourse style would be interrupted awkwardly by the last two hortatory units (5:22–6:9; 6:10–6:20), which do not begin with οὖν. Fifth, since διό in 4:25 functions similarly to οὖν in 4:17; 5:1, they are most likely functioning similarly, and διό cannot signal resumption.

Even if the resumptive view is wrong, it is only wrong in that it lacks the inferential or conclusive aspect of the units' relationships. In the sense that the uses of οὖν help us process a return to the hortatory mainline, they are resumptive in that sense. But to ignore the implied assumptions required to make the inferred directive speech acts coherent, and to miss the RESULT–MEANS relationship between the units, would cause us to miss the flow of thought that is the key to the semantic and the pragmatic structure of Division 2.

Thus, I view οὖν in 4:17 as signaling that the directive of 4:17–24 is based on the directive to unity in 4:1–16, with the implied assumption that the Gentiles avoiding their former sinful lifestyle is necessary to maintaining church unity. If they would maintain unity, then they must avoid the Gentile lifestyle.

---

[30] See discussions in Steven Runge, *Discourse Grammar of the Greek New Testament: A Practical Introduction for Teaching and Exegesis* (Hendrickson, 2010), 43–48; Stephen H. Levinsohn, *Discourse Features of New Testament Greek: A Coursebook on the Information Structure of New Testament Greek*, 2nd ed. (SIL International, 2000), 126.

[31] Larkin, *Ephesians*, 86; Best, *Ephesians*, 416; Lincoln, *Ephesians*, 276; Baugh, *Ephesians*, 357; Hoehner, *Ephesians*, 582; Thielman, *Ephesians*, 295–296.

[32] For evidence in hortatory discourse of minority languages of the Philippines, see Robert E. Longacre, *Discourse, Paragraph, and Sentence Structure in Selected Philippine Languages* (Summer Institute of Linguistics, 1968), 1:152–158.

The Discourse Structure of 4:25–5:14

Ephesians 4:25–5:14 has the most difficult discourse structure, with few commentators agreeing on any of the unit boundaries, as Figure 10.1 shows.[33]

UBS[5]	NA[28] EGGNT	THGNT	BHGNT	Hoehner	Best	Clark	Thielman
4:25–5:5	4:25–5:2	4:25–28 4:29–30 4:31–32 5:1–2 5:3–5	4:25–4:32 5:1–5	4:25–32 5:1–6	4:25–5:2	4:25–32	4:25–5:2
5:6–20	5:3–14	5:6–14	5:6–14	5:7–14	5:3–14	5:1–6 5:7–14	5:3–7 5:8–14

Figure 10.1: Proposed Unit Boundaries in Ephesians 4:25–5:14

What is clear is that 4:25 begins a new unit and 5:14 closes a unit. Otherwise, analyses diverge. The unit beginning at 4:25 may end at 4:32; 5:2; or 5:5.[34] Ending at 5:5 is an idiosyncratic and unfounded decision. Those who conclude the unit at 5:2 do so because they take 5:1–2 ("Therefore, be imitators of God as beloved children...") as a direct inference from 4:32. However, the combination of οὖν plus the imperatives γίνεσθε and περιπατεῖτε in 5:1–2 naturally opens a new unit. Also, 4:32 refers twice to "one another," which is a fitting conclusion to a section focused on loving and not sinning against one another. The first unit is therefore 4:25–4:32.

Διό (4:25) signals that the forthcoming directive speech act follows naturally from his previous directive to no longer live as the Gentiles. The entire unit contains ten commands and prohibitions (with an implied eleventh in v. 29b) that, if followed, would ensure that they leave their Gentile lifestyle behind. Based on the macrorule of generalization, and on the Judeo-Christian idea that love of neighbor is the second greatest commandment (Lev 19:18; Matt 22:39), the commands and

---

[33] EGGNT = Merkle, *Ephesians*. BHGNT = Larkin, *Ephesians*. Hoehner = Hoehner, *Ephesians*. Best = Ernst Best, *Ephesians*, ICC (T&T Clark, 1993); Clark = Clark, *Analyzing and Translating*, 253–269; Thielman = Thielman, *Ephesians*.

[34] Larkin (*Ephesians*, 95), Clark (*Analyzing and Translating*, 265), and Sellin (*Epheser*, 378–379) end it at 4:32; NA[28], Merkle (*Ephesians*, 145), Best (*Ephesians*, 442), and Thielman (*Ephesians*, 291) end it at 5:2; UBS[5] ends it at 5:5. THGNT oddly marks 4:25, 29, 31; 5:1, 3 with ekthesis. Sellin (*Epheser*, 52) presents a unique chiastic structure in Division 2, but again it lacks correspondence in the A and B elements.

prohibitions can be generalized into the proposition "renounce sin and love your neighbor." The phrase "as God in Christ loved you" (v. 32) should be included in the macrostructure as well, because it is relevant for the interpretation of the next unit.

Although many commentators and versions include 5:1–2 with the preceding verses, it should start a new unit for several reasons. First, we have seen convincing reasons for closing the previous unit with 4:32. Second, the strongest argument for keeping 5:1–2 with the preceding is that the οὖν in 5:1 signals an inference from 4:32 to 5:1–2 (rather than from all of 4:25–32). It is true that the phrase "as God in Christ forgave you" in 4:32 prompts the command in 5:1 to "be imitators of God as beloved children, and walk in love, just as Christ also loved us." But 4:32 is better taken as a "discourse pivot,"[35] which is a clause that concludes a unit but contains at least one idea that persists into the next unit. Colossians is filled with discourse pivots, so Paul is capable of using them. Third, if the unit boundary is between 5:2 and 5:3, then 5:3–14 becomes a random assemblage of commands with an indiscernible structure. If instead 5:1–2 is taken as a general command that is specified by 5:3–14, there is a simple and obvious discourse structure. So the unit should begin at 5:1.

Some break up 5:1–14 by beginning a new unit at 5:6 or 5:7. Verse 6 begins with asyndeton and the imperative μηδεὶς ἀπατάτω. Verse 7 begins with οὖν plus an imperative (γίνεσθε), which commonly signals a new section, and supposedly with one of the five collocations of οὖν with περιπατέω in chs. 4–6.[36] But οὖν is actually not collocated with περιπατέω, as each occurs in its own sentence as part of a two-pronged (negative-positive) exhortation. Also, there is too much evidence for keeping vv. 6–7 together, rather than either of them beginning a new unit. Verse 5 says those characterized by vices will not inherit the kingdom. Verse 6 follows as an inference from v. 5: "[therefore], let no one deceive you with empty words; because of these things (ταῦτα) the wrath of God is coming on the sons of disobedience." The antecedent for ταῦτα in v. 6 is the vices of v. 5, so the cohesion plus the coherence relation keep them together. The οὖν in v. 7 is local, relating only vv. 6–7; since God's wrath is coming on the sons of disobedience, they should therefore (οὖν) not be partakers with them (αὐτῶν)—the antecedent of αὐτῶν being the sons in v. 6.[37] So again, cohesion and coherence demands that vv. 6–7 stay together. Thus, vv. 5–7 belong together in the same unit.

Once the decision is made to keep vv. 5–7 together, it is difficult to find any other unit breaks in 5:1–14. When vv. 1–2 are included in the unit, a basic structure

---

[35] Richard Watson Todd, *Discourse Topics*, P&BNS 269 (John Benjamins, 2016), 72.

[36] Clark, *Analyzing and Translating*, 266; Hoehner, *Ephesians*, 667–668.

[37] Similarly, Merkle, *Ephesians*, 163; Larkin, *Ephesians*, 113; Hoehner, *Ephesians*, 668; Lincoln, *Ephesians*, 326; Baugh, *Ephesians*, 427; Thielman, *Ephesians*, 335. Hoehner strangely acknowledges the local nature of οὖν in v. 7 but begins a new unit there.

is clear and evident. Verses 1–2 provide the main command to imitate God and walk in love as Christ did. Verses 3–4, introduced by δέ signals the negative contrast to the preceding command: six vices must not even be named among them. This two-pronged (positive-negative) command is then supported by vv. 5–14, a string of verses that involve increasingly deeper semantic subordination. The imagery shifts from virtue–vice in 5:3–7 to darkness–light in 5:8–14. The unit concludes with an enigmatic citation of a hymnic line, a melded OT quotation (e.g., Isa 26:19 and 60:1), or something else.[38] The entire unit is again a directive speech act based on the preceding directive to renounce sin and love one's neighbor: if they are to achieve that, they must imitate God and Christ through love and forgiveness.

Ephesians 5:15–21

The next unit begins in 5:15 with a programmatic οὖν plus imperative βλέπετε and a close collocation of οὖν with περιπατέω, which has begun a new unit in 4:1–3, 17; 5:1–2. The semantic fields of the controlling ideas switch from virtues and vices and light and darkness (5:1–14), to wisdom and Spirit (5:15–21).

The controlling command comes in v. 15: "Therefore, watch carefully how you walk, not as unwise, but as wise." Verse 16 provides a specific (but not exhaustive) means of obeying this command: "making the most of the time." They should do so because (ὅτι) "the days are evil." From this fact, vv. 17–18 infer (διὰ τοῦτο) two commands, both expressed as two-pronged negative-positive commands:

(1) Do not be foolish,
    but understand what the will of the Lord is.
(2) And do not get drunk with wine, for that is debauchery,
    but be filled with the Spirit

The final command to "be filled with the Spirit" is then modified by five participles, seemingly expressing the means (again, not exhaustively) by which they may do so:

(1) speaking to one another with psalms and hymns and spiritual songs;
(2) singing and
(3) praising in your hearts to the Lord;
(4) giving thanks always for everything;
(5) submitting (ὑποτασσόμενοι) to one another in the fear of Christ.

---

[38] See the commentaries for discussion, e.g., Hoehner, *Ephesians*, 686–688; Best, *Ephesians*, 497–500.

As with the preceding unit, the controlling idea appears first followed by ever-increasing semantic subordination. These five means of being filled with the Spirit should be done because the days are evil, which means they should do their best to make the most of their time, which is one of the ways they can walk wisely.

Some take this unit as a resumption (signaled by οὖν) of the exhortation in 4:1–3.[39] Others take this unit as a direct inference from 5:8–14.[40] I have already presented my problems with the former view. The latter view suggests that the macrostructure of 5:8–14 (which would be "walk as children of light and do not participate in darkness") is the basis for an inference that they should "walk wisely by being filled with the Spirit." It does not seem, however, that the command to walk wisely is a necessary or coherent inference from the directive to walk as children of light (5:8–14), or even from the directive to imitate God and Christ by loving and forgiving one another (5:1–14). From a semantic standpoint it is hard to relate the ideas using a coherence relation, so the two units seem to function as parallel commands, perhaps as flip sides of the same coin: imitate God and Christ and also walk wisely in the Spirit. If love and forgiveness are collapsed into love, then the two main ethical concerns in 5:1–21 are love and wisdom. Love is motivated by God in Christ, and wisdom is granted by the Spirit. The οὖν of this section, then, best functions to signal a return to the hortatory mainline, and the contents of the units constrain me to view 5:1–14, 15–21 as parallel exhortations that complement one another.

"Submission" and the Transition into the Household Code

My analysis assumes the unit beginning at 5:15 ends at v. 21, and grammatically, this seems to be the case, since "submitting" (ὑποτασσόμενοι) in v. 21 is simply the fifth of a series of participles modifying "be filled with the Spirit" (5:18). Moreover, v. 22 begins with a nominative of direct address, αἱ γυναῖκες ("wives"), which often begins a unit, and which clearly begins the following five sub-units of the household code:

Οἱ ἄνδρες (5:25)
Τὰ τέκνα (6:1)
Καὶ οἱ πατέρες (6:4)
Οἱ δοῦλοι (6:5)
Καὶ οἱ κύριοι (6:9).

---

[39] Larkin, *Ephesians*, 121–122; Hoehner, *Ephesians*, 690–691; Best, *Ephesians*, 502 says this is a new step in the argument, building on the preceding units.

[40] Lincoln, *Ephesians*, 341; Thielman, *Ephesians*, 355.

Under this view, those who are to submit to one another in v. 21 are those being addressed in 5:15–20, namely, believers generally.

Despite this evidence, many versions and commentators prefer to end the previous unit at 5:20 and take 5:21 as the opening verse of the household code.[41] The main reason is that the verb ὑποτάσσω fits well within the content of the household code. The command to wives is actually verbless and requires an implied imperatival form of ὑποτάσσω, which some scribes supplied in their manuscripts.[42] This implied command provides a link between vv. 21–22. Ὑποτάσσω also occurs in v. 24, "but as the church submits (ὑποτάσσεται) to Christ, so also wives to their husbands." In 6:1, children are told to obey (ὑπακούω) their parents, and in 6:5 slaves are told to obey (ὑπακούω) their masters; ὑπακούω is nearly synonymous with ὑποτάσσω.[43] A second and third reason to take v. 21 with the household code are (2) the distance of ὑποτασσόμενοι from the command "be filled with the Spirit" (v. 18), which could suggest that the participle is functioning more independently with an imperatival force, and (3) a possible inclusio of "fear": mutual submission should happen "in the fear (φόβος) of the Lord" (v. 21) and wives should "fear" (φοβέω) their husbands (v. 33).[44]

These arguments are not powerful enough, however, to overcome the reasons for keeping v. 21 with vv. 15–20. The participle ὑποτασσόμενοι is far from the command in v. 18, but it is only fifteen words (one participial phrase) later than the preceding participle (εὐχαριστοῦντες), which no one tries to include in the household code.[45] Participles also rarely, if ever, act as independent

---

[41] It probably does not help with objective evaluation that UBS5 begins a new section labeled "Wives and Husbands" with v. 21, putting a period at the end of v. 20 and starting v. 21 with an indentation and a capitalized Ὑποτασσόμενοι. NA28 does the same, but without any section heading. THGNT includes v. 21 with vv. 15–20 and starts a new paragraph with v. 22, but for some reason puts a semi-colon at the end of v. 20, which still serves to separate the fifth participle from the preceding four. Benjamin L. Merkle helpfully notes that he found no critical Greek text prior to NA26 (1979) that started the household code at 5:21 ("The Start of Instruction to Wives and Husbands—Ephesians 5:21 or 5:22?" BibSac 174 [2017]: 191). Among the early manuscripts, Alexandrinus leaves a small space between 5:21–22, signaling a minor disjunction, and starts a new paragraph at 5:25. Sinaiticus uses ekthesis at 5:21 and 5:22, perhaps suggesting the transitional role of 5:21.

[42] Ὑποτάσσεσθε (present active imperative 2nd person plural) is found in D F G sy, while ὑποτασσέσθωσαν (present active imperative 3rd person plural) is found in A I P Ψ 0278 33 81 1175 1739 1881 al lat co. The reading lacking a verb is found in a few of the earliest manuscripts (𝔓46 B Cl Hiermss) and is the more difficult reading, and thus likely original.

[43] Louw-Nida includes them both under the semantic field of "Obey, Disobey" (36.12–30).

[44] For an examination of these two reasons and further sources, see Merkle, "Start of Instruction," 181–182.

[45] See a similar argument made about the distance of εὐχαριστοῦντες (Col 1:12) from the preceding verb περιπατῆσαι (1:10), with three intervening participles. Some try to start a new

imperatives, and should never be taken as such if there is a verb which it may appropriately modify.[46] The "fear" inclusio argument ignores another use of φόβος in 6:5, and also ignores the difference in person to be feared: "the Lord" in 5:21; "the husband" in 5:33; "your masters" (implied by the prepositional phrase) in 6:5. As for the conceptual fit between ὑποτάσσω and the household code, and the lexical repetition of ὑποτάσσω in v. 21, 22 (implied), and 24, such evidence does not mean that v. 21 must be included within the household code unit. It is possible and not obviously wrong to consider it the beginning of the household code. But it is more likely that v. 21 is simply another discourse pivot (cf. 4:32), with the concept of submission transitioning and persisting into the new unit, which itself begins with a specific instance of ὑποτάσσω in v. 22.[47]

Verse 21, then, simultaneously (1) concludes 5:15–21 as the final result of being filled with the Spirit and (2) evokes the next topic in Paul's mind, namely, the household code, which begins with the directive for wives to submit to their husbands. In oral conversation, one might have said it this way:

> Be filled with the Spirit...submitting to one another in the fear of the Lord. [Pivot] Speaking of submitting, [new topic] wives, submit to your husbands...

The Household Code: Ephesians 5:22–6:9

Whereas 4:1–5:21 contain directives to believers generally, the household code gives commands to three domestic pairs, each addressed in turn, with a main command that is further explained or supported:

---

sentence with εὐχαριστοῦντες because of its distance from περιπατῆσαι, but do not explain why the distance of the preceding participle δυναμούμενοι (1:11) is not also too far from περιπατῆσαι. See ch. 12, "Colossians," p. 394.

[46] On the history of research on imperatival participles, see Ervin Starwalt, *A Discourse Analysis of 1 Peter*, SKG (Fontes, 2020), 11–16.

[47] Many commentators refer to this verse as a hinge or pivot. A few representatives include Merkle, "Start of Instruction," 180; Mark J. Keown, "Paul's Vision of a New Masculinity (Eph 5:21–6:9)," *Colloquium* 48, no. 1 (2016): 49–50; Sellin, *Epheser*, 437. It is a contentious matter whether the hinge nature of v. 21 means that it simply leads to the first thought of the household code (wives submitting to husbands) or whether the idea of submission governs the entire household code. There are good reasons for both positions, and this essay is not the place to examine them. Sellin in a mediating position admits the participle is modifying "be filled with the Spirit," but also takes v. 21 as an introduction to the household code and begins a new unit there. He concludes aptly that "the *Haustafel* ethic is in this respect not set apart from spiritual-liturgical life. There is no fundamental separation of worship and ethic" (*Epheser*, 437).

Wives, submit to your own husbands as to the Lord (5:22)[48]
Husbands, love your wives (5:25)
Children, obey your parents in the Lord (6:1)
And fathers, do not provoke your children to anger (6:4)
Slaves, obey your fleshly masters (6:5)
And masters, do the same to them, giving up threatening (6:9).[49]

How this unit relates to the preceding is difficult to determine. Based on my analysis above, the shared lexeme ὑποτάσσω, explicit in v. 21 and implied in v. 22, creates a tail-head linkage, whereby the mention of the word ὑποτάσσω evokes the first sub-unit of the next topic. The household relationships provide specific instances of walking wisely and being filled with the Spirit. What Paul calls on wives, children, and slaves to do are not atypical (submit, obey, and obey, respectively). However, the motivation for doing so is distinctly Christian and Christological ("as to the Lord...in the Lord...as to Christ...their Lord and yours is in heaven"). Moreover, fulfilling these commands requires being filled by the Spirit. For Paul, "none is righteous," "no one understands," and "whatever does not proceed from faith is sin" (Rom 3:10, 11; 14:23). To obey these commands within the Christian household is not a simple task; but when they are done, they are specific instances of walking wisely in the Spirit.

Ephesians 6:10–20 as a Peroratio

I argued earlier that τοῦ λοιποῦ in 6:10 could be taken as "from now on" or "finally," but in either case the unit is semantically a final exhortation in series with "walk in love and wisdom" (5:1–14, 15–21), and pragmatically a *peroratio*. Aristotle said a *peroratio* should be paratactic in style with no connecting particles, e.g., "I have spoken; you have heard; you know the facts; now give your decision" (*Rhetoric* 3.19.6). Quintilian said it should be short, lest it become a second speech (*Institutio Oratoria* 6.1). Ephesians 6:10–20 exhibits these features. While it is not necessary to suggest that Paul had rhetorical categories in mind, or definitely had rhetorical training, he likely had some intuition of oratory practices.

A true *peroratio* would recapitulate the facts of the entire discourse, but there is disagreement about whether Eph 6:10–20 recapitulates facts from Division 1, Division 2, or the entire epistle.[50] Figure 10.2 lays out the lexical and conceptual parallels.

---

[48] The verb ὑποτάσσεσθε (2nd plural imperative "submit") must be supplied.

[49] The meaning of "the same" is not clear. See the options in Best, *Ephesians*, 580; Lincoln, *Ephesians*, 423; Hoehner, *Ephesians*, 813–814.

[50] Recapitulation of mainly chs. 1–3: Best, *Ephesians*, 585. Recapitulation of mainly chs. 4–6: Robert A. Wild, "The Warrior and the Prisoner: Some Reflections on Ephesians 6:10-20," *CBQ* 46, no. 2 (1984): 284–98; Recapitulation of the entire epistle: Thielman, *Ephesians*, 411–412;

Ephesians 6:10–20	Parallels in Ephesians
τῷ κράτει τῆς ἰσχύος αὐτοῦ (6:10)	τὴν ἐνέργειαν τοῦ κράτους τῆς ἰσχύος αὐτοῦ (1:19)
ἐνδυναμοῦσθε (6:10)	τὸ ὑπερβάλλον μέγεθος τῆς δυνάμεως (1:19)
	τὴν ἐνέργειαν τῆς δυνάμεως αὐτοῦ (3:7)
	δῷ ὑμῖν κατὰ τὸ πλοῦτος τῆς δόξης αὐτοῦ δυνάμει κραταιωθῆναι (3:16)
	τὴν δύναμιν τὴν ἐνεργουμένην ἐν ἡμῖν (3:20)
ἐνδύσασθε τὴν πανοπλίαν τοῦ θεοῦ (6:11) ἐνδυσάμενοι τὸν θώρακα τῆς δικαιοσύνης (6:14)	ἐνδύσασθαι τὸν καινὸν ἄνθρωπον (4:24)
τὰς μεθοδείας τοῦ διαβόλου (6:11) τοῦ πονηροῦ (6:16)	τὸν ἄρχοντα τῆς ἐξουσίας τοῦ ἀέρος (2:2) τὴν μεθοδείαν τῆς πλάνης (4:14) μηδὲ δίδοτε τόπον τῷ διαβόλῳ (4:27)
αἷμα καὶ σάρκα (6:12)	σάρξ (2:3 [x2], 11 [x2], 14; 5:29, 31; 6:5; 12)
τὰς ἀρχάς, πρὸς τὰς ἐξουσίας, πρὸς τοὺς κοσμοκράτορας τοῦ σκότους τούτου, πρὸς τὰ πνευματικὰ τῆς πονηρίας (6:12)	ὑπεράνω πάσης ἀρχῆς καὶ ἐξουσίας καὶ δυνάμεως καὶ κυριότητος καὶ παντὸς ὀνόματος ὀνομαζομένου (1:21) ἵνα γνωρισθῇ νῦν ταῖς ἀρχαῖς καὶ ταῖς ἐξουσίαις (3:10)
ἐν τοῖς ἐπουρανίοις (6:12)	πάσῃ εὐλογίᾳ πνευματικῇ ἐν τοῖς ἐπουρανίοις (1:3) καθίσας ἐν δεξιᾷ αὐτοῦ ἐν τοῖς ἐπουρανίοις (1:20) συνεκάθισεν ἐν τοῖς ἐπουρανίοις ἐν Χριστῷ Ἰησου (2:6) ἵνα γνωρισθῇ νῦν ταῖς ἀρχαῖς καὶ ταῖς ἐξουσίαις ἐν τοῖς ἐπουρανίοις (3:10)
δυνηθῆτε ἀντιστῆναι ἐν τῇ ἡμέρᾳ τῇ πονηρᾷ (6:13)	αἱ ἡμέραι πονηραί εἰσιν (5:16)
περιζωσάμενοι τὴν ὀσφὺν ὑμῶν ἐν ἀληθείᾳ (6:14)	τὸν λόγον τῆς ἀληθείας (1:13) καθώς ἐστιν ἀλήθεια ἐν τῷ Ἰησοῦ (4:21) κτισθέντα ἐν δικαιοσύνῃ καὶ ὁσιότητι τῆς ἀληθείας (4:24) λαλεῖτε ἀλήθειαν ἕκαστος μετὰ τοῦ πλησίον αὐτοῦ (4:25) ἐν πάσῃ ἀγαθωσύνῃ καὶ δικαιοσύνῃ καὶ ἀληθείᾳ (5:9)
ἐνδυσάμενοι τὸν θώρακα τῆς δικαιοσύνης (6:14) τοῦ εὐαγγελίου τῆς εἰρήνης (6:15)	κτισθέντα ἐν δικαιοσύνῃ (4:24) ἐν πάσῃ ἀγαθωσύνῃ καὶ δικαιοσύνῃ καὶ ἀληθείᾳ (5:9) χάρις ὑμῖν καὶ εἰρήνη (1:2) τὸ εὐαγγέλιον τῆς σωτηρίας ὑμῶν (1:13)

Lincoln, *Ephesians*, 430–433; Baugh, *Ephesians*, 526; Thorsten Moritz, *A Profound Mystery: The Use of the Old Testament in Ephesians*, SNT 85 (Brill, 1996), 181–183; Sellin, *Epheser*, 472, but he sees more recapitulation of chs. 4–6.

	συμμέτοχα τῆς ἐπαγγελίας ἐν Χριστῷ Ἰησοῦ διὰ τοῦ εὐαγγελίου (3:6)
	Αὐτὸς γάρ ἐστιν ἡ εἰρήνη ἡμῶν (2:14)
	ἵνα τοὺς δύο κτίσῃ ἐν αὐτῷ εἰς ἕνα καινὸν ἄνθρωπον ποιῶν εἰρήνην (2:15)
	εὐηγγελίσατο εἰρήνην ὑμῖν τοῖς μακρὰν καὶ εἰρήνην τοῖς ἐγγύς (2:17)
	ἐν τῷ συνδέσμῳ τῆς εἰρήνης (4:3)
τὸν θυρεὸν τῆς πίστεως (6:16)	πίστις (1:15; 2:8; 3:12; 3:17; 4:5, 13); πιστεύω (1:13, 19) ἀκούσας τὴν καθ᾽ ὑμᾶς πίστιν ἐν τῷ κυρίῳ Ἰησοῦ (1:15) ἐστε σεσῳσμένοι διὰ πίστεως (2:8) προσαγωγὴν ἐν πεποιθήσει διὰ τῆς πίστεως αὐτοῦ (3:12)
τὴν περικεφαλαίαν τοῦ σωτηρίου (6:17)	χάριτί ἐστε σεσῳσμένοι (2:5, 8)
τὴν μάχαιραν τοῦ πνεύματος (6:17)	πνεῦμα (1:13, 17; 2:2, 18, 22; 3:5, 16; 4:3, 4, 23, 30; 5:18; 6:17, 18)
διὰ πάσης προσευχῆς καὶ δεήσεως προσευχόμενοι (6:18)	μνείαν ποιούμενος ἐπὶ τῶν προσευχῶν μου (1:16) κάμπτω τὰ γόνατά μου πρὸς τὸν πατέρα (3:14)
περὶ πάντων τῶν ἁγίων (6:18)	ἅγιος (1:1, 4, 13, 15, 18; 2:19, 21; 3:5, 8, 18; 4:12, 30; 5:3, 27; 6:18)
ἵνα μοι δοθῇ λόγος (6:19)	τὸν λόγον τῆς ἀληθείας (1:13)
γνωρίσαι τὸ μυστήριον τοῦ εὐαγγελίου (6:19)	τὸ μυστήριον τοῦ θελήματος αὐτοῦ (1:9) ἐγνωρίσθη μοι τὸ μυστήριον (3:3) νοῆσαι τὴν σύνεσίν μου ἐν τῷ μυστηρίῳ τοῦ Χριστοῦ (3:4) τίς ἡ οἰκονομία τοῦ μυστηρίου τοῦ ἀποκεκρυμμένου (3:9) τὸ μυστήριον τοῦτο μέγα ἐστίν (5:32)
πρεσβεύω ἐν ἁλύσει (6:20)	Παῦλος ὁ δέσμιος τοῦ Χριστου (3:1) μὴ ἐγκακεῖν ἐν ταῖς θλίψεσίν μου ὑπὲρ ὑμῶν (3:13)

Figure 10.2: Recapitulation of Ephesians 1:3–6:9 in the Peroratio

Some of these lexemes and concepts are more specific to the discourse world of Ephesians (such as spiritual powers, mystery, gospel of peace, the heavenlies), while some are more generally Christian and would be expected to appear in the epistle (prayer, gospel, saints, Spirit, faith, righteousness, flesh, truth). Especially when the latter category is ignored, the *peroratio* contains significantly more recapitulation of the ideas in chs. 1–3, but there are enough ideas from chs. 4–6 to see the *peroratio* summarizing the entire epistle. In any case, chs. 1–3 are intricately connected to chs. 4–6 by functioning as its basis or grounds. Paul could have chosen to make the exhortations in 4:1–5:20 in terms of spiritual warfare, as he does here, but instead he chose to focus on the need for Jew and Gentile unity, for imitating God by avoiding vice and walking in love, and for walking wisely in the Spirit. These concrete, practical exhortations are grounded on the spiritual realities expressed in chs. 1–3. So even though the *peroratio* is couched in cosmic warfare language, it still aptly concludes the entire epistle.

In accord with Aristotle's stylistic suggestions, the style of Ephesians 6:10–20 is far more paratactic than in preceding sections, which exhibit much recursive nesting of phrases and a frequent use of discourse particles. In 6:10–20, there are only two discourse particles (ignoring ὅτι, v. 12, and ἵνα, vv. 13, 19, 20), namely, διὰ τοῦτο in v. 13 and οὖν in v. 14. There are four main commands in vv. 10–14, and even the elaborative v. 12 recites a list of the powers, each introduced by πρός, which allows for a powerful rhythm when read.

ἐνδυναμοῦσθε ἐν κυρίῳ καὶ ἐν τῷ κράτει τῆς ἰσχύος αὐτοῦ.
ἐνδύσασθε τὴν πανοπλίαν τοῦ θεοῦ
    πρὸς τὸ δύνασθαι ὑμᾶς στῆναι πρὸς τὰς μεθοδείας τοῦ διαβόλου·
    ὅτι οὐκ ἔστιν ἡμῖν ἡ πάλη πρὸς αἷμα καὶ σάρκα, ἀλλὰ
    πρὸς τὰς ἀρχάς,
    πρὸς τὰς ἐξουσίας,
    πρὸς τοὺς κοσμοκράτορας τοῦ σκότους τούτου,
    πρὸς τὰ πνευματικὰ τῆς πονηρίας ἐν τοῖς ἐπουρανίοις.
διὰ τοῦτο ἀναλάβετε τὴν πανοπλίαν τοῦ θεοῦ,
    ἵνα δυνηθῆτε ἀντιστῆναι ἐν τῇ ἡμέρᾳ τῇ πονηρᾷ
    καὶ ἅπαντα κατεργασάμενοι στῆναι.
στῆτε οὖν

Beyond these four imperatives, the final imperative is modified by a number of participial clauses of roughly similar length that may have a punchy rhetorical effect when read (vv. 14–16a).

περιζωσάμενοι τὴν ὀσφὺν ὑμῶν ἐν ἀληθείᾳ
καὶ ἐνδυσάμενοι τὸν θώρακα τῆς δικαιοσύνης
καὶ ὑποδησάμενοι τοὺς πόδας ἐν ἑτοιμασίᾳ τοῦ εὐαγγελίου τῆς εἰρήνης,
ἐν πᾶσιν ἀναλαβόντες τὸν θυρεὸν τῆς πίστεως,

Starting with v. 16b, the style begins to loosen up and the syntactic style returns. The semantic structure of the entire section is a four-fold command to take up arms against the spiritual powers, followed by an enumeration of the seven means of doing so:

ἐνδυναμοῦσθε ... ἐνδύσασθε ... διὰ τοῦτο ἀναλάβετε ... στῆτε οὖν
περιζωσάμενοι, ἐνδυσάμενοι, ὑποδησάμενοι, ἀναλαβόντες,
δέξασθε, προσευχόμενοι, ἀγρυπνοῦντες.[51]

This section therefore functions well as a *peroratio*. It has paratactic, punchy phrasing; it recapitulates facts especially from chs. 1–3 but also some from chs. 4–6; and it makes an emotional and urgent call to spiritual warfare, capping off the hortatory concerns.

Pragmatically, this unit is probably the second most important of the epistle. The τοῦ λοιποῦ suggests it is semantically the final and perhaps the most climactic of the three most general exhortations to love, wisdom, and warfare. Ultimately, though, the reason for these directives is that they are the means to achieving the maintenance of unity in the body (4:1–3), which is the ultimate (or *telic*) pragmatic concern of the epistle. This understanding of the letter's pragmatic structure brings the disparate realms of the epistle's discourse world together. Concerns include cosmic rebellion, cosmic subjection, and individual as well as corporate salvation on the one hand (1:3–3:21; 4:8–10), and halakhic, practical, worldly exhortations on the other (4:1–7; 4:11–6:9). The way Paul structures his most prominent ethical directives (love–wisdom ⬌ spiritual warfare) unites both realms.

Maintaining unity in the church involves such mundane concerns as forgiving one another, loving one's spouse, submitting to parents, and forsaking Gentile vices. But behind all this, they must remember that their former Gentile lifestyle was due to subjection to cosmic powers (2:1–3). Christ has overcome them (1:20–23; 3:10–11; 4:8–10), and so they must identify with their king in the fight and take up arms along with him until the war is done (6:10–20). Both realms threaten the Jew-Gentile unity wrought by the Spirit: lack of love and wisdom, and the cosmic influence of the kingdom of Satan. Of course, the realms intermingle: often, fighting against the kingdom of the evil one simply means not lying (4:25), avoiding fornication and crude talk (5:3–5), and seeking unity with fellow believers (4:1–3). Paul directs against both threatening realms in order to urge them to protect what was so central to his mission and calling, namely, the grafting of the Gentiles into God's people, who are now marked by faith in Christ (2:8–10), not by the symbolic cutting of the skin (2:11–12).

---

[51] The imperative δέξασθε in v. 17 should be taken as one of the seven means of standing firm. Paul probably intrudes in the participial list with the imperative because the human mind can only keep around seven items activated at a time, and after an imperatival phrase, four modifying participial phrases, and a phrase expanding on "faith," it would be too heavy a cognitive load to continue with more participial phrases. See George Miller, "The Magical Number Seven, Plus or Minus Two," *Psychological Review* 63, 81–97; Edward K. Vogel, Geoffrey F. Woodman, and Steven J. Luck, "Storage of Features, Conjunctions, and Objects in Visual Working Memory," *Journal of Experimental Psychology: Human Perception and Performance* 27, no. 1 (2001): 92–114.

11

PHILIPPIANS

THOMAS W. HUDGINS & J. GREGORY LAWSON

Introduction

There are two major problems with discourse analysis as a field of study: (1) terminology and (2) methodology. Neither is all that clear. With respect to the former, discourse analysis is a technical field and, as a result, has a very technical vocabulary. Increasingly aware of the handicap this vocabulary poses, researchers who perform discourse analyses sometimes include glossaries and—believe it or not—those glossaries are sometimes unintelligible even to native speakers of the same language. And, with respect to the latter, discourse analyses sometimes lack—or so it can seem—a clear investigative plan that would allow other researchers to reproduce the study or apply the same steps to similar research problems in different contexts with scientifically stable results. No branch has a firm method. One reason is because branches of discourse analysis have principles, tools, and strategies, not methods; method belongs to the researcher. The primary aim of this study is not the analysis itself, but rather to overcome these two weaknesses and hopefully give readers an understandable and replicable approach to analyzing the letters of the New Testament.

Methodology

Research begins not with a method but rather a question or series of related questions. A researcher wants to know something in particular. He or she sets out on a quest for answers. Discourse analysis is positioned to help answer a plethora of different investigative inquiries. Is a letter authentic? For example, if an individual is named as the author in the letter introduction, did that person actually write it? This comes up with a handful of letters of the New Testament, such as Ephesians, Colossians, but not so much for Philippians. Is a particular pericope within a discourse original? An issue does arise here with Philippians, mainly because some scholars have questioned the shift in tone in the third chapter and have argued that it is incongruent with the rest of the letter. And what is the purpose of a letter? And what about its structure and logical flow? And where does the author place the most emphasis? What about shifts in thoughts, or the types of signs utilized in the discourse to accomplish the author's purpose? Discourse analysis is useful for all of these questions and more.

The primary goal in analyzing any historical document is to identify its creator's intent and interpret the contents of that document in light of that intent. Secondary studies might not deal directly with original intent (e.g., perception studies), but artifacts of history are inseparable from their creators. New Testament texts are no different. Our primary research question is: What was Paul's purpose for writing a letter to this particular Philippian community? Our secondary research questions are: How does Paul utilize imitation appeals to engage his audience and how are those arguments structured in relationship to one another? In the present analysis, we want to identify the author's purpose via the mainline material and then draw some observations about the rest of the letter. As we move past the mainline material, we are going to notice that Paul makes increased appeals to imitation—compared to his other letters—and we will pay special attention to these appeals in our analysis. The following represents a methodological template for doing a discourse analysis of a New Testament letter:

1. Determine the discourse type.
2. Identify mainline material.
   a. Identify any immediate mainline material in the discourse. This should be front and center throughout the analysis. In other words, the researcher should be willing to add to the list of mainline material throughout the study if warranted.
   b. Isolate that mainline material from the remainder of the discourse content.
   c. Isolate the letter introduction and letter conclusion from the rest of the letter.
3. Identify units (e.g., paragraph groupings, paragraphs), sentences (SVO), clauses, and phrases.
4. Evaluate the progression and types of arguments within the letter and how they support the author's purpose.

We want to cultivate the skill of synthesizing the relationship of same-level discourse units to one another—synthesizing the larger discourse units with the other larger discourse units, and smaller ones to smaller ones, as we move through the text. Before moving into the analysis, it might be helpful to offer some brief comments about the first three steps in this method.

Determine Discourse Type

We begin here because discourse type sets some natural parameters for interpretation. Robert E. Longacre has identified a number of discourse types, but the following are the most general categories: Narrative, Prophetic, Procedural, Behaviorial, and Expositional.[1] They provide a healthy constraint for researchers so they invest their time and efforts in the most efficient way and with the greatest success at correctly evaluating a text. Longacre discussed this in the following way:

> The reason for insisting on text type and its corresponding template as a logical starting point in textual analysis is to insure that we are not barking up the proverbial wrong tree as we begin. A narrative, for example, has a narrative movement and it is fruitless to analyze it as if it were a scientific paper, a food recipe, or a piece of logical argumentation. . . . When we say that a text has narrative movement, we expect to find that it is built on a narrative template, a conceptual scheme which in broad outline is as old as Aristotle. . . . If we find a text to be a piece of exhortation, we expect to find it built on a hortatory template with cognitive components which are probably universal: Authority of the exhorter; Situation/Problem; Command element(s); Motivation.[2]

Also, what signals and ultimately constitutes mainline and supporting material is different depending on discourse type; what is mainline in narrative discourse might not be what is mainline in prophetic discourse and almost certainly not what is mainline in behavioral discourse. For example, the aorist is the most common tense in Greek narrative discourse. Deviations from that norm are one signal that special attention is required and it could indicate that material is mainline.

Behavioral discourse is only a general category. Letters as a type of discourse can fall under at least two of Longacre's general categories. And there are different types of letters. Some are informational, and some are corrective in nature. The amount of emotion they have can vary significantly, as can the amount of

---

[1] Robert E. Longacre, *The Grammar of Discourse*, 2nd ed. (Springer Science + Business Media, 1996). See chapter 1 "Monologue Discourse: Typology and Salience." He classifies prophecy as a subcategory of narrative, which makes sense, but it is so different than a story that it probably does warrant its own category.

[2] Robert E. Longacre, *Holistic Textlinguistics* (SIL, 2003), 4.

information. They can be more or less personal, ideological or theoretical or re-
flective, etc.; they can express how things were, how they are, how they will be,
how they could be, and how they should be. They can address problems and
attempt to solve them, just like they can cause and advance problems. My point
in mentioning all this is that identifying a discourse as a letter in general will give
a certain set of parameters by which that discourse should be interpreted. When
the kind of letter is identifiable, the researcher is able to draw some conclusions
about the text and it inevitably advances the study of its content.

Identify Mainline Material

Longacre includes an analysis of an Arthur Hailey novel (*The Final Diagnosis*) in
his essay entitled "Holistic Discourse." In the analysis, he recounts how he and a
colleague once discussed the novel's macrostructure. It was her opinion that one
of the characters, Joe Pearson, was of such significance to the storyline that "the
macrostructure of the whole novel should be centered on him, i.e., that it should
be conceived to be 'The sad story of the fall of Dr. Pearson.'"[3] Longacre responded, "Too many parts of the novel would be left uncaptured in such a macrostructure for it to serve such a general purpose."[4] That statement helps frame the discussion about mainline material. Here is one question we can ask when we are
thinking about the purpose of a discourse and its mainline material: "Is anything
left uncaptured in such a macrostructure?"

Determining what is prominent in discourses is important. In a discourse
analysis on John 17, I [Thomas] rejected the three-fold division of Jesus' prayer,
the one based on who Jesus prayed for: (1) himself, (2) immediate disciples, and
(3) future disciples.[5] When I asked, "Is anything left uncaptured in such a macrostructure?" I realized that the content of Jesus' prayer was eclipsed. People re-
membered who Jesus prayed for in his prayer, but they did not remember much
about what he prayed for. That was problematic. So, I argued that greater attention should be given to Jesus' requests and his final commitment at the end of
the prayer. These constitute the mainline material. By giving more structural
significance to them, the content of Jesus' prayer received the attention it deserved. John wanted his audience to know what Jesus prayed for, and who he
prayed for was secondary in nature.

Longacre says that certain tenses, aspects, and moods can be characteristic
of particular types of discourse, and, as a result, we can identify the mainline of

---

[3] Longacre, *Holistic Textlinguistics*, 7.

[4] Ibid., 7.

[5] Thomas W. Hudgins, "An Application of Discourse Analysis Methodology in the Exegesis
of John 17," *Eleutheria* 2:1 (2012): 24–57.

a discourse by identifying those particular features within a discourse.[6] According to him,

> In any discourse type there is a main line of development and further elements which supplement/support the main line. In narrative text there is a storyline of punctiliar sequential happenings reported in sentences whose main verb(s) are some sort of past tense, completive aspect, or a special narrative tense (Biblical Hebrew, many African languages). In hortatory text there is a line of exhortation carried by imperative or modal forms which command, suggest, or urge some action. Everything else in the hortatory text supplements or support the line of exhortation. Other discourse types also have main line elements and additional elements. All of this can be tersely summarized as on-the-line versus off-the-line elements which are subject to morphosyntactic and/or lexical identification. On-the-line elements dominate off-the-line elements in local-span (paragraph analysis).[7]

Philippians and the rest of Paul's extant letters are corrective in nature. We can make a strong argument that the same is true of all the letters of the New Testament. Paul's letters are responses to specific challenges facing particular communities. Whatever the problems, Paul believed they warranted some instruction, guidance/exhortation, and sometimes even a rebuke from him personally. His goal in these letters was to influence some sort of change within the community, to correct something about their behavior as participants of the New Covenant. When we identify the change that he addressed, then we have identified the purpose of the letter. Mainline material in his letters is what he tells them to do and who he tells them to be/become. Everything else is supplemental. As Longacre pointed out, in hortatory text we need to identify the imperatives and other constructs that function in this manner. Doing so will allow us to isolate the mainline material from the supplemental material and then analyze the microstructures through the lens of the macrostructure.[8]

---

[6] Longacre, *The Grammar of Discourse*, 3. There are additional markers of mainline material beyond just tense, aspect, mood, or combinations of the three.

[7] Robert E. Longacre, "The Discourse Strategy of an Appeals Letter," in *Discourse Description: Diverse Linguistic Analyses of a Fund-Raising Letter* (John Benjamins, 1992), 127n6.

[8] In their study on Romans, Robert Longacre and Wilber B. Wallis raise a number of questions: "What is the main line of development? And what is embedded? These in turn tie into other questions: What is the fundamental thrust and purpose of the book? What are the developmental sidelines?" ("Soteriology and Eschatology in Romans," *JETS* 41:3 [1998]: 367). They identify the purpose of the entire letter in Rom 15:14–16, introduced by the words ἔγραψα ὑμῖν ("I have written to you"). We might point out that they do not say that *is* the purpose, but that the purpose "is best seen in 15:14–16" (367). The distinction is important since purpose is evident throughout discourse content. Mainline material is never the only place purpose is

Identify Units, Sentences, and Clauses

There are two ways to approach the text at this point. The researcher can go from the top to the bottom or from the bottom to the top. In top-down analyses, the researcher identifies paragraphs first and works his or her way to clauses all the way to words and morphemes. In bottom-up analyses, the researcher identifies the smallest units of microstructure and draws connections until arriving at the completed unit. Each is looking for relationships. In the formation of paragraphs, we are looking for relationships via discourse markers (δέ, οὖν, γάρ, etc.). In the formation of sentences, we are looking for relationships between subjects, verbs, objects, and additional linguistic information the author choses to include; if an adjective, for example, the noun it modifies; if a participle, the finite verb to which it is connected; etc.[9]

The easiest way for a bottom-up analysis is to identify all of the finite verbs within a discourse, i.e., verbs of independent clauses as opposed to verbs that are restricted by subordinating conjunctions or participles, etc. It is unnecessary to begin the study all the way at the bottom (i.e., at morphemes or individual words). It is better to identify the clauses, finite and non-finite, and then be in a position where their relationships can be easily analyzed.

Macrostructure

Some words and constructs in discourse serve as the context of the rest of the letter. All parts of a discourse are related and therefore they both have and act as context. Consider the following sentence: "But even if I am being poured out as a drink offering upon the sacrifice and service of your faith, I rejoice and share my joy with you all" (Phil 2:17). There are two basic parts to this sentence: "But even if I am being poured out as a drink offering upon the sacrifice and service of your faith" and "I rejoice and share my joy with you all." The latter is what we call the finite clause because it contains the finite verb. In other words, it contains the portion of the sentence that is able to stand alone. The first part of the sentence is not able to do this. An apodosis is always more important than a protasis; the protasis is how the author wished to shade his or her apodosis and, of course, the two represent the complete idea. But note: Not all parts of discourse are equal

---

present. But mainline material is the place that most directly signals purpose for an audience. Here is one more interesting comment they make in their analysis: "This passage, which is probably a key to the whole epistle, presumably implies the preeminence of hortatory material over persuasive, expository and predictive elements" (368).

[9] For a discussion on co-textual levels of discourse, see Jeffrey T. Reed, *A Discourse Analysis of Philippians: Method and Rhetoric in the Debate over Literary Integrity*, JSNTSup 136, ed. Stanley E. Porter (Sheffield Academic, 1997), 42–51.

with regard to their force, focus, and the attention they demand, just like not all parts of a compound sentence are equal.[10] The easiest demonstration of this is to compare the letter opening and letter closing of an ancient letter with any part of its body. For example, "Paul and Timothy, slaves of Jesus Christ, to all the saints in Christ Jesus who are part of the community in Philippi, including the overseers and deacons" (Phil 1:1) is not more important than the pericope in Phil 2:5–11 describing how Jesus humbled himself, took the form of a slave, died a death on a cross, and was subsequently exalted by God the Father. To use some modern imagery, the envelope is never more important than the letter it carries. And for this reason, we have to identify what part of a discourse is more important than the rest. Through which part or parts will we understand the rest, and, in the end, the whole?

Paul's letters are situational and corrective. Since he is responding to specific challenges—from his perspective—we can expect some request(s) for change within the discourse. These requests help the researcher understand the situation from Paul's perspective. The following represent all of the requests or exhortations within the discourse:

1. τοῦτο προσεύχομαι (1:9)
2. μόνον ἀξίως τοῦ εὐαγγελίου τοῦ Χριστοῦ πολιτεύεσθε (1:27)
3. πληρώσατέ μου τὴν χαρὰν (2:2)
4. τοῦτο φρονεῖτε ἐν ὑμῖν (2:5)
5. τὴν ἑαυτῶν σωτηρίαν κατεργάζεσθε (2:12)
6. πάντα ποιεῖτε (2:14)
7. ὑμεῖς χαίρετε καὶ συγχαίρετέ μοι (2:18)
8. προσδέχεσθε αὐτόν (2:29)
9. τοὺς τοιούτους ἐντίμους ἔχετε (2:29)
10. χαίρετε (3:1)
11. βλέπετε (3:2 [3x])
12. συμμιμηταί μου γίνεσθε (3:17)
13. σκοπεῖτε τοὺς οὕτως περιπατοῦντας (3:17)
14. στήκετε (4:1)
15. παρακαλῶ (4:2 [2x])
16. συλλαμβάνου αὐταῖς (4:3)
17. χαίρετε (4:4 [2x])

---

[10] Moisés Silva has used the illustration of a chessboard with its pieces distributed. He suggests that the location of each chess piece on the board may not actually reflect the state of a particular match. Instead, he says, "there is a dynamic relationship among the pieces that reveals the true 'meaning' of the game" (*God, Language, and Scripture: Reading the Bible in the Light of General Linguistics* [Zondervan, 1990], 45).

18. τὸ ἐπιεικὲς ὑμῶν γνωσθήτω (4:5)
19. μηδὲν μεριμνᾶτε (4:6)
20. τὰ αἰτήματα ὑμῶν γνωριζέσθω (4:6)
21. ταῦτα λογίζεσθε (4:8)
22. ταῦτα πράσσετε (4:9)
23. Ἀσπάσασθε πάντα ἅγιον (4:21)

Figure 11.1: Requests and Exhortations in Philippians

Identifying all of the requests not only helps uncover the situation Paul was addressing within a community, but it also helps identify material that has been disconnected from mainline material. Take 2:2–4 for example. Our translations generally reflect a series of imperatives in these verses: (1) "have this way of thinking," (2) "do nothing out of selfish motives," (3) "consider others as more important," (4) "do not just look out for your own interests." The problem is this completely disconnects the way Paul phrases the single request: "make my joy complete" (2:2). Everything that follows is subordinate and should be considered supplemental. If we follow the way the translations present the information, the positive elements ("having the same mind . . .") are presented as subordinate while the negative is presented as finite.

Not all of these requests are equal either. When we think about mainline we need to think about it from the standpoint of the discourse as a whole and the discourse sections. We should not assume that Paul gives a single request for change that captures everything about the situation he hopes to address in the community. He could, but it is not necessary. He could address a number of specific problems with individual requests for each one. He could also provide a single request for change that is broad enough to include all of the other specific requests. The requests should be considered individually and collectively. Requests can be direct or indirect, and they appear in discourse as more than just imperatives. For example, the first request in the letter is indirect. Paul tells the Philippians about one of his prayers ("And this I pray . . ." 1:9). The request is to God, but the Philippians would hear this and understand the content of Paul's prayer as something he hopes the community will allow God to accomplish by their submission and pursuit of the same goal, namely that they would be marked by love, knowledge, discernment, that they would approve things that are excellent, that they would be sincere and blameless, and that their lives would reflect the righteousness that had been given to them (1:9–11). But this is indirect since the request is made to God, not to the Philippians. One example of a request not in the indicative mood occurs in 4:2; instead of Paul telling Euodia and Syntyche something like "Live in harmony" (with the imperative mood), he frames the request as "I urge Euodia and I urge Syntyche to live in harmony in the Lord."

Consider the first three direct requests in Philippians: (1) "live as citizens…" (1:27–30); (2) "make my joy complete . . ." (2:1–4); (3) "have the way of thinking…" (2:5–8). The first direct request is actually the first imperative in the letter. And when we compare it to the remaining requests in the letter, it becomes clear that this one captures Paul's central issue and the remaining requests, for the most part, unpack some element contained therein.

Paul tells the Philippians that he wants them to live in a particular way. He chooses the verb πολιτεύομαι instead of one of the other behavior/lifestyle lexemes (e.g., ζάω, περιπατέω), drawing a connection to the city's special Roman status and their special status as citizens of heaven (3:21). The significance of the appeal is marked by Paul's use of μόνον. He is addressing a single way of living, not just an aspect of what their lives should be. It is *the only way* they should live. The phrase "in a manner required by the gospel of Christ" (Phil 1:27) further specifies how they should live. Paul keeps the gospel front and center, as he has in the letter up to this point and as he will moving forward ultimately to the problems addressed in the rest of the letter. The remaining clauses fixed to the request contain Paul's explanation of what such a life involves: to stand firm (1) in one spirit, (2) in one soul, (3) striving together for the faith of the gospel and (4) not being intimidated by opposition. The importance of unity is seen in the use of ἑνί/μιᾷ and the συν- prefix. There are two pairs: (1) the phrase "in one spirit" reminds the Philippians of their shared status before God (vertical), and the other phrase, "with one soul," their relationship to one another (horizontal); (2) the participial clause "striving together for the faith of the gospel" indicates their primary mission, and the other, "not being intimidated," their united resolve as they encounter false teachers or persecution while carrying out that mission.[11]

What happens if we take a look at the next two direct requests? Do they further explain the first direct request, or are they unrelated thematically?

In the second request, Paul refers to κοινωνία πνεύματος, similar to what is expressed in the phrase ἐν ἑνὶ πνεύματι; τὸ αὐτὸ φρονῆτε, σύμψυχοι, and τὸ ἓν φρονοῦντες, similar to [ἐν] μιᾷ ψυχῇ. These alone are sufficient for demonstrating the parallels between the first two requests, the second being an elaboration on the first. So what does it mean to be living in a way that is required by the gospel? What does it look like to be standing firm together on mission to see people believe the gospel while resisting any opposition along the way? The second request adds how there should be love, affection, and compassion on display as a united community. Paul highlights not being selfish but esteeming the interests of others as more important than one's own. That Paul draws their attention

---

[11] The συν- prefix should be understood as applying to the second participle as well even though not present.

here tells us that he believes there is an issue of disunity caused by not treating others as more important than oneself. He could have used an imperative and told them to stop being selfish, but instead he makes a softer appeal that links their actions to his joy, another way of highlighting unity. He addresses unity throughout the letter by mentioning the community's fellowship with Christ, their partnership with Paul, their partnership with Timothy, and with one of their own, Epaphroditus. This is all growing to Paul's acknowledgment of a known dispute between two individuals in the community (4:2–3). For the request in 1:27–30 to be realized, Paul believes the disunity existing between these two women must be neutralized. When Paul arrives at the place in his discourse where he urges them to "live in harmony in the Lord," they will have these first two requests (and what follows) as the backdrop to understand what they need to do and why it matters so much. For example, if the community is divided about a problem between these two individuals (Paul never addresses the specific problem), how will they not be alarmed by opponents (persecutors or false teachers)? Living in harmony in the Lord becomes another aspect of living in a manner required by the gospel.

The third request (2:5–8) is the first direct appeal to imitation in the letter.[12] There are other appeals to imitation within the letter, both implicit and explicit. But here Paul tells the Philippians to "share the same way of thinking" that Jesus exhibited by becoming a slave and being obedient to the point of death (2:5). The imperative φρονεῖτε echoes what is expressed in the phrase [ἐν] μιᾷ ψυχῇ from the first request and τὸ αὐτὸ φρονῆτε, σύμψυχοι, and τὸ ἓν φρονοῦντες in the second request. Paul does not tell the Philippians to be imitators of Christ, which would have been similar to the appeal in Eph 5:1 ("be imitators of God"). He maintains the focus on unity by making the second direct appeal to imitation with the συν- prefix (συμμιμηταί μου γίνεσθε) and acknowledging two groups: "those [the first group] who are walking according to the pattern" that the Philippians "have in us [the second group]" (3:17). Jesus' example in 2:5–8 is an expansion of what it looks like to regard others as more important than oneself (request 2) and ultimately what it looks like to live as heavenly citizens in a manner required by the gospel (request 1); it was Jesus' desire to see the world believe in him and experience the forgiveness of their sins that drove him to the cross, and he was undeterred in his mission despite experiencing the ultimate opposition. Closer examination of Paul's requests reveals that 1:27–30 is the mainline of the discourse whole.

---

[12] For a discussion on implicit and explicit appeals for imitation, see Hudgins, "Paul's Unique Appeal for Mimesis in Gal 4,12," in *Nova et Vetera: Philological Studies in Honor of Professor Antonio Piñero*, ed. Israel M. Gallarte and Jesús Peláez, EFN 11 (Córdoba: El Almendro, 2016), 399–412.

The whole of the letter must be understood through this lens. The remainder of the requests in the letter are also mainline, but they offer a fuller picture of the issue identified in 1:27–30.

Microstructures

If we isolate Paul's opening (1:1–2) and closing (4:21–23), we have the body of the letter (1:3–4:20). You might have heard about how Paul likes to treat theological matters first in his letters before transitioning to practical matters. He obviously does this in his letter to the Romans (1–11; 12–16) and Ephesians (1–3; 4–6). But that is not as apparent in his letter to the Philippians. Thinking along those lines can actually be a hindrance in your study of this letter. He does move from the more general issue of the problem of unity within the community (1:27–30) to a specific problem between two individuals toward the end of the letter (4:2–3).

We can take a look at the beginning of the letter body and get a picture for how to start identifying sentences and grouping them together into units and, in doing so, distinguishing them from previous and subsequent material. There are a total of 87 sentences in the letter, three of which are found in the letter closing. The first three sentences (1:3–7, 8, 9–11) in the letter belong to Paul's thanksgiving. The primary exception to this custom is in Paul's letter to the Galatian communities, but he also opts to not include one following the letter opening in 2 Corinthians. The thanksgiving pericope serves as the introduction to the letter body.[13] In Philippians, Paul begins by expressing his thanks (εὐχαριστῶ) and then a request/want, which in Philippians is marked as a prayer (προσεύχομαι). His other letters look different in structure and content, but you can see something of a pattern if you look closely (Figure 11.2):

	Philippians	Romans
Thanks	1:3–7 "I give thanks"	1:8 "I give thanks"
Divine Witness	1:8 "God is my witness"	1:9–10 "God is my witness"
Request/Want	1:9–11 "This I pray: ..."	1:11–12 "I long to see you"

Figure 11.2: Thanks and Request Patterns in Philippians and Romans

---

[13] For a detailed discussion, see Peter Arzt-Grabner, "Paul's Letter Thanksgiving," in *Paul and the Ancient Letter Form*, ed. Stanley E. Porter and Sean A. Adams (Brill, 2010), 129–158; see also, Raymond F. Collins, "A Significant Decade: The Trajectory of the Hellenistic Epistolary Thanksgiving," in *Paul and the Ancient Letter Form*, 172. He discusses the differences between Paul's earlier letters and his later letters, which is a helpful exercise when we think about discourse function.

In Romans, for example, the thanksgiving begins in 1:8. There is a mention of prayer connected to the divine witness clause, but at least part of the content of those prayers is identified in the two verses that follow, which we have marked as the request/want, namely that Paul wants to see this community and help it to be firmly established in the faith. We can group these three sentences together because they follow traditional introductions to letter bodies in extant Greek manuscripts. The use of δέ signals that there is a transition to a new idea with v. 12, signaling a new paragraph.[14] So, the letter opening transitions to the letter body, which is introduced by a letter thanksgiving:

Letter Opening (1:1–2)
Letter Body (1:3–4:20)
    Letter Introductory Thanksgiving (1:3–11)
    (δέ) transition to new idea
    . . .
    . . .
    . . .
Letter Closing (4:21–23)

The next step is to identify the remaining sentences in the letter body and mark which ones belong together (Figure 11.3).

There are six units (paragraph groupings) total within the letter body. The first (1:3–11) is marked by the transition to the letter body with εὐχαριστῶ. The second, fourth, and sixth units are marked by the use of δέ. The third unit is identifiable by the switch to the imperative, the mainline in the letter, closely associating it with the preceding unit; Paul discusses the advance of the gospel, in particular the way that he is leading his life—even in prison—and then tells the Philippians to live their lives together in such a way that advances the gospel ("striving together for the faith of the gospel"). And the fifth unit, the largest of the six, is marked by the use of τὸ λοιπόν.

---

[14] See Steven E. Runge, *Discourse Grammar of the Greek New Testament: A Practical Introduction for Teaching and Exegesis*, LBRS (Hendrickson, 2010), 28ff. (especially p. 31: "it includes the added constraint of signaling a new development . . . represents the writer's choice to explicitly signal that what follows is a new, distinct development in the story or argument"). A serious student of the New Testament is going to continue in their study of the Greek language—and we do not mean the paradigms. We learn Greek best when we study it *in use*, not as it appears in a table. As we encounter parts of speech (e.g., tense, voice, mood, aspect, and in this case, conjunctions) that we are unfamiliar as to their discourse function or range of meaning and interpretive possibilities depending on the context, we need to investigate.

	1:1–2	---	**Letter Opening**
1	1:3–7	εὐχαριστῶ	
2	1:8	[ἐστιν]	**Unit 1**
3	1:9–11	προσεύχομαι	
4	1:12–14	βούλομαι	
5	1:15–17	κηρύσσουσιν	
6	1:18a	[ἐστιν]	
7	1:18b	[ἐστιν]	
8	1:18c	χαίρω	
9	1:18d	χαρήσομαι	**Unit 2**
10	1:19–20	οἶδα	Transition marked by δέ
11	1:21a	[ἐστιν]	
12	1:21b	[ἐστιν]	
13	1:22a	[ἔσται]	
14	1:22b	συνέχομαι	
15	1:23–24	συνέχομαι	
16	1:25–26	οἶδα	
17	1:27–30	πολιτεύεσθε	
18	2:1–4	πληρώσατέ	
19	2:5–11	φρονεῖτε	**Unit 3**
20	2:12	[]	Transition marked by the use of
21	2:13	ἐστιν	the imperative
22	2:14–16	ποιεῖτε	
23	2:17	χαίρω and συγχαίρω	
24	2:18	χαίρετε and συγχαίρετέ	
25	2:19	ἐλπίζω	
26	2:20	ἔχω	
27	2:21	ζητοῦσιν	
28	2:22	γινώσκετε	
29	2:23	ἐλπίζω	
30	2:24	πέποιθα	
31	2:25–26	ἡγησάμην	
32	2:27a	ἠσθένησεν	**Unit 4**
33	2:27b	ἠλέησεν	Transition marked by δέ
34	2:28	ἔπεμψα	
35	2:29a	προσδέχεσθε	
36	2:29b–30	ἔχετε	
37	3:1	χαίρετε	**Unit 5**
38	3:2a	βλέπετε	Transition marked by τὸ λοιπόν
39	3:2b	βλέπετε	

40	3:2c	βλέπετε
41	3:3–4a	ἐσμεν
42	3:4b–6	[]
43	3:7	ἥγημαι
44	3:8–11	ἡγοῦμαι
45	3:12a	[]
46	3:12b	καταλάβω
47	3:13	λογίζομαι
48	3:14	διώκω
49	3:15a	φρονῶμεν
50	3:15b	ἀποκαλύψει
51	3:16	[]
52	3:17a	γίνεσθε
53	3:17b	σκοπεῖτε
54	3:18–19	περιπατοῦσιν
55	3:20–21	ὑπάρχει
56	4:1	στήκετε
57	4:2	παρακαλῶ
58	4:3	ἐρωτῶ and συλλαμβάνου
59	4:4a	χαίρετε
60	4:4b	ἐρῶ
61	4:4c	χαίρετε
62	4:5	γνωσθήτω
63	4:6a	μεριμνᾶτε
64	4:6b	γνωριζέσθω
65	4:7	φρουρήσει
66	4:8	λογίζεσθε
67	4:9a	πράσσετε
68	4:9b	ἔσται

69	4:10	ἐχάρην
70	4:11a	[]
71	4:11b	ἔμαθον
72	4:12a	οἶδα
73	4:12b	οἶδα
74	4:12c	μεμύημαι
75	4:13	ἰσχύω
76	4:14	ἐποιήσατε
77	4:15–16	οἴδατε
78	4:17a	[]
79	4:17b	ἐπιζητῶ

Unit 6
Transition marked by δέ

80	4:18a	ἀπέχω	
81	4:18b	περισσεύω	
82	4:18c	πεπλήρωμαι	
83	4:19	πληρώσει	
84	4:20	[]	
85	4:21a	ἀσπάσασθε	
86	4:21b	ἀσπάζονται	**Letter Closing**
87	4:22	ἀσπάζονται	

Figure 11.3: Sentences and Units in Philippians

Letter Opening (1:1–2)
Letter Body (1:3–4:20)
    Body Opening (1:3–11)
    Body Proper (1:12–4:9)
        Body Head (1:12–2:30)
            Subsection 1 (1:12–26)
            Subsection 2 (1:27–2:18)
                Subunit A (1:27–30)
                Subunit B (2:1–11)
                    Part a (2:1–4)
                    Part b (2:5–11)
                Subunit C (2:12–18)
            Subsection 3 (2:19–30)
        Body Subpart (3:1–4:9)
            Subsection 1 (3:1)
            Subsection 2 (3:2–4a)
            Subsection 3 (3:4b–11)
            Subsection 4 (3:12–16)
            Subsection 5 (3:17–21)
            Subsection 6 (4:1–9)
                Subunit A (4:1)
                Subunit B (4:2–3)
                Subunit C (4:4–7)
                Subunit D (4:8–9)
    Body Closing (4:10–20)
Letter Closing (4:21–23)

Figure 11.4: The Structure of Philippians

Each of these sections of the letter can be broken down into smaller units, e.g., paragraphs. For example, the third unit (1:27–2:18) containing the change Paul hopes to see in the Philippian community is divisible into sub-units (smaller group-ings of paragraphs) and paragraphs. The use of οὖν in 2:1 indicates a logical connec-tion between 1:27–30 and what follows.[15] The next discourse marker (ὥστε) appears in 2:12, which helps us identify 2:1–11 as a subunit. Within it, we find two exhorta-tions: πληρώσατέ μου τὴν χαράν (2:1–4, v. 2) and τοῦτο φρονεῖτε ἐν ὑμῖν (2:5–11, v. 5). David Alan Black provides the breakdown of the letter above in Figure 11.4.[16]

Each of these discourse units should be explained in relationship to one an-other, paying attention to cohesion and logical flow and looking for "peaks" in the discourse. "Peaks" are deviations from what is normal or expected in a par-ticular discourse. For our purposes, though, we want to pay special attention moving forward to imitation in Paul's letter to the Philippians.

The Discourse Function of Imitation Appeals

Direct and indirect appeals to imitation in Paul's letter to the Philippians must be viewed in light of 1:27–30, the mainline of Paul's discourse. Paul includes more appeals to imitation in this letter than the rest and he develops these ap-peals robustly. There are three direct appeals. The first is found in the third unit. Paul tells his audience to "share the same way of thinking" as Jesus had when he took on human flesh and was put to death on the cross (2:5–8). The second is found in the middle of the fifth unit: "Join together in being imitators of me, and pay attention to those who are walking just like the example you have in us" (3:17). Jesus is given as the pattern to follow in the first. In the second, Paul com-bines two appeals, one to imitate him and the other to imitate others. How might the Philippians know if someone is a good example to follow? Paul tells them to follow those whose lifestyles—and we can add "shared way of think-ing"—match the pattern they have in "us," referring, we should assume, to those examples described within the discourse (Jesus, Paul, Timothy, and Epaphrodi-tus). Since we have already taken a look at the appeal in 2:5–8, we should turn the remainder of attention to the remaining direct appeals to imitation and some of the indirect appeals found throughout the letter.

Appeals to imitation are one mark of paraenetic discourse. Paul uses them like no other New Testament figure. In his letter to the Galatian communities,

---

[15] See Cynthia Westfall, "Οὖν in the New Testament: The Minimal Semantic Contribution of a Discourse Marker," in *The Language and Literature of the New Testament: Essays in Honor of Stanley E. Porter's 60th Birthday*, ed. Lois K. Fuller Dow et al., BIS 150 (Brill, 2016), 284–302.

[16] David Alan Black, "The Discourse Structure of Philippians: A Study in Textlinguistics," *NovT* 37, no. 1 (1995): 16–49.

Paul included just one direct appeal to imitation (Gal 4:12), and its syntax has been the subject of unending discussion. First Corinthians contains two direct appeals to imitation, in which Paul encourages those believers to follow his example (Figure 11.5):

4:16–17	"Therefore, I exhort you: Be imitators of me. For this reason I have sent Timothy, who is my beloved and faithful child in the Lord, and he will remind you of my ways which are in Christ, just as I teach everywhere in every community."
11:1–2	"Be imitators of me, just as I am an imitator of Christ. Now I praise you because you remember me in everything and hold firmly to the traditions, just as I delivered them to you."

Figure 11.5: Direct Appeals to Imitation in 1 Corinthians

But even in these appeals the connection to the example of Jesus and those of Paul's closest co-laborers is evident. The appeal, though, is specifically to Paul's own example, not to the group which we see in the Thessalonian letters (1 Thess 1:6; 2 Thess 3:7, 9). Not only did Paul remind Timothy to follow his example (2 Tim 3:10–11), he also told Timothy that he should present himself as an example to believers (1 Tim 4:12). There are no direct appeals to imitation in Paul's letter to the community in Colossae, arguably because he never visited that community (Col 2:1) and they had not had the opportunity to personally see the way that he and his team lived. The same occurs in Hebrews, and even though many of them would have known who Paul was, he chose to not use his own example because he had not served among them. Instead, he points them to the example of their own leaders (13:17) and others who "are inheriting the promises" (6:12). Appeals to imitation, direct and indirect (or explicit and implicit as I [Thomas] refer to them elsewhere), are integral to Paul's letters. So, how does he use them in his letter to the Philippians?

Imitation appeals are woven throughout Philippians, being found in every rhetorical division except the letter closing. Remember that audiences, including the Philippians, could potentially read over implicit appeals without recognizing them as such. The author embeds them within the discourse to reinforce his theme or purpose. Paul introduces his letter to the Philippians with Παῦλος καὶ Τιμόθεος δοῦλοι Χριστοῦ Ἰησοῦ ("Paul and Timothy, slaves of Christ Jesus"). Paul includes the names of members of his team in half of his letters, but his choice here is no accident. Maybe the Philippians could sense what was coming in the letter, but maybe not. Still, Paul is including information here that is an appeal, albeit an indirect one. When he tells the Philippians to follow his example and those who follow the group's example, there is no question that the Philippians would recall the way Paul chose to open his letter: Jesus took on the form of a slave (2:7), Paul and Timothy identify themselves as slaves, therefore everyone in their community should practice identifying as slaves. To consider oneself as a slave is to position oneself in such a way that the needs and interests of everyone else become by default more important than one's own. The letter introduction is just one example of an implicit appeal.

So, keeping the mainline material front and center in our analysis, we can survey the letter and identify just some of the appeals to imitation, paying attention to where they occur in the logical flow of the letter and taking note of how they contribute to the audience's understanding of the mainline (Figure 11.6):

Letter Opening (1:1–2)
> Paul pairs his name with Timothy and identifies them as "slaves of Christ" (1:1). Paul does this to illustrate the same way of thinking that Jesus exhibited (2:5, 7), a necessary component to being united together in striving to see people believe the gospel (1:27).

Letter Body (1:3–4:20)
> **Body Opening** (1:3–11)
> > Paul demonstrates how he cares for the Philippian believers: He prays for them all in all his prayers (1:4); he says they are in his heart (1:7) and that he longs for them all (1:8); he places them all on his level (i.e., he does not present himself as being over them or better/more important than them) when he says they are all "partakers of grace" (1:7); this is similar to Jesus' being made in the likeness of men (2:7).
>
> **Body Proper** (1:12–4:9)
> > *Body Head* (1:12–2:30)
> > > *Subsection 1* (1:12–26)
> > > > Paul presents the first negative example in this section of the letter, contrasting his example that has resulted in what he will call "the faith of the gospel" (1:27) with those who "preach Christ out of envy and strife" (1:15). The only way worth living (1:27) only happens when envy, strife, and selfish ambition are absent. By Paul mentioning it here, the community will hopefully realize that those in whom envy and strife are present have more in common with false teachers than the pattern of Jesus.
> > > >
> > > > Paul draws attention to his own way of thinking in 1:21 ("for to me . . .") and explains a difficult decision in his life: to be with Christ is obviously better than anything else. But Paul puts the needs and interests of the Philippians above his own, saying it is "more necessary for your sake" (1:24; cf. 2:3).

Subsection 2 (1:27–2:18)

   Subunit A (1:27–30)

      This comes right after Paul has explained how he is putting the needs of the Philippians above what he says is "much better" for him. If he puts their needs above his own, hopefully that will serve as leverage in persuading the community to live the only way worth living.

   Subunit B (2:1–11)

      Part a (2:1–4)

         See previous discussion.

      Part b (2:5–11)

         Direct Appeal: Paul tells the Philippians to share the same way of thinking that Jesus exhibited by taking on human flesh and dying on the cross.

   Subunit C (2:12–18)

      Paul tells them to prove themselves by living blameless and innocent lives; the exhortation is similar to 1 Tim 4:12, but instead of showing themselves to be examples, they show themselves to be "lights in the world" (2:15). To Christians, examples; to the world, lights. This parallels the focus on "striving together for the faith of the gospel" (1:27).

      Direct Appeal: Paul concludes the subunit with an explicit appeal to imitation, telling them to "rejoice in the same way and share your joy with me" (2:18). The manner of rejoicing (τὸ αὐτό) to which he refers is found in v. 17.

Subsection 3 (2:19–30)

   Two examples are given in this section: Timothy (2:19–23) and Epaphroditus (2:25–30). Again, these are implicit appeals to imitation. Paul does not say "imitate Timothy." But he does illustrate much about the mainline through the examples. Timothy is called a "kindred spirit" (ἰσόψυχον), pulling from lexemes found in the first and second requests. Timothy is concerned for the interests of the Philippians as much as Paul. And Timothy is contrasted with everyone else (an embellishment) who are just concerned about their own interests. And he is committed to the "furtherance of the gospel," a reminder of the mainline "striving together for the faith of the gospel."

   Epaphroditus' example highlights the unity Paul wants to see in the community and especially the two women mentioned in 4:2. He is called "brother," "co-laborer," and "fellow soldier" (2:25). And he is more concerned about the Philippians than he is concerned about staying with Paul. He was committed to partnership in the gospel so much that he risked his life, knowing the work he was participating in was all about seeing people believe the gospel. In coming close to death, he exhibited the same way of thinking that Jesus had who went beyond the point of death, experiencing death on a cross. Within the Epaphroditus example, Paul gives another implicit appeal via his own example: when God has mercy on one member of the community, he has mercy on all the members of the community, just like Paul experienced God's mercy by restoring Epaphroditus' health. Even the way Paul describes Epaphroditus' mission to Rome reflects the mainline—he nearly died serving the Philippians by acting as their ambassador.

Direct Appeal: The expression "hold in high regard" (ἐντίμους ἔχετε) in 2:29 refers to how the Philippians should respect and imitate Epaphroditus' example, not how they should shower him with gifts or treat him better than they treat other people in the Philippian community. He does not deserve more honor than other believers, but his example deserves greater attention and should be elevated as worthy of emulation. Again, a direct appeal to imitation concludes the section.

Body Subpart (3:1–4:9)

Subsection 1–4 (3:1–16)

Direct Appeal: Paul spends a significant amount of time contrasting his way of thinking with the lifestyles of those he calls "dogs, evil workers, and false circumcision" (3:2), all terms for false teachers. This section anticipates the contrast with those who do not walk according to the pattern of Paul and his colaborers that follows the second and last direct appeal to imitation. He describes the mindset of someone who truly believes he or she is a slave of Jesus: not boasting in their human privileges or accomplishments and not striving to attain more; instead considering them on par with street refuse and boasting only in the privilege to know Christ. And he tells them to have this same way of thinking (3:15), echoing again the first three requests. "The same way of thinking" refers specifically to his example in 3:4–14. The direct appeal to imitation concludes these three sections.[17]

Subsection 5 (3:17–21)

Direct Appeal: Paul tells the Philippians to join together in following his example. He links them together with the συν- prefix,

---

[17] The contents of v. 16 could be another direct appeal to imitation, but the syntax is not as straightforward, so the analyst should mark it and go back for a closer look later.

and he links his example and the other three positive ones provided in the letter to those in their own community who are living the way that is required by the gospel. The appeal pulls together all of the examples found within the letter: (1) Jesus, (2) Timothy, (3) Epaphroditus, (4) Paul, (5) those walking according to the pattern found in 1–4, and (6) those whose lifestyle marks them as an enemy of the cross.

The last sentence of the paragraph begins with γάρ and the reminder that the Philippian believers' citizenship is in heaven (see 1:27 and the request πολιτεύεσθε). The eschatological portion of that sentence contrasts humility with glory, reflecting the example set forth by Jesus who humbled himself and was eventually super exalted by God the Father.

Subsection 6 (4:1–9)

Subunits A (4:1)

Direct Appeal: The Philippians are told to "stand firm in the Lord" (see 1:27, where Paul identifies this as the single report he wants to receive about them) and Paul links himself to them with the strongest language possible: "my beloved brothers and sisters, my joy, my crown, my beloved [brothers and sisters]." The use of οὕτως signals this is an appeal to imitation.

Subunit B (4:2–3)

Paul addresses a significant issue of disunity between two women. Their conflict had apparently been the source of distracting the rest of the community from living for the faith of the gospel. He reminds them how they used to be living for it, using the same language (ἐν τῷ εὐαγγελίῳ συνήθλησάν) found in 1:27–28. There is a significant amount of group talk in these two verses. Paul enlists the help of two individuals, making them co-laborers in bringing peace to the situation, and then a larger group he identifies as "the rest of my co-laborers." The implication is these two women are not considered co-laborers so long as they are engaged in this dispute and not living for the faith of the gospel.

Subunit C (4:4–7)

The request in v. 5 is broad enough to include being an example within the believing community and at the same time lights in the world (similar to 2:15).

Subunit D (4:8–9)

Direct Appeal: Paul tells the Philippians to join together in following his example one more time. This time he uses

four verbs to describe how an example is given: learn, receive, hear, and see. These two verses are similar to the
third request: Both have a conditional sentence, although
the order is reversed (in this one the apodosis appears first)
and the content is distinct (in this one the protasis mentions excellence and praiseworthiness). Even though Paul
does not include his other examples in this appeal (e.g., it
does not say "in us" but "in me"), he does link the appeal to
God's presence in their lives.

Body Closing (4:10–20)

Paul provides his own way of thinking as an example to the Philippians in this
section, this time with respect to their gift and how Paul has learned contentment in times of have and times of have not. The "striving together" element is
present, for example, in 4:13. Paul chooses not to go at it alone, but relies on
God to give him strength as he pursues the mission of seeing people believe
the gospel. Collaboration is also tied to the gift that the Philippians sent by
way of Epaphroditus. This church out of all the other churches (4:15–16) is to
Paul what Timothy is among all his co-laborers (2:20–21).

Letter Closing (4:21–23)

The letter ends with a reminder of unity. Everyone is greeting one another. By
mentioning those of Caesar's household Paul is able to close the letter with a
reminder, subtle as it is, to the only way worth living: "striving together for the
faith of the gospel." Paul had mentioned how he was committed to this mission even while imprisoned, and the result was that he could see members of
the praetorian guard believe the gospel (1:13). Technically, he had not told
them that they had believed, just that everyone, including them, had heard.
When he closes the letter here, he calls them "saints."

Figure 11.6: Appeals to Imitation in the Mainline of Philippians

This content analysis easily demonstrates the cohesion within the letter's different units. Even the shift in tone that begins in 3:1 (unit 5) is not so much a
problem once its contents are considered through the lens of the mainline material.
Paul understands that there are threats from within the community as much as
there are threats from beyond. We can see that in 1:27–30, for example, with the
mention of opponents and suffering. The shift in tone in 3:1 is attributed more to
Paul's disdain for those he considers "enemies of the cross," not so much because
of how he feels about the Philippians. He had already witnessed the influence of
false teachers on the other side of the Bosporus.

Conclusion

What we have provided above is just one example of how you can move through a letter discourse and flesh out the mainline material in the various sections of the letter. Identifying the parts of the letter first, by paying special attention to discourse markers, helps see the progression of the author's argument. In the case of Paul's letter to the Philippian believers, the mainline request shows up in every section of the letter. His appeals to imitation, explicit and implicit, never lose sight of the first direct request in the letter, where we find the first occurrence of the imperative. That request via the use of μόνον was set apart as the single most important request in the letter. It is the only way to live or, you could say, the only thing that matters. Keep in mind that this is just a model. The letters of the New Testament are distinct in style and content, but hopefully this model will be of some benefit as we work through them.

The principle of identifying mainline material, specifically the requests an author makes in material that is corrective in nature, should bear the same fruit in the rest of Paul's letters and those of Peter, James, Jude, and John. Begin with the discourse type. Why? Because different discourses have different types of characteristics, especially markers of mainline material. Mark and analyze any obvious mainline material within the discourse. Then proceed to the structure of the discourse. You can start from the top and identify the larger units before you take a look at sentences and clauses and phrases. Or you can go through and identify all of the finite verbs and the sentences to which they belong, and then you can group them all together into discourse units based on the discourse markers utilized by the author. From there you can analyze the smaller units of discourse—groups of paragraphs, individual ones, clauses and phrases—or you can focus your attention on the relationship of the larger sections. We would recommend taking a look at some of the more technical approaches within this volume on discourse analysis and putting into practice some of their principles within the framework of this methodology. Be eclectic. Mix and match. But make sure you can explain what it is you want to research. Then build a methodology that will help you answer the specific questions you have about the discourse.

12

COLOSSIANS

TODD A. SCACEWATER

Colossians was written by the apostle Paul during an imprisonment (1:1; 4:18), most obviously the same imprisonment during which he wrote Ephesians, since the linguistic parallels between the two epistles are so numerous. But the parallels are not exact, and often the same language is used in different ways, so that either the same author used similar ideas in a fairly free variance in the two letters, or a later author tried to imitate the style and ideas of Colossians.[1] Some do reject Paul's authorship of Colossians, but they are far fewer than those who object to Paul's authorship of Ephesians. It is safe enough to assume for this DA that Paul wrote it from his Roman imprisonment around AD 60–62, probably within days or weeks of writing Ephesians, either before or after.

The occasion for the writing has seemed clear to most, namely, that he is addressing "the Colossian heresy" as it is often called. Research on Colossians has centered on the nature of this teaching (or "philosophy," Col 2:8), with J. B. Lightfoot generally taken as the starting point. He supposed the teaching was a mixture of Essene Judaism and a form of Gnosticism.[2] Since Lightfoot, other theories have been that the teaching was a form of Hellenistic mystery cult, Jewish syncretism with paganism or philosophy (either Middle Platonism or cynicism),

---

[1] Most critical commentary introductions cover the parallels and discuss the implications, to which I refer to the reader for the evidence.

[2] J. B. Lightfoot, "The Colossian Heresy," in *Conflict at Colossae: A Problem in the Interpretation of Early Christianity*, ed. F. O. Francis and W. A. Meeks (SBL and Scholars Press, 1975), 13–59.

Jewish-Christian mystical asceticism, or some other combination of religious, cultural, and philosophical teaching.[3] A DA of Colossians need not solve this problem, as it will be more concerned with how Paul goes about addressing this issue in the epistle as a whole. I will present my own view, but whether I am correct has little to no effect on the macrostructure of the epistle. More significantly, I will argue tentatively that the Colossian philosophy was a major reason for sending the letter, but not the ultimate reason. Paul may have a communicative purpose that relates more to his own situation than to theirs.

Methodology

My methodology in this essay will be the same as in my Ephesians chapter, to which I refer the reader. The main difference between Ephesians and Colossians is that we have much more pragmatic information, because we know that Paul was writing about a specific teaching in Colossae, to exhort them to continue in the faith they originally received (Col 2:6–7). This knowledge allows us to presume at least one high-level speech act, that of persuading his audience to reject the false teaching and persevere in the true teaching. Of special interest in a DA of Colossians, then, is to examine how each unit contributes as micro speech acts toward the larger communicative purpose. While I will formally determine semantic macrostructures for each unit, I will more informally discuss the pragmatic function of the higher-level units.

Macrostructure

In contrast to Ephesians, which divides rather neatly into chs. 1–3 and 4–6, Colossians may be split into four tightly linked divisions. Excluding the standard introduction and closing (1:1–2; 4:18), the letter body includes preparatory and grounding discourse (1:3–2:3), a polemic against the Colossian philosophy (2:4–3:4), hortatory material on how to live instead (3:5–4:1), and closing instructions to further his communicative purpose (4:2–4:17). Of note for this proposed structure is the transitional role of 2:4–5; 3:1–4; and 4:2–6, on which basis I say the parts are tightly linked. Paul also uses a number of "discourse pivots," which are clauses that conclude a unit but contain at least one idea that persists into the

---

[3] Just a few of the recent influential monographs on the issue, many of which provide excellent histories of the debate, include Adam Copenhaver, *Reconstructing the Historical Background of Paul's Rhetoric in the Letter to the Colossians*, LNTS 585 (T&T Clark, 2018); Ian K. Smith, *Heavenly Perspective: A Study of the Apostle Paul's Response to a Jewish Mystical Movement at Colossae*, LNTS 326 (T&T Clark, 2006); Clinton E. Arnold, *The Colossian Syncretism: The Interface between Christianity and Folk Belief at Colossae*, WUNT II/77 (Mohr Siebeck, 1995).

next unit.[4] The result is a unified, cohesive document that transitions smoothly from one topic to the next, and from one division to the next.

Divisions 2–3 function together to provide the prohibitions and commands (i.e., Paul's negative and positive concerns). Pragmatically, these divisions are more prominent than Division 1 (1:3–2:5) because they are more central to his communicative purpose. Semantically, they are more prominent because, although Division 2 opens with asyndeton, it is clear that Divisions 2–3 are grounded by the discourse in Division 1. Division 4, which has two units (4:2–6, 7–17) differs in the semantic and pragmatic macrostructure of the letter. Semantically, it contains final commands and greetings that are common components of the ending of Paul's epistles, and therefore may be classed as a conclusion, which is less prominent than the letter body. From the pragmatic perspective, though, Division 4 may be more integral to Paul's communicative purpose than has been realized. For many reasons argued below, Paul may be enlisting further support for his own ministry, much as in Romans. If so, then his polemic against the philosophy and exhortations for appropriate Christian living are auxiliary speech acts that prepare for his primary speech act of subtle persuasion toward ministry cooperation in 4:7–17. Paul writes to ensure that the Colossians stay true to Christ as they received him (2:6) so that they will remain healthy in their faith, both in theology and praxis, so that even though they have not met Paul, they may participate fruitfully in his ministry.

The semantic macrostructure of Colossians may be constructed by combining the lower-level macrostructures of each unit into higher levels in a hierarchical fashion, using macro-rules to reduce the information, and using coherence relations to relate the units and divisions. The following macrostructures are based on a detailed exegesis of Colossians, but exegetical conclusions vary, and so my proposals may (and certainly could) be refined or improved.

Division 1 (1:3–2:3)

1:3–8	"We thank God for your faith, hope, and love, which we heard about through Epaphras, and which are increasing in you and in all the world."
1:9–12	"We keep praying that you would be filled with knowledge about God, in order that you might live as a believer should, giving thanks to the Father."
1:13–20	"The Father redeemed us and reconciled all things through Christ, who is preeminent over the first and the new creation, because all things were created through him and because God's fullness dwells in him."

---

[4] Richard Watson Todd, *Discourse Topics*, P&BNS 269 (John Benjamins, 2016), 72.

1:21–23   "You were reconciled to God through Christ's sacrifice despite your hostility toward him, in order he might present you blameless before himself if you remain faithful to the gospel, of which I am a minister."

1:24–29   "I rejoice to struggle for your sake and the church's, as God's servant, to fully preach the gospel in order to present every person mature in Christ."

2:1–3   "I want you to know about my struggles for your sake in order that your hearts might be encouraged so that you are united in love and toward the knowledge of Christ."

Of these six units, the first four group together, as do the next two. Within the first four units, the prayer (1:9–12) is most semantically prominent because 1:3–8 is its basis and all of 1:13–23 is an elaboration on the concept of "Father" in v. 12, with 1:21–23 being a specific application to the audience of soteriological terms in 1:13–20. Among the last two units, 1:24–29 is more prominent, since 2:1–3 is provided as an explanation (γάρ) of why he wrote what he did in 1:24–29. 1:24–2:3 is connected to the preceding four units by a tail-head linkage. The phrase οὗ ἐγενόμην ἐγὼ Παῦλος διάκονος (1:23) allows Paul to pivot from the gospel to his own preaching of the gospel and, by implication, his own suffering on *their* behalf through his apostolic ministry of preaching (1:24).

Although the 1:3–23 and 1:24–2:3 are linked, there is no explicit discourse marker, and it is difficult to see how the topics of 1:3–23 and 1:24–2:3 relate. It may be that Paul wanted to ensure that he addressed both issues of Christ's supremacy and his own apostolic ministry on their behalf, in order to lay the groundwork for his two main concerns in writing the epistle (on which, see below, "The Semantic Versus the Pragmatic Macrostructure"). The two groups of units therefore stand in series, with neither being more prominent as both are essential to his communicative purposes.[5]

The hierarchy of the units for Division 2 may be expressed as:

$$(1{:}3{-}8 \therefore (1{:}9{-}12 \rightarrow (1{:}13{-}20 \rightarrow 1{:}21{-}23))) + (\mathbf{1{:}24{-}29}\ /\ 2{:}1{-}3)^6$$

The resulting macrostructure of Division 1 is "We keep praying that you would live as a believer should, giving thanks to the Father who saved you through

---

[5] John Callow relates them in the same way, but does not connect the two points to Paul's communicative purposes (*A Semantic and Structural Analysis of Colossians*, 2nd ed. [SIL International, 2002], 35).

[6] Key: → indicates elaboration or specification, which is semantically less prominent. Bold indicates prominence. / indicates "explained by."

Christ by the gospel, of which I am a minister. And I rejoice in my ministerial sufferings for your sake and the church's, which I hope will encourage you."

Division 2

2:4–5 "What I am about to say, I say in order that you will not be deceived by sophistry, and I hope it will be effective even though only through letter."

2:6–7 "Continue in the faith that you were originally taught."

2:8–15 "Be careful that no one captivates you with their false teaching, because Christ embodies God's full presence, as do you because you are united to and made alive with Christ."

2:16–17 "Do not let anyone judge you regarding earthly rituals, because they are supposed to point us to Christ."

2:18–19 "Do not let those who delight in mystic visions of heavenly worship disqualify you from the faith, because they have abandoned Christ."

2:20–23 "It is senseless to belong to the body of Christ and yet submit to regulations associated with spiritual powers whom Christ has defeated."

3:1–4 "Desire heavenly things, not earthly things, because you died with Christ and your future resurrection is secure in him."

The polemic (Division 2) opens with a hedging introduction that prepares his audience for a shift from (1) praise of their faith and discussions of his apostolic sufferings for them to (2) chastisement for their possible acceptance of a deceptive religious philosophy. The introduction is less prominent than the body of the polemic. The polemic begins with positive commands (2:6–7), continues with three prohibitive units (2:8–15, 16–17, 18–19) and a grounding unit (2:20–23), and closes with a hinge that sums up the polemic with a positive and negative command (3:1–4). These units are connected by asyndeton or by οὖν (which occurs only in 2:16 and 3:1, both after lengthy preceding units that need the οὖν to signal a return to the hortatory mainline). Since 3:1–4 sums up the polemic and is connected by οὖν, it draws on the preceding unit and is therefore more semantically prominent. The two-fold command to think on heavenly things and not earthly things is also more general than the specific preceding directives, which is also a sign of its semantic prominence. Pragmatically, though, the concern is clearly laid out in 2:8 that they not be taken captive by philosophy and empty deceit, and the entire polemic is intended to promote this concern, so 2:8–15 is the most prominent directive speech act of Division 2. Said otherwise, every unit of the polemic functions to enhance the effectiveness of the directive in 2:8.

The hierarchy of the Division may be expressed as follows:

$$|| \ 2{:}4{-}5 \ || \ ((2{:}6{-}7 + 2{:}8{-}15 + 2{:}16{-}17 + 2{:}18{-}19) \ / \ 2{:}20{-}23) \ \therefore \ \mathbf{3{:}1{-}4}^{7}$$

The resulting semantic macrostructure is "Continue in the faith you originally received and reject any deceptive teaching regarding earthly rituals and mystic visions, because you belong to Christ, who has defeated the spiritual powers associated with such regulations. So, desire heavenly things, not such earthly things."

Division 3

3:5–11   "Renounce sinfulness because you are part of the new creation, where Christ is what matters most."

3:12–17   "Live according to your new nature, especially showing love, peace, and thankfulness."

3:18–4:1 "Fulfill your relational obligations at home in the Lord."

Division 3 contains three units of positive directives. The first two units elaborate on the positive and negative commands in 3:1–4, "desire heavenly things" and "not earthly things." The third unit opens with asyndeton and, like the household code in Ephesians, seems to be a specific example of carrying out 3:5–17. The Division can be represented as follows:

$$(3{:}5{-}11 + 3{:}12{-}17) \ \rightarrow \ 3{:}18{-}4{:}1^{8}$$

The resulting macrostructure is "Renounce sinfulness and live according to your new nature as part of the new creation. And do so specifically in the home."

Division 4

4:2–6   "Pray for our ministry, and act wisely and graciously as your rejection of false teaching leads to disputes."

4:7–17   "I and my co-workers send greetings to you and to the church in Laodicea, with whom you should exchange letters."

Division 4 divides into two units, the first a sort of pseudo-*peroratio* (as argued below) and the second a smattering of final greetings and interpersonal

---

[7] Key: || # || indicates hedging. + indicates a continuation of the hortatory mainline. / indicates "grounded by." ∴ indicates the inferential and summary nature of 3:1–4.

[8] Bold indicates prominence. → indicates specification.

commands that do not relate to the Colossian situation. Since both units have a concluding function, they stand together in Division 4, but the former is more semantically prominent since it closes the body, while 4:7–17 closes the entire epistle as a formulaic epistolary unit. The macrostructure of Division 4 may be "Pray for our ministry, act wisely and graciously as you reject false teaching, and greet the brothers for us, including those of Laodicea, with whom you should exchange letters."

The Semantic Versus the Pragmatic Macrostructure

Semantically, the most prominent unit of the epistle is 3:1–4. It is the most general exhortation of the polemic, it is inferentially drawn from all of the preceding polemic, and it is the basis for the elaborative commands that follow in Division 3. As part of the hortatory portion of the epistle, it is automatically more prominent than the grounding discourse in 1:3–2:3. Since Division 4 has a summary and a closing function, it should not be more prominent than the concerns of the body. Thus, everything flows toward and then out of 3:1–4. The general concern to think about things of heaven, where Christ is, rather than earthly things summarizes well the concern of the letter, aimed at a teaching that emphasized earthly regulations promoted by malevolent heavenly beings who have already been defeated by Christ. The macrostructures of the Divisions should be combined as follows:

(Division 1 \ (**Division 2 → Division 3**)) » Division 4[9]

We may propose the following semantic macrostructure for Colossians: "We want you to live worthily as people saved by the Father through his preeminent Son according to the gospel, of which I am a minister suffering for you. Therefore, desire heavenly things where Christ is, not earthly regulations promoted by the defeated spiritual powers. Do so by renouncing your old nature and living according to your newly created nature, even in the home. Finally, pray for us, be wise and gracious, and greet the brothers for us."

The pragmatic structure differs in that different units are more important for his communicative purpose. The main difference is that (so I will argue) Division 4 is the most pragmatically prominent, even if Paul's purpose there is veiled by his rhetoric. When I discuss 4:7–17 in detail later, I will argue that addressing the Colossian heresy is a subsidiary concern for Paul. His ultimate goal in writing the letter may be to recruit more partners (at Colossae and Laodicea) to support his

---

[9] Key: \ indicates "is the grounds for." Bold indicates prominence. → indicates "is elaborated by." » indicates conclusion.

Gentile mission, much as he did with Romans. He needs more Asian churches to support his ministry, both there and abroad, but he needs *healthy* churches that have not succumbed to false teaching. Support for this view includes the way he tries to establish rapport with the Colossians in 1:3–2:3, his sly rhetoric in 4:7–17, and what we know about Paul and his need for church support of his mission.

Division 1 is still grounding discourse, and is therefore the least prominent, but we may now see how Division 1's two topics in series lay the groundwork for Paul's ultimate and penultimate communicative purposes (in Division 4 and 2, respectively). Section 1:3–23 (especially in 1:13–20) provides the most pointed motivation for the audience to reject the Colossian philosophy and stay true to Christ (his penultimate purpose). Section 1:24–2:3 (especially 1:24–29) prepares the audience for what I am proposing to be his ultimate communicative purpose, recruiting the Colossians and Laodiceans as ministry partners. His discussion of his apostolic ministry on their behalf is supposed to prepare for his subtle recruitment of them by encouraging them (2:2), by establishing rapport via his sufferings for them, and by implicitly connecting Colossae to the universal church, which contains Paul's other partner churches.

Division 2 serves his penultimate communicative purpose of dissuading them from accepting the Colossian teaching. While 3:1–4 is the most semantically prominent unit of Division 2, the more specific units of the polemic are more central to his communicative purpose. That is, if they obey the commands in 3:1–4, they will obey anything entailed by it, and it is these specific concerns of 2:6–19 that lead Paul to pen 3:1–4.[10] In other words, what he *really* wants is for them to reject the false teaching. So pragmatically, 2:6–19 as a series of four commands are the most prominent in Division 2.

Division 3 as a hortatory division is more prominent than Division 1, but less prominent than Division 2, since it could be omitted and Paul's main concern would still be addressed. Divisions 2–3 should be most closely grouped together since they contain the hortatory mainline.

If my view of what Paul is trying to do with his discourse is correct, then we might summarize the pragmatic macrostructure of Colossians by saying that Paul writes to the Colossians to exalt Christ as preeminent over the spiritual powers and to relate his apostolic struggles on their behalf, so that he can convince them to reject the false teaching and continue in the faith as they received it, so that ultimately he might recruit further partner churches to support his

---

[10] I argued for the same relationship between the hortatory units in Ephesians, where Eph 4:1–3 is the most pragmatically prominent because it is the most specific and relates to the prominent concern of unity in the epistle, while 5:1–21 contains the most general commands and are therefore more semantically prominent. If they obey the commands in 5:1–21 to be loving and wise, it is entailed that they will obey the call to unity in 4:1–3,

ministry. Such a view does not nullify the discussions about the centrality of the Colossian philosophy for Paul's communicative purpose, but it does claim a more ultimate purpose in writing that connects the letter more concretely to Paul's own mission. This view might better explain why he writes to a church he does not know, and might also possibly explain why he sends Ephesians as (purportedly) a circular letter to the Asian churches when it contains similar content to Colossians: it was a further part of his recruiting effort.[11]

Microstructures

The proposed macrostructure must now be supported by an examination of the microstructures.

Colossians 1:3–8

The first unit is a typical thanksgiving from Paul for his recipients (1:3–8). It is marked as a unit both by the fact that it constitutes one sentence (though note the semi-colon at the end of v. 6 in NA[28]) and by the διὰ τοῦτο that begins a new unit in 1:9. This pattern of thanksgiving/blessing transitioned to prayer διὰ τοῦτο is paralleled in Ephesians 1:3–14, 15–23 (cf. Phil 1:3–8, 9–11 transitioned by καὶ τοῦτο).

Paul gives thanks to God whenever he prays for the Colossians, because he has heard through Epaphras of their faith in Christ and their love toward all the saints, which they have because of the hope laid up for them in heaven. They heard about this hope in the gospel message, which Epaphras preached to them initially, and which is also "bearing fruit and growing" in "all the world" (1:6). Although Paul writes about hope as a causal basis for their love (διὰ τὴν ἐλπίδα), it is fair to see the trio of faith, hope, and love as semantically grounding his thanksgiving. The mention of "the gospel" leads to increasing subordination of clauses, so that the core thoughts of this unit are at the beginning.

Colossians 1:9–12

The structure of 1:9–12 is fairly simple without too many levels of subordination. It begins in v. 9 with διὰ τοῦτο, which transitions from the thanksgiving

---

[11] I admit this final claim about Ephesians lacks any evidence within Ephesians and is only a suggestion. But it would make sense of the general nature of Ephesians, which suggests no specific reason for sending the letter. Supposing that he wanted to promote health within the Asian churches, especially between Jews and Gentiles, coheres with my proposal here that he is trying to promote church health among prospective partner churches.

to Paul's intercession for the Colossians. It is because of "this," i.e., the faith, hope, and love that he has heard about from Epaphras, that he says he never ceases praying for them. The content of his prayer is that they would be filled with the knowledge of God's will. This core of the prayer is then modified by six clauses. The means (ἐν) of being filled is "all wisdom and spiritual insight." The purpose of being filled is "to walk worthily of the Lord to fully please him."

There are then four participial clauses that modify either πληρωθῆτε or περιπατῆσαι. If the former, then they express the result of being filled, and they would be the most prominent ideas of the unit. If the latter, they express the means by which they walk worthily, in which case the περιπατῆσαι purpose clause is the most prominent. The latter is preferable for several reasons. First, the first two participles are coherent as results of being filled with the knowledge of God's will, but the third and fourth are less obviously so. Second, it might be strange to have the infinitive περιπατῆσαι intervening between πληρωθῆτε and four participial phrases modifying it. Third, all four function coherently as means of walking worthily, so this position is probably the best.[12] So Paul's ultimate purpose in praying for the Colossians is that they would walk worthily to fully please the Lord.

This prayer is made "because of" (διὰ τοῦτο, 1:9) the faith, hope, and love he heard about from Epaphras. That is, because he has heard they represent Christ in "all the world," he wants them to walk in a manner fully pleasing to the Lord and represent him well.[13] They can walk worthily by continuing to bear fruit and grow in the knowledge of God, by being strengthened with God's power, and by giving thanks to the Father (1:10–12). That the intercession builds directly on the thanksgiving is further evident from the linguistic correspondence between the two units:

---

[12] Some have argued that εὐχαριστοῦντες is equivalent to confessing or blessing, as in a Jewish *berekah*. They begin a new sentence and unit with either εὐχαριστοῦντες or with μετὰ χαρᾶς just before it (NA[27] does the latter). Eduard Lohse argues εὐχαριστοῦντες is "only loosely attached to the preceding verses" (*Colossians*, 32–33). George Cannon follows Lohse, especially since he believes 1:12–14 is preformed material, so he feels that he needs to detach εὐχαριστοῦντες from περιπατῆσαι (*The Use of Traditional Materials in Colossians* [Mercer University Press, 1983], 12–19). There is really no basis for seeing εὐχαριστοῦντες as only "loosely connected" to the preceding verses without also seeing the preceding participle δυναμούμενοι similarly. There is also insufficient evidence for establishing 1:12–14 as a preformed piece. The language does evoke OT themes (v. 13) and Christian confessional language (v. 14), as Andreas Lindemann observes (*Der Kolosserbrief*, ZB [Theologischer Verlag Zürich, 1983], 22). But Paul's letters are soaked with OT and Christian confessional language, so the case for 1:12–14 being preformed is weak and unverifiable. See further criticisms in Thomas J. Sappington, *Revelation and Redemption at Colossae*, JSNTSup 53 (JSOT Press, 1991), 193–197.

[13] Already, then, there is a hint of the coming polemic: succumbing to the false philosophy would not represent him well, nor would it please the Lord.

ἀκούσαντες (1:4)	ἠκούσαμεν (1:9)
ἀφ᾽ ἧς ἡμέρας (1:6)	ἀφ᾽ ἧς ἡμέρας (1:9)
ἐπέγνωτε (1:6)	ἐπίγνωσιν; ἐπιγνώσει (1:9, 10)
καρποφορούμενον	καρποφοροῦντες
καὶ αὐξανόμενον (1:6)	καὶ αὐξανόμενοι (1:10).[14]

Colossians 1:13–20

It is difficult to decide what to do with vv. 13–14. Grammatically, if we take relative pronouns to indicate the continuation of a sentence, then vv. 13–16 (through ἐξουσίαι) are all part of a long complex sentence beginning with Διὰ τοῦτο in v. 9.[15] If we read a single sentence from v. 9 to v. 16, then it would be its own unit. However, there are at least two reasons not to divide the text in this way. First, relative pronouns offer elaboration on a concept already activated in the discourse, so semantically they may signal the beginning of a new elaborative unit. Second, while the grammatical "sentence" of vv. 9–16 could be viewed as a unit, this would clearly create an awkward (and surely wrong) division of the text in the middle of the "Christ Hymn" of 1:15–20. The hymn has a balanced poetic structure, as we will see, and should not be divided.

If we will not divide by grammatical structure, then we should divide by semantic structure. A clear shift of topic and reference occurs between vv. 12–13.[16] Verses 9–12 contain the content of his prayer and refer to the actions of the recipients in the second plural (πληρωθῆτε). Verse 13 shifts to the first plural ("he rescued us") and focuses fully on the Father. The dative phrase describing God in v. 12 (τῷ πατρὶ τῷ ἱκανώσαντι ὑμᾶς εἰς τὴν μερίδα τοῦ κλήρου τῶν ἁγίων ἐν τῷ φωτί) wraps up the content of his prayer, but also creates a lead-in to further elaborate on "Father" in v. 13. Both the concept "Father" and the phrase "in the light" evoke the thoughts of v. 13, that the Father is "the one who rescued us from the domain of darkness and transferred us into the kingdom of the Son whom he loves." Once the Son is mentioned, he gets his own elaboration: "in whom we have redemption, the forgiveness of sins" (1:14). Supposing the hymn was preformed, whether planned or not, the mention of Christ's work evokes the hymn and Paul continues elaborating on Christ in poetic fashion. While the hymn focuses on Christ in vv. 15–18, and while he is still in view instrumentally in vv. 19–20, the agent of the actions in vv. 19–20

---

[14] Cannon, *Traditional Materials in Colossians*, 146. Cf. the relationship between Eph 1:3–14 and 15–23.

[15] Murray J. Harris is incorrect to take 1:9–14 as a unit based on his claim that it is one sentence (*Colossians and Philemon*, EGGNT [Eerdmans, 1991], 28). The ὅς and ὅτι beginning vv. 15 and 16 continue the sentence as further elaboration on ᾧ in v. 14.

[16] This switch is seen also by Callow, *Colossians*, 38

switches to the Father.[17] This switch-reference provides a chiastic structure based on participant reference, which further supports taking vv. 13–20 as a unit:

Father (v. 13)
    Son (vv. 14–18)
Father (vv. 19–20).

Additionally, vv. 13, 20 both have the Son as the intermediate agent and use the aorist tense-form, adding to the chiastic effect.[18]

Verses 13–20 are therefore a unit, which from a semantic perspective elaborates on the concept of "Father" mentioned in v. 12, and the Son through whom he acts. The elaborations function to motivate them to give thanks (because of who he is and what he has done *through his Son*), and as a result to walk worthily and fulfill his prayer for them. The elaborations are also important for the pragmatic structure, in which this theology, Christology, and soteriology lay motivational grounds for his polemic in Division 2. In particular, his emphasis on Christ's preeminence over the spiritual powers provides powerful undergirding for his later association of the Colossians with the victorious Christ, and their necessary dissociation from the defeated spiritual powers (2:15, 20; 3:1 especially).

Studies on this hymn are endless, so I will restrict my analysis of the contents to three relevant observations. First, the significance of this hymn for Paul's polemic (and thus for Colossians' pragmatic macrostructure) is notable. M. Gordley found up to nineteen lexical links and six possible thematic links between the hymn and the rest of the Colossians.[19] Second, assuming the theological content of the hymn was either known by or agreeable to the Colossians, it also serves to build his rapport with an audience he had not met in person (2:1). Third, however one divides the hymn, the two instances of "creation" should be taken to refer to the old creation (1:15) and the new creation (1:18), which sets up for the later hortatory distinction between heavenly things and earthly things (3:1–4), which correlate respectively to life in the old creation (3:5–11) and the new creation (3:12–17).[20]

---

[17] Technically, the agent of dwelling in v. 19 is "all the fullness" (πᾶν τὸ πλήρωμα), but the parallel expression in 2:9, ἐν αὐτῷ κατοικεῖ πᾶν τὸ πλήρωμα τῆς θεότητος σωματικῶς ("in him dwells all the fullness of deity bodily) shows that "fullness" in 1:19 is a metonym for the Father. The semantic field of πληρ- is pervasive throughout Colossians (1:9, 19, 25, 2:9, 10 4:17), typically related to God's filling Christ or believers, or dwelling in them.

[18] Callow, *Colossians*, 39.

[19] Matthew E. Gordley, *The Colossian Hymn in Context: An Exegesis in Light of Jewish and Greco-Roman Hymnic and Epistolary Conventions*, WUNT/II 228 (Mohr Siebeck, 2007), 264–267.

[20] Col 1:18 refers to the new creation because (1) ὅς ἐστιν ἀρχή is elaborated by πρωτότοκος ἐκ τῶν νεκρῶν; (2) for Paul, the resurrection is God's first act of new creation (2 Cor 5:17). See also N. T. Wright, *Colossians*, TNTC (IVP, 1986), 74.

Colossians 1:21–23

The next unit (1:21–23) is marked by a break from the hymnic structure of 1:15–20 and by a fronted ὑμᾶς to signal a switch of focus to the recipients. It seems that the mention of reconciliation at the end of the hymn (v. 20) leaves something to be desired for Paul. That God reconciled (ἀποκαταλλάσσω) "all things" (1:20) is a bit general and ambiguous, and that this reconciliation happened διὰ τοῦ αἵματος τοῦ σταυροῦ αὐτοῦ is intelligible enough but still makes a strange image (a cross bleeding). So in vv. 21–22, he begins with καί to signal an additional point that his recipients, specifically, have been reconciled (ἀποκαταλλάσσω), even while they were estranged. This happened ἐν τῷ σώματι τῆς σαρκὸς αὐτοῦ διὰ τοῦ θανάτου ("by his fleshly body through his death," 1:22), a more concrete image than in 1:20. This reconciliation happened in order to present the Colossians "holy and without blemish and blameless before him," which can only happen "if indeed" they remain established and firm in the faith and not shifting from the hope of the gospel which they heard, "which was preached in all creation under heaven, of which I, Paul, became a servant" (1:23).

This condition (εἴ γε) gives the first hint that there might be a potential or actual problem among the recipients. But he quickly tempers the possibility by referring to the hope of "the gospel which you heard," which alludes back to his thanksgiving for their hearing (i.e., "obeying") of the gospel in 1:5–6. While the condition of faithfulness momentarily foreshadows the polemic ahead, Paul first needs to build some more rapport with his audience. He could have ended his sentence with "the gospel which you heard," or even after "which was preached in all creation under heaven," but he appends an additional clause ("of which I, Paul, became a servant") to create an opportunity to discuss his apostolic struggles for them.

Colossians 1:24–29

Using his mention of becoming a servant of the gospel as a lead-in, he says he rejoices in his sufferings "for your sake" and continues with a parallel universalized claim (connected by καί) that he is also compensating in his flesh for what is lacking of the sufferings of Christ "for the sake of his body."[21] Paul thereby connects his apostolic mission and sufferings with the Colossians and the universal

---

[21] The phrase ἀνταναπληρῶ τὰ ὑστερήματα τῶν θλίψεων τοῦ Χριστοῦ is difficult but probably means he is compensating for the sufferings Christ would have suffered had he taken on the apostolic task himself. See uses of ἀνταναπληρόω in Demosthenes, *Symm.* 17.4; Apollonius Dyscolus, *De Constructione* 3.365.3; 4.487.1; 2.158.1; 1.21.5; Claudius Ptolemaeus, *Syntaxis mathematica* 1.1.16; *Harmonica* 1.11.50; Clement, *Strom.* 7.12.77.

body, which connects the two together through his apostolic mission and through Christ, being the "head of the body" (1:18). This rhetorical move is perhaps intended to bridge the gap between Paul and the Colossians, since he had not met them personally. It also implicitly connects the Colossians to Paul's other partner churches by grouping them all together in "the body."

The mention of the body/church then initiates the first of three topic shifts via tail-head linkage using a relative pronoun (ἧς, v. 25; οἷς, v. 27; ὃν, v. 28, whose antecedents are "church," "saints," and "Christ" respectively). The final expansion on Christ allows him to circle back around to his apostolic ministry to proclaim Christ for the ultimate purpose of presenting every person mature in Christ (1:28). Again, he could stop here, but continuing to build rapport with his recipients, he adds "unto which I also toil, struggling according to his working that he works powerfully within me" (1:29). The piling on of concepts of struggling, toiling, working, and God's power form a nice inclusio with the concepts of suffering and tribulation that began the unit (1:24). Throughout the unit, he emphasizes that his mission is:

ὑπὲρ ὑμῶν (1:24)
ὑπὲρ τοῦ σώματος αὐτοῦ (1:24)
εἰς ὑμᾶς (1:25)
πάντα ἄνθρωπον (1:28, 3x)

The three-fold use of "every person" in 1:28 emphasizes again that the Colossians are a part of the larger body, which Paul serves, so even though he hasn't met them, he is still striving for their benefit. That his ultimate goal is to present every person mature in Christ echoes the prominent concern of 1:3–23, that they "walk worthily of the Lord unto all pleasing" (1:10). He not only prays that they would do so, but he toils and struggles to make that happen.

Colossians 2:1–3

Paul continues with a long supporting sentence explaining why he has spoken at length about his apostolic struggle for them, despite the fact that he has met neither them nor their neighboring Laodiceans in person. He wants them to know about his apostolic struggle, commissioned by God, in order that they might be encouraged toward two results: (1) being united in love, and (2) [having] all the riches of the full assurance of understanding, *that is*, the knowledge of the mystery of God, *namely*, Christ.[22] In short, he wants his ministry to encourage

---

[22] Some take the ἵνα clause to express the purpose of Paul's struggling, e.g., Harris, *Colossians*, 80; Douglas J. Moo, *The Letters to the Colossians and to Philemon*, PNTC (Eerdmans,

them, which will result in unity and knowledge of Christ. He is thereby helping to fulfill his own prayer that they continue increasing in the knowledge of God (1:10), which will help them walk worthily (1:10). In 2:3 he appends that in Christ are hidden all the treasures of wisdom and knowledge, perhaps a brief allusion toward the following unit, which will turn to the problem of wisdom and knowledge in Colossae.

Colossians 2:4–23

We now come to the polemic against the Colossian heresy, which is the main purpose for Paul writing Colossians. The structure of this section depends on four factors. First, what is the referent of τοῦτο in v. 4? Second, how does the polemic divide into units? Third, what is the function of 2:20–23? Fourth, what is the function of 3:1–4? I will answer these questions in order.

The Function of τοῦτο in 2:4

The unit beginning at 2:1 may end at 2:3 or 2:5. Asyndeton occurs between 2:3 and 2:4, with the latter beginning "I say this (τοῦτο) in order that no one may delude you with persuasive rhetoric." Τοῦτο in 2:4 can be prospective, in which case 2:4 begins a new unit, or retrospective, in which case 2:4–5 belong with 2:1–3. If retrospective, τοῦτο's antecedent could be v. 3, vv. 1–3, or any stretch of text as far back as 1:3. Whatever τοῦτο refers to, it must be sufficient and effective for the expressed purpose, namely, "in order that no one may delude you with persuasive rhetoric." Ideally, whatever the referent of τοῦτο, it should contain ideas relevant to the "persuasive rhetoric" used by the false teachers in Colossae; only then could it contribute to keeping them from being deceived. Verse 3's phrase "all the treasures of wisdom and knowledge are hidden in Christ" probably relates in Paul's mind to the Colossian philosophy, but is far too limited to accomplish his stated purpose of keeping them from being deceived. Verses 1–3 refer to his struggles for them and to the wisdom and knowledge in Christ. His apostolic struggles are related to build rapport, not to support an argument against the false teachers, so vv. 1–3 still seems too limited. If τοῦτο is retrospective, then it must refer back to most of the preceding discourse that provides grounds for his coming polemic, including especially the Christ hymn, which, as we saw, contains ideas related to the Colossian heresy. Commentators are virtually unanimous that τοῦτο is retrospective and take one of these three views.

2008), 165. But it seems more natural to take ἵνα as expressing the purpose of his desire for them to know about his struggle. In other words, he is providing justification for what could seem like a self-exalting digression in the previous unit.

However, I think τοῦτο functions better prospectively, pointing ahead to the polemic for multiple reasons. First, 2:4 is at least a pivot, making the first explicit statement of his pastoral reason for writing the letter and transitioning to the main sections to tackle the Colossian philosophy (2:8–23).[23] Second, the following content in 2:6ff. is far more appropriate for and effective at keeping them from being deceived by empty rhetoric, because 2:6–23 actually takes on the philosophy directly. Third, a prospective reading is more in line with Paul's rhetorical strategy that we have traced so far. Colossians 1:3–2:3 has all served to create a common bond between Paul and his recipients, whom he has never met (2:1), and has served to provide theological motivation for his coming polemic. These previous units are therefore grounding, or warranting units, and it is his polemic that he will "say in order that no one will deceive you by persuasive rhetoric." Fourth, taking both the ἵνα clause and γάρ clause in v. 5 as fronted hedging remarks makes a good transition from the warranting units to the polemic. This transition is sensitive, moving from common ground to contested ground, so he tells them first why (ἵνα) he is going to say what he will say in 2:6ff. (in order that no one will deceive them). He then explains (γάρ) why he will tell them "this" (the coming polemic): because even though he is absent, he is with them in the Spirit, meaning that even from afar he may still encourage and admonish them.[24] These two hedging statements indicate that he is about to transition into sensitive discourse related to teaching in their region, and inform them of the purpose of the following discourse and that he believes he can appropriately do so even from afar. Finally, the οὖν in 2:6 functions better as resuming the beginning of his admonition in 2:4, from which he digressed to hedge, than it does as an inference from 2:5 or from a larger preceding context.[25] The exhorta-

---

[23] See J. D. G. Dunn, *The Epistles to the Colossians and to Philemon*, NIGTC (Eerdmans, 1996), 132–133; Hans Hübner, *An Philemon, an die Kolosser, an die Epheser*, HNT 12 (Mohr Siebeck, 1997), 74; McKnight, *Colossians*, 212. These take τοῦτο as retrospective, but see the prospective function of 2:4 as a whole.

[24] Some claim that τοῦτο with ἵνα always refers to what precedes, citing John 5:34 as evidence. See T. K. Abbott, *Epistle to the Ephesians and to the Colossians*, ICC (T&T Clark, 1897), 242; J. B. Lightfoot, *Saint Paul's Epistles to the Colossians and to Philemon: A Revised Text with Introductions, Notes, and Dissertations* (MacMillan & Co., 1879), 175. But if Paul is hedging with the ἵνα and γάρ clauses, then τοῦτο can certainly refer forward. In fact, if we remove v. 5, then v. 4, 6 read coherently and τοῦτο is more obviously prospective. Taking v. 5 as a further hedge explains the seeming incoherence when taking vv. 4–6 together. This kind of complex hedging often occurs in natural conversation, especially if the speaker does not want the receiver to misunderstand, or if the speaker knows the receiver may not be very receptive. F. F. Bruce follows C. F. D. Moule in taking ἵνα as imperatival, which is unnecessary (*The Epistles to the Colossians, to Philemon, and to the Ephesians*, NICNT [Eerdmans, 1984]), 92.

[25] On the inferential and resumptive uses of οὖν, see ch. 10 of this volume, p. 349. John Eadie follows Calvin by taking οὖν as an inference from the final phrase of v. 5, "rejoicing to see

tion in v. 6 ("walk in Christ as you received him," i.e., continue in the original gospel teaching; cf. Gal 1:6) is the beginning of the content of τοῦτο from v. 4.[26]

The Structure of the Polemic

The polemic is structured by the initial hedging introduction, followed by 4 units that each begin with an imperative.

οὖν ... ἐν αὐτῷ περιπατεῖτε (2:6)
Βλέπετε μή τις ὑμᾶς ἔσται ὁ συλαγωγῶν (2:8)
Μὴ οὖν τις ὑμᾶς κρινέτω (2:16)
μηδεὶς ὑμᾶς καταβραβευέτω (2:18)

The command in 2:6 is the positive side of the polemic. Having already established that their faith, hope, and love is being made known abroad (1:3–8), he exhorts them to continue walking in the same faith and according to the same gospel that they originally received. That this is the meaning of "as you received Christ" (2:6) seems clear from the parallel "being firm in the faith you were taught" (ἐδιδάχθητε, 2:7).

The next unit has no connecting conjunction (2:8–15), and so is taken as in series with the previous unit, but now laying out the negative side of his exhortation. "Watch out that there is not one who takes you captive by philosophy and empty deceit..." (2:8). This philosophy is according to the traditions of men and according to the spiritual powers (στοιχεῖα), and not according to Christ. This contrast alludes back to the Christ hymn and its distinction between Christ's preeminence and his superiority over the spiritual powers (1:16). They should not be taken captive by this philosophy for three reasons, signaled by ὅτι (v. 9) ... καί (v. 10) ... καί (v. 13). First, "in him dwells bodily all the fullness of deity" (v. 9). Second, "you are filled in him, who is the head of every ruler and authority." The

---

the order and firmness of your faith in Christ" (*A Commentary on the Greek Text of the Epistle of Paul to the Colossians*, 2nd ed. [1856; repr., Zondervan, 1957], 124). On this basis, he exhorts them to walk in Christ as they received him. Such a view is coherent, but it ignores the discourse structure. The final phrase of v. 5 is the most embedded clause of the verse. The mention of their firm faith acts as a fitting conclusion to the hedging (one last gesture of common ground) and also acts as the lead-in to the polemic, in the same way that οὗ ἐγενόμην ἐγὼ Παῦλος διάκονος of 1:23 is the most subordinate clause of the verse but concludes the unit and acts as a lead-in to his discussion of his apostolic struggle on their behalf.

[26] While I have not found anyone else who interprets τοῦτο as prospective, some do begin a new unit with 2:4, including Harris, *Colossians*, 86; Lightfoot, *Colossians*, 175; NAB. Also, most commentators hedge their retrospective interpretation as probable and generally discuss the possibility of a prospective view.

fullness (πλήρωμα) of God dwells in Christ, and believers are filled (ἐστὲ πεπληρωμένοι) in Christ, thereby receiving God's fullness via union with Christ. Third, "although you were dead...God made you alive with Christ, by forgiving us all our sins." They should not squander such new life and God's presence within them by succumbing to a false philosophy. Verses 14–15 elaborate on the concept of forgiveness of sins from v. 13 and are not semantically prominent in this unit, but Christ's defeat of the spiritual powers in 2:15 is significant for his rhetorical purpose, developing Christ's preeminence over spiritual powers from 1:16 and laying the groundwork for portraying as ridiculous their preference for the spiritual powers over Christ (2:20–23).

The next unit is simple and begins with an οὖν that functions well as resuming the exhortations given in vv. 6, 8 (the long expansion in vv. 9–15 creates a need for Paul to signal a return to the hortatory mainline). This third command is "Do not let anyone judge you," followed by a list of five elements that seem to be part of the false teaching: food, drink, feasts, new moons, and Sabbaths (2:16). These are all "a shadow of things to come, but the body belongs to Christ" (2:17).[27]

The final unit is introduced via asyndeton because there was not much elaboration in 2:16–17. The command in v. 18 is "Let no one disqualify you," while the cause of disqualification is the *crux interpretum* of the letter. The two main controversies surround the phrases θρησκείᾳ τῶν ἀγγέλων and ἃ ἑόρακεν ἐμβατεύων. Is ἀγγέλων an objective or a subjective genitive? That is, are angels being worshiped or doing the worshiping? And what is the meaning of ἐμβατεύω, and what type of participle is it? The rest of the verse, εἰκῇ φυσιούμενος ὑπὸ τοῦ νοὸς τῆς σαρκὸς αὐτοῦ, gives the result of seeing the θρησκείᾳ τῶν ἀγγέλων by ἐμβατεύων, namely, that they are vainly conceited by their fleshly minds. Rhetorically, the result that they are vainly conceited, and his description of their minds as fleshly, functions as grounds for not letting anyone judge them for not participating in such rituals.

Without any pretensions of providing a forceful argument, I believe the best interpretation is that the false teachers delight in the lowliness of the angels and their worship of God, which things they have seen by entering into *the heavenly temple*, resulting in their vain conceit. Ἐμβατεύω was used in the initiation rites of contemporary mystery religions to speak of initiates entering the inner sanctuary of the god after preliminary rites.[28] The truncated nature of the phrase

---

[27] Many versions render σῶμα as "substance" (ESV; NASB), "reality" (NLT; NET), or "essence" ("das Wesen," Schlachter 2000), which brings out the meaning but ruins the imagery. "Body" corresponds to "shadow," in that the body is the reality or substance that casts the shadow. Some translations do render σῶμα as "body" (Reina Valera 1995, "cuerpo"; Louis Segond 1910, "corps").

[28] See especially Martin Dibelius, *Die Isisweihe bei Apuleius und verwandte Initiations-Riten* (Heidelberg: Carl Winters, 1917), 30–39; Wesley Carr, "Two Notes on Colossians," *JTS* 23 (1973):

supports this interpretation because it suggests a fixed expression for a known rite.[29] Jewish preoccupation with the heavenly court worshiping God is well known, while Jews worshiping angels is rarely found in our extant literature.[30] The five aspects of the teaching in 2:16 are all connected to the temple in Jewish literature. "Food and drink" probably refers to purity laws, which were necessary for purity to enter the heavenly temple.[31] The triad of Jewish feasts, new moons, and Sabbaths (which they seem to have insisted on observing) is a formula in the LXX always connected with the temple.[32] The prohibitions not to touch (ἅπτω) or taste (γεύομαι) were likely intended to keep the visionaries clean so they could enter the heavenly temple.[33] Finally, θρησκεία, refers to worship in temples in many Jewish and Greco-Roman contexts.[34] Even if this interpretation is incorrect, it has little to no effect on the macrostructure of the letter.

The Function of 2:20–23

Verses 20–23 are clearly still part of the polemic, even containing specific dogmas: "Do not handle; do not taste; do not touch" (v. 21). But the unit begins with a protasis ("if [εἰ] through death with Christ you were freed from the spiritual powers of the world…"), which looks forward to the rhetorical apodosis τί ὡς ζῶντες ἐν κόσμῳ δογματίζεσθε ("why do you submit to regulations as those who live in the world?"). There is therefore no explicit connection between this unit and the preceding.

499–500; Arnold, *The Colossian Syncretism*, 104–157; Petr Pokorný, *Der Brief des Paulus an die Kolosser*, 122–124. Dibelius inferred that the Colossian teachers were entering into *visions*, but Carr and Arnold refined Dibelius's view by showing that the verb is connected with entering a sacred space or a temple, particularly in contemporary mystery religions (Arnold).

[29] Eduard Schweizer, *Der Brief an die Kolosser*, EKKNT 12 (Benziger: Neukirchener, 1994), 124.

[30] In fact, Isa 6 and Revelation are biblical examples of heavenly beings worshiping God. The Qumran liturgy *Songs of the Sabbath Sacrifice* demonstrates a lively belief around the first century, at least among that sect, of worship by angels in a heavenly court.

[31] See, e.g., 1QH III, 20–23; Philo, *Plant.* 163; *Ebr.* 127, 131, 138; *Spec.* 1.150; *Moys.* 2.21–24, 66–78; Jos. *Ap.* 2.102–108; 11Q19 (= 11QT) XLVII, 3–4; and 4Q400 fr. 1 I, 14; Heb 9:8–14.

[32] 1 Chron 23:31; 2 Chron 2:3; 8:13; 31:3; 2 Esd. 5:51–53; Neh 10:33; Isa 1:13–14; Ezek 45:17; Josephus, *Ant.* 11.77; *J.W.* 5.230; Philo, *Spec.* 1.168. Cf. also Ezek 44:24; 46:3; 1 Macc 1:39; 1:45; Philo, *Spec.* 1.182; 2.140, 144–145; m. Šebu. 1:4–5; 1QS X, 3–7; Hos 2:11; Jdt 8:6; 1 Macc 10:34. For these references, see G. K. Beale, *Colossians*, BECNT (Baker Academic, 2019) in his comments on 2:8–23.

[33] These terms are used to refer to ritual purity or impurity in Lev 5:2 and likewise 19 other times in Leviticus; so also Num 19:11, 16, 21–22; 31:19; Deut 14:8; Hag 2:13; Let. Aris. 142, 162; 2 Macc 6:18–20.

[34] Philo, *Legat.* 298, 232; Sib. Or. 8:380; Clementine Homilies, Homily 10, chap. 22; Dionysius of Halicarnassus, *Roman Antiquities* 2.63; Dio Cassius, *Roman History* 26.87; 49.22; Sextus Empiricus, *Outlines of Pyrrhonism* (= *Pyrrhoniae hypotyposes*) III.220; Herodian, *Hist.*, *Ab excess divi Marci*, 5.6.2; Chaeremon Frag. 10 (3x).

The rhetorical question in v. 20 is clearly intended to function as an argument.[35] The Colossian teaching is "according to the spiritual powers" (κατὰ τὰ στοιχεῖα, 2:8), but Christ has defeated them (2:15) and is ontologically superior to them (1:16). Therefore, it is irrational to submit to regulations connected to these powers. After v. 21 lists the regulations (likely not exhaustive), vv. 22–23 expand on them to denigrate them as corrupt, worldly, unwise, and worthless. These descriptions further support Paul's warnings not to fall prey to such teaching.

The Hinge Function of 3:1–4

Unit 3:1–4 seems at first unrelated to the polemic, but for several reasons it probably is still addressing the Colossian teaching, but in a transitional manner. First, εἰ οὖν συνηγέρθητε τῷ Χριστῷ opening 3:1 echoes εἰ ἀπεθάνετε σὺν Χριστῷ in 2:20, whose section supports the main exhortations of the polemic. Second, Paul immediately qualifies his exhortation to seek and set their minds on "the things above" with the phrase "where Christ is seated at the right hand of God." This qualification may try to distinguish true heavenly thoughts, directed toward Christ at the right hand, from false heavenly cultic visions.[36] It also evokes the dichotomy between teaching that is κατὰ τὰ στοιχεῖα τοῦ κόσμου versus teaching that is κατὰ Χριστόν (2:8). Third, the "earthly things" (3:2) may refer to the δόγματα, the things that they submit to "as those living in the world" (2:20). Despite these good reasons for including 3:1–4 with what precedes, it is difficult to separate 3:1–4 from the following units, especially those beginning similarly with οὖν plus an imperative (3:5, 12).

It is best to see 3:1–4 as a hinge, so that it wraps up the polemic in a positive way (while still implicitly denigrating the teaching) while also opening up the positive hortatory section (3:5–4:1).[37] Aside from simply summing up the polemic,

---

[35] Callow (*Colossians*, 108–109) claims the question in 2:20 has the sense of a prohibition, so he translates it as an imperative, "Therefore do not submit to regulations." Gregory Christopher similarly takes it as a "mitigated imperative" ("A Discourse Analysis of Colossians 2:16–3:17," *GTJ* 11, no. 2 [1990]: 205–220). But this view skews Paul's rhetorical strategy here to provide support for his commands by implying how ludicrous their siding with the spiritual powers would be in light of what he has already said about their inferiority and submission (1:16; 2:15).

[36] Dunn takes this as "obvious" (*Colossians*, 200).

[37] For this reason, I am formally excluding it from the polemic proper, much as I would exclude a *peroratio* from a text's body, but since it is a hinge unit, the exclusion is more heuristic than anything. Similarly seeing 3:1–4 as a hinge are R. McL. Wilson (*Colossians and Philemon*, ICC [T&T Clark, 2005], 234); Schweizer (*Colossians*, 171); Pao, *Colossians*, 205. Markus Barth and Helmut Blanke claim 3:1–4 recapitulates statements from chs. 1–2 in order to prepare for the paraenesis in 3:5ff., yet is distinct from ch. 2 and does not refer to the Colossian teaching at all (*Colossians: A New Translation with Introduction and Commentary*, AB 34B, trans. Astrid B. Beck [Doubleday, 1994], 391–392). But how can 3:1–4 recapitulate chs. 1–2 without alluding to the false teaching at all?

it also presents a stark contrast of "two ways." They can either seek the things above, where Christ is, and appear with him in glory, or they can seek the things below, and by implication, not appear with him in glory.[38] This unit, then is a call for decision. If they are to choose Christ above, they must abandon the things below, specifically the shadowy regulations according to the spiritual powers.

Since this unit is a hinge, it goes with what precedes and with what follows, and will therefore be important to include in the following discussion on the hortatory section.

The Structure of the Hortatory Units

The two positive hortatory units (2:6–7; 3:1–4) enclose the polemic with a positive vision of what the recipients *should* do if they are not to follow the false teachers. The rest of the hortatory units continue with further exhortations and prohibitions that are not obviously related to the Colossian philosophy (3:5–4:1).

The discourse structure of 3:1–4:1 is difficult to discern because there are nine imperatives (3:1, 5, 8, 9, 12, 15 [x2], 16, 17 [implied]). Three of these imperatives are coupled with οὖν (3:1, 5, 12), and such a construction often signals a new unit, but some of the other imperatives could start a new unit as well. Another difficulty is that, while 3:1–4 still relates to the polemic, 3:5–17 are more generally applicable. Our choices are (1) to divide the 17 verses into three units, each beginning with οὖν plus an imperative; (2) to divide into nine exhortations, creating a list with some exhortations elaborated more than others; (3) to include some imperatives into larger units via semantic relationships, creating anywhere between four to eight units. I believe (1) is the best approach because οὖν + imperative is such a strong boundary marker, and because the imperatives that do not begin one of these three units fit coherently within the framework of the initial command.

That 3:1–4 is a unit is clear. The οὖν in 3:1 resumes the hortatory mainline of the polemic (2:6, 8, 16, 18) and builds on the preceding directives by developing a further line of action. The twin commands in 3:1, 2 ("seek the things above" and "think about the things above, not earthly things") express a parallelism that binds them together. Γάρ connects v. 3 with vv. 1–2, as does ἀπεθάνετε ("you died," v. 3), which is the conceptual antecedent to συνηγέρθητε ("you were raised," v. 1). The repetition of ἡ ζωὴ ὑμῶν ("your life") binds vv. 3–4 together, while Χριστός ("Christ") appears in vv. 1, 3, 4. There is an eschatological richness to the unit as well, given its emphasis on the past (you died, you were raised), the present (seek and set your mind on things above; your life is hidden with Christ), and the future (you will be revealed with him).

---

[38] McKnight, *Colossians*, 288.

The next unit begins with οὖν plus νεκρώσατε. Οὖν signals a return to the hortatory mainline following the lengthy grounds in vv. 3–4, further developing the exhortation in an inferential manner to the next directive. If they will obey 3:1–2, for starters, they must therefore "put to death your earthly members" (3:5), an apparent synecdoche of cause for effect, which Paul clarifies concretely by listing the vices that their worldly members produce. The phrase "earthly members" (τὰ μέλη τὰ ἐπὶ τῆς γῆς) is a direct allusion to "not earthly things" (μὴ τὰ ἐπὶ τῆς γῆς) from 3:2, showing that in 3:5–11 Paul is elaborating specifically on the negative portion of the directive in 3:1–2.

Verses 6–7 elaborate on the vices listed. The imperative in v. 8 (ἀπόθεσθε) could suggest a new unit, but the opening (νυνὶ δὲ) signals a temporal contrast to the end of v. 7 ("when you lived in them") and thus belongs with it. The parallel structure of vv. 5, 8 ("put to death vices," "put off vices") also suggests that v. 8 belongs with vv. 5–7. The imperative in v. 9 ("do not lie to one another") belongs in this unit as listing another vice that needs to be put to death. The following participles are grammatically dependent on "do not lie," but since lying was only one of the many vices, the participles should be viewed semantically as providing the reason for putting away vices generally: "because you have put off (ἀπεκδύομαι) the old man with his deeds, and because you have put on (ἐνδύω) the new man, who is being renewed in knowledge according to the image of the one who created him."[39] Believers are new creations, part of the new creation inaugurated by Christ's resurrection (1:18) and participated in by virtue of union with Christ (2:10; cf. 2 Cor 5:17). As a result, ethnicity and social status are no longer ultimate, but Christ is (Col 3:11).

The third hortatory unit (3:12–17) elaborates specifically on the positive part of the command in 3:1–2, "seek heavenly things."[40] The initial οὖν signals a development in the discourse such that 3:12–17 provides a parallel to 3:5–11; both together specify what the commands in 3:1–2 look like practically. The initial command is to put on (ἐνδύω) virtues, which is the counterpart of putting away (ἀποτίθημι) vices (3:8) and putting off (ἀπεκδύομαι) the old man (3:9). The contrast between putting on and putting off suggests that Paul is still operating with

---

[39] Ἀποτίθημι, used in v. 8, means "to take off clothes" (e.g., Acts 7:58), and is extended metaphorically to express the removal of something (Rom 13:12; Eph 4:22, 25; Heb 12:1). Ἀπεκδύομαι also means "to strip off clothes," and was used metaphorically in 2:15 of Christ disarming the rulers and authorities. Ἀπεκδύομαι is found in the NT only in these two instances. Ἐνδύω means literally "to put on clothing" (Matt 27:28; Mark 15:20; 15:22) and can be extended metaphorically to express receiving or being completely identified with something (Luke 24:49; Rom 13:14; 1 Cor 15:53; 2 Cor 5:3).

[40] That 3:5–11 and 3:12–17 elaborate specifically on "the things below" and "the things above," respectively, is also observed by Allan R. Bevere, *Sharing in the Inheritance: Identity and the Moral Life in Colossians*, LNTS 226 (T&T Clark, 2003), 199.

the framework of the old creation and the new creation, which is further evoked by the re-use of ἐνδύω:

ἐνδυσάμενοι τὸν νέον τὸν ἀνακαινούμενον (3:10)
ἐνδύσασθε οὖν, ὡς ἐκλεκτοὶ τοῦ θεοῦ ἅγιοι καὶ ἠγαπημένοι (3:12)

So, being part of the new creation by being "raised with Christ" (3:1) is just as much the conceptual grounding of the command in 3:12 as for the one in 3:5.

The rest of the unit provides the results of and specification of putting on virtue as part of the new creation. The result is that they will bear with and forgive one another (3:13). Verses 14–15 specify that putting on virtue includes putting on three further virtues: love, peace, thankfulness. Two uses of καί connect these three commands, making this one compound sentence with Paul's three foremost concerns for the Colossians as part of the new creation.[41] Verse 16 further specifies that life in the new creation includes allowing the word of Christ to dwell in them richly in communal worship. Additionally (καί), v. 17 adds that new creational life is not limited to community worship; rather, "whatever you do, in word or deed, do everything in the name of the Lord Jesus."

The semantic relationships I have posited suggest that 3:12–17 is one unit, but there are also many cohesive ties that provide corroboration. Communal terms in 3:13–16 include ἀλλήλων, ἑαυτοῖς, σύνδεσμος, ἐν ἑνὶ σώματι, and ἑαυτούς. The concept of thankfulness appears in 3:15 (εὐχάριστοι) and 3:17 (εὐχαριστοῦντες). Λόγῳ in v. 17 may partially relate to the teaching and admonishing in v. 16. The mention of Christ/Jesus binds together vv. 15–17 (peace of Christ, word of Christ, name of the Lord Jesus) while the mention of God binds together vv. 12, 16, 17. Conceptually, the ethical and virtue-oriented nature of the commands in 3:12–17 also binds them together.

The Function of the Household Code

Following the negative-positive elaboration on 3:1–2 in 3:5–17, Paul abruptly drops in a household code with no grammatical tie to the preceding units. He places it in a similar location to the code in Ephesians, namely, just before the final letter body unit. If Colossians was written before Ephesians then this is the first extant Christian household code.

---

[41] This approach solves the common problem that if love is Paul's concern "above all," then the two exhortations in v. 15 seem like random appendages (e.g., Dunn, *Colossians*, 235; Wilson, *Colossians*, 265). Love still gets its pride of place at the front of the three commands, as elsewhere in Paul's writings (Gal 5:22; 2 Cor 13:11; Eph 6:23; 2 Tim 2:22).

The content of the code is simple and addresses wives, husbands, children, fathers, slaves, and masters in that order, just as in Ephesians. The commands are as follows:

> Wives, submit to your husbands;
> Husbands, love your wives;
> Children, obey your parents;
> Fathers, do not provoke your children;
> Servants, obey your masters sincerely;
> Masters, treat your slaves justly and fairly.

The command to servants receives the most elaboration (3:22–25), while the other five commands each have only one elaboration clause.[42] Also of note is that the Colossian code uses κύριος seven times, demonstrating that Paul is not inserting a formulaic code for its own sake, but is providing Christ-oriented instruction for the home, which is in line with his attempts throughout the letter to point the audience away from vain philosophy and toward Christ.

Since the code is a self-contained unit and has no grammatical tie to 3:17 or 4:2, its relation to the surrounding units is unclear. Some have noticed that, if the code were extracted, one could read coherently from 3:17 to 4:2 without any problem.[43] As a result, some suggest that it is a traditional, self-contained unit that has been inserted at this point, without explaining why.[44] Many commentaries ignore discussing the connection at all. Of those who do discuss it, some try to relate the contents of the code to the historical situation or the preceding text in Colossians, but with no explanation of the relationship to adjacent units.[45] More on track are those who argue that the code is an application of the command in 3:17 to "do everything in the name of the Lord Jesus."[46] This proposal is supported by three types of cohesive ties. (1) The name

---

[42] By contrast in Ephesians, wives get three verses, husbands nine, children three, fathers one, slaves four, and masters one. So the code in Colossians is much shorter than that in Ephesians, and while the slaves do get most of the same instruction, they are given comparably more attention in the Colossian code. But this comparison is not pertinent to Colossians' discourse structure if it was written first.

[43] Eduard Lohse, *Colossians and Philemon*, Hermeneia, trans. William R. Poehlmann and Robert J. Karris (Fortress, 1971), 154; J. M. G. Barclay, *Colossians and Philemon*, NTG (Sheffield, 1997), 67–68.

[44] Eduard Lohse, *Colossians*, 154; Robert G. Bratcher and Eugene A. Nida, *A Translator's Handbook on Paul's Letters to the Colossians and to Philemon* (United Bible Societies, 1977), 92.

[45] Chrysostom, "Homily X," in *NPNF* 1:303; Eadie, *Colossians*, 256; Harris, *Colossians*, 177.

[46] Jerry L. Sumney, *Colossians*, NTL (Westminster John Knox, 2008), 238; Eduard Schweizer, *The Letter to the Colossians: A Commentary*, trans. Andrew Chester (Augsburg, 1982), 221; Barth and Blanke, *Colossians*, 429, 474; Scot McKnight, *The Letter to the Colossians*, NICNT (Eerdmans, 2018), 335, who says it is "at least arguable" that the household code "is a

of the Lord (κύριος) in 3:17 is repeated seven times in the code. (2) Πᾶς appears vv. 17 (x2), 20, 22. (3) The phrase ὃ ἐὰν ποιῆτε (addressed to slaves in 3:23) echoes 3:17's πᾶν ὅ τι ἐὰν ποιῆτε.

It seems clear enough that the code somehow relates to 3:17, but it also relates more widely to 3:12–17 as a unit. The command to "put on love" (3:14) is applied to husbands and wives in 3:19, while perhaps the "peace of Christ" (3:15) is applied when fathers do not provoke their children to anger, creating domestic peace (3:21). Conceptually, 3:12–17 is about virtue and ethics in the wider community, while 3:18–4:1 is about virtue and ethics in the home. That community worship and the home are closely juxtaposed would have been fitting to early believers, who met almost exclusively in homes.[47] Thus, the units function together to explicate what it means to "seek the things above," i.e., to live virtuously as newly resurrected creatures in Christian community (3:12–17) and in the home (3:18–4:1). The new creation has broken into this world and people are part of it insofar as they are in Christ. Being a new creation does not mean escaping the social and relational realities of the world, but rather finding transformed ways of existing in them. The strong links between 3:17 and the code suggest that 3:17 is another discourse pivot, in which the concept that carries over is doing everything in the name of the Lord.

To help summarize my proposed structure of 2:4–4:1, Figure 12.1 diagrams the structure and the connections between the units.

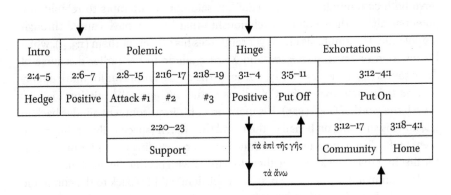

Figure 12.1: The Structure of the Colossian Polemic and Hortatory Units

---

development or illustration of 3:17." But before this, he compares Paul's train of thought to the order in the song of a mockingbird. "At some point the searcher says, 'This bird does not follow any rules; we are better off appreciating the notes in all their variety.'"

[47] See similar thoughts in Dunn, *Colossians*, 242–246. In the most general terms, if Aristotle was any indication of how first century Christians thought, then the home was the foundation of community (*Pol.* I).

A Colossian Peroratio?

The final letter body unit returns to commanding believers generally, which could cause a problem for my structure of the hortatory section. But this unit distinguishes itself from 3:1–4:1 in several ways. First, it recapitulates various themes of the letter (see below), functioning similarly to a *peroratio* like Eph 6:10–20, but without the emotive or syntactic qualities of a *peroratio*. Second, it steers away from the two-fold ethical scheme of 3:1–17 and returns to concerns about Paul's mission along with some general commands to help guide them in their situation. Third, because it reconnects the Colossians to Paul by inviting them to pray for his ministry, it functions to lead in to the final salutations in 4:7–18, and therefore belongs more with what follows than with what precedes.

This unit contains three main commands:

Τῇ προσευχῇ προσκαρτερεῖτε (4:2)

Ἐν σοφίᾳ περιπατεῖτε πρὸς τοὺς ἔξω (4:5)

ὁ λόγος ὑμῶν πάντοτε ἐν χάριτι (4:6)

Paul commands them to continue in prayer, praying together but also for "us" (Paul, Timothy, and perhaps any other co-workers), that God would create more opportunities for preaching Christ, the mystery, and that he would preach it as he should. There are several parallels here to earlier parts of the letter, which serve both as reminders of what Paul has said and as attempts to rebuild any potential rifts in their potential relationship that he may have caused through his polemic. The emphasis on prayer reinforces his prayer for them (1:3, 9), while his mention of λόγος, μυστήριον, and Χριστός allude to his earlier discourse of these topics (1:5, 15–20, 25, 26, 27; 2:2; 3:16). His desire for prayer for more opportunities to preach invites the Colossians to fuel his apostolic mission to "fully preach the word of God" (1:25). His mention of his imprisonment alludes back to 1:24 and his suffering on behalf of them and the church (specifically, his imprisonment [4:18]). This command to continue in prayer, including prayer for his team, is the first hint that Paul is inviting them to partner with his Gentile mission.

His command to "walk (περιπατέω) in wisdom" alludes back to the command to "walk in him" (ἐν αὐτῷ περιπατεῖτε, 2:6), and also wraps up the letter's heavy emphasis on "wisdom." He prayed that they would be filled with wisdom (1:9); he admonishes everyone with wisdom (1:28) and urges that they do the same (3:16); wisdom is in Christ (2:3), but not in the false teaching (2:23).[48] Finally he sums up here that they should be wise πρὸς τοὺς ἔξω ("toward outsiders"), possibly a final

---

[48] Apart from the explicit uses of "wisdom" is the plausible Wisdom Christology in the Christ hymn. Aside from the commentaries on 1:15–20, see, e.g., Christopher A. Beetham, *Echoes of Scripture in the Letter of Paul to the Colossians*, BIS 96 (Brill, 2008), 113–141.

pejorative jab at the false teachers, to whom Paul wants to return the favor by disqualifying them (cf. 2:18).

The third command is that their "word" (λόγος) should be gracious, so that they might know how they "must answer each person." Here λόγος may denote preaching as it does in v. 3, connecting their ministry with his, or it may simply mean their every-day conversations. The apologetic nature of this advice, in the context of the letter, seems like a final word on how to go about applying his exhortations. If they reject the false teaching, they will come to theological and perhaps social blows with the teachers.[49] When they engage, they should be gracious, as is fitting for those who have put off the old man.

In sum, these three exhortations recap themes from the epistle fairly well, although not comprehensively. The unit lacks the emotional appeal of a *peroratio* and the style is more syntactic than paratactic, so it is probably not fair to label Col 4:2–6 as a *peroratio*. It does, however, bring the exhortations to a close by inviting the Colossians to contribute to his apostolic ministry through prayer, exhorting them to walk in the wisdom found in Christ, rather than in the philosophy of men, and to engage that philosophy graciously.

Final Greetings

Paul gives his final greetings in 4:7–18.[50] This section may be taken solely as a formulaic ending to an epistle. However, the fronted τὰ κατ' ἐμὲ πάντα, which Paul uses to signal a topic shift in v. 7, may be another hint that he is subtly working on his recruiting effort. Having already solicited their prayers for his ministry (4:3), he is now going to send Tychichus and Onesimus to them since he, as a prisoner, cannot visit them personally (2:5; 4:18). It seems they do not know Tychichus, since Paul has to vouch for him, but they likely knew Onesimus, Philemon's runaway slave from Colossae. Sending these men will reinforce his attack of the false teaching, but will also build further rapport with the Colossians by giving them his apostolic presence via his co-workers. They will bring news of "us" (ἡμῶν), that is, of Paul and his ministry partners, which will encourage their hearts, thus ensuring that his apostolic ministry has his desired effect

---

[49] Similarly, Barth and Blanke, *Colossians*, 457–458.

[50] Cannon (*Traditional Materials in Colossians*, 160–163) distinguishes between a formal epistolary analysis and a thematic analysis. In the former, the "body closing" usually includes (in Paul's letters) a desire that he be present with his readers in person or through a representative. For this reason, he includes 4:7–9 in the "body closing." But in his thematic analysis, he observes a topical shift from vv. 2–6, 7–9, and concludes the "main argument" with v. 6. My concerns align with his thematic analysis, which trace topics and their development and shifts, rather than his formal epistolary analysis. Although the two are not mutually exclusive, they may conflict when one rigidly forces units into structural paradigms.

(ἵνα παρακληθῶσιν αἱ καρδίαι αὐτῶν, 2:2). Sending Onesimus was strategic but risky. He is a Colossian who has joined Paul's mission, thus setting an example Paul wishes they would imitate, but his status as a (runaway) slave might not make him the most desirable to imitate. Yet, Paul was risking his freedom to send him back (see Philemon), so he must have felt it was a worthy gamble. Is it possible that Paul felt that sending Onesimus back would establish further rapport and trust with the Colossians?[51] That Paul sends these two men, and particularly Onesimus, does suggest he is working to establish a good relationship with the Colossians so they will contribute to his ministry. Paul is more explicit about this intent in Rom 15:24.

The rest of the greetings are sent on behalf of Paul's various co-workers: Aristarchus, Mark, Jesus Justus, Epaphras (from Colossae like Onesimus), Luke, and Demas. In the interspersed comments, various themes from the letter are recapitulated in order to reinforce them. His description of Epaphras uses language evocative of Paul's own striving and praying for them:

Epaphras's Ministry	Paul's Ministry
ἀγωνιζόμενος, πόνον (4:12, 13)	ἀγῶνα (2:1)
ὑπὲρ ὑμῶν ἐν ταῖς προσευχαῖς (4:12)	περὶ ὑμῶν προσευχόμενοι (1:3) ὑπὲρ ὑμῶν προσευχόμενοι (1:9)
πεπληροφορημένοι ἐν παντὶ θελήματι τοῦ θεοῦ (4:12)	πληρωθῆτε τὴν ἐπίγνωσιν τοῦ θελήματος αὐτοῦ (1:9)
ὑπὲρ ὑμῶν καὶ τῶν ἐν Λαοδικείᾳ καὶ τῶν ἐν Ἱεραπόλει (4:13)	ὑπὲρ ὑμῶν καὶ τῶν ἐν Λαοδικείᾳ καὶ ὅσοι οὐχ ἑόρακαν τὸ πρόσωπόν μου ἐν σαρκί (2:1)

Figure 12.2: Verbal Allusions between Descriptions of Paul's and Epaphras's Ministries

The implication of Paul patterning the description of Epaphras's care for them after his own is either to suggest that Epaphras imitates Paul's ministry to them, or vice versa. In the former case Epaphras, another Colossian, is set forth as a model for the recipients. If imitating a slave is not desirable, then certainly they will respect Epaphras, through whom the gospel initially came to them. If Paul is suggesting that he has joined in Epaphras's concern for the Colossians, then he is attempting to continue developing rapport with them. In either case,

---

[51] Unless he had already been freed by Philemon at this time; but it seems to me that Paul sent Philemon and Colossians together through Tychichus and Onesimus, given the similar names listed in the final greetings of the two epistles. Note otherwise a newer unique argument by Vicky Balabanski that Onesimus was not from Colossae, but possibly from Rome ("Where is Philemon? The Case for a Logical Fallacy in the Correlation of the Data in Philemon and Colossians 1.1-2; 4.7-18," *JSNT* 38, no. 2 [2015]: 131–150).

it seems his comments about Epaphras are further subtle rhetoric seemingly designed to recruit their partnership.[52]

In 4:15–16, Paul greets also the brothers in Laodicea, and commands that they exchange epistles with them and have each read the other's. This greeting, combined with his mention of the Laodiceans earlier in 2:1, implicitly brings them into the epistle as secondary recipients. Paul may command that they exchange letters because he is concerned that the false teaching may spread (or is spreading) outside Colossae. But particularly his seemingly random inclusion in 2:1 of Laodicea as another church on whose behalf he is striving suggests that Paul wants to recruit their partnership as well. Greeting them here will establish rapport, and his subtle recruiting rhetoric will be passed on to them as they exchange letters with the Colossians. Since his mission is to "fulfill the word of God" (1:25), he will certainly need all the assistance he can get.

Finally, Paul gives an instruction for Archippus, a Colossian (or at least someone in Colossae), to ensure that he fulfills the ministry that he received in the Lord (βλέπε τὴν διακονίαν ἣν παρέλαβες ἐν κυρίῳ, ἵνα αὐτὴν πληροῖς, 4:17). The command is a clear allusion to his own διάκονος κατὰ τὴν οἰκονομίαν τοῦ θεοῦ τὴν δοθεῖσάν μοι εἰς ὑμᾶς πληρῶσαι τὸν λόγον τοῦ θεοῦ (1:25). Is Paul treating Archippus as a synecdoche for the Colossian congregation, trying further with his final word to meld their mission together with his own? Combined with the rest of the evidence, this suggestion is more than possible.

Conclusions

A DA of Colossians has revealed a tightly linked epistle, carefully constructed to address a particular sensitive situation. The letter needed to be crafted carefully with pastoral (or apostolic) sensitivity, tactful establishing of rapport, convincing argumentation, reassurance of his goodwill toward and confidence in them, and ultimately with direct invitations to join in his ministry as well as many subtle hints that they should do so. Semantically, 3:1–4 is the most prominent unit of the epistle, capping off the polemic and being specified by the rest of Division 3. Pragmatically, Paul's rhetoric throughout seems to be aiming at bringing the Colossians and Laodiceans into his network of partner churches so that he can "fully preach the word of God" (1:25). If so, then the pragmatic macrostructure has his intention to recruit their partnership as the most prominent communicative intent, while his polemic is an auxiliary speech act intended to ensure their spiritual health required to be useful in his mission.

---

[52] Somewhat similarly, Dunn notes the parallels and says "Presumably it was important that their own apostle should be seen by them to share the same concerns for them as Paul himself..." (*Colossians*, 280).

The two main problems with this view are that, first, it is unprovable since I am "reading between the lines" by detecting subtle rhetoric. Second, pragmatic macrostructures are composed of a main speech act with auxiliary speech acts supporting it, but it is unclear whether Paul's subtle rhetoric amounts to an actual persuasive speech act (persuading them to join his mission), or whether it is simply laying the groundwork for a future explicit invitation to participate in his mission. In the latter case, the main speech act would be the polemic in Division 2, while his purported desire to recruit them would be a "secondary concern," however one might classify that in a DA. I prefer to view the two concerns logically: why did he write the letter? To address the philosophy. But why did he want to address the philosophy? Why waste time and resources on the Colossian church specifically, and why randomly mention Laodicea twice? Because his ultimate concern was to add healthy churches to his mission. And in that sense, his recruiting intentions were ultimate and thus stand in the most prominent place in the pragmatic macrostructure.

The only lamentable conclusion is that I do not believe my DA has contributed anything to the debate about the nature of the Colossian philosophy. I had hoped to make some observations that would contribute, but my DA did not uncover anything novel. It is certainly possible there is more than I have noticed that would be helpful, and further research on the discourse of Colossians could certainly keep this question in mind.

13

---

1 THESSALONIANS

DANIEL PATTE

F
irst Thessalonians is addressed by Paul, Silvanus, and Timothy (Paul's companions) to the church at Thessalonica. From the detailed references to the circumstances of the Thessalonians' conversion, we conclude with most commentators that the letter was written shortly after (let us say four to six months after) Paul's missionary activities in that city. At the time of the writing, Paul was probably in Corinth, since the reference to Athens in 1 Thess 3:1 seems to indicate that he is no longer there.

On the basis of the account of Acts about Paul's missionary journeys, this letter is usually dated in 50/51.[1] But because of the theological and Christological views expressed in it, I think this letter should be dated even earlier, more specifically, before the Jerusalem assembly and the conflicts between Paul and the Jewish Christians which was the occasion of this meeting.[2]

In 1 Thess 2:2 we learn that Paul came to Thessalonica from Philippi, where he was persecuted. After establishing the church in that city (1:5–6), he left. He does not speak directly about the circumstances of his departure, unless 2:15–16 can be taken as an oblique reference to the Jews' driving him out and preventing him from speaking to the Gentiles "in Thessalonica," even though this city is not

---

[1] See Daniel Patte, *Paul's Faith and the Power of the Gospel: A Structural Introduction to the Pauline Letters* (Fortress Press, 1983), 352–360.

[2] C. Lüdemann in *Paulus, der Heidenapostel*, vol. 1 (Vandenhoeck & Ruprecht, 1980) reaches similar conclusions about the date of this letter on the basis of a very different type of research.

mentioned. Yet Paul might be referring to another situation (his persecution in Philippi, for instance) rather than to the situation in Thessalonica. At any rate, it is clear that he was not able to stay as long as he would have liked in order to establish the church on stronger foundations. Thus, he attempted several times to return, but without success: "Satan hindered us" (2:18). Finally, he sent Timothy to them from Athens "to establish you in your faith and to exhort you" (3:2). The Thessalonians were themselves persecuted by their "countrymen" (2:14), and he was afraid they would forsake their recently and incompletely established faith. When Paul writes, Timothy has returned to him with good news (3:6).

If we now compare this information with the account in Acts 17:1–10, we learn that Paul had to make a secret escape from Thessalonica because of a plot of the Jews against him. The Jews were "jealous" (Acts 17:5) of his missionary success among the Gentiles who attended the Synagogue (also called the God-fearers, people who were not yet Jewish proselytes but on their way to becoming proselytes). This fits well what we have found in the letter, with one important exception. While Paul is clearly saying that the church in Thessalonica is made up of pagans converted from idol worship (1 Thess 1:9) and thus of Gentiles, in contrast Acts assumes that the church included both Jewish and Gentile converts as a consequence of Paul's preaching in the Synagogue ("as was his custom" [Acts 17:2–4]). But there is nothing in Paul's letters to suggest that this was Paul's practice. This does not exclude the possibility that Gentile God-fearers had also been converted and that this brought about the hostility of the Jews against Paul's missionary activity. In 1 Thess 1:6 and 2:2 we find reference to a tense situation ("much affliction," "great opposition"), which was the occasion for Paul to warn the Thessalonians "that we were to suffer affliction; just as it has come to pass, and as you know" (3:4). But this later persecution suffered by the Thessalonians was apparently not directly from the hands of the Jews, but rather from those of their "countrymen."

Thus Paul wrote this letter to a young church that he had to abandon after a brief period of missionary activity. Yet he seems to have remained with them for several months, because the Philippians had the time to send gifts to him on at least two occasions (Phil 4:15–16). This does not necessarily contradict the account in Acts, which does not say how long Paul was in Thessalonica, but only how long he preached in the Synagogue.

Paul was concerned about this church's ability to withstand persecutions which broke out after his departure. Unable to go there himself, he sent Timothy to strengthen them and to encourage them in their faith (1 Thess 3:2). Upon receipt of good news about them (3:6) he writes to them. In effect, the goal of this letter is the same as that of Timothy's visit: strengthening them further in their faith. There is no specific problem (no false doctrine to fight against, no opponents teaching a wrong gospel) that he needs to correct. Paul simply addresses a young church which is still taking its first steps in the Christian life and needs to be guided and strengthened.[3] This is a pastoral letter of a missionary separated from recent converts.

Commentators unanimously agree that this letter was written by Paul, although some scholars argue that 1 Thess 2:13–16 is a non-Pauline addition. This view stems from the fact that this passage is violently anti-Semitic and thus in contradiction with other teachings of Paul about the Jews. It also seems to break the literary organization of the letter. The latter objection will be answered as we study Paul's argument. Against the former, it can be said that even though we might deplore such anti-Jewish statements (and their illegitimate use as a justification for anti-Semitic attitudes), they are understandable from somebody who was suffering persecution from the Jews. At any rate, our study will show that it is not an anti-Semitic but an "anti-persecutor" statement. Therefore, I view the entire letter as from Paul.

Methodology

The main purpose of this reading is to identify the passages which in this text are undergirded by fundamental convictions, that is, those which express the relation of the believers to the divine or, to use Paul's terminology, which most directly strengthen and confirm the Thessalonians in their faith. These are the statements which warrant the validity of the main argument.[4] A few remarks

---

[3] This view of the purpose and the circumstances of 1 Thessalonians is shared by most commentators; see esp. E. Best, *A Commentary on the First and Second Epistles to the Thessalonians* (Harper & Row, 1972), pp. 16–22. Others maintain that there were opponents in Thessalonica which Paul had to confront. See, e. g., W. Schmithals, *Paul and the Gnostics* (Abingdon Press, 1972), chap. 3, esp. pp. 154–55.

[4] For the role of warrants in an argument, see S. Toulmin, *The Uses of Argument* (Cambridge University Press, 1958). Yet in what follows we use a model that is more general than the one proposed by Toulmin. We want to refer to a general principle of structural organization which can be found at work in any discourse (narrative as well as any types of didactic discourses). Except in the case of very simple (and very short) discourses, there are several discourse levels. One level is the primary level. A secondary level is based upon the interpretations of the value of the primary level. A tertiary level is based upon the interpretation of the secondary level, and so on. Each level manifests a certain cluster of convictions (a certain part of the semantic universe). This can be understood by noting that, for instance, a secondary level necessarily presupposes values different from those of the primary level, since it interprets (i.e., attributes certain values to) the primary level. According to the type of discourse, the fundamental convictions are found on one or the other level. See D. Patte and A. Patte, *Structural Exegesis: From Theory to Practice* (Fortress Press, 1978), chaps. 2, 3, 4. In the case of didactic discourses (such as 1 Thessalonians) we have determined that the level formed by the warranting statements is the primary level and manifests the

about the general characteristics of the letter will help us understand how to identify them.

This letter is part of an ongoing dialogue: Paul, Silvanus, and Timothy are the "we," and the Thessalonians are the "you." As a stage of this dialogue, the letter establishes its own time-frame. The present of the letter—the dialogic present— is a reference point in time in terms of which a past and a future are posited as times which are *not* those of the dialogue. It also establishes its own "space"— the dialogic space—which includes what is directly related to "we" and "you" and thus an "outside space" which includes everything else. In a first approxima- tion we can recognize two dimensions or textual levels in this letter:

1. The level of the dialogue proper, which we shall call the *dialogic level*. It is made up of statements referring to the "present" interaction between "we" and "you." This level commands the unfolding of the overall argument of the letter.

2. Another textual level, which we shall call the *warranting level*, is formed of the statements that belong to other time and "space" frames such as past interac- tions between "we" and "you" and events which involve neither "we" nor "you." These statements do not make the main argument of the dialogic level progress. They are extraneous to it, but they play an important role in it. In fact, they es- tablish the validity of the dialogic level; they are warrants for it. To put it another way, the dialogic level is based upon the statements of the warranting level. For instance, at that level we will find former teachings of Paul serving as the basis upon which new teachings can be unfolded. On this warranting level the fun- damental convictions are found, while on the dialogic level there are only sec- ondary convictions.

This last assertion can be understood when we consider another general characteristic of 1 Thessalonians. Its dialogic level aims at *causing* the Thessalo- nians *to do* certain things such as leading a sanctified life. But how does one cause somebody to do something? There are two conditions:[5]

---

fundamental convictions, while the main argument, which is based upon the interpretation of the values of that primary level, manifests secondary values. See D. Patte, *Aspects of a Semiotics of Didactic Discourse* (Urbino, Italy: Center for Semiotic Studies, 1980). Both these publications propose precise criteria for the identification of these levels. We propose here a simpler approach which produces sound results, even though scholars will want to verify them by using the more sophisticated method. For simplicity's sake we shall speak of only two levels: a warranting level and a dialogic level. In fact, there are three levels in this text. What we call the warranting level actually involves two levels: a primary level found mostly in 1:3–2:16, and a secondary level found mostly in 2:17–3:6. The dialogic level is therefore a tertiary level based upon the interpretation of the value of both the primary level and the secondary level. Because the fundamental convictions are found on the primary level, we shall study this part of the text in greater detail.

[5] Through this example I express the two dimensions of the competence of a subject which Greimas calls "semantic competence" (having the knowledge necessary to perform the

1. One needs to explain to (or to teach) that person *how to do it*, that is, the various steps that one must take in order to do this action. This is what the dialogic level of the letter does. It explains how to have a sanctified life.

2. One needs to *convince* that person to do it, by showing why it is desirable, necessary, good, and so on, and why the instructions can be viewed as valid. This is the warranting level. In 1 Thessalonians it establishes the necessity of a sanctified life and the validity of the instructions by referring both to the fundamentals of the Christian faith accepted by the Thessalonians and to Paul as an example who implements this faith in his life.

The warranting level therefore has two functions: it establishes the fundamental convictional pattern which sets the believers in the right relationship with God (see esp. 1 Thess 1:3–2:16); and it proposes examples of the way in which this pattern can be applied. In the present case, Paul expresses how he applied this pattern in his own behavior (esp. in 2:17–3:6). Thus, the warranting level should not be construed as made up of a series of assertions verifying the validity of individual exhortations. Rather, it is providing the overall basis for the entire dialogic level, even though given parts of the warranting level are more directly related to specific parts of the dialogic level.

These brief remarks are enough to guide our reading of 1 Thessalonians.[6] By reviewing the overall argument of this letter, we will first identify how the dialogic and warranting levels are interrelated. We will note especially the textual elements which belong to the warranting level to be studied later in greater detail.

Macrostructure

This letter, in order to be a convincing discourse, needs to (re)establish a relationship between the addresser, Paul, and the addressees, the Thessalonians. The dialogic level, which includes the exhortations, posits and then takes for granted this relationship. The warranting level establishes the reality and the validity of this relationship. Yet, as we soon discover by reading the introduction and the conclusion, this relationship is not merely an "I-you" relationship but rather a complex relational network which forms the dialogic space and also defines who are the "I" and the "you."

---

action) and "modal competence" (having the will—which can also be an obligation—to perform the action). See "Competence" in A. J. Greimas and J. Courtés, *Semiotics and Language: An Analytical Dictionary* (Indiana University Press, 1982). For a discussion of the way in which this twofold competence is established, see A. J. Greimas, "pour une sémiotique didactique," *Bull.* 7 (1979); and Patte, *Aspects of a Semiotics of Didactic Discourse*, 1–20.

[6] For a more detailed account of my methodology, see Daniel Patte, "Method for a Structural Exegesis of Didactic Discourses. Analysis of 1 Thessalonians," *Semeia* 26 (1983): 85–129.

The salutation, "Paul, Silvanus, and Timothy, to the church of the Thessaloni-ans in God the Father and the Lord Jesus Christ" (1 Thess 1:1), indicates that this letter is addressed by Paul, Silvanus, and Timothy, "we," to the Thessalonians, "you," who are in a relationship with "God the Father" and the "Lord Jesus Christ." The dialogue is opened by a greeting: "Grace to you and peace." It continues with a thanksgiving: "We give thanks to God always for you all, constantly mentioning you in our prayers" (1:2). This shows that "we" is also in a relationship with "God" (through prayers). Furthermore, through this relationship with God, Paul and his companions are also in a relationship with the Thessalonians.

The conclusion of the letter, 1 Thess 5:23–28, reasserts the same dialogic space and specifies it. In 5:28 the greeting "grace to you" is repeated and made more explicit: "the grace of our Lord Jesus Christ be with you." It is a blessing establish-ing the Thessalonians in a good (right) relationship with the Lord Jesus Christ. The other part of the greeting, "peace," is also specified in 5:23: "May the God of peace himself sanctify you wholly." "Peace" expresses the establishment of the relationship of the Thessalonians with God, a relationship which implies sanctifi-cation. How can one who is in relationship with God not be holy? Furthermore, it is clear that the Lord Jesus Christ and God take the initiative for their relationship with the Thessalonians. Similarly, in 5:26–27 "you" is further defined: it involves "all the brethren" and not merely a few leaders. "Brethren, pray for us" (5:25), which echoes the prayer by Paul for the Thessalonians (1:2), shows that "you" and "we" are in a symmetrical relationship. They have the same status before God and the Lord Jesus Christ. Both Paul (and his companions) and the Thessalonians are established in their true identity ("we" and "you" as Christian brethren in dia-logue) through their relationship with God. But Paul did take the initiative in es-tablishing this "we-you" relationship. These two passages of the dialogic level posit a relational network which can be represented as a triangle. Both "we" and "you" involve a group. Even though this is in many ways a personal letter (as is clear from a few verses [2:18; 3:5; 5:27] where Paul writes in the first-person singular), Paul presents himself as associated with Silvanus and Timothy ("our brother and God's servant in the gospel of Christ" [3:2]). Similarly, he expects the Thessalonians to conceive themselves as associated with "all the brethren." The identity of the in-dividual Christian cannot be conceived outside of a relationship with brothers and sisters (i.e., with people who have the same status). Furthermore, such a rela-tionship in each of the groups, as well as the "we-you" relationship, exists only if each is in relationship with God and the Lord Jesus Christ. We can represent the relational network which forms the space of the dialogue as in Figure 13.1.

Thus, the introductory salutations and the conclusion posit a relational net-work among Paul, the Thessalonians, God, and the Lord Jesus Christ as the "space" (the partial semantic universe) in which the dialogue takes place. (For convenience, from now on we will say "Paul" to designate "Paul, Sylvanus, and

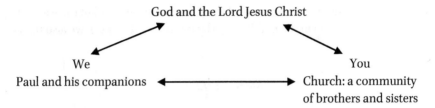

Figure 13.1: Relational Network in the Dialogue Space of 1 Thessalonians

Timothy.") This network involves the convictional pattern which characterizes Paul's faith and, in his view, also the Thessalonians' faith.[7]

In the context of this relational network the exhortations to a sanctified life (the bulk of the material in 1 Thess 3:7–5:22) can take place. These exhortations all belong to the dialogic level. For instance, consider 4:1: "*We* beseech and exhort *you* in the *Lord Jesus*...to please *God*." This exhortation is set in the present dialogic relation of "we" and "you" and involves relations to the Lord Jesus and God. Consequently, only if this relational network is accepted as true, real, and good by the Thessalonians will they perceive these exhortations as valid and trustworthy and thus as expressing what they will want to do. In other words, the Thessalonians will be true partners of Paul in this dialogue only if they perceive themselves in this relational network. Similarly, Paul can be this person he presents—a joyful and thankful Paul—only if this relational network actually exists and is perceived as good, that is, if the Thessalonians are truly in the right relationship, on the one hand, with God and Jesus and, on the other hand, with Paul as defined by this network.

Paul's thankfulness suggests that, as far as he is concerned, these relations do exist and that they are valid and good. He is convinced that the Thessalonians stand fast in their faith, but his pastoral concern for this young church under persecution pushes him to strengthen them in their faith, to reassert this faith rather than merely to presuppose that they have it. Thus the first part of the letter (which belongs to the warranting level) is devoted to reasserting the validity of the network of relations among Paul (and his companions), the Thessalonians, and the Lord Jesus and God, and to expressing what justifies his thankfulness

---

[7] In interpreting the salutation and closing of the letter, Best (*Commentary on Thessalonians*, 60–64, 242–47) follows the traditional procedure of historical-critical commentators who look for historical and theological content in key words or phrases of the text. Thus, such questions as the following are raised: Who was Silvanus? What does the word *ekklēsia* (church) mean for Paul? Do the terms spirit, soul, and body imply a tripartite psychology? Why does Paul speak of "grace and peace"? The latter two terms are unpacked with reference to Paul's theological ideas, that is, salvation, sanctification, wholeness, justification and so on. The relational network among Paul, the Thessalonians, God and the Lord Jesus Christ is thus neglected as a meaningful feature.

which he proclaims at the beginning of the letter (1:2), at the end of the warranting section (3:7ff.), and in the middle of it (by inserting the phrase "we also thank God" [2:13]).

Microstructures

The Typological Pattern of Paul's System of Convictions (1 Thess 1:3–3:6)

The entire first part (1 Thess 1:3–3:6) belongs, generally speaking, to the warranting level. In a first approximation we can distinguish two parts in this passage.

In 1 Thess 1:3–2:16 (and other verses interspersed throughout the letter) the warranting level establishes the validity of the relational network expressed in 1:1–2 (and 5:23–28). Its constitutive elements belong to a time frame other than the dialogic present, and even though they involve the same central personages (the Thessalonians and Paul), these are not set in the present we-you relationship. There is nevertheless in this part of the letter a series of phrases which belong to the dialogic level and are there as constant reminders that this material is presented to reassert the convictional basis for the rest of the argument. I refer to phrases like "remembering" (1:3), "we know" (1:4), "as you know" (1:5, 2:2, 5, 11), "you remember" (2:9), and "you are witnesses" (2:10).

Another part of the warranting level, 1 Thess. 2:17–3:6, has a slightly different function. It explains why Paul can be thankful. Consequently, it affirms the validity of the Thessalonians' faith and that this relational network is implemented both in the Thessalonians' life and in Paul's life.

We conclude that the purpose of the first part of the letter is to express what establishes and demonstrates that both Paul and the Thessalonians are in the right relationship with God and in the right relationship with each other. On this basis the exhortations found in the rest of the letter will be compelling for the Thessalonians.

In the Right Relationship with God: The Election (1 Thess 1:3–10)

In 1 Thess 1:3–10 we find a series of elements which, for Paul, are demonstrations of the reality and validity of this relationship. The warranting material is clearly broken up into discrete units by the use of phrases which belong to the dialogic level.

1. *The Thessalonians' behavior (1:3)*. "Your work of faith and labor of love and steadfastness of hope in our Lord Jesus Christ." We find here the triad which for Paul is characteristic of Christian life (5:8; cf. also 1 Cor 13:13, Gal 5:5–6, etc.). Note that faith, love, and hope are manifested in concrete behavior ("work," "labor," "steadfastness," or "endurance"). This first element of the warranting level is

introduced by the phrase of the dialogic level "remembering before our God and Father."

2. *God's action vis-a-vis the Thessalonians (1:4–5a).* "We know," a phrase of the dialogic level, introduces a second element of the warranting level. The Thessalonians are "beloved by God," "he has chosen" them by intervening in Paul's proclamation of the Gospel which was "not only in word, but also in power and in the Holy Spirit and with full conviction" (1:5a). Thus Paul's proclamation involved the intervention of God (manifestations of his power, possibly in miracles, and of his Holy Spirit).

3. *The Thessalonians' response to Paul's ministry (1:5b–6).* The next element of the warranting level is once again introduced by the phrase "you know." They "received the word in much affliction, with joy inspired by the Holy Spirit." As such they are "imitators" of Paul and of the Lord.

The response of believers in Macedonia and Achaia to the Thessalonians' faith: 1:7–8. In this element, which is not actually separated from the preceding, the Thessalonians are said to be an "example" or, better, a "type" for these believers.

4. *The message about Jesus (the kerygma; 1:9–10).* This last element is introduced by a phrase of the dialogic level: "they report," which implies, "we know." Jesus the Son of God will come from heaven; the "living and true God" raised him from the dead; he is the deliverer "from the wrath to come." We should note that all these elements are presented as related to the Thessalonians; they have turned to, and serve, the "living and true God," and they wait for his "Son from heaven."

The phrases which interrupt the development of the dialogic level allow us to identify these elements. But their identification is only approximate, and it does not show how they are interrelated. In most cases these elements seem to be merely juxtaposed and to be written down as Paul happens to remember them. Yet we can note that in this passage everything is related to the Thessalonians' experience, to which Paul directs the attention of the readers. Furthermore, Paul makes it clear that God intervened in their experience. Consequently, they are "chosen" by God. This already indicates that, for Paul, election is something *which happens in the believers' experience* rather than something established in the past. This important aspect of Paul's system of convictions sets his faith over against the Pharisees' faith. But then, in Paul's system of convictions, what is the place of this conviction about the election of the believers? And what is the distinctive convictional pattern which characterizes it? We begin elucidating it by considering how Paul relates the Thessalonians' experience to his own ministry, to the believers in Macedonia and Achaia, and to the Lord Jesus. Paul expresses this interrelation by means of two terms: "imitators" and "example" (as they are usually translated). We need to consider what kind of relations these terms refer to.

The Thessalonians are said to be "imitators of us and of the Lord" (1 Thess 1:6). What does this mean? Note that they are said to be imitators of Paul and the Lord because they "received the word in much affliction, with joy inspired by the Holy Spirit" (1:6). We again find the term "imitators" in 2:14: "For you, brethren, became imitators of the churches of God in Christ Jesus which are in Judea; for you suffered the same things from your own countrymen as they did from the Jews." From this we can conclude that Paul uses the term "imitator" in a sense quite different from the modern sense of this term. What makes the Thessalonians "imitators" of others is not that they follow their example (although they also do this), but that the same things *happened* to them.[8] When they received the word, two things happened to them: they were in affliction, that is, other people inflicted suffering upon them; and they were joyful, but this joy was a gift from the Holy Spirit and not their own doing. Similarly, in 2:14 they are imitators because they were persecuted by their countrymen. Thus, if they are imitators of Paul and of the Lord, it is first of all because what happened in their experience is similar to what happened in Paul's experience and in the Lord's experience, and only secondarily because of what they did (receiving the word and acting accordingly).

The Thessalonians are also said to be an "example," or in a literal translation a "type," for the believers of Macedonia and Achaia. "Type" is a technical term for Paul, which we can understand when we note that the Thessalonians are a "type" for the same reasons they were imitators. The text reads, "...for you received the word in much affliction, with joy inspired by the Holy Spirit; *so that* you became an example [literally, "type"]..." (1 Thess 1:6–7). Thus they are not so much a model to follow but rather a "type," that is, what happened to them is typical of what happens to those who receive the word, and thus their "experience" prefigures what will happen to other believers.

We now have an idea of how Paul perceives the relations among the various elements of this passage. There is an essential similarity among the experiences of Christ, of Paul, of the Thessalonians, and of the believers of Macedonia and Achaia, so much so that any one of these persons or groups can be said to be an imitator of those who precede him or them and a type of those who follow him or them in the unfolding of events.

In order to understand better this imitator/type relation among the Thessalonians' experience, Christ's experience, Paul's experience, and the Macedonian believers' experience, we will examine how Paul describes each of them. In a

---

[8] Best (*ibid.*, 112–13) stresses that Paul does not mean the Thessalonians were conscious imitators of the Judean churches but rather that they reacted in a similar manner (they endured) to similar pressures (persecution). But as we shall see such comments do not fully explain the relationship Paul perceives between the Thessalonians and the churches of Judea.

first approximation (which we shall refine as we progress) we can note that each of them involves three elements.

In the case of the Thessalonians' experience these three elements are (not necessarily in this order): receiving the word about the living and true God and acting accordingly (1 Thess 1:3, 9b; cf. also 1:6); suffering (1:6); and the intervention of God (at work in Paul's proclamation), which is thus an election by God (1:4), and through his Spirit (1:6). In the case of Christ we can presuppose that he received the word (since he is God's Son, he is in the right relationship with God), he suffered (he died [1:10; 4:14], he was killed by the Jews [2:15]), and God intervened and raised him (1:10). In the case of Paul, we simply know that God intervened in his experience (in his ministry [1:5]). The following verses say that he suffered (2:2) and that he received the Gospel and acted accordingly (2:4–5). In the case of the believers of Macedonia and Achaia, we know only that they are believers and thus that they received the word. But in view of the preceding types which prefigure what their experience will be, they should expect both suffering and God's intervention.

Another experience is mentioned: the experience of the believers at the end of time. Again we find the three elements: the believers are those who have received the word; they will be suffering the wrath (1 Thess 1:10) of God (cf. 5:9); God will intervene through the intermediary of his Son coming from heaven to deliver the believers (1:10).

These elements could form a chronological succession, a history: Jesus died and was raised; he appeared to Paul, who thus was elected to be Apostle to the Gentiles; Paul preached the Gospel to the Thessalonians, who thus were elected; the news of their faith is proclaimed throughout Macedonia and Achaia, and thus the believers of these regions are strengthened in their faith; and, at the end of time, Christ comes back from heaven to deliver the believers from the wrath to come. The text indicates clearly that Paul had in mind this historical development according to which one stage can take place only because the preceding stages have taken place and open the possibility for the next stages. But Paul does not present these elements in their chronological order. Such a presentation would have shown that for him the chronological and causal relations of this succession would establish the validity and the truth of the Thessalonians' faith. This would have implied either that the divine is discovered in a predetermined unfolding of history from its starting point (in the case of our text, Jesus) to its end (the Parousia) or that a complete and final revelation is found in its starting point (Jesus) and thus that the rest of the chronological succession is an implementation of this revelation in new situations.

Again, Paul does not ignore the historical development which links the experience of the believers on the one hand to Jesus and on the other hand to the Parousia. We will see that he perceived these stages as forming a sacred history which prolongs the sacred history of the OT. At the same time, he sees (and emphasizes) among the elements of this history another kind of relationship, namely, a certain identity among them. What happens to the Thessalonians is the "same thing" that happened to Jesus, Paul, and the churches of Judea. This two-fold understanding of the relations among Jesus, Paul, the Thessalonians, the Macedonian believers, and the believers at the Parousia is also reflected in his concepts of "imitator" and "type." On the one hand, the Thessalonians are imitators of Paul and the Lord because they *do* the same things they did: receiving the word, loving, hoping. The fact that the Thessalonians follow them as models is an expression of the historical link between them and those who preceded them. The same could be said about the statement that the Thessalonians themselves are models to be followed by the believers of Macedonia and Achaia. On the other hand, the Thessalonians are imitators of Paul and the Lord (and types for the Macedonians) because what happens to them is like what happened to Paul and the Lord (and what will happen to the Macedonian believers). In this case the historical, chronological, and causal link is discarded. The respective natures of the events/situations are compared and found to be equivalent. Since Paul does not stress in any way the chronological order of these various experiences, he makes it clear that this second kind of relation is primary for him, at least in this letter. In other words, he emphasizes the fundamental equivalence of these experiences.

It is also clear that he emphasizes the Thessalonians' experience. This suggests that the validity and truth of the Thessalonians' faith is found first in their own experience, where there is everything needed for establishing the truth of their faith. It is the experience of being chosen by God who intervened with power and with his Holy Spirit, and of having a joy inspired by the Holy Spirit in the midst of afflictions. Because of what happened in their lives, they are in the right relationship with God. Thus we can anticipate that Paul's experience and Jesus' experience simply verify the validity of the Thessalonians' experience. It is valid because it is of the same type as Paul's experience and Jesus' experience.

This provisional conclusion has far-reaching implications, since it means that the Thessalonians' faith is not centered on Jesus but on their own experience and what happened in it. More generally, it means that, according to Paul's faith, it is in the believers' experience that the convictional pattern is established for them. We have reached this provisional conclusion by noting that Paul focuses the attention of his readers on their own experience.

A first objection could be raised: this emphasis on the Thessalonians' experience was demanded by the thanksgiving literary form. But this emphasis is not accidental. Paul could have expressed his thankfulness about the Thessalonians' faith while focusing the readers' attention, for instance, upon Jesus' death and resurrection. This would have meant that he conceived of their faith—their right relationship with God—as primarily established by the events concerning Jesus. Such is, for instance, the pattern in Ephesians. In such a case, faith would be primarily an appropriation of the message about Jesus' death and resurrection, as the Pharisees appropriated the Sinai covenant, but a study of the organization of the argument in 1 Thessalonians shows that this is not how he sees their faith. It is not because of what happened to Jesus, nor because of what Jesus did, that the Thessalonians are in the right relationship with God. Rather, it is because of what happened in their own experience. To put it in terms of our discussion of Pharisaic Judaism, Jesus is not the complete and final revelation of their election (their chosenness). There is a new revelation to the Thessalonians.

But do not these last statements contradict what Paul writes about Christ in other letters? I have addressed this issue elsewhere with respect to Philippians and central texts of Romans and 1 Corinthians.[9] But in reading 1 Thessalonians we cannot reach any other conclusion. In fact, this letter says very little about what happened to Jesus and what he did in the past. It mentions that he was killed by the Jews (1 Thess 2:15), but no particular significance is attached to his death. Paul simply says that Jesus was killed as the prophets were and as Paul and the Thessalonians are persecuted. There is no mention that he "died for our sins" and thus that his death establishes the believers in the right relationship with God. Actually his death is mentioned in only three other passages of the letter. In 1:10 and 4:14 his death is mentioned merely to point out that God raised him from the dead. What is significant is his resurrection.

What then is Christ's role? It is a *present* and *future* role, as is clear in 1 Thess 1:10, "Jesus who delivers us from *the wrath to come*," and in 4:14, "through Jesus, God *will bring* with him those who have fallen asleep." The third reference to his death (5:10) also indicates that it is a future role. Christ "died for us so that whether we wake or sleep we might live with him" (5:10). As the context shows, this means that whether the believers are alive or dead they will be saved from God's wrath at the end of time. Again, Christ will bring about this salvation as the resurrected one (the believers will live with him), but in order to be the resurrected one who will save us, he needed to die. Thus he "died for us." This is all that our text says when one does not project on it what Paul writes in other letters.[10] The other passages about Christ in this letter also emphasize his future

---

[9] Patte, *Paul's Faith and the Power of the Gospel*, chs. 5, 7, and 8.

[10] According to Best (ibid., 217–18), 5:10 *does* focus attention on the salvific effects of Christ's death in the past: "Though salvation is future it is irrevocably bound to Jesus 'who died for us'; the exalted Lord who achieves salvation for us is the crucified Jesus." Verse 10 is the only place in the letter where Paul gives an explicit interpretation to the death of Jesus. For Best, the phrase used by Paul in this instance "recalls many others," such as Romans 5:6, 8; 14:15; 2 Cor 5:15. "It implies that through Christ's death we are aided and that in respect of salvation. Its casual introduction without any explanation of how Christ's death does benefit

salvific role. At the end of time he will come (cf. 2:19; 5:23) from heaven to "deliver us from the wrath to come" (1:10; cf. also 5:9) by taking the believers (both those who are alive and those who died) with him to heaven (4:17). Thus, one of the characteristics of the believers' attitude is "hope in our Lord Jesus Christ" (1:3).

Christ also has a role in the *present* experience of the believers. To begin with, as the resurrected Christ, he is the Son of the Father (1 Thess 1:10) and is with God in heaven ("sitting at the right hand of God" [Ps 110:1], a verse which was used by the early church to explain and make sense of the resurrection[11]). Therefore, he is Lord, the Lord of the believers, and as such he has authority over them, and Paul links his exhortations to the authority of the Lord Jesus (4:1). Furthermore, the resurrected Christ, the Lord, also intervenes (or is expected to intervene) in the present experience of the believers as God does. So we read in 3:11–12 this prayer of Paul: "Now may our God and Father himself, and our Lord Jesus, direct our way to you; and may the Lord make you increase and abound in love...." The intervention of God in the present life of the believers is associated, or even identified, with that of Christ. This helps us understand the strange statement found in 1:10: "Jesus who *delivers* us from the wrath to come." He delivers us *in the present*. The tense could easily be overlooked, since it is clear from the phrase "wrath to come" as well as from other passages that this deliverance will take place at the Parousia, that is, in the future. But the present tense indicates that this is the permanent function of Christ and that in a certain way it already takes place, although it will be fully carried out only in the future. Indeed, the wrath has already begun to come (on the Jews [2:16]). Furthermore, Paul uses technical terminology to speak about the present suffering and tribulations of the believers, which indicates that these are part of the sufferings expected at the end of time. And therefore, the ability to persevere joyfully despite these tribulations might also be viewed by Paul as a present (and preliminary) deliverance from the wrath to come. Indeed, this ability is given to the believers by an intervention of God through his Holy Spirit (1:6). The end is close at hand. Paul so much expects to be alive at the time of the Parousia ("we who are alive, who are left until the coming of the Lord" [4:15]) that during his missionary activity among the Thessalonians he did not teach them anything about what happens to those who die before that time (cf. 4:13).

---

men shows that it was a phrase well known to the Thessalonians." The assumption, then, is that we are to "fill in" the meaning of the phrase here with the content quarried from other Pauline and early Christian texts. But as Best himself notes, "salvation is future" according to 1 Thessalonians. Saying that it is past (achieved on the cross, as Best implies) contradicts Paul's letter. This future salvation is indeed "bound to Jesus who died for us," but it is because Jesus is a type of the believers both in the present and in the future.

[11] B. Lindars, *New Testament Apologetic* (SCM Press, 1961), 44–51; D. Hay, *Glory at the Right Hand: Psalm 110 in Early Christianity* (Abingdon Press, 1973).

All this suggests that in 1 Thessalonians the believers are not established in the right relationship with God through something which happened in the past (e.g., Jesus' death or the event of his resurrection in the past), but rather through what happens in their present experience which involves interventions of God, of the Holy Spirit, and of the resurrected Christ as Lord. Jesus' past experience (his death and resurrection) and Paul's experience guarantee the validity of their experience insofar as it follows the same type or pattern as theirs. In effect, Jesus' and Paul's experiences prefigure the Thessalonians' experience in the same way as their experience prefigures what will be that of the believers of Macedonia and Achaia, as well as the believers' experience at the time of the Parousia (we shall come back to this). The decisive events which establish them in their faith and thus in the right relationship with God and the Lord Jesus Christ take place in their own experience. In Jewish terminology, the Thessalonians have been chosen, elected by God (1 Thess 1:4), to be his servants (1:9) or, better, his "co-workers" (as Paul says of Timothy [3:2]; RSV: "God's servants") not because they appropriated a past election from the time of the Exodus or from the time of Jesus. They themselves are directly elected by God, who intervenes in their lives.

We should also note that Jesus Christ is a special kind of type. He might be viewed as the central type, since any new act of God can be viewed as Christ-like and even as manifestation of the resurrected Christ. Only when we have a more complete picture of Paul's system of convictions will we be able to understand Christ's uniqueness.[12] But it remains that Jesus Christ is a type, a promise (and not a complete and final revelation).

The preceding verses have warranted one part of the dialogic space, the relationship of the Thessalonians with God and the Lord Jesus Christ (the resurrected Christ). The place of Paul in this relational network remains largely undefined. The following passage specifies it.

Paul's Relationship to the Thessalonians (2:1–12)

The Thessalonians' experience is closely interrelated with Paul's, indeed, their experience includes Paul's ministry among them. Through his proclamation of the Gospel "in power and in the Holy Spirit and with full conviction" (1 Thess 1:5) God's call was manifested to them. This new section of the warranting level emphasizes this dimension of their experience and also the relation between their experience and Paul's, that is, the relation "we-you" of the dialogic space. On the basis of our reading of 1:3–10 we can now proceed more quickly.

As was the case in 1 Thess 1:3–10, this passage of the warranting level includes phrases of the dialogic level which emphasize certain elements of Paul's

---

[12] See Patte, *Paul's Faith and the Power of the Gospel*, 232–296.

and the Thessalonians' experience. The phrase "you know" is related to the Thessalonians' response to Paul's ministry in 2:1 (cf. 1:9) and to Paul's persecution in Philippi (2:2). The phrase "God who tests our hearts" (2:4; comparable to "as God is witness"), which expresses a present relationship with God and thus belongs to the dialogic level, is related to the affirmation that Paul's message was entrusted to him by God and was proclaimed to please God and not humans. This is reinforced by "as you know," in 2:5a, which points out that these are not words of flattery. "As God is witness" (2:5b) emphasizes that this is neither a disguised expression of greed nor an attempt to seek glory. On the contrary, Paul is both like a baby among them and like a nurse (2:6–8). The phrase "you remember" in 2:9 underscores that he worked night and day in order to avoid burdening them. The phrase "you are witnesses, and God also" in 2:10 calls his readers' attention to the holiness of his behavior among them. Finally, the phrase "for you know" in 2:11 is related to Paul's fatherly attitude toward the Thessalonians.

In order to understand how these components are interrelated, we consider successively those which concern Paul's experience prior to his interaction with the Thessalonians (Paul's own experience) and those which concern his ministry among the Thessalonians (Paul as part of the Thessalonians' experience). What does Paul say about his experience prior to his ministry in Thessalonica? Very little. He writes, "We have been approved by God to be entrusted with the gospel" (1 Thess 2:4a). He also states that he proclaimed and still proclaims the Gospel to other people, as well as to the Thessalonians (2:6; cf. also 2:4b, which is a general statement about his proclamation of the Gospel). Despite their conciseness, these statements include the three elements we have found to be the characteristic pattern of the Thessalonians' experience: suffering; God's intervention in his experience (in order to test and approve Paul and thus to establish his true identity, i.e., his identity as "apostle of Christ" [2:6]); and receiving the word and acting accordingly.

The description of his ministry in Thessalonica demonstrates that it is a manifestation of God in the Thessalonians' experience. Thus he declares that his message is "the gospel of God" (1 Thess 2:2) and not human, false, or greedy words (2:3, 5). He links his courage (in preaching the gospel despite great opposition) to God (having "courage in our God" [2:2]). He also emphasizes that his conduct among them was "holy and righteous and blameless" (2:10). This suggests the meaning "holy and righteous as God is." And he moves on to speak about "how, like a father with his children, we exhorted each one of you" (2:11). "Like a father," that is, like God the Father. Through his ministry Paul is indeed a manifestation of God for the Thessalonians. Using his terminology, we can say that Paul in his ministry is "imitator" of (or fulfillment of) the type "God in relation to somebody" (that is, with his Son, Jesus [1:10]). And thus, in the dialogic space, Paul (and his companions; "we") have authority over the Thessalonians, "you." Paul has the authority to exhort, to encourage, and to charge them.

In his ministry, Paul is also the fulfillment of the rest of the type "God in relation to somebody," that is, he is also the child under the authority of the Father, and as such he is concerned "to please God" (and "not to please men" and not to seek a benefit for himself [1 Thess 2:4–6]). He writes, "We could have made demands on you, but we were babies among you" (2:7). (This is, in my view, the best translation of this verse, including the word "babies" found in very good Greek manuscripts, rather than "gentle" found in other manuscripts[13]) This describes Paul in his relationship with the Father. Yes, Paul and his companions are apostles of Christ; they have authority. Yet at the same time they are children in their relationship with God, and thus they are like babies among the Thessalonians.

This brings about another metaphor: "As a nurse [nursing mother] taking care of her children [and giving them her own milk], so, having a strong affection for you, we were ready to share with you not only the gospel of God but also our own selves [or, our own life]" (1 Thess 2:7b–8, my translation; I have added the parenthetical phrases to clarify the meaning). Concretely this means that Paul shared his life with them by working night and day rather than being a burden to them (2:9).

Thus Paul is in the following relationship with the Thessalonians: he is an apostle, called and tested by God, in whose ministry among them God manifests his power and his Holy Spirit (1 Thess 1:5); but he is so as a child, submitted to and willing to please God the Father, and therefore he is a child with them, he is their brother (2:9); he is also a nursing mother who gives of herself (and who, in the family structure of that time, was submitted along with the children to the authority of the father); yet, in all this, he is a manifestation of God among them, and thus a father with his children. Paul is all this at the same time!

This is certainly a confusing use of metaphors, which we can better understand with the help of the imitator/type pattern we found in 1 Thess 1:3–10. Conversely, these metaphors will help us to perceive more clearly the relations which characterize this pattern and to complement the description we have

---

[13] While admitting that the reading "infants" has better manuscript evidence than the reading "gentle," Best prefers the latter on the grounds (1) that it fits in well with Paul's defense; (2) that "infants" would be an image which Paul elsewhere considers pejorative (1 Cor 3:1); and (3) that the reading "gentle" does not require a sudden inversion of metaphor as the former does (*Commentary on Thessalonians*, 10). However, swift and dramatic changes in metaphor are quite common in Paul's writings. For example, all the following metaphors are used in one short passage (2 Cor 3:1–5:2): letters written on our hearts, servants of a new covenant, a veil over the old covenant, a treasure in earthen vessels, the earthly tent which is our house, and ambassadors for Christ. We shall see why Paul "mixes" metaphors in our passage.

proposed above on the basis of 1:3–10. So we need to clarify the elements of Paul's, Jesus', and the Thessalonians' experience which correspond to the four metaphors.

Paul's experience involves: (1) Suffering, declaring to the Thessalonians the Gospel in the face of great opposition (persecution) because he has "confidence and assurance in God" (1 Thess 2:2) and sharing with them his own life (or his own being). This is the nurse metaphor. (2) Being approved by God to be entrusted with the Gospel; having a ministry in which God manifests his power. This is being an apostle. (3) Being in a child/father relationship with God, pleasing God and not humans. (4) Having a father-like authority to exhort, to encourage, and to charge.

As such, Paul's experience is the fulfillment of the type "Jesus," or in other words, he is an imitator of Jesus. Jesus' experience involves suffering and "dying for us" (1 Thess 5:10); God's intervention, the resurrection; the Father/Son relationship between God and Jesus; and Jesus as Lord (with the authority of God).

The Thessalonians' experience is, in turn, the fulfillment of both Paul and the Lord Jesus as types; that is, they are imitators of Paul and of the Lord. It involves: suffering and spreading their faith (the Gospel [1 Thess 1:7–8]) by their "work of faith, labor of love, and steadfastness of hope" despite persecutions; being called by God, having joy inspired by the Holy Spirit; being beloved by God their Father and being Paul's brothers; and being a "type" for the believers in Macedonia and Achaia.

As suggested earlier, Paul sees these three situations—Paul's, Jesus', and the Thessalonians'—as equivalent. In each of them there is the full manifestation and establishment of the right relationship with God. This is why Paul can direct his readers' attention to their own experience. But this also means that for Paul the various components of Jesus' experience, his own experience, and the Thessalonians' experience can be, and should be, understood together. As we saw, this is what he does in Galatians when speaking of his experience in terms of the Galatians' experience, and vice versa. Taking into account the equivalence of each of these components allows us to formulate some hypotheses and questions concerning Paul's system of convictions.

1. *Sharing One's Life with Confidence.* We shall make two observations concerning the correspondence of the first element of Paul's, Jesus', and the Thessalonians' experience.

When interpreting the meaning of his own experience, Paul knows the kerygma (proclamation) about Jesus. For him, as we suggested, the kerygma is a type of what will happen or happens to him as a believer. Thus he can perceive his own suffering (persecution) as equivalent to Jesus' suffering. But if this is so, he can then expect that God will intervene, as he did in the case of Jesus (when God raised Jesus from the dead). Thus Paul describes his suffering as follows:

"But though we had already suffered and been shamefully treated at Philippi, as you know, we had courage [confidence and assurance] in our God to declare to you the gospel of God in the face of great opposition" (1 Thess 2:2). So Paul "had confidence and assurance in God" (our effort to render the term usually translated "having courage" [2:2]). Could this mean that his confidence and assurance are based on the conviction that Jesus' experience as a whole is a type, a promise (Gal 3:22: "What was promised to faith in Jesus Christ") of what will happen and happens in Paul's experience? Jesus faced "great opposition," but God intervened. This is a promise that the same will be true in Paul's case. Similarly, in the Thessalonians' case, what does "work of faith" mean? Could it mean work in the confidence and assurance based on the promises manifested in Jesus' experience and Paul's experience?

Paul's attitude toward the Thessalonians in the context of persecutions can be described as sharing his own life with others (like a nursing mother). And Paul does this by working night and day (1 Thess 2:9). This could readily correspond to the Thessalonians "labor of love" (1:3). The exhortations of the dialogic level suggest it further. In 4:9–12, after stating that they do not need to be taught anything about love, he nevertheless exhorts them to work with their hands to "command the respect of outsiders, and be dependent on nobody." This is what the labor of love should entail, as they already know and manifest by their own behavior. Furthermore, in 5:14–15 Paul writes, "Encourage the fainthearted, help the weak, be patient with them all. See that none of you repays evil for evil, but always seek to do good to one another and to all." This could be summarized "Share yourself with others."

In Jesus' experience all this corresponds to Jesus "dying for us" (1 Thess 5:10). This should not be understood here as a sacrificial death for our sins (dying vicariously instead of the sinners). Rather, Jesus is sharing his life with us even up to death, a work of love comparable to Paul's proclamation of the Gospel despite persecutions and to the Thessalonians' labor of love.

2. Approved and Elected by God. Because of the correspondences among the various experiences, we can conclude that on the one hand, the joy inspired by the Holy Spirit during the Thessalonians' afflictions (1 Thess 1:6) and their election by God (1:4), and, on the other hand, God's approval of Paul (2:4) and the manifestation of God's power in his ministry (1:5), are equivalent to God's resurrection of Jesus. Thus Jesus' resurrection would be both a manifestation of God's power and an election. This would confirm our suggestion that, in Paul's view, through the resurrection Jesus became the Lord. Jesus is the Christ, the Lord, because God raised him not only *from* the dead but also *to* heaven, so that he might sit at his right hand. As we noted above, Paul's view of Jesus' death and resurrection seems to be based on the interpretation of those events as fulfillment of Ps 110:1: "The Lord says to my lord: 'Sit at my right hand, till I make your enemies your footstool.'" According to this interpretation of the early Palestinian church, the resurrection is the vindication of Jesus and also his election (and establishment) as the Lord. Similarly, the interventions of God in the Thessalonians' and Paul's experiences are resurrection-like events, events through which they are delivered from death like situations and through which they are elected, chosen for a specific vocation.

3. *Having Authority.* Similarly, the equivalence of the authority of Jesus as Lord, of Paul as apostle with a father-like authority, and of the Thessalonians as "type" for other believers is clear. The Thessalonians are Lord-like or apostle-like figures for other people.

So, this passage further establishes and defines the convictional pattern we found earlier. It does not add anything to our understanding of the believers' experience at the Parousia, except for the brief comment that this will involve participating in God's kingdom and glory (1 Thess 2:12). In other words, the believers will then be fully Lord-like.

The Scope of the Type/Imitator Pattern (2:13–16)

In this passage, already discussed in part, we find the same pattern again. The attention is focused on the Thessalonians' experience (1 Thess 2:13). Paul emphasizes that they are imitators of the churches in Judea (2:14) as well as implicitly of the Lord Jesus, of the prophets, and of Paul (2:15), since all of them have "suffered the same things" from their respective fellow citizens. We need only add two remarks.

First, the type/imitator pattern is expanded to include two additional stages: the churches in Judea and the prophets (of the OT). Second, despite the diatribe against the Jews (2:16), the convictional pattern demands that this same harsh judgment be applied to the persecutors at each stage of the pattern, that is, to the Gentile fellow citizens of the Thessalonians as well as to the Jews (in the same way that in the letter to the Galatians both the Gentile idolaters and the Jews are under a curse). Thus, this passage is not, in Paul's mind, anti-Semitic but rather "anti-persecutor."

Application of the Type/Imitator Pattern to New Situations (1 Thess 2:17–3:6)

This passage, which recounts both Paul's efforts to go back to Thessalonica and Timothy's visit, shows what Paul did as a result of his evaluation of the Thessalonians' situation as described in 1 Thess 1:3–2:16. It presupposes the fundamental convictional pattern we have elucidated and therefore expresses less fundamental convictions. Actually, it shows how Paul applies this pattern to new situations. Yet, once again we find the phrase "as you know," which signals the presence of another element of the fundamental warranting level. I am referring to 3:3b–4, where Paul mentions that he had told them beforehand that they would suffer affliction. This had already been said once, but his explanation of this in 3:5 brings a new dimension. The afflictions are associated with the Tempter (also called Satan [2:18]). The afflictions are the manifestation of a satanic power which can eventually cancel the manifestation of God's power (and thus Paul's labor would be in vain"). This begins to confirm our suggestion that the manifestation of God in the believers' (Thessalonians' and Paul's) experience is resurrection-like. Anticipating what we shall find in other letters, we can say that, in the same way that the resurrection is the overcoming of death by the power of God, so the election of the believers as well as the joy inspired by the Holy Spirit in the midst of persecution is the overcoming of an evil power. In light of our reading of Galatians, we can also say that this evil power which is overcome by the manifestation of God's power in the conversion of the believers is a power of bondage.

Similarly, 1 Thess 2:19–20 involves elements of the fundamental warranting level (the rhetorical question form has the same role as the phrase "as you know"). The Thessalonians are described as Paul's "hope," "joy," "crown," and "glory." Thus, he says that he will be able to boast of them "before our Lord Jesus at his coming." In other words, in Paul's experience the Thessalonians' conversion and faithfulness, which manifest that he is indeed an apostle with a father-like authority over them, is equivalent to the glory and the Lord-like position (cf. the crown) that he will have at the Parousia. They are his hope in the sense that they already prefigure what he will receive then. This suggests that while, for Paul, hope is the expectation of that which is not seen (Rom 8:24), it is *not* a blind expectation. Rather, it is based upon manifestations in the believers' experience, of things which are like—or, better, which are of the same nature, which are preliminary manifestations of—what is hoped for. Thus, this passage expresses the interrelationship of Paul's experience and the Parousia experience of the believers as conceived according to his convictional pattern.

About the rest of this passage we need only say that it is clearly the application to a new situation of the convictional pattern which had been previously established. In his concern for the Thessalonians, Paul is like a nursing mother to them (worrying about them and willing to sacrifice himself by being left alone in Athens [1 Thess 3:1]), but also like a father, since he wants to strengthen them in their faith and to exhort them. He does so through Timothy (3:2), because he himself was "hindered by Satan" (cf. 2:18). Similarly, Timothy's report about the faithfulness of the Thessalonians shows that they are themselves applying the convictional pattern to the situation of persecution in which they find themselves.

Implementing the Faith (1 Thess 3:7–5:22)

The rest of the letter belongs almost entirely to the dialogic level, which expresses how to carry out this faith in various concrete situations, that is, how to apply the convictional pattern in their daily life. First, Paul states in 1 Thess 3:7–13 how he applies this pattern in the present of the letter. He repeats in many ways what he has already expressed about the time he was without news from them (2:17–3:5), but adds now the dimension of thankfulness. This involves a veiled exhortation to lead a loving, perfect, blameless Christian life following Paul's example.

Then we find exhortations to a life free from immorality. This passage involves references to elements of his former teaching which belong to the warranting level (4:2, 6b–8) and which we have already found in other forms. This is followed by an exhortation to love (4:9–12), which also includes elements of the warranting level (4:9b–10a) that we have discussed above. Then Paul gives the Thessalonians a new teaching about the fate of those who died in 4:13–18 (with a brief reference to Jesus' death and resurrection).

The following exhortations to watchfulness (in the expectation of the Day of the Lord, which may come at any time [5:1–11]) also involve a reference to a former teaching on this matter (5:2–5). This shows that Paul included in his proclamation of the Gospel extensive teaching about the Parousia experience. But he primarily emphasized the relation between the believers' present experience and the Parousia. They are "children of light" who can hope (1:3; 1:10; 2:12; 2:19–20) because in their present there are prefigurations of what will be given to them at the end of time. But they have to be watchful. In the present there are people under the wrath of God (the Jews [2:16] and also possibly people under the power of the Tempter [3:5]), "children of darkness" who prefigure those who will be under the wrath of God at the end of time.

Finally, we find a series of exhortations about various issues (5:12–22). We need to emphasize only those found in 5:19–21a: "Do not quench the Spirit, do not despise prophesying, but test everything." These words presuppose that, for Paul, in the present of the believers and through the action of the Spirit, new revelations are received. They should not be neglected or set aside even though they always need to be tested.

Paul's Faith as Manifested in 1 Thessalonians (4:13–18)

The teaching of Paul concerning those who died (1 Thess 4:13–18) once more displays the pattern we found in 1:3–2:16. It applies the convictional pattern to a situation which heretofore had not been integrated into the Thessalonians' system of convictions (or semantic universe). As such, this passage gives us the opportunity to review the results of our reading of this letter.

The Thessalonians are ignorant concerning the fate of the Christians who died. This means that Paul failed to give them any instruction on the topic. But of what precisely were they ignorant? This is not clear. Were they ignorant of everything about the resurrection of the dead? The statement of 1 Thess 4:13 seems to imply that they are without hope for those who died. Yet the following verses do not emphasize the resurrection in itself but rather that "God will bring with him those who have fallen asleep" (4:14b), that is, that the dead, after being resurrected will participate in the Parousia. They will be taken to heaven by Christ, together with the believers who are alive (4:17). At the Parousia, those who are alive will not precede those who are dead (4:15). Did the Thessalonians already know about the resurrection of the dead and merely not know how the resurrected believers will participate in the events of the Parousia? This seems to be the case. To be "without hope" is not to be ignorant of a doctrine (here, about the resurrection of the dead) but to be unable to perceive the correspondences of one's experience (which includes death) with, on the one hand, the promise (type) which Jesus' experience is and, on the other hand, the ultimate fulfillment at the Parousia. Paul then shows them what it is to hope.

Paul establishes his teaching about the resurrection by referring to Jesus' death and resurrection in 1 Thess 4:14. As Jesus died, these believers died. As Jesus rose from the dead and to heaven at the right hand of God (see again our discussion of 1:10), God will bring these believers to him in heaven. This presupposes that he will also raise them from the dead (4:16). Therefore, the experience of the dead believers at the Parousia corresponds to and fulfills the promises contained in Jesus' experience. Yet, this correspondence, and therefore these promises, are not valid for everybody. They apply only to the believers, to those who died in Christ (4:16) or through Christ (a possible reading of 4:14). Whatever else the phrase "dead in Christ" means, it expresses that the believers' death corresponds to Jesus' death. Once the correspondence between this element of the believers' and Jesus' experiences is established, the correspondence between the other elements of their respective experiences is also established. So there is hope for the believers.

This is how the convictional pattern of Paul's faith is applied to new situations and how he incorporates them into his system of convictions. These remarks about 1 Thess 4:13–18 also underscore that the most characteristic feature of this convictional pattern is the establishment of correspondences among various experiences (or situations). Furthermore, these experiences are not merely duplications of each other. In each there is something new. Each involves a specific election and vocation (those of Jesus, Paul, and the Thessalonians are not identical). Therefore, none of these experiences can be viewed as a complete and final revelation. Rather, each is the promise or type of new revelations in new situations. Only one of these experiences can be viewed as absolute: the

Parousia experience (that is, the experience at the end of time). But even though it is expected soon, this experience is still in the future. In the present there are only relative revelations, revelations which apply to specific believers in specific situations.

Consequently, what establishes specific believers in the right relationship with God is what happens in their own experience. Since Paul addresses the Thessalonians, he focuses most of his attention on their experience and on God's manifestation in it, and therefore also on his ministry among them. Jesus' experience as well as Paul's own experience (and the experience of the churches in Judea) are secondary for the Thessalonians' faith, even though these experiences have an important role in ascertaining the validity of the Thessalonians' experience. Their experience cannot stand on its own. It is not an absolute. It is valid only insofar as it is related to other experiences either in the past or in the future.

For Paul the convictional pattern which characterizes the faith of the believers is centered on their experience (this is where they are established in the right relationship with God). But it has a threefold dimension, which Paul expresses by means of the three concepts "faith, love, and hope" (1 Thess 1:3 and 5:8). In light of our reading of this letter, we can propose the following three hypotheses regarding the meaning of these concepts.

1. The concept of "hope" clearly expresses the relations of the believers' experience to future experiences and especially to the Parousia experience. Hope is identifying events or situations of one's experience which are preliminary manifestations (types) of what will be manifested in other people's experience (the Macedonians [1 Thess 1:7]) in the near future, as well as, more fully, at the time of the Parousia. In Paul's experience, the faithful Thessalonians are his hope, his crown, his glory, that is, preliminary manifestations of what will be at the Parousia (2:19–20). Hope therefore involves identifying, in one's present experience, the preliminary manifestations of the Parousia and waiting with confidence for the ultimate manifestations.

2. Similarly, we can suggest that Paul's concept of "faith" (not to be confused with faith as a phenomenon which includes convictions about what Paul calls "faith," "hope," and "love") could express the relations of the believers' experience with past experiences (especially Jesus' but also Paul's, the Judean churches', and the prophets' experiences). "Faith" is identifying, in one's experience, events or situations which are fulfillments of what has been manifested in Jesus' or Paul's or the Judean churches' or the prophets' experiences (the types). Because of this correspondence, having faith means being at one with Jesus or with Paul or with the Judean churches or with the prophets. Could it be that the phrase "in Christ" is used in part to express that such a relationship is acknowledged by the believers? They are "in Christ" because, in their experience, there are Christ-like events.

The elements in one's experience discovered through faith as fulfilling the promises contained in the types Jesus and Paul, as well as in other types, are actually the same elements discovered through hope as being preliminary manifestations of what will be in the future and at the Parousia. Thus, in Paul's experience, the Thessalonians through their conversion are the fulfillment of the promises contained in Jesus' experience as well as preliminary manifestations of what will be Paul's crown and glory at the Parousia. By the discovery, through faith and hope, of the relations of these elements of one's experience with past and future experiences, one is established in the right relationship with God. In other words, it is by considering what God has done in Jesus' and Paul's experiences, as well as what he is beginning to do in the experience of others (the Macedonians) and what he will do at the Parousia, that one is established in the right relationship with God. Through faith (and hope) one is established in the right relationship with God; that is, one discovers one is chosen by God, elected by God. In other words, it is only when one takes into account how God acted, is acting, and will act in the experience of other people that one can be in the right relationship with God. This does not occur when one's attention is focused exclusively on one's own relationship with God and on what God does in one's life.

3. Paul's concept of love could then express how this pattern (of the right relationship with God established through faith and hope) is applied in all the situations of one's own experience. It should not come as a surprise that the application of the faith and hope pattern to the believers' experience defines this experience as a specific kind of relationship with other people, love, for it is clear from our reading of 1 Thessalonians that a believer's experience is not a private experience. We are far from a view of religious experience (common in our culture) according to which a believer is in relationship with the divine by him or herself, through an individual, interior (mystical) encounter with the divine. For Paul, a believer's (religious) experience involves other people. Without even speaking of the Thessalonians' interrelation among themselves, we have noted that, at least, Paul was part of the Thessalonians' experience. And Paul is a necessary part of the Thessalonians' religious experience. Where did they discover manifestations of God? First of all, in Paul, in whom God manifested his power. Indeed, their conversion involved the discovery of God in Paul's ministry. Faith is not merely believing that God intervened in the past and will intervene in the future in other people; it is also the discovery that God manifests himself in somebody else who is part of one's present experience. The Thessalonians first discovered God at work in Paul, and this was for them an election (1 Thess 1:4–5). Only afterward did the Thessalonians experience God's intervention in their own private lives (e.g., the intervention of the Holy Spirit [1:6]). As a consequence of such a faith, the believers cannot but see themselves in a special relationship with those (or the one) in whom they discover God at work. Thus the

Thessalonians' "love" Paul (3:6), but now Paul is exhorting them to love one another as they already do (4:9–10) and also to "esteem . . . very highly in love" those who labor among them and are over them in the Lord (5:12–13). The inevitable question is: could it be that, according to Paul's system of convictions, the Thessalonians are in the same relation among themselves as they are with Paul? In other words, could it be that, through faith, they also discover God at work in their sisters and brothers? Could it be that love is this attitude that one has toward persons in whom one discovers God? My study of the rest of Paul's letters has confirmed that this is the case, despite the puzzling fact that Paul also appears to ask the Thessalonians to love nonbelievers (3:12; 5:15).[14]

A last tentative remark about love, love as imitation of those who preceded the believers in the faith. Through hope and faith the believers are "imitators" of those who preceded them (the prophets, Jesus, the churches in Judea, Paul) and "types" of those who will follow them (the Macedonian believers, the believers at the end of time), because what happens to them is the same thing which happened or will happen to those who preceded them or will follow them. Yet through love the believers are "imitators" of those who preceded them and whose example they follow. As they did, the believers implement their faith in their daily life. They receive the word (1 Thess 1:6), they turn to God from idols, they serve God (1:9), and they love one another and all people (3:12).

The convictional pattern of Paul's faith includes the same elements as the convictional pattern of the Pharisees' faith, although the patterns themselves are quite different. I have argued elsewhere that in the Pharisees' faith there are two dimensions: (1) the election and the vocation is established once and for all in the biblical (past) sacred history. To be the Chosen People, the Pharisees only need to appropriate this past election by "entering into Scripture." (2) The way to walk (the halakah) involves carrying out this vocation in any new cultural situations by following the example of the biblical personages viewed as models and by fulfilling the commandments which need constantly to be reinterpreted so that they might be coextensive with life.[15]

For Paul, the election and the vocation are discovered, through faith and hope, in the believers' experience. The revelatory acts of God, which are calls (elections), are to be found in the experience of the believers either in the recent past or in the present. Thus, Paul writes, "He who calls you is faithful" (1 Thess 5:24), not "He who called you in the time of the Exodus or of Jesus' death and resurrection." God acts (performs revelatory acts) in the present as he did in the past. These acts are calls, elections, and also vocations. Through faith and hope (which allow them to view events of their experience as God's acts, as elections),

---

[14] Patte, *Paul's Faith and the Power of the Gospel.*
[15] Ibid., 87–121.

the believers discover that they are called to be God's Chosen People. This also involves a vocation, the vocation to serve God (as the Lord Jesus and as Paul the apostle did and do). In all this, Jesus, Paul, and others who preceded the believers are types whose experiences help them to discover their election and vocation.

Once this election and vocation are established, the believers must carry out their vocation. Because their vocation is not exactly the same as the vocations of those who preceded them, their way of carrying it out involves new dimensions. But those who preceded them—Jesus and Paul in this letter—are examples, models, that they can and should follow, as the Pharisees followed the examples of Abraham, Moses, and other biblical personages.

14

2 Thessalonians

Michael Aubrey

1. Preliminaries

This essay attempts a brief discourse analysis of Paul's second letter to the Thessalonians. Its author, however, has a background in syntax and semantics rather than the more established approaches to discourse analysis. The analysis attempted here is from someone not entirely engaged with the concept of grammar "above the sentence." Instead, I consider sentence grammar and discourse grammar as the same grammar. What cognitive science, generally, and linguistics, specifically, has taught about language processing tells us that human beings engage with language in a more-or-less linear manner: processing one sentence at a time. What has come before, in the minds of the reader (and what is about to come in the mind of the author) exists not as sentences, but as concept, image, and symbol—to borrow a turn of phrase from Langacker.[1] Discourse is, itself, *language-in-use*. As such, any functional approach to studying language and grammar, to the extent that it is usage-based, ought to be able also to account for discourse structure. As Langacker puts it,

> Discourse is the use of language. Conversely, a language resides in conventional patterns of usage. These patterns, learned from countless instances of

---

[1] Ronald W. Langacker, *Concept, Image, and Symbol: The Cognitive Basis of Grammar* (Mouton de Gruyter, 1990).

use in discourse contexts, are subsequently applied in producing and under-standing further discourse. It is the old, familiar story of the chicken and the egg.[2]

It is no accident that much of usage-based linguistics is framed in terms of discourse. Syntactic patterns of word order are conventionalized through infor-mation flow. Even English's fairly strict Subject-Verb-Object constituent order is a conventionalized version of the movement from information presumed that audience knows (the subject) to the asserted new information (the verb and object) in the traditional topic-comment structure.[3] This is the principle of natu-ral information flow—the tendency in communication to move from old infor-mation to new.[4] English, for example, has a wide variety of formal constructions for getting around its otherwise strict word order in order to adjust clause struc-ture to the needs of this information flow.

- Dummy subject constructions: There once was a prince.
- Passive constructions: The prince was attacked by a knight.
- It-cleft constructions: It was the knight who had previously kidnapped the princess.

In these sentences we find discourse and sentence grammar happening all at once. The dummy subject construction is used to present brand new information when a speaker has no ability to rely upon previous context or shared knowledge of people or events—hence its common use as a means of beginning stories. Pas-sive constructions provide a means of separating the ordering position of new or old information from the expectations that the subject and the agent are one and the same. In passive constructions, English speakers prefer the agent in the *by-phrase* to be the newest piece of information, while the subject being acted upon tends to be an already established participant. The *it-cleft* construction provides a means for the speaker to shift the topic from the *prince* to the *knight*. Sentence grammar constructions drive the development of the discourse.

Finally, there is the *princess*. Her status as new information makes sense at the end of the *it-cleft* construction. Yet, her existence in the story is somehow also expected, or at least, unsurprising. The other two participants: *prince* and *knight* were both introduced with an indefinite article: "*a*." They were brand new and thus it would have seemed odd in the story if the definite article "*the*" had

---

[2] Ronald W. Langacker, *Cognitive Grammar: An Introduction* (Oxford University Press, 2008), 457.

[3] See Knud Lambrecht, *Information Structure and Sentence Form: Topic, Focus, and the Mental Representations of Discourse Referents*, CSL 71 (Cambridge University Press, 1994), 221–228.

[4] Steven E. Runge, *A Discourse Grammar of the Greek New Testament: A Practical Introduc-tion for Teaching and Exegesis* (Hendrickson Press, 2010), 187–189.

been used. "There once was the prince," sounds foreign to English speakers as the beginning of a story. This is not the case for "the princess." Despite being brand new, the definite article does not sound strange here. Definiteness is chiefly a question of participant reference. Introducing a participant "activates" that participant. Once active in the mind of the audience, reference can be made using the definite article to signal: "this is the same prince as before."[5] So why does it seem so natural for *princess* to also receive the definite article here? Simply: as participants, "prince," "princess," and (to a perhaps lesser extent) "knight" all come from shared conceptual scene: introducing or activating "prince" and "knight" activates the larger frame of the genre of the story: *the fairy tale*. Activating part of the frame makes the entire frame with all that it entails accessible to the audience.[6] All these basic principles are relevant, also, to New Testament Greek, as well as several others. But out of considerations of space, the focus below is on these topics: information structure and flow, word order, definiteness, frame semantics, participant reference, and activation.

A comment needs to be made, additionally, about the structure of texts. In narrative, which letters and epistles are not, it often feels like a relatively simple matter to separate out the mainline narrative story from the contextualizing, offline information.[7] The various genres of non-narrative present a much more

---

[5] Stephen Levinsohn describes two basic default principles for definiteness with people in Greek: (1) to introduce and activate a new participant by name, a speaker uses an anarthrous noun phrase, while (2) to refer to an already active participant, a speaker uses an articular noun phrase. See Stephen Levinsohn, *Discourse Features of the Greek New Testament* (SIL International), 148–167 for a fuller discussion of definiteness and participant reference in Greek.

[6] As an alternative example, consider the sentences: "John entered his house. A book was on the table." The noun "table" is already activated by the larger frame that "house" activates. Similarly, there would be little need to introduce other elements such as "chair," "couch," "door," "window," or "kitchen" using the indefinite article. All of these are elements of the "house" frame and would naturally receive the definite article instead. See: Allan M. Collins and Elizabeth Loftus, "A Spreading-Activation Theory of Semantic Processing," *Psychological Review* 82 (1975): 407–28; Karen Sullivan, *Frames and Constructions in Metaphoric Language*, CAL (John Benjamins, 2013), 64–76; and Alan Cienki, "Frames, Idealized Cognitive Models, and Domains," in *The Oxford Handbook of Cognitive Linguistics*, ed. Dirk Geeraerts and Hubert Cuyckens (Oxford University Press, 2007), 170–187. The terms "frame," "scene," "script," and "schema" are often used interchangeably (Cienki, "Frames," 173).

[7] "Feels" is a key word here; there is little simple about it. Nevertheless, distinctions in tense and aspect in narrative often contribute to a sense of stability in separating out the storyline from its context. See Livia Polanyi-Bowditch, "Why the Whats are When: Mutually Contextualizing Realms of Narrative," Berkeley Linguistics Society 2 (1976): 59–77; Monika Fludernik, "Narratology and Literary Linguistics," in *The Oxford Handbook of Tense and Aspect* (Oxford University Press, 2012), 75–101, and Stephen H. Levinshon, "Verb Forms and Grounding in Narrative," in *The Greek Verb Revisited*, ed. Steven E. Runge and Christopher J. Fresch (Lexham Press, 2016), 163–183.

complicated situation. While in narrative discourse, tense and aspect are central devices for organizing a text,[8] in non-narrative discourse, connectives, finiteness, and complex constructions like subordination become central for authors and speakers creating structure in their discourse.[9] The difference between the mainline and offline material is also scalar rather than absolute. We see this regularly in Paul's letters, where excurses and elaborations create their own miniature mainlines before Paul comes back to whatever his central focus might be. Connectives, in particular, form the structural rigging for shifts between topics in a manner that helps orient the reader between continuity and change in discourse.

Finally, a couple notes on how I deal with non-discourse questions are in order. First, because of space constraints, I leave numerous non-discourse-oriented issues without comment. A good example is the phrase τοῖς μὴ ὑπακούουσιν τῷ εὐαγγελίῳ ("the ones who did not obey the gospel/good news") in 2 Thess. 1:8, which in any other context would otherwise deserve substantial examination—obedience to the good news strikes a chord of dissonance that yearns for a fuller exploration, especially given how commonly unremarked it is in major commentaries. Unfortunately, such an examination must be left for another time and place. Second, the past three decades have seen an ongoing rise of secondary literature examining the nature and structure of languages with active-middle voice systems, such as Greek, as compared to active-passive systems, such as English.[10] I have taken the opportunity, then, to explore alternative glosses to verbs that have traditionally been rendered in translation as

---

[8] Paul J. Hopper, "Aspect between Discourse and Grammar," in *Tense-aspect: Between Semantics & Pragmatics*, ed. Paul J. Hopper (John Benjamins, 1982), 3–18.

[9] Steve Runge, "The Contribution of Verb Forms, Connectives, and Dependency to Grounding Status in Nonnarrative Discourse," in *The Greek Verb Revisited*, ed. Runge and Fresch, 221–272.

[10] The literature on middle voice is vast, but some of the important contributions include: M. Klaiman, *Grammatical Voice* (Cambridge University Press, 1991); Suzanne Kemmer, *Middle Voice* (John Benjamins, 1993); Linda Manney, *Middle Voice in Modern Greek* (Amsterdam: John Benjamins, 2000), Robert M. Dixon and Alexandra Y. Aikhenvald, eds., *Changing Valency: Case Studies in Transitivity* (Cambridge University Press, 2000); Carl W. Conrad, "New Observations on Voice in the Ancient Greek Verb," https://pages.wustl.edu/files/pages/imce/cwconrad/newobsancgrkvc.pdf (accessed January 17, 2017); Rutger Allan, *Middle Voice in Ancient Greek* (Brill, 2003); Åshild Næss, *Prototypical Transitivity* (John Benjamins, 2007); Ricardo Maldonado, "Middle as a Basic Voice System," in *Studies in Role and Reference Grammar*, ed. Lilian Guerrero, Sergio Ibáñez, and Valeria Balloro (Mexico City: UNAM, 2009), 69–109; Rachel Aubrey, "Motivated Categories, Middle Voice, and Passive Morphology," in *The Greek Verb Revisited*, ed. Runge and Fresch, 563–625; and Rachel Aubrey, *Hellenistic Greek Middle Voice, Semantic Event Structure and Voice Typology* (Thesis, Canada Institute of Linguistics and Trinity Western University, 2020).

English passives. I hope this endeavor encourages new ways of thinking about how we can understand and interpret another language's voice expressions in English.

2. A Discourse Analysis of 2 Thessalonians

Reading the mail of strangers may often feel like a fraught affair. There are necessarily events, people, and information shared between the authors and the audience to which we, as readers, do not have access. Despite how familiar Paul might be to readers of the New Testament, between Acts and his other letters, we are still merely snooping in on the relationship between himself and the church at Thessalonika. We do not have their shared knowledge, and this affects our ability to process how Paul activates shared ideas, concepts, and events.

The letter itself can be split into two sections. In addition to the formal greetings, the letter has two expressions of thanksgiving: the first at 1:3–4 and the second at 2:13. These two sections function to frame the primary purpose for writing this letter. The first expresses thanksgiving before the authors lay out prohibitions and warning with regard to how the church understands Christ's return and the eschatological events surrounding that final judgment in order to encourage and alleviate troubled readers. The second thanksgiving balances out those prohibitions and warnings with more thanksgiving before reframing those warnings in a positive manner: Do not be shaken or deceived vs. stand firm. These two thanksgivings also illustrate the complex relationship in nonnarrative between the foreground/mainline thrust of a letter and its background/offline context. The thanksgiving sections are background relative to the main teachings, but each thanksgiving itself has its own internal line of thought as well. In this way, letters represent complex, layered discourses. The second chunk of the letter, 3:1–15, focuses on practical issues: prayer needs and behavior correction. Finally, Paul concludes the letter in 3:16–17.

2.1. Letter Preliminaries: Addresses and Greetings.

Letter-writing has its own script. This was as true two thousand years ago as it is today. The Greco-Roman letter structure establishes a minimum of two participants from the beginning: speaker and audience. This effectively locates the letter genre within the domain of dialogue/monologue, rather than narrative proper, since the discourse is framed in terms of two interlocutors: first-person (speaker) and second-person (audience). These two are then introduced by a nominative case participant and a dative case participant, which positions a trajectory of transfer from nominative (sender) to dative (recipient).

1–2 Παῦλος καὶ Σιλουανὸς καὶ Τιμόθεος τῇ ἐκκλησίᾳ Θεσσαλονικέων ἐν θεῷ πατρὶ ἡμῶν καὶ κυρίῳ Ἰησοῦ Χριστῷ· χάρις ὑμῖν καὶ εἰρήνη ἀπὸ θεοῦ πατρὸς καὶ κυρίου Ἰησοῦ Χριστοῦ.[11]

Paul and Silas and Timothy, to the Church of Thessalonika in God our Father and the Lord Jesus Christ. Grace and peace to you from God the Father and the Lord Jesus Christ.

Both sender and recipient, here, are plural groups. Thus, here in 2 Thessalonians 1:1, the speakers are "Paul, Silas, and Timothy," respectively. We may make the reasonable judgment that when the first-person singular is used, it refers to Paul only. Similarly, the audience is also a group: "the church at Thessalonika in God our father and the Lord Jesus Christ." All second-person verbs and pronouns in this brief letter are plural, so it is also safe to assume that the authors are directing the entirety of their message to the whole church, though the authors do call out a smaller group within the congregation in chapter 3. Thus, Paul's standard greeting, "Grace to you and peace from God the Father and the Lord Jesus Christ." Note that the greeting shares a syntactic structure with the address: like the letter itself moving from nominative sender to dative recipient, so do the nominative grace and peace move from God and Christ to the dative pronoun ὑμῖν, "you."

2.2. Thanksgiving and Instruction

Following the initial greeting, the first section of the letter's body goes from 1:3 through 2:17. This section is constituted by three smaller sections. First is the writers' thanksgiving prayer (1:3–12). Second is their discourse on the Lord Jesus Christ's return (2:1–12), which expounds on themes introduced in the prayer. In addition to the content segmentation (prayer vs. exposition), the shift from chapter one to chapter two is also reflected in structural differences: 1:3–12 moves from thought to thought primarily through various forms of subordinating constructions with far fewer clear independent clauses, while 2:1–12 organizes itself with smaller independent clauses. The third section is 2:13–17, in which Paul and his coauthors give thanks for the Thessalonians once more before summarizing the purpose of the letter with a final positive command and benediction.

2.2.1. First Thanksgiving

3–4 εὐχαριστεῖν ὀφείλομεν τῷ θεῷ πάντοτε περὶ ὑμῶν, ἀδελφοί, καθὼς ἄξιόν ἐστιν, ὅτι ὑπεραυξάνει ἡ πίστις ὑμῶν καὶ πλεονάζει ἡ ἀγάπη ἑνὸς ἑκάστου πάντων ὑμῶν εἰς

---

[11] The Greek text used here is the SBLGNT: Michael W. Holmes, *The Greek New Testament: SBL Edition* (Lexham Press; Society of Biblical Literature), 2011–2013.

ἀλλήλους, ὥστε αὐτοὺς ἡμᾶς ἐν ὑμῖν ἐγκαυχᾶσθαι ἐν ταῖς ἐκκλησίαις τοῦ θεοῦ ὑπὲρ τῆς ὑπομονῆς ὑμῶν καὶ πίστεως ἐν πᾶσιν τοῖς διωγμοῖς ὑμῶν καὶ ταῖς θλίψεσιν αἷς ἀνέχεσθε.

3 We are obliged to give thanks to God constantly for you, brothers and sisters, just as it is deserving, that your faith is flourishing the love of each and every one of you toward each other, such that we ourselves boast about you among the churches, about your patient perseverance and faith in all your persecutions as well as in the oppression that you are bearing

The prayer of thanksgiving comes from all three senders and introduces themes central to the first, larger section of the letter's body. This expression of thankfulness establishes an interpretive frame for Paul's following exhortation and encouragement.

The first-person plural pronouns in 3–4, function exclusively, referring only to the senders of the letter, as evidenced by the contrast with the second-person pronouns: περὶ ὑμῶν, "concerning you," and ἡ πίστις ὑμῶν, "your faith," and ἡ ἀγάπη ἑνὸς ἑκάστου πάντων ὑμῶν εἰς ἀλλήλους, "of each and every one of you toward each other." The thanksgiving is structured around abstract concepts about the audience (again, cf. περὶ ὑμῶν). Concepts like *faith* and *love*, are readily made definite because they belong to a group of abstract entities that are always accessible, even if they are not overtly activated by a speaker.[12] That they are new topics in the discourse is reflected in the VERB-SUBJECT constituent order—the default for newly asserted information.[13] The coordination of these two intransitive clauses also has significance for the discourse: each time faith is mentioned in chapter 1, it comes coordinated with some manifestation. Here in 1:3 it is faith and reciprocated love in the church community. In 1:4 it is patient endurance / steadfastness. In 1:11, it is desire for generosity. In addition to the fact that Paul is genuinely thankful for the Thessalonians' love, he also wants them to associate these behaviors with ἡ πίστις. Faith is not merely belief or assent to theological truth (though it is that, too: 2 Thess 2:13), but the acting on that truth: love one another, patiently persevere, show generosity. By coordinating these with πίστις at the beginning of the letter, they become part of faith's frame of reference and are readily reactivated again when πίστις is mentioned later.

---

[12] For πίστις "faith, trust," and ἀγάπη, "love," specifically, their accessibility for definiteness marking emerges from the existing relationship between speaker and audience, on the one hand, and between audience and God, on the other. Because Christian relationships presume trust and love, the concepts are already accessible. Sullivan observes that, "extremely basic" lexical items tend to be associated with a large number of domains (*Frames and Constructions*, 109). The concepts to which such items refer are readily accessible across wide variety of contexts.

[13] Levinsohn, *Discourse Features*, 29–30.

The connective ὥστε is often described in terms of result, but it is also often used in the papyri for elaboration of a point and these two are not mutually exclusive. This is true, not only of its use with indicative finite verbs (e.g. 1 Cor 3:7), but also with infinitives.[14] Especially in letters, the distinction between independent and dependent clauses grows weaker. That is, ὥστε has both a semantic function, but also serves as a marker of text segmentation.

Paul and his co-authors continue to emphasize the relationship between (1) behavior and (2) the growth of the church's faith: patient perseverance and faith, except now it is framed in terms of external forces at work as well: oppression and persecution.

5 ἔνδειγμα τῆς δικαίας κρίσεως τοῦ θεοῦ, εἰς τὸ καταξιωθῆναι ὑμᾶς τῆς βασιλείας τοῦ θεοῦ, ὑπὲρ ἧς καὶ πάσχετε

—*evidence of God's just judgment for your worthiness of God's kingdom, which is also why you are suffering.*

Ἔνδειγμα τῆς δικαίας κρίσεως τοῦ θεοῦ can either be construed as an appositional construction (known in linguistics as a right-dislocation) or as an independent non-verbal clause.[15] Both interpretations of the syntax create discontinuity in the discourse. This question is not insignificant, but the more interesting part of its syntax is its definiteness.

Up until this point, there are been very few indefinite noun phrases. We had the address and greeting, which introduce all the essential participants: Paul, Silvanus, & Timothy, God the Father, and Jesus Christ, but everything in vv. 3–4 was treated as given or already known by the audience: their faith, their love, their patient perseverance, their persecution and oppression—all introduced with definite articles. Paul, Silvanus, and Timothy know that the Thessalonians know these things. This is all grounding for their main purpose.

This noun phrase, ἔνδειγμα τῆς δικαίας κρίσεως τοῦ θεοῦ, on the other hand, is effectively the first piece of brand-new information in the letter. Whether an appositional NP ("noun phrase") or a non-verbal clause, it functions as the lynchpin that connects the known experiences of the audience to the message of the writers. In a sense, everything they have said in the thanksgiving is grounding for this assertion in v. 5.[16] The scope of the proof/evidence likely covers most

---

[14] See P.Oxy 268, line 6, for example.

[15] The question of case for ἔνδειγμα is moot. If a right-dislocation, either nominative or accusative is perfectly grammatical. If a non-verbal clause, then it is necessarily nominative.

[16] The idea that ὅ ἐστιν should be supplied, as described by BDF §480(6) is predicated on non-Greek assumptions about how verbless clauses function—"because English or German

of v. 4: "patient perseverance and faith in all your persecutions as well as the oppression that you are bearing," since the ἐν πᾶσιν NP καὶ NP construction in v. 4 expresses the context (via the container schema evoked by the preposition ἐν) of the Thessalonians' perseverance and faith.

This new assertion also introduces a specific frame of reference. The writers describe the Thessalonians' experiences as a courtroom where evidence is presented for the guilt or innocence of defendants and where God is the judge of worthiness. This is a frame that, along with the themes of persecution and oppression already introduced, firmly plants Paul's thanksgiving section here into the genre of apocalyptic literature.[17] The middle-passive καταξιωθῆναι, "to be worthy" plays into this courtroom frame. While lexicons suggest the glossing "consider worthy,"[18] this represents a much weaker sense than what the context deserves. The active καταξιόω certainly can communicate a simple weighing of options, such as in Josephus's *Ant.* 11.135, where Esdras does not consider horses necessary (οὐ κατηξίωσεν ἱππεῖς). But in legal contexts, the verb more overtly denotes a causative change of state in the object of the clause: a declaration of worthiness or a passing of judgment of worthiness, such as in 3 Macc 3:21, where Ptolemy Philopater judges the inhabitants of Coelsyria and Phoenicia worthy of Alexandrian citizenship. Here in 2 Thessalonians, God the righteous judge weighs the evidence of persecution and oppression to decide who is worthy of God's kingdom.

6–7a εἴπερ δίκαιον παρὰ θεῷ ἀνταποδοῦναι τοῖς θλίβουσιν ὑμᾶς θλῖψιν καὶ ὑμῖν τοῖς θλιβομένοις ἄνεσιν μεθ' ἡμῶν

since it is just before God to recompense to those who oppress you: oppression, and to you the afflicted: relief along with us

The authors also describe God's judgment as just and they elaborate on that. Note, it is not only the Thessalonians who stand in judgment. Persecution and oppression are two-participant events. Thus, if persecution and oppression constitute the evidence, they necessarily do so not only for those persecuted, but also for those who persecute: observe the contrast between the active τοῖς θλίβουσιν and the middle τοῖς θλιβομένοις. And it is just to render judgment toward each group accordingly.

---

would require the inclusion of the relative pronoun and auxiliary verb, surely all languages do," entirely misses how languages with verbless clauses function.

[17] Persecution, judgment, and final destruction are foundational thematic elements in Jewish apocalyptic literature; see J. J. Collins, ed., *Apocalypse: The Morphology of a Genre*, Semeia 14 (Scholars Press, 1979), 28.

[18] See BDAG & G-E.

7b–10a ἐν τῇ ἀποκαλύψει τοῦ κυρίου Ἰησοῦ ἀπ' οὐρανοῦ μετ' ἀγγέλων δυνάμεως αὐτοῦ 8 ἐν φλογὶ πυρός, διδόντος ἐκδίκησιν τοῖς μὴ εἰδόσι θεὸν καὶ τοῖς μὴ ὑπακούουσιν τῷ εὐαγγελίῳ τοῦ κυρίου ἡμῶν Ἰησοῦ 9 οἵτινες δίκην τίσουσιν ὄλεθρον αἰώνιον ἀπὸ προσώπου τοῦ κυρίου καὶ ἀπὸ τῆς δόξης τῆς ἰσχύος αὐτοῦ 10 ὅταν ἔλθῃ ἐνδοξασθῆναι ἐν τοῖς ἁγίοις αὐτοῦ καὶ θαυμασθῆναι ἐν πᾶσιν τοῖς πιστεύσασιν, ὅτι ἐπιστεύθη τὸ μαρτύριον ἡμῶν ἐφ' ὑμᾶς, ἐν τῇ ἡμέρᾳ ἐκείνῃ.

at the appearance of the Lord Jesus Christ from heaven with his mighty angels in fiery flames, giving out punishment to those who do not know God and do not obey the good news of our Lord Jesus Christ. Such as these will pay a penalty of eternal destruction separated from the presence of the Lord and from the glory of his strength, when he comes to receive honor among his saints and receive admiration among all who believe.

The second half of vv. 7–10 continues the courtroom frame, shifting from the evidence and verdict to the carrying out of punishment and reward. Here the authors introduce more overtly apocalyptic elements to the courtroom. This is a natural shift since future and final judgment is a central motif in apocalyptic literature. Structurally, vv. 7–8 function simply as an elaboration of Paul's courtroom image, but he quickly and actively leans into the eschatological themes already hinted at. Still, while this small piece of text feels like a brief divergence from the topic, it has a larger discourse function signaling to the reader the central issues on the minds of Paul and his coauthors that they intend to bring to fore in chapter 2. This material is supplemental and contextual for the mainline of their encouragement and thanksgiving here, but it is also so central to their goals that they cannot help in vv. 9–10 but to create a miniature future-referring narrative with its own small storyline inside the thanksgiving section, yet not entirely part of it either. It consists only of a single mainline event: the paying of their penalty, which is placed in a temporal context, when Jesus comes to receive glory and honor.[19]

10b–12 ὅτι ἐπιστεύθη τὸ μαρτύριον ἡμῶν ἐφ' ὑμᾶς, ἐν τῇ ἡμέρᾳ ἐκείνῃ. εἰς ὃ καὶ προσευχόμεθα πάντοτε περὶ ὑμῶν, ἵνα ὑμᾶς ἀξιώσῃ τῆς κλήσεως ὁ θεὸς ἡμῶν καὶ

---

[19] Despite the use of θη morphology here with these two verbs, ἐνδοξασθῆναι and θαυμασθῆναι, they are not passives (Aubrey, "Motivated Categories"). Nearly all translations suggest a rendering "be glorified" (e.g. NIV, NASB, ESV) and a handful even go as far as to make ἐν τοῖς ἁγίοις αὐτοῦ into an expression of the passive agent (e.g. the CSB, "by his saints"). The traditional passive glosses for ἐνδοξασθῆναι and θαυμασθῆναι, "be glorified" and "be marveled at," present an otherwise highly dynamic scene as bare states in unnatural English. The renderings here, "receive honor" and "receive admiration," attempt to continue the more dynamic scene presented by Paul and do better justice to the voice morphology.

πληρώσῃ πᾶσαν εὐδοκίαν ἀγαθωσύνης καὶ ἔργον πίστεως ἐν δυνάμει, ὅπως ἐνδοξασθῇ τὸ ὄνομα τοῦ κυρίου ἡμῶν Ἰησοῦ ἐν ὑμῖν, καὶ ὑμεῖς ἐν αὐτῷ, κατὰ τὴν χάριν τοῦ θεοῦ ἡμῶν καὶ κυρίου Ἰησοῦ Χριστοῦ.

For our testimony was entrusted to you on that day. To that end, we also pray for you constantly, that our God might declare you worthy of his calling and effectively satisfy every desire for generosity and faithful deeds, so that the name of our Lord Jesus might receive glory in you and you in him, according to the grace of our God and the Lord Jesus Christ.

The final clause in v. 10 begins with ὅτι but is not directly subordinate to the immediately preceding clause.[20] Jesus is not coming because the Thessalonians believed. Rather Paul is picking up his line of thought from vv. 5–7. The Thessalonians are among those who will be judged worthy of the kingdom and receive relief from their suffering because when Paul and his co-writers entrusted their testimony to the Thessalonians, they took it to heart. And to that end they also pray—not that suffering, oppression or persecution might cease, but that the Thessalonian church might continue to act faithfully and generously.

2.2.2. *Do Not Be Troubled or Deceived*

1–2 Ἐρωτῶμεν δὲ ὑμᾶς, ἀδελφοί, ὑπὲρ τῆς παρουσίας τοῦ κυρίου ἡμῶν Ἰησοῦ Χριστοῦ καὶ ἡμῶν ἐπισυναγωγῆς ἐπ' αὐτόν, εἰς τὸ μὴ ταχέως σαλευθῆναι ὑμᾶς ἀπὸ τοῦ νοὸς μηδὲ θροεῖσθαι μήτε διὰ πνεύματος μήτε διὰ λόγου μήτε δι' ἐπιστολῆς ὡς δι' ἡμῶν, ὡς ὅτι ἐνέστηκεν ἡ ἡμέρα τοῦ κυρίου.

Now, we ask you, brothers and sisters, regarding the coming of our Lord Jesus Christ and our gathering to him, that you do not become hastily shaken from your mind nor troubled either by spirit, message or letter such as by ours, as that the Day of the Lord is arrived.

The pivot from prayer to instruction is immediately reflected in the appearance of δὲ in 2:1. With only eleven instances of δὲ in this letter, the first occurs here at the first natural shift in content.[21] The authors frame their instruction as request, softening the instruction that rhetorically and pragmatically leans toward a command. Here the shift is to Paul's central purpose with the letter, confronting what appears to be bad teaching or confusion about

---

[20] BDF §456(1) observes, "Subordination with ὅτι and διότι is often very loose (cf. διό, ὅθεν §451(5, 6)), so that it must be translated 'for.'"

[21] The majority of this letter's use of δὲ is in chapter 3, where Paul moves more rapidly and covers a larger variety of topics.

eschatological events and the return of Christ. These two verses also provide an important external context for the letter: at least some in the Thessalonian church are disturbed by the possibility that the Day of the Lord is already here.[22] We now see the full effect of Paul's miniature future-referring narrative about Christ's return in chapter two. While it seemed out of place in the thanksgiving back in chapter 1, it had a larger communicative purpose of getting ahead of the specific issue for the Thessalonian church: the Day of the Lord is still in the future.

The source of these worries is a little obscure in precisely the kind of way we would expect in reading someone else's mail. That Paul, Timothy, and Silvanus use διά, rather than ἀπό ἐκ or παρά in the string of possible origins is notable. Every language's prepositions prefer to be used in particular and idiosyncratic ways and these tendencies are quite strong.[23] As such, διά, which necessarily activates a channel/path image frame, cannot refer to the actual source of the idea, but only to an intermediary source. For that reason, the common rendering of this verse, particular the δι' ἡμῶν toward the end as "from us" (ESV, NIV, NRSV, NASB) is misleading. It is not impossible that Paul and his associates are referring to communication from others who are pretending to be them. BDAG even cites the possible parallel from Diodorus Siculus, 33.5.5, ἔπεμψαν ὡς παρὰ τῶν πρεσβευτῶν ἐπιστολήν ("they sent a letter which purported to come from the emissaries"). But this analysis does not solve the choice of διά, which cannot denote a source in the way that παρά, ἐκ or ἀπό can. The better understanding of their meaning here is not: "troubled either by spirit, a word, or a letter purportedly from us [but it isn't], but instead: "troubled ... either by spirit, message, or letter as by ours [but that isn't our meaning]." That is, the Thessalonians have misunderstood what he has previously communicated to them.[24]

3–4 μή τις ὑμᾶς ἐξαπατήσῃ κατὰ μηδένα τρόπον· ὅτι ἐὰν μὴ ἔλθῃ ἡ ἀποστασία πρῶτον καὶ ἀποκαλυφθῇ ὁ ἄνθρωπος τῆς ἀνομίας, ὁ υἱὸς τῆς ἀπωλείας, ὁ ἀντικείμενος καὶ

---

[22] ἐνίστημι refers to the coming or arrival of a person, thing, or event. The aorist describes such a coming/arrival as a means of moving forward narrative: ἡνίκα γοῦν ὁ ἕβδομος ἐνιαυτὸς τῆς ἐνδείας ἐνέστη "So when the seventh year of feminine came" (Philo, On Joseph 261), but the perfect has a strong preference for non-narrative, such as direct speech, dialogue, and letters to refer to fully-realized comings/arrivals: hence we find translation such as "is here," "is arrived," or "has arrived" to be common.

[23] See especially Silvia Luraghi, On the Meaning of Prepositions and Cases (John Benjamins, 2003), for an excellent comprehensive discussion of conventional usage of prepositions in Ancient Greek. In that vein, Gordon Fee (God's Empowering Presence: The Holy Spirit in the Letters of Paul [Hendrickson, 1994], 71–74) is by far the best analysis of the preposition usage in the exegetical literature on this passage.

[24] For larger discussion of this analysis, see Fee, God's Empowering Presence, 74.

ὑπεραιρόμενος ἐπὶ πάντα λεγόμενον θεὸν ἢ σέβασμα, ὥστε αὐτὸν εἰς τὸν ναὸν τοῦ θεοῦ καθίσαι ἀποδεικνύντα ἑαυτὸν ὅτι ἔστιν θεός.

Do not let anyone deceive you in any way. For unless the rebellion comes first and the man of lawlessness appears, the son of destruction, the adversary who exalts himself over every so-called god or object of worship, such that he should take a seat even in the temple of God.

With the basic instruction already introduced more politely in the form of a request in vv. 1–2, the authors have created the social capital for a more direct injunction, here with an aorist subjunctive + μή aorist subjunctive prohibition. They ground this prohibition with a clear chronology: rebellion and the man of lawlessness (ἄνθρωπος τῆς ἀνομίας) must appear first (ἀποκαλυφθῇ).[25] Whoever this is, the writers take pains to depict him with titles and distinguishing behaviors. The fact that this person has, up till now, gone unmentioned, while still receiving definiteness marking, suggests that Paul, Timothy, and Silvanus expect their audience to know who they are referring to already, at some level. Still, the fact that they feel the need to devote so much space to elaborating about him suggests that they also believe that the definite article itself is not sufficient to fully activate this participant in the Thessalonians minds. This is a *definiteness description*, which functions to help the audience access and activate in their minds a participant of otherwise low accessibility, [26] perhaps as a result of time passed since the writers were physically present in Thessalonika. In turn, this implies that the description chosen for this person is a relevant and, to some extent, known by the Thessalonians. As such, this is not new teaching for the Thessalonian church, if it was, he would have been introduced without a definite article.

5–6 οὐ μνημονεύετε ὅτι ἔτι ὢν πρὸς ὑμᾶς ταῦτα ἔλεγον ὑμῖν; καὶ νῦν τὸ κατέχον οἴδατε, εἰς τὸ ἀποκαλυφθῆναι αὐτὸν ἐν τῷ ἑαυτοῦ καιρῷ·

Do you now remember that I spoke to you these things? And now you know what is holding him back so that he might appear in his own time.

Paul makes this fact quite clear in vv. 5–6 by interjecting here. This is the first time he takes the reins of the letter's content to emphasize his point: these are things that Paul himself taught the Thessalonians.[27] Verse 6 continues in a similar

---

[25] This is a spontaneous process middle.

[26] Mira Ariel, *Accessing Noun Phrase Antecedents* (Routledge, 1990), 34–36.

[27] It seems possible that everything from here up to the next major section of the letter is Paul alone. It is not until 2:13 that we see another 1PL verb.

fashion, with Paul telling them what they already know as a means of reminding them. This is an effective didactic technique, since repetition of information is effective for long-term memory retention, but it also leaves us out of the loop as readers of another's mail, since we have no access to the full context of his in-person instruction on the topic. Cognitively, the function of this (almost certainly) briefer discussion/reminder is to reactivate the original teaching in their minds—activating part of the frame activates the entire frame. As in v. 3 above and in verse 8 below there is no grammatical reason for ἀποκαλυφθῆναι to be treated as "be revealed" rather than "appear" the middle-passive verbs in each case are ambiguous. The former, the traditional gloss, is more product of misunderstandings of Greek voice than of actual semantic need.

7–8a τὸ γὰρ μυστήριον ἤδη ἐνεργεῖται τῆς ἀνομίας· μόνον ὁ κατέχων ἄρτι ἕως ἐκ μέσου γένηται. καὶ τότε ἀποκαλυφθήσεται ὁ ἄνομος...

For the secret of lawlessness is already active; only until the one who currently restrains him is out of the way. And then the lawless one will appear...

The γὰρ in v. 7 signals an elaboration on vv. 5–6, strengthening Paul's point. The noun phrase subject split in two by the verb has a highlighting effect on τὸ μυστήριον; this is a new and perhaps unexpected way of referring to the man of lawlessness, who will appear later. The noun μυστήριον (secret/hidden) and the verb ἀποκαλύπτω (appear/reveal) form a clear set in this passage relative to τῆς ἀνομίας "of lawlessness." It also seems likely that, since Paul has successfully reminded his audience of previous teaching, his instructions beginning with this γὰρ are new information: Paul wants not only to remind his audience about what he taught, but now also to expand on it. The lawless one is active, but presently held back by some unstated force or person who will eventually no longer be in the picture. Then, and only then, will the lawless one appear.

8b–10 ...ὃν ὁ κύριος Ἰησοῦς ἀνελεῖ τῷ πνεύματι τοῦ στόματος αὐτοῦ καὶ καταργήσει τῇ ἐπιφανείᾳ τῆς παρουσίας αὐτοῦ, οὗ ἐστιν ἡ παρουσία κατ' ἐνέργειαν τοῦ Σατανᾶ ἐν πάσῃ δυνάμει καὶ σημείοις καὶ τέρασιν ψεύδους καὶ ἐν πάσῃ ἀπάτῃ ἀδικίας τοῖς ἀπολλυμένοις, ἀνθ' ὧν τὴν ἀγάπην τῆς ἀληθείας οὐκ ἐδέξαντο εἰς τὸ σωθῆναι αὐτούς·

... whom the Lord Jesus will execute by the breath of his mouth, annihilating him in the appearance of his arrival, whose coming is in accordance with the Deceiver's efforts with all power and deceitful signs and wonders, as well as every type of evil deception for those who are perishing because they rejected the love of the truth for their salvation.

Now, remember: the entire thrust of Paul's words here are building off two key instructions: (1) Do not be shaken/troubled and (2) Do not be deceived. The first relative clause that modifies ὁ ἄνομος (the lawless one) is in service to that first communicative purpose. Now that Paul has given them the facts, he gives them the reason why they have no need to be shaken or troubled. Jesus' return will bring the end of the lawless one. The second relative clause modifying ὁ ἄνομος fills the second purpose: the lawless one's actions, empowered by the Deceiver do false miracles to deceive those who are perishing. The reference to τοῖς ἀπολλυμένοις (those who are perishing) also reactivates the other recipients of God's judgment in 1:6–9, namely, those who are oppressing the Thessalonian church and who will pay the penalty of eternal destruction. Finally, note the constituent order of the last relative clause: τὴν ἀγάπην τῆς ἀληθείας, "the love of truth" is fronted before the verb drawing more attention to it as the focal part of the assertion in the clause. This has a similar effect as speaking it louder or marking it in italics in writing would in English.

11–12 καὶ διὰ τοῦτο πέμπει αὐτοῖς ὁ θεὸς ἐνέργειαν πλάνης εἰς τὸ πιστεῦσαι αὐτοὺς τῷ ψεύδει, ἵνα κριθῶσιν πάντες οἱ μὴ πιστεύσαντες τῇ ἀληθείᾳ ἀλλὰ εὐδοκήσαντες τῇ ἀδικίᾳ.

For this reason, God sent them an active deception, so that they will believe the lie in order that they would be condemned—all who do not believe the truth, but instead took pleasure in wickedness.

The καὶ διὰ τοῦτο that begins vv. 11–12 frames God's actions here as a consequence for not accepting the gospel (the love of the truth), while also serving as a final summary of what these unbelievers will experience. Their unbelief is itself a divinely sent delusion that will lead those who have rejected the truth and enjoyed wickedness to their final punishment. This final pronouncement ties everything back to the first thanksgiving, where Paul, Timothy, and Silvanus gave thanks for their suffering and oppression as proof of the righteous judgment of God.

2.2.3. Second Thanksgiving

13–14 Ἡμεῖς δὲ ὀφείλομεν εὐχαριστεῖν τῷ θεῷ πάντοτε περὶ ὑμῶν, ἀδελφοὶ ἠγαπημένοι ὑπὸ κυρίου, ὅτι εἵλατο ὑμᾶς ὁ θεὸς ἀπαρχὴν εἰς σωτηρίαν ἐν ἁγιασμῷ πνεύματος καὶ πίστει ἀληθείας, εἰς ὃ ἐκάλεσεν ὑμᾶς διὰ τοῦ εὐαγγελίου ἡμῶν, εἰς περιποίησιν δόξης τοῦ κυρίου ἡμῶν Ἰησοῦ Χριστοῦ.

Now then, we are obliged to give thanks to God always for you, brothers and sisters dearly loved by the Lord, because God has chosen you to be the first fruits for salvation in sanctification of spirit and in true faith, for which he called you through our gospel to acquire the glory of our Lord Jesus Christ.

Here we have our second piece of text segmented by δέ, returning the reader back to thanksgiving. Similarly, the first-person plural ὀφείλομεν brings the content of the letter back to all three authors. This thanksgiving is brief, a single expression of thanks followed by a single reason. They are thankful for the Thessalonians because God chose them for salvation. The phrase ἐν ἁγιασμῷ πνεύματος καὶ πίστει ἀληθείας ("in sanctification of spirit and true faith"), with its indefinite noun phrases, raises questions of participant reference. The noun ἁγιασμός is eventive, related to the transitive verb ἁγιάζω, "to consecrate, sanctify," which raises the question of whether the genitive πνεύματος is the agent of consecration, which would refer to the Spirit ("in sanctification by [the] Spirit"), or the patient/recipient of the consecration, referring to the Thessalonians' souls being consecrated ('in sanctification of [your] spirit'). While the person of the Holy Spirit has not been overtly activated in the discourse by the authors,[28] it is at least possible, in principle, that the Spirit's relation to the Godhead naturally activates the Spirit as a participant.

However, the Thessalonians' souls should be preferred as the referent of πνεῦμα, from the perspective of discourse structure and participant reference. If the 1 Thessalonians usage of πνεῦμα is relevant to the authors' and the audience's shared knowledge, then Paul appears to prefer to introduce the Spirit as a participant in the same way one would expect any other person. The first two references are definite, but overtly specified by the addition of ἅγιος (1 Thess 1:5, 6) only then does Paul shift to referring to the person of the Spirit with the definite article as is natural for Greek participant reference.[29] Here, Paul has made no such effort to overtly specify πνεύματος as the πνεύματος ἁγίου, as he did in his previous letter to this church. The phrase ἐν ἁγιασμῷ πνεύματος might be referentially ambiguous if taken entirely in isolation, but within the larger discourse, its referent is naturally the Thessalonians' spirit.

2.2.4. Stand Firm

15 ἄρα οὖν, ἀδελφοί, στήκετε, καὶ κρατεῖτε τὰς παραδόσεις ἃς ἐδιδάχθητε εἴτε διὰ λόγου εἴτε δι' ἐπιστολῆς ἡμῶν.

So then, brothers and sisters, stand firm and hold fast to the received instruction that you were taught either by our words or letters.

This much shorter sentence in v. 15 closes out the teaching of Paul, Silvanus, and Timothy. The complex connective ἄρα οὖν marks a transition and new paragraph,

---

[28] The noun πνεῦμα only occurs two other times in this letter and neither of those refer to the Holy Spirit.

[29] Levinsohn, *Discourse Features of the Greek New Testament*, 150.

but also signals to the reader that they should not expect a change in content from what has come before.[30] The word order here stays with default verb-initial orderings without drawing extra attention to the participants for special focus marking. And indeed, v. 15 simply functions as a positive summary of what they want the Thessalonian church to take away from their writing. Note that the authors' main focus began at 2:1–2 with two negative commands (do not be shaken/troubled and do not be deceived), but they chose to conclude on a much more positive and encouraging note: Stand firm; hold fast to the teaching you have received from us. Each of these function in parallel with the negative commands earlier in the discourse: *do not be shaken* = *stand firm* and *do not be deceived* = *hold fast to what we have taught.*

Similarly, with prepositional phrases, they conclude as they began. As in 2:1–2, there is a repetition of διὰ λόγου and δι' ἐπιστολῆς, but this time the authors do not refer to themselves in the same way (ὡς δι' ἡμῶν), but use a clear source expression in the bare genitive. Just as with the negative and positive commands, the repetition here serves to reactivate and reinforce the primary instruction of the letter in their conclusion, before Paul, Silvanus, and Timothy move to their blessing.

16–17 Αὐτὸς δὲ ὁ κύριος ἡμῶν Ἰησοῦς Χριστὸς καὶ θεὸς ὁ πατὴρ ἡμῶν ὁ ἀγαπήσας ἡμᾶς καὶ δοὺς παράκλησιν αἰωνίαν καὶ ἐλπίδα ἀγαθὴν ἐν χάριτι παρακαλέσαι ὑμῶν τὰς καρδίας καὶ στηρίξαι ἐν παντὶ ἔργῳ καὶ λόγῳ ἀγαθῷ

Now, may our Lord Jesus Christ himself and God our Father, who has loved us and given an eternal encouragement and a good hope in his favor, encourage your hearts and strengthen you in every good word and good deed.

In some of Paul's letters, the benediction or blessing appears at the end as part of his final greeting, such as in in 2 Cor 13:11–14. They could have simply ended the letter here with the expected final greetings that come with ancient letters. Other times, a blessing serves a segmenting function in Paul's letters in addition to a concluding one. This is found in in Eph 3:14–21 and 1 Thess 3:11–13. The change in content again coincides with the appearance of δέ. The two participants, Jesus and the Father, receive striking over-specification that suggests a formally established pattern. Many note the use of intensive αὐτὸς appears to be a structural part of these formal blessings as it is repeated elsewhere.[31] That may certainly be true, but its structural role is a direct result of its highlighting function:

---

[30] Runge, *Discourse Grammar*, 43.

[31] Charles E. Wanamaker, *The Epistles to the Thessalonians: A Commentary on the Greek Text* (Eerdmans, 1990), 270. Examples of this include Paul's previous letter to this church at 1 Thess 3:11 and 5:23 and then at the end of this one at 3:16.

it is special and important that the Lord Jesus Christ would encourage their hearts. It is a personalization strategy.[32] In a different, but comparable vein, God the Father receives a lengthy attributive description of his character and actions. These additional characterizations function to highlight to the reader (1) it is significant that Jesus himself would encourage them and that (2) God the Father has exactly the character for encouraging them exactly as they need it. A father who loves them and gives eternal comfort is precisely the kind of father that encourages a church to stand firm and not be shaken or troubled.

2.3. Prayer Requests & Instruction

The final chapter of 2 Thessalonians shifts its tone from long complex sentences of teaching and instructional discourse to much shorter sentences. Instead of complex embeddings of relative clauses, participles, and complements across a single sentence, the authors use short sentences. Indeed, even when they desire to provide more elaboration of their point (as in 3:6–11), they choose independent clauses with inferential connectives such as γάρ. Additionally, with regular changes in topic or attention, there is also a noticeable increase in their use of δέ for marking shifts in their discussion. Indeed, eight of the eleven instances of δὲ occur in this last chapter. These two structural patterns create an entirely different reading experience.

3:1–3 Τὸ λοιπὸν προσεύχεσθε, ἀδελφοί, περὶ ἡμῶν, ἵνα ὁ λόγος τοῦ κυρίου τρέχῃ καὶ δοξάζηται καθὼς καὶ πρὸς ὑμᾶς, καὶ ἵνα ῥυσθῶμεν ἀπὸ τῶν ἀτόπων καὶ πονηρῶν ἀνθρώπων, οὐ γὰρ πάντων ἡ πίστις. πιστὸς δέ ἐστιν ὁ κύριος, ὃς στηρίξει ὑμᾶς καὶ φυλάξει ἀπὸ τοῦ πονηροῦ.

Finally, pray for us, brothers and sisters, so that the word of the Lord may spread and be honored just as it also did for you, and also so that we might be delivered from evil and wicked people. For not everyone has faith! Yet the Lord is faithful; he will strengthen you and guard you from the evil one.

With the shift to their final words (τὸ λοιπὸν), the writers shift attention from the Thessalonians to themselves, their challenges, and ministry in order to request prayer. This reflects an effective strategy for reciprocity: we pray blessings for you and then we request your own prayers for our needs.

4–5 πεποίθαμεν δὲ ἐν κυρίῳ ἐφ' ὑμᾶς, ὅτι ἃ παραγγέλλομεν καὶ ποιεῖτε καὶ ποιήσετε. ὁ δὲ κύριος κατευθύναι ὑμῶν τὰς καρδίας εἰς τὴν ἀγάπην τοῦ θεοῦ καὶ εἰς τὴν ὑπομονὴν τοῦ Χριστοῦ.

---

[32] BDAG, αὐτός, 1d.

Now, we are certain in the Lord about you that, what we are directing you in, you are doing and you will continue doing. May the Lord direct your hearts toward the love of God and toward the patient endurance of Christ.

The δέ here reflects a change in topic and a shift in the attention back to their readers. By expressing confidence in the Thessalonians, the authors prime their audience to be more receptive to the instruction in v. 6. Praising them creates an opening for instruction that perhaps some of them might find a little more challenging.

6 Παραγγέλλομεν δὲ ὑμῖν, ἀδελφοί, ἐν ὀνόματι τοῦ κυρίου ἡμῶν Ἰησοῦ Χριστοῦ στέλλεσθαι ὑμᾶς ἀπὸ παντὸς ἀδελφοῦ ἀτάκτως περιπατοῦντος καὶ μὴ κατὰ τὴν παράδοσιν ἣν παρελάβοσαν παρ' ἡμῶν.

So we give this direction to you, brothers and sisters, in the name of our Lord Jesus Christ, that you should avoid any Christian family member who lives irresponsibly and not according to traditions passed down from us.

Then comes that specific command—the δέ reflecting the change in discourse from talking about the Thessalonians' life and character to instructing them about it, vis-à-vis, a specific problem in their congregation. The preposition ἀπό is partitive, calling attention to a subgroup within the Thessalonian church that the congregation needs to distance themselves from. While this group is part of the church, it is still a new participant and, as such, is anarthrous. The modifier παντός (any) expresses indefinite quantification, which makes the whole phrase παντὸς ἀδελφοῦ ἀτάκτως περιπατοῦντος "any Christian family member who lives irresponsibly" closer to the domain of irrealis. The authors are not yet overtly saying that there are such believers, *yet*. They take an indirect tact first here in vv. 6–10.

7–10 αὐτοὶ γὰρ οἴδατε πῶς δεῖ μιμεῖσθαι ἡμᾶς, ὅτι οὐκ ἠτακτήσαμεν ἐν ὑμῖν οὐδὲ δωρεὰν ἄρτον ἐφάγομεν παρά τινος, ἀλλ' ἐν κόπῳ καὶ μόχθῳ νυκτὸς καὶ ἡμέρας ἐργαζόμενοι πρὸς τὸ μὴ ἐπιβαρῆσαί τινα ὑμῶν· οὐχ ὅτι οὐκ ἔχομεν ἐξουσίαν, ἀλλ' ἵνα ἑαυτοὺς τύπον δῶμεν ὑμῖν εἰς τὸ μιμεῖσθαι ἡμᾶς. καὶ γὰρ ὅτε ἦμεν πρὸς ὑμᾶς, τοῦτο παρηγγέλλομεν ὑμῖν, ὅτι εἴ τις οὐ θέλει ἐργάζεσθαι μηδὲ ἐσθιέτω.

For you yourselves know how essential it is to imitate us since we didn't conduct ourselves negligently among you and gifted food we did not eat; rather with toil and labor, night and day, we were working to not be a burden on any of you—not that we weren't free to do so, rather that we might provide for you ourselves as an example. As well, when we were with you, we were giving the following instruction: "If anyone does not want to work, then neither should he eat."

In their elaboration of this command, our three authors still do not go straight to criticizing anyone in particular. They instead appeal to the Thessalonians' own experience of how they saw Paul, Timothy, and Silvanus live before them. Observe the word order here. First there is a simple negative assertion of how they behaved. They then follow that up with specifics. The authors place in front of the verb the behaviors they want to emphasize for their readers: "*gifted food* we did not eat" and "*with toil and labor, night and day,* we were working."

The interjective οὐχ + complement clause construction emphasizes that their behavior before them was entirely voluntary. The customs of the society certainly allowed such arrangements.[33] But Paul, Timothy, and Silvanus genuinely cared about the example they were setting to the churches they established, as Paul also emphasized to another church in 1 Corinthians 9. And then with another γάρ, elaborating on their elaboration, they provide not only an example of their behavior, but remind the church of the specific instruction they had already given on the very issue.

What effect does this all of this have? First of all, back in v. 6, Paul and his coauthors have already activated a participant without directly calling them out. Without saying right at the beginning, "we have heard reports about these people," they have their audience already thinking of specific people. Further, by taking their time in laying out in close, emphatic detail all the efforts that Paul, Timothy, and Silvanus put into not only teaching responsible living, but also actively modeling it, they are drawing out the discussion. By talking about themselves on responsibility, they are giving the Thessalonians plenty of time to process and reflect on (1) their own behavior and (2) the behavior of their brothers and sisters in Christ. They are letting the guilty simmer uncomfortably as this letter is being read publicly in the congregation.

11–12 ἀκούομεν γάρ τινας περιπατοῦντας ἐν ὑμῖν ἀτάκτως, μηδὲν ἐργαζομένους ἀλλὰ περιεργαζομένους· τοῖς δὲ τοιούτοις παραγγέλλομεν καὶ παρακαλοῦμεν ἐν κυρίῳ Ἰησοῦ Χριστῷ ἵνα μετὰ ἡσυχίας ἐργαζόμενοι τὸν ἑαυτῶν ἄρτον ἐσθίωσιν.

For we hear that some people among you are living irresponsibly, doing no work, but just being intrusive meddlers. People like this we direct and exhort in the Lord Jesus Christ that in quiet they work and their own food they should eat.

After dragging out the entire question, this γάρ clause finally gets to the point. The previous γάρ clauses had not advanced the argument, but only filled in more details about the instruction. This one, however, does. The γάρ is still

---

[33] See Paul Millett, "Patronage and Its Avoidance in Classical Athens," in *Patronage in Ancient Society*, ed. Andrew Wallace-Hadrill (Routledge, 1989), 15–47.

functioning normally to flesh out what precedes.[34] But it also provides the payoff for the tension the authors were building up in vv. 6–10.

The indefinite pronoun τινὰς represents a change in the accentuation of the text. Much like the accented forms of the personal pronouns (e.g. accented ἐμέ vs. enclitic με), τὶς has emphatic (accented) and non-emphatic (unaccented) forms.[35] I believe either the accented or the enclitic are possible here. The expected position of the second-position enclitic is identical to the focal constituent position in Greek syntax. This has the potential to introduce ambiguity as to which one should be preferred. This judgment is discourse significant. It is the difference between treating τινας as merely in its normal second position,[36] on the one hand, or treating τίνας as fronted and focal constituent, on the other. This second reading makes sense of the build up to this verse where the authors have delayed directly calling out the group of lazy Thessalonians. In this reading, the participle περιπατοῦντας is splitting the noun phrase τινὰς ... ἐν ὑμῖν in two, which is itself a strategy for drawing focus to a participant.[37] To render it colloquially, it is as if Paul, Timothy, and Silvanus are saying: "We hear that *cough* SOME PEOPLE *cough* among you are living irresponsibly." Then, having called them out, the authors speak to these lazy busybodies directly, fronting specific phrases for emphasis: IN QUIET they should work and THEIR OWN FOOD they should eat. These constituent order choices should be viewed as all the more striking and jarring due to the slow build up to direct rebuke in vv. 6–10.

13–15 ὑμεῖς δέ, ἀδελφοί, μὴ ἐγκακήσητε καλοποιοῦντες. Εἰ δέ τις οὐχ ὑπακούει τῷ λόγῳ ἡμῶν διὰ τῆς ἐπιστολῆς, τοῦτον σημειοῦσθε, μὴ συναναμίγνυσθαι αὐτῷ, ἵνα ἐντραπῇ· καὶ μὴ ὡς ἐχθρὸν ἡγεῖσθε, ἀλλὰ νουθετεῖτε ὡς ἀδελφόν.

---

[34] Runge, *Discourse Grammar*, 52

[35] See for example Acts 8:34, where accented τινός is contrastive with ἑαυτοῦ: περὶ τίνος ὁ προφήτης λέγει τοῦτο; περὶ ἑαυτοῦ ἢ περὶ ἑτέρου τινός; "About whom is the prophet speaking? About *himself* or about *someone else*?" or 1 Cor 10:19, τί οὖν φημι; ὅτι εἰδωλόθυτόν τί ἐστιν, ἢ ὅτι εἴδωλόν τί ἐστιν; "What am I suggesting? That food sacrificed to idols is something? Or that an idol is something?" Another example, from the LXX is Sirach 48:16, τινὲς μὲν αὐτῶν ἐποίησαν τὸ ἀρεστόν, / τινὲς δὲ ἐπλήθυναν ἁμαρτίας "Some of them did what was acceptable, but some [others] increased sins." Still, emphatic/contrastive τὶς is still relatively unusual. It is certainly a linguistic innovation compared to Classical Greek, which would use ἔνιοι. Even in the Koine period this usage is rare.

[36] As BDF §473 observes, "The old rule, observable in Greek and cognate languages, that unemphatic (enclitic) pronouns and the like are placed as near the beginning of the sentence as possible, applies also to the NT."

[37] See A. M. Devine and Laurence D. Stephens, *Discontinuous Syntax: Hyperbaton in Greek* (Oxford University Press, 1999), 36–44.

Brother and sisters, you must not grow weary in doing what is right. Now if some do not obey our message through this letter, take not. Do not associate with them so that they might feel shame. Also do not treat them as enemies, instead admonish them as Christian family.

The authors shift back (hence the δέ) to speaking to the larger congregation to conclude with a general exhortation to press on doing what is right. The next clause is also introduced by the postpositive δέ, transitioning from that general exhortation to a specific action for dealing with lazy or irresponsible believers: separate from them so that they experience shame. Despite the shift to a prohibition in v. 15, the καί reflects the continuity in the instruction. These believers are not enemies, so do not treat them as such. Instead, warn them as brothers and sisters—ἀλλά points to a positive alternative.[38]

2.4. *Final Blessing & Farewell*

16–18 Αὐτὸς δὲ ὁ κύριος τῆς εἰρήνης δῴη ὑμῖν τὴν εἰρήνην διὰ παντὸς ἐν παντὶ τρόπῳ. ὁ κύριος μετὰ πάντων ὑμῶν. Ὁ ἀσπασμὸς τῇ ἐμῇ χειρὶ Παύλου, ὅ ἐστιν σημεῖον ἐν πάσῃ ἐπιστολῇ· οὕτως γράφω. ἡ χάρις τοῦ κυρίου ἡμῶν Ἰησοῦ Χριστοῦ μετὰ πάντων ὑμῶν.

May the Lord of Peace himself, give you peace through all times and in all places. The Lord be with all of you. This greeting is in my own hand, "From Paul," which is the mark in all my letters, just as I write. The grace of our Lord Jesus Christ be with you all.

These last three verses function as the final formal element of the ancient letter, which Paul expands on in characteristically theological ways. His benediction or blessing again uses αὐτός for emphasizing and personalizing the Thessalonians believers' relationship with Christ. And Paul takes extra pains to associate the instruction and contents of this letter as being from his own, effectively providing brief commentary on his own writing. He concludes in his traditional manner: the grace of our Lord Jesus Christ be will you all.

3. *Concluding Notes*

This is a letter about specific issues in the Thessalonian church. The manner that particular topics are introduced as assumed and given information says much about what the writers expected their readers to already understand. But the

---

[38] Runge, *Discourse Grammar*, 55–56.

larger message is, nevertheless, fairly simple and continues to be applicable to-day. Do not be shaken or be troubled by news about the future. Do not be deceived by teaching that diverges from what you have learned from Paul and his fellow missionaries. Instead stand firm and hold fast to what you have been taught. As well, live responsibly and guide those who are lazy or reckless in their lifestyle back to one that works hard. May the grace of our Lord Jesus Christ be with you all.

15

THE PASTORAL EPISTLES

ISAIAH ALLEN

The Pastoral Epistles (hereafter, "PE") have been received by the church as personal letters from the apostle Paul to his junior colleagues Timothy and Titus and their respective communities in Ephesus and Crete. They contain early Christian instructions for church leaders.

In the modern era, scholars began to express doubt about their traditional provenance and to speculate about their origins. A variety of proposals have been argued, but the evidence is inconclusive—every point seems to have its counterpoint. A common assumption is that they were composed by one pseudonymous author as a fictional collection. Luke Timothy Johnson sounds a caution against foreclosing on the question, however:

> Little real discussion of the issue of authenticity still occurs. But I remind the reader that this consensus resulted as much from social dynamics as from the independent assessment of the evidence by each individual scholar. For many contemporary scholars, indeed, the inauthenticity of the Pastorals is one of those scholarly dogmas first learned in college and in no need of further examination.[1]

Even without giving the question extended critical energy, assumptions regarding provenance underlie any reading. Interpreting passages from the

---

[1] *The First and Second Letters to Timothy: A New Translation with Introduction and Commentary*, AB 35A (Doubleday, 2001), 55.

PE without at least tacitly subscribing to some conclusion (often furnished by another, trusted scholar) about their compositional history is virtually impossible.

If the PE are a fictional letter collection, the most plausible form of the single-document hypothesis takes Titus as the initial letter. Their canonical order may not represent their original order. Titus's longer epistolary introduction (1:1–4) and organizational simplicity suggest that it might have come first. In which case, Titus introduces the entire collection.[2] Titus and 1 Tim reflect the *mandata principis* (imperial orders) genre adapted to church use.[3] Placing the solemn and intimate 2 Tim at the end of the collection instead of the center is fitting if it is indeed end-of-life testamentary literature.[4] Pursuing this line of thought further requires several debatable assumptions. Increasingly, diverse scholars contend that the prevalent single-document hypothesis is mistaken.[5]

Surveying PE scholarship, I. Howard Marshall noted, "A number of writers are emphasizing the individuality of the Pastorals as three separate compositions."[6] These scholars represent various cross-sections of opinion on authorship. One of them, James W. Aageson, says that he "takes seriously the literary and conceptual world of each of the individual letters as discrete documents that have integrity in their own right." He continues, "This is not the case in much scholarship on the Pastorals. They are often treated as a Pastoral corpus, which

---

[2] The Muratorian Fragment, perhaps the oldest known canon list, places Titus before 1 and 2 Tim. Some scholars suggest an alternative ordering but note that manuscript evidence is thin, e.g., Jerome D. Quinn, *The Letter to Titus: A New Translation and Commentary and an Introduction to Titus, I and II Timothy, the Pastoral Epistles*, AB 35 (Doubleday, 1990), 2–3; I. Howard Marshall, *A Critical and Exegetical Commentary on the Pastoral Epistles*, ICC (T&T Clark, 1999), 1–2. Both scholars order their commentaries with Titus first.

[3] Johnson discusses the *mandata principis* genre proposal. See *First and Second Letters*, 137–42. For examples, see Stanley Kent Stowers, *Letter Writing in Greco-Roman Antiquity*, LEC 5 (Westminster, 1986), 103–4.

[4] Philip H. Towner argues that 2 Tim lacks typical features of the genre. See *1–2 Timothy & Titus*, IVPNTC 14 (InterVarsity, 1994), 156. Benjamin Fiore acknowledges that 2 Tim does not follow expected patterns of testamentary literature but asserts that the designation has hermeneutic value. See *The Pastoral Epistles: First Timothy, Second Timothy, Titus*, ed. Daniel J. Harrington, SP 12 (Liturgical Press, 2007), 8–9.

[5] See, e.g., Rüdiger Fuchs, *Unerwartete Unterschiede: Müssen wir unsere Ansichten über die "Pastoralbriefe" revidieren?* (Wuppertal: Brockhaus, 2003); Jens Herzer, "Zwischen Mythos und Wahrheit: Neue Perspektiven auf die sogenannten Pastoralbriefe," *NTS* 63 (2017): 428–50; I. Howard Marshall, "The Pastoral Epistles in Recent Study," in *Entrusted with the Gospel: Paul's Theology in the Pastoral Epistles*, ed. Andreas J. Köstenberger and Terry L. Wilder (B&H Academic, 2010), 268–312, at 304–308.

[6] Marshall, "Pastoral Epistles in Recent Study," 308.

disguises the substantive differences between them."[7] Philip H. Towner argues that the single-document hypothesis has been an obstacle to the cogent interpretation of these letters.[8] It amalgamates their distinct polemics, yields an artificial PE community, and stultifies their theological and moral instruction.

The commentary below treats the PE in canonical order and works primarily with the text of the biblical book at-hand. The author is referred to as *Paul* and the addressees as *Timothy* and *Titus*, respectively, in accordance with their canonical presentation. There is little doubt that these letters were crafted to be read aloud with members of the recipients' congregations present.[9]

This analysis focuses on the logical-semantic structure of these epistles from the book to the paragraph level. Rather than interpret passages, it highlights features of discourse structure that have bearing on interpretation. The critical intentions of this work are as follows:

- Describe how each paragraph relates to the whole and to its surrounding discursive context.
- Identify logical-semantic structures that have significance for interpretation.

For this reason, conventional modern inquiries (e.g., composition history, women's roles, stage of ecclesial development, proto-Gnosticism, absolute and relative literary chronology) are relativized.

Methodology

Discourse analysis (DA) labels a range of approaches. Acknowledging the variety, Stanley E. Porter urged critics to wait-and-see. Every discipline, he argued, takes time to achieve technical and philosophical precision and standardization.[10] Practitioners nurture this maturing process by clarifying their terms and identifying their schools of thought. The axes below represent one typology of the discipline in which no analyst truly occupies the extreme. The present analysis leans toward the second of each comparison.

---

[7] James W. Aageson, *Paul, the Pastoral Epistles, and the Early Church*, LPS (Hendrickson, 2008), 16.

[8] Philip H. Towner, *The Letters to Timothy and Titus*, NICNT (Eerdmans, 2006), 27–36.

[9] See comments at 1 Tim 6:21b.

[10] See Stanley E. Porter, "Discourse Analysis and New Testament Studies: An Introductory Survey," in *Discourse Analysis and Other Topics in Biblical Greek*, ed. Stanley E. Porter and D. A. Carson, JSNTSup 113 (Bloomsbury Academic, 1995), 14–35, at 18–19. Stephen W. Pattemore summarizes the development of DA in *Souls under the Altar: Relevance Theory and the Discourse Structure of Revelation*, UBSMS 9 (United Bible Societies, 2003), 4–16. He argues that Relevance Theory provides critical parameters for DA. See ibid., 16–45.

Axes of Emphasis

Determinacy—Stable or Dependent? Some analysts emphasize the stable semantic values of words and syntactical constructions and how they contribute
predictably to the discourse contexts in which they appear. Others emphasize
context dependency.

Scale—Micro or Macro? Logical-semantic relationships structure discourse at
every level. Some analysts focus on lexemes and syntax at the phrase, clause, and
sentence level. Others include features that operate from the paragraph to the
whole-book level.

Outcome—or Interpretation? Some analysts endeavor to uncover the semantic core of words and constructions by piercing through the accumulations of
interpretive history and naïve linguistic pedagogy. They articulate something
akin to a grammar of discourse.[11] Most, however, use DA hermeneutically (including translators).

Eclecticism—Words-and-Syntax-Only or All-of-the-Above? Some analysts favor
specific aspects of formal linguistics—the visibly observable, consistently defin-
able features of language (e.g., morpheme, lexeme, syntax). Others also incorporate and evaluate diverse prominence markers, semantic frames, literary forms,
and other discourse features for their influence upon interpretation.

Parameters—Pure or Modified? Some analysts simply label their approach
DA. Others employ a distinct philosophy of language or hermeneutic theory that
provides parameters for their analysis or an external factor for interpretive decisions.[12] Relevance Theory (RT) has this function in the analysis below.

Relevance Theory and Discourse Analysis

Relevance Theory is the dominant species of linguistic pragmatics with roots in
philosophical linguistics and branches in cognitive linguistics. It assumes the

---

[11] E.g., Steven E. Runge, *Discourse Grammar of the Greek New Testament: A Practical Introduction for Teaching and Exegesis*, Lexham Bible Reference Series (Hendrickson, 2010); Stephen H. Levinsohn, *Discourse Features of New Testament Greek: A Coursebook on the Information Structure of New Testament Greek* (SIL International, 2000); idem, "Some Constraints
on Discourse Development in the Pastoral Epistles," in *Discourse Analysis and the New Testament: Approaches and Results*, ed. Stanley E. Porter and Jeffrey T. Reed, JSNTSup 170 (Sheffield:
Sheffield Academic, 1999), 316–33; Robert E. Longacre, *The Grammar of Discourse*, 2nd ed.
(Plenum, 1996).

[12] E.g., Relevance Theory guides Stephen W. Pattemore's practice. See *The People of God in
the Apocalypse: Discourse, Structure, and Exegesis*, SNTSMS 128 (Cambridge University Press,
2004). Structuralism guides Lucinda A. Brown's practice. See "Asceticism and Ideology: The
Language of Power in the Pastoral Epistles," *Semeia* 57 (1992): 77–94.

underdeterminacy of linguistically encoded speech, insisting that hearers must *infer* meaning from incomplete semantic representations. Theorists accept that words have conventional semantic force, but they argue that such does not constrain authorial use. In context, words have *ad hoc* meanings, and no concept is fully lexicalized.[13]

Authorial intention is the chief constraint upon meaning, not previous uses, which interest conventional lexicographers and grammarians. RT emphasizes the context-dependency of meaning, which requires an appreciation of discourse structure, hence the complementarity of the disciplines. Inference is not a license for eisegesis; it is the process by which hearers discern speaker intentions.

As with any approach, an eisegete can label their method *discourse analysis* and have no interest in what the text conveys. RT provides critical parameters to the practice of DA, because RT is interested in *ostensive inferential communication* and understands speaker intention to be of utmost importance in the interpretive enterprise.[14]

Features of This Analysis

Understanding how passages relate to their larger contexts is one of the most important contributions of DA. Large-scale logical-semantic relationships at the book and multi-paragraph levels are frequently neglected, illustrated by a genuine greeting card with the quotation, "We bless you in the name of the Lord! (Psalm 129:8)."

To discern the structure of the PE, the following analysis examines a variety of textual evidence for unit boundaries and cohesion (e.g., recurrence, prominence, synonyms, antonyms, conjunctions, particles, themes, literary forms, and the products of previous study). It recognizes that discourse consists of smaller semantic units that combine in logical-semantic relationships into larger semantic units in a logical hierarchy to form a cohesive and coherent discourse.[15]

Constituent organization charts visualize the arrangement of semantic units and provide pithy titles as simplified summaries of their relationships and contents. They are interpretively non-committal. Richard J. Erickson is not alone in

---

[13] See Gene L. Green, "Lexical Pragmatics and the Lexicon," *BBR* 22 (2012): 315–33; Dan Sperber and Deirdre Wilson, "Pragmatics," in *Oxford Handbook of Contemporary Philosophy*, OHO (Oxford University Press, 2007), 468–504, at 485–490.

[14] See Billy Clark, *Relevance Theory*, CTL (Cambridge: Cambridge University Press, 2013), 112–19; Robyn Carston and Seiji Uchida, ed., *Relevance Theory: Applications and Implications*, P&B 37 (John Benjamins, 1998), 298.

[15] See Robert E. Smith and John Beekman, *The Literary-Semantic Analysis of Second Timothy*, ed. Michael F. Kopesec (SIL International, 1981), 1.

noting that most logical-semantic relationships are binary in nature.[16] Therefore, units at every level are typically divided into two parts. Some large subunits are further divided in separate graphs. These charts are not to scale.

Discerning unit boundaries and relationships is a dialectic process, what relevance theorists call *mutual adjustment*.[17] Clues at one level illuminate structure at another level. Evidence accompanies each explanation of unit cohesion and structure, but it cannot be exhaustive or explicitly negate every alternative. The rationale for every decision should be transparent, some requiring more comment than others.

The relationships between units are reasoned generalizations, even though particular clauses may suggest an alternative semantic logic. For instance, a paragraph functioning as the imperative result of an argument may also exhibit an interchange of problems and solutions. Such is to be expected in natural language. These rational proposals are not intended to negate other reasonable claims.

To make this commentary amenable to general use, the analysis below attempts to balance standard descriptive language with more technical language.[18] Discourse unit labels follow David R. Bauer and Robert A. Traina's scheme—the main units of books are *divisions*; the main units within divisions are *sections*; and the main units within sections are *segments*.[19] Other designations (e.g., paragraph, clause) should be intuitive.

Although logical-semantic relationships could be delineated further, even to the word level, the analysis below focuses on discourse structure only as deep as the paragraph level. Some small-scale items of significance that illuminate or are specially illuminated by aspects of discourse structure, however, do bear comments.

This analysis is organized sequentially so that any comments relevant to a specific passage will be found under the reference for that unit and its larger context. This arrangement reduces the need to flip pages back-and-forth to locate pertinent comments.

The UBS[5] text is used. Where its editors have left a variant reading in brackets (e.g., [καί], Titus 1:10), it is excluded.

---

[16] Richard J. Erickson, "The Damned and the Justified in Romans 5:12–21: An Analysis of Semantic Structure," in *Discourse Analysis and Other Topics in Biblical Greek*, ed. Porter and Carson, 282–307, at 286.

[17] See Clark, *Relevance Theory*, 148, 242.

[18] Different schools also use different jargon, and Moisés Silva's critique of DA "restating the obvious using unnecessarily forbidding terminology" gives one pause. See "Discourse Analysis and Philippians," in *Discourse Analysis and Other Topics in Biblical Greek*, ed. Porter and Carson, 102–6, at 103.

[19] David R. Bauer and Robert A. Traina, *Inductive Bible Study: A Comprehensive Guide to the Practice of Hermeneutics* (Baker Academic, 2011), 143–44.

Like any books in the NT, the PE contain passages with a contentious history of interpretation. To focus on the discourse, dialogue with the secondary literature has generally been excluded. Although DA may freshly illuminate their interpretation and help readers to sidestep overworn lines of debate (e.g., regarding Paul the misogynist, Paul the bigot, Paul the anti-Semite, the complexity or simplicity of church organization), it cannot promise solutions to long-standing impasses.

1 Timothy

In discerning the logical-semantic structure of 1 Tim, it is relatively easy to answer the questions of cohesion and division—Where do units begin and end? What holds units together? The golden question has to do with the issue of development—Which subunits belong together in larger segments? How do units relate to one another? Several kinds of evidence must be examined—e.g., grammatical, topical, literary-aesthetic.

The conjunction δέ, appearing 30 times in 113 verses, signals a relation of generic development. The less frequent logical conjunction οὖν (2:1, 8; 3:2; 5:14) connects paragraphs and signals consequence. Other conjunctions (e.g., ἀλλά, γάρ) hold units together by connecting clauses and sentences, but these latter conjunctions do not operate on the paragraph or macro-structural level in 1 Tim. In all cases, the semantics of specific units determine the exact nature of their relation to each other more than the conjoiner or lack thereof (asyndeton).

The body of 1 Tim (1:3–6:21a) is the largest and highest-level division. The opening (1:1–2) and closing (6:21b) are high-level, but not particularly large, divisions. The body can be partitioned into two sections (1:3–4:5 and 4:6–6:21a).

In a personal correspondence in which a senior minister instructs a junior colleague, the absence of second-person singular imperatives in the first half (1:1–4:5) and their predominance thereafter (4:6–6:21) is significant. Other features signal the cohesion of material in the first half, including the backward-looking general discourse deictic ταῦτα (*these things*, 4:6), suggesting that a shift occurs at 4:6 in the body, where Timothy's own actions are directly addressed to accomplish the vision that Paul portrays earlier.

Some indirect or implicit imperatives toward Timothy are sprinkled throughout the letter (e.g., ἵνα παραγγείλῃς, *in order that you might command*, 1:3; ἵνα στρατεύῃ, *in order that you might fight*, 1:18; μὴ ἐπιπλήξῃς, *do not scold*, 5:1), but they either do not have the force or purpose of a direct imperative or are rendered in non-imperative form for other reasons and actually follow the general non-imperative-to-imperative structure between the letter's halves.

Patches of third-person imperatives and indirect imperatives—i.e., infinitives or participles with an imperative or moral force (e.g., 2:1, 8 [x2], 9; 3:1)—

cluster as cohesive elements in specific units. These units include the worship and worship decorum guidelines in 2:1–12; the overseer and deacon guidelines in 3:2–12; the widow guidelines in 5:4–16; and the instructions for slaves in 6:1–2a. A few imperatives fall outside these clusters to serve other rhetorical purposes.

The demonstrative pronoun οὗτος (neuter plural ταῦτα, *these things*, 3:14; 4:6, 11, 15; 5:7, 21; 6:2; also, Ταύτην [τὴν παραγγελίαν], 1:18; cf. 6:11) is used heavily in the latter part of 1 Tim as a backward-looking (anaphoric) discourse deictic that functions as a point of departure for a new segment. It is typically a concise means of pointing at what was said earlier, without delimiting how far back it points. Paul frequently uses it to wrap up one segment while shifting to a new topic or concern. Deixis is not contained in a single kind of word, such as οὗτος, but this word is of strategic importance for grasping the larger structure.

First Timothy features a handful of transitional paragraphs where segment partitions become somewhat ambiguous (1:18–20; 3:14–16; 4:6–10, 11–16; 6:11–16, 20–21a). They serve both as generalizing summaries of the previous material and as points of departure that prepare for what follows. So, instead of a structure where one unit cleanly abuts another with a single transparent logic-semantic relationship between them, 1 Tim presents a somewhat more opaque structure with multiple semantic and logical links to what precedes and follows. After analyzing more than thirty scholarly opinions regarding the structural outline of 1 Tim, it appears that most disagreements with respect to structure pertain to whether they group these transitional paragraphs with the preceding or the following material.[20] It is good to recognize that some leeway on this matter is justified by the writing style. These small units are important and meaningful, but from the standpoint of logical-semantic structure, they are transitional.

1:1–2

The somewhat brief epistolary opening of 1 Tim is preparatory of the entire letter body. It may be the most obvious structural feature of the book. As an introduction, it is not unusual. It marks the document as a letter and evokes the more narrow genre designation some scholars have identified as *mandata principis* (imperial orders) applied to the church.[21] The phrase, *by the command of God our Savior* (1:1), points to two important themes in the book. The first is ethical obedience to Paul's, Timothy's, and the congregational leadership's endowed authority (see, e.g., 1:11, 18; 2:7; 3:4–5; 4:11–16; 5:17–22; 6:20). The second is the role of

---

[20] Richard C. Blight compares about twenty different outlines in *An Exegetical Summary of 1 Timothy* (SIL International, 2009).

[21] Luke Timothy Johnson, *Letters to Paul's Delegates: 1 Timothy, 2 Timothy, Titus* (Trinity Press International, 1996), 114.

1 Tim 1:1-6:21								
1:1-2 Epistolary Introduction	1:3-6:21a Letter Body (*Mandata Principis*)							**6:21b Closing Greeting**
	1:3-4:5 Description of Church Community Ideals				4:6-6:21a Consequential Responsibilities and Imperatives for Timothy			
	1:3-3:13 The Way Things Ought to Be (with contrast between negative and positive)	3:14-4:5 Rationale for Teaching "These Things"			4:6-16 Timothy's Role, Righteousness, and Relationship to the Church	5:1-6:21a Dealing with Various Church Members		
	1:3-20 Problems and Promises with Troublemakers	2:1-3:13 Worship and Leadership in the Church	3:14-16 Divine Mystery	4:1-5 Human Hypocrisy	4:6-10 Timothy as Virtuous Pastor	4:11-16 Timothy as Ordained Example	5:1-6:2a Propriety among Household Constituents	6:2b-21a Shunning Arrogance, Controversy, and Greed

Figure 15.1: Constituent Organization of 1 Timothy

God as savior. Several commentators highlight how distinct these themes seem in comparison to other Pauline writings.[22] The present analysis does not attempt to adjudicate such discussions but recognizes significant *internal* consistency regarding Paul's ethical reasoning in 1 Tim and a recurring concern for people's salvation (see, e.g., 1:15; 2:3–4, 15; 4:10, 16).

Although only a few verses are formally governed by this epistolary structure (1:1-2, 6:21b), it is significant. Unlike more homiletical epistles, such as Ephesians or Hebrews, 1 Tim carries the sensibility of a personal correspondence throughout.

The expression, *my loyal child in the faith* (1:2), prepares readers for the character of the letter body, which always holds the intimate relationship between Paul and Timothy and their history together in view (see, e.g., 1:18; 4:14–16; 5:22–23; 6:11–12, 20). Although the details of *faith* remain undeveloped in this spare opening, it subtly introduces a significant theme in 1 Tim by metaphorically locating the relationship of the protagonists (Paul and Timothy; see the agonistic theme in 1:18; 4:10; 6:12). Faith is not a fringe issue in this letter but is significant throughout (see, e.g., 1:4, 5, 14, 16, 19; 2:7, 15; 3:9, 13, 16; 4:1, 6, 12; 5:8; 6:10, 11, 12, 21).[23]

---

[22] See, e.g., Margaret Davies, *The Pastoral Epistles* (Sheffield Academic Press, 1996), 41–43; W. Hulitt Gloer, *1 & 2 Timothy-Titus*, ed. Scott Nash, SHBC (Smyth & Helwys, 2010), 23, 28, 125; Donald Guthrie, *The Pastoral Epistles: An Introduction and Commentary*, 2nd rev. ed., TNTC 14 (InterVarsity, 1990), 70.

[23] This list of pertinent references is not exhaustive. Consider the recurrence of πιστὸς ὁ λόγος and equivalents (*faithful is the word*, 1:15; 3:1; 4:9), instances where persons are referred to as *believers* or *believing* (1:12; 3:11; 4:3, 10; 5:16; 6:2), and other uses (e.g., *pledge*, πίστις, 5:12).

1:3–6:21a

The letter body of 1 Tim contains critical instructions about various aspects of church life, leadership, and opposition, but Paul conveys them with the tenderness of a caring mentor. Glimpses of Paul and Timothy's relationship and shared history recur. A shift from description (1:3–4:5) to imperative (4:6–6:21a) seems to govern the structure of this largest division of the letter. It is common to perceive a sequential shift from the declarative to the imperative, theological claim to ethical injunction, or "gift and task" in Pauline writing.[24] What is happening in 1 Tim is slightly different. Paul outlines proper order in the church as regards opposition (1:3–20), worship (2:1–15), and leadership (3:1–13), and then he shifts to more directly address Timothy's pastoral role in implementing this vision of the church.

Second-person singular imperative verbs appear in 1 Tim thirty times—all of them in the second major section (4:6–6:21a). Although a handful of indirect or implicit imperatives also appear throughout the letter, this grammatical feature plays a significant logical-semantic structural role.

Several of the issues Paul raises in the first section (1:3–4:5) appear in the second, but with a more narrow and direct focus on Timothy's part in shaping the community. At this level, the relationship between the first section and the second is one of particularization with causation—that is, general descriptions for the church congregation (1:3–4:5) provide rationale for specific, consequential instructions primarily for Timothy (4:6–6:21a).

1:3–4:5

This first major section of the letter body addresses three broad topics, but two semantic structural features point to a partition between chapters one and two. First, the initial topic Paul addresses as early as 1:3 (which suggests urgency) is opposition—a negative problem for the church, whereas the next two items (worship and leadership) essentially present positive aspects of church life in Ephesus. Antagonism (1:3–20) does not belong in the community, whereas, in contrast, prayerful worship (2:1–15) and qualified leadership (3:1–13) do. Therefore, in the presentation of issues, Paul deals with one negative and two positive issues. The two positive issues exhibit similar structural features, including the highlighting of topical pertinence to males and females. This presentation also prepares the reader for more detailed discussion, particularly of specific male and female constituencies, in the body's second major section (4:6–6:21a).

---

[24] Thorvald B. Madsen, II, "The Ethics of the Pastoral Epistles," in *Entrusted with the Gospel*, ed. Köstenberger and Wilder (B&H Academic, 2010), 219–40.

The last segment (3:14–4:5) of this first major section functions as a summary and point of departure. By mentioning his own travels and potential delay, Paul reinforces the urgency of Timothy following through with his instructions while creating a prominent break in the flow of the section. He touches on the previous topics in brief, summary form. His discussion of worship (2:1–15) is evoked by *how one ought to behave in the household of God* (3:15), which also foreshadows later ethical material (esp. 5:1–6:2a). His discussion of leadership (3:1–13) is echoed by his framing of *the mystery of piety* (3:16a; cf. 3:9). Then, after outlining essential claims of the gospel in well-placed traditional material (3:16), he dwells on the implications (eschatological and demonic), nature (hypocrisy and greed; cf. 6:3–5), and form (ascetic and exclusionary) of the opposition he introduced at the beginning of the segment (4:1–5; cf. 1:3–20).

1:3–3:13

Figure 15.2 details an additional level of structure, because the logical-semantic relationships in this segment are somewhat more complex than those in later segments. This large segment addresses three topics for Timothy's community: antagonism (1:3–20), worship (2:1–15), and leadership (3:1–13). The first topic is generally framed as a problem that requires proper teaching (1:8–11), God's grace (1:14), and Timothy's courage and calling (1:18–19a). The second two topics are framed in generally positive terms. Therefore, the structure of this segment involves interrogation (i.e., problem with solution)[25] with contrast between a negative circumstance and two positive practices—worship and leadership. Paul links the problem of 1:3–20 with the positive practices of 2:1–3:13 by way of his first consequential οὖν (*so*, 2:1) in the letter, suggesting that he sees constructively engaging in practices of worship and enlisting good leaders as appropriate responses to contention.

1:3–3:13 The Way Things Ought to Be (with contrast between negative and positive)						
1:3–20 Problems and Promises with Troublemakers			2:1–3:13 Worship and Leadership in the Church			
1:3–17 The Problem with Opposition and Its Solution		1:18–20 Encourage-ment for Timothy with Sober-ing Examples	2:1–15 Instructions Regarding Corporate Worship		3:1–13 Instructions Regarding Church Leadership	
1:3–7 The Nature of the Opposition	1:8–17 Corrective Insight and Hopeful Example		2:1–7 General Evangelistic Worship	2:8–15 Instructions for Men and Women	3:1–7 Bishops	3:8–13 Deacons

Figure 15.2: Paragraph-Level Detail of 1 Timothy 1:3–3:13

---

[25] See Bauer and Traina, *Inductive Bible Study*, 113–14.

1:3–20

Paul immediately starts the body of this letter by outlining a significant problem in the Ephesian church to which he will return (4:1–3, 7–9; 6:3–5, 20-21a). Although raising the issue of antagonism so early in this relatively long letter might otherwise threaten discouragement, the bulk of this segment (1:3–20) is instructive and positive. It is grounded in solid reasoning about the positive place of law and argument (1:8–11), the promising example of Paul's own testimony (1:12–17), and the memory of Timothy's calling (1:18–20; cf. 4:11–16). Nevertheless, Paul's focus is on the problem of opposition throughout this segment as he concludes it by bringing up the sobering examples of Hymenaeus and Alexander (1:20). Note, however, that, even with these negative examples, Paul's aim is redemptive (*so that they may learn*, 1:20). When Paul presents this problem, he does so with profound hope.

1:3–17

This segment presents the Ephesian Christian community's main problem—people teaching opposing doctrine (1:3–7)—and places it into perspective through correct teaching (1:8–11) and instructive personal example (1:12–17). This same general structure of instruction and example is echoed in the complementary conclusion (1:18–20) of the broader segment to which this portion belongs.

1:3–7

In this paragraph, the first of the letter body, Paul presents an urgent issue—the problem of people advancing contrary doctrine (ἑτεροδιδασκαλέω, 1:3; lit. *teaching otherwise*; also 6:3). Paul uses words to describe what people were unduly attending to that speak less to its content and more to its form and function (*myths, genealogies, speculation*, 1:4; *meaningless talk*, 1:6) in contrast to that of Paul and Timothy's own instruction (*love*, 1:5). We know less about *what* they were teaching and more about *why* Paul opposed it—it was speculative (ἐκζήτησις, 1:4), misleading (ἀστοχέω, 1:6), empty (ματαιολογία, 1:6), ignorant (μὴ νοοῦντες, 1:7), and potentially ruinous.

1:8–17

This segment, linked to the previous with developmental δέ (1:8), provides rationale and perspective to the problems Paul presented in the first paragraph. It contrasts with the general tone of that previous paragraph (1:3–7), wherein Paul outlined some problems that Timothy faced in Ephesus. Paul outlines the complementary relationship of law and gospel—what is contrary to law is contrary to gospel and sound teaching (1:8–11). He then presents his own testimony as an example of what the *grace of our Lord* (ἡ χάρις τοῦ κυρίου ἡμῶν, 1:14) can accomplish, even in the most vicious opponent (1:12–17).

1:8–11

Paul presents reasoning about the proper use of the law and the place of argument which contrasts with the previous broad strokes with which he painted those who teach useless doctrines (1:3–7). The law (by which Paul probably means Torah or the Jewish Scriptures available to the Christian community in Ephesus), as an object of doctrine, is not for frivolous speculation but for community thriving, for life and death matters, and for the gospel (1:11).

A long list appears in 1:9–10 of persons who do acts that contrast with those of the *innocent* (1:9, before the list) and with *sound teaching* (ὑγιαινούσῃ διδασκαλίᾳ, 1:10; lit. *healthy doctrine*, after the list). The following facts characterize this list and the type of entries it features. Several of the PE's famous *hapax legomena* appear in this list. A shift in the list occurs from the general and attitudinal to the particular and behavioral—from *lawless and insubordinate, godless and sinful* (1:9) to *sodomites, slave traders, liars,* and *perjurers* (1:10). This is not a conventional vice list, enumerating undesirable or repugnant attitudes or behaviors; it is a list of people characterized by such attitudes and behaviors.

Paul's reason for framing the list in this way is a matter of interpretation, but it is peculiar and it sets up a parallel between these people and Paul's personal examples—himself, *a blasphemer, persecutor, and man of violence* (1:12–17) and *Hymenaeus and Alexander*, who were also blasphemers (1:20).

1:12–17

In this paragraph, Paul presents his personal testimony of redemption as a profound and hopeful example of how even Timothy's worst opponents can be redeemed. This paragraph is closely tied to the previous by way of biographical and teleological contrast—that is, Paul's life turned out drastically different from the destination that Timothy's opponents are travelling toward. He was one of them, but God's grace radically transformed him; hence, the mid-segment benediction (1:17)! He exults in God's overflowing grace and personally gives hope for Timothy's most difficult responsibility.

1:18–20

This paragraph concludes the initial discussion of dealing with contrarian doctrinaires. Generalizing what came before (1:3–17) as *this instruction* (Ταύτην τὴν

παραγγελίαν, 1:18), the opening phrase also creates an inclusio between the cognates παραγγέλλω (*I instruct*, 1:3) and παραγγελία (*instruction*, 1:18), holding the
larger unit together. As a discourse deictic, *this instruction* points back and opens
the present paragraph (1:18–20) as a segment summary with specific examples.
These named individuals (*Hymenaeus and Alexander*, 1:20) provide a sobering
contrast to the hopeful tone of Paul's own testimony (1:12–17). The structure of this
small paragraph reflects the general structure of the segment it concludes (1:3–
17)—problem with solution (a.k.a. *interrogation*) followed by personal example.

Paul sets the paragraph apart from the previous material by the meta-
comment (*I am putting before you*, 1:18). The generalization *this instruction* (1:18)
also serves as a point of departure, and this paragraph is syntactically and logically linked with the following paragraphs by the consequential conjunction οὖν
(2:1, 8). First Timothy 1:18–20 is, therefore, transitional. It relates to the previous
paragraphs by way of generalization (*this instruction*, 1:18) and summary example
(*Hymenaeus and Alexander*, 1:20) and to the following paragraphs by way of preparation. The themes of faith and faithlessness link the paragraph to what precedes
(1:4, 12, 13, 19[x2]), while the theme of a good or bad conscience links it with material before and after (1:5, 19[x2]; 3:9; 4:2) in the first major division (1:3–4:5).

2:1–3:13

This large segment contains two mid-sized segments with distinct topics but a
similar structure. In the previous segment (1:3–20) Paul dealt with opposition,
giving himself as a hopeful example of what can come when opponents are converted (1:12–17) and Hymenaeus and Alexander (1:20) of the consequences of
opponents virtually lost. The character of 2:1–3:13, however, is not about dealing
with opposition as much as the orderly arrangement of worship (2:1–15) and
management (3:1–13).

In three strategic and telling places, Paul uses the comparative adverb
ὡσαύτως (*likewise*, 2:9; 3:8, 11), which signals a recurring structure throughout this
large segment. Its comparative effect can also be seen in 5:25. With comparisons,
an implicit contrast must obtain and *vice versa*. An important interpretive question is *What is the nature of the comparison and contrast between the items?*

In 2:9, ὡσαύτως signals a comparison between men and women. Among the
points of comparison are the fact that Paul is referring to the conduct of Christian believers in a corporate worship setting, that both men and women are worshipping agents, that the conduct of persons of both genders is described and
delimited by church authorities, that even worship behavior should be modified
on the basis of community impressions (cf. 1 Cor 14:26–40).

In 3:8, ὡσαύτως signals a comparison between *bishops* and *deacons*. The job
responsibilities may differ between the largely administrative role of bishops

and the largely service role of deacons, but they are only fragmentarily written and largely taken for granted as *contextual assumptions* held by Paul and Timothy.[26] For the most part, the two lists of required attributes mirror one another. The ὡσαύτως reinforces the similarity of bishops and deacons as positions of leadership, trust, and public representation. It would be anachronistic to assume an inappropriate level of rigidity, but generally bishops seem to come to their roles *from* a place of public esteem (3:7) whereas deacons seem to come to their roles *toward* a place of public esteem (3:13).

In 3:11, ὡσαύτως signals a comparison between the character of deacons in general and of *women* (γυνή) in particular. Although the expected genitive pronoun (*their*, αὐτῶν) is not present to provide certainty, *women* here may refer to the *wives* (same Greek word) of male deacons. Some have argued, however, that *women* refers to female deacons.[27] That deacons are in view throughout the paragraph (3:8–13) is suggested by the resumption of the qualifications list in 3:12. Regardless of whether women were expected to fill such ministry roles alongside men, Paul had slightly different, albeit complementary, expectations for these women. For example, Paul mentions that these women should be serious (σεμνός, 3:8, 11) and pay special attention to slander (cf. 5:13).

The lists of personal qualities in 3:1–13 hardly mention job-specific tasks or skills; rather, Paul points to aspects of character. Scholars must draw on historical and literary backgrounds to debate whether being the *husband of one wife* (3:2, 12) equally excluded unmarried men, divorced men, women, or other categories from service as clearly as it excluded polygamists. Paul may have intended to require some of the characteristics in this list *where applicable*. For instance, one cannot govern his children (3:4, 12) without having any, but we usually do not take Paul to mean that children are a requirement for ministry. On the other hand, qualities such as *serious* (3:8, 11), *temperate* (3:2, 11), and not greedy (3:3, 8) seem to be more universally applicable. Rather than enumerating exact conditions for leadership without remainder, these lists may portray composite sketches of ideal leaders.

2:1–15

This segment is primarily about corporate worship and the appropriate activities, behaviors, conduct, and decorum. A consequential οὖν (*so*, 2:1) connects the

---

[26] For explanation of *contextual assumptions*, see Sperber and Wilson, "Pragmatics," 469–75, 478–84; Clark, *Relevance Theory*, 141.

[27] See, e.g., Susan E. Hylen, "Women διάκονοι and Gendered Norms of Leadership," *JBL* 138 (2019): 687–702; Jennifer H. Stiefel, "Women Deacons in 1 Timothy: A Linguistic and Literary Look at 'Women Likewise ... ' (1 Tim 3.11)," *NTS* 41 (1995): 442–57.

first paragraph of this segment (2:1–7) with the transitional paragraph before-hand (1:18–20), and another οὖν (2:8) connects the second paragraph (2:8–15) to the first. The outline of worship propriety (2:1–2) with rationale (2:3–7) present-ed in 2:1–7 has its consequential development (2:8–11) with rationale (2:12–15) in 2:8–15.

2:1–7

This sub-segment begins with an indirect imperative (meta-comment with em-phatic prioritization) that is applicable to entire church assemblies, not simply to Timothy—*I urge, therefore, first of all* (2:1). Paul goes on to indicate the proper business of the church—prayer of all kinds for all kinds of people, especially public leaders, regardless of affiliation. The purpose (ἵνα), however, circles back onto the Christian community—*so that we might carry on* (2:2). But, it is not simply a live-and-let-live mindset. Two factors strongly suggest that the prayers are intended toward conversion, rather than mere civility.[28] First, the epexegeti-cal relative clause (*who desires everyone to be saved*, 2:4) and the hymn that Paul presents (2:5–6, esp. *who gave himself a ransom for all*) points toward redemp-tion. Second, Paul inserts that aspect of his own vocation that points to the con-version of Gentiles (2:7). The deictic *unto which* (εἰς ὅ, 2:7) points to Christians' participation in God's world-saving mission (2:4–6), which includes this ministry of prayer in corporate worship (2:1–2).

   The prayers of men and women in the community had an end in mind, and it was not to insulate the church from discomfort and difficulty; rather, it was to accomplish God's mission of reconciling the world to himself. This explains why Paul's selection of the traditional material (2:5–6) includes the refrain *there is one mediator between God and humankind.*

2:8–15

This sub-segment takes the church's mission, as it is expressed and engaged through corporate worship, as the rational basis (οὖν, 2:8) for a certain kind of culturally attuned behavior. In two ways, these paragraphs exhibit a semantic shift from general injunction toward particular, personal preference and prac-tice. First, we see five all-inclusive words *everyone* or *all* (πάν, 2:1, 2[x2], 3, 6), as well as broad references to *humankind* (ἄνθρωπος, 2:5) and *the nations/Gentiles*

---

[28] Appreciation for the civil importance of *piety* (εὐσέβεια, 1 Tim 2:2; 3:16; 4:7, 8; 5:4; 6:3, 5, 6, 11; 2 Tim 3:5, 12; Titus 1:1; 2:12) notwithstanding. See T. Chrisopher Hoklotubbe, *Civilized Piety: The Rhetoric of Pietas in the Pastoral Epistles and the Roman Empire* (Baylor University Press, 2017).

(ἔθνος, 2:7). This is followed by more specific reference to *men/husband* (ἀνήρ 2:8, 12) and *women/wife* (γυνή, 2:9–12) with Adam and Eve presented illustratively. Second, Paul begins with a general indirect imperative for the church (παρακαλέω, *I urge*, 2:1), which is followed by a wish expression (βούλομαι, *I wish*, 2:8) then a more idiosyncratic description of his own practice (οὐκ ἐπιτρέπω, *I do not permit*, 2:12).

Paul offers an illustration based on Adam and Eve's temptation, fall, and redemption to reinforce his position, and scholars have been debating the point he was trying to make ever since.[29] In terms of logical-semantic structure, the δέ (*moreover*, 2:12) indicates that Paul's own practice and the illustration from Genesis together (2:12–15) provide rational grounds for his advice (2:8–11). The γάρ (*for*, 2:13) indicates that his understanding of the Adam and Eve narrative serves as rationale for his own practice. Paul makes a series of additions in this argument, using δέ in an atypical fashion three times in these four verses (2:12–15) when the average use is one in four (find concentrations of δέ also in 1 Tim 1:8–9; 3:4–7; 4:7–8; 5:4–13; 6:6–10).

3:1–13

This segment is about people who are designated, probably through a somewhat informal local community procedure (cf. 1:18–19a; 4:11–16, esp. 14; 5:22; 6:12), to serve in specific capacities in the church. Many commentators discuss the church's presumed state of organizational development at the time of writing. Given the uncertainty of the exact historical setting from which this letter emerged, from the standpoint of the discourse, two assumptions will aid interpretation. First, the PE in general and 1 Tim in particular exhibit a good measure of flexibility and informality regarding specific positions, interchanging terms and allowing for several plausible interpretations. Second, the community to which Paul wrote had a sufficiently strong sense of these ministry roles that he did not need to describe the duties and responsibilities as much as the qualifications and character. The latter point makes exegesis somewhat difficult for modern readers, because no one today knows exactly what those bishops and deacons did. History and archaeology, biblical testimony, other ancient literature, and so forth must illuminate the issue.

---

[29] Illuminating and pertinent examples include Elna Mouton and E. J. van Wolde, "New Life from a Pastoral Text of Terror?: Gender Perspectives on God and Humanity in 1 Timothy 2," *Scriptura* 111 (2012): 583–601, doi:10.7833/111-1-38; John R. Master and Jonathan L. Master, "Who Is the 'Woman' in 1 Timothy 2?," *MJTM* 10 (2008): 3–21; Bruce Barron, "Putting Women in Their Place: 1 Timothy 2 and Evangelical Views of Women in Church Leadership," *JETS* 33 (1990): 451–59; Theresa L. Tinkle, "Subversive Feminine Voices: The Reception of 1 Timothy 2 from Jerome to Chaucer," in *Gender & Power in Medieval Exegesis* (Palgrave Macmillan, 2010), 17–47.

3:1–7

A bishop (ἐπισκοπῆς/ἐπίσκοπος, 3:1–2; lit. *overseer*) seems to have had a steward-ship role (cf. Titus 1:7, where *bishop*, ἐπίσκοπος, and *household steward*, οἰκονόμος, are paralleled). That is, the bishop was likely responsible for the operational as-pects of the church assembly, such as (please pardon the anachronisms) meeting place, schedule, hospitality, coordinating guests, communication, public rela-tions, decorum, worship order, and so forth. Paul compares the role of a bishop with the role of a parent (3:4–5), which is suggestive of the possible head-of-household relationship a bishop was to have with respect to a congregation. The extent to which this kind of relationship with the church was unique to bishops is mitigated by the fact that *managing their children and their households well* (3:12; cf. Titus 2:5) is similarly an attribute of good deacons. Nevertheless, this requirement, in the case of bishops but not in the case of deacons, is coupled with a comparison between managing their own household and managing God's church (3:5). This suggests that the same quality is required for different reasons.

In 3:2, Paul lists seven positive attributes that should characterize bishops, and in 3:3 he lists four contrasting negative attributes that bishops should not have, inserting *gentle* in contrast to *violent* as an additional positive attribute. The positive list may show slight development from the general and characteris-tic (*above reproach, married only once*) to the specific and behavioral (*hospitable, an apt teacher*). Because this positive list culminates with teaching, we may un-derstand that bishops were trusted stewards of doctrine. But, direct teaching may not have been a primary responsibility, given that the characteristic of be-ing *able to teach* (διδακτικός, 3:2) would seem an unnecessary requirement of a person accepting teaching duties—*à la* "the head coach must have a knowledge of sports." First Timothy shows a repeated concern for public impressions (2:2; 3:7, 13; 4:11–16; 6:1, 12; cf. 5:24–25), and *to have a good testimony* [μαρτυρία] *from outsiders* (3:7) is a required attribute.

3:8–13

The structural parallels between 2:1–15 and 3:1–13 include how Paul moves from general (*all*, πᾶν) to particular (*men, women*; ἀνήρ, γυνή) and how he marks paral-lels between bishops and deacons (3:8) and men and women (2:9; 3:11) both in the worship and in this leadership segment using the same comparative adverb (ὡσαύτως; cf. Titus 2:3, 6). The differences he articulates pertaining to each cate-gory function in a tandem context of mutual complementarity. The writer and original readers would likely take for granted that the typical nominee for a role as bishop or deacon would be male, hence the enumeration of some requirements in male perspective (e.g., *husband of one wife*, 3:2, 12). Attunement to such cultural norms may not have constituted a universal rule, but the portrayal of ministry here is predominantly masculine.

3:14–4:5

The two sub-units that comprise this segment (3:14–16 and 4:1–5) seem unrelated on the surface, but there are three features that make them cohere. First, they are joined by a discourse level developmental δέ (4:1). In 1 Tim, δέ usually functions on a larger scale than the sentence, appearing once in every four verses on average, and marking development between entire paragraphs. What this common but subtle conjunction signals is that the writer thinks that more must be said in order for the reader to grasp the full significance of what precedes. That is why *moreover* is a common translation for δέ. In some instances, the more colloquial *What's more ...* might be appropriate. The nature of the development depends upon the logical-semantic relationship between the material before and after δέ.

Second, the two segments are complementary as a summary of the issues raised in the first segment (1:3–3:13) of the first section (1:3–4:5). Paul evokes the issues of congregational behavior (2:1–15) with *how one ought to behave in the household of God* (3:15), and issues of leadership (3:1–13, esp. *mystery*, v. 9) with *the mystery of piety* (3:16). He highlights the character, implications, and error of Timothy's opposition—first addressed in 1:3–20—in the last paragraph (4:1–5).

Third, several semantic connections tie 4:1–5 more to the preceding material than to what follows—*conscience* (1:5, 19; 3:9; 4:2), *prayer* (2:1; 4:5), *thanksgiving* (2:1; 4:3, 4), and *knowing the truth* (2:4; 4:3), for instance.

3:14–16

Like 1:18–20, this paragraph functions transitionally and has multiple ties to what comes before and after. The theme of *mystery* (μυστήριον, 3:9, 16) connects this paragraph to previous material. The backward-looking generalization with meta-comment *I am writing these things to you* (ταῦτά σοι γράφω, 3:14) seems to encompass everything that came before or perhaps the entire letter. But, these latter features also function as a point of departure, and δέ (4:1) signals continuity and development with the following paragraph.

4:1–5

In the PE, Paul's interest in the eschaton generally has two aspects. Most frequently, he is speaking about Christ's coming (ἐπιφάνεια)—sometimes with ambiguity as to whether he refers to the first and/or second coming (1 Tim 3:16; 6:14; 2 Tim 1:10; 4:1, 8; Titus 1:3; 2:11, 13; 3:4). The second aspect is the expectation and experience of treacherous times for believers, to which he briefly alludes in a few instances, as he does here (1 Tim 4:1; 2 Tim 3:1; 4:3). He is using the notion of ultimate things to accentuate the seriousness of the problematic opposition (1 Tim 1:3–20) and likely drawing on prior dialogues in the community that featured this topic.

By mentioning *lying spirits* and *demons* (4:1), he associates the opponents' doctrine with evil non-human agents, which Derek Brown has argued is a theme in 1 Tim (cf. 1:20; 3:6–7; 5:15).[30] Good non-human agents also appear in the letter (4:1; 5:21; see also *justified* [*in/by the S/s*]*pirit*, ἐδικαιώθη ἐν πνεύματι, 3:16). The issue of asceticism (*forbidding to marry and to receive foods*, 4:3) does not appear except here as a rare glimpse into the content of the troublemakers' doctrine. Nevertheless, eating and marriage are in the background of several passages (e.g., 3:2, 12; 5:3–16, esp. 11–12, 17–18, 23; 6:6–8, 17). The issue of the condition of a person's conscience, recurrent only in the letter body's first section, culminates here with the vivid description of *people whose own conscience has been seared* (4:2; cf. 1:5, 19; 3:9).

4:6–6:21a

Although this section addresses several broad issues, what sets it apart quite clearly from the previous one (1:3–4:5) is its interest in what healthy doctrine and a healthy church require of Timothy as a leader. A handful of indirect and implicit orders for Timothy and church members pepper the first section (e.g., 1:3, 18; 2:1, 8), but all thirty of the explicit and direct second-person singular imperatives in 1 Tim appear in this second section (4:6–6:21a). So, Paul shifts perspective toward the distinct implications for Timothy of his foregoing discussion of church order.

When Paul resumes topics in this second section, he tends to relate them to Timothy's leadership role. For instance, Paul speaks about acts of congregational worship in 2:1–15, but he speaks of Timothy *reading, exhorting,* [*and*] *teaching* in 4:13, which are presumably acts he would perform in the same setting. Paul outlines qualifications for church leaders in 3:1–13, including that bishops should not be novices (3:6), but in this final section he instructs Timothy not to participate too hastily in ordaining a person (5:22). Whereas Paul speaks about the hypocritical and mistaken position of misled asceticism in 4:3–5, he directs Timothy toward specific gastronomic practices in 5:23. Further, telling Timothy, *No one*

---

[30] Derek Brown, "Satan: The Author of False Teaching in the Pastoral Epistles" (paper presented at the SBL Annual Meeting—Program Unit: Disputed Paulines, Atlanta, November 30, 2015).

should despise your youth (4:12), sounds a related personal note characteristic of this section.

In this section, Paul emphasizes Timothy's role as teacher with respect to Paul's instructions (4:6, 11, 13, 16; 6:2b). Paul himself has been a model (2:7), and other leaders, *bishops* (ἐπίσκοπος, 3:2) and *elders* (πρεσβύτερος, 5:17), have been expected to engage in teaching. The problem with the troublemakers largely had to do with their presumptive teaching (1:3, 7; 4:1; 6:3), but this section now highlights Timothy's role in addressing that issue.

4:6–16

The focus of this segment is Timothy, his teaching role (*sound teaching*, 4:6, *encourage and teach these things*, 4:11, *attend to reading, exhortation,* [*and*] *teaching*, 4:13, *take heed to yourself and* [*the/your*] *teaching*, 4:16), and his modeling responsibility (*become an example to the faithful*, 4:12, *so that all may see*, 4:15). Paul turns decidedly from concerns with the church more generally (1:3–4:5) to a personal focus on Timothy. His job, if he wants to be a good servant (*deacon*, διάκονος, 4:6) of Christ Jesus, is to share Paul's vision of the church (*these things*, ταῦτα, 4:6) with the church. Such teaching was to be an extension of Timothy's personal faith and calling in contrast to what preoccupied others (4:7–8).

Elsewhere in 1 Tim, Paul provides instructions about propriety in the Christian family (a.k.a. *the household of God*, 3:15; cf. 3:4–5; 5:1–6:2a), worship (2:1–15; cf. 4:13), and attitudes toward wealth (2:9; 3:3, 8; 4:12; 5:6, 17–18, 6:3–10, 11, 17–19). But, by beginning this second section of the letter body in this way, Paul ensures that the premise of Timothy's leadership is the integrity of his character and calling, founded in God's grace (esp. 4:14–16). In this sense, 4:6–16 is introductory for 5:1–6:21a by laying a foundation for Timothy's authority.

4:6–10

The discourse deictic *these things* (Ταῦτα, 4:6) seems to point back at everything that came before in the letter. This paragraph begins to make everything that Paul has talked about and will talk about personal to Timothy. By using first-person plural verbs (*we toil and struggle ... we hope*, 4:10; cf. *fight*, 1:18[x2]; 6:12[x2]), Paul draws Timothy into a spiritually and morally deep collegiality. What is true of God's grace and calling in Paul's life (see 1:12–14) extends to his *true child* (γνησίῳ τέκνῳ, 1:2).

Although the *faithful is the word* (πιστὸς ὁ λόγος, 1:15; 3:1; 4:9; cf. 2 Tim 2:11) formula is typically a forward-looking meta-comment, there is some ambiguity as to what exactly Paul is pointing to in his use here in 1 Tim 4:9 and also in Titus 3:8. In contrast to other uses of the formula, the immediately preceding material in these two contexts is more pithy, poetic or liturgical than what follows. Further, conjunctions and first-person conversational speech that appear in the immediate context afterward (γάρ, 1 Tim 4:10; Titus 3:8b) suggest that this phrase is not pointing to material that follows it. Regardless, the phrase functions transitionally, whether as a concluding endorsement (likely) or as an introduction.

4:11–16

A discourse deictic opens this paragraph—Paul orders Timothy to encourage and teach *these things* (ταῦτα, 4:11; cf. 1 Tim 4:6; 5:7; 6:2b). Because this instance of ταῦτα appears toward the beginning of the section characterized by second-person singular imperatives (4:6–6:21a), it seems that the vision Paul had been expressing of how the church ought to be (1:3–4:5) is the content that Timothy is to promote. What follows is Timothy's specific role in catalyzing this ideal into a reality.

The focus of this paragraph remains on Timothy, but Paul shifts to encompass Timothy's calling and character. *These things* (4:11) is both forward- and backward-looking toward everything that Paul had earlier characterized as *how one ought to behave in the household of God* (3:15). Here we glimpse something of Timothy's biography—his *youth* (4:12), his practices (4:13), his ordination (4:14). Paul's expectations of Timothy are very high. Timothy's credibility and success in his role depend upon God's grace, Paul's commendation, and his own unimpeachable example.

Several instances of the deictic pronoun οὖτος appear in this paragraph, pointing both outside and inside the paragraph. In 4:15, Paul tells Timothy to *practice these things* (ταῦτα); *remain in these things* (τούτοις). The context, in which Paul is calling Timothy to set an example, and the direct imperative suggest that Paul is applying the previous instructions more narrowly and personally to Timothy's life and ministry. In 4:16, Paul tells Timothy that if he does *this* (τοῦτο), it will lead to redemptive outcomes for himself and his hearers. This οὖτος likely points back specifically to Paul's commands, first, that Timothy personally integrate the values and practices he had outlined into his own life (4:15a) and, second, that Timothy teach those ideals to the church (4:11).

5:1–6:21a

In this large segment, Paul zooms back out to view the broader church body. As he did in an earlier segment (2:1–3:13), he provides a block of teaching on the body at-large (5:1–6:2a; cf. 2:1–15) and a block of teaching on its prominent and influential members (6:2b–21a; cf. 1:3–20 negative and 3:1–13 positive). This constitutes a movement from general (albeit internally delineated) population to specific constituency. The angle of view, however, is on how these instructions for the church require Timothy's specific administration. Many of the second-person singular imperative verbs are predicated upon Timothy's position of authority and trust—for example, *rebuke, encourage*, 5:1, *honor*, 5:3, *command*, 5:7, *enroll*, 5:9, *preclude*, 5:11, *accept*, 5:19, *reprove*, 5:20, *guard*, 5:21, *lay hands upon*, 5:22; *command*, 6:17, *guard*, 6:20.

Paul can use *these things* (ταῦτα) to point across the letter and generalize a swath of instructions for a point of departure (e.g., 3:14; 4:6, 11; cf. 1:18), but he uses the deictic more narrowly in 5:7 and 21. Grammatically, ταῦτα could take a broad referent, but the contexts suggest that Paul is mainly pointing to his ongoing instructions regarding widows (5:3–16) in 5:7 and his instructions regarding elders (5:17–20, 24–25) in 5:21. He highlights Timothy's role in the oversight of care for widows in the congregation and in addressing leadership issues.

5:1–6:2a

This segment (5:1–6:2a) evokes the general form of a household code with some interesting exceptions. First, instead of parents, children, and slaves within a nuclear, blood, legal, or traditional household, the household is comprised of church members who occupy various social categories—e.g., older and younger men and women (5:1–2; relative to Timothy's age?), older and younger widows (5:3–16), elders who are church leaders (5:17–20, 24–25), Timothy himself (5:21–23), and slaves (6:1–2a). These features of the household list and even its general order parallel the household list in Titus 2:1–10 in which an excursus to Titus appears toward the end (2:7–8) just before instructions for slaves (2:9–10).[31] Although the code in 1 Tim is much longer than Titus's code, the structure is similar and the comparison, not only with traditional household codes but with another code for the metaphorical household of God, is illuminating.

Second, the outsized amount of material—roughly half of the section—devoted to instructions surrounding widows, their families, and the church (1 Tim 5:3–16) is peculiar. Paul must have thought that issues surrounding the care of widows were a significant problem in Timothy's community. Within the church's household code, Paul repeatedly distinguishes between the responsibilities of legal kin versus spiritual kin (5:4, 8, 14, 16).

Each paragraph within this quasi-household-code takes up a different sector of the Christian family—older and younger men and women (5:1–2), older and younger widows (5:3–16), elders (5:17–20; plus resumptive comments, 5:24–25), Timothy (5:21–23), and slaves (6:1–2a). Household codes were intended to serve the purposes of masters, not bind obligations upon them, so they primarily addressed the attitudes and behaviors of social subordinates.[32]

---

[31] See comments at Titus 2:1–10 and 3:1–2 (under *Submission*).

[32] See, e.g., arguments in Aristotle, *Pol.* 1:1253b; Josephus, *Ag. Ap.* 2:206

Extensive instructions for husbands, fathers, and masters were unusual in the Greco-Roman world.[33]

The oath formula and first-person metacomment in 5:21 give emphasis and prominence to the material aimed personally at Timothy. New Testament household codes (e.g., Eph 5:21–6:9; Col 3:18–4:1; Titus 2:1–10; 1 Pet 2:18–3:7) are typically organized according to members' relationships with one another, especially with the head of household (*pater familias*), and ordered according to descending social status and proximity to headship or authority.[34] That is, the further down the list a person falls, the lower their relative status and the further from power they are, and *vice versa*. If the fictive household code is generally organized by analogy to this structure, then the choice to place Timothy (1 Tim 5:21–23; cf. Titus 2:7–8) near the end may imply a subversion of normal social ordering within the church, especially if he might otherwise be viewed (organizationally) as the head of household.

Paul refers to himself, his calling, and his partners in mission in terms of servanthood, which embraces the implication of a lower social position—for Paul, see 1 Tim 1:12 (see also 2 Tim 4:11; Titus 1:1); for Timothy, see 1 Tim 4:6 (see also 2 Tim 2:24; 4:5). He thereby reinforced a perception of equality among church members that defied external social norms. Because Timothy is supposed to view himself as a brother to the younger men and women and a son to the older men and women (1 Tim 5:1–2), his place as a child in the household code is understandable, but it upends the expectation that the leader of a group would rule by fiat and demand personal deference. Instead, Paul instructs familial gentleness (e.g., 5:1–2).

6:2b–21a

Parallel with his usage in 5:7 and 5:21, the backward-looking deictic *these things* (ταῦτα, 6:2b) generalizes Paul's instructions but with a specific contextual emphasis. He is mainly pointing to the household-oriented instructions that he just completed (5:1–6:2a). Afterward, Paul opens this segment with a double contrast that affects an indirect comparison: First, he contrasts his and Timothy's own doctrine—of which the letter is representative—with that of those who *teach otherwise* (ἑτεροδιδασκαλέω, 6:3), resuming the theme of opposition from the beginning of the letter (ἑτεροδιδασκαλέω, 1:3)—a prominent single recurrence. In

---

[33] Some propose that 1 Tim is organized as a household code, but only 5:1–6:2a truly bears the marks of the literary form. See David E. Aune, *The New Testament in Its Literary Environment*, LEC 8 (Westminster John Knox, 1987), 196; James S. Jeffers, *The Greco-Roman World of the New Testament Era: Exploring the Background of Early Christianity* (IVP Academic, 1999), 86–87, 228–29.

[34] See discussion in Marshall, *Pastoral Epistles*, 231–6.

turn, he contrasts the doctrine of these opponents with *the sound words of our Lord Jesus Christ and the teaching that accords with piety* (6:3). By virtue of this double contrast, Paul and Timothy's own teaching is implicitly characterized as sound and devout.

Paul then ascribes to the opponents a list of negative personal attributes (6:4a) and the attitudes and behaviors they produce (6:4b–5). Among them is greed, which Paul then expands upon with a teaching on contentment that has a more general-audience applicability. So, in 6:6–10 Paul develops the topic of greed, which appears at the end of a list of the opponents' negative attributes 6:2b–5. While the topic of greed (6:6–10) is more narrowly concentrated than the vice list (6:3–5), the congregational applicability is broader.

When Paul tells Timothy to *flee these things* (ταῦτα φεῦγε, 6:11), he narrowly points back to the wasteful controversy and corrosive greed discussed in 6:3–10. Throughout the letter, Paul considers these pursuits to be unfitting for church leaders (*teaching otherwise*, ἑτεροδιδασκαλέω, 1:3, 6:3; *being puffed up*, τυφόομαι, 3:6, 6:4; *[speculative] debate*, [ἐκ]ζήτησις, 1:4; 6:4; *uncontentious/word-contention* ἄμαχος/λογομαχία, 3:3, 6:4; [idea of greed] ἀφιλάργυρος/φιλαργυρία, 3:3, 6:10; etc.). He tells Timothy to run the other way (φεύγω) and *pursue* (διώκω) a different set of interests (6:11b)—complementary behaviors from exact opposite verbs.

In 6:11–16, Paul does not mention greed but sets up a more general contrast between the opponents, who represent *these things* (ταῦτα) that Timothy is supposed to *flee* (φεύγω, 6:11a), and Timothy himself. While running away from what negatively characterizes the opponents, Timothy is to run toward or *pursue* (διώκω; also *persecute*) a short list of positive virtues (6:11b). Among these virtues, Paul develops some more than others elsewhere—*righteousness* (1:9; 3:16; 6:11), *piety* (2:2; 3:16; 4:7–8; 5:4; 6:3; cf. 1:9; 2:10; 6:5–6, 11), *faith* (1:2, 4, 5, 11, 12–14, 16, 19; 2:7, 15; 3:9, 11, 13, 16; 4:1, 3, 6, 10, 12; 5:8; 6:2, 10, 11, 12, 21; for additional uses of *faith* language, see 1:15; 3:1; 4:9; 5:12; etc.), *love* (1:5, 14; 2:15; 4:12; 6:2, 11), *endurance* (ὑπομονή, 6:11; cf. Titus 2:2; ὑπομένω, 2 Tim 2:10, 12; ὑποφέρω, 3:11; κακοπαθέω 2:9; 4:5), *gentleness* (1 Tim 6:11; cf. 2 Tim 2:25; Titus 3:2). Like an earlier paragraph containing Paul's own autobiography, this paragraph climaxes in a benediction with *amen* (1 Tim 6:16; cf. 1:12–17).

As in the segments that dealt with influential people earlier in 1 Tim, greed and deceitfully using the social standing that comes from observed piety to gain material wealth are the negative attitudes and actions that Paul instructs Timothy to address, especially in 6:5b, 9–10 (cf. 3:3, 8). In 6:17–19, Paul resumes the topic of wealth but outlines positive attitudes and actions.

Verses 20–21a serve a summary function for the entire letter body, but especially of the issue of opposition (cf. 1:3–20; 4:1–3, 7; 5:20; 6:3–5). What Paul briefly alludes to as *falsely called knowledge* (6:20) may have a more specific technical meaning in relation to the opposition in Ephesus, given that the same outcome obtains in 6:21a as 1:6 (*deviate*, ἀστοχέω in both verses), where the concern began.[35] The concern with professors of mislabeled knowledge (6:20–21a; a.k.a. *those who teach otherwise*, 6:3) in the beginning and end of this segment brings the letter full circle to Paul's initial concern with misled and misleading speculators (1:3–7).

Some commentators consider the final charge to Timothy (6:20–21a) part of the closing. The vocative address sets it apart from the previous paragraph. Because the final charge to Timothy (6:20–21) recapitulates themes and material from earlier (e.g., 1:6, 20) and because direct address is not reserved in this letter for epistolary features (cf. 1:18; 6:11), only the final greeting (*grace be with you*, 6:21b) is strictly epistolary in nature.

6:21b

The epistolary conclusion in 1 Tim is extremely brief, essentially amounting to a closing greeting. Although no travelogue appears here, where one might be expected, Paul mentioned his plans to visit in 3:14–15. Two additional aspects of the greeting should be noted in terms of the semantic structure of the book. First, it is a Christian greeting. The *grace* that Paul mentions here echoes the significant instances of *grace* language earlier in the letter—in the opening (1:2) and during his testimony (1:14)—and accounts of divine action (e.g., 1:12–17; 3:16; 4:4–5, 14; 6:6–8, 13–15).

Second, the pronoun *you* here is plural, probably the only explicit grammatical indicator that 1 Tim was written to be heard by Timothy's community. Of course, there are many indicators throughout that 1 Tim was written to a community—for instance, the numerous third-person plural imperatives which were undoubtedly meant to be "overheard" and the shift from general instructions (1:3–4:5) to particular mandates (4:6–6:21a).

This one final word (ὑμῶν, 6:21b) signals the way the entire book is to be read. The first major section of instruction is given under Paul's direct authority; in the second major section, Paul publicly charges Timothy to administer the church in specific ways thereby securing the endowment of authority to Timothy and, by extension, to Timothy's designees. This final word addresses the audience to this exercise and explicitly manifests that Paul expects them to support his mandates.

---

[35] See Jens Herzer, "Was ist falsch an Der 'fälschlich so genannten Gnosis'?: Zur Paulusrezeption des Ersten Timotheusbriefes im Kontext seiner Gegnerpolemik," *EC* 5 (2014): 68–96.

2 Timothy

Second Timothy is personal and intensely intimate. Paul does not disguise his affection for his colleagues (e.g., 1:2, 16–18; 2:1; 4:11, 19–22), sugar-coat his trouble with the antagonistic or disloyal (e.g., 1:15; 2:9, 17–18; 3:11; 4:9–10, 14–15, 16), or ignore his feelings about his own death (e.g., 4:6–8). In every case, however, he expresses a trust and resolve (e.g., 1:12; 2:19; 3:9, 11; 4:17–18) that he urges Timothy to embrace (e.g., 1:13–14; 2:1–4, 22; 3:14–15; 4:1–5). In making this appeal for Timothy to *guard the deposit* (1:12, 14), Paul even brings Timothy's (and perhaps his own, 1:3) family of origin into discussion (see 1:3–7; 3:14–16). Paul's confidence in the midst of persecution is that the victory is ultimately with *God, who saved us* (1:8–9). The last *times* (3:1), nonetheless, call for strategy (1:3–2:13) and resolve (2:14–4:8).

Some commentators note that this personal letter sounds something like a testament. At points, Paul appears to think that he has time left (e.g., 1:4; 4:9–13, 21) but that he is preparing for his own departure (4:6–8). Because discourse functions differently between genres, attending to its testamentary aspects is appropriate. The genre may signal how specific words and phrases are to be taken. There is debate as to the value of seeing 2 Tim as a testament, however, given that the features of testamentary literature are not strong throughout.[36] The label has been given mainly in recognition of the circumstance the letter evokes, not in view of literary features that point to this genre. Acknowledging the end-of-life dimension to some of Paul's expressed concerns, the analysis below reads 2 Tim as a personal letter of exhortation to his junior colleague, Timothy, not as a final testament.

The basic outline of 2 Tim takes account of its average-sized epistolary opening (1:1–2), lengthy conclusion (4:9–22), and body (1:3–4:8). Some commentators consider various portions of the letter body's initial paragraph (1:3–7) to be part of a customary letter opening (e.g., the thanksgiving and blessing, 1:3–4). Two factors suggest that this material belongs equally to the main letter body. First, the theme of succession that Paul begins in 1:3 is prominent throughout the letter. Second, conjunctions, dependent clauses, and topical development keep the entire paragraph (1:3–7) so cohesive that a break might seem artificial.

The letter body is then divided into two parts: The first (1:3–2:13) focuses on the succession theme and strategy that seems urgent to Paul. The second (2:14–4:8) focuses on the obstacles that Paul sees to advancing the mission of the church with their solutions as the rationale for the preceding strategy of succession planning. Some themes obtain throughout the letter, however. These include suffering persecution, faithfulness and disloyalty, and God's ultimate victory.

---

[36] See comments about genre in the Introduction and at 2 Tim 1:1–2.

2 Tim 1:1-4:22							
1:3-4:8 Letter Body—Keeping the Faith				4:9-22 Letter Conclusion			
1:3-2:13 Trustees of the Gospel		2:14-4:8 How and Why We Fight		4:9-18 Travel and Team Instructions		4:19-22 Greetings and Blessing	
1:3-2:7 Trusted Timothy and Others	2:8-13 Gospel Premises and Promises	2:14-3:17 Troublemakers Internal and External	4:1-8 Resolve to Fight and Endure	4:9-15 Instructions and Information	4:16-18 Concession and Consolation from the Lord	4:19-21 Greetings All Around	4:22 Final Blessing

(left margin, vertical) 1:1-2 Epistolary Intro

Figure 15.3: Constituent Organization of 2 Timothy

1:1–2

The epistolary opening marks the genre of 2 Tim as a personal letter. Because Paul refers to his own death (4:6–8), some have pointed to *final testament* as a sub-genre, but this designation may distort how one reads the very vital instructions in the rest of the letter.[37] Paul does not dwell on his passing any more than on the unstoppable nature of the *promise of life that is in Christ Jesus* (1:1). There are several points in the letter in which, through a recurrence of the logical-semantic structure of concession, he expresses the imperturbable nature of God's grace—*I suffer hardship, ... but the word of God is not chained* (2:9); *if we are faithless, he remains faithful* (2:13); *they are upsetting the faith of some, but God's firm foundation stands* (2:18–19); *these people ... oppose the truth, but they will not make much progress* (3:9); *what persecutions I endured, yet the Lord rescued me* (3:11); *no one came to my support, ... but the Lord stood by me* (4:16–17; see also 1:8–10; 4:8).

The initial introduction of several concepts in these opening verses is sparse, awaiting further development. The concept of *will* or *purpose* appears a few times and conveys aims that can be aligned with God's will or not (*will*, θελήμα, 1:1; 2:26; *desire*, θέλω, 3:12; *purpose*, πρόθεσις, 1:9; 3:10). Because of its somewhat idiomatic nature, one might not expect the blessing, *grace, mercy, peace* (1:2) to anticipate much development, but each of these concepts does receive attention. *Grace* develops as an expression of God's generosity and activity in the lives of Christians (1:6–7, 9; 2:1; 4:8, 22; see also *thankful*, 1:3; *unthankful*, 3:2) and can be seen throughout the letter, even where -χαριτ- roots do not appear. Other topics that first find expression in these introductory verses include Paul as *apostle* (see 1:11), part of an important succession planning theme in the letter; *the*

---

[37] True examples of testamentary literature are typically fictionalized long after the death of the subject, and virtually no examples exist of a testament being written to mimic the form of a contemporary personal letter.

promise of life (see 1:8–11; 2:11; 3:10–12; 4:1), a précis of Paul's gospel; and Timothy as a beloved *child* (see 1:5; 2:1; 3:14–15).

Ancient personal letters often featured thanksgivings and reminiscences at the beginning, so it is appropriate to consider 1:3–5 as part of the epistolary introduction, as some have done. Because of this opening material's substantial ideas, which prefigure the central themes of faithfulness and passing on the gospel to a new generation of believers, and because of its cohesive grammatical features and tight logical connection to the injunction *re-ignite the gift* (1:6), it belongs just as well with the body proper. It nevertheless serves an introductory function.

1:3–4:8

This division comprises the letter body. The greetings, travelogues, and personal instructions of 4:9–22 have bearing upon the letter as a whole but are materially distinct from the body's pastoral content. Paul's critical message to Timothy here is to keep the faith and not to become fatigued (like the soldier, athlete, and farmhand in 2:4–6) on account of the pressures around him. Strategically, Paul focuses on the importance of passing on the faith, outlining a remarkable lineage that includes Paul's *ancestors* (1:3), Timothy's *grandmother Lois* and *mother Eunice* (1:5), Paul himself (1:6, 11–14), and Timothy's own protégés (2:1–2). As much as anything else, Timothy's looming departure from the church in Ephesus (4:9) may have called for such a strategy.

Paul encourages Timothy to fight opposition and suffer persecution—first, because it is virtuous (1:8, 16; 2:3, 12, 15; 4:5); second, because of Paul's example (1:12; 2:9–10; 3:10–11; 4:6–7); and third, because it is inevitable (3:1, 12). The concept of not being ashamed almost invariably accompanies this theme of persecution as a micro-structural relationship of concession. This theme is so prominent in the letter that it is no wonder that Paul also mentions persecution in his concluding personal instructions and benediction (4:15, 18).

The body of the letter may be divided into three concerns for Timothy and his community. First, Paul is concerned with preserving the faith both at a personal and a corporate level and the strategy of passing it on to trustees just as Timothy has been entrusted (1:3–2:13). For this purpose, Paul outlines Timothy's own faith lineage (1:3–7), instructs him to entrust others with the doctrine (1:8–2:7), and reprises essential aspects of the gospel (2:8–13).

Second, he is concerned with wasteful and erosive internal doctrinal conflicts (2:14–26). The issue bleeds into 3:1–8, as well, connected with developmental δέ (3:1), but the primary opponents in 3:1–8 seem to be outside the Christian community. The internal conflicts hinder Paul's first concern with staying firm in the faith personally and passing it on corporately. Despite the prominence of the concept of suffering of various kinds and sources in 2 Tim, Paul basically frames the issue as a problem (2:14–19) that has a solution (2:20–26). This problem-solution logical-semantic structure may be referred to as *interrogation*.[38]

Third, Paul is concerned with troublemakers who persecute him and others in the church either as external enemies of the faith or as infiltrators with wrong motives (*wicked people and imposters*, 3:13). He is resolved and admonishes Timothy to endure the suffering for the sake of the gospel and sound doctrine (4:3–5; cf. 1:13). Paul describes the persecution, where it comes from, and the scriptural solution as matters of fact (3:1–17, esp. *all who want to live devoutly in Christ Jesus will be persecuted*, 3:12). This segment (3:1–17), which is concerned with external opposition, mirrors the logical-semantic structure of interrogation exhibited in the previous segment (2:14–26), which, by contrast, was concerned with internal conflict. Basically, Paul outlines factors in the problem of opposition (3:1–9), then he outlines factors in the solution—these include his example, the Lord's power to rescue, acceptance of the inevitability of opposition, Timothy's resolute participation, the credibility of Timothy's sources for faith, and the equipping capacity of Scripture (3:10–17).

In light of the concerns Paul outlines, he resolves to instruct Timothy to follow his example and endure whatever challenges might come as Timothy implements all aspects of his instructions—*carry out your ministry fully*, 4:5. This generalization of the specific instructions Paul had given and the reiteration of Paul's role as example (4:6–8; cf. 1:8; 2:1–3; 3:10–11) brings the final segment of the letter body (4:1–8) full circle. So, this final segment of exhortation, emphatically marked with an oath meta-comment (4:1), functions as hortatory causation.[39] In other words, it is Paul's logical conclusion to all of the problems and solutions that came before, given in the form of a cluster of imperatives—nine second-person singular imperative verbs in one paragraph (4:1–5).

1:3–2:13

This section addresses the issue of carrying the Christian faith and doctrine (a.k.a. *deposit*, παραθήκη, 1:12, 14) into the next generation. Paul begins with Timothy's own biography—initial deposits involved pivotal people in his life (*Lois, Eunice, Paul*, 1:5–6). He follows with an appeal for Timothy to *join* [*him*] *in suffering* (συγκακοπαθέω, 1:8) and continues by talking about Christ's work (1:9–10), Paul's own calling (1:11), and the trust Paul has suitably placed in someone (ᾧ, *in whom*, 1:12; he speaks elliptically; *Timothy?*). The next paragraph instructively presents negative and positive examples of trusted colleagues (1:15–18). Then,

---

[38] Bauer and Traina, *Inductive Bible Study*, 113–14.
[39] Ibid., 106–7.

Paul explains and illustrates the strategy and models for entrusting other worthy people with this ministry (2:1–7). The remainder of the segment (2:8–13) carefully conveys the contents and consequence of the *deposit* (1:12, 14; i.e., the *gospel*, 1:8–10, and *sound words* [*doctrine*], 1:13).

This section contrasts with the following one in terms of structure. Whereas 2:14–4:8 features a recurrence of the logical-semantic relationship of interrogation (see 2:14–26 and 3:1–17), this section (1:3–2:13) interchanges what could be considered a solution—passing on the faith—with issues of persecution (see e.g., 1:8, 16; 2:3, 9, 11) and disloyalty (see e.g., 1:15; 2:12–13), which are not the problems that passing on the faith solves. The actual problem—the erosion of faith in individual and corporate life—is implicit throughout. So, Paul's instructions in this section (1:3–2:13) are a pivotal, strategic, preemptive, but also an indirect solution to an implicit problem.

One might refer to the logical-semantic relationship between this segment and the next as one of *hortatory substantiation*.[40] That is, Paul prescribes a course of action for Timothy in the present segment (1:3–2:13), but he outlines the reasons for this approach more vividly in the following segment (2:14–4:8, including that Paul's own time is short, 4:6–8).

1:3-2:13 Trustees of the Gospel			
1:3-2:7 Passing on the *Parathēkē*		2:8-13 Gospel Premises and Promises	
1:3-7 Biography—Gifts to Timothy	1:8-2:7 Strategic Trust	2:8-10 Gospel Contents and Consequence	2:11-13 Gospel Confidence
	1:8-18 Paul's Trusted Colleagues / 2:1-7 Consequential Strategy		

Figure 15.4: *Paragraph-Level Detail of 2 Timothy 1:3–2:13*

1:3–2:7

This segment is characterized by the theme of trust and the perpetual endowment of the Christian faith from one person to the next. The lineage of gift and reception includes Paul's *ancestors, Lois, Eunice, Paul, Timothy,* and ultimately *God* (1:3–7). Paul receives from Christ and trusts to Timothy (1:8–14), empowered by the Holy Spirit. Paul and Timothy have trusted others—including Phygelus, Hermogenes, and Onesiphorus—with lessons learned (1:15–18). To the point, Paul instructs Timothy to entrust other worthy people and presents some illustrative models for Timothy's own and for the new trustees' relationship to their ministry and recruiter (2:1–7).

---

[40] Ibid., 107.

Although imperatives and indirect imperatives that call for faithful endurance under pressure appear earlier in this segment (e.g., 1:8, 13, 14), this last paragraph (2:1–7) represents the culmination of Paul's strategy for the sustainability of the Christian community in Ephesus (note that Paul expects Timothy to depart, 4:9). So, there is a general chronological progression from the past (1:3–7), through the present (1:8–18), and into the future (2:1–7).

1:3–7

Ancient letters frequently had a small note of thanksgiving and prayer near the beginning. Paul follows this formal feature (1:3–4), which leads into some aspects of Timothy's biography that are critical to Paul's message. First, Timothy's faith and spiritual lineage (1:5); second, his gifting and ordination in relation to Paul (1:6); third, Timothy's (and Paul's) divine endowment and empowerment (1:7). This paragraph represents the first impression of a theme of passing on the faith that characterizes the larger segment. Paul places Timothy's past into view as a prototype of what he will ultimately instruct Timothy to accomplish—passing on what he had heard from Paul (2:1–2).

1:8–2:7

In this segment, Paul shifts from the intimate, personal, and spiritual (1:7) to the public, corporate, and collegial (1:8–2:7). Although they are in jeopardy (hence the ubiquitous refrain of persecution and chains; e.g., 1:8, 12, 16; 2:3), the Christian community depends upon those who have been entrusted with the gospel—Paul (1:8–9, 11), Timothy (1:12–14), and others (1:15–18; 2:1–2).

1:8–18

This segment portrays Paul, his trusted colleagues (worthy and unworthy), and the triune God who empowers them as trustees and agents of the gospel.[41] Paul expands the circle of trust outward from himself and Timothy (1:8–14) toward others (1:15–18), which admits that not all who are trusted are trustworthy. This awareness is critical for where Paul wants to take Timothy next—a call to expand the circle of trusted colleagues further for the sake of the gospel (2:1–2).

---

[41] Paul does not explicitly address trinitarian theology, but the structure of 2 Tim 1:8–14 is illuminating. Paul asserts that *the power of God* (1:8) is the essential resource needed to face suffering and that *the grace given to us in Christ Jesus* (1:9) and *the appearing* [ἐπιφάνη] *of our Savior Christ Jesus* (1:10) are essential to gospel ministry. Finally, he acknowledges that *the help of the indwelling Holy Spirit* (1:14) is pivotal to success.

1:8–14

The consequential conjunction οὖν (1:8) connects this large paragraph with the introductory material preceding it (1:3–7). Specifically, on account of the kind of *spirit [Spirit?] God has given us* (1:7) and on account of Timothy's biography (1:3–7), Paul orders him not to be *ashamed of the testimony of our Lord* (1:8) or of Paul, even if he is a *prisoner. Rather* (ἀλλά), Timothy is to *join [Paul] in suffering for the gospel* (1:8b). Paul briefly outlines some of the claims of the gospel (1:9–10) and describes his vocation relative to the gospel (1:11–12a). The remainder of the paragraph has to do with Paul entrusting the gospel (1:8, 10) and sound doctrine (1:13) to a capable trustee (1:12–14; cf. 1 Tim 6:20).

Although interpreters typically take Paul's *the one in whom I have put my trust* (2 Tim 1:12) to refer elliptically to God or Christ,[42] the context suggests another option. The unasked question is, *in whom has Paul put his trust?* The surrounding verses point in a relatively clear direction—Paul is referring to Timothy as a trustee of his *gospel* and *sound words [doctrine]* (1:8, 10, 13). Throughout the letter, Paul bolsters Timothy's confidence and staying power, because Paul believes in him (or has no other choice). Timothy is Paul's trusted confidant in Ephesus. For the sake of Timothy's community, Paul vouches for his calling and capacity even as he commands him to *guard the good deposit that has been entrusted* (1:14).

There is such a precise verbal comparison between the one Paul elliptically says that he trusted *to guard* [φυλάσσω] *my [Paul's] deposit* [παραθήκη] (1:12) and Timothy, whom Paul instructs to *guard* [φυλάσσω] *the good deposit* [παραθήκη] (1:14) that Paul may be referring to the same person that he stationed in Ephesus with the responsibility of stewarding the church (cf. *O, Timothy, guard* [φυλάσσω] *the deposit* [παραθήκη], 1 Tim 6:20). Other possibilities exist, including that Paul emphasizes God's power to *guard* (2 Tim 1:12) as he calls Timothy to *guard through the indwelling Holy Spirit* (1:14) or that *my [Paul's] deposit* (1:12) refers to gifts of God (e.g., gospel and sound doctrine) that Paul is holding in trust by God's power.

1:15–18

This brief paragraph presents examples of Paul's (and Timothy's) trusted colleagues—contrasting bad examples (*all the ones in Asia, Phygelus and Hermogenes*, 1:15) with good (*the household of Onesiphorus*, 1:16–18). These examples are in keeping with the topic of passing the *deposit* (παραθήκη, 1:12, 14) of the *gospel* (1:8, 10, 11) and *sound teaching* (1:13) down to the next generation. *Lois, Eunice,*

---

[42] E.g., Guthrie, *Pastoral Epistles*, 149; Marshall, *Pastoral Epistles*, 710; Towner, *1–2 Timothy & Titus*, 166.

Paul, and *Timothy* have been the explicit custodians of the faith until now (1:3–14), but Paul is about to instruct Timothy to expand that circle to other trustworthy stewards (2:1–7). These examples inspire both hope and caution.

2:1–7

This paragraph has two purposes. First, it culminates Paul's strategic vision and command for passing the *deposit* down, a theme that began with Paul's ancestors (1:3) and Timothy's forebears (1:5–6). Now Timothy is to continue the legacy by entrusting others with *the things that you [Timothy] have heard from me [Paul]* (2:2).

Second, Paul illustrates the relationship of the workers (*soldier, athlete, farmhand*,[43] 2:3–6) to their work and their leaders. BDAG and some translations associate this reference to γεωργός (*farmworker*) with a definition that implies owning land, but each illustration is of a social subordinate, suggesting that the person in view here is a farmworker, not a farm-owner.

Each illustration makes a different point, so they are not parallel. They combine to illustrate various aspects of being entrusted with the gospel—necessary focus and the aim of pleasing the right person, propriety in conduct as a condition of success, and the expectation of a reward for diligence. Verse seven invites the reader not to hurry these analogies into a facile interpretation but to allow the Lord to illuminate them—good hermeneutical advice in general!

2:8–13

This segment is comprised of a paragraph that succinctly reiterates a few critical points of *my [Paul's] gospel* (2:8). Paul immediately points to a negative outcome to himself (persecution) and two reasons he endures suffering: evangelical—*so that they also may obtain salvation* (2:10)—and existential—because *the word is faithful* (πιστὸς ὁ λόγος, 2:11).

The traditional material in 2:11–13 that follows the introductory endorsement *faithful is the word* (2:11) is a list of general conditionals that imply that each consequence is based in the faithfulness of God (esp. v. 13). In case there were any questions about the content of the *deposit* (1:12, 14) that Paul seeks to transfer, this segment (2:8–13) articulates some of the key claims. Of course, this is not the only place in the letter where Paul discusses some details of his proclamation (see e.g., 1:1, 9–10; 2:19; 4:1, 8).

---

[43] See BDAG, 196.

2:14–4:8

This section addresses two problems that are causing trouble for Paul, Timothy, and the church. One is primarily an internal issue—conflict that squanders and erodes the faith of individuals and communities (2:14–26). The other is primarily an external issue—opposition that attacks and disrupts the Christian community (3:1–17). Both segments exhibit the same logical-semantic structure of interrogation (problem-solution).

The issues addressed here differ from that addressed in the first section (1:3–2:13). Whereas Paul's instructions regarding passing on the deposit in the first section simply constitute good practice, his instructions in this second section respond to negative circumstances. In the first section, Paul may have been addressing an implicit, potential, and subtle problem (e.g., eroding personal and corporate faith). In the second section, the problems are explicit, current, and palpable.

The final segment (4:1–8) of this section exhibits features that increase its prominence. Verse one begins with an emphatic first-person meta-comment and oath (*I solemnly urge you in the presence of God*) and proceeds with an epexegetical relative clause that speaks of ultimate judgment. Verse two starts a cluster of imperatives. The initial paragraph (4:1–5) is the hortatory culmination of the entire letter body as it mentions in general terms all of the issues Paul addressed earlier (e.g., *proclaim the message*, 4:2; *do the work of an evangelist*, 4:5; cf. 1:3–2:13; *convince, rebuke, encourage*, 4:2; *turn away from hearing the truth and wander away to myths*, 4:4; cf. 2:14–26; *unfavorable* [*times*], 4:2; *endure suffering*, 4:5; cf. 3:1–17). Paul's example (4:6–8) again provided rationale and encouragement to follow his instructions.

2:14-4:8 How and Why We Fight					
2:14-3:17 Troublemakers Internal and External				4:1-4:8 Resolve to Fight and Endure	
2:14-26 Wasteful and Erosive Internal Conflict		3:1-17 Painful Opposition from *Wicked People and Imposters* (3:13)		4:1-5 Timothy's Ministry	4:6-8 Paul's Example
2:14–19 Problem— Ruinous Wrangling	2:20-26 Solution— Riddance of Wrangling	3:1-9 Problem— Fact of Wickedness	3:10-17 Solution— Factors for Endurance		

Figure 15.5: Paragraph-Level Detail of 2 Timothy 2:14–4:8

2:14–3:17

The ταῦτα (*these things*, 2:14) that Paul orders Timothy to remind the church of looks back (anaphoric) across the entire first section of the letter, but especially the material closest to this deictic. It functions as a point of departure that generalizes everything that Paul has been saying—Timothy's background (1:3–7), Paul and Timothy's custodianship of the gospel (1:8–14), their record with colleagues (1:15–18), Timothy's duty to engage other gospel trustees (1:15–2:7), and especially the contents and consequence of the gospel (2:8–13). Aside from the mentions of persecution that Paul interspersed, *these things* were generally positive. Now, Paul talks about where things have been going wrong for the Christian community. He begins this segment by telling Timothy to *remind* them of *these things*, because he hopes that they will be part of solving the problems he is about to outline.

The break between this and other major units is signaled by Paul's use of διαμαρτύρομαι (*to solemnly testify* or *warn*, 2:14; 4:1). In this instance, Paul advises Timothy to instruct the community with all solemnity, even using an oath formula (*in the presence of the Lord*, 2:14). Later, Paul will use this very oath formula in the first person (4:1) to present his final charge to Timothy in light of the issues he addresses in this segment (2:14–3:17).

Although each paragraph has its own complexities, the general logical-semantic structure of this segment is a recurrence of interrogation. Internal problems are presented in 2:14–19. This is not without a measure of response to the issue of conflict—Timothy's personal preparation (2:15) and the inscribed claims (2:19) play a part in mitigating the issues of *wrangling over words* (2:14), *profane chatter* (2:16), and their ruinous outcomes. The solutions to these issues come in 2:20–26—*ridding oneself of these* troublemaking behaviors (2:21), shunning *youthful passions* and pursuing the listed virtues (2:22), *repentance* (2:25), etc.

External problems are presented in 3:1–9. This paragraph is almost completely comprised of adverse circumstances. The solution to such damaging opposition comes in 3:10–17—continuing in the faith, trusting those *from whom* (παρὰ τίνων, 3:14; genitive, plural, inclusive gender) he learned it (an allusion to Lois and Eunice, 1:5; cf. 3:15), and recognizing the provenance and power of Scripture (3:16). The list of solutions may not be exhaustive or systematic, but it comes from a place of credibility and passion—Paul's own life experience, calling, and faith and his deep affection for Timothy.

2:14–26

The two paragraphs of this segment (2:14–19 and 2:20–26) are held together by at least three discourse features. The first is the logical semantic relationship of interrogation, where the first paragraph outlines a multidimensional problem and the second outlines a multidimensional solution.[44] To the extent that

---

[44] See Bauer and Traina, *Inductive Bible Study*, 113–14.

portions of the solution come in the form of imperatives that Timothy is to enact (*flee, pursue,* 2:22; *put aside,* 2:23), one might call this relationship *hortatory interrogation.*

The second is the conjunction δέ (2:20), which signals that Paul sees 2:20–26 as a development from 2:14–19. After presenting the largely problematic contents of the first paragraph, he offers the hopeful, yet stern, guidance of the second. The tenderness of Paul the pastor can be seen here as he speaks about such difficult intracommunal issues using imagery (2:20–21), sympathy, and optimism.

The third is the backward-pointing deictic *from these things* (ἀπὸ τούτων, 2:21). By this phrase, Paul is almost certainly pointing back at the troublesome behaviors outlined in 2:14–19—e.g., *wrangling* and *chatter.* One becomes useful by putting aside such futile and empty pursuits.

2:14–19

In this paragraph, Paul is just as concerned with the outcomes of internal conflict as he is with the behaviors. He uses more words describing the trouble it causes than describing the behaviors it involves. What Timothy is to remind the church of (i.e., *these things,* 2:14) is the preceding material, especially the gospel outline provided in 2:8–13. This *deposit* (1:12, 14) of *truth* (2:15, 18, 25; 3:7, 8; 4:4) and *sound teaching* (1:13; 4:3) is the premise for calling the church away from *wrangling over words* (λογομαχέω, 2:14; lit. word-fighting), *profane chatter* (βεβήλους κενοφωνίας, 2:16; lit. profane empty-sounds), and *missing the mark with respect to truth* by making false claims (2:18).

The initial injunction against *wrangling over words* (2:14) comes before Paul's order for Timothy to studiously prepare himself for a ministry of the *Word* (2:15) and may be a general representation of the various kinds of internal conflict (2:16–18), characterized as they are by verbal malpractice. The final verse of the paragraph provides a sharp contrast to the pugnacious, empty, irreverent, malignant, false, and upsetting words of troublemakers—God's words stand firm (2:19).

2:20–26

Rather than using the illustration to follow his claim, Paul leads with the household utensil imagery (2:20–21). This opens the paragraph with whimsy and optimism (*ethos*). Each instruction that follows (2:22–26) is paired with a rationale—*shun* and *pursue ... pure heart* (2:22), *put aside ... kind to everyone* (2:23–24), *correcting opponents ... they may escape* (2:25–26). This constitutes a recurrence of hortatory substantiation.

3:1–17

Paul attributes the specific kinds and occasions of persecution—generalized as *distressing times*—partly to the time they are living in or approaching (3:1). He later talks about his own time being short (4:6–8), but here he is speaking eschatologically. Given the scarcity of eschatological material in 2 Tim, this reference is probably focused on the topic of persecution and not meant to make broad claims about the end times.

3:1–9

By saying *know this* (3:1; imperative cataphoric deictic meta-comment), Paul points to the virtually prearranged nature of what is transpiring. He explains *that in the last days will come* what he generalizes as *distressing times* (3:1), thus setting the topic for the paragraph. In other words, even this hardship they are facing is not outside of God's oversight.

Paul lists a long and unique collection of reprehensible attributes, attitudes, and behaviors (3:2–5). More than any individual item, its bulk has a sickening effect, and he closes it with a curt consequential command—*avoid them* (3:5). He then provides contemporary and [apocryphal] historical examples along with profiles of their victims and inevitable failure (3:6–9).

3:10–17

The solution to wickedness and opposition, most of which seems to come from outside the church, involves the following: observe Paul's example in character and experience (3:10–11); recognize the Lord's power and prerogative to rescue (3:11b); accept that persecution is commensurate with *living devoutly in Christ Jesus* (3:12) and that deceit begets deceit (3:13); but, in contrast to the general degradation (3:13), remain faithful to the doctrine (3:14a); honor your forebears in the faith (3:14b–15) and the gift that they gave above all—the holy scriptures (3:16–17; climax signaled by superlative language—*All scripture*, comprehensive value, *everyone, every good work*).

This paragraph represents, in the *ad hoc*, occasional nature of letter-writing, Paul's response to the problem of prolific wickedness and persecution. In a discursive logical-semantic sense, it may be labelled a *solution*, but Paul does not claim that this response will make the wickedness or persecution stop—quite to the contrary (3:1, 13). What he does claim is that God's justice and redemption ultimately prevail and that such difficulty is not a reason to give up the faith but a motive to remember the reasons we hold it in the first place—even *from childhood* (3:15).

4:1–8

This last paragraph of the letter body comes with several signals of prominence. First, a meta-comment using the verb διαμαρτύρέω (*I solemnly testify* or *warn*, 4:1; cf. 2:14). This is completed by an oath formula (*in the presence of God and Christ Jesus*, 4:1). Invoking both divine names makes it even more emphatic (cf. 2:14). A lengthy, compound epexegetical participial clause (*who is about to judge* ..., 4:1) adds to the weight of the oath. This oath is followed by nine second-person singular imperative verbs in verses 2 and 5. Intermediate reasoning (*for* [γάρ] *the time is coming* ..., 4:3–4) appears between these verses.

Paul's charge is about resolve, not a strategy for making the problems simply go away, but about carrying on with the calling they had been given in the first place (cf. 1:11–12a). That is why Paul's example is fitting here (4:6–8). If Timothy follows Paul's instructions, he may expect the same dignity.

4:9–22

After Paul's climactic charge (4:1–8), he abruptly (with asyndeton) signals a shift to epistolary closing (4:9–22) with primarily travelogue, technical, and formal material. There is no clearer break between any of the letter's units. The section is, nevertheless, filled with echoes of key themes from 2 Tim.

4:9–18

Conveying the material in this segment certainly was a critical reason for writing 2 Tim, but it is distinct from the body proper for the following reasons: First, it is of a different character than the previous material, being primarily technical (i.e., about physical objects, geographic places, and specific activities) and personal (i.e., not about Timothy's relationship and actions with respect to his congregation as much as Timothy's relationship and actions with respect to Paul and other colleagues).

Second, much of the material here and in the greeting below (4:20–21a) may be characterized as travelogue, which typically appears at the end of the epistolary form. So, this segment is part of the formal structure rather than the theological, ethical, and argumentative thrust of the letter, even though it coheres with the message and values of the letter body. The distinction is only made on structural grounds.

Whereas the first paragraph (4:9–15) of this segment is generally actionable on Timothy's part—featuring several imperative verbs with interspersed explanation—the second paragraph (4:16–18) is background in which Paul explains his attitude about several issues—disappointment, persecution, peril, and God's temporal consolation and ultimate salvation. This even stirs a benediction

(4:18b). The relationship between these paragraphs seems to be hortatory sub-stantiation—command, followed by cause.

4:19–21

The greetings here are an expected part of a personal letter. The insertion of a plea for Timothy to *come before winter* (4:21a) after a brief geographic census of two select colleagues (4:20) gives them an in-the-moment feel. Paul still pre-serves order, however; he starts by greeting individuals himself (4:19; for Onesiphorus, who is again mentioned with his household; cf. 1:16–18); he ends by sharing individual and group greetings from others (4:21).

4:22

This final blessing includes a micro-logical-semantic development from particu-lar to general—a blessing for Timothy (*the Lord be with your spirit*) and a bless-ing for his community (*grace be with you*, plural).[45]

Titus

Titus, the shortest of the PE, has the most straightforward logical-semantic organi-zation of the grouping. It nevertheless conveys a deep gospel logic. The epistolary opening (1:1–4) and closing (3:12–15) clearly frame but also illuminate the letter body (1:5–3:11). Paul has two major concerns with the church at-large in Crete—leadership (1:5–16) and propriety in God's household (2:1–15)—before he addresses the believers more generally (3:1–11). Throughout the letter, he is concerned with submission, ethno-religious division, and Christians' good works. Other concerns, such as Titus's ministry and esteem (e.g., 1:5, 13; 2:1, 7–8, 15b; 3:1, 8) are interspersed.

The chart below outlines the logical and topical divisions of Titus, its book-level units, and their relation to one another. Titus has relatively clear themes and observable boundary-marking features that signal the beginning, ending, and internal shifts of sub-units. As Andreas J. Köstenberger puts it, "The various proposals regarding the structure of Titus ... reveal a certain amount of consen-sus."[46] This outline of Titus is not innovative. It recognizes 1:1–4, 1:5–16, 2:1–15, 3:1–11, and 3:12–15 as its major units. Few would disagree with its main contours.

Discourse features in the Greek text reinforce these major breaks in Titus. The body (1:5–3:11) begins after a relatively substantial salutation (1:1–4) with the

---

[45] See comments at 1 Tim 6:21b.

[46] Andreas J. Köstenberger, "Hermeneutical and Exegetical Challenges in Interpreting the Pastoral Epistles," in *Entrusted with the Gospel*, ed. Köstenberger and Wilder, 1–27, at 15.

standard features of a Greco-Roman epistolary opening. The break between 1:4 and 1:5 is clear based on the conclusion of the salutatory blessing (1:4b), the topicalization affected by the left-dislocation of 1:5a (*This is the reason I left you in Crete*), and the topical resumption of the following ἵνα clause (*in order that ...*, 1:5b). The abrupt shift into travelogue, final instructions, and greetings with asyndeton (3:12–15) is not an unusual way to conclude a personal correspondence. It clearly separates the epistolary ending from the body, even though important themes from the body still find expression in the conclusion (e.g., *good works*, 3:14, *faith*, 3:15).

Because of the clarity of the breaks between units, the analysis below will focus more on the development of themes as they weave through the letter. Headings that treat these themes appear under references that feature a significant expression of the theme in question—*the courtroom semantic frame, moral topics, submission, Jewish religious culture*, and *division*.

Titus 1:1–3:15							
1:1–4—Epistolary Opening; Testimony, and Greeting	1:5–3:11 Main Body—"straighten out what remains and appoint elders" (1:5)						3:12–15—Epistolary Closing; Travelogue, and Greeting
	1:5–16—Particular Instructions Regarding Leaders with Contrast		2:1–15—Particular Household Instructions with Substantiation and λάλει Inclusio (vs. 1, 15)		3:1–11—General and Substantiatory Instructions for All Christians		
	1:5–9—Good Leaders Appointed to Serve	1:10–16—Bad Leaders Taken to Court	2:1–10—Specific Categories in God's Household (the Church)	2:11–15—Gospel Substantiation	3:1–7—Reminders and Reasons	3:8–11—Consequential General Imperatives	

Figure 15.6: Constituent Organization of Titus

1:1–4

Commentators note the relative length of Titus's epistolary introduction (1:1–4) and offer various hypotheses. Marshall critiques the proposal that it was written to introduce a faux collection: "This hypothesis depends completely on prior assumptions."[47] It certainly introduces the Epistle to Titus well, however. Exceptional themes that Paul develops later in the body find their first expression here—e.g., Paul as *servant* (1:1) and the theme of submission; *piety* (1:1) and the theme of religious and moral instruction; the *unlying God* (1:1, 2) and the theme of *truth* (1:1); *revelation* (φανερόω) at an appropriate time (1:3) and redemptive acts of divine grace; *common* (κοινός) *faith* (1:4) and the equal standing of those in Christ.

---

[47] Marshall, *Pastoral Epistles*, 112, n. 3.

1:5–3:11

The logical-semantic relationship of the body is one of generalization with re-currence of substantiation. Paul addresses concerns toward specific groups in the church (people of influence, 1:5–16, and specific social categories, 2:1–15) and provides rationale, then he delivers instructions and rationale for the body in general (3:1–11). Blocks of gospel summary in 2:11–14 and 3:3–7 elucidate the logic behind Paul's instructions in each respective section. Some specific thematic examples:

- Paul's recurrent concern with submission (see heading below) in the first chapters (e.g., ἀνυπότακτος, *insubordinate*, 1:6, 9; cf. 1 Tim 1:9; and cognate ὑποτάσσω, Titus 2:5, 9) finds general expression in *be subject* (ὑποτάσσω, 3:1).
- His interest in *good works* for leaders (e.g., 1:16; 2:7) also shifts toward a more general audience (2:14; 3:1, 8, 14).
- He names specific categories of people in the first two chapters—*elders* (1:5–9), *the circumcision* (1:10), older men and women (2:2–3), younger women and men (2:4–6), Titus himself (2:7–8), and *slaves* (2:9–10). But, the third chapter refers to *them* (3:1), *ourselves* (3:3), *we* (3:7), and *those who have trusted in God* (οἱ πεπιστευκότες θεῷ, 3:8)—i.e., the whole church.

1:5–16

The topic of addressing leadership problems holds this segment together. On the one hand, 1:5–9 portrays a vacuum of good leadership that Titus must fill by sanctioning leaders of impeccable character. On the other hand, 1:10–16 portrays the harmful influence of people who have presumed the prerogatives and social influence of leaders but without proper accountability, scruples, or healthy doc-trine. Whereas Paul instructs Titus to deal with the broader church population under the rubric of a household code in 2:1–10; in the present segment, Paul ad-dresses leadership as a discrete issue.

The two pericopes that comprise 1:5–16 describe two kinds of leaders by con-trasting them along corresponding lines. These correlations suffice to demonstrate the strong complementary nature of these two pericopes (1:5–9 and 1:10–16). The following list of features is not exhaustive, but it demonstrates cohesion—a con-tinuous concern for good and bad leaders and what to do about them:

- A good leader's children should not be prone to the accusation of being *insubordinate* (1:6); the presumptive leaders were *insubordinate* (1:10).
- Elders were to *have faithful children* (1:6); the troublemakers were *faith-less* (1:15).

- Elders were compared to *God's household steward* (1:7); troublemakers *disrupt entire households* (1:11).
- Good leaders would not *crave shameful gain* (1:7); troublemakers assumed leadership roles *for the sake of shameful gain* (1:11).
- Elders were to engage in *teaching* (1:9); disruption in Crete resulted from the troublemakers' *teaching* (1:11–12).
- Good elders held to *the doctrine of the faithful word* (1:9); troublemakers were *empty[-word]-speakers* (1:10).
- Properly sanctioned leaders were to *rebuke* (1:9) those who contradicted; Paul told Titus to *rebuke* (1:13) the troublemakers sternly.
- Sanctioned leaders encourage the church *in healthy teaching* (1:9); the hope for duly corrected troublemakers is being *healthy in the faith* (1:13).
- The *love for good* (1:8) that elders are to exhibit starkly contrasts with Paul's final, biting judgment against the troublemakers; they were *unfit for every good work* (1:16).

The conjunction γάρ (1:10) marks a clear logical relationship between the paragraphs. This relationship may be called hortatory substantiation. In other words, the material governed by γάρ (1:10–12) is the reason that Paul presents for his prior instructions (1:5–9). The conjunction γάρ can govern a small or large amount of material from a single clause or sentence to a paragraph. Here, it seems to be connecting multiple verses. The presence and activity of a group of primarily Jewish troublemakers (*especially the ones from the circumcision*, 1:10–12) are the explicit bases for placing elders of Paul's description in each town (1:5–9) and for the consequential instructions of *rebuke* (1:13a) and the rationale (1:13b–16).

The Cretan quotation (1:12) is contextually relevant as a salient example of leadership malpractice. Harmful speech was the problem that Paul identified as characteristic of the presumptive leaders whom he called *empty-talkers and deceivers ... whose mouths must be stopped* (1:10–11). His description raises the question, *What were they saying that was so objectionable?* Paul answers by quoting what *someone said* (εἶπέν τις, 1:12a).

The troublemakers were not vicious in a generic moral sense; their disruptions (*upsetting entire households*, 1:11) constituted leadership malpractice. In such a context, Paul exposes one of their most divisive and misleading declarations—the Cretan quotation (1:12b). Context suggests that the speaker was one of the (predominantly Jewish) troublemakers (1:10–11).[48] This slur against the Cretans (1:12) accuses them of permanent, intrinsic, overall degradation.

---

[48] For an argument against Paul using a direct quotation from Epimenides, see Isaiah Allen, "Paul the Bigot? Reading the Cretan Quotation of Titus 1:12 in Light of Relevance Theory" (PhD Diss., Middlesex University, 2019), 1–46.

Within the paragraph that focuses on bad leaders (1:10–16), Paul appears to echo themes from the Cretan quotation in order to characterize the trouble-makers instead. Paul's original readers were cognizant of the ethno-religious nature of the contentions in Crete and thus would not have been oblivious to the irony of the associations Paul made. Grasping the significance of these concep-tual associations for Crete's Jewish Christians (1:10, 14) is critical for modern readers. Paul exposed the ones who called the Cretans *liars* (1:12b) and character-ized them as people who reject the *truth* (1:14). He prepared original readers with his epistolary greeting where *truth* (1:1) and *un-lying* (1:2) appear in reference to Paul's message and God.

Whereas the troublemakers regarded the Cretans with disdain as *evil beasts* (1:12b), which has implications of uncleanness, Paul said that it was rather *to the defiled and faithless that nothing is clean* (1:15) and that these troublemakers, barring restoration (1:13b), were *detestable* or *abominable* (1:16). Restoration seems to have been the goal (*in order that they may be healthy*, ἵνα ὑγιαίνωσιν, 1:13b); that is, Paul's intent was not to leave the troublemakers in their de-praved condition.

The Courtroom Semantic Frame

In the first chapter of Titus, several words and information structures suggest that Paul was activating the type-scene of a courtroom. He uses words from a juridical domain (e.g., *testimony, true, accusation, convict*, 1:13; *confess, deny*, 1:16), and he structures information forensically. The sequence establishes both his own and the troublemakers' character (1:1–4, 10–11), makes an accusa-tion (1:12), swears an oath (1:13a), then renders a verdict and a sentence (1:13b). Establishing *pathos* for specifically forensic purposes may be one of the rea-sons the epistolary introduction of Titus is remarkably longer than the other PE. By evoking a legal proceeding in a semi-official correspondence (perhaps modelled after imperial *mandata principis*) that would be read aloud and in-tentionally overheard by the named addressee's community, Paul makes the trial public.

When Paul mentioned *testimony* (μαρτυρία, 1:13), he also evoked other key components of this type-scene, activating *witnesses, judges, offenders*, and *prose-cutors* in a sort of *Gestalt* complex cognitive entity. The word *reason [accusation]* (αἰτία, 1:13) also corresponds to the activation of a courtroom frame. Because the conceptual frame of juridical proceedings was in plain view, his assertion of *true* (ἀληθής, 1:13) acquired a more specific thrust than it would without other com-ponents of the frame. Pragmatically, it became a verdict.

Paul introduced a second-hand quotation (1:12) as from an unreliable witness of whom he had already established the untrustworthy character. Paul was the μάρτυς (*witness*) of the μαρτυρία (*testimony*). It is plausible that, if Paul was swearing on his own report that someone was disparaging Titus's missionary congregants, then it is Paul's witness, not the so-called prophet's, that he asserted as *true*.

The text is ambivalent on a matter that some prominent interpretations assume—namely, that the *testimony* (1:13) Paul pronounces as true is that borne by a Cretan poet. They suppose that Paul ratifies the substance of the quotation—that Cretans, in fact, are intrinsically morally defective. Such interpretations may gloss over the semantic thrust of μαρτυρία (*testimony*, 1:13) and the courtroom frame that Paul seems to have been activating.

If the signals of courtroom proceedings mean that Paul was presenting arguments against a group of unsanctioned leaders and essentially accusing them of misdemeanors against other believers, then the meta-comment (*this testimony is true*, 1:13a) may refer to Paul's own testimony. Paul presented a case against the most shocking and blatant offenders among the troublemakers—those who justified their presumption on the basis of age-old ethnic stereotypes. Ethno-religious bigotry was a stinging example of the leadership problems in Crete.

The simple recurrence of the topic of truth and lies in Titus accentuates the courtroom scene contextually, because occurrences cluster in 1:10–16 and because concerns with truth and falsehood correspond in specific ways to the setting of a courtroom. Within the quotation, Cretans were called *liars* (1:12), but Paul disclosed the most salient disagreement between truth and reality in the crescendo of his remarks about the troublemakers—*they profess to know God, they nevertheless deny [him] by their works* (1:16). Whereas Paul called his testimony *true* (1:13), he characterized some of the troublemakers' *works* (1:16) as promoting commandments of people who reject the *truth* (1:14). Overly concerned with peripheral religious works, they nullify their capacity to do *any good work* (1:16) by their harassment of the Cretans. These collocated contrasts are striking. Paul opened the Epistle to Titus with his own unique salutation as a servant of the *unlying* (1:2) God whose purpose includes spreading the knowledge of the *truth* (1:1).

Paul topicalized *ones who are defiled and unbelieving* (1:15), suspending them in a δέ development clause. By means of this left-dislocation, he accentuated the self-condemning effects of judging people's redemptive status on an ethno-religious basis. It is only those sorts of people who find that *nothing is clean* (1:15). Simply reversing the order without changing the grammar yields a more syntactically neutral or unmarked way of organizing the information: *nothing is clean to ones who are defiled and unfaithful*. But, Paul placed the information in a cause-and-effect order. *Why did the troublemakers see their Cretan brothers and sisters as unclean?* It was because the troublemakers themselves were *defiled and unfaithful*.

2:1–15

This segment is held together by the logical relationship of the household (of God) code (2:1–10) with the gospel rationale that follows (2:11–14) and is completed with a concise but intriguing charge to Timothy (2:15). The conjunction γάρ (2:11) marks (not makes) the logical-semantic relationship between these sub-units as hortatory substantiation.

An inclusio marks the beginning and ending boundaries of the segment. Paul first contrasts Titus's speech with the presumptive leaders' speech (σὺ δὲ λάλει, *you however [are to] speak*, 2:1); he then completes the inclusio by instructing him to *speak these things* (ταῦτα λάλει, 2:15).

As an alternative to the troublemakers' *myths* and *commandments* (1:14), Titus is to pronounce the logic of the Christ-life (i.e., the Christian gospel, 2:11–14). In contrast to a faith that is preoccupied with observing specific ethnic, religious, or cultural traditions and shunning others, the Christian gospel reorients faith and proclamation around the person and work of God. Titus 2 has the highest concentration of *soundness/health* (-ὑγιε-) language in the New Testament (2:1, 2, 8). The ethically-oriented instructions Paul gives Titus to propound in 2:1–10 constitutes sound doctrine as much as the more theologically-oriented gospel summary of 2:11–14.

2:1–10

In terms of literary form, this segment has the structure and development of a household code (2:1–10). Titus is to teach standards of personal, inter-personal, and communal behavior. While Titus did this, he was to assert and rely on his authority among the churches of Crete by virtue of Paul's commission. Paul portrays Titus as a model (τύπον, 2:7) for the entire congregation.

This is not a conventional code that addresses a hereditary, legal, or traditional household. The relations of people in this household are metaphorical—believers in Crete are fictive kin. The categories Paul mentions do not comprise a comprehensive code because significant familial relations are absent. The only explicit relations are between older and younger women (2:3–4), between younger women and their own husbands and children (2:5), between Titus and younger men (2:6–7), and between slaves and their own masters (2:9–10).

Unsurprisingly, Paul placed instructions regarding slaves where they would normally appear in a household code—at the end (2:9–10). And, as expected, submission was a requirement for slaves. Paul places Titus after the center of the code, where children (unaddressed) and slaves belong, which raises the interpretative question, *What are the dynamics of Titus's relations with the rest of the church members?*

The household of God was a recognized metaphor for the church, so this code, applied to the church, reinforced the metaphorical environment of God's household and the call toward specific dispositions (prominently, submission; see heading below) in all types of relationships.[49]

Moral Topics

At the center of Paul's moral concern are practices of right *teaching* (1:9[x2]; 2:1, 3, 7, 10) and *submission*, the personal qualities of σώφρων (*sensible*, 1:8; 2:2, 5; cognates in 2:4, 6, 12) and σεμνός (*serious*, 2:2, 7), and a number of φιλο- root prefix words (*loving [appropriately]*, 1:8[x2]; 2:4[x2]; 3:4, 15). The spread of these virtues across every social category that Paul addresses yields a remarkable comparison among the expectations of each group. In other words, what Paul expects of one category of people has a high degree of correspondence to what he expects of otherwise contrasting groups, including leaders and slaves, women and men, young and old, Jew and Gentile.[50]

This correspondence is particularly visible through an explicit comparative connective adverb that Paul used in Titus to move from one category to another (ὡσαύτως, 2:3, 6)—*older men ... likewise ... older women; younger women ... likewise ... younger men.* The comparison was not just in the fact that Titus was to give instructions to each group but in the kind of instructions he was to give. The Cretan quotation (1:12), incidentally, represents a different set of moral concerns than Paul himself presents in the rest of Titus, where gluttony, laziness, and general debauchery are not broached.

The expectations of every member of the household parallel the requirements of good leaders. Paul indicates that submission, non-contentiousness, and un-greediness are specific qualities to look for among those in higher-status positions. Titus's leadership segment (1:5–16) and household code (2:1–10) feature striking correspondences between submission or the lack thereof (ὑποτάσσω, 2:9; cf. ἀνυπότακτος, 1:10), talking back or contradicting (ἀντιλέγω, 2:9; cf. 1:9), and inappropriate gain (νοσφίζομαι, 2:10; cf. αἰσχροκερδής, 1:7; αἰσχροῦ κέρδους χάριν, 1:11). Servants must be good; despots [δεσπόται, 2:9] ought to be gooder! or so to speak.

The comparison demonstrates that Paul expects the Christian community to exhibit, for instance, submission from the top to the bottom of the social ladder—an attitude the presumptive leaders in Crete did not share (1:10; 3:9–11). The requirements of a true leader were precisely those of servanthood—in contrast to the aggrandizing behavior of the antagonists. The code applies comparable

---

[49] See comments at 1 Tim 5:1–6:2a.

[50] The overlap of moral expectations among groups is remarkable. It echoes such a core Pauline doctrine as the radical equality of persons before God (see 1 Cor 12:13; Gal 3:28; Col 3:11; Rom 10:12).

values to all people—even Paul, who begins the letter by identifying himself within the category of *slave* (δοῦλος, 1:1; see 2:9).

2:11–15

This segment includes one of two profound gospel summaries in Titus (2:11–14 and 3:3–7) that explicate the moral logic of the letter. They answer the question *Why does Paul give these instructions?* But, the logic is not merely philosophical rationale for good conduct or reasonable justification for obeying Paul's instructions. Rather, they are the moral results of transforming grace.[51] As far as Paul's gospel is concerned, the Cretan believers are made righteous and clean (2:11-15 and 3:3–7, esp. δικαίως in 2:12 and καθαρίσῃ in 2:14; cf. λουτροῦ in 3:5), even though troublemakers portrayed them as intrinsically morally deficient (1:10–12).

The gospel summary (2:11–14) begins the generalizing phase of Titus's body structure (*all*, 2:11, 14; *a people*, 2:14), but it builds specifically on the instructions of 1:5–16 and 2:1–10. Issues of *piety* (2:12; cf. 1:1), *sanity* (2:12; cf. 1:8; 2:2, 4, 5, 6), and *purity* (2:14; cf. 1:15–16), for instance, correlate to concerns earlier in the book more than later. Both summaries have all Christians in view, but the one in 3:3–7 is somewhat less tied to specific points from the preceding segments. Both may incorporate traditional material.

Paul wraps up this section (1:5–2:15) with a charge to Titus that points back at all that went before (ταῦτα, *these things*, 2:15) and a curious caveat—*no one should scorn you* (2:15b). The troublemakers may have looked at Titus's Gentile ethnicity as an excuse not to show him deference (Gal 2:1–3; cf. 1 Tim 4:12, where Timothy's youth was the issue). To them, he was inherently an inferior and an unacceptable leader. The underlying prejudice of the Cretan quotation (Titus 1:12) made any Gentile unacceptable as a leader. To the troublemakers in Crete, Titus was no better than a Cretan; because what was at issue for them was the Cretans *qua* Gentiles, not *qua* Cretans.[52]

3:1–11

In this segment, Paul discusses matters of relevance for the general church populace—submission to authorities and courtesy to everyone (3:1–2), the gospel of life-change (3:3–7), and the value of good works verses the worthlessness of controversy (3:8–11). The gospel of life-change provides a rationale for the instructions

---

[51] For a discussion of the moral logic of Titus, see Allen, "Paul the Bigot?" 205–33.

[52] For an exposé on how interpretive history has distorted ancient opinions about Cretans, see ibid., 23–32.

that surround it as well as those that came before—an interchange of exhortation, rationale, and exhortation.

3:1–2

The theme of submission comes to a general culmination applicable to the entire congregation here. Earlier instances of the theme involved specific subjects and their appropriate object of deference—e.g., Paul to God (1:1), children of elders to their parents (1:6), rebels toward Titus or Paul (1:10), young wives to their husbands (2:5), and slaves to their masters (2:9). Now Paul instructs Titus that Christians' submission and obedience are foundational for *good works* (3:1). Perhaps Paul perceives an evangelistic or testimonial dimension. In addition to submission, there is a theme of tolerance and cooperation among the general church populace (3:2).

Submission

Paul repeatedly instructs subjection, not self-aggrandizement, within the household of God. One of the strongest themes throughout Titus is submission. This theme emerges from the portrayal of social relationships evoked by many occurrences of Greek words that feature -ταγ- roots (ἐπιταγή, *command* [n], 1:3; 2:15; διατάσσω, *command* [v], 1:5; ἀνυπότακτος, *insubordinate*, 1:6, 10; ὑποτάσσω, *submit*, 2:5, 9; 3:1) and from specific words sharing that semantic domain such as ἐνκρατής (*disciplined*, 1:8), ἐξουσία and πειθαρέω (*authority* [*figure*] and *obey*, 3:1).

The theme of submission does not follow a superiority-and-inferiority scheme but an equals-in-humility program that applies to the entire constituency of the church, including Paul himself. Unlike the social dynamic that the troublemakers promoted, where others were inferior, submission commits all uses of power and freedom to the service of others.

Note the initial prominence of Paul as a *slave* (δοῦλος, 1:1) of God and the ideal leader portrayed as a *household steward* (οἰκονόμον, 1:7, a category of slave or servant). Notice also that attributes customarily associated with subordinates, such as slaves, are expected even of leaders in God's (ideal) household. For instance, *submission*, *un-greediness*, and *not-talking-back* all appear as expectations of the general church population. These qualities appear both in the household code for slaves (2:9–10) and in the leadership discussion (1:7–10) as desired traits. The troublemakers, however, exhibit the opposite qualities, being *contradictory* and *insubordinate* (ἀντιλέγω, 1:9; cf. 2:9; ἀνυπότακτος, 1:10). When Paul says, *Slaves should be submissive ... pleasing ... and not talk back* (δούλους... ὑποτάσσεσθαι ... εὐαρέστους εἶναι, μὴ ἀντιλέγοντας 2:9), he is repeating several of the key qualities expected of those who execute authentic leadership roles with integrity. They are to instantiate the values of submission and sensibility, just as Titus was to be a model for them (τύπον, 2:7; cf. 1 Tim 4:12; Phil 3:17; 2 Thess 3:9).

Paul's expectations of slaves and his general expectations of all Christians parallel one another remarkably. In this segment regarding general instructions for all Christians, Paul urges *showing all gentleness* (πᾶσαν ἐνδεικνυμένους πραΰτητα, Titus 3:2); while in the segment of the household code regarding slaves, he urges *showing all good faith* (πᾶσαν πίστιν ἐνδεικνυμένους ἀγαθήν, 2:10)—remarkably parallel.

3:3–7

This testimonial gospel summary (3:3–7) is logically tied to the previous exhortation (3:1–2) by the conjunction γάρ. Inasmuch as that exhortation is general in nature, this summary may also be considered a rationale for the entire moral logic of the book. Regardless, Paul does not present here reasons for Christian morality as much as he presents a bi-partite typology of redemption—before (ἦμεν γάρ ποτε, *at one time we were*, 3:3) and after (ὅτε δὲ, *but when*, 3:4).

The shift in this relative chronology is marked by a developmental δέ in verse 4 that punches above its weight class. Paul portrays the common Christian testimony as a before-and-after life. The pivot is not human decision and action but divine. Specifically, the turning point is the appearance (ἐπιφαίνω) of *the goodness and lovingkindness of God our Savior* (3:4)—likely a circumlocution for the Christ-event. The Christ-event in Titus is signified in the language of epiphany (1:3; 2:11, 13; 3:4; cf. 1 Tim 3:16; 6:14; 2 Tim 1:10; 4:1, 8).

Being *disobedient* (ἀπειθής) and *serving* (δουλεύω) *all kinds of passions and pleasures*, as well as the other listed attributes, characterized us (Titus 3:3), even Paul, before the kindness and love of God our savior *appeared* (ἐπιφαίνω, 3:4) and prior to *rebirth* (παλιγγενεσία, 3:5). The troublemakers' behaviors occupy the pre-conversion end of the submission-insubordination continuum. The problem with these opponents is expressed but not rooted in false doctrine; it is rooted in a failure of faith.

In Christian conversion, the categories of difference that were once available for ethnic and cultural othering are no longer applicable to one's new status in Christ. This inapplicability seems central to the Epistle of Titus, especially as expressed in 3:3–5. When Paul articulated the redeeming purpose of Jesus's *self-giving* work (3:3–7; see also 2:11–14, esp. ἔδωκεν ἑαυτὸν, 2:14), he expressed the logic of the gospel that undergirded his whole vision of human redemption—the reason he could see Jews and Gentiles as equals before God.

3:8–11

This paragraph begins with a *faithful is the word* (πιστὸς ὁ λόγος, 3:8) formula which may point back to the more poetic gospel summary of 3:3–7.[53] The first verse of exhortation is positive with purpose and rationale—*insist ... in order that* (ἵνα) ... *these things are profitable* (3:8); the rest are negative with rationale—*shun ... because* (γάρ) *they are unprofitable ... rebuke ... seeing that ...* (εἰδὼς ὅτι, 3:9–11). The δέ in v. 9 signals the complementary nature of this contrasting exhortation (pos. and neg.) with its recurrent structure of hortatory substantiation.

Paul gave specific instructions to Titus in dealing with a divisive person (3:9–11). Such persons correspond to the main category of troublemakers that concerned Paul. Their interests are not generic but have the same ethnoreligious associations as named and evoked earlier (1:10–16). They divided and were divided from the Pauline church. Paul seems to have been concerned with one main category of troublemakers.

Jewish Religious Culture

Troublemakers in Crete were not all Jewish even though Paul asserted that *the ones from the circumcision* (1:10) were prominent among them. Jewish religious culture clearly featured prominently among opponents of Titus, but Paul did not find Jews themselves or Judaism itself to be problematic. Paul was combatting distortions of Judaism as much as of his Christian gospel.

Marginal matters had become central for Paul's opponents (e.g., 3:9). Instead of bearing fruit of a religious or spiritual nature, their behaviors had produced ethno-religious class stratification. The epistle portrays a vacuum of leadership (1:5); and some Cretan Christians felt pressured to attend to various interests of a Jewish religious provenance (1:10, 14; 3:9–11), while others held to Paul's transformative gospel to the Gentiles (2:11–14; 3:3–7).

Some Jewish believers and their sympathetic associates instilled the native Cretan believers with an ethno-religious inferiority complex analogous to those in congregations the Apostle Paul dealt with elsewhere in the NT.[54] The essential substance of their message was that those who would not go in for the trappings of Jewish religious culture (e.g., *circumcision*, 1:10; *Jewish myths and commandments of men*, 1:14; *vain controversies and genealogies and strife and quarrels pertaining to the law*, 3:9) could not be Christians of the first order. Paul was concerned with attitudes and practices that were used to denigrate Gentile Christian religious

---

[53] See comments at 1 Tim 4:6–10.

[54] See Acts 15:1–9; Rom 2:25–29; 4:14; Gal 2:14–16; 3:2–8, 25–29; 5:6–12; Phil 3:2.

status. To gain a following, the troublemakers may even have deprecated the people whom Paul left Titus in Crete to nurture.

The contingent most likely to ridicule, shame, and disparage Cretan Christians on account of general moral faults (e.g., gluttony or laziness, 1:12) was one that advocated strict ascetic dietary laws and proto-gnostic moral scruples.[55] So, whereas Paul addressed one set of character traits, his opponents were preoccupied with another, which happened to be reflected in the Cretan quotation (1:12).[56]

The troublemakers expanded a power differential in Titus's community by driving a wedge of bigotry and ethno-religious hierarchy between Jewish and Cretan Christians within the church. So, Paul was concerned for the members of his vulnerable missionary congregation as well as for the integrity of the gospel.

Division

Several observations suggest the prevalence of ethno-religious tensions in the Cretan church. A theme of division is present throughout the epistle, even though Paul did not mention a *divisive person* (αἱρετικὸν ἄνθροπον, 3:10) until late in the letter. The concept of division, us/them distinctions, in/out contests, and the dynamics of superiority and inferiority are present throughout. Titus himself was likely a collateral target of such prejudices (2:15).

We cannot tell precisely what theological propositions the troublemakers taught, because Paul expresses his concern with them in terms of their social effect upon the church (e.g., *upsetting whole houses*, 1:11). Heresy causes or exacerbates division and animosity; so, in this sense, the Cretan quotation (1:12) is an expression of heresy even though its semantic representation does not strike the modern reader as holding much theological content.

Heresy has come to mean straying from an established dogma, but heterodoxy is only one aspect of division. The modern impulse to identify this or that particular heresy from a known line-up of heterodoxies is anachronistic. Paul hoped that Titus could restore the presumptive leaders (*in order that they might*

---

[55] See, e.g., Jay Twomey, *The Pastoral Epistles through the Centuries*, BBC (Wiley-Blackwell, 2009), 224; William D. Mounce, *Pastoral Epistles*, WBC 46 (Thomas Nelson, 2000), 402; Jouette M. Bassler, *1 Timothy, 2 Timothy, Titus*, ANTC (Abingdon, 1996), 27–28; Charles K. Barrett, *The Pastoral Epistles in the New English Bible*, New Clarendon Bible: New Testament (Clarendon, 1963), 127, 145.

[56] Some perceive more harmony between the moral concerns of the quotation and the rest of Titus. See Reggie M. Kidd, "Titus as Apologia: Grace for Liars, Beasts, and Bellies," *HBT* 21 (1999): 185–209; Riemer A. Faber, "'Evil Beasts, Lazy Gluttons': A Neglected Theme in the Epistle to Titus," *WTJ* 67 (2005): 135–45. Allen interacts with their arguments in "Paul the Bigot." 28–29, 35, 160, 182.

be healthy in the faith, 1:13b). He was protecting the community's tenants as much as its tenets!

The heart of the problem in Crete does not seem to have been a matter of lining up theological ideas in the wrong fashion. It was the social and behavioral outcomes of division that were unacceptable. The gospel that Christ accepts people without regard to conventional tokens of status confounds the attempts of superiority groups to place additional demands upon converts. Christ is the agent of acceptance and his ruling cannot be overturned: Jews and Gentiles are equals in grace.

3:12–15

Paul moves immediately into this epistolary closing by talking about travel plans. It is not unusual for the formal components of a letter to lack explicit conjoiners (asyndeton) with the rest of the letter. Although this conclusion is set apart structurally, some themes are echoed or reinforced in these final words— especially Christians' *good works* (e.g., 1:16; 2:7, 14; 3:8, 14) and the community of faith (e.g., 1:1, 4, 13; 2:10; 3:8, 15). Although the address (1:1–4) and Paul's speech throughout the letter indicate an individual primary audience, the *you* (3:15) in the final greeting is plural, suggesting that Paul expected Titus's community to "overhear" these instructions and witness Paul's sanction of Titus's authority (esp. 2:15).[57]

---

[57] See comments at 1 Tim 6:21b.

16

PHILEMON

DAVID L. ALLEN

The Chomskyian revolution in linguistics had one glaring weakness: it failed to break away from its Bloomfieldian presupposition that the sentence was the highest level of linguistic consideration. As a result, the sentence as a linguistic unit was overemphasized without regard to context, thus eliminating the possibility of determinable structure (grammar) beyond the sentence level.

Modern linguistic theory is now recognizing that we may (and indeed must) talk about the structure of meaning beyond the sentence level, just as we can talk about the structure of clause and sentence. The name given to this branch of linguistic study is textlinguistics,[1] or, more familiarly, discourse analysis. Formerly the Cinderella of linguistics, discourse analysis has been recently elevated, if not to the position of princess, at least to that of lady-in-waiting.

In an attempt to show the rightful place of discourse analysis in the study of linguistics as a whole, we may view language as a two-story, split-level house. The basement of the house is linguistics proper—the study of the basic elements of communication such as phonology, morphology, grammar, etc. Most split-level houses have a basement entrance, but it is not the main entrance. The first floor of the house we may call discourse analysis. This is the linguistic study of the text as a whole. The main entrance to our house of language is normally the first floor since it is here that most people enter any given text they read. One

---

[1] For a helpful survey of the field and excellent bibliography see Robert de Beaugrande and Wolfgang Dressler, *Introduction to Text Linguistics* (Longman, 1981).

reads an entire story, letter, article, etc. without meticulous analysis of the phonology and morphology of each word or the grammatical analysis of each sentence. Yet at any given point, the reader/hearer of a discourse may stop and engage in minute analysis in any of these areas. The top floor of our split-level, two-
story house may be called text theory. This is the interdisciplinary intersection of
such disciplines as psychology, sociology, anthropology, etc. in the study of texts.
The post-Bloomfieldian era has seen a flurry of activity taking place on the first
and second floors of the house of language.

Discourse analysis offers those of us interested in biblical exegetics one of the
most exciting, challenging, and fruitful methodological frontiers on the contemporary linguistic landscape. Yet despite the progress discourse studies have
made in the last thirty years, OT and NT scholars alike have been, with few exceptions, reluctant to employ it.[2] One is hard pressed to find a recent commentary which approaches the text from a discourse perspective.

---

[2] See Richard J. Erickson, "Linguistics and Biblical Language: A Wide-open Field," *JETS* 26,
no. 3 (1983): 257–63 for an excellent discussion of the present state of affairs. Several linguists
have seen to it that commentators are not without the tools to practice discourse analysis.
John Beekman and John Callow's *Translating the Word of God* (Zondervan, 1974) and (with
Michael Kopesec) *The Semantic Structure of Written Communication* (Summer Institute of
Linguistics, 1981) present a model for discourse analysis that has been widely used by SIL International. *Translating the Word of God* was one of the earliest works available to the biblical
scholar which sought to analyze the larger semantic units of a biblical text, but because of its
title it has been greatly neglected (interestingly enough, the foreword was written by Harold
Greenlee). Wilbur Pickering's *Framework for Discourse Analysis* (Summer Institute of Linguistics, 1978) offers a discourse analysis of Colossians. He presently serves as a translation consultant at SIL, and in the preface to his book he acknowledges his debt to Beekman, Callow,
Longacre, and others. Timothy and Barbara Friberg, also associated with Wycliffe Bible Translators, served as editors for the *Analytical Greek New Testament* (Baker, 1981), an important
work which provides a grammatical tag for every word of the Greek New Testament. These
tags provide the exegete with linguistic information essential for determining the discourse
function of large sections of text. The value of their work will be illustrated in my analysis of
Philemon. J. P. Louw (*Semantics of New Testament Greek* [Scholars Press, 1982]) presents a
method of colon analysis not unlike the propositional approach of the Beekman-Callow model. Likewise, Nida, Louw, Snyman, and Cronje (*Style and Discourse* [Bible Society of South
Africa, 1983]) provide the methodological tools for New Testament discourse analysis. David
Alan Black's *Linguistics for Students of New Testament Greek: A Survey of Basic Concepts and
Applications* (Baker, 1988) is a successful nontechnical effort at dealing with the interrelations
between linguistics and NT Greek grammar. Finally, Peter Cotterell and Max Turner's *Linguistics and Biblical Interpretation* (InterVarsity, 1989) is an excellent introduction to the relevance
of linguistics for biblical exegesis. In addition, several journals have for some time now highlighted a discourse-oriented approach to the biblical text: *Linguistica Biblica, Neotestamentica,
The Bible Translator,* and *Journal of Translation* (formerly *Journal of Translation and Textlinguistics*), to name four.

Methodology

Robert Longacre, a colleague of Harold Greenlee, has taught linguistics at the University of Texas at Arlington since 1972 and, having been an international field consultant for SIL, has applied discourse analysis to numerous languages with fruitful results. The purpose of this article is to apply the specific tagmemic[3] method/model of discourse analysis as developed by Longacre to the hortatory text of Philemon in an attempt to explicate its structure and macrostructure. Paul's epistle furnishes a classic example of the way an author makes use of mitigation in attempting to impose a course of action upon someone else.

Space does not permit a thorough analysis of Longacre's approach to discourse (see bibliography for his major works).[4] However, a summary would be in order. The foundation of the tagmemic model is twofold: (1) the notion of the distinction between function-slot and filler-set, and (2) the integrating of the two into a functional unit called the tagmeme.[5] From this base, Longacre develops a model of discourse analysis which posits the following three aspects for any discourse: constituency structure, texture, and macrostructure.

First, all texts have constituency structure, that is, they are composed of paragraphs, sentences, clauses, and phrases. Longacre's brand of tagmemics does away with intermediate levels above the sentence such as section, chapter, and sentence cluster within a paragraph. Rather, he posits discourse, paragraph, and sentence, plus recursion, as being the three basic units necessary to any discourse.[6] Thus,

> Any string of paragraphs that belong together can be shown to have the structure of a discourse of a recognizable type; and ... any string of sentences that

---

[3] For a discussion of tagmemics, see Philip W. Davis, *Modern Theories of Language* (Prentice Hall, 1973), 173–216; Robert E. Longacre, "Discourse," in *Tagmemics I: Aspects of the Field*, ed. Ruth Brend and Kenneth Pike, Trends in Linguistics, Studies and Monographs 1 (Mouton, 1976), 1–44; Kenneth Pike, *Linguistic Concepts: An Introduction to Tagmemics* (University of Nebraska Press, 1982).

[4] The most complete presentation of Longacre's approach is given in his *Grammar of Discourse* (Plenum, 1983). Application of his method to biblical texts can be seen in Robert E. Longacre, "The Discourse Structure of the Flood Narrative," *JAAR* 47, Supplement B (1979): 89–133; idem, "Exhortation and Mitigation in the Greek Text of the First Epistle to John," *Selected Technical Articles Related to Translation* 9 (1983): 3–44; idem, "Interpreting Biblical Stories," in *Discourse and Literature*, ed. Teun van Dijk, CTS 3 (John Benjamins, 1985), 169–85; idem, *Joseph: A Story of Divine Providence: A Text Theoretical and Textlinguistic Analysis of Genesis 37 and 39–48* (Eisenbrauns, 1989). His work on biblical texts has had only limited exposure in the world of Old and New Testament studies.

[5] Longacre, *Grammar of Discourse*, 270.

[6] Ibid., 271–72.

belong together can be shown to constitute a paragraph of recognizable type. ... Thus the constituents of a discourse are discourse level slots which are filled either by a paragraph or an embedded discourse (with the latter ultimately composed of paragraphs as well). Similarly, the constituents of a paragraph are paragraph level slots which are filled by sentences or paragraphs (with the latter ultimately composed of sentences as well).[7]

Longacre has developed a taxonomy of paragraph types to be used in the analysis of a text's constituency structure.[8] By "paragraph" he means a structural rather than an orthographic unit. In the analysis of Philemon below, I will attempt to segment the epistle into sentences and paragraphs and then justify the segmentation linguistically.

A second feature of texts according to Longacre is "texture," which he further defines under the two rubrics spectrum and profile.[9] Spectrum is the term applied to the analysis of various levels of information relevance in a given discourse. A metaphor derived from optics, it suggests that a text has a clause structure revealing a cline of information that ranges from foregrounded (primary) events to backgrounded (secondary/tertiary) events.[10] It is Longacre's contention that the verb forms/clause types of any language can be hierarchically ranked in a manner relevant to the main line of development in a given text type. Hence, in narrative discourse, clauses with the simple past tense would tend to be the most salient (prominent), while the most static (backgrounded) clauses would tend to have stative verb forms ("to be," etc.). Expository discourse has a verb-rank scheme that is the inverse of narrative so that the two static forms (equative verbs, etc.) would rank the highest. Hortatory discourse would have command forms (imperatives, etc.) at the apex of the verb cline, while participial and nominal clauses would be backgrounded. In my paragraph analysis of Philemon (a piece of hortatory discourse), I will treat sentences whose main verb(s)/clause(s) are imperatives or other command forms or command surrogates as structurally dominant and those of lower rank as structurally ancillary. This main line versus ancillary ranking of clauses/sentences will likewise allow us to determine which paragraph(s) are more salient (thematic) in the epistle.

In addition to spectrum, a text also has profile, the term used to describe the development of plot or theme. A grammatical profile of a given discourse is deduced

---

[7] Ibid., 272.

[8] Longacre, "The Paragraph as a Grammatical Unit"; idem, *An Apparatus for the Identification of Paragraph Types*, NL 15 (Summer Institute of Linguistics, 1980).

[9] Robert E. Longacre, "A Spectrum and Profile Approach to Discourse Analysis," *Text* 1, no. 4 (1981): 332–59; idem, "Verb Ranking and the Constituent Structure of Discourse," *JLAS* 5 (1982): 177–202.

[10] Robert E. Longacre, "Spectrum."

from clearly marked features in the surface structure. NT epistolary genre is marked by a well-defined opening (salutation), body, and finis (conclusion/benediction). Furthermore, since few discourses are spoken or written on a uniform level of excitation, Longacre posits the notion 'peak as a further element in a text's profile. He defines peak as any episode-like unit set apart by special surface structure features and corresponding to the Climax or Denouement in the notional [deep] structure."[11] Peak is essentially a "non-routine zone of turbulence"[12] in the surface structure of a discourse. Peak is marked by such features as rhetorical underlining, concentration of participants, heightened vividness (shift in the nominal/verbal balance, tense, third person to second or first, etc.), change of pace (shift to short crisp sentences/paragraphs or to a long run-on type of sentence/paragraph structure), change of vantage point and/or orientation, and so on.[13] In my analysis of Philemon it will be shown how peak is marked in the most salient paragraph of the epistle.

Finally, a text has macrostructure—the main point or theme of the discourse. This can be arrived at by the analysis of the interplay between the constituency structure and the texture (particularly the verb-rank scheme) for the particular text. In one sense, the macrostructure is logically prior to the other two features of text in that an author has in mind what he wants to communicate before he structures this information into the finished product, a spoken or written text.

Longacre's model may be illustrated by the diagram below (Figure 16.1) in which the two-way arrows are to be read as "mutually supports and is mutually dependent upon":

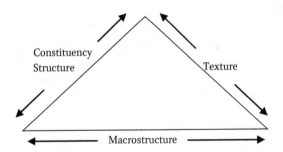

Constituency Structure

Texture

Macrostructure

Figure 16.1: Longacre's Discourse Model

---

[11] Longacre, *Grammar of Discourse*, 24.
[12] Ibid., xvii.
[13] Ibid., 349–351, 25–38.

Macrostructure

Philemon as Hortatory Discourse

The Epistle to Philemon provides a fertile field of investigation into the nature of hortatory discourse.[14] In hortatory discourse, the basic schema seems to be problem, command, motivation. In Philemon, motivation precedes problem and command. Actually, the text is long on motivation with mitigated exhortation (command surrogates) and short on overt commands. This will be seen in the paragraph structure of the book, as the most salient command form (imperative) does not occur until v. 17.

Perhaps some word should be said about participant identification and the communication situation in Philemon. The letter was written by the Apostle Paul to an individual named Philemon, a Christian who lived at Colossae and who was probably led to faith in Christ through the ministry of Paul. Philemon owned a slave, Onesimus, who had run away and apparently had met Paul in Rome. There Onesimus became a Christian, and now Paul has dispatched him and this letter back to Philemon at Colossae. The purpose of the letter is to exhort Philemon to forgive Onesimus and to receive him back without retribution. Secondary participants are mentioned in the text but play no significant role.[15]

This letter provides a fascinating background for the study of sociolinguistic factors.[16] One of the most serious offenses known in the ancient world was for a slave to run away. Consider the difficulty in writing a letter in that day and time requesting pardon for a runaway slave, particularly in light of the possibility that he had been guilty of theft as well. Paul had to ask Philemon to excuse his own presumption in detaining Onesimus for so long. Furthermore, he had to avoid all appearance of dictating terms to his friend which easily could have defeated his purpose. Paul employs psychological tact while at the same time not sacrificing his apostolic authority. His method is subtle, adroit, delicate. The Book of Philemon is a classic example of the use of mitigated exhortation.

---

[14] Consult J. H. Roberts, "Filemon in Diskussie: Enkele Hoogtepunte in die Sand van Sake" ("Philemon in Discussion: Some High Points in the State of Research"), *Scriptura* 21 (1987): 24–50.

[15] For further information on the background of Philemon consult Eduard Lohse, *Colossians and Philemon*, trans. William R. Poehlmann and Robert Karris, Hermeneia (Fortress, 1971); P. T. O'Brien, *Colossians and Philemon*, WBC 44 (Word, 1982) and their respective bibliographies.

[16] For an excellent discussion of the sociological factors in Philemon, consult Norman R. Petersen, *Rediscovering Paul* (Fortress, 1985), esp. 65–78, 89–109, 131–34, and 287–302.

Sentence and Paragraph Segmentation

Before the text can be segmented into paragraphs, the sentences must be identified.[17] In Greek discourse this is not always an easy task. One must beware of
simply accepting the sentence closure of the printed Greek text. A relative pronoun may often be functioning as the beginning of a new sentence (cf. ὃν in v. 12).[18]
I propose that the text be segmented into the following twenty-two sentences:

Sentence number	Verse numbers	Sentence number	Verse Numbers
1	1–2	12	17
2	3	13	18
3	4–5	14	19
4	6	15	20a
5	7	16	20b
6	8–9	17	21
7	10–11	18	22a
8	12	19	22b
9	13	20	23
10	14	21	24
11	15–16	22	25

The following is the paragraph segmentation which I posit for Philemon and
will attempt to justify linguistically below:

Paragraph number	Sentence numbers	Verse numbers
1	1–2	1–3
2	3–5	4–7
3	6–11	8–16
4	12–16	17–20
5	17–19	21–22
6	20–22	23–25

The letter of Philemon fits the usual tripartite structure of NT epistles. There
is an introductory salutation: paragraph 1; body: paragraphs 2–5; and closure:

---

[17] In this analysis, I am primarily interested in the inter-sentential and inter-paragraph relations. Intra-sentential, intra-clausal, and other lower-level matters are not dealt with here
unless they shed light on a high-level relation. Clause, phrase, and word studies are handled
quite well by the commentators.

[18] A. T. Robertson, *A Grammar of the Greek New Testament in the Light of Historical Research*, 4th ed. (Broadman, 1934), 443.

paragraph 6. Since both the salutation and closure are fairly fixed forms of letter writing, I will simply comment on their contribution to our understanding of the total letter without offering a diagrammed paragraph analysis of them.

Microstructures

Structure of the Salutation

Characteristics of opening salutations is their lack of finite verbal forms. Thus a literal reading would be "Paul, a prisoner of Christ Jesus and Timothy our brother to Philemon our beloved one and fellow-worker" (v. 1). The chief purpose of a salutation is to identify the writer, the reader, sometimes the location of the reader, and to offer greetings. It is interesting that Paul does not identify himself as an "apostle" in the salutation, perhaps due to the nature of his request. Rather, he chooses the phrase a prisoner of Christ. The full rhetorical and sociolinguistic implications of this choice are not apparent until the entire letter has been read.[19]

Since the letter is addressed to Philemon, why is there specific mention in the salutation of his family and the church which met in his house? It would appear that while Paul intended this as a personal letter, he also intended that this matter have a special message to the local church as well. Indeed, whatever Philemon's response to the return of Onesimus, the church would know, and this bit of added "pressure" may be accounted for on the basis of the sociolinguistic factors evident in the epistle. Notice the shift from the singular personal pronouns throughout the epistle to the plural use of ὑμῶν and ὑμῖν in v. 22.

The structure of the salutation appears to be an expository CO-ORDINATE paragraph[20] with two sentences of equal weight, sentence 1 (vv. 1–2) and sentence 2 (v. 3). Some form of the verb write is probably to be understood in sentence 1, while the optative πληθυνθείη 'let it be multiplied' would give the sense of sentence 2: "May grace and peace . . . be multiplied to you."

The body of the epistle consists of paragraphs 2–5. It has very definite boundaries which mark it off from the salutation and the closure. The use of the performative εὐχαριστῶ (v. 4) is the first occurrence of a finite verb in the letter.

---

[19] See John L. White, "The Structural Analysis of Philemon: A Point of Departure in the Formal Analysis of the Pauline Letter," in *Society of Biblical Literature Seminary Papers* (Scholars Press, 1971), 1:1–47.

[20] Longacre posits a finite set of twenty-four semantic paragraph types, many of which are used in the analysis of Philemon. These are discussed and illustrated in Robert E. Longacre, "The Paragraph as a Grammatical Unit," in *Discourse and Syntax*, ed. Talmy Givón, SSS 12 (Academic Press, 1979), 115–34; idem, *Apparatus*; idem, *Grammar of Discourse*. With each type that occurs in Philemon, I will offer a brief definition from Longacre.

An expression of thanksgiving to God for the recipient is indicative of the beginning of the body of the letter. Body closure is marked by the verb ἀσπάζεταί 'to greet' at the beginning of paragraph 6, followed by the names of those sending greetings.

The Structure of Paragraph 2 (vv. 4–7)

Paragraph 2 (vv. 4–7) also has definite boundaries. The performative verb εὐχαριστῶ marks paragraph onset while the vocative ἀδελφέ at the end of v. 7 marks paragraph closure. The repetition of the notion of "love for the saints" in vv. 5 and 7 serves almost like an inclusio to give cohesion to the paragraph. Traditionally, this THANKSGIVING paragraph has been separated from the body proper. For purposes of this analysis, however, I am considering "body" to refer to everything other than the formulaic salutation and closure.

I believe this paragraph (see Figure 16.2) is best described as an EXPOSITORY REASON paragraph whose TEXT[21] is composed of sentences 3–4 (vv. 4–6) and its REASON of sentence 5 (v. 7). The TEXT (vv. 4–6) itself embeds a SIMPLE paragraph with an INTRODUCTION (vv. 4–5) and

	TEXT: SIMPLE PARAGRAPH
vv. 4–5	INTRODUCTION: Εὐχαριστῶ τῷ θεῷ μου πάντοτε μνείαν σου ποιούμενος ἐπὶ τῶν προσευχῶν μου, ἀκούων σου τὴν ἀγάπην καὶ τὴν πίστιν, ἣν ἔχεις πρὸς τὸν κύριον Ἰησοῦν καὶ εἰς πάντας τοὺς ἁγίους.
v. 6	TEXT: ὅπως ἡ κοινωνία τῆς πίστεώς σου ἐνεργὴς γένηται ἐν ἐπιγνώσει παντὸς ἀγαθοῦ τοῦ ἐν ἡμῖν εἰς Χριστόν.
v. 7	REASON: χαρὰν γὰρ πολλὴν ἔσχον καὶ παράκλησιν ἐπὶ τῇ ἀγάπῃ σου, ὅτι τὰ σπλάγχνα τῶν ἁγίων ἀναπέπαυται διὰ σοῦ, ἀδελφέ.

Figure 16.2: Philemon 4–7 (E): REASON Paragraph

TEXT (v. 6). The INTRODUCTION (vv. 4–5) is a REASON sentence with v. 4 the main clause and the reason introduced by the participle ἀκούων in v. 5: "I give thanks … because I hear … " Γάρ in v. 7 introduces a sentence subordinate to the preceding two sentences because semantically the clause that supplies a reason is subordinate to the clause it explains.[22]

---

[21] Longacre uses the term TEXT to identify the most salient part of a paragraph, i.e., that which carries the most semantic weight. His paragraph types are identified by the semantic function of the least-weighted member. Hence, a REASON paragraph is one in which the most important information is conveyed in the TEXT portion of the sentence or embedded paragraph rather than in the REASON portion.

[22] The conjunction γάρ is always considered by Friberg and Friberg, *Analytical Greek New Testament*, 834 (for semantic reasons) to introduce a subordinate clause/sentence in the Greek NT.

A REASON paragraph encodes efficient cause or reason for an action. A SIMPLE paragraph is one in which there is one sentence in its body but which may also contain a second sentence that initiates or terminates the paragraph.[23] Verses 4–5 serve as the INTRODUCTION to the STATEMENT of v. 6.

There is an exegetical problem in v. 6 with the conjunction ὅπως. Is it to be related to μνείαν σου ποιούμενος or ἣν ἔχεις, or can it be construed as the beginning of a new sentence with the main verb (προσεύχομαι) left unexpressed? I agree with Louw that the latter of these constructions is the best option and have posited a new sentence beginning with v. 6.[24]

Having made v. 6 the beginning of a new sentence, a reason must be offered for analyzing it as the most salient piece of information in the embedded SIMPLE paragraph (vv. 4–6). Friberg and Friberg give the conjunction ὅπως a hyperordinating-conjunction tag in v. 6, which raises its position on the semantic scale of prominence.[25] Traditional Greek grammar recognizes two clausal relationships: coordinate and subordinate. On the basis of semantic analysis rather than syntactical, Friberg and Friberg have added a third logical possibility: superordination. A superordinate conjunction introduces a clause that is more prominent than the one to which it is related.[26] Since I have analyzed v. 6 as the beginning of a new sentence, its relationship to the previous sentence (vv. 4–5) is one of superordination because the content of the prayer is more salient than the reason for the prayer. Furthermore, it is only after we have read the entire epistle that the function of v. 6 in the overall discourse becomes clear. The content of Paul's prayer is an ever-so-mild hint of the full-blown exhortation to come in v. 17. Thus, I have analyzed this embedded SIMPLE paragraph (4–6) as INTRODUCTION (vv. 4–5) and TEXT (v. 6).

The verb structure of this paragraph further warrants describing it as basically EXPOSITORY. After the initial εὐχαριστῶ, the verb forms are mostly relational in nature and very low on the transitivity scale. This paragraph is highly descriptive of Philemon's Christian character, and thus we have verbs and verbals like "to hear," "to have" (twice), and "to become." The final verb in the paragraph is a perfect passive ("has been refreshed") that appears in a subordinate ὅτι clause. No command forms or command surrogates occur.

Paragraph 2 has both an overt and a covert function in the epistle. Since it is EXPOSITORY (containing no overt or mitigated command forms), it functions to express to Philemon the reason that Paul thanks God for his Christian behavior. This explains why there are so many TEXT–REASON relationships embedded in

---

[23] Longacre, *Apparatus*, 6.

[24] Louw, *Semantics of New Testament Greek*, 118–19.

[25] Friberg and Friberg, *Analytical Greek New Testament*, 657.

[26] Ibid., 833–34.

the sentence structure as well as in the overall paragraph. However, I believe we can surmise a further function lying behind this paragraph, a covert function. That function is to prepare Philemon for the request which Paul plans to make in v. 17. Mention is made of his love and faith toward all the saints, his fellowship of faith which leads to the knowing and doing of all that is good, and the statement that the innermost beings of the saints have been refreshed because of him. Paul's employment of σπλάγχνα in v. 7 rhetorically prepares Philemon for his request (note its use also in vv. 12 and 20). Church (1978: 24) highlights the rhetorical effectiveness of this term on Philemon by noting that "if Philemon refreshes the very hearts of the saints (v. 7); and, if Onesimus is Saint Paul's very heart (v. 12); then, to refresh Paul's very heart, Philemon must refresh Onesimus (v. 20)."[27] Semantically, paragraph 2 serves a covert purpose of setting the stage for Paul's request.

Structure of Paragraph 3 (vv. 8–16)

Paragraph 3 (vv. 8–16) is a hortatory AMPLIFICATION paragraph with the mitigated command form "beseech." The following considerations led to the suggestion of the paragraph boundaries between vv. 8 and 16. First, the conjunction διό in v. 8 signals a new paragraph. The appearance of the conjunction οὖν in v. 17 marks a new paragraph at that point as well. The topic of conversation shifts in v. 8 to Onesimus and to Paul's justification to Philemon for the reasons that Onesimus should be received again as a Christian brother. Finally, there is an inclusio formed by the phrase ἐν χριστῷ at the beginning of v. 8 and the phrase ἐν κυρίῳ at the end of v. 16. This phrase does not occur anywhere else within this paragraph.

I take this paragraph to be a hortatory AMPLIFICATION paragraph whose TEXT consists of vv. 8–9 and an AMPLIFICATION in vv. 10–16 (see Figure 16.3). The amplification portion of the paragraph reflects multiple levels of embedding. For example, the AMPLIFICATION paragraph (vv. 10–16) embeds a COMMENT paragraph whose TEXT is vv. 10–14 and COMMENT vv. 15–16. The TEXT of that COMMENT paragraph also embeds an AMPLIFICATION paragraph whose TEXT is vv. 10–11 and AMPLIFICATION vv. 12–14. This AMPLIFICATION paragraph further embeds a REASON paragraph whose TEXT is v. 12 and REASON vv. 13–14. Finally, the REASON paragraph embeds an ANTITHETICAL paragraph with THESIS (v. 13) and ANTITHESIS (v. 14).

Four paragraph types are identified in this large paragraph: AMPLIFICATION, COMMENT, REASON, and ANTITHETICAL. AMPLIFICATION and COMMENT paragraphs fall under the general head of EMBELLISHMENT paragraphs according to Longacre.[28] The

---

[27] F. F. Church, "Rhetorical Structure and Design in Paul's Letter to Philemon," *HTR* 71 (1978): 17–33.

[28] Longacre, *Apparatus*, 14.

AMPLIFICATION paragraph employs a set of two or more sentences to develop a theme by bringing in additional information in each successive sentence. The result is a "circling-in-on-the-target" type structure. Notice how vv. 10–11 further amplify vv. 8–9. The COMMENT paragraph involves the speaker or writer in some personal observation of his own.[29] Notice how vv. 15–16 function in this way. The REASON paragraph has been discussed above. The ANTITHETICAL paragraph encodes contrast, frustration, or expectancy reversal.[30] This is marked among other ways in the surface structure of Greek by the use of δέ as in v. 14. Paul desired to keep Onesimus with him, but he would not do so without Philemon's consent. Notice that semantically v. 14 is a further explication of ἀνέπεμψά in v. 12, so that v. 14 furnishes the ANTITHESIS to v. 13, and together the two function as the REASON for the statement of v. 12.

vv. 8–9   TEXT: διὸ πολλὴν ἐν Χριστῷ παρρησίαν ἔχων ἐπιτάσσειν σοι τὸ ἀνῆκον διὰ τὴν ἀγάπην μᾶλλον παρακαλῶ, τοιοῦτος ὢν ὡς Παῦλος πρεσβύτης νυνὶ δὲ καὶ δέσμιος Χριστοῦ Ἰησοῦ.

         AMPLIFICATION: COMMENT PARAGRAPH

           TEXT: AMPLIFICATION PARAGRAPH

vv. 10–11   TEXT: παρακαλῶ σε περὶ τοῦ ἐμοῦ τέκνου, ὃν ἐγέννησα ἐν τοῖς δεσμοῖς, Ὀνήσιμον, τόν ποτέ σοι ἄχρηστον νυνὶ δὲ [καὶ] σοὶ καὶ ἐμοὶ εὔχρηστον.

             AMPLIFICATION: reason paragraph

v. 12   TEXT: ὃν ἀνέπεμψά σοι, αὐτόν, τοῦτ' ἔστιν τὰ ἐμὰ σπλάγχνα.

               REASON: ANTITHETICAL PARAGRAPH

v. 13   THESIS: ὃν ἐγὼ ἐβουλόμην πρὸς ἐμαυτὸν κατέχειν, ἵνα ὑπὲρ σοῦ μοι διακονῇ ἐν τοῖς δεσμοῖς τοῦ εὐαγγελίου.

v. 14   ANTITHESIS: χωρὶς δὲ τῆς σῆς γνώμης οὐδὲν ἠθέλησα ποιῆσαι, ἵνα μὴ ὡς κατὰ ἀνάγκην τὸ ἀγαθόν σου ᾖ ἀλλὰ κατὰ ἑκούσιον.

vv. 15–16   COMMENT: τάχα γὰρ διὰ τοῦτο ἐχωρίσθη πρὸς ὥραν, ἵνα αἰώνιον αὐτὸν ἀπέχῃς, οὐκέτι ὡς δοῦλον ἀλλ' ὑπὲρ δοῦλον, ἀδελφὸν ἀγαπητόν, μάλιστα ἐμοί, πόσῳ δὲ μᾶλλον σοὶ καὶ ἐν σαρκὶ καὶ ἐν κυρίῳ.

Figure 16.3: Philemon 8–16 (H): AMPLIFICATION Paragraph

     This is the most involuted paragraph of the book in terms of structure. Paul is not yet ready to command, but he uses some clear command surrogates which extenuate exhortation to Philemon.

---

[29] Ibid., 16.
[30] Ibid., 10.

Paul informs Philemon at the outset that he has a specific request to make of him, but the content of the request is deferred until a bit later. In vv. 10–16, Paul gradually clarifies the content of his request. The structure of this paragraph reflects the very reserved way in which Paul approaches Philemon with his request. Almost every statement is a further AMPLIFICATION on the preceding statement: I beseech you ... I beseech you for Onesimus ... I beseech you for Onesimus whom I have begotten in my bonds. ... The result of this kind of structure gives the impression of "circling in on the target." Furthermore, the verb which Paul chooses for receiving Onesimus (ἀπέχῃς) is in the subjunctive mood, the mood of potentiality, and this is the only subjunctive in the entire paragraph (the only other one in the book up to this point is γένηται in v. 6).

The sociolinguistic relationships in this paragraph become quite interesting upon study. Up to this point, Paul has not made any effort to remind Philemon of his authority as an apostle or to command him on the basis of that authority. However, all of this changes in vv. 8–9 as Paul says: "Wherefore, although I have much boldness in Christ to charge you [to do] that which is fitting, yet because of love, I rather beseech, being such a one as Paul, an old man and now also a prisoner of Christ Jesus." Here we see Paul pulling rank on Philemon, although in a very mitigated fashion. He informs Philemon that although he could charge him to do the right thing, yet he chooses rather for love's sake to beseech or encourage him to do what is right. Both the infinitive ἐπιτάσσειν 'to charge' and the main verb παρακαλῶ 'I beseech' are examples of mitigated command. Paul must get Philemon's attention but yet not come on too strong too soon. Notice the preposed διὰ τὴν ἀγάπην in v. 9 (before the verb παρακαλῶ, which gives emphasis to "love" and deemphasizes the exhortation. Through the repetition of the verb παρακαλῶ in v. 10 "Paul pulls Philemon's heartstrings not once, but twice."[31] Note that Onesimus is not mentioned until the end of the clause (v. 10). Thus, a literal rendering would be: "I beseech you concerning my own son, whom I have begotten in my bonds, Onesimus."

Wickert interprets the participle ὤν in v. 9 as a concessive participle and thus begins a new sentence at v. 9b: "Although I am none other than Paul . . . I beseech." In this way vv. 8–9a are rhetorically balanced with vv. 9b–10 by means of tautological parallelism.[32] However, it seems best, following Lightfoot, to take τοιοῦτος ὤν with the preceding sentence and construe the resumptive παρακαλῶ as the beginning of a new sentence.[33]

---

[31] Church, "Rhetorical Structure," 26.

[32] U. Wickert, "Der Philemonbrief—Privatbrief oder apostolisches Schreiben?" in *ZNW* 52 (1961): 235.

[33] J. B. Lightfoot, *Saint Paul's Epistles to the Colossians and to Philemon* (Zondervan, 1959), 338.

Paul continues in v. 11 with a comment about the profitableness of Onesimus to both himself and Philemon. Onesimus's name means "profitable"—hence the play on words which Paul employs in v. 11. Verse 12 states the fact of Paul's having sent Onesimus back to Philemon, and perhaps there the verb receive is to be supplied in the context. The text reads: "Whom I have sent to you, him, that is my own heart." We may have here a case of mitigation through ellipsis. Paul is not yet ready to command Philemon as he does in v. 17. It is also possible that no verb is to be supplied, and Paul simply further identifies Onesimus through a somewhat broken construction as "him, that is my own heart."

Verse 13 may be interpreted as a covert request on Paul's part that Philemon allow Onesimus to remain with him as his assistant in the gospel. Paul does not overtly request this, but he does mention the fact of his own intent to this effect. Paul did not presume upon Philemon's generosity in this area and thus sent Onesimus back to him. Note the statement in v. 14, "but without your opinion I was willing to do nothing, in order that not as by way of necessity the good of you might be, but rather by way of [being] voluntary." How cleverly Paul inserts this idea, perhaps with the intent that Philemon will agree not only to forgive Onesimus and receive him back, but even more, may free him completely to serve alongside of Paul.

Thus, the clause structure of this paragraph again reveals no overt imperatives. Nevertheless, by means of skillful use of mitigation, Paul covertly begins to apply the pressure in preparation for the overt command about to be definitized in v. 17.

Structure of Paragraph 4 (vv. 17–20)

Verses 17–20 constitute the fourth major paragraph and what I consider to be the PEAK of the book. I take this to be a hortatory PARAPHRASE paragraph, which further embeds a SIMPLE, COMMENT, and REASON paragraph, whose TEXT is v. 17, containing the most salient verb in the epistle: προσλαβοῦ.

SIMPLE, COMMENT, and REASON paragraph types have been defined above. The PARAPHRASE paragraph states the same thing in a different way. It can have a generic–specific type of structure in which sentence 1 would give the general information while sentences 2–N would give details, or vice versa where sentences 1, 2, and following would encode the details and sentence N would give a summary.[34]

In Philemon 17–20, vv. 17–19 compose the TEXT while v. 20 gives a PARAPHRASE of the text (see Figure 16.4). The TEXT embeds a COMMENT paragraph whose TEXT is v. 17 and COMMENT vv. 18–19. This COMMENT paragraph further embeds a SIMPLE

---

[34] Longacre, *Apparatus*, 14–15.

paragraph with v. 17 as the TEXT. This paragraph (composed of a single sentence) contains the most salient verb in the epistle and provides a concise statement of the macrostructure of Philemon: "Receive him as you would receive me." The COMMENT paragraph further embeds a REASON paragraph whose TEXT is v. 18 and REASON v. 19. This paragraph informs Philemon that he can charge anything to Paul's account because he has written it with his own hand and will repay any debt. Finally, v. 20 contains a PARAPHRASE paragraph with the most salient verb being the imperative ἀνάπαυσόν 'refresh', and thus it is tagged as the TEXT.

TEXT: COMMENT PARAGRAPH

      TEXT: SIMPLE PARAGRAPH

v. 17   TEXT: εἰ οὖν με ἔχεις κοινωνόν, προσλαβοῦ αὐτὸν ὡς ἐμέ.

      COMMENT: REASON PARAGRAPH

v. 18   TEXT: εἰ δέ τι ἠδίκησέν σε ἢ ὀφείλει, τοῦτο ἐμοὶ ἐλλόγα.

v. 19   REASON: ἐγὼ Παῦλος ἔγραψα τῇ ἐμῇ χειρί, ἐγὼ ἀποτίσω· ἵνα μὴ λέγω σοι ὅτι καὶ σεαυτόν μοι προσοφείλεις.

PARAPHRASE: PARAPHRASE PARAGRAPH

v. 20   PARAPHRASE: ναί ἀδελφέ, ἐγώ σου ὀναίμην ἐν κυρίῳ.

            TEXT: ἀνάπαυσόν μου τὰ σπλάγχνα ἐν Χριστῷ.

Figure 16.4: Philemon 17–20 (H): PARAPHRASE Paragraph

This paragraph is clearly marked in the surface structure by the use of οὖν in v. 17. There is a shift at v. 17 from the indicative mode to the imperative mood, and then v. 21 shifts back to the indicative.

The following surface-structure features mark this paragraph as the PEAK of the book. First, there is a definite shift in the verb structure. Up until this point, there has been no imperative used. However, here at the PEAK of the book and within the confines of only four verses, three command forms appear. The most salient of the three appears in v. 17 and gives a unique summary of the book: "Receive him [Onesimus] as you would receive me." Furthermore, there are no less than eleven verbs in this paragraph, and not one of them is a verbal (participle or infinitive). In the preceding paragraph of eight verses there are only seventeen verb forms, and five of those are verbals. There is a wide range of mode shift in these four verses as well, including the use of the imperative, indicative, and optative modes.

The sentence structure of this paragraph is different from the preceding material in that Paul shifts to short, almost staccato, sentences with very few preposed and postposed clauses. This added "punch" is further magnified by the increase in finite verb forms. All of these features combine to mark vv. 17–20 as the peak of the book.

In this paragraph all the stops are pulled out, in that Paul is overtly "twisting the arm" of Philemon to comply with his command. The sociolinguistic factor of mitigation seen in the previous paragraphs is all but abandoned here as blunt imperatives occur. Furthermore, Paul reminds Philemon how he owes even his own being (probably a reference to his salvation) to Paul. The structure at this point is interesting. The clause ἵνα μὴ λέγω has an imperatival sense, though it is not a surface-structure imperative. It is actually embedded in a postposed sentence margin following the independent clause "I will repay." Thus Paul employs a further argument for Philemon to receive Onesimus back.

The only example of the first-person optative to express a wish in the NT occurs in v. 20: ὀναίμην 'let me benefit.' This in turn is followed by a final independent clause with an overt imperative ἀνάπαυσόν 'refresh,' harking back to what was stated in v. 7. Thus Paul is found to play notes all up and down the scale of verb salience for hortatory Greek discourse in an effort to sway Philemon to accept Onesimus.

Structure of Paragraph 5 (vv. 21–22)

The final paragraph to be studied is found in vv. 21–22 (see Figure 16.5). I take it to be a hortatory SIMULTANEOUS paragraph with a covert command form in the first sentence and an overt imperative in the second. There is a certain balance between the two sentences that is further shown by the use of the coordinating conjunction δὲ at the beginning of v. 22.

| v. 21 | SIMULTANEOUS 1: πεποιθὼς τῇ ὑπακοῇ σου ἔγραψά σοι, εἰδὼς ὅτι καὶ ὑπὲρ ἃ λέγω ποιήσεις. |
| v. 22 | SIMULTANEOUS 2: ἅμα δὲ καὶ ἑτοίμαζέ μοι ξενίαν· ἐλπίζω γὰρ ὅτι διὰ τῶν προσευχῶν ὑμῶν χαρισθήσομαι ὑμῖν. |

Figure 16.5: Philemon 21–22 (H): SIMULTANEOUS Paragraph (Closure of Body)

Under the heading of "temporal paragraphs," Longacre posits two types: those that encode chronological sequence and those that encode simultaneity or overlap.[35] In English, overlap may be marked in the surface structure by "meanwhile," "at the same time," or a preposed adverbial clause introduced by "as." Philemon 22 is introduced by the adverbial ἅμα 'at the same time' which is the surface-structure device that here encodes the notion of temporal overlap. Paul's thought may be summarized as "I have written knowing that you will do beyond what I have asked [namely, receive Onesimus back], and at the same time [of your receiving Onesimus] prepare a place for my lodging [prepare to receive me as well]."

---

[35] Ibid., 8–9.

The paragraph boundary between vv. 20–21 is not as clear as other places and has led some to consider v. 21 as part of the preceding paragraph. Its relation to that paragraph would then be some sort of summary statement. While I agree it is a summation, I do not believe this to be an accurate way of analyzing the text for the following reasons. There is not a single nonfinite verb form in vv. 17–20, yet v. 21 begins with the participle πεποιθώς. This does not mean, of course, that v. 21 could not go with the preceding paragraph, only that in my opinion it is more likely that it does not. Furthermore, the scope of the ἔγραψά in v. 21 harks back, not only to the command of the preceding paragraph, but also to the entire epistle up to this point. Such summation probably merits a new paragraph.

The only overt imperative in this paragraph is found in v. 22, in which Paul asks Philemon to prepare lodging for him. This imperative is clearly not of the same nature as the preceding three, and thus without question we are in a new paragraph by v. 22. However, there is a covert command in v. 21 embedded in the postposed ὅτι clause. After the salvo of imperatives in the preceding paragraph, there is no need for Paul to continue the appeal with another imperative. Rather, he in effect mitigates a command by saying, "I know that you will do beyond what I have asked." Although the main verb in this sentence is the performative ἔγραψα, it does not convey the most prominent information. In the case of v. 21, what is grammatically subordinate (the ὅτι clause) is semantically prominent. The same kind of thing occurs in 1 John 2:1–6, where v. 1a reads ταῦτα γράφω ὑμῖν ἵνα μὴ ἁμάρτητε. Longacre identifies this as a hortatory REASON paragraph whose TEXT is vv. 1–2 and REASON vv. 3–6. He notes that the REASON portion of the paragraph goes with μὴ ἁμάρτητε rather than the ταῦτα γράφω. The sense of the paragraph is "don't sin, because ..." The command element is expressed in a postposed ἵνα clause, but it semantically dominates the paragraph.[36] Hence, 1 John 2:1–6 is hortatory, though it appears upon first blush to be purely expository.

Thus Philemon 21–22 is a hortatory SIMULTANEOUS paragraph which functions as closure for the main body of the epistle by summarizing again Paul's request via mitigation and adding an additional request to prepare lodging for an impending visit by the apostle.

Final greetings are expressed in vv. 23–25, and, due to their formulaic nature, they need not detain us here. Paul appends a list of the names of people who are apparently with him at the time of writing and who send their greetings to Philemon. The closing sentence of this paragraph expresses the usual benediction of grace.

---

[36] Longacre, "Exhortation," 9.

Macrostructure, Constituent Structure, and the Texture of Philemon

We are now ready to deduce an overall macrostructure for Philemon based on the above analysis. Excluding the salutation and finis which open and close the epistle in a formal manner, paragraph 2 (vv. 4–7) semantically functions as what we might call grounds 1, while paragraph 3 (vv. 8–16) semantically functions as grounds 2 for the (thematic and most salient) exhortation of paragraph 4 (vv. 17–20). The most salient clause of paragraph 4 (and of the entire epistle) is v. 17. Paragraph 5 (vv. 21–22) summarizes and mitigates the exhortation of paragraph 4, makes a secondary request to prepare lodging, and serves as closure for the main body of the epistle. Thus, from the most-prominent clause in the epistle according to my analysis the following macrostructure can be deduced: "Receive Onesimus as you would receive me."

The "constituent structure" of Philemon contains twenty-two sentences which comprise six paragraphs. Paragraphs 1 and 6 comprise the salutation and closure and have not been analyzed in this study. The middle four paragraphs (body) exhibit multiple layers of embedding and reveal the hierarchical structure of Philemon. Second, the "texture" of Philemon reveals the development of theme and shows how the verb scheme of Philemon fits that of hortatory discourse. The PEAK of this epistle is vv. 17–20, with v. 17 containing the most salient clause in the entire piece. This information yields a viable macrostructure for the text.

The interfusion of discourse analysis with traditional exegesis serves to explicate the meaning of Philemon so that we are allowed to account for the textual features in a more thorough and holistic way. The result of my analysis shows the epistle to be a carefully written document which reflects Paul's rhetorical art in handling a delicate situation. The Epistle to Philemon is a beautiful piece of mitigated arm-twisting!

17

HEBREWS

CYNTHIA LONG WESTFALL

W hat is Discourse Analysis? Simply put, Discourse Analysis (DA) involves the analysis of units of naturally-occurring language in its social contexts. DA typically focuses on written or vocal language above the sentence level but may also include signs. It is an approach rather than a methodology, and though clearly linguistic as a field of study, it is synthetic by nature in practice.[1] It draws on and informs work from such diverse fields as psychology, speech-language pathology, informatics, computer science, philosophy, biology, human anatomy, neuroscience, sociology, anthropology, acoustics, cultural studies, international relations, communication studies, and translation studies. That is to say, in practice a discourse analysis may utilize insight or methodological tools from any relevant discipline to achieve a number of different goals.

Any of the above disciplines may provide a lens through which patterns above the sentence level are analyzed in a biblical text. There are an unlimited combination of features that can be analyzed for a number of reasons. I have been primarily interested in using discourse analysis as a means of identifying the structure or organization of a text and how that structure relates to its meaning, which

---

[1] George Brown and George Yule, *Discourse Analysis*, CTL (Cambridge University Press, 1983) is still a solid introduction to DA, though the field has expanded since 1984. Another source that is helpful, particularly on the scope of DA, is Deborah Tannen, Heidi E. Hamilton and Deborah Schiffrin, eds., *The Handbook of Discourse Analysis*, 2nd ed. (Wiley Blackwell, 2015). See also James Paul Gee and Michael Handford, *The Routledge Handbook of Discourse Analysis* (Routledge, 2012).

involves building a mental representation of the text that is grounded in the formal features of the discourse.[2] In my book, *A Discourse Analysis of the Letter to the Hebrews*, I used this approach as a means to solve one of the book's most difficult critical issues: the structure of the discourse.

SFL Linguistic Theory and DA

I have adopted Halliday's Systemic Functional Linguistics (SFL) as my linguistic theory for DA. However, I utilize other linguistic insights used in DA that can be compatible with and integrated into SFL theory.[3] SFL studies how real language is used to communicate in social interaction (the functional element), and treats language as a network of systems, or interrelated sets of options for making meaning. The battle cry of SFL linguistics is "Trust the text!"[4] I assume that the biblical text has coherence, relevance, cohesion, and prominence which are basic properties that define a text.

Halliday and those who follow him analyze the features of language according to features that are realized in three metafunctions or categories of meaning: the Ideational, the Interpersonal, and the Textual, which correspond to Field, Tenor, and Mode, terms that specify the context of situation and the functional variety of a language.[5] I therefore have a three-fold analysis, in which the Textual metafunction is associated with the patterns of cohesion that group or "chunk"

---

[2] For a description that enables one to arrive at a mental representation of the text, see R. A. Dooley and S. H. Levinsohn, *Analyzing Discourse: A Manual of Basic Concepts* (SIL International, 2001), 51–53.

[3] For an introduction to SFL, see M. A. K. Halliday and Christian M. I. M. Matthiessen, *Halliday's Introduction to Functional Grammar*, 4th ed. (Routledge, 2014). For a brief summary of discourse analysis of the New Testament based on SFL, see J. T. Reed, *A Discourse Analysis of Philippians: Method and Rhetoric in the Debate over Literary Integrity*, SNTSup 136 (Sheffield Academic Press, 1997), 16–122. For a fuller description of my model as illustrated by various New Testament texts and as applied to Hebrews, see Cynthia Long Westfall, *A Discourse Analysis of the Letter to the Hebrews: The Relationship between Form and Meaning*, LBS 297 (T&T Clark, 2005), 28–87.

[4] The argument behind this statement is that the analysis of language should be textually based, and that form and meaning are inseparable. Trusting the text involves the assumption that the author has a purpose in the way he or she structures the text and that the formal features reflect meaning and should affect interpretation. See John Sinclair and Ronald Carter, eds., *Trust the Text* (Routledge, 2004). John Sinclair first summarized SFL's textually based approach in an earlier article: "Trust the Text" in *Advances in Systemic Linguistics: Recent Theory and Practice*, ed. M. Davies and L. Ravelli, OLS (Pinter, 1992), 5–19.

[5] One of the revisions in this article of my original approach is to associate the terms Textual, Ideational and Interpersonal with the first three steps in my methodology rather than Mode, Field and Tenor.

the discourse, the Ideational metafunction is associated with the topics within the units/subunits established by patterns of cohesion, and the Interpersonal metafunction is associated with prominence within the units/subunits, which, taken together with the topic, will be most closely associated with the message or thesis of the author in each part. That being said, the project of determining the structure of the discourse falls under the category of the Textual metafunction, in which the other two metafunctions play a supportive role.

Some who apply SFL to biblical studies conflate DA with Register Analysis. While both SFL-based DA and Register Analysis will look at a text above the sentence level and tend to analyze a given text according to Halliday's three metafunctions, Halliday would distinguish between the two. Register Analysis, as Halliday and Hasan define it, is consistent with their approach to SFL. Their focus is on what a given text tells us about the language. Register Analysis is a theory that focuses on the language—on how the features of language change in different contexts (such as in a bank, church, classroom), so that it is comparative and intertextual in goal and method, since it views a given text in its relationship with and to other texts that have similar functions in similar contexts, and is thus by definition related to corpus linguistics and intertextuality. Discourse analysis, on the other hand, views the text as an artifact and is interested primarily in the meaning of the text above the sentence level, and how the system of language, the context of culture and the context of situation contribute to the interpretation of the text.[6] Therefore, while I stay within the theory, I have collected tools from others who have done Discourse Analysis with a focus on the text as an artifact, and perhaps I will appear to have more in common with Critical Discourse Analysis.

In *A Discourse Analysis of the Letter to the Hebrews*, I concentrate on the formal features of the text to demonstrate how the author uses formal features to communicate meaning at the discourse level. This is not to suggest that the context of situation and culture do not play a crucial role in the interpretation of Hebrews or any text. To the contrary, I am a strong advocate of the linguistic principle that words have meaning in context—textual, cultural and situational. On the other hand, one of the tenets of SFL is that the author/speaker's choice of grammar and words have meaning, and the patterns of a language's grammar and lexis are both formed by culture and impact the culture—language is a social semiotic and, among other things, the text points to its situational context through reference, deixis, and its register. I proceeded with my analysis with the

---

[6] This difference in focus led in part to Norman Fairclough's move out of SFL and his founding of Critical Discourse Analysis (CDA), which focuses on the meaning of the text in social practice and power structures, but retains an association with SFL theory. See Norman Fairclough, *Critical Discourse Analysis: The Critical Study of Language* (Routledge, 1995).

thesis that the patterns of the author's choices of grammar and vocabulary would have meaning at the discourse level and those patterns should constrain and frame our interpretation of their meaning in the context of culture and situation as a starting point. I have distilled my analysis and my concluding mental representation of the text.

Methodology and Procedure

The simplest way to describe my methodology for the analysis of the structure or organization of a discourse is that it is based on formal and semantic patterns of continuity and variation in the grammar and lexis, which group the text into units (cohesion), and the identification of semantic chains to find the topic and highlight material as important for the reader (prominence). The textual aspect of the cohesion of the text determines how the author chunks the text though continuity and variation. Each chunk becomes the basic unit in which the ideational aspect of the topic is determined and the interpersonal aspect of how the author engages the reader through prominence to focus the central clause or point that he or she is making. While this all requires the reader's interpretation, the author guides the reader through the choice of grammar and lexis. Developing a mental representation of the text similarly is an interpretive exercise, but consists of recognizing the cohesion between the parts and the whole through an analysis of the patterns of continuity/repetition and variation.

Analytical Procedure of the Microstructure

In my book, I employ a four-step methodology to analyze the structure of the discourse at and above the sentence level in the text, working through the text in a linear manner.[7]
1. Grouping with patterns of cohesion and variation (textual)
2. Identifying topics within the groupings (ideational)
3. Locating patterns of prominence and main clauses (interpersonal)
4. Determining the relationship to the co-text (cohesion at the discourse level)

While I cannot explain in detail all the formal and semantic data in the text that are used to analyze each of these discourse functions, I can refer you to my *Discourse Analysis of the Letter to the Hebrews* where there is an attempt to describe in detail the various devices that authors used to create cohesion, topics

---

[7] This requires some preliminary observation and hypotheses of what constitutes a section in the discourse, but the process should be self-correcting by the end and should test the preliminary determination of each unit of study for analysis.

and prominence in a unit and at the level of discourse. However, I can briefly explain the steps of analysis. In this analysis, the message of each subunit is clarified and summarized in the fourth step instead of a discussion of the relationship of each unit to the discourse as a whole. I reserve the discussion of the relationship of the parts to the whole for the final section on the macrostructure of Hebrews.

Cohesion of the Passage

The first step is to locate the way that the author groups or chunks the text above the sentence level into subunits, units and sections. This is done through analyzing the cohesion patterns.[8] Cohesion refers to how an entire discourse hangs together, but we may also detect cohesion patterns that group the text at lower levels in the discourse. In our textual analysis and translation work in texts that belong to cultures and languages of which we are not native speakers, our embedded linguistic assumptions will mislead our interpretation. Cohesion patterns in the Greek should be the foundation and basis of our paragraph and section structures, rather than starting with the location of breaks (driven by Western assumptions of paragraph breaks) or our intuitive (or learned) notions about "topic."[9] In Greek the author creates cohesion with patterns of continuity. The sentence structure is the starting point for determining cohesion.[10] Above the sentence level, an author glues sentences together into units with a number of strategies that utilize repetition of formal and semantic features.[11] Cohesion patterns create units with spans and cohesive ties but an author also uses sequencing, staging, and logical relationships. In a complementary way, the author also uses variation of formal and semantic features to group the discourse. Grouping with variation is done with a shift in patterns, and also with features that are marked or emphatic (such as the nominative of direct address). However, the

---

[8] For theory and description of cohesion, see M. A. K. Halliday, and R. Hasan *Cohesion in English* (Longman, 1976). See also Westfall, *Hebrews*, 30–31, 37–55.

[9] This methodology and approach is in direct contrast with the text-linguistic approach of Mark Taylor, whose "cohesion analysis" has the starting point of "cohesion shift analysis," where the first step discerns where the shifts or breaks occur based on shifts in predetermined "cohesion fields." However, there is no rigorous methodological attention given to the actual patterns of cohesion and continuity in the fields. See Mark Edward Taylor, *A Text-Linguistic Investigation into the Structure of James* (T&T Clark, 2006), 42–43, 45–58.

[10] Sometimes commentators' notions about the topic override the basic sentence structure, and a commentary, translation or even the editors of the critical Greek text will begin a paragraph or even a section in the middle of a sentence. The integrity of clause complexes should be respected as a rule of thumb.

[11] See Westfall, *Hebrews*, 39–55, which demonstrates relationships between grammar and lexis and grouping.

author also uses variation in the discourse to create prominence. Therefore, patterns of continuity in the discourse must be given priority over variation or discontinuity at the beginning of the process.[12] The assumption of the coherence of a discourse means that the text is relevant and it makes sense. Discrete units will form cohesive ties with each other to reinforce and clarify a relationship between them that makes sense.

Topic of the Passage

"Topic" refers to what a speaker or writer is talking about within a given unit of analysis. This is arguably the most important step because our sense of the topic is the interpretive frame that we place on the discourse.[13] When we place subheadings in our translations or commentaries, they often become more powerful than the text itself. However, there has been little control on what counts for evidence in the identification of topics—it appears to be primarily an intuitive process in most translations and commentaries and even in some discourse analyses.

Only after we identify how the author chunks or groups the discourse are we in a position to identify topics in each unit, or answer the question: What is a discourse unit about? What accounts for all of the data or information in the unit? Often this involves (1) the identification of semantic and identity chains of the participants and how they interact with each other, (2) the process chains (verbs and verbal elements) and/or (3) the linear information flow.[14] For example, two individuals or groups may be compared and evaluated—is the point of the comparison merely establishing superiority of one over the other or does the

---

[12] This is in contrast with Guthrie's methodology, because his first step is to locate "cohesion shifts," in a variety of formal and semantic "cohesion fields" which calculates the variation or breaks in the discourse. Furthermore, shifts in topic and "genre" are considered to be part of the variation, so preconceived notions about topic and discontinuity in the "genre" (exposition and exhortation) are included at the first step which creates a somewhat circular process. Also, the method tends to confuse prominence with a "break" in the discourse. See George Guthrie, *The Structure of Hebrews: A Text-Linguistic Analysis*, BSL (Baker Books, 1994). But also see Taylor, *Structure of James*, 9.

[13] See Brown and Yule, *Discourse Analysis*, 140: "There are, of course, many ... easily recognisable thematisation devices used in the organisation of discourse structure. Placing headings and sub-headings within a text is a common thematisation device in technical or public-information documents .... What these thematisation devices have in common is not only the way they provide 'starting points' for paragraphs in a text, but also their contributions to dividing the whole text into smaller chunks. This 'chunking' effect is one of the most basic of those achieved by thematisation in discourse."

[14] For a description and illustration of semantic chains and identity chains, see Westfall, *Hebrews*, 49–53. For a description of different forms of repetition, see Michael Hoey, *Patterns of Lexis in Text*, DEL (Oxford University Press, 1991), ch 3.

linear information flow indicate that the author is using the comparison to make a point drawn from the comparison?

However, there are times that other factors may play a large role in identifying the topic, for instance, when the reader cannot identify clear semantic chains. Besides being organized around a topic, the units and sections can be organized around an episode, a character, the pattern of an inductive proof, or other features such as a repeated element of a phrase or a group of commands. There are formulaic discourse structures such as a problem-solving procedure, an instruction manual, recipe formats or stereotypical scenes, stories and characters. Describing the information flow takes into account the linearization of the unit, including the starting point and the end point. The starting point is the "theme" in that it connects back with the previous discourse and serves as a point of departure for further development. The end point or destination concludes the unit and points the way forward to the rest of the discourse. The function of the starting point and ending point can be consistent with the occurrence of prominence in the discourse.

Prominence of the Passage

Authors utilize an assortment of emphatic elements and techniques both to chunk or group the text and to create contours in its patterns of emphasis or focus.[15] Prominence describes the author's emphasis or focus above the sentence level and is signaled by formal and semantic features which elevate a given feature or set apart content.[16] Clusters of emphatic features place the emphasis on one sentence over another and highlight clauses or clause complexes as being "main" or "central."[17] Prominent clauses are both highlighted by emphatic formal

---

[15] One of the more confusing aspects of prominence or "emphasis" for the Greek student is to find that commentators will correctly say that an element is emphatic (or marked) in the Greek, but there are so many features identified as emphatic that it is difficult to adjudicate between the prominent features or use the information in any kind of coherent interpretation. The fact is, every phrase, sentence and passage is contoured with features that create emphasis and focus, but in my methodology, prominence is reserved for the author's emphasis or focus above the sentence level in a way that acknowledges this contouring but focuses on the central sentences that contribute to and form the global patterns.

[16] Note that this definition carefully allows a broad understanding of prominence that goes beyond how emphasis or focus functions in the structure of a discourse, and can also refer to, for example, the motivated use of a marked grammatical feature at the discourse level that communicates meaning. See M. A. K. Halliday, "Linguistic Function and Literary Style: An Enquiry into the Language of William Golding's 'The Inheritors,'" in *Literary Style: A Symposium*, ed. Seymor Chatman (Oxford University Press, 1971), 330–368.

[17] For a further description of prominence, see Cynthia Long Westfall, "A Method for the Analysis of Prominence in Hellenistic Greek," in *The Linguist as Pedagogue: Trends in the*

features and form a semantic relationship with the rest of the passage so that they will reflect the purpose of the unit. The formal features include marked choices and variation in grammar, the use of discourse markers, conjunctions, word order, deixis, the use of emphatic words or phrases and repetition. Semantic prominence involves devices such as the use of extra words, vividness, crowding the stage, the use of certain figures or concepts that the author assumes are of particular interest to the readers, and the use of logical relationships that distinguish between mainline material and support material. Authors highlight the clauses that are central with clusters of these features that create "zones of turbulence."[18] One clause will therefore be more prominent in a paragraph or section than another on the basis of the confluence of these emphatic indicators.

Message of the Passage

In this study, the relationship between the parts and the whole is deferred to the final description of the macrostructure of Hebrews. Instead, the analysis of each passage will conclude with a more transparent explanation of how cohesion, determination of topic and prominence indicate the message that the passage contributes to the whole. In one sense, this step is redundant because the location of the central clause through the analysis of prominence will usually be the message that the author is stressing and bringing to the readers' attention through various strategies. However, the history of interpretation of Hebrews indicates the necessity of giving a more cogent explanation of how the central clauses that are prominent in each passage are precisely related to the topic of the passage to which they are connected through cohesion patterns.

Procedure for Demonstrating the Analysis of the Microstructure

The application of the four steps will be demonstrated by working through Hebrews 1:1–4:16 as a sample, passage by passage, and summarizing the findings of each step. Sub-headings are given for each passage that signal the content/message, but it must be stressed that in the actual analysis, the passage was established in each case by the patterns of cohesion apart from any notions of topic or content. Once the passage was determined it established a domain to determine the topic, prominence and message. The limited sample should be

---

Teaching and Linguistic Analysis of the Greek New Testament, ed. Stanley E. Porter and Matthew B. O'Donnell (Sheffield Phoenix Press, 2009), 75–94.

[18] "Zones of turbulence" is a term introduced by Robert E. Longacre, *The Grammar of Discourse*, 2nd ed. (Plenum Press, 1996), 38.

adequate to display how the entire discourse was analyzed, which in turn provided the data to build the macrostructure of the text.

The Macrostructure of Hebrews: A Mental Representation of the Text

In *A Discourse Analysis of the Letter to the Hebrews,* as mentioned above, my fourth step was to establish the relationship of each passage with the rest of the discourse. As Brown and Yule have stated, "the Text creates its own context."[19] The co-text is the text that surrounds the passage, and the interpretation of any text in constrained by its co-text. The recognition of cohesive ties on the formal and semantic levels between a text and its co-text is a study of both the text's coherence and cohesion. It contributes directly to understanding the place of a passage in the general structure of a text and locating the text's global themes.

Once an analysis of the entire discourse was completed, the determination of the final design requires quite a bit more interpretation than the analysis of each passage. Yet the four steps that reflect the metafunctions are applied at the discourse level, and the findings in each passage provide the data. Patterns of cohesion must be analyzed at the discourse level—such as the patterns of repetition of entities, vocabulary and formal features. Central discourse themes are established from the consideration of the topics of each passage and the cohesion patterns of repetition. The most prominent or central sentences of each passage must be collocated and their relative prominence evaluated and established at the discourse level. Summarizing the final design can be an art, but the final design must correspond to the data. The final section of this paper provides a mental representation of the entire text.

Analysis of the Microstructures of Hebrews

Let's Pay Attention to the Message of God's Ultimate Messenger (1:1–2:4)

Textual Cohesion of 1:1–2:4

Hebrews 1:1–2:4 contains three subunits that are clearly defined by their grammatical patterns. The point of departure of the discourse in 1:1–4 consists of a periodic sentence. It is followed by a well-defined span of quotations from the LXX in 1:5–14, and then another periodic sentence in 2:1–4. The conjunctions that join the subunits at 1:5 and 2:1 signal their logical relationships. The span of quotations in 1:5–14 is joined with a γάρ which indicates that they are support

---

[19] Brown and Yule, *Discourse Analysis*, 50.

material for 1:1–4. The periodic sentence in 2:1–4 is introduced with διὰ τοῦτο, which is consistent with a conclusion based on preceding grounds. An analysis of the lexical patterns indicates an unusually high level of cohesion between the three parts: there are three participant chains in each unit (God, the Son, and angels/messengers) that interact with the process chain of speech in all three units. Furthermore, the process of speech is discontinued in 2:5. Therefore, the cohesion patterns in the grammar, the conjunctions and the lexis establish 1:1–2:4 as the first unit or domain in which we may determine a topic and plot the contours of prominence.

Topic of 1:1–2:4

To determine the topic of 1:1–2:4, we are again assisted by the three primary participant chains: God is a subject/actor in each subunit, who interacts with the Son and/or messengers (i.e., angels) through the process chain of speech. They are identified as God's messengers in 1:1–2, 4; 2:2. The function of angels as God's messengers is constrained in 1:1 and 2:2 to refer to one of the various ways and means with which God has spoken to the ancestors. God's communication to and through the Son is grammatically the focus (1:1, 2:1), and is in contrast with God's communication to angels/messengers in each subunit. The topic may be summarized as: *the Son is God's ultimate messenger*, which is explicit in the point of departure in the finite clause of the opening periodic sentence in 1:2: in these last days God has spoken to us through his Son. This topic accounts for all of the text in 1:1–2:4.

Prominence in 1:1–2:4

While the point of departure in 1:1–4 is elegant and emphatically places the focus on the Son, the finite verb clause in 2:1 is the most prominent clause in the unit.[20] The function of the conclusion signaled by διὰ τοῦτο is prominent, and there is an accumulation of marked constructions and a 'crowded stage' in 2:2–4 (author and recipients, angels, Jesus, eyewitnesses/apostles and God). Furthermore, the

---

[20] Significantly, Cotterell and Turner agree in their linguistics-based analysis: "The most prominent element in 2.1–4 is the *Exhortation*. Everything else in the paragraph turns around this. But the 'therefore' with which 2.1 commences shows that chapter 1 is already furnishing other grounds for the exhortation in this paragraph. A similar analysis of the first chapter would show its most prominent nucleus to be the statement that God has finally spoken in a Son (1.2) who is supreme over the angels (2.4). This, then, provides the *grounds* for the *exhortation* to hold all the more firmly to what was announced by the Son, rather than to what was merely announced through angels." Peter Cotterell and Max Turner, *Linguistics and Biblical Interpretation* (InterVarsity Press, 1989), 221.

information given in 2:1, as well as its support material in 2:2–4, gives the point of the topic and the purpose of the comparison with angels: therefore, we must pay greater attention to what the Son declared to us.[21]

Message of 1:1–2:4

The message that emerges from the analysis of the combination of topic and prominence of the passage is not the superiority of Christ per se, nor any threat from angels or Judaism, but the prominent exhortation in 2:1 which accounts for the material in each of the three subunits: Let's hang on to the message/confession that we received from Jesus. The Son is God's ultimate messenger in 1:1–4. The point of the contrast with angels in 1:5–14 is made explicit in 2:2: if the message of angels was important, how much more so is the message from the Son. This message is confirmed with repetition through paraphrase in 4:11 and 10:22: the point of departure for the discourse sets the stage for the first unit, and the first unit sets the stage for the first section of the discourse. The author will use this as grounds for 3:1: the author's description of Jesus as God's ultimate messenger grounds the command to think of Jesus as the ultimate apostle of the faith. The structure of the unit may be summarized as follows:

Point of departure: God has ultimately spoken through his Son (1:1–4)
Subunit: The Son is greater than God's previous messengers (1:5–14)
Conclusion: Let's hold on to the things we have heard from the Son (2:1–4)

Jesus Identified with Humanity to Become our High Priest (2:5–18)

Cohesion of 2:5–18

Discourse markers and cohesion patterns form three subunits in 2:5–9, 2:10–13 and 2:14–18 into one unit. The unit is framed by the exhortation in 2:1–4 with the shift in 2:5 and the command in 3:1, which contains a pivotal shift. The first subunit in 2:5–9 contains a quotation of LXX Ps 8:5–7 with its interpretation. It is introduced with a contrastive δέ and a spatial shift from Jesus' enthronement above the angels to his incarnation below the angels. The interpretation of the quotation is signaled in 2:8b as support material with γάρ, but moves quickly to an emphatic declaration in v. 9, in which Jesus is introduced as the fulfillment of

---

[21] In contrast, Swetnam finds a second "announcement of the theme" in 2:3a–4 in James Swetnam, "Form and Content in Hebrews 1–6," *Bib* 53 (1972): 368–85; see 374. But the information in 2:3a–4 is support material. By definition, an announcement should be the most prominent sentence in the near co-text in order to signal the readers, as is the case in 3:1.

the references to humanity in the psalm quoted in 2:8–9: he was made lower than the angels in his suffering and death which are the means of his enthronement. The interpretation of Ps 8 is discontinued in 2:10, but the following subunit in 2:10–13 is signaled as support material with γάρ, and forms cohesive ties with Jesus in 2:9: his suffering and his kinship with humanity is supported by a string of quotations (LXX Ps 22:22; Is 8:17, 18). The final subunit in 2:14–18 is joined with ἐπεὶ οὖν, which signals a summary of Jesus' unity with humanity in his physical nature (flesh, blood and death), together with a conclusion marked with ὅθεν in 2:17. His unity/identification with humanity qualifies him to be a merciful and faithful high priest.

Topic of 2:5–18

The topic of 2:5–18 is Jesus' identification with humanity, which is signaled in all three subunits. In contrast to the angels (2:5), it is humanity that God has destined to rule the world to come, as is shown from the author's quotation of LXX Ps 2:8–9.[22] However, the author points out that we do not yet see this destiny fulfilled for humanity (2:8). Rather, we see that Jesus, who was made to identify with humanity's lower position through his suffering and death, fulfilled human destiny when he was crowned with glory and honor (2:9). In 2:10–13, the author argues that Jesus' identification with humanity by suffering is fitting theologically and biblically. Finally, in 2:14–18, he summarizes that Jesus shared death and suffering with humanity in order to become a merciful and faithful high priest, which is new information.

Prominence in 2:5–18

The patterns of prominence follow the development of the topic of Jesus' identification with humanity. The introduction of Jesus in 2:9 is most heavily

---

[22] The reference to humanity (ἄνθρωπος, υἱὸς ἀνθρώπου) entails a double understanding of the way the author utilizes the psalm, almost like a pun. It is common to assume that every reference to the "son of man" in the NT must be understood as a messianic title, but υἱὸς ἀνθρώπου was a common idiom for "human being" in Greek and is its meaning in the LXX. The author uses it both ways with rhetorical skill. To make sense of the author's line of argument, first it should be read with the traditional Jewish understanding as a reference to humanity and human destiny, then in v. 9 as applied to Jesus, as was common in the Christian tradition. See Craig Blomberg, "'But We See Jesus': The Relationship between the Son of Man in Hebrews 2:6 and Verse 9 and the Implications for English Translations," in *A Cloud of Witnesses: The Theology of Hebrews in Its Ancient Contexts*, ed. Richard Bauckham et al. (T&T Clark, 2008), 88–99. For further discussion of "son of man" see Cynthia Long Westfall, "The Human One: A Controversial CEB Translation Choice," *Open Theology* 2 (2016): 895–906.

marked with grammatical, lexical and interpersonal patterns and places emphasis on the introduction of the topic: Jesus as the fulfillment of LXX Ps 2:8–9.[23]
This is the first time that the name of Jesus is mentioned in Hebrews, which resolves a tension—the reader has been waiting to hear his name. The summary
and conclusion of the unit in 2:17–18 are clearly but moderately prominent in
comparison to the immediate context (2:9 and 3:1) but provide new information
that is certainly salient (engages the interest of the reader): the author makes the
surprising and unexpected point that Jesus was made to identify with humanity
to become a high priest to make atonement, whose human experience helps the
readers in their time of need. But the unit is building in prominence to climax in
3:1 with a more marked conclusion to both units (1:1–2:4; 2:5–18).

Message of 2:5–18

The point of 2:5–18 is the conclusion in the finite verb clause of 2:17: that Jesus was made a high priest on the basis of his identification with humanity. This
passage provides the grounds for the command in 3:1 to think of Jesus as the high
priest of our confession in the same way that 1:1–2:4 provides the grounds for the
command in 3:1 to think of Jesus as our apostle. The identity of the readers as
partners with Jesus in his heavenly calling in 3:1 is also introduced explicitly in
this passage (2:10), and in his partnering (κεκοινώνηκεν) with humanity in 2:14, so
that the identity of the readers also flows out of Jesus' identification with humanity. He will shift the focus to this partnership specifically in 3:1–6. The structure of the unit may be summarized as follows:

> Point of departure: Jesus' exalted position is based on his humanity (2:5–9)
> Subunit: Jesus is fully identified with believers (2:10–13)
> Conclusion: Jesus identified with humanity to become a merciful and faithful
> high priest (2:14–18)

Pivotal Summary and Discourse Orientation in 3:1

Though the command to the readers in 3:1–2 forms a subunit as a grammatical
sentence, there is a very interesting phenomenon. The command in 3:1 is marked
with ὅθεν which is consistent with a conclusion. The command itself forms
strong cohesive ties with the topic of 1:1–2:4 (Jesus is an apostle in the sense of

---

[23] The prominence in 2:8c–9 should be apparent in English translation, but for a breakdown of the formal features that mark 2:9 in the Greek, see the analysis of prominence in
Westfall, *Hebrews*, 106–7.

being God's ultimate messenger),[24] the message of 2:5–18 (Jesus is a high priest), and emphatically fronts the identity of the readers as holy partners in Jesus' calling (e.g., 2:10 in which he is bringing many sons and daughters to "glory").[25] This indicates that 3:1 concludes both units with a command to think about Jesus' identity with two titles (apostle and high priest) and emphasizes the readers' identity as partners in Jesus' calling. However, the dependent participial phrase in 3:2 has no cohesive ties with the previous text other than the tie of Jesus who must be the grammatical subject of the participle ὄντα. Rather, v. 2 unambiguously introduces 3:3–6 and thus forms a cohesive unit with the following text, which clearly has a different topic. Much ink has been spilled arguing about whether 3:1 goes with 1:1–2:18, or with 3:2–6.[26] The question is where one should place "the break." I want to emphasize that this is a translation question that is driven by an intuitive European linguistic understanding of what constitutes a paragraph and the necessity of locating a break. The author does not choose to make a break, but rather he uses a pivotal transition which maintains cohesion and resists division. This characterizes the author's style, and can already be detected in 2:5, where angels are used in the transition to the new unit, but entails an explicit spatial shift from Jesus' high status above the angels to a lower status in which he is below the angels in the quotation (2:7) and the interpretation of the psalm (2:9).[27]

---

[24] The title "apostle" in 3:1 has been a conundrum for both readers and commentators. It is often confused with the NT technical term used for the twelve disciples and one who possesses the spiritual gift in the Pauline epistles. However, the application of the technical term to Jesus has no precedent in the NT and does not discernably contribute to the argument, but rather distracts and confuses. On the other hand, if ἀπόστολον is understood in its more generic sense as a messenger as it occurs in Second Temple and Hellenist literature (see BDAG 122), it makes sense in the context of the discourse. The numerous references to God's messengers and the emphatic identification of Jesus as one whom God spoke through in these last days provide the necessary constraint. Consequently, ἀπόστολον forms strong cohesive ties with the topic of 1:1–2:4, and particularly the first finite verb clause of the letter in 1:2. See Westfall, *Hebrews*, 112–13.

[25] If Jesus shares with humanity, those whom he leads will have a partnership (μέτοχοι) in his calling/destiny/glory.

[26] See Westfall, *Hebrews*, 115 for scholars who argue that 3:1 "looks backward" (a minority position notwithstanding the inferential conjunction ὅθεν), and those who argue that 3:1 "looks forward" (based on the content of 3:2–6).

[27] The cohesive ties formed by the refences to angels have led some with European linguistic assumptions to mistakenly assume that Jesus' superiority to angels is a topic that unifies 1:5–14 and 2:5–18, but that causes 2:1–4 to be off topic and does not fit the contrast between the two passages. The comparison with angels is quickly backgrounded in 2:5–18, and superiority is not the point. Others want to talk about the author using "stitch words" to tie the "breaks" between units together. The linguistic theory of cohesion is a more powerful explanatory tool

Therefore, the function of 3:1 as a conclusion to 1:1–2:18 focuses the readers' attention on their own identity and the two identities for Jesus that have been established in the preceding two units:

1:1–2:4	Think about Jesus as our apostle
2:5–18	Think about Jesus as the high priest of our confession
3:1	You (holy siblings) are partners in Jesus' heavenly calling

Most are aware that the high priesthood of Jesus is the dominant topic of the material in the center of the discourse (4:14–10:19), and I have demonstrated that the point of departure is Jesus as a messenger/apostle (1:1–2:4). Note that the identity of Jesus as high priest highlights and arguably subsumes the relationship of this title to Jesus' message/confession, and his high priesthood is not mentioned again until 4:14 so that the author keeps the focus on Jesus as a messenger until 4:14. In the final third of the book (10:24–13:25), the focus is on believers whereas Jesus is notably backgrounded (missing until 12:2).[28] I will argue in the macrostructure section that 3:1 is discourse deixis in which the author signals the readers on how to follow the structure and argument of the discourse.

We are Jesus' Partners/House (3:1–6)

In the macrostructure, I will argue that 3:1–4:16 form the second unit in the first section (1:1–4:16). However, for this paper's strategy, I will use a more inductive approach to the analysis that will lead us to that conclusion, subunit by subunit.

Cohesion in 3:1–6

This unit is determined by high level of cohesion in vv. 2–6 created by the repetition of "house" (οἶκος repeated 6x) which consists of a correlation between two houses, one of which includes the readers (hopefully) and the other being the wilderness generation. There is also a correlation between the identity chains of Jesus and Moses, introduced in 3:2. The parallels in the correlation (in which Jesus is like Moses) involve the relationship of Moses and Jesus respectively to their "house."[29]

---

of the author's use of repetition and recognizing cohesive ties leads us to appreciate the author's development of a virtually seamless structure.

[28] The many scholars who argue that Jesus' high priesthood is the theme of the epistle fail to convincingly explain the final three and a half chapters, let alone the first and second person exhortations that dominate the discourse.

[29] The correlation (ὡς καὶ Μωυσῆς emphasizes how Jesus is *like* Moses) is the focus in 3:2, and yet the topic and message is often mistakenly identified as "Jesus is superior to Moses," which is reflected in the subheadings of translations such as the NIV. However, Jesus' superiority

There are also contrasts in the honor that each should receive from their house as well as their respective identity in relationship to the houses. But, as in 2:1–4, the contrasts serve to strengthen the readers' response to the exhortation in 2:7—how much more is expected of Jesus' house! The direct correlation between Jesus and Moses is discontinued in 3:7, though the correlation between the houses provides the grounds for 3:7–19 (signaled by διό) and the exhortation in 4:1.

Topic of 3:1–6

The fact that οἶκος is reiterated so many times without pronominalization highlights "house," reflects its semantic weight and therefore is the key to the topic. In addition, the author places himself and the readers in the same category as "house" at the endpoint of the passage in 3:6b, in such a way that it defines the readers' partnership in 3:1, which is the fronted theme and point of departure. Therefore, the topic is the readers' partnership with Jesus, which is redefined as "house" and described through a correlation of Jesus' house with Moses' house. It accounts for the entire passage.

Prominence in 3:1–6

The most prominent point in the passage is 3:1, not only because of numerous formal indicators of prominence, but also because of its semantic relationship with the rest of the discourse. The author addresses the readers directly for the first time with the nominative of direct address. The description of the readers and Jesus is salient by definition, but the prominence is increased by the author's piling on of "extra words" to describe the readers and Jesus. The command to "think intently" creates further interpersonal involvement with information that could have been presented as a proposition. The identities of the readers and Jesus introduced in 3:1 are elaborated in 3:2–6. But in addition, 3:1 provides a summary for the first two chapters and we will see that it introduces the new topic for the rest of the section. But the passage is also concluded prominently in 3:6b by the return to direct references to himself and readers (1st person plural pronoun and verbs) in a restatement of the partnership, consistent with a conclusion of the comparison.

Message of 3:1–6

While the topic is the readers' partnership with Jesus (redefined as his "house"), the primary message is the establishment of an analogy between two

---

cannot account for the content, and scholars must argue for a deviation in 3:4! See William Lane, *Hebrews 1–8*, WBC 47A (Word, 1991), 72.

houses: the readers and the Israelites of the wilderness generation. But the obligation of Jesus' house to honor Jesus (holding on to confidence and hope) is much greater than the obligation of Moses' house to honor Moses. This analogy provides the grounds for the exhortations in 3:7–4:1, and the argument about the rest in 4:1–10. Therefore, 3:1–6 will be treated as a subunit that provides the point of departure for the larger unit.

Do Not Harden Your Hearts to Jesus' Voice (3:7–19)

Cohesion in 3:7–19

The subunit is framed by a quotation of LXX Ps 94:7–11 and the well-defined unit in 4:1–10. The unity of this section is not challenged in scholarship, though its relationship to 3:1–6 is definitely an issue.[30]

Topic in 3:7–19

The topic of this subunit is constrained by 3:1–6: the comparison between Jesus' relationship with his house and Moses' relationship with his house lays the groundwork to draw a further correlation or comparison between the houses. The readers and the Israelites are dominant identity chains that interact with the identity chains Jesus, God and Moses.[31] The process chain of hearing remains active from 1:1–2:4, 3:1 which defines the required response to the messenger in these last days—Jesus our apostle (1:1, 3:1), and the partnership of the readers with Jesus from 3:6 is what is highlighted and rephrased in 3:14: we are his partners if we hold on to the confidence to the end. The constraint of 3:1–6 similarly indicates that it is Jesus who the author presents as our apostle who is continually speaking on behalf of God, and his voice must not be resisted (cf. 12:25–27 for a recapitulation). The primary process chain is the metaphor of "hardening the heart," which is repeated and paraphrased by words from semantic domains such as rebellion (L-N 39.40), sin (L-N 88.118) and the opposite of trust or reliance (L-N 31.89), but the author represents all of them as antonyms to "hearing" as in LXX

---

[30] Those who argue a "Moses theme" in 3:1–6 are at a loss to explain the supposed logical leap in 3:7. As Paul Ellingworth observes, 3:7 "does not follow smoothly on 3:6" (*The Epistle to the Hebrews: A Commentary on the Greek Text*, NIGTC [Eerdmans, 1981], 213). Thus, the identification of "Jesus' superiority over Moses" creates incoherence in both the short passage itself and with the context of the passage, which is a sure sign that the topic has been misidentified.

[31] The assertion that Jesus and God are not dominant identity chains may seem counterintuitive, but one can confirm it by simply counting the references to subjects/actors. See my analysis of the formal features in Westfall, *Hebrews*, 121–122.

Ps 94.[32] The topic continues to be the readers' partnership with Jesus which must be expressed by hearing his voice, the alternative to hardening their hearts.

Prominence in 3:7–19

Normally, a quotation is marked as support material with γάρ which is not prominent by definition. However, in this case, 3:7–8 is unusually marked as high level material with διό. The prohibition in v. 8, "do not harden your hearts," is emphatically and directly applied to the readers and repeated. The triad of commands in vv. 8, 12 and 13 form a prominent span in which vv. 12 and 13 develop the command in v. 8 not to harden their hearts. Nevertheless, the rhetorical questions in vv. 16–18 also create interactive involvement with the readers, and place prominence on the destination of the unit, which is marked with the first person plural and provides a summary: we see that the wilderness generation failed to enter "the rest" because of unbelief. This leads to the prominent exhortation in 4:1, which is marked as a conclusion and provides the point of the correlation of the houses.

Message in 3:7–19

In 3:1–6, the author established that the readers belong to Jesus' house in the same way as the Israelites belonged to Moses' house. The message is that the readers are responsible to respond to Jesus' voice just as the Israelites were responsible to listen to God's word through Moses—the author stresses that they face the same consequences if they disobey. However, this correlation between the two houses grounds the exhortation in 4:1, which is marked as a conclusion with οὖν, and it may be argued that 4:1 is the central sentence that functions as a conclusion and provides the message for 3:7–19. The structure of 3:1–4:1 may be summarized as follows:

Point of departure: Jesus' house corresponds to Moses' house (3:1–6)
Subunit: Do not harden your hearts to Jesus' voice like the Israelites (3:7–18)
Conclusion: Let's make sure that no one fails to enter the rest (4:1)

Pivotal Conclusion and Point of Departure in 4:1

In another surprise move, the author exhorts the readers with a conclusion marked by οὖν that is based on the content of the psalm and the correlations be-

---

[32] For understanding how an author may create semantic domains and his/her own categories by "placing words in the same pile," see Cynthia Long Westfall, "Blessed Be the Ties That Bind: Semantic Domains and Cohesive Chains in Hebrews 1.1–2.4 And 12.5–8," *JGRChJ* 6 (2009): 203–205.

tween the readers and the Israelites. He exhorts them with a hortatory subjunctive to make sure that no one misses "the rest" (let's be afraid in case anyone seems to fall short). He indicates that when they hear and respond to Jesus' voice, the readers have the same opportunity and destination of rest that the Israelites had (which clearly raises questions that the author will answer in 4:2–10). The exhortation therefore provides a conclusion to 3:7–18 but it also provides a seamless transition to the following unit in 4:1–16, in which he justifies his conclusion in 4:1 and provides a "proof" that the rest is still open, and concludes with a triple exhortation that repeats the main themes of the discourse.

There is a Rest/Let's Enter It (4:1–10)

Cohesion in 4:1–10

The unit is framed by the hortatory subjunctive exhortation in 4:1 and the paraphrase or repetition of that exhortation in 4:11. The exhortation in 4:1 is supported by an indicative span that consists of a structured defense or a proof of the premise that the rest is still open. The unity of 4:1–10 is virtually undisputed since it is characterized by an unusually high level of lexical and semantic cohesion.

Topic of 4:1–10

The correlation between the readers and the Israelites continues in 4:1–10. There is a strong semantic chain in which the readers and Israelites are the recipients of preaching and the subjects of hearing. However, the dominant topic is the entrance to God's rest, which should be the result of hearing the preaching. In 4:1, the author teasingly argues, "Since the promise of entering his rest remains..." and bases the exhortations in 4:1 and 4:11 on that assumption. This is a proof after the statement of the assumption that the rest is still open—the readers can still enter God's rest when they respond in faith to the apostle's message.

Prominence in 4:1–10

The most prominent element in 4:1–10 is the exhortation in 4:1 in terms of its position, support and development by the preceding and following discourse, its emphatic marking with οὖν and its marked grammar. The restatement of 4:1 in v. 11 significantly builds its prominence. The proof in 4:2–10 is support material, with some emphasis in vv. 2–3.

Message in 4:1–10

The message to enter the rest is the prominent exhortation which the rest of the unit supports. This message accounts for all the material in the unit and is restated in 4:11: let's be afraid in case anyone seems to fall short of the rest. It can be summarized together with v. 11 as "let's enter the rest," and can be considered the destination of the combined units of 3:1–6 and 3:7–19. While there may be interpretive and logical problems, the structure of the passage is quite simple as follows:

> Point of departure: Let's make sure that no one falls short of the rest (4:1)
> Subunit: There is a rest still open for the people of God (4:2–10)

Pivotal Section Conclusion and Point of Departure for Central Section in 4:11–16

Cohesion of 4:11–16

Commentaries recognize that the hortatory subjunctive in 4:11 restates 4:1, and therefore it must be linked to 4:1–10.[33] However, structural and functional unity bind the three hortatory subjunctive exhortations in 4:11–16:

> Therefore, let's make every effort to enter the rest (4:11)
> Therefore, let's hold fast to our confession (4:14)
> Therefore, let's draw near to the throne of grace (4:16)

They occur in close proximity forming a triad that is reinforced with repetition of features and grammatical patterns that would particularly hang together with rhetorical impact when read out loud. Therefore, there is a very high level of formal cohesion that binds 4:11–16 into a unit. However, there is little overt lexical cohesion within the unit except for the first-person plural span referring to the identity chain of the author and readers that binds the passage together in opposition to the immediate contexts.

On the other hand, there is high lexical and semantic cohesion between the passage and the rest of the discourse, particularly between the first two exhortations and the preceding discourse and the third exhortation and the central section. The first exhortation for "us" to enter the rest together with the support material on the nature of the word of God (4:11–13) summarizes or recapitulates the

---

[33] The exhortations in 4:1 and 4:11 are often considered to form an inclusio (a closed unit), while 4:14–15 obviously initiates the topic of high priesthood. However, that strands 4:12–13 outside of any structure, and the hortatory subjunctive to draw near to the throne of grace in 4:16 immediately appears to veer off the topic of Jesus' high priesthood.

message in 3:1–4:10, repeating the exhortation in 4:1.[34] The second exhortation in 4:14–15 summarizes or recapitulates 1:1–2:18. The exhortation repeats or paraphrases the exhortation in 2:1–4 for "us" to hang on to the confession or message we received from Jesus. Its support material, which is given as the reason to hang on to the confession, summarizes and reactivates the high priesthood of Jesus introduced in 2:5–18. Finally, the third exhortation provides new information about "us" drawing near to the throne of grace. This is the point of departure for the central section, is restated in its conclusion in 10:19–22, and occurs within the section.

Topic of 4:11–16

The topic of 4:11–16 is best described as having a discourse level textual function. It is a summary of commands that paraphrase three discourse themes that may be described as physiological behavior patterns that are spatial and involve the body: move forward, hold on, draw near. The triad is restated in 10:19–25 (stimulating each other to love and good works in 10:25 replaces making sure that no one misses entering the rest in 4:11 to represent movement forward). We will see in the discussion on the macrostructure that these three themes account for the entire discourse with the possible exception of the formal epistolary closing in 13:17–25.

Prominence in 4:11–16

Each of the three exhortations are prominent, with marked grammatical features, emphatic discourse markers (three uses of οὖν!), salience and formal parallelism. Even the parts marked as support material are so semantically salient that some scholars think that they are the focus. The effect is cumulative, so that this unit is the most prominent part of the discourse so far.

Message of 4:11–16

The three exhortations represent topic sentences that function at the global level of the discourse. The unit of 4:11–16 is something like a thesis statement, though its location in the discourse does not follow Western expectation for composition. This demonstrates there is a pattern in which the message of Hebrews is

---

[34] That exhortation is supported by a description of the word of God in 4:12–13, which has been established as the motivation to enter the rest (3:7, 15; 4:2, 7), and has also been the continual focus since 1:1 in Jesus as God's messenger/apostle of what we have heard (2:1–4), our confession (3:1), and now the call to enter the rest.

given in the exhortations, particularly the exhortations utilizing the first plural (usually hortatory subjunctives), whereas the material that is often referred to as the "exposition" or teaching material is consistently marked as support material for the exhortations. Another pattern that has been repeated three times is that major transitions are accomplished with pivotal transitions that both conclude or summarize the preceding material and introduce the following material seamlessly so that there are not the kind of "breaks" in the discourse that we need to have in our English translations.

The analysis above of Hebrews 1:1–4:16 demonstrates the DA methodology and significantly lays the groundwork for the following description of the macro-structure of the discourse.[35]

Macrostructure of Hebrews: A Mental Representation of Hebrews

The following is the concluding mental representation of Hebrews, based on the application of SFL-based methodology. I will show the features that indicate the mental representation of the discourse. Then I will show an outline of how the parts in Hebrews relate to the whole book in a coherent design that is memorable.

Discourse Deixis in 3:1: Three Discourse Topics

The first major discourse feature occurs in 3:1. Hebrews begins with two descriptions of Jesus as God's messenger and our high priest. There is nothing particularly unusual about the first description of Jesus as God's ultimate spokesperson (1:1–2:4). However, there must have been something unusual about the second description of Jesus as our high priest (2:5–18) because later on, the author will offer an extensive proof of the validity of the description (5:1–10:25).

The command in 3:1 concludes the two units in 1:1–2:18, creating a subsection by combining them into one statement. The author commands the readers to think of Jesus in terms of the two roles of apostle (which is related to the function of Jesus as messenger) and high priest in conjunction, but at this point in the discourse, he presents the function of apostleship and messenger as primary and places the high priesthood of Jesus in a supportive role—he is portrayed as the high priest of the message, so that the focus on message and messenger in the first section is not lost. Later in the central section Jesus' high priesthood will be the primary focus which the message supports.

The command in 3:1 not only concludes and combines the first two units, but

---

[35] For my analysis of the rest of the microstructures of Hebrews, see my *Discourse Analysis of the Letter to the Hebrews*, 140–296.

it is also discourse deixis and staging, indicating the organization and themes of the discourse by stepping outside of the structure.

The three sections of the discourse correspond with the three topics introduced in 3:1:

1:1–4:16	Consider Jesus as our apostle
4:11–10:25	Consider Jesus as our high priest
10:19–13:25	You are partners in Jesus' heavenly calling

Therefore, the author is informing the readers about what they can expect in the following co-text.

The presentation of Jesus as God's ultimate messenger (1:1–2:4) and the preliminary basis of Jesus' priesthood in 2:5-18 respectively ground the application of the titles of apostle and priest to Jesus. While the first unit of the discourse exhorts the readers to "hang on" to the content of the confession of their faith, which was given by Jesus in the past, the rest of the first section is concerned with a second aspect of Jesus' apostleship, which is his current communication to his people. In 3:1–4:10, the author presents Jesus as still speaking (cf. 12:24–25), and his people choose either to resist him and harden their hearts, or to respond in faith and enter his rest.

After 10:18, the discourse focus shifts from Jesus as the primary figure to the recipients, and works out the implications of Jesus' priesthood and secondarily his apostleship in terms of the readers' lives and responsibilities. The readers share in Jesus' heavenly calling as priests (10:18–22) and their lives are reframed as a ministry of worship and service (12:28–29), where love and good works are the sacrifices that they offer (13:1–16). Their location is with Jesus and with all of God's heavenly hosts and the believers from the past (12:18–24), and their struggles are a festival competition that takes place in heavenly Jerusalem (12:1–17, supported by 10:26–11:40).

Discourse Peaks in 4:11–16 and 10:19–25 and the Tripartite Structure & Message

The tripartite division of Hebrews is formally based on the two thematic discourse peaks in 4:11–16 and 10:19–25, which are formed by triads of hortatory subjunctives. The topic structure of the three sections is indicated by discourse deixis in 3:1, which states the discourse topics of Jesus as an apostle/messenger (1:1–4:16), Jesus as a high priest (4:11–10:25), and the partnership of the readers with Jesus (10:19–13:25). The discourse topic structure is supported by the local topic structure and semantic patterns in the units of each of the sections.

The most marked relationship between 4:11–16 and the co-text is the formal and semantic parallels that are formed with 10:19–25.[36]

4:11–16	10:19–25
Σπουδάσωμεν ... εἰσελθεῖν	προσερχώμεθα
κρατῶμεν τῆς ὁμολογίας	κατέχωμεν τὴν ὁμολογίαν
προσερχώμεθα ... τῷ θρόνῳ	κατανοῶμεν ἀλλήλους εἰς παροξυσμὸν

Figure 17.1: Semantic Parallels between Hebrews 4:11–16 and 10:19–25

The connection between 4:11 and 10:24–25 is less transparent, but that is because of the metaphoric nature of the language of entering the rest in 4:11. The concerns that involve entering the rest have many parallels with the concerns of stimulating one another towards love and good works. There is an explicit pastoral concern in both commands that is absent from the other two and there is movement towards a goal. That is not to say that making sure that everyone enters the rest is fully synonymous with stimulating one another to love and good works, but that they significantly overlap semantically, so that practicing love and good works is part of the behaviour that is consistent with making an effort to enter the rest, as is pressing on to maturity and racing for the goal with perseverance.

The Repetition of the Hortatory Subjunctives and the Three Themes

The patterned use of the hortatory subjunctive occurs at major discourse shifts and functions as a transition from one unit to the next, so the hortatory subjunctives are both the destination and point of departure of the surrounding units— they tend to function as pivots for the units they join and thus belong to both units. Besides the triplets of hortatory subjunctives in 4:11–16 and 10:19–25, the central section contains only one hortatory subjunctive and one imperative in the main text (two imperatives occur in citations in 8:5 and 8:11). This is because the central section has a sustained argument that demonstrates Jesus' high priesthood. The argument spans five and one half chapters, and has its climactic destination in the hortatory subjunctive in 10:22, where the readers are exhorted to draw near to God on the basis of Jesus' high priesthood.

The indicative spans of text, often referred to as the "exposition" or "theological passages" are consistently signaled as support material with the conjunction

---

[36] Although Nauck did not include 4:11 as part of the parallel between these two passages, he bases his structure on an inclusio between 4:14–16 and 10:19–26 in W. Nauck, "Zum Aufbau des Hebräerbriefes" in *Judentum Unchristentum Kirche: Festschrift für Joachim Jeremias*, ed. Walther Eltester (Alfred Töpelmann, 1960), 203–204. Guthrie agrees with the connection in *Structure of Hebrews*, 17–19, 35, 114.

γάρ at the beginning of each indicative unit or span. The indicative passages support the hortatory subjunctives, or sometimes imperatives or volitional statements. This holds true, whether the indicative spans are relatively short or very long. When the indicative passages are processed as support material for the mainline hortatory subjunctives, the mainline material accounts for the indicative passages. However, if the indicative passages are treated as mainline material, much of the so-called exhortation passages appear to be off-topic deviations.

The hortatory subjunctives are consistently signaled with inferential conjunctions, such as οὖν, as prominent central sentences, summaries and backbone material in relationship to their co-text. When an indicative sentence is signaled with οὖν or another inferential conjunction such as ὅθεν, it is a central sentence in an indicative span, but it does not display high prominence or thematic persistence that is characteristic of the hortatory subjunctives and certain imperatives. Its semantic domain and its domain of prominence is local, though it may contain a motif that is picked up later—often in the hortatory subjunctive summarizing conclusions. The prominence of any given indicative clause is significantly lower than the hortatory subjunctive that it is associated with.

The topics do not determine the message of the text. Rather, they support the message of the text, which the Hebrews author generally places at the end of the passage and marks with an inferential conjunction. The message or thesis is carried by the formulaic occurrence of the hortatory subjunctive (plus the first-person plural command in 2:1).

LET'S HOLD ON	LET'S GO FORWARD	LET'S DRAW NEAR
2:4 It is necessary for us to pay attention to the things we hear	4:1 Let's be afraid that one of you may fall short of the rest	4:16 Let's draw near to the throne of grace
4:14 Let's hold on to our confession	4:11 Let's make every effort to enter the rest	10:22 Let's go into the Holy of Holies
10:23 Let's hold on to the confession of our hope	6:1 Let's press on to maturity	12:28 Let's have grace and let's worship/serve God as priests
	10:25 Let's consider how to stimulate each other to love and good works	13:12 Let's go to Jesus outside of the camp
	12:1 Let's run the race	

Figure 17.2: Formulaic Occurrences of the Hortatory Subjunctive

The occurrence of the hortatory subjunctive involves thematic repetition so that each occurrence is linked to one of three themes: "let's hold on to the confession," "let's go forward spiritually," and "let's draw near to God." The themes "let's hold on to the confession" and "let's draw near to God" are fairly easy to recognize, but the theme "let's move forward spiritually" is paraphrased throughout the discourse with a variety of metaphors that combine the two concepts of pursuing a goal with pastoral service. The last hortatory subjunctive in 13:15 is difficult to categorize, because it incorporates all three of the themes: "Let's continually offer up a sacrifice of praise to God, that is, the fruit of lips that confess his name. Do not neglect to do good and to share what you have, for such sacrifices are pleasing to God." The themes of accessing God's presence, confession and doing good and possibly love (which were identified as spiritual goals in 10:24) are wrapped together in a discourse summary that depicts the believers' priesthood.

Climax of the Discourse in 12:1–29

The climax of the discourse is in ch. 12, where the author of Hebrews has reframed the believers' daily existence as located in the Holy of Holies in the sanctuary in heavenly Jerusalem where they access God and serve him. In their service, they maintain their confession and offer their praise and life actions as a sacrifice. The subunit in 12:19–28 describes the bigger picture of where the stadium and race in 12:1–18 is located. Through a series of contrasts, the author describes their location as heavenly Jerusalem, the context in which they are in the presence of all other faithful beings in a festival assembly and in which they access God. Their access to God is described as priestly service. The context and the description of access are consistent with the command to approach God in the Holy of Holies in 10:19–22. Therefore, the three discourse themes of hanging on to the confession, the pursuit of spiritual goals and drawing near to God are all placed in the context of the believers' location in heavenly Jerusalem. They must function in reference to their identities as athletes, celebrants and priests in God's kingdom.

This is the most prominent unit in the discourse. The most prominent point in the unit is its conclusion, which is the double hortatory subjunctive command to serve God as priests through grace in heavenly Jerusalem (12:28). The prominence of the rest of the unit exponentially contributes to the prominence of the conclusion. This is particularly evident in the rhetorical devices and the semantic prominence in the series of three contrasts and apocalyptic imagery in 12:18–27. The unit, and particularly the command to access God as priests is the climax of the discourse.

This unit forms bonds with the other units in the discourse. The presence of all of the faithful participants in the discourse is significant. The most striking relationship of the unit with the co-text is the confluence of the three discourse themes in the unit. In the climax, the two discourse themes of the pursuit of spiritual goals and hanging on to the confession support the third discourse theme of access to God. This comes as no surprise since it applies the new information that is given in the discourse (2:5–3:1; 5:1–10:18).

Conclusion of the Discourse 12:28–13:16

The conclusion of the discourse is 12:28–13:16, followed by personal commands and a blessing.[37] The focus is on the readers and their partnership with Christ as priests: what their responsibilities are and how they function in relationship to the "camp"—the social and religious structures of their society. After establishing the believers' priesthood and the context of their ministry, the author explains how they concretely apply the concept of the priesthood to their situation. They are to live every aspect of their lives as priests, so that all doing good and sharing is part of their priestly identity. Their nourishment is drawn from sound teaching and hanging on to the confession. Their priestly service is "outside the gates" of the spatial, social and religious structures; their ministry is not confirmed by place or position. Their entire existence has been reframed and given significance and dignity that is not dependent on circumstances.

How the Parts Relate to the Whole: An Outline

The outline of the discourse has certain limitations because the discourse is not compartmentalized, the mainline material tends to come at the end of the units, and the hortatory subjunctives are pivotal in nature. Most of the hortatory subjunctives provide a conclusion to the preceding unit and the point of departure for the subsequent unit. The author often marks the hortatory subjunctive unit as a conclusion with an inferential conjunction, but also expands the sentence with information that introduces the next unit, so that the hortatory subjunctive units look forwards and backwards. In the following outline, *these pivotal passages are included in both adjacent units*. In the following outline, hortatory subjunctives are also identified as "theme" except for the triple occurrences in 4:11–16 and 10:19–25, which are placed on the margin. The indicative spans are consistently identified as "background," and the foreground imperatives and performatives are identified as "foreground."

---

[37] Similar to Lane, who writes: "13:1–21 furnishes the conclusion to the homily" in William Lane, *Hebrews 9–13*, WBC 47 (Word, 1991), 497.

Hebrews: How to Find God in Our Time of Need

I. Consider Jesus as the apostle of our confession (1:1–4:16)
- A. Let's hold on to the message that our apostle gave us (1:1–3:1)
  - 1. Let's pay attention to the message of God's ultimate messenger (1:1–2:4)
    - a. God has spoken through his son (1:1–4)
    - b. The son is greater than God's previous messengers (1:5–14)
    - c. Let's hold on to the things we have heard from the son (2:1–4)
  - 2. Jesus is a merciful and faithful high priest (2:5–18)
  - 3. Partners in a heavenly calling; think of Jesus as an apostle and high priest (3:1–2)
- B. Let's respond to Jesus' voice today and enter the rest (3:1–4:13)
  - 1. Unlike the Israelites, let's respond to his voice and enter the rest (3:1–4:1)
    - a. We are Jesus' house, like the Israelites were Moses' house (3:1–6)
    - b. If you hear his voice, do not harden your hearts like the wilderness generation (3:7–15)
    - c. Moses' followers did not enter the rest because they lacked faith (3:16–19)
    - d. Let's be afraid lest one of you may miss the rest (4:1)
  - 2. Since the promise of the rest is still open, let's try to enter (4:1–13)
    - a. There is still a Sabbath rest for God's people (4:2–10)
    - b. Let's make every effort to enter the rest (4:11–16)

Thematic peak (4:11–16)
Let's make every effort to enter the rest
Let's hold on to the confession
Let's draw near to the throne of grace

II. Consider Jesus as the High Priest of our Confession (4:11–10:25)
- A. Let's press on to maturity with new teaching about Jesus' priesthood (5:1–7:4a)
  - 1. Draw near to the throne of grace (4:11–16)
  - 2. Jesus is a high priest according to the order of Melchizedek (5:1–10)
  - 3. We have a new teaching about Melchizedek, but you are too immature (5:11–14)
  - 4. Let's press on to maturity (6:1–3)
- B. The new teaching results in access to God
  - 1. Through advanced teaching, let's press on to maturity, building on the foundation (6:1–3)
  - 2. Teaching must result in persistence and growth (6:4–8)
  - 3. We want you to show diligence to inherit the promises (6:9–12)
  - 4. Teaching about hope and God's oath and promise gives you access to God (6:13–7:4a)
- C. Let's draw near to God (7:4b–10:25)
  - 1. Jesus is a priest according to the order of Melchizedek (7:4–28)
    - a. Think about how great Melchizedek was! (7:4)
    - b. A defence of Jesus' priesthood according to the order of Melchizedek (7:4b–28)
  - 2. Jesus' priesthood cleanses us and qualifies us to serve as priests (8:1–10:18)
    - a. Jesus' priesthood, covenant, tabernacle and sacrifice (8:1–13)
    - b. Jesus' ministry in the tabernacle cleanses the conscience of the believer (9:1–14)
    - c. Jesus' death inaugurated the new covenant and removed sins once for all (9:15–28)
    - d. Jesus' sacrifice fulfilled perfected believers forever so there is no more sacrifice (10:1–18)
  - 3. Let's draw near to God in the Holy of Holies (10:19–25)

Thematic Peak (10:19–25)
Let's draw near to God in the Holy of Holies and serve him as priests
Let's hold on to the confession
Let's consider how to motivate one another to love and good works

III. We are partners in Jesus' heavenly calling (10:19–13:16)
- A. Let's run the race (10:19–12:2)
  - 1. Let's consider how to motivate one another with love and good works (10:19–25)
  - 2. Sin is a hindrance to progress and leads to judgment (10:26–31)

      3.   You need endurance to move forward (10:32–39)

      4.   Faith is modelled by action-events in the lives of people from the past (11:1–40)

      5.   Let's run the race with faith and endurance (12:1–2)

  B.   Let's serve God as priests in heavenly Jerusalem (12:1–28)

      1.   Let's run the race with discipline (12:1–17)

          a.   Life viewed as a race in heavenly Jerusalem (12:1–2)

          b.   The believers' suffering is like athletic training (12:3–11)

          c.   Strengthen weak limbs, make straight paths and pursue the goals of peace and righteousness (12:12–17)

      2.   Climax: Let's serve God as priests in heavenly Jerusalem (12:18–29)

          a.   Your location is heavenly Jerusalem where all the faithful are present and Jesus is speaking (12:18–24)

          b.   Do not resist Jesus' voice (12:25–27)

          c.   Let's serve God as priests through grace in heavenly Jerusalem (12:28–29)

  C.   Conclusion: Let's go to Jesus and offer sacrifices of love, good works and sharing (12:28–13:16)

      1.   Let's serve God as priests through grace (12:28–29)

      2.   Offer good works and sharing (13:1–9a)

      3.   It is good to be strengthened by grace (13:9b–12)

      4.   Let's go to Jesus and offer sacrifices (13:13–16)

Closing—Draw strength from relationships with your leaders and community (13:17–25)

18

JAMES

WILLIAM VARNER

I n teaching DA to students over the years, I have often remarked that discourse analysis is better described than defined. I also have reminded them that discourse analysts have been better at applying the method to actual texts than in theorizing about them. Functional discourse analysts, rather than looking at what is theoretically possible in a language, study the actual language used in naturally occurring texts. This study of "language in use" is the basis of the discourse analysis methodology that I have employed in the following analysis of the Letter of James. To put it simply, when humans perceive that a discourse "makes sense" to them, it generally means that there is some theme that flows through the discourse that allows them to recognize it as cohesive rather than as a group of unrelated words.

Methodology

How does such an approach to language work in actually analyzing discourse? There are three important principles that form the basis of DA of texts, including the NT.

1. Grammar beyond the sentence
2. Role of cohesion
3. Function of prominence

The first principle, *grammar beyond the sentence level*, is perhaps the most distinguishing tenet of discourse analysis. Sadly, much traditional biblical exegesis, while always nodding its approval on the importance of *context*, has often-times ignored this principle in practice. The analysis of words and clauses is constrained by the perspective of the larger discourse in which they are found. It is helpful to view all the linguistic elements of a text as comprising different "levels of discourse," with individual words on the bottom level and then clauses, clause complexes, sentences, paragraphs, and the entire discourse on the ascending levels, similar to a pyramid.[1] Longacre describes the levels from the top-down as "discourse, paragraph, sentence, clause, phrase, word and stem."[2]

The second principle, *cohesion,* is a means of linking clauses and sentences into larger syntactical units and refers to the various ways which readers make sense of a text. Specifically, cohesion occurs where the interpretation of some element in the discourse is dependent on that of another. Cohesion is so important that O'Donnell makes the following observation, "Many treatments of discourse analysis are in reality simply discussions of cohesion. In many ways it is the simplest area of discourse analysis to understand."[3]

The third feature of discourse analysis is the function of linguistic prominence. The contrast between cohesion and prominence is as follows. Lexical and grammatical ties function as a cohesion of similarity, while prominence functions as a cohesion of dissimilarity.[4] In other words, an author uses language to set apart certain entities from other entities of the discourse. The reader's attention is drawn to important topics in the discourse, then supported by less prominent material. This prominence functions to set aside certain ideas as more semantically or pragmatically significant than others.

Macrostructure

So how does this theory of discourse analysis apply to the Letter of James? For over four centuries, discussion about the structure of James' letter has been greatly influenced by two influential Germans: Martin Luther in the sixteenth century and Martin Dibelius in the twentieth century. Both could see no coherent structure in the book. While there were others who voiced exception to the views of the two Martins, their influence has dominated the discussion.

---

[1] Stanley Porter utilizes the figure of a pyramid with "word" as the base and successive levels as "phrase," "sentence," "pericope," and finally "discourse" as the cap of the pyramid (*Idioms of the Greek New Testament* [Sheffield Academic, 1992], 298).

[2] Robert E. Longacre, *The Grammar of Discourse*, 2nd ed. (Plenum Press, 1996), 291–94.

[3] Matt O'Donnell, *Corpus Linguistics and the Greek of the New Testament* (Sheffield Phoenix, 2005), 156.

[4] Jeffrey T. Reed, *A Discourse Analysis of Philippians: Method and Rhetoric in the Debate over Literary Integrity*, JSNTSup (Sheffield Academic, 1997), 385.

Luther's comment about James being "a right strawy epistle," as compared to other NT writings, is his most well-known comment on the book. His views about the style and structure of James, however, were equally negative. Discounting apostolic authorship, Luther concluded that the author must have been "some good, pious man, who took a few sayings from the disciples of the apostles and thus tossed them off on paper."[5]

Furthermore, in his erudite commentary, Dibelius concluded from his form critical analysis that James contained no overall thematic or structural unity.[6] He did acknowledge that three individual treatises (2:1–13; 2:14–26; 3:1–13), which he called "the core of the writing," were coherent in their diatribal style. But the rest of the book, however, was primarily composed of loosely arranged sayings, sometimes connected by catch words, in the style of what Dibelius referred to as Jewish paraenesis.[7] Dibelius' influence on later writers is undeniable and pervasive.[8]

Among recent writers who have discerned some measure of coherence in the epistle's structure, many often stress the key role of chapter one in serving as a sort of "table of contents" for the rest of the book.[9] Despite this recent trend toward seeing greater coherence, Taylor and Guthrie recently concluded that "no consensus has emerged concerning the details of the book's organization."[10]

I am convinced that a discourse analysis of this book that gives attention both to how authors indicate prominence and to how they group their messages offers fresh hope that we can then uncover the structure of this little book and its ensuing overall message.

We have previously covered the topics of prominence and we now suggest that the most prominent paragraph, which I call the discourse "peak," is James 3:13–18. This paragraph with its appeal to divine and human wisdom as polar

---

[5] For the two quotations see *Luther's Works* (Concordia, 1972), 35:362, 397.

[6] Martin Dibelius, *James: A Commentary on the Epistle of James*, rev. Heinrich Greeven; trans. M. A. Williams (Fortress, 1976), 34–38.

[7] Ibid., 1–10.

[8] For discussion of the literary structure and genre of James, see Luke T. Johnson, *The Letter of James*, AB 37A (Doubleday, 1995), 11–25; Peter H. Davids, "The Epistle of James in Modern Discussion," *ANRW II* (25.5): 3621–45; Mark E. Taylor, "Recent Scholarship on the Structure of James," *CBR* 3, no. 1 (2004): 86–115.

[9] Johnson, *James*, 15; Richard Bauckham, *James: Wisdom of James, Disciple of Jesus the Sage* (Routledge, 1999), 68–73. Douglas Moo opts for "an overall concern" rather than a structured theme. That concern is James' desire for spiritual "wholeness" (*The Letter of James*, PNTC [Eerdmans, 2000], 44, 46).

[10] Mark E. Taylor and George H. Guthrie, "The Structure of James," *CBQ* 68.4 (2006): 681–705. For recent efforts in this area, see the thorough study by Luke Cheung, *The Genre, Composition and Hermeneutics of the Epistle of James* (Paternoster, 2003) and M. E. Taylor, *A Text-Linguistic Investigation into the Discourse Structure of James*, LNTS 311 (T&T Clark, 2006).

contrasts focuses James' call to his readers to choose the lifestyle of a "friend of God." By recognizing this thematic peak, a reader can also better develop a mental representation of the discourse. "By reducing the flow of the texts to polar opposites, dialectical discourse not only clarifies the issues; it also serves as an aid to memory."[11]

How does this macrostructural approach view the book in its microstructural sections? I suggest that the collocation of imperative commands with nominatives of direct address (most often ἀδελφοί, "brothers") is the cohesive tie that James utilizes to group his discourse into sections. Each discrete section, introduced in this way, signals a new group of semantically related information as well. Occasionally, this grammatical tie functions simply as a span within a section (5:7–10) and a lexical semantic chain within that section indicates this to be the case. The thematic second person imperative in each section serves as the central clause with the following indicative clauses and/or clause complexes providing support for the mainline imperatival command. There may be additional imperatives (often in the third person) that expand further the command of the central clause/sentence and are then further supported by a series of indicative clauses. The main thrust of each section, in accord with the overall theme in the discourse peak in 3:13–18, is an appeal to readers to follow the divine viewpoint ("wisdom from above") by obeying the imperatival command that he has delivered. Consequently, his readers are exhorted to reject any human viewpoint ("wisdom not from above") about the ethical demands in the section.

According to this proposal, the main sections of the book can be displayed as follows in Figure 18.1 on the next page.

In this analysis, there are fourteen sections of the discourse in addition to the epistolary prescript. Each of these contributes its own unique semantic development of the main theme—namely, demonstrating behavior that accords with divine wisdom. Three of the sections begin with a rhetorical question rather than with an imperative (2:14–26; 3:13–18; 4:1–10). The first passage (2:14–26) could be viewed as a consequential application of the section beginning in 2:1, particularly continuing the theme of partiality as applied to the poor.

Section 4:1–10 begins with a question and immediately follows the thematic peak of the discourse (3:13–18). Commentators have noted that there are many verbal similarities in these passages and often take them as two sections of the same unit.[12] I suggest that 4:1–10 is a sub-unit of 3:13–4:10 and should also be considered the hortatory peak of the discourse. This is evidenced by the concentration of ten imperatives in 4:7–10.

---

[11] K. J. Tollefson, "The Epistle of James as a Dialectical Discourse," *BTB* 27, no. 2 (1997): 63.

[12] Johnson, *James*, 267–69.

Section	Nominative of Address	Imperative Command/ Rhetorical Question
1:2–15	ἀδελφοί μου	Πᾶσαν χαρὰν ἡγήσασθε
1:16–18	ἀδελφοί μου ἀγαπητοί	Μὴ πλανᾶσθε
1:19–27	ἀδελφοί μου ἀγαπητοί	Ἴστε plus ἔστω
2:1–13	ἀδελφοί μου	μὴ ἐν προσωπολημψίαις ἔχετε
2:14–26	ἀδελφοί μου	Τί τὸ ὄφελος
3:1–12	ἀδελφοί μου	Μὴ πολλοὶ διδάσκαλοι γίνεσθε
3:13–18	ἐν ὑμῖν THEMATIC PEAK	Τίς σοφὸς καὶ ἐπιστήμων
4:1–10	ἐν ὑμῖν HORTATORY PEAK	Πόθεν πόλεμοι καὶ πόθεν μάχαι plus 10 impvs in 4 :7–10
4:11–12	ἀδελφοί	Μὴ καταλαλεῖτε ἀλλήλων
4:13–17	οἱ λέγοντες	Ἄγε νῦν
5:1–6	οἱ πλούσιοι	Ἄγε νῦν ... κλαύσατε
5:7–11	ἀδελφοί	Μακροθυμήσατε plus 4 impvs
5:12–18	ἀδελφοί μου	μὴ ὀμνύετε
5:19–20	ἀδελφοί μου	γινωσκέτω

Figure 18.1: Sections in James

This explanation of the linearization of James pays attention to the special way that he indicates prominence by the use of peak. It also notes the ways that he uses the grammatical resources of his language to group his discourse to most effectively communicate the details of the theme embodied in his peak. With this approach, his readers can better develop a mental representation of the discourse at all levels. Finally, if his readers heed his exhortations, they will then become "whole" persons in their undivided loyalty to God.

Having completed an analysis of the letter from the top down by discovering its macrostructure, any discourse analysis commentary should also analyze from the bottom up the successive microstructure levels of clauses, clause complexes, and paragraphs. Such a commentary should examine in detail the way in which James maps to each individual section of his discourse his overall theme of living according to heavenly wisdom rather than earthly wisdom. Our anticipation is that the lowest levels of this discourse will support and illustrate the overall theme conveyed by its highest levels.[13]

---

[13] Kenneth Tollefson analyzes how James "uses binary opposition to instruct or persuade the reader/listener in some new element of truth that would otherwise be difficult to obtain." Tollefson, "James as Dialectical Discourse," 62–69.

As noted, Luther thought that James borrowed a few ideas from the apostles and thus "threw them on paper." If he could have gotten past his misunderstanding of the "faith-works" issue in chapter two, he could have discovered a remarkable structural unity in the book. Discourse analysis can help us uncover that structure.

I again stress the key to its seemingly disparate order is through (1) recognizing James' overall call to be "whole" and not divided, and then (2) through viewing 3:13–18 as its peak and its call to follow wisdom from above and not from below. Recognizing the segments introduced with "brothers" plus an imperative or question also suggests that there is a structure and progression in this epistle.

The choice between the two wisdoms is conveyed by the use of polar opposites consistent with the Jewish "two ways" approach to ethics. To his readers who think they can have it both ways, James issues the scathing denunciation of being "double-minded" or literally "double-souled"—an adjective he may have coined (1:8; 4:8). In the paragraph following his thematic peak (4:1–10, which I argue is the hortatory peak of the book and also introduced by a rhetorical question), James calls for a change from being double-minded to purifying our hearts (4:8), which is consistent with another of James' themes, that of perfection. Early in his letter he tells us that our goal in all of this is to be "perfect and entire, lacking nothing" (1:4). To be perfect (τέλειος) is not to be sinless but to be whole. In other words, we are not to be divided people marked by doubleness but rather to exhibit singleness.

I again stress that James employs a cohesive device that cements his hortatory written discourse together: his use of the direct address word "brothers" accompanied by either an imperative command or by a rhetorical question. The following outline of James indicates where those paragraphs begin, each of which introduces a new topic as well. The two topics introduced, not by "brothers" but by a rhetorical question, serve as the two peaks (thematic and hortatory) that convey the main themes of the letter in the prominent way. Our task is to discern how each paragraph develops its topic along the lines of the behavior condemned (earthly wisdom) and the behavior commended (heavenly wisdom). The goal is to recognize that wholeness, maturity, and their consequent peace (3:18) will be the result of his hearers and readers making the wise choice of heavenly wisdom.

I suggest the following outline (i.e., macrostructure) of the letter, based on its hortatory character. Bold points indicate their prominent roles as the thematic and hortatory peaks of the discourse. It is this outline that will form the structure of the discourse analysis that follows in Figure 18.2.

1. Be Joyful in Trials	1:2–15
2. Do Not Be Deceived about God's Goodness	1:16–18
3. Become a Good Hearer/Doer of the Word	1:19–27
4. Do Not Show Favoritism	2:1–13
5. Show Your Faith by Your Works	2:14–26
6. Be Consistent in Your Speech	3:1–12
7. Follow the Wisdom of God	**3:13–18**
8. Become a Friend of God	**4:1–10**
9. Do Not Speak Against One Another	4:11, 12
10. Do Not Plan Presumptuously	4:13–17
11. You Rich Should Treat the Poor Justly	5:1–6
12. Wait Patiently for the Lord's Coming	5:7–11
13. Do Not Swear but Pray	5:12–18
14. Convert the Erring Brother	5:19, 20

Figure 18.2: Outline of James

Microstructures

1. Be Joyful in Trials: 1:2–15

Trials and Maturity (*1:2–4*). The first major division of the letter is 1:2–15. This decision is based on the conviction that the coupling in 1:2 of a nominative plural of direct address (ἀδελφοί) with an imperative command (ἡγήσασθε) signals a new section. This combination of a nominative plural (most often ἀδελφοί) plus a command appears again in 1:16. Not only do the presence of these formal discourse markers confirm that 1:2–15 is the first main paragraph, but the theme that runs throughout this section (trials) indicates that it is to be viewed as a discrete unit. Although it functions as a self-contained section, the paragraph can be broken down into four smaller subparagraphs (1:2–4; 1:5–8; 1:9–11 and 1:12–15). In 1:2–4 James offers counter intuitive advice to consider trials as joy because they are part of the process God uses to produce endurance and maturity in us.

Wisdom and Faith (*1:5–8*). This section displays some unique characteristics, but it is still linked to the previous section by the word λείπεται which connects the thought with the closing word of 1:4, λειπόμενοι. The obvious conclusion is that wisdom (σοφίας) is necessary to help complete and make whole the individual facing trials, the main concern of the previous paragraph. The verb αἰτείτω ("he should request") introduces the subject of prayer, which dominates the rest of the section since each clause explains both how one should pray for wisdom and what are the hindrances to praying for wisdom. The concept of wisdom runs through the paragraph, but it is the effective praying for wisdom that is its permeating theme. There is no definition of wisdom yet, but in 3:13–18, the thematic peak of the letter, heavenly wisdom from above is contrasted with earthly wisdom from below by their binary-opposite behaviors. This subsection then concludes with a brief and negative description of the "double-souled" person in 1:8.

Poor Man, Rich Man (1:9–11). This small sub-paragraph reveals a clear linkage with the preceding paragraphs. The postpositive δέ connects and contrasts the humble brother with the double-minded person just mentioned in 1:8. There is also a semantic link with 1:2 where the "brothers" are exhorted to "consider it all joy" when they encounter trials. In 1:9 an example of one of those brothers is exhorted to boast (positively) in an example of those trials, i.e., being lowly. Just as it may sound strange to exhort someone to be joyful in trials, so it is also counterintuitive to exhort someone when he is being lowered to boast (καυχάσθω), and also to exhort someone in a higher status to boast when they are lowered. Another link with the preceding verses appears in the last clause of this paragraph, where it is said that "the rich man will fade away in the midst of his pursuits." This statement parallels both in structure and in thought what is affirmed at the conclusion of 1:8: "a double-minded man is unstable in all his ways." Although the terms for "ways" are different, some versions translate πορείαις αὐτοῦ in 1:11 as "his ways," thus indicating an even closer parallelism to the ὁδοῖς αὐτοῦ ending 1:8.

Blessing for Those Who Pass the Test (1:12–15). James 1:12–15 is the fourth paragraph in 1:2–15. He has never abandoned the topic of being tested and learning to respond properly. It is best to view 1:2–15 as variations on a single theme, with 1:2–4 and 1:12 helping to span the entire section. Thus 1:12 introduces the fourth section of 1:12–15. This is because of the six occurrences of the πειρα-word group in these four verses that bind them together with the preceding verses. The passage is introduced in 1:12 by the first of two uses of μακάριος in the chapter (see also 1:25), and concludes with a climactic reference to death at the end of 1:15. Other verbal connections with 1:3–4 are the ὑπομένει and δόκιμος in 1:12. Furthermore, the description of one who shows constancy under trial as "blessed" completes the thought expressed in 1:2—namely, that we must count it "entirely joy" when we encounter all kinds of trials. The passage thus completes an inclusio that begins in 1:2 and ends in 1:15.

2. Do Not Be Deceived about God's Goodness: 1:16–18.

The paragraph opens with the collocation of a nominative of direct address (or vocative plural), ἀδελφοί μου ἀγαπητοί, and a negated imperative, πλανᾶσθε, that is fronted for emphasis. Other such negated commands accompanying ἀδελφοί are in 2:1; 3:1; 4:11; and 5:9. With this repeated pattern, James provides cohesion to his composition and also advances the subjects by successive shifts in topics.

While semantic links between these paragraphs should not be ignored, the collocation of the address with the imperative introduces enough of a semantic shift that suggests the beginning of a separate paragraph, with 1:19–27 as the closing paragraph. In 1:16–18 James desires that his readers not be led astray from a faith commitment that God only gives good gifts.

3. Become a Good Hearer/Doer of the Word: 1:19–27

Hearing and Doing (1:19–21). The governing command in these verses is James' expectation to spend more time listening and less time speaking and getting angry because anger does not equal righteousness (1:19–20). He then expects his readers to stop sinning and be open to actually live out God's message (1:21–22). James reinforces his message with life-related examples: people who merely listen to God are like a person who forgets what he looks like in a mirror (1:23–25), people who do not control what they say reveals a lot about their religion (1:26–27).

Deceived or Blessed? (1:22–25). In this paragraph, James develops another of the triadic virtues mentioned in 1:19. Having developed the expression, "slow to anger" in 1:20–21, he now expounds the command to be "quick to hear" in this section. The one who truly receives the word that is able to save him (1:21) is also the one who should become a "doer" of the word, not just one who "hears" it. The two primary clauses (1:22, 25) bookend the paragraph and function as an inclusio with a cognate noun and verb (1:22, ποιηταί; 1:25, ποιήσει). The secondary clauses comprise a parable about a person who forgets what he looks like in the mirror (1:23–24). The parable illustrates from real life the meaning of "deceiving yourselves" (1:22b), and contrasts this self-deception with the hearer/doer who will be blessed because of his obedience to the word (1:25).

Real Religion (1:26–27). The third subparagraph (1:26–27) of the larger section (1:19–27) concludes the threefold command in James 1:19: "every person must be quick to hear, slow to speak, slow to anger." James has elaborated on being "slow to anger" in 1:19–21. He expanded the idea of being "quick to hear" in 1:22–25. Now he applies what it means to be "slow to speak" in 1:26–27. This exhortation also introduces themes yet to be discussed. In chapter 2 James further develops how we must be "quick to hear" what the Torah and the Lord Jesus say about the poor (2:1–5) and to put what we have "heard" to "work" in 2:12–26. In 3:1–12, he exhorts us to be "slow to speak" through analogies illustrating the dangers of an uncontrolled tongue. In 3:13–4:10, he warns that a failure to be "slow to wrath" displays devilish wisdom manifested in conflicts among the congregations. 1:26–27 thus functions both anaphorically (looking back), as it recalls 1:19, and then cataphorically (looking forward) as it anticipates chapters 2 through 4.

4. Do Not Show Favoritism: 2:1–13

Partiality in Practice (2:1–4). This paragraph (2:1–4) is bracketed by its opening and closing with two independent, primary clauses, the first conveying a command (2:1) and the second asking a rhetorical question (2:4). The first of those clauses opens with Ἀδελφοί and an imperative. When this combination signals a new topic, as is the case in 2:1, it serves as one of the twelve main divisions of the letter (e.g., 1:2, 16, 19). The second primary clause (2:4) is actually the apodosis (the "then" clause) of a long conditional clause (2:2–4). The protasis (the "if") of the conditional clause contains five secondary clauses, each containing a subjunctive verb introduced by the single ἐάν that initiates 2:2. These conditional clauses effectively convey the inconsistency of discriminatory behavior in light of Jesus' teaching.

Honoring Those God Honors (2:5–7). This section begins with the familiar nominative of direct address, ἀδελφοί μου, combined with the fronted imperative verb, Ἀκούσατε which functions as a meta-comment that calls attention to the question that follows. That rhetorical question effectively points out the fact that the discriminators against the poor are not following God's examples of choosing the poor as heirs of His kingdom. Furthermore, their behavior insults the very name by which these poor believers are called!

The Royal Law (2:8–9). James 2:8–13 comprises the third and final subparagraph within the larger unit beginning at 2:1 and concluding at 2:13. The literary linkage between the sections is made clear by the use of the verb προσωπολημπτεῖτε in 2:9, which recalls the noun προσωπολημψίαις in 2:1.

In this, the last subparagraph (2:8–13), acts of partiality are shown to be inconsistent with a saying from the Torah (Lev 19:18, regarding loving one's neighbor) that is also a saying from Jesus (Matt 22:39). James, therefore, calls it a royal or "kingly" law (2:8). James 2:1–13 is a skillful midrashic treatment of Lev 19:12–18, the use of which continues at later points in his letter as well (Jas 4:11; 5:4, 9, 12, 20). We deal with 2:8–9 and 2:10–13 separately as further subsections of 2:8–13. The reason for the break is that 2:8–9 deals with the "kingly law" (νόμον ... βασιλικὸν), while 2:10–13 deals with the "whole law" (ὅλον ... νόμον).

The Whole Law (2:10–13). This second part of the overall section of 2:8–13 is marked by a change from discussing the "royal law" to a broader discussion of "the whole law." The description of those who break the "kingly law" as transgressors (2:9b) leads to this section (2:10–11) that explains and elaborates what is intended by the expression, "transgress the law." The postpositive γὰρ in 2:10 explains that even if someone could obey all the laws but one, he or she has still become guilty of all of them (γέγονεν πάντων ἔνοχος). Then in 2:11, James will illustrate his apparently severe point by citing the sixth and seventh words of the Mosaic Decalogue, namely the prohibitions against adultery and murder. The law is a whole and breaking one command still makes a person a law transgressor.

James develops further his discussion of partiality in 2:10–13 by issuing two imperatives in 2:12, with each command introduced by οὕτως. He concludes with two aphorisms conveyed by the indicative mood in 2:13.

5. Show Your Faith by Your Works: 2:14–26

A Parable of the Poor (2:14–17). Two distinct discourse markers set this second main paragraph of the chapter apart from the first paragraph (2:1–13). One is the use of the nominative of direct address in the words ἀδελφοί μου plus the introduction of a new topic, the inseparable alliance of faith and deeds (2:14). The paragraph, however, is not isolated from its previous context, because it brings together three themes that were previously introduced: (1) hearing/doing (1:22–25); (2) discrimination (2:1); and (3) the poor (2:5). Although James 1:22–25 stressed the importance of not only hearing but also doing the word, it is in this passage that the theme of faith and actions finds its most complete treatment. Hearing implies faith and James uses πίστις sixteen times, and eleven of them are in 2:14–26. He uses ἔργον (deed) fifteen times, and twelve appear here, each time in the plural. Nine of these uses of ἔργον appear in close connection with πίστις—a combination that occurs nowhere else, although the theme of a behavior that must match one's profession permeates the book.

A Debate about Deeds (2:18–19). There is a great irony in the interpretation of James 2:18–19. James is concerned that the kind of faith which is his special concern in this letter must not be separated from its appropriate accompanying deeds. That living faith is not just creedal—an affirmation of a doctrinal truth—but manifests itself in deeds. The challenge in 2:18–19 is a simple one: when is James "speaking" during the brief but spirited exchange of the diatribe, and when is his "interlocutor" speaking? And when do they switch? James is opposing two false ideas: (1) that faith can be separated from works (or as I prefer "deeds"); and (2) that faith is defined simply by a creedal affirmation. Now how does James work that out in the diatribal form of debate that emerges in 2:18 and continues to the end of the chapter?

Patriarchal Proof (2:20–23). The passage opens with a harsh address to the author's debate partner (ὦ ἄνθρωπε κενέ). The way the question is posed effectively introduces his final argument. This involves two well-known exemplars from Israel's past history, each of whom illustrates his point that a person is justified not by a faith that is alone but by a faith that is accompanied by the appropriate deeds (2:24). The following examples are persuasive to a person who is willing (Θέλεις) to accept them. Abraham is discussed in 2:20–23 and Rahab in 2:24–25, with each being introduced by a restatement of the overall topic of 2:17–26—namely, that a faith that is unaccompanied by the appropriate deeds is first "dead" (2:17), then "useless" (2:20), and finally "dead" again (2:26).

Matriarchal Proof (2:24–26). At this point James shifts from addressing the interlocutor in the second person singular (βλέπεις in 2:22) to the second person plural (ὁρᾶτε) and also drops the dialogue with his debate partner. The address is no longer "you [sing.] see," but rather "you [pl.] see." The shift to another verb for "see" is probably due to his focus being shifted from his opponent in debate now to his readers. For the second of three times in this paragraph (see the rhetorical questions in 2:21 and 25), James declares that a "person" (ἄνθρωπος) is justified by works (ἐξ ἔργων). The choice of the generic noun for "person" may be due to the fact that he is about to introduce a "matriarch" as the second of his two prime exemplars.

6. Be Consistent in Your Speech: 3:1–12.

All commentators agree that 3:1–12 is a separate section, being introduced by the familiar ἀδελφοί μου plus the imperative Μὴ ... γίνεσθε, and then concluded by a series of agricultural analogies (3:11–12). This passage shares verbal links with both earlier and later ideas in the book. The most obvious semantic link is with 1:26, where reference is made to "not bridling" (μὴ χαλιναγωγῶν) one's tongue, in that 3:2 uses the same rare verb to describe the person who controls his tongue as "able also to bridle [χαλιναγωγῆσαι] the entire body." The command "slow to speak" in 1:19 is elaborated here in 3:1–12. James also will continue his emphasis on speech ethics by his later warnings not to speak against a brother (4:11), not to speak presumptively about the future (4:13), and not to swear (5:12).

Taming the Tongue (3:1–2). In 3:1–2 a new topic is introduced—namely, the great role played by teachers in the assemblies of Jesus-believers with their subsequent great responsibility. This responsibility relates to the teacher's obvious use of the tongue as the instrument for speaking and teaching. This topic of speech is described first by vividly illustrating both the powerful and positive effects of such a small member in one's body (3:3–5a). The consequent negative influence of the tongue—great in relation to its tiny size—is illustrated in 3:5b–12. In both of these sections, some quite colorful rhetorical figures are drawn from both the animal and natural worlds in the created order. In addition to these colorful analogies drawn from the world of nature, James also utilizes a rich intertexture by drawing from both Jewish wisdom literature and also from the sayings of Jesus, both of which he adapts for his own purposes. James effectively argues that his readers should give serious consideration before assuming the responsible "job" of becoming a teacher.

Small but Powerful (3:3–5). James calls attention to three examples of small things in nature that have large effects. The bit/bridle, the rudder, and the tongue are here mentioned as being alike in one thing: they are multum in parvo in their power. Each is comparatively small, but each produces great effects. To help visualize the structure of this section, notice the following analysis and the prominent role of the orienters ἴδε and ἰδού.

A Wildfire and a Wild Beast (3:6–8). Because the rhetorical thrust and the message of this smaller section within the larger 3:1–12 are so intertwined and intended to be experienced as a whole, it is difficult to micro-analyze every individual word and clause. Therefore, the "message" of this section and the next section (3:9–12) clearly overlap. Therefore, any attempt to lay out the message of 3:6–8 must also clearly coincide at times with what follows in the next section. James effectively utilizes examples form nature to expound the effective dangers of an uncontrolled tongue.

A Strange Mixture (3:9–12). James continues his practice of employing asyndeton by means of a series of primary clauses. There are eight of them in 3:9–12, and only two of the clauses are linked by a conjunction (καί in 3:9). The only participle in the passage (γεγονότας) introduces an embedded attributive clause, also in 3:9b. The admonition against being double in the use of one's tongue (3:9–10) is then followed by three rhetorical questions, each drawn from the nature of springs and vineyards (3:11–12a). The paragraph is concluded with an aphorism in 3:12b: "A salt pond cannot yield fresh water." The obvious use of ellipsis (omitted words that are implied) in these last verses indicates that he is drawing his argument to a rhetorically intensive and effective conclusion. He understands that his readers will identify the missing words and that they will know the obvious answer to the questions that are articulated with the negative particles μήτι and μή. That answer to these questions is: "No, these things can't be true!" Likewise, this tongue cannot be employed for contradictory purposes—namely, to bless God and others while also to curse God and others.

7. Follow the Wisdom of God: 3:13–18

Wisdom Shown By Behavior (3:13). This passage (3:13–18) has special linguistic features that set it apart from other paragraphs along with its semantic function of conveying the essential message of the entire letter. The paragraph has verbal ties with both previous and subsequent material, thus serving as a transitional section but also functioning as a summation of the entire discourse. The semantic content of this paragraph conveys the main themes of the book. He expresses here the essence of his overall message that his readers must embrace a lifestyle that is based on the wisdom that descends from God above, and that consequently they must reject any forms of antiwisdom that arises from a human viewpoint only. It is my argument that each distinct paragraph of the book displays the recognizable stamp of that overall message.

Unwise Behavior Comes from Below (3:14–16). The next three verses (3:14–16) introduce a negative tone, because James loves portraying the oppositions of actions through his ethical exhortations. The Jewish "two ways" tradition could also be invoked here, as he describes the characteristics of antiwisdom by means of a vice list. He never calls this behavior a type of wisdom, but he does state, "this is not the wisdom that comes down from above, but is earthly, unspiritual, demonic" (3:15).

Wise Behavior Comes from Above (3:17–18). The striking contrast of the following list of virtues in 3:17 is evident by its emphasis on the harmony and peace that is conveyed by the words that characterize behavior that descends from "above." These attributes of heavenly wisdom perhaps are intended to recall the personification of wisdom in Prov 8:22–36. The Greek reader can recognize rhetorical flourishes that were heard in the oral reading of the book to its original hearers. Six consecutive words beginning with epsilon appear in rapid sequence: ἡ δὲ ἄνωθεν σοφία πρῶτον μὲν ἁγνή ἐστιν, ἔπειτα εἰρηνική, ἐπιεικής, εὐπειθής, μεστὴ ἐλέους. Furthermore, the second, third, and fourth words rhyme by ending with a similar sound: -ή, -ής, -ής. This is followed by three words that are initiated by an alpha: καὶ καρπῶν ἀγαθῶν, ἀδιάκριτος, ἀνυπόκριτος. This intentional alliteration contrasts aurally in a graphic manner with the preceding vice list, which has no such alliteration. The contrast of the sounds conveys an oral message about the difference between the behavioral disharmony that comes from below and the harmonious order of the behavior that descends from above.

8. Become a Friend of God: 4:1–10

A War in the Members (4:1–3). James 4:1–10 has features that both connect it closely with the previous paragraph and also distinguish it as the next separate paragraph in the book. Connecting it with 3:13–18 are the following features: (1) 4:1 begins with a rhetorical question like in 3:13. (2) Its initial question ends with the phrase ἐν ὑμῖν in 4:1 as in 3:13. (3) The verb ζηλοῦτε in 4:2 echoes its cognate noun ζῆλον in 3:14, as evidence that the behavior that is condemned in 4:1–3 comes not from above but from below.

We have entered, however, a section that differs from the three so-called "treatises" that precede it (2:1–12; 2:13–26; 3:1–12). Not only is the tone more severe in this section, but James has introduced the expression ἐν ὑμῖν (3:13 and 4:1) which he will continue to use in 5:13, 14, and 19. He also begins to use the consequential conjunction οὖν at this very point (4:4, 7, 17; 5:7, 16), which indicates that he is now dealing with specific situations within the communities addressed. The function of the οὖν is to transition to the expected ethical application rather than for logical development of his argument—the way it often appears in the Pauline writings.

Recognizing this new way of addressing his readers can also help explain why James waits until 3:13–4:10 to expound the thematic and hortatory peaks of his discourse. While everything that has preceded this passage can be also viewed in light of the polar opposite behaviors he portrays, from this section onward he exposes that wrong behavior more closely and fervently than he has before. One might imagine a preacher initially discoursing about general issues that affect all congregations, but then becoming more specific as he moves into problems that he knows are prevalent in his own parishioners' lives.

Adultery and Bad Friendships (4:4–6). In the second of the three sections in 4:1–10, the serious charges introduced in 4:1–3 by the "prophet" James reach a rhetorical crescendo. By a series of questions concluded with a scriptural citation, his diatribe powerfully portrays the central thrust of his argument— namely, that one must finally decide whose friend one actually is: the world's or God's. In keeping with the idea that 3:13–18 contains the thematic peak of the book (following wisdom from above and not from below), this passage equates the choosing of heavenly wisdom with being God's friend. Making the opposite choice, however, will result in being opposed and resisted by God, who will become our enemy.

Divine Submission and Humility (4:7–10). This third section (4:7–10) of the larger paragraph (4:1–10) includes some stylistic links with the first section (4:1–3). These links highlight how the quotation in 4:6 looks both backward and forward, as previously noted. There were eleven second person plural present indicative verbs in 4:2–3, while 4:7–10 contain nine second person plural aorist imperatives, one third person singular imperative, and one future indicative verb expressing the fulfillment of the preceding commands. These structured sets of eleven clauses both compare and contrast the reproach of the beginning section in 4:1–3 with the call to repentance at its end in 4:7–10. This evident contrast between the two passages is emphasized stylistically by these changes in tense and mood.

4:7–10 consists of a series of imperatives that press even further for a decisive choice between these two contradictory philosophies of life, one based on pleasing self and the other based on pleasing God. This can be illustrated by the following analysis of their overall structure. Three couplets of imperatives (7b–9) are framed by two other imperatives dealing with submitting oneself to God (7a, 10), thus forming a fivefold structure.

9. Do Not Slander One Another: 4:11, 12

There is an apparent disjunct in these verses with the previous harsh charges in 4:1–10. Verbal and semantic connections with what precedes, however, are not totally absent. For example, the sin that is condemned in 4:11–12, namely sinful slander, can be viewed as simply an outward result of those selfish motives that are the actual causes of those conflicts and divisions that are so strongly condemned in 4:1–3. While the passage does begin with an address to the "brothers," the exhortation is still quite a strong one, since it declares that the slanderer places himself at God's level and His law rather than submitting to both. How then and why does James combine this affectionate address with such a stern warning about slander?

10. Do Not Plan Presumptuously: 4:13–17

The passage is directly related to the following paragraph due to their identical openings (Ἄγε νῦν 4:13; 5:1). Moreover, these sections are also semantically connected by the topic of wealth. To be sure, those strongly admonished in 4:13–17 are not explicitly said to be "rich," but their extensive travel plans mentioned in 4:13 imply that they are well-off, and their expressed intention certainly is to "make money." Both paragraphs, 4:13–17 and 5:1–6, do not condemn wealth as such, but they do criticize "people of the world" for simply leaving God and His values (heavenly wisdom) out of their course of life. However, while the rich in 5:1–6 are condemned, the merchants in 4:13–17 are exhorted to change their attitudes. It is not their wealth that James criticizes, but their boastful presumption.

The overall meaning of 4:13–17 is the foolishness of making confident plans apart from unforeseen circumstances. The vivid portrayal of "merchants" whose plans are altered by unknown developments can be appreciated even by unbelievers. The challenge to the interpreter is how that topic is conveyed syntactically through clauses which are strangely complex in their structure. What is James attempting to do with his choice of words here, and how does his language function to fulfill his intended purpose?

11. You Rich Should Treat the Poor Justly: 5:1–6

Woe Because They Hoard Wealth (5:1–3). James issues a series of rapid-fire condemnations (as is his style) against the rich. But these are not simply rich people as such—they are rich oppressors of their own day laborers. An imperative clause followed by a call to mourn is then followed by a series of six indicative clauses describing the results of mislaid trust in riches. The three perfect verbs describe the state in which the rich find themselves, while they are attempting to enjoy their riches. Then two future clauses describe what will take place during their judgment, while a final clause looks back to what they have done to deserve this condemnation.

Woe Because They Steal and Murder (5:4–6). The linguistic and semantic characteristics of Jam 5:1–3 apply also to 5:4–6, but even more intensely. The "meta-comment," Ἄγε νῦν, opened 5:1, while 5:4 opens with a similar "orienter" (ἰδού) that directs the reader to the words that follow. The strong accusatory tone directed toward the rich in 5:1–3 is actually heightened in 5:4–6. The personification of their corroded riches by their "testifying" and "eating" flesh in 5:3 is developed further by the day laborers' defrauded wages crying out against their heartless employers (5:4). Eschatological themes were earlier expressed by future tenses (5:3), allusions to Isaiah (5:1, 3), and reference to the "last days" in 5:3b. These themes are stressed in the same ways in 5:4–6 by references to a future judgment and a clear allusion to the "day of slaughter" by Jeremiah.

12. *Wait Patiently for the Lord's Coming: 5:7–11*

The internal structure of 5:7–11 indicates that a slight transition occurs between 5:7–9 and 5:10–11. The passage is introduced by the imperatival clause in 7a: Μακροθυμήσατε οὖν, ἀδελφοί, ἕως τῆς παρουσίας τοῦ κυρίου. Two following subsections each share the following features. Both utilize the imperative ἰδοὺ (5:7b, 9b/5:11), as was the case in the previous paragraph (5:4), where this "orienter" called attention to the cries of the day laborers. Here, James three times employs it to call attention to the patience of the farmer, the role of the judge, and the blessedness of the prophets. The exemplar of patience in the first section is the farmer, while two exemplars of patience/endurance in the second section are the prophets and Job. Finally, two similar descriptions are made about the Lord's coming in the first section (His coming is near and He is at the door), while in the second section two factual statements are added about the Lord's character (He has a purpose and He is compassionate/merciful).

13. *Do Not Swear but Pray: 5:12–18*

Let Your Yay be Yay (5:12). There are some good reasons for considering 5:12 as marking a turn to the final section of this "homiletical letter." First is the use of the formula Πρὸ πάντων ("above all"). Whether or not it has specific contextual significance, such a phrase may serve in epistolary convention to signal a final series of remarks. Second, the negative command (μὴ) has initiated other major portions of James' composition (2:1; 3:1; 4:11). We suggest that the expression is pointing out a prominent theme in the book, namely the utter importance of one's word as being trustworthy. The analysis revealed below indicates how James arrests the attention of his readers, and then delivers two imperative commands, one that is negative and in the second person plural plus one that is positive and in the third person singular. The first command about the reliable nature of one's words is elaborated by three neither/nor accusatives, and the second is elaborated by a purpose/result clause containing an implicit threat of judgment.

Prayer, the Sick, and Elijah (5:13–18). It has been argued that 5:12 functions as a sort of stand-alone transition to the conclusion of this Diaspora encyclical, which now begins with 5:13. Conclusions of ancient letters often mentioned the recipients' health and a prayer, and this is consistent with the references to both health and prayer in 5:13–18. James, however, does not conform exactly to the way in which those matters are usually treated. He is concerned with internal and communal matters as is evidenced by his use of ἐν ὑμῖν in 5:13, 14, 19 and ἀλλήλοις and ἀλλήλων in 5:16. He introduces the topic of prayer in 5:13 and he develops prayer as the main theme in the paragraph through 5:18. There are eight verbs—προσεύχομαι (5:13, 14, 17, 18), εὔχομαι (5:16), ψάλλω (5:13), προσκαλέω (5:14), and ἐξομολογέω (5:16)—and four nouns—ὄνομα (5:14), εὐχή (5:15), δέησις (5:16), and προσευχή (5:17)—that share the same semantic field (LN, 33). The paragraph first presents prayer as it is practiced in the community (5:13–16) and then describes the specific praying of Elijah as an exemplar (5:17–18).

14. Convert the Erring Brother: 5:19, 20

This final paragraph opens with ἀδελφοί—the fifteenth occurrence of this nominative of address and the tenth time that it inaugurates a new paragraph (1:2, 16, 19; 2:1, 14; 3:1; 4:11; 5:9, 12, 19). This address preceding the protasis of a conditional clause is combined with an imperative (γινωσκέτω) preceding the apodosis of the clause in 5:20. Commentators have generally overlooked that this is only the second time that James fronts the ἀδελφοί μου, which normally is preceded by the imperative command. The placing of the address here and in 2:1 serve as an inclusio for the two paragraphs that open and close the body of the letter with chapter 1 serving as a sort of table of contents.

One should recall the "two ways" theme as the basis of James's entire appeal as evidenced by the peak paragraph in 3:13–18 with the wisdom from above and that from below. This finds a clear illustration with the reference to the "erroneous way" in 5:20 and the "truthful way" in 5:19. The hope offered for the erring brother to "be returned" at the end of a sometimes harsh and confrontational letter are a reminder to its readers about the hope of forgiveness, restoration, and reconciliation.

Conclusion

At this point, the skeptical reader may justly ask the question: "So what?" So what is the hermeneuetical and exegetical take away of such an approach to the Epistle of James? When we get down to the nitty gritty of the linguistic details and the settling of sepecific issues, how does discourse analasis really help? Let me suggest just two examples that come to mind as I have worked through James in my own discourse commentaries on the book.[14]

---

[14] William Varner, *The Book of James, A New Perspective: A Linguistic Commentary Applying Discourse Analysis* (Kress Biblical Resources, 2010). For a more detailed commentary following the same "discourse" methodology, see William Varner, *James: A Commentary on the Greek Text* (Fontes, 2017).

1. Is James 1:19 a command or a statement? Every commentator wrestles with the rare form Ἴστε in James 1:19. Is the form a perfect imperative: "*Know* this my beloved brothers (ἀδελφοί μου ἀγαπητοί)? Or is the form a perfect indicative: "*You know*, my beloved brothers..." A good argument can be made for either and either can make sense in the verse and context. When we recognize, however, that there is the possible collocation here of an imperative command with the nominative of address (ἀδελφοί), and that a new topic is being introduced at this point (being a swift hearer and a slow speaker), then the pattern discerned throughout the separate sections of James points, in my opinion, to the Ἴστε being an imperative and not an indicative.

2. Who is resisting in James 5:6? Commentators have also wrestled with whether the clause ending 5:6 (οὐκ ἀντιτάσσεται ὑμῖν) is a question or a statement. In other words should it be: "He does not resist you" or "Does he not resists you"? Furthermore, who is the subject of the verb, the poor "righteous one" (preceding context) or the Messiah (also referred to as τὸν δίκαιον in other texts). From a broader discourse perspective, I have argued that the statement is a question and that "God" is the subject asking the question ("Does He not resist you?"). This conclusion is based on the only other occurrence of this verb in James appearing in 4:10 where "God resists (ἀντιτάσσεται) the proud." Furthermore, James's penchant for asking challenging questions in his overall diatribal style argues that it could be a question here addressed to the proud landowners who oppress their day laborers (5:1–5).[15]

These are just two of many other examples of exegetical issues that can have light shed on them when we look to the larger discourse context of individual passages in a book.

---

[15] See William Varner, "Who Is Resisting – The Righteous One or Someone Else?: James 4:6 and 5:6," in *New Testament Philology: Essays in Honor of David Alan Black*, ed. Melton B. Winstead (Pickwick, 2018), 1–13.

19

1 PETER

ERVIN STARWALT

First Peter is preeminently a text about suffering as a Christian, suffering for doing the right thing, the thing that pleases God. The letter is a hortatory or commanding text. Peter calls these believers to think in a certain way and to live in a way that pleases God, even if they must do so in the midst of great difficulty. This chapter attempts to lay out the message of Peter to these believers, a message with three themes that dominate in the text: the favorable standing the recipients have before God as his people, that they are to be about doing good, and the issue of suffering.

What follows is a discourse analysis of this letter. First the methodology is given so the reader can follow the analysis more clearly. Texts are hierarchical structures with some portions being more prominent than others. In addition, texts also exhibit different features depending on the type of text they are; exhortation has some differing features from that of exposition. Neither are texts typically flat: they are not merely a list of things or events. Typically, a text moves to a climax and a longer text may have several climatic sections within it. Furthermore, there is the issue of the global thematic idea that controls the writing and the read or hearing of a text. These sorts of issues and some other related analytical issues are addressed in the section on method.

Next after looking at method, we will address the global controlling theme, often called macrostructure. In order to arrive at a macro-statement, we will need to look at the climatic or peak paragraphs in the text. These maximally prominent paragraphs tell the reader what is really important, what the thrust of the letter is. There are four peak paragraphs in 1 Peter.

After this, we will look at the evidence found in the surface features of the text that confirm that these four paragraphs are truly peak. Thus, various markers of peak are discussed, features situated within the paragraph and in contrast to the flow of thought up to that point.

Lastly, we will consider the issue of suffering. Peter does not immediately directly address the fact that these believers are suffering. Not until chapter four does he finally tell these believers that suffering is normal. It is not that suffering is completely ignored until chapter four, but it is in chapter four that it becomes a focal issue. So having surveyed the scope of this analysis, we move on to method.

Methodology

The method employed in this discourse analysis of 1 Peter begins with the basic assumption of how to approach a text as expressed by Longacre, namely "that language is language only in context."[1] What he means is that one cannot understand the meaning of a sentence without its context, a context that most naturally resolves most ambiguities in interpreting the sentence.[2] Thus sentences or verses or clauses are studied in relation to other sentences or verses that they may be related to in a hierarchy of meaning.

Hierarchy

The primary tool used to look at the hierarchy of meaning in 1 Peter is that of semantic structural analysis, more specifically the model presented by Longacre. He presents an extensive catalogue of semantic relations that (1) occur between clauses within a sentence and then (2) that occur between sentences and groups of sentences or paragraphs.[3] Such semantic catalogues are not unique to Longacre; several other scholars have semantic catalogues that they suggest can aid in understanding a text.[4] The purpose of such an analysis is to establish the relations that exist between the elements of the text in a very conscious and intentional

---

[1] Robert E Longacre, *The Grammar of Discourse*, 2nd ed. (SIL, 1996), 1.

[2] Ibid.

[3] Longacre, *The Grammar of Discourse*. See chapter four for clausal relations and chapter five for relations between sentences and paragraphs.

[4] See for example John Beekman and John Callow, *Translating the Word of God* (SIL, 1974); Mildred L. Larson, *Meaning Based Translation: A Guide to Cross-language Equivalence*, 2nd ed. (University Press of America, 1998); Kathleen Callow, *Man and Message: A Guide to Meaning-Based Text Analysis* (University Press of America, 1998); and George H. Guthrie and J. Scott Duvall, *Biblical Greek Exegesis: A Graded Approach to Learning Intermediate and Advanced Greek* (Zondervan, 1998). While the terminology or labels may differ, they all are doing the same sort of thing.

way. We shall be primarily looking at the relationships that exist between sentences and paragraphs. Any two sentences that cluster together form a paragraph which in turn may combine with another sentence or paragraph to form a larger paragraph and even continue upward to form a section of a text.

Semantic relations within a paragraph are not flat. That is, a paragraph is not just a sequence of sentences all of which are equally prominent or salient. Typically within a local span of text some sentence will be more prominent, forming a hierarchy of meaning. If this were not true, processing communication would be most difficult indeed. If all things are equal, they might well be also equally unintelligible or at least quite difficult to decipher. For example, teachers of developmental English talk about the topic sentence as that which controls the organization of the paragraph. The rest of the paragraph develops or supports the topic sentence.[5] Longacre and Hwang in their discussion of this hierarchy of meaning use the term salience and discuss salience ranking schemes. A salience ranking scheme ranks the "continuum verbs and clauses of a text so as to reflect the salient (highly prominent) mainline information down to the lowest supportive information."[6] In other words, one element dominates and is supported or developed by others. So the text exhibits salience. Sentences of higher salience dominate the paragraph.

In analysis presented here, the semantic relationship of different elements, clauses or paragraphs, is categorized with the dominating element labeled Thesis, showing that it is the most salient. Of course, both elements may be equally salient. For example, we may have coordinate Theses in which the propositions or paragraphs are equally salient. Consider for example:

Light is good. Darkness is bad.

Here are two equivalent Theses in a contrastive relation. Both are equally salient. But consider again the following:

Light is good. I can see where I am going.

Here the claim "light is good" is the Thesis supported by the following sentence. More support could be given: "I don't stumble when I walk or step into a

---

[5] Writing Tutorial Services: WTS Writing Guides: Paragraphs and Topic Sentences, Indiana University Bloomington: http://wts.indiana.edu/pamphlets/paragraphs.shtml (accessed July 3, 2017). One can write a paragraph without a topic sentence if the topic is inferable. But the writer needs greater skill to successfully write such a paragraph.

[6] Robert E. Longacre and Shin Ja J. Hwang, *Holistic Discourse Analysis*, 2nd ed. (SIL, 2012), 223.

pothole." In other words, the dominant proposition is that light is good, and the second sentence provides support. The second or further supporting sentences are less salient. Various semantic relations can occur in the development or support of a Thesis: conditionality, causation, circumstance, paraphrase, illustration, identification, and comment, just to name a few.[7]

Text-Type

Another important theoretical issue is that of genre or text-type. Longacre identifies four basic notional[8] text-types: narrative, procedural, behavioral, and expository. He considers two basic features which give him the four text-types: contingent temporal succession and agent orientation.[9] Figure 19.1 gives the basic outline of how the four basic text-types are organized.

	+ Agent Orientation	- Agent Orientation
+ Temporal Succession	Narrative	Procedural
- Temporal Succession	Behavioral	Expository

Figure 19.1: Longacre's Text Types

A narrative is organized by contingent temporal succession plus agent orientation. There is a sequence of events involving an agent. A procedure has a temporal orientation but without a focus on an agent. Procedural texts are written for anybody to follow, so the agent is not in focus. Behavioral texts have agent orientation but are arranged logically—not by means of temporal succession. For example hortatory, a type of behavioral text, gives commands to an agent with the hope that the agent will comply. Finally, exposition is minus for both features, being logically arranged and without an agent in focus. He also considers two more features: +/- tension and +/- projection. This results in a sixteen-cell layout of notional discourse types.[10] For example, a behavioral text that has + projection is a hortatory text, someone wants somebody to do something. Eulogy would be – projection.

---

[7] See Longacre and Hwang, *Holistic Discourse Analysis*, 217–221 for a brief summary of possible relations. See Longacre, *The Grammar of Discourse*, chapters 3 and 4 for a more extensive presentation.

[8] By notional Longacre means universal features we expect to find in languages everywhere. See Longacre and Hwang, *Holistic Discourse Analysis*, 220 for a definition of the term and 38 and 39–42 for a discussion of the realization of these notional structures in a particular language. This notional understanding provides a starting point for discovering the emic, language-specific system in a language.

[9] Longacre, *The Grammar of Discourse*, 9–11.

[10] Ibid., 10.

Climax and Peak

A hortatory text with argument is + tension, reflecting that some sort of difficulty or struggle must be overcome in order for the command to be appropriately responded to. Without the struggle there is no tension. Most of us are used to tension in a narrative where the story builds to a climax, the place of highest tension with high interest and complication.[11] In Longacre's model the term climax refers to an underlying notional structure that is thought to be universal, found in all languages.[12] A climax will manifest in different ways depending upon the language and genre of text or even the author. This surface manifestation is referred to as peak. In other words, a climax will have some sort of surface level expression; it could be longer or shorter sentences, different types of verbs, rhetorical underlining, and so on. Basically the discourse analyst is looking for some sort of change of pattern.[13] In non-narrative text these surface level markings typically occur "at the culminating exhortation, or argument, or the most adequate explanation."[14] Hortatory texts can build to a climax, reflecting the struggle or difficulty of responding to the commands. A longer text can contain more than one underlying climatic structure or surface level peaks. For example, Longacre in his analysis of 1 John identifies four surface level peaks, two doctrinal and two ethical.[15] Peter's text also has multiple peaks.

Mainline and Motivational Material

The point of all of this is that we cannot approach a text without an awareness of what genre it belongs in. A hortatory text such as 1 Peter cannot be analyzed the same way as a narrative text in the Gospels. The mainline or backbone of the text is different. The mainline of a hortatory text is commands, imperative verbs and other commanding forms. A hortatory text with tension will have a considerable amount of exposition where relational and static verb forms are typical.[16] In fact, a text with a majority of expository verb types may still be classified as hortatory. Longacre and Hwang comment that it is not count that is determinative, but the weight.[17] Exposition embeds within the text in support of the command(s). The more difficult the command, the greater will be the need for supporting material to back it up.

---

[11] Longacre and Hwang, *Holistic Discourse* Analysis, 212.

[12] This does not mean that there are not texts that have no tension or cultures that may prefer –tension or episodic texts. Longacre's model acknowledges this with its –tension category.

[13] See Longacre, *The Grammar of Discourse*, 38ff. for a list of peak marking devices; see below.

[14] Longacre and Hwang, *Holistic Discourse Analysis*, 220.

[15] Longacre, "Towards an Exegesis of 1 John Based on the Discourse Analysis of the Greek Text," in *Linguistics and New Testament Interpretation*, ed. David Allen Black (B&H, 1992), 279ff.

[16] Longacre, "Towards an Exegesis of 1 John," 278.

[17] Longacre and Hwang, *Holistic Discourse* Analysis, 174.

However, we must not suppose that because certain material only supports the mainline commanding form, it is not important. The author presents such material so as to make the commands more reasonable and thereby more likely to be acted upon. We might term supporting material as motivational: its purpose is to motivate the audience to action. 1 Peter 2:19–25 is a good example of such a supporting motivational text. After commanding believing slaves to submit to their masters, even bad ones in 2:18, Peter goes on for the rest of the paragraph to support the command. He tells them that God commends suffering for doing good and then goes on to give the example of Christ's suffering. The command to submit is a difficult one, so Peter extends considerable support to motivate these recipients of his letter to obey the command. This pattern of command plus motivation is repeated several times over. In short, 1 Peter is a hortatory text with a considerable amount of embedded exposition.

Hortatory Template

A hortatory text typically follows a basic four-pronged template: (1) establishment of authority, (2) problem(s) presented, (3) command forms, mitigated or not, and (4) motivational material that supports the commands.[18] Some authors might elide the appeal to authority, but not Peter. He is an apostle (1:1) and a witness of Christ's passion (5:1). Issues or problems are presented throughout the text, primarily stemming from the fact that these believers are suffering; they are being persecuted because they are Christians. Commands and motivational material are interspersed throughout as well. The backbone of the text is its command forms, usually finite imperative verbs plus other forms used to indicate commands: the performative verb plus the infinitive, the participle in certain instances, adjectives (occurring at peak), and in some places a commanding structure with the command form elided (again at peak). Participles, adjectives, and elision can be used to diagnose surface level peak marking since they are not the normal forms for the command line.

Macrostructure

A well-formed text has a basic global idea or thrust that structures its message, a view of the text as a whole, often called the macrostructure.[19] Callow

---

[18] Robert E. Longacre, "The Discourse Strategy of an Appeals Letter," in *Discourse Description: Diverse Linguistic Analyses of a Fund-raising Text*, ed. William C. Mann and Sandra A. Thompson (John Benjamins, 1992), 110. Ervin R. Starwalt, *A Discourse Analysis of 1 Peter*, SKG (Fontes, 2020), 8–9.

[19] Longacre, *The Grammar of Discourse*, 4, 33; Longacre and Hwang, *Holistic Discourse Analysis*, 218.

in reference to macrostructure, but referring to it as theme, says that, "The theme is prominent material which moves the message forward towards the communicator's goal. It is the framework of message development."[20] The concept of a macrostructure has a cognitive basis. It involves a reduction of complex information to a manageable or comprehensible form.[21] The text producer or reader ignores certain details in order to conceptualize the point of text.[22] When the text gets large or complex enough that memory no longer can handle processing it, a reduction that involves both reduction and synthesis occurs. Without it the text would lose its coherence and we would never be able to process a text that went beyond our short-term memory.[23] A macrostructure is derived from the microstructures and is necessary for interpreting the microstructures.[24]

How do we identify the macrostructure? Van Dijk suggests various ways in which the macrostructure is signaled. There may be key words or thematic sentences or nominalized themes.[25] He gives a process for arriving at a text's macrostructure. It first involves deleting material that is locally relevant, while retaining the globally relevant. Next come generalization and abstraction from details to form a more general concept from which a new proposition must be formed.

How then is this applied to 1 Peter? First, online material is vitally important for getting the gist of the book. That means we need to pay close attention to the commanding backbone of the text. Much of the supporting material can be ignored. But we also need to realize that what might be seen as typically supporting material can be promoted to mainline. We will argue such for 2:4–10 below. Moreover, peak feature in a paragraph can give it extra prominence in the text, forming a backbone of sorts of the mainline. So peak paragraphs in 1 Peter give us a good picture of where the text is going and what Peter's goal is in his letter.[26] Longacre also proposes that noticing where peaks occur and what come before and after them is a good way to arrive at the message of a book.[27] Thus to establish the macrostructure of 1 Peter, we must look closely at the peak material in 1 Peter.

---

[20] Callow, *Man and Message,* 231.

[21] Teun A. van Dijk, *Text and Context: Explorations in the Semantics and Pragmatics of Discourse* (Longman, 1977), vi.

[22] Ibid., 4.

[23] Ibid., 8–12.

[24] Ibid., 13, 26.

[25] Ibid., 27, 88.

[26] See ibid., 102–103.

[27] Longacre, "Towards an Exegesis of 1 John," 279.

Indicators of Peak

How then does one determine what is peak in the text? Longacre refers to peak as a zone of turbulence where the routine pattern is broken. He gives a list of features that may signal peak. There may be rhetorical underlining by means of parallelism or paraphrase. In narrative, it may be encoded by means of the crowded stage, where all the participants suddenly are on stage at once. Correspondently, in a hortatory text we could also add the convergence of significant themes, themes coming together on the mainline (which we will see below). It could involve unusual verb forms in the peak paragraph. In certain paragraphs in 1 Peter, for example, participles and adjectives occur with imperatival force. It could involve something as simple as a change in sentence length.[28] Simply put, we are looking for a change in pattern. The place to look for such surface features in a hortatory text is at concluding exhortations and in key supporting material or motivational material.

Chunking the Text

Finally, a comment on how the text was analyzed. Here we first consider the basic unit or structure that was considered in order to determine the basic semantic analysis as presented below. This is followed by a look at how the letter segments into sections and subsections, a macrosegmentation concern.

Basic Unit of Analysis

The basic unit for analysis as presented here is roughly the sentence as represented by a full stop, a period, a question mark, or a colon.[29] It might be argued that the colon marks only part of a sentence, but the purpose is to segment the text into manageable units and observing the colon as marking a unit helps to do that. It is possible to analyze a text clause by clause.[30] However that would add more detail, more than is needed to get the idea of how the text is functioning. This does not mean that clausal relations are not important, but rather that at times they are not in focus in the present analysis, especially if they are part of the inner working of a larger unit that is in a semantic relationship to another unit. Neither does this mean that internal clauses are to be automatically ignored. They can be very helpful in figuring out the function of the larger unit.

---

[28] See Longacre, *The Grammar of Discourse*, 38–48 for his discussion of peak marking features.

[29] See Starwalt, *A Discourse Analysis of 1 Peter*, 5–8 for a fuller explanation of the method used.

[30] Steven Runge, ed., *The Lexham Discourse Greek New Testament* (Lexham Press, 2008–2014) does an analysis that includes clausal relations.

UBS[4] and UBS[5] are the texts consulted, with primacy given to UBS[4] for doing semantic analysis. UBS[5] often has less punctuation. For example, UBS[5] punctuates 1:3–9 as a single sentence while UBS[4] has five, counting the colon as a full stop. Thus, UBS[4] punctuation provides the opportunity for a more detailed semantic analysis of the text without considering every clause.[31]

Macrosegmentation of 1 Peter

The next concern is how to segment the text into sections. The text is analyzed as having a body introduction (1:3–2:10), a body middle (2:11–4:11), and a body conclusion (4:12–5:11).[32] 1:1–2 gives a fairly formulaic opening of the letter and 5:12–14 an equally formulaic closing. Peter's use of the vocative adjective *beloved* (ἀγαπητοί) helps to segment part of the text, specifically the last two sections. Vocatives often signal a transition.[33] In addition, the vocatives are coupled with a commanding form to further signal the start of the last two sections: the performative plus the infinitive in 2:11, *I-exhort you . . . to abstain* (παρακαλῶ . . . ἀπέχεσθαι) and the imperative in 4:12, *don't you-be-surprised* (μὴ ξενίζεσθε). "This coupling of the vocative is a common stylistic device in the New Testament for indicating a new start in the argument."[34] Further indication that the vocative *beloved* indicates a new start is that the vocative plus the command in 2:11 follows a lengthy OT quote which closes out the section of 1:3–2:10 in a climactic fashion,[35] and that in 4:12 it follows a doxology.[36]

The first section of 1:3–2:10 divides into two subsections: the opening praise of God which is motivational followed by a hortatory section beginning in 1:13 that is distinguished by the imperatives that occur: the recipients are commanded to hope (1:13), to be holy and fear God (1:14–16 and 4:17), to love one another (1:22) and to desire God's word (2:1–3). The last portion of the second subsection, 2:4–10, is a climatic motivational unit, closing out the section. More will be said about this unit below.

---

[31] It would be fair to call this a pragmatic convenience. Nothing theoretical is implied.

[32] See Starwalt, *A Discourse Analysis of 1 Peter*, 25–27 for the structural understanding of the letter as presented in this section.

[33] See Starwalt, *A Discourse Analysis of 1 Peter*, 26; Robert E. Longacre, "Exhortation and Mitigation in First John," *Selected Technical Related to Translation*, no. 9 (December 1983), 7, 30; and Barth L. Campbell, *Honor, Shame, and the Rhetoric of 1 Peter*, SBLDS (Scholars Press, 1995), 99.

[34] Starwalt, *A Discourse Analysis of 1 Peter*, 26. See also J. Ramsey Michaels, *1 Peter*, WBC 49 (Word, 1988), 115. Cf. Rom 12:1; 1 Cor 1:10.

[35] William Joseph Dalton, *Christ's Proclamation to the Spirits: A Study of 1 Peter* (Pontifical Biblical Institute, 1965), 76.

[36] Thomas R. Schreiner, *1, 2 Peter, Jude*, NAC 37 (B&H, 2003), 216.

The second section, the body middle (2:11–4:11) also consists of two units. The first subsection (2:11–3:12) exhorts these believers to do good in social hierarchical relations. Peter exhorts believers to be submissive to authorities (2:13–14), slaves submissive to masters (2:18) and wives submissive to their husbands (3:1). Husbands are commanded to treat their wives with consideration and honor (3:7). All the previous commands have been to those in the weaker position in the hierarchy, but now the husbands are commanded to act in such a way that they will not take advantage of their wives. Finally, this subsection climaxes with commands to all believers (3:8–12): all should be of one mind, sympathetic, loving, tender hearted, humble, not returning evil for evil, but rather blessing. Then Peter quotes Psalm 34:12–16 to give scriptural support to the commands: God looks favorably on those doing right, but he is against those who do evil. Thus, ends this subsection.

The next subsection (3:13–4:11) continues the idea of doing good. Following up on the quote in the psalm that God is for the righteous and against evil doers, Peter asks who would harm one zealous for good (3:13). Expected answer, no one. But then Peter affirms that harm is a possibility (3:14a): even if you should suffer (πάσχοιτε),[37] you are blessed. Then he commands them to not fear their persecutors (3:14b). Rather they are to set apart Christ in their hearts (3:15a), always ready to give a defense or explanation of their hope with gentleness (3:15b–16). The next command comes in 4:1: they are to have the attitude of Christ toward suffering. And finally, to close out this section, Peter tells them that the end of all things is near (4:7a). He then follows with a series of exhortations: be sensible and disciplined in prayer (4:7b), loving (4:8), hospitable (4:9), minister as good stewards (4:10), and lastly, speak God's words and minister in his strength (4:11). Thus, this section ends with a flurry.

The final section (4:12–5:11) is analyzed as having three subsections. The first subsection (4:12–19) opens with the vocative, as noted above, which is followed by a command: Peter tells his addressees to not think it strange if they suffer. Then again in 4:19 Peter gives another command: they are to commit themselves to the Lord in doing good in the midst of suffering. In 5:1–5 Peter first charges the elders to shepherd the flock willingly, not lording over their charges. Young men on the other hand are to submit to the elders. Then in the final subsection comes a series of related commands. Peter now addresses everyone telling them first of all to humble themselves before God in casting their cares upon him (5:6–7).[38] Next they are commanded to be sober and watchful because of their enemy the

---

[37] The optative here suggests a more remote possibility. See Daniel B. Wallace, *Greek Grammar Beyond the Basics* (Zondervan, 1996), 484.

[38] See Schreiner, *1, 2 Peter, Jude*, 240 for an explanation of the participle *casting* (ἐπιρίψαντες) as instrumental giving how believers are to humble themselves.

devil (5:8). In conjunction with the command to be watchful, these believers are directed to resist the devil (5:9). Then, 5:10–11 terminates the subsection; in fact it terminates the letter.[39] Peter ends his letter by affirming that God, who has called these suffering believers though Christ, will strengthen them; and lastly he closes with a brief doxology: to him be power forever.

Macrostructure

A good place to start in determining the macrostructure of 1 Peter is to first consider those paragraphs that exhibit peak features: 2:4–10; 3:9–12; 4:7–11, and 4:12–19. In this section we consider the cumulative thrust of these four paragraphs, leaving the microanalysis that establishes them as peak for the next section. Peter follows a general pattern of presentation in his letter. Typically, in each section or subsection he builds toward a climax except in the case of 4:12–19 which begins its section.[40]

2:4–10 climaxes the section of 1:3–2:10. It is a doctrinal or motivational peak. The passage focuses on the reception of the living stone, Jesus, by these believers. With extensive citations or allusions to the OT, this paragraph hammers home that God has chosen them; they are his people. So a part of the gist of this book is that in Christ the recipients belong to God as his chosen people.

3:8–12 is the climatic paragraph for the section of 2:11–3:12. Doing good is thematic in this section, even in difficult situations that a slave or wife might encounter. This peak paragraph focuses on how the believers are to conduct themselves. Within the church they are to be like-minded, sympathetic, loving, compassionate, and humble (3:8). Apparently considering outsiders in 3:9, Peter tells them not to return evil for evil or insult for insult, but they are instead to bless. The passage thus tells believers how to honor all,[41] believers and unbelievers.[42] The last command appears to paraphrase all the rest: bless. So from this paragraph we see that Peter wants this church, in attitude and action, to bless insiders and outsiders.

Next follows 4:7–11 climaxing the section of 3:13–4:11. Peter asserts that the end is near. He has just finished making a comment about judgement in 4:4–6.[43] In that circumstance he gives a series of commands: be sober-minded and self-controlled in prayer; love; be hospitable; and minister as God has gifted you including the

---

[39] See Peter H. Davids, *The Frist Epistle of Peter*, NICNT (Eerdmans, 1990), 194, and Schreiner, *1, 2 Peter, Jude*, 244 for comments on the terminating function of this paragraph.

[40] See below in section 3 for an explanation for considering this paragraph as exhibiting peak features.

[41] Following the command in 2:17.

[42] Starwalt, *A Discourse Analysis of 1 Peter*, 78–81.

[43] See Schreiner, *1, 2 Peter, Jude*, 210.

speaking of God's words. The good works that are in focus here are those that build up the body of Christ: again prayer, love, hospitality, and ministry of various types. Peter wants these people to care for each other in the believing community in the mist of their circumstance. He is still emphasizing the theme of doing good.

Last of all comes the opening paragraph of the section of 4:12–5:11, namely, 4:12–19. Peter opens this paragraph, commanding his addressees not to be surprised by persecution. Instead they are to rejoice in sharing in Christ's suffering (4:13). Again in 4:16 he tells his audience that if they suffer they ought not to be ashamed. Rather they should glorify God in Christ's name if they suffer as Christians. The final command of this paragraph comes in 4:19 where Peter commands those who suffer according to God's will to commit themselves to a faithful creator in doing good. This is the point of the paragraph.

To intent of the letter might be stated thusly: Reminding these believers that they are God's people in Christ, Peter calls them to do good in honoring others by blessing them, to do good by praying, loving, and ministering to those in the house of God, and finally in their suffering to commit themselves to God doing good. In fact the whole letter may be summarized in 4:19: Let those who are suffering according to the will of God commit themselves to a faithful creator in doing good.[44] Now we turn to a closer analysis of these four paragraphs.

Microstructures

As presented above, the macrostructure analysis taken here suggests four key paragraphs to be looked at more closely: 2:4–10, 3:8–13, 4:7–11, and 4:12–19. These four paragraphs exhibit surface level features of peak. "How so?" it may be asked. To answer that question, we look at the flow of thought relative to these passages as well as a microanalysis of each paragraph. The analysis of each paragraph is followed by a display of the semantic structure of the paragraph. Readers may wish to consult the display at the end of the discussion to have a visual to aid in following the argument.

Doctrinal Peak: 1 Peter 2:4–10

Ellicott understands 2:4–10 to form a doctrinal climax in 1 Peter, observing that 1:3–12 and 2:4–10 form a doctrinal inclusion around the hortatory portion of 1:13–2:3 where the recipients are commanded to hope on the grace that comes when Christ is revealed (1:13), not to be conformed to their former desires, but rather to

---

[44] The section below on the salience of suffering will argue that this is indeed the gist of the letter.

be holy (1:14–15), to fear or reverence the father (1:17), to love one another fervently (1:22), and to crave the pure spiritual milk (2:1–3).[45] These are the online commands in this hortatory text.

In the sentence comprising 2:1–3, Peter commands his audience to desire spiritual milk which appears to be a command based on the mention of God's word in 2:25. These believers are to earnestly desire pure spiritual milk so that they might grow into salvation, if they have tasted that the Lord is good. Then supporting motivational material follows in 2:4–10. The command in 2:1–3 finds its primary support in the motivational material of 2:4–10, although it may be argued that the praise of God for his wonderful provision of salvation sits behind it as well, if Ellicott's assertion is correct that the commands of this section are bracketed by supporting or motivational material.

What follows in 2:4–10 is a discussion of Christ's centrality and the believers' status before God. This expository material is essential support of not only the command in 2:1, but also of the whole text. Surface level peak marking features promote this paragraph from being merely supportive. Peter states here information that these believers must know, understand, and believe if they are to be able to do what he asks of them in this epistle. Three features indicate the peak nature of the material. First, there is a convergence of lexical terms and concepts in the paragraph, a crowded lexical or conceptual stage of sorts.[46] One term is *holy*, ἅγιος (2:5, 9; cf. 1:15–16, 19, and 22). Second is *believe*, occurring as a noun or verbal, πίστις and πιστεύω (the noun occurring in 1:5, 7, 8, 9, 21 and the verbal in 1:8 and in 2:6, 7 in this paragraph). Third there is (*dis*)*obedience*, ἀπειθέω (2:8) set against ὑπακοή (1:14, 22). Fourth is *word*, λόγος (2:8; cf. 1:23 and 2:2 if the metaphor is counted as referring to the *word*). Fifth is a cluster of words referring to God's selection of these believers as his own: *chosen*, ἐκλεκτός (2:9; cf. 1:1) and *call*, καλέω (2:9; cf. 1:15). In fact, Peter is emphatic about God having chosen his readers: They are a chosen race, a royal priesthood, a holy nation, a people for his possession.[47] There are a whole cluster of terms and metaphors at play here. Finally come the terms related to moral and ethical behavior:[48] *mercy*, ἐλεέω, is mentioned twice in 2:10; it may be seen as an outgrowth of *grace*, χάρις (see 1:13). As can be seen, 2:4–10 is lexically and conceptually dense.

---

[45] John H. Ellicott, *1 Peter: A New Translation with Introduction and Commentary*, AB 37B (Doubleday, 2000), 407–408.

[46] See Longacre, *The Grammar of Discourse*, 40; Ellicott, *1 Peter*, 407 notes this convergence of motifs.

[47] This emphasis on their special relationship with God would be important to those struggling with persecution and perhaps questioning their relationship to God because of it. It forms an important motivational basis for the commands that will continue throughout the text.

[48] See L&N, 1:742, 750.

The second feature signaling that this paragraph is a doctrinal or motivational peak is the concentration of OT quotes or allusions. The text has some twenty-nine citations from or allusions to the OT,[49] establishing that through Christ these believers are truly God's own people. In addition, this paragraph contains the highest number of "stone" quotations in the New Testament.[50] We will look at the structure of the paragraph while noting the use of OT quotes.

The paragraph is analyzed as follows. First it is observed that the paragraph stands in support of the commanding sentence of 2:1–3: believers are to desire the pure spiritual milk if they have tasted that the Lord is good, v. 3 itself referring to Ps 34. So the commanding sentence forms the thesis of the larger unit of 2:1–10. This thesis is hortatory followed by a larger expository paragraph that consists of several embedded paragraphs. Perhaps we might visualize the structure as a group of nested paragraphs, one inside the other before it. First the sentence of vv. 4–5 provides a comment on the word *lord* that the end v. 3. The comment in v. 4 says that these believers have come to Christ, the living stone, who was rejected by men (Ps 118:22), but who was elect and precious to God (Isa 28:16). The sentence continues in v. 5 to state how these believers as living stones have become a spiritual community so as to be a holy priesthood (Ex 19:6; Is 61:6) that offers spiritual sacrifices to God. This sentence of vv. 4–5 in turn forms the thesis of an attestation[51] paragraph. That is, the rest of the passage gives the evidence for the claim being made about Jesus and his people in vv. 4–5, using many OT scriptures to support the claim. V. 6 quotes Isa 28:16, stating that God has placed in Zion an elect and precious stone; those believing in him shall not be put to shame. This statement in turn forms the thesis for what follows: the statement is amplified in vv. 7–8a. We may summarize the material here: God honors those who trust Christ, who form the basis of the believing community, but Christ, on the other hand offends unbelievers (Ps 118:22 and Isa 8:140). Of note here is the use of δέ[52] at the end of 7a, signaling the shift from the discussion of believers to a statement about Christ's reception by unbelievers: Jesus, the stone whom the unbelieving rejected, has become the cornerstone (Ps 118:22). This sentence continues to the end of v. 8a. Here Jesus is described as a stone of stumbling and a rock of offence (Isa 8:14). Then v. 8b provides a brief comment

---

[49] This count comes from the apparatus of UBS[5] which lists both MT and LXX quotes or allusions; this is more than Ellicott, *1 Peter,* 407–408 observes, but he still notes an extensive number, referring to them as collages of quotations.

[50] D. A. Carson, "1 Peter," in *Commentary on the New Testament Use of the Old Testament,* ed. G. K. Beale and D. A. Carson (Baker Academic, 2007), 1028.

[51] Attestation refers to giving evidence for something.

[52] See Steven E. Runge, *Discourse Grammar of the Greek New Testament: A Practical Introduction for Teaching and Exegesis* (Lexham Press, 2010), 31ff. for a discussion of the discourse function of δέ.

on the unbelievers: The Gospel offends unbelievers because God has appointed them to such. Finally, v. 9 moves on to the next point which paraphrases the previous position of these believers. Again, δέ appears introducing the sentence. Leaving the issue of unbelievers behind, now the status of believers is addressed. In summary, they are God's chosen people. As evidence for this, the OT is referenced sixteen times or so.[53] This is an amazingly dense cluster of OT references, driving home that these believers are truly God's people. Then v. 10 summarizes v. 9, stating that they were once not a community, but now they are since God had mercy upon them (Hos 2:23; 1:6, 9; 2:1).

The third feature indicating peak is the use of paraphrase.[54] Verses 9–10 paraphrase and amplify the statement of 7a, which states that there is honor for those who believe, reflecting the previous statement of v. 6 that those who believe will not be put to shame—an eschatological statement.[55] In vv. 9–10 Peter says the same thing over and over, but in different ways: in v. 9 these believers are referred to as a chosen race, a royal priesthood, a holy nation, and a people for God's own possession. Then in v. 10 all this is paraphrased in a summary stating that they are now God's people: they are a people who formerly were not a people, but now are God's people, who did not receive mercy but now have received mercy. Such repetition signals the importance of what Peter is saying. As he hammers his message home with a barrage of OT references, he further hammers what he says with repetition.

So in summary, 2:4–10 speaks of the centrality of Christ (vv. 4, 5 and 6). Verses 4, 7, and 8 speak to the rejection of Christ, of his rejection of those who do not believe (v. 8). This Christ who has been rejected, but whom these believers have received, has been raised by God and honored. He is the key person for the formation of the Christian community; he is the cornerstone (v. 4). Then starting with v. 5 the text elaborates how these believers have been made into a key people, a spiritual community made by God and one that pleases God. The rest of the passage establishes that these believers are chosen by God; they are chosen to proclaim the mighty deeds of God (v. 9). Those who once were not a people are now God's chosen people (v. 10).

Finally, it may be observed that within this expository portion of the text, a hint appears of the suffering (or persecution) that will be addressed more directly later in the epistle. In 2:8 Peter tells us that Christ offends unbelievers; the

---

[53] The UBS⁵ apparatus lists in sequence as it follows the argument of the sentence, citing both the Hebrew and the LXX: Isa 43:20; Deut 7:6, 10:15; Exod 19:6, 23:22; Isa 61:6; Exod 19:6, 23:22; Isa 43:2; Exod 19:5, 23:22; Deut 4:20, 7:6, 14:2; Isa 43:12, 42:12.

[54] See Longacre, *The Grammar of Discourse*, 39 for a discussion on the use of paraphrase for rhetorical underlining to signal an important part of a text; see 76–82 and 113–114 for a discussion on various types of paraphrase.

[55] See Michaels, *1 Peter*, 104.

gospel offends unbelievers. Thus, they reject Christ and his gospel. What can these believers expect? But at this point Peter does not address the suffering of these believers directly, though he does later in the book. Furthermore, also embedded with this paragraph in v. 9b is something that will become more thematic in the material that follows: God has chosen them so that they might proclaim his virtues.[56] A semantic outline of 1 Pet 2:1–10 follows below in Figure 19.2. The command in 2:1–3 is the fourth command in this section; thus, it is labeled THESIS 4. Ordinarily this would indicate that what follows is subordinate to the command, but for the reasons given above the exposition itself is peak, the only expositional peak in the text.

THESIS 4: Comment ¶ [57]
   THESIS: 2:1–3: So get rid of all evil and all deceit and hypocrisy and envy...
  Comment: Attestation ¶
     THESIS: 2:4–5: So as you come to him, a living stone rejected...
    Evidence: Result ¶
       THESIS: 2:6: For it says in scripture, *"Look, I lay in Zion a stone...*
      Result: Amplification ¶
       THESIS: Comment ¶
         THESIS: 2:7–8a: So you who believe see his value...
         Comment: 8b: They stumble because they disobey...
       Amplification: Summary ¶
         THESIS: 2:9: But you are a chosen race...
         Summary: 2:10: You once were not a people...

Figure 19.2: Semantic Structure of 1 Peter 2:1–2:10

First Hortatory Peak: 3:8–12

In order to follow how the paragraph of 3:8–12 functions, we need to review the construction of the section that it terminates, 2:11–3:12. Figure 19.3 lays out the flow of thought in this section.[58]

---

[56] See Davids, *The First Epistle of Peter*, 92–93 and Schreiner, *1,2 Peter, Jude*, 115–116 for a discussion on this purpose clause.

[57] This semantic outline is based on Starwalt, *A Discourse Analysis of 1 Peter*, 142–143. Indenting shows relative salience or prominence. The English translation used in the semantic displays is that of the *NET Bible* (Biblical Studies Press, 1996–2017). The electronic database from which both the Greek and English in the displays come is that of BibleWorks 10.

[58] See Starwalt, *A Discourse Analysis of 1 Peter*, 55. The display indenting does not reflect salience; each paragraph has a thesis that consists of an online command. The indenting is given as an aid to visualizing the generic-specific relations occurring in the section.

> 2:11–12 Avoid fleshly lusts; do good
>> 2:13–17 (Doing good more specifically involves that all) Submit, love, fear, <u>honor</u>
>>> 2:18–25 (Honor more specifically involves that) Slaves submit to masters
>>> 3:1–6 (Honor more specifically involves that) Wives submit to their husbands
>>> 3:7 (Honor more specifically involves that) Husbands understand and honor their wives
>>> 3:8–12 (Honor more specifically involves that) Believers be compassionate and bless others

Figure 19.3: Flow of Thought in 1 Peter 2:11–3:12

This section consists of six hortatory paragraphs, the first signaling the beginning of a new section of the text by means of the vocative, *beloved,* that introduces v. 11. In this verse Peter uses the performative verb, *I-exhort,* παρακαλῶ, plus the infinitive *to-abstain,* ἀπέχεσθαι, to state the command: abstain from fleshly lusts which war against the soul. This states the negative injunction followed by the positive command in v. 12, the participial construction, *having good conduct.* Good conduct or doing good becomes thematic for all that follows.[59] It is the generic command for all that follows. Peter in this section moves up and down the generic-specific hierarchy.[60]

The second hortatory paragraph begins with the imperative verb *submit* to human intuitions (2:13–14) followed by support for the command (2:15–16). This command to submit forms the first thesis of the paragraph. The paragraph ends with its second thesis given in v. 17, a hinge verse. In rapid succession Peter gives four commands by means of four finite imperative verbs: *honor all, love the brethren, fear God, honor the king.* The sentence forms an inclusio of an even number of elements which puts the ends, *honor,* in focus.[61] In fact this verse acts as a climax to the paragraph, a marked one at that. Verse 17 signals a shift in the generic-specific hierarchy: submission is no longer prominent, rather honor is. Thus the rest of the section deals with how one honors others in various hierarchical relationships: submission for slaves (2:18) and wives (3:1); and for husbands (3:7), understanding and honor toward their wives. This is how those in the various stations do good; they honor.

---

[59] Starwalt, *A Discourse Analysis of 1 Peter,* 56; see Michaels, *1 Peter,* 117.

[60] Starwalt, *A Discourse Analysis of 1 Peter,* 55–60.; see Longacre, *The Grammar of Discourse,* 80 for a brief overview of generic-specific relations.

[61] See Starwalt, *A Discourse Analysis of 1 Peter,* 62; John Beekman et al. *The Semantic Structure of Written Communication,* 5th ed. (SIL, 1974), 120 state that sandwich structures with an even number of elements tend to give prominence to the outer elements.

Now the climax of this section comes in 3:8–12. This paragraph has peak features. It is analyzed as follows. First it opens with *finally*, τὸ τέλος, indicating a close to this section. The sentence composed of 3:8–9 opens with five adjectives used in an imperatival fashion: *of one mind* or *harmonious*, ὁμόφρονες; *sympathetic*, συμπαθεῖς; *having brotherly love*, φιλάδελφοι; *tender hearted*, εὔσπλαγχνοι; and *humble*, ταπεινόφρονες (all in v. 8). Then in v. 9 comes the negative command not to return evil for evil or insult for insult via the participle used for the command, μὴ ἀποδιδόντες, followed by the positive command given by the participle *blessing*, εὐλογοῦντες. The flourish of unusual terms in the place of finite imperatives points to the peak nature of this sentence.[62] These two verses form the thesis of the paragraph (composed of vv. 8–12). Then 3:10–12 gives evidence supporting the commands in vv. 8–9, a quote from Psalm 34:12–16. The first sentence (vv. 10–11) forms the thesis of the evidence given, stating that the one wishing to see good days should avoid evil and pursue peace. The next sentence (v. 12) gives further evidence, evidence for the evidence in vv. 10–11. Why avoid evil and pursue peace? The answer: because God takes care of those who do what is right, but is against evil doers.

Five imperatives plus an infinitive used imperatively occur in vv. 10–11. First the quote gives three negative commands: let him *keep*, παυσάτω, his tongue from evil; let his lips *not speak*, μὴ λαλῆσαι, deceitfully; and let him *turn*, ἐκκλινάτω, from evil. This last negative command opens the next point that begins the negative and goes on with the positive: what is that person to do? Let him *do*, ποιησάτω, good and *seek*, ζητησάτω, peace and *pursue*, διωξάτω, it— peace that is. This part of the quote is command-laden and moreover it is replete with repetition, basically saying the same thing again and again but in different ways—all further signs that this paragraph climaxes this section; it is a peak.[63] Figure 19.4 gives the overall semantic structure of 3:8–12.

THESIS 4: Attestation ¶[64]
    THESIS: 3:8–9: Finally, all of you be harmonious, sympathetic...
    Evidence: Attestation ¶
        THESIS: 3:10–11: For the one who wants to love life...
        Evidence: 3:12: For the eyes of the Lord are upon the...

Figure 19.4: Semantic Structure of 1 Peter 3:8–12

---

[62] See Longacre, *A Grammar of Discourse*, 38–48 for different ways a text may mark peak.

[63] Again see Longacre, *The Grammar of Discourse*, 38–48 for how texts may mark peak; Ellicott, *1 Peter*, 617 appears to consider that a climax happens here, but rejects the idea, seeing this paragraph as a minor conclusion in Peter's line of thought. In one sense he is right; this is not the climatic paragraph of the book; rather it is the climax of this section of the book; see Starwalt, *A Discourse Analysis of 1 Peter*, 78–81.

[64] See Starwalt, *A Discourse Analysis of 1 Peter*, 81 for this display.

Second Hortatory Peak: 4:7–11

1 Peter 4:7–11 closes out another portion of the letter, 3:13–4:11. Three paragraphs make up this part of the letter. In the first paragraph, 3:13–3:22, the doing good theme turns to the issue of suffering, suffering for doing the good. Picking up on the terms *good* and *bad* that are used in the quotation of Psalm 34 in 3:10–12, Peter asks in 3:13, "Who will harm you if you are a zealot for the good?" Expected answer: no one. However, in 3:14a Peter gives a correction to the expected answer (note the ἀλλά) by affirming that if you might suffer, you are blessed. The reality of suffering is held somewhat in abeyance by means of the optative verb for suffer (πάσχοιτε).[65] The question and its answer form an introduction to the paragraph.

Next the sentence comprising vv. 14b–16 gives a series of commands which form the thesis or core of the paragraph. Beginning in v. 14b Peter commands these believers first not to fear their persecutors via two negative subjunctives, *do not fear nor be troubled* (μὴ φοβηθῆτε μηδὲ ταραχθῆτε); then in v. 15a he uses the imperative telling them to *sanctify* (ἁγιάσατε) Christ in their hearts. In v. 15b they are told to be ready to give a defense of their hope, but in v. 16 with gentleness and reverence with a good conscience.[66] Thus vv. 14b–16 give the online commands that pertain to attitude and conduct toward possible antagonists.

What follows in v. 17 supports the commands by telling them that it is better to suffer for doing good than for doing evil, if God so *wills* (θέλοι), again the optative verb, which evokes the most remote possibility. The rest of the paragraph, vv. 18–22, gives the reason why it is better to suffer for doing the good. These believers are to be motivated by what Christ has done for them, suffering for sin so that they might have access to God and because of Christ's victorious status over all.

So in summary the thesis of this paragraph is contained in the commands: these believers are not to fear those who might do harm to them, but rather they are to sanctify Christ in their hearts, meaning that he is to be lord.[67] Having done so, they will be open to the further injunctions: to be ready to give an answer to those who ask about their hope, and to do it in a gentle way, maintaining a clear conscious. Christ's death and resurrection, his provision of salvation, and his victory set the stage for what follows.

The following paragraph, 4:1–6 opens with the inferential conjunction *therefore*, οὖν, signaling a return to the hortatory mainline after the supporting material of

---

[65] The use of the optative here has caused some consternation among some commentators; these believers are suffering. Cf. Ellicott, *1 Peter*, 662; see below on the salience of suffering.

[66] Achtemeier, *1 Peter*, 233n54 and 235 sees these propositions as giving the way in which believers are to sanctify Christ in their hearts; Ellicott, *1 Peter*, understands these propositions following the imperative to be imperatives even though they are not formally imperatival. Either way it is an elaboration of sanctifying Christ in the heart.

[67] See the NIV, NET, NAS, and NLT, all of which translate the idea in this fashion.

3:18–22.[68] Peter is drawing an inference from the previous motivational material, especially 3:18–22 where Christ's victory through his suffering, death, and resurrection is presented. Since Christ has suffered, believers should be ready to do the same.[69]

Peter, based on Christ's suffering, commands believers in 4:1 to *put on* (ὁπλίσασθε) the same way of thinking. Thus, the sentence of 4:1–2 forms the online thesis and the following, vv. 3–6 give further support for doing so.

Finally comes the last paragraph of the section, 4:7–11. This paragraph resembles that of 3:8–12. In 3:8–12 Peter uses a series of adjectives and participles to fill imperative slots. "Here imperative verbs are followed by participles, an adjective, a participle and two clauses that have the command portion elided. The command forms . . . suggest that the argument is coming to a climax and that this paragraph serves to close out this section."[70] Furthermore the paragraph closes with a doxology. Another feature that stands out in this paragraph is the scarcity of supportive or motivational material. Other than the opening and quite short statement in 4:7a, supportive material is given only in two places in postposed clauses: 4:8 and 4:11b. This reveals a shift in paragraph structuring: the two previous paragraphs, 3:13–21 and 4:1–6, have more ample supportive material. 3:13–21 has a reason paragraph supporting the commands not to fear but rather to revere Christ. Within the reason, Peter embeds further supporting comments. Then in 4:1–6, first comes the command to think about suffering the same way as Christ. Next follows a supporting reason with embedded comments rendering further support.

Two primary features indicate that this paragraph closes out the section. First we may note that 4:12 begins with the vocative *beloved* (Ἀγαπητοί), indicating that 4:12 begins a new section just as the same vocative opened the section of the text beginning in 2:11. Second 4:1 opens the statement with the conjunction δέ indicating that the text has moved now to a new point from the previous material.[71] In addition, Peter says, "The end of all is near." The lexical item *end* (τέλος) has appeared once before to signal the close of a section of this letter in 3:8.

In 4:7a, the phrase *the end has drawn near* ". . . gives the circumstance that should motivate the readers to respond to the commands that follow."[72] This

---

[68] For the inferential conjunction see Jakob K. Heckert, *Discourse Function of Conjoiners in the Pastoral Epistles* (SIL, 1996), 94–96; Daniel B. Wallace, *Greek Grammar Beyond the Basics: An Exegetical Syntax of the New Testament* (Zondervan, 1996), 673.

[69] Schreiner, *1,2 Peter, Jude*, 199.

[70] Starwalt, *A Discourse Analysis of 1 Peter*, 99.

[71] Again see Runge, *Discourse Grammar of the Greek New Testament*, 31ff. for a discussion of the discourse function of δέ.

[72] Starwalt, *A Discourse Analysis of 1 Peter*, 99.

sentence is the opening remark, setting up the online commands that follow.[73] The rest of the paragraph is analyzed as thesis, consisting of online commands.

This thesis is composed of four coordinate theses: (1) 4:7b, (2) 4:8, (3) 4:9, and (4) 4:10–11. The fourth thesis is more complicated, organizing the commands here in a generic-specific relationship: the generic command is given in v. 10 followed by two more commands in v. 11 that may be considered more specific applications of the command of v. 10. The structure of the paragraph is analyzed as follows.

Following the introductory circumstantial statement that the end is near comes the first finite imperative statement in 4:7b, thesis 1. Peter commands believers to be *sensible* (σωφρονήσατε) and *sober-minded* (νήψατε) for prayer. These two verbs appear to be quite similar in meaning. Some take this construction to be a hendiadys that rhetorically underscores that the readers must maintain self-control of themselves.[74] Since the two verbs are so close in meaning and appear as a compound verbal phrase, we take the two imperatives as forming one statement, one thesis. "This thesis with its finite imperative verbs initiates what appears to be a series of commands, even though the grammatical constituents of all the following theses are not finite imperatives."[75]

The second coordinate thesis occurs in 4:8. Peter marks the prominence of this thesis by the way he introduces it: he says *above all* (πρὸ πάντων).[76] What follows is the participle *having* (ἔχοντες) that appears to be used imperatively to command them to have earnest love for each other. A brief statement of reason is given in the postposed subordinate clause stating that love covers a multitude of sins.

The third coordinate thesis comes in 4:9 Here the recipients of the letter are told to be *hospitable* (φιλόξενοι) to one another without grumbling. Here we see an adjective used to indicate a command.

Next comes the fourth coordinate thesis, one having a more complicated presentation. In 4:10 readers are exhorted to serve one another as good stewards according to their gifting. The commanding element is the present participle *serving* (διακονοῦντες). This is a generic thesis, giving a broader command that is fleshed out in more detail in what follows in 4:11. In v. 11 two specific coordinate ways are commanded (or we might say the general command gets amplified). In both specific theses no verbal element is present. To represent what is commanded more literally we put the null sign in the verb slot. First, they are told that if anyone *speaks* (λαλεῖ), Ø as the oracles. Second if anyone *serves* (διακονεῖ),

---

[73] See Longacre, *The Grammar of Discourse*, 111 for a discussion of circumstance relations.

[74] Starwalt, *A Discourse Analysis of 1 Peter*, 100; see Achtemeier, *1 Peter*, 294; Daniel C. Arichea and Eugene A. Nida, *A Translator's Handbook on the First Letter from Peter* (United Bible Societies, 1980), 138; for a different view see Michaels, *1 Peter*, 245.

[75] Starwalt, *A Discourse Analysis of 1 Peter*, 100; cf. 3:8–12.

[76] Ibid.

Ø as from the strength which God provides. Then a postposed clause gives the reason for ministering thusly: so that God might be glorified. Finally, in a final postposed clause comes the doxology: to him is the glory and power forever.

In summary the thesis of the paragraph begins with finite imperatives (4:7b), then an imperatival participle follows (4:8), then an adjective (4:9), next a participle again (4:10) followed by an elision twice (4:11) where what might fill the expected imperatival verbs slot is left out. As the paragraph progresses, more and more surface elements of the command structure fall out, although the whole thesis may be seen to be imperatival. As the paragraph progresses the commands come in ever more rapid-fire cadence, with tension mounting until the end. It is almost as if Peter cannot get the commands out fast enough. None of the commands appear to have been intended to be more salient.[77] Thus Peter ends this section in a climatic fashion. A display of the paragraph's structure follows in Figure 19.5.

Circumstance ¶[78]
    Circumstance 4:7a: For the culmination of all things is near.
THESES: Coordinate ¶
    THESIS 1: 4:7b: So be self-controlled and sober-minded...
    THESIS 2: 4:8: Above all keep your love for one another fervent...
    THESIS 3: 4:9: Show hospitality to one another without complaining.
    THESIS 4: Generic-Specific Paraphrase ¶
    GENERIC THESIS: 4:10: Just as each one has received a gift, use it...
    SPECIFIC-THESIS: Coordinate ¶
        THESIS 1: 4:11a: Whoever speaks, let it be with God's words.
        THESIS 2: 4:11b: Whoever serves, do so with the strength...

Figure 19.5: Semantic Structure of 1 Peter 4:7–11

Peak' 4:12–19 (Denouement)

The next section may be analyzed as having three subsections: 4:12–19, 5:1–5, and 5:6–11.[79] The first culminates with the command for believers, in dependence

---

[77] One may argue that in a generic-specific relationship, elements are not equal, that the generic dominates the specific. However, for example, Peter uses this device in 2:17, giving the generic command to honor followed by the specifications of following this command in 2:18, 3:1, and 3:8 which are clearly mainline commands, all equally salient. Again, see Longacre *The Grammar of Discourse*, 80, 113ff. for a discussion of generic-specific relations and of paraphrase structures.

[78] The semantic diagram comes from Starwalt, *A Discourse Analysis of 1 Peter*, 102–103.

[79] See Starwalt, *A Discourse Analysis of 1 Peter*, 113 for an overview of this last section.

upon God, to persist in doing good in the face of persecution. The inferences of this more general command, do good, are given next. Here Peter turns to consider how doing good plays out in the church, addressing the conduct of both leaders and followers. Humility is essential. Finally, in 5:6–11 Peter states some implications of his OT quote from Proverbs 3:34: God resists the proud but gives grace to the humble. If this is so, believers must submit to God who will enable them to resist their real enemy, a supernatural one, the devil.

As previously noted, 4:12–19 begins with the vocative *beloved*, indicating the opening of this final section of the letter.[80] The previous peaks analyzed occur at the end of their sections. Here a paragraph that begins a section exhibits peak features. In fact, we will argue that this is a different sort of peak, calling it peak prime (Peak'), the denouement of the letter. Usually the term is used in reference to narratives. For example, the online Oxford Dictionaries defines denouement as, "The final part of a play, film, or narrative in which the strands of the plot are drawn together and matters are explained or resolved.[81] Longacre and Hwang give the following definition: "from French 'loosen' or 'untie it'; notional slot of a narrative discourse after climax where a crucial event happens making possible a resolution or a way out of difficulty."[82] We may characterize denouement as a certain type of peak, hence the label of Peak'. It will have the surface level features of peak.[83]

But here we are not dealing with narrative, but with a hortatory text. What then are the signs of peak in this paragraph? First, three major themes merge in this paragraph: persistence in doing good, utter dependence upon God as the children of God, and the issue of suffering or persecution for one's faith. In this paragraph these themes converge, creating a thematically crowded stage.[84] 4:19 is where the letter has been headed: commit yourself to the faithful creator in doing good in your suffering. Second, the six imperative verbs of the paragraph of 4:12–19, eight verses long, suggest peak.[85] That is a high concentration of

---

[80] Davids, *The First Epistle of Peter*, 164; Michaels *1 Peter*, 257

[81] *English Oxford Living Dictionaries*, https://en.oxforddictionaries.com/definition/denouement (accessed August 14, 2017).

[82] Longacre and Hwang, *Holistic Discourse Analysis*, 214.

[83] See Longacre, *The Grammar of Discourse* for an example and brief discussion of denouement in narrative. The notional structure is the underlying structure of an argument; it is considered to be universal, though it may appear in the surface level of different texts of different languages in various ways. See Longacre and Hwang, *Holistic Discourse Analysis*, x–xi, 56–57, and 97 for notional and surface feature correlations in narrative; and see 169ff. where they discuss specifically hortatory texts considering the hortatory template, text organization, peak, and so on.

[84] See Longacre, *The Grammar of Discourse*, 40 for crowded stage in narrative.

[85] UBS⁴ has eight sentences while UBS⁵ has seven.

imperatives. Third, the paragraph is an inference paragraph, the first major paragraph to be so structured. That is, the thesis or main point of the paragraph is delayed until the end.[86] The issue of suffering is now online; this paragraph is the most extensive portion of text which has the innocent suffering of these believers so in focus.[87]

The structure of the paragraph is analyzed as follows. 4:12–13 forms the thesis of a reason paragraph, giving two commands. As Peter is prone to do, he gives the negative first followed by the positive command (cf. 3:14–15 and 2:11–12). He first tells them to *not be surprised* (μὴ ξενίζεσθε that they suffer, picking up on the reaction of unbelievers to these believers in 4:4: they are *surprised* (ξενίζονται) that the believers no longer participate with them in activities as they used to do. Then follows the positive corrective: rather they are to rejoice (χαίρετε). The postposed ἵνα clause gives the purpose for such rejoicing: that they may have even greater joy when Christ appears.

4:14 then in addition gives the supporting reason for rejoicing: if you are reviled in the name of Christ, you are blessed (μακάριοι) because the spirit of glory and God rests upon you. This motivational sentence does not move the hortatory argument forward, but rather buttresses what has come before it. The next verse, 4:15, is analyzed as a warning: for let not any of you suffer as a murderer, thief or evildoer or busybody. The conjunction γάρ here suggests that the argument has not moved on, but rather that this imperative somehow supports the previous statement that they are blessed if reviled for Christ because the spirit abides on them.[88] There is some difficulty in understanding a supporting function here due to the imperative verb. Some argue for a different use of γάρ here, seeing the conjunction as marking an inference.[89] This would make v. 15 the next command and not a command supporting v. 14. This problem in no way mitigates the effect of the imperative as a peak marking feature. In fact, the unusual structure could be seen as another way of marking peak by using a more difficult or ambiguous construction here. Nevertheless, we analyze 4:15 as a warning. If they really want to be sure that they are blessed, that the spirit rests upon them, they must avoid these things.

Δέ introduces the next sentence, 4:16. While some see a contrastive coordination with v. 15 here,[90] the conjunction δέ here is taken to mark development to

---

[86] Starwalt, *A Discourse Analysis of 1 Peter*, 104.

[87] Ibid.

[88] See Runge, *Discourse Grammar of the New Testament*, 51ff. and Steven H. Levinsohn, *Discourse Feature of the Greek New Testament*, 91 for the use of γάρ; and see the analysis in of 4:15 in Runge, *The Lexham Discourse New Testament* for an analysis of the use of γάρ that fits with the analysis here; see also Achtemeier, *1 Peter*, 309 and Kelly, *The Epistles of Peter and Jude*, 188.

[89] So Danker, *Lexicon of the New Testament*, s.v. γάρ.

[90] Schreiner, *1, 2 Peter, Jude*, 218.

more relevant material.[91] In other words, the warning is now left behind and the text has returned to and advances the issue of suffering as a Christian. Peter states two commands, again a negative one first followed by the positive: if you suffer as a Christian, *do not be ashamed* (μὴ αἰσχυνέσθω), but rather *glorify* (δοξαζέτω) God in this name.

4:16 forms the thesis or the head of the next embedded paragraph, a reason paragraph. The reason comes in v. 17a: because (ὅτι) the time has come to begin the judgement with the house of God. Then a comment is made upon the term *judgement* (κρίμα): and if first with us, what is the end of those being disobedient to God's gospel? Finally, Peter gives scriptural evidence for his statement, citing Prov 11:31: And if the righteous are hardly saved, what becomes of the ungodly and sinners? Thus 4:17a–18 gives support to the commands of 4:16.

Inference ¶
    THESIS Coordinate ¶
        THESIS 1 Reason ¶
            THESIS: 4:12–13 Dear friends, do not be astonished that a trial by
                fire is occurring among you...
            Reason: Warning ¶
                THESIS: 4:14 If you are insulted for the name of Christ...
                Warning: 4:15 But let none of you suffer as a murderer...
        THESIS 2 Reason ¶
            THESIS: 4:16 But if you suffer as a Christian...
            Reason: Comment ¶
                THESIS: 4:17a For it is time for judgment to begin...
                  Comment: Attestation ¶
                  THESIS: 4:17b And if it starts with us, what will...
                  Attestation: 4:18 And if the righteous are...
THESIS: 4:19 So then let those who suffer according to God's will entrust...

Figure 19.6: Semantic Structure of 1 Peter 4:12–19

4:19 opens with *therefore* (ὥστε) introducing a statement that is a conclusion that is to be drawn from the preceding material in the paragraph.[92] Suffering again is an issue in the formation of the thesis of this sentence as in vv. 12–16. Verse 19 relates back not only to the previous sentence, but also to this theme of suffering that runs through the paragraph.[93] Here in v. 19 the three themes merge

---

[91] Starwalt, *A Discourse Analysis of 1 Peter*, 107; see Levinsohn, *Discourse Features of New Testament Greek*, 112 for the use of δέ in non-narrative texts.

[92] L&N, 1:783–784.

[93] Starwalt, *A Discourse Analysis of 1 Peter*, 108–109; Schreiner, *1, 2, Peter, Jude*, 229.

being explicitly stated: suffering/persecution, doing good, and dependence on God. Figure 19.6 above outlines the semantic structure of the paragraph.

The Salience of Suffering in 1 Peter

Three major themes converge in 1 Pet 4:19, but only two of them go mainline early in the letter. Believers are exhorted to do good throughout the letter: they are to be holy (1:15), to have good conduct (2:13), to render honor appropriately (2:17), to bless (3:9), and on again throughout the letter Peter exhorts the recipients of his letter to good behavior. In other words, doing good is mainline early on throughout the text. Next is the theme of being God's own people. Peter addresses these believers as the elect of God (1:1) and follows this by exclaiming that God is to be blessed for the wonderful gift of salvation he has given them (1:3–12), indicating that they are of the family of faith. This eulogy of God forms the basis of the commands that follow throughout the text.[94] But the preeminent passage, establishing God's relationship to these Christians is that of 2:4–10. With reference after reference to OT passages, Peter concludes that they are God's people; his mercy rests upon them. As already asserted, the preponderance of OT quotes or allusions and other features of the paragraph point to this paragraph being promoted to mainline, even though it contains no command. It is more than just mainline; it is peak. Thus God's relationship to his people is established early in the letter, receiving consideration in the mainline of the letter. They truly are God's own.

In contrast, the issue of suffering is approached much more cautiously. Peter does not immediately broach the issue of suffering as a Christian directly. In other words, he takes his time in promoting the issue of their suffering to mainline status. In those places where it surfaces as part of the mainline (2:18 and 3:19), the normalcy of suffering is not established. Not until chapter four does suffering as a believer become part of the command line. There Peter tells believers that suffering is normal.

Peter first mentions suffering in 1:6–7, in the midst of commenting on these believers' joyous reception of the salvation that God has provided. They are joyous even though they must suffer for a short time. The focus of the paragraph (1:3–12) is on the blessed God and the wonderful salvation he has given these believers. The comment on suffering is buried lower down in the salience structure of the paragraph. The paragraph may be seen as a series of nested paragraphs. Starting with a call to bless God, Peter structures the paragraph with a

---

[94] Ellicott, *1 Peter*, 329. Jobes, *1 Peter*, 79 describes 1:3–12 as persuasive, meaning that it is meant to affect attitude. No commands are given; rather it forms the basis for the following commands.

series of result or comment paragraphs. The first nested paragraph in vv. 6–7 gives the result of the circumstance[95] laid out in vv. 3–5, followed by a comment on Christ in vv. 8–9, followed by a comment on the prophets' role in this salvation in vv. 10–11, and finally followed by a comment on the prophets of old. The paragraph may be outlined as follows in the diagram below.

Thesis: 1:3–5 May God be blessed for ...

    Result: 1:6–7 In which (salvation) you rejoice ... though suffering briefly.

        Com.: 1:8–9 Whom you love, not seeing.

            Com.: 1:10–11 Salvation prophets prophesied ... The sufferings of Christ and glory.

                Com.: 1:12 They ministered, not for themselves, but for you— angels want to know.

Figure 19.7: Semantic Structure of 1 Peter 1:3–12

In 1:11 the suffering of Christ is also mentioned, but at this point it too is buried down in the hierarchy of the text.

Following this opening motivational paragraph, Peter gives a series of five commands, starting with 1:13 extending to 2:1–3. Only in the supportive material of one command is there any mention of suffering, the suffering of Christ. The believers are commanded to have reverent conduct in 1:17 and the supporting reason is that they were redeemed by the blood of Christ (1:19). 2:4–10, as previously asserted is on the mainline and is a doctrinal peak. There, the suffering that is mentioned is that of Christ. In 2:4 Christ is rejected by men and then again in 2:7 Christ is the stone the builders rejected. 2:8 continues the idea, describing Christ as a stone of stumbling. Here again the suffering of Christ is being alluded to; suffering of these believers is not being directly addressed. It might be deduced that believers' suffering could be the occasion of such an extensive and emphatic discussion of their standing before God, that they are emphatically his own people.

Next follows a section that is thematically held together by the call for these believers to do good. In 2:11–12 they are commanded to avoid fleshly lusts and to have good conduct among the non-Christians. The command to submit to governmental authority follows in 2:13; a reason given in 2:15 is that by doing so they might silence the foolish ignorance of nonbelievers by doing good. Again, a backdrop of hostility can be deduced from this reason given for good conduct, but again the reason is supportive of the command. Suffering is thematic but not yet online.

Next, 2:17 is analyzed as a hinge verse. 2:11–12 gives a generic command to do good. A specific way to do so is to submit to rulers. Now the idea of honor comes

---

[95] This could also be read as a comment structure.

into focus: honor all, love the brethren, fear God, honor the king.[96] From this verse to 3:12 the idea becomes that of honoring others in a hierarchical culture, a notion reflected in this section. Those of lower status and most likely to be abused are mentioned first, namely slaves and wives. Peter gives considerable support to the commands directed to these two, perhaps reflecting the difficulty of the commands. He gives little support to the commands to the husbands since they are in more of a position of power. Basically, Peter tells them not to take advantage of their position. Then finally Peter addresses everyone without any indication of one's position in the culture.

So then slaves are to honor masters by submitting (2:18), wives their husbands by submitting (3:1), husbands their wives by treating them with consideration and showing them honor (3:7), and finally all are to honor by being united, being sympathetic, showing brotherly love, being compassionate, being humble, and by not returning evil for evil, but rather blessing (3:8–9). The mainline here is carried by the participles which explicate a specific way of honoring.[97]

SPECIFIC-THESIS 1: Reason ¶

   THESIS: 2:18 Slaves, be subject to your masters with all reverence...

   Reason: Amplification ¶

      THESIS: 2:19 For this finds God's favor, if because of conscience...

      Amplification: Contrast ¶

         Contrast: 2:20a For what credit is it if you sin and are mistreated and endure it?

         THESIS: Reason ¶

            THESIS: 2:20b But if you do good and suffer...

            Reason: Comment ¶

               THESIS: 2:21–23 For to this you were called, since Christ also suffered for you, leaving an example for you...

               Comment: Reason ¶

                  THESIS: 2:24 He himself bore our sins in his body...

                  Reason: 2:25 For you were going astray like sheep...

Figure 19.8: Semantic Structure of 1 Peter 2:18–2:25

---

[96] See Starwalt, *A Discourse Analysis of 1 Peter*, 68–82. for a more extended analysis of the structure of 2:17–3:12.

[97] 2:18 uses five adjectives to command the desired behavior which form part of the mainline. But this verse, as explained above, is part of a peak closing out the section of 2:11–3:12.

The command to the slaves is qualified: they are to submit not only to good masters but also to bad ones (2:18). Then 2:19 gives a reason for the command: one finds favor with God for suffering unjustly because one is mindful of God. Then further down in the paragraph the thought is amplified: there is no credit for suffering for sinning, but suffering for doing good is commendable (2:20). Next in 2:21–23, the reason why or support for the statement that suffering for doing good is laudable is found. It is that Christ also suffered, thereby giving the believer (in this case the believing slave) an example to follow. See the following display for the structure of the paragraph. Again, the command to the slaves is labeled specific thesis because it is an instantiation of honoring.

As can be seen from the display the issue of suffering is primarily embedded within the command to submit to good or bad masters. It is not certain that one will have a bad master. Nevertheless, the supporting material addresses the plight of the slave who has a bad master. The supporting material is extremely important thematic material, calling on the slave to follow the example of Christ, a call that will be stated more forcefully later in the letter (4:1).

Next, Peter addresses the wives (3:1–6), telling them to submit to their husbands, even unbelieving husbands. The issue of suffering for their faith is addressed in the last verse of this paragraph, buried within the supporting material that provides motivation for following the command. As may be seen in the display below, the command of 3:1–2 is commented upon in vv. 3–4. Verse 2 ends with a statement about conduct and 3:3–4 picks up on the word for conduct and makes a statement about it, stating that it is the gentle and quiet spirit that God values. Then support for this statement follows in a reason paragraph. Peter discusses the conduct of the holy women of old, finally telling these women not to be afraid at the very end of the supporting reason in v. 6. So while possible suffering is acknowledged, it is buried in the supportive material. It is not mainline.

THESIS 2: Comment ¶
    THESIS: 3:1–2 In the same way, wives, be subject...
    Comment: Reason ¶
        THESIS: 3:3–4 Let your beauty not be external...
        Reason: 3:5–6 For in the same way the holy women...

Figure 19.9: Semantic Structure of 1 Peter 3:1–6

Next comes the third thesis in 3:7, which gives some commands to husbands. The supporting or motivational material is minimal with no hint of any discussion of suffering. The husbands within the family were in a position of power. The exhortations here deal with the possible misuse of their position on the family.

Finally 3:8–12 closes this section of 2:11–3:12. Having more recently given commands to slaves, wives, and husbands, Peter now addresses the whole church.[98] As observed above, this is a peak paragraph with its five adjectives and two participles used imperatively. The five imperatival adjectives (*be-likeminded, sympathetic, loving the brethren, compassionate,* and *humble*) address the sort of attitudes or traits that result in good conduct. The adjectives look at attitudes that need to be exhibited within the believing community. The following participles address behavior, that which is forbidden and promoted. They are not to return (μὴ ἀποδιδόντες) evil for evil or insult for insult but rather they are to bless (εὐλογοῦντες). The two participles appear to address more directly how to honor those outside the community; they are to bless. This is not to deny that insults occur among believers.[99] Thus suffering and how Christians are to respond has become part of the mainline argument here. In fact, the commands are more than just mainline propositions; they occur at peak which may be characterized as primary mainline (i.e., as the mainline of the mainline). Still yet, up to this point Peter does not indicate, as he does later, the normalcy of suffering for all. Instead, the beginning of the next section of the letter will call into question the normalcy of Christian suffering.

In 3:13 Peter asks the rhetorical question: who will persecute you if you as zealous for the good? This question follows the quote from Ps 34:12–16, which asserts that God is for the righteous but against evildoers. So the expected answer is that no one should persecute someone for doing the right and good thing. But Peter corrects that assumption in 3:14a. The verse opens with the conjunction ἀλλά,[100] suggesting that a correction is coming. Peter modifies the assumption emanating from 3:13 by telling these believers that even if they should suffer (πάσχοιτε), they are blessed. The optative normally indicates that something is more remote. An optative verb also occurs in 3:17 where Peter affirms that it is better to suffer for doing good if the will of God *desires* (θέλοι) such.

A few observations are in order here. First, both uses of the optative occurs in non-mainline material. 3:14a is part of the introductory material leading up to the commands in 3:14b–15: they are not to be afraid but must sanctify Christ in their hearts. 3:17 itself is a supportive statement, giving affirmation to the previous commanding unit starting in 3:14 and extending to 3:16. They are told to reverence

---

[98] Ellicott, *1 Peter*, 600.

[99] Ellicott, *1 Peter*, 602 argues that v. 9 has outsiders in view. Michaels, *1 Peter*, 175 asserts that this verse primarily addresses believers' relations with outsiders. Schreiner, *1, 2 Peter, Jude,* 164 sees the possibility that relations with both believers and the outside community are in view here. All see this verse as addressing how the church is to respond to outside persecution. The question is the scope of the commands.

[100] See Runge, *Discourse Grammar of the Greek New Testament,* 55ff. for a discussion of the discourse function of this conjunction.

Christ and to be ready to give an apology with meekness for their faith, always having good conduct. Such good conduct will put unbelievers to shame. 3:17 buttresses the commands, and itself is buttressed by 3:18: because Christ suffered for the unjust. So the discussion concerning remoteness of suffering is found in supportive or introductory material, not online.

Second the use of the optative has led to considerable discussion as to why it is used at all. The contents of the letter clearly indicate that these believers are suffering. Is the suffering really a remote possibility, or is it remote eschatologically, or is it that such suffering is not constant?[101] Achtemeier also considers the idea that the optative here may be used to soften the discussion of a sensitive topic for these believers who are suffering.[102] This is the understanding of the optative taken in this work. Suffering became mainline in 3:9. But its normalcy was not indicated there. Peter is slowly revealing to his readers the extent and nature of suffering. But he does not rush to the full revelation yet. That might be too painful.

The section of 3:13–3:22 closes out with a discussion of how Christ suffered for the unjust and of his resurrection and victory. 4:1 then opens with a command: Since Christ suffered in the flesh, have the same attitude. These people are commanded to think about suffering as Christ did. The imperative signals that suffering has become mainline here. But the story does not end here. The normalcy of suffering becomes fully mainline in 4:12–4:19, the denouement of the letter. This paragraph draws together three major themes: that they are God's people, the necessity to do good, and the fact of suffering. 4:12 then supersedes the optatives of 3:14a and 3:17. Suffering is normal. The believers are commanded not to think suffering strange. Rather, they are to rejoice in suffering for Christ (v. 14). Finally, in 3:19, all of it is drawn together: let those who suffer according to the will of God commit themselves to a faithful creator in doing good. As observed before, three major themes converge in this paragraph. If we look at the structure of the text, we can see that while suffering is never ignored, it is not fully addressed until chapter four. The topic slowly rises in the salience of the text, at first being addressed in supportive material, but ever rising until ultimately the commands of 4:12 and 4:19 come. It is normal. Commit yourselves to your creator.

Conclusion

As can be seen, 1 Peter is a deceptively complex letter. Peter carefully establishes certain themes in the text before stating clearly that suffering is normal and that

---

[101] See Achtemeier, *1 Peter*, 230–231 for a survey of several explanations.

[102] Achtemeier (ibid., 230) rejects this option, seeing the suffering as not contentious.

believers must persist in doing good in the face of persecution. All this is predicated on the fact that they are truly God's own people. The text goes in cycles and culminates each section in a climax that has peak marking features. They are God's people; they are called to humbly do good; they are to be self-controlled and sober-minded for prayer, to love one another, to be hospitable, and to minister to one another in God's power; and finally in the midst of suffering they are to commit themselves to their faithful creator in doing good. It is within the last peak, the denouement, that what might be termed the macro-statement comes. It is where the text has been heading and forms the basis for all that Peter is about as he addresses these believers.

20

2 PETER

CHRISTOPHER J. FRESCH

1. Methodology

At its core, discourse analysis is interested in how language is *used*, i.e.,
how a piece of linguistic data *functions* and thus how it is cognitively processed.[1] As Gillian Brown and George Yule state, "In discourse analysis, as
in pragmatics, we are concerned with what people using language are doing, and
accounting for the linguistic features in the discourse as the means employed in
what they are doing."[2] Or, as Barbara Johnstone simply puts it, "The basic question a discourse analyst asks is 'Why is this stretch of discourse the way it is? Why
is it no other way? Why these particular words in this particular order?'"[3]

My purpose in this article is to demonstrate how the central concerns of discourse analysis can be helpfully applied in an analysis of the text of 2 Peter, primarily with regard to the linguistic structure of the letter and to the communicative functions of the grammatical choices made by the author. Of course, these
two considerations are informed by and affect each other. That is, there is a circular relationship between grammar and discourse. What one does grammatically has consequences for the structure of the discourse and the interpretation
of it. At the same time, what one intends to achieve with a discourse and how

[1] Gillian Brown and George Yule, *Discourse Analysis*, CTL (Cambridge University Press, 1983), 1, 25.
[2] Ibid., 26.
[3] Barbara Johnstone, *Discourse Analysis*, 2nd ed. (Blackwell Publishing, 2008), 9.

one conceives of their readers has consequences for the grammatical decisions being made.[4] Owing to this, the discourse analyst would do well by beginning their study of a given text simply by becoming well acquainted with and immersed in the text. As one reads and becomes more familiar with the text's structure by experiencing it firsthand, there are a number of interrelated features, both structural and grammatical, that ought to be noted. In what follows, I detail some of those features and considerations that are especially relevant to my analysis of 2 Peter.

First, one should determine the discourse type of the text. One can do this by paying attention to whether a text is +/-contingent temporal succession, +/-agent orientation, +/-projection, and +/-tension.[5] According to Robert Longacre's and Shin Hwang's etic scheme of notional discourse types, these parameters result in the following grid of four broad discourse types, each one then divided into four narrower types (Figure 20.1):[6]

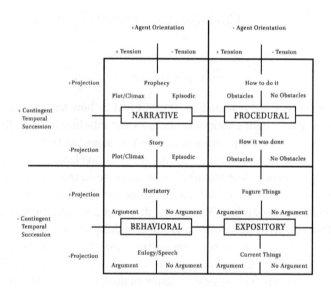

Figure 20.1: Etic Scheme of Notional Discourse Types

As one reads 2 Peter, it becomes evident that it is a hortatory discourse, a

---

[4] So also Michael Hoey, *Textual Interaction: An introduction to written discourse analysis* (London: Routledge, 2001), 61; Robert E. Longacre and Shin Ja J. Hwang, *Holistic Discourse Analysis*, 2nd ed. (SIL International, 2012), 1; Ronald W. Langacker, *Cognitive Grammar: A Basic Introduction* (Oxford University Press, 2008), 492.

[5] Longacre and Hwang, *Holistic Discourse Analysis*, 34–37.

[6] Ibid., 37.

type of discourse that urges and exhorts.[7] A hortatory discourse exhibits the following four general parameters:[8]

1. -Contingent Temporal Succession: The purpose of hortatory discourse is not to describe a series of temporally related events but rather to speak directly to the recipient and affect their behavior.
2. +Agent Orientation: Since the aim of hortatory discourse is to urge and exhort its recipient, it is agent-oriented, i.e., it frequently refers to the agents of the actions that the discourse producer wishes to see enacted or stopped.
3. +Projection: The actions described in a hortatory discourse are anticipated or future, rather than having already occurred.
4. +Tension: Given that a hortatory discourse aims at affecting behavior, there is often a tension between current behavior and hoped-for behavior or between the exhorted behavior and perceived threats to it. A hortatory discourse can be +tension or -tension, though the former is more typical.

Understanding the parameters that shape hortatory discourse helps one recognize what such a discourse is setting out to do. This in turn aids the analyst in determining the salience of macro- and micro-features for achieving the discourse's goals as well as for providing a structure. In addition, by contrasting it with other discourse types, the analyst is reminded to read hortatory discourse *qua* hortatory discourse and not to impose expectations on it based on other discourse types.

Second, once the discourse type is identified, one can reasonably expect certain types of content that are closely connected to it. Longacre and Hwang posit four structure slots that are usually found in hortatory discourse, all of which naturally extend from the parameters for hortatory discourse given above:[9]

1. The authority and credibility of the text producer
2. Indication of the problem/situation
3. One or more command elements (whether brusque or mitigated)
4. Motivation for obeying (essentially threats or promises)

Based on Longacre's structure slots, the reader of 2 Peter can already perceive a general structure forming (Figure 20.2; note that discourse types can skew,[10]

[7] Ibid., 169–70, 217.
[8] The following draws heavily from ibid., 34–37.
[9] Ibid., 171. It is not a requirement that these slots occur in a particular order or be confined to one place within the discourse.
[10] Ibid., 38–39.

which does occur in 2 Peter as the author moves into expository discourse on a few occasions):[11]

Ref.	Structure Slot	Ref.	Structure Slot
1:1	Authority and credibility of the text producer	2:1–3	Indication of the problem/situation
1:2	Command element (mitigated)	2:4–10a	Motivation
1:3–4	Motivation	2:10b–22	Expository Discourse
1:5–7	Command element (imperative)	3:1–3a	Command elements (mitigated)
1:8–9	Motivation	3:3b–7	Indication of the problem/situation
1:10a	Command element (imperative)	3:8	Command element (imperative)
1:10b–11	Motivation	3:9–10	Expository Discourse
1:12	Expository Discourse	3:11–13	Motivation
1:13–15	Expository Discourse	3:14–16	Command elements (imperatives)
1:16–21	Authority and credibility of the text producer	3:17–18a	Command elements (imperatives)

Figure 20.2: Discourse Structure of 2 Peter

Third, given the nature of hortatory discourse, one should expect imperative verbs and mitigated exhortations to be the primary types of verbs in the foreground of the discourse. Steven Runge writes,

> Hortatory discourse typically consists of theme line exhortations with expository material serving as the ground or support for them. Prototypically, hortatory expressions like those using imperative mood are part of the theme line of the discourse, though they may be found in supportive material to reinforce theme line exhortations.[12]

---

[11] Note that, with regard to the motivation for obeying slots, one must determine via context whether the motivation is connected to that which precedes or follows. My analyses of macro- and micro-structures later in the chapter will address this for each slot.

[12] Steven E. Runge, "The Contribution of Verb Forms, Connectives, and Dependency to Grounding Status in Nonnarrative Discourse," in *The Greek Verb Revisited: A Fresh Approach for Biblical Exegesis,* ed. Steven E. Runge and Christopher J. Fresch (Lexham Press, 2016), 232. So also, Longacre and Hwang, *Holistic Discourse Analysis,* 174–75; Robert E. Longacre, "Towards

Foreground, Runge's "theme line," is content that moves the main ideas of the discourse forward. It is that material, which, in the words of Paul Hopper and Sandra Thompson, supplies "the main points of the discourse" and comprises "the backbone or skeleton of the text, forming its basic structure."[13] Since the purpose of hortatory discourse is to effect and encourage certain behaviors in its recipients, it makes sense that exhortations are the default forms for its foreground. Given this, at the onset of a discourse analysis of 2 Peter, it would be beneficial to single out the commands and mitigated exhortations within the letter, as this offers a reasonable picture of the text's skeleton. Figure 20.3 does so, and while it does not show all of the foreground material of 2 Peter, it does include much of it (except 1:19–20, which is a mitigated exhortation backgrounded within a relative clause).

Ref.	Content	Ref.	Content
1:2	"**May** grace and peace **be multiplied** to you in the knowledge of God and of Jesus our Lord."	3:8	"<u>Beloved</u>, **do** not **let** this one thing **escape** your notice ..."
1:5–7	"**Add** to your faith excellence, etc."	3:14–15a	"Therefore, <u>beloved</u>, since you are waiting for these things, **do your best** to be found in peace without spot or blemish before him, and **regard** our Lord's patience as salvation."
1:10	"Therefore, <u>brothers and sisters</u>, **make every effort** to make your calling sure."		
1:19–20	"We have the prophetic word as an altogether reliable thing, to which **you do well** to pay attention.... **understanding** this above all: ..."	3:17	"So, <u>beloved</u>, since you know beforehand, **be on guard** that ..."
3:1–3	"<u>Beloved</u>, I am already writing this as a second letter in which **I am waking up your sincere mind with a reminder to recall** the things foretold by the holy prophets ... **understanding** this above all: ..."	3:18	"**Grow** in the grace and knowledge of our Lord and Savior Jesus Christ."

Figure 20.3: Commands and Mitigated Exhortations in 2 Peter

an Exegesis of 1 John Based on the Discourse Analysis of the Greek Text," in *Linguistics and New Testament Interpretation: Essays on Discourse Analysis,* ed. David Alan Black with Katharine Barnwell and Stephen Levinsohn (B&H, 1992), 277–79.

[13] Paul J. Hopper and Sandra A. Thompson, "Transitivity in Grammar and Discourse," *Language* 56 (1980): 280–81.

Fourth, one should take note of background information. According to Hopper and Thompson, background is "that part of a discourse which does not immediately and crucially contribute to the speaker's goal, but which merely assists, amplifies, or comments on it.... the backgrounded clauses put flesh on the skeleton, but are extraneous to its structural coherence."[14] Background information fills out the picture, providing the reasons for and motivations behind the foreground. As such, it is no less important than the foreground information, but it does exist in a hierarchically subordinated relationship to the foreground. This is crucial to understand as one seeks to analyze the flow of a discourse and provide a structure for it. One key indicator of background information, though by no means the only indicator, is the particle γάρ. Runge writes, "The use of γάρ marks what follows as supporting what precedes. It strengthens the preceding theme rather than advancing or building upon it."[15]

Fifth, one ought to look for and take note of grammatical features typically present at boundaries between discourse units. As thematic groupings, discourse units internally exhibit thematic continuity. The seams between them tend to occur, quite naturally, in contexts of thematic discontinuity, that is, at changes in time, place, action, and/or participants.[16] In addition, there are a number of grammatical features that either explicitly signal discourse boundaries or tend to appear at them. In this way, both the discourse-grammatical features of the text and the nature of the content work together to mark movement forward to new, distinct developments. In what follows, I will briefly detail a few of those grammatical features that are relevant to our present purposes.

Discourse markers, as I have written elsewhere, "signal the structure of the discourse and instruct the reader on how to process new linguistic material in relation to the wider context.... They assist and guide the reader in their processing and comprehension, clarifying discourse relations."[17] While many languages contain a plethora of discourse markers that serve a variety of roles, most will include some that signal breaks between discourse units.[18] *Koine* Greek is no exception. The discourse marker δέ "signals a new segment, a distinct information unit"[19] and can occur with a broad scope, thus introducing a new development

---

[14] Ibid.

[15] Runge, "Grounding Status in Nonnarrative Discourse," 242–43.

[16] Robert A. Dooley and Stephen Levinsohn, *Analyzing Discourse: A Manual of Basic Concepts* (SIL International, 2001), 35–37. So also Hoey, *Textual Interaction*, 55–56.

[17] Christopher J. Fresch, "Discourse Markers in the Septuagint and Early *Koine* Greek with Special Reference to The Twelve" (PhD Diss., University of Cambridge, 2015), 2.

[18] For a survey of some boundary-marking discourse markers cross-linguistically, see ibid., 55–58.

[19] Ibid., 58. See also Steven E. Runge, *Discourse Grammar of the Greek New Testament: A Practical Introduction for Teaching and Exegesis* (Hendrickson, 2010), 28–36; Stephen H.

within the discourse, with a moderate scope, thus introducing a new subtopic or the next part of an argument or scene, or with a narrow scope, sectioning out small steps or segments.[20] Similarly, οὖν also signals a distinct information unit but explicitly marks its host utterance and what follows as maintaining a certain amount of continuity with some preceding material in the discourse (whether directly preceding or resuming an earlier theme-line that was interrupted by background material).[21]

Points of departure are nominal or adverbial constituents placed before the verb to indicate a switch to a new topic or to provide a frame of reference for what follows.[22] While points of departure can and do occur within discourse units, they often appear at their beginnings, since they are markers of thematic discontinuity.

Another feature to pay attention to is the use of vocatives. Stephen Levinsohn argues that vocatives "are found at the beginning of units and in connection with key statements such as nuclear propositions."[23] While Levinsohn notes that their use does not necessarily signal a discourse boundary, they can provide evidence for one.[24]

Back-reference devices such as tail-head linkage also often occur at discourse boundaries. Tail-head linkage, as described by Levinsohn, "involves the repetition, in an adverbial or participial clause at the beginning (the head) of a new sentence, of the main verb and other information that occurred in the previous sentence (the tail)."[25] Tail-head linkage can be used to highlight forthcoming significant information and/or as a point of departure at the beginning of a new discourse unit.[26] Similar to vocatives, tail-head linkage often occurs at discourse boundaries, but its use is not restricted to discourse boundaries. Levinsohn also notes the use of summary statements "to unite together the information they

---

Levinsohn, *Discourse Features of New Testament Greek: A Coursebook on the Information Structure of New Testament Greek*, 2nd ed. (SIL International, 2000), 112–14.

[20] Fresch, "Discourse Markers," 58–59. See also Kathleen Callow's helpful discussion of long-, short-, and intermediate-span uses of δέ in Kathleen Callow, "The Disappearing Δέ in 1 Corinthians," in *Linguistics and New Testament Interpretation: Essays on Discourse Analysis*, ed. David Alan Black, Katharine G. L. Barnwell, and Stephen H. Levinsohn (Broadman Press, 1992), 184–88.

[21] See Christopher J. Fresch, "The Peculiar Occurrences of οὖν in Septuagint Genesis and Exodus," in *XV Congress of the International Organization for Septuagint and Cognate Studies, Munich, 2013*, ed. Wolfgang Kraus, Martin Meiser, and Michaël van der Meer (Society of Biblical Literature, 2016), 458–59; Runge, *Discourse Grammar*, 43–48.

[22] Levinsohn, *Discourse Features*, 7–8.

[23] Ibid., 278.

[24] Ibid. See also the helpful discussion of vocatives in 1 John in Longacre, "1 John," 272–76.

[25] Levinsohn, *Discourse Features*, 197.

[26] Ibid., 197, 280–81.

summarize and thereby indicate that the preceding material should be treated as a block, over against what is to follow."[27] These can occur both at the beginning and end of discourse units.[28]

Lastly, orienters are statements in which "speakers stop saying what they are saying in order to comment on what is going to be said, speaking abstractly about it."[29] Given the break that naturally occurs when a speaker stops what they are saying to comment on what they are about to say, orienters are often used at the beginning of discourse units.[30]

Of course, boundaries in discourse can occur without any overt marker (though this is typically not the case). As Richard Hurtig urges, attention must be paid not only to overt markers but also to the topical structure of the discourse.[31]

2. Macrostructure of 2 Peter

Delimiting the macrostructure of 2 Peter is no simple task. There is widespread disagreement with regard to its genre and whether its structure is determined by Greek rhetoric. For instance, Richard Bauckham sees in 2 Peter certain aspects that conform to the epistolary genre, though he notes ways in which it diverges from the epistolary format. Bauckham also posits the farewell speech/testament genre for 2 Peter, given the ethical admonitions and the revelations of the future within the letter, though he notes here too how the author breaks with the genre's conventions.[32] The resulting structure for Bauckham, then, begins and ends as a letter, but the body alternates between apologetic sections and sections fitting to the testament genre.[33] Jerome Neyrey acknowledges the letter form of 2 Peter but states that such "appears to be merely the literary fiction in which the author's remarks are cast,"[34] owing to how the author diverges from letter-writing conventions. Neyrey also perceives characteristics pertaining to a farewell

---

[27] Ibid., 277.

[28] Ibid.

[29] Runge, *Discourse Grammar*, 101.

[30] Stephen H. Levinsohn, "Self-Instruction Materials on Non-Narrative Discourse Analysis," http://www-01.sil.org/%7Elevinsohns/NonNarr.pdf (accessed 26 October 2018), 101. They can also be used to highlight forthcoming material. On this, see Runge, *Discourse Grammar*, 105–16. The two uses are not mutually exclusive. Note that Runge uses the term "metacomment" for "orienter."

[31] Richard Hurtig, "Toward a Functional Theory of Discourse," in *Discourse Production and Comprehension*, ed. Roy O. Freedle, Discourse Processes: Advances in Research and Theory 1 (Ablex Publishing Corporation, 1977), 94–96.

[32] Richard J. Bauckham, *Jude, 2 Peter*, WBC 50 (Thomas Nelson, 1996) 131–35.

[33] Ibid.

[34] Jerome H. Neyrey, *2 Peter, Jude: A New Translation with Introduction and Commentary*, AB 37C (Yale University Press, 1993), 111.

address.[35] More important for him, though, is the proposed rhetorical structure of 2 Peter. Neyrey observes three major rhetorical movements: *exordium* (1:3–15), *probatio* (1:16–3:13), and *peroratio* (3:14–18).[36] It should be noted that this proposed structure is interrupted by a *digressio* in 2:10b–22.[37] Peter Davids, like Neyrey, regards 2 Peter as following a rhetorical structure of *exordium*, *probatio*, and *peroratio* (with the interrupting *digressio*).[38] In addition, while noting the similarities with and differences from the typical letter form, he regards the book as having been composed as a letter but being a sermon or speech at its core.[39] He further regards the letter as a farewell speech but argues, contra Bauckham, that it does not share enough characteristics with testaments to be classified as one.[40] Contrasting with these views, Gene Green regards 2 Peter as a genuine epistle, specifically as a combination of the advisory and vituperative letter types.[41] He argues that neither the rhetorical-structure theory nor the testament-genre theory are viable, given that the former must be adjusted significantly to fit 2 Peter into it and the latter overlooks the lack of testamentary features in the letter and ignores the many aspects of the letter that are not testamentary.[42] Green thus proposes a macrostructure of greeting (1:1–2), body (1:3–3:18a — in which there is a subdivision of opening, middle, and closing), and letter closing (3:18b). Lastly, Thomas Schreiner likewise calls a rhetorical structure into question, stating that it is unclear whether the letter actually conforms to such.[43] He then suggests a structure of five major movements (1:1–2; 1:3–11; 1:12–21; 2:1–22; 3:1–18).[44]

What one decides on these issues will affect how one delimits 2 Peter's macrostructure. Of course, at the same time, such decisions cannot be made apart from an analysis of 2 Peter's constituent parts and the insights gleaned by reading through it and experiencing it as it unfolds. My purpose here is not to convey a sense of futility; rather it needs to be recognized that just as the whole informs the parts, so the parts inform the whole.

---

[35] Ibid., 112–13.

[36] Ibid., 113–18.

[37] Ibid., 116.

[38] Peter H. Davids, *The Letters of 2 Peter and Jude,* PNTC (Apollos, 2006), 143–45.

[39] Ibid., 143, 145.

[40] Ibid., 145–49. Michael Green also raises doubts as to whether 2 Peter can be called a testament or even regarded as having been influenced by the tradition. Michael Green, *2 Peter and Jude,* TNTC 18 (IVP Academic, 1987), 46.

[41] Gene Green, *Jude and 2 Peter,* BECNT (Baker Academic, 2008), 164, 167–70.

[42] Ibid., 165–67.

[43] Thomas R. Schreiner, *1, 2 Peter, Jude,* NAC 37 (B&H, 2003), 281. As an example, Schreiner points specifically to the digression in 2:10b-22, noting that "such a long digression calls into question whether the proposed analysis fits."

[44] Ibid., 282.

There is an additional difficulty in determining the structure of 2 Peter. The author often seamlessly transitions from one idea to the next. This results both in discourse units that do not break where one would expect (e.g., 1:1–12 is one macro-unit, even though one would normally expect two macro-units, given the letter format: 1:1–2 and 1:3–12) and in relatively high thematic continuity between discourse units. Bauckham describes the latter phenomenon well in his discussion of 2 Pet 2:1–3a: "The author of 2 Peter dislikes abrupt transitions, and his mention of the false prophets of OT times (2:1a) is designed to effect a smooth transition from the discussion of OT prophecy (1:20–21) to the prediction of the false teachers (2:1b–3a)."[45] As discussed above, new discourse units naturally occur in contexts of thematic discontinuity. Thus, high thematic continuity makes detecting discourse boundaries more difficult.

* * * * *

In what follows, I provide a macrostructure of 2 Peter based on principles of discourse analysis. Such an analysis cannot explain every facet of the letter, but it produces a structure that is drawn from the demands of the linguistic features present and based on the nature of the information presented.[46] Not only does this provide a grammatically-based representation of the flow of the discourse, but it also sets necessary boundaries for discussions of rhetoric (whether rhetorical features or structuring) and exegesis. Based on the considerations detailed in this section, the following macrostructure can be posited for 2 Peter:

Ref.	Macro-Units
1:1–12	Greeting and Exhortation to Grow in the Knowledge of Jesus
1:13–2:22	The Author's Intent to Remind and The Reminder: Beware of False Teachers
3:1–10	The Reminder: Beware of Scoffers
3:11–16	Waiting for the Day of the Lord and What to do in the Meantime
3:17–18	Summative Exhortations and Doxology

Figure 20.4: Macro-Units of 2 Peter

2.1. Introduction: Greeting and Exhortation to Grow in the Knowledge of Jesus: 1:1–12

Overall, this unit is a mixture of foreground and background material—mostly commands and the motivations for those commands. Much of the unit centers thematically on the initial exhortation to grow in knowledge.

---

[45] Bauckham, *Jude, 2 Peter*, 236.

[46] It should also be noted that the analysis presented here is not all that discourse analysis offers. Rather, it is a starting point for further work to be done and insights to be drawn.

While it is tempting to separate 1:1–12 into two macro-units, 1:1–2 and 1:3–12, the grammatical features require it to be regarded as one. The transition between vv. 2–3 is the first instance of the author's seamless style. One would normally expect a clear break between the letter introduction and the main body,[47] but the author instead moves from the salutation to the readers' motivation for adhering to the salutation (by means of the particle ὡς). In this way, the author clearly indicates that the salutation is not only a greeting but is also meant to be taken as an exhortation to the readers:

> May grace and peace be multiplied to you in the knowledge of God and of Jesus our Lord because his divine power has bestowed on us everything needed for life and godliness through the knowledge of the one who called us in his own glory and excellence....

By expressing a desire that the audience grow in their knowledge of God and of Jesus, and since it is through that knowledge that they will live a godly life, the author thereby encourages the readers to actively pursue such growth. Granted, it is a mitigated command, but it expects action on the part of the readers nonetheless. That this is the expectation is made all the more clear in the rest of the unit (detailed in §3.1).

Most commentators and English translations regard v. 11 as the end of this unit and v. 12 as the start of the next. However, v. 12 begins with the discourse marker διό, which signals an inference but *not* a development or a break in the macrostructure of the text.[48] That is to say, διό does not occur at discourse seams (at least not typically) but rather instructs the reader to read its host utterance as an inference *within* the unit already unfolding. Note also that whereas there is a change in verb tense between vv. 12 and 13 (discontinuity of time), the future tense is maintained between vv. 11 and 12. To take v. 12 as the beginning of a new, distinct unit, then, would ignore the language used, especially given the absence of any explicit discontinuity or boundary markers. Instead, in this verse, the author comments on the background information of v. 11 (which, along with the content of v. 10b, provides the motivation for adhering to the exhortation in v. 10a), expressing their intention to remind the readers of the motivating reasons to make their calling and election certain.

---

[47] Cf. 1 Peter 1:2–3.

[48] See Stephen H. Levinsohn, "'Therefore' or 'Wherefore': What's the Difference?" in *Reflections on Lexicography: Explorations in Ancient Syriac, Hebrew, and Greek Sources,* ed. Richard A. Taylor and Craig E. Morrison, PLAL 4 (Gorgias Press, 2014), 329–30.

2.2. *The Author's Intent to Remind and The Reminder:*
Beware of False Teachers: 1:13–2:22

By using δέ at the beginning of v. 13, the author signals a distinct movement within the discourse. In addition, the author opens with a metacomment (δίκαιον ... ἡγοῦμαι) as well as a change in time (future orientation in vv. 10–12 to present in v. 13). This cluster of discourse features encourages the reader to process v. 13 as the beginning of a new discourse unit.

The use of ὑπομνήσει evinces the author's seamless style. It picks up on the concept of "reminding" already brought up in v. 12 by ὑπομιμνῄσκειν. However, despite this connection, the contents to which ὑπομιμνῄσκειν and ὑπομνήσει refer are not the same. The reminder in v. 12 pertains to the motivations to make one's calling and election certain (vv. 10–11). The content of the reminder in v. 13 is not stated, but if it were coextensive with that to which ὑπομιμνῄσκειν refers, one would expect ὑπομνήσει to be articular, as the article would mark ὑπομνήσει as a known, identifiable referent.[49] The absence of an article suggests that the referent of ὑπομνήσει is new information. In addition, as already discussed, the author has clearly marked a discourse boundary between vv. 12 and 13, which would create the expectation for a shift in topic.

As to the question of to what content ὑπομνήσει in 1:13 refers, similarities and parallels in ch. 3 provide insight. In similar fashion to 1:13, the author states in 3:1 the desire to *wake up* the readers *with a reminder* (διεγείρω ὑμῶν ἐν ὑπομνήσει τὴν εἰλικρινῆ διάνοιαν). According to 3:2, the reminder is that the readers remember the words foretold by the prophets and the commandment of the apostles of the Lord. The content of the reminder is then specified in 3:3—that the readers know firstly that blatant scoffers will come in the last days—[50]and discussed further in the following verses. Similarly, after the announcement of a reminder in 1:13–15, 2 Peter 2 begins with the shared knowledge of an imminent threat, false teachers who will arise among the readers. Granted, there is intervening material between 1:13–15 and ch. 2, but none of it is foreground information and thus cannot be the reminder. 2 Peter 1:16–21 is background material, serving to bolster the author's credibility, particularly in contrast to the teachers and scoffers

---

[49] Steven E. Runge, "The Greek Article: A Cognitive-Functional Approach" (paper delivered at the Evangelical Theological Society 2013 Annual Meeting, Baltimore, MD, 20 November 2013).

[50] Not all commentators agree on the content of the reminder in 3:1–3, but what I have proposed above fits best with the grammar of the dependent participial phrase in 3:3. See also Davids, *2 Peter and Jude*, 260–63. Further, this can be defended by reference to Jude 17–18, given the heavy borrowing between 2 Peter and Jude: "Now, you, dear ones, recall the words foretold by the apostles of our Lord Jesus Christ, namely that they said to you, 'In the end time, scoffers will come, going according to their ungodly desires.'"

to be discussed. Given the nature of the intervening material as background and given the clear parallels to 2 Peter 3, one can reasonably posit that the content to which ὑπομνήσει in 1:13 refers is the warning about false teachers in ch. 2.[51] The thematic connection between the reminders in chs. 1 and 3 is clear: they both remind the readers of threats to their faith, whether in the form of false teachers or scoffers who dispute the promise of the Lord's return.[52]

2.3. The Reminder: Beware of Scoffers: 3:1–10

2 Peter 3:1 marks another prominent boundary within the discourse. The author uses a cluster of features: the vocative ἀγαπητοί, an orienter (the entire verse), a participant shift from third person to first person, a shift in time from past to present, a topic shift from those who abandoned the faith to the author's commenting on the nature of the letter being written, and asyndeton.[53] Each one, on its own, may suggest a new macro-unit. Together, they leave no doubt.

Similar to 1:13–2:22, this unit is concerned with a threat to the believing community. In the previous discourse unit, the threat was false teachers who may mislead some within the community. Here, the author predicts scoffers who will cast doubt on the promise of the Lord's return and then presents an argument against them.

2.4. Waiting for the Day of the Lord and What to do in the Meantime: 3:11–16

Again, the author demonstrates a seamless style, using the day of the Lord, mentioned in v. 10, as a jumping off point to encourage the readers in godly behavior in the meantime. Verse 11 contains a few features that encourage the reader to understand this section as a new macro-unit. First, the genitive absolute (τούτων ... πάντων λυομένων) is preposed, thereby calling attention to itself as a new frame of reference.[54] In addition, it serves as a summary statement,

---

[51] Note too the similarities between 2 Peter 1:13; 2:1–17 and Jude 3–13.

[52] It is no wonder, then, that the author places so much weight on growing in the knowledge of Jesus in the first and final discourse units. Given the nature of the threats with which the author is concerned (false teaching and calling into question the Lord's return), growth in the knowledge of Jesus would provide the best defense against them.

[53] Asyndeton implies that the host utterance is either a part of the same unit as what preceded or is not a part of the same unit as what preceded. Levinsohn, *Discourse Features*, 118.

[54] I should note that Levinsohn (*Discourse Features*, 187–89) regards sentence initial participles as indicating "continuity of situation" in contrast to points of departure (188). While I am inclined to agree with his position that preposed participial clauses do convey a certain amount of continuity (at least over against other types of preposed adverbial clauses) and that such would motivate their usage, I believe he presses the distinction too far and in a way that is at odds with cognitive processing. A preposed participial clause is still placed in a pragmatic position in the sentence that denotes topical prominence, and it necessarily acts in such a way

thereby effecting a transition to a new block. Second, there is a significant change in the nature and theme of the discourse. In vv. 1–10, the author was concerned with reminding the readers about the threat of scoffers, dismantling their arguments, and reassuring the readers of the Lord's return. In vv. 11–16, on the other hand, the author moves away from the topic of the scoffers and reassuring the readers of the Lord's return and to current expectations of the readers. Third, following the Tyndale House Greek New Testament, v. 11 is introduced by οὖν (instead of the οὕτως in the NA²⁸).⁵⁵ This discourse marker is particularly well-suited here, as it signals a break in the discourse but also explicitly indicates a connection to the preceding material. These features together indicate a new macro-unit—one that draws from the preceding macro-unit but is nevertheless a major development in the discourse.

2.5. Summative Exhortations and Doxology: 3:17–18

The author ends the letter with a summative section containing two exhortations and a doxology. In addition to the discourse marker οὖν, the author indicates the new discourse unit by beginning v. 17 with the vocative ἀγαπητοί and a switch to a new frame of reference, προγινώσκοντες, from the previously posited grounds for the author's exhortations, ταῦτα προσδοκῶντες in v. 14. In addition, there is a distinct thematic shift between 3:11–16 and 3:17–18. The former is broad in its perspective. It exhorts the audience to be found without spot or blemish and to regard the Lord's patience as salvation while waiting for the new heavens and new earth. The final unit, however, returns to the letter's narrower perspective, threats to the believing community and how the readers should defend against them.

---

as to update or change the frame of reference for the reader. This conveys at least some level of discontinuity, and it would be processed as such by a reader or listener. (This, then, makes good sense of the plethora of occurrences where a preposed adverbial participle is collocated with δέ, as the discourse marker most naturally occurs in contexts of discontinuity.) The motivation to use a participle rather than another adverbial clause would be, in light in Levinsohn's work, to indicate explicitly the connections between what precedes and what follows. As such, a preposed adverbial participle is well-suited either to continue a discourse unit or to begin a new one. What is crucial is that one look to the linguistic context, both in terms of theme and other discourse features, in order to determine how the discourse is structured in any given instance.

⁵⁵ This is not the place for a text-critical discussion. Suffice it to say for our present purposes, the following was conveyed to me by Dirk Jongkind, editor of THGNT, in a personal communication on Sept. 18, 2018: "The main reason [for choosing οὖν] is the breadth of external evidence. None of the various variants that have οὕτως added has very good support, and the fact that οὕτως wanders a bit through the various variations (some of which with minimal support) shows that the word may even have entered the tradition multiple times."

The second exhortation, αὐξάνετε δὲ ἐν χάριτι καὶ γνώσει τοῦ κυρίου ἡμῶν καὶ σωτῆρος Ἰησοῦ Χριστοῦ, is worth mentioning here. The author's last words before the doxology are that the readers should "grow in the grace and knowledge of our Lord Jesus Christ." This effectively forms an inclusio with the beginning of the letter (after the indication of author and recipient in 1:1) in 1:2: χάρις ὑμῖν καὶ εἰρήνη πληθυνθείη ἐν ἐπιγνώσει τοῦ θεοῦ καὶ Ἰησοῦ τοῦ κυρίου ἡμῶν. In this way, not only does it provide a fitting end to the letter, but it also reinforces one of the primary exhortations of the letter, that the readers grow in the knowledge of Jesus. It is this knowledge that leads them toward the godly lives they are to live and that helps guard them against the threats of false teachers and scoffers.

3. Analysis of Microstructures

3.1. 1:1–12

These verses contain a number of elements central to hortatory discourse. 2 Peter 1:1 introduces the author and establishes their authority and credibility. This is then followed by three foregrounded command elements, each one followed by motivations for it.

3.1.1. 1:2–4

Verse 2 contains foreground material. The optative πληθυνθείη expresses the author's wish that grace and peace be multiplied for the readers in the knowledge of God and of Jesus, but it functions as a mitigated exhortation. The author does not simply hope that this will be the case but expects the readers to actively pursue this knowledge.[56] Verses 3–4 provide background material, motivation for the exhortation in v. 2. Note the cohesive links[57] between these verses and how they progress:

---

[56] As discussed below, this is made all the more clear by the content in vv. 5-8, which commands the readers to undertake certain actions that lead to growth in the knowledge of Jesus.

[57] Cohesive links are those elements of a text that explicitly direct the reader in the construction of a coherent mental representation of the text. See Wilbert Spooren, "Structuring Texts: Text Linguistics," in *Cognitive Exploration of Language and Linguistics*, ed. René Dirven and Marjolijn Verspoor, CLiP 1 (John Benjamins, 2004), 184–86; Ted Sanders and Wilbert Spooren, "Discourse and Text Structure," in *The Oxford Handbook of Cognitive Linguistics*, ed. Dirk Geeraerts and Hubert Cuyckens (Oxford University Press, 2007), 918–19.

v. 2: May grace and peace be multiplied for you <u>in the knowledge of</u> <u>God and of Jesus,</u>

> v. 3: **because** through <u>this knowledge of the one who called us</u> <u>in his own glory and excellence,</u> his divine power has given us <u>all things for life and godliness,</u>

>> v. 4a: through <u>which (i.e., all things for life and godli-</u> <u>ness),</u>[58] he has given us <u>the precious and greatest</u> <u>promises,</u>

>>> v. 4b: **so that** through <u>these things (i.e., the</u> <u>precious and greatest promises)</u>, you would become sharers of the divine nature.

Thus, for the author, growing in the knowledge of God and of Jesus leads, ultimately, to becoming partakers in the divine nature. The foreground material is the initial exhortation, and everything that follows supports it by explaining to the readers why pursuing such knowledge is vital.

3.1.2. 1:5–12

By using δέ in v. 5, the author signals a new, distinct chunk of discourse. One must examine the context and other discourse features to determine at what level of the discourse this new segment occurs. The exhortation (ἐπιχορηγήσατε ἐν τῇ πίστει ὑμῶν τὴν ἀρετήν ...) conveys a shift to a new action in the foreground. At the same time, there is an absence of any major shifts in time, place, or participants. In addition, the presence of καὶ αὐτὸ τοῦτο explicitly links this section to the preceding one. Owing to these features together, the reader is instructed to understand v. 5 as the beginning of a distinct movement *within* the larger macro-unit. Verse 5 is the next step in the argument being built.

The content of vv. 5–7 is rhetorically structured, exhibiting a κλῖμαξ, or *gradatio*, figure. As Galen Rowe explains, "Climax is an ascending order of thought through successive phrases, in which the last word of the preceding phrase is

---

[58] One could argue that the antecedent of ὧν is ἰδίᾳ δόξῃ καὶ ἀρετῇ (so Schreiner, *1, 2 Peter, Jude*, 293; Davids, *2 Peter and Jude*, 171; Green, *Jude and 2 Peter*, 184). Although these terms are closer in proximity to ὧν, proximity is not a sufficient argument. Taking ἰδίᾳ δόξῃ καὶ ἀρετῇ as the antecedent disrupts the progressive momentum that the author is building (note too how, in the structure I posit, each direct object subsequently becomes the object of the preposition διά). Moreover, it is more likely that v. 4 builds on the main idea of v. 3, the predication, than on adverbial modifiers within the topical information that links v. 3 to v. 2.

repeated as the first word of the next phrase. The effect is that of climbing a ladder."[59] The use of δέ to connect each phrase is effective, as its function to mark distinct units slows the discourse down and requires the reader to give extra attention to each successive phrase. Since the reader is being exhorted to supply each of these attributes to their faith, it is understandable that the author would want to ensure that the reader focused on each one individually. It is worth noting that, between the rhetorical arrangement of these verses and the nature of the content, there is no doubt that vv. 5–7 constitute a peak in the discourse, that is, climactic material characterized by a turbulent or irregular surface structure.[60]

Verse 8 is connected to vv. 5–7 by γάρ and is thus background material that supports the preceding foreground information. In this case, it provides the motivation for obeying the command of vv. 5–7. This motivation is of particular interest given the themes of the letter so far. Verse 2 exhorted the reader to grow in the knowledge of God and Jesus. This was then followed by motivations for such a pursuit. Verses 5–7 link back to the argument of vv. 2–4, commanding the reader "for this very reason" to supply their faith with the attributes listed. Thus, up to this point, the reader's growth in knowledge has been the controlling theme. It is no surprise, then, to read in v. 8: "For if these things are present in you and are increasing, then they will not make you idle nor unfruitful *in the pursuit of the knowledge of your Lord Jesus Christ.*" The readers' growth in the knowledge of Jesus thus bookends the positive exhortations and motivations that open the book.

Verse 9 continues the motivation of v. 8 with another γάρ. However, the motivation here is negative, expressing what one who lacks the attributes of vv. 5–7 looks like. Verse 10a begins with διό, which effectively places its host utterance in the foreground,[61] particularly given the accompanying imperative, and frames the exhortation as an inference of vv. 8–9. Verse 10b, another clause introduced by γάρ, provides the motivation to follow the command of 10a to make one's calling and election certain, and this is followed by yet another γάρ (v. 11), providing further motivation. Verse 12 then ends the unit with another διό, signaling the author's conclusion, based on vv. 10–11, that they will continue to remind the readers of these things.

3.2. 1:13–2:22

This section can be divided into two major movements. In the first, 1:13–21, the author mentions the intent to rouse the audience with a reminder but first provides

---

[59] Galen O. Rowe, "Style," in *Handbook of Classical Rhetoric in the Hellenistic Period, 330 B.C.-A.D. 400*, ed. Stanley E. Porter (Brill, 1997), 130.

[60] Longacre and Hwang, *Holistic Discourse Analysis*, 53–54, 173–74.

[61] See the discussion in Levinsohn, "'Therefore' or 'Wherefore',"" 329.

a defense of their credibility and authority. In the second movement, 2:1–22, the reminder is given and explicated.

3.2.1. 1:13–21

This unit contains a block of foreground information (vv. 13–15) and a block of background information (vv. 16–21). The first block is expository meta-commentary. The second provides reasons as to why the readers should heed the author.

As discussed in §2.2, v. 13 contains a cluster of features that signal a break in the overall discourse. The author comments on what is being written and presents the first point of this new unit — they want to stir up the readers with a reminder. This is felt to be an immediate need, given the author's imminent death predicted in v. 14. This leads to the second point, introduced by δέ, in v. 15: the author will make every effort that, after their death, there will be a testimony of these things for the readers.

Contrary to expectation, the author does not move directly to the stirring reminder. Verse 16 is introduced by γάρ, signaling the content as background information. This background material is qualitatively different from other background material observed in the letter so far, given that it does not follow an imperative and thus does not fill the motivation structure slot of hortatory discourse. Instead, it fills the authority and credibility of the text producer structure slot. Thus, before presenting the content that prompted the letter, the author discerns the need first to defend their authority and credibility, presumably to ensure that the readers do in fact listen. In this way, v. 16 (and what follows) answers the assumed question, "Why should we listen to you?"

The author's first defense is that they were an eyewitness to the majesty of Jesus. Therefore, their initial teaching of the Lord's power and return was based on their eyewitness account, not on craftily devised fables. This is further supported in the following verses. Verse 17, introduced by γάρ, and v. 18, connected to v. 17 by καί, provide evidence of the author's status as an eyewitness.[62]

Verse 19 also begins with καί, but given its content, the verse must be understood as connecting to v. 16 as a second defense of the author's credibility and authority.[63] Whereas the first defense stated the author's status as an eyewitness, the second posits the possession of the altogether reliable prophetic word. The author encourages the readers to pay attention to the prophetic word and then further elaborates on this mitigated exhortation (ᾧ καλῶς ποιεῖτε προσέχοντες ...) with a subordinate participial adverbial clause in v. 20 (τοῦτο πρῶτον γινώσκοντες ...).

---

[62] See also the discussion of these verses in §3.3.1 below.

[63] Note the shift from relating *past* events in vv. 16-18 to describing the *present* possession of the prophetic word in v. 19.

The participial clause states that no prophecy comes about through one's own (the prophet's) creation. Verse 21 provides further support for the claim in verse 20, as is clear by the use of γάρ, arguing that prophets spoke from God.

3.2.2. 2:1–22

Chapter 2 comprises a distinct unit within the 1:13–2:22 macro-unit. That said, there are two discernible movements, 2:1–10a and 2:10b–22. Verses 2:1–3 provide an indication of the problem/situation and are followed by a block of motivating material in vv. 4–10a. In vv. 10b–22, the author engages in expository discourse that further supports the purpose of the letter by critiquing the false teachers.

3.2.2.1. 2:1–10a. There is a cluster of features indicating a break in the discourse between 1:21 and 2:1. First, the author uses δέ at the beginning of 2:1 to signal the beginning of a new, distinct unit. Given the context of use, this δέ has a broad scope, but the thematic connections between 1:13–21 (announcement of the reminder) and 2:1–22 (the reminder itself) encourage one to take the new unit as a movement within the overarching macro-unit, rather than as a new macro-unit itself. Second, despite the thematic connections, there is a clear topic shift from 1:13–21 to 2:1–10a. In the former, the author announces the intention to remind the readers but then provides a defense of their authority and credibility. In 2:1–10a, the reminder, the prediction of false teachers and the dangers they will present, is given. Third, related to the previous, new participants are introduced to the discourse, false prophets and false teachers, the latter of which become a primary topic for what follows. Fourth, similar to tail-head linkage, the author effects a transition by repeating an aspect of what directly preceded (false prophets who arose within Israel, though not discussed in 1:20–21, is easily retrievable encyclopedic information that was activated by 1:20–21) and using it as a jumping off point for what follows.[64] These features together make clear that this is a major step in the structure of the discourse. One could chart this macro-unit up to 2:1–3 as in Figure 20.5 below.

Note how the false teachers are introduced in 2:1. Under normal circumstances, one would expect the introduction of a new topic to be foregrounded within the sentence and, if necessary, a backgrounded anchoring device to facilitate the new topic's introduction. In this way, the following could have conceivably begun the new unit:

Ὡς δὲ ἐγένοντο καὶ ψευδοπροφῆται ἐν τῷ λαῷ, καὶ ἐν ὑμῖν ἔσονται ψευδοδιδάσκαλοι
Now, just as false prophets also arose among the people, false teachers will also arise among you.

---

[64] Again, one can observe here the author's seamless style.

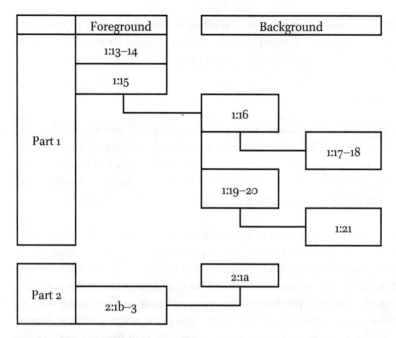

Figure 20.5: The Macro-structure of 2 Peter 1:13–2:3

This would have the benefit of introducing the coming of the false teachers as brand new information whilst anchoring it to the assumed encyclopedic information that false prophets arose in Israel. However, instead, the author writes:

> Ἐγένοντο δὲ καὶ ψευδοπροφῆται ἐν τῷ λαῷ ὡς καὶ ἐν ὑμῖν ἔσονται ψευδοδιδάσκαλοι
> Now, false prophets also arose among the people, just as false teachers will also arise among you.

The prediction of false teachers among the letter's readers is placed within a comparison, thereby backgrounding it and indicating that is known, or assumed to be known, information. On the face of it, this is an odd way to package the information, unless the prediction of the false teachers was already known by the letter's recipients. Given this, the grammar of 2:1 thus provides further support for the conclusion above that the reminder announced in 1:13 is the prediction of false teachers. A reminder, by definition, refers to known information.

As the above chart demonstrates, v. 1 is comprised of background and foreground information. The statement that false prophets arose does not move the discourse forward but serves to ground what follows. As already stated, the comparative clause, by its very nature, is also background information. The comparison is then followed by a continuative relative clause. Such clauses tend to be preceded by information that is backgrounded in relation to the relative clause itself.[65] Given this and given that this portion of discourse is moved forward by future tense-forms (see vv. 2–3), it can be confidently posited that the relative clause is the first instance of foreground material within this new unit.

Verses 1–3 fill the indication of the problem/situation structure slot. They acknowledge the threat of false teachers to the readers, a threat which would naturally lead the author to exhort the readers to grow in the knowledge of Jesus, as happens at the beginning and end of the letter. The threat is conveyed force-fully through the preposing of nominal constituents (πολλοί in 2:2 and πλαστοῖς λόγοις in 2:3) and the postposing of a verb (βλασφημηθήσεται in 2:2) for focal prominence.[66] Note as well the preposing of ἐν πλεονεξίᾳ in 2:3 as a frame of reference, effectively coloring the statement that follows. The author communicates the seriousness of the threat in no uncertain terms.

Verse 3 ends with a claim that the judgment against the false teachers is not idle and their destruction is not sleeping. This is then supported in vv. 4–10a, background material introduced by γάρ. However, this background information serves more than one purpose. While it does support the claim in v. 3, it also fills the motivation structure slot. The author uses the supportive content as an opportunity to encourage the readers by stating that not only does God bring destruction to the wicked, but he also delivers the godly from their trials. This, then, motivates the readers to continue in faithfulness, particularly when the false teachers arrive. Note how vv. 4–8 act as a crescendo as the reader waits for the apodosis to the lengthy, complex conditional. Such an effect makes the resolution in v. 9 — οἶδεν κύριος εὐσεβεῖς ἐκ πειρασμοῦ ῥύεσθαι, ἀδίκους δὲ εἰς ἡμέραν κρίσεως κολαζομένους τηρεῖν — all the more satisfying and conclusive.

The two occurrences of δέ in vv. 9 and 10 merit brief mention. In v. 9, the δέ signals a distinct unit that forms the second half of the apodosis. The δέ is especially well-suited here given the discontinuities between 9a–b, namely, a topic switch (εὐσεβεῖς to ἀδίκους) and the different actions undertaken by the Lord (ῥύεσθαι and εἰς ἡμέραν κρίσεως κολαζομένους τηρεῖν). The δέ in v. 10 occurs with a smaller scope, introducing an additional nominal element that specifies a subgroup of the ἀδίκους, those who pursue fleshly desires and who despise authority that especially deserve the Lord's judgment.[67] The discourse marker is not necessary,[68] but its use makes good sense. The presence of δέ correlates well with topic shifts, and the content of v. 10a does constitute one, although it

---

[65] Levinsohn, *Discourse Features*, 191.

[66] Focus, or focal prominence, is that which is most salient in a clause and can be pragmatically marked through a variety of shifts to word order, based on the information structure of the clause. See ibid., 7, 29–70; Runge, *Discourse Grammar*, 181–205, 269–85.

[67] Given the logic of the letter and the purpose of the current unit, this subgroup comprises the false teachers of 2:1-3.

[68] Cf. similar contexts of use, but without δέ, in 1 Tim 4:10; 5:17; 2 Tim 4:13; Titus 1:10.

is not characterized by high discontinuity. Moreover, by signaling a small break for the reader as they process, the author slows the discourse down, thereby drawing extra attention to the shift in v. 10a. The author has good reason to do so, given that the subgroup introduced in v. 10a is the primary topic for the rest of the chapter.

3.2.2.2. 2:10b–22

The author uses the rest of chapter 2 to further detail the false teachers' sins and the dangers they represent. These verses are not a new unit structurally; they provide background information that serves to flesh out 2:10a. This is evinced by the nature of the information. No part of 2:10b–22 moves the hortatory discourse forward. Instead, these verses elaborate on the character and on the actions of the false teachers.[69] It is important information, but it supports the author's case rather than moving it forward along the theme-line.

There are no overt features that signal the thematic shift between vv. 4–10a and vv. 10b–22. The material itself is clear enough. Verses 4–10a were concerned with providing support for v. 3, and v. 10b starkly moves away from that kind of material and to a critical description of the false teachers. Verse 10b does begin with asyndeton, but, in this context, asyndeton only indicates that what follows is a part of the same discourse unit as what preceded.[70]

In verses 10b–11 the author describes the insolence of the false teachers by contrasting the way they blaspheme "the glorious ones" with the behavior of angels. Verses 12–17 move to a related but different concern, the sinful actions of the false teachers and the certainty of their judgment.[71] To effect this movement, the author renews the false teachers as the topic (after v. 11, in which the angels were the topic) with a preposed οὗτοι,[72] which also serves as a cohesive link to the preceding, and couples it with a δέ to indicate a break between distinct blocks.

Within vv. 12–17, there are a few features worth special mention. First, many elements are preposed for focal prominence, e.g., ἡδονήν, ἐν ἡμέρᾳ (embedded), ὀφθαλμοὺς (+ μεστοὺς μοιχαλίδος καὶ ἀκαταπαύστους ἁμαρτίας), καρδίαν γεγυμνασμένην πλεονεξίας. This draws extra attention to the accusations and heightens the

---

[69] Note the many copular and present tense indicative verbs within these verses. Such verb forms are not typically those in the foreground of hortatory discourse. They are typical for the foreground of expository discourse (Longacre and Hwang, *Holistic Discourse Analysis*, 189). However, given that 2 Peter is, as a whole, a hortatory discourse, the foreground of expository material will not necessarily be in the foreground of the letter.

[70] See the discussion in Levinsohn, *Discourse Features*, 118.

[71] Note how their judgment bookends vv. 12-17 with ἐν τῇ φθορᾷ αὐτῶν καὶ φθαρήσονται in v. 12 and οἷς ὁ ζόφος τοῦ σκότους τετήρηται at the end of v. 17.

[72] Regarding points of departure involving renewal, see ibid., 12-14.

emotion of the passage. Second, also contributing to the emotion of the passage, is the change of reference to the false teachers as κατάρας τέκνα in v. 14. Changes of reference are not necessary to convey content, but they cause the reader to update their mental representation of the referent with the new expression, thereby altering the way the reader perceives the referent.[73] Third, the author uses subtle lexical links that connect to previous parts of the letter, demonstrating how closely knit together the letter is and contributing to its global coherence. In v. 14, the false teachers' hearts are trained for πλεονεξίας; in 2:3, it is in their πλεονεξία that they will exploit the readers. Also in v. 14, the author effects a contrast between those who are enticed by the false teachers and the letter's audience, describing the former as ἀστηρίκτους and the latter, in 1:12, as ἐστηριγμένους in the present truth.[74] In v. 15, the false teachers are said to forsake the right ὁδόν; in 2:2, the author writes that because of the false teachers, the ὁδός of truth will be slandered. In v. 17, upon reading that the ζόφος of darkness is reserved for the false teachers, the reader will likely recall the prior occurrence of this lexeme in 2:4, especially given that both verses are similar thematically in that they are concerned with judgment. One would be justified in wondering whether the author is implicitly comparing the false teachers and their judgment to the sinful angels and their fate. Lastly, the preposed οὗτοι in v. 17, like the occurrence of the pronoun in v. 12, renews the topic after the digression about Balaam and his donkey.[75]

Verses 18–19a are introduced by γάρ, signaling the content as supportive, background material to the content of v. 17. There are notable lexical links to other parts of the letter in these verses as well. In v. 18, δελεάζουσιν is used to describe the false teachers' activity. This connects back to 2:14 (δελεάζοντες ψυχὰς ἀστηρίκτους). Also in v. 18, the author writes that the false teachers entice with fleshly desires and licentiousness (ἐπιθυμίαις σαρκὸς ἀσελγείαις). The former echoes 2:10, where the author, referring to the false teachers, states that those who go after the flesh in defiled desire (ὀπίσω σαρκὸς ἐν ἐπιθυμίᾳ μιασμοῦ) are especially deserving of judgment. The latter connects to 2:2, where the author predicts that many will follow the false teachers' ἀσελγείαις. In addition to the lexical links, the author reuses some of the vocabulary from 1:4 (ἐπιθυμίαις, ἀποφεύγοντας, φθορᾶς). While simple reuse of vocabulary would not typically merit a mention, it may demonstrate that the content of 1:4 is on the author's mind. This is important to note because it is explicitly recalled in v. 20.

---

[73] Runge, *Discourse Grammar*, 354.

[74] Thus, it would be reasonable to posit that there is an underlying caution in 2:14, namely, to remain established so as to not become unestablished and therefore be enticed by the false teachers.

[75] Unlike v. 12, though, v. 17 does not move to something new but rather is a part of the current unit. Because of this, v. 17 exhibits asyndeton instead of a δέ.

Verse 19b is also introduced by γάρ and is thus presented as supporting information to the preceding. Likewise, v. 20 is introduced by γάρ and supports v. 19b. Up to this point, the discourse has primarily been about the false teachers. In v. 20, however, the author takes the notion of enslavement from v. 19b and turns it into a description of those believers who are enticed by the false teachers.[76] Note that the author recalls 1:2–8 here. In 1:2–8, the knowledge of God and Jesus was described as ultimately leading to sharing in the divine nature (1:4), which is connected with escaping from the corruption of the world (ἀποφυγόντες τῆς ἐν τῷ κόσμῳ ἐν ἐπιθυμίᾳ φθορᾶς). In 2:20, the author laments those who have escaped the defilements of the world (ἀποφυγόντες τὰ μιάσματα τοῦ κόσμου) through the knowledge of Jesus, only to be enticed by the false teachers. Presumably, this is at least one of the reasons the author began and ends the letter with the exhortation to *grow* in the knowledge of God and Jesus. If the readers grow in that knowledge, there is less of a chance that they will be enticed by the false teachers. Lastly, vv. 21–22 are also introduced by γάρ. These verses support v. 20 by fleshing out and defending the author's claim in v. 20.[77]

3.3. 3:1–10

The next macro-unit moves to the second threat to the believing community, scoffers who will cast doubt on the promise of the Lord's return. It can be divided into two further units: 3:1–7, in which the author deals primarily with reminding the readers about the scoffers and dismantling their arguments, and 3:8–10, in which the author reassures the readers that the day of the Lord will indeed come.

3.3.1. 3:1–7

Verses 3:1–3a fill a command element slot. The author conveys three mitigated commands: that the readers wake up, remember the foretold words of the prophets and the commandment of the apostles, and (therefore) know that scoffers will come in the last days and attempt to cast doubt on the Lord's return. Following this, vv. 3:3b–7 comprise an indication of the problem/situation. The author details the threat posed by the scoffers and then offers an argument against them.

In addition to the boundary markers in 3:1 discussed above, there are a few features that bear special mention. Within the quoted material of v. 4, the scoffers question the promised return of the Lord, thereby implying that he will not

---

[76] Note the repetition of ἡττάομαι between vv. 19b and 20.

[77] Note the mention of τὴν ὁδὸν τῆς δικαιοσύνης in 2:21, which recalls ἡ ὁδὸς τῆς ἀληθείας in 2:2.

return. This foreground material is immediately followed by background information in 3:4b, introduced by γάρ, that provides support for the implied assertion that the Lord will not return. In vv. 5–7, the author offers background expository discourse, introduced by γάρ, that explains the error of the scoffers. The author moves to a second proof in v. 7, which is marked as the next step in the argument by δέ. Along with the δέ, there is a topic switch to the current heavens and earth (οἱ δὲ νῦν οὐρανοὶ καὶ ἡ γῆ), which are preposed to draw attention to them as the new topic.

It is also worth noting that the issue raised by the scoffers in v. 4 is the Lord's coming, his παρουσίας. This occurrence of παρουσίας links to its use in 1:16 and provides additional insight into what the author is doing there. While vv. 1:16–21 are comprised of a defense of the author's authority/credibility, the first defense (vv. 16–18) serves a secondary purpose. In 1:16, the author states that they made the Lord's power and coming (παρουσίαν) known to the audience not by following clever myths but by their own eyewitness account. This is then further supported in vv. 17–18. In light of 3:4 and the fact that 3:8–10 is concerned with reassuring the readers that the Lord will indeed come, one can observe that, in addition to defending the author's authority/credibility, 1:16–18 also preempts the threat of the scoffers. The author, knowing the issues they intend to address in the letter, definitively establishes the certainty of the Lord's coming well before even mentioning the scoffers. In other words, it would seem likely that since the author knew that the question of the Lord's coming would come up, they provided a strong defense of it early on.

3.3.2. 3:8–10

The following features in v. 8 indicate a step forward in the discourse:

1.   The discourse marker δέ signals a break between units.
2.   There is a change in the discussion topic. Verses 5–7 discussed the fate of creation, presenting it as an argument against assumptions made by the scoffers. Verses 8–10 are concerned with assuring the readers of the Lord's coming.
3.   Given the hortatory nature of the letter as a whole, the imperative λανθανέτω likely indicates a return to foreground material, as well as to hortatory discourse.
4.   The presence of the vocative, ἀγαπητοί, suggests a discourse boundary.

These features together leave no doubt that the author has moved to something new. However, while such a clustering of features could suggest a new macro-unit, the content of vv. 8–10 indicates that these verses are a distinct unit within the current macro-unit. From the beginning of this macro-unit, the author has been concerned with warning the readers about the scoffers and providing a defense against them. In vv. 5–7, the author left the foreground to argue against the foundational assumption of the scoffers that nothing has changed since creation. This is background material because, though important, it is not the main point. It does not address the actual claim made by the scoffers. This is done in vv. 8–10 where the foreground is resumed. It is here that the author responds to the scoffers' implied assertion in v. 4 that the Lord's promised coming will not take place. The author assures the audience that the Lord will indeed fulfill his promise and explains to them that the reason the Lord has not yet come is due to his patience. Thus, vv. 8–10 demonstrate a high level of thematic continuity with the preceding and constitute a crucial piece of the current macro-unit.

There are a number of discourse features within these verses. In v. 8, Ἓν ... τοῦτο is preposed for focal prominence, drawing attention to this most salient part of the sentence. This points forward to the content clause marked by ὅτι, thereby creating anticipation for it.[78] There is a cohesive link between λανθανέτω in v. 8 and λανθάνει in v. 5 that sets up a contrast between the two groups. The scoffers forget, but the readers are commanded not to forget. Verses 9–10 are background information, containing expository discourse wherein the author explains what is meant by v. 8. The occurrence of τῆς ἐπαγγελίας in v. 9 explicitly links to ἡ ἐπαγγελία in v. 4, indicating that the content of vv. 8–10 is a direct rebuttal to the scoffers. Verse 9 also links to v. 7 by way of the related lexemes ἀπολέσθαι (v. 9) and ἀπωλείας (v. 7). Verse 7 brought up the destruction of the ungodly. Verse 9 revisits this and indicates that the destruction can be avoided by those who repent. In addition, after the second ἀλλά, πάντας is preposed for topical prominence — as the topic switches from τινας —, and εἰς μετάνοιαν is preposed for focal prominence, thereby drawing extra attention to it as the most important part of the focus domain. In v. 10, there are two occurrences of δέ. The first marks v. 10 as a distinct step in the argument. Whereas v. 9 provided a defense of the Lord, explaining why he had not yet come, v. 10 moves forward to assure the readers that he will come. The δέ collocates well with this discontinuity in topic and with the discontinuity in time (v. 9 – present; v. 10 – future). To understand the use of the second δέ, it is important to consider how the three final sentences relate to each other:

1a.   οἱ οὐρανοὶ ῥοιζηδὸν παρελεύσονται,

1b.   στοιχεῖα δὲ καυσούμενα λυθήσεται,

2.   καὶ γῆ καὶ τὰ ἐν αὐτῇ ἔργα εὑρεθήσεται

---

[78] On forward-pointing devices, see ibid., 61–71.

This is not a simple list of three events. The first two sentences together convey one event with two distinct parts. The third sentence posits a second event, likely one that is a result of the first. In other words, the first two sentences work together to communicate a complete picture of what will happen on the day of the Lord to all of creation apart from the earth. The use of δέ between these signals the second sentence as distinct information *within that event* (note the topic switch from οὐρανοί to στοιχεῖα). The author then uses καί to connect the third sentence to the whole complex that is sentences 1–2 to describe the second event, i.e., what will then take place on the earth. Had all three sentences instead been connected by καί, the reader would have been required to process them as three separate events.[79]

3.4. 3:11–16

In v. 11 the author refers to the content of v. 10 and uses it to ground material in vv. 11–13 that serves as background motivation for the exhortations in vv. 14–16.

The main idea of vv. 11–12 is conveyed by the question in v. 11: ποταποὺς δεῖ ὑπάρχειν ὑμᾶς. The rest of these two verses are backgrounded relative to this core. In v. 13, δέ signals a small step within this. Verses 11–12 framed the audience's waiting with the day of the Lord and the destruction it would bring on creation. Verse 13 provides a contrast, indicating that the author and readers are, in fact, waiting for a new heavens and a new earth.[80] This is a development in thought between vv. 11–12 and v. 13 and is structured accordingly by δέ.

In vv. 14–16, the author exhorts the readers, based on the motivating material of vv. 11–13 (v. 13 especially), to do their best to be found without spot and without blemish before God (v. 14) and to regard the Lord's patience as salvation. In many ways, these verses serve as the culmination of the author's teachings, as they recall earlier parts of the letter and exhort the readers in how they are to live in the here and now.

In v. 14, διό indicates that what follows is not a new unit and is an inference based on the preceding. Following διό, the vocative ἀγαπητοί works well. Though it does not co-occur with a discourse boundary as vocatives often do, it occurs at a pivotal moment within the unit, as the author moves from motivation to

---

[79] The absence of the third sentence in v. 12 ostensibly confirms this analysis. The author does not convey [First Event (Part 1/Part 2) and Second Event] in v. 12 but only repeats the first two sentences (with some lexical changes). Given this, there is no need to use δέ to distinguish the nature of the information in order to ensure the first two sentences are understood as one event comprised of two parts instead of as two completely separate events.

[80] Note that καινοὺς ... οὐρανοὺς καὶ γῆν καινὴν is preposed for focal prominence. Its relative clause is not preposed because, as Levinsohn writes, "If a complex constituent is in focus, it is normal for only part of it to precede the verb." Levinsohn, *Discourse Features*, 57.

commands. After ἀγαπητοί, ταῦτα προσδοκῶντες is preposed before the verb to provide a point of departure that links to the preceding content and frames what follows.[81] Verse 14 also recalls other parts of 2 Peter. By exhorting the readers to be found without spot and without blemish (σπουδάσατε ἄσπιλοι καὶ ἀμώμητοι αὐτῷ εὑρεθῆναι), the author provides a contrastive cohesive link between them and the false teachers, who were described as σπίλοι καὶ μῶμοι in 2:13. Further, εὑρεθῆναι links to εὑρεθήσεται in 3:10. The earth and every work in it will be found on the day of the Lord. Verse 14 details how the readers are meant to be found in the meantime.

In v. 15, the author commands the readers to regard the Lord's patience as salvation. This recalls 3:9, where the author explained that the Lord's patience was due to his desire that none should perish but that all would come to repentance. Note the correspondences:

v. 9: μακροθυμεῖ εἰς ὑμᾶς μὴ βουλόμενός τινας ἀπολέσθαι ἀλλὰ πάντας εἰς μετάνοιαν χωρῆσαι

v. 15: καὶ τὴν τοῦ κυρίου ἡμῶν μακροθυμίαν σωτηρίαν ἡγεῖσθε

The preposed topic switch in v. 15, τὴν τοῦ κυρίου ἡμῶν μακροθυμίαν, connects to the mention of God's patience in v. 9. The preposed focal element, σωτηρίαν, effectively sums up the latter part of v. 9 ("not wanting any to perish but that all would come to repentance"). In v. 9, the author explained the reason for God's patience. In v. 15, the author uses that explanation to explicitly instruct the readers in the way they are meant to regard the Lord's patience.

In vv. 15b–16, the author links his commands with those of the apostle Paul. These verses are backgrounded within dependent clauses and thus do not contribute to the development of the theme-line of the discourse, but they do serve to further bolster the credibility of the author (by associating himself with Paul) as well as provide a critique against opponents. First, note how the author demonstrates a concern to present Paul in a positive and authoritative light. Paul is introduced not simply as Παῦλος but as ὁ ἀγαπητὸς ἡμῶν ἀδελφὸς Παῦλος. The author wants to ensure that the readers think of Paul in terms of ἀγαπητὸς and ἡμῶν ἀδελφός.[82] Note, too, that ὁ ἀγαπητὸς ἡμῶν ἀδελφὸς Παῦλος is fronted before the verb to indicate the topic switch. After the new topic is introduced,

---

[81] Note too how well suited ταῦτα προσδοκῶντες is to chapter 3. It sets the readers sights on the present and assumes a period of waiting, during which there are things to be done. This creates a barrier between the readers and the scoffers. If the readers think of the present as a period of waiting in which there is work to be done, they are less likely to be swayed by the scoffers whose tactic is to sow doubt and impatience regarding the Lord's coming.

[82] Runge labels this "thematic highlighting," a type of overspecification. See Runge, *Discourse Grammar*, 321–24.

another fronted element occurs, κατὰ τὴν δοθεῖσαν αὐτῷ σοφίαν. This is pre-posed to mark it as the most salient piece of information within the sentence. The author is drawing attention not only to Paul's wisdom but that this wis-dom was bestowed upon him, thereby highlighting Paul's authoritative insight. Second, the author uses this connection with Paul's letters to indicate a prob-lem and immediately critique it. The problem is that those who are ignorant and unstable (οἱ ἀμαθεῖς καὶ ἀστήρικτοι) distort Paul's writings as well as the rest of the Scriptures. The critique is presented both at the onset — they are *ignorant* and *unstable* — and at the end — their distortions lead to their own destruction.

The full force of the phrase οἱ ἀμαθεῖς καὶ ἀστήρικτοι in v. 16 is felt when the reader observes its connections to other parts of the letter. By using ἀστήρικτοι, the author takes the same critique of those who are enticed by the false teach-ers in 2:14 and applies it to the opponents. Not only are those who are enticed unstable, but so are the opponents! Also, as with 2:14, there is a contrast be-tween the ἀστήρικτοι mentioned here and the audience, who were described as ἐστηριγμένους ἐν τῇ παρούσῃ ἀληθείᾳ in 1:12. There is thus an implicit directive to remain established and not to become unstable. The mention of the ἀμαθεῖς does not have an explicit connection like ἀστήρικτοι does, but there is an im-portant theme that has been crucial to the author's concerns with which ἀμαθεῖς would appear to connect: growing in the knowledge of Jesus. The au-thor began the letter with an exhortation to grow in such knowledge, as it leads to living a godly life, through which one receives God's promises, which results in becoming a partaker of the divine nature. Moreover, the threats against the faithful community are those things against which knowledge forms a shield — false teachers who entice with empty words (2:18) and scoff-ers who cast doubt on the Lord's promised return (3:4). The author therefore encourages the readers to grow in the knowledge of Jesus by demonstrating that ignorance leads to destruction. Furthermore, it makes good sense that the author would refer both to ignorance and instability. First, the two are neces-sarily tied together. One cannot be established without having knowledge in which to establish oneself. Conversely, one can have knowledge but can still be susceptible to being enticed (2:20) if they are not established (2:14). Second, given this and given the message of the letter as a whole, these two character-istics together present the antithesis of what the author hopes for the readers. The opponents in 3:16 have no knowledge of Jesus nor are they firmly estab-lished. Their ignorance and their lack of foundation led them astray, which results in them leading others who are ignorant and unstable astray. The au-thor wants the readers to be aware of this and to embody the opposite charac-teristics as them. Owing to this, the content of the concluding remarks in vv. 17–18, to which we now turn, is of no surprise.

3.5. 3:17–18

Verses 17–18 return to the foreground and effectively sum up the overall concern of the letter, that the readers heed the forewarning and resist threats to the community by remaining firm and by growing in the grace and knowledge of Jesus. The οὖν is especially well-suited to a summative exhortation, as it signals both the movement to something new and the continuity with the rest of the letter. Note, too, the use of preposed points of departure in v. 17 that evince coherence with the rest of the letter. In v. 17a, προγινώσκοντες refers to the content of the letter itself as well as to the words of the prophets and apostles about which the author sought to remind the readers. In v. 17b, τῇ τῶν ἀθέσμων πλάνῃ συναπαχθέντες effectively sums up the threats to the community discussed in the letter, the false teachers[83] and the scoffers.

The transition between macro-units is seamless, as the author just mentioned the threats to the community, οἱ ἀμαθεῖς καὶ ἀστήρικτοι, in the background material of v. 16. This allows the author to easily pick up on the themes of ignorance and instability and provide the readers with their final exhortations. First, the author commands the readers to be on guard so as not to be led into the error of the lawless and thereby fall from their steadfastness (τοῦ ἰδίου στηριγμοῦ). Note the link between στηριγμοῦ here and ἐστηριγμένους in 1:12 and the contrast with the ἀστηρίκτους in 2:14 and the ἀστήρικτοι in 3:16. The second command is given in v. 18 and is introduced by δέ, indicating the next step within the present unit. The readers are commanded to grow in the grace and knowledge of Jesus. The mention of knowledge is especially important.[84] By growing in knowledge, the readers will not be like the ἀμαθεῖς of v. 16. Taken together, if the readers are guarded so as to remain firm and if they grow in the grace and knowledge of Jesus, then they will represent everything the ἀμαθεῖς καὶ ἀστήρικτοι are not, and they will not be susceptible to being led astray by empty words (2:14, 18). From the beginning of the letter to its end, this is the goal of 2 Peter. It is an hortatory discourse that seeks to exhort its readers towards right knowledge and being well established in that knowledge, so that they are unswayed when the false teachers and scoffers inevitably come.

---

[83] It is also worth noting that the false teachers were described in 2:18 as τοὺς ἐν πλάνῃ ἀναστρεφομένους.

[84] As discussed in §2.5, this forms an inclusio with 1:3. Furthermore, it connects with the author's claim in 1:8 that, by following the command of vv. 5-7, the readers will not be unfruitful or idle in their pursuit of the knowledge of Jesus.

21

Johannine Epistles

Ernst Wendland

"The ways of analyzing the structure of 1 John are almost as numerous as its exponents..."[1]

"...it seems preferable to regard the Epistle as being composed of a series of connected paragraphs whose relation to one another is governed by association of ideas rather than by a logical plan."[2]

Introduction

The challenge facing anyone attempting to analyze the Johannine literature is that, despite the relative simplicity of the Greek text, the structural organization of the discourse itself is quite difficult to discern due to its cyclical, repetitive nature. A "logical" sequentially-developed arrangement is clearly not followed, and no credible concentric formation of significant length has yet been proposed.[3] Some commentators claim that the epistle does not manifest

---

[1] Stephen S. Smalley, *1, 2, 3 John*, WBC 51 (Word Books, 1984), xxxiii.

[2] I. Howard Marshall, *The Epistles of John*, NICNT (Eerdmans, 1978), 26.

[3] See, for example, Nils W. Lund, *Chiasmus in the New Testament* (Hendrickson, 1942); John H. Welch, *Chiasmus in Antiquity* (Gerstenberg Verlag, 1981). There is, to my knowledge, one

any specifiable structure: "A curious circumstance about the letter is that it seems to have no divisions."[4] In an earlier study of 1 John,[5] I considered the general content, style, and purpose of the epistle,[6] but in the present investigation I will focus more pointedly on the discourse structure of the Greek composition in order to suggest how this dimension might contribute to our perception of the letter's overall design and, as a result, a better understanding of the author's fervent pastoral message to the faithful—then and now.[7]

In the next section, I will summarize my form-functional methodology for the study of biblical (OT/NT) discourse. This leads to the centerpiece of the present investigation, namely, a detailed examination of the entire Greek text of John's epistles.[8] The aim will be to demonstrate how this bottom-to-top approach enables

---

possible exception (though debatable), namely, the concentric structure manifested in 2:18–28 (see below).

[4] R. C. H. Lenski, *The Interpretation of the Epistles of St. Peter, St. John, and St. Jude* (Wartburg, 1945), 373—but see later below.

[5] Ernst R. Wendland, "'Dear Children' Versus 'the Antichrists': The Rhetoric of Reassurance in 1 John," *Neotestamentica* 41, no. 1 (2007): 173–219. See this study for my perspective on the theological and ethical semantics of this epistle.

[6] In this study, four primary stylistic-rhetorical features of 1 John were singled out for special examination and exemplification: recursion, contrast, focus, and mitigation. These interrelated stylisic devices were viewed as enabling the author to clearly and forcefully express his chosen "rhetoric of reassurance" whereby he sought to strengthen and encourage the addressed community of believers which was being threatened by false teachers. John's message, which majors on the three major themes of faith, love, and obedience in relation to the central truth about Jesus Christ, the Son of God (3:23), is also traced in the form of "speech-acts" as it is synonymously and systematically recycled for emphasis throughout the epistolary discourse (ibid., 198–202).

[7] The text of 1 John—variously classified by scholars as a general epistle, a sermon, a pastoral tract, an instructional "enchiridion," or simply a theological "writing" or essay—begins with an elaborate personal "testimony" concerning the validity of its contents (1:1–4), and it ends with a pronounced emphasis on "knowing" the "*truth*" about "eternal life" (5:13–20). For a discussion of these and other genre classifications in relation to 1 John, see the following: Ruth B. Edwards, *The Johannine Epistles* (Sheffield Academic Press, 1996), 34–35; Thomas F. Johnson, *1, 2, and 3 John*, NIBC (Hendrickson, 1993), 13; Grace E. Sherman and John C. Tuggy, *A Semantic and Structural Analysis of the Johannine Epistles* (SIL, 1994), 6; Marianne M. Thompson, *1–3 John* (InterVarsity, 1992), 18. For a detailed discussion of different methods of analyzing a biblical text, see Dean B. Deppe, *All Roads Lead to the Text: Eight Methods of Inquiry into the Bible* (Eerdmans, 2011); for a shorter comparative survey of several discourse methodologies (with outlines) applied to 1 John, see Birger Olsson, "First John: Discourse Analyses and Interpretations," in *Discourse Analysis and the New Testament: Approaches and Results*, ed. Stanley E. Porter and Jeffrey T. Reed (Sheffield Academic Press, 1999), 369–391.

[8] Several significant text-critical issues will be noted, but not much attention will be given to background (isagogical) and intertextual issues (for these, see Wendland, "Rhetoric of Reassurance," 173–176 and the works cited in the Reference section). Thus, the focus of the present

us to structure each letter in terms of three basic levels of verbal organization, that is, with respect to (1) putative oral-aural "utterances" (spoken lines), (2) groups of topically related utterances (epistolary "paragraphs"), and (3) sets of thematically related paragraphs ("sections"). In a parallel column alongside the Greek paragraph units, explanatory notes are included to provide reasons for my proposed demarcation of the discourse, which may then be evaluated for credence in relation to the original. It is hoped that this approach will offer a testable and/or defendable scheme for each structural unit individually and in relation to others that precede or follow it in the epistle. After this central textual display, the overall composition of 1 John epistle is summarized and briefly compared with several alternative proposals.[9] In conclusion, the practical implications (pros and cons) of this method of discourse analysis will be summarized.

Methodology

First John is an "epistle" in the sense that it was a verbal discourse *written* (1:4; 2:1, 14, 26; 5:13) and circulated for *reading*-proclamation to specific audience groups, who are frequently addressed by vocative expressions. However, in terms of its principal genre, this text is more precisely classified as an "expository-hortatory homily," a rather passionate, recursive pastoral composition intended to encourage steadfast confessional discipleship in word and deed in the face of strong "anti-christian" opposition. Since a vigorous reinforcement of the faithful was necessary, the author employed an appropriate literary style to suit his essentially twofold paraenetic purpose—that is, involving basic didactic *instruction* (edifying and reminding) and earnest pragmatic *reassurance* (encouraging and admonishing). John's teaching thus focuses on Christology, upon which is based his exhortation, which features Ecclesiology, or "fellowship"—both motivations being summarized both at the beginning (1:1–5) and ending (5:18–20) of this epistle. Various aspects of these two macro-themes are manifested in the cyclically patterned organization of the discourse structure, with key topics arranged recurrently like beads on a multifaceted thematic string, rather than some

---

study will be on the original Greek text itself and how it is shaped and arranged to form a coherent and cohesive communicative whole.

[9] Perhaps, in the end, some readers will be led to make a conclusion similar to that found in the following report: "In a 1956 *JBL* article on John's gospel, one Pierson Parker makes the intriguing statement that 1 John makes almost as much sense read backward as it does read forward. This is evidence that the letter's contents are 'disconnected' and that the letter reads like 'an old man's anxious exhortations to his flock.' Perhaps it's evidence of something else, not an old man's anxiety, but his cunning, his deliberate construction of a letter that reads forwards, backwards, and from the middle" (Peter Leithart, accessed November 2, 2017 at: http://www.patheos.com/blogs/leithart/2007/12/structure-of-john-2).

sequentially unfolding, "logical" plan (which is why every proposed topical out-line differs from the next).[10]

In brief, my methodology seeks to identify four principal aspects of discourse structure, namely, its breaks, bonds, bounds, and bumps.[11] The "breaks" are points where we note a shift or discontinuity with respect to form (e.g., shift to direct speech), content (e.g., a new topic), and/or function (e.g., an example given to illustrate a prior exposition). The "bonds" of a text are literary elements that contribute to the "cohesion" (form) and/or "coherence" (content) of a posited structural unit, such as a "paragraph" of prose. The breaks and bonds operate together to establish the initial and final "bound[arie]s" of a unit, while the "bumps" (projections) refer to places in the text where we note a convergence of stylistic features, thus indicating a semantic "peak" and/or an emotive "climax" (usually involving a Christological assertion of some type).

The following then is a literary-structural compositional analysis of John's First Epistle,[12] followed by a similar study of 2 and 3 John. The Greek text has been demarcated "oratorically," that is, segmented in terms of *paragraph* units grouped, roughly thematically, into larger *sections* and displayed in the form of putative lineal *utterance* units (breath-spans) to facilitate (and visually represent) an oral-aural proclamation of the text.[13] Often these lines of poetic prose

---

[10] Some would call this a "spiral"-shaped construction (W. Hall Harris III, "Structure and Purpose of 1 John," accessed on 11/22/2017 at: https://bible.org/seriespage/4-structure-and-purpose-1-john)—or, on the other hand, a text "lacking any major divisions based on content" (Johnson, *1, 2, and 3 John*, 16), an opinion which the present study clearly indicates is not the case.

[11] For additional information regarding this methodology, including a more detailed application, see Ernst R. Wendland, *Translating the Literature of Scripture: A Literary-Rhetorical Approach to Bible Translation* (SIL, 2004), 229–245 and Ernst R. Wendland, *LiFE-Style Translating: A Workbook for Bible Translators*, 2nd ed. (SIL, 2011), 126–149.

[12] A "literary-structural" analysis is a bottom-up/top-down methodology that seeks to determine the principal compositional units of a text, that is, its larger "structure," by means of a multifaceted stylistic (formal) and rhetorical (functional) examination, beginning with the individual utterances and their linguistic constituents, and moving up the ladder of verbal organization to encompass larger elements—paragraphs and sections. Once the entire "discourse"—viewed as a macro-speech-act—has been carefully demarcated in this manner, the process is reversed, analyzing the complete text "downwards" to evaluate and test how well the various structural units are seen to complement and interconnect with one another to comprise a coherent (formal) and cohesive (semantic) whole, thus effecting what is posited as being the author's intended communicative purpose(s).

[13] The proposed lineation is of course a hypothetical reconstruction based on my perception of how the Greek text might be orally articulated in a public performance—with the individual line breaks determined by: (a) the syntax, (b) content, (c) sound patterning, (d) prose rhythm, (e) breath pauses, and/or (f) assumed dramatic effect. "The lineation tells the reader how to hear, see, and understand the poem. As the central formal principle of verse, lineation establishes the auditory and semantic patterns of the poem. The overall formal power

pattern together synonymously, augmentatively, or contrastively in a manner reminiscent of Hebrew lyric parallelism.[14] In addition, prominent lexical-conceptual recursion (mainly exact or synonymous, but occasionally contrastive) is indicated by <u>underlining</u> the main words concerned, while certain reiterated "function words" (conjunctions, prepositions, etc.) are **boldfaced**, and notable tail-head "hook expressions" are italicized as well as ***boldfaced***. Important text-critical matters are summarized in footnotes.[15] Periodic Christological confessions are automatically, in view of the message of the epistle as a whole and the author's assumed communicative intention, regarded as thematic "peaks" and highlighted by gray shading within the text.

There are five main types of "discourse marker" ("communicative clue")[16] that indicate five distinct aspects of compositional structure in keeping with the methodology described above: unit-initial *Aperture* (A), unit-final *Closure* (C), unit-internal *Bonding* (B), unit-adjacent transitional *Juncture* (J), or a periodic topical *Peak* point (P).[17] These markers operate together and serve to establish

---

of the poem cannot be achieved if lineation is done carelessly" (Diana Gioia, "Thirteen Ways of Thinking About the Poetic Line," accessed 06/01/2018 at http://danagioia.com/essays/writing-and-reading/thirteen-ways-of-thinking-about-the-poetic-line). However, with respect to "poetic prose," as I consider 1 John to be, I would say rather that the auditory, semantic, and syntactic patterns of the text establish the lineation. For further documentation and illustration of this and related methodologies, see "Notes on the 'Sonic Structure' of Paul's Epistle to Philemon" in Ernst. R. Wendland, *Orality and Scripture: Composition, Translation, and Transmission* (SIL, 2013), ch. 8; cf. also Margaret Ellen Lee and Bernard Brandon Scott, *Sound Mapping of the New Testament* (Polebridge Press, 2009); T. V. F. Brogan, "Line," in Roland Green, ed., *The Princeton Encyclopedia of Poetry & Poetics*, 4th ed. (Princeton UP, 2012), 801–803; Ernst R. Wendland, "Comparative Rhetorical Poetics, Orality, and Bible Translation," in *Translating Scripture for Sound and Performance: New Directions in Biblical Studies*, ed. J. A. Maxey and E .R. Wendland (Cascade Books:, 2012), ch. 7. The only Bible translation that I have noted which displays the text of 1 John in this formatted way is the *New Jerusalem Bible*; however, its utterance lineation differs from mine since it is based upon the English text, not the Greek.

[14] John Breck called attention to "antithetical statements" in 1 John, observing that "in many cases they can be divided into couplets, suggesting the influence Hebrew poetry exercised on the Johannine author" (*The Shape of Biblical Language: Chiasmus in the Scriptures and Beyond* [St. Vladimir Press, 1994], 27).

[15] Cited from the text notes of the *New English Translation* (NET) or Rodger Omanson, *A Textual Guide to the Greek New Testament* (Stuttgart: German Bible Society, 2006).

[16] "Communicative clues" are "stylistic properties...[that] guide the audience to the intended interpretation" of a text (Basil Hatim and Jeremy Munday, *Translation—An Advanced Resource Book* [Routledge, 2004], 65).

[17] From one perspective, discourse "peaks," may be identified as "punctiliar," that is, centering upon one or two suitably marked passages, e.g., 1 John 2:12–17 (hortatory) and 18–27 (doctrinal) (Robert E. Longacre, "Towards an Exegesis of 1 John Based on the Discourse Analysis of the Greek Text," in *Linguistics and New Testament Interpretation: Essays on Discourse*

the main thematic and/or pragmatic segments, or interior boundaries, of the letter (paragraphs and sections). The abbreviations for these markers will be used throughout the text analysis below in the right-hand column. The most important discourse constituent is the unit- beginning (aperture), which may be indicated by several literary structural features, for example: a vocative,[18] imperative, asyndeton,[19] a formula, a new topic, and the reiteration of lexical items or concepts found at the onset of a preceding unit (technically termed structural "anaphora"). These distinguishing characteristics work in concert to reveal and/or to support the textual divisions being posited. Thus, a weak "aperture" may be confirmed by a previous strong indication of "closure," for example, the second element of an "inclusio" that demarcates the preceding unit, or the repetition of lexical material that concludes the arrangement of a prior unit (termed structural "epiphora").[20] Furthermore, the more diagnostic features that converge at a proposed structural border, the more credible and convincing that boundary is—and will presumably sound aurally to an audience (e.g., 1:4). Prominent thematic and/or formal (artistic-rhetorical) elements may appear together at a structural border or within a delineated unit to mark and emphasize a discourse "peak" point.

Following the textual analysis, I will provide a discourse outline of 1 John based on the section and paragraph titles from the analysis. In conclusion, I will present data from the textual analysis to suggest a way forward in the debate over the structure of 1 John.

A final note: since the following investigation focuses on the organizational form of 1 John (also 2–3 John), many significant issues pertaining to exegetical interpretation and theological-ethical meaning are not addressed;[21] for such matters, a much larger commentary-like exposition would be required. This is not to suggest, however, that the present study has little or no hermeneutical value for pastors, theological students and New Testament scholars. The path towards interpreting the detailed content of any biblical text must always arise from an

---

Analysis, ed. David Alan Black [B&H Academic, 1992], 279). Alternatively, they may be viewed, like I do in 1 John, as being "progressive" in nature, that is, unfolding as a periodically emphasized thematic notion and/or pragmatic objective that extends throughout the entire text.

[18] The importance of the vocative as an initiating structural device is supported by Longacre, "Towards an Exegesis," 272–276.

[19] "Asyndeton," the lack of a conjunctive expression, is a very low-level marker of aperture in 1 John since it occurs so often elsewhere in the text. However, it does create a conceptual pause in the discourse, especially when preceded by an utterance that does begin with a conjunction.

[20] For a more detailed explanation of these structural devices and their function in biblical texts, see Wendland, *Translating the Literature of Scripture*, 125–130.

[21] For an overview of the latter aspects of meaning along with selected stylistic features, see Wendland, "Rhetoric of Reassurance," passim.

accurate understanding of its constituent linguistic forms—both small (the phonological soundscape) and large (the overall compositional arrangement). My structural exploration primarily engages these discourse-defining, demarcative formal features.

Epistolary PROLOGUE:	*Proclaiming the Word of Life* (1:1–4)

1:1 "Ο ἦν ἀπ' ἀρχῆς, ὃ <u>ἀκηκόαμεν</u>,
ὃ <u>ἑωράκαμεν</u> τοῖς ὀφθαλμοῖς <u>ἡμῶν</u>,
ὃ <u>ἐθεασάμεθα</u> καὶ αἱ χεῖρες <u>ἡμῶν</u>
   ἐψηλάφησαν,
περὶ τοῦ λόγου τῆς <u>ζωῆς</u> —
2 *καὶ* ἡ <u>ζωὴ</u> <u>ἐφανερώθη</u>,
καὶ <u>ἑωράκαμεν</u> *καὶ* <u>μαρτυροῦμεν</u>
καὶ <u>ἀπαγγέλλομεν</u> ὑμῖν τὴν <u>ζωὴν</u>
   τὴν αἰώνιον
ἥτις ἦν πρὸς <u>τὸν πατέρα</u> καὶ
   <u>ἐφανερώθη</u> ἡμῖν —
3 ὃ <u>ἑωράκαμεν</u> *καὶ* <u>ἀκηκόαμεν</u>
   <u>ἀπαγγέλλομεν</u> <u>καὶ ὑμῖν</u>,
ἵνα <u>καὶ ὑμεῖς</u> <u>κοινωνίαν</u> ἔχητε μεθ'
   <u>ἡμῶν</u>·
καὶ ἡ <u>κοινωνία</u> δὲ ἡ <u>ἡμετέρα</u> μετὰ
   <u>τοῦ πατρὸς</u> *καὶ* <u>μετὰ</u> τοῦ υἱοῦ
   αὐτοῦ Ἰησοῦ Χριστοῦ·
4 *καὶ* ταῦτα <u>γράφομεν ἡμεῖς</u>[22]
ἵνα ἡ χαρὰ <u>ἡμῶν</u>[23] ᾖ πεπληρωμένη.

- there is distinctive front-shifting of multiple direct object clauses within a climactic parallel syntactic pattern in v. 1 (A)
- reiterated verbs of two main semantic sets—of physical witnessing of and verbal testifying to "the w/Word of life" (B)—a case of deliberate topical ambiguity, referring equally to "Jesus Christ" (v. 3) and the Christian "message" (v. 5)
- several of the major themes of this epistle are foreshadowed in this Prologue (J), namely, the importance of eyewitness testimony (e.g., 5:6–12); Jesus Christ's personal instruction of his disciples,also to be proclaimed by them (4:2, 5:6); eternal life made available through Christ (5:11–12); human-divine, faith-based fellowship (1:6–7); cf. "joy" (intertextual link: 2 John 12; 3 John 4, J)
- an internal parenthesis (v.2) manifests the various Christological topics which intertextually connect this epistle with the Prologue and Conclusion of John's Gospel (1:4;

---

[22] The reading ἡμεῖς ('B' rating) "has the support of good quality manuscripts of the Alexandrian text-type. ... It seems likely that copyists changed the subject pronoun ἡμεῖς to the indirect object pronoun ὑμῖν, which is expected after the verb γράφομεν (we write)... (Omanson, *A Textual Guide*, 503).

[23] NET text note: A number of mss, some of them important (A C K P 33 81 1505 1739 pm syh bo), read ὑμῶν (humōn, "your") rather than ἡμῶν (hēmōn, "our"), which is found in somewhat better witnesses (א B L Ψ 049 1241 pm syp sa). Although the majority of Byzantine minuscules are split between the two readings, *Textus Receptus* (TR) reads ὑμῶν. It is possible that ὑμῶν represents a scribal assimilation to John 16:24. As far as the immediate context is concerned, either reading could possibly be original, since the recipients have already been

20:31) (P); this macro-theme resonates throughout 1 John
- a sequence of 12 occurrences of καί ("and"), many utterance-initial, occur within a single Greek sentence in vv. 1–4 (B)
- a pair of concluding ἵνα ("that") clauses announce the purpose of this epistle, which is prominently pragmatic (ethical) as well as conceptual (Christological) in nature (C)
- a progressive build-up to the revelation of "his son, Jesus Christ" (v. 3) (P)
- the metatextual communication formula "these things we write" (paralleling "we proclaim also to you" in v. 3) occurs at the end of this opening paragraph (C), rather than at the beginning (e.g., 2:1)

Epistolary **BODY** of Paraenesis— Exhorting Believers:	The TESTS of True Christology and Genuine Discipleship (1:5–5:20)
A. *Walking in the Light by Loving One Another—Not the World* (1:5–2:17)	**1. The need for confessing the darkness of our sins (1:5–10)**
5 Καὶ ἔστιν αὕτη ἡ <u>ἀγγελία</u> ἣν <u>ἀκηκόαμεν</u> ἀπ' αὐτοῦ καὶ <u>ἀναγγέλλομεν</u> ὑμῖν, ὅτι ὁ θεὸς <u>φῶς</u> ἐστιν καὶ <u>σκοτία</u> ἐν αὐτῷ οὐκ ἔστιν οὐδεμία. 6 ἐὰν <u>εἴπωμεν</u> ὅτι <u>κοινωνίαν</u> <u>ἔχομεν</u> μετ' αὐτοῦ καὶ ἐν τῷ <u>σκότει</u> <u>περιπατῶμεν</u>, ψευδόμεθα καὶ οὐ ποιοῦμεν τὴν ἀλήθειαν·	• v.5 overlaps in content with the Prologue (Καὶ "resumptive"; cf. vv.2–3— also in terms of mode of communication, "hearing" ἀκηκόαμεν) (J), thereby forging a conceptual progression as well as a new beginning (A) • Καὶ ἔστιν αὕτη ("And this is") is a formulaic "opener"; cf. 2:25; 3:25; 5:4, 11, 14 (A) • there is an interweaving of three main semantic complexes that are

mentioned in 1 John 1:2 (ὑμῖν, humin) and 1 John 1:3 (ὑμῖν), while it might seem more natural for the author to be concerned about the fulfillment of his own joy than his readers'; (cf. 2 John 4, 2 John 12; 3 John 3). Overall, the first-person pronoun is preferred on both external and internal grounds.

7 ἐὰν δὲ ἐν τῷ <u>φωτὶ</u> <u>περιπατῶμεν</u>
ὡς αὐτός ἐστιν ἐν τῷ <u>φωτί</u>,
<u>κοινωνίαν ἔχομεν μετ'</u> ἀλλήλων
καὶ τὸ αἷμα Ἰησοῦ τοῦ υἱοῦ αὐτοῦ
   καθαρίζει <u>ἡμᾶς</u> ἀπὸ πάσης <u>ἁμαρτίας</u>.
8 ἐὰν <u>εἴπωμεν</u> ὅτι <u>ἁμαρτίαν</u> οὐκ ἔχομεν,
   ἑαυτοὺς πλανῶμεν,
καὶ ἡ ἀλήθεια οὐκ ἔστιν ἐν <u>ἡμῖν</u>.
9 ἐὰν <u>ὁμολογῶμεν</u> τὰς <u>ἁμαρτίας</u> <u>ἡμῶν</u>,
   πιστός ἐστιν καὶ δίκαιος
<u>ἵνα ἀφῇ ἡμῖν τὰς ἁμαρτίας</u>
καὶ καθαρίσῃ <u>ἡμᾶς</u> ἀπὸ πάσης <u>ἀδικίας</u>.
10 ἐὰν <u>εἴπωμεν</u> ὅτι οὐχ <u>ἡμαρτήκαμεν</u>,
   ψεύστην ποιοῦμεν αὐτὸν
καὶ ὁ λόγος αὐτοῦ οὐκ ἔστιν ἐν <u>ἡμῖν</u>.

contrastive (also chiastic, vv. 6–7) in character: light and darkness, truth and falsehood, sinning and forgiving (B)—also:

- an internal sequence of three paired conditional sentences, each beginning with a false assertion (perhaps made by John's opponents, the "antichrists," 2:18): "if we say that" (ἐὰν εἴπωμεν ὅτι) in vv. 6, 8, and 10, which is followed by its consequence, with reference to "lying"; after the first two negative constructions, the corresponding contrastive positive truth is declared (ἐὰν [δὲ], "[but] if") in vv. 7 and 9 (B)—the third positive occurrence being found foregrounded at the onset of the next paragraph in 2:1 (P, J)

- the central Christological theme recurs as an emphatic assertion at the end of v. 7 ("and the blood of Jesus..."), being later reinforced in the second half of v. 9 (P)

- the manifold parallelism manifested by these verses structures the text linearly, as in the case of biblical Hebrew poetry (B)

- the final negative claim (v.10) is not immediately followed by its positive counterpart (which is postponed until after the direct address and exhortation in 2:1) (C)

- the paragraph thus concludes with a jarring implied warning to all false teachers: they make God a liar! (10b-c) (C)

2. Christ is the Advocate who deals with our sinfulness (2:1–2)

2:1 Τεκνία μου,
ταῦτα γράφω ὑμῖν
ἵνα μὴ <u>ἁμάρτητε</u>.
καὶ ἐάν τις <u>ἁμάρτῃ</u>,
<u>παράκλητον ἔχομεν πρὸς τὸν πατέρα</u>
Ἰησοῦν Χριστὸν δίκαιον,
2 καὶ αὐτὸς ἱλασμός ἐστιν περὶ τῶν
<u>ἁμαρτιῶν ἡμῶν</u>,
οὐ περὶ τῶν <u>ἡμετέρων</u> δὲ μόνον
ἀλλὰ καὶ περὶ ὅλου τοῦ κόσμου.

- vocative opener plus asyndeton, and a metatextual formula, "these things I am writing to you" (A); cf. 1:4 (J)
- the concept of "*sin*" (ἁμαρτ-) is initially foregrounded by a pair of seemingly incompatible clauses: "that you (pl.) do not sin—and if anyone does sin…" (A)
- the latter forms a topical-syntactic overlap with the close of the preceding paragraph (1:10), thus concluding the paired series of hypothetical clauses begun in 1:6 (J)[24]
- this immediately leads to an expanded expression of the central Christological profession of the epistle, given as "reassurance" (παράκλητον ἔχομεν) for believers (vv. 1b–2) (P)
- the segment climaxes in an all-inclusive salvific assertion (2b–c) (C)

3. Knowing Jesus means keeping God's commands (2:3–6)

3 Καὶ <u>ἐν τούτῳ γινώσκομεν ὅτι</u>
<u>ἐγνώκαμεν</u> <u>αὐτόν</u>,
ἐὰν <u>τὰς ἐντολὰς αὐτοῦ</u> <u>τηρῶμεν</u>.
4 ὁ λέγων ὅτι "Ἔγνωκα <u>αὐτὸν</u>
καὶ <u>τὰς ἐντολὰς αὐτοῦ</u> μὴ <u>τηρῶν</u>
<u>ψεύστης</u> ἐστίν,
καὶ <u>ἐν τούτῳ</u> ἡ ἀλήθεια οὐκ ἔστιν·
5 ὃς δ' ἂν <u>τηρῇ</u> <u>αὐτοῦ τὸν λόγον</u>,

- the new topic of "knowing" (no lexical overlap here) is syntactically foregrounded ("And in this we know that…"), followed by another conditional clause (ἐάν)—cf. 2:1, structural *anaphora* (A)
- the relative construction of v.4 ("the one who says") initiates a parallel, contrastive sequence that runs throughout the paragraph (cf. v. 5a, 6a) (B)

[24] I recognize that it is tempting (with considerable scholarly support) to include 2:1–2 in the preceding strophe by virtue of the conditional (ἐάν) construction of v. 1 that semantically attracts v. 2 along with it. I affirm the obvious overlap in meaning, but feel that the disjunctive literary features that initiate v. 1, as noted above, require a new structural beginning—one that similarly highlights of content of this short strophe. For a counter argument, see Deppe, *All Roads*, 2–3.

ἀληθῶς ἐν τούτῳ ἡ ἀγάπη τοῦ θεοῦ
τετελείωται.
<u>ἐν τούτῳ</u> γινώσκομεν ὅτι <u>ἐν αὐτῷ ἐσμεν</u>·
6 <u>ὁ λέγων ἐν αὐτῷ μένειν</u>
ὀφείλει καθὼς ἐκεῖνος <u>περιεπάτησεν</u>
καὶ αὐτὸς <u>περιπατεῖν</u>.[25]

- lexical recursion involving "obedience" appears throughout the unit (B)
- a conceptual peak is found in the lengthy exhoration that introduces the thematic concept regarding God's love (5b), emphasized by "truly" and a repetition of "in this we know that..." (P)
- the reference to "walking as (Jesus) did" in terms of "his commands" (4–6) implicitly anticipates the subject of the next unit (J)

4. Introduction of the new-old command (2:7–8)

7 Ἀγαπητοί, οὐκ <u>***ἐντολὴν καινὴν*** γράφω</u>
<u>ὑμῖν</u> (a) ἀλλ' <u>ἐντολὴν *παλαιὰν*</u> (b) ἣν
εἴχετε ἀπ' ἀρχῆς·
ἡ <u>ἐντολὴ</u> ἡ <u>*παλαιά*</u> (b') ἐστιν ὁ λόγος ὃν
ἠκούσατε.
8 πάλιν <u>ἐντολὴν *καινὴν* γράφω ὑμῖν</u> (a')
ὅ ἐστιν <u>ἀληθὲς</u> ἐν αὐτῷ καὶ ἐν ὑμῖν,
ὅτι ἡ <u>σκοτία</u> παράγεται
καὶ τὸ ***φῶς*** τὸ <u>ἀληθινὸν</u> ἤδη φαίνει.

- a vocative preceded by asyndeton and followed by a lengthy lineal chiastic construction (a-b=b'-a') (B), including the metatextual formula ("I am writing to you"), marks the onset of this new paragraph (A)—cf. vv.3–4 (structural *anaphora*) (A)
- the "old-new ***command***" is not explicitly explained until v.10a, but it concerns "truth" as revealed in "the light" as opposed to "the darkness"—now recalling the teaching of 1:5–10 (C)

5. We overcome the darkness of sin by loving one another (2:9–11)

9 <u>ὁ λέγων ἐν τῷ ***φωτὶ*** εἶναι</u>
καὶ <u>τὸν ἀδελφὸν αὐτοῦ μισῶν</u>
<u>ἐν τῇ σκοτίᾳ ἐστὶν</u> ἕως ἄρτι.
10 <u>ὁ ἀγαπῶν τὸν ἀδελφὸν αὐτοῦ</u>
<u>ἐν τῷ φωτὶ μένει,</u>

- the subject of ethical, behavioral "***light***" is now discussed in detail (J, A)
- prominent lexical recursion, including paired antithetical assertions set within participial constructions (e.g.,

---

[25] "The manuscript support for the omission [of *houtws*] is strong, and it is possible that *houtws* was added as a correlative with the preceding *kathws*. On the other hand, it is possible that *houtws* is original but was dropped for stylistic reasons..." (Omanson, *A Textual Guide*, 504). The present text reading is given a 'C' (doubtful) rating.

καὶ σκάνδαλον ἐν αὐτῷ οὐκ ἔστιν·

11 ὁ δὲ <u>μισῶν</u> <u>τὸν ἀδελφὸν αὐτοῦ</u>

<u>ἐν τῇ σκοτίᾳ ἐστὶν</u>

καὶ <u>ἐν τῇ σκοτίᾳ</u> περιπατεῖ,

καὶ οὐκ οἶδεν ποῦ ὑπάγει,

ὅτι ἡ <u>σκοτία</u> ἐτύφλωσεν τοὺς ὀφθαλμοὺς

αὐτοῦ.

12 <u>*Γράφω* ὑμῖν</u>, <u>τεκνία</u>,

   ὅτι ἀφέωνται ὑμῖν αἱ ἁμαρτίαι διὰ τὸ

     ὄνομα αὐτοῦ·

13 <u>*γράφω* ὑμῖν</u>, <u>πατέρες</u>,

   ὅτι <u>ἐγνώκατε</u> τὸν <u>ἀπ' ἀρχῆς</u>·

<u>*γράφω* ὑμῖν</u>, <u>νεανίσκοι</u>,

   ὅτι <u>νενικήκατε τὸν πονηρόν</u>.

14 <u>*ἔγραψα* ὑμῖν</u>, <u>παιδία</u>,

   ὅτι <u>ἐγνώκατε</u> τὸν <u>πατέρα</u>·

<u>*ἔγραψα* ὑμῖν</u>, <u>πατέρες</u>,

   ὅτι <u>ἐγνώκατε</u> τὸν <u>ἀπ' ἀρχῆς</u>·

<u>*ἔγραψα* ὑμῖν</u>, <u>νεανίσκοι</u>,

   ὅτι <u>ἰσχυροί ἐστε</u>

καὶ ὁ λόγος τοῦ θεοῦ ἐν ὑμῖν μένει

καὶ <u>νενικήκατε τὸν πονηρόν</u>.

---

v.9–10), gives cohesion to the entire paragraph (B)

- the negative side of the topical polarity (light and love—*darkness and hatred*) is underscored through repetition and figurative redundancy ("the darkness has blinded his eyes") at the end (P) (C)

6. Poetic pastoral encouragement for the faithful (2:12–14)

- the metatextual formula "I am writing to you" also initiates paragraphs at 2:1 (also "little children") and 2:7, thus exemplifying structural *anaphora* (A) and conceptual linkage (J)
- in this segment "I write/wrote to you" (pl.) (asyndeton) is consistently followed by a ὅτι object clause (6x), which, along with extensive lexical repetition, produces a very rhythmic unit (B)
- two parallel sets of three addressees and distinct forms of the verb "write" (γράφω— ἔγραψα) divide the paragraph into two sub-sections (12–13/14), but lexical recursion smoothes over the potential perception of a break in the text (B)
- the final ὅτι clause (14f) is extended thereby distinguishing the end of the sequence; the key pragmatic notion "you have defeated the evil one" is also repeated to mark the point of conclusion (C).
- the topical peak in v.14g (P) makes a distinctive, but condensed reference to Jesus Christ (cf. 1:1–4) and re-introduces the key concept of "remaining" (2:6, 10) (μένει) (J)

7. Don't love worldly things! (2:15–17)

15 Μὴ <u>ἀγαπᾶτε</u> <u>*τὸν κόσμον*</u>
μηδὲ τὰ ἐν τῷ <u>κόσμῳ</u>.
ἐάν τις <u>ἀγαπᾷ</u> τὸν <u>κόσμον</u>,
<u>οὐκ ἔστιν</u> ἡ <u>ἀγάπη</u> <u>τοῦ πατρὸς</u> ἐν αὐτῷ·
16 ὅτι πᾶν τὸ ἐν τῷ <u>κόσμῳ</u>,
<u>ἡ ἐπιθυμία</u> τῆς σαρκὸς
καὶ <u>ἡ ἐπιθυμία</u> τῶν ὀφθαλμῶν
καὶ ἡ ἀλαζονεία τοῦ βίου,
<u>οὐκ ἔστιν ἐκ τοῦ πατρός</u>,
ἀλλὰ ἐκ τοῦ <u>κόσμου</u> ἐστίν·
17 καὶ ὁ <u>κόσμος</u> παράγεται
καὶ <u>ἡ ἐπιθυμία</u> αὐτοῦ,
ὁ δὲ ποιῶν τὸ θέλημα τοῦ θεοῦ
μένει <u>*εἰς τὸν αἰῶνα*</u>.

- asyndeton and a direct prohibition contrastively renews the topic of *"love"* (J) to initiate this paragraph (A); inter-paragraph conceptual linkage within the section is also created by the semantic set of **sin** and its associates: "darkness" (2:11), "wicked one" (2:14), "world" (2:15), "lusts" (2:17), with "antichrist" then linking up with the following section (2:18) (J)
- "love" for "the Father" is opposed to "lust" (ἐπιθυμία) for "the world" as the author's admonition against sinful desires continues (B)
- the paragraph concludes with a final contrast between the transitory things of earthly life and the ever-living person, who loves (implied) aright and shows it by doing "God's will" (C)
- the notion of "remaining" (μένει) recalls the close of the preceding paragraph (2:14)—structural *epiphora* (J) (C)

B. *Warning Against Antichrists* (2:18–27)[26]

18 Παιδία, <u>*ἐσχάτη ὥρα* ἐστίν</u>,
καὶ καθὼς ἠκούσατε ὅτι <u>ἀντίχριστος</u>
ἔρχεται,[27] καὶ νῦν <u>ἀντίχριστοι</u> πολλοὶ

1. Antichrists versus anointed ones (2:18–21)

- a new paragraph and discourse "section" begins distinctively with asyndeton, a vocative, a formulaic temporal indicator, a temporally related

---

[26] It is possible to posit a chiastic-concentric arrangement that extends from 2:18–28, one having minor text-critical significance involving πάντα in v. 20 (cf. Wendland, "Rhetoric of Reassurance," 204–205). However, based on my current structural analysis I view v. 28 as being a hinge passage that properly initiates a new section, 2:28–3:10.

[27] "Most minuscules include the definite article ὁ after ὅτι, but the article is probably a scribal addition under the influence of v. 22, where the article is used with ἀντίχριστος (antichrist)..." (Omanson, *A Textual Guide*, 505).

γεγόνασιν·

ὅθεν γινώσκομεν ὅτι <u>ἐσχάτη ὥρα ἐστίν</u>.

19 <u>ἐξ ἡμῶν</u> ἐξῆλθαν,

ἀλλ’ οὐκ ἦσαν <u>ἐξ ἡμῶν</u>·

εἰ γὰρ <u>ἐξ ἡμῶν</u> ἦσαν,

μεμενήκεισαν ἂν <u>μεθ’ ἡμῶν</u>·

ἀλλ’ ἵνα φανερωθῶσιν

ὅτι οὐκ εἰσὶν πάντες <u>ἐξ ἡμῶν</u>.

20 καὶ ὑμεῖς <u>χρῖσμα</u> ἔχετε ἀπὸ τοῦ ἁγίου

καὶ <u>οἴδατε</u> πάντες·

21 οὐκ ἔγραψα ὑμῖν

ὅτι οὐκ <u>οἴδατε τὴν ἀλήθειαν</u>,

ἀλλ’ ὅτι <u>οἴδατε αὐτήν</u>,

καὶ ὅτι πᾶν <u>ψεῦδος</u> ἐκ <u>τῆς ἀληθείας</u> οὐκ

   ἔστιν.

22 τίς ἐστιν ὁ <u>ψεύστης</u>

εἰ μὴ <u>ὁ ἀρνούμενος</u>

ὅτι <u>Ἰησοῦς οὐκ ἔστιν ὁ χριστός</u>;

<u>οὗτός ἐστιν ὁ ἀντίχριστος</u>,

<u>ὁ ἀρνούμενος τὸν πατέρα</u> καὶ <u>τὸν υἱόν</u>.

23 πᾶς <u>ὁ ἀρνούμενος</u> τὸν υἱὸν

οὐδὲ <u>τὸν πατέρα</u> ἔχει·

<u>ὁ ὁμολογῶν τὸν υἱὸν</u>

καὶ <u>τὸν πατέρα</u> ἔχει.

24 ὑμεῖς <u>ὃ ἠκούσατε ἀπ’ ἀρχῆς</u>,

<u>ἐν ὑμῖν μενέτω</u>·

idea (*"last hour"*; cf. "forever" in v. 17d, J), which is connected chiastically with the new topic concerning the "antichrist[s]" (A)

- true disciples, in paired topical contrast (note the 3 ἀλλ’-s) with "antichrists," are identified by two features: (a) they have not left the fellowship (18–19), and (b) they have received an "anointing" by the "Holy One" (P), which is manifested by their "knowing" the "truth" (20–21) (B)

- the paragraph concludes with a metatextual formula "I did not write to you" (οὐκ ἔγραψα ὑμῖν) (cf. 1:4), a repeated reference to "(not) knowing the truth,"; and final graphic contrast "every lie," presumably concerning Christ, as propounded by the "antichrists" (C)

2. How to identify antichrists (2:22–23)

- a rhetorical question, asyndeton, and lexical overlap with *"liar"* (J) initiates a new paragraph (A)

- reference to "the *antichrist*" (v. 22) recalls (J) and expands upon the beginning of the preceding paragraph (*anaphora*) (A)

- chiastic and parallel constructions build up to a climactic antithetical Christological confession in v.23, in sharp contrast to those in the camp of "the antichrist" (P)(C)

3. How to remain in divine fellowship (2:24–25)

- a foregrounded, contrastive (i.e., to the "liars," v.22) "**you**, pl." (ὑμεῖς) and

ἐὰν <u>ἐν ὑμῖν μείνῃ ὃ ἀπ' ἀρχῆς ἠκούσατε</u>,
καὶ ὑμεῖς ἐν <u>τῷ υἱῷ</u>
καὶ ἐν <u>τῷ πατρὶ</u> <u>μενεῖτε</u>.
25 καὶ αὕτη ἐστὶν <u>ἡ ἐπαγγελία</u> ἣν αὐτὸς
   <u>ἐπηγγείλατο</u> ἡμῖν,
τὴν ζωὴν τὴν αἰώνιον.

- a pointed recall of v.7 (structural *anaphora*) initiates another short paragraph (A)
- lexical reiteration again forms the cohesive backbone of this unit (B)
- reference to "the promise" in v.25, foregrounded by "this is" (αὕτη ἐστὶν), recalls the close of a prior paragraph (2:17) (structural *epiphora*) (C)

4. Manifest your Christian anointing by remaining in Christ (2:26–27)

26 Ταῦτα ἔγραψα ὑμῖν
περὶ τῶν πλανώντων ὑμᾶς.
27 καὶ ὑμεῖς <u>τὸ χρῖσμα</u>
<u>ὃ ἐλάβετε ἀπ' αὐτοῦ</u>
<u>μένει ἐν ὑμῖν</u>,
καὶ οὐ χρείαν ἔχετε
ἵνα τις <u>διδάσκῃ ὑμᾶς</u>·[28]
ἀλλ' ὡς <u>τὸ αὐτοῦ χρῖσμα</u>
<u>διδάσκει ὑμᾶς</u> περὶ πάντων,
καὶ <u>ἀληθές ἐστιν</u>
καὶ <u>οὐκ ἔστιν ψεῦδος</u>,
καὶ καθὼς <u>ἐδίδαξεν ὑμᾶς</u>,
<u>μένετε ἐν αὐτῷ</u>.

- mention of "writing these things to *you*" occurs at the onset of prior paragraphs, e.g., 2:1, 7, 12; also the synonymous ("those leading you astray") τῶν πλανώντων and ("the deceiver") ὁ ψεύστης (2:22) (structural *anaphora*) (A)
- lexical juncture (hook-word)—*"remain"* (J)
- connection with the preceding paragraph is made through reference to "remaining" (2:24), while a connection with the opening paragraph of this section in forged by the reference to "anointing" (v. 22) (J)
- lexical parallels and contrasts continue within the paragraph (B)
- there is a conceptual build-up to the final conclusive imperative [*not indicative!—cf. v. 28*] ("remain in him" μένετε ἐν αὐτῷ); note also the repetition of "lie" (ψεῦδος, v.21, structural *epiphora*) (C)

---

[28] "The translation of the second half of this verse is difficult since it is not clear how the text should be segmented, whether it should be taken as a single sentence or as two..." (Omanson, *A Textual Guide*, 506; cf. Smalley, *1, 2, and 3 John*, 125–126).

C. *Live as Children of God by Avoiding Sin* (2:28–3:10)

28 Καὶ νῦν, *τεκνία*,

μένετε ἐν αὐτῷ,

<u>ἵνα ἐὰν φανερωθῇ</u> (a)

<u>σχῶμεν παρρησίαν</u> (b)

καὶ <u>μὴ αἰσχυνθῶμεν</u> (b') ἀπ' αὐτοῦ

<u>ἐν τῇ παρουσίᾳ αὐτοῦ</u> (a').

29 ἐὰν <u>εἰδῆτε ὅτι</u> <u>δίκαιός</u> ἐστιν,

<u>γινώσκετε ὅτι</u> πᾶς ὁ ποιῶν τὴν

   <u>δικαιοσύνην</u>

ἐξ αὐτοῦ γεγέννηται.

3:1 Ἴδετε ποταπὴν ἀγάπην δέδωκεν ἡμῖν

   ὁ πατὴρ

ἵνα *τέκνα θεοῦ κληθῶμεν*,

καὶ *ἐσμέν*.

διὰ τοῦτο ὁ κόσμος <u>οὐ γινώσκει ἡμᾶς</u>

ὅτι <u>οὐκ ἔγνω αὐτόν</u>.

2 ἀγαπητοί, νῦν *τέκνα θεοῦ* <u>ἐσμεν</u>,

καὶ οὔπω <u>ἐφανερώθη</u> τί <u>ἐσόμεθα</u>.

οἴδαμεν ὅτι ἐὰν <u>φανερωθῇ</u>

ὅμοιοι <u>αὐτῷ</u> <u>ἐσόμεθα</u>,

ὅτι ὀψόμεθα <u>αὐτὸν</u> καθὼς <u>ἐστιν</u>.

3 καὶ *πᾶς ὁ ἔχων* τὴν ἐλπίδα ταύτην

<u>ἐπ' αὐτῷ</u> <u>ἀγνίζει</u> ἑαυτὸν

καθὼς <u>ἐκεῖνος</u> <u>ἁγνός</u> <u>ἐστιν</u>.

4 *Πᾶς ὁ ποιῶν* τὴν <u>ἁμαρτίαν</u>

1. God's children act righteously (2:28–3:1)

- a key-word vocative "children" (τεκνία) and lexical overlap with v.27 ("*remain in him*") (J), coupled with a subsequent chiastic arrangement in the last four lines of v.28, announce this new paragraph and section, one that focuses on the notion of "**children of God**" (A)

- the initial term τεκνία is paraphrased in the middle of this paragraph (29c) and then made theologically explicit and highlighted by emphatic lexical ordering and lineal patterning at its conclusion (3:1a–c), which explains "having been born" (ἐξ αὐτοῦ γεγέννηται) in v.29c (B) (P)

- the final negative assertions regarding "the world" reinforce the thematic notion of "knowing" (e.g., 2:29–3:1, B) cf. 2:3) and strongly (probably deliberately) recall John's Gospel (15:21, 16:3; cf. also 2:3) (C)

2. God's children will be like him (3:2–3)

- initial epistolary vocative with "now" (νῦν) (A), asyndeton, and lexical-thematic overlap ("*we are children of God*") (J)

- there is a prominent referential line ("him") pointing back to "the Father" (ὁ πατὴρ) (3:1a) (J) (B)

- this short paragraph concludes with the dramatic, "hope"-filled notion of being "purified" by/like God (C) (P)

3. God's children avoid sinning (3:4–6)

- the notion of "*everyone who* is doing sin" sharply contrasts with "everyone

καὶ τὴν <u>ἀνομίαν</u> ποιεῖ,

καὶ ἡ <u>ἁμαρτία</u> ἐστὶν ἡ <u>ἀνομία</u>.

5 καὶ οἴδατε ὅτι ἐκεῖνος ἐφανερώθη

ἵνα τὰς <u>ἁμαρτίας</u> ἄρῃ,

καὶ <u>ἁμαρτία</u> ἐν αὐτῷ οὐκ ἔστιν.

6 πᾶς ὁ ἐν αὐτῷ μένων

οὐχ <u>ἁμαρτάνει·</u>

πᾶς ὁ <u>ἁμαρτάνων</u>

<u>οὐχ ἑώρακεν αὐτὸν</u>

<u>οὐδὲ</u> ἔγνωκεν αὐτόν.

7 τεκνία, μηδεὶς πλανάτω ὑμᾶς·

ὁ ποιῶν τὴν <u>δικαιοσύνην</u> <u>δίκαιός</u> ἐστιν,

καθὼς ἐκεῖνος <u>δίκαιός</u> ἐστιν·

8 <u>ὁ ποιῶν τὴν ἁμαρτίαν</u> ἐκ τοῦ <u>διαβόλου</u>

ἐστίν, ὅτι ἀπ' ἀρχῆς ὁ <u>διάβολος</u>

ἁμαρτάνει.

εἰς τοῦτο <u>ἐφανερώθη</u> ὁ υἱὸς τοῦ θεοῦ

ἵνα λύσῃ τὰ ἔργα τοῦ <u>διαβόλου</u>.

9 πᾶς <u>ὁ γεγεννημένος ἐκ τοῦ θεοῦ</u>

<u>ἁμαρτίαν οὐ ποιεῖ</u>,

ὅτι σπέρμα αὐτοῦ ἐν αὐτῷ μένει,

καὶ οὐ δύναται <u>ἁμαρτάνειν</u>,

ὅτι <u>ἐκ τοῦ θεοῦ γεγέννηται</u>.

10 ἐν τούτῳ <u>φανερά</u> ἐστιν <u>τὰ τέκνα τοῦ</u>

<u>θεοῦ</u>

καὶ <u>τὰ τέκνα τοῦ διαβόλου·</u>

πᾶς ὁ <u>μὴ</u> ποιῶν δικαιοσύνην

<u>οὐκ ἔστιν ἐκ τοῦ θεοῦ</u>,

καὶ ὁ <u>μὴ</u> ἀγαπῶν τὸν ἀδελφὸν αὐτοῦ.

having this hope" and with the "pure person" of the preceding verse (J); the conceptual break here (reflecting back to 2:29, J) is reinforced by asyndeton (A)

- the semantic string explicitly referencing "sin" dominates this paragraph (B)
- paired negative assertions forcefully conclude the unit in a chiastic arrangement (C); these reflect back contrastively to the preceding paragraph, and similarly anticipate the following unit (3:2) (J)

4. God's children versus the Devil's (3:7–10)

- a familiar vocative (cf. 2:28), coupled with asyndeton and a strong prohibition, begins the paragraph (A)
- the focal expression "*one doing righteous-ness*" (7) patently contrasts with "the sinner" of the preceding verse (v. 6c; cf. 8a) (J) (A)
- a progressive, internal thematic contrast (involving antithetical parallelism, e.g., v. 9) between the children/works of the Devil and those of the "children of God" creates coherence within the paragraph (B)
- the sudden introduction of "the Son of God" to "undo the works of the Devil" (v.8) represents the theological peak of this paragraph (P)
- the thematic distinction between respective "children," with an emphasis now on the negative diabolical group, the non-lovers (cf. 2:9, 4:8), concludes the paragraph and section as a whole (C)

D. *Love One Another as Christ Commanded* (3:11–3:24)

11 Ὅτι αὕτη ἐστὶν ἡ ἀγγελία
ἣν ἠκούσατε ἀπ' ἀρχῆς,
ἵνα ἀγαπῶμεν ἀλλήλους ·
12 οὐ καθὼς Κάϊν ἐκ τοῦ <u>πονηροῦ</u> ἦν
καὶ <u>ἔσφαξεν</u> τὸν <u>ἀδελφὸν αὐτοῦ</u>·
καὶ χάριν τίνος <u>ἔσφαξεν</u> αὐτόν;
ὅτι τὰ ἔργα αὐτοῦ <u>πονηρὰ</u> ἦν,
τὰ δὲ τοῦ <u>ἀδελφοῦ αὐτοῦ</u> δίκαια.

1. Do not act like Cain! (3:11–12)

- the beginning of this, again contrastive *"love"*-centered section (cf. v.3:10e—J) has expressions that reflect prior units, e.g., 1:5, 2:7, 2:24 (structural *anaphora*); also "this is the message..." occurs at 1:5 (also *anaphora*) (A); the initial "For" (Ὅτι) is viewed as asseverative Hebraic usage, "Indeed...!"
- some commentators (e.g., the NET notes) consider v.11 to mark the onset of the second half of the discourse due to its similarity with 1:5; thus, "walking in the light" (1:5–7) means that "we should love one another" (3:11); however, many prominent thematic topics are common to both halves, such as the command to "walk in love" (cf. 2:7–11)
- after the initial thematic exhortation, concerning the already "heard" fellowship test of "love" (11c), the striking, contrary example of Cain is introduced, perhaps for shock effect (B)
- the contrastive, unit-ending concept "righteous" (δίκαια), with implicit reference to Abel, concludes this brief section-opening paragraph (C)

2. A hater is a murderer (3:13–15)

13 μὴ θαυμάζετε, ἀδελφοί,[29]
εἰ <u>μισεῖ</u> ὑμᾶς ὁ κόσμος.
14 ἡμεῖς οἴδαμεν ὅτι μεταβεβήκαμεν

- a forceful imperative plus asyndeton and vocative is John's standard unit opener, now followed by a new warning—*"brothers,"* (you must)

---

[29] "Some good manuscripts do not have the conjunction καὶ (and) at the beginning of this verse. It is difficult to decide whether καὶ was added by copyists in order to provide a closer connection to what has already been written in the preceding verses ot whether it was accidentally omitted" (a 'C' rating; Omanson, *A Textual Guide*, 507). The same problem occurs at 3:19 and 5:1.

ἐκ τοῦ <u>θανάτου</u> εἰς τὴν ζωήν,

ὅτι <u>ἀγαπῶμεν</u> τοὺς <u>ἀδελφούς</u>·

ὁ μὴ <u>ἀγαπῶν</u> <u>μένει</u> ἐν τῷ <u>θανάτῳ</u>.

15 πᾶς ὁ <u>μισῶν</u> τὸν <u>ἀδελφὸν</u> αὐτοῦ

    <u>ἀνθρωποκτόνος</u> ἐστίν,

καὶ οἴδατε ὅτι πᾶς <u>ἀνθρωποκτόνος</u>

οὐκ ἔχει *ζωὴν* αἰώνιον ἐν αὐτῷ <u>μένουσαν</u>.

- expect the world's hatred! (A)
- more typical, paragraph-internal lexical reiteration and overlapping (B)
- the shocking possibility of "remaining" forever excluded from "eternal life" as a "murderer" closes the segment, with implicit reference to Cain at the beginning of the section in v. 12 (*inclusio*) as well as the conclusion of the preceding section in 3:10 (structural *epiphora*) (C)

3. Christ's example should be our guide (3:16–17)

16 ἐν τούτῳ ἐγνώκαμεν τὴν <u>ἀγάπην</u>,

ὅτι <u>ἐκεῖνος</u> <u>ὑπὲρ ἡμῶν</u> <u>τὴν *ψυχὴν*</u> αὐτοῦ

    <u>ἔθηκεν</u>· καὶ <u>ἡμεῖς</u> ὀφείλομεν <u>ὑπὲρ τῶν</u>

    <u>ἀδελφῶν</u> <u>τὰς *ψυχὰς* θεῖναι</u>.

17 ὃς δ' ἂν ἔχῃ τὸν βίον τοῦ κόσμου

καὶ θεωρῇ τὸν <u>ἀδελφὸν αὐτοῦ</u> χρείαν

    ἔχοντα καὶ κλείσῃ τὰ σπλάγχνα αὐτοῦ

    ἀπ' αὐτοῦ,

πῶς ἡ <u>ἀγάπη</u> τοῦ θεοῦ μένει ἐν αὐτῷ;

- the asyndetic, formulaic "in this we have known" followed by a key Johannine concept ("*life*") is similar to the onset of an earlier paragraph (2:3) (*anaphora*) (A)
- we "have life" (v. 15d) because "that one gave his life for us" (v. 16) (J)
- the close thematic comparative parallelism of v.16 expresses the seminal principle of brotherly substitution (P)
- the prosaic exhortation of v. 17 leads up to a penetrating, *negative* anticipating rhetorical question (C)

4. Loving unburdens one's conscience (3:18–20)

18 Τεκνία, μὴ *ἀγαπῶμεν* λόγῳ

μηδὲ τῇ γλώσσῃ

ἀλλὰ ἐν ἔργῳ καὶ <u>ἀληθείᾳ</u>.

19 ἐν τούτῳ <u>γνωσόμεθα</u> ὅτι ἐκ τῆς

    <u>ἀληθείας</u> ἐσμέν,

καὶ ἔμπροσθεν αὐτοῦ πείσομεν <u>τὴν</u>

    <u>καρδίαν ἡμῶν</u>

- an asyndetic vocative followed by the core concept "*love*," now *negativized* in the cohortative form begins the paragraph (A)
- the hook word "love" links up with v. 17d (J)
- prominent internal lexical cohesion (B)

20 ὅτι ἐὰν καταγινώσκῃ ἡμῶν ἡ καρδία,
ὅτι μείζων ἐστὶν ὁ θεὸς τῆς καρδίας ἡμῶν
καὶ γινώσκει πάντα.

- the explicit mention of "God" at the end in v. 20 parallels its occurence at the close of the preceding paragraph (v. 17, structural *epiphora*) (C)

5. Living in the love command (3:21–24)

21 ἀγαπητοί, ἐὰν ἡ καρδία μὴ
    καταγινώσκῃ ἡμῶν,[30]
παρρησίαν ἔχομεν πρὸς τὸν θεόν,
22 καὶ ὃ ἐὰν αἰτῶμεν λαμβάνομεν ἀπ'
    αὐτοῦ, ὅτι τὰς ἐντολὰς αὐτοῦ τηροῦμεν
καὶ τὰ ἀρεστὰ ἐνώπιον αὐτοῦ ποιοῦμεν.
23 καὶ αὕτη ἐστὶν ἡ ἐντολὴ αὐτοῦ,
ἵνα πιστεύσωμεν τῷ ὀνόματι τοῦ υἱοῦ
    αὐτοῦ Ἰησοῦ Χριστοῦ
καὶ ἀγαπῶμεν ἀλλήλους,
καθὼς ἔδωκεν ἐντολὴν ἡμῖν.
24 καὶ ὁ τηρῶν τὰς ἐντολὰς αὐτοῦ
ἐν αὐτῷ μένει καὶ αὐτὸς ἐν αὐτῷ·
καὶ ἐν τούτῳ γινώσκομεν ὅτι μένει ἐν
    ἡμῖν,
ἐκ τοῦ πνεύματος οὗ ἡμῖν ἔδωκεν.

- another vocative (cf. v.18) and a double key term overlap ("*heart*" and "*God*") in chiastic order (J) initiates a new paragraph (A)
- the renewed notion of "confidence" before God reflects 2:28 (structural *anaphora*) (A)
- the Christological exhortation of v.23, which is introduced by "this is" (cf. 1:5, 3:11) and bounded by "command" (ἐντολὴ), is thereby emphasized, thus highlighting the three central tests of Christian discipleship: *faith—love—obedience* (P)
- a prominent demonstrative sequence with reference to "him/his" (B)
- unexpected mention of the "(Holy) Spirit" concludes this longer paragraph and the section as a whole with a notable Trinitarian allusion (J) (C)

E. *Test the Spirits by Their Confession* (4:1–6)

4:1 Ἀγαπητοί, μὴ παντὶ πνεύματι
    πιστεύετε, ἀλλὰ δοκιμάζετε τὰ
    πνεύματα
εἰ ἐκ τοῦ θεοῦ ἐστιν,
ὅτι πολλοὶ ψευδοπροφῆται ἐξεληλύθασιν

1. How to discern a false spirit (4:1–3)

- a standard vocative + asyndeton + lexical overlap ("*spirit-*," J) + chiasmus + imperative (prohibition) initiates a new section, one that emphasizes true versus false **speaking**

---

[30] "It is hard to determine whether the pronoun ἡμῶν is original and was later deleted by copyists who considered it unnecessary [since it is found in many manuscripts as the object of the verb καταγινώσκῃ], or whether it was not original but was later added to agree with the usage of the preceding verses" (a 'C' rating; Omanson, *A Textual Guide*, 509).

εἰς τὸν κόσμον.

2 ἐν τούτῳ γινώσκετε τὸ πνεῦμα τοῦ
   θεοῦ·

πᾶν πνεῦμα ὃ ὁμολογεῖ Ἰησοῦν Χριστὸν
ἐν σαρκὶ
ἐληλυθότα ἐκ τοῦ θεοῦ ἐστιν,

3 καὶ πᾶν πνεῦμα ὃ μὴ ὁμολογεῖ τὸν
   Ἰησοῦν
ἐκ τοῦ θεοῦ οὐκ ἔστιν·
καὶ τοῦτό ἐστιν τὸ τοῦ ἀντιχρίστου,
ὃ ἀκηκόατε ὅτι ἔρχεται,
καὶ νῦν *ἐν τῷ κόσμῳ ἐστὶν* ἤδη.

and **hearing**, while the warning against false teachers, only briefly mentioned in the preceding section (3:7) is now elaborated upon (A)

- new information about "false prophets" (v. 4:1d) is in the end linked up with old news concerning "the antichrist" (v. 3c, cf. 2:22) (B)
- the center of this paragraph features a crucial contrast in theological ("spiritual") perspectives (2–3) (B)
- the central Christological point is marked by the formulaic introduction "in this you know" (v. 2a, cf. 2:29, 3:24) (P)
- the close of this unit is distinguished by the emphatic reiteration of a disturbing warning of *immediate* temporal relevance "now...already" (νῦν...ἤδη) (v. 3e; cf. 2:18) (C)

2. The S/spirit of truth enables God's children to overcome every false spirit (4:4–6)

4 ὑμεῖς *ἐκ τοῦ θεοῦ ἐστε*, τεκνία,
καὶ νενικήκατε αὐτούς,
ὅτι μείζων ἐστὶν ὁ ἐν ὑμῖν
ἢ ὁ ἐν τῷ κόσμῳ·

5 αὐτοὶ ἐκ τοῦ κόσμου εἰσίν·
διὰ τοῦτο ἐκ τοῦ κόσμου λαλοῦσιν
καὶ ὁ κόσμος αὐτῶν ἀκούει.

6 ἡμεῖς ἐκ τοῦ θεοῦ ἐσμεν·
ὁ γινώσκων τὸν θεὸν ἀκούει ἡμῶν,
ὃς οὐκ ἔστιν *ἐκ τοῦ θεοῦ* οὐκ ἀκούει ἡμῶν.
ἐκ τούτου γινώσκομεν τὸ πνεῦμα τῆς
   ἀληθείας καὶ τὸ πνεῦμα τῆς πλάνης.

- a back-shifted vocative and a contrastive paralleled topical overlap (*"out of..."* J) announce this new paragraph beginning, with its new, encouraging, confidence-building theme: "you (*emphasized*) have defeated them!" (A)
- reference to the contrasting "spirits" of the preceding paragraph, introduced by the formulaic "from this we know" (ἐκ τούτου γινώσκομεν), rounds out the present unit, which is also distinguished by longer utterance length (C)
- there is extensive internal lexical overlapping, including three occurrences

of the contrasting phrases "in/from the world" and "from God" (B)

F. *We Love Because God Loves* (4:7–21)

7 Ἀγαπητοί, ἀγαπῶμεν ἀλλήλους,
ὅτι ἡ ἀγάπη ἐκ τοῦ θεοῦ ἐστιν,
καὶ πᾶς ὁ ἀγαπῶν ἐκ τοῦ θεοῦ
  γεγέννηται
καὶ γινώσκει τὸν θεόν.
8 ὁ μὴ ἀγαπῶν οὐκ ἔγνω τὸν θεόν,
ὅτι ὁ θεὸς ἀγάπη ἐστίν.
9 ἐν τούτῳ ἐφανερώθη ἡ ἀγάπη τοῦ θεοῦ
  ἐν ἡμῖν,
ὅτι τὸν υἱὸν αὐτοῦ τὸν μονογενῆ
ἀπέσταλκεν ὁ θεὸς εἰς τὸν κόσμον
ἵνα ζήσωμεν δι' αὐτοῦ.
10 ἐν τούτῳ ἐστὶν ἡ ἀγάπη,
οὐχ ὅτι ἡμεῖς ἠγαπήκαμεν τὸν θεόν,[31]
ἀλλ' ὅτι αὐτὸς ἠγάπησεν ἡμᾶς
καὶ ἀπέστειλεν τὸν υἱὸν αὐτοῦ ἱλασμὸν
περὶ τῶν ἁμαρτιῶν ἡμῶν.

1. God's love culminated in sending his Son (4:7–10)

- a vocative, a cohortative thematic verb ("let us love [one another]") and lexical overlap ("*he is* [*not*] *of God*" – cf. v. 4, *anaphora*) (J) mark the onset of this new paragraph and section, one that again centers upon the godly "love" of Christlike fellowship (A)
- one overlapping lexical-conceptual chain (v. 7) builds up to another (v. 8), both of which are combined in the end (v. 9) (B)
- God's love being preeminently displayed in the sending of his Son to the world is a recurrence of the Christological confession of 1 John— the paralleled repetition (vv. 9–10) producing one of the most prominent thematic-theological assertions of this epistle, cf. 2:1–2 (P)
- the extensive reiteration and conceptual significance of vv. 9–10 also distinguish the conclusion of this paragraph (C)

2. Loving one another follows God's example (4:11–12)

11 ἀγαπητοί, εἰ οὕτως ὁ θεὸς ἠγάπησεν
  ἡμᾶς, (a) καὶ ἡμεῖς ὀφείλομεν
  ἀλλήλους ἀγαπᾶν (b)
12 θεὸν οὐδεὶς πώποτε τεθέαται· (c)

- conceptual overlap ("*God loves us*," J) coupled with a typical asyndetic vocative, initiates this short paragraph; the topic of 3:16 and 4:7 is

---

[31] "The manuscript evidence is equally divided between the perfect tense ἠγαπήκαμεν (we have loved) and the past tense (aorist)...(we loved). It seems more likely that copyists would have changed the perfect tense to the aorist in order to agree with the following verbs in the aorist..." (a 'B' text rating; Omanson, *A Textual Guide*, 510).

ἐὰν <u>ἀγαπῶμεν</u> ἀλλήλους, (b')

ὁ <u>θεὸς</u> <u>ἐν ἡμῖν</u> *μένει* (a')

καὶ ἡ <u>ἀγάπη</u> αὐτοῦ <u>ἐν ἡμῖν</u> τετελειωμένη

    ἐστιν.

13 Ἐν τούτῳ γινώσκομεν

ὅτι ἐν αὐτῷ *μένομεν* καὶ αὐτὸς ἐν <u>ἡμῖν</u>,

ὅτι ἐκ τοῦ πνεύματος αὐτοῦ δέδωκεν

    <u>ἡμῖν</u>.

14 καὶ <u>ἡμεῖς</u> τεθεάμεθα καὶ μαρτυροῦμεν

ὅτι ὁ πατὴρ ἀπέσταλκεν τὸν <u>υἱὸν</u> σωτῆρα

    τοῦ κόσμου.

15 ὃς ἐὰν ὁμολογήσῃ

ὅτι Ἰησοῦς ἐστιν ὁ <u>υἱὸς</u> τοῦ <u>θεοῦ</u>,

ὁ <u>θεὸς</u> ἐν <u>αὐτῷ</u> <u>μένει</u>

καὶ <u>αὐτὸς</u> ἐν τῷ <u>θεῷ</u>.

16 καὶ <u>ἡμεῖς</u> ἐγνώκαμεν

καὶ πεπιστεύκαμεν *τὴν ἀγάπην*

ἣν ἔχει ὁ <u>θεὸς</u> ἐν <u>ἡμῖν</u>.

Ὁ <u>θεὸς</u> *ἀγάπη* ἐστίν,

καὶ ὁ <u>μένων</u> ἐν τῇ <u>ἀγάπῃ</u>

ἐν τῷ <u>θεῷ</u> <u>μένει</u>

reproduced here (*anaphora*) (A)

- the paragraph topic of "love" contin-ues emphatically from beginning to end in a chiastic arrangement (B)
- the thought of "love being made com-plete" recalls 2:5 and anticipates 4:17 (C)

3. Loving God means confessing his Son (4:13–16b)

- lexical overlap in the verb *"remain"* (cf. v. 12c) (J), this thematic concept being foregrounded by the preced-ing formulaic "In this we know that..." (Ἐν τούτῳ γινώσκομεν ὅτι) (cf. 2:3; 3:24) (A)
- the central (literally) focus of this paragraph is on loving God by mak-ing a strong Christological confession with crucial implications for "us" (every Christian) (B); it culminates in the rhythmically expressed v. 15 (P)
- the unit concludes with the corollary to the preceding—juxtaposing God's love for "us" (believer-confessors) (C)
- the two initial verbs of v. 16, "we have come to know and to believe" could represent a hendiadys describ-ing a single composite action (cf. NET note), but each is set off in the text display as part of a separate ut-terance, under the assumption that this is how they would have been emphatically articulated orally here at the close of this paragraph

4. God's love casts out all fear (4:16c–18)

- considerable lexical-conceptual overlap, again involving the fore-grounded notions of *"God"* and *"love"* (J), constitute another major

καὶ ὁ θεὸς ἐν αὐτῷ μένει.

17 ἐν τούτῳ τετελείωται ἡ ἀγάπη μεθ'
    ἡμῶν, ἵνα παρρησίαν ἔχωμεν ἐν τῇ
    ἡμέρᾳ τῆς κρίσεως,
ὅτι καθὼς ἐκεῖνός ἐστιν
καὶ ἡμεῖς ἐσμεν ἐν τῷ κόσμῳ τούτῳ.
18 φόβος οὐκ ἔστιν ἐν τῇ ἀγάπη,
ἀλλ' ἡ τελεία ἀγάπη ἔξω βάλλει τὸν
    φόβον, ὅτι ὁ φόβος κόλασιν ἔχει,
ὁ δὲ φοβούμενος οὐ τετελείωται ἐν τῇ
    ἀγάπη.

- theological assertion, once again lexically and poetically expressed
- v.16c–f is a corollary to v.15: a confession of faith in Christ and manifested in love results in fellowship with God (A) (P)
- the multifaceted topic of "love" is featured again throughout this paragraph (B)
- the paradox of "love" conquering all "fear" highlights the close of this unit (C)

19 ἡμεῖς ἀγαπῶμεν,
ὅτι αὐτὸς πρῶτος ἠγάπησεν ἡμᾶς.
20 ἐάν τις εἴπῃ
ὅτι Ἀγαπῶ τὸν θεόν,
καὶ τὸν ἀδελφὸν αὐτοῦ μισῇ,
ψεύστης ἐστίν·
ὁ γὰρ μὴ ἀγαπῶν τὸν ἀδελφὸν αὐτοῦ (a)
ὃν ἑώρακεν, (b)
τὸν θεὸν ὃν οὐχ ἑώρακεν (b')
οὐ δύναται ἀγαπᾶν. (a')
21 καὶ ταύτην τὴν ἐντολὴν
ἔχομεν ἀπ' αὐτοῦ,
ἵνα ὁ ἀγαπῶν τὸν θεὸν
ἀγαπᾷ καὶ τὸν ἀδελφὸν αὐτοῦ.

5. Loving God means loving one's brother (4:19–21)

- lexical overlap in the key term "*love*" (J), which is expressed in various ways, including the use of antithetical chiasmus (v.20), continues throughout this closing paragraph of section F (B)
- the focus of discussion (+ asyndeton) returns to the reason why "we love" (cf. paragraphs F, 1–2) (A)
- the paragraph and section concludes with a reference to the fundamental "love command," foregrounded by "and this" (cf. 2:7–8) (C)

G. Believe in God's Son and Accept God's Testimony (5:1–12)

5:1 Πᾶς ὁ πιστεύων
ὅτι Ἰησοῦς ἐστιν ὁ χριστὸς
ἐκ τοῦ θεοῦ γεγέννηται,
καὶ πᾶς ὁ ἀγαπῶν τὸν γεννήσαντα
ἀγαπᾷ καὶ τὸν γεγεννημένον ἐξ αὐτοῦ.
2 ἐν τούτῳ γινώσκομεν

1. Someone "born of God" loves— trusts—and obeys, thus demonstrating discipleship (5:1–5)

- the sub-theme of being "born of God" is resumed (cf. 2:29, 3:9, 4:7) (A)
- although the subjects discussed are somewhat different, the main theme dealing with "*God*" and

ὅτι <u>ἀγαπῶμεν</u> τὰ <u>τέκνα τοῦ θεοῦ</u>,
ὅταν τὸν θεὸν <u>ἀγαπῶμεν</u>
καὶ τὰς <u>ἐντολὰς αὐτοῦ</u> ποιῶμεν·[32]
3 αὕτη γάρ ἐστιν ἡ <u>ἀγάπη</u> τοῦ θεοῦ
ἵνα τὰς <u>ἐντολὰς αὐτοῦ</u> τηρῶμεν,
καὶ αἱ <u>ἐντολαὶ αὐτοῦ</u> βαρεῖαι οὐκ εἰσίν,
4 ὅτι πᾶν τὸ <u>γεγεννημένον ἐκ τοῦ θεοῦ</u>
<u>νικᾷ τὸν κόσμον</u>.
καὶ αὕτη ἐστὶν ἡ <u>νίκη</u>
ἡ <u>νικήσασα τὸν κόσμον</u>,
ἡ <u>πίστις</u> ἡμῶν·
5 <u>τίς δέ ἐστιν ὁ νικῶν τὸν κόσμον</u>
<u>εἰ μὴ ὁ πιστεύων</u>
ὅτι Ἰησοῦς ἐστιν ὁ υἱὸς τοῦ θεοῦ;

6 Οὗτός ἐστιν ὁ ἐλθὼν δι' <u>ὕδατος</u> καὶ
   <u>αἵματος</u>, Ἰησοῦς Χριστός·
οὐκ ἐν τῷ <u>ὕδατι</u> μόνον
ἀλλ' ἐν τῷ <u>ὕδατι</u> καὶ ἐν τῷ <u>αἵματι</u>·
καὶ τὸ <u>πνεῦμά</u> ἐστιν τὸ μαρτυροῦν,
ὅτι τὸ <u>πνεῦμά</u> ἐστιν ἡ ἀλήθεια.
7 ὅτι <u>τρεῖς</u> εἰσιν (a) οἱ *μαρτυροῦντες*
   (b),[33]

"love" is continued from the preceding paragraph (J)

- internal lexical overlapping (believe, born, love, obey command, conquers) knits the paragraph into a coherent unit; the central trio of tests for true discipleship co-occur: *love, faith,* and *obedience* (B)
- the unit culminates thematically (P) in a rhetorical question (C)
- the ending of this paragraph is also distinguished by a Christological *inclusio* (v. 5c; cf. v. 1b) (C)

2. Three testimonies to Christ's humanity and divinity (5:6–8)

- reference to "Jesus **Christ**" creates a topical connection with the preceding paragraph (J)
- lexical cohesion is created through "water," "blood," and "spirit"—a threefold figurative witness to the Incarnation (B)
- the paradox that these three "are [intended] for the one/single [testimony]"

---

[32] "The external evidence is rather evenly divided between the verbs ποιῶμεν (we do) and τηρῶμεν (we keep). This is the only time in the Johannine writings that the words "do his commandments" occur, but the words "keep his commandments occur nine times. It seems likely, therefore that ποιῶμεν is original and was changed to τηρῶμεν in order to agree with common usage in the Johannine writings (see v. 3 and also 2.3, 4, 5; 3.22, 24)" (a 'B' text rating; Omanson, *A Textual Guide*, 512).

[33] NET text note: "Before τὸ πνεῦμα καὶ τὸ ὕδωρ καὶ τὸ αἷμα (*to pneuma kai to hudōr kai to haima*), the TR reads ἐν τῷ οὐρανῷ, ὁ πατήρ, ὁ λόγος, καὶ τὸ ἅγιον πνεῦμα, καὶ οὗτοι οἱ τρεῖς ἕν εἰσι. 1 John 5:8 καὶ τρεῖς εἰσιν οἱ μαρτυροῦντες ἐν τῇ γῇ ("in heaven, the Father, the Word, and the Holy Spirit, and these three are one. 1 John 5:8 And there are three that testify on earth"). This reading, the infamous *Comma Johanneum,* has been known in the English-speaking world through the KJV. However, the evidence—both external and internal—is decidedly against its authenticity. ... The oldest ms with the *Comma* in its text is from the 14th century (629), but the wording here departs from all the other mss in several places. The next oldest mss on behalf of the *Comma,* 88 (12th century) 429 (14th) 636 (15th), also have the reading only as a marginal

8 τὸ <u>πνεῦμα</u> καὶ τὸ <u>ὕδωρ</u> καὶ τὸ <u>αἷμα</u> (b'),
καὶ οἱ <u>τρεῖς</u> εἰς τὸ ἕν εἰσιν (a').

makes a chiastic confessional statement that concludes this short paragraph (C)

3. God's testimony in his Son gives life (5:9–12)

9 εἰ τὴν <u>*μαρτυρίαν*</u> τῶν ἀνθρώπων
λαμβάνομεν, <u>ἡ μαρτυρία τοῦ θεοῦ</u>
μείζων ἐστίν,
ὅτι αὕτη ἐστὶν <u>ἡ μαρτυρία τοῦ θεοῦ</u>
ὅτι <u>μεμαρτύρηκεν</u> περὶ <u>τοῦ υἱοῦ αὐτοῦ</u>.
10 <u>ὁ πιστεύων</u> εἰς <u>τὸν υἱὸν τοῦ θεοῦ</u>
ἔχει τὴν <u>μαρτυρίαν</u> ἐν αὐτῷ.[34]
<u>ὁ μὴ πιστεύων</u> τῷ θεῷ
ψεύστην πεποίηκεν αὐτόν,
ὅτι οὐ <u>πεπίστευκεν</u> εἰς τὴν <u>μαρτυρίαν</u>
ἣν <u>μεμαρτύρηκεν</u> ὁ θεὸς περὶ <u>τοῦ υἱοῦ</u>
<u>αὐτοῦ</u>.
11 καὶ αὕτη ἐστὶν ἡ <u>μαρτυρία</u>,
ὅτι <u>ζωὴν</u> αἰώνιον ἔδωκεν ὁ θεὸς ἡμῖν,
καὶ αὕτη <u>ἡ ζωὴ</u> ἐν <u>τῷ υἱῷ αὐτοῦ</u> ἐστιν.
12 <u>ὁ ἔχων</u> <u>τὸν υἱὸν</u>
<u>ἔχει τὴν ζωήν</u>·
<u>ὁ μὴ ἔχων</u> <u>τὸν υἱὸν</u> <u>τοῦ θεοῦ</u>
<u>τὴν ζωὴν</u> οὐκ <u>ἔχει</u>.

- the notion of "***testimony***" is expanded upon, now presenting "our" response to and blessing derived from the preceding Christological facts (J), which we have guaranteed "from God" (A)
- there is much lexical overlapping throughout the paragraph (testimony, God, Son, believe, life) (B)
- the topical peak in the argument may be the shocking negative assertion in the middle: "a liar (focus) he has made him (God)!" (v. 10d) (P)
- this relatively long paragraph concludes with the paralleled identification of "the Son [of God]" with "life" (v. 12; cf. v. 10a) (C)

H. *Concluding Commands* (5:13–21)

13 Ταῦτα ἔγραψα ὑμῖν
ἵνα εἰδῆτε ὅτι <u>ζωὴν ἔχετε</u> αἰώνιον,
τοῖς πιστεύουσιν εἰς τὸ ὄνομα τοῦ υἱοῦ
    τοῦ θεοῦ.

1. Pray in confidence! (5:13–15)

- the crucial concept of "***having*** [eternal] *life*" forms the juncture between these two final epistolary sections, G and H (J)

---

note (v.l.). The remaining mss are from the 16th to 18th centuries. Thus, there is no sure evidence of this reading in any Greek ms until the 14th century (629), and that ms deviates from all others in its wording; the wording that matches what is found in the TR was apparently composed after Erasmus' Greek NT was published in 1516..."

[34] "Good manuscripts support the reading with the reflexive pronoun *en heautw* (in himself [*that is*, in the one who believes in the Son of God]). Most minuscule read ἐν αὐτῷ (in him [*that is*, in the Son of God])." The manuscript evidence favors the former reading, and "the translation should make it clear that the pronoun refers to the Christian believer and not to Jesus" (a 'B' text rating; Omanson, *A Textual Guide*, 513).

14 καὶ αὕτη ἐστὶν ἡ παρρησία
ἣν ἔχομεν πρὸς αὐτόν,
ὅτι ἐάν τι αἰτώμεθα κατὰ τὸ θέλημα
αὐτοῦ ἀκούει ἡμῶν.
15 καὶ ἐὰν οἴδαμεν ὅτι ἀκούει ἡμῶν
ὃ ἐὰν *αἰτώμεθα*,
οἴδαμεν ὅτι ἔχομεν τὰ *αἰτήματα*
ἃ *ᾐτήκαμεν* ἀπ' αὐτοῦ.

16 ἐάν τις ἴδῃ τὸν ἀδελφὸν αὐτοῦ
ἁμαρτάνοντα ἁμαρτίαν μὴ πρὸς
θάνατον,
αἰτήσει, καὶ δώσει αὐτῷ ζωήν,
τοῖς ἁμαρτάνουσιν μὴ πρὸς θάνατον.
ἔστιν ἁμαρτία πρὸς θάνατον·
οὐ περὶ ἐκείνης λέγω ἵνα ἐρωτήσῃ.
17 πᾶσα ἀδικία ἁμαρτία ἐστίν,
καὶ ἔστιν ἁμαρτία οὐ πρὸς θάνατον.

18 Οἴδαμεν ὅτι πᾶς ὁ γεγεννημένος ἐκ
τοῦ θεοῦ οὐχ ἁμαρτάνει,
ἀλλ' ὁ γεννηθεὶς ἐκ τοῦ θεοῦ τηρεῖ
αὐτόν,[35]

- the formulaic phrase "These things I wrote to you" occurs also at the start of an earlier paragraph (2:26); moreover, the concept of "confidence" (παρρησία), now with reference to the assertion of v. 13, is found near or at the beginning of these units—2:28, 3:21, 4:17 (structural *anaphora*) (A)
- lexical repetition underscores the great assurance that believers have in divinely answered prayer (cf. 3:21) (P) (C)

2. Admonish sinners! (5:16–17)

- the disciple's essential activity of "*asking*" (prayer) carries over from the preceding paragraph (J)
- now the "asking" concerns intercession with regard to "sinning" and possible "death" (B)
- the short paragraph concludes with a minor chiasmus (ἁμαρτία ἐστίν // ἔστιν ἁμαρτία) and the words of implicit warning: "unto death" (πρὸς θάνατον)! (C)

3. Remember the teachings of this epistle! (5:18–20)

- the general (thematic) topic of "*sinning*" is continued (J)
- the central truth that God's children (those "begotten by God") do not sin

---

[35] NET text note: Here a textual variant for ὁ γεννηθείς (ἡ γέννησις, hē gennēsis) has suggested to some that the passive participle should be understood as a noun ("fathering" or perhaps "birth"), but the ms evidence is extremely slight (1505 1852 2138 latt [syh] bo). This almost certainly represents a scribal attempt to clarify an obscure phrase. (2) "The One fathered by God [Jesus] protects him [the Christian]." This is a popular interpretation and is certainly possible grammatically. Yet the introduction of a reference to Jesus in this context is sudden; to be unambiguous the author could have mentioned the "Son of God" here, or used the pronoun ἐκεῖνος (ekeinos) as a reference to Jesus as he consistently does elsewhere in 1 John. This interpretation, while possible, seems in context highly unlikely. (3) "The one fathered by God

καὶ ὁ πονηρὸς οὐχ ἅπτεται αὐτοῦ.

19 οἴδαμεν ὅτι ἐκ τοῦ θεοῦ ἐσμεν,

καὶ ὁ κόσμος ὅλος ἐν τῷ πονηρῷ κεῖται.

20 οἴδαμεν δὲ ὅτι ὁ υἱὸς τοῦ θεοῦ ἥκει,

καὶ δέδωκεν ἡμῖν διάνοιαν

ἵνα γινώσκωμεν τὸν ἀληθινόν·

καὶ ἐσμὲν ἐν τῷ ἀληθινῷ,

ἐν τῷ υἱῷ αὐτοῦ Ἰησοῦ Χριστῷ.

οὗτός ἐστιν ὁ ἀληθινὸς θεὸς καὶ ζωὴ αἰώνιος.

21 Τεκνία, φυλάξατε ἑαυτὰ ἀπὸ τῶν εἰδώλων.[36]

recalls (2:1) and the section that begins there (cf. 3:6) (A)

- lexical cohesion with respect to key terms initiated by three occurrences of "we know" distinguishes this concluding paragraph (B)
- the Body of this epistle concludes with an extensive, emphatic, confidence-building, "truth"-stressing Christological confession (P), which then forms an *inclusio* with the Prologue (macro-structural envelope) (C)

4. Guard against all "idolatry"! (5:21)

- a vocative that introduces a comprehensive, corporately challenging

[the Christian] protects himself." Again a textual problem is behind this alternative, since a number of mss (א Ac P Ψ 33 1739 𝔐) supply the reflexive pronoun ἑαυτόν (heauton) in place of αὐτόν in 1 John 5:18. On the basis of the external evidence this has a good possibility of being the original reading, but internal evidence favors αὐτόν as the more difficult reading, since ἑαυτόν may be explained as a scribal attempt at grammatical smoothness. From a logical standpoint, however, it is difficult to make much more sense out of ἑαυτόν; to say what "the Christian protects himself" means in the context is far from clear. (4) "The one fathered by God [the Christian] holds on to him [God]." This results in further awkwardness, because the third person pronoun (αὐτοῦ, autou) in the following clause must refer to the Christian, not God. Furthermore, although τηρέω (tēreō) can mean "hold on to" (BDAG 1002 s.v. 2.c), this is not a common meaning for the verb in Johannine usage, occurring elsewhere only in Rev 3:3. (5) "The one fathered by God [the Christian], he [God] protects him [the Christian]." This involves a pendant nominative construction (ὁ γεννηθεὶς ἐκ τοῦ θεοῦ) where a description of something within the clause is placed in the nominative case and moved forward ahead of the clause for emphatic reasons. This may be influenced by Semitic style; such a construction is also present in John 17:2 ("in order that everyone whom You have given to him, he may give to them eternal life"). This view is defended by K. Beyer (Semitische Syntax im Neuen Testament [SUNT], 1:216ff.) and appears to be the most probable in terms both of syntax and of sense. It makes God the protector of the Christian (rather than the Christian himself), which fits the context much better, and there is precedent in Johannine literature for such syntactical structure (cf. Omanson, *A Textual Guide*, 514).

[36] The ἀμήν "is the result of liturgical usage in which this text was read aloud in worship services" Omanson, *A Textual Guide*, 515; cf. NET text note: "Most, later mss (P 𝔐) have ἀμήν (amēn, "amen") at the end of this letter. Such a conclusion is routinely added by scribes to NT books because a few of these books originally had such an ending (cf. Ro 16:27; Ga 6:18; Jud 25). A majority of Greek witnesses have the concluding ἀμήν in every NT book except Acts, James, and 3 John (and even in these books, ἀμήν is found in some witnesses). It is

prohibition concerning God's "children" in relation to "idolatry" (εἰδώλων – i.e., all anti-Christian, sinful, discipleship-stifling behavior: the lack of *love, faith, obedience*) forms the letter's dramatic, paraenetic epilogue! (C)

Discourse Outline of 1 John

If we extract all of the section and included paragraph titles from the preceding text analysis, the following discourse outline emerges:

Epistolary **PROLOGUE:**   *Proclaiming the Word of Life* (1:1–4)

Epistolary **BODY** of Paraenesis—Exhorting Believers

The TESTS of True Christology and Genuine Discipleship (1:5–5:20)

A. *Walking in the Light by Loving One Another—Not the World* (1:5–2:17)

1. The need for confessing the darkness of our sins (1:5–10)
2. Christ is the Advocate who deals with our sinfulness (2:1–2)
3. Knowing Jesus means keeping God's commands (2:3–6)
4. Introduction of the new-old command (2:7–8)
5. We overcome the darkness of sin by loving one another (2:9–11)
6. Poetic pastoral encouragement for the faithful (2:12–14)
7. Don't love worldly things! (2:15–17)

B. *Warning Against Antichrists* (2:18–27)

1. Antichrists versus anointed ones (2:18–21)
2. How to identify antichrists (2:22–23)
3. How to remain in divine fellowship (2:24–25)
4. Manifest your Christian anointing by remaining in Christ (2:26–27)

---

thus a predictable variant. Further, the earliest and best witnesses, along with several others (א A B Ψ 33 323 630 1505 1739 al sy co), lack the inoffensive particle, rendering its omission as the authentic reading.

C. *Live as Children of God by Avoiding Sin* (2:28–3:10)	1. God's children act righteously (2:28–3:1)
	2. God's children will be like him (3:2–3)
	3. God's children avoid sinning (3:4–6)
	4. God's children versus the Devil's (3:7–10)
D. *Love One Another as Christ Commanded* (3:11–3:24)	1. Do not act like Cain! (3:11–12)
	2. A hater is a murderer (3:13–15)
	3. Christ's example should be our guide (3:16–17)
	4. Loving unburdens one's conscience (3:18–20)
	5. Living in the love command (3:21–24)
E. *Test the Spirits by Their Confession* (4:1–6)	1. How to discern a false spirit (4:1–3)
	2. The S/spirit of truth enables God's children to overcome every false spirit (4:4–6)
F. *We Love Because God Loves* (4:7–21)	1. God's love culminated in sending his Son (4:7–10)
	2. Loving one another follows God's example (4:11–12)
	3. Loving God means confessing his Son (4:13–16b)
	4. God's love casts out all fear (4:16c–18)
	5. Loving God means loving one's brother (4:19–21)
G. *Believe in God's Son and Accept God's Testimony* (5:1–12)	1. Someone "born of God" loves—trusts—and obeys, thus demonstrating discipleship (5:1–5)
	2. Three testimonies to Christ's humanity and divinity (5:6–8)
	3. God's testimony in his Son gives life (5:9–12)
H. *Concluding Commands* (5:13–21)	1. Pray in confidence! (5:13–15)
	2. Admonish sinners! (5:16–17)
	3. Remember the teachings of this epistle! (5:18–20)
	4. Guard against all "idolatry"! (5:21)

The preceding outline gives us a topical-thematic arrangement for 1 John, but not one that can be easily or "logically" summarized. Furthermore, it is a structural proposal that will undoubtedly not agree in many respects with the discourse frameworks to be found in commentaries, NT introductions, and study Bibles, even on the broader "sectional" level, as already noted at the beginning of this study. Thus, it will not profit us to further describe, evaluate, and critique the differences that present themselves here (or, indeed, for the enclosed "paragraph" units, where even more diversity is apparent). Every Bible translator, teacher, student, or commentator must therefore assess the results for themselves, using the diagnostic criteria and analytical procedures given in support of each structural proposal in close comparison with the method that they happen to be applying to the Greek text.

One possible reason for this widespread lack of organizational agreement will be suggested below, but to begin with, the following observation might be put forward for consideration. My hypothesis is simply that this epistle was not only written down (probably by a scribe) with ultimate *aural proclamation* in view, but it was also conceived and mentally constructed orally, more-or-less on the spot as the Apostle John composed his text aloud. This would account for the rather large amount of reiteration of ideas as well as the text's formation in terms of measured utterance units (i.e., limited by breath/speech-spans), as shown on the detailed discourse display above. Perhaps the entire text could be divided roughly into two parts at 3:11, where John reiterates the fact that "this message is the [same] one which we/you heard from him [Jesus Christ] from the very beginning" of the Gospel proclamation ministry:

A. Καὶ ἔστιν αὕτη ἡ ἀγγελία ἣν ἀκηκόαμεν ἀπ' αὐτοῦ... (1:5)
B. Ὅτι αὕτη ἐστὶν ἡ ἀγγελία ἣν ἠκούσατε ἀπ' ἀρχῆς... (3:11)

In a sense then, the author was simply recycling the chief points of his pastoral homily along with certain significant additions in the second half of the letter—a basic but effective compositional style that follows the Semitic poetic preference for A-B type parallelism of thoughts, involving similarity as well as contrast. That would be a broad bird's-eye view of the epistle as a whole.

More specifically then, I might close with a few comments regarding the more detailed organization of the letter and why there is so much disagreement, on the one hand, among commentators with regard to a structural outline of 1 John—and, in contrast, a number of simple proposals for setting things right. Accordingly, quite a few scholars of yesteryear suggest that the discourse structure of 1 John features a threefold reiteration of the "three tests" of a valid Christian profession: faith (doctrinal), obedience (moral), and love (social). R. C. H. Lenski, for example, posits three cycles that cover these sections of the epistle: 1:5–2:28, 2:29–4:6, and 4:7–5:12.[37] I do not dispute the presence and the

---

[37] Lenski, *The Epistles of St. John*, 366–367. For a similar outline, see Donald W. Burdick, *The Letters of John the Apostle* (Moody, 1985) 88–90.

importance of these three themes in the letter, but I do not feel that the text can be quite so neatly demarcated in terms of its structure. The third section in particular is difficult to differentiate as evidenced by the titles that are suggested, e.g. "Closer correlation of righteousness, love, and belief."[38] Then too the internal sections are often rather arbitrarily set up and labeled, e.g., "Sonship demands love of fellow believers, 3:10b–24."[39] In this case, the discourse unit proposed is too long, its beginning being more accurately fixed at 3:11, and it includes a distinct segment that does not deal specifically with "sonship," i.e., 3:19–24.

The problem here is that these seemingly precise, but inaccurately defined and designated text units may confuse or mislead unsophisticated readers with regard to the author's intended organization of ideas and the unfolding development of his argument. A greater difficulty is that the attempt to apportion the text into clearly differentiated units of content leads one to overlook or ignore the prominent sequence of overlapping Christological propositions that runs throughout the entire work, simply because they do not happen to fit into a given larger topical category.

It may be more accurate, therefore, to describe overall arrangement of 1 John—*not* as a "spiral," a "winding staircase," or an "inverted pyramid or cone," as is commonly the case,[40] —but rather as the dynamic *armature* of a motor which is characterized by a central metal core situated between the poles of a magnet and wrapped with coils of wire. When an electric current is introduced into the wire, the core begins to rotate rapidly due to the magnetic field that is set up thereby creating a powerful force (torque). Such is the ever-changing, but always didactically familiar discourse of 1 John. Thus, a better way perhaps to display the text's organization is to view the sequence of Christological assertions as the foundational "nucleus" around which revolves a variety of individual pericopes that pertain primarily to the macro-themes of "obedience" and "love"—but which include a number of topics of distinct but related interest, especially in the first two and the final chapters.

The following diagram is a crude attempt to present a paradigmatic display of the overlapping and interwoven formal organization of content in 1 John, i.e., the "expression" of its semantic "substance." In the central horizontal "core" is listed the series of Christ-oriented doctrinal passages, most of which are associated with "faith" (or its opposite), and revolving around this preeminent nucleus is the sequence of ethical topics which are listed in lettered order and identified on the right, including "other" concepts that are closely related to "love," "obedience," and/or "Christ"—whether by semantic association, antithesis, or cause/ effect.

---

[38] Ibid., 87.

[39] Ibid., 89.

[40] Some suggestions of commentators listed by ibid., 86, 91.

LOVE	CHRIST	OBEDIENCE	OTHER	*Topical Description of Contextual Unit*
	1:1–2		a	a: divine fellowship and testimony (1:1–4)
	1:7, 9	b		b: we ought to walk in the light (1:5–7)
	—		c	c: we should confess our sins (1:8–10)
	2:1–2	d		d: we must obey God's commands (2:1–8)
e	—			e: show light and love your brother (2:9–11)
	2:12		f	f: victory in knowing God/Christ (2:12–14)
g	—			g: do not love the world (2:15–17)
	—		h	h: revelation of antichrist[s] (2:20–23)
	2:22–23		i	i: knowing the truth/Christ (2:20–23)
	2:28	j		j: remain faithful in your anointing (2:24–28)
	3:2, 8	k		k: God's children do right/avoid sin (2:29–3:10)
l	3:16			l: we should love one another (3:11–18)
	3:23	m		m: assurance through obedience (3:19–24)
	4:2		n	n: discerning the S/spirit of truth (4:1–6)
o	4:9–10			o: we love because God loved us (4:7–16)
p	4:14–15			p: love is fearless and unfeigned (4:17–21)
q	5:1, 5			q: victorious love is built on faith (5:1–5)
	5:6		r	r: true testimony about God's Son (5:6–12)

	5:11–12		s	s: reassurance of answered prayer (5:13–15)
	5:13		t	t: the sin that does/not lead to death (5:16–7)
	5:20		u	u: knowledge that we are God's children (5:18–20)
	5:21	v		v: keep away from all idolatry/antichrists! (5:21)

Figure 21.1: Paradigmatic Display of Content Organization in 1 John

The preceding is not offered as the complete answer to the compositional mystery of the structure of 1 John, but at least it does offer a different—and verifiable—perspective on how the author has expertly fashioned the text in order to effectively carry out his fervent pastoral communicative purposes. The sustained thread of theologically interrelated dogmatic assertions provides a unified "directive" (paraenetic) aim for the whole, i.e., how Christians are to confront the crisis posed by the false-teaching/living antichrists, and gives both *cohesion* (surface *texture*) as well as *coherence* (deep *structure*) to the entire message. The schema proposed above gives special prominence to the doctrinal component of this epistle, namely, the person and work of "Jesus Christ, the Son of God" (3:23; 5:20), but this is because of the demonstrable importance of this axiomatic truth to John's message as a whole. It is also interesting to observe that almost a quarter of the verses which comprise this book include some significant Christological statement (i.e., 26/115). In correspondence with the antithetical assertions that are evident throughout the text, the letter also closes on a strikingly contrastive (hence most memorable!) note (v): thus an "idol" is anything (of the antichrist [2:22], the world [4:5], or the devil [3:11]) pertaining to our faith or practice that would lead us away from a vibrant fellowship and life with Christ and his heavenly Father (1:3; 5:20—the "great" *inclusio!*).[41]

Conclusion

I believe my methodology to be sound, but in the case of 1 John I am certainly in no position to claim that my structural analysis and resultant proposal for the

---

[41] In the context of the discourse as a whole, the seemingly misplaced reference to "idols" at the end of 1 John turns out to be very much "in place" and a graphic way for the Elder to leave his readership with something very colorful and concrete to remember: This prohibition calls to mind the First Commandment (Exodus 20:4–6, 23) and its juxtaposition with a confession of "Jesus Christ" (5:20) also stresses the deity of their Lord and Savior. Thus, anyone who would deny Jesus in word or deed also denies the Father (cf. 2:22–23)—hence his/her idolatry

organization of the epistle cannot be contested either on the text's macro- or micro-level. As already noted, this is due primarily to the elaborate repetitive nature of this oral-based composition and the (deliberate) semantically-enriched lexical and syntactic expressions employed by the apostolic author. I will close then with a brief listing of the main pros and cons of my analytical approach as applied above:

Pros:

1) the entire Greek text is sequentially examined from an oratorical perspective;
2) a systematic, potentially testable method for postulating structural units is employed;
3) this then provides the basis for a thorough text-based exegesis, interpretation, and subsequent practical (e.g., homiletical) application;
4) the detailed structural analysis identifies and gives new exegetical insights into the letter's prominent stylistic and rhetorical features, for example:
   a) poetic, including sonic, patterns of integrated form and meaning, involving exact and synonymous repetition along with antithetical contrast;
   b) "semantic density"[42]—deliberate superfluity of lexical meaning (e.g., "make/do," "remain," "walking," "loose," "seed")—as well as semiotically "significant" syntactic features, i.e., allowing for several compatible construals, such as:
      i) the anaphoric and/or cataphoric reference of demonstrative pronouns (e.g., 2:10, 3:8, 3:10);
      ii) the manifold usage of *hoti* ("causal" and/or "objective," e.g., 2:8, 2:21, 3:20, 5:9; also *hina* (4:21);
      iii) the genitive case (e.g., "objective" and/or "subjective," e.g., "love of God" in 3:17, 5:3);
      iv) second–person plural present indicative and/or imperative verbs (e.g., 2:29);
      v) other syntactic constructions with several possibly convergent interpretations (e.g., 4:2, 18–19; 5:1, 4, 16, 18);
      vi) occasional occurrence of debatable segmentation of the Greek text into sentences, with consequent implications for translation (e.g., 2:27, 3:2);
   c) the presence of overlapping structural units, producing textual cohesion (form) and coherence (content);
   d) frequent allusion to John's Gospel (thus entailing the prominent factor of intertextuality);

---

[42] See E. R. Wendland, "'What Is Truth?' Semantic Density and the Language of the Johannine Epistles, with special reference to 2 John," *Neotestamentica* 24, no. 2 (1990): 301–333.

e)   the possible inclusion of deliberate "parentheses," usually prominent Christological assertions—which are thereby highlighted (e.g., 1:2, 3:1–3);

f)   the use of word-order variations (front- or back-shifting) for emphasis (topicalization, focalization)—and recognizable only in the original text;

5)   a discourse outline of the entire Greek text is presented, which allows for a critical, comparative examination of the proposed structural arrangement with alternatives put forward by others, and with special reference to disputed boundaries and associated topical headings, e.g., 3:1, 5:1, 5:4–5, 5:6 (compare, for example, the notes for these in the *New English Translation*).

Cons:

1)   carrying out this type of rigorous textual analysis is rather strenuous and time-consuming;

2)   after completion, it also requires a close comparison with other discourse proposals;

3)   many potentially debatable points remain due to the nature of John's recursive, allusive style, and so, in short, my various construals certainly do not provide the unequivocal "final answer!"

In conclusion then, as in the case of the proverbial plum pudding, so also it goes for any discourse analysis of the Scriptures: Its "proof"—or relative value—can be determined only in the actual eating thereof. That is to say, it requires a careful, consistent, and comprehensive effort to apply one method or set of procedures in critical comparison with another in relation to a complete biblical book or distinct pericope.[43] Despite the relative uncertainty of some of the results, one thing is certain: Analysts will always benefit, in more ways than one, from this precise study-reading experience in terms of their understanding of, and appreciation for the Word of God as written—and also as the text was hypothetically proclaimed as well!

---

[43] Any discourse analysis of a literary text, whether secular or scriptural, benefits from the application of several approaches and multiple perspectives, as noted with examples in Olsson ("First John," 389).

Discourse Structure and Notes for 2 John

The organization of 2 John is not difficult to discern, and the text includes a number of the key concepts found in 1 John and indeed the Gospel of John as well.[44] Excluding the opening salutary material (vv.1–3) and formulaic epistolary farewell (vv.12–13), the letter body may be divided roughly into two major portions that express "commendation," on the one hand (vv.4–6), and pastoral "cautioning," or warning, on the other (vv.7–11). Thus, the addressees—the "dear lady" and her "children" (probably referring to a Christian congregation and its members)—are first praised for remaining faithful to the "truth," presumably the central Christological teachings of the Gospel and first Epistle, and demonstrating this by showing "love" and "obedience" within the community. In the second part of the epistolary body then, they are strongly warned against "the deceivers," namely, the itinerant (vv.10–11) false teachers who would lead them away from the true "teaching of [from/about] Jesus Christ" (v.9). Similar stylistic (literary-rhetorical) devices to those of 1 John appear to demarcate the discourse into its constituent paragraphs, as shown in the analytical display below.

Epistolary SALUTATION

1 Ὁ πρεσβύτερος ἐκλεκτῇ κυρίᾳ καὶ τοῖς
  τέκνοις αὐτῆς,

οὓς ἐγὼ ἀγαπῶ ἐν <u>ἀληθείᾳ</u>,

καὶ οὐκ ἐγὼ μόνος

ἀλλὰ καὶ πάντες οἱ ἐγνωκότες τὴν
  <u>ἀλήθειαν</u>,

2 διὰ τὴν <u>ἀλήθειαν</u> τὴν μένουσαν ἐν ἡμῖν,

καὶ μεθ' ἡμῶν ἔσται εἰς τὸν αἰῶνα·

Christological BENEDICTION

3 ἔσται μεθ' ἡμῶν χάρις ἔλεος εἰρήνη
  παρὰ θεοῦ πατρός, καὶ παρὰ Ἰησοῦ
  Χριστοῦ τοῦ υἱοῦ τοῦ πατρός, ἐν
  ἀληθείᾳ καὶ ἀγάπη.

Christian love is based on the truth (1–2)

- a formulaic opener by the writer to his addressees initiates 2 John (A)
- a laudatory description of the addressees with manifold reference to "(the) truth" (a subtle allusion also to Christ?) rounds out the salutation (B)
- this initial paragraph of the epistolary Prologue concludes (C) with a climactic assertion (P) (v. 2b)

Christ makes truth and love possible (3)

- a chiastic lexical reiteration joins the Prologue's Address to its Blessing: "with-us + it-will-be (2b) // it-will-be + with-us" (3a) (J)
- marked word order distinguishes the onset of this short paragraph (A)
- key theological terms (grace, mercy,

---

[44] For a study of these lexical connections (intertextuality) and proposals for the mutually-supporting semantic (propositional) as well as pragmatic (speech-act) structures of this epistle, see Wendland, "What Is Truth," 301–333.

peace, truth, love) highlight this benediction (B), which ends in John's keynote—"love" (P/C)

Walking in truth, love, and obedience (4–6)

- another chiastic arrangement of ideas mark the overlap (J) between the Prologue and the Body of this letter: "from God [the] Father + in truth // in truth + from the Father"
- introduction of the authorial "I" ("I rejoiced") begins this first segment of the epistolary Body (A)
- the author's joy introduces his first major appeal, namely, to continue faithfully to follow in the "love-command," an entreaty that features an iteration of concepts that are familiar already from 1 John (B)
- closure (C) of this paragraph is marked by an end of the sequence of repeated ideas

Epistolary BODY—A

4 Ἐχάρην λίαν ὅτι εὕρηκα
ἐκ τῶν τέκνων σου περιπατοῦντας *ἐν*
    ἀληθείᾳ, καθὼς ἐντολὴν ἐλάβομεν
    παρὰ τοῦ πατρός.
5 καὶ νῦν ἐρωτῶ σε, κυρία,
οὐχ ὡς <u>ἐντολὴν</u> καινὴν γράφων σοι
ἀλλὰ ἣν εἴχομεν <u>ἀπ᾽ ἀρχῆς</u>,
ἵνα <u>ἀγαπῶμεν</u> ἀλλήλους.
6 καὶ <u>αὕτη ἐστὶν ἡ ἀγάπη</u>,
ἵνα <u>περιπατῶμεν</u> κατὰ τὰς <u>ἐντολὰς</u>
    αὐτοῦ· <u>αὕτη ἡ ἐντολή ἐστιν</u>,
καθὼς ἠκούσατε <u>ἀπ᾽ ἀρχῆς</u>,
ἵνα ἐν <u>αὐτῇ περιπατῆτε</u>.

Warning: Watch out for deceivers! (7–8)

- A obvious shift in topic and tone indicate the movement to the twofold "warning" section of the Body (A)
- the only topical connection (J) is with the *first* epistle's condemnation of the deceptive, Christ-disparaging teaching of the "antichrist"
- the first warning, involving a dramatic contrast beween "losing" and "gaining" the gracious "reward" of faith, concludes the paragraph (C)

Epistolary BODY—B1

7 ὅτι πολλοὶ <u>πλάνοι</u> ἐξῆλθον εἰς τὸν
    κόσμον,
οἱ μὴ ὁμολογοῦντες Ἰησοῦν <u>Χριστὸν</u>
ἐρχόμενον ἐν σαρκί·
οὗτός ἐστιν ὁ <u>πλάνος</u> καὶ ὁ <u>ἀντίχριστος</u>.
8 βλέπετε ἑαυτούς,
ἵνα μὴ <u>ἀπολέσητε</u> ἃ εἰργασάμεθα,
ἀλλὰ μισθὸν πλήρη <u>ἀπολάβητε</u>.[45]

---

[45] In an earlier study of 2 John, I posited v. 8 as being the center of a concentric topical structure that includes the entire epistle (Wendland, "What Is Truth," 329). In the present study then it was difficult to determine whether v. 9 should be incorporated as part of the paragraph covering vv. 7–8, or leading off the new paragraph of vv. 9–11. I now feel that the notion of "teaching" lends support to the latter structural arrangement.

Epistolary BODY—B2

9 πᾶς <u>ὁ προάγων</u>

καὶ μὴ μένων <u>ἐν τῇ διδαχῇ</u> τοῦ *Χριστοῦ*

θεὸν οὐκ ἔχει·

<u>ὁ μένων ἐν τῇ διδαχῇ,</u>

<u>οὗτος καὶ τὸν πατέρα</u>

<u>καὶ τὸν υἱὸν ἔχει.</u>

10 εἴ τις ἔρχεται πρὸς ὑμᾶς

καὶ <u>ταύτην τὴν διδαχὴν</u> οὐ φέρει,

μὴ λαμβάνετε αὐτὸν εἰς οἰκίαν

καὶ χαίρειν αὐτῷ μὴ λέγετε·

11 <u>ὁ λέγων</u> γὰρ αὐτῷ χαίρειν κοινωνεῖ

τοῖς ἔργοις αὐτοῦ τοῖς πονηροῖς.

CLOSURE

12 Πολλὰ ἔχων ὑμῖν γράφειν

οὐκ ἐβουλήθην διὰ χάρτου καὶ μέλανος,

ἀλλὰ ἐλπίζω γενέσθαι πρὸς ὑμᾶς

καὶ στόμα πρὸς στόμα λαλῆσαι,

ἵνα ἡ χαρὰ ὑμῶν πεπληρωμένη ᾖ.

FAREWELL

13 Ἀσπάζεταί σε τὰ τέκνα τῆς ἀδελφῆς

σου τῆς ἐκλεκτῆς.

Warning: Don't welcome false teachers! (9–11)

- v. 9 acts as a transitional "hinge" that links the two warnings of the second section of the epistolary Body
- the second half of v. 9 highlights the contrary, in this case positive truth (P)
- the author's warning concerns those who pervert "the teaching" about Christ—presumably who he is (his nature) and what he was born to do (his work) (B); believers are not to offer brotherly hospitality to such itinerant false teachers
- the false teacher (v. 9) and "the one who" (3x in vv. 9–11) "welcomes" him (v. 11) are foregrounded at the beginning and ending of this paragraph, which concludes with a final emphatic reference to their "wicked deeds" (C)

I hope to visit you soon in joy (12)

- a sudden return to familiar, formulaic epistolarly language reveals the initiation of the closing portion of this letter (A)
- the conclusion of the formula ends the paragraph (C)

Greetings from fellow believers (13)

- the final farewell wish clearly indicates the ending of 2 John (A–C)

Discourse Structure and Notes for 3 John

A perceptible similarity in content, style, and structure would suggest that 3 John may have been written about the same time as 2 John—but now to an individual believer name Gaius. Several verses would indicate that Gaius was a respected leader in the church (e.g., vv. 3–5), who was facing the same same sort of opposition in the form of false teachers as the "chosen lady" of 2 John and also the addressees of 1 John. As in the case of 2 John, the central "body" of 3 John may be divided into two main portions: The first offers positive encouragement to Gaius to remain faithful in "the truth" and the practice of mutual Christian "love" (vv. 3–4), and at the same time to continue to support fellow evangelists and apologists who were also proclaiming "the Name" of Christ (vv. 5–8).

The second portion of the letter then focuses on countering a prominent errorist named Diotrephes, who was proudly seeking an exalted position for himself and thereby causing great confusion and consternation among the Christian communities (vv. 9–10). One way to offset such heretics was to support true teachers, like Demetrius, who is strongly commended (vv. 11–12). 3 John concludes in the same way as the second epistle, namely, with a promise that "the elder," undoubtedly the Apostle John (v. 1), would try to make a personal visit soon for the purpose of encourging "the church" (v. 13–14; cf. 2 John 12).

Christological GREETING

1 Ὁ πρεσβύτερος Γαΐῳ τῷ <u>ἀγαπητῷ</u>, ὃν ἐγὼ <u>ἀγαπῶ</u> ἐν ἀληθείᾳ.

Unity based on Christian love and truth (1)

- the distinct epistolarly greeting features two central Christological concepts of the Johannine corpus of writings—"love" and "truth"

Benediction

2 Ἀγαπητέ, περὶ πάντων εὔχομαί σε <u>εὐοδοῦσθαι</u> καὶ ὑγιαίνειν, καθὼς <u>εὐοδοῦταί</u> σου ἡ ψυχή.

A wish for health and well-being (2)

- the notion of "love" creates a lexical overlap with the author's benedictive well-wish for his addressee (J)
- the dominant topic of personal "health" in this short unit sets the stages for the subsequent comparative discussion of spiritual well-being in the letter's Body (B)

Epistolary BODY—A1

3 ἐχάρην γὰρ λίαν ἐρχομένων *ἀδελφῶν*
καὶ μαρτυρούντων σου τῇ <u>ἀληθείᾳ</u>,
καθὼς σὺ ἐν <u>ἀληθείᾳ</u> <u>περιπατεῖς</u>.
4 μειζοτέραν τούτων οὐκ ἔχω <u>χαράν</u>,
ἵνα ἀκούω τὰ ἐμὰ τέκνα ἐν <u>τῇ ἀληθείᾳ</u>
<u>περιπατοῦντα</u>.

Epistolary BODY—A2

5 Ἀγαπητέ, πιστὸν ποιεῖς
ὃ ἐὰν ἐργάσῃ εἰς τοὺς *ἀδελφούς*
καὶ τοῦτο ξένους,
6 οἳ ἐμαρτύρησάν σου τῇ ἀγάπῃ ἐνώπιον
ἐκκλησίας,
οὓς καλῶς ποιήσεις προπέμψας ἀξίως
τοῦ θεοῦ·
7 ὑπὲρ γὰρ τοῦ ὀνόματος ἐξῆλθον
μηδὲν <u>λαμβά</u>νοντες ἀπὸ τῶν ἐθνικῶν.
8 ἡμεῖς οὖν ὀφείλομεν ὑπο<u>λαμβάν</u>ειν
τοὺς τοιούτους,
ἵνα συνεργοὶ γινώμεθα <u>τῇ ἀληθείᾳ</u>.

Epistolary BODY—B1

9 Ἔγραψά τι τῇ *ἐκκλησίᾳ*·
ἀλλ' ὁ φιλοπρωτεύων αὐτῶν Διοτρέφης
οὐκ <u>ἐπιδέχεται ἡμᾶς</u>.
10 διὰ τοῦτο, ἐὰν ἔλθω,
ὑπομνήσω αὐτοῦ τὰ ἔργα ἃ ποιεῖ,
λόγοις πονηροῖς φλυαρῶν ἡμᾶς,
καὶ μὴ ἀρκούμενος ἐπὶ τούτοις
οὔτε αὐτὸς <u>ἐπιδέχεται τοὺς ἀδελφοὺς</u>
καὶ τοὺς βουλομένους κωλύει

Praise for faithfully "walking in the truth" (3–4)

- 3 John includes many of the same topics as 2 John, as manifested also in the onset of the epistolary Body (A)
- the key thematic concepts of this first paragraph are repeated in a paralleled manner: JOY—TRUTH—WALKING (B)

Support fellow teachers working for the truth (5–8)

- the vocative "Beloved" functions as a common paragraph-opening frame in 3 John (vv. 1, 2, 5, 11) (A)
- reference to "the brothers" creates a unit-initial connection (*anaphora*) with the preceding paragraph (J, A)
- reference to "the truth" creates a unit-ending connection (*epiphora*) with the preceding paragraph (J, C)
- the related concepts of "truth"-based doctrinal fellowship and fraternal hospitality link the various lines of this paragraph (B), which is high-lighted at its close (P, C)

Resist the errors of Diotrephes (9–10)

- an overt reference to "writing to the church" (v. 6, J) initiates the second, contrastive section of the Body, as John moves from *commendation* to *condemnation*, from welcoming brothers in faith, to someone who does not—namely, Diotrephes! (A)
- mention of "the church" begins and ends this paragraph (*inclusio*) (A, C)
- a rhythmic, conjunctive syntactic

καὶ ἐκ τῆς <u>ἐκκλησίας</u> ἐκβάλλει.

Epistolary BODY—B2

11 Ἀγαπητέ, μὴ μιμοῦ <u>τὸ κακὸν</u>
<u>ἀλλὰ</u> <u>τὸ ἀγαθόν</u>.
<u>ὁ ἀγαθοποιῶν</u> ἐκ τοῦ θεοῦ ἐστιν·
<u>ὁ κακοποιῶν</u> οὐχ ἑώρακεν τὸν θεόν.
12 Δημητρίῳ <u>μεμαρτύρηται</u> ὑπὸ πάντων
καὶ ὑπὸ αὐτῆς τῆς <u>ἀληθείας</u>·
καὶ ἡμεῖς δὲ <u>μαρτυροῦμεν</u>,
καὶ οἶδας ὅτι ἡ <u>μαρτυρία</u> ἡμῶν <u>ἀληθής</u>
   ἐστιν.

CLOSURE

13 Πολλὰ εἶχον <u>γράψαι</u> σοι,
ἀλλ' οὐ θέλω διὰ μέλανος
καὶ καλάμου σοι <u>γράφειν</u>·
14 ἐλπίζω δὲ εὐθέως σε ἰδεῖν,
καὶ *στόμα πρὸς στόμα* λαλήσομεν.

FAREWELL

15 Εἰρήνη σοι.
<u>ἀσπάζονταί</u> σε <u>οἱ φίλοι</u>.
<u>ἀσπάζου</u> <u>τοὺς φίλους</u> κατ' ὄνομα.

string highlights the sin of Diotrephes in conclusion (P, C)

Support true leaders, like Demetrius
(11–12)

- an initial vocative, "Beloved" (A)
- contrastive thematic concepts set in chiastically-arranged poetic prose begin the second paragraph of part two of the epistolary Body (A)
- "Demetrius" (front-shifted focus) is the positive antithesis of Diotrephes with regard to "testifying to the truth," a Johannine thematic axiom that is emphasized through poetic expression, a theme that concludes two earlier paragraphs (vv. 4, 8; structural *epiphora*) (P, C)

I hope to visit you soon to talk (13–14a)

- the formulaic epistolary closure of 3 John nearly repeats that of 2 John (A, C)

Greetings from fellow believers (14b)

- even the concluding farewell with "greetings" is poetically phrased (C)
- the final "by name" (reflecting also "mouth to mouth" in v. 14) underscores the notion of interpersonal fellowship that John emphasizes is the vital result of preserving "the truth" of Christological teaching and living among believers

Conclusion

One aim of the present study has been to demonstrate in a practical, text-centered way the value of systematic discourse analysis in biblical studies. This is but one essential tool among many others for enabling one to dig more deeply and confidently into the major (structural) and minor (sentential) forms of the orginal text of Scripture. As a result, the attentive student (at whatever academic level) will most certainly mine a great treasure of meaning in terms of both understanding the intended message and also appreciating the excellent literary (artistic-rhetorical) manner, or style, in which it is expressed. The latter, formal constitution, including the conjectural manner of proclaiming (orating) the text publicly, is arguably part of the author-intended communicative significance of God's Word. Speaking for myself, while diligently working through these Johannine epistles in the Greek text once again, I was greatly encouraged by the fact that, along with other fundamental Christological truths, through faith in the Son of God I am assured that I "have eternal life" (1 John 5:11–13). On the other hand, I have also been admonished not to take this gracious status lightly, but personally to become ever more vigilant to "keep [myself] from idols!" (1 John 5:21).

22

JUDE

DAVID J. CLARK

Methodology

T his chapter will propose an analysis of the letter of Jude based primarily on the syntax of the Greek sentences, especially the changes in the person of verb forms, and paying close attention also to lexical recursions and other rhetorical features, not least markers which have proved significant in the discourse analysis of other biblical books.[1] The presupposition of this analysis is that this letter is a coherent literary unit, put purposefully by an author or redactor into the form in which we have it today. It is thus likely to be basically well structured, but not necessarily perfectly structured. Even though the present form of the text incorporates citations from or allusions to other sources, scholars have to deal with the letter as it now stands, and so questions relating to sources or authorship will not be discussed. The Greek text cited is that of Nestle Aland (27th revised edition of 1993) with punctuation adjusted (very significantly adjusted in some places) to reflect the discourse analysis. The issue is also raised whether discourse analysis may have a contribution to make in the field of textual studies.

Glosses of the Greek words are taken as much as possible from the RSV, but where it uses different English words to translate the same Greek word, one of its variants will be used consistently in order to show the repetition in the Greek. The RSV word order may be changed, together with other alterations as deemed

---

[1] This essay incorporates the results first presented in my "Discourse Structure in Jude," *BT* 55, no. 1 (2004): 125–137, used by kind permission of the current *BT* editor, Dr. Stephen Pattemore.

necessary to let the glosses reflect the Greek structure more closely. The result is neither elegant nor natural but fits the purposes of this analysis.

Sample analyses of the letter's structure by several earlier scholars are recorded, but they all appear to be impressionistic in nature and do not offer any principles of analysis. The present analysis differs from all of them and is based on explicitly linguistic criteria. Some more recent analyses are also considered, but again, the one presented here differs from all of them.

Macrostructure

Since the analysis inevitably contains a lot of detail, a summary of the results is presented at the beginning as an indication of the destination to which the discussion will lead. The subsequent discussion will show the reasoning behind the decisions made. In summary form the outline is as follows:

A.   1–2 Greetings
B.   3–23 Main body
        B1. 3–6 1st person main verbs
                B1a. 3–4
                B1b. 5–6
        B2. 7–16 3rd person main verbs
                B2a. 7–8
       B2b. 9–10
                B2c. 11–13
                B2d. 14–16
       B3. 17–23 2nd person main verbs
                B3a. 17–19
                B3b. 20–23
C.   24–25 Doxology

Figure 22.1: The Macrostructure of Jude

Macrostructural Markers

There is no problem at all in delimiting the opening and closing greetings, vv. 1–2 and 24–25 respectively. All scholars are in agreement that these short passages fall within the expectations of the ancient Christian letter form. When these greetings are isolated, vv. 3–23 are left as the body of the letter.[2] There is much

---

[2] This terminology is borrowed from Daniel C. Arichea and Howard A. Hatton, *Handbook on the Letter from Jude and the Second Letter from Peter* (United Bible Societies, 1993).

less agreement about how these verses are structured, so this is where the main interest of the present analysis lies. Earlier analyses appear to be based on intuitive evaluations of the content rather than on formal criteria, so the challenge is to see if there are objective structural markers that point to one analysis rather than another.

Below are given four fairly random examples of analysis.[3] The differences are displayed in chart form below.

James	Guthrie	Leahy	Arichea & Hatton
1–2	1–2	1–2	1–2
3	3–4	3–4	3–23: 3–4
4			
5–7	5–7	5–16: 5–7	5–7
8–11	8–19: 8–10	8–16	8–16
	11		
12–13	12–13		
14–16	14–16		
17–19	17–19	17–23: 17–19	17–23
20–23	20–23	20–23	
24–25	24–25	24–25	24–25

Figure 22.2: Four Analyses of the Structure of Jude

James splits vv. 3–23 into eight short paragraphs, beginning at vv. 3, 4, 5, 8, 12, 14, 17, and 20. Guthrie has four paragraphs, beginning at vv. 3, 5, 8, and 20, though he subdivides vv. 8–19 into five shorter units, beginning at vv. 8, 11, 12, 14, and 17. Leahy has only three paragraphs, beginning at vv. 3, 5, and 17, though he subdivides the latter two into two smaller units each, beginning at vv. 5, 8, 17, and 20. Arichea and Hatton keep vv. 3–23 together, but subdivide into four shorter units beginning at vv. 3, 5, 8, and 17. There is thus fairly broad agreement about where the divisions fall, but surprising diversity about the relative importance assigned to them.

In the analysis of other biblical books, a vocative has proved to be a common marker of a new unit, and there are several occurrences of the vocative ἀγαπητοί (beloved) in Jude, at vv. 3, 17, and 20, so it is reasonable to suppose that a new unit or sub-unit is likely to begin in each of these verses. Even so, that still leaves vv. 3–16 to be analysed, nearly sixty percent of the whole letter.

---

[3] Montague Rhodes James, *The Second Epistle General of Peter and the General Epistle of Jude* (Cambridge University Press, 1912); Donald Guthrie, *New Testament Introduction: Hebrews to Revelation* (Tyndale, 1962); Thomas W. Leahy SJ, *The Epistle of Jude*, JBC (1968), 2:378–380; Arichea and Hatton, *Handbook*.

Another potential marker of a new (sub-)unit is the interjection οὐαί, which serves this function elsewhere, most notably in Matt 23:13–36.[4] So it seems likely that the same interjection in v. 11 will also be an opening marker at some level, but even if this is accepted, it still leaves vv. 3–10 to be analysed.

Microstructural Markers

NA[27], UBS[4], all four analyses mentioned above, all available English versions, and almost all versions available in fifteen other languages begin a new paragraph or other unit at v. 8, and it is easy to start by assuming that this must be a correct division. However, v. 7 begins with ὡς (as) and v. 8 with Ὁμοίως (so), a combination which rings mental bells. In some Old Testament texts, there are places where a lengthy comparison is built around the terms כַּאֲשֶׁר (ka'äsher, "as") and כֵּן (kên, "so"), for instance Zec 8:12–13, 14–15.[5] So could this not be a similar example here in Jude? Although written in Greek and not Hebrew, the letter of Jude is heavily influenced by OT writings, and the present passage is actually dealing with an OT example, that of Sodom and Gomorrah. The Greek does not offer any compelling reason why v. 7 has to be linked with v. 6, so why should it not be linked with v. 8 instead? This has the effect of making an explicit comparison of the false teachers who "defile the flesh" with the people of Sodom and Gomorrah, who "indulged in unnatural lust" and now "serve as an example" of punishment.

If this view of the structure is accepted, it entails an adjustment of the punctuation in NA[27] and UBS[4], so as to place a full stop at the end of v. 6 and a comma at the end of v. 7, rather than the other way round as at present. It is not at all obvious on what principles the editors of NA[27] and UBS[4] have decided where and what kind of punctuation marks to place in their texts. Although the two editions are claimed to be identical in terms of their wording, they are by no means identical in their punctuation, their identification of citations, and even their paragraphing, but neither states clearly how they have arrived at their decisions in such matters, so they must be open to question.

For examples of punctuation differences in Jude, we can note the following:

1. In vv. 9, 10, and 12, NA[27] begins the sentences with a capital letter, whereas UBS[4] does not.
2. In v. 9, NA[27] has a colon after εἶπεν (said), and by using italics identifies the following three words as a citation, whereas UBS[4] has a comma and does not identify any citation.

---

[4] See David J. Clark, *Analyzing and Translating New Testament Discourse*, SKG (Fontes, 2019), 83–85.

[5] See David J. Clark, "Discourse Structure in Zechariah 7.1–8.23," *BT* 36, no. 3 (1985): 328–335.

3. In v. 14, NA²⁷ has a colon after λέγων (saying), and begins the following direct speech with a small letter, whereas UBS⁴ has a comma after λέγων and begins the direct speech with a capital letter.
4. In v. 18, NA²⁷ has a colon after ὑμῖν (to you), and begins the (presumably indirect) quotation with a small letter, whereas UBS⁴ has no colon and begins the (presumably direct) quotation with a capital.
5. In v. 20, NA²⁷ begins a new paragraph, whereas UBS⁴ does not.
6. In vv. 10, 12, 16, and 22, NA²⁷ indicates by the use of a larger space what we might call new sub-paragraphs whereas UBS⁴ begins a new sentence at each of these places, but only in v. 16 does the new sentence begin with a capital letter.

This amounts to over a dozen differences in a mere 25 verses. If there is any rationale for these variations it remains opaque. Such examples are multiplied vastly in the entire NT, and they do have discourse implications that affect both exegesis and translation. The conclusion that seems unavoidable is that decisions on these matters have been made on a largely impressionistic basis, and this was confirmed in a personal communication from Prof. Bruce Metzger, one of the editors of both NA²⁷ and UBS⁴. Although this is in one way rather alarming, it does give the discourse analyst more confidence in proposing a change in the punctuation that is based on some objective evidence.

Let us now come back to the question of whether ὡς (as) and Ὁμοίως (so) can be credibly treated as a pair like כַּאֲשֶׁר (ka'äsher, "as") and כֵּן (kên, "so"). Rather surprisingly, there appears to be no other example exactly like this in the NT. The regular pair of adverbs used in comparisons is καθὼς... οὕτως... (Luke 11:30; 17:26; John 3:14; 12:50; 14:31; 15:4; 2 Cor 1:5; 8:6; 10:7; Col 3:13; Heb 5:3). In the LXX there seems to be only a single example of ὡς... ὁμοίως..., in Prov 1:27, and one example of the very similar οὕτως... ὁμοίως..., in Esth 1:18. But even one clear example is sufficient to prove that the combination, though unusual, is possible. In a personal communication, Prof. Johannes Louw considered that the analysis of Jude 7–8 as a single sentence balanced around the combination ὡς... Ὁμοίως... is quite acceptable. It may also be noted that the verses are further linked by the occurrence of σάρξ in both.

The Precise Meaning of Ὁμοίως Μέντοι

A further question arises about the adverb μέντοι (RSV "yet") that follows Ὁμοίως in Jude 8. Lust, Eynikel, and Hauspie show only five occurrences of this word in the LXX, all in Proverbs (5:4; 16:25, 26; 22:9a; 26:12), and state that the meaning is "mostly adversative."⁶ All these examples are indeed clearly adversative. Louw

---

⁶ J. Lust, E. Eynikel, and K. Hauspie, *Greek-English Lexicon of the Septuagint* (Deutsche Bibelgesellschaft, 1996), s.v. ὁμοίως.

and Nida treat μέντοι together with πλήν as "markers of contrast" (89.130), and this fits well with five of the eight occurrences of μέντοι in the NT (John 4:27; 7:13; 20:5; 21:4; 2 Tim 2:19).[7] They treat the occurrence in James 2:8 as more affirmative (§89.136), and that in John 12:42 as "a marker of an implied clause of concession" (§89.75). It is noteworthy that in this one context the whole phrase is ὅμως μέντοι, rather similar to Ὁμοίως μέντοι in Jude 8 (which Louw and Nida do not mention). Moulton and Milligan note that Hort also argued that μέντοι in James 2:8 "retains its original force of a strong affirmation."[8] Liddell and Scott (under μέν B.II.4.b) give numerous classical examples of μέντοι carrying the sense of "eager or positive assent."[9] There seems to be no reason why it could not have this sense in Jude, reinforcing ὁμοίως with the meaning "in the same way indeed."

Arndt and Gingrich state that μέντοι is "mostly adversative" and give the same five NT verses as Louw and Nida as exemplifying this sense.[10] They give the meaning in James 2:8 as "really, actually," and say a little curiously that in Jude 8, the meaning is "weakened to but," though they adduce no supporting evidence. For the combination ὅμως μέντοι in John 12:42, they offer yet, despite that. However, when they deal with ὅμως, they cite all the three NT examples (John 12:42; 1 Cor 14:7; Gal 3:15), and after offering the meaning all the same, nevertheless, yet, they go on to argue that the two Pauline examples should perhaps better be linked with the older form ὁμῶς, with different accentuation, and taken to mean equally, likewise (compare Liddell and Scott). If two of the three occurrences of this word are taken that way, why not the third, especially in combination with μέντοι taken as affirmative? It thus seems at least arguable that the sense of ὅμως μέντοι in John 12:42 may be affirmative like that in James 2:8, with the meaning "likewise indeed." This would imply that the statement in John 12:42 refers back only to 12:41 rather than to 12:37–40. The paragraph would then be understood to be saying that although the majority of people did not believe in Jesus, a few saw his glory "in the same way, indeed" as Isaiah did, and so believed. Does not such an understanding give more point to the next comment in 12:42b–43 that these people did not make a public confession of their faith because "they loved the glory of men more than the glory of God"?

Lust, Eynikel, and Hauspie give five occurrences of ὅμως in the LXX (2 Macc 2:27; 14:18; 15:5; 4 Macc 13:27; 15:11) and state the meaning as yet, nevertheless. This seems very clear in four of the five cases, but in 2 Macc 14:18, one might perhaps

---

[7] L&N, §89.130.

[8] James Hope Mouton and George Milligan, The Vocabulary of the Greek Testament (Hodder and Stoughton, 1957), 397.

[9] Henry George Liddell and Robert Scott, A Greek-English Lexicon (Clarendon Press, 1953), s.v. μέν B.II.4.b.

[10] William F. Arndt and F. Wilbur Gingrich, A Greek-English Lexicon of the New Testament and Other Early Christian Literature (University of Chicago Press, 1952), s.v. μέντοι.

make a case for reading ὁμῶς and taking the sense as affirmative. However, the uncertainty over the meaning of the previous verse makes the situation indecisive.

The end result of this digression is that while there is only a small amount of evidence to support the analysis of ὡς ... Ὁμοίως ... in Jude 7–8 as a single sentence, there is no evidence against it, and this analysis therefore adopts it. Among recent versions in European languages, the French *Traduction Œcuménique* and the Russian Cassian have the whole of vv. 5–15/5–16 in a single paragraph, thus supporting a closer link between vv. 7 and 8 than is usual, and the Italian Common Language version *Parola del Signore* actually begins a new paragraph at v. 7, thus separating it from v. 6 more sharply than is usual. However, *Parola del Signore* also begins a new paragraph at v. 8 and does not link vv. 7 and 8 closely.

Further Considerations

Thus far, then, the following divisions appear: 1–2, 3–6, 7–10, 11–16, 17–19, 20–23, and 24–25. The next question is whether there are any other breaks that should be recognised, and finally what relative importance should be attached to the various breaks. In examining the first question, it can be observed that after the initial introduction of the false teachers as τινες ἄνθρωποι (certain people) in v. 4, they are thereafter referred to only as οὗτοι (these, in vv. 8, 10, 12, 16, 19) with no noun, which is probably rather disparaging. In each of these occurrences, οὗτοι begins the second half of a comparison or contrast. A recognition of this repeated rhetorical balance leads to the identification of other breaks at vv. 9 and 14. The occurrence of οὗτοι in v. 8 supports the view that this verse is the second half of a unit, and should be joined with v. 7 rather than with v. 9. Furthermore, it can be noted that two units now end with the words ζόφος (nether gloom) and τετήρηκεν/τετήρηται (kept, vv. 6 and 13). While two occurrences of a collocation hardly amount to a formula, it is encouraging to see that the collocations do occur at similar places in their paragraphs, as this lends some *a posteriori* support to the paragraph divisions.

When attention is turned to the verbs, it become clear that through the letter there is a movement in the dominant verbs in the various sections from first person in vv. 3–6 to third person in vv. 7–16 to second person in vv. 17–23. The expression "dominant verbs" is used because it is not the case that every finite verb in each of the three sections is in the same person. But in vv. 3–6 παρεισέδυσαν γάρ (for they slipped in) in v. 4 is clearly dependent on the first person clause ἀνάγκην ἔσχον γράψαι (I found it necessary to write) in v. 3, and the verbs ἀπώλεσεν (destroyed) and τετήρηκεν (kept) in vv. 5 and 6 are in a subordinate clause. In vv. 7–16 all the finite verbs are third person. In v. 18 the third person verbs ἔλεγον (they said) and ἔσονται (there will be) are in subordinate clauses. The only real exception to the pattern is εἰσιν (are) in v. 19, and this is probably to be explained by its link with οὗτοι (these) as part of the repeated contrasts noted above. It is also significant that taking v. 7 with v. 8 instead of v. 6 strengthens rather than weakens the pattern of change in the person of the dominant verbs.

Detailed Display

In any language, the verb forms are likely to hold the most vital keys to discourse structure, and so in assessing the relative importance of the different breaks, the changes of person are to be given greater weight than other factors. Taking the highest level break as that between the opening and closing greetings and the body of the letter, the change of person will then mark the second level breaks, and other factors will mark third level breaks. The outline is displayed more fully as follows:

============ indicates a major break
=-=-=-=-=-=-= indicates a medium break
---------------------- indicates a minor break

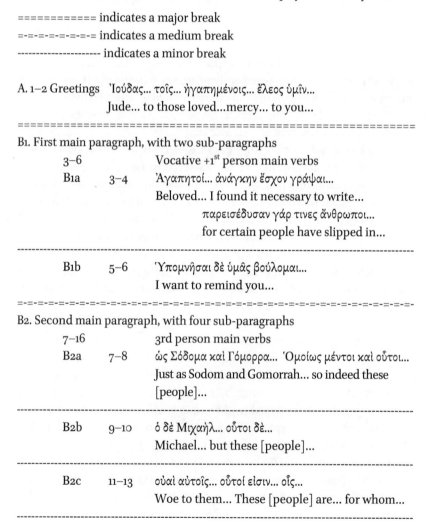

A. 1–2 Greetings Ἰούδας... τοῖς... ἠγαπημένοις... ἔλεος ὑμῖν...
                  Jude... to those loved...mercy... to you...
===

B1. First main paragraph, with two sub-paragraphs
        3–6   Vocative +1st person main verbs
        B1a   3–4   Ἀγαπητοί... ἀνάγκην ἔσχον γράψαι...
                           Beloved... I found it necessary to write...
                                   παρεισέδυσαν γάρ τινες ἄνθρωποι...
                                   for certain people have slipped in...

        B1b   5–6   Ὑπομνῆσαι δὲ ὑμᾶς βούλομαι...
                           I want to remind you...
=-

B2. Second main paragraph, with four sub-paragraphs
        7–16   3rd person main verbs
        B2a   7–8   ὡς Σόδομα καὶ Γόμορρα... Ὁμοίως μέντοι καὶ οὗτοι...
                           Just as Sodom and Gomorrah... so indeed these
                           [people]...

        B2b   9–10   ὁ δὲ Μιχαὴλ... οὗτοι δὲ...
                           Michael... but these [people]...

        B2c   11–13   οὐαὶ αὐτοῖς... οὗτοί εἰσιν... οἷς...
                           Woe to them... These [people] are... for whom...

B2d   14–16   Προεφήτευσεν δὲ... Οὗτοί εἰσιν...

                          [Enoch] prophesied... These [people] are

=-=

B3. Third main paragraph, with two sub-paragraphs

        17–23   Vocatives, with 2nd person main verbs

B3a   17–19   Ὑμεῖς δέ, ἀγαπητοί, μνήσθητε... Οὗτοί εἰσιν...

                          But you, beloved, remember... These [people] are...

B3b   20–23   ὑμεῖς δέ, ἀγαπητοί... ἑαυτοὺς... τηρήσατε...

                          But you, beloved,... keep yourselves...

                          καὶ οὓς μὲν ἐλεᾶτε... οὓς δὲ σῴζετε... οὓς δὲ ἐλεᾶτε...

                          have mercy on some... save others... have mercy on others...

==

C. 24–25 Doxology   Τῷ δὲ δυναμένῳ... μόνῳ θεῷ σωτῆρι... δόξα...

                          To him who is able... to the only God our saviour... glory...

Figure 22.3: Detailed Display of Jude's Structure

This display incorporates one third level break not previously identified, namely that between vv. 4 and 5. There is no overpowering reason to propose this break. The new first-person verb phrase Ὑπομνῆσαι δὲ ὑμᾶς βούλομαι (I want to remind you) in v. 5 suggests a change of topic from vv. 3–4, though this is a rather subjective judgement. However, the results of making this break are aesthetically gratifying. Not only do sections B1 and B3 now have two sub-paragraphs each, but there is a lexical echo from Ὑπομνῆσαι (remind) in B1b to μνήσθητε (remember) in B3a. There is also an eschatological note in both these sections. Moreover, sections B1a and B3b both contain references to faith, which is not mentioned elsewhere in the letter. There is thus a low-key chiastic link between sections B1 and B3. Overall, this ends with a 2-4-2 pattern in section B, with all the four sub-paragraphs in B2 showing the οὗτοι (these) in their second half. The other οὗτοι in B3 (v. 19) balances τινες ἄνθρωποι (certain people) in B1 (v. 4).

Comparisons and Contrasts

Three other studies of Jude deserve comparison. The first is by Lauri Thurén.[11] While this analysis is not without interest, it does bring its own set of presuppositions

---

[11] Lauri Thurén, "Hey Jude! Asking for the Original Situation and Message of a Catholic Epistle," *NTS* 43 (1997): 451–465.

and often undefined rhetorical categories. Moreover, it reaches no clear conclusions, and thus can offer no real help to exegetes or translators. Ideally an analysis of the type attempted above, one that looks in detail at the text and its formal structure should precede efforts to apply more subjective categories. Such analysis could offer some relatively objective limits to the application of rhetorical categories, and if it proposes results that conflict with those arising from other approaches, then there is the prospect of further dialogue as to why this should be, and what the differences imply for future methodology.

The second study is a much more positive one by Ernst R. Wendland.[12] Wendland gives a brief summary of the rise and fall of Rhetorical Criticism (RC) under the initial influence of Classical Rhetoric (CR). He is well aware of "the imprecise (hence often debatable) use of the detailed technical categories and terminology, the frequent lack of any alternative perspective on the overall organisation of a given discourse, and an often undiscriminating application of the classical rhetoric framework...."[13] He goes on to examine in some detail the analysis of Jude along CR lines by Duane F. Watson.[14] In comparison with the four outlines given above, Watson's analysis is closest to that of James, the main difference being that Watson links v. 11 with vv. 12–13 rather than with vv. 8–10. While Wendland recognises that it can be helpful to analyse Jude on these CR principles, he insists that the conclusions "do not tell the whole story" and he particularly objects to Watson's view that the text must be interpreted *only* by CR methodology.[15]

Wendland goes on to study the analysis of Richard J. Bauckham along RC rather than CR lines, though Bauckham himself does not use this terminology.[16] In comparison with the outlines given above, Bauckham's is closest to that of Guthrie, though more detailed in that he separates v. 16 from vv. 14–15, and v. 19 from vv. 17–18. Wendland then explains why he prefers the conclusions of Bauckham at all the major points where they differ from those of Watson, namely on "the organisation and function of vv. 3–4, 17–19, and 20–23."[17]

Wendland next offers his own analysis of the text in the form of "an extended chiasm, or 'introversion,' that spans the entire text. This is not viewed as... displacing the consecutively organised patterns presented above, but rather

---

[12] Ernst Wendland, "A Comparative Study of 'Rhetorical Criticism', Ancient and Modern – with Special Reference to the Larger Structure and Function of the Epistle of Jude," *Neotestamentica* 28, no. 1 (1994): 193–228.

[13] Ibid., 203.

[14] Duane F. Watson, *Invention, Arrangement, and Style: Rhetorical Criticism of Jude and 2 Peter*, SBLDS 104 (Scholars Press, 1988).

[15] Wendland, "Comparative Study," 206.

[16] Richard Bauckham, *Jude, 2 Peter*, WBC 50 (Word, 1983).

[17] Wendland, "Comparative Study," 207.

as constituting another—a complementary—level of rhetorically shaped discourse organisation."[18] Since a chiasmus is better displayed than described, its outline is reproduced below.

A Epistolary introduction (v. 1)
  B Salutation (v. 2)
    C Purpose introduced (v. 3)
      D Motivation (v. 4)
        E Reminder (vv. 5–7)
          F Description -- heretics (v. 8)
            G Extracanonical example (v. 9)
              H Description -- heretics (v. 10)
                I Woe oracle (v. 11)
              H' Description -- heretics (vv. 12–13)
            G' Extracanonical prediction (vv. 14–15)
          F' Description -- heretics (v. 16)
        E' Reminder (vv. 17–18)
      D' Motivation (v. 19)
    C' Purpose elaborated (vv. 20–21)
  B' Commission (vv. 22–23)
A' Epistolary conclusion (vv. 24–25)

Wendland's chiastic pattern focusses on the semantic content more than the syntactic form which is the focus of the present study, but the two are by no means incompatible. If Wendland were to accept the proposal to link v. 7 with v. 8 rather than v. 6, it would actually strengthen the balance of his chiastic pattern by removing the only place where it has to put three verses into one unit. Verse 7 in fact fits his label for unit F (Description) better than it does his label for unit E (Reminder).

Wendland concludes his article with a section on the contemporary relevance of the study of biblical rhetoric, and draws on his experience as a Translation Consultant in Central Africa to show its relevance for Bible translation. Though that is not a topic for the present volume, it is certainly one that deserves to be explored and developed in much greater detail with respect to all biblical books. As Wendland says, "No single method of investigation is sufficient unto itself to satisfactorily accomplish such a multifaceted task."[19] What has been attempted here is perhaps a small part of a prolegomenon to that task.

---

[18] Ibid., 210.
[19] Ibid., 225.

The third work is by Charles Landon.[20] This assesses the Greek text of Jude from the perspective of thoroughgoing eclecticism, and on that basis constructs a text differing from that of UBS⁴/NA²⁷ at 21 points. It is worth asking whether discourse analysis has any contribution to bring to the field of textual decisions. It is after all one of the various factors that must come into play in a holistic view of the text, and an eclectic approach more than any other should theoretically be willing to take account of such additional evidence. In the case of Jude, there are some considerations arising from the analysis presented above that may be germane to textual issues, but there are few places where they would lead to direct opposition to the recommendations of Landon. Even if his recommendations were accepted *in toto*, it would make no difference to the major features of the present analysis.

The following comments are limited to two categories of text: (1) those places where Landon differs from the text of NA²⁷/UBS⁴ and on which discourse analysis may make a contribution to the debate; and (2) those places where Landon's comments may find either support or opposition from discourse considerations. The comments below mark with an asterisk (as Landon does) those places where he differs from UBS⁴, and use his numerical notation for referring to each place.

*5.3 For the omission of [ὁ] before κύριος, Landon's arguments by analogy with the anarthrous κύριος in vv. 9 and 14 look sound, but his adducing of κύριος in v. 4 as anarthrous seems highly questionable, since it is there part of a compound nominal phrase τὸν μόνον δεσπότην καὶ κύριον ἡμῶν Ἰησοῦν Χριστὸν.

*6.1 Landon prefers δὲ to the τε in UBS⁴. He cites the occurrences of δὲ in vv. 1, 14, and 24 in support, claiming that "In places where τε or δὲ would be optional, Jude always prefers δὲ" (p. 78). However, he overlooks the fact that in Jude, δὲ does not come twice in one sentence unless it is part of a balanced pair or triplet, as in vv. 8 and 23. If δὲ is read in v. 6, this would be its second occurrence in the sentence that began in v. 5, and it would not be part of a balanced pair or triplet. This is an argument in favour of retaining τε, especially if a full stop is placed at the end of v. 6. This makes the example of the angels in v. 6 co-ordinate with the example of the people rescued from Egypt in v. 5, which is surely more appropriate than implying a contrast, however mild. It is noteworthy that Landon nowhere discusses punctuation. Even though there is little of it in the manuscripts, the consideration of where it is best placed in printed editions of the NT should surely form part of textual discussions. The placement of punctuation can have a significant impact on the overall perception of textual structure, and this should not be excluded as a factor in an eclectic approach.

---

[20] Charles Landon, *A Text-Critical Study of the Epistle of Jude*, JSNTSup 135 (Sheffield Academic Press, 1996).

*6.6 A Greek text that depends on a retroversion from a quotation of a Latin father is surely weakened when it changes the word order of the Latin original (*sanctorum angelorum sub tenebras* > ὑπὸ ζόφον ἁγίων ἀγγέλων). Moreover, the anarthrous collocation ἁγίων ἀγγέλων is unparalleled in the New Testament. At Luke 9:26, there is the phrase τῶν ἁγίων ἀγγέλων, but this is not anarthrous. The anarthrous phrase ἐνώπιον ἀγγέλων ἁγίων is found in Rev 14:10, but in this case the word order is different. We must judge that in this instance, by not looking at the wider implications of his proposal, Landon has failed to make his case. Indeed his very proposal of a conjectural emendation goes against the principle of Elliott that he cites with approval in fn 253 on p. 132. Furthermore, there are discourse arguments against this conjectural reading. The introduction of ἁγίων ἀγγέλων into v. 6 creates a gratuitous ambiguity, since the sentence already contains ἀγγέλους. Landon himself admits that this would have caused confusion (p. 84). And in v. 9, Michael is introduced with an article as ὁ ἀρχάγγελος, which very probably marks him as a new participant. This would hardly have been necessary if he had already been referred to implicitly in v. 6 as one of the ἁγίων ἀγγέλων.

7.1 The proposal in the present analysis to begin a new sentence at the beginning of v. 7, balancing ὡς here with ὁμοίως in v. 8 supports the reading of a single occurrence of ὡς.

7.2 The view that τούτοις refers forward to οὗτοι in v. 8 is surely not necessary if Landon's proposal 6.6 is rejected. Arguments cited by Landon in favour of this view would be weakened if the proposal of a full stop at the end of v. 6 is accepted.

8.1 The existence of the A variant ὅμως for ὁμοίως is interesting, and perhaps offers some support for the present suggestion to link v. 7 with v. 8 rather than v. 6. However, as argued above, it would be preferable to accentuate the A variant as ὁμῶς, understood in the sense of "likewise."

8.5 If, as Landon argues, the antecedent of δόξας here is the ἁγίων ἀγγέλων that he wants to read in v. 6, then surely one would expect an article with δόξας since this would then no longer be new information. Is this not a further argument against reading ἁγίων ἀγγέλων in v. 6?

*15.1 Against Landon's preference for "a stylistically polished formula," one could argue that introducing the root ἀσεβ- a fourth time into one sentence is hardly conducive to stylistic polish! But this, like most stylistic arguments, is rather subjective.

*17.1 A purely discourse argument against a present imperative here is that an aorist is needed to balance the corresponding aorist imperative τηρήσατε in v. 21. If this were recognised by copyists, it is hardly incredible that it should have been recognised by the original writer.

*19.1 Landon wants to include the reflexive pronoun ἑαυτοὺς after ἀποδιορίζοντες. Part of his argument in favour of this reading is that there is an "antithetical parallel between v. 19 and v. 20, to which ἑαυτοὺς in v. 19 is essential" (p. 126). From a discourse perspective the real parallel is between vv. 20–21 and v. 17, so that this part of Landon's case cannot be given much weight. Moreover, Liddell and Scott offer only one other occurrence of this verb, in Aristotle's Politics 1290b26. There is no reflexive in the Aristotle passage, as is hinted at by the fact that in citing Jude 19 they add "(sc. ἑαυτοὺς)." So it appears that there is no example of this verb with a reflexive pronoun in the whole of Greek literature. If so, the case for adding the reflexive here is surely weakened.

*22–23.1 In favour of the NA^{27} reading with the three clauses, one could argue that it produces an A-B-A pattern with the imperative verbs. Since such a pattern is not central in the structure of the letter as a whole, this is not a strong argument.

*24.1 Landon's proposed reading would introduce another NT *hapax legomenon* into the text of Jude with ἀγνευομενους (not, as he prints it on p 150, ἀγνευομενους). Linking a participle with two adjectives and claiming that the result "is a striking example of triadic illustration" (p. 135) seems to be going beyond the evidence. Moreover, Liddell and Scott do not cite any examples of this verb being used in the passive, though they do print some references without citing them.

*24.3 The proposal to omit ἀμώμους here is necessitated by the decision taken at 24.1 to include it there. The weakness of the reasoning there militates against accepting Landon's recommendation here.

*25.1 The inclusion of σοφῷ here is not strictly comparable with the phrase in Rom 16:27 because in that place there is no additional noun following θεῷ. The phrase μόνῳ σοφῷ θεῷ σωτῆρι ἡμῶν sounds distinctly overloaded.

*25.3 The addition of αὐτῷ is certainly no improvement to a book that is supposed to be in good style, neither is the repetition of δόξα and κράτος.

Conclusion

Finally, the entire NA^{27} text of Jude, laid out in accordance with the above analysis, is printed below. The sign + indicates that the following line is a continuation line.

1 Ἰούδας Ἰησοῦ Χριστοῦ δοῦλος, ἀδελφὸς δὲ Ἰακώβου,
   τοῖς ἐν θεῷ πατρὶ ἠγαπημένοις
   καὶ Ἰησοῦ Χριστῷ τετηρημένοις κλητοῖς·
2 ἔλεος ὑμῖν καὶ εἰρήνη καὶ ἀγάπη πληθυνθείη.
==

3 Ἀγαπητοί, πᾶσαν σπουδὴν ποιούμενος γράφειν ὑμῖν +
                     περὶ τῆς κοινῆς ἡμῶν σωτηρίας
ἀνάγκην ἔσχον γράψαι ὑμῖν
    παρακαλῶν ἐπαγωνίζεσθαι τῇ ἅπαξ παραδοθείσῃ τοῖς ἁγίοις πίστει.
4 παρεισέδυσαν γάρ τινες ἄνθρωποι,
        οἱ πάλαι προγεγραμμένοι εἰς τοῦτο τὸ κρίμα,
        ἀσεβεῖς,
        τὴν τοῦ θεοῦ ἡμῶν χάριτα μετατιθέντες εἰς ἀσέλγειαν
        καὶ τὸν μόνον δεσπότην καὶ κύριον ἡμῶν Ἰησοῦν Χριστὸν +
        ἀρνούμενοι.

----

5 Ὑπομνῆσαι δὲ ὑμᾶς βούλομαι
        εἰδότας ὑμᾶς πάντα
    ὅτι [ὁ] κύριος ἅπαξ λαὸν ἐκ γῆς Αἰγύπτου σώσας
      τὸ δεύτερον τοὺς μὴ πιστεύσαντας ἀπώλεσεν,
      6 ἀγγέλους τε τοὺς μὴ τηρήσαντας τὴν ἑαυτῶν ἀρχὴν
            ἀλλὰ ἀπολιπόντας τὸ ἴδιον οἰκητήριον +
        εἰς κρίσιν μεγάλης ἡμέρας δεσμοῖς ἀϊδίοις ὑπὸ ζόφον τετήρηκεν.

=-

7 ὡς Σόδομα καὶ Γόμορρα καὶ αἱ περὶ αὐτὰς πόλεις +
        τὸν ὅμοιον τρόπον τούτοις ἐκπορνεύσασαι [τούτοις = angels in 6]
            καὶ ἀπελθοῦσαι ὀπίσω σαρκὸς ἑτέρας,
    πρόκεινται δεῖγμα,
        πυρὸς αἰωνίου δίκην ὑπέχουσαι,
8 ὁμοίως μέντοι καὶ οὗτοι ἐνυπνιαζόμενοι σάρκα μὲν μιαίνουσιν, [οὗτοι = men in 4]
                       κυριότητα δὲ ἀθετοῦσιν,
                       δόξας δὲ βλασφημοῦσιν.

----

9 ὁ δὲ Μιχαὴλ ὁ ἀρχάγγελος,
        ὅτε τῷ διαβόλῳ διακρινόμενος διελέγετο περὶ τοῦ Μωϋσέως σώματος,
    οὐκ ἐτόλμησεν κρίσιν ἐπενεγκεῖν βλασφημίας
    ἀλλὰ εἶπεν, Ἐπιτιμήσαι σοι κύριος.
10 οὗτοι δὲ
        ὅσα μὲν οὐκ οἴδασιν
    βλασφημοῦσιν
        ὅσα δὲ φυσικῶς ὡς τὰ ἄλογα ζῷα ἐπίστανται,
    ἐν τούτοις φθείρονται.

----

11 οὐαὶ αὐτοῖς,
        ὅτι τῇ ὁδῷ τοῦ Κάϊν ἐπορεύθησαν
            καὶ τῇ πλάνῃ τοῦ Βαλαὰμ μισθοῦ ἐξεχύθησαν
            καὶ τῇ ἀντιλογίᾳ τοῦ Κόρε ἀπώλοντο.

12 οὗτοί εἰσιν οἱ ἐν ταῖς ἀγάπαις ὑμῶν σπιλάδες συνευωχούμενοι ἀφόβως,
    ἑαυτοὺς ποιμαίνοντες,
    νεφέλαι ἄνυδροι ὑπὸ ἀνέμων παραφερόμεναι,
    δένδρα φθινοπωρινὰ ἄκαρπα δὶς ἀποθανόντα,
    ἐκριζωθέντα,
    13 κύματα ἄγρια θαλάσσης ἐπαφρίζοντα τὰς ἑαυτῶν αἰσχύνας,
    ἀστέρες πλανῆται
    οἷς ὁ ζόφος τοῦ σκότους εἰς αἰῶνα τετήρηται.

---

14 Προεφήτευσεν δὲ καὶ τούτοις ἕβδομος ἀπὸ Ἀδὰμ Ἑνὼχ λέγων,
    Ἰδοὺ ἦλθεν κύριος ἐν ἁγίαις μυριάσιν αὐτοῦ
        15 ποιῆσαι κρίσιν κατὰ πάντων
    καὶ ἐλέγξαι πᾶσαν ψυχὴν περὶ πάντων τῶν ἔργων ἀσεβείας αὐτῶν
                ὧν ἠσέβησαν
           καὶ περὶ πάντων τῶν σκληρῶν
                ὧν ἐλάλησαν κατ' αὐτοῦ ἁμαρτωλοὶ ἀσεβεῖς.
16 Οὗτοί εἰσιν γογγυσταὶ μεμψίμοιροι κατὰ τὰς ἐπιθυμίας ἑαυτῶν πορευόμενοι,
    καὶ τὸ στόμα αὐτῶν λαλεῖ ὑπέρογκα,
    θαυμάζοντες πρόσωπα ὠφελείας χάριν.

=-=

17 Ὑμεῖς δέ, ἀγαπητοί, μνήσθητε τῶν ῥημάτων τῶν προειρημένων +
        ὑπὸ τῶν ἀποστόλων τοῦ κυρίου ἡμῶν Ἰησοῦ Χριστοῦ
        18 ὅτι ἔλεγον ὑμῖν·
        [ὅτι] Ἐπ' ἐσχάτου [τοῦ] χρόνου ἔσονται ἐμπαῖκται
           κατὰ τὰς ἑαυτῶν ἐπιθυμίας πορευόμενοι τῶν ἀσεβειῶν.
19 Οὗτοί εἰσιν οἱ ἀποδιορίζοντες,
    ψυχικοί,
    πνεῦμα μὴ ἔχοντες.

---

20 ὑμεῖς δέ, ἀγαπητοί, ἐποικοδομοῦντες ἑαυτοὺς τῇ ἁγιωτάτῃ ὑμῶν πίστει,
        ἐν πνεύματι ἁγίῳ προσευχόμενοι,
21 ἑαυτοὺς ἐν ἀγάπῃ θεοῦ τηρήσατε
        προσδεχόμενοι τὸ ἔλεος τοῦ κυρίου ἡμῶν Ἰησοῦ Χριστοῦ +
        εἰς ζωὴν αἰώνιον.
22 καὶ οὓς μὲν ἐλεᾶτε διακρινομένους,
23 οὓς δὲ σῴζετε ἐκ πυρὸς ἁρπάζοντες,
    οὓς δὲ ἐλεᾶτε ἐν φόβῳ μισοῦντες καὶ τὸν ἀπὸ τῆς σαρκὸς ἐσπιλωμένον χιτῶνα.

==

24 Τῷ δὲ δυναμένῳ φυλάξαι ὑμᾶς ἀπταίστους
        καὶ στῆσαι κατενώπιον τῆς δόξης αὐτοῦ ἀμώμους ἐν ἀγαλλιάσει,

25 μόνῳ θεῷ σωτῆρι ἡμῶν διὰ Ἰησοῦ Χριστοῦ τοῦ κυρίου ἡμῶν
   δόξα
   μεγαλωσύνη
   κράτος
   καὶ ἐξουσία
      πρὸ παντὸς τοῦ αἰῶνος
      καὶ νῦν
      καὶ εἰς πάντας τοὺς αἰῶνας,
        ἀμήν.

23

REVELATION

STEPHEN PATTEMORE

T he structure of John's Apocalypse is much disputed.[1] Apart from the obvious structuring techniques of the numbered septets, the book is full of other potential groupings and key words and phrases which have led to a vast number of proposed schemes, which incorporate or subvert or nuance the overt shape given by the septets. It would be passing arrogant to propose another structure as definitive and final and it is not my intention to do so here. Nor do I want to suggest a methodology to trump all others. I do want to explore the implications of Relevance Theory, a pragmatic communication theory, and how they interact with other more established criteria of structural analysis.

Methodology

I will not describe either Discourse Analysis or Relevance Theory (hereafter "RT") in any detail.[2] Rather I want to introduce my relevance-guided discourse analysis of the Apocalypse by considering the interest that both disciplines have in context.

Stanley Porter, introducing discourse analysis, stresses the importance of context. Noting the "appreciable distance between the world of the New Testament and the modern world" he comments:

---

[1] This essay is an adaptation and abbreviation of central chapters in my fuller discourse analysis of Revelation: Stephen Pattemore, *Souls Under the Altar: Relevance Theory and the Discourse Structure of Revelation*, UBSMS 9 (UBS, 2003).

[2] For a discussion of the various meanings of "Discourse Analysis" see ibid., 3–16. On Relevance Theory see ibid., 16–45.

Whereas there is increasing awareness in many sub-disciplines of New Testament study regarding the importance of understanding the complexities of context, many of these studies have not addressed the attendant linguistic issues.[3]

In a footnote on the word "context" he states, "Context itself is a difficult term to define, but here it is meant to include at least the sociological, literary, historical, theological and, certainly, linguistic worlds out of which the text(s) emerged."[4]

It is this interest in total context that he finds discourse analysis to address. Speaking of different models of text-linguistic analysis he says:

> each defines language usage in terms of its social-semiotic function. In other words, language is seen as an instrument or tool for communication and social interaction. Within a framework of actual usage, language establishes a reciprocal relationship with its setting or context.[5]

Similarly, Jeffrey Reed's description of discourse analysis stresses its importance as study of language in use and focuses on its pragmatic and socio-rhetorical force.[6]

These interests (in context, real language usage, and the pragmatic effects of text) are all shared by RT. But at the heart of all pragmatic analysis is the issue of context, and it is here that many conventional discourse approaches have difficulties.[7] RT complements and completes conventional discourse approaches in this respect.

Regina Blass took the RT pioneered by Diane Blakemore and applied it to discourse analysis.[8] Beginning from Sperber and Wilson's understanding of the

---

[3] Stanley E. Porter, "Discourse Analysis and New Testament Studies: An Introductory Survey," in *Discourse Analysis and Other Topics in Biblical Greek,* ed. Stanley E. Porter and D.A. Carson, JSNTSup 113 (Sheffield Academic Press, 1995), 14–15. The lead-in quote is on p. 14.

[4] Ibid., 15n3.

[5] Ibid., 20.

[6] Jeffrey T. Reed, "Discourse Analysis as New Testament Hermeneutic: A Retrospective and Prospective Appraisal," *JETS* 39 (1996): 233–237.

[7] See the discussion of Gillian Brown and George Yule, *Discourse Analysis,* CTL (Cambridge University Press, 1983), and Robert de Beaugrande and Wolfgang Dressler, *Introduction to Text Linguistics* (Longman, 1981) in Pattemore, *Souls Under the Altar,* 45–51.

[8] Regina Blass, *Relevance Relations in Discourse: A Study with Special Reference to Sissala* (Cambridge University Press, 1990); see Diane Blakemore, *Semantic Constraints on Relevance* (Blackwell, 1987); idem, "Organization of Discourse," in *Language: The Socio-Cultural Context,* vol. 4 of *Linguistics: The Cambridge Survey,* ed. Fredrick J. Newmeyer (Cambridge University Press, 1988), 229–250.

importance of the entire cognitive context for understanding communication, she focused on the interpretation of entire discourses, including the contribution of discourse structure to discourse meaning. These are not inherent in the text, thought of as a set of linguistic signs (oral or written), but emerge from the interaction between the text and the context.[9]

Neither cohesion (surface-level, grammatical relationships) nor coherence (deeper, meaning-based relationships) offer a satisfying explanation of the way discourses are understood because they fail to take into account the total context: "what is crucial to discourse comprehension is the recognition of relevance relations, which are relations between the content of an utterance and its context."[10]

"Topic," a problematic concept for discourse analysts, cannot be identified from the text in isolation:

> Brown and Yule seem to envisage the interpretation of text as like doing a jigsaw puzzle. What they ignore is that in the case of text there are two 'pictures' involved. One is in the mind of the speaker, the other will be in the mind of the hearer, and they are not necessarily the same. In processing a text, the speaker is concerned about which picture the hearer will construct and takes his assumptions into account. It cannot be assumed that every text provides enough content for anyone who reads it to activate the right context, or that a discourse analyst will be able to complete the puzzle. Neither picture nor context is fixed in advance, and there is no reason to think that the text itself provides all the necessary clues. There is no one-to-one relation between the content of the text and the intended context, and...the identification of a topic depends on context as well as on content.[11]

Despite an interest in context, many discourse analyses lack an adequate definition of context and an adequate model to describe and predict the choice and limitation of context, which takes place in any communication. Here Blass repeats for extended discourse what Sperber and Wilson established in the case of shorter utterances, and which may be summed up as follows:

(1) Context is neither simply the "context of situation" (a vague and ill-defined notion) nor the co-text, but the sets of mental representations (including of situation and co-text) which forms the cognitive environment within which a text is processed.

---

[9] Blass, *Relevance Relations*, 9–10: "Discourse analysis can therefore not be a purely linguistic matter; it necessarily involves an analysis of the role of context in the interpretation process."

[10] Ibid., 24.

[11] Ibid., 27–28.

... I am not rejecting the view that physical, social and cultural factors play a major role in utterance interpretation. Of course they do. I am claiming, however, that they affect interpretation by affecting the individual's assumptions about the world.[12]

(2) This cognitive environment is not pre-selected or given but is constructed in the course of the hermeneutic process in order to maximize relevance.

> The notions of contextual effect and processing effort are very important for discourse analysis. As a discourse proceeds, the hearer works out the contextual effect of the newly presented information in a context retrieved or derived from memory and perception. These contextual effects and new assumptions then become part of the context in which later stretches of the discourse are processed. Selection of a context will be affected by the twin aims of minimizing processing effort and maximizing contextual effect. Thus relevance theory suggests an answer...for the problem of context selection, which... has defeated so many pragmatic theories.[13]

(3) The initial context gives access to ever widening circles of context as parts of the discourse are processed which themselves give access to further assumptions and to knowledge derived from both perception and memory. This expansion of context, however, is not unrestrained but subject to the principle of relevance. Just sufficient context will be activated to obtain optimal relevance for the text being processed.

A cognitive and dynamic understanding of context combined with the principle of relevance therefore provides precisely what is lacking in many discussions of discourse analysis.

Rather than a concern simply for the surface structure of a discourse, Blass argues that discourse analysis is a process of retracing the hearer's steps in understanding the text:

> I do not share Brown and Yule's view that data-based discourse analysis is something quite different from the investigation of the hearer's task in processing... to me, discourse analysis is nothing else *but* tracing the hearer's part in understanding utterances ...[14]

When it comes to the question of how to "do discourse analysis" within the framework of RT, Blass only begins to open the door on the wider possibilities of

---

[12] Ibid., 31.

[13] Ibid., 53.

[14] Ibid., 11 (emphasis hers).

her theoretical position. However, she does provide certain important starting points, largely made with respect to narrative discourses, but which clearly have wider validity.

First, bringing RT to bear on the understanding of discourse does not involve abandoning previous ways of looking at and analysing text, but instead sharpens their focus. For example, "staging," "peak," or "climax" can be used to partition the discourse.[15]

Secondly, it is meaningful to talk of the paragraph structure of a discourse and the connectivity that creates it, including both cohesion and coherence, but more as well. What defines text units is now identity or similarity of cognitive environment. Text units are units of relevance, and these establish a continuity of context passing it from one to the next.[16]

Finally, we can examine a whole discourse for its relevance. This is both a unifying concept for the discourse and an orienting principle for its various component parts:

> In the case of a planned narrative, for example, it seems reasonable to assume that the speaker tries to optimise relevance over the narrative as a whole. In this case one could talk of the narrative as a whole as consistent or inconsistent with the principle of relevance...every part of a narrative must be there for a reason, and within relevance theory there are only a few possible reasons to consider: either it must be relevant in its own right, or it must contribute to the relevance of later stretches of discourse.[17]

In one sense the whole effort of biblical exegesis and hermeneutics could be described as discourse analysis—an attempt to follow the cognitive processes of the earliest readers. But here we are particularly concerned with the structuring of a text. What makes certain parts of the discourse cohere with each other more than with other parts? Using the insights of RT, it is now clear that the structural units which contribute to meaning at every level, from the smallest to the whole text, can be defined as sections of text over which there is an optimization of relevance. Hierarchical and coordinate relationships between structural units will also be such as to optimize relevance for the complex of such units being considered.

The drive to understand texts within the pragmatics of real communication leads to the principle of relevance as the primary criterion for discourse structure.[18]

---

[15] Ibid., 59.

[16] Ibid., 78.

[17] Blass, *Relevance Relations*, 79.

[18] On the application of RT to discourse analysis see further C. Unger, "The Scope of Discourse Connectives: Implications for Discourse Organisation," *JLing* 32 (1996): 403–38. For a

In analysing a biblical text, we are primarily seeking to uncover the relevance to the original readers, which might be called synchronic relevance. However, we do it, of necessity, from within our own cognitive environment and there are considerations of this diachronic relevance which inevitably affect our view. The hope of insights into the relevance perceived by the original readers rests on several assumptions. Fundamentally we assume that human thought processes, in particular logical and inferential processes, are to some degree universal and unbounded by local and temporal conditioning. Thus what appears to us as a logical or inferential relationship we assume would have appeared so to first century readers/hearers as well. Second, we assume that we can reconstruct enough of the cognitive environment of the first readers/hearers to make meaningful statements about their probable perceptions of relevance. Blass has argued also for the validity of hypothetical contexts if we can show that they lead to optimal relevance for the text.[19] In fact we must often work with cognitive environments which are a mix of evidenced and hypothetical contextual assumptions. The test of our hypotheses will be the degree of relevance obtained for the text.[20] There remains an unavoidable degree of opacity of the original context, however, in that we don't know what we don't know. We can construct positive aspects of contexts with a greater or lesser degree of probability, but we have no way of knowing what additional parameters, whether features of the situational environment, or earlier texts, or relational assumptions, have simply disappeared without trace.

These considerations have some implications for the way we analyse discourse:

(1) The context within which the structure of a text is understood is composed of the co-text, the situational context, the intertextual relationships, *as they have become a part of both author's and audience's mental geography*.

(2) Text units, or integral text-sequences, are units over which relevance is optimised. This applies to both large and small units.

(3) Relationships perceived between text units are those relationships which optimise relevance. This means that significant contextual effects are experienced for acceptably low processing effort.

(4) More complex relationships should only be postulated where there is a failure to account for the presence of a particular feature by means of linking to the most readily accessible cognitive environment.

---

defence of the RT approach to the study of discourse structure see D. Wilson, "Discourse, Coherence, and Relevance: A Reply to Rachel Giora," *JPrag* 29 (1998): 57–74, who writes in reply to criticisms by Rachel Giora, "Discourse Coherence and Theory of Relevance: Stumbling Blocks in Search of a Unified Theory," *JPrag* 27 (1997): 17–34.

[19] Blass, *Relevance Relations*, 31.

[20] The validity of this test rests, of course, on the fundamental assumption described above.

(5) The significance of discourse markers is always that which optimises relevance. This means, for example, that in Revelation μετὰ ταῦτα ("after these things") does not always operate on the same level. The referent of "these things" will be such as to maximize cognitive effects for minimal processing effort.

Macrostructure

We begin with the structure of the Apocalypse on the largest scales, covering the whole book, and attend to a little more detail at the beginning and ending of the book.

The Integrity of the Apocalypse as a Single Discourse Unit

"A unit of text is a unit of relevance if relevance is optimised over it."[21] Blass's dictum leads us first to examine the Apocalypse as a whole unit. The assumption of its integrity as a text entails the assumption that relevance is optimized by considering the unit of communication begun in Rev 1:1 to proceed continuously and finish at Rev 22:21. Both the integrity and the completeness of this text unit can be challenged. Is it a single or a composite unit, whether by juxtaposition or interpolation of independent text units?[22] Is it complete in itself, or is it part of a larger text?

Neither the integrity nor the completeness of the text of the Apocalypse is significantly threatened by any external textual evidence.[23] Yet we must examine internal evidence of its integrity.[24] Few scholars today accept such speculative source-critical analyses as those of Charles, Boismard, or Ford, yet the question must still be asked as to whether the whole text coheres as a

---

[21] Blass, *Relevance Relations*, 80.

[22] An *edited* text, even if it was a composite, and even if some component parts could be shown to have their own self-contained integrity, would presumably still exhibit a degree of relevance over the whole text, due to the editor's communicative intent.

[23] See David Aune, *Revelation 1–5*, WBC 52A (Word, 1997), cxxxiv–clx, for a detailed treatment of the text of Revelation. Fragmentary manuscripts can clearly be ignored for this purpose.

[24] That Revelation should be treated as a unit on its own might be challenged by consideration of its place within "Johannine literature" and within the canon of the NT. While the former may have implications for relevance relations, it is too controverted to take into account in this study. See R. H. Charles, *The Revelation of St. John*, ICC (T&T Clark, 1920), 1:xxix–l, and S. S. Smalley, *Thunder and Love: John's Revelation and John's Community* (Word, 1994), 57–73, for different accounts. As for its place in the canon, we may assume, given its unique textual history, that it stood alone for some considerable period. For references see Stephen Pattemore, *The People of God in the Apocalypse: Discourse, Structure and Exegesis*, SNTSMS 128 (Cambridge University Press, 2004), 1n1. Nevertheless, its canonical position will considerably affect the way its relevance is perceived today.

unit.[25] The first and most significant challenge to this is the shift in communication situation between 1:3 and 1:4. In 1:1–3 an anonymous author addresses an equally anonymous audience, referring to John in the third person, whereas 1:4–22:21 presents, at least formally, a unified communication situation in which a specific person ("John") addresses a specific group of people (the Asian churches) using a well-known form of communication, the letter.[26] It is, however, unlikely that 1:1–3 is simply added to a pre-existing letter.

First, although there is no closing section with the same communication situation as 1:1–3, the semantic content of the initial verses is strongly echoed in 22:6–7.[27] Even if 1:1–3 was deliberately composed to reflect 22:6–7, this would still argue that the text as we receive it is a carefully edited unit. The fact that this closure is on a different communication level emphasizes the integration of the whole. Furthermore, there are occasional loosely-connected text sequences within 1:4–22:21 which appear to belong to the same communication level as 1:1–3, that of author to audience.[28]

Gregory Beale has emphasized the structuring role of the words ἃ δεῖ γενέσθαι ἐν τάχει (1:1 echoed in 22:6) as an allusion to Dan 2:28–29, 45, which enhances the relevance of the whole being a single unit.[29] The frequency of

---

[25] Charles, *Revelation,* 1:l–lix; II, 144–154; R. P. Boismard, "«L'Apocalypse», ou «Les Apocalypses» de Saint Jean," *RB* 56 (1949): 507–541; J. M. Ford, *The Revelation of John,* AB 38 (Doubleday, 1975), 39–46. Aune, *Revelation 1–5,* cv–cxxxiv, provides an updated summary of source critical hypotheses and presents his own. This is critiqued by A. Yarbro Collins, "Source Criticism of the Book of Revelation," *BR* 43 (1998): 50–53. However one judges the likelihood of any of these hypotheses, the immediate task is to examine the coherence of the text as it has reached us.

[26] J. M. Ross, "The Ending of the Apocalypse," in *Studies in New Testament Language and Text: Essays in Honour of George D. Kilpatrick,* ed. J. K. Elliott (Brill, 1976), 338–344, tentatively suggests that the epistolary closing may not be original, and, even more tentatively, prefers the reading of 2329 which ends the book with Ἀμήν, ἔρχου κύριε Ἰησοῦ μετὰ τῶν ἁγίων σου. ἀμήν. Though manuscripts witness some uncertainty of wording, most scholars accept that an epistolary ending is original. See, for example, B. M. Metzger, *A Textual Commentary on the Greek New Testament,* 2nd ed. (Deutsche Bibelgesellschaft/UBS, 1994), 690–691; Aune, *Revelation,* 1239–1241.

[27] See ibid., 1148–1149. Analyses which treat 1:1–3 (or 1:1–8) as prologue and 22:6–21 as epilogue ignore the difference in communication situation. Such, for example, are Ugo Vanni, *La struttura letteraria dell'Apocalisse,* 2nd ed., Aloisiana 8a (Morcellianai, 1980), 171–72; Jan Lambrecht, "A Structuration of Revelation 4, 1–22, 5," in *L'Apocalypse johannique et l'Apocalyptique dans le Nouveau Testament,* ed. J. Lambrecht, BETL 53 (J. Duclot, 1980), 78–79; F. D. Mazzaferri, *The Genre of the Book of Revelation from a Source-critical Perspective,* BZNW 54 (de Gruyter, 1989), 334.

[28] For example, 13:9–10 and 14:12.

[29] G. K. Beale, *The Book of Revelation,* NIGTC (Eerdmans, 1999), 136–141, 152–161. See Pattemore, *Souls Under the Altar,* 86–87. See also the treatment by Vanni, *Struttura,* 116–19.

Danielic allusion throughout the book suggests that Daniel forms an important and readily accessible part of the mutual cognitive environment. The author of the Apocalypse assumes that his text is heard against a knowledge of Daniel. Therefore, the closure obtained by the use of the words at the beginning and end of our text is reinforced by evoking similar closure in Daniel 2. Dan 2:28 refers to θεὸς ἐν οὐρανῷ ἀποκαλύπτων μυστήρια which is evoked by the title of the Apocalypse itself. This allusion and inclusio identifies the whole Apocalypse as the content of God's revelation regarding his sovereignty over human history and empire.

Secondly, Rev 1:1–3 refers meta-referentially to the rest of the Apocalypse. No other NT document is so interested in itself as a document, or in the process of its own writing.[30] This interest begins with the non-verbal title, 1:1–2, and is then focussed by the reference in 1:3 to τοὺς λόγους τῆς προφητείας and τὰ ἐν αὐτῇ γεγραμμένα. The command to write occurs twelve times in the visions of the Apocalypse,[31] but it is in the closing section that the meta-reference to the book itself or its contents is again prominent. Here references to "this book" or "this prophecy" or the like occur at 22:7, 9, 10, 18, 19. Again, the fact that this time the introspective interest is on different communication levels, none of which are the same as that of 1:3, reinforces the integration of 1:1–3 with the whole, as each level shares this perspective. Most marked of the meta-references in ch. 22 are the warnings of 22:18–19, which explicitly guard the integrity and closure of the book. While formally they are embedded speech within the letter of John to the churches, semantically and functionally they most closely correspond to the blessing of 1:3. They are strongly evocative of Deut 28–29, with its meta-referential focus.[32]

Finally, we can note that it is in 1:1–3, not in the formal letter opening at 1:4, that we find the characterization of the author, which in other NT letters is part of the letter opening.

The Two Primary Divisions of the Text

Despite the unity argued above, the difference between the communication situation of the first three verses and that of the rest of the book, shifting from third

---

[30] In Revelation, 17 out of 29 occurrences of forms of γράφειν are meta-referential, while the remainder refer to items within the visions themselves. None refer to the OT. By contrast in the rest of the NT, over 50% of occurrences of γράφειν refer to the OT and less than a third are meta-referential. The other Johannine writings are the closest to Revelation in this regard.

[31] Γράψον occurs at Rev 1:11, 19; 2:1, 8, 12, 18; 3:1, 7, 14; 14:13; 19:9; 21:5; and only twice elsewhere in the entire NT (Luke 16:6–7).

[32] Note especially Deut 28:58, 61; 29:20–21. See also K. Vanhoozer, *Is There a Meaning in This Text? The Bible, the Reader and the Morality of Literary Knowledge* (Apollos, 1998), 174–177.

person to first person reference to John, appears puzzling. And although the macarism in 1:3 is closely echoed by that of 22:7, there is also a significant difference. While those who hear and those who keep the words of the book are referred to on several occasions, only at 1:3 do we have a reference to the reading of the book, an event which objectifies the whole text. This reinforces the impression that 1:1–3 both stands outside and is closely integrated with the remainder of the Apocalypse. So, is one of these communication levels a literary fiction? Is John both author of the letter and narrator of the Apocalypse, and are the narratees precisely the members of the seven churches? In this case John has framed his letter to give the impression that the seven churches are part of a wider audience. Or is the letter from John a literary fiction, never intended specifically for those churches? Both options result in a loss of relevance. There appears no logical reason to justify the first, and the second means that the high degree of local detail in the messages from the risen Christ diminishes rather than increases the relevance of the whole.[33]

But there is another explanation. The apparent change in communication situation, where John is first referred to in the third person and then in the first, is a generic feature of both prophetic and apocalyptic literature. Numerous examples can be adduced in both canonical and deutero-canonical books.[34] With such a strongly evidenced cognitive environment, we can affirm both that the entire text is intended as a communication from an individual (we will continue to call him John) to a particular group of people, and that it is intended to be seen in continuity with the prophetic and revelatory literature with which the audience would have been familiar.

Since it is the letter body, the bulk of the text, which will occupy most of our attention, it is worth noting briefly at this point that the Introduction, 1:1–3, is itself a composite structure, consisting of a title statement (1:1–2), a complex

---

[33] Some writers downplay the importance of the epistolary framework. Adela Yarbro Collins, *The Combat Myth in the Book of Revelation*, HTRDR 9 (Scholars Press, 1976), 6–7, dismisses it as "superficial" and of "secondary importance." David Hellholm, "The Problem of Apocalyptic Genre and the Apocalypse of John," *Semeia* 36 (1986): 47, does not give adequate attention to the standard components of the epistolary form. Lambrecht, "Structuration," 78–79, divides the book into three major parts, 1:1–3 1:4–22:5 and 22:6–20, overlooking both the letter structure and the plague angel sequences. Ernst Wendland, "7 X 7 (X7): A Structural and Thematic Outline of John's Apocalypse," *OPTAT* 4 (1990): 375, appears to ignore the overall letter form and treats 1:4–20 as introducing the 7 messages. In contrast see B. W. Snyder, "Triple-Form and Space/Time Transitions: Literary Structuring Devices in the Apocalypse," in *SBL Seminar Papers 1991*, ed. E. H. Lovering, Jr. (Scholars Press 1991), 440–50, who gives the epistolary form equal status with the apocalyptic and prophetic modes, arguing that it identifies the intended audience of the book.

[34] Isa 1:1 cf. 6:1; Jer 1:1–2 cf. 1:4; Dan 7:1 cf. 7:2. Hos 1:1–8 cf. 3:1; Mic 1:1 cf. 1:8; Hab 1:1 cf. 1:2; Zech 1:7 cf. 1:8; *1 En.* 1.1 cf. 1.2; 12.1 cf. 12.3; 13.1 cf. 13.3; 37.1 cf. 37.2.

noun clause with no main verb, and a macarism (1:3), typically as a participial clause.[35]

It is interesting to note that on the two major levels of communication,[36] which are the levels most involved with the "real world," there is no reference whatsoever to any member of what might be termed the "opposition" – human or spiritual forces of evil. They are consigned to lower levels of the discourse.

Untangling the Endings of the Major Text Levels

The Apocalypse is characterized by a series of discrete beginnings and a single, composite and convoluted ending.[37] It is relatively easy to identify where the major subdivisions of the text begin. The text begins at 1:1, the letter at 1:4, the letter body at 1:9, and the vision description at 1:10. But it is much more difficult to disentangle their endings. We have already seen that although the introduction has no corresponding communication situation at the end, it is strongly reflected in an embedded communication situation. And not only is the ending of the whole text identical with the ending of the letter, but the end of the vision description is intertwined with the end of the letter body. Although 1:4–6 is relatively well defined as the formal letter opening, corresponding to the formal closure in 22:21, the situation is less clear for 1:7–8 and 22:6–20, resulting in considerable divergence in scholarly opinion as to how to analyse the ending. As far as 22:5 everyone is agreed that we are still in the vision description. But of 22:6–20, how much constitutes the "epilogue"?[38] Some of the data needs to be reviewed briefly:

---

[35] For a more detailed analysis of the introduction see D. Hellholm, "The Visions He Saw or: To Encode the Future in Writing. An Analysis of the Prologue of John's Apocalyptic Letter," in *Text and Logos: The Humanistic Interpretation of the New Testament: Essays in Honour of Hendrikus W. Boers*, ed. J. Theodore W. Jennings (Scholars Press, 1990), 109–46. Here Hellholm has overcome some of the difficulties of his earlier presentation, but the result is complex and hard to follow.

[36] That is the level of the narrator and narratees of the Apocalypse, and that of the sender and recipients of the letter.

[37] The open-ended nature of much of Revelation is noted by Elizabeth Schüssler Fiorenza, "Composition and Structure of the Book of Revelation," *CBQ* 39 (1977): 360; Lambrecht, "Structuration," 87.

[38] The most common view is to take the epilogue as 22:6–21: Lambrecht, "Structuration," 78–79; Vanni, *Struttura*, 107–15; Wendland, "7 X 7," 386; Mazzaferri, *Genre*, 334; Yarbro Collins, *Combat Myth*, 19; Hellholm, "Problem," 52; Snyder, "Triple-Form," 443; U. Vanni, "Liturgical Dialogue as a Literary Form in the Book of Revelation," *NTS* 37 (1991): 348–72. Others take the epilogue as beginning at 22:8 (E. Lohmeyer, *Die Offenbarung des Johannes*, HNT 16 [Mohr Siebeck, 1953], 2); at 22:10 (Aune, *Revelation 1–5*, c; *Revelation 17–22*, 1195); or at 22:12 (C. H. Giblin, *The Book of Revelation: The Open Book of Prophecy*, GNS 34 [Liturgical Press, 1991], 16–17).

- 22:6 is closely linked to what precedes it (Καὶ εἶπέν μοι, cf. 22:1 Καὶ ἔδειξέν μοι) but the meta-reference, ἃ δεῖ γενέσθαι ἐν τάχει, is also a mark of closure with 1:1 on the highest communication level.
- 22:7, at least on the surface, appears to represent a change of speaker, but the macarism itself closely echoes 1:3.
- 22:8 is clearly defined as a break by the renominalization of John in the first person (cf. 1:4, 9) and the meta-reference of ταῦτα. Yet there is also a strong anaphoric link to the preceding sections in the mention of the angel.
- 22:10 appears to continue the same communication situation as 22:6–7, 9 but also contains a meta-reference to the whole book, echoing 1:3.
- 22:12 returns to the same communication situation as 22:7, but the whole section 22:12–20 reflects many features of 1:4–8. These include the direct speech of the deity (Jesus: 22:12, 16 cf. God: 1:8) through John to the audience, the use of Ναί and Ἀμήν in affirmation or response, the coming of Jesus, the alpha and omega statements, the explicit reference to the churches and to the Spirit.

But the major problem is the variety of voices heard through 22:6–21 and the difficulty in assigning them to John, the angel or Jesus.[39] Relevance considerations have potential to shed some light on the problem, especially the contention that the context within which an utterance is interpreted is a subset of the mutual cognitive environment of author and audience. Consider the way the communication situations presented by the text contribute to the cognitive environment.

The communication situation established at the beginning of the letter is between John and the seven churches, with God and Jesus as external elements (e.g. 1:4–7). But the voice of God, with messenger formula, breaks into the conversation (1:8) and this begins to force open the communication situation. This process continues when Jesus directs John to write to the "angels" of the churches. Here, on the surface, the communication situation of John → churches is preserved, since the whole account is a report of what John saw and heard. Yet the direct address of Jesus to each of the churches, and the challenge to hear "what the spirit says to the churches" imposes a Jesus → churches communication axis. This is precisely what is happening in the ending, especially 22:12–20 but also anticipated in 22:7. Only 22:21 is unambiguously on the level of John → churches. The effect of this is to integrate the external communication situation, in which John's letter is being read to the assembled church, with the text-internal communication situation, where the angels, God, and Jesus are communicating with John. The "confusion" of voices is not the result of inept editing, but a deliberate shattering of the boundaries of the text, so that the vision account

---

[39] See M. Eugene Boring, "The Voice of Jesus in the Apocalypse of John" *NovT* 34 (1992): 334–359; Vanni, "Liturgical Dialogue"; Michaels, "Revelation 1:19."

becomes not merely an account of what John saw, which the audience is called to consider objectively, but a story which involves the audience themselves, during which they hear the words of God and Jesus to them.

Does the audience have cognitive assumptions that form a context for understanding such a crossover of communication modes? Understanding that the cognitive environment includes both textual and situational presuppositions, helps. If the immediate context of hearing the letter is the church gathered for worship, then there is also the strong expectation that they are there to hear the voice of Jesus.[40] The likely mode through which this happened was Christian prophecy.[41] The voice of the prophet carries the message of Jesus. Furthermore, the Pauline letter form carries implications of *author-ity* and the textual mediation both of the authorial presence (cf. 1 Cor 5:3–5) and the voice of the Lord (cf. 1 Cor 7:10).[42] The letter form, and the description of the text as prophecy, then, are not a confusion of generic categories, but a deliberate communicative technique. In the words of the letter from John to the churches, God, Jesus, and the Spirit are communicating directly to the gathered church. This is both appropriated and delegated speech, in Wolterstorff's terminology.[43]

But is it possible to trace a meaningful structure to this convoluted ending? The variety of attempts thus far warn against any claim to final status for a new proposal. However an examination of Rev 22:6–21 shows not only that the passage is strongly linked to every major section of the Apocalypse, but also that it appears to parallel in reverse order several of the opening text sequences.

As we have already observed, 1:1–3 finds strong closure with 22:6–7. But equally clearly, 22:6–9 is the final scene of the angelic revelation which begins at 21:9 and which closely parallels in form that of 17:1–19:10. Thus 22:6–9 corresponds closely to 19:6–10 and, despite the embedded voice of Jesus, rightly belongs with the vision section. But the formal letter opening, 1:4–6, is matched by a formal closing in 22:21.

Superficially 22:10–11 appears to continue the same communication situation as 22:6–9.[44] But on the other hand, the command in 22:10 not to seal the book forms a fitting semantic closure to 1:11, at the very beginning of the revelatory

---

[40] Cf. Matt 18:20, ἐκεῖ εἰμι ἐν μέσῳ αὐτῶν.

[41] See Boring, "The Voice of Jesus," and the discussion in D. Hill, *New Testament Prophecy* (Marshall Morgan & Scott, 1979), 160–185.

[42] Yarbro Collins, *Combat Myth*, 7, notes that G. Bornkamm, "On the Understanding of Worship" in *Early Christian Experience* (Harper & Row, 1969), 169–179, esp. 171–173, compares the ending of Revelation to liturgical formulae in 1 Cor 16:20–24, with the implication that the reading was a prelude to the celebration of the eucharist. See also Lohmeyer, *Offenbarung*, 179.

[43] Nicholas Wolterstorff, *Divine Discourse: Philosophical Reflections on the Claim that God Speaks* (Cambridge University Press, 1995), 37–57.

[44] Verse 6, Καὶ εἶπέν μοι...v. 9, καὶ λέγει μοι... v. 10, καὶ λέγει μοι.

experience, where John is commanded to write what he sees in a book. This suggests that 22:10–11 may be on the same communication level as 1:9–11.

At 22:12 the voice of Jesus breaks in unannounced. It is possible to construe the whole of what follows in 22:12–20 as the voice of Jesus, with a few responses: Jesus speaks (vv. 12–16); response (v. 17a); Jesus speaks (vv. 17b–20a); response (v. 20b). Thus, this passage corresponds most closely to 1:7–8, where the voice of God similarly alternated with responses.[45]

This analysis results in an outline structure for the epistolary part (1:4–22:21) which is broadly chiastic:

1:4–22:21 Letter
A 1:4–6 Formal letter opening
  B 1:7–8 Prophetic messages and response
    C 1:9–22:11 Letter body
    C1 1:9–11 Prologue to vision reports—audition of command to write
      C2 1:12–22:9 Vision reports
    C1' 22:10–11 Epilogue to vision reports—audition of command not to seal
  B' 22:12–20 Prophetic messages and response
A' 22:21 Formal letter closing

But this chiasm is rather more superficial than others which have been proposed.[46] Furthermore, there are features which tell against any attempt rigidly to divide up the closing section.[47]

Discourse Structure Diagrams

Discourse structure diagrams, beginning here, resulting from the discussion of the issues will display the text delimited into text sequences, whose boundaries and titles are in bold-face type. Hierarchical subordination of text sequences is indicated in two ways. First, each new layer is indented from the text sequence

---

[45] But, as noted above, the voice of Jesus has already been heard at 22:7, embedded in the final vision report. This is one of the features which binds the whole ending together.

[46] See references in Pattemore, *Souls Under the Altar*, 63 n. 12.

[47] These include (1) the strong binding effect of meta-level focus on the book itself at 22:7, 9, 10, 18, 19; (2) references to the coming of Jesus at 22:7, 12, 17, 20; (3) the renominalization of John, which last occurred at 1:9 introducing the vision, occurring at 22:8, embedded in the end of the angelic revelation 21:9–22:9; (4) the only two occurrences of κύριος Ἰησοῦς in the book, at 22:20b (directed to Jesus) and 22:21 (directed to the churches); (5) macarisms ocurring at 22:7 and 22:14; and (6) the inclusion in the closing prophetic messages (in 22:14–20) of many features which come from the final vision sequence (21:9-22:9), perhaps most notably the city and the tree of life.

of which it is a subsequence. In addition, a sequence label (in brackets before the text reference) indicates the position this text occupies in the overall structure. The whole text is considered a zero-grade sequence, made up of two first grade sequences (1) 1:1–3, and (2) 1:4–22:21.[48] The first of these is composed of two second grade subsequences (1.1) 1:1–2, and (1.2) 1:3, and so on. To avoid these strings of numbers becoming unreadable, succeeding diagrams will each show the detailed structure of a part of the whole only, and sequence labels will be abbreviated. Generally, the analysis only goes as far as paragraph level and reference is made to other works which provide a more detailed analysis. On a few occasions, where the outcome may be significant for the overall structure or argument, paragraphs are analysed further.

The text-delimitation has been done with respect to several significant features which are shown under the sequence label, with the same indentation. These include:

Delimiters: textual signals which mark off the text sequence. These may be lexical, syntactic, semantic or formal. Initial and final delimiters are separated by a semi-colon. The final delimiters may be features of the end of the current text sequence, or of the beginning of the following one (when they are enclosed in square brackets.)

Communication axis: refers to the source and target of the text sequence as a communication unit. A given communication axis automatically applies to all text sequences which are hierarchically subordinate to the sequence. Only new embedded communication axes are listed for subordinate sequences.

Personal reference: human, divine or spiritual beings named in the text sequence at the level being analysed but not acting in it. Those only occurring at lower levels, are not listed.

Dramatis personae: participants who are described as performing some action within a sequence. These are distinct from the poles of the communication axis, and from the persons only referred to in the text sequence.

Spatial signals: locations or directions of movement in space characteristic of the sequence.

Temporal signals: locations or directions of movement in time characteristic of the sequence.

Not all features will be significant for any particular text sequence. Features which only apply to a sub-sequence are not normally listed in the description of the major sequence to which the sub-sequence is subordinated. Question marks indicate uncertainties. Round brackets are explanatory notes.

---

[48] See Discourse Diagram 1. The grade of the sequence equals the length of label string.

(0) 1:1–22:21 APOCALYPSE

Delimiters: Ἀποκάλυψις... (=text opening); text ending (=letter closing)[49]

Communication axis: Author → audience

Personal reference: God, his servants, his angel, John, Jesus Christ, the reader, the listeners.

  (1) 1:1–3 Introduction

  Delimiters: Ἀποκάλυψις ..., 3rd person ref. to John; [Ἰωάννης (letter opening), 1st person ref.]

  Communication axis: *Author → audience*

    (1.1) 1:1–2 Title

    Delimiters: Ἀποκάλυψις ...; asyndeton

    Personal reference: Jesus Christ, God, his servants, his angel, John

    (1.2) 1:3 Macarism

    Delimiters: asyndeton; [Ἰωάννης (letter opening)]

    Personal reference: the one who reads, the ones who hear and keep

  (2) 1:4–22:21 Letter

  Delimiters: Ἰωάννης (letter opening); letter closing

  Communication axis: John → seven churches in Asia

  Personal reference: John, seven churches, God, Jesus Christ, the seven spirits

    (2.1) 1:4–6 Formal letter opening

    Delimiters: Ἰωάννης (letter opening); ἀμήν [Ἰδοὺ (prophetic message)]

    (2.2) 1:7–8 Prophetic messages and response

    Delimiters: Ἰδοὺ; [Ἐγὼ Ἰωάννης (renominalization)]

    Communication axes: Deity (→ John) → churches; audience → deity[50]

    (2.3) 1:9–22:11 Letter body

    Delimiters: Ἐγὼ Ἰωάννης; final delimiter ambiguous

    Communication axis: John → churches

      (2.3.1) 1:9–11 Prologue to vision reports—audition of command to write

      Delimiters: Ἐγὼ Ἰωάννης; [Καὶ ἐπέστρεψα βλέπειν]

      Communication axes: John → churches, voice → John

      Personal reference: God, Jesus, seven churches (named)

      Dramatis personae: John, voice

      Spatial signals: Patmos

      Temporal signals: The Lord's day

      (2.3.2) 1:12–22:9 Vision reports

      Delimiters: Καὶ ἐπέστρεψα βλέπειν... καὶ ... εἶδον; end of visual components.

      Communication axes: John → churches, deity (→ John) → churches

      Dramatis personae: John, one like Son of Man, angels

      (2.3.3) 22:10–11 Epilogue to vision reports—audition of command not to seal

---

[49] See UBS[5], NA[28], for the omission of the final ἀμήν.

[50] Multiple communication axes strictly imply further subdivision. I am not showing these here.

Delimiters: καὶ λέγει μοι; ['Ἰδού (asyndeton)]

Communication axes: John → churches, angel? → John

Personal reference: evildoers, the filthy, the righteous, the holy

Dramatis personae: John, angel?

(2.4) 22:12–20 Prophetic messages and response

Delimiters: 'Ἰδού (asyndeton); ['Η χάρις ... letter closing formula)]

Communication axes: Jesus (→John) → churches; churches → Jesus

Personal reference: those who wash their robes, list of outsiders, angel, David, hypothetical person who adds or takes away,

Dramatis personae: Jesus, Spirit, bride

(2.5) 22:21 Formal letter closing

Delimiters: 'Η χάρις; text ending

Communication axis: John → churches

Personal reference: The Lord Jesus, the saints

Figure 23.1: The Discourse Structure of Revelation

Broad Structure of the Central Visionary Section (1:12–22:9)

Moving inwards, we will now examine the discourse structure of the central section, 1:12–22:9, the report of John's visions. The essential unity of the section is
supported by several features. First, the section is bracketed by the command in
1:11, ῝Ο βλέπεις γράψον εἰς βιβλίον, and the prohibition in 22:10, Μὴ σφραγίσῃς τοὺς
λόγους τῆς προφητείας τοῦ βιβλίου τούτου. The only intervening meta-referential
uses of βιβλίον come in 22:7, 9, at the very end of the vision report, where the integration of communication situations is taking place. Every other occurrence is a
reference to something seen in the vision. Clearly, the things which John sees,
which are to be the subject of his book, include the whole vision narrative. Not
only is there no closure of the book following 3:22, but there are close connections
between the contents of the messages to the churches and the remainder of the
book.[51] Thus 1:9–11 is preparatory to the whole visionary experience, which is all
therefore anchored in the "real" space-time world on Patmos, on the Lord's day.

Nevertheless, there are strong reasons for seeing a fundamental division between 1:12–3:22 and 4:1–22:9.[52] First, there are several surface-level discourse

---

[51] See Austin Farrer, *The Revelation of St. John the Divine* (Clarendon, 1964), 83–86; J. Sweet,
Revelation (SCM, 1979), 44–45. Note also Schüssler Fiorenza's suggestion, "Composition," 364,
of the relationship of chs. 1–3 with chs. 19–22.

[52] Wide support for this division comes from, among many others, Hellholm, "Problem,"
48; Ekkehardt Müller, *Microstructural Analysis of Revelation 4–11*, AUSDDS 21 (Andrews University Press, 1996), 200–202; Aune, *Revelation 1–5*, c; Lambrecht, "Structuration," 79;
Wendland, "7 X 7," 376; Vanni, *Struttura*, 171–172.

markers which delimit the two subsections. The concept of what John *sees* has already been given meta-referential status in the title at 1:2 (ἐμαρτύρησεν ... ὅσα εἶδεν), and again in the instruction to write in 1:11, as we have seen. Now εἶδον is first used with structural significance at 1:12, and then not again until 4:1.[53] Furthermore, its use in 4:1 is as part of what will become an important cataphoric marker of new visionary material, εἶδον, καὶ ἰδοὺ ... Preceding this at 4:1 is the phrase Μετὰ ταῦτα used here for the first time as a structural meta-referential marker. Similar usage, to locate subsequent action or vision with respect to a preceding sequence, occurs in John's narrative at 7:9, 15:5, 18:1 and 19:1, while at 9:12 and 20:3 it is in embedded speech and operates at a somewhat different level, though still to relate elements within the world of the vision. Here at 4:1, the ταῦτα would most easily refer to the whole sequence of vision and audition stretching from the previous use of εἶδον in 1:12. But μετὰ ταῦτα occurs twice in 4:1, the second time in the clause δείξω σοι ἃ δεῖ γενέσθαιb μετὰ ταῦτα. This evokes contextual allusion to both 1:1 and 1:19.[54] Thus the double use of the formula here in 4:1 accomplishes at least two things. It links 4:1 back to the title in much the same way as the first vision sequence is linked. But it also integrates two time sequences, the sequence within the world of the visions, where μετὰ ταῦτα marks the relationship of the following material with what has preceded it, and the sequence in the world of the author and audience, where μετὰ ταῦτα marks the relationship of the events represented by the *whole* vision sequence to the author's present. Nothing in 1:12–3:22 has moved the temporal frame of reference from the author's present and hence 4:1 marks a significantly new stage in the revelation.

Spatial location is another major difference between the two sub-sections. John is on Patmos, in the spirit, when he hears a voice *behind him* and *turns* to see the owner of the voice (1:10, 12). Following the vision (1:12–16) the remainder of the section consists of what John heard. Nothing in all of this has moved him, in reality or "in the spirit," from his location on Patmos. But at 4:1 his attention is seized (εἶδον, καὶ ἰδοὺ) by the sight of a door *in heaven*, and he is invited to "come up." Although he does not relate an ascent, the location of subsequent visions is *in heaven*.[55]

Two features of 4:1–2 link directly the prologue to the vision reports, particularly 1:10: the references to John being ἐν πνεύματι (4:2) and to ἡ φωνὴ ... ὡς

---

[53] Its use at 1:17 is anaphoric and subordinate to 1:12, serving merely to resume the narrative of action after the description of what John saw.

[54] 1:1, δεῖξαι... ἃ δεῖ γενέσθαι ἐν τάχει; 1:19, ἃ μέλλει γενέσθαι μετὰ ταῦτα. As noted previously, Beale has persuasively argued that this pattern of usage sets up Daniel 2 as a structural template for the whole book.

[55] Οὐρανός occurs 51 times from 4:1 to the end, eighteen times as the precise phrase ἐν τῷ οὐρανῷ. The only prior occurrence was an anticipatory reference at 3:12.

σάλπιγγος (4:1).[56] But there is a distinct *lack* of lexical and semantic linkage between the body of the first vision section and the beginning of the second. While the messages to the churches have many points of contact with subsequent parts of the second vision, very little of the throne-room scene of chapters 4 –5 is anticipated in chs. 2–3.[57]

Last, but by no means least, of the features which compel us to analyze the central vision report in two related but distinct sections, is the change in communication situation which takes place. Although on one level John relates his vision continuously from 1:12 to 22:9, throughout the early part it is the seven churches, the real (implied) recipients of the document, who are very strongly in focus. John relates his vision of Christ, and this includes a report of what Christ instructed him to write to the seven churches. Yet although formally reporting, he is in fact obeying the instruction, communicating the message of Christ to the churches. Furthermore, the messages in chs. 2–3 are specifically directed to the churches, as exemplified by the seven specific churches. Thus, the function of John's reporting, as has been noticed previously, is to shatter the "box" into which a vision report is often placed. By means of the vision report being read to the assembly, not only the words of John, but the words of Jesus are directed to the churches. Thus, while the surface level communication situations are these:

John → text (Jesus → John) → lector → churches

What is happening is more like:

Jesus → (John → text → lector) → churches

The communication situation is turned inside out. Nothing occurs on such a scale in 4:1–22:9. With the exception of a few verses where they may be directly addressed, the implied audience does not feature at all.[58] John simply relates the

---

[56] The latter is parallel to the similar anaphoric reference to the voice at the start of the first vision section, 1:12.

[57] The most significant parallels are: falling down in worship (2:5 cf. 4:10; 5:8); the seven spirits of God (3:1 cf. 4:5; 5:6); seven stars (2:1; 3:1 cf. 4:5; 5:6); Jesus conquers (3:21 cf. 5:5); crowns (2:10; 3:11 cf. 4:4, 10); throne of God, Christ (3:21; cf. 4–5 passim); clothed in white garments (3:4, 5 cf. 4:4); an open door (3:8, 20; cf. 4:1); holy (3:7 cf. 4:8; 5:8); David (3:7 cf. 5:5). The more numerous connections with later passages will be examined in due course. On the paucity of direct linkage between chs. 1–3 and 4–5 see further R. D. Davis, *The Heavenly Court of Judgement of Revelation 4–5* (University Press of America, 1992), 19.

[58] The verses concerned are 13:9–10, 18; 14:12; 16:15; 17:9a; 19:6b; 20:5b–6; 22:7.

sequence of visions which he sees "in heaven."[59] The relationship between the implied audience, so prominent in 1:12–3:22 (as well as in the outer envelope), and the elements of the visions John sees, is expanded on in Pattemore, *People of God*.

Features of the First Major Vision Report (1:12–3:22)

Discussion of the structure of the messages to the churches will be brief. It is uncontroversial and has been frequently analysed.[60]

The general communication situation has been discussed above. But note that the repeated phrase ὁ ἔχων οὖς ἀκουσάτω τί τὸ πνεῦμα λέγει ταῖς ἐκκλησίαις has two implications. First, although each message is addressed to an individual "angel," they are clearly intended to be heard by all, hence the same communication situation covers all. Secondly, it establishes an ambiguity, where the words of Jesus to the churches are also the words of the Spirit.[61]

Two features regarding the personal references in this section are worthy of note. First, it is here, within the vision report and not in the outer epistolary layers, that we encounter *specific* reference to the people of God who constitute the "churches in Asia." The "angel" of each church is a rhetorical device which has aroused discussion.[62] But the text in each case quickly moves to reprimand and applaud the church members themselves for their actions and attitudes, and in some cases to encourage change or maintenance of these attitudes. Secondly, it

---

[59] Mazzaferri, *Genre*, 338–339, follows Kempson in claiming primary structural significance for the phrase ἐν πνεύματι (1:10; 4:1; 17:3; 21:10), resulting in "four principal literary divisions... 1:9–3:22; 4:1–16:21; 17:1–21:8 and 21:9–22:5." But note that while the first two are initiatory (ἐγενόμην ἐν πνεύματι), ἐν πνεύματι in the last two describes an existing state and they are therefore subordinate to the occurrence at 4:1. Further, placing so much weight on this phrase ignores other significant intervening markers. Snyder, "Triple-Form," 445–449, suggests only that the phrase indicates important transitions in space and possibly time. Christopher Smith, "The Structure of the Book of Revelation in Light of Apocalyptic Literary conventions," *NovT* 36 (1994): 373–393, presents a more sophisticated version of this structuring plan. His final outline (392) is very useful in displaying what might be called "pneumatic locations" of the book. But the disjunctions between textual, literary, and narrative sequences in the section labeled "*In the Spirit" in Heaven*' (essentially 4:1–16:21 + 19:11–21:8) are severe and must raise the question of whether such a structure can be consistent with the principle of relevance.

[60] For example, Wendland, "7 X 7," 375–376; Aune, *Revelation 1–5*, 119–124; Beale, *Revelation*, 224–228; W. H. Shea, "The Covenantal Form of the Letters to the Seven Churches," *AUSS* 21 (1983): 71–84; Vanni, *Struttura*, 175–181.

[61] See A.-M. Enroth, "The Hearing Formula in the Book of Revelation," *NTS* 36 (1990): 598–608; Beale, *Revelation*, 236–239.

[62] See for example, Aune, *Revelation 1–5*, 108–112, and references there; also Enroth, "Hearing Formula."

is at this level that first mention of human and spiritual opposition occurs. They are absent from the outer communication situations. Here we find reference to Satan as the power behind human opponents of the Christians both within and without the church, and the devil in his familiar role of tester and accuser. External opposition is focussed on those described as "the synagogue of Satan."[63] Internal tension centres around the person of self-styled apostles, Jezebel and her followers, the Nicolaitans and perhaps Balaam (though it is less clear whether the name refers to a contemporary individual or is merely used to characterize a teaching). These people are clearly part of the Christian community, but equally clearly are not addressed by the author, forming instead a foil of error over against which John calls the churches to faithfulness. But in the case of Thyatira and Sardis there would appear to be a further distinction implied among those who receive the letter, between those who are caught up in error and those who are not (2:24; 3:4). Furthermore, there are the repeated challenges to the audience to hear, and the promises to those who conquer, which imply another potential distinction within the communities addressed, between those who will respond appropriately and those who will not. This is a complex picture.

We can now expand our presentation of the overall discourse structure, to include the detail of the first major vision sequence. Note that only part of the text of Revelation is displayed, and the sequence labels are abbreviated. Figure 23.2 shows the structure of a third-grade sequence, (2.3.2) 1:12–22:9. The text sequence labels are shown beginning with a full-stop, which means that the sequence labelled (.1) is actually sequence (2.3.2.2.1). In this way the relationship of text sequences within one part of the text are obvious without the string being too unwieldy.

This figure concentrates on the vision reports proper, giving the detail of only the first one. The whole figure is a third-grade sequence, each set of numbers being preceded by 2.3.2

1:12–22:9 **Vision reports**

Communication axis: John → churches

    (.1) 1:12–3:22 **John's vision of Jesus on Patmos**

    Delimiters: Καὶ ἐπέστρεψα … καὶ … εἶδον; [Μετὰ ταῦτα εἶδον, καὶ ἰδού]

    Dramatis personae: John, one like son of man

    Personal reference: seven churches, angels of seven churches

    Spatial signals: ἐπέστρεψα

---

[63] It is sometimes suggested that these are Judaizing Christians. See, for example, S. Goranson, "Essene Polemic in the Apocalypse of John," in *Legal Texts and Legal Issues. Proceedings of the Second Meeting of the International Organization for Qumran Studies, Cambridge 1995*, ed. M. Bernstein, F. García Martínez, and J. Kampen, STDJ 23 (Brill, 1997), 453–460.

(.1.1) 1:12–16 John sees Jesus

Delimiters: εἶδον; [Καὶ ὅτε εἶδον]

(.1.2) 1:17ab Reaction and response

Delimiters: Καὶ ὅτε εἶδον; λέγων

    (.1.2.1) 1:17a John falls down

    (.1.2.2) 1:17b Jesus places his hand on John

(.1.3) 1:17c–3:22 The words of Jesus[64]

Delimiters: [λέγων]; [Μετὰ ταῦτα εἶδον, καὶ ἰδού]

    (.1.3.1) 1:17c–20 The words of Jesus to John

    Delimiters: [λέγων]; [Τῷ ἀγγέλῳ...]

    Communication axis: Jesus → John

    Personal reference: seven churches, angels of seven churches

    (.1.3.2) 2:1–3:22 The words of Jesus to the churches through John

    Delimiters: Τῷ ἀγγέλῳ... [Μετὰ ταῦτα εἶδον, καὶ ἰδού]

    Communication axis: Jesus → (John) → churches; spirit → churches

        (.1.3.2.1) 2:1–7 Message to Ephesus

        Delimiters: Τῷ ἀγγέλῳ... (and the same for each message)

        Personal reference: angel of church in Ephesus, self-styled apostles, Nicolaitans, God

        (.1.3.2.2) 2:8–11 Message to Smyrna

        Personal reference: angel of church at Smyrna, so-called Jews (= synagogue of Satan), the devil

        (.1.3.2.3) 2:12–17 Message to Pergamum

        Personal reference: angel of church at Pergamum, Satan, Antipas, Balaam, Balak, children of Israel, Nicolaitans

        (.1.3.2.4) 2:18–29 Message to Thyatira

        Personal reference: angel of church at Thyatira, son of God, Jezebel, those who commit adultery with her, her children, the rest in Thyatira, Satan, the nations, my father

        (.1.3.2.5) 3:1–6 Message to Sardis

        Personal reference: angel of church at Sardis, my God, a few names not blemished, my father, his angels

        (.1.3.2.6) 3:7–13 Message to Philadelphia

        Personal reference: angel of church at Philadelphia, David, synagogue of Satan (=self-styled Jews), earth-dwellers, my God, holy city =New Jerusalem

        (.1.3.2.7) 3:14–22 Message to Laodicea

        Personal reference: angel of church at Laodicea, God, my father

---

[64] Hellholm, "Problem," 48, does not place the messages to the churches hierarchically under the vision, but in fact they are subordinate to the vision sequence.

(.2) 4:1–22:9 John's vision of "things which must happen after this" in heaven[65]

Delimiters: Μετὰ ταῦτα εἶδον, καὶ ἰδού; end of vision reports

Communication axis: John → churches (occasionally author → audience or Jesus → ?)

Dramatis personae: John, angels

Spatial signals: in heaven

Temporal signals: Μετὰ ταῦτα

Figure 23.2: Vision Reports in Revelation 1:12–22:9 with Detail on the First Report

Broad Structure of the Second Major Vision Report (4:1–22:9)

Integrity and Major Subdivisions

The integrity of 4:1–22:9 as a unit of relevance is established both externally and internally. Externally it is delimited from the preceding and following text sequences in ways that have already been discussed. Internally two features are prominent throughout. First is the mode of narration, which is characterized by the first-person aorist forms εἶδον and ἤκουσα. Only two out of forty-five occurrences of the former (1:12, 17), and one out of twenty-seven of the latter (1:10) are outside the bounds of this major text sequence. Second is the single perspective, evident in nearly every sub-section, which could best be described as a relationship to heaven and to the earth. Οὐρανός occurs in each of chs. 4–21 except ch. 7, and the only occurrence outside these limits is an anticipatory reference in 3:12. Most characteristically, action is seen and heard to take place ἐν τῷ οὐρανῷ or something comes ἐκ τοῦ οὐρανοῦ.[66] Not only does this whole text sequence share this perspective, but the other sequences lack it completely. Connected to the "heavenly" perspective is a view of the whole earth, as if from outer space, which also permeates the text sequence. References to the earth outside of this section are rare and anticipatory, and point to groups of people rather than to the earth itself.[67] Here the earth is frequently the object of some action or something moves εἰς τὴν γῆν.[68] Only rarely is action said to take place explicitly ἐπὶ τῆς γῆς.[69]

---

[65] Ibid., 48–49, presents essentially the same analysis, except that his main division ends at 22:5.

[66] The difference between the perspectives expressed by these two prepositional phrases is itself interesting. There is one occurrence of εἰς τὸν οὐρανὸν (10:5). Interestingly, the location of action in or coming from heaven is not a feature of the Greek book of Daniel. There, heaven occurs either in the phrase "the God of heaven" (especially in ch. 4) or is a spatial marker internal to the description of the visions (again most common in ch. 4).

[67] Kings of the earth (1:5); tribes of the earth (1:7); dwellers on the earth (3:10).

[68] 5:6; 6:13; 8:5, 7; 9:1, 3; 11:6, 18; 12:4, 9, 13; 13:13; 14:19; 16:1, 2. There are single occurrences only of ἐκ τῆς γῆς (13:11) and ἀπὸ τῆς γῆς (14:3).

But a perspective closely tied to the earth is implicit in many other locative expressions. There is also a significant interest throughout on the peoples of the earth.[70] The cosmic perspective is enhanced by the frequent linking of heaven and earth.[71]

While the unity of this major text sequence, comprising the greater part of the book, is apparent, its complex internal structure is both easy to observe and difficult to delineate with precision. Some scenes are clearly demarcated by their content or form, for example the vision of two witnesses (11:1–13); the vision of the woman and the dragon (12:1–18); the vision of the two beasts (13:1–18); the two visions with angel guides (17:1–19:10 and 21:9–22:9). While others, such as the numbered sequences of seals, trumpets and vials, appear to be straightforward, their precise limits are notoriously controversial. And the hierarchical relationship of different visionary text sequences is most problematical.[72]

Several words or phrases offer themselves as surface-level discourse markers.[73] There are nine occurrences of μετὰ ταῦτα, but closer examination shows that these perform various functions. Twice the phrase relates the events described in the totality of the visions to the real-time of John's present (1:19 and 4:1, second occurrence). This is the usage which is strongly evocative of the phrase in Dan 2:29, 45 (Th).[74] Twice it is internal to a vision, relating events in

---

[69] 7:1; 10:2, 5, 8. But note also 20:8, 9.

[70] Kings of the earth: 6:15; 17:2, 18; 18:3, 9; 19:19; 21:24. Dwellers on the earth: 6:10; 8:13; 11:10; 13:8, 14; 14:6; 17:2, 8. Merchants of the earth: 18:3, 11. Great ones of the earth: 18:23. Metonymy for peoples of the earth: 6:8; 11:6; 13:3; 14:3.

[71] 5:3, 13; 10:6; 14:7; 20:11; 21:1 (twice).

[72] Hellholm, "Problem," 49 reads ἔσωθεν καὶ ἔξωθεν in 5:1, with 025, 046 fam 1006, 1611, 1854, 2050 and the majority of Byzantine texts, in place of ἔσωθεν καὶ ὄπισθεν (see Aune, *Revelation 1–5*, 322 for details). Hellholm then assigns 6:1–22:5 to the contents of the heavenly scroll, a fourth-grade sequence, and divides it into two fifth-grade sequences, the *scriptura exterior*, 6:1–7:17, and the *scriptura interior*, 8:1–22:5. By contrast Schüssler Fiorenza, "Composition," 363, assigns 4:1–9:21; 11:15–19; 15:15–16:21; 17:1–19:10 to the "seven-sealed scroll," 10:1–15:4 (without 11:15–19) to the "little scroll" of ch. 10, and 19:11–22:9 to a final distinct section. Vanni, *Struttura*, 249 and Lambrecht, "Structuration," 85–86, nest the three plague sequences within each other, as does Aune, *Revelation 1–5*, c-cv. Wendland, "7 X 7," divides the text into seven scenes, which requires incorporating the whole text to 22:21. (His sevenfold structures internal to the scenes are often equally forced.)

[73] Schüssler Fiorenza, "Composition," 362, points out that "these 'dividing marks' do not occupy such a clear position in the outline of Revelation that the author could have intended to indicate the structure of his work with them. The author does not divide the text into separate sections or parts, but *joints* units together by interweaving them with each other..." (italics hers). The second point is well made. But "divisions" of the book certainly exist and I will argue here that some of the markers *are* intended to indicate transition from one to another.

[74] The only other occurrences in the Greek of Daniel are a single use in the real-world time sequence (1:5, Th) and a similar use but within the vision-world time sequence (7:6, OG).

the sequence of vision time, not to John's time (9:12; 20:3). Twice it is a relatively low-level marker within the first angelic vision sequence (18:1; 19:1). This leaves three occurrences where it is potentially of major significance within the time frame of John's visionary experience (4:1; 7:9; 15:5) and of these the last is possibly down-graded by a paratactic καί. At both 4:1 and 7:9 the phrase combines with other discourse markers to form the sequence μετὰ ταῦτα εἶδον, καὶ ἰδού. Once only (7:1) there is μετὰ τοῦτο εἶδον, where the singular τοῦτο appears to have less scope than the plural ταῦτα.

I have already noted the frequency of εἶδον which, along with ἤκουσα, creates the continuity through the whole of 4:1–22:9. Both εἶδον and ἤκουσα draw attention to a new feature, shifting the focus, or the breadth or depth of vision, from the previous segment but still within the same perspective.[75] Both most commonly are immediately preceded by καί in clause-initial position.[76] The preponderance of conjunctive καί in Revelation is enormous, and it is the default conjunction for linking elements of the same vision segment.[77] This gives a paratactic, Hebraic flavour to the narrative. It combines with εἶδον or ἤκουσα to form a somewhat higher level of discourse connective as already described. Ἰδού most often occurs in direct speech as a marker of semantic emphasis or attention. In narrative, however, combined with εἶδον, it draws emphatic attention to a new visual component.[78] Εἶδον, καὶ ἰδού thus marks a stronger shift in focus than εἶδον by itself. On three occasions (4:2; 12:3; 19:11) καὶ ἰδού heads the second clause of a sentence, as part of a high-level complex shift to a new discourse segment. We can thus suggest an approximate hierarchy of discourse connectives, with the first mentioned generally causing the strongest break in flow:

---

[75] Εἶδον and ἤκουσα also appear to have another narrative function. The continuity of perception represents the visionary's perspective and this keeps the visionary himself within the audience's view. Meadowcroft (personal communication), pointed this out with its parallels to Daniel 7. See T. J. Meadowcroft, *Aramaic Daniel and Greek Daniel: A Literary Comparison*, JSOTSup 198 (Sheffield Academic Press, 1995), 208–209.

[76] Εἶδον 32/45 occurrences; ἤκουσα 17/27 occurrences. Occasionally they are separated from the καί by an intervening phrase. Not uncommonly they occur in anaphoric relative clauses, referring back to an earlier vision or audition.

[77] Καί occurs 1123 times in Revelation, on average nearly three times per verse. This contrasts with other normally common conjunctions: δέ (7 times), οὖν (6 times, only once outside of chs 2–3), ἀλλά (8 times, once outside chs. 2–3). There are no occurrences of μέν, but γάρ is slightly more common with 16 widely spread occurrences.

[78] This may also be true of the first occurrence, at 1:7, in a prophetic speech. Both usages of ἰδού are common in the Old Greek text of Daniel, but in Theodotion the use in direct speech as a marker of semantic emphasis is rare (3:92, 8:19, 11:1). Much more common is its use to draw attention to a new visual stimulus. On the discourse functions of ἰδού see R. Van Otterloo, "Towards an Understanding of 'Lo' and 'Behold': Functions of ἰδού and ἴδε in the Greek New Testament," *OPTAT* 2 (1988): 34–64.

μετὰ ταῦτα εἶδον, καὶ ἰδοὺ
καὶ εἶδον, καὶ ἰδοὺ; (clause) καὶ ἰδοὺ; μετὰ ταῦτα (εἶδον OR ἤκουσα)
καὶ (...) εἶδον; καὶ (...) ἤκουσα; μετὰ τοῦτο εἶδον
καὶ

Based on these markers alone, we would expect to find major new segments
or sub-segments beginning at 4:1–2; 7:1; 7:9; 12:1–3; 14:1; 14:14; 19:11. However, the
picture is much more complicated than this. The numbered sequence of seals
imposes a structure which overrides the breaks at 7:1 and 7:9. But when the seals
are considered together with the trumpets, the break at 12:1 is reinforced. 12:1 also
introduces another discourse delimiter, the appearance of a σημεῖον ... ἐν τῷ
οὐρανῷ, which occurs again in 12:3 and 15:1.[79] For the time being, therefore, I will
consider 4:1–11:19 as a single text sequence, with a question-mark hanging over
the status of chapter 7 and the two major discourse breaks in it.[80] The decision to
close this sequence at 11:19, however, needs some defence.

Revelation 11:19 as a Hinge Verse

Müller argues that the use of ἐν τῷ οὐρανῷ and ὤφθη in 11:19 links it closely to 12:1,
and that it is in some ways comparable to the throne scene of chs. 4–5, providing an
introductory worship scene for the bowl series, as those chapters did for the seals.[81]

---

[79] Ralph J. Korner, "'And I Saw...': An Apocalyptic Literary Convention for Structural Identification in the Apocalypse," *NovT* 42 (2000): 160–183, has outlined a discourse structure
based on a hierarchy of discourse markers which are, in descending order of significance (162),
the "space/time referent," μετὰ ταῦτα εἶδον and καὶ εἶδον (καὶ ἰδοὺ). However, his approach has
a tendency to oversimplify the distinctions between variants. He takes no account of the
many other markers of discourse structure mentioned in the discussion above.

[80] This basic division is supported (in different eras) by Henry B. Swete, *The Apocalypse of
St. John* (Macmillan, 1911), xxxix–xli and Yarbro Collins, *Combat Myth*, 28–31. K. A. Strand,
"Chiastic Structure and Some Motifs in the Book of Revelation," *AUSS* 16 (1978): 401–408, argues that the main turning point in the book comes between chs. 14 and 15, rather than between chs. 11 and 12. However, the evidence he adduces, in particular the way in which the
"Evil Hierarchy" is introduced from 12:3 and then punished in the reverse order, only serves to
emphasize the essential unity of the sequence. J. A. du Rand, "A 'Basso Ostinato' in the Structuring of the Apocalypse of John?" *Neot* 27 (1993): 299–311, finds that references to "the Christ-
event" bind three major subdivisions, chs. 1–3; 4–11; 12–22 into a unity. On the other hand, the
schemes proposed by Hellholm and Schüssler Fiorenza (see n. 72 above) both fail by the principle of relevance. At least from our admittedly distant perspective in time, there are no elements in the text or its context that would lead to these particular structures presenting themselves to the hearer as optimally relevant. The use of ἐν πνεύματι to obtain a different division
has been mentioned above (n. 59 above).

[81] Müller, *Microstructural Analysis*, 325–331. So also K. A. Strand, "The 'Victorious Introduction' Scenes in the Visions in the Book of Revelation," *AUSS* 35 (1987): 267–288.

The first point may be granted, but could equally be explained as part of John's interlocking technique.[82] The second is most unlikely, as this single verse is both too short and too far distant from the bowls to be in any way comparable to the throne scene of chs. 4–5, which leads immediately to the opening of the seals. Chapter 15 itself provides a suitable, immediate introduction to the bowl series. Aune supports the linking of 11:19 to ch. 12 with a number of arguments of varying degrees of cogency.[83] Whether the thunders open or close scenes is admittedly ambiguous.[84] The suggestion that at 8:5, 11:19 and 16:18–21 they close the seals, trumpets and bowls, corresponding to their opening appearance in the throne-room scene, is at least as likely as any other. The further argument that the opening of the heavenly temple functions to open a scene, corresponding to the open door in heaven (4:1) and the open heavens (19:11), is weightier. But in both those cases a perfect participle is used to describe an existing state of affairs. In 11:19 an aorist indicative suggests an action seen by John in the vision.[85] In fact the closest link to 11:19 comes not in chs. 12–14 but in 15:5.[86]

The most interesting argument, from a relevance perspective, in favour of linking 11:19 to ch. 12, is Aune's suggestion (without using RT terminology) that Isa. 66:6–7 is the cognitive environment which provides the structural clues.[87] However, if RT allows this argument to be heard, it also disposes of it. Nothing in 11:19 would lead to accessing Isa 66:6 as a possible context of interpretation. Revelation does have a "voice from the temple," but in 16:1, 17, not 11:19. And if the Isaianic context is suggested retrospectively when the audience hears 12:5 (or 16:1), then it must be said that it requires far more processing effort than other more accessible contexts, built from the text of Revelation itself. The temple is completely absent from 12:1–14:13.

The feature of 11:19 that is totally new and unexpected is ἡ κιβωτὸς τῆς διαθήκης. This is one of only two references to this cultic object in the entire NT and raises a significant problem for the relevance of this verse. What co-text or context is accessible within which to make sense of this reference?[88] Or, more to

---

[82] See section 5.4 below.

[83] D. E. Aune, *Revelation 6-16*, WBC 52b (Word, 1998), 661–662.

[84] See also Vanni, *Struttura*, 141–148; Lambrecht, "Structuration," 93–95; Richard Bauckham, *The Climax of Prophecy: Studies on the Book of Revelation* (T&T Clark, 1993), 199–209.

[85] 11:19 ἠνοίγη; cf. 4:1, ἠνεῳγμένη; 19:11, ἠνεῳγμένον.

[86] Aune treats 11:19 as introducing 12:1–17. If it is introductory it should be to 12:1–16:21 or even 12:1–22:9.

[87] Isa 66:6, φωνὴ ἐκ ναοῦ (cf. Rev 11:19); Isa 66:7, ἔτεκεν ἄρσεν (cf. Rev 12:5).

[88] Bauckham's suggestion, *Climax*, 203, that it "must be the throne of God which chapter 4 describes," offers an interesting possibility, but the associations cannot be said to be very strong. Rev 7:15 has made the connection between the throne and the sanctuary, but the ark of

the point in our current structural study, are there cognitive environments that give it structural significance?

First, it is closely linked with all the other furnishings of the tabernacle.[89] Among these is the θυσιαστήριον which has been prominent in Revelation 6–11, but disappears from sight along with the temple, before two final mentions in chs. 14 and 16.[90] Secondly, when the tabernacle is set up, the ark is screened from sight by a κατακάλυμμα τοῦ καταπετάσματος.[91] And in one of the most fascinating references, 2 Macc 2:4–8, Jeremiah is said to have hidden the ark, with the tent and the altar of incense, in a cave and sealed (ἐνέφραξεν) the entrance, declaring that the place would remain unknown until God gathered his people and the glory of the Lord and the cloud would appear (ὀφθήσεται). The ark, covered, hidden or sealed, linked to the appearance of the glory of God and the cloud (recalling both the initial installation of the tabernacle and the dedication of Solomon's temple) are all motifs quite coherent with the text sequences preceding 11:19 and not at all with those immediately following it. Thirdly, when the ark is established in its tent outside Jerusalem in 1 Chr 16, Benaiah and Jahaziel were appointed "to blow trumpets regularly" before it (1 Chr 16:6), providing a further link back to the trumpet sequence of Rev 8:2–11:18.[92] It must be acknowledged that these possible contexts for understanding the significance of the ark are somewhat distant. Nevertheless, the principle of relevance suggests that such a prominent feature will prompt the audience to investigate possible contexts until adequate contextual effects are found. One of these contextual effects, I suggest, is the association of 11:19 primarily with what precedes it.

Finally, regarding 11:19, it must be stressed that although there is little connection to 12:1–14:13, thereafter the links begin to be formed again, until 15:5–8 brings us strongly back to the same context. Furthermore, the end of the bowl septet, 16:17–21, not only repeats the thunder and lightning, but expands on both the earthquake and the hail. It is almost as though the entire bowl sequence is an expansion on 11:19. It seems likely that John uses it as a joint or hinge, to close the temple scene opened in 11:1, as well as the whole trumpet series, and to provide

---

the covenant is never explicitly described as a throne in the OT and the ναός is not mentioned in the throne-room vision at all.

[89] Note especially Exodus chapters 25–26, 31, 37–40, and the only other NT occurrence, Heb 9:4. The tabernacle is called a σκηνή τοῦ μαρτυρίου, Exod. 40:34–35; cf. Rev 15:5.

[90] The references are Rev 6:9; 8:3, 5; 9:13; 11:1 and then 14:18; 16:7.

[91] Exod 40:21. In our text the ark is part of the ἀποκάλυψις.

[92] This is part of the close association of the ark with David, pointed out by S.-M. Kang, *Divine War in the Old Testament and in the Ancient Near East,* BZAW 177 (Gruyter, 1989), 208–212, an association which strengthens the conclusion that 11:19 closes the section which explicitly names its main protagonist "the Lion of the tribe of Judah, the Root of David" (5:5).

a link forward to ch. 15 where the main narrative will resume and the temple will become the dominant spatial marker.

Broad Outline of 12:1–22:9

The audience hearing the reading of the Apocalypse will almost certainly have perceived a major new section beginning at 12:1, a section whose structure of "great signs" will go on to include the bowl sequence. Yet at the same time, the return to the temple and all its associated phenomena will have had the effect of bracketing 12–14 and linking the bowls closely with the earlier septets, though not as closely as the trumpets are linked to the seals.[93]

The occurrences of σημεῖον μέγα … ἐν τῷ οὐρανῷ are an obvious structuring device. But 12:3 clearly does not introduce a new sequence since the story of the woman and the story of the dragon are inextricably linked. If 15:1 is parallel to 12:1, it also stands as a title over the whole of 15:1–22:9, since, except for the interlude 19:11–21:8, the plague-bearing angels are significant actors throughout. In 15:1–16:21 they are the principal actors, but one of their number is the angelic guide in each of the vision journeys, 17:1–19:10 and 21:9–22:9, which define the main outlines of the remainder of the central vision section.[94] This leaves ch. 14 hanging. With its pairing of significant discourse markers (Καὶ εἶδον, καὶ ἰδού, 14:1, 14) introducing two quite different sections, one largely retrospective in its linkages, the other largely, though not entirely, prospective, it stands as something of a bridge between the text sequences 12:1–13:18 and 15:1–22:9.

Overlaps and Interlockings

Despite the degree of coherence evidenced by these subsections, there are several features which cross the boundaries. In fact John sometimes introduces an anticipatory reference to something which will become the focus of a later vision, so that the vision sequences are more like the links of a chain than a discrete linear sequence.[95] For example, the beast is mentioned at 11:7 and is then focal in 12:1–14:13, links to the next sequence at 15:2, becomes focal again in ch. 17 and links again into the penultimate sequence at 19:19; 20:4, 10. The first and second

---

[93] Giblin, *Revelation*, 15, considers the seventh trumpet to include 11:15–15:8 and to be composed of a sevenfold chiasm, focused on 14:1–5. This is intriguing but I suggest that it is a pattern which would be imperceptible to the hearer and overrides significant structural discontinuities.

[94] Mazzaferri, *Genre*, 338–339, argues, against Kempson, that the σημεῖον connects 12:1–15:1, not 12:1–16:21 but does not notice that 15:1 itself is connected, not only to the whole of 15–16, but with the rest of the Apocalypse, as far as 22:9, by the device of the plague-bearing angels.

[95] Schüssler Fiorenza makes a similar point (see note 73 above).

sequences are also linked by the songs of victory at 11:15–18 and 12:10–12. Babylon is mentioned at 14:8, again in the next section at 16:19, before it becomes focal in chs. 17–19. The connection of wine and wrath is made (in two different ways) at 14:8, 10 and is picked up again in the next section at 14:19 and 16:19. The blood of the saints is first explicit at 16:6, then again at 17:6, 18:24. The bride links 19:6–9 with 21:2 and 21:9. Thus the theme of the marriage of the Lamb spans the penultimate section of unnumbered visions. Jerusalem, the holy city, strongly connects the final two sections (21:2 and 21:10). The throne of God, which was the centre of all action in chs. 4–11 moves somewhat to the background, until 19:4, and the heavenly temple is the point of reference in the section 14:14–16:21. The elders and the living creatures, prominent in the throne scene, also recede into the background and after 7:13 are only mentioned at a couple of significant junctures.[96] Many more examples could be adduced of lexical and semantic strands woven through the whole section, but these are the main chaining motifs and are a warning not to expect to find a watertight, logical structure within this major section of the text.[97]

At this point we can view the overall structure of the second major vision section.

Figure 23.3 gives the broad outline of the second vision narrative. Every section number is preceded by 2.3.2.2. The whole diagram represents a fourth-grade sequence.

4:1–22:9 John's vision of "things which must happen after this" in heaven
(.1) 4:1–11:19 Vision of throne room, leading on to the 7 seals and 7 trumpets
Delimiters: Μετὰ ταῦτα εἶδον, καὶ ἰδού; thunder etc. [Καὶ σημεῖον μέγα ὤφθη ...]
Spatial signals: in heaven, from heaven, around/before/beside the throne
(.1.1) 4:1–7:8 Heavenly worship and the first six seals
Delimiters: Μετὰ ταῦτα εἶδον, καὶ ἰδού ; [Μετὰ ταῦτα εἶδον, καὶ ἰδού]
Spatial signals: in heaven, around/before the throne
(.1.2) 7:9–11:19 Heavenly worship and the seventh seal
Delimiters: Μετὰ ταῦτα εἶδον, καὶ ἰδού; [Καὶ σημεῖον μέγα ὤφθη ἐν τῷ οὐρανῷ]

---

[96] Living creatures: 14:3, 15:7, 19:4. Elders: 14:3, 19:4. Note that the throne of God also becomes focal again at 19:4, having had only two mentions (12:5 and 16:17) since the end of ch. 11.

[97] Schüssler Fiorenza, "Composition," 360, notes that the "technique of *intercalation*... makes a diagramming of the successive sections of Revelation almost impossible." It is not entirely clear how she distinguishes between "interludes" and "intercalations," so that the name intercalation should perhaps be reserved for what she calls a "double intercalation" (p. 361), in which two text sequences are interlocked (the term used by Yarbro Collins, *Combat Myth*, 16–19) in the form [A__A][B][A][B__B]. This feature certainly means that the linear displays of structure are far from satisfactory in showing the structure of Revelation.

Temporal signals: Μετὰ ταῦτα

Spatial signals: in heaven, from heaven

Dramatis Personae: great crowd, angels, living creatures, elders, bowl angels, strong angel

(.2) 12:1–22:9 Signs and visions in heaven

Delimiters: Καὶ σημεῖον μέγα; end of vision reports

Communication axis: vision narration broken by author → audience asides

Dramatis Personae: Lamb, beast

Spatial signals: πόλις

(.2.1) 12:1–14:20 Signs and visions of conflict

Delimiters: Καὶ σημεῖον μέγα ὤφθη ἐν τῷ οὐρανῷ; [Καὶ εἶδον ἄλλο σημεῖον]

Spatial signals: in heaven, on the earth

Dramatis Personae: dragon, beast, people of God, Lamb

(.2.2) 15:1–22:9 Signs and visions of judgment and victory, involving plague angels

Delimiters: Καὶ εἶδον ἄλλο σημεῖον; end of vision narration

Dramatis Personae: plague angels

(.2.2.1) 15:1–16:21 From the temple – 7 bowls of plagues

Delimiters: Καὶ εἶδον ἄλλο σημεῖον; [Καὶ ἦλθεν εἷς ἐκ τῶν ἑπτὰ ἀγγέλων]

Spatial signals: out of the temple

(.2.2.2) 17:1–19:10 First vision sequence with angel-guided journey—Babylon

Delimiters: Καὶ ἦλθεν εἷς ἐκ τῶν ἑπτὰ ἀγγέλων; final interaction with angel

Spatial signals: into the wilderness, the throne (ch.19)

(.2.2.3) 19:11–21:8 Unnumbered sequence of visions

Delimiters: end of first angelic journey; beginning of second

Spatial signals: in heaven, on earth, the throne (20:11, 21:3)

(.2.2.4) 21:9–22:9 Second vision sequence with angel-guided journey—New Jerusalem

Delimiters: Καὶ ἦλθεν εἷς ἐκ τῶν ἑπτὰ ἀγγέλων; end of vision sequence

Spatial signals: a great, high mountain, out of heaven

Figure 23.3: Discourse Structure of the Second Major Vision Section (4:1–22:9)

The End of the Beginning

We have examined the overall structure of the book of Revelation, looked at the beginning and the ending in a little more detail, and then analysed its major subdivisions. Already at this level of detail we can see that of the four numbered septets, the first (churches) stands apart in the first vision sequence, while the latter three are all in the second. Of these the seven trumpets clearly function as the detail of the seventh seal. But the bowls are separated by significant higher-level sequences and attempts to find the same nested linkage do not represent the way the text as we have it works. There is much more detail which could be examined using the same principles. On closer examination, some of the un-numbered septets which have been proposed have little relevance-based evidence. For example, the set of visions between the two angel-guided journeys are more likely to number four than seven. Those interested in pushing inwards from seventh- to fourteenth-grade text sequences can refer to the latter part of Pattemore, *Souls Under the Altar*. RT does not replace other pragmatic-semantic methodology but proves to be a useful way to test the credibility of some proposed structural schema.

Select Bibliography for Discourse Studies

The following list of works is not exhaustive. They include studies on the nature of discourse by linguists as well as studies by biblical scholars applying insights about the nature of discourse to biblical literature. I have tried to select works that have been especially influential in discourse studies as well as works that introduce the state of the field, its history, or both. If I could choose only one book with which the completely uninitiated could begin profitably, I would suggest the very brief overview by Widdowson (2007). I have not included textbooks on disciplines or theories that have fed into and shaped discourse studies. Candidates would have been textbooks on semantics, pragmatics, grammar, cognitive linguistics, functional grammar, information structure, Relevance Theory, Systemic Functional Linguistics, and more. The reader will encounter these disciplines and theories in the literature listed below and may pursue them at will.

Beaugrande, Robert de and Wolfgang U. Dressler. *Introduction to Text Linguistics*. Longman, 1981.

Beekman, John, John Callow, and Michael Kopesec. *The Semantic Structure of Written Communication*. 5th rev. Summer Institute of Linguistics, 1981.

Bergen, Robert D., ed. *Biblical Hebrew and Discourse Linguistics*. Summer Institute of Linguistics, 1994.

Bhatia, V. K., John Flowerdew, and Rodney H. Jones, eds. *Advances in Discourse Studies*. Routledge, 2008.

Black, David Alan, Katharine Barnwell, and Stephen H. Levinsohn, eds. *Linguistics and New Testament Interpretation: Essays on Discourse Analysis*. Broadman Press, 1992.

Blakemore, Diane. *Relevance and Linguistic Meaning: The Semantics and Pragmatics of Discourse Markers*. CSL 99. Cambridge University Press, 2002.

Blass, Regina. *Relevance Relations in Discourse: A Study with Special Reference to Sissala*. CSL 55. Cambridge University Press, 1990.

Bodine, Walter Ray, ed. *Discourse Analysis of Biblical Literature: What It Is and What It Offers*. SBLSS. Scholars Press, 1995.

Callow, Kathleen. *Man and Message: A Guide to Meaning-Based Text Analysis*. University Press of America, 1998.

Carson, D. A. and Stanley E. Porter, eds. *Discourse Analysis and Other Topics in Biblical Greek*. JSNTSS 113. Sheffield Academic Press, 1995.

Clark, David J. *Analyzing and Translating New Testament Discourse*. SKG. Fontes, 2019.

Coulthard, Malcolm. *An Introduction to Discourse Analysis*. Longman, 1985.

Dooley, Robert and Stephen H. Levinsohn. *Analyzing Discourse: A Manual of Basic Concepts*. SIL International, 2001.

Fischer, Kerstin, ed. *Approaches to Discourse Particles*. Studies in Pragmatics 1. Elsevier, 2006.

Gee, James Paul and Michael Handford, eds. *The Routledge Handbook of Discourse Analysis*. Routledge, 2012.

Givón, T. *Coherence*. John Benjamins, 2020.

Grimes, Joseph E. *The Thread of Discourse*. Mouton, 1975.

Guthrie, George H. *The Structure of Hebrews: A Text-Linguistic Analysis*. Brill, 1994.

Halliday, M. A. K. and Raqaiya Hasan. *Cohesion in English*. Longman, 1976.

Harris, Zellig. "Discourse Analysis." *Language* 28, no. 1 (1952): 1–30.

Harweg, Roland. *Pronomina und Textkonstitution*. Fink, 1968.

Heckert, Jakob K. *Discourse Function of Conjoiners in the Pastoral Epistles*. Summer Institute of Linguistics, 1996.

Hoey, Michael. *Patterns of Lexis in Text*. DEL. Oxford University Press, 1991.

Hoey, Michael. *Textual Interaction: An Introduction to Written Discourse Analysis*. Routledge, 2001.

Johnson-Laird, P. N. *Mental Models*. Cambridge University Press, 1983.

Johnstone, Barbara. *Discourse Analysis*. 2nd ed. Blackwell, 2008.

Lambrecht, Knud. *Information Structure and Sentence Form: Topic, Focus, and the Mental Representations of Discourse Referents*. CSL 71. Cambridge University Press, 1994.

Levinsohn, Stephen. *Discourse Features of New Testament Greek: A Coursebook on the Information Structure of New Testament Greek*. 2nd rev. ed. SIL International, 2021.

Long, Fredrick J. Koine Greek Grammar: A Beginning-Intermediate Exegetical and Pragmatic Handbook. Accessible Greek Resources and Online Studies. Wilmore, KY: GlossaHouse, 2015.

Longacre, Robert E. *Discourse, Paragraph, and Sentence Structure in Selected Philippine Languages*. Summer Institute of Linguistics, 1968.

Longacre, Robert E. *The Grammar of Discourse*. Plenum, 1983.

Longacre, Robert E. *Hierarchy and Universality of Discourse Constituents in New Guinea Languages*. Georgetown University Press, 1972.

Longacre, Robert E. *Joseph: A Story of Divine Providence*. 2nd ed. Eisenbrauns, 2003.

Longacre, Robert E. and Frances M. Woods. *Discourse Grammar: Studies in Indigenous Languages of Colombia, Panama, and Ecuador*. 3 vols. Summer Institute of Linguistics and the University of Texas at Arlington, 1976–1977.

Longacre, Robert E. and Shin Ja J. Hwang. *Holistic Discourse Analysis*. 2nd ed. SIL International, 2012.

Louw, Johannes P. *Semantics of New Testament Greek*. Semeia Studies. Fortress, 1982.

Mann, William C., Christian M. I. M. Matthiessen, and Sandra A. Thompson. "Rhetorical Structure Theory and Text Analysis." *ISI/RR-89-242* (1989): 1–60.

Mann, William C. and Sandra A. Thompson, eds. *Discourse Description: Diverse Linguistic Analyses of a Fund-raising Text*. John Benjamins, 1992.

Paltridge, Brian. *Discourse Analysis: An Introduction*. 2nd ed. CDS. Continuum, 2012.

Pattemore, Stephen W. *The People of God in the Apocalypse: Discourse, Structure, and Exegesis.* SNTSMS 128. Cambridge University Press, 2004.

Pattemore, Stephen W. *Souls under the Altar: Relevance Theory and the Discourse Structure of Revelation.* UBSMS 9. United Bible Societies, 2003.

Porter, Stanley E. and Donald A. Carson, eds. *Discourse Analysis and Other Topics in Biblical Greek.* Sheffield Academic Press, 1995.

Porter, Stanley E. and Jeffrey T. Reed, eds. *Discourse Analysis and the New Testament: Approaches and Results.* JSNTSup 170. Sheffield Academic Press, 1999.

Read-Heimerdinger, Jenny. *The Bezan Text of Acts: A Contribution of Discourse Analysis to Textual Criticism.* JSNTSup 236. Sheffield Academic Press, 2002.

Reed, Jeffrey T. *A Discourse Analysis of Philippians: Method and Rhetoric in the Debate over Literary Integrity.* JSNTSup 136. Sheffield Academic Press, 1997.

Runge, Steven E. *Discourse Grammar of the Greek New Testament: A Practical Introduction for Teaching and Exegesis.* Hendrickson, 2010.

Schiffrin, Deborah. *Discourse Markers.* SIS 5. Cambridge University Press, 1987.

Starwalt, Ervin Ray. *A Discourse Analysis of 1 Peter.* SKG. Fontes, 2020.

Tannen, Deborah, Heidi E. Hamilton, and Deborah Schiffrin, eds. *The Handbook of Discourse Analysis.* 2nd ed. Wiley Blackwell, 2015.

Taylor, Mark E. *A Text-Linguistic Investigation into the Discourse Structure of James.* LNTS 311. T&T Clark, 2011.

Terry, Ralph Bruce. *A Discourse Analysis of First Corinthians.* Summer Institute of Linguistics, 1995.

Todd, Richard Watson. *Discourse Topics.* P&BNS 269. John Benjamins, 2016.

van Dijk, Teun A., ed. *Handbook of Discourse Analysis.* 4 vols. Academic Press, 1985.

van Dijk, Teun A. *Macrostructures: An Interdisciplinary Study of Global Structures in Discourse, Interaction, and Cognition.* Erlbaum, 1980.

van Dijk, Teun A. *Studies in the Pragmatics of Discourse.* De Gruyter, 1981.

van Dijk, Teun A. *Text and Context: Explorations in the Semantics and Pragmatics of Discourse.* Longman, 1977.

van Dijk, Teun A. and Walter Kintsch. *Strategies of Discourse Comprehension.* Academic Press, 1983.

Varner, William. *The Book of James, A New Perspective: A Linguistic Commentary Applying Discourse Analysis.* Kress Biblical Resources, 2010.

Wendland, Ernst R., ed. *Discourse Perspectives on Hebrew Poetry in the Scriptures.* UBSMS 7. United Bible Societies, 1994.

Westfall, Cynthia Long. *A Discourse Analysis of the Letter to the Hebrews: The Relationship between Form and Meaning.* LNTS 297. T&T Clark, 2005.

Widdowson, H. G. *Discourse Analysis.* OILS. Oxford University Press, 2007.

Wirth, Jessica R., ed. *Beyond the Sentence: Discourse and Sentential Form.* Karoma, 1985.

CPSIA information can be obtained
at www.ICGtesting.com
Printed in the USA
BVHW051218160721
612127BV00013B/1027/J